WHERE THE LAND MEETS THE SEA

WHERE THE LAND MEETS THE SEA

FOURTEEN MILLENNIA OF HUMAN HISTORY AT HUACA PRIETA, PERU

EDITED BY TOM D. DILLEHAY

University of Texas Press   *Austin*

Publication of this book was made possible in part
by a generous subsidy from Vanderbilt University.

LIBRARY OF CONGRESS CATALOGING-IN-
PUBLICATION DATA

Names: Dillehay, Tom D., editor.
Title: Where the land meets the sea : fourteen millennia of
human history at Huaca Prieta, Peru / edited by Tom D.
Dillehay.
Description: First edition. | Austin : University of Texas
Press, 2017. | Includes bibliographical references and index.
Identifiers: LCCN 2016038507
ISBN 978-1-4773-1149-3 (cloth : alk. paper)
Subjects: LCSH: Huaca Prieta Site (Peru) | Archaeological
expeditions—Peru—Chicama River Valley. | Excavations
(Archaeology)—Peru—Chicama River Valley. | Chicama
River Valley (Peru)—Civilization. | Indians of South
America—Peru—Antiquities. | Human ecology—Peru—
Chicama River Valley—History.
Classification: LCC F3429.1.C486 W54 2017 |
DDC 985—dc23
LC record available at https://lccn.loc.gov/2016038507

doi:10.7560/311493

In memory of Duccio Bonavia (1935–2012)

Photo taken in 2011 at Huaca Prieta, Peru

CONTENTS

FIGURES

APPENDICES

TABLES

PREFACE

This volume reports the results of investigations conducted in the lower Chicama Valley on the north coast of Peru where the Preceramic sites of Huaca Prieta, Paredones, and others are located. Huaca Prieta was first excavated in 1944 and 1945 by the late Junius B. Bird of the American Museum of Natural History (AMNH). At the time, his research at the site was a good example of productive archaeological work conducted within the framework of the types of issues studied and methodologies of the era. After Bird's work at Huaca Prieta, no additional research was carried out at Huaca Prieta until our study began in 2006.

Permission to excavate sites in the lower Chicama Valley was granted by the Instituto Nacional de Cultura (now called the Ministerio de Cultura) in Lima, Peru. Our research was greatly facilitated by archaeological colleagues associated with the regional office of these institutions in Trujillo, especially César Gálvez Mora, the director of archaeology there. Our research in the study area also was supported logistically by colleagues of the Fundación Wiese at the nearby El Brujo Museum, also located in the lower Chicama Valley. We are also grateful to Ricardo Morales of the Huaca de La Luna Project in the Moche Valley for lending us the scaffolding to recut and profile the high walls of Bird's unit HP-3.

Our interdisciplinary research in the valley was funded principally by the National Science Foundation, the National Geographic Society, Becky and Spence Wilson, and the Vanderbilt University Discovery Research program. We sincerely thank these institutions and individuals for supporting our research over the past ten years.

The logistics of performing the groundwork in the research area are complicated. Personnel of the Municipalidad de Magdalena de Cao helped us to obtain a large crew of local workers, many of whom had prior excavation experience at the Moche pyramid site of Huaca Cao Viejo. During the course of the project we employed more than sixty individual workers from the local community.

The professional archaeological crew besides Duccio Bonavia and myself consisted of Gabino Rodríguez, Gerson Levy-Lazzarus, Daniel Fernandes Moreira, Marilaura López Solís, José Saavedra, Carol Rojas, Liz Ramírez, Carlos Zapata Benítez, Greg Maggard, Phil Mink, Brian McCoy, Curtis McCoy, and Patricia Netherly. In addition to the archaeologists, numerous specialists intermittently joined the project for specialty studies; their names and affiliations are presented in each chapter that they authored.

Colleagues who provided valuable advice and conversation about early sites during the project were César Gálvez, Jesús Briceño, Santiago Uceda, Claude Chauchat, and Enrique Vergara Montero.

Social life for the crew centered around the rustic restaurants in the small village of Magdelena de Cao, where we also lived during the field seasons. The local people there were gracious and fun hosts, with whom we shared many good times, including a few feasts on weekend nights.

Special thanks are extended to Teresa Rosales Tham, director of the archaeological laboratory at the Universidad Nacional de Trujillo, and to Víctor Vásquez, director of the Arquebios Laboratorio. All excavated artifacts and ecofacts from our project are currently housed at the Universidad Nacional de Trujillo.

I also thank Patricia Netherly, who worked for two years with me to bring this manuscript together. She not only filled a few gaps left behind by the unexpected death of Duccio Bonavia but also read the entire manuscript, pointing out omissions, redundancies, inconsistencies, and faulty syntheses. Her efforts were significant in achieving the final version of this book. Special thanks are extended to Paige Silcox and Kristin Benson for their invaluable help in bringing the manuscript together, especially for working with the references, tables, and figures. Iris Bracamonte made the lithic drawings. Several photographs of artifacts that we excavated from Huaca Prieta,

which have been presented at several national and international meetings, have made their way onto the Internet and are often erroneously listed under different contexts attributed to other sites and other places. I also thank Sumru Aricanli and Charles Spencer of the American Museum of Natural History for facilitating our study of the Huaca Prieta Collection in the Department of Anthropology.

A special kind of recognition goes to my good friend and colleague Duccio Bonavia, who died of a heart attack while we were in the field at Huaca Prieta in 2012 carrying out research. Duccio was extremely well versed in the empirical record of the Preceramic and other periods in Andean archaeology. He is sorely missed by all of us.

Although Duccio is the co-author of several chapters in the book, I did not add him as co-editor and co-author on some chapters because I was not sure that he would have agreed with all of the themes covered in the book, particularly those dealing with social and ontological issues. In this regard Duccio was a well-focused techno-environmentalist and cultural materialist. This volume is dedicated to him.

As mentioned at the end of chapter 1, the project members presented detailed reports and analyses of all excavated archaeological and ecological materials. Unfortunately, the complete set of those reports, even in their most abbreviated versions, was more than double the amount of material that any press was willing to publish. I spoke with eleven different presses to attempt to find one that would publish all of the data, but none agreed. The only one willing to publish the majority of the data and interpretive chapters was the University of Texas Press, to which we are extremely grateful. But even there we had limits. As a result of having to cut back on the details of some databases, I decided to reduce the size of the chapters describing the excavated cultural materials (chapters 11 and 12) and the settlement patterns (chapter 13). More detailed information on these data and several appendices reporting on specialty studies (pollen, shell analysis, lithic microuse-wear analysis, soil chemistry, GPR [ground-penetrating radar] study, textiles, tables, and other voluminous data) were placed online at https://my.vanderbilt.edu/huacaprieta/.

Finally, I wish to thank Casey Kittrell of the University of Texas Press for accepting this manuscript and for working with us to bring this long and complex project to fruition. We also thank the members of the staff at the press, especially Lynne Chapman, the manuscript editor, and Kathy Lewis, the copy editor, for their support and for their work in improving the manuscript and also bringing it to publication.

Inevitably, I have omitted someone or some entity that deserves mention. I ask that you accept my sincere apology for this.

The archaeological record of the pre-pottery mound at Huaca Prieta on the north coast of Peru consists of innumerable broken pieces, deliberately smashed, torn, snapped, cut and fractured objects, and segmented and partially defined spaces and architectural elements. All of these represent snippets and venues of stratigraphically and behaviorally arranged human fragments, most of which are archaeologically coherent, while others are incoherent. As a result, the mound is constituted by thousands of small upward and outward building episodes created within confined spaces, each reflecting slightly different recursive behaviors in structure and content. Nearly all objects composing the mound—the shells, textiles, stone tools, food remains, stone vessels, gourds, and human skeletons—are fractured or broken. How do we explain these thousands of fractured pieces, some of which are discarded trash, a few of which are broken by natural processes, but many of which were deliberately fractured as the result of human action. How do we understand the meaning of the hundreds of individually differentiated and circumscribed spaces? Is it more than just social, economic, and political behavior? What forces give cohesion to these fragments and spaces? The cause-and-effect relations almost always employed by archaeologists to explain the character of complex sites (random deposition; domestic activity; technological, economic, social, ritual, and other behaviors) simply do not account for the majority of broken pieces at Huaca Prieta.

Besides containing material fragments and segmented spaces, Huaca Prieta is a dark mound, which contains ash and billions of specks of charcoal revealing numerous burning episodes throughout time. Thus the name *prieta* (black). Curiously, in stark contrast, the mound also exhibits an unusually high amount of salt crystals resulting from pouring enormous quantities of seawater onto the structure. How do we explain this unusual archaeological presence of the by-products of fire and water, two contrasting yet apparently complementary elements in nature?

Lighting areas at night, cooking, and burning trash or using water to dampen areas or to extinguish fires cannot explain the excessive amounts of charcoal and salt in the mound. Or were fire and water representing cooperative coexistent or antagonistic forces within the ancient world of these coastal people? Certainly something about charcoal and salt/fire and water at Huaca Prieta encapsulates their respective and contradictory powers of destruction and creation. The elements of fire and water represent transition and transformation, changes or flows from one physical state to another. Did fire and water, as metaphysical icons of transition and fluidity, help figuratively shape the contours of socially constructed relationships between people and their natural world in this coastal setting? Do these elements and the contradictory forces that they represent in nature reflect important aspects of the cosmology and ontology of these past peoples? That is, do these elements metaphorically embody sociocultural knowledge and an understanding of the physical and social worlds of the coastal Andes at this early time? Are the mound and its history (now conceived primarily as an archaeological place in a natural setting after a long period of ritual use) an accumulation of thousands of individual or group life histories represented by the numerous fragmented objects deliberately deposited in special places by the living during those ritual episodes and by the dead buried there? Were these episodes enacted by a socially segmented society constituted by various dispersed littoral and inland household communities involved primarily in ritual at Huaca Prieta? What are the combined social and ontological meanings of the elements and episodes constituting the site? These are questions that most archaeologists ignore because they are empirically difficult to measure and explain. In the case of Huaca Prieta, however, they must be explored in terms of why and how these elements and episodes were constructed and transformed and what they might have meant to the societies producing them over time.

CHAPTER 1

RELEVANCE

Tom D. Dillehay

INTRODUCTION

The development of stable communities and food-producing cultures of farming and animal husbandry has often been described as the most important change in all of human history. These developments, generally known in archaeology as the Neolithic period, are usually thought of as a time when people practiced farming and possessed a similar set of material traits such as pottery, larger houses, storage surplus and facilities, permanent cemeteries, and elaborate craft goods. Several different social and environmental theories have been offered to explain why these transformations occurred, none of which have been satisfactory for all regions of the world and especially for cultural anomalies that do not neatly fit within traditional portrayals. One such anomaly is the prepottery Andes, where maritime, agricultural, and pastoral economies evolved simultaneously to establish the independent development of civilization beginning around 10,000 years ago.

For many decades, Andean archaeology was viewed as one of the least informative places to provide insight into the rise of ancient civilizations. Machu Picchu and the Inka civilization have been well known for a long time, but they were late cultural developments compared to early states in regions such as China, the Middle East, and Southeast Asia. The pre-Inka period and especially the earlier prepottery period in the Andes were often ignored by archaeologists working in other areas of the world, generally viewed as a long interlude during which little worthy of note occurred. This began to change over the past four decades. Researchers have compiled enough evidence on what is called the Preceramic or Archaic period in the Central Andes, dating from ~11,400 to 4000 years ago, to demonstrate early complex society. This approach contrasted with previous views, which argued that pottery and agriculture evolved parallel to each other and were required for a sedentary, food-producing, and food-storing strategy that eventually led to increased social complexity. Recently, however, the Andes have been seen less as a backwater cultural region and more as a key region of the early emergence of proto-urbanism, great art styles, political hierarchy, and variable strategies of food production. In fact, many globally significant food crops have come from this region, including potatoes, corn, beans, peanuts, chile peppers, avocados, tomatoes, quinoa, and others. In addition, the offshore waters of the Pacific coast from south Ecuador to central Chile are some of the richest in the world, providing an abundance and diversity of seafood. The richness of marine life found along the Pacific shore of Peru and its potential as a permanent food source provided the basis for Michael Moseley's (1975) hypothesis for the maritime foundations of Andean civilization. This hypothesis stated that a Preceramic sedentary lifeway, monument building, social inequality, corporate labor, and population growth were supported by an economy based primarily on marine resources from ~5500 to 4000 cal BP (Moseley [1992] later gave more emphasis to the role of plants in this economy).

Research on ancient civilizations along the coast of the Central Andes has a long history, revealing some of the world's earliest and most elaborate maritime societies, including the Chinchorro mummies of north Chile and south Peru dated between ~7000 and 4500 years ago and the slightly later Preceramic mound cultures from southern Ecuador to central Peru, with broad spectrum economies based on fishing, gathering, and farming. These latter cultures are best known by sites such as the Valdivia settlements of Real Alto Loma Alta in southwest Ecuador and Caral, Aspero, Salinas de Chao, Huaca Prieta, and others of coastal Peru. Understanding these early coastal cultures is important, because Peru is one of the few areas in the world where the coalescence of once separate maritime, agricultural, and pastoral economies set in motion long-term biological and cultural transformations that led to increased social complexity and food production and later the independent development of preindustrial states and urbanism.

One large early coastal site in particular, Huaca Prieta, has been a unique candidate for understanding these developments. The dark nature and oddly shaped, elongated, oval form of its mound, set against a contrasting landscape of the desert on one side and the Pacific Ocean on the other, has long intrigued archaeologists, perhaps more so than its potential contribution to understanding the rise of Andean civilization. But the importance of Huaca Prieta goes well beyond this contribution. As one of the world's sites with the longest human occupation, spanning more than fourteen millennia, and one of the most complex prepottery coastal sites ever, Huaca Prieta's significance is global.

This volume explores the origins and impacts of Huaca Prieta and other Preceramic sites located nearby. It presents analysis of the large body of interdisciplinary data derived between 2006 and 2013 from archaeological research at Huaca Prieta, Paredones, a nearby contemporary mound, and several Preceramic domestic sites in the lower Chicama Valley (figs. 1.1 and 1.2), where people lived with changing social and environmental circumstances over the past ~14,500 calibrated ^{14}C years BP. Although Huaca Prieta was occupied intermittently between ~14,500 and 7500 cal BP, it was permanently used as a ritual and mortuary mound between ~7800 and 3500 cal BP and occasionally afterward to the early colonial period as a cemetery. Although the site contains late Pleistocene to early Holocene cultural deposits, the interdisciplinary data presented here pertain primarily to the 7800 to 3500 cal BP period when the mounds at Huaca Prieta and Paredones were built.

Pioneering archaeological excavations conducted at Huaca Prieta by the late Junius Bird of the American Museum of Natural History in the mid-1940s revealed that the site had some of the densest, temporally longest, and deepest middle to late Holocene maritime cultural deposits in the world (Bird 1948a, 1948b, 1963a, 1963b; Bird et al. 1985). (The site also was one of the first to be radiocarbon dated by Willard Libby's radiocarbon laboratory.) Huaca Prieta measures ~29 m high in some places, ~65 m wide, and ~162 m long, with more than ~190,000 m³ of below-ground

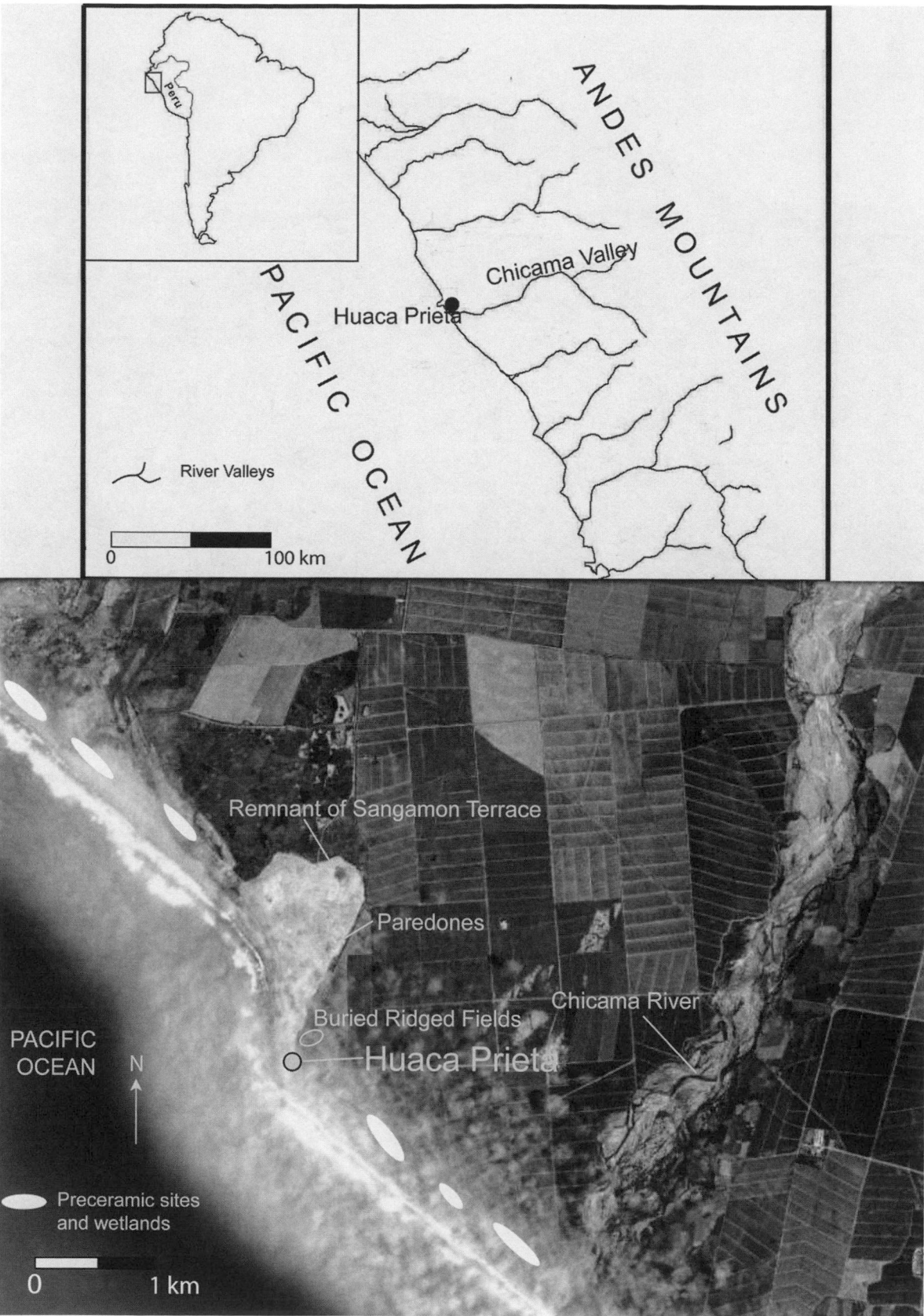

FIGURE 1.1. Location of the lower Chicama Valley and the archaeological sites on the north coast of Peru.

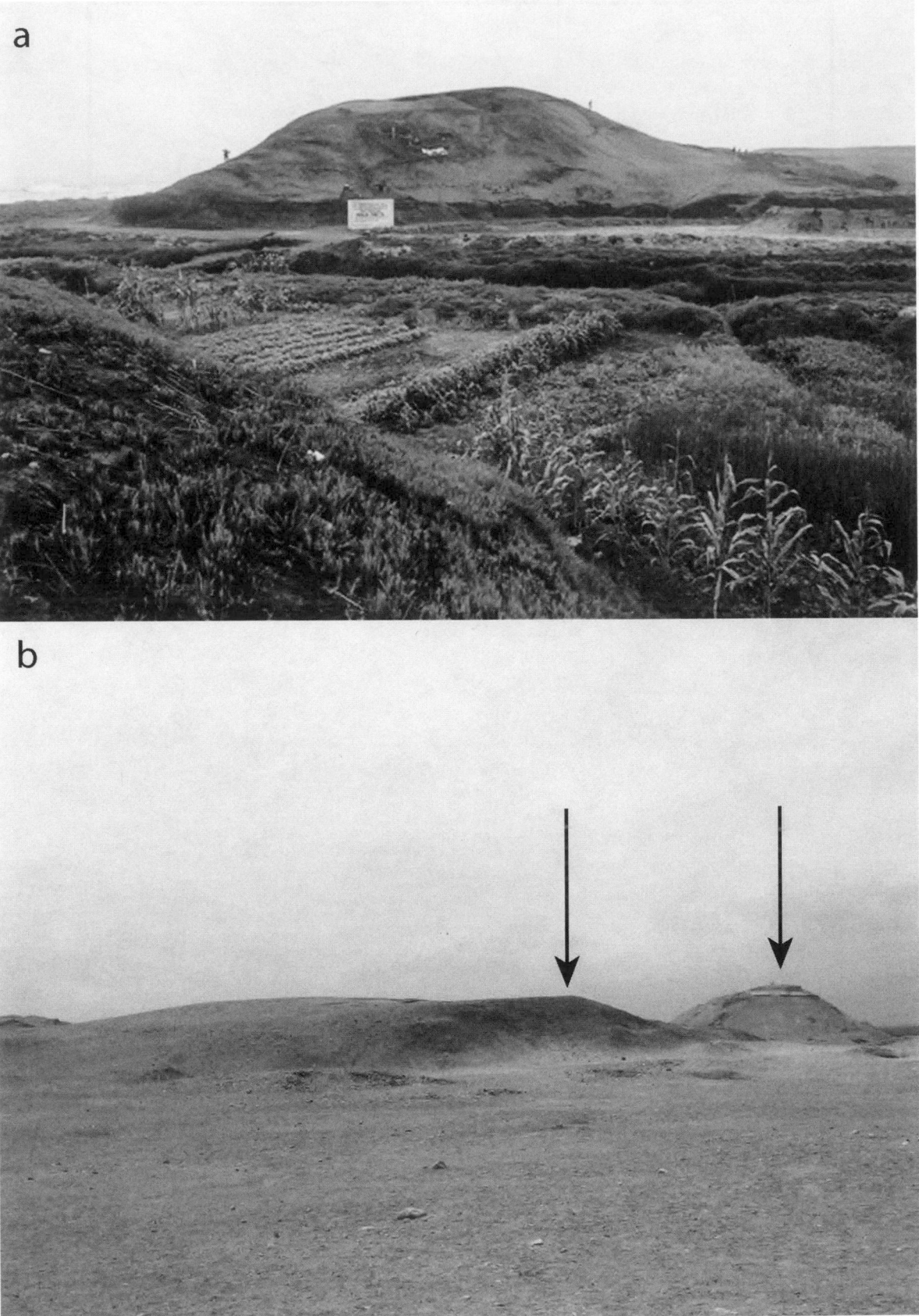

FIGURE 1.2. General views: *a*, Huaca Prieta looking to the northeast (the Pacific Ocean is on the other side of the mound; note the present-day household gardens in the wetland to the left); *b*, Paredones (*left arrow*) and the eastern side of the Sangamon terrace looking to the north (the El Brujo or Cao Viejo mound of the Moche period is in the background [*right arrow*]).

and above-ground deposits. Bird's archaeological study of Huaca Prieta indicated different strategies of marine foraging and initial farming over time, as evidenced by changes in intrasite spatial patterns, construction of permanent structures on the upper mound, placement of human burials, and a wide variety of food resources and material technologies. The most developed technology was cotton weaving and netting, which is the earliest documented so far in the New World and one of the earliest in the world (Bird and Mahler 1951–1952). The site's weavers devised a sophisticated art style with various visual (Bird et al. 1985) and nonvisual designs. Art was also exhibited through etched gourds (Bird 1963a), sculpted blocks of polychaete tubes (mineralized sediment formed by tube-dwelling marine worms), and cobbles painted with red hematite.

The Preceramic use of Huaca Prieta was previously thought to date between ~5500 and 3500 cal BP. It was considered to have been only an occupational and burial mound (Bird et al. 1985). Our recent research, however, shows that the site was initially a late Pleistocene to early Holocene campground. With the beginning of mound construction around 7500 cal BP, its primary function shifted to ritual and mortuary events (Dillehay et al. 2012b). Located on the southern tip of a remnant Pleistocene terrace on the present-day Pacific littoral, the site had direct access to multiple resource zones: marine, littoral, brackish and freshwater wetlands, desert and grassland plains, and Andean foothills. What has not been well understood until now, however, is how the site's inhabitants exploited a wide range of resources across these zones yet always focused on marine resources, how they developed early social complexity, why the site is composed of hundreds of segmented spaces and thousands of intentionally and unintentionally broken material remains, and what the wider ontological meaning of all of this is. I say "ontological," because the anomalous appearance of the mound and its varied art styles and mortuary practices were very different from anything else at the time in the Andes as well as in the Americas and must have been related to ideology, religion, or cosmology or the beginnings of one or more of these. (Because it is nearly impossible to determine which of these institutions may be relevant or whether all of them existed at this

early time, I prefer to bundle them together and simply call them "ontology.")

Paredones is a later, smaller Preceramic mound related to Huaca Prieta and the domestic sites but with a different history, economy, and archaeological record. It does not have the same stratigraphy, size, diversity, and quantity of deliberately broken material seen at Huaca Prieta. Paredones is about 60 m long, 40 m wide, and 6 m high. It dates intermittently from ~10,500 to 3800 cal BP, but primarily between ~6500 and 3800 cal BP, and is located ~500 m north of Huaca Prieta on the eastern edge of the terrace once overlooking a large wetland. It was initially an occupational site that later became a mound associated mainly with ritual and the preparation of plant foods.

As developed in this book, the ritual economy at Huaca Prieta involved primarily maritime products, while the ritual economy at Paredones was centered on farming and wild plants. The location of the two mound sites on different but closely positioned edges of the Sangamon terrace, one overlooking the sea and the other overlooking inland wetlands, indicates orientation toward different ecological zones and economies. Associated with both sites are roughly contemporaneous Preceramic household mound sites scattered along the terrace, the littoral, and the interior wetlands. These sites must have been the residences of people who built and used the two mounds. What makes all of these sites so important to world archaeology is that at this early time they collectively represent a local population of related people with simultaneously developed economies of fishing and shellfish gathering, farming, wetland foraging, and camelid husbandry, all juxtaposed and apparently specialized along the littoral and in the nearby wetlands of the lower Chicama Valley. (From a cultural geographical perspective, in this study the littoral zone is the part of the ocean that is close to the shore; it extends from the high water mark to shoreline areas that are permanently submerged and includes the intertidal zone, the beach and dune formations, and the estuaries and lagoons located ~0.5 to 2.0 km inland from the dunes. It does not include the entire lower valley from the Andean foothills to the shoreline, an approximate distance of 10 to 15 km. The inland coastal area includes the lower and middle valley desert and the Chicama River draining it, which encompass a distance of roughly 40 km from the estuaries and lagoons behind the shoreline to the middle valley.)

Although the local Preceramic population underwent dramatic shifts over time, other societies in the Andean region experienced similar changes. But no other known mounds near the scale and type of architectural and stratigraphic structure recorded at Huaca Prieta were constructed during this period. The structural nature of Huaca Prieta appears to be without parallel for this period not only in the Andes but in the Americas at large. It clearly exemplifies a different aspect of early mound building and in some ways compares better with early monuments elsewhere in the world, particularly the earthen mounds of North America (Milner 2005) and western Europe (Bradley 2007), than with the Preceramic stepped-platform mounds on the north-central coast of Peru, such as Caral, Aspero, Salinas de Chao, Bandurria, Huaricanga, and others (for example, Chu Barrera 2011; Haas and Creamer 2012; Moseley 1992; Shady S. 2004).

The end of Preceramic mound building at Huaca Prieta and Paredones was a conscious act between 3800 and 3500 cal BP. Later an adobe-brick mound of the early ceramic period (~3800–3000 cal BP), named Cupisnique, was built immediately north of Huaca Prieta. The people living there occasionally used the far northeastern end of Huaca Prieta for various activities, as evidenced by the presence of Guañape-like and Cupisnique ceramics. Huaca Prieta then became an occasional burial platform for certain individuals from this period to the colonial era. People continued to live in the area, but their society and culture changed significantly. Why these changes occurred is not clear. Perhaps an increased reliance on domesticated crops introduced new technologies and ideas that were incompatible with earlier ones. We know that the trend for coastal people at the end of the Preceramic period was toward a more intensified agricultural economy that combined domesticated plants and a mixed economy of terrestrial and maritime resources. Or perhaps it was caused by the arrival of new peoples and ideas into the area.

In summary, Huaca Prieta has been one of the best known yet least understood early maritime-related mound sites in the world. It was built

at an unusually fertile location on the southern point of an ancient terrace overlooking the Pacific Ocean and a series of rich wetlands. Its significance was not static: it varied over time according to the needs of a wide-ranging residential population, a changing socioeconomic landscape, and an evolving natural landscape. The impacts of these changes are read in the physical environment of the site, from its development as a maritime/wetland forager campsite to a large mound used primarily by fisherfolk for a variety of ritual practices. At the contemporary site of Paredones, a different history is evidenced within this setting. It related primarily to farming but also complemented, and was complemented by, the maritime ritual economy and activities at Huaca Prieta.

THE 2006–2013 RESEARCH PROJECT

With the exception of Bird's excellent study of the cotton textiles, the remainder of Huaca Prieta's archaeology has received little detailed study. Over the years, several archaeologists have addressed the function of the site (for example, Bird et al. 1985; Tellenbach 1997; compare Rick 1990). Bird thought that it was a residential site built up over time by discarded midden debris, house remains, and human burials. He was partially correct, because the premound phase is intermittently habitational from the late Pleistocene to the middle Holocene period (~14,500–7500 cal BP: Dillehay et al. 2012a, 2012b). Michael Tellenbach believed that the site was ceremonial, not occupational. He did not specify the nature of the ceremonies and had no hard evidence to support his idea; he thought that the mound presented an unusual type of architecture and content (mainly its black charcoal content) for a domestic site. In reviewing Bird's 1985 publication, John Rick (1990) questioned the function of the "houses" identified by Bird, noting that they were far too small for domestic use, generally being no more than 1.2 m in height. Terrence Grieder (1997: 108) also thought that Bird misinterpreted the houses, which he saw as shallow shaft tombs. We later demonstrate that these structures are indeed small chamber tombs, not houses, and that most of the history of Huaca Prieta is associated with nonmortuary and mortuary ritual, not residence.

Based on a cursory study of Huaca Prieta, on its previously little known function, and on our long-term interest in the site, the late Peruvian archaeologist Duccio Bonavia and I decided to reexcavate the site. In 2006 we began an interdisciplinary project in the lower Chicama Valley to gain a better understanding of the dynamic interrelationships among maritime and wetland foraging, farming, mound building, social complexity, and changing environments within the context of local landscape. A primary goal was to understand the reasons for the prolonged differential development among various sites in the study area and why Huaca Prieta was such an unusual and outsized Andean mound built by a society with little apparent social differentiation. Key pieces of the explanation come not only from the site itself but from Paredones and the house mound sites and from the human and landscape history of wider coastal and highland regions in the Andes.

We knew that it would be an interdisciplinary challenge to investigate these sites and their paleoecology. Having had archaeological experience at large earthwork mounds in the eastern United States and in southern Chile and at mounded platform sites in Peru, I anticipated that the size and nature of the stratigraphy would require slow, detailed excavation in multiple off- and on-mound areas and experienced personnel to record the paleoecological, geological, and archaeological details. Thus several geologists who had worked around the world with tsunamis, El Niño events, and riverine and coastal geomorphology and several Brazilian archaeologists with experience in excavating highly stratified, large, and deep *sambaquis* (large shell mounds) who had worked previously with me in Chile joined the project. In addition, a large interdisciplinary research team composed of geneticists, soil chemists, various macro- and microfaunal and floral experts, geophysicists, geologists, and various other specialists worked with the project (see chapter 3).

Based on interdisciplinary collaboration, the specific goals of the project were (1) to restudy the previous excavations of Bird; (2) to provide detailed stratigraphic, geological, and chronological data for new and different excavated areas of Huaca Prieta and other Preceramic sites; (3) to collect soil samples, plant, animal, and other remains

from various sites for reconstruction of subsistence strategies; and (4) to obtain various paleoecological samples at sites and across the valley to reconstruct past environments and climates. The project resulted in a wide variety of well-preserved organic and inorganic materials that required studies by more than fifty specialists drawn from different countries.

In addition to working at Huaca Prieta and Paredones, the project conducted a nonsystematic, opportunistic survey of Preceramic domestic sites from Malabrigo to Huanchaco, a littoral and inland coastal strip of ~30 km in length and between ~2 and 3 km inland, and worked with interdisciplinary teams to reconstruct the physical setting of the local paleoecology. These sites contain well-preserved archaeological and paleoecological records that offer insight not only into the dynamically linked social and natural systems of the littoral and coastal desert but also into some beginnings of early Andean civilization in this region. A better understanding of these issues affords comparison with similar and dissimilar processes in other areas of the world where long-term, in situ transformations occurred during the late Pleistocene to middle Holocene periods (for example, Barker and Goucher 2015).

Although the project addressed a wide range of research questions, targeted excavations exposed an extensive stratigraphic picture of Huaca Prieta, Paredones, the domestic sites, and geological areas between them. The removal of nearly 500 m³ of sediment from these sites and areas revealed new information regarding the internal structure and construction methods in building the mounds and the use of the local environment. These excavations were extensive and deep and along with Bird's prior work at the site represent ~4% of Huaca Prieta's total size and ~6% of the total volume of Paredones. Our work demonstrated a complex internal stratigraphy indicating that the mounds were consistently and gradually built over a long time. Subsequent coring and test pits by project geologists in off-mound areas defined the geological and geomorphological setting and provided a framework for reinterpreting the construction chronologies and functions of the mounds. Taken together, these data present a long chronology of all excavated sites. Examining this chronology in relation to the history of the sites provides the basis for theorizing about wider social, cultural, and demographic processes.

Finally, in carrying out archaeological and informal ethnoarchaeological research over the past four decades with the indigenous Mapuche of south-central Chile, we have learned that it is essential to draw on the knowledge of present-day local people to gain insights into short-term environmental impacts and traditional technological and subsistence practices. Our project at Huaca Prieta worked in a similar way by consulting with local fishers who still use the one-person reed raft (*caballito*) to fish offshore, elderly women who still grow reeds to make mats for flooring and for the side walls of houses, farmers who still farm small plots in the wetlands to sustain traditional crops, hunters who still set up bamboo blinds in shallow lagoons to capture pelicans and other birds, and littoral families who rush with buckets and fish nets to capture fish stranded in shallow backwater lagoons by overnight storms. In short, many individuals in the study area still carry out various behaviors of a Preceramic-like lifeway, which need to be recorded and utilized by archaeologists before they disappear. This is what we have attempted to do. Some of the results are presented throughout this volume, which focuses almost exclusively on the Preceramic use of the sites under study. Data recovered for the later ceramic periods will be published in a later volume.

THE NATURAL AND DEMOGRAPHIC SETTING

Huaca Prieta and Paredones are situated on a terrace platform 2.5 km long. The terrace is a freestanding remnant of the once much larger Sangamon terrace dating back to the Pleistocene period (see chapter 5 and appendix 1). The terrace contains a record of long-term human settlement defined most conspicuously by five large mounds, called the El Brujo Complex, dating from the long Preceramic period to the colonial era, and by extensive domestic and burial areas. It represents one of the largest spatially contiguous (if not largest by volume) collections of diverse mounded architecture in Peru. Other, spatially discrete mounds surround the terrace on the nearby floodplain of the lower Chicama Valley.

Huaca Prieta is situated on the southern tip of the terrace, where it overlooks the ocean immediately to the west (Dillehay et al. 2012b). The Paredones site is located at the eastern edge of the terrace overlooking an old lagoon setting. Here the floodplain is wide and the old riverbed follows an alluvial depositional regime with gravel and sediments laid down since the beginning of the early Holocene, forming the valley fill (see chapter 5). Through time, the river has meandered less, with the final premodern regime characterized by a braided pattern that appeared about 1000 years ago. With the transition to this pattern, the river migrated to the southern side of the valley, where it is located today. Its course is impounded between the sandy bluffs of Cerro Campana on the south and former meander belts and old lagoons on the north. Farther north, these wetlands depend on groundwater instead of the river and dominate the area between the coast and the nearby Andean foothills. The foothills and lower cordillera to the east consisted of desert, arid grasslands, upland dry forests, and semihumid montane forest above 1800 m above sea level (masl) (see chapters 4–5).

Yet the study of Huaca Prieta and Paredones cannot be contained within the boundaries of the physical site settings themselves. In defining the reasons for site locations and functions, they are not entirely the result of natural features along the coast. Huaca Prieta was placed in relation to other sites in much the same way that these sites were probably positioned in relation to each other. For instance, our opportunistic archaeological survey in the lower Chicama Valley indicates that stylistically similar artifacts found at Huaca Prieta and Paredones have a much larger range and are also found at several Preceramic household sites located along the full length of the terrace and on low, littoral dune formations as far as 25 km to the north near the town of Malabrigo (several km to the south near Cerro Campana) and at least 3–4 km inland (fig. 1.1). Radiocarbon dating and diagnostic artifacts show that most of these sites were in use during the same periods as Huaca Prieta and Paredones (see chapter 6).

These outlying domestic sites are associated with individual wetlands in the lower valley and along the coastline, which suggests that the Preceramic littoral society contained subdivisions, perhaps small, at least spatially and probably socially segmented residential communities that were economically specialized. Within these subdivisions, clusters of house mounds and burials within these communities appear to represent even smaller social groupings. The spacing of these sites across the landscape in relation to certain topographical features (such as wetlands and dune formations) and to Huaca Prieta and Paredones also suggests ideas about subsistence practices and about connections with their surrounding natural world.

Furthermore, the data from the mound and domestic sites indicate that the population of the Chicama coast and surrounding region grew throughout the Preceramic period. Growth was likely the result of both natural increase and immigration, as perhaps suggested by the increased presence of offerings of diverse exotic items and foods at Paredones and especially Huaca Prieta, which might represent pilgrimages to the area and/or contacts with outsiders via exchange networks. A response to this growth may have been changing worldviews to bring about greater social integration as expressed in the construction and continued expansion of the mounds and the appearance of symbolic artwork on textiles, gourds, sculpted polychaete tubes, and painted stones as well as the thousands of small, circumscribed individual rituals performed at Huaca Prieta over a period of more than 4000 years.

THE MOUNDS AND THEIR SOCIAL SETTING

Opinions are divided about what early mound architecture may indicate about past societies in the Andes (see Burger and Salazar 2012). Several explanations can be proposed for the commencement of mound building in the littoral and inland coastal regions of Peru during the late Preceramic period between 5200 and 4500 cal BP. There is a general consensus that this phenomenon reflects the emergence of early coastal economic strategies focused on both food crops and marine resources with concomitant changes in population sizes, demography, settlement, and mobility patterns. Some archaeologists have argued that these shifts were the result of complex, long-term interactions between environmental changes and associated social responses by early coastal societies

(for example, Moseley 1992). Others theorize that mound building was a component of a political economic system that resulted from the actions of a few aggrandizing individuals or groups regulating resources and controlling labor (for example, Haas and Creamer 2012). In this sense, mound size and form are suggested as relative indicators of social power, with larger mounds generally representing people that are more powerful. These and other opinions are dubious in the setting of this study because there are no archaeological indicators of elite housing, accumulation of wealth and status items, and burials associated with Huaca Prieta and Paredones, which would be expected if formal leaders and powerful persons or groups existed. As discussed later, no formal leadership and authority, even if ephemeral, appears to have been necessary to coordinate the scattered, diverse social groups that built and used them at these two sites. Based on the stratigraphy and on highly circumscribed activity areas, most ritual and other events at these sites involved very few people. Also, no hard evidence suggests the existence of large-scale, formally organized public ceremonies or even expansive public spaces.

Although these and other opinions are important for identifying the social, economic, and environmental conditions involved in early mound building, they deal with variables that only involve part of the archaeological record and thus are not a focus of this study. We require an understanding of the Huaca Prieta and Paredones sites beyond their socioeconomic and techno-environmental features, entailing a new paradigm that considers the possible ways in which people viewed and made up their social and physical worlds (for example, Ingold 2000; Lathrap 1984). In addition to socioeconomic power, some architectural and other material expressions are thought to represent ontological knowledge and practice, such as excessively high contents of charcoal from ritual fires and salt crystals derived from deliberately pouring large amounts of saltwater on the mound. This suggests that the opposing forces of fire and water played important roles in formulating the cosmological and ideological foundations of the Huaca Prieta society and that some rituals and decisions were perhaps created by divine or special groups. We thus consider the inferred material and ontological contexts for the mounds at these two sites. The ontological contexts are believed to be more specifically related to themes of deliberate fragmentation and burning of nearly all material culture (such as cutting, tearing, smashing, and breaking things) and the presence of the charcoal and salt at Huaca Prieta. Hence this stance approaches mound building from the perspective that the architecture was a shared icon to the regional population, which was configured within a system of meanings that had deep history in the spatial patterning of social organization, ancestors, and cosmology. This system must have worked both consciously and unconsciously to integrate local social or kin groups from multiple places and backgrounds in the Chicama Valley with their natural or nonhuman world but also with other peoples from the distant Andean mountains to the east and probably from the tropical lowlands farther north and also to the east (Dillehay et al. 2012b).

Although the majority of the early cultigens at Huaca Prieta and Paredones came from distant regions, the cultural origins of these sites are clearly based along the Pacific littoral of South America. For instance, the maritime economic tradition and the pebble tool industry at the site are defined as early as 13,000 cal BP at several coastal localities extending from southern Ecuador to central Chile (Sandweiss 2014). Some cultural elements such as the technologies of gourd decoration and cotton weaving at Paredones and Huaca Prieta, respectively, seem to have spread to later Preceramic monumental sites of the interior valleys on the north and central coasts of Peru (Caral, Aspero, and others; see Haas and Creamer 2012; Shady S. 2004; Williams 1985). Some of the geometric designs appearing on textiles and gourds from Huaca Prieta, dated between ~6000 and 4000 cal BP, are somewhat reminiscent of those depicted on 5000-year-old ceramics at Valdivia sites located farther north in south coastal Ecuador (see Bischof 1999) and 4000- to 3000-year-old textiles and ceramics at early Formative period sites of coastal Peru (Bird et al. 1985; see chapter 12). Between ~4500 and 4000 cal BP, shared architectural features in the form of entry ramps and sunken circular plazas or forecourts are evidenced between Huaca Prieta and the later Preceramic sites of the coastal interior. The majority of these interior sites, however, have

few or no visual arts, no painting, and no carving such as that seen on the textiles, gourds, stones, and polychaete blocks at Huaca Prieta. Moreover, the mixture of exotic cultigens adopted at Huaca Prieta and Paredones throughout the Holocene period are typical of many of these later coastal sites and also of most early Formative sites located on the north and central coasts of Peru and on the western slopes of the Central Andes (Dillehay and Piperno 2014). These later sites, however, seem not to have the same diversity and abundance of cultigens documented at Huaca Prieta and Paredones. In short, prior to ~4500 cal BP, Huaca Prieta and Paredones were quantitatively and qualitatively different from the interior coastal sites and from anything else in the Andes before them. More research is required to gain a better understanding of the historical and cultural relationships between the interior coastal sites and littoral sites such as Huaca Prieta and Paredones. One suggestion has been that littoral sites may have been "coastal [littoral] satellite villages to monumental inland [coastal] sites" (Pringle 2001), providing marine foods in return for cotton and other inland products, but no hard evidence supports this interpretation. Besides, cotton and most other food crops can be grown close to the littoral, as they are today, depending on soil conditions. At present we can only surmise that the late Preceramic littoral and coastal sites were linked not only through economic exchange networks but through a wider religious if not ontological system of beliefs and ritual practices. The term "ritual" in this study means "a sequence of activities involving gestures, words, and objects, performed in a sequestered place [such as the early mound sites discussed here], and performed according to a set sequence" (Bell 1997: 138–139). (See chapter 6 for definitions of the archaeological indicators of rituals, nonritual or commensal feasting, and domestic food consumption.)

In this book we propose a different, if not new, historical model of the development of the lower Chicama Valley and the north Peruvian coast. Though speculative at times, it uses both archaeological and analogical data to suggest a context of social, economic, and ontological practices based primarily on cooperation and deliberation. Occasionally drawing on ethnographic analogs (Descola and Pálsson 1996; Geertz 1973; Viveiros de Castro

1998), we develop the thesis that the ontology, social organization, and economy of the Huaca Prieta area were designed to balance natural and social forces (of which human action was a component), as opposed to aggrandizing an elite component of society. In this view the Huaca Prieta and Paredones society was fundamentally a vehicle for both the ontological and economic management of its social and natural worlds. Competition and the accumulation of individual power possibly happened, but the society was structured to achieve balance and harmony. Our approach allows for the permanent presence of a few powerful individuals, although individualism was probably tempered by group-oriented structures and practices. This perspective requires an understanding of Huaca Prieta and Paredones not as representative of an individual family, site, or group, a measure of social control, or the manipulation of a corporate labor force. Rather, we argue that these sites were components of special places embedded in a transgenerational ontological system that facilitated social and economic integration and, when possible, environmental harmony and a congruent built landscape. As discussed in the following chapters, the archaeological record of these sites reflects a stable coexistence of interdependent specialized maritime foraging, wetland foraging, and farming groups in the lower valley, most likely around a segmented kinship system perhaps composed of at least two different social groups that provided the structure for local social and economic life. This supposition is strongly supported by the material record of textiles, basketry, gourds, foods, and other assemblages, all of which point to at least two different yet complementary operating technologies as well as symbolic and economic systems.

The idea of the Pacific littoral and the adjacent desert coastal plains of Peru as nodes of early Andean civilization was at one time considered odd and challenging. As stated earlier, the region does not fit within global stereotypes of Neolithic society and emergent civilization. Many of the expected features of this society, such as pottery, elaborate houses, storage facilities, and incipient craft production, were not present at the time when the permanent maritime and farming communities described here developed in the lower Chicama Valley. This society had no writing systems and provides no clear evidence of elites, hierarchy, leadership, social ranking, and other expected characteristics of an emerging civilization. Although Huaca Prieta and the other sites under study here do not conform to these traditional expectations of early social complexity, our research shows that the study area is one of several probable geocultural facets of an Andean prism of independent complex development. Other Preceramic nodes (sites with similar or dissimilar types of archaeological evidence) occur elsewhere in various coastal and highland settings of the Andes.

ORGANIZATION OF THE BOOK

Chapter 2 presents the theoretical background employed to explain the data and patterns. Chapter 3 describes the research design and methods at sites and the history of research at Huaca Prieta and provides general background materials related to the nature of the sites and their wider relevance. Chapter 4 focuses on the paleoenvironmental study of the project. Although prior work has emphasized the mound at Huaca Prieta, little attention has been devoted to the landscape and modification beneath and around it. Chapter 5 presents the geology of the lower valley. Chapter 6 discusses the results of the chronology and radiocarbon dates from sites. Chapter 7 describes the fieldwork done at Huaca Prieta, Paredones, and the outlying sites. Earlier scholars have only used radiocarbon dates for a general understanding of the chronology of the mound. Here we consider temporal and functional implications of stratigraphic relationships. Chapters 8 through 12 analyze the material records from sites, including the architecture and spatial patterns, floral, faunal, lithic, textiles, basketry, and others. These data provide essential grounding for models of how and possibly why the sites were built and used and how they are interrelated. Chapter 13 discusses the settlement pattern of outlying domestic sites and their possible relations to Huaca Prieta and Paredones.

Using the concepts and data presented in chapters 1 to 13, chapter 14 presents an empirical model of mound construction. The model supports a long, multistage construction chronology.

This chapter also provides a synthetic model of the sites on the Sangamon terrace describing a history of the social and economic developments centered on the sites. Chapter 15 explains these data in relation to the theoretical framework of the organizational structure laid out in chapters 1 and 2. Each of the nineteen appendices at the end of the book focuses on a specific database, ranging from the results of ground-penetrating radar to burned wood studies to starch grain and isotope analyses.

Finally, as mentioned in the preface, we significantly reduced the book length and the number of figures and tables due to contractual limits. Most such reductions were made in chapters report-ing on the material culture and floral and faunal remains. This resulted in brief analyses of certain databases, such as artifact description, inventory, and provenience data: specifically, highly detailed quantitative studies of lithic, wood, gourd, shell, and bone materials. A more in-depth Bayesian analysis of the numerous radiocarbon dates from the project also was not possible. More detailed reports on these aspects of the project are planned for the future. As a result, we have placed additional textual, photographic, and statistical information online at https://my.vanderbilt.edu /huacaprieta/.

CHAPTER 2

FOUNDATIONAL UNDERSTANDINGS

Tom D. Dillehay

INTRODUCTION

What gave rise to the long histories at Huaca Prieta and Paredones and what brought about continuities and changes within them? At a more theoretical level these questions pose a challenge: how to integrate these sites into areal and sub-regional narratives in the Central Andes. Recent theoretical approaches such as centers of origins/core areas, interaction spheres, and polycentric and core-periphery models do not provide satisfactory insights into the late Preceramic world of these sites, where various socioeconomic interactions, acculturation, and demic diffusion were all active at different temporal and spatial scales. An alternative approach, a different paradigm for the study area, is needed to identify the specific socio-ecological contexts of intergroup and intragroup interactions. This approach focuses primarily on the nature of economic, social, and settlement organization and the introduction of exotic goods (such as cultigens) and stylistic designs as socially situated processes related to the integration of groups. We also give special consideration to the ontological implications of this organization and process and the legacy of Huaca Prieta and Paredones in Andean cultural history.

The diversity and complexity of the Preceramic period in coastal Peru bring into question a number of concepts that have dominated current interpretations of early complex societies in the Central Andes. The late Preceramic period has been broadly defined as a supraregional network of contacts focusing on the procurement and circulation of raw materials and on sociopolitical/ritual interaction among rising ceremonial centers (for example, Kaulicke 2010; Lumbreras 1972; Moseley 1992). Unfortunately, very few excavated sites have provided the sampling diversity and resolution of datasets that are required for a plausible reconstruction of the social structure, economic practices, spatiotemporal transformations, and diverse local manifestations of the late Preceramic period, so we are often left with more guesswork than data-supported interpretations. That is, except for a few ideas about architectural features (such as sunken circular plazas and platform mounds), we have few hard data to support the proposition that outward similarities in economic and ceremonial practices translated into effective social, economic, political, and ideological interregional linkages. The apparent movement of people, material culture and ideas, and architectural styles of the period suggests contacts among different communities and areas. We have no hard or circumstantial evidence, however, to support centralized political networks or elite ruling groups controlling this movement on either a regional or interregional level. In the absence of formal political entities such as polities, I believe that the material, social, and symbolic resources available to most Preceramic societies were mobilized primarily across local and regional boundaries in response to specific socioeconomic activities whose overriding concern was the maintenance of cohesion and the reproduction of individual communities and their kinship and household group identities. This is expected during a period that saw major restructurings of worldviews and of economic and social relations along the Pacific coast. At this time many of the constituent elements of early food-producing societies were gradually established in diverse environmental settings and ecological contexts (Dillehay 2011b; Sandweiss 2014).

The central position given to the formation of Preceramic coastal communities in Peru is borne out by the role reserved for material culture. It appears that cotton textiles and nets at Huaca Prieta, for example, were not focused primarily (or solely) on domestic clothing and fishing, respectively, in a strict sense (see chapter 12). Instead they likely formed active ingredients in rituals directly associated with the definition of transgenerational kin/community group identities. A similar argument also can be made for the prominent role of decorated gourds in social exchange in the context of consolidating local kinship-based relations. With regard to

the circulation of more utilitarian objects, such as exotic seafood and cultigens, a strong case can be made that these were items of an organized interregional exchange network (see chapter 10 and appendix 4). It seems likely that such material items were invested with multiple layers of local domestic and nondomestic meanings, kinship relations, and acts of individual groups that formed the fabric of rituals and ontologies of origin embraced by local communities, which could have been shared within and between different coastal and inland areas. Such a perception views Preceramic exchange as a social reality that, in the words of Maurice Godelier (1999: 40), probably "combined many aspects of social practice and numerous institutions characteristic of the society," thus enabling "the society to represent itself (to others and to itself) as a whole."

Another point is the economic basis of the coastal Preceramic societies. We know something about foods and their attendant ritual and feasting domains during this period (see Hastorf and Johannessen 2009; Pearsall 2015), but very little about the social contexts in which foodstuffs were produced, processed, consumed, circulated, and valued. Seeds and marine shells have often been used in the quest to identify areas of origins and centers of cultural ascendancy in the process of gaining social complexity (Piperno 2011b; Sandweiss 2014). Less pragmatic research has been dedicated to the social impacts of changes in food procurement and production strategies, especially with regard to any restructuring of the management of marine and land resources and household and kin relations. In addition, once we move away from the level of the individual site, where recording contextual association is less feasible, the resolution of the archaeological record becomes too coarse to allow us to engage fully in broad-scale intersite explanations. Once again, too few Preceramic sites have been well excavated and their remains studied and published in detail.

Thus a major purpose of this volume is to reconstruct and explain the maritime and terrestrial subsistence and settlement patterns of the Huaca Prieta area. Three primary questions guide this research. How and why did the human landscape change through time? To what extent were subsistence, settlement, social, and mortuary patterns shaped by a changing human population and economic specialization and by cooperation and/or by competition over resources? What economic, social, and other factors (for example, ontological) can account for the early emergence of mound building, social complexity, and a mixed economy of maritime and wetland foraging, farming, and possibly low-level animal husbandry in the study area?

COMPLEXITY

Terms such as "complex foragers" (marine or terrestrial) have been based in large part on indicators of sedentism, higher population density, intensive exploitation of local resources including cultigens, incipient social differentiation and complementary organizational components, and the development of symbols to express ideological concerns. Recent research reveals that forager behavior is not simply a product of adaptations to specific natural environments but also a response to elements of sociopolitical strategies and intergroup social relations (for example, Kuijt 2012; Russo 2009; Sassaman and Anderson 1996). Foraging mobility, which is viewed as an adaptive strategy that evens out spatial resource variability, is also seen as a social strategy aimed at accessing regional information and maintaining social networks (Gamble 2013). Mound building by complex foragers, including some practicing farming, can be viewed as either egalitarian or nonegalitarian projects that integrated groups, enhanced group identity, and/or ritually and spatially separated groups from the outside world (for example, Milner 2005; Sassaman 2008). That is, mound building was essential for the creation of a sense of community among dispersed foragers who were incorporating crops and needing a permanent place to integrate. Studies also suggest that some foragers actively reproduced and transformed their own histories through daily and commemorative acts at monuments (Thomas 2014). Such monuments often served communities for many generations as the burial places of founding ancestors and as a continuing focus for public ritual beyond the household and community levels. These ideas thus identify complex forager behaviors not simply as responses to the natural environment but also as strategic choices in which intersocietal relations are critical variables.

A starting point of social complexity may be the intensification of alliance relationships, increased levels of organization and social obligation, surpluses for ceremonial activities, including feasting, and monument building (compare Bender 1978; Dietler 2001; Hayden 2001; Trigger 1990). Other options may result from competition among aspiring elites, information management, control over non-kin labor, political competition, demographic pressure and environmental stress, and increased reliance on plant or other foods (compare Ames 1985; Fitzhugh 2003; Hayden 2001; Pearsall 2003), including marine resources (Kidder and Sassaman 2009; Randall and Sassaman 2010).

The Central Andes is one of the few areas of the world where social complexity and the initial pulses toward independent civilization developed early, between at least 7500 and 5000 cal BP (for example, Dillehay 2004; Moore 2014; Moseley 1992). A major aspect of this development was complementary foraging and sedentism, which allowed societies simultaneously to maximize the exploitation of multiple and closely juxtaposed maritime, inland, and/or highland resource zones and to aggregate socially in certain favorable places. Within a millennium or two of the first domestication of plants and animals, between ~11,000 and 8000 cal BP, some people lived in sedentary communities that derived food from various combinations of farming, animal, and/or marine resources. Once these and other combinations appeared, significant social and cultural changes ensued. These changes manifested themselves in different ways from one part of the Andes to another, but several cross-cultural convergences suggest that similar processes occurred in different places and that sedentary strategies eventually were incorporated within mobile foraging ones (and vice versa) to lead to more complex and complementary societies (Núñez and Nielsen 2012; Dillehay et al. 2004). One area where this complementarity occurred was at Real Alto and other Valdivia sites on the south coast of Ecuador and at Huaca Prieta, Alto Salaverry, La Paloma, Chilca, Asia, and other sites in north to central coastal Peru. Increased social complexity at these and other sites is indicated by domestic structures, by specialized edifices such as low mounds or platforms, and occasionally by elaborate craft objects (such as clay figurines, gourds, and textiles). After ~4500 cal BP specialized mounds or monumental buildings became increasingly large and sophisticated like those at the sites of Caral, Aspero, Piedra Parada, Las Haldas, Bandurria, Salinas de Chao, Ventarón, El Paraíso, and Buena Vista (for example, Benfer 2012; Engel 1966a; Fung Pineda 1969). Such edifices indicate to many archaeologists a hierarchical social structure, intensified economies, specialization within a system of exchange and redistribution of goods, status, privilege, community-level power, and, when present, human burial patterns indicative of increased social differentiation.

In particular reference to the late Preceramic monuments of coastal Peru (~4500 cal BP) mentioned above, they were partially designed to divide, separate, and elevate above other physical positions and to host special, probably public activities within communities. Most striking is the scarcity of convincing archaeological evidence at these locales to suggest the rise of individual elites and leadership in the form of elaborate housing and burials and the accumulation of individual (or even group) wealth and prestige goods. These came later at larger, more complex, planned town and preurban sites during the terminal Preceramic and the following early Formative period (~4500–3500 cal BP). In the mixed maritime/horticultural foraging communities of the preceding middle Preceramic period (~8000–4500 cal BP) on the Peruvian littoral and arid coastal plains, it is apparent that diverse paths were taken to social complexity and to various scales of interaction between different types of communities with distinct economic combinations and community and burial patterns. Sites like Huaca Prieta and Paredones represent at least one, if not two, of these different paths. It is apparent at these sites that individual or small-group leadership and wealth accumulation were not yet developed or at least manifested materially. It also is apparent, as mentioned in chapter 1, that traditional models of early monumentality and emergent complex society in the Andes do not work to explain the rise and development of sites like Huaca Prieta and Paredones. Other models must be sought, which is one of the goals of this study.

Although no uniform method of human burial apparently was used during the middle to late Pre-ceramic period, attention was paid to the positioning of the body and to the objects left with it. Ornamental objects adorn burials at Preceramic sites like Chilca, La Paloma, Asia, Huaca Prieta, Bandurria, and others. Representational artwork was expressed occasionally: for example, clay figurines at Aspero and Caral and geometric designs on cotton textiles and carved gourds at Huaca Prieta. Whatever their meaning, these and other objects suggest increased attempts to understand, categorize, control, and reproduce the natural and social surroundings and, along with burial patterns, to express self-identity and other identities. Although concepts of afterlives, the control of death, and possibly ancestor worship may be implied in these patterns, little clear evidence suggests the employment of mortuary patterns to display social ranking and leadership. Particularly important, however, is the Chinchorro tradition in southern Peru and mainly northern Chile (Arriaza et al. 2008), which dates between ~7500 and 3500 cal BP and is associated with a maritime economy, separate burial places for the dead, and extraordinary funerary practices focused on mummification of the dead. Collectively, the particulars of early burial practices at Chinchorro and other sites (such as La Paloma) suggest that these early communities created new social and ancestral geographies along the Central Andean coast through the construction of structured settlements and integrative mortuaries.

The relationship between burial practices and social differentiation is complex, however (O'Shea 1984). The disposition of the dead not only is the outcome of the social identity and personhood of the dead but may also reflect the social aspirations of kin or religious/ideological proscription. From the perspective of ritual process, the remains found in a burial need to be viewed as the material traces of a long and sometimes incomplete process in which a once-living person is transformed to a "safe" dead person or ancestor (Bloch and Parry 1982; Hertz 1960). Ethnographic studies are clear in illustrating how manipulating the dead can be a powerful means of negotiating identities and that burials are not merely passive reflections of social order, especially in special places like mounds and monuments, but also community and cross-generational histories (see chapter 15).

Finally, one of the most difficult and important

challenges facing Andeanists is the task of disentangling past human responses to changes in both physical and social environments. Geoclimatic processes can occur serially and may generate potentially challenging changes in the landscape as well as induce transformations in the socioeconomic organization of both past and present human populations. Documenting the frequency, duration, and severity of such impacts is important to our understanding of the long-term dynamics of the interaction between social and natural systems in the study area. Equally important is understanding the changing material culture of the social system and what it implies about social, economic, and ontological dynamics over several millennia within the local environment.

SOCIO-ECOSYSTEMS

Our research is broadly situated within the field of human ecodynamics (Kirch 2005; McGlade 1995; Redman 2005), in which archaeology plays a key role by providing data on the long-term development of human socio-ecosystems. With Christopher Barton ct al. (2004: 254), we view human society as "constantly reshaping the intertwined cultural and natural components of the socio-ecological landscape on which its members and their descendants must operate." Here we are interested in these components and how they materially manifested their place in the environment and in positioning the lower Chicama Valley within a wide range of human and environment interactions that characterize the Preceramic period.

Space and time are key attributes in this approach, since people reacted in relation to the microenvironments available, none of which were static. Space is primarily related to economic intensification: human labor may be traded for spatial efficiency, resulting in changes in mobility as well as increases in the intensity and duration of occupation (Richerson et al. 2001). For example, increase the amount of work undertaken at a single location and more people can be sustained without the need to move to new places. This is especially important in resource-rich areas like the littoral of Peru, which has some of the highest and most diverse marine life in the world. Time is also significant, because measuring economic intensi-

fication and occupation intensity depends on estimates of the duration of site use. Understanding the relationships between space and time requires the evaluation of separate lines of evidence. In the Central Andes, for example, where public buildings make an early appearance, it is not their presence alone that indicates permanent settlement but the combination of the stratigraphic character, structures, economic practices, and the material culture that they contain. The investment in nonportable site furniture and the nature of trash disposal also imply the degree of site use and permanency, as human groups may be quasi-mobile yet create structures that long outlast the duration of a single occupation.

Turning to another topic related to ecosystems, given the rich floral and faunal database of our project, we feel compelled to comment on a popular approach in foraging studies, which we do not apply here. Over the past few decades several optimal foraging strategy and human behavioral ecology models have been applied to complex hunter-gatherer societies, with mixed success. These models have attempted to predict dietary and land-use patterns of hunter-gatherers (for example, Hawkes and O'Connell 1981; Winterhalder and Kennett 2006). We agree with the basic assumptions of these models that foragers operate to maximize the overall rate of energetic return. But we have several problems with the empirical analysis of these models for our study area. First, they are established primarily for domestic sites not for ritual, specialized food production/preparation areas, and burial localities like Huaca Prieta and Paredones. Second, these models pertain to terrestrial not marine and mixed foraging and farming practices. There is also the matter of economic specialization and exchange, which can present different figures on return rates, patch choices, and other variables linked to procurement strategies. Collecting and applying data for these approaches is also highly subjective. Given these nonconformities, uncertainties, and subjectivities, we prefer to estimate what percentage of the diet for each cultural phase at each site is given to marine, farming, and wetland foraging.

In summary, one goal of this study is to understand the interactions between Preceramic human populations and the coastal environments that allowed the local socio-ecosystem to develop substantial resilience, as evidenced by the continued presence of humans in the area over fourteen millennia. This does not necessarily imply that these systems never experienced occasional states of instability and vulnerability, however. Both archaeological and paleoecological evidence are used to understand these interactions and to define the material history and meaning of human adaptive responses, including development of specific settlement-subsistence regimes and of sociopolitical and ideological systems (for example, mortuary ritual) that were essential to resilience in this area. In this regard, we expand the socio-ecosystemic approach to consider the symbolic and ontological implications of materiality.

MATERIAL CULTURE AND MEANING

In recent years the interplay between structure and agency within human networks has given more attention to the relationships among culture, society, and nature (for example, Boivin 2008; Tilley and Bennett 2004). This interplay has been examined from different paradigmatic approaches. More concern especially has been given to relationships between social constructionism and postmodernism on the one hand and realism and scientific objectivism on the other. These relationships were brought to the forefront by cultural studies (Foucault 1972: compare Lakoff and Johnson 2003). These studies questioned the true knowledge gained about the natural world, however, when nearly everything in it is semiotically (for example, Preucel 2010) and thus socially "constructed" through languages, signs, and symbols, which are arbitrary and fleeting (Shanks and Tilley 1992).

In turn, this premise has been questioned over the past decade. Michel Foucault, in particular, made a significant contribution when he reconsidered the conceptual distinction between the physical world and that of humans (see Latour and Porter 1993: compare Descola 2005) and between culture and nature. He and others began to shift an epistemological question—how can we get to the truth and what is the truth?—to an ontological one—how do knowledge and understanding come about and how and why do people perceive them the way they do? How is this knowledge used and what does it mean? This shift entailed a

concern not just with ideas, signs, symbols, and meanings but with knowledge as a physical, circulating and conflicting process, especially in regard to cultural materialism. Largely as a result of this shift, practice, network, and interaction theories developed in the social sciences (Latour 1999) and in archaeology to study the meaning and movement of people and things, to identify social, technological, and ideological knowledge, and to analyze how these were constructed and negotiated to bring about change in both the social and natural worlds.

Influenced by these and other approaches, especially cultural materialism, archaeologists began to view material objects as meaningfully constructed, as symbols and semiotics, manipulated by social actors to attain certain ends, such as acquiring or legitimating status, contesting power, marking an ethnic identity, negotiating identity, and establishing a society's ontology (Hodder 1982: 85–86; Preucel 2010). Material culture thus was viewed as a reflection of various aspects of society. Yet it was also realized that there is more to material culture and the nature of things than meaning, reflection, symbolism, and semiotics (Jones 2005). Material culture also "transforms, rather than reflects, social organization according to the strategies of groups, their beliefs, concepts and ideologies" (Hodder 1982: 212). And material culture serves along with social actions to establish adaptive cycles and resilience within society (Redman 2005).

As a result of these approaches, cultural materialism in anthropology and, by extension, archaeology has recently become more antiessentialist, relational, and interactional in understanding the intertwined social and physical worlds (Latour 2004). Culture/nature and the human/nonhuman are things perceived to represent a continuum rather than a rupture from one world to another—they represent a single commingled world. Appreciating the human/nonhuman as lying on a continuum goes beyond just stating that both are implicated in knowing and conceptualizing the world. The continuum also involves worldviews or ontologies and how these affect and are affected by social relations and people's relations with the natural world. For instance, in most Amerindian ontologies, animals, plants, mountains, and rivers are perceived as social actors as much as humans and treated in equal terms (Boddy and

Lambek 2013). Although archaeologists acknowledge the role of nonhumans in constituting culture, they seldom take nonhuman "things" into account. Archaeologists tend to see these as passive resources, economic elements, indicators of past climate and environment, techno-facts, eco-facts, and so forth. That is, archaeologists are less "devoted to how societies and cultures are constructed and to analyze the real building material . . . involved in their construction . . . [they] should pay more attention to the material agents that constitute the very condition of possibility for those features we associate with social order, structural durability and power" (Olsen 2010: 5).

Though archaeologists speak of institutions, social relations, power, technologies, roles, and situations, these are not just entities created only by humans. They are interactive entities composed of things and different elements. This implies that to describe a social structure, a thing, a basket, or a mound, we cannot exclude the exploitation of resources by society members; the extraction, use, manipulation, and interaction with raw materials; the weight of a monument on the landscape; and how its placement enhances or interrupts the flow of natural organisms in that specific locale. One goal of interaction theory in archaeology has been to bridge the gap between aspects of the "human" and the "natural" worlds. Yet, despite this recent understanding, archaeology still heavily privileges the human side of things. Biology and nature are usually relevant insofar as they have an effect on the environment, economy, and technology. Saying that "interaction" and "practice" theories, for instance, encompass the physical environment is fine, but it still does not suggest how the gap between nature and culture can be bridged to form a continuum. The precise interplay between, on the one hand, processes within the local environment and, on the other hand, interpersonal and institutional relations between humans and how humans view and utilize these relations—aspects of ontology—remains underconsidered by archaeologists.

A value of considering an ontological relationship among humans, the environment, and archaeological things is that it attempts to give equal emphasis to the mutually affecting, intertwined human, material, and natural world. Although archaeology cannot approach all aspects of a society's ontology, it can attempt to explain the context of material things and the possible relationships and meanings between them within both the human and natural world. This is a major goal of this study.

ONTOLOGY AND MATERIALITY

Ontology generally posits a conceptual framework upon which all sociocultural possibilities and fabrics of being are predicated (compare Descola 2005; Harris and Robb 2012; Kockelman 2014). As a branch of philosophy, it also is considered to be the science of what is, of the kinds and structures of objects, properties, events, processes, and relations in every area of reality. It concerns how sociocultural knowledge and understanding of the physical and social worlds come about, how and why people perceived them the way they do, how this knowledge is used and what it means, and, for our purpose, why and possibly how it was materialized. Within this understanding, social scientists (for example, Descola 2005; Kockelman 2014; Latour 2004; Viveiros de Castro 1998) have analyzed the ways in which social configurations produced different sets of relationships, cultural logics, material worlds, and ontologies.

The specific use of ontology here more closely fits Paul Kockelman's (2014: 3) definition: views of existence in the world that are "ensembles of assumptions regarding the underlying constitution of, or salient, patterns in the world." He sees ontologies acting as "sieves" through which information flows, with some details sifted out and others allowed through. His framework provides a theorized account of the rootedness of meaning as it emerges in interactions (among human or other agents) against the backdrop of infrastructures, institutions, and cultural materialism—the relatively unrecognized semiotic contexts that make more foregrounded meanings possible.

The relationship between ontology and materiality is especially important because what things are—in practical and cultural terms—has pragmatic consequences that affect their social function and meaning. Ontological understandings can also affect the types of social relations and the interplay between structure and agency. At Huaca Prieta, for instance, our ontological understanding of materials and things (such as sediment, stone, and artifacts) contained in the mound is not just an epiphenomenal problem; it addresses various aspects of the foundations and meaning of the society itself. The archaeological record of things at Huaca Prieta (and Paredones) reflects a society intensively interacting with various natural elements in the local environment over several millennia, which implies that many different things must have been interacting with various peoples that had different meanings and ontologies rooted in these interactions.

As people's varying ontologies sifted out some things and allowed others through, things could have become other objects and had diverse functions and meanings for different individuals, different segments within the society, and different societies over time. From one perspective, an ontological approach to these things attempts to "decenter" them to various possible practices, meanings, and outcomes (Law 2008; compare Law and Mol 2002; Mol 2002). That is, things or objects do not always exist in and of themselves but also through multiple situated practices that are constructed by humans and can have different meanings. In other words, the object can always be constituted, reconstituted, and enacted in relation to various other things and settings through local ontologies. Our description of the archaeological practices or enactments at sites thus is a description of the ontology of the possible multiple uses and meanings of an archaeological object, not just its perceived central or primary practice or meaning. For example, the mound at Huaca Prieta may have been initially built solely for ritual purposes associated with specific things, practices, and meanings. But the mound was later associated with the practices of both a ritual and mortuary place, which amplified its practices and meanings historically. That is, over a period of several millennia the internal spatial and stratigraphic record and the fragmented or whole material content of Huaca Prieta reflect thousands of recursive behavioral episodes, material depositions, and building and ritual moments, not all necessarily associated with the same practices and meanings. But these episodes must have been sieved through different or similar ontologies through time. Above all, they collectively formed a cohesive, coherent, and meaningful archaeological material record at the site.

FRAGMENTS, FRACTALS, AND MEANINGS

Different meanings and practices can be considered to represent differences or divided practices and meanings in the world of human subjects. In this world, both subjects and objects are split and categorized, heterogeneous and multiple. If subjects depend on webs of relations for their existence, so do material things or objects; and these webs consist of both humans and nonhumans. Subjects and objects are for the anthropologist John Law (2002) "fractional coherences," the state of being more than one but less than many or associated with more than one practice and meaning. Law believes that objects are simultaneously coherent and incoherent, single and multiple. In nature, the typical example of a fractal is the form of a coastline, which is broken up into many different forms (and uses by human social systems and natural ecosystems) but is also a unified biological and geographic entity. Although a broken or fractal coastline has many forms and practices and meanings associated with it, it is still a single, coherent object or thing. Through the idea of fractional coherence, Law follows the metaphor of the "bulletin board," which is a singular object that juxtaposes snippets or fragments of text and pictures without implying an obvious coherence or singularity. Yet the snippets hold together as sociocultural messages on the bulletin board.

In Law's model, fractional coherence is derived from fractals in biology, which views a fractal as a repetitive pattern, having multiple practices and possible meanings. Fractals are infinitely complex patterns that are self-similar across different scales. In other words, repeating a simple process over and over in an ongoing feedback loop creates and re-creates them. The idea is similarity, repetitive segmentation, or recursiveness. A thing or object does not need to exhibit *exactly* the same structure or practice at all scales, but the same "type" of structures and practices appear on all scales. A fractal thus is a thing that displays self-similarity on all scales. Fractal patterns with various degrees of self-similarity and scale have been studied in images, structures, and sounds and found in nature (Tan et al. 2009), technology (Hu et al. 2012), art (Eglash 1999), law (Stumpff 2013), and organizational structures. In fact nature is full of fractals: trees, rivers, coastlines, mountains, clouds, seashells, hurricanes, and so forth. Although the individual properties of these things are different, they also are structurally similar and the way they are differently perceived and filtered in and out of human society relates to ontologies.

Most organizational structures of human society are reproduced in a piecemeal, step-by-step recursive, diachronic fractal manner (*sensu* Law 1991). For example, fractal patterns have been found in the paintings of American artist Jackson Pollock. While Pollock's paintings appear to be composed of chaotic drippings and splatterings, computer analysis has found fractal patterns in them and in the paintings of Max Ernst (Ozhovan et al. 1993). Furthermore, cybernetist Ron Eglash (1999) has found fractal geometry and mathematics in African art, games, divination, trade, and architecture. Fractals and multiples also have been considered in different ways in archaeology and in fragmentation theory (Chapman 2000; Brown et al. 2005, especially as it relates to broken artifacts, repetitive settlement and urban patterns, and nonlinear and irregular spatial and material forms; Burkle-Elizondo and Valdez-Cepeda 2006).

As stated at the outset of chapter 1, similar patterns exist in the stratigraphy, structure, and material composition of the fragmented materials and segmented spaces of the Huaca Prieta archaeological record. Like Law's bulletin board, the site is composed of thousands of individual behavioral "snippets" inferred from thousands of individual stratigraphic layers, ritual spaces, and fragmented artifacts that are held together to characterize a single structurally and physically coherent place and archaeological site, most of which represent recursive step-by-step ritual actions over time resulting in similar behavioral deposits, some probably with different meanings. We presently do not know the precise principles of the ritual and socioeconomic organization that formed this record through time and gave it material cohesion, but some practice, guiding or "sieving" ontology, or cosmology must have influenced such similar or recursive forms cross-generationally over several thousand years.

In summary, both the social and natural worlds (and their material manifestations) are made of many different sorts of things that are brought into a complex fractal or fragmented alignment and coherence. One thing can recursively dissolve into many things that may have many uses and meanings or multiplicity. The world is defined by multiplicities, multiple distributions of subjects, and multiple distributions of objects throughout time and space—throughout history. These distributions accumulate and overlap in time and space just as they do in archaeological sites like Huaca Prieta. An object in a site (a textile or a mound, for instance) thus is not just a singular entity but a fractal or fragmented texture of partially coherent and partially coordinated enactments, some intentional and others unintentional. Sometimes they consolidate themselves to make coherences. And sometimes they do not.

OBJECTS AND ARCHAEOLOGY

Objects and their world are not always totally knowable; nor are our archaeological descriptions or reflections of the social and physical worlds. We do not always know the strategies of distribution and coordination required for multiple objects (like gourds, lithics, or mounds) to hold together, to be "more than one but less than many" (Law 2002: 3). Nor do we know when an object comes apart or is discarded because it is no longer useful or it breaks. What results archaeologically is a "mapping" of its life history, the taphonomy of the object, with all sorts of archaeologically constructed technical and social practices associated with it that collectively constitute its multiple diachronic functions and meanings. These functions, practices, and meanings often can be divided and multiplied—such as making a pottery vessel, gifting it, and smashing it during a ceremony.

An advantage of thinking in terms of fractional coherence for this archaeological study is that it is possible to consider social and/or material entities (such as monuments, lithics, food, and site boundaries) without implying any essence or necessity. The attempt is to follow the works, the practices, the meanings, and the life histories of human groups, material things, and symbols that enter into linking them to the intertwined social and physical world of the lower Chicama Valley. Whether we are dealing with the natural or the social world, objects or artifacts come into existence—and break, disappear, or are discarded—with the work and practices in which they were produced and used, thus (for our purposes) resulting in an archaeological site. A goal of the use of objects or things may have differed from one practice to another (for example, a gourd vessel could have been a storage container, a burial offering, or a drinking vessel), so the reality and use of the object can multiply. The human body, the object, the technology, the nonhuman, and other factors are all more than one individual entity. The important questions for the study of Huaca Prieta are how and why so many of the archaeological objects in them are deliberately fractional or fragmented pieces and contextually related, and why they are coherent and associated with repetitive ritual patterns. This returns us to the thousands of individual use floors, fills, and artifact fragments and thus behavioral episodes composing Huaca Prieta. What do these individual seemingly chaotic pieces and instances, all constituting a singular archaeological site or "bulletin board," mean? Even if some or all objects differed from one practice and one floor and ritual space to another, there were relations between these practices and spaces within the Preceramic coastal society and among the human actors and the physical things within it. Multiple objects in the site can and did fragment, thus creating multiplicities, or they came together somehow. Attending to the multiplicity of this reality opens up the study of their wider use, their practice, their meaning, and thus their ontology within the social and natural world of the lower Chicama Valley.

That is, objects were not just constructed, signified, used, and discarded by multiple practices; they also were enacted by those practices. For instance, despite any design and functional differences among various public monuments across a local landscape, they can be connected historically and culturally. We can argue that most people at the time of construction and use of a specific mound like Huaca Prieta would perhaps have possessed only vague, unmarked senses of what its mound signified. Yet there must have been a cross-generational or panregional transmission of ideas about the site and what it meant to people. Although the special knowledge about the functions and meanings of the mound would perhaps have been inhibited by any temporal and spatial gaps in its construction (albeit few exist at Huaca Prieta), given its place in the physical

world people still must have had an idea of what it meant and how to construct it. Local people in the Chicama Valley today know that the site has a special meaning, which they do not specifically know, and that it was built differently from other monuments in the area, as indicated by its dark appearance. Local shamans still periodically come to the site at night to carry out rituals associated with celestial legends. Recognition of the special place and meaning of ancient mounds also is true of the present-day Mapuche population in south-central Chile, which knows little about the meaning of *kuel* (artificial) mounds on their lands. In communities where these mounds still are used in public ceremony, however, shamans and ritual priests understand their history and meaning (Dillehay 2007, 2014). That is, the Mapuche know that a single mound is an accumulation of hundreds of ritual events and enactments through time and space that represent the past, present, and future. Although these mounds have been and in some areas still are in ritual use today, their form and place in public ceremony are transgenerational: their meaning relates to a deeply rooted ontology and oral tradition of historical interactions between people and sacred landscapes.

The ubiquity of mound building in the Central Andes was probably established in transgenerational mythologies and oral traditions by at least the early fourth millennium BP and has repeatedly been carried forward through time. If not, mounds or *huacas* would not be so consistent in form, place, and social and ideological meaning in the Andes. The specific meaning of a mound and its linkage to a particular group and place may have been forgotten through time. It may have become just a collective enterprise or memorial in society, but it still has a place in history and a physical presence on the landscape even though it may have become an "inalienable" or impersonal object to today's society (Weiner 1992; compare McAnany 1998; Kovacevich and Callaghan 2013) that now belongs to memory and to a collective history. (According to Annette Weiner [1992], what makes a possession inalienable is its exclusive and cumulative identity with a series of related users through time or across many generations, not just one generation. In this way inalienable possessions are transcendent things such as heirlooms that are kept and accumulate real or fictive biographies through time.) Even though inalienable objects like monuments and heirlooms may take on different meanings and social practices, they also can provide a sense of well-being, self-awareness, order, routine or repetition, orientation, tradition, and "ontological security." When a mound such as Huaca Prieta is repetitively built and used by multiple generations of users, most or all of whom built individual segmented spaces, performed rituals, and deposited broken or fragmented things within it, it too became a transcendent thing. It is an accumulation of the life histories of different generations and their material expressions in a single place. Its continued construction and use required memory, continuity of technology skills, and an operational sequence, repetitiveness, or routine across many generations. As Anthony Giddens (1991: 60–61) has noted: "Routine is integral . . . to the institutions of society, which are such only through their continuity. . . . [The continuity of mound-building can be explained as an attempt of keeping routines alive, which are linked to the making of the community.] It is precisely in these critical circumstances when routines are more necessary to maintain *ontological security*" (my emphasis).

FRACTIONAL COHERENCE, REPETITION, AND ACCUMULATION

John Chapman (2000: 32) has developed a routinized "narrative of social practices" within archaeological materiality by focusing on several interrelated principles ("fragmentation," "enchainment," inalienability," and "accumulation") that are useful to our attempt to explain the content and structure of the Huaca Prieta mound. Fragmentation is the intentional breakage or burning of objects before the end of their useful lives, the dispersal of these fragments, and their deliberate deposition rather than random discard. Most objects at Huaca Prieta are scored and snapped gourd fragments, deliberately cut and torn textile fragments, smashed stone tools, animal bones, shells and human bones, and so forth. That is, most of these objects were probably made or gathered for the specific purpose of being fragmented and deliberately interred (see chapters 11 and 12). Chapman argues that fragmentation is pervasive across all artifact categories, including human remains. Fragmentation plays a critical role in his notion of "enchainment," a process by which a linkage of social relations or enactments is repetitively constructed through the dispersal of "inalienable" items (*sensu* Weiner 1992) imbued with personal qualities. Accumulation involves the assembling of sets of inalienable objects that are relatively devoid of intimate individual or personal connotations. In following Chapman, the interplay between fragmentation and accumulation (via recursive practices in the same place or site) is a critical aspect of understanding the meaning of cultural and social change and the composition of many deliberately fragmented artifacts in archaeological sites, in this case Huaca Prieta.

Chapman also considers the transgenerational biographies of objects by revising Weiner's (1992) notion of inalienability. He connects it with his concept of enchainment, by which people are not autonomous individuals but are interconnected through the possession and use of material objects and the properties (such as raw materials) composing them. To Chapman, objects and human burials in sites are material things gathered from disparate places and different times, enchaining objects and people together across time and space in networks of cohesive reciprocal relationships and transgenerational meanings. In contrast with anthropological treatments of inalienable objects, in which whole artifacts are preserved and safeguarded, Chapman (2000: 44) makes the argument that each part of a fragmented object "stands not only for the rest of the artifact but . . . [for those] persons concerned with the exchange." In this way, individuals become "individual" or "fractally" connected or enchained with others through the extension, deposition, and accumulation of fragmented artifacts in a site, with transgenerational burial places and/or ritual mounds serving as primary examples of this process. For Chapman, inalienability is thus about the acquisition and accumulation of biographies or life histories that are represented by objects over time or across generations. In other words, "The notion that fragments of objects transmit not only the symbolism of their complete, once-intact form but also the enchained, or fractal, connotations of past makers and owners would account for a wide variety of fragmentation behavior" (Chapman 2002: 39). He provides the example of the *Spondylus* shell ornaments that made their way from the Aegean through central Europe during the early Neolithic, acquiring many "biographies" along the way. Apachetas are an example in the Andes. These artificial shrines along roads are composed of an accumulation of thousands of rocks (or other objects) brought by travelers and pilgrims passing through a distant or unknown area and placing an heirloom, an inalienable object of their homeland and journey, on the shrine for safe passage and to leave an identity marker. Each rock is not only a biography of the individual pilgrim or traveler but also an accumulative enchainment or repetitive act of all people passing by, who become enchained historically and thus form a fractionally coherent material or archaeological place, a "bulletin board of meanings" in the words of Law.

In sum, for our purpose, Chapman's argument is that selected material fragments represent transgenerational social linkages between people and places, each of which has a biography or life history of its own. By breaking and distributing the various broken pieces of an object and deliberately discarding them in certain places, people and places become connected or enchained. All people, whether the living depositing objects or the dead buried with broken offerings, have a piece of the other and of the other's life history. The objects then become relational, providing a "definition of the self in relation to others" (Brück 2006: 84) across generations. In essence, by connecting and enchaining these objects and thus people, societies empower them with mnemonic, metaphorical, and metonymic meaning. Furthermore, by accumulating or depositing enchained objects, they become "sets" or groups that store social capital and harmony and serve as identity markers (Gamble 2007: 144). Social capital implies an obligation, a social and economic reciprocity either between two or more individuals or perhaps across multiple generations of kin groups, which ultimately serves to integrate communities.

Thinking in terms of these concepts and issues, we can ask: does the deliberate fragmentation of many textiles, gourds, human skeletal parts, other objects, and ritual spaces at Huaca Prieta represent enchained transgenerational heirlooms or biographies and the accumulative enchainment of the living with the dead and other objects in the mound? Was the mound an inalienable object composed of hundreds of repetitive ritual episodes transcending multiple generations and accumulating multiple kinship or social group biographies? Who are the dead buried in chamber tombs at Huaca Prieta who are different, at least in terms of their articulated skeletal remains and place of burial, from the disarticulated and articulated bodies found in domestic middens and in the fill between floors in the mound? The notion of the enchained living and dead users at Huaca Prieta requires the acceptance of a fundamental view of this Preceramic society as essentially "collectivist." Individuals were involved in a web of binding transgenerational social and economic relationships by accumulating and placing objects in specific family or social group spaces in the mound for the memory and perpetuity of society. That is, the mound is an accumulation of hundreds, if not thousands, of individual and group life histories represented by the dead buried there, by the scattered human bones tossed in middens and fills, and by the numerous fragmented objects deliberately deposited by the living during ritual episodes. Were these relationships enacted by a socially segmented society constituted by various dispersed littoral and inland household communities? Were textiles, gourd vessels, baskets, and human skeletons deliberately fractured and their parts distributed and deposited as a way of building or sustaining a partitioned historical identity and biography of related users or owners within a society whereby the role of kinship was an organizing function? Was all of this a major accomplishment, organizing principle, and legacy of the Huaca Prieta society and part of its ontology: a collectivist principle of segmented kin groups? These questions are of interest as we examine the material record of sites in the study area and what it might mean.

Finally, in addressing the meaning of deliberately torn, cut, smashed, and broken materials in the mound at Huaca Prieta, we do not want to lose sight of the unintentionally broken objects there as well. These are portions of the lithics, shells, faunal and floral remains, natural rocks, and other things that were unintentionally fractured or damaged due to use and discard. Unintentionally broken objects, primarily shellfish remains, quantitatively dominate the archaeological record at the site, but it is the deliberately broken ones that are most significant symbolically and contextually. They primarily are fragments of textiles, baskets, gourds, and shell that appear in nearly all offerings and across all segmented and circumscribed ritual spaces and on the zigzag footpaths that served as entry and exit points to the mound. We know that they were intentionally fragmented because they have scored or marked areas for cutting, breaking, and snapping them apart (see chapters 7, 11, and 12).

AN EARLY SEGMENTED ANDEAN SOCIETY

As mentioned in chapter 1 and developed in chapters 14 and 15, the settlement pattern of Preceramic household communities in the study area is dispersed in the deltas and along inland terraces and shorelines of the wetlands of the lower Chicama Valley. This pattern, the individually circumscribed ritual spaces in the Huaca Prieta mound, and the economic specialization evidenced at Huaca Prieta and Paredones collectively suggest a segmented or segmentary system of socioeconomic organization. When Meyer Fortes and E. E. Evans-Pritchard (1940) first used the word "segmentary" in their typology for the Ngoni of Africa, they referred exclusively to major groups similar in form to lineages. To them, a segment was "one of an indefinite number of parts comprising a whole in which one part is like another in structure, or composition, and function" (White 1959: 143), a description similar to the fractal systems described earlier except that in this context they are social.

In following Fortes and Evans-Pritchard, a critical characteristic of segmentary societies is that segmentation develops continually. Every person is a potential founder of a new segment. Although a segment once formed tends to persist in time, more and more segments of lower and smaller order are all the while potentially being formed within it. Most importantly, the system is governed by the same repetitive principles at all scales or levels. Thus in some way it can be seen as a coherent and recursive fractal system, that is, a group formed in a specific way at one level (such

as a single house mound) may become another level or a social or residential group (such as a cluster of house mounds). Thus at any one time the constancy of past formation is reflected in the present and recursive uniformity of the social and settlement organization. Fortes (1949: 13) states: "It means that the same units of a particular force are, like cause, associated together into larger units of the same general foray and these again associated into still larger units of analogous or identical form, and so on up to the limits of the system . . . the principles operating on one level presuppose the principles operating on a lower level." The arrangement of segments relative to one another is with few exceptions "fixed, repetitive, and enduring. The residential system was a growing one and not merely a static division of the population inherited from the past." The process of continual formation of segments, which Raymond Firth (1951: 250) called the "branching or rambling process," is diagnostic of a segmentary society, the type of society that we believe existed along the littoral of the lower Chicama Valley during the Preceramic period (see chapters 13 and 14). To a large extent, as argued later, the demographic aspect of a segmented settlement system in the lower valley may have been positioned to exploit different ecological habitats, to create specialized maritime, wetland, and farming communities, and to establish resource exchange between them.

CONCLUSION

This discussion on concepts relevant to the concerns of this study provides an overview of some current issues related to the Preceramic period in the Central Andes and specifically to the study area here. The data from Huaca Prieta, Paredones, and other sites provide evidence for social, demographic, and economic patterns during the early to late Preceramic period on the north coast of Peru. At Huaca Prieta we find architectural and ritual repetitiveness and fragmented artifacts. These elements of the archaeological record seem to have had little economic significance and played no obvious role in the social sphere. A new paradigm is required to explain this type of record. As we discuss in more detail later, the fragmentation of key material items (especially textiles, gourds, and the mound itself at Huaca Prieta, the three material categories that consistently show more symbolic expression) was involved in the creation of new social and ontological forms. This preoccupation with fragmentation and repetitiveness must have transformed social groupings and the way in which people economically and demographically organized themselves and interacted with the environment.

CHAPTER 3

RESEARCH DESIGN

Tom D. Dillehay

The intent of the Huaca Prieta Project was to study the long-term dynamics of the social and natural systems of a mixed maritime/wetland foraging and farming society on the north coast of Peru. Huaca Prieta and Paredones contain well-preserved archaeological and paleoecological records that offer insights not only into varied early social and ecological interactions between ~14,500 and 3500 cal BP but also into the beginnings of early Andean civilization in the region. How people at these sites adapted to environmental changes and what factors led to increased social complexity and to a complementary multizone economy are two specific subjects of study.

The project had several research interests. First, to study whether the sites were first occupied by maritime foragers and later developed into ritual and residential localities employing a mixed foraging and farming economy. Second, to determine the extent to which Huaca Prieta was a special place operating within a broader complex of residential sites along the littoral of the Chicama Valley, with the mound at the site serving as a node for private and public rituals and off-mound and outlying domestic localities serving as support and participant populations. Third, to document whether Huaca Prieta was built for transitory use, rituals, and mortuary practices. In this regard, was depositional activity at the site commemorative in character? Were preparing floors, burning things, and placing burials a means of venerating the mound, its component elements, and the past activities that took place there? Fourth, to gain a better understanding of the long-term socioeconomic, architectural, and technological changes from ~14,500 to 3500 cal BP, including the rise, growth, and abandonment of Huaca Prieta and Paredones, transformations in funerary practices, and the context of cotton textile and fishnet, gourd, basketry/matting, and other artifact discard at the sites and their relations to site activities. Fifth, to define a firm and more widespread chronological sequence for the sites and their internal features and building phases. Sixth, to clarify the linkage of Huaca Prieta and Paredones to off-mound geological contexts and environs in order to correlate site use sequences with climatic and environmental events and to study the paleolandscape history, particularly to identify any evidence of tsunami and El Nino deposits. And seventh, to understand the social structure of Preceramic sites in the study area and to speculate on the possible relationship between people's ontologies and sociocultural transformations.

As part of the project's research design, we studied the collection of archaeological and paleoecological materials excavated by Bird at Huaca Prieta and housed at the American Museum of Natural History, New York. During the project's field seasons from 2006 to 2013, Bird's earlier excavations were cleaned, restudied, and remapped. We also screened his entire large backdirt pile, which was just east of the mound; once it had been screened, we used it to fill in the HP-3 trench to prevent its further erosion. In his two largest excavations, HP-3 (which measured ~25 m long and ~12 m deep at the northeast center of the mound) and HP-2 (which measured ~12 m long and ~3 m wide on the west side of the mound), we recut and redrew all of Bird's stratigraphic profiles. This entailed more than 5000 individual profile measurements (see chapters 6 and 7). Our project also placed 32 individual test pits (between 2 by 2 and 2 by 3 m in size, 2–5 m in depth), three trenches (for example, 1 by 15 and 2 by 25 m in size, 5–20 m in size, and 2–20 m in depth), and 30 block excavation units (4 by 4 and 10 by 18 m in size, 3–20 m in depth) at varying depths, which totaled more than 732 m³ of newly excavated deposits at Huaca Prieta and Paredones and places between them (fig. 3.1). In our deepest excavations (in Bird's HP-3 unit and our Units 15/21), we reached the culturally sterile buried surface of the Sangamon terrace, which was approximately 30 m below the top of the mound in these two units. We also constructed Harris Matrices for the HP-3 trench and for Units 2 and 22 (see chap-

ter 7). Restudy of Bird's units and new excavations revealed a highly complicated series of thousands of circumscribed floor, use-surface, retention berm, and fill sequences indicative of deliberate and planned mound construction. We initially interpreted four building phases of the mound, beginning in ~7500 and ending in ~3500 cal BP (Dillehay et al. 2012b), and a long premound phase that spanned the early Holocene period. Due to our more recent excavations in 2011 to 2013, Phase I now includes the late Pleistocene and the early Holocene subphases that date from ~14,500 to 7500 cal BP.

The specific purpose of the excavations was (1) to provide detailed stratigraphic, paleoecological, geological, and chronological data for new and different areas of Huaca Prieta, Paredones, and other sites; (2) to collect flotation samples and plant and animal remains for a precise reconstruction of the past ecology, resource zone(s) exploitation, seasonality of occupation, chronology, and subsistence strategies; and (3) to collect artifact and feature data from in situ stratigraphic positions to determine variable site functions and meanings. The sites also were completely mapped (fig. 3.1). Subsurface deposits around the base of the mounds and at nearby off-mound localities were examined through cursory conductivity and GPR studies.

We obtained more than 150 new radiocarbon and optically stimulated luminescence (OSL) dates from various strata at several sites. The dates were processed at the University of Arizona AMS (Accelerator Mass Spectrometry) lab, Beta Analytic, Inc., Oxford University Laboratory, the National Oceanic and Atmospheric Administration (NOAA), and the Universidade de Sao Paolo. These dates range in age from ~14,500 to 3400 cal BP in the deeper premound and basal mound levels on the north, east, and south sides of Huaca Prieta to ~5900 to 3800 cal BP for basal and upper deposits on the west side. The latter time range generally agrees with the ¹⁴C dates previously obtained by Bird for his units HP-2 and HP-3. Our project also processed off-mound radiocarbon dates for outlying Preceramic residential areas, which ranged between ~7500 and 3500 cal BP and generally coincide with the primary phases of mound construction of Huaca Prieta. Dates for

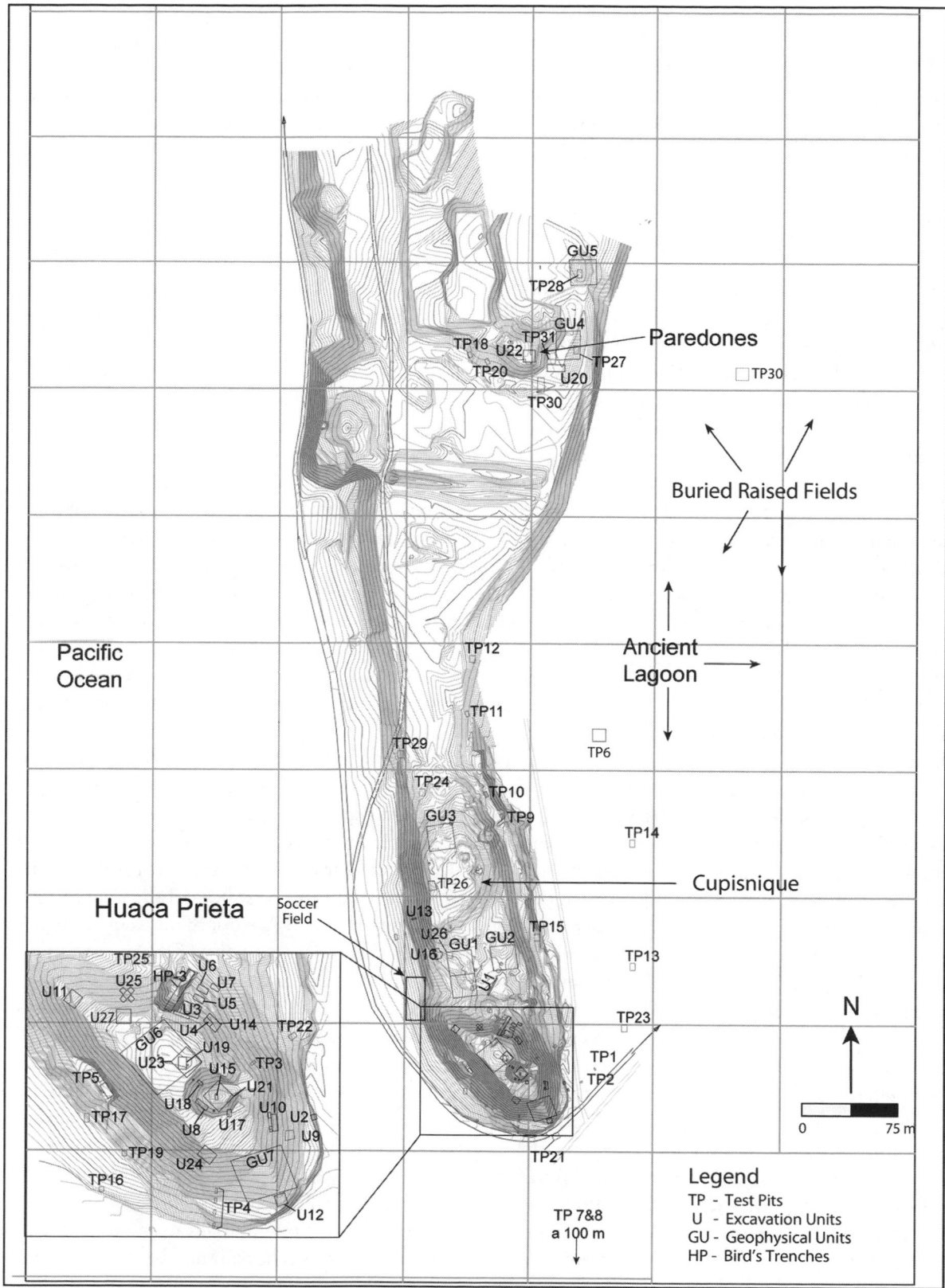

FIGURE 3.1. The Huaca Prieta Project map of Paredones, Huaca Prieta, the Cupisnique mounds, surrounding topographic features, and all excavation units, test pits, and geophysical quadrants.

the Paredones mound reveal its construction from ~6500 to 4000 cal BP, contemporary with later activity at Huaca Prieta. One ^{14}C date on a chile pepper seed in premound deposits at Paredones assayed ~10,578–10,285 cal BP (see chapter 6), suggesting early premound activity there.

APPROACH TO SITE MAPPING AND ARCHAEOLOGICAL EXCAVATION

Several problems were considered in developing an excavation strategy. The palimpsest perspective on the character of stratigraphy commonly attributed to earthen mounds similar to Huaca Prieta and Paredones tends to view the deposits in coarse arbitrary partitions and thus samples the record, assuming an overall homogeneous distribution of the remains. Huaca Prieta and Paredones are different, however, and contain highly heterogeneous and truncated strata. The research strategy thus took into account (1) the low-speed volume accumulation of the mounds due to the large amount of residues produced by food preparation, consumption, and deposition and the innumerable amount of individual burning and depositional episodes that they contain; (2) the abundant vertical and horizontal extension of thousands of small circumscribed deposits; (3) the prevalence of an artificial plaster covering the mound layers that sealed the archaeological remains, which enabled us to distinguish repetitive short-term building moments; and (4) the accumulation of offerings and debris from mortuary and other rituals or for intermittent occupation. This complexity imposed the need to develop a specific interdisciplinary methodology for the analysis and interpretation of the archaeological evidence. Thus we focused on the relevance of a methodology detecting the microstratigraphy of the sites and consequently the need to employ a sampling method that covered a wide area of multiple-use episodes.

In 2006 we surveyed and began mapping the study area. In 2007 we recut and profiled Bird's HP-3 trench on the north side of the mound at Huaca Prieta and conducted preliminary subsurface testing in other mound and off-mound areas of the site. The published profile of the trench was very general and difficult to relate to the exposed walls at the time (Bird et al. 1985: fig. 20). Once we recut the walls, we excavated deeper, reaching the undisturbed buried surface of the Sangamon terrace and the habitational midden deposits below. We also excavated farther west of Bird's deepest excavation in the trench. Our deeper excavation in the northwest corner of the trench was ~2 m below Bird's deepest level, which he indicated by placing old newspapers and clothing at the base of his trench, and ~1.0 m farther west and into (or behind) his "retaining wall" no. 1 (see fig. 7.5). Bird must have thought that he had reached culturally sterile sediment in the trench. This was partially true, because he terminated his excavation where he had reached a culturally sterile conglomerated layer at the buried surface of the Sangamon terrace. But we excavated through this 35–50 cm thick, culturally sterile layer along the northwest border of the HP-3 trench (see fig. 11 in Bird et al. 1985) and below and behind retaining wall no. 1, finding several thin, stratigraphically intermittent, burned, and deeper habitation lenses that dated to the terminal Pleistocene and early Holocene periods (see chapter 7). We carried out similar procedures of probing deeper into presumed culturally sterile sediments in 41 other areas on and off the Huaca Prieta and Paredones mounds and recovered earlier premound evidence in seven of them (Units 2, 9, 12, 15/21, 20, 22, and Test Pit 22), indicating how sparse and dispersed (or possibly disturbed) the older, deeper premound cultural deposits are.

New and extensive units also were excavated in areas where Bird did not work, such as the south, southeast, and southwest sides of the mound (our Units 1–19 and 23–25), the sunken circular plaza on the upper south end of the mound, and the far north side, in addition to numerous off-mound areas between Huaca Prieta and the Cupisnique mound and between the Cupisnique and Paredones mounds (figs. 3.1 and 3.2). We placed units and trenches in or near Paredones (Units 20, 22, and 30 and Test Pits 18 and 27–29); we also recut and profiled Bird's units in the Cupisnique mound. We cored and cleaned several looter's holes and drainages across the entire Sangamon terrace and in the off-mound cane fields to the east (fig. 3.3). It was hoped that these new excavations would yield enough data across and off the terrace for analysis of a wider Preceramic presence in the study area and for reconstruction of the paleoecology of the area.

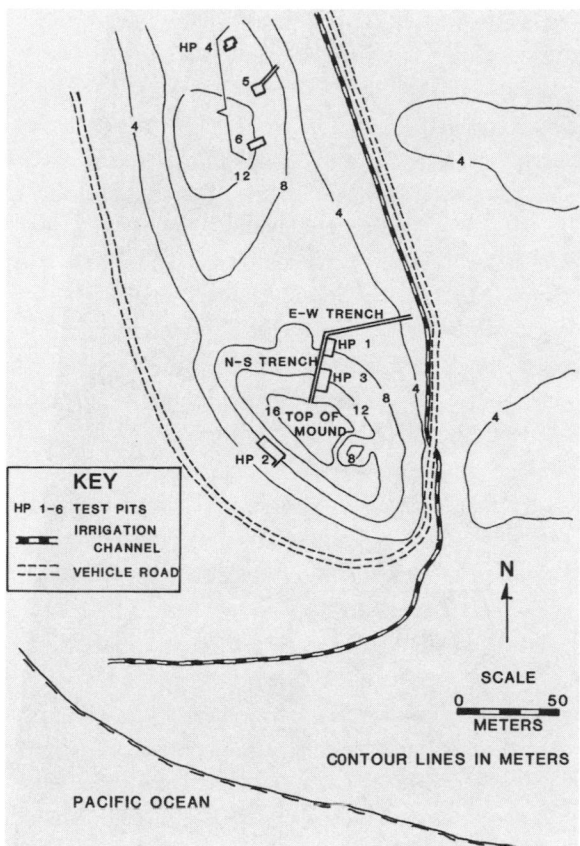

FIGURE 3.2. Bird's map of Huaca Prieta, showing his excavation units.

FIGURE 3.3. Aerial view of Huaca Prieta and outlying areas taken in the 1940s, including mounded features east of the site in the cane fields (see Bird et al. 1985: 6).

The method used to produce the contour map for the sites was a Total Station data collector and Trimble GPS system set up in the middle of the wider study area. Twenty-two elevation lines were run to the base of the mounds. The first line was set up with grid north and the rest of the lines were made at 22.5-degree intervals between, around the mounds and off-mound areas. Six of the lines began at the edge of the top of the mounds. The lines were run off the edges of the mound; elevations were taken at 1 m intervals along each line. A total of 1122 elevation readings was recorded for the entire study area (see fig. 3.1).

Following the completion of the elevation lines, the locations of Bird's excavations on the mounds were recorded. It was occasionally difficult to define the precise limits in his excavations because many of them had eroded over the past sixty-five years. Modern-day looting and other activities also have heavily eroded the large semi-circular "looter's hole" on the south end of Huaca Prieta and other excavated units as well.

The mounds (as seen in fig. 3.1) are decidedly elongated ovoids. There is a hint of the entry ramp at Huaca Prieta that is visible on the detailed topographic drawing (fig. 3.4). The summit of the mound, while eroded in some places, reveals a roughly rectangular shape, with the long axis running slightly east of north. The highest part of the mound consists of a flat, eroded ridge that extends east to west across the top. The highest reading was at the northern end of the ridge, with an elevation of ~28.9 masl and 29.2 m above the present-day ground surface to the east of the mound. The original height of this mound, just as at Paredones, is difficult to estimate because of the uneven nature of the ground at the base of the mound and erosion of the summit due to reuse over time and constant wind erosion. The south side of the mound has an elevation of ~19.8 masl. The top of the central area of the Huaca Prieta mound is flat except the southern end that declines to the south, where the sunken looter's hole is located, and the northern end that slopes to the north. While there is a gradual slope of the

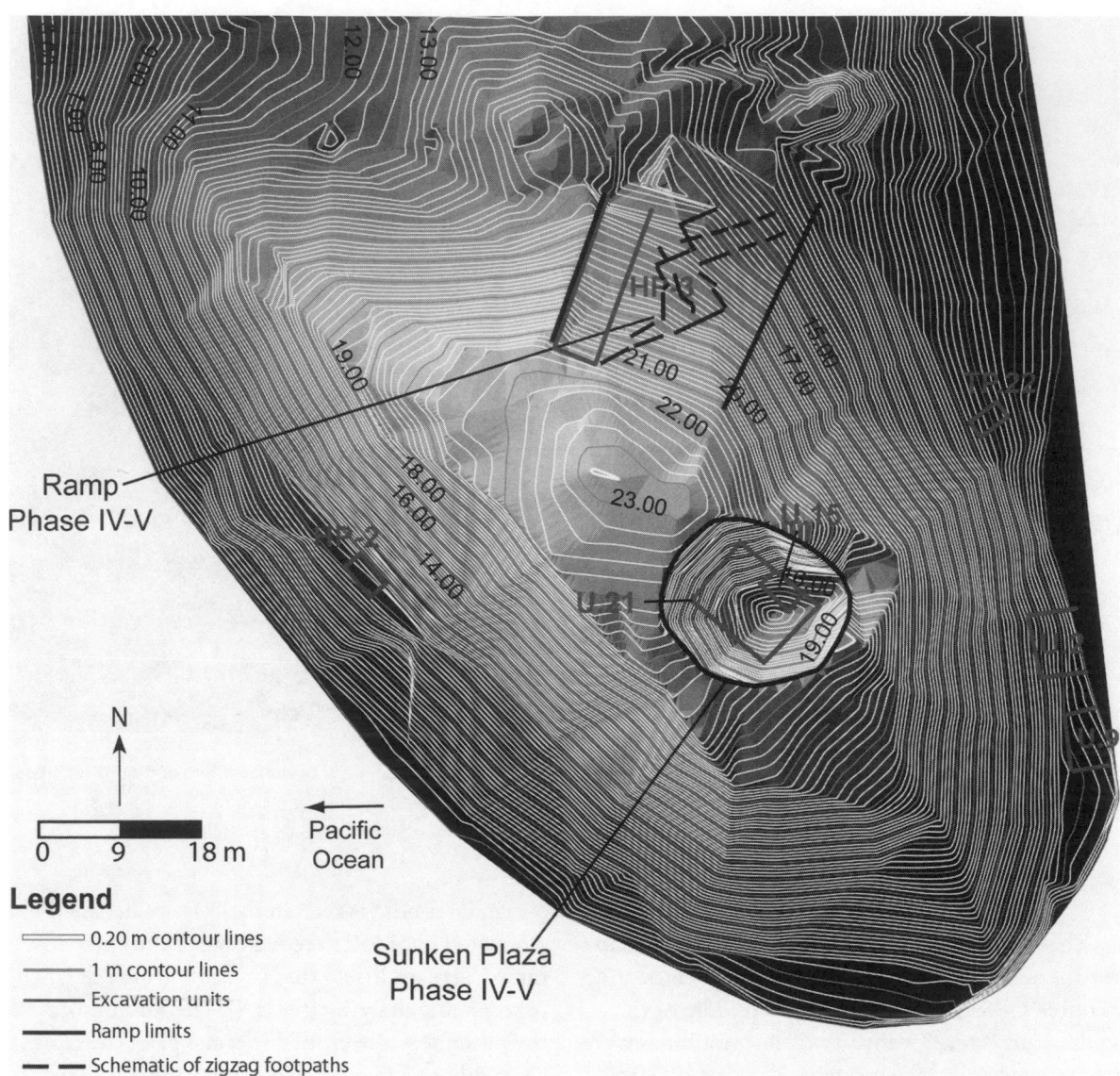

FIGURE 3.4. Detailed topographic map and main features, including schematic of the zigzag footpaths on the ramp at Huaca Prieta.

upper portion of the northeast side defined as a later entry ramp, this feature is notable, orienting the mound east to slightly northeast.

SITE EXCAVATIONS

A total of thirty excavation units were placed in and around Huaca Prieta and Paredones. In addition, thirty-two test pits and eighty geological cores were excavated. Eight units were excavated through the depths of artificial mound layers to sterile sediments at the base of Huaca Prieta. Four units were excavated to sterile sediments in Pare-

dones and five between the two sites. All outlying test pits were also taken to sterile deposits in the terrace. In our Units 2, 12, 15, 19, 20, 22, and 23 and in Bird's HP-2 and HP-3, we excavated to depths varying between 5 to 31 m below the top of the mound and into the buried cultural deposits contained in the upper levels of the Sangamon terrace. Premound habitation middens were found in only a few of these (see chapters 6 and 7). Several other units were excavated to sterile sediment in and around Huaca Prieta and Paredones, but no late Pleistocene to early Holocene midden deposits were found. When sterile soil was penetrated, two to five 1.0 m deep and 6 cm wide auger holes were placed in each unit to test whether deeper cultural deposits were present. Most excavation units off of the Huaca Prieta mound were designed to answer specific questions related to site stratigraphy, features, or architecture and were terminated at depths of 2 to 8 m (see chapter 7). Other than stone structures, features such as pits, postholes, and hearths were scarce in excavated units at Huaca Prieta and Paredones. Although this was good for recording and interpreting the profiles, it resulted in a low frequency of formal feature recovery. All use surfaces, floors, and fills were recorded in detail; and, with the exception of shell debris, all artifacts and features were piece-plotted. All excavated sediments were screened.

We also inspected the cut walls of 23 drainages, irrigation canals, and roadcuts constituting a total distance of 14.2 km in the cane fields east of the study area. The profiles of and tossed debris around 234 looter's holes on the Sangamon terrace and in outlying domestic sites also were examined.

Relative to spatial analysis, the point-plotting of ecofacts (especially shell debris) was impossible given that we excavated more than 1,000,000 items, but all were recorded within 2 cm levels (especially floors and use surfaces) and within quarter-m units. All screening was done with 0.25 and 0.5 cm mesh using 1 by 2 m hand-shaker screens. Because natural levels were difficult to distinguish within deeper premound and off-mound layers, we excavated in 15 cm arbitrary layers. Otherwise, all other excavations in the mounds followed floor and fill sequences. Profiles of two of the most diagnostic walls of each excavation unit were drawn. All four walls of all excavation units were photographed, as well as use surfaces, floors, and features. Numbers were assigned to the excavation units in the order in which they were excavated. Due to the extent of the depth and slope angle of the mound, it was necessary to cut larger benches and units in order to access the deeper levels in units reaching the old terrace surface below. All excavation units were backfilled upon completion.

Excavation procedures followed standard protocols of data recording. The excavation and survey team for each two- to three-month (six days a week) field season was composed of eight profes-sional archaeologists and thirty to forty workers equipped with data recording forms compatible with project software, including Excel, GIS, and ArcInfo. Information from a wide variety of excavation forms was entered into the database on laptops in the field laboratory. All materials recovered from the excavations were washed, catalogued, classified in the field, and then stored permanently at the archaeological laboratory of the Universidad Nacional de Trujillo.

INTERDISCIPLINARY ARCHAEOLOGICAL RESEARCH

In general, excavations at the sites have revealed a pattern of relatively extensive and dense depositions and activity areas that indicate multiple burning, ritual episodes, mortuary practices, and/or food preparation and consumption of the same locations by small groups. These kinds of associations, combined with the analysis of faunal and floral remains, more than 350 flotation samples (each ~0.7 cubic m in size) studied, and spatial data from floors and features afforded an opportunity to examine changes in site function and temporality. Analysis of these data addressed significant gaps in our understanding of subsistence strategies, resource exploitation, seasonality, activity areas, and community patterns that were instrumental in examining how diverse groups may have pursued resource use strategies through time. mtDNA and stable isotope analyses of human skeletal remains provided potential data on dietary practices, kin groupings, and migration. Specific methods employed by each discipline are presented in the individual chapters and appendices.

A typological and functional analysis of excavated and surface-collected cotton nets and weavings, gourds, reed mats and baskets, lithics, and other materials from all sites was performed. Jeff Splitstoser and initially William Conklin studied the cotton textiles and nets; James Adovasio and Jeff Illingworth examined the rush matting and basketry; Duccio Bonavia and I studied the majority of the other artifacts, including my low- and high-power microscopic examination of individual tool edges for use-wear polishes, striations, and other indicators to assess tool function. Tiffiny Tung, Jessica Blair, Raúl Tito, and Cecil Lewis performed the mtDNA analysis on human bone remains.

Steven Goodbred, Mario Pino, Claudio Latorre, Michael Ramírez, Rachel Beavins, and Andre Oliveira Sawakuchi studied the geology and paleoecology. Several specialty studies were undertaken: starch grains and phytoliths by Dolores Piperno and José Iriarte, respectively; human skeletal remains by John Verano and Anne Titelbaum; geochemistry and isotope analyses of fish otoliths by Philippe Béarez, Elise Dufour, and Olivier Trombret; chile peppers by Katherine Chiou and Christine Hastorf; all other faunal and floral remains were studied by Teresa Rosales Tham and Víctor Vásquez. Pollen samples were analyzed by Linda Scott Cummings. Soil chemistry samples were studied by the Soil Chemistry Laboratory at the University of Kentucky. GPR analyses were carried out by Phillip Mink and Greg Maggard. Teresa Franco examined marine shells (*Semele* sp.) for seasonality of use. Jeixin Wei and Fred Andrus performed isotope study of marine shells. Jan Wouters and Ana Claro studied the indigo dyes of textiles. Jeff Illingworth, Jack Williams, and Michelle Farley examined other dyes. Isabel Rey identified the charcoal from sites. Alexander Grobman and Duccio Bonavia studied the maize remains. André Oliveira Sawakuchi performed OSL dating assays. Larisa DeSantis and Robert S. Feranec examined isotopes of human teeth. Patricia J. Netherly aided in the translation, compilation, and write-up of the faunal and floral reports presented by Vásquez Sánchez and Rosales Tham (2008, 2010). Unfortunately, due to heavy salt saturation of some organic materials (human bone in particular), we were unable to derive positive results from genetic, strontium, and other studies (see chapter 6 and appendix 17).

SAMPLING THE EXCAVATED CULTURAL DEPOSITS

All excavated archaeological deposits were dry-sieved by 2.5–5 mm screens or were treated by water flotation for the extraction of organic remains and artifacts. The integrated use of soil micromorphology, bulk, and routine soil samples was also undertaken. The sampling strategy involved the removal of bulk samples of five to ten liters from every excavated sediment context.

These samples generally represented less than 20 percent of the total volume of context excavated. Sediments of all features were sampled 100 percent. Extra bulk samples were chosen for specialty analyses from organic rich in situ deposits (for example, starch grains, phytoliths, and pollen). Routine samples of ~0.3 liters were taken from bulk samples for sedimentary analysis. A column sample of small soil samples was also taken through the in situ deposits identified in all units from the surface to the underlying sterile subsoil. The samples consisted of approximately 30 cc of sediment taken at 1.0 m contiguous intervals from individual profile sections, for pollen, phytoliths, starch grains, and detailed sedimentary analysis.

We collected 350 flotation samples (0.7 m^3 each) from excavated use-surfaces and floors within all excavation units. Tools, carbon samples, and any clusters or offerings of macrobotanic specimens were individually piece-plotted and collected. Analysis of recovered macro- and micro-botanical materials and other debris from intact subsurface deposits allowed for new insights into resource procurement and use of specific micro-environmental zones. Analysis of flotation samples also allowed for the identification of floral and faunal resources to specific zones and for tracking changes in resource use/exploitation. Changes in the frequency of targeted species or the appearance of new species were correlated with changes in site technologies, location of sites, recorded climatic changes, and seasonality of site occupation, which provided new avenues for understanding shifts in foraging patterns and paleoenvironmental shifts.

Charcoal was sorted from 5 mm dry sieved residue and excessively charcoal-saturated samples at Huaca Prieta, Paredones, and domestic sites. All charcoal identifications were checked against the botanical literature and studied (modern reference materials were from collections in the Universidad Nacional de Trujillo). The charcoal fragments were generally identified to genus, with the number of fragments and weight in each sample for each genus recorded.

When selecting a portion of charcoal for radiometric assay, care was taken to choose only the outer parts of burned stems in an effort to avoid induced time lag due to any old wood. We took 99 percent of the samples from burned stems of short-lived bushes (e.g., *Bunchosia armeniaca*, *Persea* sp., *Schinus molle*, *Annona* sp., *Pouteria* sp.) or from corncobs (see chapter 6 and appendices 2 and 5).

SITE SURVEY

Opportunistic archaeological survey was carried out along the littoral zone from Malabrigo ~20 km north of Huaca Prieta to Cerro Campana ~6 km south of the site. We also surveyed selected areas into the interior along the finger-like wetlands running from the east near the Pan-American Highway to the sea (see chapter 13). Many of the interior areas had been destroyed by bulldozers and deep plowing to level the land for sugarcane fields and by draining and infilling most wetlands for cattle grazing. We estimate that about 50 percent of the Preceramic and other sites had been destroyed or heavily modified. Furthermore, some of these latter areas could not be surveyed because some private landowners did not grant permission to enter their lands. In total, we registered and photographed thirty-two Preceramic sites and observed lithic scatters in disturbed areas that we thought represented others, although there surely are more to be recorded by more extensive survey. When a new site was encountered, we assigned it a valley number. We collected a sample of surface artifacts from each site, took its GPS location, examined the stratigraphy in any looter's holes present, and calculated site areas based on these surficial and subsurficial data. We also walked numerous canal drainages and road cuts searching for buried cultural deposits. Several of these findings are discussed briefly in chapters 5, 7, and 13.

PALEOENVIRONMENTAL AND GEOLOGICAL ANALYSES

Because of the monumental scope of mound construction at Huaca Prieta and the large sand-duned, raised agricultural fields to the east of the site (see fig. 7.32), we focused the geological studies on the lower valley (see chapter 5 and appendix 1). No prior empirical data existed about the geomorphological setting and premound contexts of Huaca Prieta, so we carried out a geological study of the Sangamon terrace under and around the mound. Geological investigation and

coring of areas away from Huaca Prieta, including the floodplain, yielded a wealth of information about the complexity of long-term human modification and preparation of the local substrates. Data from this project also provided a secure point from which to evaluate other aspects of the archaeological database. The geological project had three underlying goals.

1. To establish the basic geological/geomorphological context of the premound and mound units of the Sangamon terrace and the wider valley setting.
2. To gauge the degree of landscape preparation done before the construction of Huaca Prieta and Paredones.
3. To understand the relationship of Huaca Prieta and Paredones to the relic Sangamon terrace, the Pacific shoreline, the Chicama River, and the surrounding lagoons.

Our specific paleoecological objectives were threefold. First, we studied natural sediments buried beneath the anthropic sediments of mounds and other sites that would indicate environmental conditions prior to a human presence. Second, we sought evidence from sediments of impacts on the valley floor that was associated with initial human settlement and related activities prior to, during, and after the deposition of the anthropic materials. And third, we sought to characterize the anthropic sediments themselves to indicate the nature of activities at and around the sites. For each of these objectives we used thin-section micromorphology of undisturbed core samples to characterize soils and sediments from site areas. This technique allowed microscopic, chemical, and isotopic identification of features and their relationship to one another, which led to our interpretation of activities and environmental conditions.

We used the stratigraphic record of sediments to reconstruct past environments in the study area, including their general character, distribution, and history of change. Sediment cores were collected with a hand-operated soil auger to a depth of 2–6 m, which encompassed the period of mound development as well as times before and after. Paleoenvironmental reconstructions also were made based on sediment textures, plant remains, weathering characteristics, magnetic susceptibility, and radiocarbon dating. All analyses were performed with instruments in Goodbred's geology lab at Vanderbilt University, including a laser-diffraction particle size analyzer and multi-sensor core logger; in Pino's lab at the Universidad Austral de Chile; and in Oliveira Sawakuchi's lab at the Universidade de São Paulo. Based on these data, we identified the nature and history of major paleoecological changes along the floodplain and delta systems of the Chicama River. A principal goal of this work was to test the hypothesis that environmental changes and major physical events were an influence on the development and/or demise of the wider Huaca Prieta community. These studies allowed for reconstructed general histories of human cultural development and physical environmental change and subsequently the correlations between them.

Sections from the excavated deposits were stratigraphically examined in great detail by both archaeologists and geologists, from Bird's excavated units and from our units and test pits, giving the opportunity to consider variations in natural and cultural deposition processes across and between the sites. Description of the exposed stratigraphic sequences used Munsell color notation and standard textural classes allowing soils and sediments on sites to be integrated as stratigraphic contexts and matrices. To support the archaeological excavation, chronological control of the stratigraphy was achieved through a series of radiocarbon and OSL measurements on charcoal from the strata (see chapters 5 and 6).

GEOPHYSICAL RESEARCH

Subsurface structures and features in off-mound areas are not always visible above the ground in the Huaca Prieta and Paredones landscape, although a few structures and small mounds have been observed among scattered occupational refuse. Located ~3 km south and ~20 km north of the mound sites are Preceramic sites associated with shoreline and wetland environments. Geophysical data were essential to the understanding of the landscape at these sites and at Huaca Prieta and Paredones. Magnetometer and electrical resistance surveys of selected off-mound areas were undertaken in 2009. These data helped to determine where to place our subsurface test pits in sites.

CONCLUSIONS

The Huaca Prieta Project was designed to explore aspects of the nature, organization, and impact of human and environmental relations in the study area. The interrelated research components of the project also were designed to generate fundamental new data concerning the history, technology, economy, paleoecology, and society of the study area during the long Preceramic period. This volume is not only descriptive and interpretative with respect to the archaeological and paleoecological data but inferential in regard to the wider social and ontological meaning of the interplay between human and nature interactions.

CHAPTER 4

THE ENVIRONMENTAL SETTING, PAST AND PRESENT

Patricia J. Netherly
and Tom D. Dillehay

INTRODUCTION

The record of human occupation of the space in which the Huaca Prieta and Paredones mound sites are located begins at ~14,500 cal BP and is intermittent for some 5000 years. Site use at Huaca Prieta is essentially continuous from about 7500 cal BP to the abandonment of the site in ~3500 cal BP, and it was later sporadically used as a burial locale by Formative to colonial period societies. At the nearby mound site of Paredones the record of occupation begins at least by 10,000 cal BP but is more consistent by ~6500 cal BP, when the mound use begins, and continues into the early Moche period. This sequence documenting a human presence over 14,000 years offers detailed information about the changing nature of the marine, littoral, and inland environments and the relationship of the human populations to the physical world in which they lived. (As mentioned in chapter 1, in this study the littoral zone is considered to be the part of the ocean that is close in-shore, extending from the high water mark to shoreline areas that are permanently submerged and including the intertidal zone, the beach and dune formations, and the estuaries and lagoons located ~0.5 to 2.0 km inland from the dunes.)

Scholars have now come to regard the physical landscape as a dynamic, ever-changing ecosystem that is continually modified in response to processes initiated by geologic or climatic conditions or by human action (Gunderson and Holling 2001; Redman and Kinzig 2003). A chronological consideration of these processes in the case of the Peruvian north coast and the Chicama Valley leads to an appreciation of the resilience of the terrestrial and marine ecosystems over time and of the flexibility of both the inland and marine-oriented human socioecological systems.

In the past, Andean archaeologists followed the trends of anthropological thinking about the relationship between human societies and the environment. Thus environmental evidence was largely ignored, beyond classifying societies as hunters, pastoralists, farmers, or fishers. Later, as subsistence became a topic of research and the transition from foraging to horticulture and eventually agriculture became a research goal, more attention was paid to the plant and faunal remains from maritime and inland contexts. The suggestive lines of investigation of late Preceramic marine-oriented societies on the central coast of Peru were begun over fifty years ago by Edward Lanning (1967a), Thomas Patterson (1971), and later Michael Moseley (1974, 1992), who suggested a path to complexity for maritime-based societies without access to up-valley agriculture. Despite the presence of stratified middens, fine-grained analysis of their constituent parts, especially plant foods, was not carried out. Studies at late Preceramic marine-oriented sites with monumental architecture such as Río Seco, Aspero, Las Haldas, Culebras, Los Gavilanes, and Chao (see chapter 2), with the exception of research at Las Gavilanes by Bonavia (1982), concentrated on the architecture with less attention to the subsistence record. Too often studies of faunal and plant remains ended with lists of identified material with chronological correlations where available. They offered no perception of the marine environment as a system or of human participation in such an environment as systemic with a potential for changing the environment through the exploitation of its resources. Working with a comprehensive environmental paradigm for linked human-ecosystems, we consider both terrestrial and marine environments.

LATE PLEISTOCENE GEOGRAPHY

Consideration of the principal geologic and climatic physical systems impacting the Chicama Valley begins ~22,000 years ago at the Last Glacial Maximum (LGM) and extends to the present (see chapter 5). During the last two stadials and interstadials of the Pleistocene, some 104,000 years, atmospheric temperature was lowered ~5°C and sea surface temperature was ~3.5°C lower than at present (Lea et al. 2000). Pleistocene rainfall patterns varied with the displacement of the Intertropical Convergence Zone south to the latitude of Ecuador (Haug et al. 2001; Hughen et al. 2000). During the Pleistocene, rainfall in the Contumazá and Otuzco highland regions to the north and south of the Chicama River watershed was probably less seasonal than it has been in the Holocene (Netherly 2011b).

The effect of the lowered temperatures and high altitude glaciation in the northern highlands resulted in the depression of vegetation zones by as much as 1000 to 1500 m (Colinvaux et al. 2000; Dillon et al. 1995; Vuilleumier 1971). As a result, below the nival zone, where lichens and moss grow on rocks, and the cold paramo grasslands (alpine tundra), the depressed biozones of the humid montane forest and seasonally dry forest were far more continuous in north to south trending bands than is presently the case (Dillon 2003a, 2003b). The impact of these conditions on the lower slopes of the western Andean cordillera has been described in detail for the Zaña Valley and the Nanchoc Quebrada (Netherly 2011b). These conditions persisted over tens of thousands of years. In the 1980s a relict stand of the humid montane forest extended from ~3200 to ~1500 masl in the upper Zaña Valley and is sustained in part by condensation of moisture from evapotranspiration from the forest itself, which falls at night as a fine rain. It can be assumed that this is also the case for the Bosque de Cachil, which lies between Cascas and Contumazá in a side branch of a tributary valley on the north bank of the Chicama River (fig. 4.1). In his biogeographic study of five relict montane forests on the western slopes of the Peruvian Andes, Michael Dillon (1994, 2003b) found that a high percentage of species in the Monteseco forest in the Zaña Valley were shared with humid forests on the western slopes of the Pichincha highlands in Ecuador, indicating that the humid montane forest was continuous or nearly so during the Pleistocene. Today the Cachil forest is much smaller and depauperate but shows the same relationship observed in the Zaña Valley. A smaller but significant percentage of species is shared with the Abiseo National Park on the eastern slopes of the Andes, indicating that a forested corridor, perhaps through Olmos, existed between the eastern and western slopes of the Andean Cordilleras (Dillon 1994; Netherly 2011b).

FIGURE 4.1. Forested foothills in the Cascas area of the upper Chicama Valley.

Studies of the dry forest biozone indicate that there are many shared species of North American origin in Panama, Colombia, Ecuador, and northern Peru as far south as the Santa River, again emphasizing the north to south continuities of this biozone during the late Pleistocene (Gentry 1995; Sarmiento 1975). Dry forests are seasonal and their biodiversity is almost as high as that of the tropical rainforest (Henderson et al. 1991). Many species have been domesticated as food crops (Piperno and Pearsall 1998; Piperno 2007). Brief emphasis is given to the dry forest here because this is the most likely corridor of exchange of the numerous exotic cultigens coming into the study area since terminal Pleistocene times (see chapter 10).

The distributions of cold-adapted flora and fauna during the height of the Pleistocene were "normal" for most species of plants and animals in both these biozones. As noted, the seasonally dry forest biozone extended over an east-to-west precipitation gradient and consequently included several discrete biotopes ranging from semiarid forest on the lower western slopes of the Andes to desert

scrub near the littoral. The Pacific coastal plain of Peru and northern Chile apparently was always arid throughout the late Pleistocene (Ortlieb 1989). For this reason the trees and shrubs growing in the lower valley away from the river and wetlands display adaptations to a climate without regular rainfall. Some, like algarrobo, have extremely long taproots that reach the water table to obtain moisture. Algarrobo forests extended to the margins of the lower valleys, entering the interfluvial zones where conditions were favorable. These stands formed their own favorable environment by bringing up groundwater and through condensation of evapo-transpiration, which created a microclimate within which other shrubs and small trees could grow.

The dry forest zone in the Chicama Valley is bounded on its western margin by parallel wetland biozones that run roughly north to south behind the Pacific beach zone: first an open-water zone of paludal wetlands fed by groundwater and occasional flooding from the river when it overtopped its banks; and merging with it a north-south band of closed wetlands with brackish water, sometimes receiving seawater delivered by high storm surges (see chapter 5). A number of genera such as *Capparis* (sapote) and algarrobo grow as trees in areas with sufficient moisture or appear as shrubs where it is more arid. On the downvalley side of the dry forest cacti can form dense stands. The fruits of several dry forest species can be eaten (Sagástegui Alva 1973).

LATE PLEISTOCENE TO LATE HOLOCENE CLIMATES

From ~25,000 years ago at the LGM, the atmospheric and marine temperatures began to rise rather abruptly in a steady warming trend with some oscillations until the onset of the Heinrich 1 event in the North Atlantic, which precipitated cooling between ~17,800 and 14,800 BP, abruptly ending in the warm, moist Bølling-Allerød chronozone between ~14,800 and 13,000 BP (Mollier-Vogel et al. 2013; Rein et al. 2005). Human groups may have entered the Chicama region (chapter 6) as they had the Nanchoc Valley between these last two periods (Dillehay 2011a, 2011b). The Heinrich I event was followed by a cool period between ~12,600 and 11,500 BP, the Younger Dryas, during which air and sea surface temperatures again dropped, but which does not appear to have affected the distribution of human populations on the northern coast of Peru (Mollier-Vogel et al. 2013; Dillehay et al. 2012b).

The earliest regional dates from the Zaña and Chaman Valleys and those from Huaca Prieta appear to corroborate this (Dillehay 2011a; Dillehay et al. 2012b). The extensive late Pleistocene and early Holocene evidence for repeated and sustained occupation of the dry forest biotopes on the lower western slopes of the Andes and for contemporary occupations at or near the littoral make it clear that both biotopes were sufficiently rich in resources to sustain human groups and were probably identified and sought out. The only date from the El Palto site in the upper Zaña Valley is ~13,800 cal BP, perhaps signaling the early presence of an intense and sustained occupation of the dry forest by populations using Paijan and Fishtail projectile points and their successors

in the nearby Chaman and Jequetepeque Valleys (Dillehay 2011a).

A similar extensive and sustained occupation was located and studied earlier in the contiguous valley of the Cupisnique River, and in the Santa María, Camotera, Cuculicote, and Camotera Quebradas on the north bank of the Chicama River (Chauchat et al. 1998; Chauchat 2006; Gálvez 2012; Gálvez et al. 2012; Briceño and Millones 2000). Most of these sites are found on terraces on alluvial fans with permanent or semipermanent watercourses or permanent springs. South of these five valleys, early human occupation in the high interfluve between Quebrada de la Guitarra in the Moche Valley and the Quebrada Las Huacas in the upper Virú Valley may have been associated with *lomas*, a seasonal cloud forest of essentially specialized dry forest species (Dillon 2003a). The number and size of these sites suggest repeated occupations (Gálvez 2012). There also are terminal Pleistocene populations with a clear adaptation to the resources of the sea and littoral. The ~10,800 cal BP Las Vegas I culture, a foraging, hunting, shellfishing culture with incipient horticulture and a unifacial lithic technology, was located in the Gulf of Guayaquil (Stothert 1985; Stothert and Ubelaker 1988). In the Zaña Valley 75 km north of Huaca Prieta is a late Pleistocene unifacial culture called Carrizal that appears to have been adapted to littoral wetlands and perhaps to the sea (Dillehay 2011a, 2011b). Groups of generalized hunters and foragers appeared on the Chicama littoral at about the same time as indicated at Huaca Prieta (see chapters 6, 7, and 9).

EL NIÑO/SOUTHERN OSCILLATION (ENSO) EVENTS

The El Niño/Southern Oscillation (ENSO) is now recognized to be the result of the coupling of atmospheric and oceanic processes that are part of the fundamental circulation of air and water on the planet (Clement and Cane 1999; Díaz and Markgraf 2000). During the glacial stadials through the LGM, it appears that the influence of the Southern Oscillation was weakened, although evidence indicates that it did not disappear altogether (Wang et al. 2005, 2008). After the Younger Dryas cool period, to the end of the Pleistocene-Holocene transition and including the early Holocene, further temperature oscillations occurred. Change was relatively rapid: sea level rose from ~120 m at the LGM to ~60 m by 10,800 cal BP and reached its present level ~5000 years later (Bard et al. 1990; Cardinal et al. 2001; Rein et al. 2005). The warming trend continued to change the distribution of the major biozones of the western slopes of the Andes, breaking up the continuous or nearly continuous bands of humid and dry forest (Dillon 1994; Dillon et al. 1995; Vuilleumier 1971). In the period from approximately ~8000 to 5000 cal BP, temperatures were warmer and the Intertropical Convergence Zone began to move north (Haug et al. 2001; Hughen et al. 2000).

For the past 5000 years ENSO events on the western coast of South America, at the eastern margin of the Pacific Ocean, have resulted from the wind-driven movement of warm waters from the western Pacific Ocean toward the Eastern Equatorial Pacific. At the same time, variations in the pattern of the prevailing westerlies affect the upwelling of cold deep water at the edge of the continent. These nutrient-rich cold waters sustain an incredibly rich marine biota. When the prevailing winds weaken, the cold Humboldt Current no longer carries cold water north. The warm tropical waters of the Ecuador Current flow southward, carrying a warm-water biota and causing the cold-adapted species to migrate, seeking cooler waters. Associated with these changes are atmospheric disturbances resulting in rainfall over the desert coast and occasional strong storms on the lower western slopes of the mountains. Cyclical patterns have been identified in these occurrences, some of which are tied to astronomical forcing (Clement and Cane 1999; Mollier-Vogel et al. 2013; Rein et al. 2005).

Mild to moderate ENSO events in the dry forest zone of the lower valley could have produced scant or moderate showers sometimes repeated over several days. Even a modest amount of precipitation could bring about major transformations in the environment. Dry branches would leaf out; herbs and grasses would grow from seed, which may have lain in the ground for years. Browsers like land snails and lizards would emerge

from estivation. Insect life would multiply and provide food for small animals, including rodents and desert foxes, which also feed on small game. If ENSO conditions persist, deer descend from the highlands, bringing with them predators, such as pumas. Shrubs and trees enter a period of rapid growth followed by flowering, fruiting, and setting seed (Cárdenas et al. 2001; Gushiken et al. 2001). Lucia Rodríguez, using tree ring analysis, plotted the growth spurts of common dry forest species (Netherly 2011a; Rodríguez et al. 1993). While many of these species are drought-resistant, only *Capparis* sp. grows continually. Even today individual farmers plant a fast-growing crop such as squash or rapidly maturing races of maize on lands at the valley margins or even between valleys that have received even one good soaking, with the expectation of obtaining a crop (Dillehay and Kolata 2004). This is an important consideration with early farmers whose normal sources of water may have been disrupted by flooding. If the rain does not continue, the populations of insects, reptiles, and small rodents crash. Snails and lizards return to estivation and the vegetation dies back, awaiting the next ENSO rains (Arntz and Fahrbach 1996; Netherly 1977).

WETLAND ENVIRONMENTS OF THE LOWER CHICAMA VALLEY

The lower part of the Chicama Valley lies between sea level and 300 m to the west of the narrow neck where the river emerges from the Andean cordillera. This roughly cone-shaped region lies within the seasonally dry forest biotope. The Chicama River, which flows east to west through the valley, has a broad bed, flowing within it as a braided stream smaller than the bed. In times of seasonal high water or flood, however, the river fills its bed, carrying sediments and debris to its mouth and to the sea. The riverbanks support a narrow zone of riparian vegetation, a separate biotope, which receives moisture from the river. The river estuary is a distinct wetland habitat found at the mouth of the river. It forms a wetland with brackish water where the river meets the sea. The estuarine zone extends along some of the back channels of more slowly flowing water with direct access to the sea. The plants and aquatic animals—largely fish, crustaceans, and mollusks—are adapted to this particular environment but may live part of their lives in a marine environment.

Between the beach, which trends north to south in the valley, and the dry forest zone lies a complex of wetlands (see chapter 5), which today are rapidly disappearing under the onslaught of expanding sugarcane cultivation. These two zones are roughly parallel but differ in the degree of salinity of the water and in the plants and animals that they support and thus the resources that they offer human populations.

Immediately adjacent to the dry forest biozone are pond-like open-water wetlands fed by groundwater and occasional flooding from the river when it overtops its banks. This biozone lies in a north to south band with freshwater fauna and plants. Birds are attracted to this biotope. Fish and other fauna can enter these wetlands when the river floods its banks. Groundwater agriculture was practiced in this biotope in the near past (Watson 1979). The plants, mollusks, and gastropods of this biotope can be distinguished from those of the adjacent and parallel wetlands lying between the freshwater wetlands and the beach, again in a north-to-south band. Here the water is brackish because groundwater may be saline so close to the beach and also because seawater from intermittent storm surges enters these wetlands (see chapter 9). Marine species, such as fish, mollusks, and crustaceans, can enter as motile adults or in the larval state and complete their life cycle in the shallow waters of the wetland. Different reeds and sedges are found in freshwater contexts than in brackish water (see chapter 10). During the late Preceramic occupation of Paredones and Huaca Prieta, these wetlands were the site of raised field agriculture, which provided secure cropping environments for permanent water table horticulture (see chapters 5 and 7). Today ephemeral watercourses cross these wetlands, which may be fed by irrigation runoff, but it is also possible that these drainages fed groundwater into the freshwater wetlands (Netherly 2011a, 2011b). Where the wetlands are extensive, the upper portion may be freshwater and the sector nearer the sea may be brackish. These biotopes extend northward from the Chicama Valley, parallel to the sea, to the area of Puémape and the now dry mouth of the Cupis-

nique River. Their presence in the past is attested by the geomorphological and sediment studies by project geologists (see chapter 5) and by the faunal and floral remains recovered in the excavations at Huaca Prieta and Paredones (see chapters 9 and 10).

The impacts of periodic ENSO events have been of varying strength and greater frequency over the past 5000 years than in the first half of the Holocene. The intermittent effect on the wetland environments, however, has depended on the degree of overbank flooding by the river. High discharge from the river scoured and perhaps reworked the channels of the estuary and impacted the riverbanks and the riverine vegetation growing on them. At the same time, dense stands of reeds and trees such as willow absorbed the force of the current, allowing floodwaters to move more slowly over the floodplain and deposit sediments. One such mega-event is reported by Goodbred et al. (see chapter 5) for the lower valley plain but at a time when the Huaca Prieta and Paredones mounds were no longer in use. It affected what must have been the lowest (most seaward) part of the dry forest zone and the wetland biozone, depositing a thick layer of rich, river-borne sediment over what had been a poor, stony, soil surface in the dry forest zone and over lacustrine strata of the wetlands. ENSO events that brought general and repeated rainfall to the lower valley, in contrast to strong, isolated storms in the upper watershed of the river, charged the water table, bringing more water into the freshwater wetlands as well as causing those closer to the sea to fill with brackish water. The raised water table might persist for several years beyond a major event, supporting these wetland areas.

LITTORAL AND MARINE ENVIRONMENTS

The rocky or sandy shores, the intertidal zones, and the open sea constitute a series of biotopes of particular interest for the Preceramic populations on the Sangamon terrace. The marine sector can be divided into a series of biozones. The Huaca Prieta and Paredones populations had access to both sandy and rocky beaches (fig. 4.2). As Moseley (1975) has noted, all the maritime societies that achieved complexity during the late Preceramic

FIGURE 4.2. The present-day shoreline and pebble beach just north of the Huaca Prieta mound (*right arrow*) and the Cupisnique mound (*left arrow*).

had access to both rocky and sandy beaches and thus a broader range of resources (compare Chu Barrera 2011; Elera 1998). The intertidal zone and the adjacent benthic zone are home to mollusks like mussels and barnacles, predators like crabs, and grazers (e.g., on seaweed) such as snails, chitons, and echinoderms (sea urchins). Seaweed and kelp provide food and a substrate for some of these creatures. The most important resources of sandy beaches are various species of clam, snails, and crustaceans (see chapter 9). Some fish are habitually found near the coast, and some (like mullet) enter the estuary and may be carried into the wetlands. Some sharks can tolerate brackish water as well and may be found in the shallow waters of the estuary or even the wetlands. Other fish prefer deeper water off the coast. Many of these species can be captured by net from the beach. Distinctly pelagic species, however, would require watercraft and specialized gear for regular capture, except for scavenging occasionally stranded individuals.

Dependent on the marine resources are the multitudes of seabirds, particularly pelicans, cormorants, and boobies. These birds nest on rocky points or islands in dense numbers. Also found on the rocky shores are the rookeries or breeding grounds of marine mammals: sea lions and seals. Although these large mammals can be taken on land, their whole adaptation is marine. The large marine mammals (dolphins and whales) are pelagic but occasionally are stranded and were scavenged in the prehistoric past.

HOLOCENE GEOGRAPHY, CLIMATE, AND HUMAN HISTORY

Fourteen thousand years ago at the end of the Pleistocene, small human groups continued to camp sporadically on the Sangamon terrace. Their inventory of food shows exploitation of the open dry forest, the estuary, and the marine environment. It is clear that the terrace, in addition to its preeminence, provided access to three important environments. The steadily rising sea level had brought the shoreline to within ~2 km of the modern sea level at ~10,000 years ago. By ~5000 years ago, sea level was at modern levels. We are not certain of the linear distance from the terrace to the sea at ~14,000 years ago, the beginning of Phase I, but it is estimated to be between 28 and 30 km, a day's walk for hardy foragers.

Changes in the marine environment brought about by rising sea level clearly influenced the movement of fauna (and humans) inland. It also moved the marine environments. Another environment affected by rising sea level was the estuary, since landforms (riverbanks) as well as the grade of the river itself were affected. But the estuarine environment, however reconfigured, remained, so the plant and animal resources would probably not have changed. The continued ENSO events in the Holocene brought occasional overbank flooding of the river, with deposition of silts and sands on the coastal plain within 1–3 km of the river. It is probable that, as the boundary between land and sea advanced, limited wetlands and seeps or springs originating in groundwater flow were present throughout this period on the inland side of the terrace.

The climate became both drier and warmer at the transition to the Holocene, but ENSO activity persisted. Sea surface temperature was some 2°C warmer than at present. After ~8000 years ago, oceanic conditions were unfavorable to ENSO development. The result on land was drier conditions and lack of flood deposits (Rein et al. 2005). These conditions appear to have persisted to ~5600 years ago (Rein et al. 2005), which is the midpoint in Huaca Prieta's history. Thereafter ENSO patterns become active again.

By ~7500 years ago, however, the rising sea level caused back flooding in the lower valley and adjacent coastal area, creating lagoons in some littoral zones (fig. 4.3). These were not fluvial floods, and chemically these open lagoons were oligotrophic. They extended some 500–1000 m inland from the modern strand line and probably well seaward of the modern shoreline. The area that could be measured was some 2.5 km². While close to the Huaca Prieta site, these lagoons were not highly productive in terms of resources. The lagoons developed around 7500 years ago and persisted about 1000 years. The age of 7500 years is concurrent with the early period of mound construction at Huaca Prieta and the age of ~6500 years corresponds with the appearance of the Paredones mound and probably with use of the former lagoonal wetlands for crop food production. By 6500 years ago, the lagoons had been replaced by transient wetlands, a time when more intensive crop production developed at Paredones (chapters 5 and 10). Thus it can be seen that the first half of the Holocene saw many changes in sea level, ENSO frequency, the location of the river mouth, groundwater flow, the location of wetlands, and the deposition of sediment by overbank riverine floods.

These developments have to be taken into consideration as we consider the environments available to the population at Huaca Prieta and Paredones. The dry forest environment, which extended to the margins of the valley and included some very specialized drought-adapted plants and animals such as *Capparis*, a fruit-bearing tree; *Tillandsia*, a fiber-producing bromeliad; and the Sechuran desert fox (*Lycalopex sechurae*). As humans expanded into the lower valley, it was at the expense of the dry forest. Nonetheless, the faunal and floral remains at Huaca Prieta indicate that this environment continued to contribute both food and artisanal resources. The lower valley still had a broad belt of gravel and sand alluvium inland from the terrace and adjacent wetlands (fig. 4.4). The megafloods that deposited thick beds of alluvium over this stony ground, seen today in the walls of irrigation canals, occurred after the abandonment of Huaca Prieta. This area became an important resource zone for the Huaca Prieta populations, who eventually began to create raised fields for cultivation, thus contributing to the eventual eutrophication and reduction of the wetlands. The estuary of the river continued to be an important source of resources, both within the lower river and over the muddy riverine deposits at the river's mouth. The riparian environment along the riverbank also continued to be a source of specific resources.

Most stable of all was the marine environment, despite the gradual encroachment on the land. It is apparent from the seabed that the lower part of the valley consisted of frequent rocky outcrops

FIGURE 4.3. The present-day brackish water lagoon near the mouth of the Chicama River.

separated by alluvial plain. The marine fauna and plants found on rocky outcrops and reefs are very different from those found on sandy bottoms. This is probably the most fundamental characterization of the plants and animals found in the nearshore sectors of the sea. Oceanographers divide the marine environment into the following categories: seabirds and sea mammals, particularly sea lions, are found on the sandy beach, while seaweed, other invertebrates, snails, and clams are found both on the beach and in the immediate subtidal zone. The rocky beach and reefs are also rich in invertebrates, including echinoderms and chitons; bivalves, including mussels; limpets; marine snails; and seaweeds. Fish are found over the seabed in both areas. The estuarine zone of the shore also has a rich fish fauna not found elsewhere. Beyond the tidal zone and the subtidal zone lies the open sea, with many species of fish in the nutrient-rich Humboldt Current. Taking these fish required the development of technological aids: hooks and lines, fishnets, and eventually watercraft.

Despite the minor transgression of the land by a rising sea level, it does not appear to have caused any major disruption of the marine focus at Huaca Pricta or of the availability of marine resources. Marine foragers sought bivalves, snails, and marine invertebrates and may have scavenged pelagic fish thrown up by high surf from storms, as fisherfolk do today. They also may have driven fish upstream from the estuary to shallow water where they could be clubbed. It is clear that sea lions and seabirds that rest and reproduce onshore were also available and taken. For the Huaca Prieta populations, the marine environment juxtaposed with the wetlands, the dry forest, and the estuary provided an unusually productive cluster of environments.

DISCUSSION

We develop the compelling prospect of linking the major late Pleistocene to late Holocene trans-

FIGURE 4.4. The coastal plains, with sandy sediments of the lower Chicama Valley and the Andean foothills in the background.

formations in the Preceramic society and culture of the northern Peruvian coast with local environmental conditions by presenting high-resolution climate and paleoenvironmental records from the Chicama Valley analyzed in chapter 5 and appendix 1, together with the paleoecological record of human diets from Huaca Prieta and Paredones (see chapters 9 and 10 and appendices 4–9), and the architectural, burial, and settlement records for the area (see chapters 6, 7, and 11 and appendix 10).

In summary, we find during the Holocene and to the present day that the desert coast of Peru was and is a high-risk environment subject to a number of transient and long-term environmental impacts, including tectonic activity resulting in uplift and earthquakes; ENSO activity that can bring rain, flooding, and periodic drought in the highlands; and long-term desertification resulting from human activity as well as aeolian sand movement. These events are limited in their effect and do not impact all valleys to the same degree. For example, dune movement is much more severe in the Jequetepeque Valley than it is in the Chicama Valley (Dillehay and Kolata 2004; Netherly 2011a, 2011b). These environmental processes present challenges to human societies and may be met with diverse responses: abandonment of an area; intensification of some subsistence strategies over others; development of social, economic, and trade relations with societies living at a distance in different environments; and the development of more social and economic complexity as a means of ameliorating risk and ensuring a supply of essential resources, particularly foodstuffs. Additionally, societies seek to ensure their survival not only through cooperation but also through their belief systems or ontology, which may be made manifest in cooperative endeavors such as the use and gradual construction of the Huaca Prieta and Paredones mounds.

CHAPTER 5

HOLOCENE GEOLOGY AND PALEOENVIRONMENTAL HISTORY OF THE LOWER CHICAMA VALLEY

Steven L. Goodbred Jr., Rachel Beavins, Michael Ramírez, Mario Pino, André Oliveira Sawakuchi, Claudio Latorre, Tom D. Dillehay, and Duccio Bonavia

INTRODUCTION

This chapter focuses on reconstructing the Holocene paleoenvironmental history of the Chicama Valley and coastal system, which has provided diverse natural resources for the Preceramic cultures at Huaca Prieta and Paredones (fig. 5.1). Here we present the results of a geological investigation of sediment cores, outcrops, and surface morphology from the coastal plain and lower valley. From these data we reconstruct the paleoenvironmental history of the study area, which represents the natural landscape and resources available to the early peoples living there.

BACKGROUND

CLIMATE AND ENSO

The north coast of Peru from 4° to 10°S receives an average of 100 mm of precipitation annually (NOAA 2012), which is hyperarid. Within the Chicama River basin and adjacent river catchments, however, the Andean highlands >2500 m in elevation receive 500–1500 mm/yr of precipitation that is delivered over ~175 days/yr, providing a perennial water source to the region (Romero et al. 2007). At these relatively slow delivery rates of 3–8 mm/day, though, surface runoff is limited outside of episodically intense ENSO-related rainfall events. Thus most precipitation enters the hydrologic system as groundwater. Fed by this highland rainfall, rivers that head at elevations >2500 m (figs. 5.1 and 5.2) generally support perennial water discharge. These fluvial systems host comparatively verdant, cultivated valleys that often extend to the shoreline and punctuate the intervening stretches of coastal desert and dune fields that define most of the north coast.

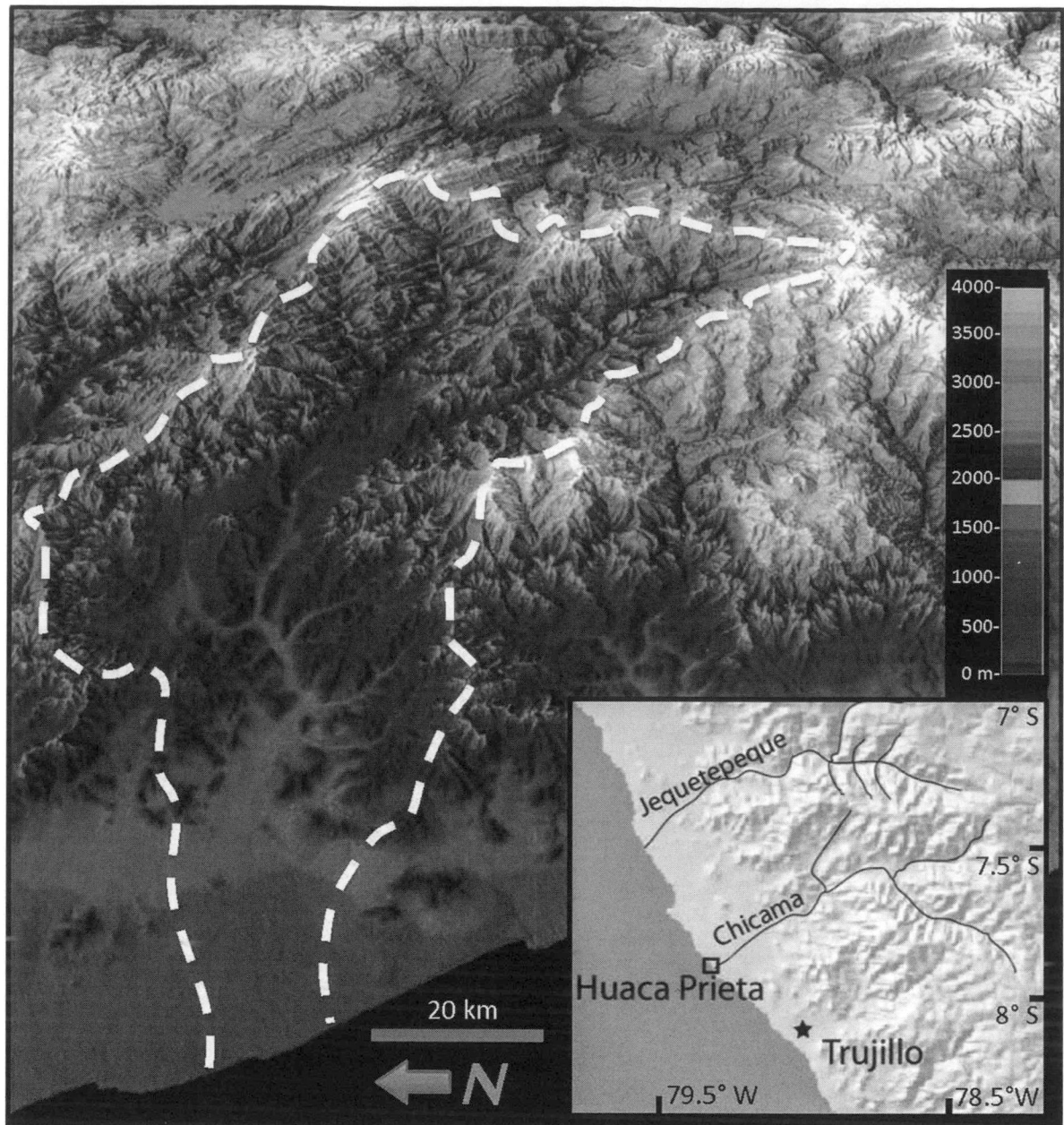

FIGURE 5.1. Oblique view of a digital elevation model (DEM) for the Chicama River catchment (*dashed line*) and regional location map (*inset*). Note the broad valleys formed in the lower catchment, where weak rocks are easily eroded. The more competent highlands define the rim of the basin, although elevations are lower than the surrounding volcanic terrains, which allow some moisture from the Amazon basin to fall in the upper catchment. Elevation data from the National Aeronautics and Space Administration Shuttle Radar Topography Mission (NASA SRTM).

Overall the regional aridity owes to a combination of the orographic barrier of the Andes, coastal upwelling, the cold Humboldt Current, and high pressure conditions in the eastern equatorial Pacific. El Niño events, bringing coastal rains and widespread flooding, occur when southeasterly trade winds weaken, allowing low pressure systems to migrate eastward across the Pacific. Historically, strong El Niño events occur on average every nine years (Quinn and Neal 1992), but paleoclimate records indicate that both the frequency and magnitude of El Niño phases have varied considerably through the Holocene (table 5.1; Moy et al. 2002; Sandweiss 2003).

Table 5.1. Overview of regional studies with results suggesting a mid-Holocene weakening of El Niño wet phases through either diminished frequency or magnitude

Study location	Proxy	Potential hiatus of weak period (ybp)	Reference
Galapagos (0.8°S)	Lake sediments (grain size)	9000–4500	Conroy et al. 2008
Galapagos (1°13′S)	Mg/Ca paleothermometry of planktonic foraminifera	8000–5000	Koutavas et al. 2002
Southwestern Ecuador (2°46′S)	Lake sediment records (inorganic clastic laminae)	Early Holocene to 5000	Rodbell et al. 1999
Southwestern Ecuador (2°46′S)	Lake sediment records (inorganic clastic laminae)	Early Holocene to 7000	Moy et al. 2002
North/central coastal Peru (4°40′S–8°55′S)	Catfish otolith $\delta^{18}O$	Prior to 5000	Andrus et al. 2002a and b
North coastal Peru (4°30′S–9°40′S)	Thermally anomalous molluscan assemblages	8000–3800	Sandweiss 2003
Offshore Peru (11°4′S)	Marine sediment organic geo-chemical markers (cholesterol and dinosterol)	8200–3900*	Makou et al. 2010
Offshore Peru (12°3′S)	Marine sediments (alkenones, photosynthetic pigments, and lithics)	8200–5600	Rein et al. 2005
Southern Peru (17°37′S)	Debris flow deposits	8400–5300	Keefer et al. 2003

*Author's interpretation of data presented in study, based on total cessation of terrestrial runoff for the period noted.

Many studies address the complex issue of ENSO variability; with growing support for the idea of diminished frequency and/or strength of El Niño events during the mid-Holocene (Conroy et al. 2008; Rein et al. 2005). But two important questions remain: first, when this hypothesized hiatus occurred and, second, what background climate conditions were during the mid-Holocene. Studies generally agree that the onset of the decline in El Niño frequency and/or magnitude occurred ~9000–8000 cal BP, with modern-day conditions established from ~5000–3800 cal BP (table 5.1). Data from a diverse range of proxies from several locations in the eastern Pacific support these findings, including offshore marine sediment records (Koutavas et al. 2006; Rein et al. 2005), paleolimnology records (Conroy et al. 2008), geoarchaeological data (Sandweiss 2003), and terrestrial El Niño flood records (Keefer et al. 2003).

Much of the current debate surrounding the issue of a mid-Holocene El Niño hiatus centers on the mean climate state during this time. Geo-archaeological evidence for warmer sea surface temperatures (SSTs) off the north coast of Peru includes the presence of thermally anomalous molluscan assemblages (TAMAs) in and around archaeological middens from ~9000–5800 cal BP (Sandweiss 2003; Sandweiss et al. 1996) as well as oxygen isotope records contained in catfish oto-liths from some of those same archaeological sites (Andrus et al. 2002a; see appendix 13). Mixed-temperate assemblages appear from ~5800–3000 cal BP, interpreted as the onset of upwelling and infrequent El Niño events, with entirely cool-water assemblages after 3000 cal BP, indicating the onset of modern El Niño frequencies. Paleo-temperatures generated from seasonal growth increments of sea catfish otoliths from some of those same sites, dated at 6500–6000 cal BP, indi-cate greater seasonality and SSTs 3–4°C warmer than present (Andrus et al. 2002a). Paleotempera-tures calculated from Mg/Ca ratios in planktonic foraminifera from the upwelling cold tongue in the Galapagos indicate a decline in seasonality from 8000 to 5000 cal BP, with cooler, more

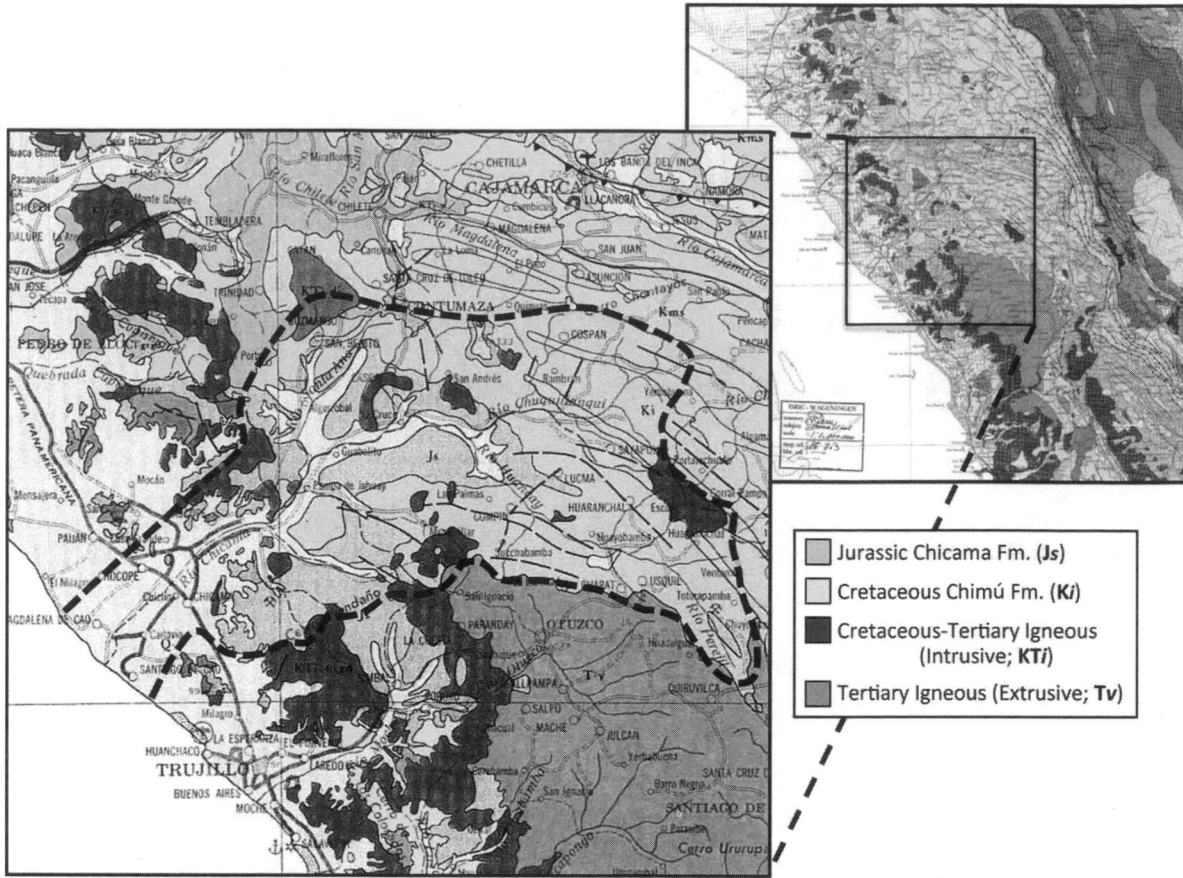

FIGURE 5.2. Geologic map of northern Peru with detailed local inset map. Dashed line traces the Chicama River catchment basin. Note that the lithology of the Chicama catchment is unique in the region, consisting of older Mesozoic sedimentary and metasedimentary rocks, compared with Tertiary-age volcanics that dominate most of the river basins north and south of Chicama. The Jurassic Chicama Formation dominates the lower catchment and consists of fractured marine shales that yield a comparatively high load of fine-grained sediment. These sediments have helped build the broad floodplains that distinguish the lower Chicama Valley from adjacent fluvial valleys. The Cretaceous Chimú Formation forms the upper portion of the catchment and consists of more competent shallow-water sandstones and limestone that form steep, high-standing mountains.

stable SSTs during this time (Koutavas et al. 2006). Numerical modeling of ENSO variability also supports the idea of a cooler eastern equatorial Pacific during the mid-Holocene (Clement et al. 2000). These results suggest that El Niño was present during this time but that El Niño and La Niña events were of smaller amplitude and frequency, with mean conditions sustaining cold SSTs and arid coasts similar to today.

These varied studies highlight the obvious spatial heterogeneity in the occurrence of ENSO phenomena, which may account for some of the discrepancies in the literature regarding the timing of the El Niño hiatus. Despite these disparities, multiple studies demonstrate that, after the onset,

a notable intensification of El Niño occurred by 3000–2000 cal BP (Conroy et al. 2008; Makou et al. 2010; Moy et al. 2002; Rein et al. 2005; Sandweiss 2003). Results from the present study show that this intensification of El Niño wet phases in the late Holocene has significant short-term impacts on the Chicama Valley and coast.

CATCHMENT GEOLOGY

The Chicama River drains terrains composed of folded, fractured metasediments of the Jurassic Chicama and Cretaceous Chimú Formations, which are locally intruded by Tertiary-age mafic

FIGURE 5.3. Photos of the upper Chicama River and catchment basin: *a*, steep, exposed bedrock with limited soil cover define the Chimú Formation of the Chicama highlands (these rocks yield limited sediment but, situated at >2000 m in elevation, serve as the main rain catchment; dissolution of limestones in the Chimú Formation also contributes to the high dissolved load of the river, which supports the carbonate-precipitating charophyte algae and abundant gastropods in downstream coastal wetlands and lagoons); *b*, rolling, soil-mantled hillslopes are typical of the mid-elevations of the Chicama catchment from 1200 to 2000 m (these areas are dominated by the Chicama Formation, with an abundance of shales that sustain soil production and arable hillside); *c–d*, the upper Chicama River is a braided, gravel bed stream that is very similar to its course further downstream at the coast (the upper reaches of the Chicama River, shown here, are incised due to long-term tectonic uplift and have eroded the terminal points of the Neogene-age fans and pediment; erosion of steep cutbanks is a major source of sediment to the river).

and felsic igneous bodies (fig. 5.2; Institute of Geology and Minerals 1975). The igneous intrusions lie principally along the front range of the Andes and dominate the catchments of the small alluvial fan systems north of the Chicama River valley. The older Chicama Formation dominates the lower elevations of the catchment (below ~1500 m) and consists of heavily folded shales interbedded with sandstone units. The shales are heavily sheared and very weak, eroding rapidly. As such, erosion of the Chicama Formation has opened broad valleys in the lower bedrock-controlled portion of the river, leaving signifi-

cant areas of arable land due to the low-gradient slopes and fine sediments derived from the shales. In contrast, the Chimú Formation that defines the highland portions the river catchment (above ~1500 m) is dominated by very competent sandstones and limestones that form steep, high-relief landforms with limited soil cover (fig. 5.3). Overall, the dominance of these Mesozoic sedimentary rocks in the Chicama River catchment is unique among north Peruvian rivers. By contrast, most river systems in the region drain younger Cenozoic volcanic rocks that are more competent and define steep, narrow river valleys (fig. 5.2).

METHODS

SEDIMENT CORING AND RADIOCARBON SAMPLING

This research was conducted through the sampling and descriptions of Holocene stratigraphy throughout the lower Chicama valley, coast, and adjacent alluvial systems (fig. 5.4a). Stratigraphy was accessed through exposed sections along river cutbanks and within irrigation ditches as well as through hand-augering of subsurface sediment to depths of 6 m. Much of the environmental history of the region is captured in riverbank exposures and associated subsurface sediments in the lower valley and adjacent coastal system (fig. 5.4b–c). Specifically, the character, origin, and relationship of these deposits were reconstructed through detailed evaluation of a coring and outcrop transect from the Chicama River mouth to ~1.5 km upstream along a 3–4 m high fluvial cutbank (fig. 5.4c). The subsurface samples were collected via sediment coring with gouge augers, using 100 cm long, 5 cm diameter or 50 cm long, 2.5 cm diameter auger heads (fig. 5.5a–b).

Radiocarbon dating was conducted on 25 samples, including wood, charcoal, organic sediment, and gastropod shells, from numerous locations within floodplain, lagoon, and shoreline settings (table 5.2). Care was taken to select high-quality, in situ samples wherever possible; the principal exceptions were two charcoal samples from sandy shoreface deposits. The charcoal samples were small, friable, and spread throughout the shoreface deposits, suggesting that they must have been locally derived and presumed to be from local fires in the nearby backdune setting. All wood, charcoal, and gastropod samples were gently washed with deionized water, dried, and weighed. Preparation of organic sediments involved drying, crushing, and weighing of bulk sediment, an aliquot of which was used to calculate organic carbon via loss–on–ignition at 450°C for 6 hours.

Most samples were measured at either the National Ocean Sciences Accelerator Mass Spectrometry Facility (NOSAMS) in Woods Hole, Massachusetts, or the Accelerator Mass Spectrometry Laboratory (AA) at the University of Arizona (table 5.2). Carbon isotopes were also measured by the lab for all samples. Radiocarbon ages were calibrated using CALIB 6.0 and the IntCal04.14C calibration dataset (Stuiver et al. 2010). No reservoir correction was applied to the gastropod samples because they represent freshwater lagoon or wetland species that are presumed to be in equilibrium with the atmospheric CO_2 reservoir. Nonmarine $\partial^{13}C$ values of −5.6‰ to −9.8‰ from these samples support this assertion (table 5.2). As a further check, all measured gastropod ages are internally consistent with adjacent organic carbon samples.

MICROFOSSILS AND STABLE ISOTOPES

Lagoonal sediments buried several meters below silty floodplain deposits consist of interbedded siliciclastic muds, organic detritus, and biogenic carbonates containing a fossil assemblage of charophyte algae, ostracods, and gastropods (fig. 5.6). Sediment samples were gently washed with deionized water over a 90 mm sieve and dried for 4 hours at 50°C. They were subsequently examined under a microscope for fossil content, with individual charophyte fruiting bodies (gyrogonites) and ostracod specimens mounted for imaging with a scanning electron microscope.

About 15–20 well-preserved gyrogonites were selected and cleaned under a binocular microscope using a fine brush and deionized water (fig. 5.6a). Treatment to remove any organic material consisted of immersing the gyrogonites in 5 mL of 10% hydrogen peroxide for 3 hours in a gentle shaker (Coletta et al. 2001). Cleaned, dried gyrogonites were weighed and placed in glass vials prior to stable oxygen and carbon analysis. Isotope analysis of ostracods consisted only of those belonging to the genus *Cyprideis* (likely sp. *torosa*) to avoid problems arising from interspecific differences (fig. 5.6d). It is also the convention to select only adult specimens for analysis, due to the fact that ostracods go through several molting stages or "instars" over their lifetime, with maximum calcification at adulthood (Armstrong and Brasier 2005). Preparation methods for ostracods for stable isotope analysis were the same as for those of the charophyte gyrogonites. Finally, 10–20 *Lymnaea* gastropods were picked from sieved sediment samples (fig. 5.6c) then gently sonicated before a final cleaning with a brush under the binocular microscope. Cleaned samples were crushed

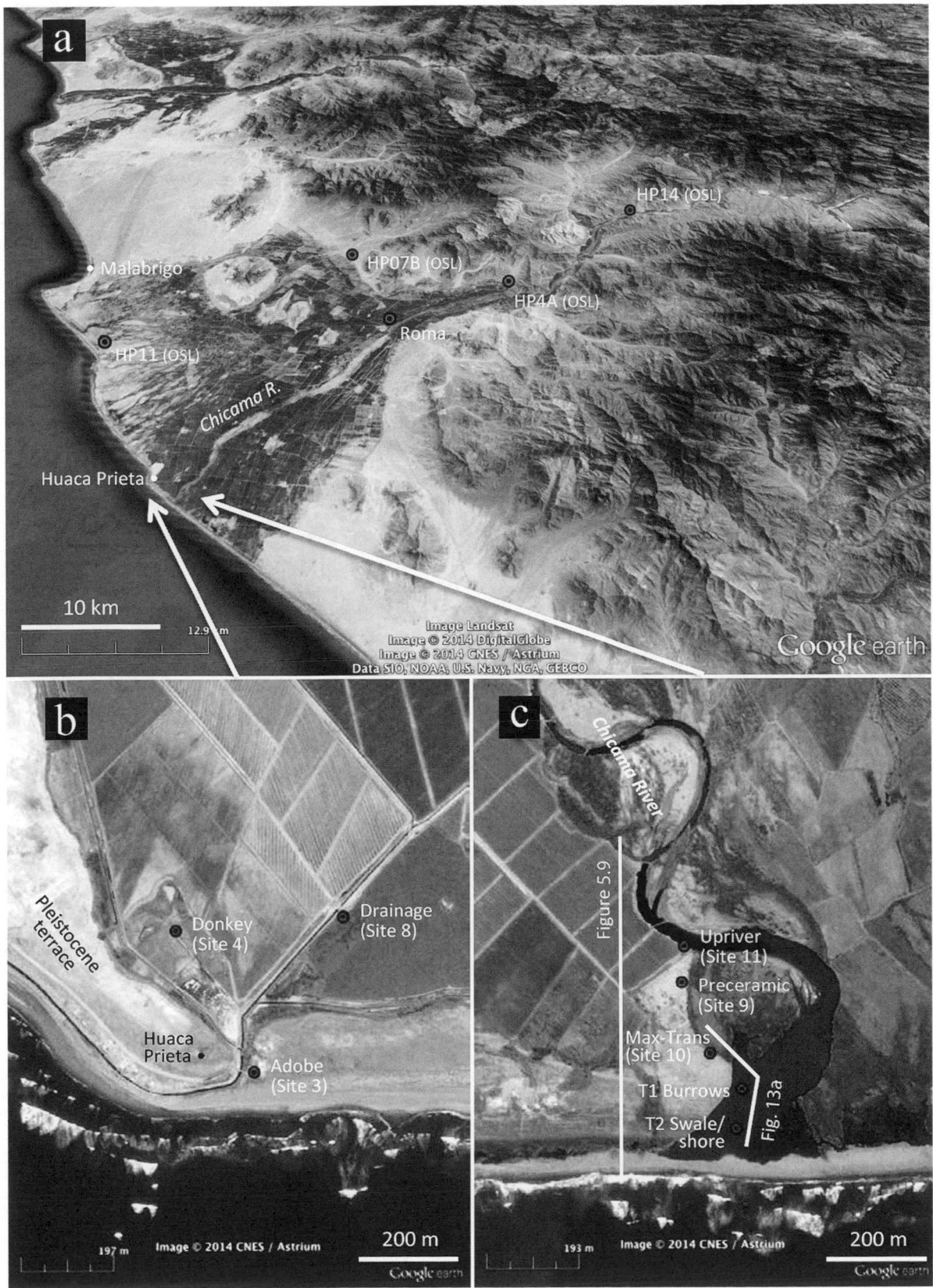

FIGURE 5.4. Google Earth maps showing sampling locations within the Chicama Valley and coastal system: *a*, north-oblique view of the Chicama River basin and coast, including location of Huaca Prieta and off-mound location of sampling sites where OSL ages were measured; *b*, location of three hand-drilled sediment cores collected adjacent to the Sangamon terrace and Huaca Prieta, which were used to correlate cultural and geological records from the mound with those from *c*, the Chicama River mouth. Sampling at the river mouth included hand cores at five locations plus mapping of the 3–4 m high cutbank exposure shown in figures 5.9 and 5.13a.

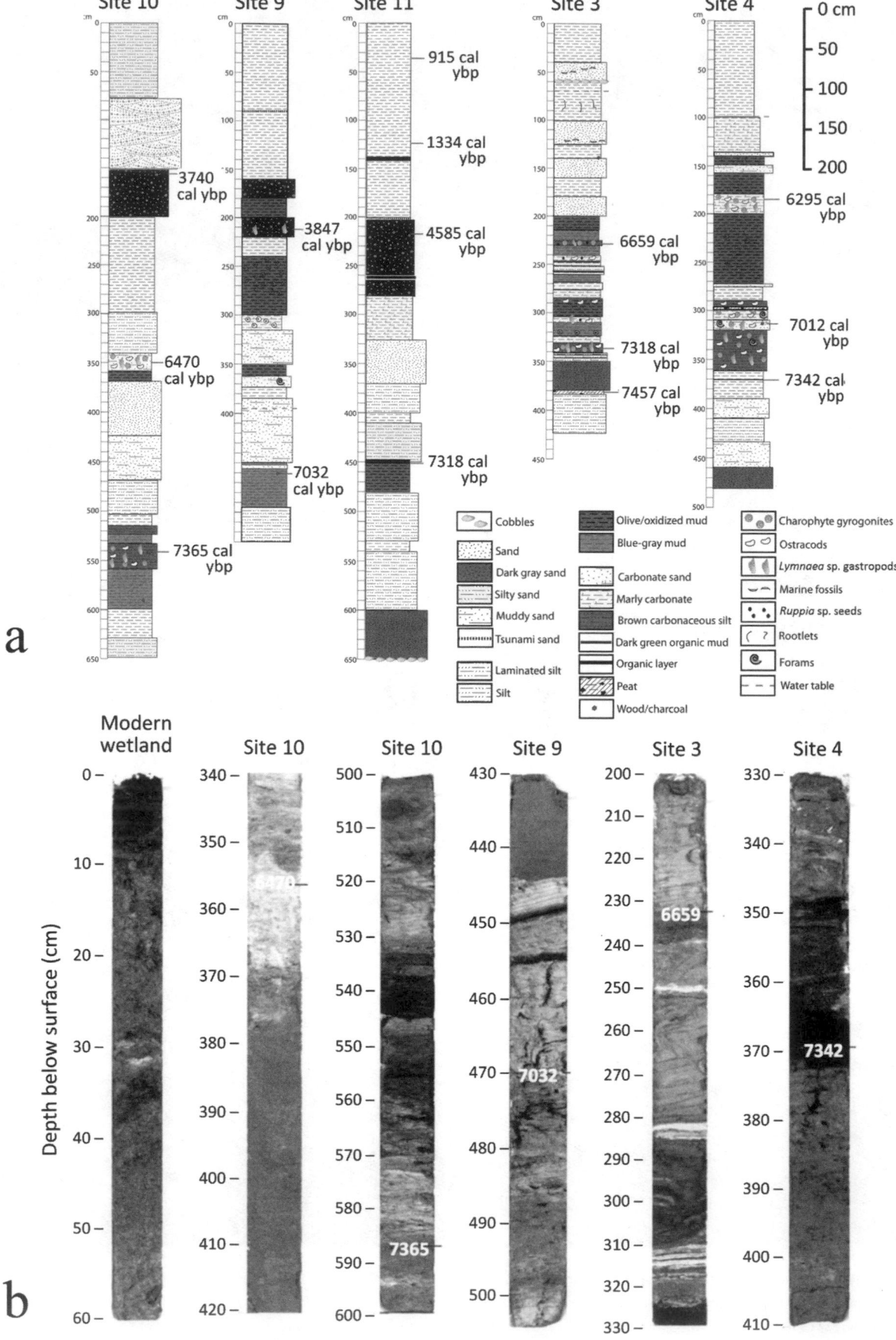

with a mortar and pestle prior to rinsing in a beaker with ethanol and drying in a 50°C oven.

OPTICALLY STIMULATED LUMINESCENCE

Sample Preparation

Samples for Optically Stimulated Luminescence (OSL) measurements were collected in aluminum tubes. Samples for gamma spectrometry measurements and radiation dose rate calculations were collected separately in plastic bags. Sample preparation for OSL measurements in coarse grained (180–250 μm or 125–180 μm) quartz grains followed standard procedures (Aitken 1998), which included (1) wet sieving to isolate the 180–250 μm grain size fraction; (2) density separation using lithium metatungstate solution at densities of 2.85 and 2.62 g/cm³ to separate light from heavy minerals and quartz from feldspar, respectively; and (3) chemical treatment of quartz concentrates with H_2O_2, HCl 3.78% to eliminate organic matter and carbonates, followed by HF 38% for 40 minutes to eliminate the outer layers of quartz grains damaged by alpha particles and remnant feldspar grains. Samples for gamma spectrometry measurements were dried, weighed, and packed in sealed plastic containers. Gamma spectrometry was performed 28 days after packing samples into sealed containers for the equilibration of radon decay.

Luminescence Measurements for Equivalent Dose Estimation

OSL measurements were made in a Risø TL/OSL DA-20 reader equipped with infrared (IR) diodes (875 nm) and blue light-emitting diodes (LEDs) (470nm) for stimulation, a Hoya-340 filter (290–370 nm), and built-in ^{90}Sr/^{90}Y beta source with a dose rate of 0.088 Gy/s. Aliquots of quartz grains were mounted in steel cups for measurements. Equivalent doses of quartz aliquots were calculated using the Single-Aliquot Regenerative (SAR) dose protocol (Murray and Wintle 2003). IR stimulation indicated significant content of feldspar in quartz aliquots even after repeated heavy liquid separation and chemical treatments. Aliquots checked under the microscope showed a significant amount of lithic fragments formed by fine-grained crystals of quartz and feldspar. Thus an IR stimulation at 60°C for 200 seconds before blue stimulation was used to bleach feldspar and measure a quartz signal in the presence of feldspar. This procedure followed the approach proposed by Jakob Wallinga et al. (2002), but using a long-time (200 seconds) IR stimulation under lower temperature (60°C). Dose recovery tests performed in aliquots bleached under sunlight were performed to set up the preheat temperature and evaluate the dosimetry capacity of the studied quartz aliquots. Table 5.3 presents the SAR protocol used for equivalent dose estimation. Sample equivalent doses were calculated through the Central Age Model (Galbraith et al. 1999).

Dose Rate

High-resolution gamma spectrometry (HPGe detector with energy resolution of 2.1 KeV and relative efficiency of 55%) was used to measure the concentrations of ^{40}K, ^{238}U, and ^{232}Th. Sample radiation dose rates were calculated using radionuclides concentrations and conversion factors by Grzegorz Adamiec and Martin Aitken (1998). Dose rate calculation used water content in samples during the time of collection, but a high range (10%) in water concentration was used due to uncertainties regarding water variation through time. The cosmic radiation dose rate was calculated according to John R. Prescott and Larry Stephan (1982).

FIGURE 5.5. (opposite) Lithologs of sediment cores and close-up photos of core sections collected near the Chicama River mouth (sites 9–11) and Huaca Prieta (sites 3–4, 8): a, lithologs reveal the complex and variable lithology of coastal river plain sediments deposited over 9000 years of Holocene environmental change (depths are below the riverbed-groundwater level, with several meters of sediment overlying these sections); b, photos of core sections show complex alternation of white to tan carbonates with brown organic layers and blue-gray fluvial muds reflecting the temporal changes in the lagoon with varying river discharge and climate (note that the photo at the left is of a surface core from a modern wetland lagoon for comparison; depths below ground surface are given in centimeters, with calibrated radiocarbon ages shown). The location of all sites is shown in figure 5.4b–c.

Table 5.2. Summary of radiocarbon samples, environmental contexts, and dating results

No.	Site	Lab sample no.	Material	δ¹⁵C	¹⁴C age BP	Cal yr BP (2σ range)	Depth* (cm)
1	Swale/shore (T2)	OS-82744	Wood charcoal	−26.4	965±20	**853** (773–908)	150
2	Swale/shore (T2)	AA-83255	Wood charcoal	−23.5	1166±40	**1017** (933–1090)	200
3	Swale/shore (T2)	AA-83253	Wood charcoal	−26.4	2043±48	**1940** (1823–2061)	160
4	Burrows (T1)	AA-83255	Wood charcoal	−21.1	2767±90	**2833** (2505–3077)	180
5	Max trans (10)	Beta244172	Organic soil (10% wt)	−19.1	2820±80	**2880** (2742–3078)	160
6	Max trans (10)	AA-83252	Wood charcoal	−25.8	3521±49	**3740** (3610–3868)	200
7	Max trans (10)	AA-83258	Gastropod (*Lymnaea* spp.)	−6.0	5739±51	**6470** (6321–6633)	350
8	Max trans (10)	OS-82737	Wood fragment	−29.9	6500±30	**7365** (7279–7428)	540
9	Preceramic (9)	AA-83257	Gastropod (*Valvata* spp.)	−9.4	3611±47	**3847** (3699–3976)	220
10	Preceramic (9)	OS-82739	Wood fragment	−27.4	6190±30	**7032** (6930–7161)	470
11	Upriver (11)	OS-82743	Wood charcoal	−19.3	1040±20	**915** (813–956)	35
12	Upriver (11)	OS-82803	Wood charcoal	−20.8	1500±20	**1334** (1300–1379)	125
13	Upriver (11)	OS-98802	Gastropod (*Valvata* spp.)	−5.6	4070±60	**4483** (4414–4778)	210
14	Upriver (11)	OS-83682	Wood charcoal	−25.6	4130±120	**4585** (4236–4860)	220
15	Upriver (11)	OS-98801	Gastropod (*Valvata* spp.)	−8.3	4390±50	**4903** (4841–5027)	260
16	Upriver (11)	OS-82742	Sediment organic carbon	−23.0	6440±30	**7318** (7258–7418)	450
17	Adobe (3)	OS-82728	Plant/wood	−26.6	1280±25	**1150** (1066–1257)	140
18	Adobe (3)	OS-86020	Gastropod (*Lymnaea* spp.)	−9.8	5900±40	**6659** (6504–6775)	230
19	Adobe (3)	OS-82727	Plant/wood	−14.7	6440±30	**7318** (7258–7418)	335
20	Adobe (3)	OS-77303	Plant/wood	−27.7	6600±35	**7457** (7416–7518)	380
21	Donkey (4)	OS-86024	Gastropod (*Lymnaea* spp.)	−7.6	5550±35	**6295** (6209–6398)	190
22	Donkey (4)	OS-77302	Wood fragment	−25.6	6180±35	**7012** (6901–7158)	315
23	Donkey (4)	OS-82735	Sediment organic carbon	−24.9	6460±35	**7342** (7266–7421)	370
24	Drainage (8)	OS-77304	Plant/wood	−24.1	6500±45	**7362** (7269–7432)	455
25	Roma	OS-99470	Wood charcoal	−24.2	2110±60	**2021** (1927–2121)	315

*Below ground surface.

**Relative to modern mean high water.

***Site is 30 km upstream along Chicama River at 165 masl.

ENVIRONMENTAL SETTINGS AND FACIES

The lower Chicama Valley, coastal system, and adjacent areas contain five major environmental settings: (1) outwash dominated alluvial environ- ments, (2) the fluvial channel-floodplain system, (3) an open-water lagoon system, (4) local palu- dal wetlands, and (5) coastal shoreface environ- ments (table 5.4). The presence and distribution of these settings have changed considerably through the Holocene, principally under the influence of

Elevation** (cm)	Facies	Environmental setting	Stratigraphic context
100	Fl-lf	Low Floodplain	Charcoal from El Niño flood deposit in swale between gravel berms
100	Fl-lf	Low Floodplain	Base of thick El Niño flood deposits between gravel berms (after T2)
165	Co-ss	Sand Shoreface	Charcoal from shoreface sand onlapping T2 tsunami surface
170	Co-ss	Sand Shoreface	Charcoal from shoreface sands just below T1 tsunami surface
190	Co-bd	Backdune	Muddy backdune swale capped by T1 tsunami surface
150	Co-bd	Backdune	Charcoal from cultural horizon in backdune; at maximum transgression
0	Lg-ca	Lagoon	Shallowest carbonate deposit below floodplain sequence
−190	Pl-lg	Lagoon	Deepest organic layer near base of lagoon deposits
130	Fl-lf	Low Floodplain	Gleysol with abundant gastropods; below Ceramic cultural horizon
−120	Pl-lg	Lagoon	Organic layer near base of lagoon deposits
315	Fl-pf	High Floodplain	Near top of high floodplain succession
225	Fl-pf	High Floodplain	Middle of high floodplain succession
140	Fl-lf	Low Floodplain	From upper gleysol beneath strong pedogenic carbonate
130	Fl-lf	Low Floodplain	From upper gleysol beneath strong pedogenic carbonate
90	Fl-lf	Low Floodplain	From lower gleysol beneath strong pedogenic carbonate
−100	Pl-lg	Lagoon	Disseminated organics near base of lagoon sequence
60	Fl-lf	Low Floodplain	Wood fragment from thick flooplain unit
−30	Lg-ca	Lagoon	Grazing gastropods from upper portion of lagoon sequence
−135	Pl-lg	Lagoon	Grass stems from organic layer in lower portion of lagoon sequence
−180	Pl-lg	Lagoon	Small wood fragment from base of lagoon sequence
60	Lg-ca	Lagoon	Grazing gastropods near top of lagoon sequence
−65	Pl-lg	Lagoon	Wood from lower portion of lagoon sequence
−120	Pl-lg	Lagoon	Disseminated organics near base of lagoon sequence
−155	Pl-lg	Lagoon	Organic matter from near base of lagoon sequence
N/A***	Fl-pf	High Floodplain	Charcoal from shallow firepit near base of thick floodplain sequence

climate, sea level, and sediment supply. Here we describe the attributes of these environments as recorded in the sediments, geomorphology, and stratigraphy of the area.

ALLUVIAL SETTINGS

Arid, rocky alluvial settings dominate the landscape regionally from the lower Andes to the coast. These environments consist of locally abundant debris cones and related mass-wasting

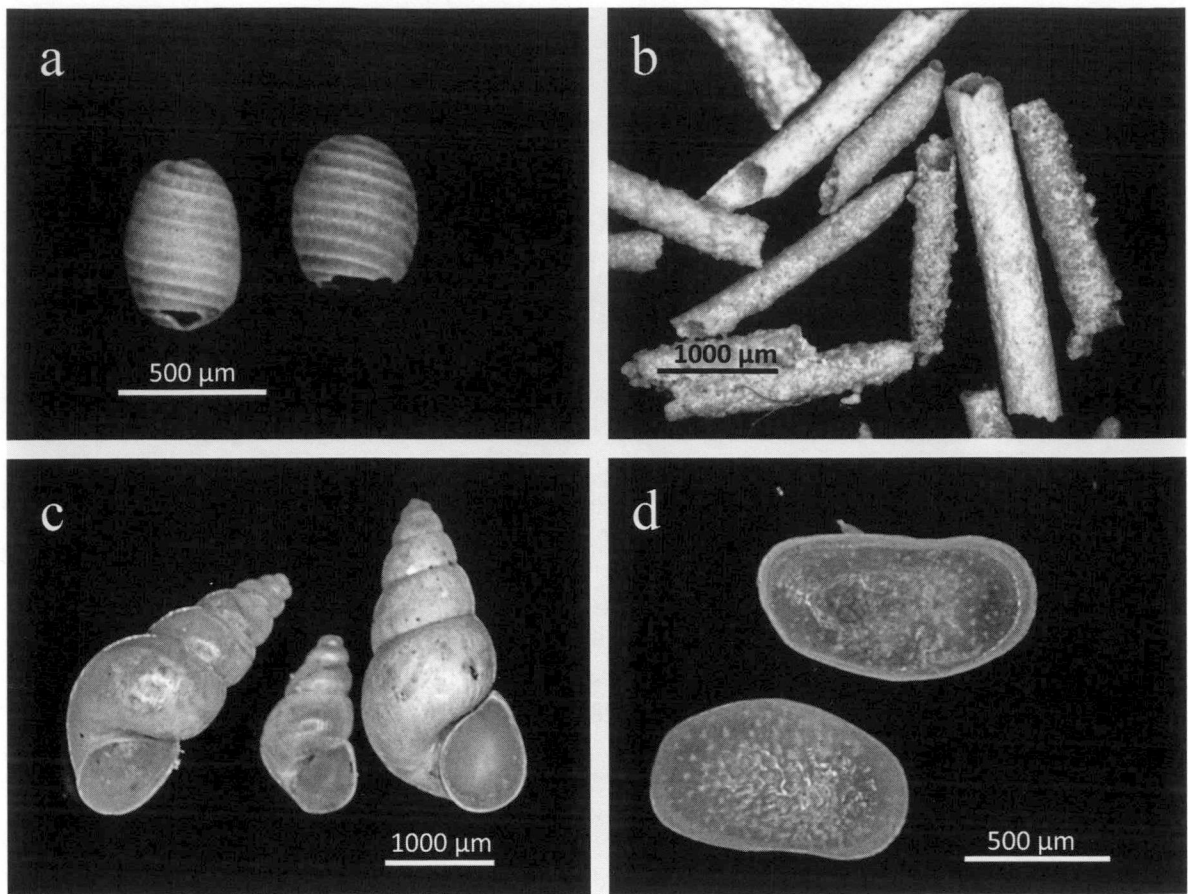

FIGURE 5.6. Light microscope images of major floral and faunal carbonates from the paleolagoon sediments: a, gyrogonites, the calcified fruiting bodies of charophyte algae, representing up to 20 percent of carbonate sediments; b, calcified stem encrustations from charophyte algae (these encrustations compose >50 percent of the carbonate deposits and often break down into fine carbonate muds); c, *Lymnaea* sp. gastropods are abundant grazers in charophyte meadows and represent up to 50 percent of the carbonate deposits; d, two examples of fresh-estuarine ostracod shells from the lagoon sequence, which are widely present and often compose up to 10 percent of carbonate deposits.

deposits that accumulate at the base of hillslopes (facies *Al-dc*; table 5.4), primarily within the arid and largely barren mountains below ~1500 m elevation. Many of the coarse, angular sediments within these debris cones are subsequently reworked into broad alluvial aprons by flash floods that are conveyed through quebrada valleys during the region's infrequent precipitation events. Such ephemeral discharge transports large volumes of poorly sorted sands and gravels that construct broad alluvial fans within nearly all mountain valley systems (facies *Al-fn*; table 5.4; fig. 5.7a). Downstream from the foothills these fans coalesce to form a vast, contiguous alluvial plain that extends roughly 20 km to the coast (fig. 5.7b).

Alluvial Fans

Shallow, braided channels that are separated by broad, flat interfluves characterize the morphology of these alluvial systems. Where the alluvial fans open to the lowland plains, these channels are poorly defined, suggesting a dominance of sheet flow and high sediment loading. Toward the coast the channels become increasingly well-defined, forming broad (200–1000 m), shallow (<2 m) braided-channel networks separated by gravelly interfluves (fig. 5.7a). During smaller, more frequent water discharge events, stream flow is generally confined to the channel and transports primarily sand and pebble-sized gravel. During large floods, however, the channels are scoured to form a cobble to boulder lag surface, and the

Table 5.3. SAR OSL protocol used for equivalent dose measurements in quartz aliquots

Step	Procedure
1	Dose (D_0, D_1, D_2, D_3, D_4, D_5, $D_6 = D_1$)
2	Preheat (200°C for 10 secs)
3	IRSL, 200 secs at 60°C
4	OSL, 40 secs at 125°C
5	Test dose
6	Preheat (160°C for 10 secs)
7	IRSL, 200 secs at 60°C
8	OSL, 40 secs at 125°C
9	Blue bleach, 40 secs at 280m°C
10	Return to step 1

Note: D_0 corresponds to the natural radiation dose; D_1, D_2, D_3, and D_4 were used to build the dose response curve; D_5 (Gy) was used to calculate recuperation; $D_6 = D_1$ was used to calculate the recycling ratio.

deposition of sand and gravel shifts to the interfluves via shallow overland flow (fig. 5.7b).

This episodic and variable discharge defines the transport regime for this gravel-dominated sedimentary facies, which generally has a low sand content and is most commonly clast supported. Where exposed in modern pits, the stratigraphy consists of 0.5–1.5 m thick bedding sets that typically fine upward from 10–25 cm sized cobbles to 2–5 cm pebble clasts with increasing sand content (fig. 5.7c). Lithology of the gravels is dominated by large quartzite clasts (70±10%) with a secondary mode of basalts (20±5%) and diverse minor components (<10%) of andesite, granodiorite, and metamorphics. These lithologies are characteristic of the Chicama and Chimú Formations that make up most bedrock in the river catchment (fig. 5.2).

EPHEMERAL WETLANDS

Between discharge events, the alluvial channel systems represent broad depressions that are 1–3 m lower than the surrounding interfluves. The channel systems are locally scoured and often backfilled with a veneer of 0.5–1 m of sand that is deposited during smaller discharge events. It is within these sandy, low-lying channel depressions that ephemeral, groundwater-fed wetlands (facies *Pl-al*; table 5.4; fig. 5.8a–c) persist during the long periods between major flood events (10^1–10^2 years). The sediments of such wetlands are not typically preserved in the stratigraphic record of the alluvial fans, but in the modern environment they consist of a simple organic-rich mollic horizon within an otherwise weakly developed sand-rich soil.

Age control is provided by four OSL dates measured on sands within the shallow stratigraphy in several alluvial fan settings, including systems both in the foothills and near the coast. All dates from widely separated sites yielded ages from last glacial to interstade, ~40,000–14,000 cal BP (table 5.5). These ages reflect the last period that the region's alluvial systems were actively depositing sediments, presumably under a wetter but still arid climate. Despite more recent discharge events during El Niño wet phases, these floods do not appear to have supported significant fan aggradation and may be largely erosional in the alluvial settings.

FLUVIAL SETTINGS

Regionally, coarse-grained alluvial deposits dominate the coastal hills and lowland landscapes (fig. 5.7). Interspersed along this arid continental margin, however, are river systems that head in the Andean highlands (>2500 m) and receive seasonal precipitation that sustains groundwater flux and perennial but highly variable river discharge. The Chicama River is such a fluvial system, which through greater, more frequent, and sustained water discharge has formed a broad (3–10 km), shallow (2–8 m) valley within the widespread gravelly alluvial terrain (fig. 5.4). During the Holocene, though, this valley was infilled through the deposition of 1–8 m of gravels, sands, and muds sourced by the river (fig. 5.9, upper part). Thus, supplied with water and sediment, this river-constructed landscape has provided a diverse and largely unique suite of environments over the last 8000 years (fig. 5.9, upper part).

CHANNEL DEPOSITS

Depositional environments within the river valley can be divided into three major facies, including coarse-grained channel deposits and two finer-grained settings within the broad floodplain. Like the region's alluvial systems, the braided channel

Table 5.4. Summary of the environmental facies and sediment characteristics found in the lower Chicama Valley, coastal system, and surrounding area

Environmental setting	Sedimentary facies	Sediment lithology	Sedimentary, geomorphic, or pedogenic structure	Artifacts, fossils
Alluvial	*Al-dc*	Clast-supported, angular, weakly stratified gravels with ≤10% sand; units are many meters thick	Desert varnish	None
	Al-fn	Mostly clast-supported, stratified, well-rounded gravels with ≤20% sand; units are many meters thick	Coarse bedding; local truncation, cut and fill	None
Fluvial	*Fl-ch*	Interstratified, rounded gravels (≥60%) and fine-medium sands (≤40%); units are many meters thick	Planar and cross stratification; imbricated gravels	None
	Fl-pf	Yellow-brown to brown, silt-dominated, loamy soils (*cambic fluvisols*); units are 1–4 m thick	Massive, tabular bedding (10–100 cm thick); columnar soil peds; weak *A* horizon	Charcoal, pottery, fire pits, and human-transported marine shells
	Fl-lf	Dark gray to gray-brown, clay to loam soils with calcic horizons (*calcic gleysols*); units are 0.5–2.0 m thick	Tabular bedding (5–30 cm thick), frequent pedogenic carbonate horizons (*K* to *Km* fabric)	Charcoal, fired clay daub, also terrestrial gastropods & human-transported marine shells (local midden)
Lagoonal	*Lg-ca*	Fossiliferous carbonate beds with interlaminated alkaline precipitate and organic layers; strata are 0.5–10 cm thick	Very well stratified; laminae to thin beds of authigenic sediment	Abundant *Charophyta* stem concretions and gyrogonites; common gastropods (≤3 mm) and ostracod valves
	Lg-fl	Massive blue-gray to olive-brown siliciclastic silt-dominated muds; strata are 10–100 cm thick	Large, tabular beds, 10–50 cm thick	Occasional crustacean or marine mollusk
Paludal (Alluvial)	*Pl-al*	Peaty to organic-rich O-horizons within sandy to silty channel outwash (*mollic cambisol*)	Surface-layer organics in otherwise poorly developed soil unit	Primarily meristems, rhizophores, and detritus from C_4 grasses

Distribution	Period of deposition	Environmental interpretation
Widespread deposits at the base of hillslopes in the hyperarid, nonvegetated hills and lower mountains	Most active up to the **latest Pleistocene**; largely inactive after ~15 ka	**Debris cones** fed by intermixed mass wasting and surface runoff
Most widespread environment defining the alluvial plains of NW coastal Peru	Very active up to **latest Pleistocene**; episodically reactivated in last ~4 ka during intense El Niño phases	**Alluvial fans** fed by large but ephemeral outwash events, forming a continuous alluvial plain between coast and uplands
Restricted to perennial river valleys and plains, almost exclusively associated with the Chicama River	Active throughout **late Quaternary** within perennial Chicama River	**Braided stream** channel and bar deposits, occurring locally as cut-and-filled within *Fl-pf*
Restricted to Chicama River valley and coastal lowlands, mostly within 3 km	**Late Holocene**; beginning ~4 ka but increasingly active after ~3 ka	Well-drained and elevated **proximal floodplain** formed by rapid overbank deposition, principally during El Niño floods
Restricted to lower Chicama River valley and coastal lowlands	**Mid–late Holocene**; mostly ~6 ka to 4 ka, but locally to present	**Low-lying floodplain** characterized by slow accretion, shallow water table, prominent pedogenic carbonates
Restricted within 500 m of modern shoreline and <3 km from Chicama River mouth	**Early–mid-Holocene**; primarily 8 ka to 6 ka at Chicama coast; found very locally to present in association with *Pl-al*	**Open-water carbonate lagoon** with authigenic algal sediments and local evaporates; interbedded with *Lg-fl*
Restricted within 500 m of modern shoreline and <3 km from Chicama River mouth	**Early–mid-Holocene**; ~8 ka to ~6 ka	**Open-water siliciclastic lagoon** fed by small-moderate river floods with clayey silt deposition; interbedded with *Lg-ca*
Widespread but local, associated with channel-scour depressions within alluvial plains (*Al-fn*), primarily near the coast	Widespread but local throughout **late Quaternary**	**Ephemeral wetlands** formed within low-lying channel scours of the alluvial outwash plains (*Al-fn*)

Table 5.4. Continued

Environmental setting	Sedimentary facies	Sediment lithology	Sedimentary, geomorphic, or pedogenic structure	Artifacts, fossils
Paludal (continued)				
(Lagoonal)	*Pl-lg*	Thin peat layers and dark-colored muds with disseminated organics; individual beds are 1–10 cm thick	Discrete laminae (peat) to diffuse organic horizons within *Lg* facies successions	Primarily C_4-grass meristems and rhizophores in peat, and C_4 detritus with organic horizons
Coastal (Shoreface)	*Co-wt*	Thinly bedded, shelly, coarse sands and pebbles; units are 0.5–1.0 m thick	Planar bedded	Abundant molluscan shell hash
	Co-ss	Planar to cross stratified, fine-to-medium sands; units are 0.5–2 m thick	Low-angle swash beds	Occasional charcoal pieces
(Aeolian)	*Co-gs*	Steeply dipping, sorted and imbricated cobbles to boulders; units are 0.5–1.5 m thick	Steeply inclined strata, 1–2 m high; strong imbrication	None
	Co-bd	Well-sorted sands as 0.5–1.5 m thick, lens-shaped deposits	Common Fe-concretion root casts	Common shallow pits with fired pottery, gravels, and charcoal; local human burials
Tsunami	*Ts-gl*	10–40 cm thick, clast-supported gravel bed (primarily cobbles) with variable sand matrix	Truncation of underlying *Co-gs* and *Co-ss* strata; weak imbrication weathering-induced spallation and shattering of clasts	Fine shell hash within sand matrix, locally infilled ghost crab burrows (*Ocypode gaudichaudii*) in underlying *Sh-ss*
	Ts-sl	1–5 cm thick, fine-sand lens within shore-proximal *Fl-pf* facies; correlative with *Ts-gl*	Thin, well-sorted sand; no structure preserved	Rare marine mollusk fragment
	Ts-ow	10–15 cm thick bed of fine-to-coarse sand within *F-lf* facies	Tabular cross-bedding; normal grading; tabular rip-ups of muddy *Fl-lf* sediments	Common marine mollusk shells (<5 mm) and shell hash

of the Chicama River is dominated by gravel-sized sediments; here, though, they are well rounded and range up to the boulder-size class (>25 cm), reflecting the river's larger discharge (table 5.4; fig. 5.9a, *Fl-ch*). Locally interspersed within these channel gravels are well-sorted sandy bar deposits, although they constitute only 5–20% of the channel units. Toward the coast, however, these sands represent an increasingly larger portion of the channel deposits within ~1.5 km of the modern shoreline, where they may compose several meters of the stratigraphy overlying the basal gravel units deposited through the last glacial period (fig. 5.9, upper part). In this case rising sea level and coastal

Distribution	Period of deposition	Environmental interpretation
Locally within and around open-water lagoon settings (*Lg*)	**Early–mid-Holocene**; primarily 8 ka to 6 ka at Chicama coast; found very locally to present in association with *Pl-al*	**Vegetated wetlands** fringing the open-water lagoon habitats (*Lg-ca* and *Lg-fl*)
Widespread shallow subtidal environment; preserved below *Co-ss* and *Co-gb* in paleoshoreface deposits	**Late Holocene**; all shoreface deposits that are preserved are <3.7 ka	**Wave-swept terrace** at base of shoreface; useful sea-level indicator
Regionally widespread, characteristic lower shoreface deposit	**Late Holocene**; all shoreface deposits that are preserved are <3.7 ka	Low-angle **sandy shoreface berm**; locally alternatives with *Co-gs* where there is adequate gravel supply
Locally restricted to shoreface settings within 2 km of Chicama River mouth	**Late Holocene**; all shoreface deposits that are preserved are <3.7 ka	**Gravel shoreface berm**; common within 2 km alongshore of Chicama River mouth (river is source of gravels)
Regionally widespread, characteristic deposit of the upper shoreface	**Late Holocene**; all shoreface deposits that are preserved are <3.7 ka	Low-lying **aeolian dunes** preserved within the strand-plain at the shoreface deposits
Observed along upper bounding surface of *Sh-gs* and *Sh-ss* deposits at Chicama River mouth	Two events recorded, ages ~2.9 ka and ~2.0 ka based on charcoal from associated *Sh-ss* facies and organic sediment from back-dune *Pl-al* facies	**Tsunami-formed truncation surface and gravel lag**; extends ~200 m from paleoshoreface
Observed in *Fl-pf* deposits within 500 m of modern shoreline at the Chicama River mouth	Two events, ~2.9 ka and ~2.0 ka, correlated with *Ts-gl* event layers	**Tsunami washover**, correlative with *Ts-gl*, extending ~200 m further inland
Preserved in *Fl-lf* deposits within 500 m of modern shoreline, 3 km north of Chicama River mouth	One event recorded, age <4 ka, presumed to correlate with either ~2.9 or ~2.0 ka events	**Tsunami washover**, apparently through low-lying outwash channel cut through dunes

transgression relaxed the river channel gradient near the coast, trapping sands in the lower fluvial system where it intersected rising base level.

One OSL age from these fluvial sands gave a date of ~14,000 cal BP, lying ~1 m below lagoon deposits dated to ~7500 cal BP (tables 5.2 and 5.5, fig. 5.9a). Thus, given this stratigraphic juxta-position and relation of the channel sands to rising base level, these sediments were most likely deposited from ~15,000 to 7500 cal BP. Overall, these facies characterize the earliest Holocene stratigraphy preserved in the region and are the first harbinger of the diverse fluvial and coastal systems that emerged after 7500 cal BP.

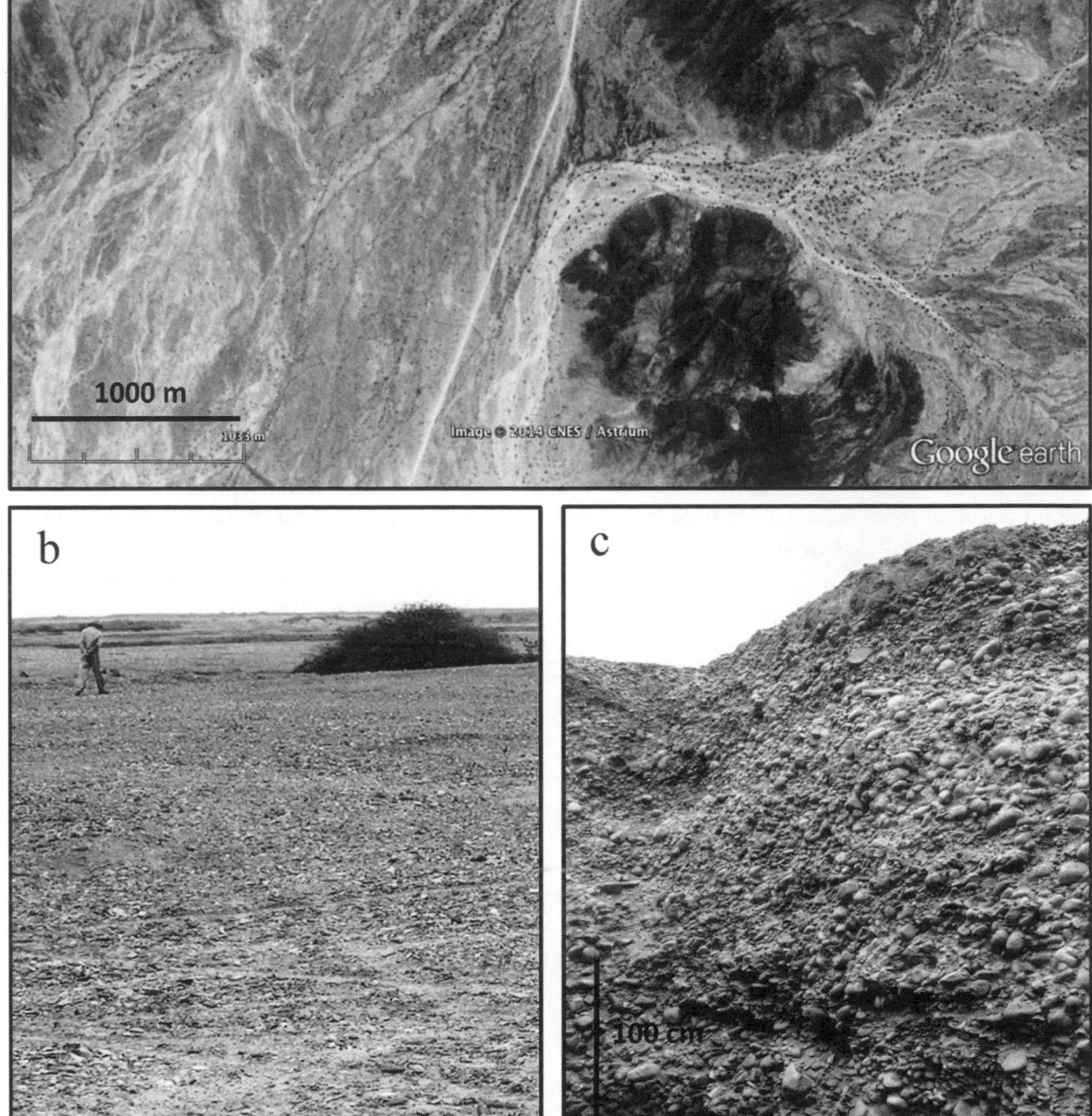

FIGURE 5.7. Images of the alluvial fan and alluvial plains that dominate the landscape outside of the Chicama Valley: *a*, Google Earth image of an alluvial fan fed by a local alluvial setting adjacent to the Chicama River; *b*, photo of the alluvial fan surface near the coast, here forming a broad interfluve, which is the barren, overwash area between the lower-lying, vegetated channels (distant area of the photo); *c*, photo of a 4-m-deep pit near *b* that was excavated into the alluvial fan, showing that the sediments are exclusively clast-supported gravels with a sand matrix. These deposits reflect the persistent arid climate of the region, which is punctuated by brief outwash floods. These alluvial settings contrast with the arable, verdant lower Chicama River Valley.

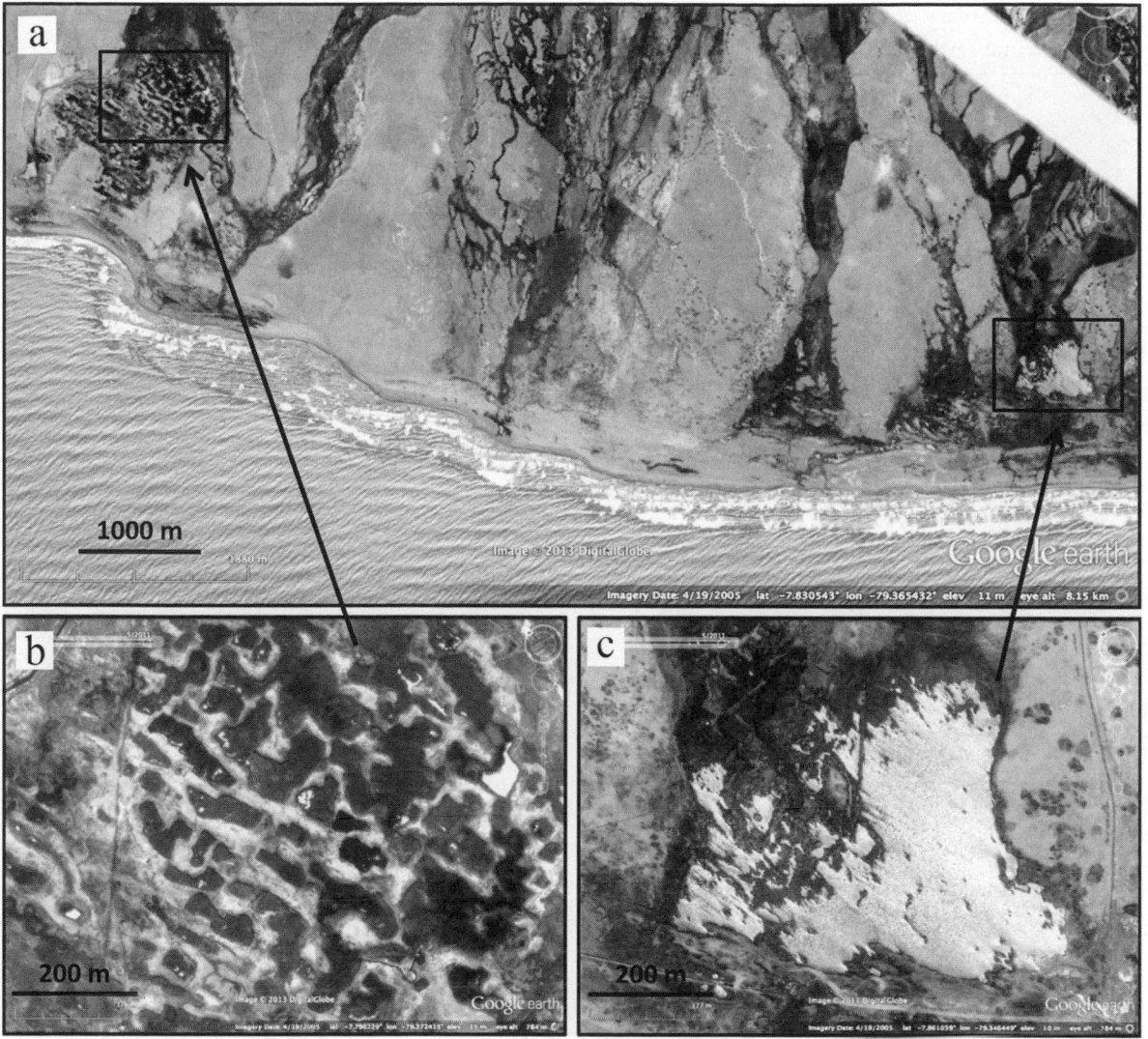

FIGURE 5.8. Google Earth images of the alluvial plain and wetlands north of the Chicama Valley: *a*, the plain consists of gravelly, barren interfluves (*Al-fn* facies) alternating with the outwash channels defined by shallow, artificial raised field platforms close to the water table and vegetated with wetland plants (*Pl-al* facies) and desert scrub; *b*, close-up image of the vegetated area on the left (north) side of *a*, showing that the area is a cultural landscape organized into terraces and raised agricultural fields; *c*, close-up image of the area on the right (south) side of *a*, showing a small open-water lagoon and a wetland fringe that locally form where channel scour has been especially deep during El Niño floods.

Overbank Floodplain

Beyond the river channel, when discharge exceeds the channel capacity during floods, overbank flow has effectively dispersed the river's finer-grained sediments to construct a vast silt-dominated floodplain (fig. 5.4a). Such floodwaters, typically occurring during El Niño wet phases, are widely broadcast over the valley given the steep gradient of the river and adjacent alluvial plains. Such

floodplain construction has extended up to 8 km away from the main channel where it everywhere constitutes the upper 1–4 m of Holocene stratigraphy (figs. 5.9–5.10). Within this floodplain setting, the local environment and associated sediments vary with distance from the river and can be differentiated into distinct facies. In this case, more proximal areas 1–3 km from the channel consist primarily of well-drained silts (loam; *Fl-pf*) compared with more clay-rich, poorly drained soils

Table 5.5. Summary of optically stimulated luminescence (OSL) dating results, including age, environmental setting, and stratigraphic context

Site	Material	No. of samples	% Overdispersion	Dose (Gy)	Dose rate (Gy/ka)	Age (years)
HP04A	Fine sand with silt	37	34	12.7±0.7	2.936±0.229	4325±414
Donkey	Fine sand	13	46	17.9±2.3	1.249±0.109	14,327±2227
HP11	Fine sand with silt, gravel	22	28	43.8±2.7	2.471±0.196	17,723±1779
HP07B	Medium-coarse sand	15	15	85.0±9.4	3.730±0.332	22,785±3233
HP14	Fine-medium sand	19	51	82.2±9.8	1.996±0.162	41,179±5940

(*Fl-lf*) that are found in areas distal from the channel (>3 km) or deeper within the stratigraphy (>2 m) (table 5.4, figs. 5–9a–d, 5.10a).

The proximal overbank facies (*Fl-pf*) includes thickly bedded, yellowish to brown silts that are generally massive in appearance and laterally contiguous for 100s of meters or more. Individual beds are 20–40 cm thick and often separated by a thin (<5 cm), weakly developed A-horizon (up to 3% wt. organics) that appears to define soil development between depositional events (figs. 5.9a–d, 5.10a). The organic content of the *Fl-pf* facies is overall much lower at 0.5–2% wt. Together, units of the *Fl-pf* facies may be >3 m thick and dominate the Holocene stratigraphy of the Chicama Valley. By comparison, sediments of the low-lying floodplain environment (*Fl-lf*) are finer grained with higher clay content (20–40%). They often develop dark soils with higher organic content (3–5% wt) throughout and well-developed calcic horizons (for example, *Bk* to *Bkm*; fig. 5.10b–c) and abundant gastropods of the genus *Valvata* (fig. 5.10a). Individual soil successions within the low-lying floodplain are typically 15–30 cm thick and overall constitute ~0.5–2 m of stratigraphy within the overbank deposits.

Cultural artifacts are common and widespread within the two overbank facies, particularly within the proximal floodplain setting. These include small fire-pits containing burned cobbles, charcoal, and ceramic fragments. These components are also found individually within the facies or locally scattered along a bedding plane.

Human-transported marine mollusks, particularly *Donax* sp. and *Tegula* spp., are also found widely within both overbank facies, although they are more common <2 km from the coast.

Overall the proximal and distal overbank deposits blanket the plains of the lower river valley and are the most widespread Holocene sediment facies. The oldest of these floodplain deposits are restricted to within ~1.5 km of the modern coast and almost exclusively consist of the low-lying floodplain facies (*Fl-lf*). Radiocarbon dates constrain deposition of this early, low-lying floodplain unit to 4903–3847 cal BP at several locations near the modern river mouth (table 5.2). The transition from low-lying to high, well-drained proximal floodplain occurs after ~3500 cal BP, with several ages from fire-pits and charcoals in the unit dating 2021–915 cal BP (table 5.2). Most of these ages are not near the base of the unit, though, which certainly extends back to at least ~3000 cal BP. Unfortunately, few dates exist from this unit upstream of the coastal area, where the proximal floodplain deposits likely develop later and may be more restricted to the late Holocene after ~2500–2000 cal BP.

In areas that are more distal from the channel or in local depressions, such as near Huaca Prieta or within shoreline swales, the low-lying floodplain setting persists into the late Holocene. Several radiocarbon dates from these areas yield ages from 1280 to 815 cal BP, indicating that the late Holocene floodplain environments of the Chicama Valley consist of high, silty, and well-drained areas

Depth below surface (m)	Facies	Environmental setting	Stratigraphic context
5.4	*Fl-pf*	Overbank levee; proximal floodplain	1 m above gravel alluvial surface (*Al-fm*)
4.5	*Fl-ch*	Braided channel	80 cm below lagoon facies (*Lg*)
0.6	*Al-fn*	Distal alluvial fan	Fine sand with silt, pebbles, and salt crust, 1 m above thick, sandy gravel units
2.4	*Al-fn*	Proximal alluvial fan	Stratified medium-coarse sand within thick, sandy gravel units
4.5	*Al-dc*	Mixed alluvial-colluvial	0.3 m above well-rounded alluvial gravel bed and 0.3 m below angular-clast debris flow

(*Fl-pf*) near the river channel, mixed with areas of lower-lying, wetter, and more clay-rich floodplain habitats (*Fl-lf*) at more distal or poorly drained locations. Overall the development of these floodplain habitats after ~5500 cal BP and especially their rapid expansion after 3500 cal BP are perhaps the most important environmental changes in the region, representing the emergence of a vast arable landscape within the generally gravelly hyperarid setting of the Peruvian coast.

LAGOONAL SETTINGS

Buried within the Chicama Valley stratigraphy near the coast is a unique, 2–3 m thick succession of sediments that represent a heterolithic mixture of fossiliferous carbonate muds and sands (*Lg-ca*) interbedded with bluish-gray to olive siliciclastic muds (*Lg-fl*) and thin organic-rich layers (*Pl-lg*; fig. 5.5b). Together these sediments represent the time-varying habitats of a shallow, open-water lagoon system (fig. 5.11a–e). Although related settings can be found in the modern environment (for example, *Pl-fl*), the thickness and extent of these deposits distinguish them in the region and represent a unique phase in the environmental history of the area (Winsborough et al. 2012). Within the stratigraphy of this lagoon succession, individual sediment strata range from 1 mm thick laminae of biogenic carbonates or organic layers to 50 cm thick fluvial mud units that together reflect shifts in hydrologic conditions of the lagoon with time. Although these deposits are all found inter-

bedded within the same lagoon setting (fig. 5.5b), they are treated here as distinct facies because each is lithologically distinct and derives from a unique source.

Within the Holocene history of the lower valley, the timing of this lagoon sequence is discrete and well constrained by radiocarbon dates (table 5.2). The initial development of the lagoon is captured at five locations, both at the river mouth and adjacent to Huaca Prieta, which yield basal ages in the narrow range of 7457–7318 cal BP (table 5.2; fig. 5.5b). The upper contact of the unit is less clear because it is transitional with low floodplain units as sediments become emergent from the lagoon. Dates from the upper lagoon sequence at three locations yield ages of 6659–6295 cal BP (table 5.2), however, which constrains the lagoon transition to a low floodplain environment to ~6300–6000 cal BP.

Carbonate Sediments

The carbonate-dominated facies (*La-ca*) consist of 50–90% calcium carbonate sediments by weight and occur as thin beds that are 0.5–10 cm thick. These sediments are primarily authigenic bioclasts that yield a clean, white carbonate deposit with occasional calcite overgrowths. The carbonates also include various admixtures of organics and siliciclastic silts that color the carbonates blackish or orange, respectively (fig. 5.11d–e). The dominant component of the carbonate minerals is the calcified stem encrustations and fruiting bodies

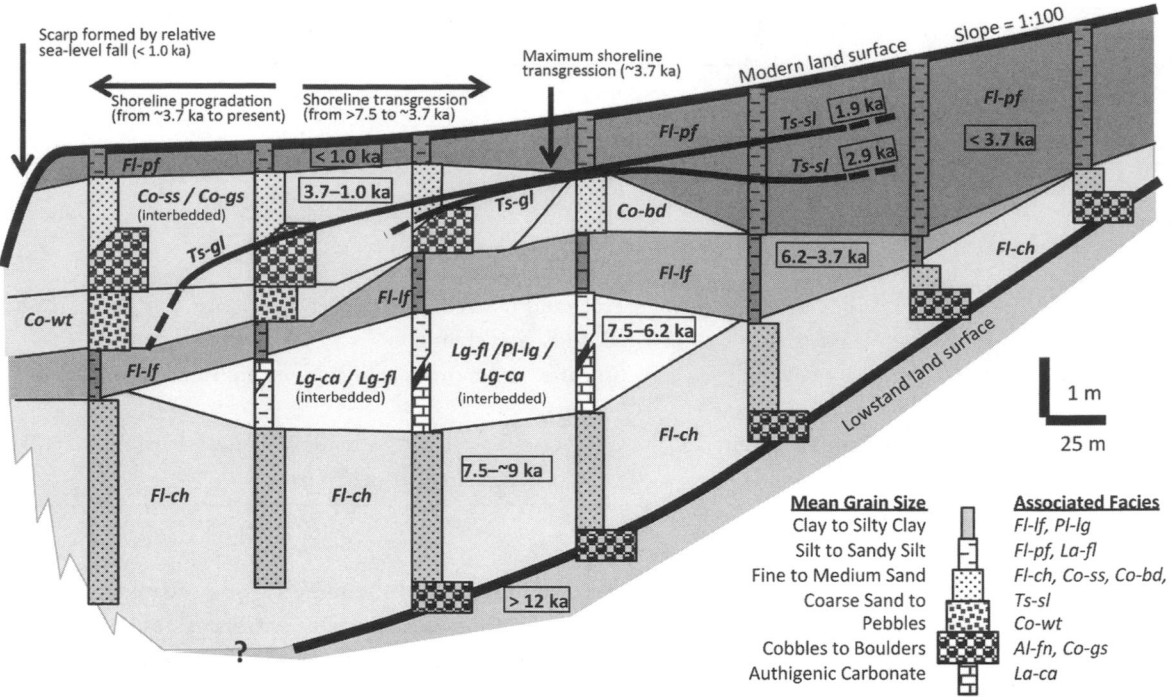

Scarp formed by relative
sea-level fall (< 1.0 ka)

Maximum shoreline
transgression (~3.7 ka)

Slope = 1:100

Modern land surface

Shoreline progradation
(from ~3.7 ka to present)

Shoreline transgression
(from >7.5 to ~3.7 ka)

Fl-pf

Fl-pf

Ts-sl | 1.9 ka

Fl-pf

< 3.7 ka

Fl-pf

< 1.0 ka

Ts-sl | 2.9 ka

Co-ss / Co-gs
(interbedded)

3.7–1.0 ka

Ts-gl

Co-bd

Fl-ch

Ts-gl

Fl-lf

6.2–3.7 ka

Co-wt

Fl-lf

Fl-lf

Fl-lf

7.5–6.2 ka

Lg-ca / Lg-fl
(interbedded)

Lg-fl /Pl-lg /
Lg-ca
(interbedded)

1 m

Fl-ch

25 m

7.5–~9 ka

Lowstand land surface

Fl-ch

Fl-ch

> 12 ka

?

Mean Grain Size

Clay to Silty Clay
Silt to Sandy Silt
Fine to Medium Sand
Coarse Sand to
Pebbles
Cobbles to Boulders
Authigenic Carbonate

Associated Facies

Fl-lf, Pl-lg
Fl-pf, La-fl
Fl-ch, Co-ss, Co-bd,
Ts-sl
Co-wt
Al-fn, Co-gs
La-ca

a

layer of pottery
sherds

2021 cal BP
(charcoal)

Fl-pf

Fl-ch

b

Fl-pf

Fl-lf

c

Fl-pf

Ts-sl

Fig. 5.10a

3611 cal BP
(*Valvata* sp.)

Fl-lf

d

Fl-pf

Fig. 5.10b

Fl-lf

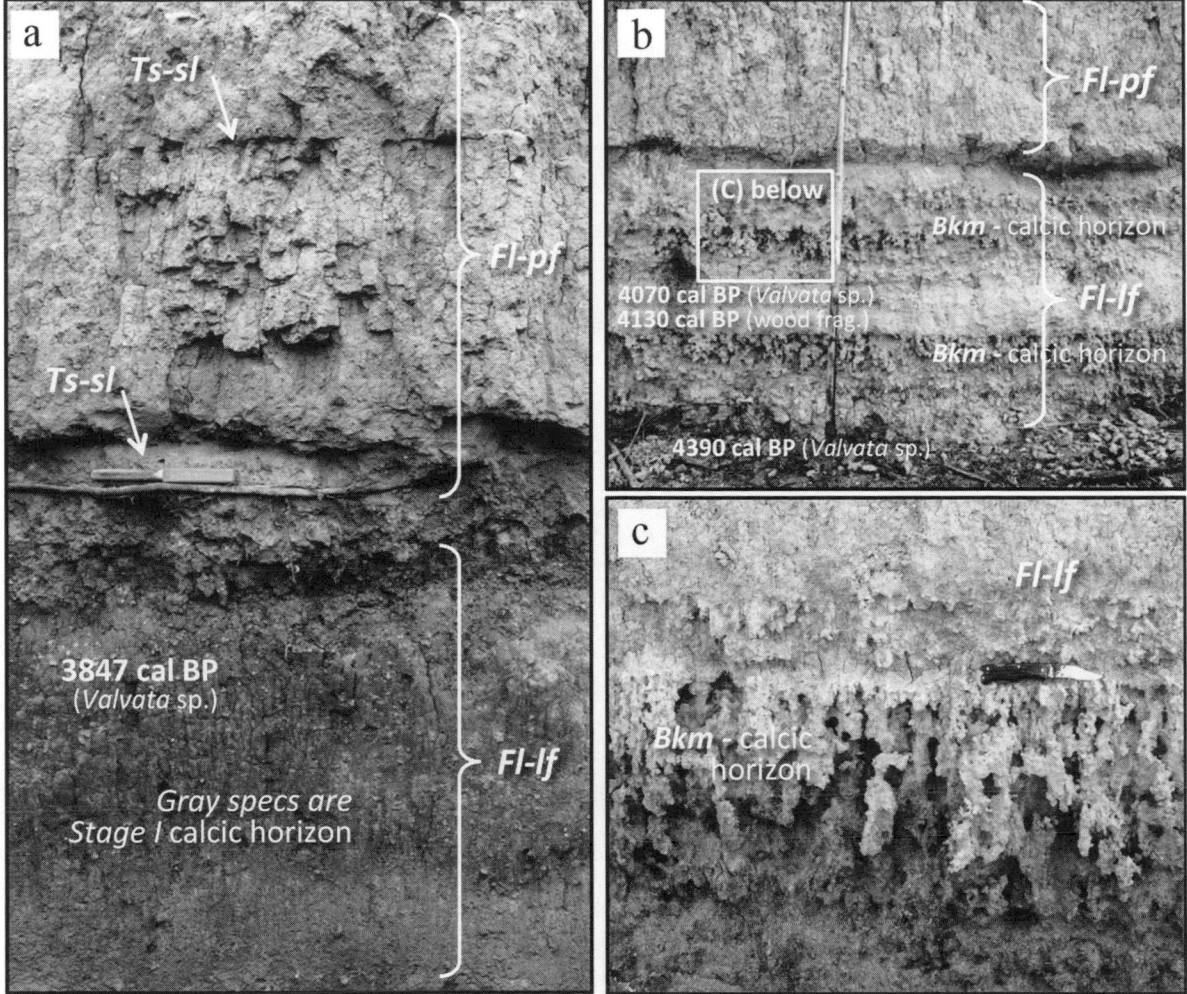

FIGURE 5.10. Close-up photos of floodplain sequence: *a*, inset from figure 5.9c contrasting the darker, organic low floodplain with Stage 1 calcic horizon with the overlying yellowish silts with prismatic beds and weak soil development (thin breaks in the upper floodplain are ~1 cm thick sand layers from the 2900 and 2000 cal BP tsunami events); *b*, inset from figure 5.9d showing two well-developed gleysols with strong *Bkm* carbonate horizons, reflecting a shallow water table, slow accretion, and abundant photosynthesis: attributes representing the paludal environmental stage during the mid-Holocene; *c*, close-up of the Stage IV calcic horizons in the low-lying floodplain facies (*Fl-lf*).

FIGURE 5.9. (opposite) Schematic cross section of the lower Chicama Valley stratigraphy across the sampling sites, showing the major facies, timing of deposition, and relative distribution through the Holocene. Location of cross section shown in figure 5.4c. Below it is a photo series of floodplain sequences within the lower Chicama River Valley. Common attributes include 2–3.5 m of silty late Holocene floodplain (*Fl-pf*) overlying older low-lying floodplain (*Fl-fl*) or fluvial channel (*Fl-ch*) deposits: *a*, thick floodplain succession from the upper valley at Roma (fig. 5.4b) showing 3.5 m of floodplain aggradation in the last 2000 years, with preserved cultural horizons; *b*, floodplain sequence showing weak soil development within the rapidly accumulating proximal floodplain (*Fl-pf*) and decimeter-scale bedding sets presumed to represent individual El Niño flood deposits (location is up-river: site 11) (fig. 5.4c); *c*, floodplain succession contrasting the darker, more organic and carbonate rich, low-lying floodplain (*Fl-lf*) with the lighter colored high floodplain, showing prismatic bed development typical of successive wetting and drying cycles in arid environments; the thin planar horizon within the upper floodplain is a ~1 cm thick sand layer (*Ts-sl*) from the 2000 cal BP tsunami event (location at Preceramic site 9) (fig. 5.4c); *d*, floodplain succession is similar to that in *c*, but with highly developed calcic horizons in the low-lying floodplain unit (*Fl-lf*); these concretions reflect the much slower accretion rates compared with the rapidly aggrading high floodplain unit (*Fl-pf*) (location ~100 m upstream of Preceramic site 9) (fig. 5.4c).

FIGURE 5.11. Photos of a modern lagoon setting near Malabrigo, 30 km north of Huaca Prieta: (*a–d*) and a buried paleolagoon deposit adjacent to Huaca Prieta (*e*). The Malabrigo site is a late Preceramic cultural setting, with ponds that provide a proxy for the paleo-lagoon setting: *a*, mixed open-water and wetland habitats are comparable to the varied carbonate, fluvial, and organic deposits of the paleolagoon sequence; *b* and *c*, ponds of different depths, with charophyte algae growing in *b* and *c* representing a shallow evaporative basin; *d*, sediments accumulating in the pond in *c*, with a thin crust of evaporites overlying several centimeters of carbonate sediment and underlain by aeolian sands; *e*, example of a buried lagoon deposit. The white carbonate at the base represents deeper (<3 m), open-water conditions; the blackish layers contain charcoal soot from local burning of wetlands; and the grayish layers represent mixed carbonates deposited at the shallow, evaporite stage.

of charophyte algae (fig. 5.6b). Charophytae is a family of submerged aquatic vegetation found in fresh to brackish water, most commonly in clear, shallow lakes in temperate regions (Jones et al. 1996). They are also found regularly in Mesozoic-age deposits in northern Peru (Jaillard et al. 1994) and at least locally at other Holocene-age sites (Winsborough et al. 2012). As calcifying species, charophytes require alkaline waters and prefer low-energy environments with little suspended sediment where they may grow in dense submerged meadows (fig. 5.11a–b). Such settings have been shown to generate 0.5 to >1 g/m² of carbonate sediment annually.

In addition to the charophytes, the carbonate deposits also host a simple fauna of tiny *Lymnaea* sp. gastropods and *Cyprideis* spp. ostracods (fig. 5.6c–d; Yen 1961). Both of these fauna contribute to sediment production and may constitute 5–20% wt of the carbonate deposits. The *Lymnaea* are 1–3 mm long grazing gastropods that are commonly associated with charophyte vegetation (Van den Berg et al. 1997). The cyprid ostracods are generally benthic dwelling and adaptable to a range of fresh to brackish waters (Heip 1976). Surprisingly, no other floral or faunal sources of carbonates were identified from the *La-ca* sediments; so together these few plants and animals define a depauperate species assemblage indicative of clear, generally low-salinity, alkaline waters in the lagoon.

Fluvial Muds

Within the lagoon deposits, the carbonate layers alternate with thicker beds of river-derived muds (*La-fl*). These siliciclastic deposits are typically 10–50 cm thick and appear to have been deposited as discrete units, presumably during flood events. As preserved in the stratigraphy, these silty muds vary from soft, blue-gray sediments that have not been subaerially exposed or desiccated to much stiffer, tan to olive sediments that have been desiccated, compacted, and mildly oxidized following deposition (fig. 5.5). These variations in the color and rheology of the deposits indicate that the lagoon periodically dried and exposed bed sediments to subaerial weathering. Such subaerial exposure may also explain the recrystallization and cementation of some carbonate beds.

The river-derived lagoon sediments are poor in fossils compared with the carbonate layers, supporting their origin as rapidly emplaced fluvial deposits. But the fluvial sediments do contain occasional fossiliferous laminae, generally dominated by ostracod shells, which may reflect seasonal to multiannual hiatuses in deposition. Locally, examples of in situ razor clams (*Ensis* sp.) and crab claws (*Brachyura* sp.) were also recovered from the sediments. These more marine-associated fauna contrast with those of the carbonate assemblage, indicating periods of brackish (mesohaline) conditions in the lagoon that require at least intermittent connections to the ocean. This assertion is further supported by the presence of seeds from the euryhaline seagrass *Ruppia maritima*, which are occasionally found within the mud units. In fact, such temporary lagoon-ocean connections may be specifically linked with the deposition of fluvial muds, because the flood discharge necessary to deliver the muds would temporarily breach the wave-built bars that normally enclose the lagoon. Such a connection would be short-lived, lasting only until wave-driven longshore transport reconstructed the shoreface barrier following the river discharge event, a process likely to take months to a few years at most.

Paludal Organics

Intermixed within the lagoon carbonates (*La-ca*) and river-derived muds (*La-fl*) are organic-rich layers (*Pl-lg*), often peaty, that are typically 0.5–5 cm thick (fig. 5.5b). This organic matter consists of degraded emergent vegetation and small-stemmed wood fragments of scrubby vegetation (Winsborough et al. 2012). The organic layers often contain *Valvata* sp. gastropods, which are commonly associated with densely vegetated, shallow, stagnant water bodies (Van den Berg et al. 1997). Considering these attributes and interbedding of the organic layers within carbonate and mud deposits, these layers appear to reflect periods of shallowing water depth that allow emergent vegetation to grow (fig. 5.11a–b). Decreased water depths might arise either through a drop in water levels or infilling of portions of the lagoon by sediments. Furthermore, because these organic layers are generally thin, we suggest that the wetland habitats are ephemeral and likely persist over

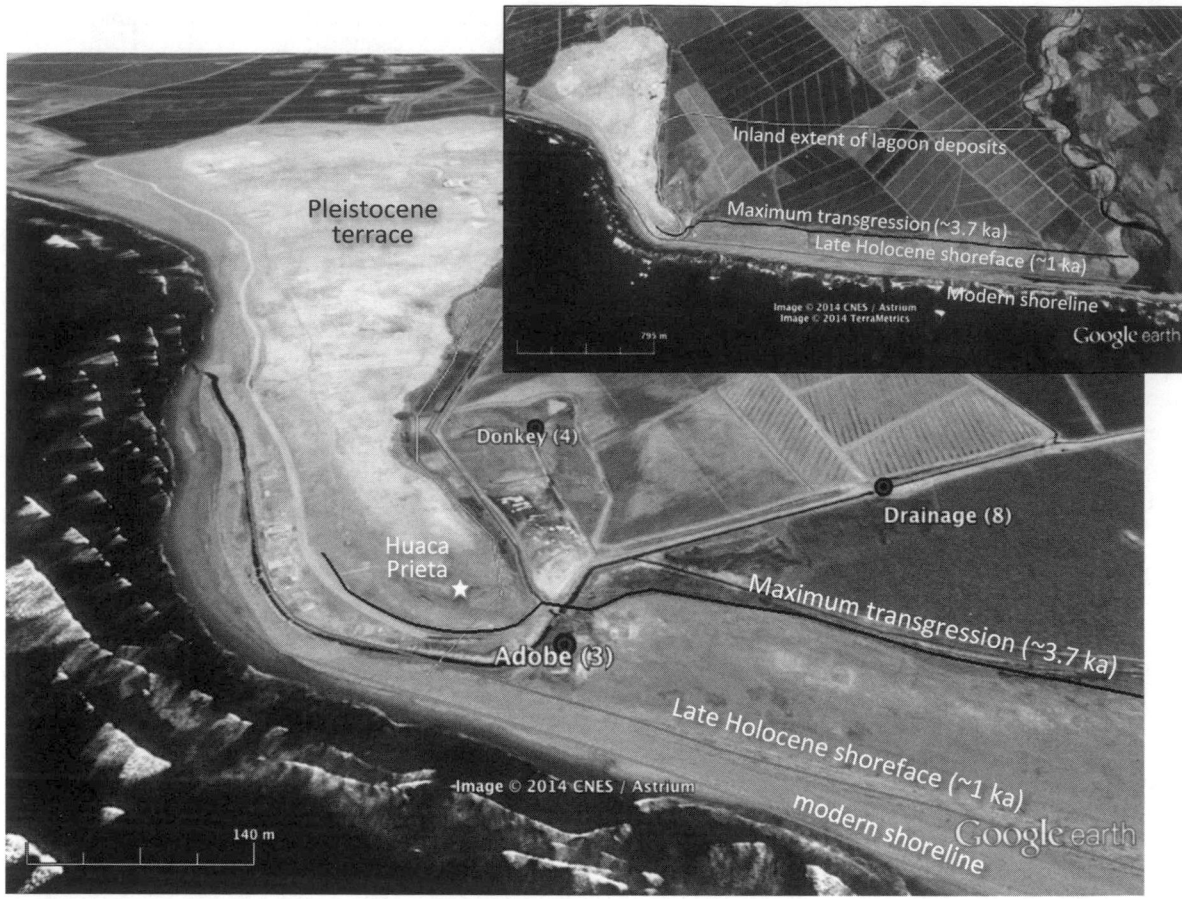

FIGURE 5.12. Annotated Google Earth images of the coastal system adjacent to Huaca Prieta and the Chicama River mouth and sampling locations (*inset*). Stratigraphy of the coastal succession shows the inland dune positioned on the gravel shoreface berm at the 3.7 ka maximum transgression, at which time the shoreline would have been at the base of the Huaca Prieta mound. This is consistent with intercalated beach deposits and mound colluvium as the base of the mound dated to this time. Following maximum transgression, the shoreline prograces to the late Holocene shoreface, before a relative sea-level fall between 500 and 1000 BP that forms a stranded shoreface and the new shoreline platform of the modern coast. These shoreline boundaries are readily traced to the river mouth, where the stratigraphy is well exposed along the river cutbank (*inset*).

relatively brief intervals (seasonal to subdecadal) during phases of wetting and drying in the lagoon.

COASTAL SETTINGS

A well-developed succession of Holocene shoreline deposits extends a few hundred meters inland of the modern coast (fig. 5.12). This coastal sequence consists of sands and abundant pebble- to cobble-sized gravels that are sourced from the Chicama River. Discharged during high flow, these sediments are subsequently reworked alongshore by the strong north-oblique wave approach (Wells 1996). Most of these northward-transported gravels are trapped at the headland

terrace where Huaca Prieta is located, and coastal deposits farther north become increasingly dominated by sand-sized sediments.

At the Chicama River mouth, a cutbank eroded along the northern channel margin in 2008 exposed an ideal cross section of these coastal deposits, revealing a dynamic history of shoreline transgression followed by long-term regression since the mid-late Holocene (fig. 5.13). Overall the coastal succession consists of ~3–4 m of sands and gravels that lie unconformably on stiff muds of the low-lying floodplain facies, reflecting transgression of the shoreline across this environment during the mid-Holocene. The most-inland extent of these shoreface deposits onlap backdune sands

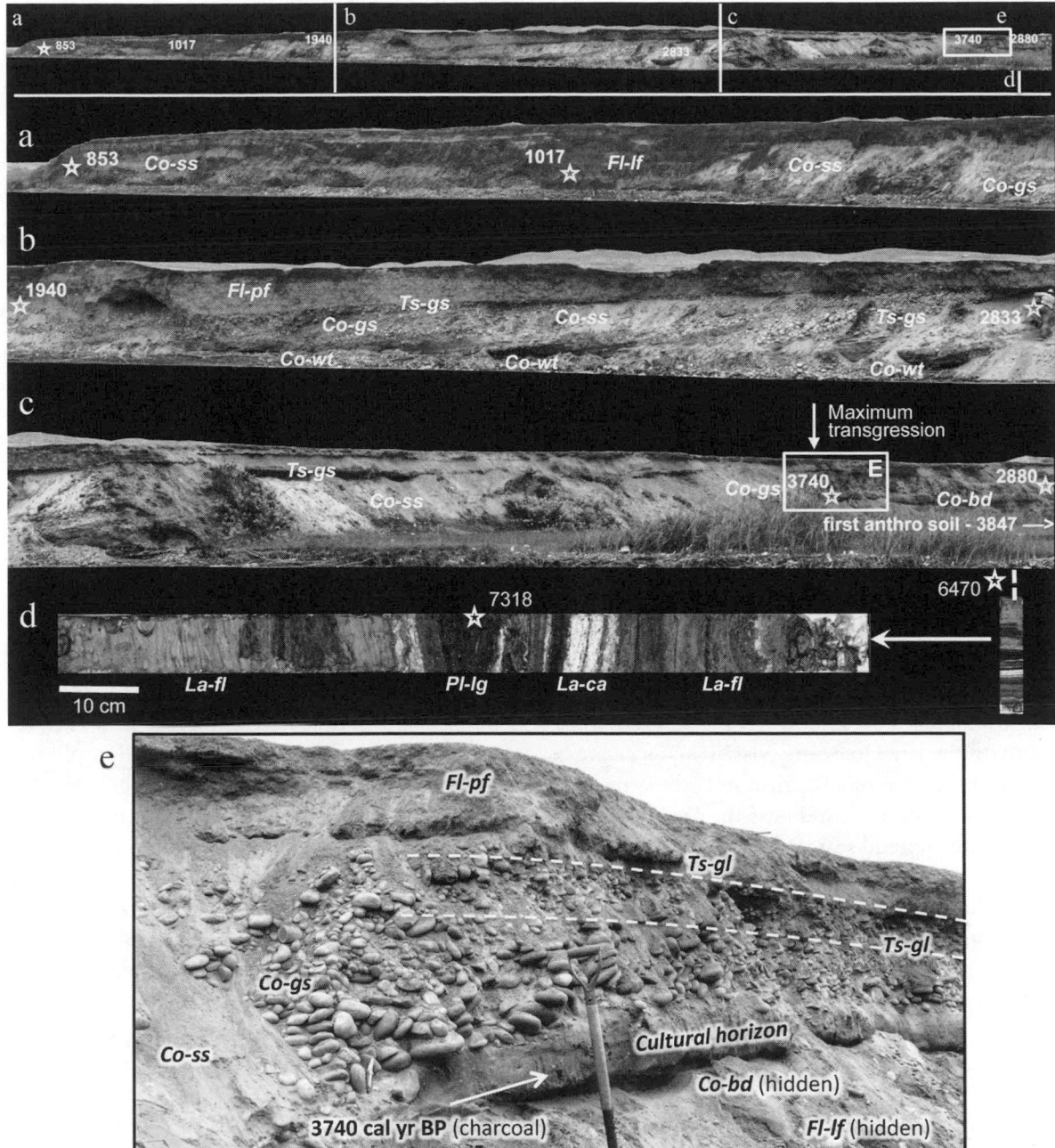

FIGURE 5.13. Composite image of coastal sections exposed along the Chicama River cutbank (location in fig. 5.4c). Full section shown in top panel is 300 m long. Facies and calibrated radiocarbon ages are shown in close-up images: a, latest Holocene shoreface sequence with increasing mud content associated with frequent El Niño floods blanketing coastal sediments; b, prograding sand and gravel shoreface deposits that are truncated by a curvilinear tsunami surface and capped by El Niño flood deposits; c, early shoreline progradation sequence (poorly exposed) with point of maximum transgression shown (the tsunami truncation surface also extends across this section); d, sediment core showing lagoon deposits that underlie the coastal sequence (the lagoon sediment begins ~1 m below ground surface in the other photos); e, maximum transgression where gravel shoreface deposits truncate and onlap a sandy cultural horizon in the backdune setting. The cultural deposit is dark red from fired clay daub and charcoal, dating to 3740 cal yr BP. The shoreface deposits are subsequently planated and reworked 50 m landward by the two tsunami events, the deposits of which lie conformably on one another. The older 2900 cal BP tsunami surface is difficult to discern in this photo but is recognized in the field by a fractured and salt-weathered cobble surface.

and mark the position of the maximum Holocene transgression about 250 m landward of the modern shoreline (fig. 5.13). From that inland position, the shoreface progrades ~150 m through the late Holocene before a drop in relative sea level in the latest Holocene (~1000 cal BP) establishes a lower shoreface terrace that extends another 50–100 m to the modern shoreline (figs. 5.12–5.13).

Wave-Swept Terrace

The basal unit of this shoreface sequence is a 50–100 cm thick deposit of coarse sands and pebble-sized gravels (Co-wt; table 5.4, fig. 5.14c). These sediments are well stratified as thin, planar beds and contain abundant sand-sized shell hash, representing deposits formed in the surf zone where breaking waves create a wave-swept subtidal terrace. The terrace intersects the base of the shoreface, where wave swash runs up to form a supratidal gravel or sand berm. Because the wave-terrace deposits are controlled by breaking waves and lie close to mean low water, they provide useful sea-level indicators (Bluck 2011; Wells 1996). In the late Holocene coastal sequence preserved at the Chicama River mouth, the wave-terrace deposits are found near the base of the outcrop and extend seaward at roughly the same elevation over the full width of the sequence (fig. 5.13). This finding indicates that sea level was largely stable from the point of maximum transgression through the period of late Holocene shoreline progradation.

Gravel and Sandy Shoreface Berms

Overlying the wave-swept terrace deposits are an alternating series of inclined gravel and sand beds that represent berms of the active shoreface at the time of deposition. The gravel shoreface deposits (Co-gs; table 5.4, figs. 5.13, 5.14a–b) consist of steeply dipping beds (15°±5°) of pebble- to cobble-sized clasts, often arranged as an upward fining unit that is 50–100 cm thick. The gravel units are interspersed with sandy shoreface deposits (Co-ss; figs. 5.13, 5.14b) that are 5–10 m wide and onlap against the gravel berms. The sands are low-angle swash beds that indicate the active shoreface. These alternating sandy-beach

and gravel-berm shoreface units reflect episodic inputs of sediment from the Chicama River during flood events. These fluvial sediments are deposited at the river mouth and subsequently reworked onshore by wave activity to form shoreface sequences (Engels and Roberts 2005; Wells 1996). The sand-sized sediments are reworked relatively quickly (months–years) to form a sandy shoreface, whereas the larger gravel clasts take years to decades to rework into the well-developed gravel berms preserved in the succession.

Aeolian Dunes

Associated with the shoreface deposits are a series of small aeolian dunes (Co-bd; table 5.4, figs. 5.13c, 5.14f) that extend ~100 m inland from the maximum transgression shoreline position. These dune sands form discrete lenses (50–100 cm thick) that are preserved between the upper and lower floodplain units (Fl-pf and Fl-lf, respectively). The backdune deposits reflect aeolian transport from the shoreface onto the adjacent floodplain by strong onshore winds (Hesse 2009). Aeolian dunes in the coastal sequence are relatively small and localized, however, suggesting that they are supply limited despite being proximal to a major fluvial sediment source. This circumstance may indicate a generally low proportion of sand in the Chicama River sediment load, especially compared with the river's abundant silts and gravels. As preserved in the stratigraphy, the backdunes are generally iron stained and partially cemented by authigenic iron oxides, the precipitation of which appear mediated by respiration in the deep root zone of densely colonizing saltgrass, Distichlis spicata (L.) (Poaceae) (fig. 5.14f). The dense grass cover is also consistent with slow dune growth due to a lack of sand supply. Overall the paucity of aeolian deposits found in the Chicama Valley likely benefited the area's human inhabitants, as large-scale mobile aeolian deposits are a major hazard to agriculture and infrastructure in other coastal regions of Peru (Dillehay and Kolata 2004).

Tsunami Surfaces and Deposits

Within the prograding coastal sequence are several unique sedimentary structures that reveal

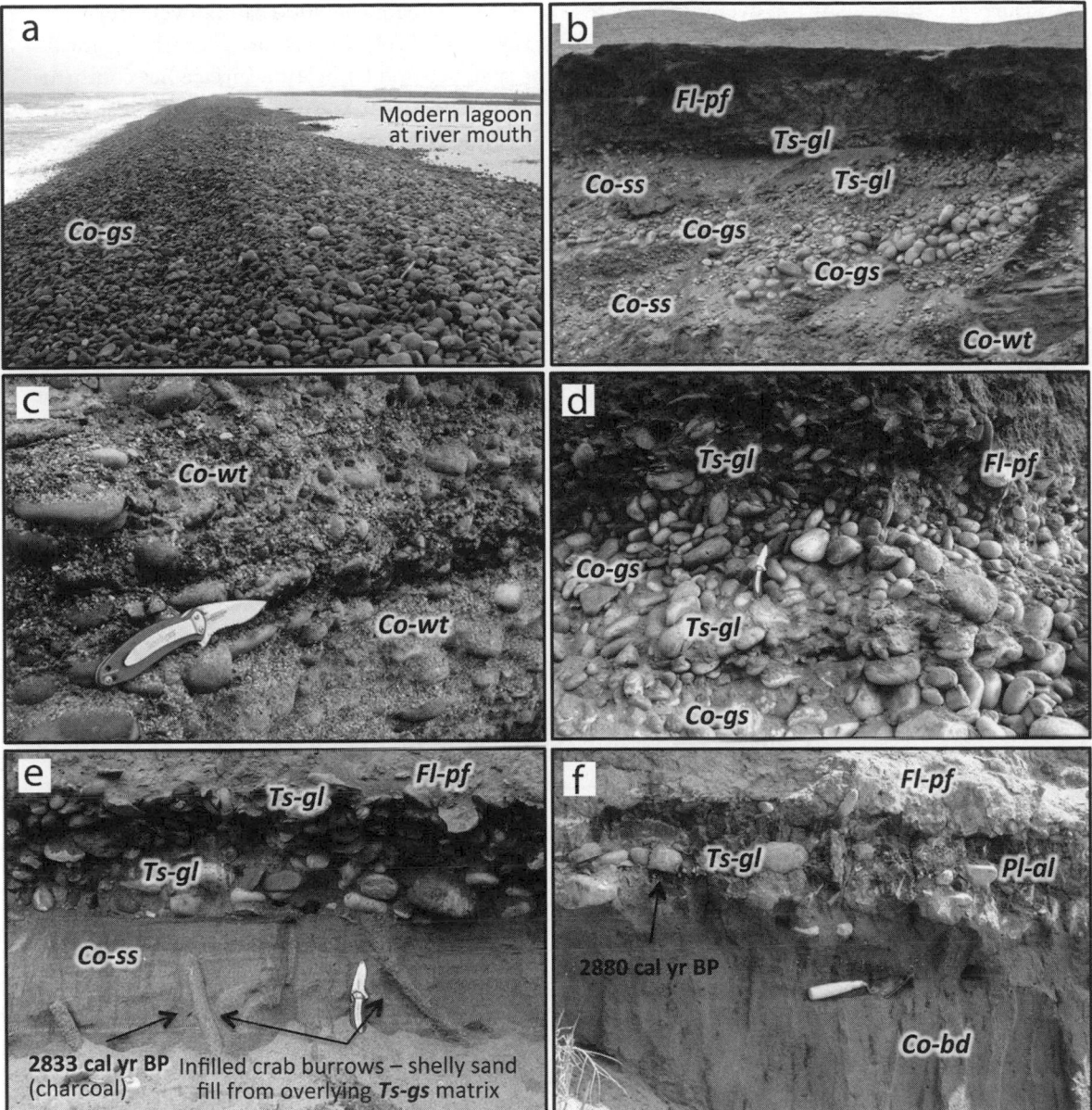

FIGURE 5.14. Modern gravel shoreface and adjacent modern river mouth lagoon and prograding coastal sequence: *a*, modern gravel shoreface and adjacent modern river mouth lagoon, which provide good proxies for the paleoenvironments preserved in the stratigraphic record (the early Holocene lagoon was much larger than the present one); *b*, prograding coastal sequence with alternating, seaward-dipping sandy (*Co-ss*) and gravel (*Co-gs*) shorefaces overlying the flat-bedded wave-swept terrace deposits (*Co-wt*); tops of the shoreface berms are truncated by the two juxtaposed tsunami gravel surfaces (*Ts-gs*); *c*, close-up, oblique photo of the gravelly wave-swept terrace deposits (*Co-wt*), with planar bedded coarse sands, shell hash, and pebble-sized gravel clasts; *d*, close-up of juxtaposed 2900 and 2000 cal BP tsunami gravel beds (*Ts-gs*); the older tsunami unit shows salt-weathering rind that indicates surface exposure prior to burial by younger tsunami deposit, while the mud-filled matrix of younger deposit is postdepositional from an El Niño flood; *e*, coarse, shelly sands from the matrix of the overlying gravel deposit (*Ts-gs*) infill open crab burrows in the fine swash-bedded sands (*Co-ss*) of the active shoreface at time of the 2900 cal BP tsunami; *f*, mud-filled swale within backdune setting (underlying *Co-bd*) with gravel layer of the 2900 cal BP tsunami.

the occurrence of two tsunami events in the late Holocene. The most apparent of these structures is a broad, curvilinear surface that crosscuts the entire coastal sedimentary succession at a shallow angle of 3°, extending from the subtidal wave-terrace deposits across the sand and gravel shore-face units and draping onto the adjacent back-shore floodplain (fig. 5.13). The surface truncates the top of older gravel shoreface beds as it extends landward, emerging at the top of the coastal succession to form the unit's upper bounding plane (fig. 5.14b). The curvilinear surface also defines a ~30 cm thick gravel bed consisting of cobbles reworked from the truncated shoreface unit (*Ts-gl*; figs. 5.13e, 5.14d–e). This reworked gravel bed extends nearly 100 m beyond the site of maximum transgression but becomes increasingly dissected due to the loss of its gravel source from the shore-face deposits (fig. 5.14f) (Nichol et al. 2003). The gravel bed also grades into a thin (1–5 cm) sand layer that extends another ~100 m into the adjacent floodplain unit (*Ts-sl*; fig. 5.10a).

The combined gravel bed and sand layer define this surface for a distance of ~200 m from the paleoshoreface (active at the time of the event) (fig. 5.9a). The surface also crosscuts 4 m of elevation, sharply truncating the tops of older shore-face berms. Finally, gravels at the top of the bed are fractured and salt-weathered, indicating that the deposit lay exposed at the surface for at least decades prior to burial by younger El Niño flood deposits (fig. 5.14b, d–e). Taken together, these attributes are uniquely consistent with a tsunami striking the Chicama coast in the late Holocene, particularly at this low latitude where tropical cyclones are absent. A charcoal fragment collected from the sandy shoreface deposits that onlap the truncation surface provides a minimum age of 1940 cal BP for the event (table 5.2; fig. 5.13b). Given that the surface was not reworked by waves, it must have been buried by these sandy shoreface deposits soon after formation, suggesting that the age of the event is just prior at ~2000 cal BP. These data may correlate with a possible tsunami identified at two sites in southern Peru at ~2250 cal BP (Spiske et al. 2013; Winsborough et al. 2012) or more likely another dated ~1980 cal BP (Spiske et al. 2013).

Clear evidence for an older tsunami is pre-served beneath the 2000 cal BP event deposit (figs. 5.13–5.14). In this case, a nearly identical gravel bed and truncation surface lies conformably beneath the younger tsunami deposit. The contact between the two beds is distinguished by the presence of a weathering horizon consisting of orange, Fe-oxidized sands formed through salt-weathering of quartzite clasts (fig. 5.14d). Tracing this surface seaward also reveals that the two event horizons separate where the older bed dips more steeply at its former shoreface (fig. 5.13b). This same separation of the two event beds occurs landward as well, where the sand layers become separated by 50–100 cm of floodplain silts inland of the maximum transgression (fig. 5.10a). The age of this earlier tsunami event is constrained by two radiocarbon ages of 2880 and 2833 cal BP, which were measured on charcoal fragments recovered in shoreface sands just beneath the gravel layer and from a backdune wetland soil onto which the thin sands and gravel are draped, respectively (fig. 5.14e–f). These dates for the older event match precisely with Junius Bird's postulated tsunami at ~2900 cal BP (Bird 1983; Bird et al 1985: 17–18).

One distinction between the two tsunami deposits is that the older gravel layer has a matrix of coarse sand with abundant fine shell hash that is distinct from the fine-grained, well-sorted sands of the underlying shoreface that it buries. In fact the shelly, coarse sands are identical to those found on the wave-swept terrace of the adjacent surf zone (*Co-wt*), sediments that would likely have been transported onshore by the wave bore. Most interestingly, these coarse, shelly sands infill burrows of the ghost crab (*Ocypode gaudichaudii*), an abundant resident of the active beach shoreface (fig. 5.14e). These crabs construct their burrows in the dry sand just above the swash zone, where the burrows will not be regularly destroyed, extending downward to the water table at 30–60 cm depth. The crab burrows therefore provide an excellent indicator of the active shoreface at the time of the tsunami event. Furthermore, as these easily collapsible burrows are only maintained by active excavation, this requires that the cobble layer and its shelly, coarse-sand matrix must have been emplaced almost instantaneously. Taken together, these attributes of the infilled burrows provide strong evidence that these sand-gravel layers and truncation surfaces record two tsunami events that struck the Chicama coast at ~2900 and ~2000 cal BP.

ENVIRONMENTAL HISTORY

The environmental history of Huaca Prieta is archived in sediments of the Chicama Valley, which contain 1–8 m of Holocene sand, mud, and carbonate sediments that were deposited within various river, floodplain, and coastal settings over the past 8000 years (fig. 5.9 upper figure). The most complete and detailed succession of these sediments is recorded in the lower valley within ~1 km of the shoreline, where the Holocene lithosome is 6–8 m thick. Inland of this area, however, Holocene sediments thin quickly to 1–3 m, representing only a veneer of late Holocene floodplain (*Fl-pf*) over the gravelly alluvial surface. By contrast, areas north and south of the valley have little to no Holocene sediment cover, containing largely older, pre-Holocene alluvial deposits (*Al-fn*) exposed at the ground surface (fig. 5.9). In relation to the Huaca Prieta site, most of the region's environmental diversity through the Holocene could be found in an area within ~4 km south of the mound and ~1 km of the modern shoreline, making the mound centrally located (fig. 5.12).

During this time the most important stages in the environmental history of the region begin with the development of a large, open water lagoon system at 7500 cal BP (table 5.6). By ~6300 cal BP the lagoon is infilled, but there is a limited geologic record until ~5000 cal BP that suggests a restricted sediment supply and presumed absence of El Niño wet phases (fig. 5.15). After 5000 cal BP, though, comes a phase of slow but clear growth of an emergent floodplain system consisting of fine muds, with disseminated organics and wetland gastropods. By 3700 cal BP this floodplain setting begins to develop more rapidly, aggrading above the water table as a high, well-drained floodplain. Floodplain development at this time also expands to include large areas upstream of the coast, blanketing the upper alluvial plane with a veneer of floodplain silts. Corresponding with this phase of rapid floodplain growth is a reversal of the shoreline tendency from transgressive to regressive (fig. 5.9 upper part), indicating an increase in fluvial sediment delivery, presumably in association with enhanced frequency and magnitude of El Niño floods. Both floodplain aggradation and shoreline progradation continue to be present.

ALLUVIAL STAGE (PRE-HUACA PRIETA [HP])

The arid Pacific slope of the Andes is defined by extensive alluvial landscapes that only episodically receive precipitation and experience active sediment transport. In the valley, OSL dating of shallow sand layers within alluvial-outwash and debris-flow deposits consistently yield ages from 40,000 to 14,000 cal BP (fig. 5.4a), indicating that these alluvial settings were most active during the last glacial period (MIS 2–3) and experienced a sharp decrease in transport and deposition prior to the Holocene. Based on these clustered dates from alluvial settings across the Chicama region, it appears that the alluvial systems have been largely nondepositional or erosional through most of the Holocene, producing no significant stratigraphic record over this time. But these alluvial surfaces have remained active despite a lack of sediment accretion, being episodically reworked by El Niño floods in the mid- to late Holocene. Scours produced by these flood events coupled with the high water table near the coast have likely supported paludal wetlands within the alluvial outwash channels over most of the Holocene (figs. 5.8, 5.11a-b). Although probably perennially present in the region, these naturally productive settings are also locally ephemeral and may not last over longer periods ($\geq 10^2$ years).

TRANSITION (HP PHASE I)

Heading into the Holocene, the earliest sediments deposited over the alluvial surface are fluvial sands (*Fl-ch*) from the Chicama River channel. These sediments are silty, fine to medium sands typically found at 6–8 m depth below the modern floodplain near the coast (fig. 5.9 upper part). The sands are nonfossiliferous and lack any mud drapes or associated overbank muds, suggesting that they represent a unit of channel and bar deposits up to several meters thick. These deposits are not found

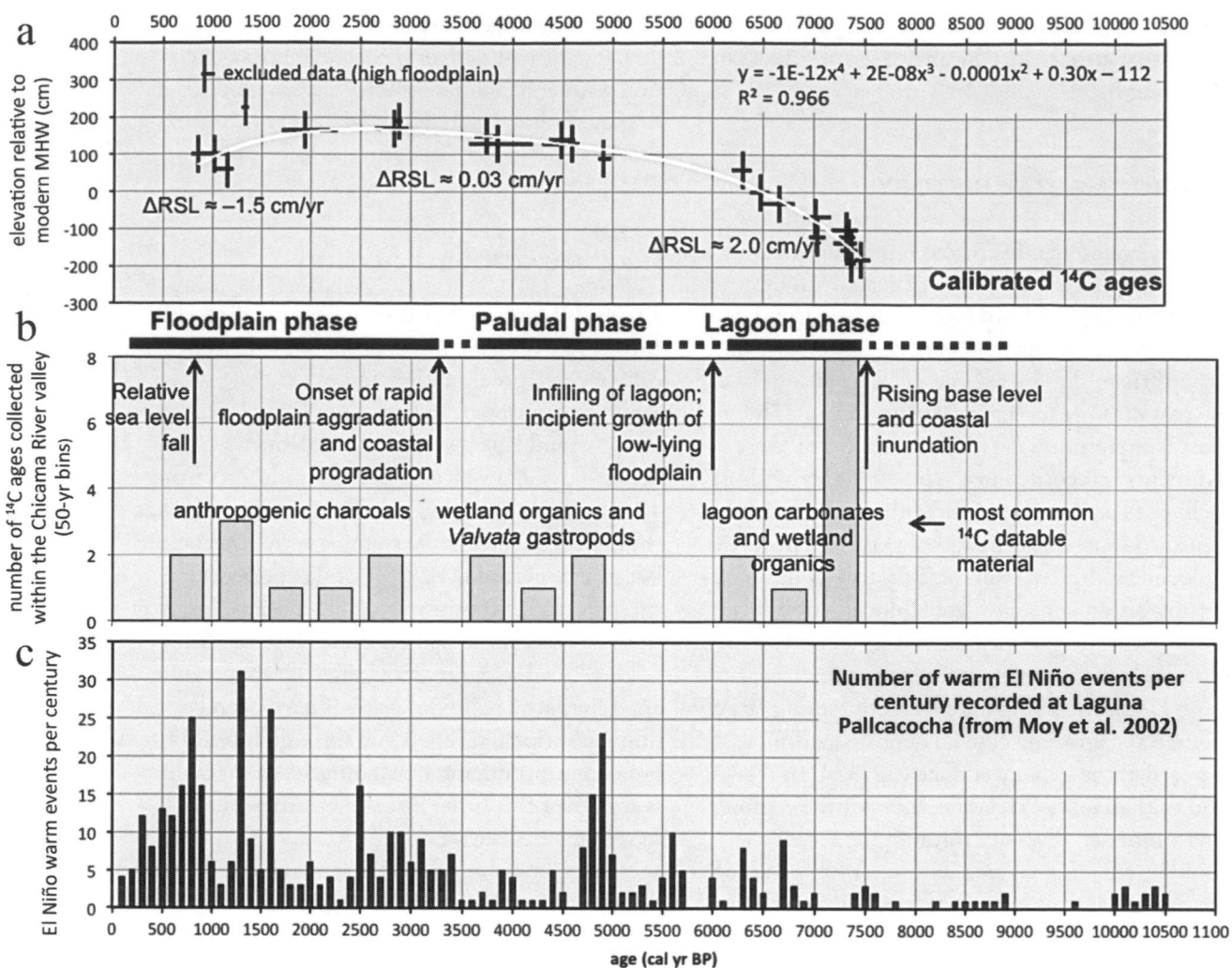

FIGURE 5.15. Data plots of Holocene radiocarbon ages from the lower Chicama Valley and coastal system (*a, b*) and frequency of El Niño wet phases through the Holocene (*c*): *a*, age-depth plot of radiocarbon ages giving a relative sea-level curve for the study area (the curve reflects general trends in sea-level and is not intended to be a high-precision sea-level curve, but trends of rapid sea-level rise up to ~6000 cal BP are evident, reaching an elevation ~2 m above present mean high water (MHW) before slowing considerably; there is no evidence for significant sea-level change from 6000 to 1000 cal BP, but evidence clearly indicates a sharp drop of 1–2 m between 1000–500 cal BP); *b*, histogram of radiocarbon ages from the study, showing clusters of ages associated with the major constructional phases of the coastal and floodplain sequences, which area also shown; *c*, frequency plot of El Niño wet phases recorded in sediments of Laguna Pallcaococha at 4500 m elevation, ~350 km SE of the Chicama River Valley. El Niño phases were reconstructed by appearance of coarse sediment deposition in the lake (Moy et al. 2002). The record shows the initial onset of El Niño phenomenon ~7000 cal BP; it remains low but variable until ~3500 cal BP, when frequency increases. A second increase in El Niño frequency occurs after ~2000 cal BP, reaching a maximum for the Holocene. The variability of El Niño recorded in Laguna Pallcaococha matches well the environmental history recorded in the Chicama Valley.

far from the central river valley, perhaps indicating that river discharge was restricted to the main channel valley and that coarse channel sands were not widely broadcast. There is no direct age control on these deposits, but they appear to lie conformably beneath the well-dated lagoon deposits and likely begin 10,000–9000 cal BP. Similar channel sands are deposited today along the lower kilometer of the river system where it intersects base level. Thus the underlying early Holocene sands may reflect a setting not unlike the modern Chicama River during normal discharge regimes (a non–El Niño year) and also presage the pending flooding of the coast by rising sea level.

Table 5.6. Summary of major environmental phases of the Chicama Valley and coastal system

Environmental phase	Start	End	Description (this study)	Cultural Phase	Start	End	Description (from Dillehay et al. 2012b)
ALLUVIAL		16,000	Latest glacial alluvial fan construction	pre–HP	13,700		Recovered simple edge–trimmed pebble flakes, several bone fish and sea lion remains, and fractured shellfish valves from these deposits
Transition	7500	7500	Fluvial sands accumulating; uncertain climate and environmental setting; seaward lagoon?	I	9000	7500	Maritime foragers and incipient gardeners; no architecture detected for this phase
LAGOON	7500	6300	Coastal inundation and development of large open–water lagoon and wetlands	II	7500	6500	First mound construction stage; the earliest mound layers were placed on the southeast flank; start of deliberate and gradual planned mounding
Transition	530	530	Poor record; lagoons infilled; slowly accreting wetlands and low–lying floodplain	III	6300	5300	Structural features are spatially and architecturally conjoined, suggesting simultaneous planned construction and use across the entire mound at this time
PALUDAL	5300	3800	Low–lying floodplains with active soil development and abundant wetland	I	5300	4100	First layers of ramp built on east side: the upper portion of the retention wall and the stepped structures in the sunken plaza
Transition (max. transgression)	3800	3500	Increased El Niño floods and riverine sediment flux; shore–line reversal to progradation	V	4100	3500	Flanks of mound to east and west were used less, with most activity limited to the flat crest of the structure; cobble–stone burial chambers were built on the upper mound
FLOODPLAIN	3500	800	Rapid floodplain construction and aggradation; widespread across valley	post–HP	3500	600	By ~3.8 kb, Preceramic use of site terminated; later Ceramic cultures from the Cupisnique to Inka periods carried out rituals and burials on top of the mound

LAGOON STAGE (HP PHASE II)

By 7500 cal BP rising sea level led to back-flooding onto the alluvial surface and inundation of the lower Chicama valley and adjacent coastal reach (figs. 5.9, upper part, and 5.15). A change from fluvial sands of the lower river to the deposition of algal carbonates, subaqueous muds, and peat horizons reflects the development of an open-water lagoon system that extended from the Pleistocene terrace at least 3 km to the modern river mouth (fig. 5.12). The lagoon deposits also extend inland 500–1000 m from the modern coastline, giving a minimum value for width of the lagoon. The observed distribution of these deposits indicates that the lagoon encompassed an area of at least 2.5 km², although it was likely much larger and extended well seaward of the modern shoreline where our observations end. Four radiocarbon dates from the base of these lagoon deposits yield a close range of ages from 7457–7318 cal BP, indicating rapid development of the lagoon system at this time (table 5.2). The lifespan of this large lagoon was relatively short at ~1000±200 years, however, with several radiocarbon dates constraining the last period of carbonate and organic deposition from 6659 to 6295 cal BP (fig. 5.15). These dates confirm that human activity at Huaca Prieta and Paredones was coincident with development of this expansive lagoon adjacent to the mound site (Dillehay et al. 2012b).

In total these early Holocene lagoon deposits are 1–3 m thick and are characterized by thick, alternating layers (5–20 cm) of algal carbonates (La-ca; primarily Charophyta) and microfossiliferous blue muds (La-fl; primarily Ostracoda) (fig. 5.5). The ecological assemblage in both lagoon facies is species depauperate, with <6 total floral and faunal species. The sediments also generally lack marine fossils, consisting primarily of freshwater gastropods, calcified charophyte stems and gyrogonites, and fresh to brackish water ostracods (fig. 5.6). The dominant carbonate producer in the lagoon deposits are charophyte algae, which are typical of fresh to brackish water conditions and depths <10 m, where they tend to grow in large submerged meadows (Andrews et al. 2004). They prefer low-energy environments with little suspended sediment, which facilitate photosynthesis, and grow best in fine-grained sediment substrates (García 1994). Also, calcifying species of charophyte, such as those in this lagoon, require alkaline water chemistry with high dissolved solids that is often reflective of a groundwater-fed hydrology.

The abundant gastropods within these deposits belong primarily to a single genus, *Lymnaea* (fig. 5.6c), which is a freshwater group with optimal living conditions at salinities <2‰ (Berezina 2003). Lymnaeids are scrapers and algivores (Thorp and Covich 2001), which is consistent with their appearance here in association with dense stands of charophyte algae. The dominant ostracod in the lagoon muds (La-fl) belongs to the genus *Cyprideis* (fig. 5.6d), which is a euryhaline group able to live in all salinities (Aparecido do Carmo et al. 1999). *C. torosa* is typically considered a brackish water species, but it also inhabits freshwater lakes and can tolerate high salinities of up to 50‰ (Smith and Horne 2002). The high proportion of round sieve pores in the *Cyprideis* specimens from Huaca Prieta, however, suggests a lagoon salinity of no more than 0.6‰. That is also consistent with the river-sourced muds (La-fl) that constitute many of the lagoon deposits and reflect episodic fluvial input to the lagoon, presumably delivered by modest river flood discharge suggested by the fine-grained nature of the sediments.

Interbedded with the carbonates and fluvial muds are thin organic layers (Pl-lg) containing detrital wood and emergent grass stems (fig. 5.5). The organic layer also often contains seeds of the common seagrass *Ruppia maritima*. Based on the sediment lithology and ecological assemblages, these units reflect a predominantly oligotrophic and oligohaline lagoon, perhaps groundwater fed, with fringing wetland vegetation, a weak to intermittent connection to the sea, and limited fluvial sediment input. Overall the sedimentary facies and ecological assemblages present in the lagoonal sediments suggest that the lagoon was freshwater to mildly brackish, with a weak to intermittent connection to the sea and episodic fluvial sediment input.

TRANSITIONAL (HP PHASE III)

After 6500 cal BP the carbonate and muddy lagoon sediments become increasingly rare in the stratigraphic record, with the youngest date of 6295 cal BP (table 5.2) near the top of the main lagoon sequence. Overlying the lagoon deposits are 1–2 m of stiff muds with well-developed soil horizons characteristic of poorly drained, seasonally saturated conditions. The emergence of these deposits begins after ~6000 cal BP, but the oldest date from the unit is 4903 cal BP (table 5.2), suggesting a possible depositional hiatus or very slow accretion from ~6000 to 5000 cal BP. Of 25 radiocarbon dates from the lower valley, none fall within 6000–5000 cal BP (fig. 5.15). After ~5000 cal BP come the prominent, well-dated soil horizons of the Paludal Stage, although these deposits too suggest continued slow sediment deposition. Thus the period from ~6300 to 5300 cal BP is considered to represent a slow, but major, environmental transition from open-water lagoon to emergent riverine floodplain. The mound at Paredones was beginning to be used ~6500 cal BP, when the lagoon disappears and converts to an ephemeral wetland and a floodplain.

The disappearance of the lagoon cannot be attributed to a fall in sea level and regression of the shoreline, however, because the coast continues to transgress for another ~1500 years, not reaching its maximum until shortly after ~3700 cal BP (figs. 5.9, upper part, and 5.15). Thus, while a rising sea level and water table led to initial development of the lagoon, the disappearance of the lagoon appears to have been forced by an increase in fluvial sediment deposition that was sufficient to outpace sea-level rise and infill the lagoon. Such an increase in fluvial sediment deposition could have occurred in response to a greater frequency or magnitude of floods. Indeed the transition from lagoon to floodplain from ~6000 to 5000 cal BP is consistent with the regional onset of El Niño–impacted climate and episodic flooding (fig. 5.15; Moy et al. 2002; Sandweiss et al. 1999).

PALUDAL STAGE (HP PHASE IV)

In the stratigraphy, the development of an incipient floodplain is recorded by sediments having well-developed soil horizons with disseminated organics, common paludal fauna (such as *Valvata* gastropods), and calcic horizons in various stages of development (for example, *Bk* layers). Together these attributes reflect seasonally wet soils and ephemeral wetlands that are characteristic of this environmental stage in the valley (figs. 5.9a–d and 5.10). Such soils are widespread near the coast but are restricted regionally, with no floodplain yet developed upstream at this time. In the coastal portion of the valley, there appear to be at least three phases of soil development within these low-lying floodplain deposits. The earliest of these soils dates to 4909 cal BP, with the middle unit yielding two ages of 4585 and 4483 cal BP (table 5.2; figs. 5.9–5.10). The earlier date overlaps chronologically with the date of a buried raised agricultural field just east of Paredones, suggesting the presence, possibly seasonal, of shallow wetlands there.

The upper soil horizon dates to 3847 cal BP (fig. 5.10a) and is the oldest stratigraphic unit near the river mouth (away from Huaca Prieta and adjacent floodplain) to contain evidence of human presence, including the presence of marine mollusk shells, centimeter-sized fired-clay daub, and allochthonous cobbles and coral fragments (figs. 5.10, 5.13e). The mollusks in these floodplain deposits are primarily *Donax* sp. and *Tegula* sp., which are common food sources and are found in clusters within the mud soil and clearly human transported. Furthermore, the presence of clay daub in these low-lying floodplain deposits, combined with the regular occurrence of Guañape pottery fragments (dated around 4200–3800 cal BP) in the overlying proximal floodplain units suggest that these deposits mark the last stage of Preceramic cultures (Dillehay et al. 2012b). Adjacent to Huaca Prieta, buried *camellones* (raised agricultural fields) within low-lying floodplain deposits date to ~5200 cal BP and indicate that people were able to engineer these saturated soil settings for agricultural use (see chapter 7).

The emergence of El Niño–driven flooding proves to be important not only for its increased sediment delivery to the coast but has several other attributes that are critical to the development of a broad floodplain in the lower valley (fig. 5.15). First, El Niño–related precipitation shifts from the highlands to the lower mountains and foothills, where strong rains and runoff cause hillslope failure and soil erosion, accounting for an increase in the fine, suspended sediment needed to construct a floodplain (Sandweiss et al. 2009). During normal climate conditions, the low runoff-rate supports more groundwater-fed discharge and a bedload dominated river system. Second, the river channel is not in equilibrium with the infrequent discharge during El Niño wet phases and thus cannot convey the floodwaters within its channel. This circumstance requires overbank flow beyond the channel, which effectively distributes fine-grained suspended sediments far from the channel, whereas the coarser bedload remains in the channel. Thus the increased erosion of fine sediments from the catchment and their effective dispersal across the lower valley are key attributes of El Niño floods compared with the perennial river discharge during normal climate conditions.

MAXIMUM TRANSGRESSION AND PRECERAMIC/CERAMIC TRANSITION (HP PHASE V)

The brief but important transition from the Paludal Stage to the Floodplain Stage is characterized by the change from a dominance of water-logged, low-lying floodplain environments to more widespread, well-drained, silty floodplains (table 5.6; fig. 5.15). The transition also coincides with maximum transgression of the shoreline, which occurs shortly after ~3700 cal BP and is followed by a shift to a regressive, prograding shoreline. The point of maximum shoreline position is ideally captured by the onlap of gravel shoreface deposits onto a truncated sandy backdune unit (fig. 5.13e). The backdune contains clear evidence of human occupation, including clay daub and fire-cemented sands, indicating that people must have been displaced by encroachment of the shoreline (fig. 5.13e). Charcoal from this backdune layer dates to ~3740 cal BP, giving a maximum age for the maximum transgression, although the gravel/dune contact appears conformable and is likely close to this age. The charcoal date from the backdune is also close to the ~3847 cal BP date from the human-occupied floodplain layer, which is located about 100 m inland, suggesting that the two layers are correlative (fig. 5.14f). These ages match the date for a gravel-sand shoreface that onlaps the base of Huaca Prieta at ~3758 cal BP. This shoreface deposit is part of numerous intercalated shoreface deposits and cultural sediment colluvium from the adjacent mound (see appendix 1).

Together these results correlate maximum

transgression at both the river mouth and Huaca Prieta, while also correlating this period with the major environmental transition from low-lying floodplain to more arable high floodplain, all occurring ~3700 cal BP. These transitions are significant to both the geological and human history of the lower valley. Up to this point in the Holocene, the shoreline had been retreating continuously landward since initial lagoon development at ~7500 cal BP, despite the onset of El Niño wet phases after ~7000 cal BP (Moy et al. 2002). Increased frequency and intensity of El Niño wet phases and associated river floods after ~3700 cal BP (fig. 5.15; Sandweiss 2003), however, drove enhanced sediment delivery sufficient to prograde the shoreline and aggrade the floodplain. This mid-Holocene intensification of El Niño is widely documented but not well constrained (table 5.1).

As noted in the Paludal Stage, this period also appears to correspond with the transition from Preceramic to Ceramic cultures, as indicated by the first appearance of clay daub in the low-lying floodplain units followed by the first appearance of Guañape-like pottery sherds in the high floodplain deposits (table 5.6). This cultural transition also marks the progressive decline in use of Huaca Prieta, which becomes effectively abandoned (except for later burials) by Preceramic cultures after 3800 cal BP (Dillehay et al. 2012b). The cultural transition and corresponding disuse of Huaca Prieta at this time correlates precisely with maximum shoreline transgression. At the river mouth, the location of maximum transgression lies ~300 m inland of the modern shoreline and at the surface is readily marked by the dune to floodplain transition (fig. 5.12). Tracing this boundary north shows that maximum transgression was located 50–100 m inland of Huaca Prieta and the Sangamon terrace. The shoreline at maximum transgression would have been at the base of the terrace and Huaca Prieta mound, which may have played a role in its decreased use around this time.

FLOODPLAIN STAGE (POST-HP)

The period after ~3000 cal BP is marked by rapid vertical aggradation of the floodplain and its alteration to an elevated, well-drained environment (figs. 5.9a–d, 5.10). This change is well reflected in the difference style and degree of soil development. The earlier low-lying floodplain deposits had well-developed soils with disseminated organics and various stages of calcic horizon growth. In contrast the overlying high floodplain shows limited soil development and a lack of concretions but does often have well-developed prismatic and columnar peds that are typical of wetting and drying in arid environments (fig. 5.10a).

This transformation also appears to correlate with the emergence of subsequent ceramic cultures (for example, Cupisnique, Gallinazo, and Salinar), an association that is reflected in the regular occurrence of small fire pits with Guañape-like pottery sherds and fractured cobbles within the thick floodplain sequences (table 5.6). Furthermore, the floodplain environment expands greatly over this time. Through most of the Holocene active sediment deposition and productive landscapes were restricted to within 1 km of the coast. Increasingly large and frequent El Niño floods in the late Holocene, however, expand sediment accumulation both up-valley and laterally away from the main channel. These areas previously consisted of gravelly alluvium, but in the late Holocene they become blanketed with silts, forming a 1–3 m thick veneer of sediments that transforms the lower valley into an arable landscape. Increasing water diversion through the use of irrigation canals may also have contributed to the expansion of the floodplain during this time (T. Dillehay, personal communication, 2010). Overall the widespread development of a silty, well-drained floodplain in the late Holocene is among the most important environmental changes over the last 8000 years.

TSUNAMIS

The prograding-shoreface sequence is interrupted at two intervals, where the tops of the gravel beach ridges are sharply truncated by well-defined curvilinear surfaces that extend >150 m across the beach-dune complex onto the adjacent floodplain (fig. 5.13). At the beach-floodplain transition, the event surfaces change from a truncated cobble lags to thin sand sheets (<5 cm) that extend another ~150 m landward. The lower of these two surfaces unconformably onlaps with a Preceramic anthropogenic horizon from the backdune area that dates ~3740 cal BP (fig. 5.13e), and is subsequently overlain by an undated ceramic-period anthropogenic horizon. Radiocarbon dates from charcoal and wetland organics (~2880 and 2833 cal BP) collected at two different locations immediately below the lower event surface and located ~3 km south of Huaca Prieta constrain its age to ~2900 cal BP. Another radiocarbon date from charcoal (1940 cal BP) within the beach sand overlying the upper surface constrains its age to ~2000 cal BP (fig. 5.13b). Both of these sharp, curvilinear truncation surfaces cum sand layers reflect tsunami waves that struck the local shoreline at ~2900 and 2000 cal BP. Origins of the tsunamis are not known, but there is no evidence for local earthquakes or uplift within the sediments, which suggests that the tsunamis may have been remotely generated. The timing of these two events falls well after Phase V at Huaca Prieta, which marks the end of mound construction (Dillehay et al. 2012b). But the older event does correspond precisely with Bird's postulated tsunami at ~2800 BP (Bird 1987). No evidence of tsunami impact was recorded at Huaca Prieta or other areas north of it on the Sangamon terrace (see appendix 1).

SEA-LEVEL FALL

Following the latest cultural activity at Huaca Prieta (post-Phase V), the shoreline continues to prograde before becoming capped by several muddy El Niño flood deposits (table 5.4; fig. 5.13). Within the last 1000 years relative sea level dropped ~1–2 (fig. 5.15), forcing the Chicama River to incise the entire mid-Holocene beach-floodplain sequence and to form a new beach-dune complex 50 m seaward and ~1–2 m lower than that of the earlier beach-terrace complex (figs. 5.13–5.14). Similarly, at Huaca Prieta a muddy El Niño flood deposit dated to ~740 cal BP lies exposed 3 m above modern sea level along the seaward side of the mound (appendix 1). The late Holocene beach terrace also lies 2 m above the modern shoreface. These data reflect an abrupt fall in relative sea level, presumably due to a tectonic uplift event, as evidenced by the large magnitude and rapid rate of change as well as the lack of any mechanism or record of eustatic fall at this time. A similar drop in relative sea level is documented at this time from the Santa beach ridge complex to the south (Wells 1996).

SUMMARY

The earliest Holocene sediments in the lower Chicama River valley are fluvial sands near the modern river mouth, beginning ~14,000 cal BP. These fluvial sands are overlain by a widespread coastal lagoon that developed along the coast at ~7500 cal BP. The lagoon was freshwater to oligohaline and supported meadows of Charophyta, a subaqueous macrophyte, and associated *Lymnaea* grazing gastropods. The lagoon also supported extensive wetlands recorded by regular organic and peat layers. By ~6300 BP the lagoon environment disappears, apparently infilled with authigenic carbonates and fluvial sediments associated with the onset of infrequent El Niño wet phases (Moy et al. 2002). By ~5000 cal BP the lower valley transitioned into a low-lying floodplain with seasonal wetlands and abundant *Valvata* gastropod grazers. These paludal settings persisted until ~3800 cal BP, when sedimentation rates began to increase significantly and build the floodplain above the water table. Around the same time, the shoreline reached its maximum inland extent 200–300 m from the modern shoreline and would have been located around the base of Huaca Prieta.

The timing of maximum transgression corresponds with the last phase of Preceramic use of the mound, suggesting that decline in human activity at the site was related to the ocean lapping at the base of the mound. Soon after the shoreline reverses its tendency and for the first time in the Holocene begins to prograde seaward. These transitions after ~3800 cal BP reflect greatly increased water and sediment discharge from the Chicama River, associated with increased frequency and magnitude of El Niño wet phases (Makou et al. 2010; Sandweiss 2003). This onset of intensified El Niño floods transforms the lower valley into a broad, arable landscape through episodic deposition of well-drained, silty loams. Rapid floodplain aggradation persisted through the late Holocene and appears to have accelerated even further after ~2000 cal BP (Moy et al. 2002), with thick decimeter-scale beds separated by weakly developed soils. These flood deposits even cap the prograding shoreface sequence, with muddy floodplain sediments overlying older shoreface sand and gravel berms.

During this phase of floodplain aggradation and coastal progradation, two tsunami events are also recorded in the stratigraphic record south of Huaca Prieta as broad curvilinear surfaces that truncate earlier sand and gravel shoreface deposits. The tsunami truncation surfaces extend over 200–300 m and grade to a thinning gravel-sand bed onto the adjacent backdune and floodplain. The two tsunami surfaces date ~2900 and 2000 cal BP, respectively, which both considerably postdate human activity at Huaca Prieta ~4000–3500 cal BP, suggesting that abandonment of the site was not related to the tsunamis (Bird [Bird et al. 1985: 17] accurately identified and dated a tsunami in the area in Cupisnique times, which would have been ~3000 cal BP). Nevertheless, the tsunamis were certainly major events and must have impacted cultures living along portions of the coast at that time. The last paleoenvironmental phase along the lower valley is a 1–2 m drop in relative sea level since 1000 cal BP. The origin and history of the base-level fall is not known, but it is reflected in the widespread shoreface berm that lies 10–50 m inland of the modern shore (see appendix 1).

In brief summary, the interdisciplinary geological research registered the type of paleoenvironment that existed in the study area roughly between the late Pleistocene and the late middle Holocene periods, with more detail given to the time span between 9000 and 3500 years ago. The major environmental impacts included radiocarbon-dated maximum Holocene transgression, two tsunamis, and several ENSO events. The only environmental events that seem to have had a major impact on the local population and activity in the Huaca Prieta area were (1) marine transgression, which probably influenced the eventual abandonment of the site area for decades or perhaps even a few centuries (see chapters 6 and 7), and (2) the development of the lagoons around 7500 cal BP when the mound at Huaca Prieta and the many of the outlying domestic sites along the littoral and into the interior began to appear, the gradual disappearance of the lagoons 1000 years later when the mound at Paredones developed, and probably crop production in the former wetlands immediately east of the terrace. Sometime after about 3500 years ago, the south point of the terrace where Huaca Prieta and the Cupisnique mounds are located was reoccupied, as evidenced by the presence of Initial Period ceramics and house structures in the deeper levels of the latter mound. We have no geological or archaeological evidence to indicate how long the hiatus between the abandonment of the mound at Huaca Prieta and reuse of the area during the Initial Period might have been. As discussed in chapters 6, 7, 14, and 15, we are not suggesting that the cumulative and short-term impacts of these events, particularly marine transgression around 3700 years ago, were the primary causes of site abandonment. These events must have had economic and demographic repercussions, however, that would have led to local social and cultural changes, shifts that we were unable to correlate clearly with any specific environmental impact through geological and archaeological analyses. None of these impacts, however, seem to have affected the long time span of human occupation along the lower Chicama Valley. As seen in chapter 9, the results from the faunal data indicate that those people using the Huaca Prieta mound always had a marine diet, although the species type and frequency occasionally changed from phase to phase. As shown in chapter 10 on plant remains, wild plants and food crops played an increasingly important role in the diet, especially at Paredones after about 6500 years ago.

CHAPTER 6

CULTURAL PHASES AND RADIOCARBON CHRONOLOGY

Tom D. Dillehay
and Duccio Bonavia

INTRODUCTION

This chapter reports on the cultural phases and chronology at Huaca Prieta, Paredones, and other sites. In total, more than 170 radiocarbon and OSL dates were obtained from 70 different mound and off-mound contexts and from geological cuts and cores. Not all intact floor and use episodes in the mounds were radiocarbon dated, which would have required several hundred chronometric measurements. But the deeper stratigraphic cuts in Units 2, 9, 12, 15/21, 16, Test Pit 22, and Bird's HP-3 at Huaca Prieta and Units 20 and 22 at Paredones were dated from the top to bottom. There is general agreement and stratigraphic alignment between Bird's dates and his schematic profile of HP-3 and our dates and stratigraphy in this same unit (see figs. 20 and 33 in Bird et al. 1985). This is significant because the dates from HP-3 and from Unit 15/21 represent the single longest dated stratigraphic profiles from the top of the mound to its deeper base just above the culturally sterile buried Sangamon terrace. All of our dates were taken on single chunks of charcoal from short-lived shrub and tree species, maize and other crop remains, or cotton textiles recovered from features embedded in floors (see chapter 3 and appendix 2). No radiocarbon samples were taken from fills, middens, or marine shells. All materials submitted for dating by Bird are reported as organics without a detailed description, so it is possible that some of his radiocarbon dates were processed on long-lived tree species. But his dates stratigraphically agree with our chronostratigraphy and seem to be correct. Given the different organic materials dated by six different laboratories over a period of six decades (the AMS laboratories at the University of Arizona, the Oxford Laboratory, Beta Analytic, Inc., the Woods Hole Oceanographic

Institute, Direct-AMS, and Bird's dates assayed by Willard Libby's laboratory in the early 1950s), the assays generally correspond and overlap chronologically and stratigraphically at the 2-sigma and 98.2% calibrated age range. All radiocarbon measures in the text are calibrated and their ± age range and lab number are given (for example, 4590±30 cal BP, AA33333); in referring to a general age range, however, only the date is provided (for example, ~2000 cal BP). The OSL dates are reported in chapter 5 on the geology of the study area.

The use of ^{14}C dates as a measure of time is subject to two critiques. It often makes occupations and phases appear longer or more uniform than may actually be the case. Radiocarbon dating also assumes an overlapping temporal continuum, although it produces points in time. Boundaries between phases and any subphases (such as early and late) are therefore arbitrary. Dates also can effectively flatten an otherwise long-term, multiple event-based sequence such as that evidenced at Huaca Prieta.

Before discussing the cultural phases at sites, it is necessary to present the terminology that we use for floors, layers, fills, and other cultural stratigraphic units. The stratigraphy, ^{14}C dates, and Harris Matrices for the primary units (HP-3, Units 2, and 22) are presented in chapter 7. Table 6.1 presents all radiocarbon dates for sites. The geological dates also are presented in this table but discussed in chapter 5 and appendix 1.

TERMINOLOGY FOR CULTURAL STRATIGRAPHY

Brief definitions of floors, use surfaces, and fills are provided for discussion of the cultural phases and archaeological findings at sites and for contextualizing the symbols used in the Harris Matrices (see chapter 7).

Floors represent human activity in highly restricted spaces and time dimensions. For instance, at Huaca Prieta they measure ~1.8 to 4 m by ~5.1 to 8 m in size and probably represent single episodes of use as suggested by their 0.5–3.0 cm thickness and by the presence of few artifacts and often no features. They form a stratigraphically discrete layer with distinct boundaries, differentiated through the uneven spatial distribution of stone walls, artifacts, faunal remains, burned areas, and other anthropogenic elements.

Table 6.1. Cultural phases and subphases and their radiocarbon time spans

Phase I:	Premound Contexts, ~14,500–7500 cal BP
	Early Subphase: ~14,500–11,400 cal BP
	Late Subphase: ~11,400–7500 cal BP
Phase II:	Incipient Mound Building, ~7572–6538 cal BP
	Early Subphase: ~7572–7000 cal BP
	Late Subphase: ~7000–6538 cal BP
Phase III:	Mound Expansion, ~6538–5308 cal BP
Phase IV:	New Architectural Ontology, ~5308–4107 cal BP
	Early Subphase: ~5308–4707 cal BP
	Late Subphase: ~4707–4107 cal BP
Phase V:	Termination, ~4107–3455 cal BP
	Early Subphase: ~4107–3800 cal BP
	Late Subphase: ~3800–3455 cal BP

There are different kinds of floors. Prepared floors are compacted and often lined with a cement-like plaster, exotic, or off-mound sediment and sometimes have small stone structures or areas defined by an alignment of stones or the placement of reed matting. Indeterminate floors are defined by unaligned stones and partial stone alignments, structures, or mats, but exotic sediments are absent.

Prepared use surfaces also exist. These are flat, compacted surfaces that were leveled but not prepared as formal floors with cement or other exotic material. They sometimes have stone alignments, features, burned areas, matting, artifacts, and other materials. Other unprepared use surfaces were leveled but have few artifacts, stone alignments, or other features and little evidence of trampling and compaction from use.

Also present are thin and thick fills between

floors and use surfaces (varying between ~5 cm to 1.5 m in thickness). One type of fill is an artificial berm composed of imbricated cobblestones, often used as a footing to support various inclined layers in the mounds (see chapter 7). Other fills are layers of loosely compacted debris that vary in thickness.

Throughout this volume "layer" is a generic term referring to a mixture of truncated floors, use surfaces, and/or fills. The term "polychaete blocks" or "tubes" refers to mineralized sediments produced by marine annelid worms that build tube dwelling blocks that were retrieved from shallow offshore waters by the Preceramic inhabitants of the littoral and used in architecture and in sculpting artwork. Cobblestones are water-rolled rocks gathered along the beach and riverbed and used in architecture too.

Finally, we consider two types of ritual contexts specifically associated with prepared and unprepared floors and use surfaces: ritual offerings and mortuary ritual contexts. Floors and use surfaces associated with circumscribed activity areas (such as exotic sediment on floors and stone-lined areas), large amounts of charcoal associated with burned plants, sea urchin spines, other items piled in discrete spaces within these activity areas, and discrete artifact clusters and offerings reflect a nonmortuary ritual. Mortuary rituals are associated primarily with small chamber tombs where burials and discrete offerings took place or secondarily with shallow, informal graves with or without offerings (see chapter 7). There are also empty chamber tombs occasionally with offerings but without human skeletons. The offerings were intentionally placed inside the tombs or graves in small discrete piles of coca leaves, various shell species, fragments of textiles, baskets, lithics, or wood, among other items. Nonritual or commensal feasting also seems to be present in a few localities. This activity is defined by less discrete spaces containing some burned material and moderate to large quantities of discarded food debris in places in and around the mounds at Huaca Prieta and Paredones. This type of activity is probably associated with mound-building activities, maintenance of the mound architecture, or other tasks. What separates all of these activities from domestic food preparation and consumption is the absence of hearths, lithic, shell, and other tools for food

preparation, discarded gourd containers with food residues inside, lightly scattered charcoal and ash, manos and grinding, food and other stains, usually house remains, and other domestic debris. Even more significant are the types of layers defining each of these activities. Ritual floors, whether prepared or unprepared, are thin and spatially discrete, usually no more than 0.5–3 cm in thickness, covering between 4 and 10 m² and often associated with aligned stones or small rooms in addition to the types of artifacts and offerings mentioned above. Layers thought to be representative of feasting activity are much less formal, usually with less defined or undefined floors and use surfaces, thus making it more difficult to estimate their thickness and extent, in addition to the material assemblages of which they are composed. Both the ritual and feasting surfaces have few, if any, intrusive features. It also is possible that some of these traits are combined to form ritual commensal feasting, but we have little clear evidence of this at Huaca Prieta. Domestic activity is perhaps the easiest to define with a wide assortment of artifacts and features, as mentioned above, and almost always involves room structures and thicker (5–20 cm), messier, dirtier floors and use surfaces with intrusive pits, hearths, and postholes, among other elements.

THE ¹⁴C CONSTRUCTION CHRONOLOGY AND CULTURAL PHASES

To provide an accurate chronological model of Huaca Prieta and Paredones, we need to know when the mounds were initiated and finished. We thus group the chronometric data by each site (see chapter 7 for discussion of dates by excavation units and all sites). Prior to discussing this chronology, the previously defined cultural phases are presented briefly (see Dillehay et al. 2012b).

An attempt was made to break down the cultural phases into more precise subphases, but this was difficult because there were not enough absolute dates and diagnostic artifacts and architecture (for example, construction of sunken plaza, ramp, and chamber tombs) across and within sites to substantiate such divisions. Whereas some phases had abundant peaks of multiple dates, gaps denote time spans for which dates were not processed for some units because they did not have diagnostic artifacts or architectural features. Nonetheless, these units were dated by relative means and, where possible, linked in the Harris Matrices by comparing the content, structure, and location of their stratigraphy to dated units within and across Huaca Prieta, Paredones, and other sites. In short, any absolute time spans and relative temporal gaps are due not to an absence of human activity but to sampling decisions whereby we did not date certain units or certain strata. Despite these issues, the stratigraphy represented by intact layers, floors, and use surfaces provides a relative chronological order for each unit and site that is arbitrarily divided into early and late subphases for each phase. The most detailed combined absolute and relative chronology is provided for Units 2, HP-3, 10, 15/21, 16, 20, and 22. Table 6.2 presents the radiocarbon dated time spans for phases and subphases. Figure 6.1 presents a plot of the calibrated radiocarbon dates from all cultural contexts of the project, revealing that most dates represent the period from ~4600–3800 years ago. This span reflects dated samples representative of both our excavation sampling strategy (which resulted in more work carried out in later phases because not all deeper contexts contained earlier cultural deposits) and the reality of more intense occupation of the sites during this period.

There are some problems with radiocarbon dates on some organic remains. As it turns out, the dates on most cotton textiles belong to a cluster of statistically similar assays generally ranging between ~4200 and 3700 cal BP. Nearly all of the dated cotton materials, including the few textiles from Bird's excavations that we assayed, were derived from the upper layers of the Phase IV entry ramp. All of these materials were unburned and saturated with a thick, salty paste consisting of salt crystals, sediment, and miscellaneous organic debris (fig. 6.2; see chapters 8 and 12 and appendices 10 and 17 for descriptions of this paste-like material), which we believe has significantly altered the dates on many materials, possibly making them slightly younger. As noted below, we have previously discussed some problems with dating unburned corn remains with soft cellular tissue that might have absorbed contaminates (for example, salt paste, fungi) through water containing younger microorganics filtering down into the mound (see Grobman et al. 2012 and chapter 12).

Certain conclusions can be drawn from the anomalous dates on the cob macroremains. There is no evidence of postdepositional disturbance at any of the three excavated sites. Thus, there is very little possibility that the younger dated samples [of corn] are intrusive. All of the dates considered reliable are entirely coherent within the radiocarbon-dated stratigraphic sequences at Huaca Prieta and Paredones and with directly associated wood charcoal dates from the same feature and floor contexts yielding the maize remains. The most reliable dates are on maize husks and charred shanks and cobs, which have a more rigid, impenetrable plant [cell] structure. This suggests the possibility that the other, more porous tissues of uncharred cobs can absorb some contaminating substance that does not affect the harder tissues of the charred tissue and husks of the maize. Finally, to be clear, we are not implying that all uncarbonized maize remains yield anonymously young dates in all environmental contexts, but this appears to be the case in this region of Peru. (Grobman et al. 2012: online supplemental material)

This condition underwent a preliminary analysis at Beta Analytic, Inc., with the following result.

With regard to possible contamination effects including from fungi, Darden Hood (Beta Analytic Inc., Miami, FL) in a personal communication to T. D. Dillehay in 2011 proposes some reasonable causes to consider: ". . . uncharred corn acts like a sponge and its integrity is too weak to withstand the pretreatments prior to removing organic contaminants. Thus, the radiocarbon (RC) pretreatments are dissolving the sample just as fast as contamination, resulting simply in reduction in sample size rather than de-contamination" and ". . . if the corn was being preferentially removed with the alkali, thereby increasing the concentration of the fungus, the date would come out younger with a higher fungus to corn ratio." (Grobman et al. 2012: online supplemental material)

It would seem that unburned, soft, porous cotton fibers were affected similarly. Although the textile dates present a case for a radiocarbon dated time span of 4200–3700 years, assays on directly

Table 6.2. All radiocarbon dates by excavation units at Huaca Prieta, Paredones, and outlying sites

Sample no.	Provenience	δ¹³C	Conventional radiocarbon	1σ (68%) calibrated age range (BP)	2σ (95%) calibrated age range (BP)	Material
Unit 2						
AA76975	Layer 3	−24.4	3535±35	3827–3696	3849–3639	Wood charcoal
Beta233650	Layer 3	−22.2	3700±40	4073–3893	4088–3844	Charred material
AA76974	Layer 5a	−24.2	3588±36	3873–3724	3956–3694	Wood charcoal
AA76973	Layer 7a	−24.0	3748±40	4137–3933	4151–3898	Wood charcoal
AA81925	Layer 7b-1	−19.1	3964±41	4418–4259	4511–4159	Wood charcoal
AA85506	First mound Layer 7c-3	−25.4	6641±49	7555–7434	7571–7424	Wood charcoal
AA76972	Premound occupation, Layer 7c-7	−23.5	6797±48	7656–7572	7680–7508	Wood charcoal
Beta233651	Premound occupation, Layer 8, base	−24.1	6920±30	7740–7660	7786–7618	Wood charcoal
Unit 3						
AA76977	Floor 2	−22.8	3530±36	3827–3693	3849–3636	Wood charcoal
Beta233649	Floor 3	−10.2	1080±40***	973–911	1052–809	Unburned corncob
AA76978	Floor 5a	−19.6	3567±40	3841–3717	3901–3643	Wood charcoal
Beta278233	Layer 2, Floor 5a	−25.5	3660±40	3972–3854	4081–3730	Charred material
AA76979	Floor 5b	−19.6	3758±40	4142–3978	4216–3901	Wood charcoal
Beta247695	Layer 8 (below Floor 6)	−20.8	4000±40	4510–4296	4520–4245	Organic sediment
Unit 7						
AA76970	Floor 1	−25.1	3649±36	3964–3841	4072–3727	Wood charcoal
Unit 8						
AA81916	Tomb 8	−17.2	3534±53	3833–3689	3892–3590	Human bone
Unit 9						
AA81922	Layer 7a, top	−22.0	3547±40	3829–3705	3876–3640	Wood charcoal
AA84168	Premound occupation, Layer 8, base	−22.8	7956±50	8931–8599	8979–8592	Wood charcoal
Unit 10						
AA81923	Structure 2, base	−25.7	3556±44	3834–3705	3895–3640	Wood charcoal
AA81919	Floor 4	−26.4	3557±40	3834–3716	3891–3642	Wood charcoal
Unit 12						
AA81929	Layer 1	−25.2	3441±39	3688–3576	3817–3480	Wood charcoal
Beta235952	Premound occupation, Unit 12, Layer 11	−25.2	9580±40	11,089–10,698	11,159–10,600	Charred juncus stalk (*Juncus* sp.)
Unit 13						
AA81920	Floor 3	−19.7	3810±41	4224–3996	4283–3974	Wood charcoal
Unit 14						
AA81921	Floor 4	−25.1	3508±40	3825–3641	3838–3588	Wood charcoal
Unit 16						
D-AMS 016633	Layer 2	−14.8	430±40	513–335	512–325	Avocado seed (*Persea* sp.)
Beta290654	House Floor 2	−23.2	5577–5330	5583–5325	4137–3892	Wood charcoal
Beta263319	House Floor 3	−11.7	830±40***	728–678	767–664	Unburned corncob
AA87665	House Floor 5	−26.1	6340±60	7306–7158	7413–7005	Wood charcoal
AA86935	Layer 13-7	−22.6	6310±33	7251–7162	7266–7021	Wood charcoal

Table 6.2. Continued

Sample no.	Provenience	$\delta^{13}C$	Conventional radiocarbon	1σ (68%) calibrated age range (BP)	2σ (95%) calibrated age range (BP)	Material
Unit 16 (continued)						
AA86632	Layer 14-6	−14.2	9230±	10,379–10,183	10,486–10,158**	Avocado seed (*Persea* sp.)
D-AMS 013332	Layer 16	−23.8	12,594±62	15,143–14,386**	15,217–14,221**	Bean seed (*Phaseolus* sp.)
D-AMS 016635	Layer 16	−13.3	12,602±35	15,025–14,810	15,188–14,641	Wood charcoal
Unit 20 (Paredones)						
AA86938	Layer 5a(6)	−11.6	1130±27***	1051–936	1055–831	Unburned corncob
AA86936	Layer 5b	−23.8	4783±31	5578–5330	5583–5324	Wood charcoal
Beta263322	Layer 6a	−9.3	1310±40***	1268–1143	1279–1076	Unburned corncob
AA86932	Layer 6b-18	−23.5	4770±35	5577–5327	5582–5321	Corn husk fragment
AA86937	Layer 6b-18	−25.8	4849±31	5589–5479	5603–5333	Charred plant material
Unit 21 (Unit 15)						
AA86941	Unit 21, Floor 2-16	−10.6	3599±29	3889–3728	3956–3704	Charred corncob
AA86931	Unit 21, Floor 3	−25.2	3638±29	3957–3838	3982–3728	Wood charcoal
AA86946	Unit 21, Floor 9	−11.9	3783±41	4148–3988	4235–3928	Charred corncob
AA75322	Unit 15, Floor 26	−29.4	5018±86	5860–5599	5911–5488	Wood charcoal
AA85507	First mound layer: Unit 15, Layer 1	−25.6	6522±54	7429–7323	7474–7268	Wood charcoal
AA75327	Premound occupation, Unit 15, Layer 3	−29.5	7226±44	8019–7947	8156–7871	Wood charcoal
Beta312771	Premound occupation, Layer 7	−24.8	9580±40	10,849–10,707	10,895–10,667	Juncus stalk (*Juncus* sp.)
Beta290621	Premound occupation, Stratum 9	−25.6	11,500±50	13,401–13,294*	13,401–13,294*	Charred wood
Beta299536	Premound occupation, Stratum 13	−28.3	11,800±50	13,757–13,517	13,794–13,459	Wood
Beta310272	Premound occupation top of Layer 13a	−22.8	12280±60	14,477–14,005[1]	14,867–13,924[1]	Deer bone
Beta310273	Premound occupation bottom of Layer 13a	−29.0	12240±50	14,184–13,991[2]	14,530–13,891[2]	Charred wood
Unit 22 (Paredones)						
AA86934	Floor 6	−13.4	4181±34	4809–4570	4821–4527	Charred corncob
Beta263988	Floor 10	−11.2	105.4±5***	132–4	133–34	Unburned corncob
Beta263320	Floor 10, Layer 14	−24.5	4590±40	5308–5062	5435–5044	Wood charcoal
Beta263321	Floor 15	−25.6	4790±40	5580–5331	5585–5325	Charred material

Table 6.2. Continued

Sample no.	Provenience	$\delta^{13}C$	Conventional radiocarbon	1σ (68%) calibrated age range (BP)	2σ (95%) calibrated age range (BP)	Material
Unit 22 (Paredones) (continued)						
AA86847#	Floor, 18	−11.6	4660±60	5463–5074	5574–5048	Corn husk fragment
Beta27823#	Floor, 18-3	−9.8	750±40***	679–571	722–563	Unburned corncob
Beta27804#	Floor, 18-3	−9.0	770±40***	720–578	729–569	Unburned corncob
Beta282127#	Floor, 18-3	−10.3	790±40***	721–662	738–572	Unburned corncob
OS86020#	Floor, 18-3	−10.3	5900±40	6734–6569	6775–6504	Corn husk and shank
AA83260	Floor 24	−26.0	5750±60	6561–6405	6640–6319	Wood charcoal
Beta343109	Premound, Sanga-mon terrace, Level 7	−19.2	9330±40	10,559–10,308	10,578–10,285	Chile pepper seed (*Capsicum* sp.)
Unit 23						
AA86930	Layer 3-1	−10.0	1760±29	1690–1557	1697–1539	Wood charcoal
AA86949	Floor 3-3	−27.1	3467±39	3704–3584	3828–3560	Wood charcoal
AA86948	Floor 11	−23.5	5059±72	5887–5652	5902–5606	Wood charcoal
Bird's HP-2						
Libby-598[3]	Test Pit 2; bottom	−22.2	4298±230	5260–4439	5462–4152	Charcoal
Beta233648	Basal mound layer: HP-2	−23.8	5110±40	5891–5745	5919–5667	Organic char-coal sediment in burned feature
HP-3						
AA81926	Layer 5	−28.0	3394±40	3634–3485	3688–3464	Wood charcoal
AA86943	Layer 14	−24.6	3806±28	4213–3999	4233–3985	Wood charcoal
AA86940	Layer 19	−25.6	3875±30	4287–4104	4406–4090	Wood charcoal
AA81924	Layer 22	−23.5	3687±40	4063–3876	4084–3838	Wood charcoal
AA81927	Layer 23	−17.3	3728±40	4084–3927	4147–3875	Wood charcoal
Beta237805	Layer 23	−12.3	3740±40	4088–3930	4150–3892	Charred corncob fragment
Beta278050	Layer 28(33)	−14.9	3740±40	4087–3931	4149–3839	Charred corncob
AA86957	Layer 35	−24.1	5020±35	5830–5598	5848–5585	Wood charcoal
AA82121	Upper Layer 52 (39)	−23.4	5980±40	6789–6676	6822–6657	Cotton yarn
AA81917	First mound layer: lower Layer 52-53	−23.8	6170±45	7154–6899	7162–6808	Wood charcoal
Beta294021	Premound occupa-tion: base Layer 54	−23.3	7000±50	7946–7840	7979–7752	Wood charcoal
Beta263318	Premound occupa-tion: Layer 55	−24.9	7000±50	7830–7703	7927–7673	Charred material
AA75321	Premound occupa-tion: HP-3 Layer 56	−28.9	7195±45	8009–7933	8040–7847	Wood charcoal
321	Layer D		2966±340	3555–2621	3905–2160	Gourds, chewed fiber, squash stems, cotton, wood, barkcloth
Beta9286	Layer E		3730±300	4422–3634	4845–3272	Gourd (*Lagenaria siceraria*)

Table 6.2. Continued

Sample no.	Provenience	$\delta^{13}C$	Conventional radiocarbon	1σ (68%) calibrated age range (BP)	2σ (95%) calibrated age range (BP)	Material
Bird's dates from HP-3						
Beta9288	Layer F		3960±100	4510–4157	4784–3989	Gourd (*Lagenaria siceraria*)
Beta9287	Layer J		3270±10	3569–3343	3692–3169	Gourd (*Lagenaria siceraria*)
318b	Layer J		3550±600	4569–3005	5446–2344	Twigs and treated huarango wood
362	Layer K		4044±300	4845–3996	5298–3648	Carbonized cattail roots
315	Layer M		3572±220	4088–3485	4423–3267	Shell
313	Layer Q		4257±250	5263–4411	5462–3999	Misc. woody plants
Cotton Textiles from HP-3 Wall Profiles						
OxA-28644	Layer 18	−22.60	3603±27	3892–3730	3960–3717 4200–4100+	Cotton textile 2008.069.01.A
OxA-28649	Layer 18	−22.69	3532±27	3827–3695	3840–3641 4200–4100+	Cotton textile 2008.070.02
OxA-28646	Layer 28	−22.52	3721±29	4081–3926	4138–3889 5000–4900+	Cotton textile 2008.075.03.A
OxA-28645	Layer 29	−23.35	3762±27	4089–3984	4150–3929 5000+	Cotton textile 2009.040.01.A
OxA-28648	Layer 29	−22.86	3749±26	4085–3982	4148–3924 5000+	Cotton textile 2009.041.01.A
OxA-28642	Layer 30	−22.97	3723±27	4081–3927	4137–3892 5200–5100+	Cotton textile 2008.077.01
Beta380897	Layer 30	−22.5	3770±30	4142–3985	4216–3928 5000+	Cotton textile 2008.088.01
OxA-28643	Layer 31	−24.47	3601±26	3890–3730	3958–3716 5200+	Cotton textile 2009.038.04
OxA-28641	Layer 32	−21.87	3724±26	4081–3928	4091–3893 5300–5200+	Cotton textile 2008.083.02.A
Beta380898	Layer 33	−23.5	3640±30	3958–3839	3984–3726 5400–5300+	Cotton textile 2008.089.01
OxA-28647	Layer 34	−23.34	3749±27	4085–3982	4148–3921 5300–5400+	Cotton textile 2008.085.01
Beta380899	Layer 44	−23.5	3620±30	3922–3778	3973–3722 5800–5700+	Cotton textile 2009.052.01.B
OxA-28650	Bird's backdirt	−22.87	3797±27	4151–3999	4228–3982	Cotton textile 2009.118.01
OxA-28650	Bird's backdirt	−22.87	3797±27	4151–3999	4228–3982	Cotton textile 2009.118.01
OxA-28651	Bird's backdirt	−21.66	3777±26	4145–3989	4220–3933	Cotton textile 2009.118.01
OxA-28652	Bird's backdirt	−22.23	3765±27	4138–3985	4152–3930	Cotton textile 2008.091.02
OxA-28849	Bird's Backdirt	−23.3	3520±30	3826–3649	3834–3639	Cotton textile
OxA-28653	Bird's backdirt	−22.55	3744±26	4084–3879	4146–3912	Cotton textile

Table 6.2. Continued

Sample no.	Provenience	δ¹³C	Conventional radiocarbon	1σ (68%) calibrated age range (BP)	2σ (95%) calibrated age range (BP)	Material
Cotton Textiles from HP-3 Wall Profiles (continued)						
OxA-28654	HP-3 Guañape/ Cupisnique levels	−23.75	2793±26	2856–2785	2923–2761	Cotton textile
OxA-28674	HP-3 Guañape/ Cupisnique levels	−23.60	2802±28	2866–2787	3200–3400[+] 2925–2764	AMNH 41.2/3493A Cotton textile
OxA-28675	HP-3 Guañape/ Cupisnique levels	−23.81	2753±28	2844–2759	3400–3200[+] 2860–2751	AMNH 41.2/3493A Cotton textile
Beta380900	Unit 3, Floor 7	−22.0	3580±30	3857–3723	3400–3300[+] 3897–3695 4100[+]	AMNH 41.2/3492F Cotton textile 2009.142.02
OxA-28676	Unit 23, Layer 4	−22.90	3740±30	4085–3975	4146–3904 4100–4000[+]	Cotton textile AMNH41.2/1599
Test Pit-3						
Beta278233	Stratum 2	−22.3	3660±40	3973–3850	4081–3730	Wood charcoal
Test Pit-5						
Beta233648	Base of pit	−22.8	5127±40	5897–5750	5919–5667	Wood charcoal
Test Pit-6						
Beta247696	Test Pit 6, base	−18.7	3350±40	3571–3464	3823–3483	Charred material
Test Pit-9						
AA86944	Stratum 2	−28.1	3334±38	3558–3455	3614–3398	Wood charcoal
Test Pit-18						
AA86932	Stratum 25	−27.2	4700±40	5460–5312	5577–5327	Wood charcoal
Test Pit-22						
AA86947	Floor 16, Fill 10	−24.0	4898±49	5644–5483	5711–5335	Wood charcoal
AA76972	Premound, occupation, Layer 15	−24.7	6770±20	7612–7566	7656–7572	Wood charcoal
Beta210862	Premound occupation, Layer 20	−27.4	9530±50	10,785– 10,594	[11,000]– 10,579	Wood charcoal
AA75326	Premound occupation, Layer 22	−26.8	10,770±340	13,096– 12,164	13,344– 11,508	Wood charcoal
Beta290620	Premound occupation, Layer 28	−28.3	11,780±50	13,732– 13,510**	13,720– 13,440**	Wood charcoal
Beta310274	Premound occupation, Layer 25 (8b)	−21.7	12,950±50	13,828– 13,554[1]	14,034– 13,301[1]	Sea lion bone

Table 6.2. Continued

Sample no.	Provenience	$\delta^{13}C$	Conventional radiocarbon	1σ (68%) calibrated age range (BP)	2σ (95%) calibrated age range (BP)	Material
Test Pit-32						
Beta233988	Base of pit	−25.2	4640±20	5438–5093	5448–5067	Wood charcoal
Cupisnique Mound, Preceramic House						
Beta233491	House floor	−25.2	6740±30	7588–7510	7615–7480	Wood charcoal
Outlying Preceramic Households						
AA75398	SN-2 House floor	−23.2	6190 ±30	7156–6949	7162–6914	Wood charcoal
AA753476	SN-3 House floor	−22.4	6310±20	7246–7165	7263–7027	Wood charcoal
Beta290762	S-2 House floor	−25.4	5377±40	6183–6005	6270–5950	Wood charcoal
Beta290668	S-5 House floor	−22.9	4689±20	5447–5313	5438–5093	Wood charcoal
Raised Agricultural Field						
Beta233988	Use floor	−21.7	4640±20	5438–5093	5448–5067	Wood charcoal
Geological Dates Associated with Appendix 1						
AA81932	Profile 2, Layer 2	−13.2	876±36	771–689	896–675	Wood charcoal
AA76986	Profile 9 Layer 3 El Niño event and tsunami	−18.5	3099±39	3338–3211	3366–3081	Wood charcoal
AA76982	Profile 2, Layer 4	−22.3	3758±40	4142–3978	4220–3900	Wood charcoal
AA76976	Profile 9, Layer 8	−22.9	4032±52	4526–4300	4780–4243	Wood charcoal
AA76984	Profile 10, Layer 6 top event tsunami	−18.0	3540±40	3828–3699	3868–3639	Wood charcoal
AA81931	Profile 14, Pino, Layer 3	−12.2	1378±36	1294–1185	1302–1177	Wood charcoal
AA86951	Profile 18, Layer 9	−19.8	3253±60	3574–3268	3618–3367	Wood charcoal
AA86939	Profile 21, Layer 2	−25.6	317±74	456–157	502–1	Wood charcoal
AA76985	THS 7 Holocene terrace	−0.9	2101±36	2096–1946	2120–1899	Sea urchin shells
AA76981	Top of Holocene terrace, THS Layer 1 north of HP	−25.2	955±64	908–765	934–688	Wood charcoal

Note: All dates calibrated using shcal04 (McCormac et al. 2004) unless otherwise noted. This calibration curve was used to correspond with same dates previously published in Grobman et al. 2012 and Dillehay et al. 2012a and b.

[ ] = calibrated range impinges on end of calibration data set. OS is the run number for radiocarbon dates of the NOSAMS facility located in the Woods Hold Oceanographic Institution.

#Dates processed on same integrated cob/shank/husk from floor 18.

*Bird's corresponding layers in HP-3 are based on study of his photographs, notes, and profile drawings.

**Calibration done on curve other than shcal04 (i.e., shcal13).

***Uncharred corncobs.

[1]Calibrated using marine 09.14c calibration curve with delta uncertainty of 725±173 (Jones 2009).

[2]Calibrated using Intcal09 calibration curve.

[3]Libby data obtained by Bird.

+14C dates on wood charcoal in layers containing dated cotton textiles.

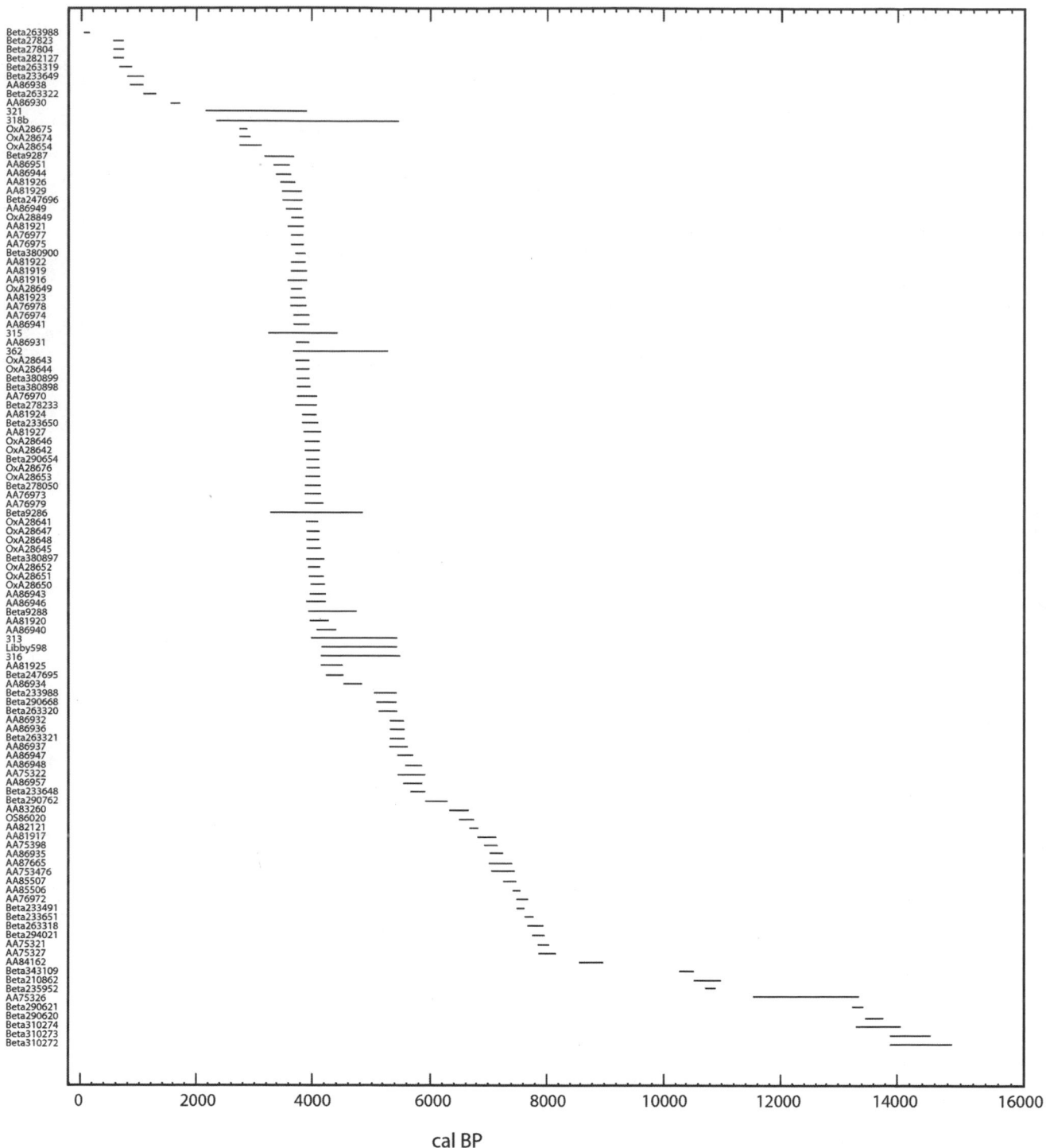

FIGURE 6.1. Plot of the majority of calibrated 2-sigma (95.4%) radiocarbon ages for all excavated sites in the study area. Geological dates are not included.

associated wood charcoal from features in the same stratigraphically intact and ordered layers place these same textiles between ~5200 and 3700 cal BP, which we believe is most likely the correct time span for those in question. Table 6.2 shows both the uncalibrated and calibrated dates on cotton textiles and the associated assays on wood charcoal and other organics. Similar problems seem to have been incurred in dating unburned fragments of basketry (see chapter 12).

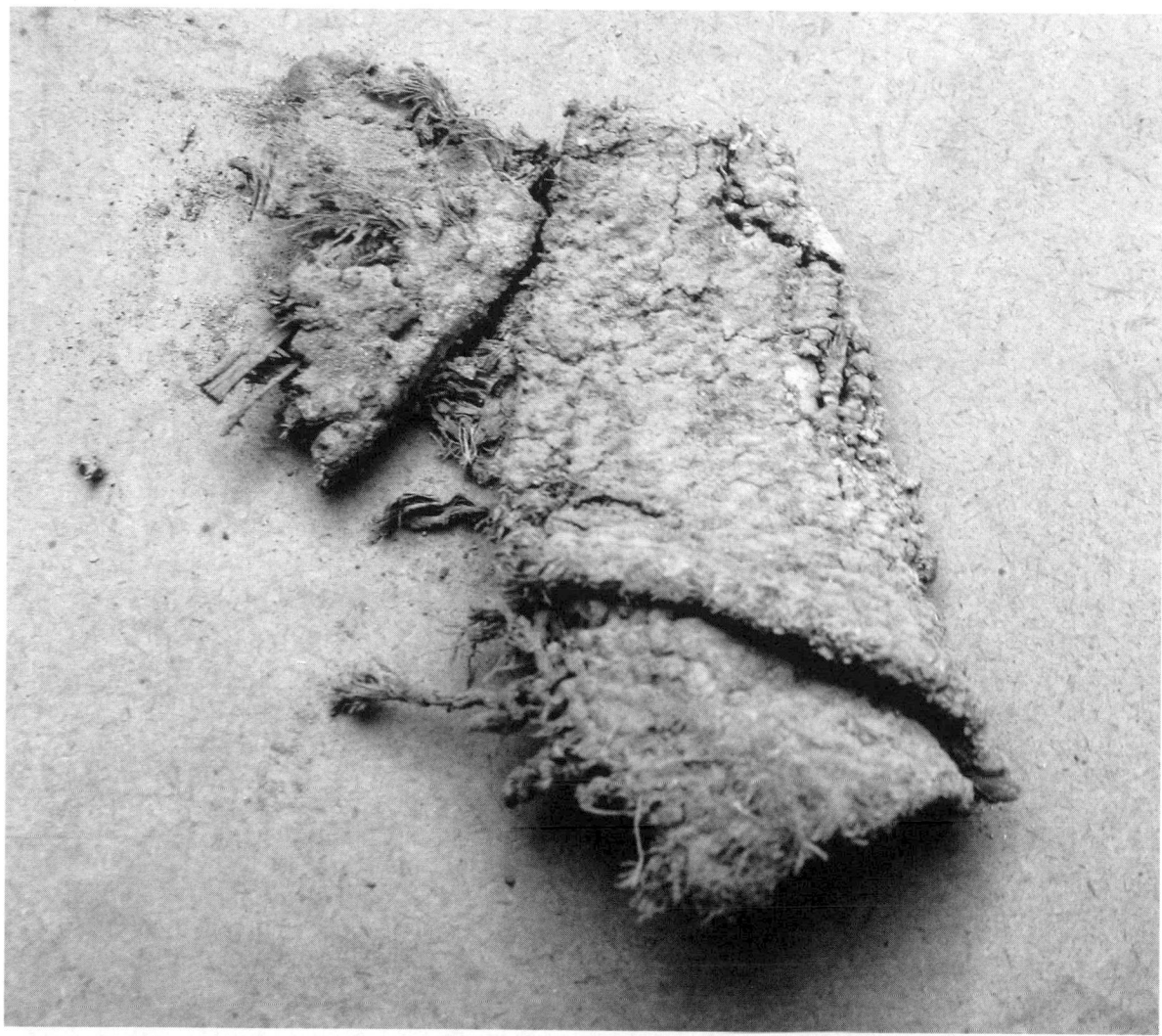

FIGURE 6.2. Textile saturated with a muddy, salty paste excavated from Stratum 32, Unit HP-3.

The older date of ~6822–6657 cal BP (AA82121) on a partially charred cotton fiber was recovered from a human burial in preramp Layer 52 at the base of Unit HP-3. This fiber was directly beneath the skeleton, which was buried ~22 m deep into the base of the mound and not covered or saturated with the salty paste found on textiles and baskets in the later, upper deposits.

Although this dating problem cannot be fully resolved without further research, we recommend that unburned, soft tissue organics saturated with a salty paste-like substance from littoral sites (if available) be dated along with directly associated wood charcoal or other organics with rigid, impenetrable cellular structures. As we experienced, thorough cleaning seems not to resolve the problem.

RADIOCARBON DATED MOUNDS AND OFF-MOUND SEQUENCES

The construction phases described below for Huaca Prieta and Paredones are based on major stratigraphic, functional, and architectural events that are radiocarbon dated within and across the mounds (Dillehay et al. 2012b). Mound building at Huaca Prieta, beginning with Phase II, did not develop from a gradual accumulation of occupation midden but from deliberate and gradual, planned mounding over a period of ~3500 years. The beginning points of the individual mound phases are represented in the form of haystacking strata whereby an artificial basal ring or layer of shingled cobblestone berms were laid out and angled to define the outer limits of the structure and to provide an architectural support-footing for the space inside to be infilled by floors, use surfaces, and floor fills (Dillehay et al. 2012b; see chapter 7). The precise premound and mound sequences have been resolved in five phases (fig. 6.1).

PHASE I: PREMOUND OCCUPATION, ~14,500–7571 CAL BP

This is an extraordinarily long phase that includes all premound deposits, most of which, especially at Huaca Prieta, were difficult to record more completely due to the depth of some deposits between 6 and 30 m below mound summits. Nonetheless, we were able to detect and define this phase across several site areas extending from Huaca Prieta to Paredones. Much more extensive excavations and especially radiocarbon dates are needed for a better definition of the character, content, and chronology of this phase. But we managed to break it down into two subphases assigned to the late Pleistocene and the early Holocene period.

Phase I previously included only the late early Holocene data and was dated from ~9000–7500 cal BP (see Dillehay et al. 2012b). We now include both the late Pleistocene and early Holocene archaeological data from an ~80 m long section of the lower southeast side of the southernmost point of the Sangamon terrace near the banks of a brackish lagoon. No architecture was detected for this phase. We now divide this phase into the late Pleistocene subphase and the early Holocene subphase.

The earliest subphase of the premound habitation midden was ~14,500 cal BP, as represented by radiocarbon dated premound contexts in Units 12 and 15/21 and Test Pit 22. The late Pleistocene habitation is dated by seven stratigraphically early early Holocene ordered assays in Units 12 and 15/21 and Test Pit 22 (see table 6.2) in the upper levels of the terrace ranging from 11,159–10,600 cal BP (Beta235952), 11,000–10,579 cal BP (Beta210862), 13,344–11,508 cal BP (AA75326), 13,420–13,260 cal BP (Beta290621), and 13,720–13,440 cal BP (Beta290620) to the lower levels from 14,034–13,301 cal BP (Beta310274) to 14,530–13,891 cal BP (Beta310273). A 10,895–10,670 cal BP date was on a charred matting fragment (listed as a charcoal fragment in table 6.2)

from Bird's backdirt pile (see chapter 7 and fig. 6.3). An early Holocene date of ~10,500 cal BP (Beta343109) also was derived from a *Capsicum* seed in a premound habitation layer in Unit 22 at Paredones (see chapter 7 and appendix 4).

Intermittent occupation during the early Holocene subphase and before initial mound construction is revealed by a series of thin midden lenses suggesting ephemeral campsites dating between ~10,000 to 7600 cal BP (AA75327, Beta263365, Beta263318, Beta294021, AA75321, and AA76972). Of the six dates for this period, two (7786–7618 cal BP [Beta233651] and 7680–7508 cal BP [AA76972]) are from a submound context in Unit 2, which is at the interfacing edge of the mound and the terrace overlooking a lagoon to the east. Cores and Unit 2 excavations penetrated alluvial sediments, but there was no in situ soil formation between the deeper sediments and the mound fill. Pino attributes the absence of a soil stratum in this area to ancient stripping and borrowing by people modifying the terrace surface. A late premound date is derived from a prepared use surface and fill in Unit 15/21 on the south side of the mound: 8156–7871 cal BP (AA75327). As mentioned above, four late Pleistocene dates (Beta290621, Beta299536, Beta210862, Beta290620) are below this date and associated with intermittent human habitation. Three premound dates are from the HP-3 unit: 8040–7847 cal BP (AA753321), 7979–7752 cal BP (Beta294021), and 7927–7673 cal BP (Beta263318). Another premound date from Unit 9 was 8979–8592 cal BP (AA84168). All premound dates are derived from circumscribed lenses of small hearths and burned stains associated with small scatters of lithics, shells, and bone remains (see chapter 7 and Dillehay et al. 2012a). These are easily distinguished from the first mound strata, which are thicker, more horizontally extensive, and associated with prepared use surfaces and fills and, more importantly, with cobblestone berms evidently designed as footings to retain the built-up mound strata. Table 6.3 shows the distribution of the number and types of features for the late Pleistocene layers, most of which are burned areas, and lithics and faunal remains from Units 9 and 15/21 and Test Pit 22 (see Dillehay et al. 2012a for more details). Finally, some places on the Sangamon terrace contain

FIGURE 6.3. Fragment of a possible mat, basket, or bag of simple twining with two-ply z-twist weft elements from Bird's backdirt pile that is radiocarbon dated between ~10,895 and 10,667 cal BP.

scatters of large, well-patinated, basalt and andesite tools that appear to be older and more like the hammerstones, choppers, and large primary flakes of the late Pleistocene Carrizal assemblage in the lower Zaña Valley (Dillehay 2011a), but these require more investigation before more can be surmised about them.

The late early Holocene premound midden deposits dating from ~10,000 to 7500 cal BP ranged between 0.5 and 1.0 cm thick. Here in situ pedogenic features were used as markers for premound deposits. It is likely that some of the conglomerated rock and sediment identified by Bird as culturally sterile in the HP-3 trench (see Bird et al. 1985: 35–43) were disturbed anthropogenic deposits related to early premound fill. The conglomerated sediments that he mentions also may have been partially obliterated by subsequent anthropogenic activity (although technically anthropogenesis is a form of pedogenesis). Furthermore, some premound fill might have been emplaced during the initial construction of

the mound. In short, human disturbance of the original terrace surface might have obscured the relationship between the observable basal mound layers and the underlying premound habitational and/or culturally sterile strata in unit HP-3, making some interpretations equivocal. Accepting this possible condition has implications for the radiocarbon sequence, as assays 8040–7847, 7979–7752, 7927–7673, 7786–7618, and 7680–7508 cal BP, although in stratigraphic order and from in situ features (such as burned areas), might relate to slight stratigraphic modification due to leveling of the terrace prior to formal mound building around 7500 cal BP. Only Units 2, 9, 12, and 15/21 and Test Pit 22 reached the bottom of the eastern and central areas of the mound and thus the original surface of the Sangamon terrace, so the older stratigraphically ordered dates from these excavations are the most useful. Like the dates mentioned above, they also derive from in situ features and thus are chronologically reliable.

Table 6.3. Feature types and distribution in the late Pleistocene and early Holocene layers of Units 9 and 15 and Test Pit 22

| Units | No. of features | Feature types | | | No. of lithics | No. of faunal remains |
		Burned sediment	Ash/charcoal/burned sediment	Ash/charcoal/burned sediment/hematite		
Unit 9						
Layer 7					2	
Layer 8a	2			2	3	2
Layer 8b	2	1		1	3	
Layer 9	1	1			3	
Subtotal	**5**	**2**		**3**	**11**	**2**
Unit 15						
Layer 4	3	2	1			4
Layer 8	2	1	1		4	11
Layer 9	3	1	2		5	14
Layer 13a	2	1		1	5	4
Subtotal	**10**	**5**	**4**	**1**	**14**	**33**
TP 22						
Layer 5a	2	1	1		5	11
Layer 8a–b	4	2	1	1	6	22
Layer 11a	3	1	2		6	9
Subtotal	**9**	**4**	**4**	**1**	**17**	**42**
Total	**24**	**11**	**8**	**5**	**42**	**77**

PHASE II: INCIPIENT MOUND BUILDING, ~7572–6538 CAL BP

Phase II represents the first mound construction stage on the southeast flank and crest of the ancient terrace near the shoreline of the lagoon. We estimate that the mound during this phase minimally measured 6–8 m high, 25–30 m wide, and 35–45 m long and consisted of several small cobblestone berms and soil layers, as evidenced in HP-3 and Units 2, 9, 12, and 15/21, and Test Pit 22. From there the mound gradually spread to the north and west along this flank, with later construction layers reaching the western edge of the terrace, as evidenced by stratigraphy and radio-carbon dates in Bird's HP-2 unit dated ~5900–5600 cal BP and in several test pits along the western edge of the mound. The use of space along the eastern flank and the crest of the terrace eventually became more restricted by the increasingly steeper-sloped sides of the mound. No stone room foundations were recovered for this phase. A few rock alignments and cane poles were excavated, however, suggesting the construction of perishable structures. Unprepared floors and use surfaces were documented along with burned areas and moderate amounts of lithics and floral and faunal remains, all suggestive of food preparation and consumption related to ritual not domestic activities (see chapter 7). Phase II arbitrarily is divided into an early subphase ~7500–7000 cal BP and a late subphase ~7000–6500 cal BP.

More specifically, overlying the lower stratum of Units 2, 9, 12, and 15/21 and Test Pit 22 and Bird's HP-2 and HP-3 units, we encountered approximately 0.5–2 m of artificially laminated organic enriched silty loams and sands that constituted the first horizontally extensive layers, which were identified as the initial mound fill episodes. These artificial fills contained thin use surfaces (1–3 cm thick) associated with charcoal, lithics, shell and fishbone, and few plant remains. In Unit 15/21 below the sunken plaza on the south-central side of the mound the first mound layer dated at 7474–7268 cal BP (AA85507). On the southeast side in Unit 2 the first layer was 7571–7424 cal BP (AA85506). The first mound layer in unit HP-3 on the northeast side of the mound dated 7162–6808 cal BP (AA81917) or a few centuries after initial construction on the south side. On the west side of the mound the basal artificial layers in HP-2 pit are 5462–4152 cal BP (Libby 598), which is Bird's assay taken in the 1950s, and our date from this same unit at 5919–5667 cal BP (Beta233648). On the north-central side of the mound as it turns toward the center point of the terrace, where the western side of Unit 23 is located, the deepest mound layers dated to 5902–5606 cal BP (AA86948), a time that roughly coincides with the expansion of the mound to the western edge of the terrace in Bird's HP-2. However, in this unit we reached a depth of only 17 m below the summit. This date thus registers only the lower middle mound layer and not necessarily the first ones. All of these dates confirm the stratigraphic phasing recorded by our excavations, which suggests that the earliest mound section was built on the southeast side of the terrace and progressed over time to the north and west.

Noteworthy here is that an early twined cotton fiber, dated at ~6822–6657 cal BP (AA82121), was recovered in Stratum 52 in the lower levels of Bird's HP-3. Bird stated that in his Test Pit 1 (see fig. 3.2), where it extends into the lower levels of the mound where he excavated near HP-3, he found "many pieces of cloth similar to . . . the oldest material in north Chile—not woven, but made by twining cotton strands" (Bird et al. 1985: 22). Although the deeper levels of his Test Pit 1 where he observed these cloth fragments are not radiocarbon dated, we estimate their stratigraphic age between ~6500 and 5500 cal BP based on our excavations in the area.

PHASE III, MOUND EXPANSION, ~6538–5308 CAL BP

During Phase III, the focus of mound construction shifted more to the crest and the western edge of the terrace. Phase III is characterized by the addition of more artificial layers, several small stone rooms placed along the eastern and western slopes of the mound and, at the end of this phase, the lower floors of the sunken circular plaza on the south side and the lower portion of Bird's retention wall no. 1, and the lower berms of the entry ramp on the northeast side. These structural features are spatially and architecturally conjoined, suggesting simultaneous planned construction and use across the entire upper third of the mound between ~5500 and 4500 cal BP. These features began to give the mound a stepped platform-like form. During this phase, the mound expanded to ~10–16 m in height in some places and ~80 m in length. For Phase III, all excavation units provided relevant chronological data, especially Units HP-3, 3–6, 9, 12, 15–21, 23, and 25. This phase is subdivided into an early subphase at ~6500–6000 cal BP and a late subphase at ~6000–5300 cal BP.

PHASE IV, NEW ARCHITECTURAL ONTOLOGY, ~5308–4107 CAL BP

Phases III and IV are separated by a yellowish sediment cap ~25 cm thick placed over most of the mound (see chapter 7). During Phase IV, the mound spread over a more extended area of old and new ground and increased in width and height, as best evidenced in Units HP-3, 3–7, 10–12, and 19–25. Further additions during this phase were the first nonberm layers of the ramp built on the northeast side, the upper portion of retention wall no. 1, the bases of retention walls nos. 2 and 3, and the rooms and other structures in the sunken plaza. The ramp addition is ~40 m long east to west and ~35 m high north to south and characterized by intervening floors and fills built over and eventually sealing all three retention walls and the first construction phases of the mound. Some of the first chamber tombs in Units 10 and 23 were built during this phase. The mound during Phase IV was roughly the size it is today, with a few new layers added in Phase V. Phase IV is subdivided into an early subphase at ~5300–4700 cal BP and a late subphase at ~4700–4100 cal BP.

PHASE V, TERMINATION OF MOUND-BUILDING AND ABANDONMENT OF RITUAL PRACTICES, ~4107–3455 CAL BP

During Phase V, the steep sloping flanks of the mound to both the east and west were used less (with most activity limited to the flat crest) and eventually abandoned. This phase dates between ~4107 and 3455 cal BP when, during the early part of this phase, more chamber tombs were added along the upper rim of the sunken plaza and on the top of the mound. More layers were added to the ramp on the northeast side. By ~4000–3800 cal BP the Preceramic use of the site terminated. People of later ceramic cultures, dating from the Guañape/Cupisnique to colonial periods (~3500–300 years ago), often buried their dead on the top of the mound, but they added no new layers or architecture.

Summit dates represent the final phase of mound building at Huaca Prieta. Five major contexts serve as termination for different stages of mound building: Units 2, 3, 10, 12, and 23. In multiple units across the mound, the last artificial layers date between 3817–3480 cal BP (AA81929) in Unit 12 to 3849–3639 cal BP (AA76975) in Unit 2 to 3849–3636 cal BP (AA76977) in Unit 3. On top of the mound, Floor 11, which is approximately 30 cm above the basal floors (12–13) in Unit 23, was dated at 3828–3560 cal BP (AA86949). A later date was recorded above this assay, but it was derived from an early Moche tomb (1697–1539 cal BP, AA86930). This phase also is subdivided with an early subphase at ~4100–3800 cal BP, the last building and capping episodes, and a late subphase at ~3800–3400 cal BP, the last Preceramic use episodes.

Disuse of the Huaca Prieta mound as a place of ceremony and ritual is estimated to have occurred sometime between 3800 and 3500 years ago. Although there is a stratigraphic hiatus between the last Preceramic use and the first ceramic use of the mound during the Initial Period (Guañape-like pottery) and subsequent Cupisnique period, as evidenced by culturally sterile lenses and a radiocarbon dated gap near the top of the mound, we are unable to determine more precisely how long this hiatus was. Archaeological evidence from the deeper levels of the Cupisnique mound immediately north of Huaca Prieta suggests a minor Preceramic occupation there that probably coincided with the use of the Huaca Prieta mound from Phase III to V and the subsequent domestic occupation of the area in the Initial Period around 3500 years ago, perhaps suggesting a hiatus of one to two centuries (see chapters 7 and 14).

CHRONOLOGICAL MODEL OF HUACA PRIETA

To account for the variation in chronological patterns at Huaca Prieta, we modeled the chronostratigraphic data where temporally different horizontal stratigraphy occurs within the mound. As the mound was expanded upward it also grew outward. The basic a priori assumption of the model is that the Preceramic use of the Huaca Prieta mound spans the time from ~7500 to 3500 cal BP. Previous research by Bird suggested a later initial site use (~5400 cal BP: Bird et al. 1985), but he did not excavate the south end of the earliest mound section and did not probe deeper into the northeast mound sector where we excavated.

Based on stratigraphic correlations and radiocarbon dates, we can posit that the construction of Huaca Prieta occurred during several phases of continuous activity. The entire mound sequence was built as thousands of episodes of blanket mantles or thin lenses of sediment laid over different surfaces, as shown in observable floors, fills, use surfaces, and other breaks in the construction sequence (see chapter 7). Phases I and II were modeled sequentially, meaning that there may or may not be any time interval between the phase boundaries, although the stratigraphy suggests a few brief hiatuses. Dates associated with the premound habitation materials serve as a beginning point for Phase I, the late Pleistocene to early Holocene period. Phase II was defined as the time of construction of the first nonoccupational or mound-building phase. Summit dates represent an important period: the termination of Pre-ceramic mound use. This date is not possible to know directly, although it can be approximated as the time of the last burning events of material on top and the last Preceramic capping episode ~3800 cal BP. Layers above this date contain early Guañape-like or Initial Period sherds. Thus, in this model, the time of construction of the mound is the time between the minimum age of Phase II and maximum age of Phase IV. The time of con-struction for the lower mound is the time between the minimum age of Phase III and the maximum age of Phase II.

PAREDONES, ~10,500 CAL BP AND ~6500–4000 CAL BP

At Paredones no formal architecture or stone alignments were detected. Although a premound layer with a *Capsicum* sp. seed dated around ~10,500 cal BP, the mound dates from ~6500–4000 cal BP. The stratigraphy of the mound is similar to that documented for Phase II at Huaca Prieta, which is characterized primarily by sedi-ment layers composed of food remains and few lithics but little evidence of domestic activity (see chapter 7 for more details). Below the mound in Units 20 and 22 are several currently undated cultural deposits that stratigraphically pertain to at least the early to middle Holocene period (see chapter 7).

At first this mound appears irregular and ran-dom, but closer inspection shows that its layout was roughly from east to west perpendicular to the eastern edge of the terrace. The mound has no apparent entranceway and no known stone archi-tecture or human burials. Its top is flat and its sides are roughly beveled, both by wind and water ero-sion and perhaps by planned design. While ~6500 years of erosion and disturbance have undoubtedly softened the contours of the mound, it probably retains most of its original shape. The west end of the mound was modified and built onto by a later Moche structure.

Excavation data suggest that the people using this locality occupied an area that was gently sloping and well drained. Compared to other localities on the terrace, it was closer to the flood-plain and raised agricultural fields to the immedi-ate east. Between ~6500 and 4000 years ago the

soils of the emerging floodplain were shallow and humid and would have been nutrient rich with inherent agricultural productivity as well as soil moisture holding capacity (see chapter 5). The juxtaposition of organic horizon features with overlying sediments indicative of cultural activity suggests that people at Paredones coincided with a period of specialized use of a particular land-scape—Preceramic field agriculture, as evidenced by raised agricultural platforms buried just east of the terrace by at least 5200 cal BP (see chapter 7).

The Paredones data are modeled as two separate areas: on mound (Unit 22) and off-mound (Units 20 and 30 and Test Pits 28 and 29). With reference to the primary site map (fig. 3.1), the boundary is as follows. Beginning west of the mound, the boundary starts near the middle of the north arm of a juxtaposed Moche structure, extends just east of a plaza associated with the Moche mound, and heads in an east-oriented line to within 35 m of the edge of the terrace. These boundaries describe a roughly ovoid space about 30 by 60 m that includes an area between at least 0.5 and 1.0 hect-ares of off-mound habitation debris, as evidenced by Test Pits 28 and 29 and GPR data (see chapter 7 and appendix 15).

Several observations can be made about this distribution. The mound appears to be delib-erately placed near the eastern edge of the ter-race. Furthermore, most of the observed asso-ciated domestic debris is to the east primarily because areas to the north, south, and west have been destroyed by subsequent mound construc-tions. Few Preceramic artifacts were found in looter's holes immediately to the south and north of the mound, but this is possibly due to exten-sive disturbance and later rebuilding of the Moche mound.

Reconstruction of the mound structure is prob-ably overly simplistic, as disturbance of its west-ern portion by Moche construction blurs its full complexity. The first documented activity on the low natural knoll of the terrace where Paredones is located was a thin layer of premound sediments about 0.5 m thick that contained sea lion bones, shell, burned areas and small rock-lined hearths, and plant remains indicative of terminal Pleisto-cene to early Holocene habitation areas (Units 20 and 22). Burned rock and patchy burned areas indicate that fires were built on this surface until it was hard and reddish. As mentioned above, a ^{14}C date on a *Capsicum* sp. seed from one burned area in Unit 22 was assayed at ~10,500 cal BP. (If more terminal Pleistocene to early Holocene cultural debris is present, it may have been destroyed by later mound activity or may be so spatially scattered that it is difficult to detect without extensive excavation.) Unit 20 is the off-mound trench that begins at the base of the Paredones mound and extends eastward to a premound domestic space. Its deeper cultural layers, Layers 5b and 6b, were dated from ~5603–5333 (AA86937) to 5583–5524 cal BP (AA86936), respectively. The premound excavations in Units 20 and 22 revealed few formal hearth structures, pits, postholes, use surfaces, grinding stones, and other debris suggestive of domestic occupation. As mentioned earlier, these layers and features are generally characterized by 2 cm thick use surfaces and fills very similar in form, structure, and content to those of late Phase II at Huaca Prieta, which dates earlier between ~7500 and 6500 cal BP. Similar strata and features were also recovered in Unit 30 and Test Pits 28 and 29 but not radiocarbon dated.

In Unit 22 on the eastern end of Paredones, mound-building began around 6500 cal BP. The entire stratigraphy of the site at this time consists of multiple intact floors ranging in thickness from 2 to 5 cm that are interspersed by 10–25 cm thick fills containing midden debris. The deeper Floors 18 to 28, however, were compact and thin (~1–2 cm thick) and with thin intervening fills (~2–5 cm thick). Floor 24 is one of the deepest and dated at 6640–6319 cal BP (AA83260). A burned corncob from Floor 18 dates at 6775–6504 cal BP (OS86020), suggesting that the lower floors were used within a relatively short time, given these overlapping ages. Several intervening dates and an assay of 4821–4527 cal BP (AA86934) from Floor 6 indicate that the mound was utilized to the end of the late Preceramic period around 4000–3800 cal BP. This is about the same time that Huaca Prieta was abandoned, although it was later used for human burials.

In summary, Paredones is a relatively moderate-sized mound built up in several continuous stages on the eastern edge of the terrace above the floodplain to the east, containing at least 28 intact superimposed floors, each heavily burned, and fills. There also are off-mound habitation features.

Mound construction was gradual and coincided with various activities at Huaca Prieta. During early Moche times, Paredones served as a place for a few burials and had a boundary wall built across its western end, demarcating it from a juxtaposed Moche structure.

UNIT 16, ~7200–4600 CAL BP

Unit 16 is a domestic site that dates from ~7200 to 4000 cal BP and is associated with a stratigraphic sequence of habitation deposits followed by house remains. Below these houses are thin lenses of early Holocene habitation debris similar to that documented at Huaca Prieta and Paredones and dated around ~7200 years ago.

Multiple house remains were grouped along the western edge of the terrace north of Huaca Prieta overlooking the ocean and beach to the west. The dated materials from Unit 16 are from feature contexts in house floors. The houses at Unit 16 represent a series of imbricated residential and burial events. Prehousehold levels of Unit 16 are associated with hearths, lithics, shells, and bone debris.

The data from Unit 16 are modeled as three discrete phases. The first phase is bound by the onset of Phase II (~7200 cal BP) and terminates before 6000 cal BP. A single piece of charcoal in a burned area in the deeper prehouse levels (Layer 13) dated at 7266–7021 cal BP (AA86935). The second phase is associated with Houses 4 and 5, Phases II–III. The early limit, Phase II, was defined by a charcoal date from the floor of House 5 (7413–7005 cal BP, AA87665). The last occupation in Phases IV and V was determined by the floor of House 2 (4780±20 cal BP, Beta290654). The upper limits were derived from the abandonment of Houses 1 and 2 in Phase V, probably sometime ~4500 cal BP.

PRECERAMIC HABITATION SITES ON THE SANGAMON TERRACE AND WETLANDS TO THE NORTH AND SOUTH

We examined several looter's pits across the entire Sangamon terrace. The deeper pits revealed dark, burned sediments, suggesting Preceramic occupation. No early ceramics were recovered from these pits. We dated two features from looter's holes in two other terrace sites, which were processed on single pieces of charcoal at 7162–6914 cal BP (AA75398) and 7263–7027 cal BP (AA753476). One of these sites was located about 200 m north of Paredones; the other was about 180 m south of Huaca Cortada situated on the northeast corner of the Sangamon terrace. Also, a single radiocarbon date 6270–5950 cal BP (Beta290762) was produced with the cleaning of a looter's pit in a Preceramic house mound located 1.0 km south of Huaca Prieta. Another date of 5438–5093 cal BP (Beta290668) was associated with a disturbed house mound near Pulpar, located about 8 km north of Huaca Prieta.

We also cleaned and profiled Bird's TP-5 on the Cupisnique mound just north of Huaca Prieta; below it we found Preceramic house remains with cobblestone foundations (see fig. 31 in Bird et al. 1985: 49). A single piece of charcoal from the deepest house floor dated to ~7500 cal BP (Beta233491). This single date and premound debris along with the deeper levels of Unit 16 suggest habitation areas possibly associated with early mound building at Huaca Prieta.

AGRICULTURAL FIELDS EAST OF THE TERRACE

The dune earthworks lying to the east of Huaca Prieta and Paredones were unknown before our work. These earthworks include five large L-shaped to amorphous dune deposits that excavations reveal are raised agricultural platforms covered by aeolian sand (see fig. 3.3). We exposed raised agricultural field underneath the dunes that are 0.5 to 1.3 m high and between 2.2 and 3.1 m wide. We could not determine their full length because we did not excavate them completely, although we estimate that they were at least 20–30 m long. Old aerial and ground photos of these features show ten of them in the 1940s, although only five are visible today. It is probable that more once existed but have been destroyed by sugarcane production. The existing dune features measure between 28 and 48 m long and 1.3 to 4.3 m high. The presence of Moche and Lambayeque rim sherds on the excavated buried surface of three excavated fields places their chronology roughly between AD 500 and 1200.

Also identified in the profiles of modern-day drainage ditches in the same area just east of the Sangamon terrace are *camellones*: raised agricultural platforms that are buried between 80 cm to 1.1 m below the present-day ground surface (see fig. 7.32). These below-ground features were observed as far away as 1 km to the east of the terrace, yet not as dense in number there as they are close to the mounds and the terrace. A radiocarbon date of charcoal embedded in the surface of one of these features was 5448–5067 cal BP (Beta233988), which coincides with the seasonal wetlands east of the terrace (see chapter 5). There also are Preceramic raised fields in a wetland about 1.5 km southeast of Malabrigo, located about 20 km north of Huaca Prieta. Goodbred and Oliveira Sawakuchi processed an OSL date for an upper, terminal-use level of a raised field there at 2200 years ago (see chapter 5).

HUACA PRIETA AND PAREDONES IN THE CONTEXT OF THE SANGAMON TERRACE

Work at Huaca Prieta, Paredones, and other sites has produced a sufficient number of radiocarbon dates to allow the creation of a moderate-scale chronometric history of the mounds. The present understanding of the cultural chronology of the Huaca Prieta and Paredones sites is built around the idea that the southern tip of the Sangamon terrace was occupied from ~14,500 through ~3500 cal BP. Five cultural phases were constructed, using radiocarbon measures from feature and floor contexts at Huaca Prieta and Paredones. Excavations also suggest that the areas of the mounds we examined were built without appreciable hiatuses.

Beginning in Phase II, Huaca Prieta was intentionally constructed as mounded architecture, designed and executed on a scale not seen in the contemporary Andean world. Soil coring and mapping indicate that the mound contains at least ~200,000 m³ of rock, debris, and sediment. Additionally, coring located the original terrace surface beneath Huaca Prieta and demonstrated that the premound unit slopes almost 1.5–1.8 m from west to east across the Sangamon terrace. The chronological analysis suggests the gradualism implicit in the construction of Huaca Prieta and Paredones. The data indicate that the construction of both mounds occurred in multiple events stretched over several millennia. Construction of Huaca Prieta probably was not necessarily conceived and executed with a single purpose and was probably undertaken without final finished dimensions, although it must have had an idealized form passed from generation to generation. Huaca Prieta initially was a ritual mound and then later became both a ritual and mortuary place. Paredones also was built gradually and later than Huaca Prieta. Paredones was constructed in a location that has a distinct history, which was associated initially with domestic activity and later with ritual and food preparation. Underlying both mounds are scattered remains of domestic activity that date to the terminal Pleistocene and early Holocene periods.

This view indicates that the context of building Huaca Prieta and Paredones was fundamentally different from (most) other construction models for other Preceramic mounds along the coast of Peru. Most archaeologists see the late Preceramic landscape of more inland coastal agricultural areas growing around a central monument, such as Caral, Aspero, and others in the Norte Chico area, for instance, all of which increased in size through time. Our analysis, however, proposes that Huaca Prieta and Paredones were the result of changes occurring in a differently developed society, one associated more with a littoral and an adjacent coastal wetland.

As described in subsequent chapters, anthropic sediments and related excavation matrices and chronologies enable fundamental questions of environment and activity associated with the use of Huaca Prieta and Paredones to be addressed. Significantly, these localities were subject to numerous periodic phases of ritual practices and food preparation and consumption. As noted above, there is evidence at both sites of extensive premound burning and disturbance of soils related to domestic activities. The earlier phases of anthropic sediment deposition reflect a subsistence strategy based on the management of marine and wetland resources and introduced cultigens.

A marked change in anthropic sediment characteristics, however, occurred between ~7500 and 3500 cal BP at Huaca Prieta and ~6500 and ~3800 cal BP at Paredones. This represents evidence of a change in activities at these sites, not only a possible widening of resource extraction to include more domestic food crop production but also increased economic specialization and complementarity between maritime foraging/fishing and agriculture and less dependence on wild foods from the wetlands, which by ~6500 cal BP had diminished significantly. A partial explanation for this specialization strategy may be continuing landscape modification in the vicinity of each site and a growing population in the littoral zone. By 3500 BP the cultural landscape consisted of a palimpsest of unique yet interrelated mounds and domestic spaces connected through a common history.

Finally, many of the cultural changes recorded above coincide with paleoenvironmental and climatic shifts documented in the study area (see chapter 5). For instance, mound building at Huaca Prieta roughly corresponds with the appearance of the lagoon just east of the terrace ~7500 cal BP. Furthermore, the onset of more intensive use of cultigens at Paredones coincides with the disappearance of the lagoons and the development of the seasonal wetlands east of the terrace around 6500 years ago. Abandonment of the two sites occurred about the same time as the development of the floodplain in the lower valley, the later building of the Cupisnique mound to the north, an increase in marine transgression with the sea closer to the mounds, and shrinkage of the wetlands. Perhaps most notable is that the abandonment of both Huaca Prieta and Paredones coincides roughly with the maximum Holocene transgression at 3700 cal BP and the ocean lapping at the western base of the Huaca Prieta mound at this time. Transgression also would have led to higher standing water in the floodplain and wetlands just east of the terrace where the raised agricultural fields were located near Paredones (see chapter 7). Although we were unable to date the time of the abandonment of the raised fields, no Initial Period ceramics were associated with them, suggesting that they were probably in disuse by ~4000 to 3500 years ago. The point here is not that the environment determined major settlement and subsistence changes but that it probably influenced some of them.

SITE DATA AND PATTERNS

Tom D. Dillehay, Duccio Bonavia, Gabino Rodríguez, Gerson Levi-Lazzarus, Daniel Fernandes Moreira, Marilaura López Solís, Paige Silcox, and Kristin Benson

INTRODUCTION

This chapter describes the nature of the cultural and paleoecological data from Huaca Prieta, Paredones, and other sites by (1) description of the excavated remains, primarily the stratigraphy, architecture, floors, use surfaces and features, and the organic and inorganic materials recovered from them, and (2) interpretation of these remains for understanding the cultural phases under investigation. The starting point of our work was at Huaca Prieta where we reexcavated several of Bird's units to understand them; we then branched into our own excavations (fig. 7.1). Most of our units were placed in areas not excavated by Bird to define the stratigraphy of different areas on and off of the mound, including the Paredones site to the north. In addition to describing the stratigraphy and general findings in each unit in each site, Harris Matrices are given for the major excavations in Huaca Prieta and Paredones. Not presented are quantitative and qualitative analyses of the faunal and floral species and artifacts recovered from excavations; these are presented in chapters 9–12.

SYNCHRONIC AND DIACHRONIC VARIATION WITHIN SITES

The archaeological and geological stratigraphy of Huaca Prieta shows that it is not a homogeneous block of sediments. In fact, it is a mound composed of thousands of vertically and horizontally discontinuous strata that represent many different use episodes. In order to understand the complexity of this vertical and lateral variability in the mound, macro- and micro-artifact and ecofact analyses were performed for all units. The same was done for all other excavated sites. Every floor and use surface shows a different artifact

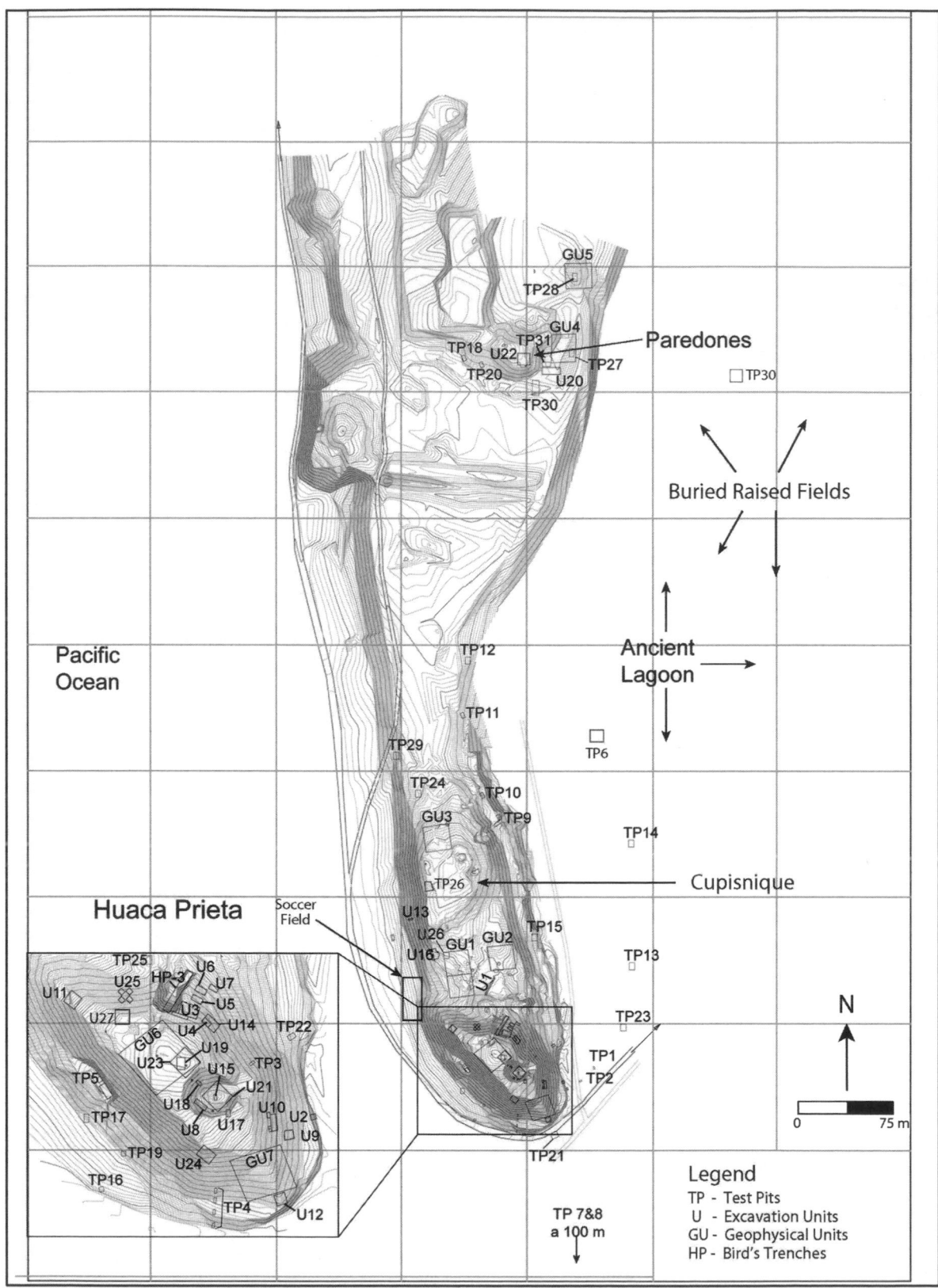

FIGURE 7.1. Map of the excavation units and test pits at Huaca Prieta and Paredones.

and sediment composition. They do not co-vary along vertical and lateral sequences; nor are they apparently caused by a particular seasonal or other organization of activities. As a result of the stratigraphic complexity in the site, we employed the Harris Matrix to major excavation units in an attempt to clarify stratigraphic relationships and to illustrate this complexity.

Refitting of a few textile, gourd, and other artifact fragments, sampling techniques and stratigraphy of units, and the establishment of detailed sequences of use episodes were designed to define interunit stratigraphic links, postdeposition processes, activity areas, intersite and intrasite circulation of products, recycling tools and other items, ritual offerings, nonritual feasting, and domestic or other preparing and consuming of food. Plotting the different artifacts and ecofacts depicted the distribution of consumed goods and related activities. The potential variability between stratigraphic units depended on the organization of activities of preparation, distribution, consumption, and deposition as well as on the recurrence and regulation of discarding residues. We can verify the recurrences and the variability in the strategies of food preparation, consumption, and discard during ritual and other activities, in the organization of space, and in the distribution of the labor effort invested in the construction and use of sites.

Harris Matrices

Harris Matrices were drawn for Unit 2 and the east and west walls of HP-3 at Huaca Prieta and Units 20 and 22 at Paredones. The first step in creating the matrices was to assign Harris numbers (H#) to all individual strata. Harris numbers were not assigned during most excavations (a different nomenclature was given in the field prior to using the Harris method). This was done later by applying numbers to stratigraphic profiles digitized from highly detailed profiles made in the field. To prevent confusion between the two nomenclatures, each individual unit, wall, stratum or layer, floor, and fill sequence in the profiles was given a discrete Harris number, with no overlapping or duplicating numbers within and across profiles. Thus the Harris Matrix profiles are much more schematically detailed and numerous, as they

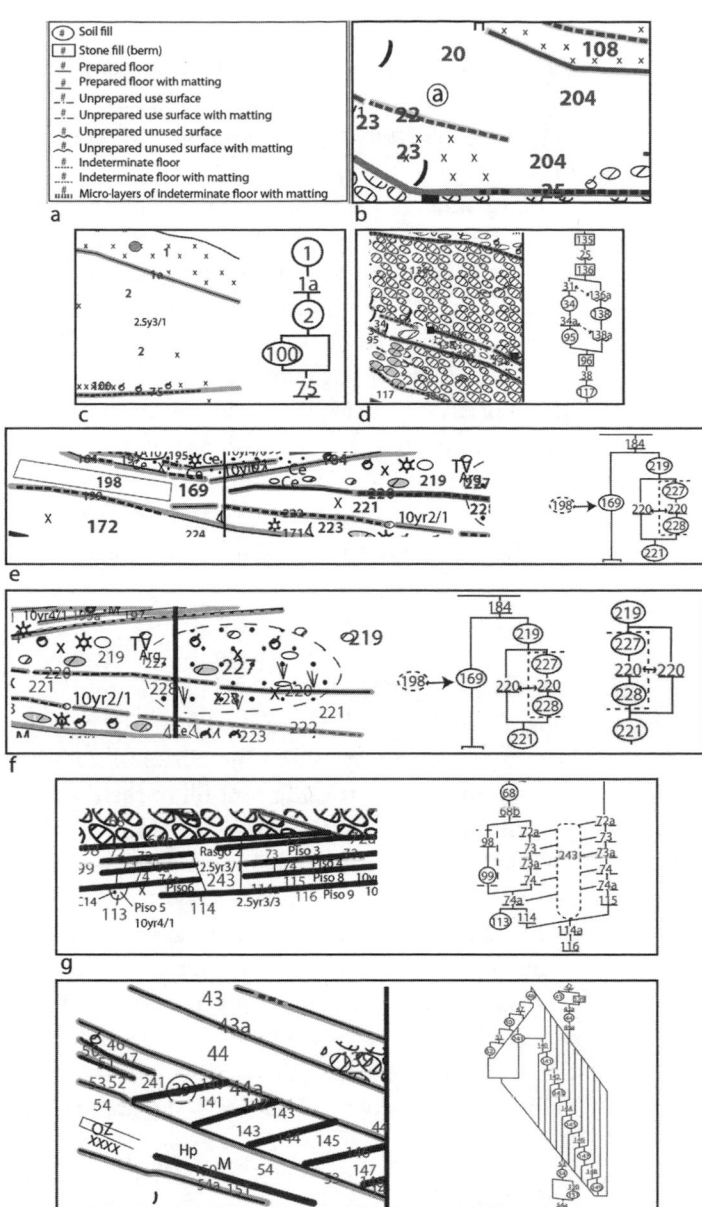

FIGURE 7.2. Symbols for Harris Matrices and illustrative explanations of strata patterns: *a–h* represent sample symbols mentioned in the text.

should be, and based upon profile drawings and photographs of the excavated stratigraphy. Figure 7.2a presents a listing of the symbols for different floor and layer types in the matrices (see chapter 3 for definitions of these types). Early versions of the profiles and Harris Matrices used shaded symbology to distinguish between various types of floors and layers, whether they contained matting, and in some profiles whether yellow clay was used. Because these variations were not discussed in detail in the following descriptions, the shading was not used in the figures included in this chapter. However, the symbology remains in the legends to illustrate the stratigraphic complexity of the site.

To maintain correspondence between the field and the Harris systems, the original working profiles presented both sets of numbers. All profiles are associated with hundreds of individual truncated strata indicative of many use episodes. When there was doubt about whether a stratum was horizontally or vertically continuous or discontinuous a new number was assigned to it. Comparison of profiles to field notes, photographs, and other sketches clarified these relationships, with the Harris numbers later combined more easily within and across sites.

Figure 7.2b illustrates an example of a new Harris number applied to a potentially continuous stratum. H#22, the dotted line, abruptly terminates, no longer distinguished from the overlying and underlying H#20 and H#23 fills. Rather than assuming that the adjacent fill to the right is a continuation of either H#20 or H#23, a new number was applied, H#204, for the thicker and conjoined fills of H#20 and H#23.

In other profiles, letter designations rather than numbers were used to prevent overlap of numbers from one profile to the next. In these cases letters were added to the numbers. For example, in the west wall profile of Bird's HP-3, a thin surface below H#1 and above H#2 was designated H#1a (fig. 7.2c).

When constructing the Harris Matrices for profiles in Huaca Prieta, the primary focus was vertical association among layers. This approach was based on the large, detailed scale of the profiles and the complicated stratigraphy, reflecting several large- and small-scale deposition, modification, and construction phases. With complex profiles over 20 m long and 20 m high, maintaining horizontal associations was unwieldy (compare Harris 1975; Paice 1991). Because of the unique nature of Huaca Prieta and the application of Harris numbers, some alterations were made to the matrix format. However, the main goal was to place each stratum into a stratigraphic sequence and to illustrate that sequence with a two-dimensional schematic diagram (Paice 1991).

Dividing the profiles into arbitrary vertical columns made construction of matrices easier and allowed the final product to be read more clearly. The width of columns varied depending on the small-scale detail of the profile; more detailed profiles or sections required narrower vertical columns, while less complicated profiles allowed for wider ones, which illustrate more horizontal association between strata. Vertical columns are denoted by vertical lines and by letter designations. For layers that extend continuously across vertical columns, the same Harris number was used in all columns.

The symbols used to show vertical associations in the matrices are straightforward. As is typical of Harris Matrices, solid vertical lines connect strata that are in direct contact, with horizontal branching in places where two strata are in direct vertical contact with one another (Harris 1975; fig. 7.2c). One variation made branched lines diagonal, particularly in places where there are a number of small, but complexly associated layers, to give a clearer impression of horizontal associations. Where possible, these lines are drawn to illustrate the sloping nature of the mound strata.

In the example from the west wall of Unit HP-3 (fig. 7.2c), the basic elements of vertical association are seen. The branched horizontal line derived from Layer H#2 connects to both Layers H#100 and H#75; in this case, it forms a box-like structure, which illustrates the staggered layering of the strata.

In terms of symbols in the profiles, soil fills are shown as a circle or ellipse around the Harris number, stone berms are distinguished by a square around the number, intruding features have a dotted surrounding symbol, and underlined numbers indicate the various types of floors or prepared surfaces. A solid line is indicative of a prepared floor, a line-dot-line indicates an unprepared use surface, a jagged line is used for unprepared and unused surfaces, and a series of dots indicates an indeterminate surface. In some places there are a number of closely stacked microstrata of the same type. These were all given a single Harris number, but the underlining symbol stacked below the number in the matrix applies to more than one layer.

When comparing vertical columns from the same profile, the same Harris number indicates a continuous layer. The symbol may change in some cases: e.g., if a prepared floor transitions to an indeterminate floor, the Harris number is the same while the solid line beneath changes to a dotted line. In places where there is a clear break in the horizontal line, a new Harris number was applied, though arrowed dotted lines connect the numbers to indicate that they may be the same layer.

In the example from the west wall of Unit HP-3, several symbols distinguishing different types of layers are seen as well as the diagonal horizontal branching that illustrates the slope of the mound. The diagonal branching is only seen where two separate strata lie horizontal to each other below a single continuous strata on a slope, in this case Layer H#31 and Layer H#136a lie below Layer H#136 (fig. 7.2d). The slope creates a vertical association between the two strata adjacent to each other and thus an important association to demonstrate. Also shown is the arrowed dotted line connecting two distinctly numbered Harris layers that are potentially the same layer.

If a change occurs in a layer within a single vertical column, a branched horizontal line is used to show where the split occurs, as if it were a new stratum, and a solid arrowed line is drawn between the two Harris numbers to indicate that it is the same stratum.

Intrusive features interrupted both the vertical and horizontal stratigraphy that made it difficult to use the methods described above. Various dotted symbols were employed to distinguish intrusions. This allowed the matrix to show the variation of intrusive layer types. Single intrusive features are shown with dotted symbols that correspond with fill type: a dotted circle indicates an intruding soil fill and a dotted square is an intruding stone fill. The example shown in figure 7.2, from the west wall, shows how a simple intrusive feature, H#198, is encased in H#169 (fig. 7.2e). This makes a vertical association between the two layers impossible, as H#169 exists both above and below H#198. Thus the clearest way to present this type of feature is to place it outside of the vertical flow of the matrix with an arrowed line indicating which layer the feature intrudes.

In cases where the intrusion is large enough to disrupt several layers and to contain its own individual stratigraphy, it is included in the vertical flow with a dotted line separating it from the general stratigraphy. These dotted lines are open

ended in cases where the intrusion continues from one vertical column to the next. In some places individual layers continue into these "intrusive" features. Continuous layers are shown both inside and outside the dotted line with the same Harris number, connected by a solid double-arrowed line.

Figure 7.2f illustrates the intrusion of H#227 and H#228 into H#220 (as shown by the solid double-arrowed line), which exist within and across the intrusion. The dotted line is open ended on the right, indicating that H#227, H#220, and H#228 continue across the intrusion and the adjacent column. Figure 7.2f also shows the intrusive feature containing H#227 and H#228. There are also lines marking the division between two vertical columns in the profile. To the right, the portions of the matrix from both columns are placed adjacent to each other so that the entire diagram for that particular feature is shown. There are other types of intruding features, such as postholes or filled-in pits. In these cases, the symbols are altered to correspond to the general shape of the intrusion to clarify its vertical and horizontal alignments.

Figure 7.2g shows an example from the west wall of Unit HP-3 where H#243 (*rasgo* or Feature 2) intrudes into several layers of unprepared use surfaces (labeled as individually numbered *pisos* or floors on the original profile). This illustrates how the symbol of H#243 was vertically elongated in the matrix to show the horizontal interruption of several presumably preexisting layers.

In summary, the primary relationship shown in all matrices is a schematic vertical alignment because the mounds are composed of very few laterally extending layers. If a vertical line in the matrix connects two layers, one is in direct vertical contact with the other. Horizontal relationships are maintained when possible, but only when they do not interfere with vertical alignments. In some places the layers are at such a small scale, and the relationships between them so complicated and discontinuous, that it becomes impossible to keep any horizontal connections spatially oriented in the matrix.

A portion of the west wall of Unit HP-3 (fig. 7.2h) shows how fitting complex small-scale stratigraphy into the matrix occupies a larger amount of space than the actual layers occupied in the site. Here a vertical line directly connects the layers in stratigraphic contact, which requires extra space on the matrix. Using diagonal lines to connect single layers with multiple layers directly below shows the horizontal associations. This technique aligns adjacent vertical columns to show their horizontal associations. The profiles shown and described below present the precise and accurate stratigraphy for each excavated unit; the Harris Matrices provide only a schematic representation of the horizontal and vertical complexity of the stratigraphy.

We begin the description of excavation units by presenting a synopsis of Bird's excavated units and then turning to those we excavated between 2007 and 2011.

DESCRIPTION OF BIRD'S MAJOR EXCAVATION UNITS

BIRD'S HP-2

Bird's HP-2 is located ~30 m west of Unit HP-3 at the base of the mound's northwest side. The original unit was ~4 m high, 3 m wide, and 12 m long (Bird et al. 1985: 29–34). Our work recorded materials in the deeper premound deposits, which were mixed with sterile sediment and thin habitation lenses (1–3 cm thick) similar to those observed at the base of HP-3 (Bird et al. 1985; Dillehay et al. 2012b) and in Units 2, 9, 12, and 15/21 and Test Pit 22. Bird dated these lenses to 5462–4152 cal BP, an assay provided by Libby in the 1950s (see chapter 6). Our excavations in the deepest levels of this unit produced a date of 5919–5667 cal BP (see chapter 6). These dates suggest that the higher west side of the terrace, which was closest to the ocean and more exposed to the strong southwest winds, was probably occupied later in time. This also indicates that the lower southeast side of the terrace, which is closest to the ancient lagoon and protected from the winds, was where the first mound layers were placed (see the discussion below). There are no supportive cobblestone berms at the base of the west side, perhaps because its west-to-east slope provided a natural berm or because it is not as high in relief from ground level as the east side. As described by Bird, the stratigraphy and artifact content in this unit consists of multiple

use surfaces and fills containing burned sediments and a wide variety of materials. The stratigraphy of HP-2 corresponds with those dating to Phases IV–V on the east side of the mound. No domestic hearths, postholes, or other debris indicative of habitation were found in this unit except the thin habitation lenses in the deeper premound levels dated before 5800 years ago.

Bird's excavation in this unit convinced him that the western half of the mound was washed away by a massive tsunami (Bird et al. 1985: 16, 30–32). He states that the excavated "face seemed to indicate that those layers ran into the mound horizontally rather than with a downward slope toward the western edge of the mound. If the mound had not been eroded away, one would expect the strata to dip toward the mound's edge" (Bird et al. 1985: 30). Bird was correct in identifying the horizontal bedding of the cultural stratigraphy but mistaken in attributing it to massive erosion whereby more than half of the mound was washed away. In fact, the strata in HP-2 are not precisely horizontal but are slightly inclined (5–15 degrees) to the west or declined (5–15 degrees) to the east, corresponding to the natural west-to-east incline-to-decline, respectively, of the underlying Sangamon terrace (see fig. 18 in Bird et al. 1985: note the horizontal strata and, in the lower levels, their declination from west [right] to east [left], which conforms to the declining angle of the underlying surface of the terrace). This does not imply that some erosion did not occur on the west side of the mound. After all, it was exposed to heavy winds and periodic wave action (we estimate no more than 2–4 m might have been lost on the west side of the mound over time), but not to the extent postulated by Bird.

BIRD'S HP-3 TRENCH

After removal of accumulated modern trash in this trench, it was clear that much damage had occurred since Bird's 1944–1945 excavations. Earth, trash, and fallen stones formed the infill of the trench. We recut, restudied, and redrew the profiles of both the east and west walls of the trench, after excavating them to a depth of ~24 m from the middle upper western slope of the mound. (Note that layers 29–38 are numerically out of order in the west wall profile;

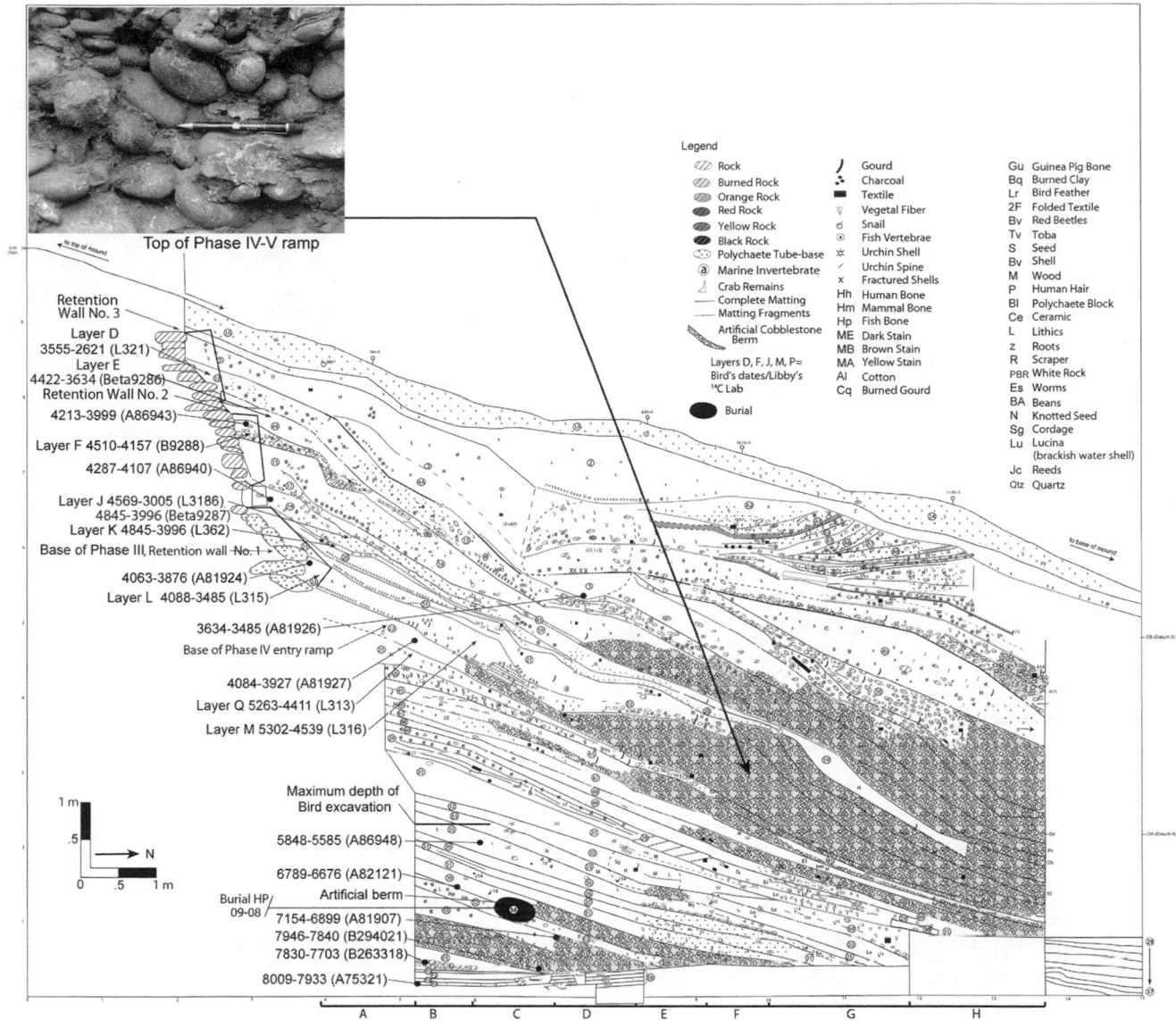

FIGURE 7.3. Profile of west wall of HP-3, showing strata, cobblestones, and mortar composing the artificial berms (inset) and radiocarbon dates. Shaded areas show the berms. Not shown are layers A2–A6 in a section 2 m farther east of the profile but still part of the HP-3 trench.

this is because they were first recorded in a test pit that we located farther east but contiguous to the HP-3 trench [see fig. 7.3]. The pit was excavated at the same time when we were recutting the trench and assigning strata numbers. When we returned to recut the trench, we skipped layers 29–38 assigned to the test pit and continued with Layer 45 immediately below Layer 26, thus the vertical sequence of Layer 26 to Layer 45. Later it was determined that layers 29–38 continued to the west underneath Layer 45, thus accounting for the sequence of Layers 45 to 38, and so forth.

Rather than renumber all layers, we retained the sequence excavated in the field.) More than 5000 data points were measured on the two walls (using high scaffolding loaned to us by the Huaca de la Luna Project in Trujillo). Underneath the rubble and trash, our excavations documented the previously unrecorded premound layers described in earlier chapters (Dillehay et al. 2012b). These deposits were thin, dark habitation lenses (0.5–1.5 cm thick) with a variety of artifact inclusions (for example, charcoal, shell, animal bones, and lithics). Figure 7.3 shows the stratigraphy and

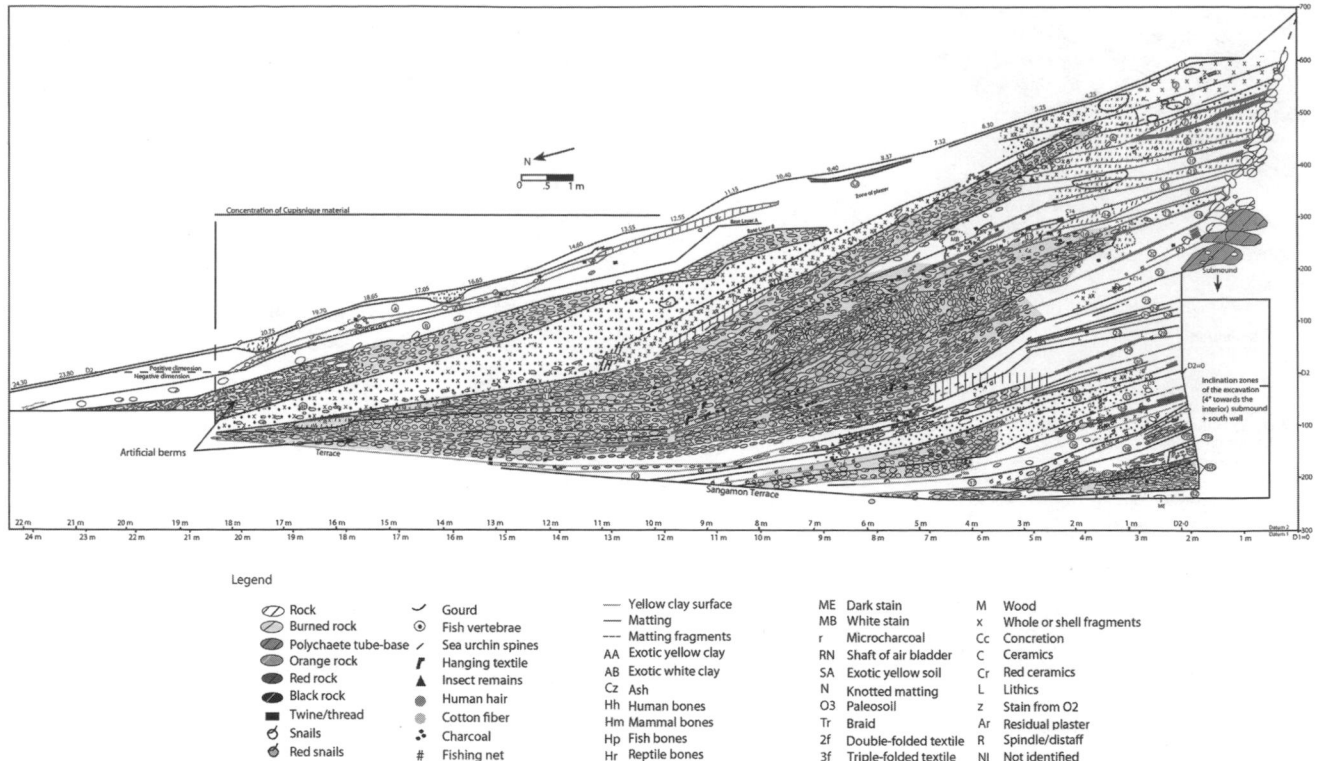

FIGURE 7.4. Profile of east wall of HP-3, showing strata, cobblestones, and mortar composing the artificial berms. Shaded areas show the berms.

radiocarbon chronology of the west wall; figure 7.4 reveals the profile of the east wall.

HP-3 became a large stratigraphic puzzle, as it proved difficult to locate the precise depth of Bird's prior excavations and to relate his stratigraphy to our profiles (see chapters 3 and 6). It also was clear that Bird had not fully (or laterally?) excavated the cultural deposits below and slightly behind retention wall no. 1 in the west face of the unit (see fig. 7.5; see figs. 20–23 in Bird et al. 1985) to the undisturbed surface of the terrace. As Bird had discovered before us, the upper layers of the trench contained intrusive Guañape and Cupisnique materials (~3700–3000 years ago).

Numerous individual floors, fills, use episodes, and stone artificial berms were recorded in HP-3. On the upper west side of the trench our excavations exposed the three retention walls first excavated by Bird. The base of retention wall no. 1 disappeared into the lower sections of the mound. The three walls extended along the east side of the mound and initially served as a series of off-setting, stacked retention walls and later as the vertical buttresses against which the Phase

IV entry ramp was constructed. (Ramp construction begins with Layer 25: see fig. 7.3.) Based on Bird's work and our excavations, we estimated the full size of the walls: the three together varied between 18 and 22 m wide and 3 to 6 m high. Prior to the construction of the entry ramp in Phase IV, the three walls were a reinforced vertical rather than a sloped side of the mound, the original purpose of which is unknown. This walled segment, which dates to Phases III and IV, clearly is not domestic related and depicts part of a previous building form. Approximately 4 m beneath the base of retention wall no. 1 were the undisturbed deposits of the first mound layers and the deeper, premound habitational lenses. Throughout the layers of the trench are articulated and disarticulated human remains (see chapter 8 and appendix 10; Bird et al. 1985).

One burial at the bottom of our excavation in HP-3 was articulated and dated to late Phase II (see chapter 8, HP09-08). Offerings consisted of several small snails and gastropods, particularly around the skull and over portions of the upper body (fig. 7.6). In addition there were thousands

Retention wall 3

Retention wall 2

Retention wall 1

FIGURE 7.5. Photograph of the three retention walls excavated by Bird in HP-3 (*top three arrows*) and the area behind the wall where we excavated into the interior and deeper (*bottom arrow*).

of burned sea urchin spines, a small white spherical stone on the northwest side of the skull, and several lithic flakes. The body was placed on a "bed" of folded cotton cloth that was ~1 m in length and 0.50 m in width and covered with a reed mat. A partially charred, loose cotton fiber was beneath the corpse and dated to 6822–6657 cal BP (see chapter 6). A layer of thick plaster covered the tomb, preserving the skeletons and cotton at this deeper level. The body was in a flexed position; the skull faced southwest. The long bones were well preserved, but the rest of the bones were fragmented as a consequence of deliberate crushing.

Bird's excavations recorded piles of stone at the base of HP-3 and in the east-extended middle layers, which he thought were tsunami deposits (Bird et al. 1985: see figs. 1 and 12). But these are artificial berms of cobblestones (locally called *chungos*), not tsunami deposits, as evidenced by the deliberate imbricated placement of thousands of similar-sized cobblestones, most with their long axes oriented up and down and not across the mound slope and with the use of mortar to hold them in place (see appendices 1 and 8, chapter 5, and fig. 7.3). Moreover, unlike natural beach berms composed of various large to small to gravel size stones, the berms at Huaca Prieta are sorted and composed of roughly the same size of stones. An artificial mortar composed of salt more than 157 and 190 times greater than the natural content of salt in the sea and in natural beach sediments was used to hold the stones in place (see appendix 8). That is, the cobblestones, which Bird thought had been tossed on the lower east side of the mound by a tsunami, were deliberately placed and imbricated there as footings to support the increasing infilled and heightened mound layers. Besides, tsunamis do not imbricate stones along their long axes and combine artifacts, high salt content, and other elements in this way. The stone berms were selectively placed along the sloping sides of the east side of the mound, as revealed by our excavations in Units 2, 6, 9, and 25 and Test Pit 22 and by their absence in the nearby Cupisnique and other mounds on the Sangamon terrace, which surely would have been covered by similar stones if a tsunami had indeed hit the coastline. In short, our excavations did not find any geological evidence of tsunami damage at the site or in any of the geological trenches and excavations elsewhere on the Sangamon terrace. However, evidence of two limited tsunami impacts were recorded on the south side of the valley and dated to ~2000 and 2900 years ago (see chapter 5).

As discussed in other chapters, we never fully understood how deeply Bird had excavated HP-3. His photographs and drawings suggest that he excavated about 3–4 m below the base of "retaining wall 1," but his published and unpublished descriptions of the unit (for example, Bird et al. 1985 and field notes housed in the AMNH) suggest that he might not have reached the sterile "conglomerated" terrace surface or at least not

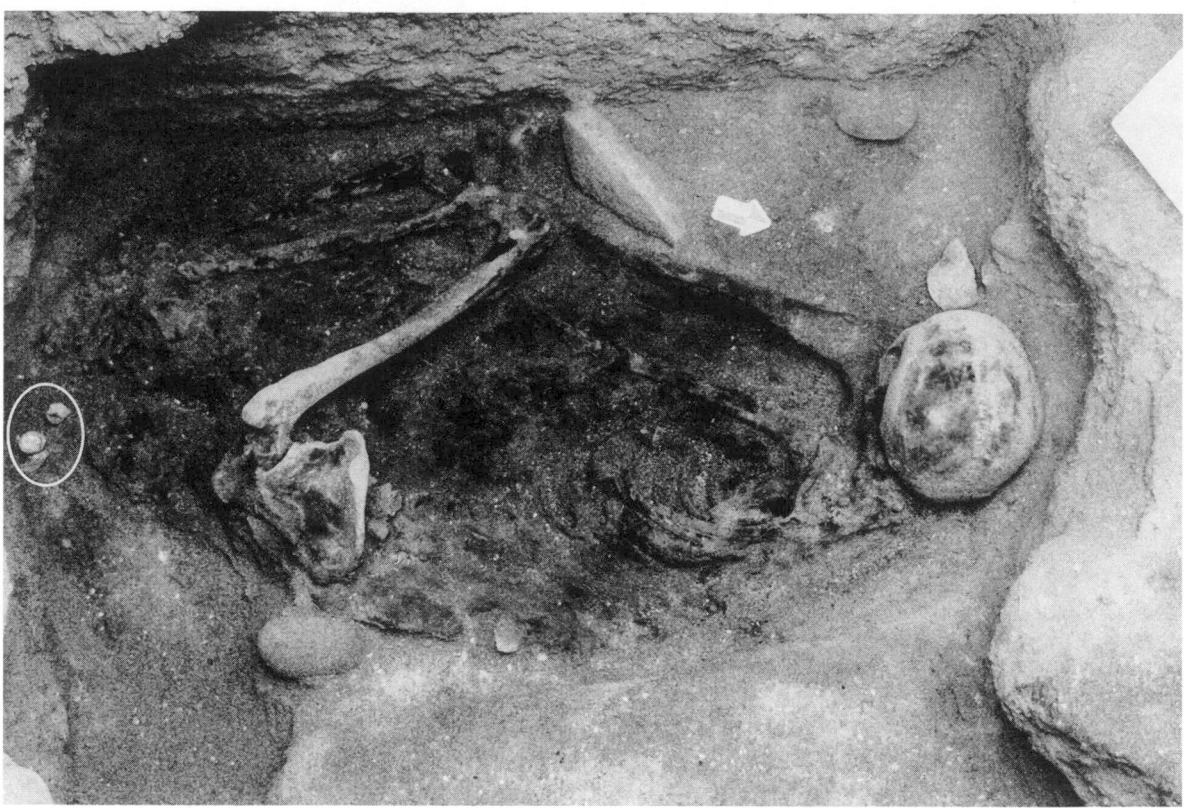

FIGURE 7.6. Burial HP09-08 near the base of HP-3. The circled area on the left shows shell offerings. Dark areas are red pigments.

reached deeply into it and into the underlying early Holocene deposits. The following description suggests that he penetrated culturally sterile strata somewhere in HP-3, TP-1, or nearby, but his figure 11 in Bird et al. (1985) indicates that he never reached these deposits. To explain, he states that Layer T at the base of HP-3 "was composed of yellowish, tramped, compact dirt and contained streaks of shell refuse, charcoal, and a few burned stones . . . The lower part of the layer was sterile. That part of the layer was yellowish and full of salt-fractured cobbles. It is apparently the disintegrated top of the conglomerate rock base upon which the mound rests." He also noted that the underlying Layer U "was dug even deeper . . . to insure that the excavations had revealed the very first human occupation . . . the percentage of split cobbles became less and the yellowish dirt . . . became harder. At the bottom of the pit the matrix was stained and not white as observed in Test Pit 1" (Bird et al. 1985: 41). We excavated four deeper areas in the base of his trench, one ~1.5–2 m into, behind, and below the base of

retention wall no. 1, where we found early Holocene habitation lenses. Of the three other areas in the trench, only one yielded older deposits. Our excavations in various units and test pits extending from Paredones to Huaca Prieta revealed that the buried natural surface of the terrace was characterized by whitish yellow to white or yellow sediments and contained few rocks, very few of which were "salt-fractured cobbles." The only fractured cobbles were those composing the artificial berms described above at the base of HP-3, which were generally void of artifacts but were clearly human-made. Approximately 2 m below what we thought was the deepest part of Bird's excavation and below and behind the base of the berms in Layers 45–47 in HP-3 we found the early Holocene deposits, which Bird apparently never reached (see fig. 7.3). (Due to the highly scattered nature of these earlier remains, it is possible that Bird's excavation simply missed them, as several of our other excavations did.) None of Bird's profile drawings, photographs, or field notes in HP-3 depict the salt-fractured cobble layers

(Bird et al. 1985: 35–43) or describe precisely in detail where he excavated deeper deposits. His drawings have no vertical scales, so it is difficult to determine the exact depth of his excavation there. Furthermore, Bird had the habit of placing old papers and clothing at the base of his excavations, which presumably marked the termination of his excavation. We found old newspapers ~30 cm below the deepest berm in HP-3, resting on top of a whitish yellow sediment that contained thin lenses of shell, lithics, and charcoal. Based on this scant information and on the spottiness of the deeper early Holocene materials along the buried surface of the Sangamon terrace, we can only presume that Bird reached sterile sediments but did not excavate deep enough to find earlier cultural materials or, again, simply excavated areas where none were present.

Finally, construction of the three retention walls and the entry ramp on the northeast side of the mound is an enigma. Figure 7.3 shows the upper deposits of the entry ramp abutted against the walls. The base of retention wall no. 1 is estimated to date around 5300–5000 cal BP or at the end of Phase III. We probed on top of the mound behind wall no. 3 and also in the adjacent Unit 3, which revealed the mound stratigraphy had been deliberately truncated to build the walls. Our work also suggests that this was the only portion of the mound modified by construction of retention walls, suggesting a different concept of mound retention than the hardened plaster coatings covering the entire mound surface. To conclude, we believe that this portion of the mound was successively truncated to build the retaining walls and then the later ramp. All three walls were built in different styles and indicate considerable damage and decay, probably resulting from the sequential construction of each wall and of the later entry ramp. The upper portions of the ramp are associated with additional chamber tombs in our Unit 10 and those revealed by Bird's excavations on top of the mound and with the sunken circular plaza on the south end of the mound, all dating in late Phase IV ~4500–4000 cal BP. Clearly, the entry ramp and plaza suggest new ideas about the form, function, and meaning of the mound, including ritual processions. The presence of portions of several stratified zigzag paths on the ramp, as described later, indicates reuse and recapping over a long period. The plaza and ramp may also indicate that people at Huaca Prieta were attempting to emulate contemporary mounds on the coast that had vertical walls, sunken plazas, and entry ramps (such as Alto Salaverry and sites in the Norte Chico area).

Harris Matrix for Unit HP-3

West Wall

Both the east and west walls of Bird's HP-3 were profiled. Since both profiles are generally similar and primarily represent the Phase IV entry ramp on the east side of the mound, only the west wall is described here (fig. 7.7). Not all columns A–H in figure 7.7 correspond with those in figure 7.3 because the stratigraphy in each profile is separated by several meters and is slightly to moderately different in each.

The west wall is made up of at least 265 individual strata, with eleven different layer types, ranging from soil fills and stone berms to prepared floors and unprepared use surfaces. At least 51 different material/artifact types form the layers, making a complex mosaic of interwoven strata. As such, the profile was divided into the eight sequential A–H columns, with column A beginning at the southern end of the profile, extending northward, down the mound to the east, to column H. Solid lines across matrix sections denote continuous strata, with dashed lines as possible discontinuous strata.

Only nine strata in the profile are continuous, though fragmented in some way. H#1, H#1a, and H#2, at the top of the profile, are the only layers that extend completely across the profile without interruption. H#1 is predominately soil, shell, rock, and vegetal fragments, while H#2 is largely a matrix of soil with less shell. H#1a is a floor layer separating H#1 and 2. Another section of strata (H#42, H#43a, H#44, and H#44a) is nearly continuous across the profile, but each is fragmented in one place or another. H#44 is the only soil fill, consisting of shell and rock in the southern end (column B) and an uneven mixture of shell, rock, and charcoal in the north end (column G). H#42 and H#43a are floors with indeterminate layers in places, and H#44a is a floor that has matting in the southern end.

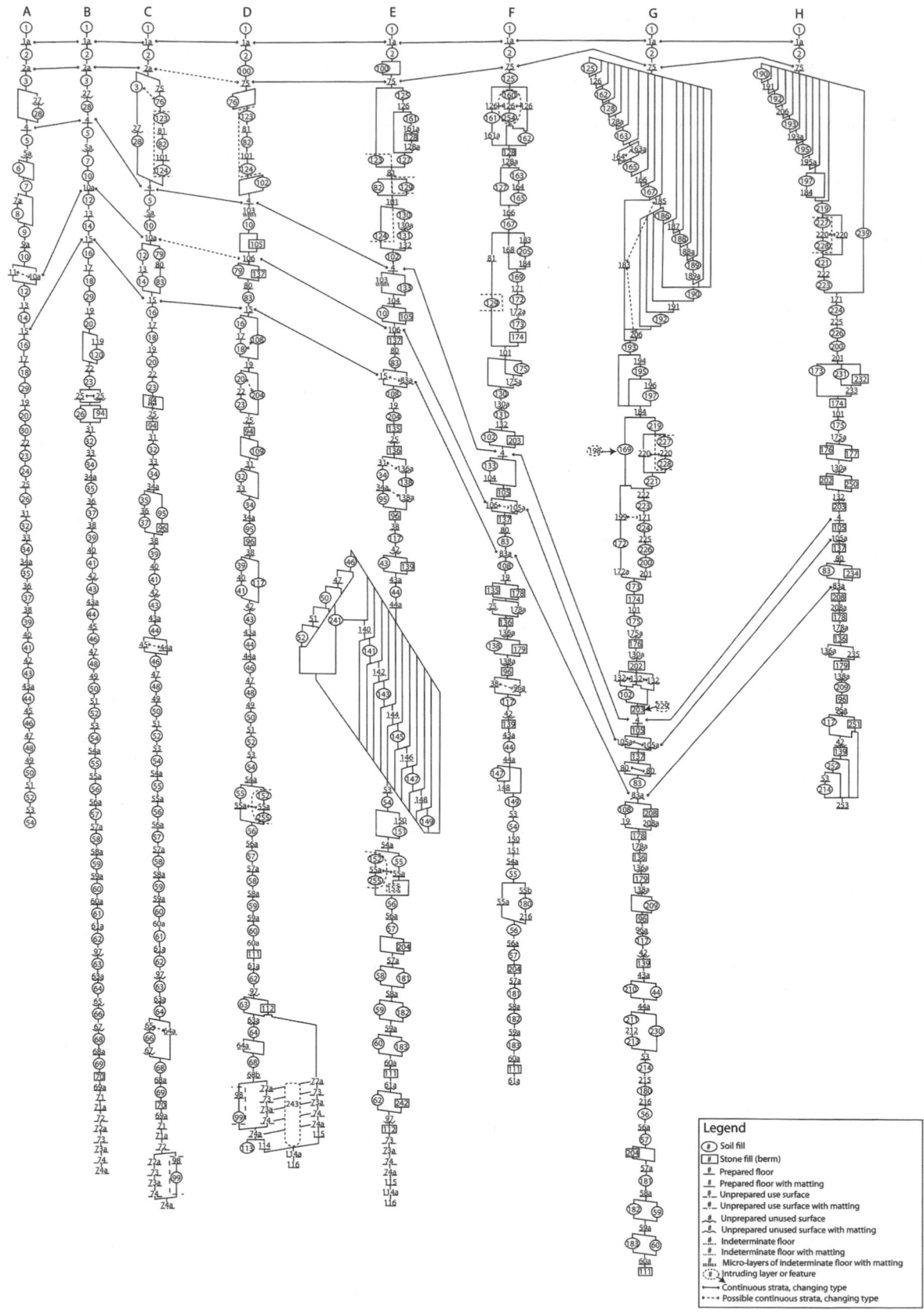

FIGURE 7.7. Harris Matrix of the west wall of HP-3.

Continuous strata are present, consisting mostly of prepared floors but also of soil fills and one unprepared floor. Although some strata are continuous, the material changes (such as shell, rock, reed, and matting), warranting a new H#, as with the series of floors H#11–10a–106–105a, H#15–83a, H#19–208a, H#25–178a, H#31–138a, and H#38–96a. These all begin in the southern portion of the profile as floors, alternating between matted use surfaces and prepared floors. H#2a–75 is fragmented by a large section of an "indeterminate" floor in the middle of the profile. Strata H#54–151 are soil layers divided by an intermediate floor, with H#54a–215 and H#55a–216 both intersected by prepared floor H#55b. H#56 is interrupted with a stone intrusion, and H#133 is a stone berm.

H#10, H#14–83, and H#46 through 52 are strata with clear interruptions. H#10 is a soil fill that begins on the south side and continues to intersect with a stone berm (H#105). Soil fills H#12 and H#14, made mostly of shell, continue into column C before interruption by H#83, a fill of mostly shell, burned sea urchin spines, and rock, before ending in a stone berm (H#234). H#46 through H#52 are an alternating series of floors and soil fills that meet H#241 in column E. This section continues, with the alternating floors/fills at an angle perpendicular to that of the slope of the mound until it meets H#149, a stratum with textile fragments. The remaining interrupted strata continue with shell and stone in H#211, H#212, and H#213, followed by H#230. The profile ends in the northern portion with H#252 and H#253.

The west wall profile also contains numerous stone berms, at least 22 in all and mostly along the base, making them the most significant strata, representing half of the profile depth in column H. A few berms are present in the southern base of columns B–F. The berms truncate other strata.

Finally, H#126–H#222 is a concentrated section, containing multiple alternating strata of every type.

CAPPING EPISODES AND A YELLOWISH SEDIMENT LAYER

The west wall profile of Unit HP-3 demonstrates several important features that are clues to the history of the northeast side of Huaca Prieta. First, we identified a silty to fine sand layer running down the full length of the unit. This layer represents a capping episode in the exterior of the mound at the end of Phase V and the beginning of the ceramic period. These sediments were buried under a later blanket mantle of a 10–44 cm thick hard plaster (Layer 2 in fig. 7.3). This suggests the presence of at least two late mound-capping stages and represents the exterior of the mound.

Second, a ~32–35 cm thick yellowish sediment layer (5Y/8) lies behind retention walls nos. 2 and 3 at a depth of ~4.6 m from the top of the mound and extends laterally over most of the mound at varying depths (not shown in figures). This layer was laid at the end of Phase IV, ~4300–4200 cal BP. Other than thick plaster coverings over the mound, which were poured several times during Phases IV and V, the yellow clay layer represents the only known effort to cover most mound areas by a single overlying sediment.

BIRD'S UNITS IN THE CUPISNIQUE MOUND

The project also profiled Bird's units (see fig. 3.2) in the Cupisnique mound to the immediate north of Huaca Prieta (fig. 7.1). Ceramics, conical adobe bricks, and domestic debris typical of the Cupisnique period were recovered. Extensive burned material observed at Huaca Prieta and Paredones was not present. The Cupisnique mound was habitational, as evidenced by grinding stones, hearths, burials, storage pits, house remains of cobblestones and adobe bricks, and other domestic debris. The deeper layers of the mound (5–7 m in depth) were defined by late Preceramic domestic debris overlaid by Guañape-like ceramics and stone-lined houses of the Initial Period and later Cupisnique ceramics and architecture. Several thin to moderately thin culturally sterile lenses were present between the upper Preceramic levels and the first ceramic levels, suggesting a brief hiatus of site abandonment at the end of the former period. No late Pleistocene or early Holocene deposits were recorded in the deeper layers, perhaps due to sampling bias and to disturbance of the original surface of the terrace by the construction of the adobe bricks constituting the mound or simply to the absence of people in this particular place during this period.

The oldest ^{14}C dates for the basal deposits under the Cupisnique mound were ~7500 cal BP (see chapter 6). This area of Bird's pits in the mound evidently was settled during the first phases of mound building at Huaca Prieta. Unit 16 and Test Pit 26, which are located at the southwest edge of the Cupisnique mound and extend underneath it to the north, yielded deep, thin midden lenses dated around 7200 cal BP (see chapter 6 and table 6.2). Both of these areas indicate that residential zones were immediately north of Huaca Prieta near the outset of its construction.

Although not clear in Bird's publications (Bird et al. 1985), the greatest concentrations of Guañape-like to Cupisnique and later Salinar, Gallinazo, and early Moche ceramics are associated with the northeast side of the mound at Huaca Prieta (the ramp area and area leading off toward the east and to the north near the Cupisnique mound). We found no evidence of a ceramic presence on top of the mound other than pottery offerings in the later tombs and none in other areas of the mound, except for two Moche pots in the upper levels of Unit 2.

DESCRIPTION OF OUR ARCHAEOLOGICAL UNITS: 2007–2013

Our excavation units are divided into four sectors, the mound at Huaca Prieta (Units 1–12, 14–15, 17–19, and 23–25), Paredones (Units 20 and 22), off-mound domestic locations (Units 13, 16 and 26), and the test pits (1–32). The cultural deposits are described in terms of layers, floors, and fills (see chapter 3 for definitions of floors, fills, and use surfaces). Although not discussed in the Harris Matrices described in this chapter, several worn zigzag footpaths on the Phase IV and Phase V entry ramp on the east side of the Huaca Prieta mound were formed primarily as a result of human traffic. They contain no special sediments or stone alignments suggestive of a formal feature. Finally, many descriptions mention faunal and floral remains, including all identifiable (analyzed in chapters 9 and 10, respectively) and unidentifiable elements that were observed and excavated. Some layer and floor nomenclature may include both numbers and letters, such as Layer 6c, which may not be specified in the quantitative and qualitative tables in

chapters 9 and 10. Combined numbered and lettered layers refer to a specific feature or sublayer.

Described below are the individual units for all four categories of excavations within the study area. Each unit is presented in terms of the layers, floors, fills, and features excavated with them in addition to brief descriptions of the artifactual, human skeletal, faunal and floral, and other remains recovered in them. Those radiocarbon dates presented in table 6.2, but not discussed in detail in that chapter, are contextualized below for each excavation unit. Finally, although they are not detailed below, the functions of all layers, floors, use surfaces, and features in all excavated units are interpreted in terms of the criteria defined for ritual, feasting, mortuary, domestic, and other activities in chapter 6.

UNIT EXCAVATIONS AT THE MOUND OF HUACA PRIETA (HP)

Reported below are the details of the excavation units and test pits at all sites. Ideally, most large-scale archaeological excavations of monumental sites with architecture and different activity zones present a concise, coherent synthesis of construction episodes, occupation surfaces, and unique, individual features keyed to the different macro-areas and cultural phases of the excavated units (Huaca Prieta, Paredones, the Sangamon terrace, and other off-mound excavated areas), along with a discussion of the spatiotemporal distribution, inferred function, and proposed significance of differential human activity as revealed in the extensive excavation program. This was done in brief in chapter 6 for each major excavated macro-area and cultural phase. But Huaca Prieta does not have a concise, coherent construction sequence like most large-scale monumental sites. Its internal structure and content, at least from an archaeological viewpoint, are anything but coherent, although its overall outward mounded structure gives the appearance of coherence. A concise and coherent description of Huaca Prieta cannot be done easily because its stratigraphy and internal activity areas are so diverse. In fact one of the major goals of this chapter is to convey the seemingly incoherent nature of the content and structure of the site, which requires detailed descriptions of the stratigraphic profiles and visuals of the major architectural features. These are provided below. Furthermore, the only major construction stages at Huaca Prieta are described for each cultural phase in chapter 6. These focus primarily on the premound domestic levels, the initial mound layers ending with the sunken circular plaza, the entry ramp, and last the chamber tombs in the later phases. Not described below are the later ceramic layers dating from the Initial Period (for example, Guañape-like to Cupisnique) to the early colonial period at Huaca Prieta. In general these are located on the northeast side and on the ramp of the mound at Huaca Prieta and are briefly described by Bird (Bird et al. 1985). A few deeper layers on the southeast side of the mound in the vicinity of Unit 2 exhibit early Guañape-like ceramics.

As mentioned in chapter 1, the focus of this book is on the middle to late Holocene period at Huaca Prieta and Paredones (~8000–4000 cal BP) and not on the late Pleistocene and early Holocene cultural deposits, which have been discussed elsewhere (Dillehay et al. 2012a). Also not described in detail is the enormous amount of fragmented matting and, to a lesser extent, basket and cordage fragments found in all levels of the mound at Huaca Prieta. The premound layers also contained fragmented matting, baskets, and cordage (see chapter 12) but in much lesser quantities and in generally poorer condition than those in the mound. Because matting is so ubiquitous at Huaca Prieta it is not listed in the following unit descriptions. Curiously, no basket, cordage, or matting was recovered from the floors at Paredones. However, as reported in appendix 12, an excessive amount of *Typha* pollen was found in floors at Paredones, perhaps suggesting that reed mats were produced at this site and then transported to Huaca Prieta and other localities for use.

HP Unit 1: This was a 1 by 15 m trench placed between Huaca Prieta and the Cupisnique mound to test the intervening stratigraphy and cultural deposits.

Layer 1, ~0–0.15 m: Layer 1 is a matrix of yellowish sandstone (10YR 8/6). The unit contains small amounts of lithics, late Moche ceramics, and marine shells. Two large ash stains (23 by 33 cm and 18 by 28 cm) at a depth of 15 cm are Features 1 and 2. Maize remains and animal coprolites were recovered from them.

Feature 1 is a layer of ash in the middle of the east wall. Feature 2 was a cluster of cobblestones and may be a tomb marker. The tomb was not excavated. Feature 3 was associated with large water-rolled stones, Moche sherds, and two wooden stakes, which were tomb markers; the tomb contained unburned but fragmented human bones.

Layers 2–3, ~0.15–0.45 m: The soil is compact and composed of sand. Materials are Moche sherds, lithics, plant remains, and shell. A human skull and a Guañape sherd were also found. This concentration of materials was Feature 4. Other materials included concentrations of cotton cordage, lithics, cornstalks, and unidentified sherds, which were Features 5 to 8. Feature 5 consisted of a concentration of various organic materials and lithics. Feature 6 consisted of animal bones, Guañape sherds, and pieces of cordage. Feature 7 consisted of a thick deposit of shell and polished blackware. Feature 8 is a compacted midden of shell, clay, animal bones, and Guañape sherds.

Layer 4, ~0.45–0.60 m: The soil texture is hard and compact with a sandstone conglomerate. Materials are distributed irregularly, with the exception of Feature 5, which extended deep into this layer and consisted of human teeth, a cotton cord, abundant shells, and utilitarian sherds. At the bottom of Layer 4 a 5 by 8 cm depression was labeled Feature 7.

In sum, Unit 1 was an off-mound area of various domestic activities from early to late ceramic periods.

HP Unit 2: Unit 2 is located in the southeast corner of Huaca Prieta. Its location relates the basal mound deposits to off-mound strata and to adjacent lagoon deposits off the terrace to the east. This unit constituted a primary chrono-stratigraphic unit (fig. 7.8), for which we constructed a Harris Matrix. The two profiles represent the south and east walls of the unit, respectively, and do not always correspond.

Harris Matrix for Unit 2

For Unit 2 the profile was divided into three columns. Stratigraphic continuity across the three columns was most prevalent in the bottom third, which are premound habitation layers (fig. 7.9). The middle layers were the most inconsistent in

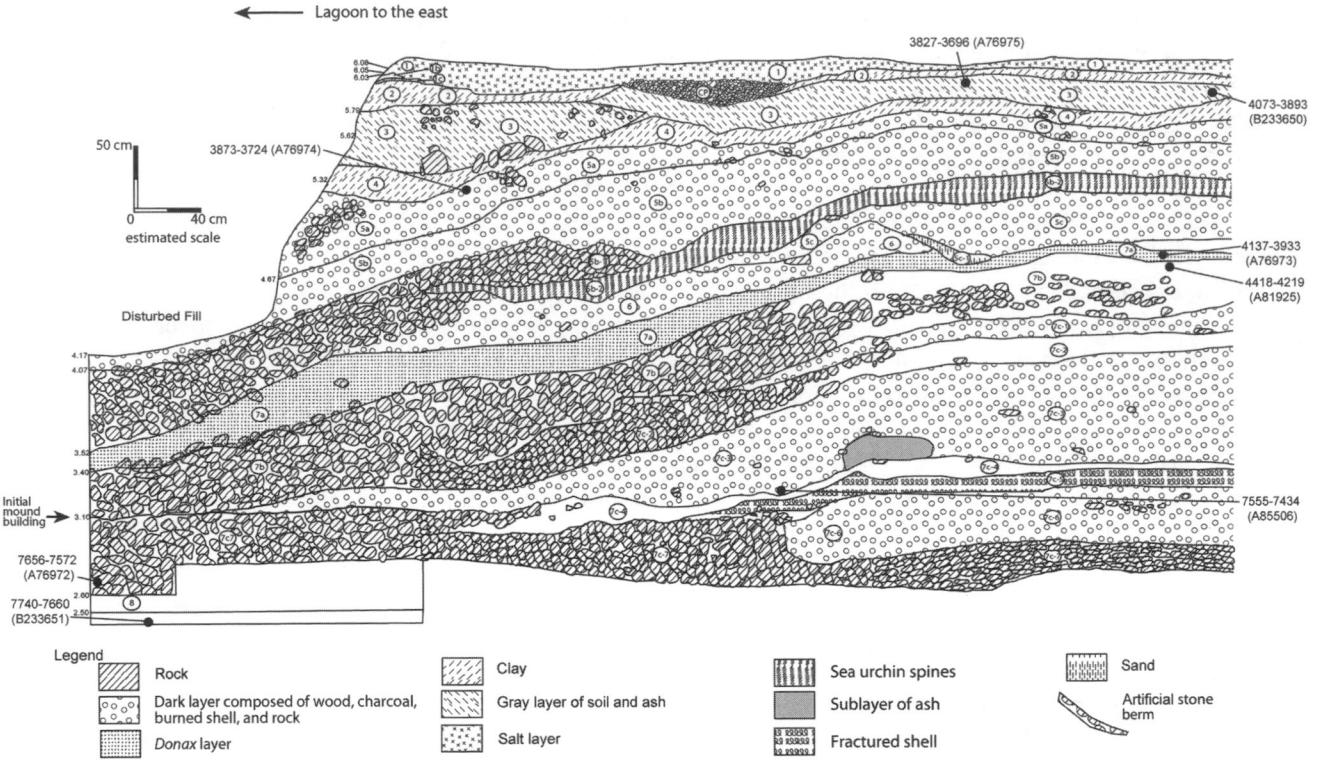

Lagoon to the east →

3827-3696 (A76975)

3873-3724 (A76974)

4073-3893 (B233650)

50 cm

0   40 cm
estimated scale

Disturbed Fill

4137-3933 (A76973)
4418-4219 (A81925)

Initial
mound
building →

7555-7434 (A85506)

7656-7572 (A76972)

7740-7660 (B233651)

Legend

Rock

Dark layer composed of wood, charcoal, burned shell, and rock

Donax layer

Clay

Gray layer of soil and ash

Salt layer

Sea urchin spines

Sublayer of ash

Fractured shell

Sand

Artificial stone berm

FIGURE 7.8. Profile of the west wall of Unit 2 with radiocarbon dates.

continuity; the upper third displayed more continuity as the slope of the mound increased in elevation toward the west.

H#301 and H#302 formed the surface of the profile. H#301 mostly consisted of soil fill with a few rocks and burned and unburned sea urchin spines. It was not continuous across the profile and terminated in a floor layer (H#408) at the bottom, where it connected with H#302, which was continuous across most of the profile. H#302 was composed mainly of burned sea urchin spines, with a few snail shells, shell fragments, and burned rock. H#409, the base of H#302, was continuous across the profile. The next layer with lateral continuity was H#330, a soil fill interspersed with fragments of matting, rock, and shell (H#407). Above H#330 was a series of thin stone berms (H#329, H#358, H#328, and H#356), each of which extended into all columns, yet none of which was completely continuous across the profile. H#357 cut across all columns and consisted of whole or fragmented shells. These layers alternated with thin prepared and unprepared floors and unprepared use surfaces (H#438, H#435, and H#433), all continuous across the majority

of the profile, while H#437 and H#432 extended across it.

Multiple stone berms of the type described for the HP-3 unit existed throughout the middle to lower profile, all of varying sizes. At 2–4 m in length, the smallest included H#359, H#354, and H#384. H#303, H#309, and H#331 were larger, cutting across multiple columns. These berms mark the beginning of mound building around 7500 cal BP and were placed on the steepest slope angle on the southeast side of the terrace. The thickest layer is H#318, a relatively uniform mixture of vegetal fibers, shells, and charcoal. Forming the base of H#318 is a series of micro-layers (H#320), a feature that continues in the middle column as H#333 and H#360 and extends into the southernmost column as H#369. The layers forming H#333 contained textile fragments.

Two layers exhibited vertical features. H#388 is a rectangular section in H#375, which contained wood. H#399 is a posthole. H#316 includes H#317, which appears to be a feature. This feature contains mammal bone, fish vertebrae, burned rock, shells, and lithics. Concentrated fills of shell compose the remaining layers, H#401, H#377,

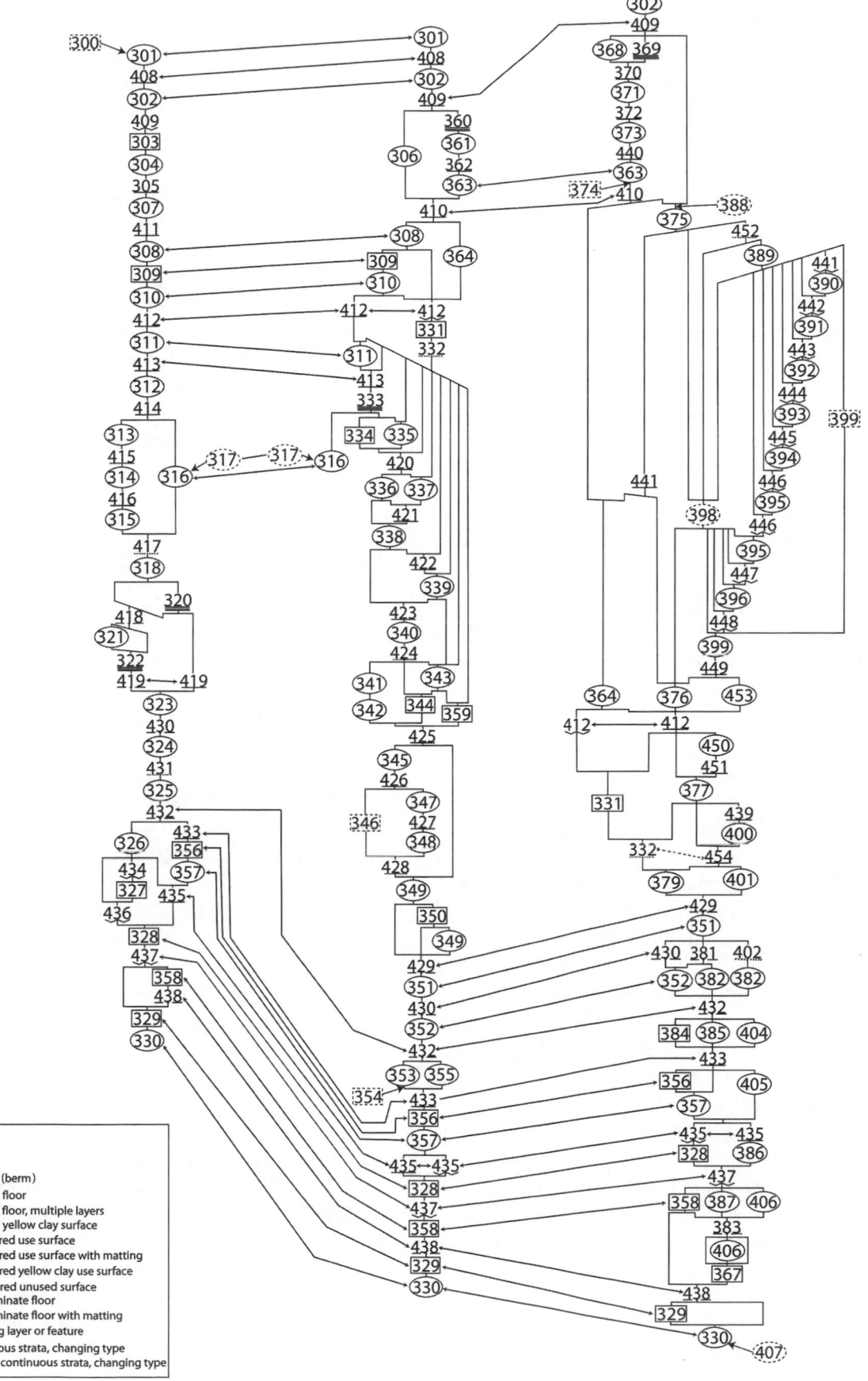

FIGURE 7.9. Harris Matrix of the east wall of Unit 2.

and H#376. Finally, a few continuous strata are observed in the upper and lower portions of the profile as opposed to the more spatially circumscribed strata seen in Units HP-3 and 20.

Layer Descriptions for Unit 2

Layer 1, ~0–0.20 m: The soil texture is compact. The layer was divided by intrusive rocks about 1.5 m wide and oriented north to south. Materials were shell, fish bones, sea urchin remains, and a copper spindle weight. It also includes plant remains in a reddened soil (2.5YR 4/1).

Layers 2–3, ~0.20–0.34 m: The soil is semicompact with lenses of a yellowish clay (10YR 8/6). Materials were shell and bone.

Layer 4, ~0.34–0.42 m: The soil is semicompact with clay; a pit exists in the west side of the unit where lumps of clay are mixed with organic fill. Materials include three Cupisnique sherds and broken shells.

Layer 5a–b1, ~0.42–1.30 m: The soil texture was soft to semicompact and dark (10YR 2/1) due to charcoal and ash. The layer contained isolated fire-reddened rocks and abundant shell, bone, and burned sea urchin spines. This layer was divided into Layers 5B, 5B1, and 5B2, characterized by micro-layers of burned rock with a large quantity of shell, sea urchin remains, and bone.

Layer 5b2, ~1.30–1.38 m: This is a feature with abundant shell and sea urchin remains associated with the rim of a late Moche jar.

Layer 5c–c1, ~1.38–1.65 m: The soil is sand. The layer contains two Moche jars and small mineral beads, bone, and shell.

Layer 6a–d, ~1.65–1.81 m: The soil is semicompact to soft, with a concentration of rocks, and a light gray to greenish yellow sediment (10YR 7/1). In places the soil is reddish in tone (2.5YR 5/3) with burned rock. Materials found are bone, shell, burned rock, wood, charcoal, gourd fragments, a plain sherd, and burned clay.

Layer 7a–b, ~1.81–2.62 m: The soil texture is semicompact and dark (10YR 2/1). Layer 7b is dense with shell, particularly *Donax* sp., and cobblestones forming the first berm layer for initial mound building in this area of the site. Bone and lithics also were recovered. A concentration of rock diminishes to the west. Materials are shell, charcoal, bone, lithics, and basket fragments.

Layer 7c1–4, ~2.62–3.25 m: Layer 7c is complex, with several sublayers down to the level of the lagoon. A thin rock layer is designated Layer 7c3. Layer 7c4 is a humid, compact soil, dark (10YR 2/1), with burned rock and abundant broken shell, bone, and lithics.

Layer 7c5–6, ~3.25–3.43 m: The soil is semicompact and dark (10YR 2/1). This layer is a shell fill. Materials are shell, bone, and lithics.

Layer 7c7–8, ~3.43–3.95 m: Layer 7c7 is a rock fill with loose, soft white clay (5YR 8/1). Materials recovered are rock, bone, shell, and charcoal. Below is a culturally sterile lens. Layer 7c8 continues to an unknown depth. Layer 8 contains several thin habitational lenses (Layers 8a–g) between 0.5 and 1.1 cm in thickness that blend into the culturally sterile carbonate clay of the lagoon.

In summary, the deeper layers of Unit 2 represent premound habitation by maritime and terrestrial foragers on the shoreline of the old lagoon lying east of the terrace during the early to middle Holocene period (see chapter 5). Afterward, this area was used for initial mound activity, with occasional placement of stone berms to prevent soil erosion in this steeper terrace area. It is not well understood why mound building began ~7500 years ago. It apparently was associated with nonmortuary rituals taking place along the eastern edge of the terrace, as suggested by the absence of hearths in Unit 2, the basal levels of Unit 9 and Test Pit 22 (discussed later) about this same time, and perhaps by the appearance of opposing sets of marine resources collected from different biozones (see chapter 9). These may have been simply rituals associated with foraging activities or social gatherings.

HP Unit 3: This 6 by 8 m unit was excavated on the eastern upper slope of the mound adjacent to and connected with the south side of Unit HP-3. Its placement revealed the southern extension of retention walls nos. 1–2 excavated by Bird along the northeast face of the mound. The stratigraphy (fig. 7.10) demonstrated at least two major episodes of wall extensions. Multiple applications of plaster repair also were documented. This unit was composed of several thick layers of floors, fills, and imbricated plaster coverings that served as retention surfaces to prevent erosion (fig. 7.11a).

Layer 1, ~.0–0.5 m: The matrix is a thick, compact plaster (15–30 cm thick), with loose soil

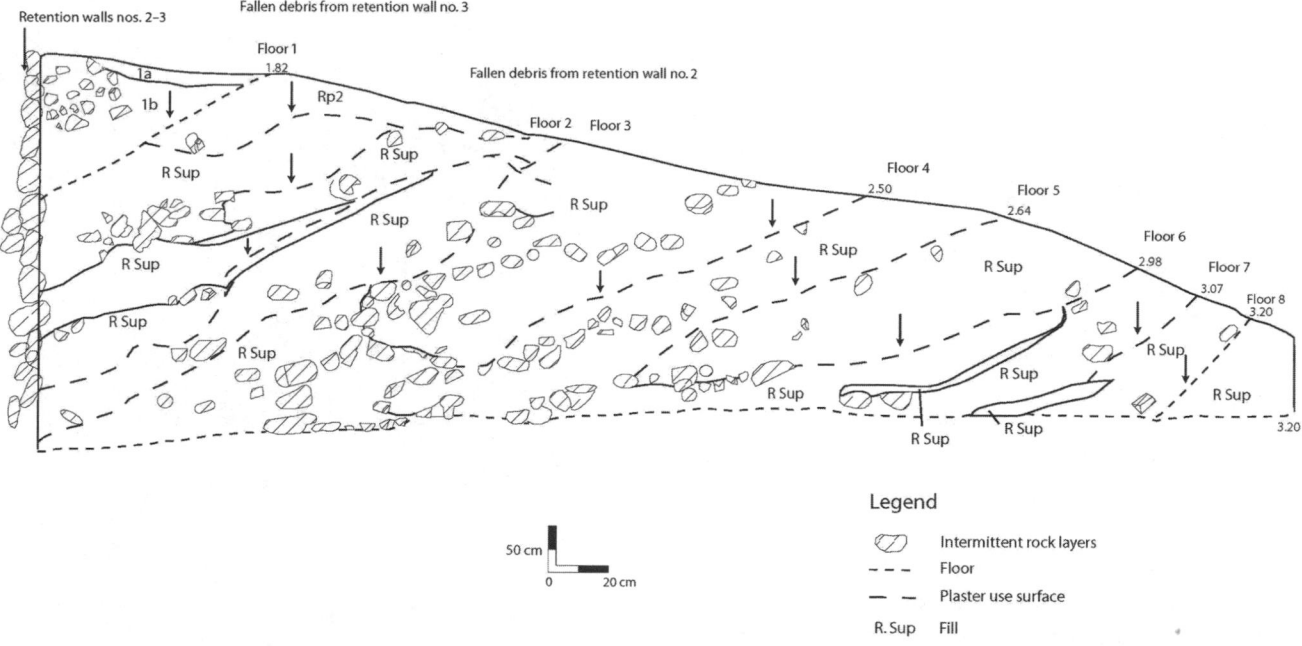

FIGURE 7.10. Profile of the east wall of Unit 3, showing floors, plaster surfaces, and fills. Note the declining plaster floor surfaces (*arrows*).

mixed with shell, burned rock, sand, and rocks. Large blocks of compact sediment and pockets of organic matter (for example, fragmentary shell, bone, plant materials), textile fragments, and reeds were also recovered. In the southwest corner was a row of large rocks set vertically, which was the southern continuation of Bird's retention wall no. 3. Pieces of folded textile fragments were excavated throughout the unit. Imbricated shingle-like sections of compact plaster composed the upper retention surface. A ^{14}C sample was assayed at 3849–3636 cal BP (AA76977).

Layer 1a, ~.0.5–0.95 m: The matrix is heterogeneous, with a loose soil mixed of rocks. Materials are rock, bone, shell, burned rock, wood, and charcoal. The soil is compact and forms Floor 1.

Layer 1b, ~.0.95–1.14 m: This is a layer of loose soil. Underneath is a compact layer of broken shell. A row of aligned rocks continues into the HP-3 trench above retention wall no. 3. Small rocks placed in a 40 cm wide semicircle are associated with the scattered remains of a child (see appendices 10 and 14).

Layer 1c, ~1.14–1.57 m: The soil is semicompact. Materials are rock, bone, shell, charcoal, bird bones, and plant remains. One reed mat is associated with rocks and plant remains, representing an offering of chile peppers, beans, and the

FIGURE 7.11. Unit 3: *a*, shingled layers of plaster (*arrows*); *b*, two whole bundles of reeds containing fragments of textiles and other materials, found at the corner of a zigzag pathway on ramp (*arrows point to knots*).

lucuma fruit placed in a small hole. This is Feature 1.

Feature 1, ~1.20 m: Feature 1 corresponds to Plasters 1 and 2 and the corner of a zigzag path. The soil is loose and ashy gray (2.5Y 4/2). Burned stones are associated with the burned sea urchin spines, human bone remains, reed mats, textiles, and a whole gourd with *Phaseolus* sp. seeds, all of which were offerings. The textiles were cut and folded (see chapter 12, part I).

The stratigraphic sequence of the feature is given below.

Base: Burned rocks placed under reed mats and a whole gourd with beans and chile peppers; placed over these were textiles and then sea cucumbers, seashells, sea urchin spines, and gourd fragments. The two reed mats are oriented northeast to southwest and resting on a worn zigzag footpath to the top of the mound near the upper part of retention wall no. 2. The mats lie over burned rocks and are associated with two unburned gourds. Textile fragments lie around the mats on burned rocks or on the edge of the mats. Three textiles are associated with Feature 1. Human hair, a temporal bone, and a mastoid bone from a human skull were found with Feature 1 (see appendix 10).

Layer 2, ~1.57–3.04 m: The matrix is heterogeneous with loose soil mixed with rock, bone, shell, wood, and charcoal. A layer of compact clay is Floor 2. In the northwest corner of retention wall no. 2 were large stones joined by a mortar of loose soil, plants, and shells. In the center of the unit was a large pelvic bone of a whale associated with rocks. Floors 2 and 3 are on the south side and Floors 4 and 5 on the lower north side. The floors are compact, dark brown (10YR 2/1), and mixed with fragments of shell and rocks. A worn zigzag path from the northwest to the southeast exists across Floor 5. A ^{14}C sample was assayed at 3901–3643 cal BP (AA76978).

Layer 3, ~3.04–3.16 m: The soil matrix is loose and mixed with rock and organic materials. In some sectors there are thin lenses of mortar with shell, rock, bone, wood, and charcoal. Large rocks form a wall of 1 to 1.2 m in height. This structure appears to be part of a staircase or entry ramp accessing the top of the mound.

Layer 4a, ~3.16–4.16 m: The layer is irregular and has a compact texture with shell, wood,

FIGURE 7.12. Section of a worn zigzag pathway on access ramp in Unit 3.

charcoal, and a green rock painted with red dots. A thick light gray (10YR 7/1) plaster covers the layer.

Layer 5, ~4.16–4.34 m: Numerous fragments of reed were concentrated in the southwest side. Materials recovered were shell, burned rock, wood, reed, charcoal, burned daub, and ground shell. Sea urchin spines and cobbles with percussion marks were found in small piles (10–23 cm wide) at the corners or turns of a zigzag path throughout the unit. Traces of a thick plaster surface represent a floor associated with a large whalebone.

Layers 6 and 7, ~4.34–5.22 m: This layer consists of loose soil placed between reed mats and Floors 6 and 7. It is a dark greenish gray (2.5YR 4/1). Materials recovered from Floor 6, which included a zigzag path, were two reed and textile bundles associated with fragments of wood, shell, gourd, and charcoal, all deposited at a southward turning corner of the path (figs. 7.11b and

7.12). Burial HP09-07 was recovered from Layer 7 (extension Unit 3N). A ^{14}C sample assayed was 4216–3901 cal BP (AA76979).

Layer 8, ~5.22–5.87 m: Layer 8 is composed of loose soil between reed mats. The soil is a dark greenish gray (2.5YR 4/1). Materials recovered were sea urchin spines, mussels, shell fragments, snails, and plant fibers. Fragments of shell and sea urchin spines were placed over a human burial in the northwest corner and associated with small piles of textiles, reed mats, red stains, and burned rocks. Floor 8 was later documented. A ^{14}C sample assayed was 4520–4245 cal BP (Beta 247695).

Eight prepared floors were defined in this unit. Gourd fragments, fragmentary shell, and charcoal were concentrated in small piles across all floors, especially where zigzag paths make turns north or south. Floors 1 and 2 have a fine-texture of a dark grayish brown (10YR 3/2). Floor 2 had fragments of mussel shells, snails, and fragmentary reeds. Materials recovered were shell, burned rock, wood, charcoal, and reeds. Numerous sea urchin spines and fish vertebrae were mixed in reddish stains. Floor 3 is compact and associated with reed mats, shells, snail shells, and loose soil. Feature 1 is composed of human bones and other remains associated with Floor 3. Floor 4 has a fine texture of a very dark grayish brown (10YR 3/2). This is a hardened surface compacted with broken shell and charcoal. Floor 5 is a compact plaster. It is 4–6 cm thick in most places and nearly absent in others, especially where the soil is loose with reed mats. A worn zigzag path from the northwest to the southeast is seen across the floor. Feature 2 is associated with this path. Floor 6 is compact and a grayish green (2.5YR 4/2). Materials recovered were rock, bone, shell, burned rock, wood, and charcoal. The floor also is associated with a plaster covering. Floor 7 is a soft, loose soil. It is a grayish green (2.5YR 5/2). Materials recovered were rock, bone, shell, burned rock, wood, gourd, and charcoal. Floor 7 was associated with textile fragments on top of reed mats that follow a northwest to southeast directional pattern, which is the same orientation found in Floor 5, indicating a prior zigzag path from the lower to the higher slope of the mound (fig. 7.12). Floor 8 is compact and loose. There is a partial human burial on a compact grayish green (2.5YR 4/2) and red (10YR 4/3) soil. Materials recovered were bone, shell, burned rock, wood, gourd, and charcoal. A textile was placed over the head of the burial.

In summary, several truncated and prepared plaster floors and unprepared use surfaces, fills, and three paths highlight this unit, indicating disturbance, reuse, and resurfacing. The plaster surfaces were layered like a shingled roof cover that generally descended in a stair-step form, as if they were poured from a container and thickly flowed and slowly dried downslope. Pockets of loose soil reveal areas where the shingled layering did not fully cover the former surface, giving the impression of a rapid build-up of the plaster surfaces. Although these layers are oriented downslope, their outer 1–2 m long edges angle upward between 25–35 degrees, an architectural technique seemingly to prevent downslope erosion of mound layers (see fig. 7.3). This technique was developed during early Phase IV and replaced the cobblestone berm, haystacking footings to hold layers in place. (A similar technique was excavated in Unit 10 for this phase.)

On these floors and plaster coverings were numerous broken shells, fragments of reed, sea urchin spines, offerings of crop foods, and scattered cobbles of burned quartzite. Most floors were associated with stratigraphically distinct zigzag paths up and down the entry ramp. There are features deposited on reed mats, fragmented shells, and torn textiles stacked in an order. The reed mats and folded textiles mark a path with offerings up the east side of the mound's entry ramp. The offerings were almost always placed where the paths turn to the north or the south.

The southwest corner contains extensions of the plaster overlying loose soil and reed mats as well as thick plaster surfaces that run up against the retention walls (nos. 2–3) to the west. This suggests that the walls were used as an anchor surface to attach the plaster and vice versa (the plaster preventing erosion of the walls). The plaster layer in this area is constructed of a succession of microlayers (2–5 cm thick) as revealed in stratigraphic cuts, suggesting multiple reuse and retention episodes. Several individual events are associated with the plaster surfaces: (1) these surfaces are associated with all floors, which are thin (1–2 cm thick) and segmented horizontally in the border of contact with retention walls; (2) reeds and shells are part of the fill between the floors and at the same time a component of the plaster; (3) the continuity of plaster in an area where the slope is between 25° and 40° is considered a retention surface; and (4) the layer of reeds indicates at least four depositional episodes of plaster associated with individual ritual events in which offerings of textiles and reed mats coincide with the deposition of the plaster and with the loose soil fills and thin floors. This was a complex unit with multiple surfaces and floors that were horizontally and vertically circumscribed spatially, which is indicative of numerous individual ephemeral events, all likely related to ritual offerings.

HP Unit 4: This unit was 2 by 4 m and placed farther downslope from Unit 3 to test whether zigzag paths existed there.

Layer 1–2, ~0–0.6 m: The soil texture was compact with a prepared floor between 10 and 15 cm thick. We found much charcoal, vertically placed wooden stakes, and several Cupisnique ceramics.

Layer 3, ~0.6–1.7 m: This is a sandy layer with broken shells and burned rock.

Layer 4, ~1.7–2.3 m: This is a compact layer with cultural debris and rock, which seems to have been used to level the area for an unknown purpose. Feature 1, a partial secondary and disturbed burial, is in this layer.

Layer 5a–d, ~2.3–2.8 m: These are a series of relatively thin fills and layers (each 2–7 cm thick) that revealed no specific function. A segment of a path was discovered at the 2.4 m level.

Unit 4 reveals a 3 m section of a diagonally worn path across a hard plaster, suggesting the presence of a zigzag path associated with Layer 5, Phase V, in Unit 3. Unit 4 also consisted of fill deposits and mottled wash deposits. Fill deposits were laminated (1–3 cm thick) and ran downslope west to east.

Feature 1: This is a tomb covered with plaster but heavily looted; it had offerings of shells and small snails. The body was placed on a textile 1 m long and 0.5 m wide. The skull has the remains of red pigment on the right side. The tomb is covered with a mat, as evidenced by fragments of reed.

HP Unit 5: This unit was located on the northeast face of the mound for the same purpose as Unit 4.

The soil texture is a mixture of shells, sand, gravel, and cultural materials. This unit had eight superimposed layers and five prepared floors. The floors are thin and not uniform horizontally. Floor 1 is composed of soil and shell fragments. Floor 2 is heterogeneous and has large rocks in the center. Floor 3 contains a thin layer of reddened rocks. Floor 4 is a slight U-shaped depression that corresponds to a Phase V zigzag path on the entry ramp. Floor 5 had shell and plant remains as offerings.

HP Unit 6: Unit 6 was located on the northeast slope of the mound for the same reasons as Units 4–5.

Layer 1, Floor 1, ~0–0.85 m: The soil texture is a fine yellow (10YR 8/6) and light gray (10YR 7/1). Fragments of Cupisnique pottery and cloth were recovered. An offering of corncobs was recovered from a shallow pit.

Layer 2, Floor 2, ~0.85–1.66 m: This surface extends throughout the unit as a crusty sand and salt with cobblestones. In the southwest corner, at ~40 cm, is a thick plaster layer with reed mats and cloth, all mixed with animal bones, gourd fragments, and charcoal. A 2 m section of a zigzag path was observed at the 1.4 m level. An offering of 168 corncobs was located in a shallow pit where the footpath turns to the southwest. One unworked piece of copper sulfate was found on the path.

HP Unit 7: This unit had the same purpose as Units 4–6.

Two use surfaces were detected, and one floor was defined with evidence for a structure with a foundation of large stones. The structure was partially dismantled and mixed with a semicompact plaster. Floor 1 is compact plaster that has a slightly worn path, suggestive of a segment of a zigzag footpath to the top of the mound.

Use Surfaces ~1–2, 0–2.1 m: The first use surface was associated with shells and small areas of ash mixed with hard pieces of plaster, as if an earlier plaster had been broken up and scattered. The second use surface is hard mortar overlying a gray sand (10YR 7/1). Use surface 1 was dated at 4072–3727 cal BP (AA76970).

HP Unit 8: The objective of excavating this unit was to clean the south sector where the sunken circular plaza is located. The excavation began with 10 cm layers in the south rim of the hole where aligned stones formed visible walls thought to be small tomb structures (fig. 7.1). One structure was excavated to a depth of 1.3 m, where an intact human skeleton was recovered that dated to Phase V (see chapter 8, HP08-01).

Feature 1: Only one feature was recovered, about 30 cm outside of the tomb to the north. It consisted of an offering of 20 coca leaves deposited in a small hole ~20 cm in diameter and 5 cm in depth. The majority of the leaves were whole.

The tomb was constructed of cobblestones, with two vertical stones supported by others laid in flat brick-like rows (fig. 7.13a–b). A plaster was used to hold the stones in place. Tomb 8 and others around the rim of the sunken plaza are semicircular or half-moon chamber tombs rather than completely circular ones like those found in Units 10 and 23. The aperture faces the center of the sunken circular plaza. The termini points of the tombs facing the center are often characterized by large vertically placed cobblestones. The area around the tomb was a thick plaster. A ^{14}C date on the skeleton was 3892–3590 cal BP (AA81916).

HP Unit 9: This unit lies south of Unit 2 on the lower skirt of the eastern edge of Huaca Prieta. This unit was placed to search for additional evidence of premound use of the eastern side of the Sangamon terrace. The lower layers yielded intermittent premound human activity of the late Pleistocene and early Holocene periods (see chapter 6 and Dillehay et al. 2012a). The feature type and brief description for Unit 9 are presented in table 6.3.

Layer 1, ~0–0.80 m: The soil is compact and a dark brown (10YR 2/1). Materials recovered were rock, reed mat fragments, bone, shell, burned rock, and charcoal. At the bottom of Layer 1 two concentrations of burned areas were recovered. Early Holocene ^{14}C dates for the deeper levels of Unit 9 were presented in chapter 6; Stratum 7 at the top of the unit dated to 3876–3640 cal BP (AA81922).

Layers 2–5, ~0.80–4.6 m: This is a compact sandy layer composed of cobbles, shell fragments, bone, and a few lithics of basalt. Each layer is separated by slight changes in the color and texture of sands ranging from dull yellowish brown (10YR 4/3) in Layers 2 and 3 to a grayish brown (7.5YR 4/2) to a very dark brown (7.5YR 2/3) in Layers 4 and 5. All layers contain varying amounts of shell, bone, vegetal, reed mat fragments, and lithic

debris. The base of Layer 5 yielded one unworked piece of copper sulfate.

Layer 6, ~4.6–5.1 m: This is a layer with thin charcoal lenses associated with shell, bone, lithics, and charcoal. Thin, intermittent layers 30 cm underneath the early Holocene levels contain shell fragments, lithic debris, reed mat and basket fragments, and ash similar in texture and stratigraphy to the early Holocene and late Pleistocene lenses excavated in Units 2, 12, 15/21, and 22. The lenses are 1–2 cm thick and represent small, circumscribed burning and probably food preparation episodes (fig. 7.14). Below this layer is a culturally sterile, whitish gray clay (10YR 8/2) situated at the edge of the old lagoon east of the terrace.

This unit contained radiocarbon-dated early Holocene materials more fully described in chapters 6, 9, 10, and 11 (see Dillehay et al. 2012a).

HP Unit 10: This unit was opened to test the middle slopes of the eastern side of the mound, which showed large horizontal cracks suggesting hollow areas below the mound's plaster surface (these cracks can also be seen on the west side of the mound: see dark spots above Bird's HP-2 excavation in fig. 17, Bird et al. 1985). Excavation revealed that the cracks are associated with unattached tomb structures underneath thick plaster coatings over this section of the mound. The unit is described in terms of several extensions due to its vertical and horizontal complexity. Three major layers, each with sublayers labeled as a1, a2, b1, b2, c1–7, and so forth were defined and associated with small chamber tombs. The profiles of all walls are shown in fig. 7.15; they do not reveal all strata discussed below because some appear and reappear in circumscribed vertical and horizontal dimensions. Figure 7.16 shows a plan view of the excavation extensions, structures, and features in Unit 10.

Layers 1a–c, ~0–0.35 m: The soil texture is semicompact with shell, stones, and charcoal. Materials recovered were shell, bone, gourds, and plants.

Four floor segments were excavated in the northwest extension near a tomb wall. Floor 1 was compact in texture with little fill and consisted of several thinner subfloors (a–c). Floor 2 was compact and dark brown (10YR 2/1). Materials were shell, bone, and organics (offerings of plant materials and charcoal). Floor 3 was compact and

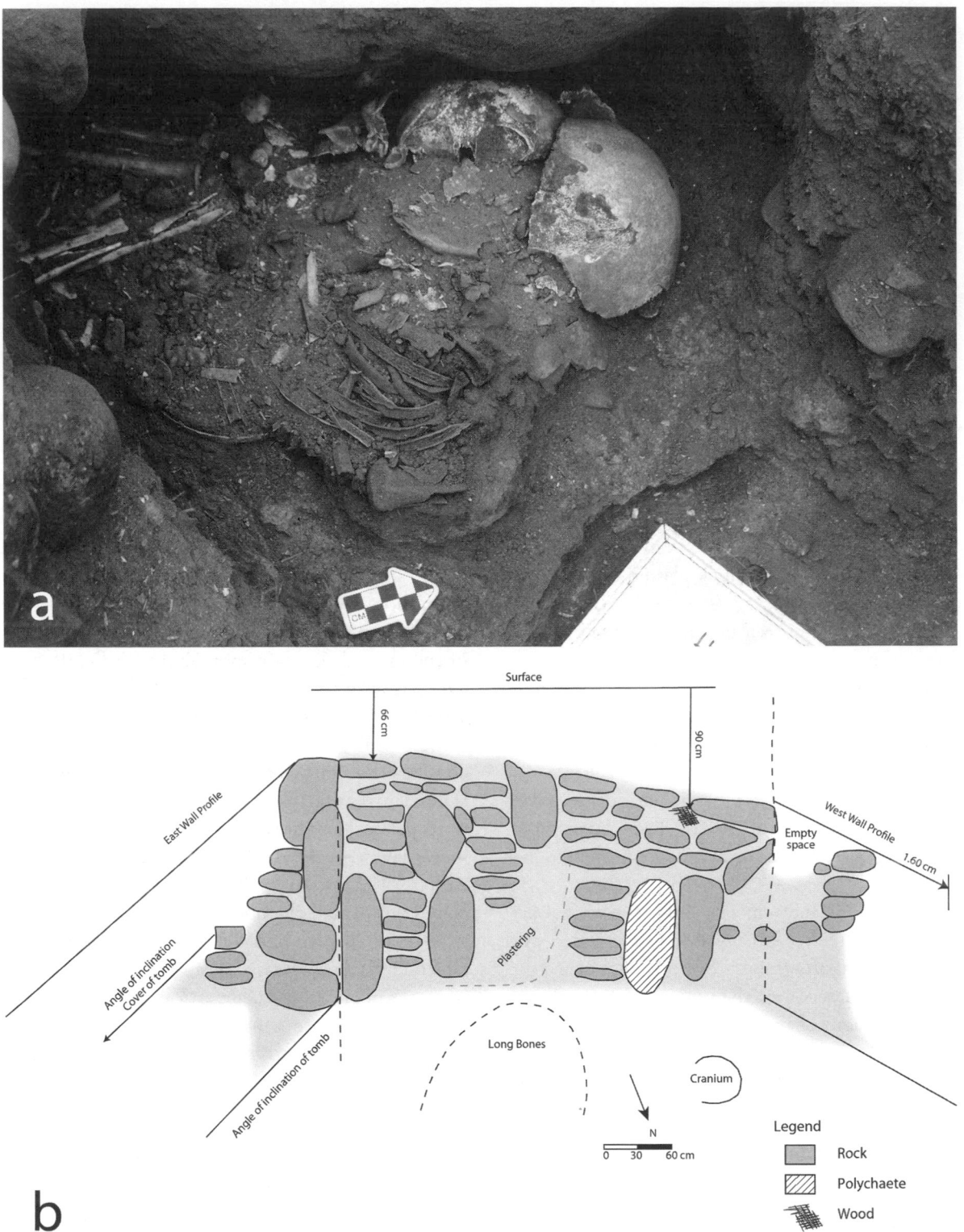

FIGURE 7.13. *a*, photograph of burial HP08-01 on the south rim of the sunken circular plaza; *b*, cobblestone architecture of Tomb 8 containing HP08-01 on the rim of the circular plaza.

FIGURE 7.14. Burned area (*arrow*) showing ash and charcoal in Layer 6 in Unit 9.

light olive brown (2.5YR 6/3). Materials include shell and other organics. Floor 4 is a stone wall emerging from under Floor 3.

Layer 2, ~0.35–0.80 m: The soil texture is compact. Materials recovered were bone, shell, sea urchin spines, plant remains, and charcoal. This layer is a light gray (10YR 7/1). Remnants of previous stone walls were observed in the north end.

Southwest (SW) Extension:

Layer 1, ~0.10–0.40 m: The soil is loose. Materials were shell, bone, and organic matter. A wall section runs diagonally from north to southwest.

Layers 2–3, ~0.40–0.80 m: The soil texture is semicompact and a milky gray (10YR 7/1). Many sublayers were found, associated with a sequence of many individual burning episodes ranging from light olive brown (2.5YR 6/3) to grayish white to gray (10YR 7/1). In the lower part of Layer 2 part of a circular wall was exposed.

Extensions SW-1 and 2:

Layer 1, ~0–0.47 m: The soil texture is loose,

with two accumulations of cobblestones in the fill. One is part of a circular wall and the other is part of a collapsed wall.

Layer 2, ~0.47–0.59 m: This layer has lenses of differently colored ash, which suggests a series of different burning events. The cultural remains were shell and animal bone.

Extension SW-3:

Layers 1–2, ~0–0.65 m: Shell, bone, plant materials, and lithics were recovered. Two circular structures were exposed. Structure 1 is 2.1 by 2.7 m in size, with irregular walls, which vary in width from 20 to 30 cm. Structure 2 is 1.80 by 1.80 m; walls vary between 20 and 30 cm in width. Both structures are built of cobblestones and blocks of polychaete blocks (see chapter 9). A compact plaster was used in the wall construction for the foundation and also as a roof to seal the tombs.

Features 1–6: Features are small individual pockets of shell (*Semele* sp.) on the floor of struc-

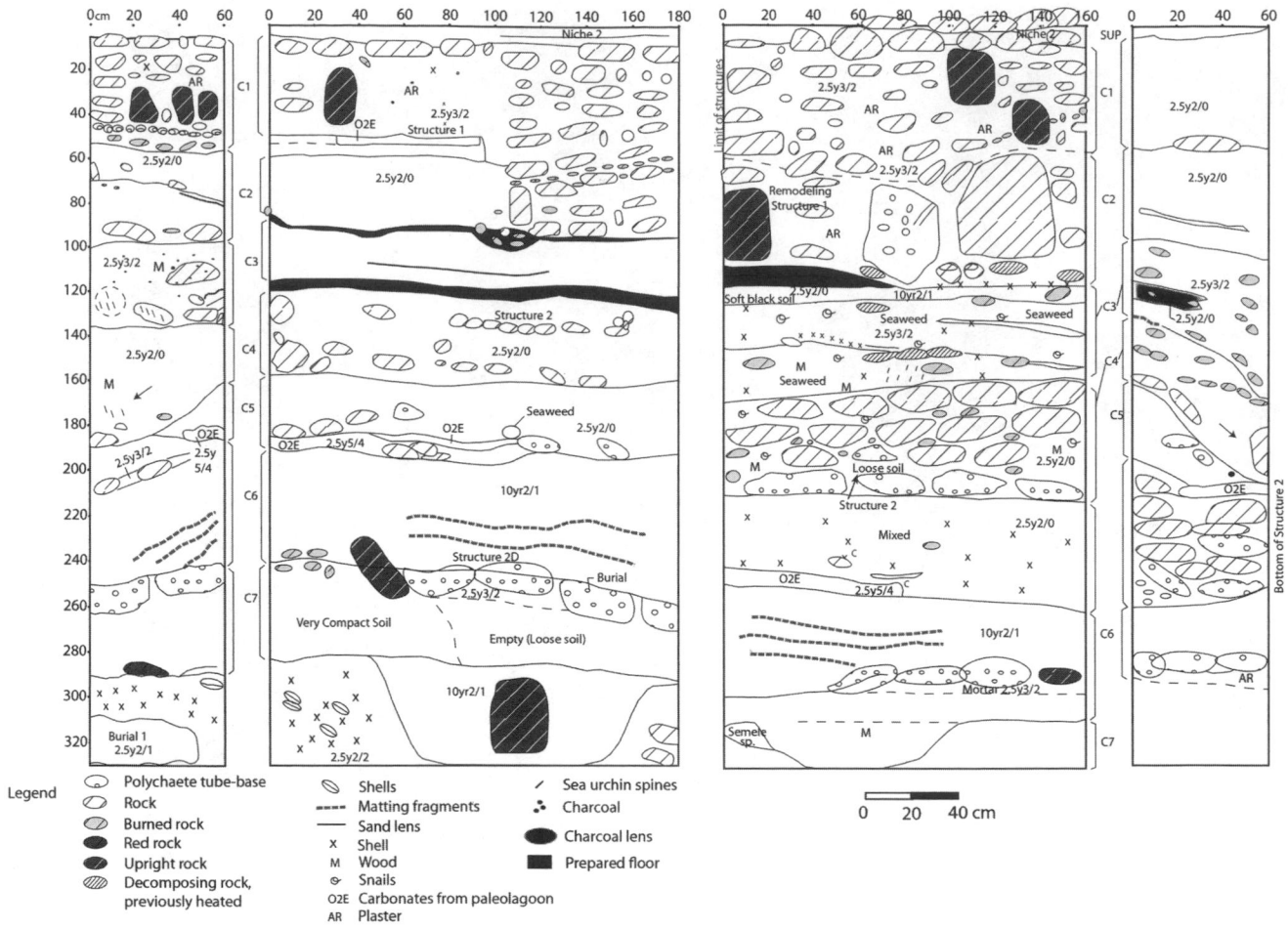

FIGURE 7.15. Profile of tomb walls and other structures in Unit 10. The two middle columns are west wall profiles; the two outer ones are north and south wall profiles, from right to left.

tures that represent funerary offerings. One adult skeleton and an infant (see chapter 8, HP09-09 and HP09-09A) were recovered in Structure 1 (fig. 7.17a–b; see chapter 8). The infant's body was in a fetal position. Some bones had shreds of textile attached, suggesting wrapping. Placed around the body were rocks of different sizes and a pocket of *Semele* sp. shells. Nearby were the remains of fragmented reed mats, which had covered the burial; the remains of reeds and wood also were found in the fill of the grave. Soil was mixed with shell, fish bones, plant remains, and charcoal. Feature 1 was a shell offering in Structure 1. Feature 2 was an offering of *Semele* sp. shell in an otherwise empty Structure 2. Feature 3 consists of shells on a prepared floor at 0.67 m. Features 4–6 at 0.78 to 0.85 m in depth contained *Semele* sp. shells. The burials dated to late Phase IV.

In summary, Unit 10 is a complex of numerous small complete and incomplete circular structures, prepared and unprepared floors, use surfaces, and other layers situated on a ledge overlooking the lower slopes of the eastern side of the mound. The structures have no entryways, and only one has burials. They are not dwellings because they are too small and only 1–1.2 m deep. They also cannot be storage structures because nothing but one adult skeleton and a fetus and/or *Semele* sp. shell offerings were found in them, in small deliberate piles. The structures are chamber tombs, as suggested by their form and the offerings of shells. One empty tomb and portions of others, which had been modified, were left open; plaster roofs sealed others. Lying underneath the structures were several partially reused and/or destroyed small, circumscribed use surfaces and tomb floors, often associated with heavily fractured plaster surfaces. The exposed wall segments and loose rock

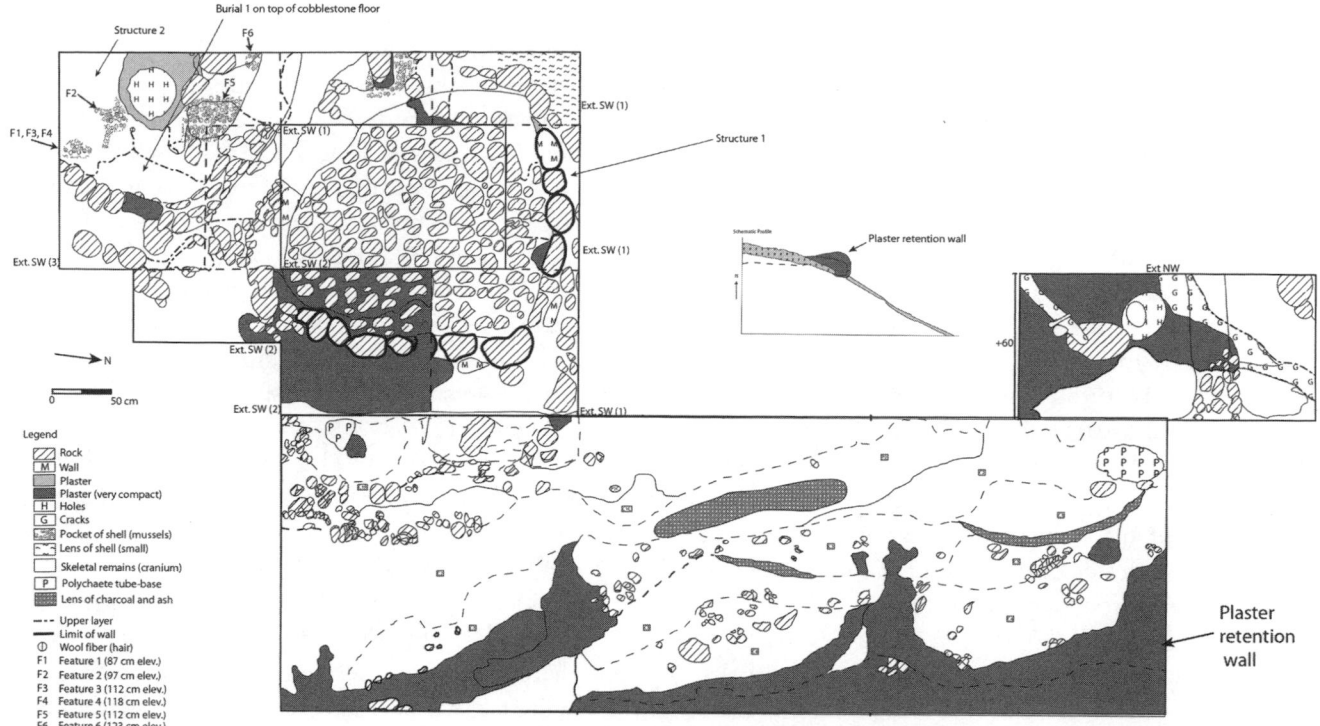

FIGURE 7.16. Plan view of excavation extensions, structures, and plaster retention wall in Unit 10.

piles also appear to represent a sequence of super-imposed structures, floors, and use surfaces that had been partially dismantled to build Structures 1 and 2. The disposition of these segments and the complete structures suggest reuse of both the space and the materials (such as stones). The base of Structure 2 was radiocarbon dated to 3895–3640 cal BP (AA81923). Floor 4 just above the base was dated to 3891–3642 cal BP (AA81919). Finally, once Unit 10 was constructed, a plaster wall was placed along its eastern edge to prevent erosion (see fig. 7.16).

HP Unit 11: This unit was excavated on the far north slope of the mound to search for the presence of a path to the top and to determine the function of this area. Portions of two structures similar to those observed in Unit 10 were recovered.

Layer 1, ~0–0.75 m: The soil texture was loose and dark gray (7YR 4/1) with charcoal, broken shell, and fishbone. A thick plaster is on the upper portion of two small stone structures, probably empty tombs similar to those in Units 10 and 23 and those excavated by Bird on top of the mound just west of his HP-3 trench (see Bird et al. 1985). The structures measure between 1.2 and 2.2 m in

FIGURE 7.17. Unit 10: *a*, two empty chamber tombs, Structures 1 and 2; *b*, Burial HP09-09 in Unit 10.

diameter and 1.3 m deep. We excavated the larger structure, which had a mortared roof. Nothing was found inside except for a few *Semele* sp. shells piled in one corner as a possible offering. It contained no skeleton.

Layer 2, ~0.75–1.5 m: This was the layer of the two partial structures.

There are two features present: an area of charcoal and ash and a wall segment.

Feature 1: The feature was a shallow lens of gray ash.

Feature 2: This is a stone wall with mortar. The wall is 30 cm high, 42 cm thick, and 2.4 m long.

No worn path was observed in this unit.

HP Unit 12: This unit had the same purpose as Unit 11, but the excavation was located on the south side of the mound. A series of floors and fills were found, but no path.

Floor 1, ~0–0.24 m: Floor 1 is compact and dark brown (10YR 2/1) with broken shells.

Floor 2, ~0.24–0.27 m: The soil texture is rough and a brownish gray (10YR 5/2). Materials recovered were shell and bone. This floor was dated to 3817–3480 cal BP (AA81929).

Floor 3, ~0.27–0.30 m: The floor is thick, with abundant shell. Materials recovered were shell, burned rock, and charcoal. The floor is dark gray (7YR 4/1) with a high quantity of charcoal and ash and a moderate amount of sea urchin spines, beans, peanuts and fruits, and shells placed in small piles. This floor was associated with a 2 m long rock alignment that demarcated a particular space.

No evidence of a footpath was observed.

There were twenty-three layers below Floor 3 that composed the bottom levels of the mound and an additional ~5.1 m of intermittent cultural deposits below the first mound layer, of which about 1.1 m extended into the natural surface of the Sangamon terrace. Layer 11 contained a bedding of juncus reeds and fragments of juncus matting. A charred matting fragment in Layer 11 (see chapter 12, part 2) dated to 11,159–10,600 cal BP (Beta235952).

HP Unit 14: This unit was excavated on the western edge of the entry ramp to search for a zigzag path. A series of floors and features and a possible segment of the path were discovered.

Floors 1–2, ~0.45–1.61 m: A thick plaster covers Floor 1, which is brownish gray (10YR 7/1) with broken shell. Floor 2 is grayish brown (10YR 5/2). The texture is compact. A well-preserved floor below this was designated Floor 2A. Materials were rocks, shell, and wood.

Four small pit features were associated with a worn path across Floor 2. The features seem to be offerings. Feature 1 was a spinal column of a large fish and burned rocks placed in a small pit (30 cm deep). Feature 2 was a deposit of shell with a gourd, also placed in a shallow pit (32 cm deep). Feature 3 consisted of *Semele* sp. shells with fragments of gourd placed in a small pit (18 cm deep). Feature 4 was a deposit of shells in a small pit (23 cm deep).

Floor 3, ~1.81 m: This floor is irregular with abundant plants. Feature 5 was a deposit of shell on the floor. A broken polished and grooved stone axe was recovered.

Floor 4, ~2.05 m: Floor 4 is brownish gray (10YR 7/1), slightly compact, with plant fibers, charcoal, and an offering of shells (fig. 7.21d below); at the base of this floor is a thin layer of fine, light olive brown soil (2.5YR 6/3). Burial 1, consisting of a few scattered human bones (see appendix 10), was below Floor 4 and was marked by a block of polychaete tubes. It is associated with plaster that forms the walls of a chamber tomb. The bones were partially covered by a textile. One ^{14}C sample was assayed at 3838–3588 cal BP (AA81921).

HP Unit 15: This unit was placed in the center of Bird's looter's pit, the sunken circular plaza on the south side of the mound, to define the stratigraphy there (fig. 7.18). Unit 15 was excavated within the spatial area of Unit 21, which was the larger excavation that exposed the stone architecture in the sunken circular plaza and below it the deeper first mound layer, which was ~5.6 m below the ground surface of the plaza area. The numbered strata in Unit 15 began at the base of Unit 21 at a depth of ~31.6 m below the highest point of the mound, where the first mound layer dated at 7474–7268 cal BP (see figs. 7.18–7.20). Thus the numbered strata of Unit 15 began at the first mound layer, at the base of Unit 21, at a depth of ~31.6 m below the ground surface of the plaza on top of the mound.

Soil texture was loose and varied from dark gray to dark brown (10YR 5/2). Materials were bone, burned rock, reed mat and basket fragments, charcoal, and lithics. The layer contained large and medium-sized rocks, which were found throughout in varying concentrations; the density of rocks was high, suggesting the presence of a disturbed or fallen structure. Material culture consisted of stone tools, burned rock, complete bird skeletons, shell, pieces of hardened white clay (5YR 8/1), fish vertebra, and a human skull fragment. This pit was taken to 8 m below the sunken surface of the plaza on the south side of the mound where late Pleistocene and early Holocene premound habitation lenses were recovered (see chapters 6, 9, and 11; Dillehay et al. 2012a). Several thin floors (1–2 cm thick) in the upper levels of this unit were excavated prior to probing deeper into the mound. These were prepared floors in the upper 40 cm of the initial Unit 15. The layers described below pertain to the later deeper probe into the mound.

Use Surfaces and Fills, Layers 1–3, ~0–.05 m (or ~5.6 m below ground surface): The soil texture is clayey and semicompact. The color is black (10YR 2/1). Materials were burned rock, reed mat fragments, and charcoal. Layer 1 is the base of the artificial mound as defined by stone berms and a rock layer (fig. 7.18). Layer 1 is dated at 7474–7268 cal BP (AA85507).

Use Surfaces and Fills, Layers 4–8, ~0.5–2.1 m: From 1.17 to 3.0 m in depth, the unit shows a fill of rocks interbedded with 13 intermittent thin layers (1–3 cm) of a fine clay sediment, which suggests a heterogeneous deposit of fills and thin use surfaces. The interface between Layers 4 and 5 is dated at 8156–7871 cal BP (AA75327).

Use Surfaces and Fills, Layers 9–13a, ~2.1–3.5 m: At the base of the unit is the disturbed surface of the Sangamon terrace that was associated with several thin habitation layers dating to the late Pleistocene to early Holocene periods. As discussed in chapter 6, these surfaces were associated with shell, bone, reed mat fragments, and lithic materials as well as with hearths and burned features indicative of early foragers. The interface between Layers 9 and 10 is dated at 13,420–13,260 cal BP (Beta290621).

Use Surfaces and Fills, Layers 14-base, ~3.5–4.1 m: These layers contained loose cultural debris of shell, undetermined bone fragments, reed mat fragments, and lithic debris, but none were associated with clear use surfaces and charcoal like those in Layers 9–13b. The base of this unit was the surface of the Sangamon terrace.

FIGURE 7.18. Strata in Unit 15, showing late Pleistocene and early Holocene levels and radiocarbon dates.

The interface between Layers 13 and 13a is dated at 13,794–13,459 cal BP (Beta299536); the upper part of Layer 13a is dated at 14,867–13,924 cal BP (Beta210272); and the lower part of Layer 13a is dated at ~14,530–13,891 cal BP (Beta310273).

HP Unit 17: This unit was excavated on the south end of the mound beyond the sunken circular plaza to test for additional chamber tombs. Several floors were recovered but no chamber tombs. Geophysical survey in the area also failed to reveal tombs (see appendix 15).

Floors 1–2 and Fills, ~.0–1.91 m: These are highly compacted black (2.5YR 2/0) floors with fragmented shells and pebbles. Floor 1 is a loose fill with charcoal, shells, and stones. Floor 2 is similar but has many sea urchin spines. Below

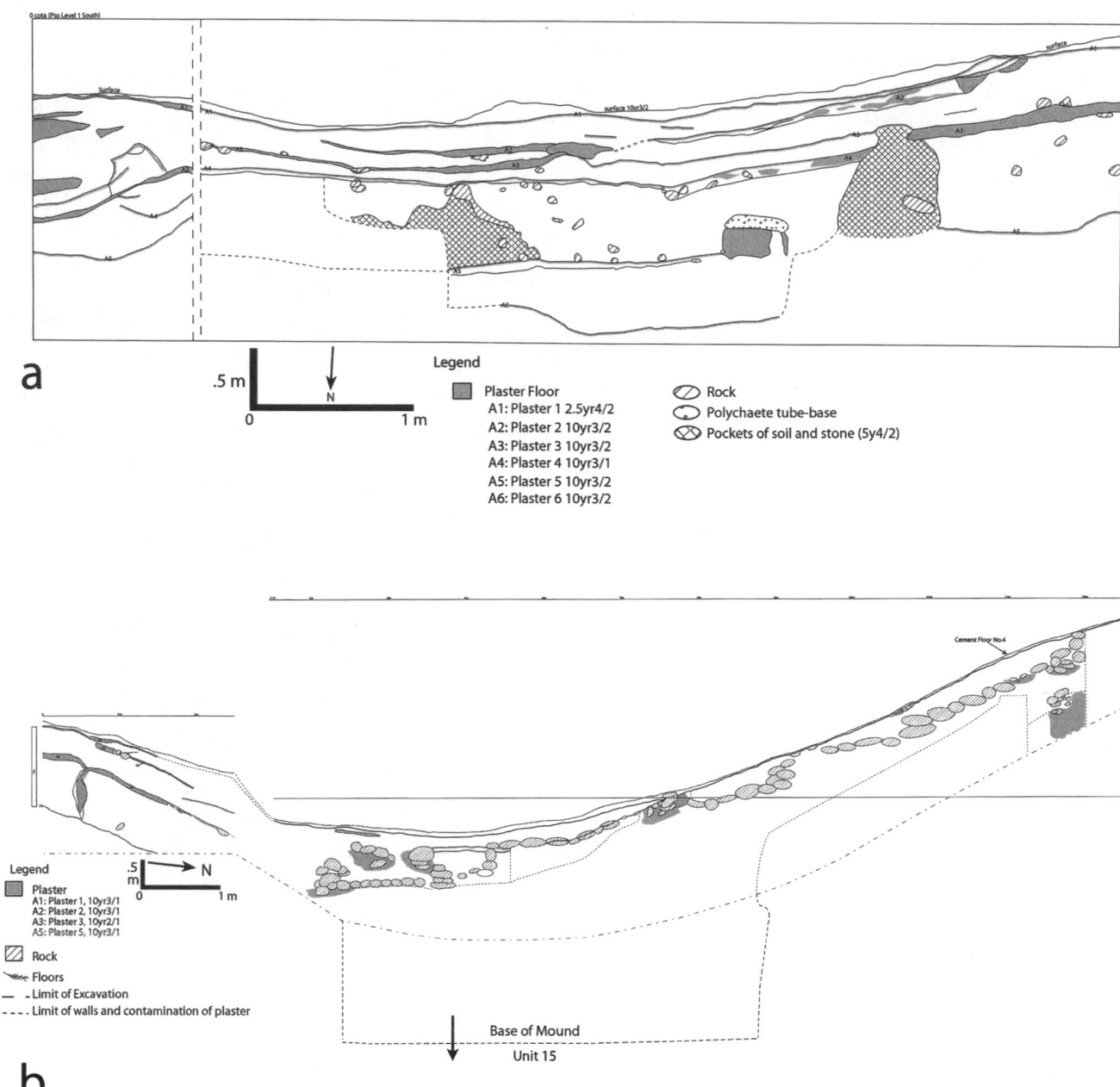

FIGURE 7.19. Unit 21: *a*, south profile of plaster floors and fills; *b*, west profile of structures and plaster and other floors.

Floor 2 are various fill layers with similar content and a dark gray sediment (5YR 3/1).

In summary, this unit produced multiple floors and fills. The material content is typical of other excavated units, revealing numerous individual burning episodes and offerings but no tombs.

HP Unit 18: This unit was initially an exploratory pit placed on the north side of the sunken looter's hole; but excavation was halted when workers exposed a wall and an underlying Moche burial, which we decided not to excavate.

HP Unit 19: This unit was opened on the top of the mound and was 1 by 5 m in size. (It was later expanded and renumbered as Unit 23.) The goal was to determine whether there were structures near the mound surface, as had been found in the sunken circular plaza. Between 10 and 20 cm in depth a layer of rocks was encountered with heavily fragmented floors. There was a wooden post associated with a partial room structure, as defined by a row of aligned stones (~0.17 m wide and 0.70 m long). Charred reed mats were piled in

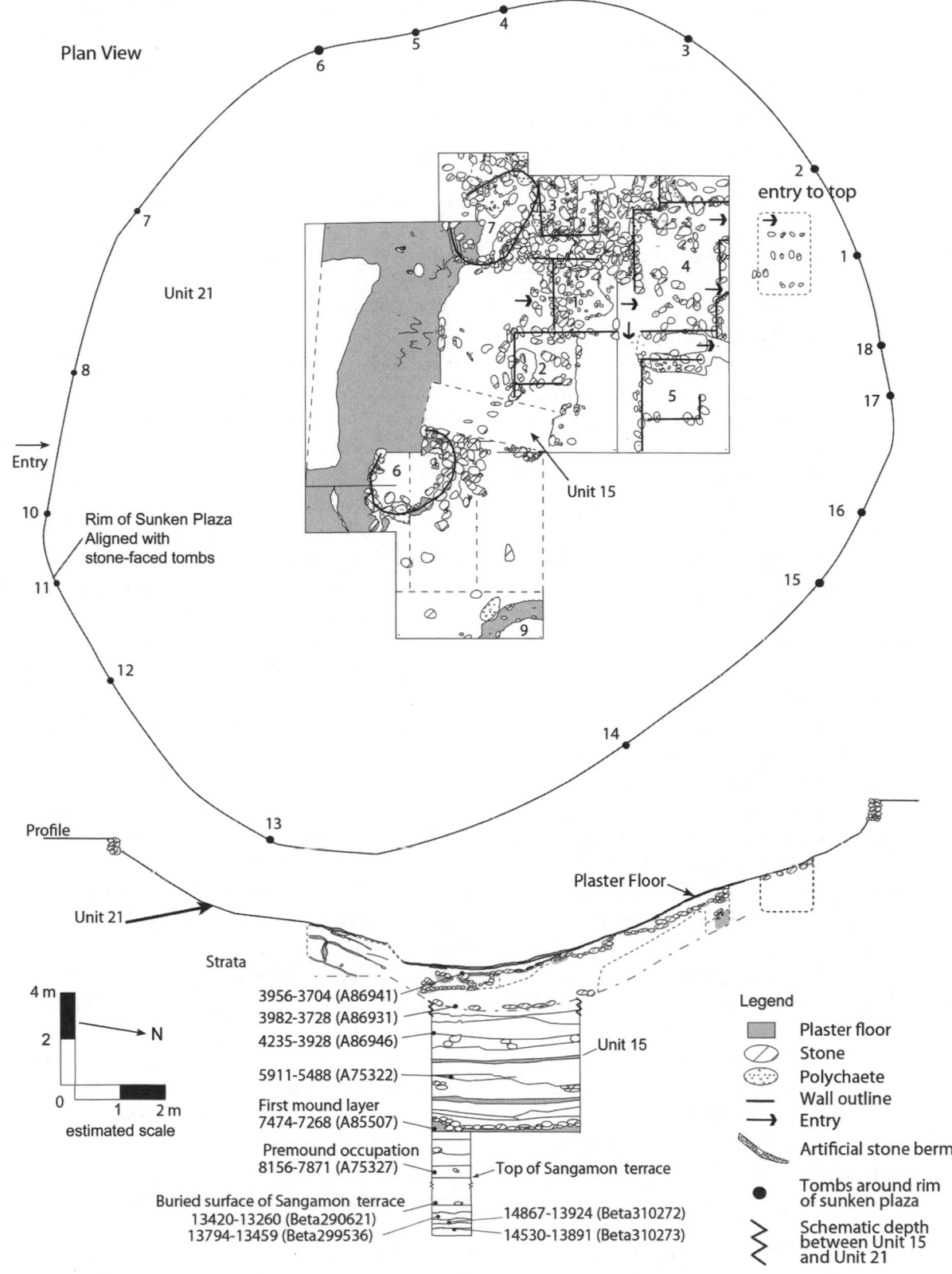

Plan View

4

5

6

3

2

entry to top

1

7

Unit 21

8

Entry

10

Rim of Sunken Plaza
Aligned with
stone-faced tombs

11

12

13

14

15

16

17

18

3

7

4

2

5

6

9

Unit 15

Profile

Unit 21

Strata

Plaster Floor

4 m

2

N

0   1   2 m
estimated scale

3956-3704 (A86941)
3982-3728 (A86931)
4235-3928 (A86946)

5911-5488 (A75322)

First mound layer
7474-7268 (A85507)

Premound occupation
8156-7871 (A75327)

Buried surface of Sangamon terrace
13420-13260 (Beta290621)
13794-13459 (Beta299536)

Unit 15

Top of Sangamon terrace

14867-13924 (Beta310272)

14530-13891 (Beta310273)

Legend

Plaster floor

Stone

Polychaete

Wall outline

Entry

Artificial stone berm

Tombs around rim
of sunken plaza

Schematic depth
between Unit 15
and Unit 21

FIGURE 7.20. Plan of structures and pathways in Unit 21 (*top*) and of the strata and radiocarbon dates in Unit 15 (*bottom*).

one area. Other organic materials included guinea pig coprolites. Below this was a solid wall of stones that reached 1.3 m in depth. The unit was reduced in size to a 1 by 2 m pit. Fills of rock and sediment were found between 1.3 and 1.8 m. At 1.8 m several loose stones and part of a wall oriented east to west were exposed. The layer yielded large quantities of charcoal, ash, burned rock, and shell and small pockets of plant food offerings. Below this layer the south side of the pit contained solid rock down to the 2.6 m level. The excavation terminated at this point.

HP Unit 21 and the Sunken Circular Plaza: After excavating Units 15 and 18, it was discovered that the Bird's "looter's pit" was actually a planned sector of the mound that was a sunken circular plaza with access to the higher portion of the mound to the immediate north. Unit 21 was excavated to determine the nature of this sunken area. The unit was a ~11 by 12 m, with multiple extensions that followed architectural walls as the excavation expanded (figs. 7.19 and 20). A series of radiocarbon dates from Floors 2 (3956–3704 cal BP, AA8641) and 3 (3982–3728 cal BP, AA86931) and from Floors 9 (4235–3928 cal BP, AA86946) to 26 (5911–5488 cal BP, AA75322) were processed. The deepest levels for this unit are discussed in the section on Unit 15. No burials were associated with the sunken part of the plaza, although the upper rim around it contained several rock-lined chamber tombs (see chapter 8).

Unit 21 has a concave surface. At 1 m deep large rocks appeared, which were aligned and formed part of a structural wall. Several excavation extensions followed this wall and others (top of fig. 7.20). Many stones were not aligned; they had fallen from walls that formed structures. Two use surfaces were found, but no prepared floors were observed in the upper layers or in the structures. Beyond the confines of the structures several plaster surfaces were laid down in and around the structures, especially on the inclined slopes of the sunken plaza, presumably to prevent erosion in the area.

The individual structures have their own entrances, which form oval to semirectangular enclosures. The structures were sealed under thick, hard plasters (6–18 cm); other structures (tombs) were built higher along the rim of the curved walls of the plaza (see Unit 8). A 60–80 cm path

up to and down from the top of the mound to the north, where Unit 23 and numerous agglutinated chamber tombs were excavated, separated two parallel structures near the upper side of the sunken plaza. This was the entry path between the plaza and the upper north end of the mound. Two rock crystals, which are exotic to the site, were placed on the path (see fig. 11.16f).

After removing the first floor, another thick plaster was exposed from 1.50 to 2.08 m; part of a semicircular structure (fig. 7.19b) also was exposed. The remains of two underlying, heavily disturbed structures (fig. 7.20: Nos. 2 and 3) formed a deeper entrance from the north end of the mound, almost exactly below the one described above. Excavations also revealed evidence for another structure (No. 4) to the northwest. Additional low collapsed walls were found to the northeast. The best-preserved structure was No. 5, with a small entryway that measured 1.7 and 2.0 m. All of these structures are semirectangular to rectangular and appear to have been agglutinated at one time. Materials associated were small rocks, hammerstones, flakes, shell, plant remains, and utilized flakes. Several offerings were found in the sunken plaza near here, including a coca leaf and two unworked pieces of copper sulfate in Structure 3 (fig. 7.21a) and a pocket of 18 coca leaves in Structure 8 (fig. 7.21b), a pelican skeleton, several piles of burned sea urchin spines, and lithics, all dating to Phase V. Three *Anadara* sp. shells, an exotic species from southwest Ecuador were found in Structure 4. Other features include a bundle of salt from Structure 6 (fig. 7.21c; see chapter 11). In total, nine thin (1–2 cm thick) and partial floors outside of the structures were exposed, revealing multiple rebuilding and reuse episodes of the plaza.

Two other semicircular structures were exposed on the highest and steepest slope to the north. These structures measure 2.0 by 1.50 m and 2.1 m by 3 m and have entryways. Several rocks also were aligned toward the northwest. Although no structures were found, many lenses of small shells in a yellowish sand (10YR 8/6) as well as lenses of ash were recovered. The semicircular structures, reed matting, gourds, offerings, and lithic tools seem to represent intermittent rituals and the remodeling of the floors and structures.

An extension was opened to the south and

FIGURE 7.21. Offerings in various units: *a*, offering of coca leaf (*right-pointing arrow*) and copper sulfate (*left-pointing arrow*) on pathway up and down the mound, Unit 21; *b*, offering of many coca leaves on floor of Structure 8, Unit 21; *c*, offering of tightly wrapped bundle of salt crystals in a cotton textile contained within a corded bag on the floor of Structure 6, Unit 21; *d*, offering of shells in Unit 14.

west of Unit 21 to reveal the sequence of the westward-trending aligned stones. Two more oval structures (Nos. 6 and 7) were found opposite each other like mirror images. These two measured ~2.1 m in diameter. Portions of other disturbed structures were observed in the unexcavated profile walls of the unit. Materials were knotted cords of cotton, lithics, and bivalves.

The sunken circular plaza has several compact floors, all of which slope steeply toward the center from the top of the mound. Access to the plaza is from the north down a stepped path from the top of the mound. The architectural design inside the plaza apparently was to construct small individual rooms and ritual spaces, agglutinated when possible, that conformed to the concavity of the plaza. The uniqueness of the plaza, which is ele-

vated by its placement on top of the mound, is its sunken, circular form, both of which reveal its planned nature and its functional integration with the rest of the mound, particularly the chamber tombs on top. Modern-day activity has partially destroyed the format of the circular plaza, eroding its sidewalls and expanding its aperture on the east side.

We cannot fully explain the presence of the aperture. It appears to be pre-Hispanic, however, because it also has a plaster covering it. We initially thought that the sunken plaza had been dug out and that the aperture was used to toss the fill downslope on the eastern side of the mound. The placement of Test Pit 3 downslope from the aperture was to see whether the deposits there were of loose debris or fill from above or were intact.

FIGURE 7.22. Unit 23: *a*, view of excavated and numbered chamber tombs on top of Huaca Prieta; *b*, view of excavated chamber tomb no. 8, showing empty floor and the top of Structure 9.

mound. The paucity of debris in and around the structures suggests ritual activity.

<u>HP Unit 23 (also Unit 19 within it)</u>: This unit was placed on the top of the mound just north of the sunken plaza. The goal was to define the presence of additional activity areas and structures and attempt to relate this area of the mound to the adjacent plaza. Nine structures interpreted as tombs were excavated (fig. 7.22a–b). They were agglutinated and similar in form and size to those excavated by Bird on the far north end of the upper surface of the mound (Bird et al. 1985: 47). They range between 1.1 and 1.2 m in depth and 1.0 to 1.8 m in width. Below the upper layer of structures were found other tombs and several layers of rock wall segments, fills, plaster surfaces, and other layers similar to those recovered in other areas of the mound for Phases III to V.

Layer 1, ~0–0.17 m: Soil texture ranges from compact to loose and is black (2.5YR 2.5/1). The layer has dull reddish stains (2.5YR 5/3) with many burned sea urchin spines and fish vertebrae alternating with blackened areas (10YR 2/1), shell, mortar, floor fragments, and lines of rock. The reddish stains are outside of the structures, while the black stains are inside. Other materials were rock, bone, shell, burned rock, wood, charcoal, plant food remains, and burned clay. A broken polished stone drinking vessel was located in Layer 2 (see fig. 11.5d). A ^{14}C sample associated with early Moche sherds in upper Layer 1 of this unit was processed at 1697–1539 cal BP (AA86930).

Fragments of Floor 1 and the hard plaster were encountered in some areas. There are two circular structures in the southern part of the excavation and a double line of rocks with thick mortar denoting a wall. A large quantity of lithics and small burned areas were piled in four discrete locations. Organic remains (such as shells, sea urchin spines, and fish vertebrae) are abundant, forming 2 cm thick layers above the rock floors of the structures. These also occur as small piles and appear to be offerings.

Layer 2, ~0.17–1.28 m: The soil is loose to compact, is reddish (2.5YR 5/3), and has dark stains (10YR 2/1) with burned and unburned sea urchin remains and fish vertebrae. Materials were bone, shell, burned rock, wood, and charcoal. Five structures and one floor were recorded.

Excavation showed that they were intact and covered by a thick plaster. It is possible that the aperture was an access route to chamber tombs on the eastern slope of the mound or that it was a sight-line from inside the sunken plaza to the sacred Cerro Cuculicote to the east, the latter suggested to us by a local *curandero* or shaman who once performed rituals at the Huaca Prieta mound ("El Shaman" Rodríguez, personal communication, 2010).

In summary, this sunken area with floors, structures, and offerings is undoubtedly Preceramic in age (see all radiocarbon dates for Unit 15/21 in chapter 6) and associated with the timing of construction of the chamber tombs in Units 10, 11, and 23 and the entry ramp on the east side of the

Floor 1, ~0.80–0.85 m: The floor has burned sea urchin remains, shell, charcoal, plant fibers, and burned rocks.

Layer 3, ~1.20–1.80 m: This layer contains use surfaces, lenses of charcoal, and a reddish black soil (2.5YR 2/1). Fragments of snails and shell, seaweed, wood fragments, plant fiber and burned rocks are found between layers of loose sand. A ^{14}C sample was assayed at 3828–3560 cal BP (AA86949).

The laminar nature of the layers and the presence of aeolian sand (0.2–.08 cm) suggest two hypotheses to explain the succession of layers. The lenses mark periods of abandonment of the structure. The lenses and charcoal stains also suggest a process of cleaning structures without removing all charcoal. Lamina of charcoal and sand are scattered outside of the structures along the entire southern edge of Unit 23, marking a sequence of multiple burning events oriented toward the stairway that descends into the sunken circular plaza.

Layer 4–5, ~1.80–2.56 m: Layer 4 is loose with compacted areas and a dark soil (2.5YR 3/2). Materials recovered were burned sea urchin spines, seaweed, charcoal, wood, blocks of polychaete tubes, stones, lenses of sand, shells, and seaweed. Layer 4 marks the transition between the first row of tombs and the second row below. Burned sea urchin spines are concentrated along the west wall of Layer 5 outside of Structure 2. Another structure with four rows of rocks forms a wall from the east toward the northeast. The base or foundation of the wall is made of blocks of polychaete tubes.

Layers 6–7, ~2.56–3.29 m: The soil is semi-compact with lenses of burned sea urchin spines. Reeds cross the unit horizontally and are fragmented. Broken mussel shell, bone, burned rock, wood, charcoal, reeds, and blocks of polychaete tubes were piled in the southern part of the layer.

Layers 8–9, ~3.29–5.1 m: These are the basal stone layers of tombs excavated in the unit. They contain a few prepared use surfaces that served as the bottom of layers of structures. Below these basal layers are a few shells and lithics.

Structure 1: The soil is loose, with concentrations of plaster below and is brownish black (10YR 2/1). A ring of stones and a dense concentration of burned sea urchin spines and fish bones were neatly piled in the center of the structure. The

structure is 1.3 m wide and 1.2 m deep. Entry is from the east.

Structure 2: Structure 2 has three walls of mortar and cobbles with a depth of 1.1 m. The soil is a brownish black (10YR 2/1). Two small burned offerings of shell are present (Features 1 and 2), aligned to the east of the entrance of this structure. Feature 3 contained burned sea urchin spines and shells with plant materials. Feature 4 had offerings of burned shell and a few small snails and fish bones separated into four small piles. The structure is 2.1 m wide and 1.3 m deep. Entry is from the northeast.

Burials: Below Structure 2 at a depth of 3.2 m is Burial 1 (see chapter 8, HP09-10), which is a small burial chamber with a child whose head is lying on the left arm. *Semele* sp. shells partially cover Burial 1. Burial 2 was recovered in Structure 3 and has a semicircular layer of mortared polychaete blocks above it. The burial dated to Phase IV.

Structure 3: The structure is composed of burned rocks and blocks of polychaete tubes. Materials were shell, burned rock, wood, and charcoal. The structure is graded into the stairway that descends to the sunken circular plaza. The structure is 1.3 m wide and 1.2 m deep. Entry is from the north.

Structure 4: This structure is a double row of rock filled with burned rock and burned areas, Features 5 and 6. Materials include rock, bone, shell, burned rock, wood, and charcoal. The burned areas are ~40 by 50 cm and contain fishbone, burned sea urchin spines, and burned rock. The structure was not completely excavated.

Structure 5: The structure is defined by low walls of mortar with one or two rows of cobbles. Cultural materials included rock, bone, shell, burned rock, wood, and charcoal. A few human bones (ribs and cranial fragments) were recovered from the floor of the structure, suggesting a secondary burial or that the skeleton had been removed. A small internal division is created by three large rocks associated with several burned rocks. The structure is 2.4 m wide and 1.3 m deep. Entry is from the west.

Structures 6 and 7: Both structures were empty but sealed with plaster, which had been cracked. Although they were not completely excavated, their interiors were empty as observed through

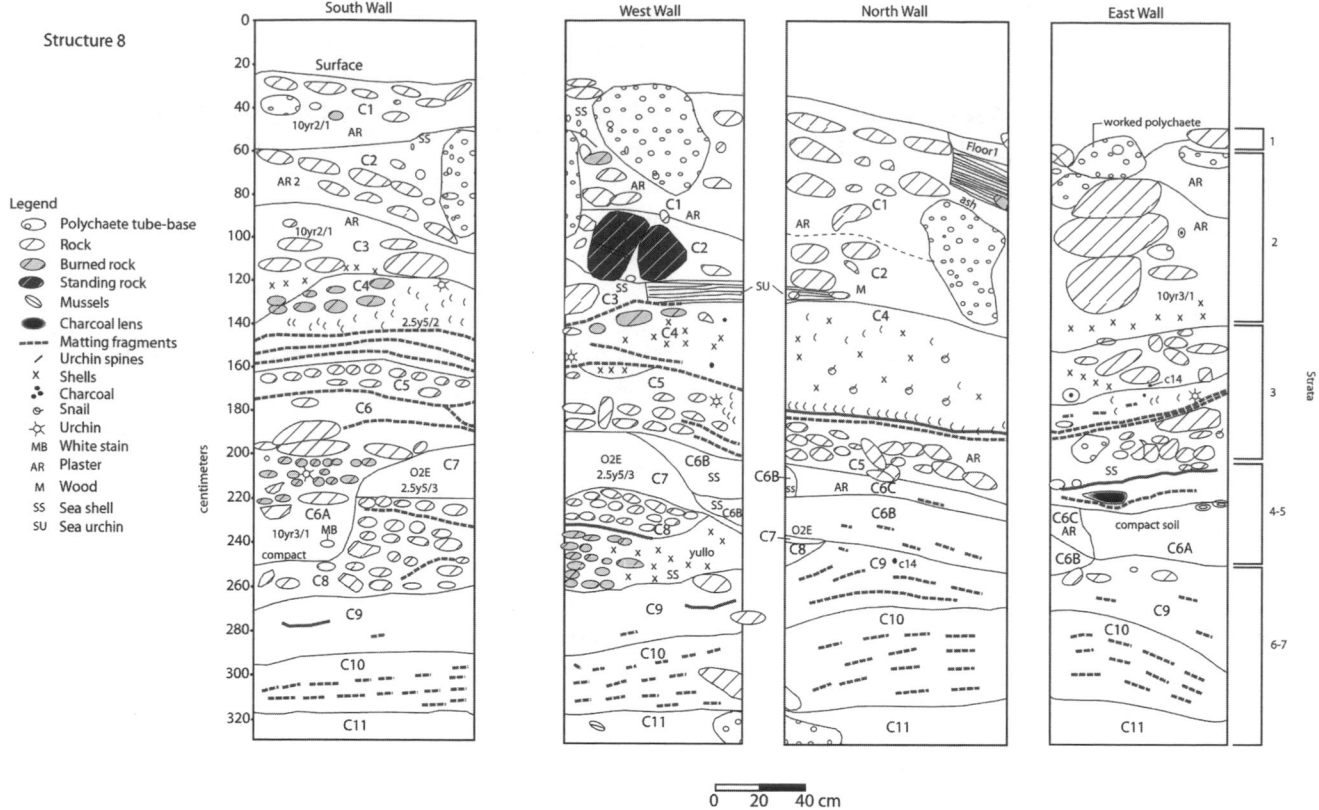

FIGURE 7.23. Profile of multiple floors and fills of Structure 8 in Unit 23.

cracks in the roofs. The structures are 1.2 to 1.3 m wide and 0.9 to 1.1 m deep.

Structure 8: The soil texture is soft and reddish (10YR 4/2), with mammal and fish bone, mortar, and burned rock. The burned rock and mortar are evenly scattered inside the structure, but the bone is concentrated to the east of it. Materials were rock, bone, shell, burned rock, wood, gourd, and charcoal. The structure is more than 3 m deep and defined by multiple layers of use surfaces and various layers and fills (C1–11), suggestive of recycled use (fig. 7.23). Entry is from the north.

Structure 9: This structure is inside of and lies below Structure 8 at a depth of 5.1 m below the mound surface. The soil is loose, with 2 to 3 thin layers of cane, below which are small piles of snail shells, broken shell, sea urchin spines, and burned rock. Materials were burned clay, charcoal, rock, shell, bone, sea urchin spines, and burned rock. The color is a reddish gray (2.5YR 5/3). A ^{14}C sample was assayed at 5902–5606 cal BP (AA86948).

In summary, it is clear that these structures

are too small to be houses. Most were covered by a plaster roof and had piled offerings (*Semele* sp. shells, snails and gastropod remains, crop foods, lithics, broken and complete shells, and seaweed) inside on the floors; other structures were empty but had offerings. Two of the nine structures were associated with complete or partial burials. This burial area clearly was associated with the sunken circular plaza and the tombs lining the circular rim above it in Unit 23, as evidenced by similar architectural features, corresponding radiocarbon dates, and a connecting pathway between them.

HP Unit 24: This 1 by 3 m unit was excavated on the upper slope of the southwest side of the mound to search for the yellow clay layer of Phase IV that possibly extended across the entire mound. The unit is characterized by several plaster coverings, floors, and fills (fig. 7.24).

Layers 1–2, ~0–0.65 m: A thick plaster, Layer 1, covered the surface. Below the plaster were pieces of polychaete tubes in Layer 2. At the base of the plaster were two layers, one a light gray (10YR 7/1) and the other a yellowish brown (10YR 8/6).

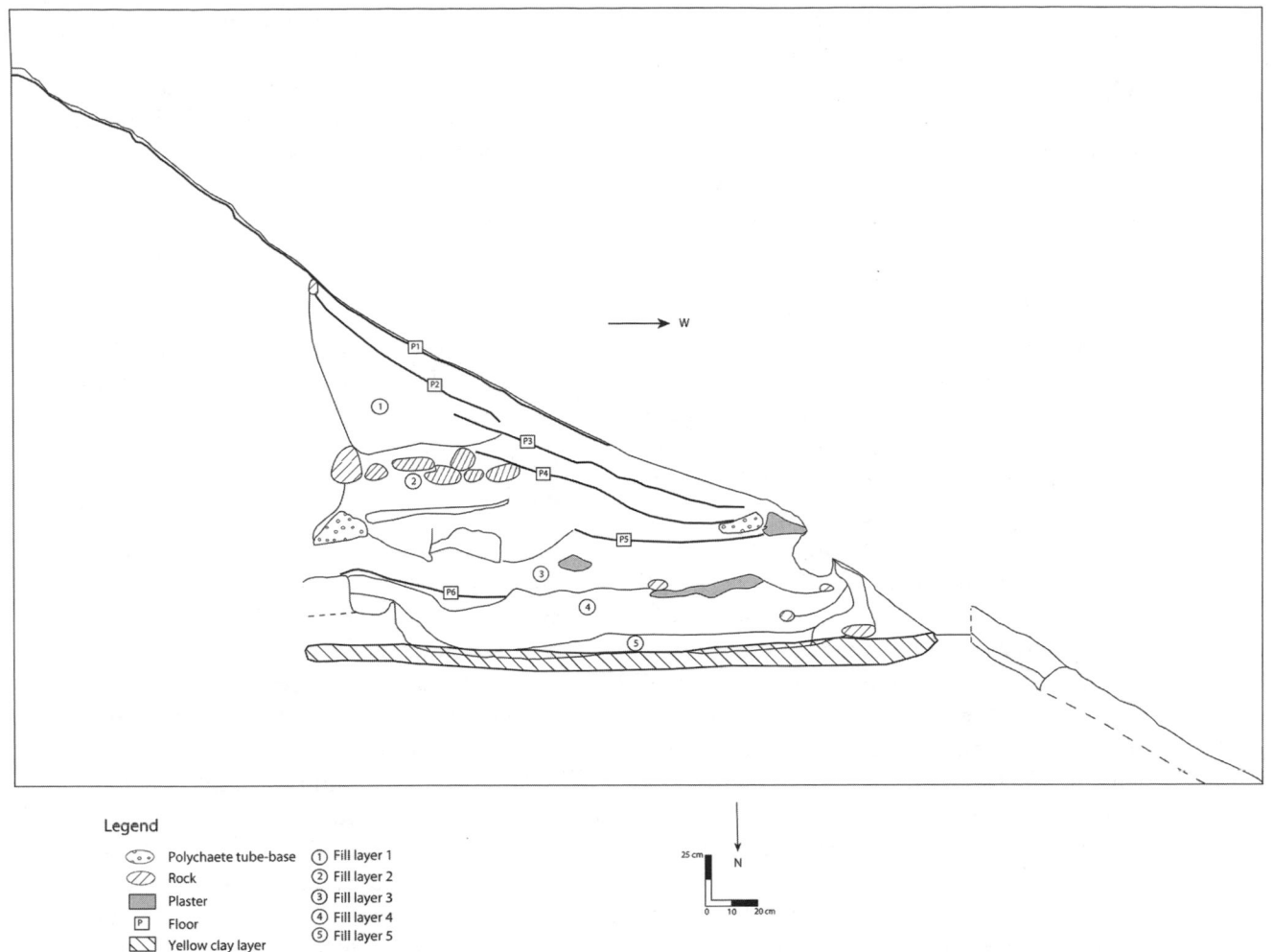

Legend

⬭ Polychaete tube-base	①	Fill layer 1
⬭ Rock	②	Fill layer 2
▬ Plaster	③	Fill layer 3
P Floor	④	Fill layer 4
▨ Yellow clay layer	⑤	Fill layer 5

FIGURE 7.24. Profile of floors and fills in Unit 24.

Shells, fish bones, and lithics were found in these layers.

Layers 3–4, ~0.65–1.27 m: Layers 3 and 4 have a compact homogeneous soil (0.8–1.7 m in depth). Materials were rock, bone, shell, and wood. Another plaster layer was below Layer 4.

Layer 5, ~1.27–1.97 m: This was filled with shell and unidentified plant remains. In the upper layer is a deposit of cemented rocks and shell. The stratigraphy closer to the interior is almost horizontal, but toward the outside it is steeply inclined and covered by a thick plaster, revealing a deliberate shaping of the mound down toward the sea and placing a protective plaster seal over it. Materials were rock, bone, and shell. The excavation ended with the discovery of the same yellow clay cap that was observed at 2.46 m in depth on the northeast side of the mound in unit HP-3.

Four thin floors (nos. 1–4) were recovered. Two were limited in thickness (~1 cm) and size (~1.3–1.4 m long and 2.1 to 2.3 m wide).

Once the yellow sediment layer between Phases III and IV was exposed, the excavation was closed (see the earlier discussion of this layer).

HP Unit 25: This 1 by 3 m unit was excavated at the elevation of the middle lower slope on the northeast side of the mound to determine whether the yellow clay layer extended here.

Floors 1–2, ~0–.24 m: The soil is compact and composed of sand, fine gravel, and gravel and is reddish gray (2.5YR 4/1). Materials recovered were shell, bone, maize, gourd fragments, wood, lithics, plant remains, and feathers.

Floors 3–4, ~0.24–0.54 m: The soil is semi-compact, composed of sand, fine gravel, gravel, broken shell, and fragments of sea urchins, and is brownish gray (5YR 5/1). Shell, charcoal, gourd fragment, reed cordage, textile fragments, and quartz rocks were recovered.

Floors 5–6, ~0.54–0.86 m: Soil of Floor 5 is semicompact and composed of sand, fine gravel, gravel, and plant remains and is reddish gray (7.5YR 4/0). Materials recovered were shell, plant remains, and gourd fragments. Soil of Floor 6 is semicompact, composed of sand, gravel, broken shell, and burned sea urchin spines, and grayish brown (7.5YR 6/2). Materials were shell, bone, plant remains, gourd fragments, and charcoal.

Floors 7–8, ~0.86–0.94 m: The soil is grayish red (7.5YR 5/2). Texture is semicompact, composed of three piles of sand, clay, and sea urchin fragments. Cultural remains were shell, bone, lithics, unidentified wood, fragments of gourd, textile fragments, and charcoal.

The yellow sediment layer was not recovered.

HP Unit 27: The objective of excavating this unit was to detect the layer of yellow clay (10YR 8/6). This yellow clay layer was not observed, however. Several floors and fills were observed to a depth of 1.67 m.

Floors 1–2, ~0–0.87 m: The soil is semicompact to compact, composed of sand, fine gravel, and gravel, and light brownish gray (5YR 7/1). Floor 2 is reddish gray (2.5YR 4/0). Materials were shell, bone, lithics, plant remains, and feathers.

Floors 3–4, ~0.87–.1.67 m: The soil texture is compact, with sand, fine gravel, gravel, clay, and charcoal.

Materials were shell, bone, a gourd fragment, and charcoal. Floors are brownish gray (5YR 5/1). Shell, textile fragments, charcoal, a gourd fragment, reed cordage, and quartz also were recovered.

HP Units 28 and 29: These two areas near Paredones were disturbed by modern activities and thus closed and covered after 0.80 m of excavation.

In summary, the Huaca Prieta mound is a highly complex stratigraphic and architectural structure unlike anything previously recorded in the Andes and in the Americas in general. Its size, form, material content, chronology, and function all suggest that a unique set of economic and social circumstances and ontological understandings produced and sustained this mound over several millennia. Perhaps most notable about this

site, from an archaeological perspective, are the thousands of individual small offerings of different local and exotic materials, the associated highly circumscribed nature of the ritual, and perhaps some nonritual feasting and other spaces making up the mound. These factors all suggest high-frequency ritual use by small groups of people. Finally, one of the most impressive aspects of the mound at Huaca Prieta is its black or dark appearance, which is the result of the enormous quantities of burned material composing it, including millions of burned and broken sea urchin spines.

UNIT EXCAVATIONS AT PAREDONES (PA)

Fewer excavation units were placed in the Paredones site because this mound was not as large and as deep as the one at Huaca Prieta. We also located several trenches and test pits around the base to connect the lower stratigraphy of the mound to the underlying terrace sediments and to test for off-mound cultural activity.

PA Unit 20: This unit was a long off-mound trench on the east side of the mound, with later extensions to define the stratigraphic linkage between the terrace and the mound (fig. 3.1). No ritual offerings were associated with this unit. All lower cultural deposits suggested domestic activity, while all upper deposits were associated with nondomestic activity of the mound.

Layers 1–2a, ~0–0.34 m: The soil texture is semicompact, a very pale brown (10YR 8/3). The matrix consists of sand, rock, ash, and fractured shell. Materials were snail shells, rock, burned rock, plant remains, and charcoal. There were traces of a hearth, burned sediment, and burned snail shells. Guañape sherds were associated with the hearth.

Layers 3–4, ~0.34–0.67 m: The soil is semicompact and light gray (10YR 7/6). Materials were animal bone, corncobs, rock, shell, and squash seeds.

Layer 5, ~0.67–0.78 m: The soil texture is loose to semicompact. It is yellowish (10YR 8/6). Materials were shell, rock, bone, and plant remains.

Layers 6a–h, ~0.78–1.3 m: This is a series of laminated use surfaces. The soil is semicompact and a brownish black (10YR 3/1), with a heavy concentration of ash. Materials were burned shells, charcoal, fish vertebrae, and plant remains. A fragment of gourd was found as well as a container lid of unbaked clay.

Layers 7–8, ~1.3–1.6 m: The soil texture is homogeneous and semicompact. Layer 7 is a dark grayish brown (10YR 3/2). Layer 8 was brownish black (10YR 5/2) with concentrations of sea lion bone, fish vertebrae, whole shells, lithics, burned rock, and charcoal. Feature 1, a hearth 25 cm long and 30 cm thick, was recovered from Layer 7. A posthole suggests the presence of a structure.

Layers 9–10, ~1.6–1.9 m: The soil is homogeneous and varies from brownish black (10YR 3/3) to brown (10YR 3/1). Materials were rock, bone, shell, and lithics. There was an abundance of sea lion bone. A second posthole was recovered. Numerous burned stains were observed.

Layer 11, ~1.9–2.1 m: The soil is homogeneous, loose, and brownish black to dark brown (10YR 3/3–10YR 3/2). Fragmented shells and red hematite were found in this layer. Layer 11 reached the culturally sterile Sangamon terrace at 2.3 m.

This is an off-mound domestic and workshop unit associated with the Paredones mound. The lower levels are characterized by lithic and faunal and floral remains suggestive of premound maritime and wetland foragers. The upper levels, beginning with Layers 5 and 6, contain maize remains and are associated with mound activity demonstrated in Unit 22.

PA Unit 22: This unit was excavated on the eastern end of the Paredones mound to examine the internal structure and content of the mound. Figure 7.25 shows the thin lamina of floors and fills and the associated radiocarbon dates. No ritual offerings were associated with this unit.

Harris Matrix for Unit 22

The unit consists of 161 individual layers and seven different types of soil fills, floors, berms, micro-layers, unspecified layers, intruding layers or features, layered floors containing matting, and possible continuous strata (fig. 7.26).

The Harris Matrix for this unit was divided into three sections, one corresponding to each profiled wall (East, South, and West). Identified in the Harris Matrix were soil fills, prepared floors,

Charred Cob
4821-4527 cal BP
(AA86934)

Wood Charcoal
5435-5044 cal BP
(Beta263320)

Corncob
133-34 cal BP
(Beta263988)

Wood Charcoal
5585-5325 cal BP
(Beta263321)

Wood Charcoal
5711-5335 cal BP
(AA86947)

Corn Husk
6775-6504 cal BP
(OS86020)

Corncob
722-563 cal BP
(Beta27823)

729-569 cal BP
(Beta27804)

738-572 cal BP
(Beta282127)

Post-bomb Date
(AA88761)

Wood Charcoal
6640-6319 cal BP
(AA83260)

FIGURE 7.25. Profile of Unit 22, showing intact floors, fills, and radiocarbon dates.

stone berms, micro-layers, unspecified flat layers, and intruding layers or features. Solid lines across matrix sections were used to denote continuous layers, and dashed lines indicate possible continuous strata.

Extending across all three walls of the profile for Unit 22 are five continuous layers. Harris Matrix number H#1000 makes up the entire top surface layer, with a floor just below it (H#1001) that extends across all profile walls. Layer H#1000 contains a few cobblestones and snail shells but mostly consists of shell fragments and a brownish gray soil (10YR 4/1) in the west wall. The next continuous stratum is H#1017 (near the middle of the profile, starting in the east wall and rising gradually as it continues into the west wall). Near the bottom of the profile are the final continuous strata, H#1048 and H#1049, a soil fill and ter-

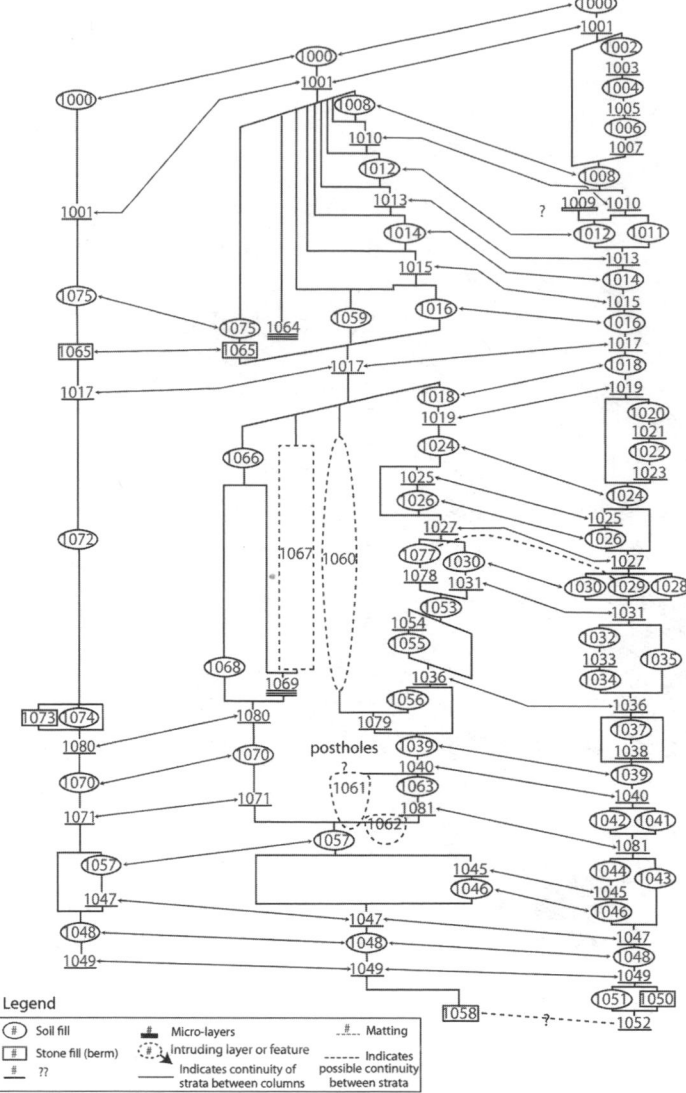

FIGURE 7.26. Harris Matrix of strata in Unit 22.

race surface, respectively. H#1048 was an irregular mixture of shell fragments, snail shells, cobblestones, and burned cobbles. H#1047 is also worth mentioning, as it extends across all three profile walls. But it stops short of extending across the entirety of the east wall and thus cannot be considered a continuous layer.

The first of three sets of potentially continuous strata are Harris Matrix numbers H#1016, H#1059, and H#1075. H#1016, consisting largely of shell fragments and snail shells, extends across the entire west wall and part of the south wall into layer H#1059, where it is interrupted by a layer of cobblestones (H#1065) that extends slightly into the east wall. In the east wall the stratum is

labeled as soil fill H#1075 and does not have the shell fragments and snail shells found in H#1016 and H#1059. But it is still bounded on the top and bottom by H#1001 and H#1017, both of which are continuous layers.

Second are layers H#1039 and H#1070, both of an irregular mixture consisting mostly of pockets of shell fragments, snail shells, and cobblestones. In the east wall H#1070 is identified in the original profile as "2c"; when it extends into the south wall, its floor (H#1071) abruptly ends. Here it is labeled as layer "8," though there is no clear divide between the two fills.

Finally, fills H#1041, H#1042, and H#1063 extend across layer 9 in the original profile, beginning at the east wall as H#1063 and containing lithics, shell fragments, cobblestones, and mammal bones. Layer 9 is interrupted by Post Hole 1 (H#1061) but continues across the rest of the south wall until the consistency of its matrix changes as it transitions into the west wall, where it is labeled H#1042. H#1042, like H#1063, is also made up of fragmented shells, lithics, mammal bones, and cobblestones. It extends into H#1041, a soil fill with a few cobblestones lining its bottom. Strata H#1040 and H#1077 are continuous in their bordering of the tops and bottoms of strata H#1041, H#1042, and H#1070, which suggests that they are potentially part of the same layer.

H#1002 through H#1007 are a stack of fills and floors in the west wall. The soil fills consist of a largely uniform matrix of shell fragments with a few snail shells in H#1002. These layers end with H#1001 coming down on their eastern slope. Following these in a similar fashion are H#1008, H#1010, H#1013, H#1014, and H#1015, a combination of floors and fills consisting mostly of shell fragments. These layers begin in the west wall and continue into the south wall, where they are terminated by the slope of H#1001.

H#1024, consisting largely of shell fragments, snail shells, and cobblestones, extends through most of the west wall and more than half of the south wall before it terminates at H#1060, an intrusive soil fill made up of shell fragments, small cobbles, and soil. This intrusive soil fill also interrupted the extension of layer H#1072. Soil fill H#1072 (2b in the original profile) begins in the east wall and extends into the south wall, where it is interrupted by a group of small cobbles

(H#1067), then becomes an intrusive soil fill (H#1060).

Finally, H#1040, an unspecified floor that extends along the entire West Wall and most of the south wall, is interrupted by Post Hole 01 (H#1061); it ends at the upslope (and terminating end) of H#1071.

There are three stone berms in Unit 22, identified as H#1065, H#1073, and H#1076. H#1065 is a loose pile of cobblestones at the junction of the east and south walls. At the north end of the east wall are stacked cobblestones making up layer H#1073, and, finally, also in the east wall is H#1076, a smaller berm at the base of the mound, above the culturally sterile layer and below H#1049.

Unlike the strata for Phases III–V at Huaca Prieta, those in Unit 22 have both discontinuous and continuous layers and floors suggestive of more lateral consistency in activity areas and less definition of individually discrete spaces. This pattern is more typical of Phase II stratigraphy at Huaca Prieta, which is associated with domestic activity, or at least food preparation and consumption, and also with less charcoal content. As reported in appendix 12, Paredones had a high charcoal content, which also gives it a dark appearance, but not to the extent observed at Huaca Prieta. Three loose human teeth (two lower right adult molars, indicating two individuals, and a third child molar, suggesting three different individuals) were found in the Paredones mound in Floors 4, 9, and 18. It is not known whether they were offerings or partial secondary burials or related to another form of mortuary behavior. The isotope analyses of the teeth reveal that they came from individuals with a high diet of plant foods, which fits the archaeobotanical and other findings at Paredones.

Floors in Unit 22

Floors 1–1a, ~0–0.16 m: Floor 1 is 2–4 cm thick, consisting of semicompact clay with gravel, sand, and small rocks. The soil is a light orange (10YR 8/4). A large amount of shell was recovered, with lesser amounts of bones, ceramics, and plant remains, including 13 diagnostic early Moche ceramic fragments, bones (a camelid mandible and avian bones), lithics, shells (mainly gastropods), and various species of bivalves. Floor 1a con-

tained fewer but similar materials. It was a pale red (10YR 5/2).

Floor 1b, 0.16–0.21 m: The soil texture varied from semicompact to loose and was brownish black (10YR 3/1). Shell was the most abundant material, followed by gourd, with lesser amounts of lithics, charcoal, and ceramics. The floor consisted of six circular areas (10–20 cm in diameter) of compact brown soil (10YR 3/4). It seems that these compacted circles were caused by the pressure of structural elements, such as footings for columns, which supported a roof.

Floors 2–3, ~0.21–0.47 m: Floor 3 is semicompact, composed of sand, ash, small stones, and broken shells. It is brownish gray (10YR 5/1). Materials consisted of bones, shell, and lithics. A human molar was recovered with a small fish vertebra and bird bones. Floor 3 is semicompact, composed of sand, fine gravel, gravel, ash, and shell. It is brownish gray (10YR 5/1). A wooden artifact, shaped like a long punching tool, was recovered. It may have been used in weaving, because it was associated with a textile (see chapters 11 and 12).

Floors 4–7, ~0.47–0.86 m: Floor 4 was semicompact, composed of sand, fine gravel, and ash. It is reddish gray (2.5YR 5/0). Remains included bone, shell, lithics, sea cucumber, plant remains, cotton threads, and animal coprolites. A lot of animal bone (from mammals, birds, and fish) was found. Floors 5–6 are semicompact and reddish gray (2.5YR 5/0). Floor 5 is composed of sand, gravel, broken shell, fragments of unburned sea urchins, ashes, and wood fragments. Floor 6 is similar, with stone lithics, bones, shells, gourds, charcoal, bean pods, and squash seeds. Fragments of gourd, with perforations for mending, were recovered in both floors. Floor 7 is semicompact and dark reddish gray (7.5YR 4/0). It is composed of sand, shell, bone, unidentified wood, bean pods, and gourd fragments. A few mammal and fish bones were recovered.

Floors 8, ~0.86–1.12 m: The soil is semicompact and black (7.5YR 2/1). The floor is composed of sand, gravel, and broken shell. Materials were shells, bones, lithics, textile fragments, charcoal, sea cucumber, and unidentified wood. Three features were found.

Features 1–3: Three hearths were identified in this floor and defined as features. All three are shallow depressions (1–2 cm) with ash and charcoal fill. Hearth 1 has a diameter of 70 cm, Hearth 2 has a diameter of 80 cm, and Hearth 3 has a diameter of 80 cm.

Floors 9–11, ~1.12–1.96 m: Floors 9 and 10 are semicompact, composed of sand, gravel, and ash, and are brownish gray (10YR 5/1). Materials include bone, lithics, gourds, cotton, plant remains, unidentified wood, and charcoal. Three hearths were located in Floor 9 and designated as Features 1, 2, and 3. A possible posthole was found at a depth of 1.96 m. Only Floor 9 had food remains, mainly shells.

Floors 12–15, ~1.96–3.27 m: Floor 12 is semicompact, composed of ash and broken shells. It is brownish gray (10YR 5/1). Materials consisted of bones, plant remains, and lithics. Floor 13 is compact, composed of sand, ash, and broken shell. It is also brownish gray (10YR 5/1). Floors 14 and 15 are similar and contain a variety of plant material.

Floors 16–19, ~3.27–5.17 m: Floor 16 is brownish gray (10YR 5/2). Materials recovered were plants and bones. Floors 17 and 18, separated by a thin sandy fill, are thick, with abundant plant remains. Floor 19 is dark gray (7YR 4/1) with a high quantity of charcoal and ash and plants, shells, and bones.

Floors 20–23, ~5.17–6.23 m: Floor 20 is a brownish gray (10YR 5/2). Materials recovered were plants, shell, and bone. Floor 21 is similar to Floor 20, with an abundance of burned rocks, bones, lithics, plants, and charcoal. Floors 22 and 23 are a dark gray (7YR 4/1) with a high quantity of charcoal, ash, and plants.

Floors 24–28, ~6.23–6.91 m: These are a series of thin floors and fills with less plant, bone, lithic, shell, and ash and charcoal. As in the case of the lower floor layers of Unit 20, a high quantity of sea lion bones were recovered. These deeper floors also contained maize remains (see chapter 10; Grobman et al. 2012).

Below these floors are early Holocene deposits that were minimally explored. They are thin lenses of charcoal, shell, bone, lithics, red hematite, and some plant remains, including a *Capsicum* sp. seed ^{14}C dated around 10,500 cal BP (see chapters 6 and 10). These premound levels are associated with marine and wetland foraging and are similar in content and structure to those in Units 2, 9, 12, 20, and HP-3.

Unit 22 represents a different type of stratigraphy from that documented in Huaca Prieta. Rather than containing discrete and discontinuous ritual spaces, it reveals a series of intact and mostly continuous floors and fills primarily associated with plant food preparation and probably with the consumption of both plant and meat from marine mammals. This unit also produced the best evidence for early maize agriculture (see chapter 10 and appendix 10; Grobman et al. 2012).

PA Unit 30: This unit lies at the southeast base of the Paredones mound and was placed to link the mound to additional off-mound domestic areas (fig. 7.27).

Layers 1–3, ~0–0.57 m: The soil texture is semicompact and brownish black (5YR 3/1), composed of sand, fine gravel, shells, Moche sherds, charcoal, burned clay, and plant remains (mainly corncobs).

Layers 4–6, ~0.57–0.85 m: The soil is semicompact and brownish black (5YR 3/1), with both fine and coarse sand, ash, and broken shell. Materials were bone, shell, burned rock, plant remains, and charcoal. Features 1–3 were small hearths (23–45 cm).

Layers 7–8, ~0.85–0.99 m: The soil texture is semicompact, composed of fine gravel, charcoal, and ash. Materials recovered were a few shells, bivalves and snails, and charcoal fragments. Layer 7 is grayish red (7.5YR 6/2), and Layer 8 is brownish black (5YR 3/1).

Layers 9–10, ~0.99–1.68 m: The soil is compact and is a dull reddish brown (5YR 4/3) to a dark red gray (7.5YR 3/4), composed of sand, gravel, ash, and broken shell. Materials were rock, bone, shell, plant remains, burned clay, and charcoal. Several stones indicative of a possible feature were associated with a patch of yellow clay.

Layers 14–18, ~1.68–2.86 m: The soil texture is semicompact and brown (10YR 3/4), composed of fine gravel, decomposed bone, and ash. Materials include shell and bone. Six articulated fish vertebrae, a large shark vertebra, and a stone mortar were recovered in Layer 18.

Layers 19–20, ~2.86–3.79 m: The soil is semicompact and is a dull yellowish brown (10YR 5/4) to dark reddish gray (7.5YR 4/1), composed of sand, fine gravel, ash, and fragments of charcoal. Materials were lithics, bone, shell, and charcoal.

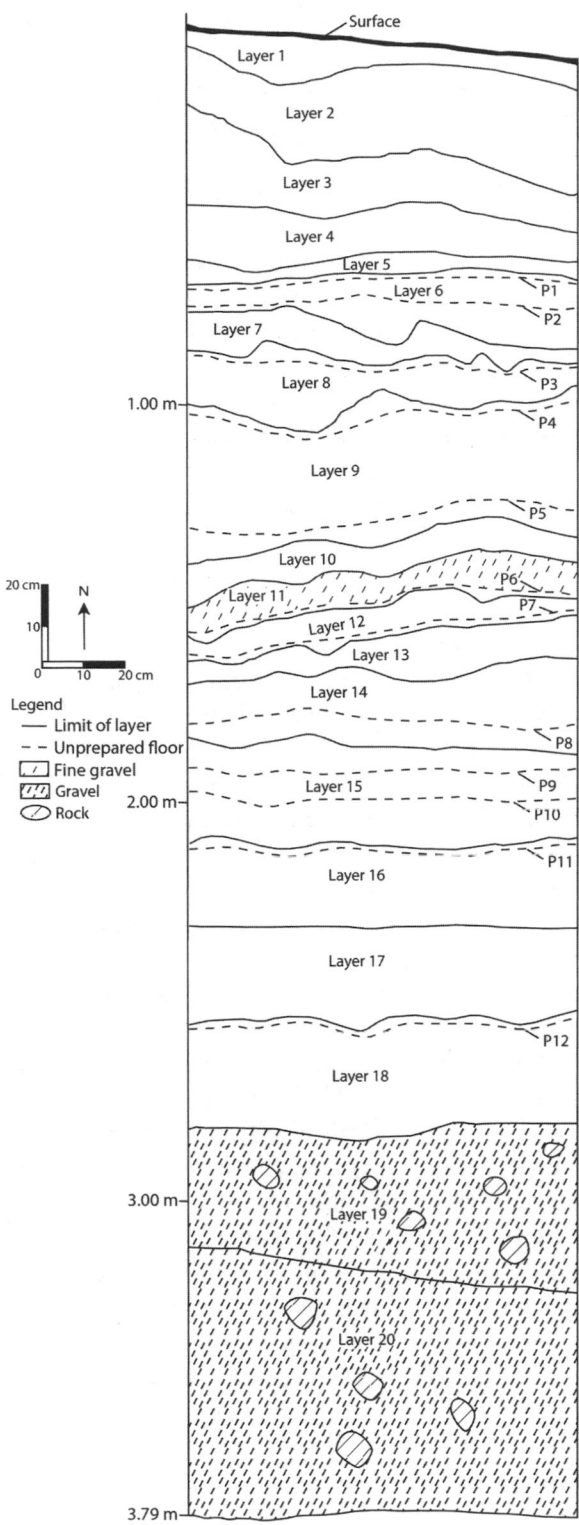

FIGURE 7.27. Profile of west wall of Unit 30.

Beneath both mounds is early domestic debris indicative of sporadic habitation by marine and wetland foragers, as evidenced by burned areas, hematite stains, and lithic, shell, and bone scatters dating from the late Pleistocene to the early Holocene (see chapters 6, 9, and 11 and Dillehay et al. 2012a). Around 7500 cal BP at Huaca Prieta and 6500 cal BP at Paredones, planned mound building began after earlier use of the underlying and off-mound areas of the terrace. The bulk of sediments in both mounds derives primarily from organic materials, the waste from food consumption, most likely related to multiple ritual and probably nonritual commensal episodes, burials, and offerings at Huaca Prieta and to food preparation and consumption at Paredones. Fuel residues are also evident as wood charcoal and coarse mineral grains indicative of excessive combustion, especially at Huaca Prieta. Throughout the history of Paredones, floors and fills spanned the entire length and width of the mound, indicating deliberate and continuous expansive surfaces, unlike the discrete, spatially circumscribed episodes and heavily truncated stratigraphy in Phases III–V at Huaca Prieta. (Phase II at Huaca Prieta also contained some continuous layering similar in content and structure to the layering at Paredones, as best represented in Unit 22.)

The consistently compacted, indurated nature of cement-like plaster and the berm footings of mortared cobbles seen in Phases III–V at Huaca Prieta do not exist extensively at Paredones, perhaps because the latter mound was no higher than ~6 m and did not require retention measures. (A few stone footings at Paredones perhaps suggest the intent to build the mound higher, but this never occurred.) Other distinctive features of Paredones are the contrasts in organic materials and the variances in the organic and inorganic components within floors and fills. Paredones contains more abundant and diverse edible plant remains and fewer marine resources than Huaca Prieta (see chapters 9 and 10). Paredones also has a high content of charcoal and thus is also a dark mound but with a lower charcoal than at Huaca Prieta and hence less dark. Unit 22 floors at Paredones contained extraordinarily high amounts of *Typha* sp., suggesting that they may have been covered with reed mats or, more likely, that reed mats were produced at Paredones for use at Huaca Prieta and elsewhere (see chapter 12 and appendix 12). Given the excellent preservation of organics at these sites, the absence of mats at Paredones supports the latter possibility. Although mats were found in abundance at Huaca Prieta, the *Typha* sp. pollen content there was considerably less. We are unsure of the kinds of rituals carried out at Paredones; they may be related primarily to the preparation of plant foods for consumption at Huaca Prieta, making the Paredones mound ancillary to activity at Huaca Prieta. Although we found no clear offerings, there was a great deal of evidence for food preparation at Paredones but no domestic debris. Layers such as house remains, hearths, postholes, food pits, lithic debitage, food waste, burials, thick use surfaces with high amounts of waste and intrusive features, and so forth were recorded at the outlying domestic sites.

Furthermore, no informal graves, formal chamber burials, or ritual offerings were present at Paredones. The small chamber tombs in Units 10 and 23, those in Bird's excavation on top of the mound, and those around the upper edge of the sunken circular plaza at Huaca Prieta are late in time, dating to Phases IV and V, and are associated with the construction of the plaza and the entry ramp.

Chapter 8 and appendix 10 present a detailed analysis of the human skeletal remains briefly reported for each excavated unit above. Thirteen human skeletons and various human bone elements were recovered from excavations in and around Huaca Prieta and in domestic Unit 16. Only human teeth were recovered from Paredones. Five fetuses and children and eight young to old adult skeletons were excavated by our project. Two adult skeletons reveal postmortem disturbance (HP09-01 and HP09-07), but this could be related to secondary burial or to later intrusive domestic activities. As with most other Preceramic mortuary practices in the Central Andes (see chapter 8), body orientation and position are variable, with skeletons oriented to the east and west and north to south and in various flexed and semiflexed positions. Most burials that we excavated also have rocks placed on and around the graves, which also is typical of Pre-

ceramic burials in the Central Andes. Red pigment was found on two adult and one child burial; Bird found it on only one adult individual. However, both Bird's and our excavations recovered red pigment from numerous textiles and baskets. Both skeletal collections reveal some nutritional stress, especially due to low amounts of Vitamins B and C for two individuals we excavated, which was not expected due to the high amount of chile pepper remains found at excavated sites. (Could these two persons have come from distant areas where chile peppers were not a dietary staple?) At least three individuals in our collection and one in Bird's assemblage had physical trauma on the bones, but this could be related to occupational hazards (such as diving and climbing on slippery rocks) rather than resulting from armed conflict or domestic violence, which are infrequent in Preceramic Andean societies. Exostoses were recorded for the majority of adult males in both skeletal collections and possibly for one female, which indicates a division of labor, with males likely diving and harvesting marine resources. In terms of age and sex patterns, Bird found twice as many female skeletons as males; we recovered an even amount for both sexes. Both collections suggest that adults were dying between the ages of 35 and 50.

Finally, although the sample sizes are limited, soil chemical analyses of floors and use surfaces within the two mounds, as well as domestic Unit 16, indicate different chemical signatures. Paredones generally contains higher percentages of organic debris, potassium, and calcium, which is generally more indicative of plant material, while Huaca Prieta and Unit 16 exhibit less organic debris, which suggests more marine products (see appendix 18). These general patterns may indicate differential discard of these remains, further suggesting different degrees of access to food products and perhaps social and other differentiation and various specialized economic tasks and activities carried out at these sites.

OFF-MOUND DOMESTIC UNITS (DU)

The excavation data at both the Huaca Prieta and Paredones mounds suggested nondomestic activity, at least after the initial layers of construc-

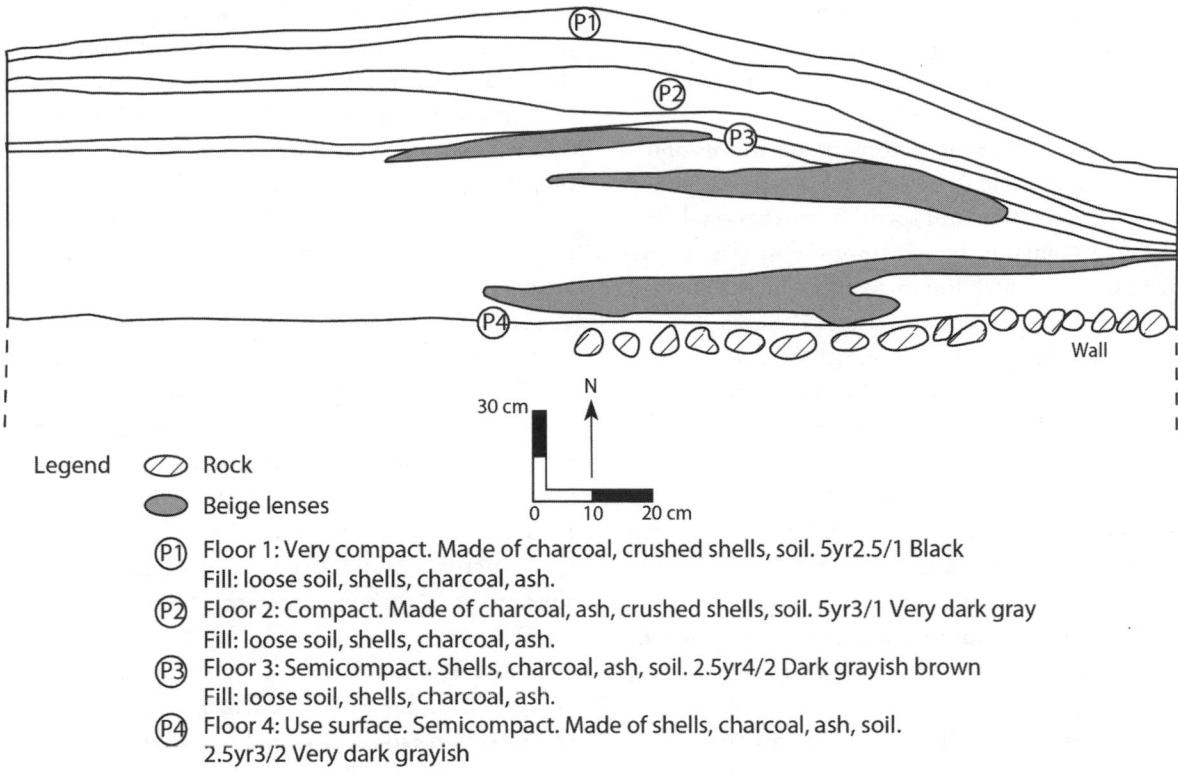

+ 0.00m

Legend

⬭ Rock

⬬ Beige lenses

30 cm

N

0 10 20 cm

(P1) Floor 1: Very compact. Made of charcoal, crushed shells, soil. 5yr2.5/1 Black
Fill: loose soil, shells, charcoal, ash.

(P2) Floor 2: Compact. Made of charcoal, ash, crushed shells, soil. 5yr3/1 Very dark gray
Fill: loose soil, shells, charcoal, ash.

(P3) Floor 3: Semicompact. Shells, charcoal, ash, soil. 2.5yr4/2 Dark grayish brown
Fill: loose soil, shells, charcoal, ash.

(P4) Floor 4: Use surface. Semicompact. Made of shells, charcoal, ash, soil.
2.5yr3/2 Very dark grayish

FIGURE 7.28. Profile of north wall of Unit 13.

tion at both sites. After reopening and cleaning Bird's excavation units at the Cupisnique mound, we discovered late Preceramic domestic debris below it. Based on this combined information and on our observations in outlying geological cores and test pits, which revealed Preceramic habitational debris scattered across various areas of the Sangamon terrace, we decided to open several off-mound test pits between the Huaca Prieta and Paredones mounds to search for domestic sites. This work also complemented our survey and testing of domestic sites north, east, and south of the Sangamon terrace. The results of these excavations are reported below.

DU Unit 13: This 2 by 2 m unit was excavated at the base of the Sangamon terrace, immediately west of the Cupisnique mound, to test for habitation debris. A series of unprepared floors, fills, and wall segments of domestic structures was found (fig. 7.28).

Floor and Fill 1, ~0–0.19 m: The soil texture is hard and compact. The color was black (10YR 2/1). Materials included bone, shell, wood, and charcoal.

Floor and Fill 2, ~0.19–0.30 m: The soil texture is hard and compact. Floor 2 is light gray (10YR 7/1). Materials were bone, shell, wood, and charcoal. A wall segment 0.87 m long was recorded here.

Floor and Fill 3, ~0.30–0.58 m: The soil texture is compact. The floor is dark gray (7.5YR 4/1) with lenses of light olive brown (2.5YR 6/3) soil. Materials were rock, bone, shell, and charcoal. A ^{14}C date of 4283–3974 cal BP (AA81920) was assayed.

Floor and Fill 4, ~0.58–0.94 m: The soil is semicompact and is gray and dark brown (10YR 2/1). A stone wall segment begins in the northeast corner and extends to the south. Materials were rock, bone, shell, burned rock, and charcoal. Several features were recorded.

Feature 1: A stone wall 1.0 m high on Floor 1 emerges from the northeast corner and extends to the west.

Feature 2: This is a concentration of rocks or a wall segment associated with Floor 1.

Feature 3: A concentration of rocks and a stone wall 0.80 m long extended across the unit. It is part of the wall found on Floor 2.

Feature 4: A wall segment (25 cm long) is found below the floor.

The discontinuous wall segments in this unit are not of a single structure and lack correspondence in direction and form. Segments on different floors apparently represent the spatial boundaries of individual domestic units that had been disturbed due to repeated use of the area. The unprepared floors are discontinuous and become less compact and change color and content across the unit, each representing a different use episode. The features and cultural debris are similar to those of the domestic units recovered in Units 16 and 26, which lie about 30 m southeast on the edge of the terrace at the southwest base of the Cupisnique mound.

DU Unit 16: This unit originally was 4 by 5 m and is located 40 m north of Huaca Prieta on the western edge of the Sangamon terrace near the Cupisnique mound (fig. 7.1). The unit consists of multiple layers, floors, houses, and burials (figs. 7.29 and 7.30). None of the burials were associated with or below house floors; all were placed in tombs outside of houses.

Layer 1, ~0–0.38 m: This layer is a compact, dark gray (2.5YR 4/1) soil. Materials include lithics, fish bones, shell, gourd, burned plants, and charcoal.

Layers 2–3, ~0.38–0.58 m: The soil is slightly compact and gray (2.5YR 4/1). Materials include shell, rock, fishbone, plant remains, charcoal, a reed rope, and wood. A few human bone fragments were recovered and dated to Phase V (see appendix 10). Layer 3 yielded three different areas of dispersed human bones indicative of secondary burials, all dating to late Phase IV.

House 1: Layers 2 and 3 presented a circular arrangement of rocks. Floor 1 was registered at 42 cm. Floor 2 was recorded slightly below at 60 cm and was defined by plaster and medium-sized rocks. It was not associated with a structure. Materials were lithics, fish bones, shell, and charcoal. Two postholes were uncovered in Floor 2. The house was ~3.8 m in diameter.

Layer 4, ~0.58–0.82 m: The soil is semicompact and a dark gray (2.5YR 4/1). Materials were fish, bird and other bones, charcoal, gourd fragments, reeds, pockets of ash, and plant remains. The remains of additional house floors and structures and three burials appeared in this layer. On the edge of the terrace just west of Structure 2 are two articulated human skeletons in shallow tombs defined by standing cobblestones and large pieces of polychaete. These are burials HP09-01 and HP09-02 (see chapter 8). Both tombs date to early Phase IV. HP09-01 is an older female associated with a possible weaving tool.

House 2: This structure was below House 1 and measured 4.5 by 4.7 m. It was radiocarbon dated to ~5583–5325 cal BP (Beta290654).

House 3: This is a structure of rocks and mud mortar; the shape is semicircular and measures ~4.4 by 5.0 m in diameter. It dates earlier than Houses 1 and 2. Floors 3 and 4 are associated with this structure. An unburned corncob produced an aberrant radiocarbon date in this layer (see chapter 6).

House 4: Structures of stone and mud mortar were found in House 4, which is contemporaneous with House 1. Burial 4 (HP09-03) was a nearly complete skeleton of a middle-aged adult female who was interred flexed, on her left side, with her head oriented toward the south. Burial 4 was associated with the exterior of the sinuous exterior wall of House 4. It measured 3.1 by 3.2 m. House 4 dates to late Phase III.

Layer 5, ~0.82–1.26 m: The layer has rocks and consolidated soil and is gray (10YR 7/1). Materials include charcoal, wood, reeds, shell, lithics, and carbonized seeds. Several partial floors were uncovered, indicating periods of reuse and disuse, each associated with varying frequencies of large pieces of polychaete of tube-base. The floor extensions ranged between 1.2 to 2.8 m in size and occasionally were associated with aligned walled segments indicating disturbed structures. This evidence indicates domestic reuse and refurbishment of the area. The floors extended to a depth of 1.26 m and cover no more than 1.5 m² in size. Three burials were recovered from Layer 5, all dating to early Phase III: HP09-04, HP09-05, and HP09-06 (see chapter 8).

House 5: To the east of Structure 4 was House 5, in the form of a semicircle, with a base of mud mortar. This house was cut on its east and

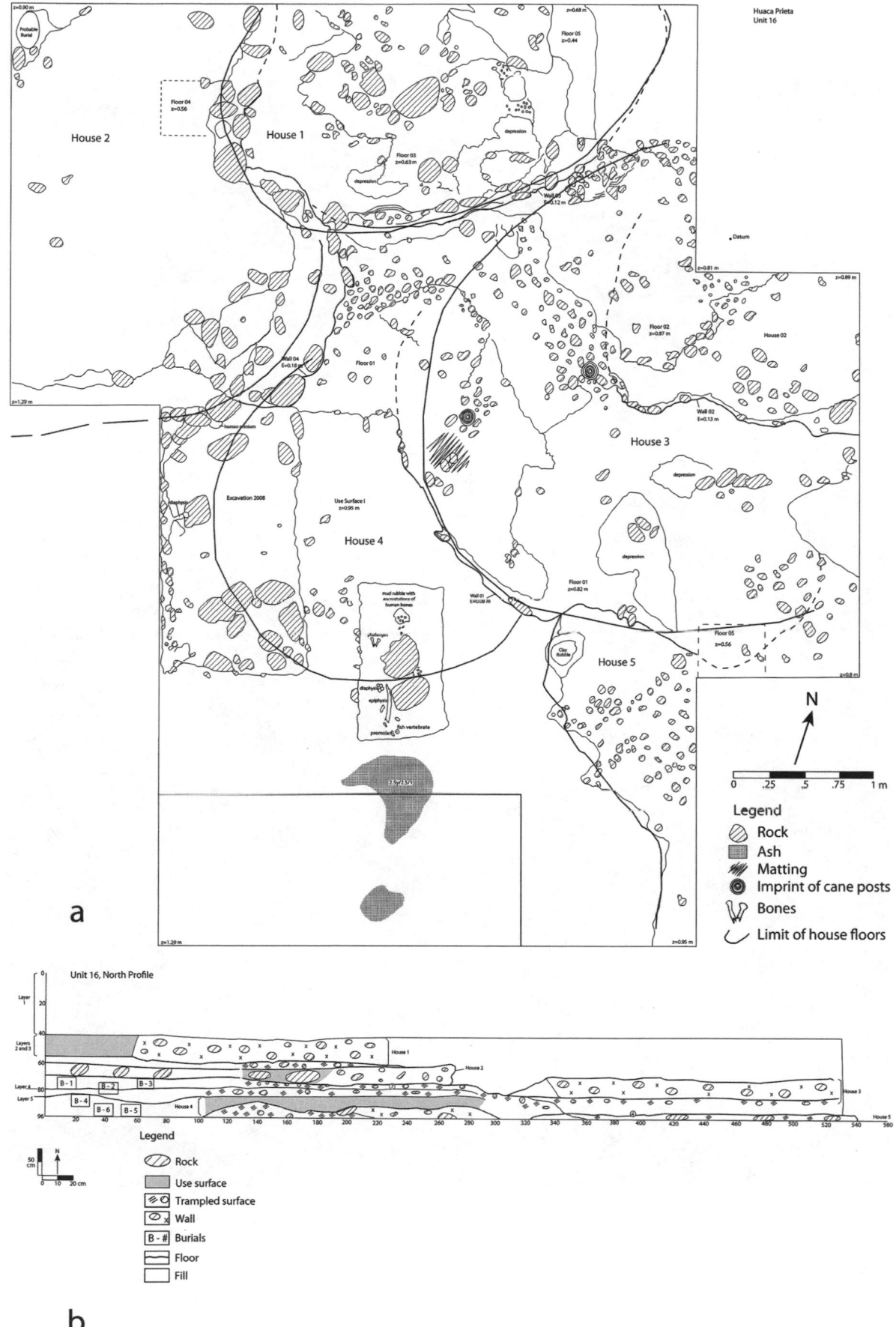

FIGURE 7.29. *a*, plan of house foundations in Unit 16; *b*, schematic profile of floors and structures in Unit 16.

FIGURE 7.30. *a*, house floors in Unit 16; *b*, burial HP09-05, showing sculpted blocks of polychaete tube-base placed on the corpse, including the squarish block with 20 depressions (*arrow*) and the anthropomorphic-shaped head.

west ends by later house walls. House 5 is the oldest and deepest structure in Unit 16. It could not be accurately measured due to partial destruction. Floors 5 and 6 were recorded in this unit. Materials were charcoal, fish bone, mammal bone, lithics, burned seeds, and gourd. Wood charcoal from a hearth dated the floor to Phase II at ~7413–7005 cal BP (AA87665), which is slightly after mound building began at Huaca Prieta.

Burial 5 (HP09-05), dating to late Phase III, was located in the southwest sector of the unit (fig. 7.30b). Five sculpted blocks of polychaete tubes covered it (see chapter 8). One block had 20 circular depressions arranged in four rows of five (see chapter 11). Two complete spheroid stones of andesite, one black and the other white, were placed next to this block. Another block was shaped into the head of an anthropomorphic figure. Three other blocks were sculpted but not in any discernible form. When the worked polychaete blocks were removed from above the skull, a concentration of interwoven reeds, shells, a reed bundle of salt crystals, and fragmentary human bones was revealed. This burial appears to be associated with a distinguished individual.

About 73 cm to the west of burial HP09-05 was a second burial (HP09-06), completely fractured and facing west. A polychaete block located next to the skull was not worked but was associated with fragments of reed and shell. This burial also dated to late Phase III.

Layer 13-7, ~1.26–2.3 m: This layer was south of the houses and had no house floor but was associated with a series of intact thin use surfaces and thick fills containing scant faunal, floral, and lithic remains. A ^{14}C sample was assayed at 7266–7021 cal BP (AA86935) on wood charcoal in a burned feature at level 1.45 m, a date that corresponds with House Floor 5.

In addition, seven other layers (numbers 13-8 to 16-5) were excavated underneath the house remains in the southwest part of this unit. These layers date to the late Pleistocene and early Holocene and are described in chapter 6. In general these layers are characterized by sparse cultural remains (burned areas and lithics and a few bone, shell, and floral remains).

In summary, five slightly imbricated small circular house foundations were found in this unit. In addition to the foundations, the excavation yielded nine human skeletons and a small quantity of implements and ornaments made of bone, stone, and shell. Eight skeletons were in open areas between foundations. Burial implements and ornaments were discovered, including two sculpted blocks of polychaete tubes and several shell ornaments. In addition, some small fragments of red pigment were found in burial deposits.

The house foundations were organized as multistructural extensions stratified into five layers in deposits of ~1.5 m thick. The circular houses were stone-lined and built of *quincha*. Each was about 4 by 6 m² in area and opened onto an open space. Most had unprepared soil floors. The multilayered foundations are the result of periodic rebuilding of the houses over a long period. Several layers of foundation are superimposed with little disjunction and the style of architecture did not change, suggesting long-lasting domestic stability in the area. Very few artifacts and animal bones remained on the floors, as the houses were probably cleaned out before rebuilding. Each house had at least one hearth (~1 m in diameter, usually located in the center of the house floors). A few stone, shell, and bone tools were found. The lower exterior surface of the remaining wall foundations and the ground next to them were sometimes heavily burned or had charcoal piled against them, indicating that outdoor cooking activities probably took place there. Debris found in the house compounds also suggests that some of the processes involved in manufacturing and resharpening tools were carried out. Marine resources and floral remains, including carbonized and uncarbonized corncobs, were also recovered.

The results of coring tests indicate that no foundations existed in the area immediately outside the unit, although additional house foundations were found a few meters to the east in Unit 26. This multihouse group likely does not form an independent cluster; it probably extends underneath the Cupisnique mound to the north.

Finally, three radiocarbon dates were assayed on avocado seeds (*Persea* sp.) and on a bean seed (*Phaseolus* sp.) from Layers 2 to 16 in Unit 16. The avocado seeds dated at 525–513 cal BP (Layer 2) and 10,486–10,158 cal BP (Layer 14), while the bean seed assayed at 15,217–14,221 cal BP (Layer 16). For this early time, the bean probably is a wild form. The avocado seed dated to 525–513 cal BP is very late and does not agree with assays from other intact strata in Layer 16 (see table 6.2).

DU Unit 26: This was a 3 by 5 m unit with an extension located just east of Unit 16. The geophysical survey indicated dark stains, which required subsurface testing (see appendix 15). The surface texture is a loose, semicompact, homogeneous soil. Materials recovered were rock and shell.

Layer 1, ~0–0.29 m: This layer is yellowish (10YR 8/6) with some reddish lenses. The surface was compact and homogeneous. Materials recovered were rock, bone, shell, and wood. Two decorated Guañape-like sherds and many unburned sea urchin spines were recovered.

Layers 2–3, ~0.29–0.84 m: A thick plaster appears in this layer, which has a large quantity of sea urchin spines. A dark gray plaster was found in part of the unit; it was yellow in another part and a light olive brown (2.5YR 6/3) in another. Several extensive burned areas (0.85–1.3 m in diameter) were recorded in Layer 3, which corresponds with anomalies observed in the geophysical survey. No house remains were found in this unit; the dark features were interpreted as workshops for food preparation associated with the domestic structures in Unit 16.

SUMMARY OF EXCAVATED DOMESTIC UNITS

In summary, the excavated data from these domestic units of the Sangamon terrace, which are located near the Huaca Prieta mound, are different in size and form from the outlying households located off of the terrace to the north and south. It is not known whether these are different social groups, perhaps more privileged than others because they reside on the terrace and near the mound, or simply a different population segment focused on different maritime resources or people who maintained the mound area. Also significant is that none of the excavated domestic units yielded the decorated gourd and other material fragments and ritual offerings recovered at Paredones and especially at Huaca Prieta. But these two sites do not contain hearths, the density of waste debris, and the wide variety of tools, postholes, and other domestic indicators observed at the residential sites of Units 13, 16, and 26 and

at the outlying residential mounds reported below and later (chapter 13).

Based on the data retrieved from cleaning Bird's pits on the Cupisnique mound, observations of Preceramic domestic debris and house structures in geological test pits and archaeological excavations in off-mound areas between the Paredones and the Cupisnique mounds and between the latter mound and Huaca Prieta, and the data from Units 13, 16, and 26, we believe that an extensive Preceramic residential village extended several hundred meters north of Huaca Prieta. Although much of this village has probably been destroyed by the construction of the Cupisnique and Paredones mounds, it also is likely that portions of this village still remain and can be exposed by deep, extensive excavation. It is probable that this village was contemporary with the Huaca Prieta and Paredones mounds and likely was the primary support for the local population associated with these mounds.

TEST PITS 1–32

The brief description of test pits below discusses their purpose, content, and chronology. As noted in appendix 15, several of the test pits were dug to examine subsurface anomalies indicated by geophysical survey, but most were designed to test for buried domestic sites possibly related to the activities recorded at Huaca Prieta and Paredones.

Test Pit 1, ~0–1.5 m: This 1 by 2 m pit was located near the southeast base of Huaca Prieta. The deposits were culturally sterile. Gravel and a large number of stones were recorded all through this deposit. None were parts of structures. The base of an old lagoon was reached at the 1.5 m layer (see chapter 5); the sediment in it was a whitish clay (5YR 8/1).

Test Pit 2, ~0–1.6 m: This pit was located 20 m south of Test Pit 1. A thin cultural deposit (15 cm thick) contained shell and rock. Underneath was a midden deposit mixed with stones, charcoal, and bones. Underneath this layer was another midden mixed with small pebbles, stones, animal bones, charcoal, and ash. These deposits were a dark gray (2.5YR 4/2). Below this layer were lagoon deposits.

Test Pit 3, ~0–2.8 m: The pit was located east

of the entryway to the sunken circular plaza on top of Huaca Prieta and approximately midway between the top of the mound and its base. The purpose of digging the pit was to test whether this area contained overburden tossed downslope as a result of looters who excavated the hole. The slope had a hard, intact, thick plaster (~25 cm thick) similar to other areas on the mound; below it were stratified, intact deposits of shell, rock, and charcoal that indicated typical mound stratigraphy, not tossed overburden. Stratum 2 at a depth of 1.1 m was ^{14}C dated at 4081–3730 cal BP (Beta278233).

Test Pit 4a–d, ~0–2.4 m: A series of four 1 by 1 m pits was placed in a northeast to southwest direction at the base of southwestern Huaca Prieta to define the stratigraphy and interface between the old beach and the mound. Midden deposits and thin slope wash were recorded. The deposits were similar in cultural composition: shell, charcoal, rock, lithics, and bones. Thin lenses of slope wash containing fractured shell and sand were intermittently dispersed in the pits, which were excavated to 2.1 m. The two lower pits contained large deposits of salt, which Pino believed were deliberately stored as caches in pits at the base of the mound (Pino, personal communication, 2009).

Test Pit 5, ~0–2.0 m: In HP-2 on the west side of the mound, we placed a 2 by 2 m pit to take the unit deeper to determine whether earlier deposits were present, as they were in Bird's HP-3 unit on the northeast side of the mound. We located the base of Bird's excavation in this area and excavated ~1.2 m deeper, finding four thin lenses of fractured shell and charcoal radiocarbon dated at 5919–5667 cal BP (Beta233648). Cultural deposits were light gray (10YR 7/1) and mixed with organic materials. Below was the buried, culturally sterile Sangamon terrace.

Test Pit 6, ~0–2.1 m: This pit was located at the southern base of a L-shaped "dune" about 100 m east of the terrace in the floodplain. It was excavated to test whether the dune was a large, above-ground, raised agricultural field, which proved to be the case. A 4 cm thick dark use surface about 4.3 m long and a dark, beveled-shape surface appeared at the 1.8 m level, which was a 5 cm thick use surface of a raised agricultural field oriented north to south. Underneath was a mixed deposit of sand; the base of the structure was made of large capillary stones to allow water

to pass through. The only artifacts recovered were two early Moche sherds. Below the base of the unit and the Moche sherds was another use surface that was burned; it yielded a radiocarbon date of 3823–3483 cal BP (Beta247696), which corresponds with the last phase of use of the Huaca Prieta mound. It is not known whether this deeper, burned surface was part of a subterranean raised field; lagoon deposits were found immediately below the deeper burned surface.

Test Pit 7, ~0–1.4 m: Pit 7 also was excavated at the base of a large above-ground dune, located 200 m north of the road that runs just south of Huaca Prieta. The context was the same as in Test Pit 6, except that no sherds were recovered. Similar cultural deposits were found at a depth of ~1.80 m, indicating that this was a raised field; we found no below-ground evidence of a raised field, although lagoonal deposits were found.

Test Pit 8, ~0–1.2 m: Two deposits were recorded, which were a mix of gravel and earth. A stone wall extended to the south and west at 0.78 m. No diagnostic artifacts were found to date this pit.

Test Pit 9, ~0–1.5 m: This 1 by 2 m pit was located on the eastern edge of the Sangamon terrace midway between the mounds of Paredones and Cupisnique. The purpose of digging it was to record buried materials associated with the terrace. A collapsed stone wall was recorded. A few burned stones, fractured shells, and charcoal were observed along with broken conical-shaped adobe bricks. Given the location of this pit, immediately north of the Cupisnique mound, the surface of the terrace appears to have been disturbed by the removal of sediments to make conical adobes for the mound. The pit was excavated to a depth of 1.5 m. An upper stratum dated to 3614–3398 cal BP (AA86944), which corresponds roughly with the abandonment of Huaca Prieta.

Test Pit 10, ~0–1.3 m: This pit was located about 40 m south of Test Pit 9 along the eastern edge of the terrace. The recovered deposits were the same as those observed in Test Pit 9. The pit was excavated to 1.3 m.

Test Pit 11, ~0–1.2 m: This 1 by 2 m unit was located at the eastern edge of the terrace but closer to the Cupisnique mound. Two complete conical adobes were found in addition to several Cupisnique sherds, postholes, and shells.

Test Pit 12, ~0–1.3 m: This pit had the same purpose as Test Pits 9–11. A midden deposit of shells, charcoal, bone, and lithics was observed between 10 and 70 cm. The deposits are not intact middens; they were redeposited at this location from elsewhere, because the strata are mixed.

Test Pit 13, ~0–1.6 m: This 1 by 2 m pit was dug in the floodplain east of the terrace for purposes of defining the local stratigraphy and searching for more buried raised fields. No fields or artifacts were recovered, but the layer served to inform geologists of the lagoon and floodplain deposits. The pit was excavated to a depth of 2.1 m, at which point white clay and carbonate deposits of the lagoon were exposed. The upper layers of the excavation unit were brown to dark brown (10YR 2/1), composed of organic sediment and sand, and the lower ones contained a whitish gray clay (10YR 7/1).

Test Pit 14, ~0–1.4 m: This 2 by 2 m pit was located about 30 m south of Test Pit 13 and served the same purpose as Test Pit 13. The same layer and sediments were recorded. No artifacts were recovered.

Test Pit 15, ~0–5.3 m: This 1 by 2 m pit was dug in the center of the looter's hole on the south side of the mound to test for intact architecture or floors. Several thin floors contained plant material, including maize (see appendix 5). The test pit was later converted to Unit 15 (see the description for Units 15/21).

Test Pit 16, ~0–1.3 m: This was a geological pit placed by Pino to examine the stratigraphy near the southwest edge of the mound. Materials were rock, shell, lithics, and burned rock. Several use surfaces were defined, indicating that the area was used for various activities during the Preceramic and later ceramic periods. A disturbed human burial, a fragmented skull, and loose human bones were found in a fill at the 0.76 m level. The bones were underneath several large rocks (see appendix 10).

Test Pit 17, ~0–1.6 m: This pit was located southwest of unit HP-2 and off the mound. It contained Moche sherds and animal bones.

Test Pit 18, ~0–2.1 m: This was a looter's hole on the southwest side of the Paredones mound. The intact floors and fills of the mound were first observed in the profiles of this unit, which led us to place a larger unit on the eastern end of the mound (Unit 20). A ^{14}C date of 5577–5327 cal BP (AA86932) was obtained from Stratum 25.

Test Pit 19, ~0–2.1 m: This test pit was located off-mound on the southwest side of Huaca Prieta. It contained intermittent deposits of natural sand and cultural materials dating from the late Preceramic to Formative times.

Test Pit 20, ~0–.90 m: This pit was located and abandoned when observed to be a disturbed looter's hole.

Test Pit 21, ~0–1.2 m: This 1 by 2 m pit was placed in the road immediately south of the southern edge of the mound. It revealed mixed mound layers and deep culturally sterile basal gravel deposits typical of those found in Unit 2 on the southeast side of the mound.

Test Pit 22, ~0–6.2 m: This 2 by 2 m pit was placed on the lower eastern slope of Huaca Prieta about 15 m from the edge of the terrace. Its purpose was to define the chronology and stratigraphy of this sector of the mound (see chapter 6 and Dillehay et al. 2012a). Intermittent late Pleistocene and early Holocene deposits were found in the deepest layers (fig. 7.31). The basal stratum dated to 13,720–13,440 cal BP (Beta290620).

Test Pit 23, ~0–1.4 m: This 1 by 2 m test pit was excavated in the floodplain east of Huaca Prieta to reveal the geological stratigraphy. It was culturally sterile and had lagoon deposits in the deeper levels.

Test Pit 24, ~0–1.4 m: This 1 by 2 m pit was placed along the far western edge of the terrace about 20 m north of the northwest corner of the Cupisnique mound. Few materials were recovered due to slumping and erosion along this edge.

Test Pit 25, ~0–1.3 m: This 1 by 2 m pit was located on the small natural knoll just north of Huaca Prieta in the space between the mound and the Cupisnique mound to the north. It yielded Moche materials to a depth of 40 cm; it was culturally sterile below.

Test Pit 26, ~0–1.2 m: This 1 by 2 m pit was placed off the western edge of the Cupisnique mound and the terrace. The purpose was to test the stratigraphy in this area. No materials were found.

Test Pit 27, ~0–1.3 m: This 1 by 2 m test pit was placed due east of the Paredones mound between the eastern edge of the mound and the terrace about 25 m farther east. This pit revealed stratigraphy and materials similar to those in the deeper layers of Unit 20.

Test Pit 28, ~0–1.4 m: This 1 by 2 m pit was located in a small, dark household mound located about 25 m north of Test Pit 27 and associated with Paredones. It yielded materials similar to those of Test Pit 27.

Test Pit 29, ~0–1.3 m: This 1 by 2 m pit was located north of Test Pit 24. It was placed on the far western edge of the terrace about 60 m north of the Cupisnique mound. The pit yielded Moche materials in the upper 40 cm; no Preceramic materials were found below.

Test Pit 30, ~0–1.6 m: This 1 by 2 m pit was placed about 150 m east of the terrace from Paredones. It revealed a portion of a raised agricultural platform buried 81 cm below the ground surface.

Test Pit 31, ~0–1.5 m: This 1 by 2 m pit was located on the northeast end of the Paredones mound. The purpose was to test the interface between the mound base and the off-mound areas. It also revealed stratigraphy and material similar to those of Unit 30.

Test Pit 32, ~0–1.2 m: This 1 by 2 m pit was placed in a buried agricultural field ~300 m east of Paredones. The field was 0.85 m high and 4.8 m wide and had a 0.4 m thick dark brown surface (fig. 7.32). A ^{14}C sample assayed at 5448–5067 cal BP (Beta233988).

In summary, the effects of the numerous test pits, clearing, and sediment definition in mound and off-mound and terrace and off-terrace deposits were compared across areas. Hearths with shallow depressions, burned stones, and charcoal and ash were observed in several off-mound test pits adjacent to Huaca Prieta and Paredones (see appendix 1), suggesting that some off-mound locations immediately west of Huaca Prieta were staging areas with many hearths and an abundance of ash and charcoal, perhaps places for lighting torches and preparing for rituals on the mounds. Other areas represent off-mound domestic activity from early to late Holocene times. Very few tools, food remains, and other domestic items were present in the test pits, however, indicating that these were not full-time residential areas. Sediment translocation to build the later adobe brick mounds north of Huaca Prieta may account for part of the disturbance of the stratigraphy in several test pits, particularly those located north of

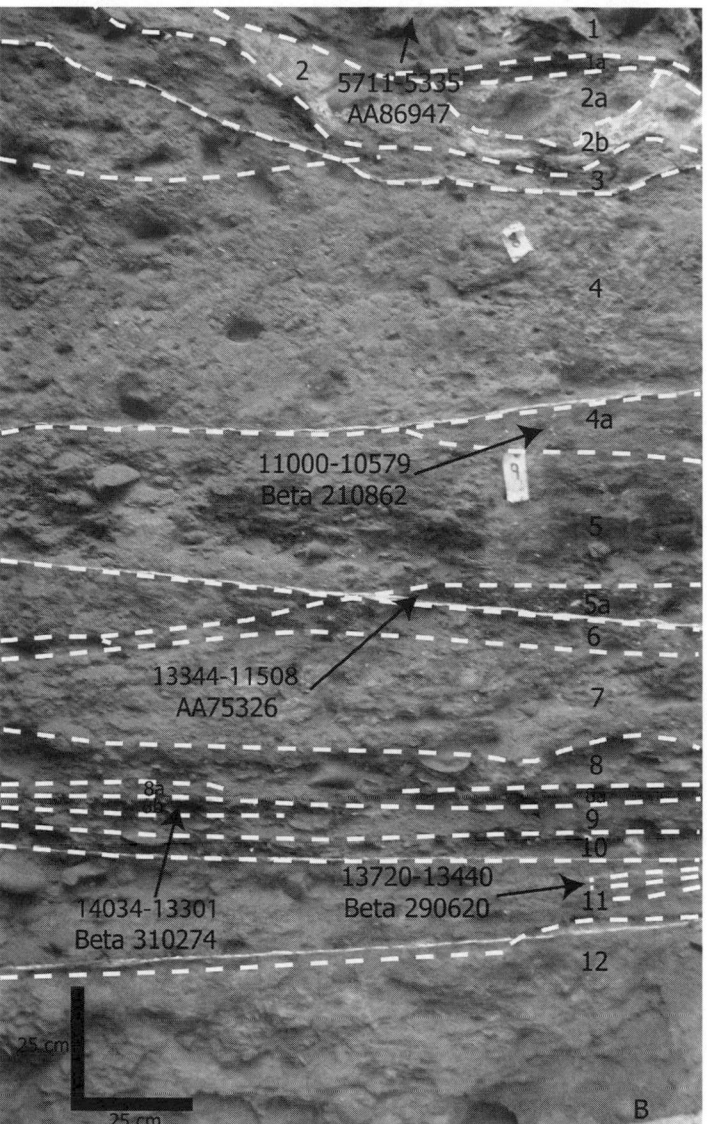

FIGURE 7.31. Profile of Test Pit 22.

Huaca Prieta and in the vicinity of the Cupisnique and Paredones mounds. Stratigraphy seen in the premound contexts of the south side of Huaca Prieta reinforces the generally undisturbed nature of the southern end of this portion of the terrace. Wall profiles from the deeper pits consisted of intact deposits and the original surface of the terrace. Test pits off of the south end of the mound also revealed the contours of an ancient stream that passed by the edge of the terrace and had been modified by modern-day drainages. Test Pits 28–31 were placed in accordance with subsurface anomalies revealed by the geophysical survey (see appendix 15).

FIGURE 7.32. Drainage ditch east of Paredones, showing part of a thin, burned surface (*arrows*) of the beveled side of a buried raised agricultural platform.

Test Pits 1, 2, 6, 7, 13, 14, and 23 were all located in the floodplain off of the terrace to the east of Huaca Prieta and Paredones. These pits and detailed examination of the cut profiles of drainage ditches reveal that the area immediately east of Paredones and Huaca Prieta was first a lagoon of varying depths (~7500–6500 cal BP) and then a shallow, seasonal wetland (~6500–4000 cal BP) (see chapter 5). The deeper, now below-ground, late Preceramic raised fields were built during this latter period, with one field dated around 5200 cal BP. We suspect that the wetlands supporting the raised fields were also associated with seasonal groundwater agriculture in areas where these types of fields were not constructed.

DISCUSSION

Based on the stratigraphic profiles and their multiple radiocarbon dates, the mounds of Huaca Prieta and Paredones were built over a long period as a series of many interconnected layers of sand, burned material (including excessive quantities of sea urchin spines), cultural debris, prepared and unprepared floors and use surfaces and their fills,

ritual offerings, human burials, and plaster retention surfaces in the case of Huaca Prieta. Huaca Prieta progressed from an early habitation area (Phase I) to a low earthen mound (Phase II) to a planned mound with stone architectural alignments (Phase III) to a large mound monument with chamber tombs, an entry ramp, and a sunken circular plaza (Phases IV–V; fig. 7.33a–b).

Within the smaller, thinner, horizontally limited ritual floors and use surfaces at both sites (fig. 7.34), people utilized a wide variety of food sources and sediments, sometimes juxtaposing different types (for example, wetland vs. littoral; tidal vs. deep sea) complementing as well as contrasting with one another (see chapter 9). One pattern of note is the large amount of burned sea urchin spines throughout all cultural deposits of Huaca Prieta from late Phase II to Phases III–V, implying that this organism played a significant role both in ritual practice as an offering, revealed by numerous small piles in tombs and ritual spaces, and as an element of the mound's architecture. The remains of this organism appear only as a minor element at Paredones. Results of the excavation at Huaca Prieta imply that ritual use and construction of the mound occurred over a long enough time for slight erosion to take place, as some strata are occasionally interspersed with thin slope wash deposits. The need for extensive plaster seals and the vertical retention walls indicate that erosion was an occasional issue during Phases III–IV, especially for the steeper and higher Phases III–V strata. Mound construction and use at both sites occurred relatively slowly and frequently.

Comparing the stratigraphic profiles between excavation units using the Harris Matrices demonstrates the difficulty of trying to create a single integrated profile with these sites. The matrices reveal that thousands of thin blanket mantles and micro-layers existed within the lower and upper elevations of Huaca Prieta, primarily defined by hundreds of discrete ritual spaces usually demarcated by stone alignments and off-mound sediments (fig. 7.34). No stratigraphic breaks from one stratum on one profile could be securely matched to another across the entire site. The mound also demonstrated little variation in source materials, with differing textured sediments and fills placed adjacent to one another in both horizontal and vertical dimensions. There also were no appre-

Phase I
Phase II
Phase III
Phase III-V
Sunken Plaza
Retention Wall
Legend
Building Phases
Terrace
Ramp
Premound Occupation
Surface of Terrace
Sunken Plaza
30 m
15 m
0
15 m
30 m
N
Phase III-IV
Sunken Plaza
Retention Wall
Phase IV-V
Ramp
Phase IV
Sunken Plaza
Phase III-V
Retention Wall
Phase IV-V
Ramp
Phase V
IVb
IIIa
IV
V
III
II
T
Retention Wall
Ramp
200 m
Pacific ocean
50 m
Lagoonal wetland
20 m
10 m
0
10 m
20 m
N
Legend:
T Terrace
I Phase I surface (premound occupation)
II Phase II surface
III Phase III surface
IV Phase IV ramp
V Phase V surface
Phase IV-V ramp
Circular sunken plaza

a

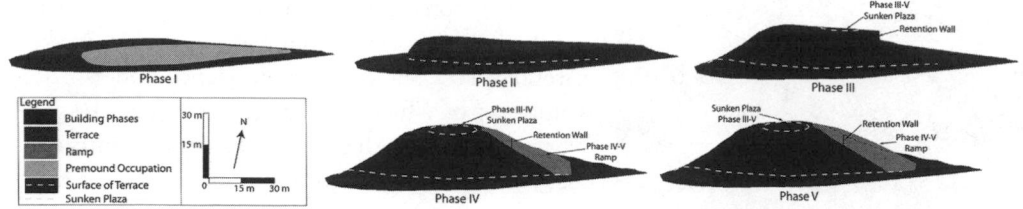

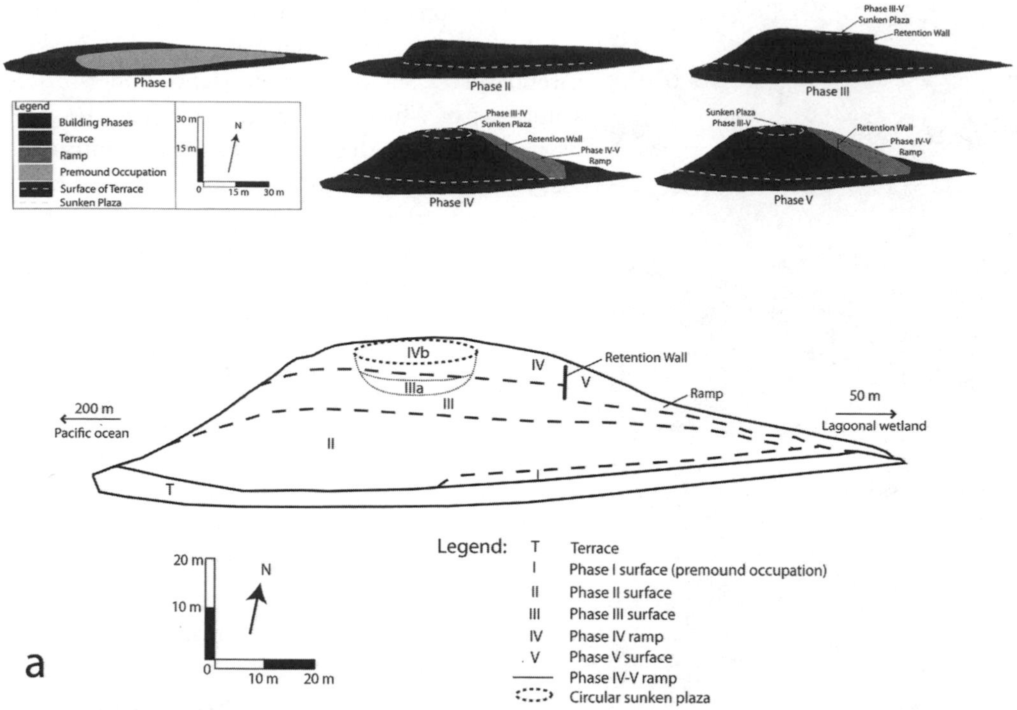

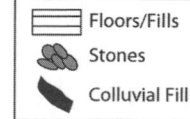

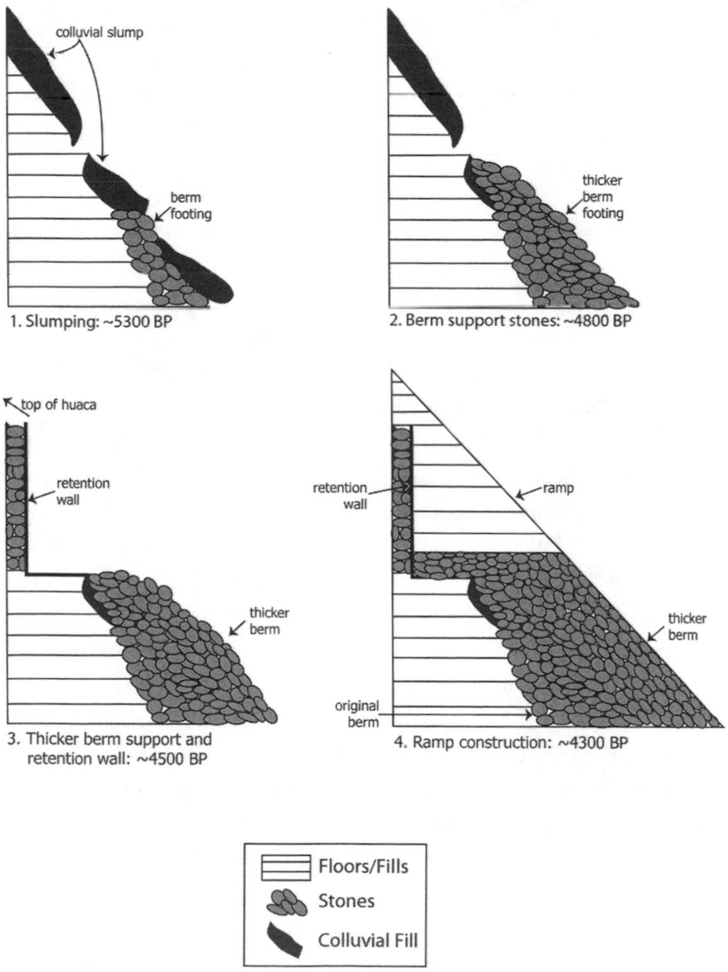

colluvial slump
berm
footing
1. Slumping: ~5300 BP
thicker
berm
footing
2. Berm support stones: ~4800 BP
top of huaca
retention
wall
thicker
berm
3. Thicker berm support and
retention wall: ~4500 BP
retention
wall
ramp
thicker
berm
original
berm
4. Ramp construction: ~4300 BP
Floors/Fills
Stones
Colluvial Fill

b

FIGURE 7.33. Schematic architectural sequences: *a*, sequence of mound building phases at Huaca Prieta; *b*, sequence of development of Phases IV–V access ramp at Huaca Prieta. (See color plates.)

FIGURE 7.34. Circumscribed ritual spaces: *a*, small circumscribed space in Unit 12; *b*, small stone aligned space in Unit 19.

and floors constituting the mound, its most distinguishable late architectural features are the sunken circular plaza, the entry ramp, and chamber tombs, all of which date to terminal Phase III to Phases IV and V. All of these features are interconnected spatially and probably functionally, as late access to the mound was on the zigzag footpaths up and down the entry ramp on the northeast side, entering the summit and the chamber tombs and dropping down the path into the sunken circular plaza on the south end. Although entrances also may have been located along the north and south slopes of the mound, we found no evidence for paths there. Prior to the construction of the Phase IV and V architecture, entrance onto the top may also have been along the more gently sloping portions of the structure. The one anomaly that we could not fully explain was the opening on the east side of the sunken circular plaza. We found no path leading to it and no debris and sediment tossed downslope to indicate that it had been dug out in later times, perhaps by the Spanish (as local rumor has it today and as Bird thought). It is also possible that an entryway existed along this eastern side, but it has now been eroded. A more likely explanation is that the opening provided a sight-line up-valley to the east to Cerro Culicote, which is known in the area as a sacred place (Cesar Gálvez, personal communication, 2009).

When Huaca Prieta reached its maximum Preceramic height near 4500–3800 cal BP, construction ceased or slowed in order for a stable suite of agglutinated chamber tombs to be built on the summit. The mound may have remained in this configuration long enough for aeolian sand to develop in small crevices between individual tombs and architectural walls (for example, Unit 23). After the site was abandoned around 3500 cal BP, the slopes remained stable due to the thick plaster cover. Sediments from the outer surfaces and edges of the west side of the mound were partially eroded as a result of storm action and perhaps high waves, but not to the extent estimated by Bird (Bird et al. 1985), who believed that more than half of the mound was washed away by tsunamis. The upper and western portions of the mound slope may have eroded slightly, but we estimate no more than 1 m or so.

We have interpreted Huaca Prieta primarily as a ritual mound and secondarily as a mortuary place.

ciable time breaks between individual depositions, although thin sandy sheet washes occasionally occur. These observations negate any hypothesis that the Huaca Prieta mound was built by simply adding sediment and debris in an unplanned lateral and/or vertical layer-cake fashion. If this was the case, then stratigraphically continuous layers should be observed across the site. The only exception is the yellow clay layer, which covers about 90% of the surface of Phase IV architecture, and the final plaster seal at the end of Phase V. Finally, the imbricated stone footings or berms for supporting mound build-up and the extensive plaster seals had been utilized since Phase II at Huaca Prieta, which indicates the planned nature of the mound.

Besides the thousands of individual use surfaces

We also have argued that the excessive burning and food and other debris at the site relate almost exclusively to nonmortuary and mortuary rituals carried out frequently by small groups of people, likely both local and nonlocal, over a long period. The archaeological evidence from floors, use surfaces, fills, and features is different in quality and quantity from the evidence in the off-mound domestic units and in the domestic sites located along the littoral zone (see chapter 13). Extremely high frequency use of the mound must have required occasional management by local people, perhaps those living in the nearby domestic Units 13, 16, and 26 and the hypothetical Preceramic village thought to exist underneath the Cupisnique and Paredones mounds. It is thus possible that some of the food debris, floors, use surfaces, and activity areas defined at Huaca Prieta might be related to stewardship residency by selected individuals, perhaps ritual specialists, who regulated access to and ritual use of the mound by others. It also is likely that some individuals lived on the site as caretakers, attending to maintenance of the mound, and that some of the food debris and midden trash was deposited by these individuals. Such an explanation would also account for some of the continuous and intensive deposition of debris at the site over time.

Given the individual nature of each of the prepared and unprepared floors and other surfaces thought to be related to frequent ritual activity by small groups of individuals, especially from the end of Phase II to the beginning of Phase V, it is difficult to estimate if there were simultaneously used surfaces either across the mound or within circumscribed areas. Each individual floor or surface tends to have a line of stones, a different sediment texture and artifact content, and/or uneven border with an adjoining floor or surface, suggesting independent construction and use. Nonetheless, give the size of the mound and the thousands of use floors and surfaces in it, there must have been moments of simultaneous use and thus some degree of stewardship of activities.

The use surfaces and floors at Paredones also retain features that are associated with activities on the landscape. Evidence shows that sand and gravel with much charcoal accumulated between the relatively thin floors and fills in Units 20 and 22. Paredones is an enigma, however; it is associated with domestic activities in the deeper pre-mound levels, but primarily with food preparation (and possibly the construction of matting for use at Huaca Prieta) and ritual activity in the middle and upper floors. Most puzzling is that the vertical accretion of Paredones was not necessary to perform domestic and other activities that occurred in the more horizontally extended Units 13, 16, and 26 and the slightly mounded outlying household sites seen along the coastline. These units and sites are different and do not contain the high amount of charcoal and decorated gourds seen at Paredones, suggesting that special burning acts were taking place primarily there and at Huaca Prieta. These sites also do not contain the numerous burned sea urchin spines observed at Huaca Prieta. Curiously, very few burned sea urchin spines were observed at Paredones, suggesting that this was a species almost exclusively associated with ritual activity and mound building at Huaca Prieta. We cannot explain the high density of burned sea urchin spines at Huaca Prieta. Two types of sea urchins have lived in the area today and in the past (see chapter 9): black and red. The vast majority of the spines are from the black sea urchin, which is highly toxic and not consumed today by local people. People do report, however, that the spines on a live black sea urchin are used to puncture infected cuts to help heal them (local fishers, communication to Duccio Bonavia, field notes, 2009). It may be that the chemistry of the black variety had something to do with its use in the plaster and mortar at the site.

Finally, there was abundant lateral space on the terrace for horizontal expansion, but the choice was made to build the Paredones mound upward within a confined area, the same choice made at Huaca Prieta. Yet, as noted above, Paredones and Huaca Prieta are different in that the former does not have the high number of individual circumscribed ritual spaces, ritual offerings, and burials observed at the latter, suggesting different types of rituals and other activities.

CHAPTER 8

BIOARCHAEOLOGY OF THE HUACA PRIETA REMAINS

Anne R. Titelbaum
and John W. Verano

INTRODUCTION

This chapter presents the findings from our examination of human skeletal remains excavated in Huaca Prieta during the 2008–2009 field seasons. Thirteen nearly complete individuals were excavated from burial contexts. Additional human remains recovered are described in appendix 10. To contextualize this sample, we compare it to the skeletal remains excavated by Bird (Bird et al. 1985; Tattersall 1985), to the study of Bird's excavated remains by Julie Farnum and Robert Benfer (2004), and to other samples of Preceramic skeletal remains from Peru, Ecuador, and Chile. Titelbaum carried out a cursory analysis of the remains of Bird's excavations, which are housed at the American Museum of Natural History, New York.

The human remains were examined during the fall of 2009 with four principal objectives:

1. To inventory the skeletal remains.
2. To assess the demographic characteristics, such as sex and age at death.
3. To determine physical characteristics, such as stature and cranial form.
4. To document pathological conditions and anomalies of the bones and teeth.

During analysis, a laboratory number was assigned to each complete skeleton, corresponding to the site, year of excavation, and skeleton number. For example, "HP08-02" indicates that the individual was excavated in 2008 and is skeleton number 2.

While some of the human remains have good preservation, others are fragmented, largely due to the effects of salt. In some cases, large salt crystals had formed in the trabecular bone and split apart the cortical bone. In other cases, a tenacious salt-and-dirt matrix adhered to the bone, causing damage and impeding analysis. Hair was recovered with some of the remains, as were textile fragments, shells, gourds, and faunal material.

METHODOLOGY

The methods used to analyze the skeletal material were in accord with established standards for data collection from human remains (*sensu* Buikstra and Ubelaker 1994). When it was helpful for observation and analysis, bones that were broken postmortem were rejoined with a bonding agent. Measurements were collected from well-preserved cranial and postcranial bones. Digital photography was used to record a reference image of each skeleton and to document pathological conditions and anomalies. A hand lens was used to magnify details of the bone surface. When possible, a well-preserved complete tooth was removed from each skeleton for DNA analysis.

SKELETAL AGE INDICATORS

Age was estimated by examining dental development (Anderson et al. 1976; Gustafson and Koch 1974; Ubelaker 1989), the morphology of the pubic symphysis (Brooks and Suchey 1990; Suchey and Katz 1986; Todd 1921a, 1921b), the morphology of the auricular surface of the ilium (Lovejoy et al. 1985; Meindl and Lovejoy 1989), postcranial development and epiphyseal closure (Buikstra and Ubelaker 1994), dental wear, and degenerative changes of the postcranial skeleton (osteoarthritis and vertebral osteophytosis). Endocranial and ectocranial suture closure (Meindl and Lovejoy 1985) was also examined and recorded where possible.

SKELETAL SEX INDICATORS

The sex of adult skeletons was assessed by the morphological features of the pelvis and by the robusticity of the cranium and mandible (Buikstra and Ubelaker 1994; Phenice 1969). Consideration was also given to the size of adult long bone epiphyses, given the observed sexual dimorphism among the sample (see "Stature and Sexual Dimorphism" below). Sexual identification is less accurate for immature remains, so the sex of sub-adult skeletons was considered "indeterminate."

STATURE

Estimation of adult living stature was calculated with the formulae of Santiago Genovés (1967), using the separate maximum lengths of the left femur and left tibia. When the left element was not measurable, the right one was used. Due to the fragmented condition of the remains, stature estimates were not possible for every individual.

PATHOLOGICAL CONDITIONS, ANOMALIES, AND TRAUMA

The cranium, mandible, dentition, and postcranial skeleton were examined for anomalies and evidence for pathological conditions and trauma. Anomalies include developmental variants and congenital absence of teeth. Pathological conditions include signs of nutritional deficiency (for example, cribra orbitalia), degenerative change (osteoarthritis and vertebral osteophytosis), abnormal size and shape, areas of active bone remodeling, and infection. Trauma refers to antemortem (healed, healing) and perimortem (unhealed) bone fractures. In addition to dental wear, teeth were examined for carious lesions, enamel hypoplasias, abscesses, and calculus.

GENERAL OBSERVATIONS

This section describes the general observations recorded for the burials that were excavated by Dillehay and Bonavia. For more detail on specific observations, refer to the description of the referenced skeleton below.

SEX DISTRIBUTION

Of the thirteen excavated skeletons, four are adult males, four are adult females, and five are sub-adults of indeterminate sex (table 8.1).

AGE DISTRIBUTION

The ages of the thirteen individuals range from fetus to older adult: fetus ($n = 1$), children

Table 8.1. Age and sex distribution

Age at Death	Indeterminate	Male	Female	Total
	Sex			
Fetus	1	—	—	1
Newborn to 11 months	—	—	—	—
1–4	2	—	—	2
5–9	2	—	—	2
10–14	—	—	—	—
15–19	—	—	—	—
Young Adult: 20–34	—	2	1	3
Middle Adult: 35–49	—	2	2	4
Older Adult: 50+	—	—	1	1
Total No. of Individuals	5	4	4	13

Table 8.2. Arthritis: Severity of expression by major joint

Joint	Mild	Moderate	Marked	Total
Shoulders	2	—	—	2
Elbows	4	—	—	4
Wrists	—	—	—	0
Ribs	1	1	—	2
Vertebrae	1	—	1	2
Hips	1	1	—	2
Knees	2	1	—	3
Ankles	—	—	—	0
Feet	2	—	1	3
Total	13	3	2	18

approximately 3–4 years of age (*n* = 2), children between 5–9 years of age (*n* = 2), young adults (20–34) (*n* = 3), middle adults (35–49) (*n* = 4), and older adult (50+) (*n* = 1), (table 8.1).

BURIAL TREATMENT

While the majority of the burials were undisturbed and complete, at least two individuals show postmortem disturbance. HP09-01, an older adult female, was a disturbed burial. While the woman's bones were not found in anatomical position, her skeleton was largely complete. In contrast, HP09-07, a middle adult male, was found in anatomical position in what appeared to be an undisturbed context; however, the bones of his right leg (femur, tibia, and fibula) are missing.

The orientation of the bodies varied. Some were buried on an approximate north-south axis, whereas others were on an east-west axis. Some individuals were buried tightly flexed, with their knees drawn toward their chests. Some were interred on their left sides, others on their right sides, and others on their backs with their legs folded toward their chest or toward the side. No correlations can be made concerning posture and position with age and sex. Inconsistent orientation has also been observed among Early and Middle Cupisnique burials from the site of Puémape, located north of Huaca Prieta, between the Chicama and Jequetepeque Valleys (Elera 1998).

As at other early sites, including Paloma, Las Vegas, Piedras Negras, and Río Seco, rocks are often placed in the graves, sometimes directly on top of the burial, and then covered with fill (Quilter 1989). This practice was also observed among 20.83% of the early Cupisnique and at least 16.67% of the middle Cupisnique burials from Puémape (Elera 1998). Among the 2008–2009 Huaca Prieta burials, three (23.08%) had rocks and/or polychaete blocks placed on or around the graves. Two burials, both children, appeared to be surrounded by rings of rocks (HP09-02, HP09-03). In contrast, one middle adult male (HP09-05) was discovered beneath a line of rocks, one of which appears to have crushed his skull.

PRESERVATION

The skeletal remains were heavily impregnated with salt, and salt crystals were present on most bones. As the bones dried in the lab, salt crystals continued to grow and were readily discernible the next morning. Most problematic was the occasional formation of large crystals that grew outward from cancellous bone and medullary cavities, causing the cortical bone to fracture (fig. 8.1a). Additionally, plaster or *argamasa* (an artificially produced mortar-like salt and dirt matrix) adhered to numerous bones. In general, if not for

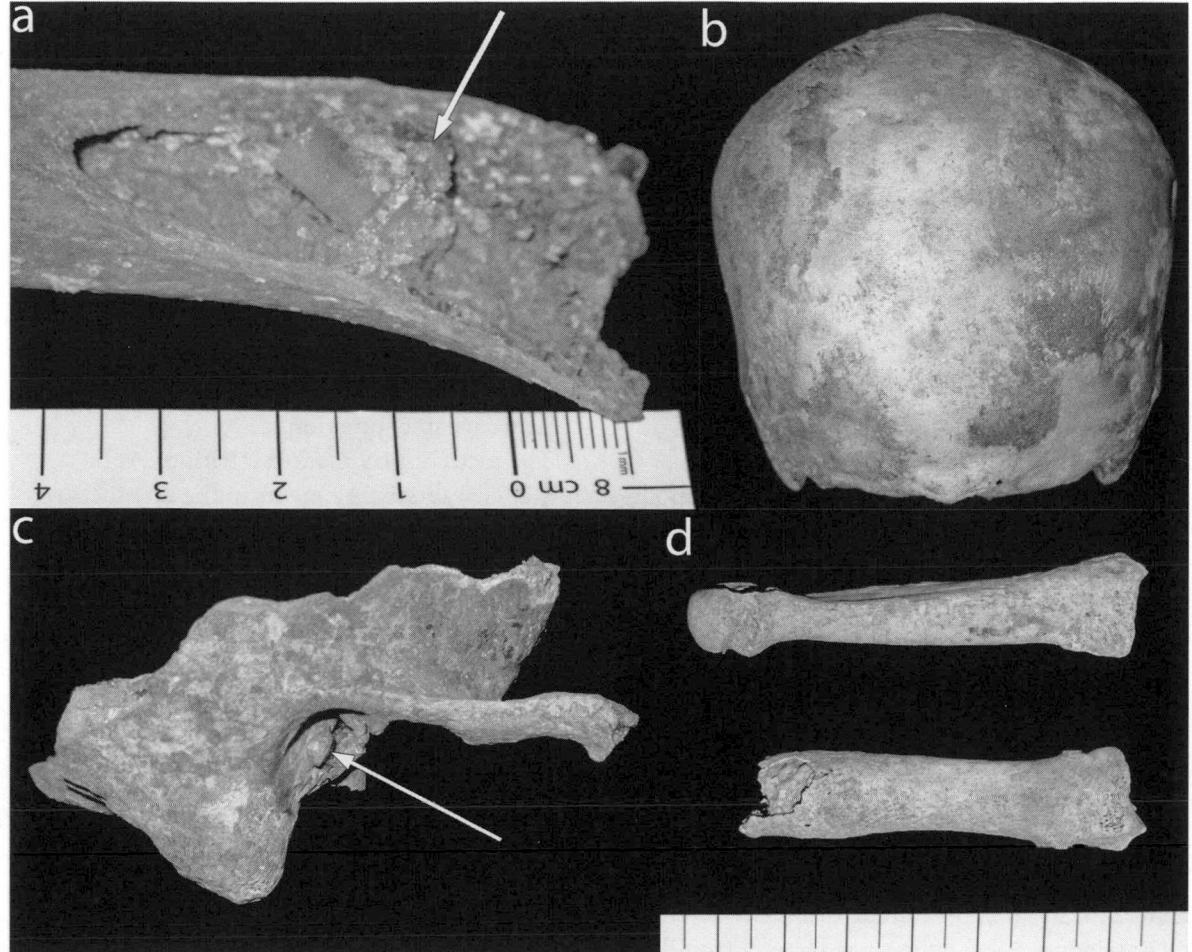

FIGURE 8.1. Elements of human skeletons: *a*, salt crystals (upper arrow) in the medullary space of a distal right humerus (HP09-05); *b*, posterior view of a cranium (HP09-07); *c*, exostosis in the external auditory meatus of a right temporal bone (HP09-05); *d*, left and right third metatarsals of HP09-01 (dorsal view).

the effects of the salt, the remains would have been in overall good condition.

RED PIGMENT

Among the burials excavated by Bird during the 1940s, red pigment was observed on the soil beneath the crushed skull of one poorly preserved individual (Bird et al. 1985). Because of the condition of the remains, the age and sex of the individual could not be assessed, and the individual was not assigned a catalog number. Bird also noted that red pigment was applied to numerous Preceramic textiles and baskets (see chapters 11 and 12 and appendix 11).

In the 2008–2009 burials, red pigment was observed on three skeletons and their surround-

ing soil matrix (also see chapter 7 and appendix 10). The individuals include a young adult male (HP08-01, ~30 years of age), a young adult female (HP09-09, ~18–25 years of age), and a child between ~3 and 5 years of age (HP09-02). The chemical composition of the pigment was identified as red hematite; a sample was taken from the soil matrix surrounding HP09-09.

The presence of red pigment in graves has been observed at other early burial sites in Peru, including Paloma and Asia (Quilter 1989) and Initial Period sites such as Caral in the Lurín Valley (Burger and Salazar-Burger 1991), Puémape in the Jequetepeque Valley (Elera 1998), Huaca El Gallo/Huaca La Gallina in the Virú Valley (Verano 1995a; Zoubek 1997), and Pampas Gramalote in the Moche Valley (Prieto 2012, 2014). The practice became more prevalent over time at Puémape: of twenty-four Early Cupisnique interments, Carlos Elera (1998) found hematite applied around the eye orbits of one adult female, whereas nine of the forty-six Middle Cupisnique burials were painted with hematite, including two infants, two children, one adolescent, two young adult females, an older adult female, and one male of unknown age. In addition, the upper surfaces of at least three rocks placed over graves were also painted (Elera 1998).

CRANIAL SHAPE

None of the skulls have intentional cultural modification, although they do show some distinctive morphology. From a posterior view, all skulls are roughly pentagonal in shape. Most have a flattened area extending from obelion to slightly below lambda (fig. 8.1b). Six skulls have slight occipital buns (HP09-01, HP09-03, HP09-04, HP09-05, HP09-07, HP09-10), and three skulls have slight metopic ridges (HP09-01, HP09-05, HP09-10). The slight ridge refers to a thickening along the sagittal midline of the frontal bone. While the ridges do not have the prominent "beaking" of the midline that is characteristic of trigonocephaly, they may represent a mild or nonsyndromic form of this condition (Kelleher et al. 2006; Shimoji et al. 2002). The slight ridge was most evident on HP09-10, a juvenile with an asymmetrically shaped skull that was about eight years old at the time of death. Skeleton HP09-05 has both a slight frontal ridge and a scaphocephalic skull with a sagittal ridge or keel. While the etiology of the ridges or keels is unknown, their development may be related to cranial robusticity (Baab et al. 2010) or bony overgrowth associated with premature fusion of cranial sutures (Aufderheide and Rodríguez-Martin 1998).

TEETH

The dentition was examined for carious lesions, enamel hypoplasias, abscesses, attrition (tooth wear), calculus, and anomalies (such as congenital absence). As recommended by J. E. Buikstra and D. H. Ubelaker (1994), the evaluation of tooth wear was based on two systems. The Smith scoring system was used for the incisors, canines, and premolars, while the Scott system was used for the molars. The Smith system has eight stages of wear, ranging from a score of "1" for unworn to polished or small facets with no dentin exposure, to a score of "8," for the complete loss of the tooth crown, with no remaining enamel. The Scott system for scoring ranges from "1," indicating that the molar wear facets are invisible or very small, to "10," where there is no enamel remaining on any quadrant of the molar, such that dentin exposure is complete, and wear has extended below the cemento-enamel junction.

The teeth display marked attrition. Probably due to abrasive elements in the diet such as sand and grit, teeth are heavily worn, resulting in exposed dentin, the use of tooth roots as occlusal surfaces, and the early and frequent loss of teeth. One individual (HP09-07) has marked dental wear on the buccal aspect of postcanine teeth and their roots, which may suggest that he used his teeth for paramasticatory purposes.

Minor accumulation of calculus is present at the cemento-enamel junctions on three individuals (HP09-01, HP09-07, HP09-08), and only two individuals have carious lesions (HP08-02, HP09-04). This is consistent with an abrasive diet low in carbohydrates and is a pattern seen at other early coastal sites (Mujica Barreda et al. 2007; Quilter 1989; Verano and Lombardi 1998; Zoubek 1997).

Congenital absence of one or more third molars was noted in three adults (HP09-01, HP09-07, HP09-09). No other dental anomalies or variants were noted.

GROWTH AND DEVELOPMENT

Numerous individuals have minor developmental variants of the axial skeleton. Several factors likely caused these variations, including genetic and environmental factors (such as maternal nutritional health) affecting embryonic and fetal development (Barnes 1994). Multiple variants are often found in one individual. While variants observed among the Huaca Prieta sample would not have compromised health or mobility, one individual presents a vertebral segmentation error that can be described as Klippel-Feil syndrome (HP09-09). Clinically, Klippel-Feil syndrome has been variably associated with deafness and musculoskeletal, genitourinary, and cardiovascular abnormalities (Tracy et al. 2004).

Among the samples, observed developmental variants of the axial skeleton include four individuals with tympanic apertures (Huschke's foramen) resulting from a developmental delay of the closing membrane of the tympanic plate (HP08-01, HP09-01, HP09-04, HP09-07); ossicles at lambda (HP09-08), asterion (HP08-01, HP09-08) and the parietal notch (HP08-01), due to delays in the closure of fontanelles; ossicles in the mid-lambdoidal suture (HP08-01); what appears to be premature fusion of cranial sutures, reflected by metopic ridges (HP09-01, HP09-05, HP09-10) and a sagittal ridge or keel (HP09-05); one partially bifurcated mandibular condyle (HP09-07); two sternal apertures resulting from the incomplete caudal cohesion of the developing sternal bands (HP09-06, HP09-08); four cases of border shifting of the vertebrae (HP09-07, HP09-08, HP09-09, HP09-10); one segmentation error of the C2–C3 vertebrae (Klippel-Feil) (HP09-09); and one instance of cleft neural arches of multiple sacral segments (HP08-02).

Developmental variants of the appendicular skeleton also were observed. Two individuals have anatomical variations of the acetabular roof of the hip joint (HP09-08, HP09-09), and three have septal apertures of the humeri (HP09-01, HP09-05, HP09-09).

NUTRITIONAL STRESS

Three minor cases of healing cribra orbitalia in the orbital roofs were seen in two children between 3 and 5 years old (HP08-02, HP09-02) and one middle adult male (35–45) (HP09-07). A number of skulls had eggshell porosity on the occipital and posterior parietals, but there were no clear cases of porotic hyperostosis. In general, cribra orbitalia and porotic hyperostosis appear to result from anemia caused by the synergistic effects of weaning, gastrointestinal infections, and the nutritional stress from a diet deficient in vitamins, such as C and B-12 (Walker et al. 2009). While a greater range of factors can account for cribra orbitalia, the absence of porotic hyperostosis among the sample suggests that the presence of cribra orbit-alia is due to factors other than a vitamin B-12 deficiency, such as vitamin C deficiency or chronic infection (Walker et al. 2009). No linear enamel hypoplasias were observed.

NONSPECIFIC INFECTION

Six individuals had active, healing, or healed inflammatory processes at the time of death. Nonspecific periosteal reactions characterized by bone deposition and occasional venous markings were observed among five individuals (HP08-01, HP09-04, HP09-05, HP09-06, and HP09-07). One individual (HP09-04) may have had a systemic infection, as multiple bones are affected. Another individual (HP09-05) has a nonspecific lesion, characterized by pitting resulting from the destruction of the cortical bone.

One individual (HP09-01) has an inflammatory reaction on the neurocranium, with proliferative bone deposition and porosity, possibly due to a scalp infection. Another (HP09-04) has a unilateral localized destructive lesion in the lacrimal fossa of the frontal bone that may be the secondary result of an infection affecting the lacrimal gland.

Two individuals (HP09-04, HP09-07) show bony reaction on the calcaneal tuberosities that likely resulted from calcaneal bursitis (Achilles bursitis). One of those individuals (HP09-04) also has calcaneal spurs that probably developed in response to plantar fasciitis (Moore et al. 2014).

Possible osteomyelitis that was active at the time of death was observed in the medial left clavicle and the sternal end of the first rib of a young adult female (HP09-09). These bones show a combination of bone formation and destruction, with possible cloacae.

TRAUMA

Antemortem and perimortem trauma was identified among three and possibly four individuals. Antemortem injuries were identified by breakage pattern and extent of healing and by areas of depression or unevenness. Perimortem trauma was identified by breakage pattern, homogeneous coloration, and small adhering bone fragments at fracture margins (Lovell 1997).

One individual (HP09-07) has a healed depression fracture on the skull, a healed fracture of the distal right ulna (parry fracture), and possible perimortem blunt force trauma to the skull. Another individual (HP09-08) appears to have perimortem skull trauma; however, the fractures are more ambiguous, and may instead be due to postmortem damage. The same individual (HP09-08) suffered rib fractures on two separate occasions, as indicated by two ribs with well-healed fractures, and one rib with proliferative woven bone that was actively being deposited at the time of death. One adult male cranium had healed fractures of both nasal bones (Unit 16, Ext. W, Layer 02, Profile W).

HP09-01 has remodeled subperiosteal bone enveloping the shaft of the left third metatarsal, with an underlying cortical bone surface that is sclerotic and irregular. Possible diagnoses include healed fracture or localized infection. The adjacent bones of the foot are normal in appearance.

OSTEOCHONDRITIS DISSECANS

Osteochondritis dissecans is characterized by focalized areas of necrosis on the convex articular surfaces of the major joints (for example, knee, ankle, elbow), resulting in the partial or complete detachment of a segment of the articular cartilage and the subchondral bone (Aufderheide and Rodríguez-Martin 1998). Clinically found in athletically active young adults between 10 and 25 years of age, osteochondritis dissecans appears to be the result of repeated low-grade microtrauma. The appearance of this lesion may foretell degenerative joint disease.

Four individuals in the sample have osteochondritis dissecans. HP09-01, an older adult female, has a lesion on the posterior lateral condyle of her left femur. HP09-04, a middle adult female, has a lesion on the lateral condyles of both tibiae. HP09-07, a middle adult male, displays bilateral lesions on the acetabula of the pelvis, a unilateral lesion on the right posterior humeral trochlea, and lesions on the superior posterior lateral left femoral condyle, the inferior anterior lateral left femoral condyle, and the lateral left tibial condyle. Since the right leg of this individual is missing, it could not be determined if the femoral and tibial lesions are unilateral or bilateral. Edward

Kostick (1963) considered the lesion on the posterior superior lateral femoral condyle (as is seen in HP09-01 and HP09-07) to be an osteochondritic imprint resulting from the hyperflexion of the knee resulting from a habitual squatting posture. Similar lesions have been reported in other Andean skeletal samples and attributed to squatting as well (Verano 2003).

DEGENERATIVE CHANGES

A variety of age-progressive degenerative and inflammatory changes to joint surfaces are generally referred to as arthritis. Throughout life, joints are subject to biomechanical loading and are affected by factors such as genetic predisposition, body mass, injury, and age.

"Osteoarthritis" refers to degenerative changes of the diarthrodal joints of the skeleton. Degenerative changes generally follow insults to the joint, and tears and loss of the articular cartilage. Ranging in their manifestation from barely discernible to severe, degenerative changes include lipping of the margins of the joint surfaces, osteophyte formation, porosity of the articular surfaces, and eburnation, which is the polish that results from bone-on-bone contact. With age there is a loss of cartilage due to wear, particularly among weight-bearing joints (such as the knee). Therefore the severity of osteoarthritis (OA) tends to increase with age.

Analysis of OA followed recommendations in Buikstra and Ubelaker (1994), for recording maximum expression. Observations are described in table 8.2 as mild (barely discernible marginal lipping, possibly with pinpoint porosity of the joint surface), moderate (sharp marginal ridge, sometimes with curved spicules, sometimes associated with coalesced surface porosity), or marked (extensive spicule formation with pinpoint and coalesced porosity, and eburnation).

The majority of OA in the 2008–2009 sample is found on the elbows and knees, with lower frequencies in other diarthrodial joints. Mild OA was observed in shoulders (HP09-01, HP09-07), elbows (HP09-01, HP09-05, HP09-07, HP09-08), hips (HP09-07), knees (HP09-01, HP09-08), feet (HP09-01, HP09-05), ribs (costal facets; HP09-01), and intervertebral aygopophyseal joints of the fourth and fifth cervical vertebrae

(HP09-05). Moderate OA was observed on ribs (HP09-07), hips (HP09-01), and knees (HP09-07). Two cases of marked OA involved the intervertebral joints of the lower lumbar vertebrae of HP09-01 and the right metatarsal-phalangeal joint of the great toe of HP09-05 (table 8.2).

Vertebral Osteophytosis: As with OA, degenerative changes of the vertebral bodies are related to activity and age and are affected by factors such as genetic predisposition, body mass, and injury. Typical degenerative change of vertebral bodies involves lipping and the growth of osteophytes. Osteophytes are bony spurs that initially extend horizontally from vertebral bodies.

Analysis of vertebral degeneration followed the standards outlined by Buikstra and Ubelaker (1994: 121–122), indicating the maximum expression. Observations are summarily described by the terms mild (barely discernible marginal lipping), moderate (elevated ring), or marked (curved spicules).

There are no instances among the 2008–2009 samples where vertebrae fused together via osteophytes. Most of the vertebral degenerative change is mild and located in the middle thoracic (HP09-01, HP09-04, HP09-07) and upper lumbar (HP09-01) vertebrae. Moderate osteophytosis is seen in the cervical (HP09-07), thoracic (HP09-08), lower thoracic (HP09-01, HP09-07), and lumbar (HP09-01, HP09-07, HP09-08) vertebrae.

EXOSTOSES OF THE EXTERNAL AUDITORY MEATUS OR CANAL

Often referred to as osteomas, exostoses that form in the external auditory (acoustic) meatus or canal of the temporal bone are benign, dense, smooth-surfaced osseous nodules. These exostoses tend to be more frequently found in adult males than in adult females at ratios as high as 6:1 (Aufderheide and Rodríguez-Martín 1998). Except for rare instances, juveniles do not have exostoses, which suggests that the growths are developmental. They are predominantly found among males, which may reflect a difference in susceptibility or the sexual division of labor (Tattersall 1985).

The cause of these growths is unresolved, as factors implicated for the etiology have not been determined experimentally. It has been suggested that repeated exposure to cold water (for example, diving or harvesting marine resources) leads to the formation of the growths (Kennedy 1986). However, an explanation of water exposure does not account for the occurrence of exostoses among some inland populations (Godde 2010). Mitchio Okumura et al. (2007) suggested that it is the interaction of temperature, wind chill, and water exposure that influence the trait's development. Other researchers report additional factors not related to water, such as systemic conditions and trauma (Hutchinson et al. 1997).

Among the 2008–2009 samples, only adult males have obvious exostoses (fig. 8.1c). And of the adult males with preserved external auditory meati (*n* = 3), all have the exostoses (HP08-01, HP09-05, HP09-7).

STATURE AND SEXUAL DIMORPHISM

Estimates of stature could be calculated for only four adult females and one adult male. Standing 162–165 cm tall, the single male was approximately 10–15 cm taller than the four females, who average 150 cm (range: 147–154 cm). While this difference in stature is consistent with what was found among Bird's Preceramic skeletal collection (Farnum and Benfer 2004), it is somewhat greater than what has been reported for other Preceramic sites (Farnum and Benfer 2004) and later north coast, highland, and modern Peruvian populations, which tend to show differences averaging only 10 cm (Verano 2003) (table 8.3).

BURIALS

This section presents detailed observations for each of the thirteen nearly complete human skeletons excavated from burial contexts during the 2008 and 2009 field seasons. The sample consists of eight adults (four males, four females), four children, and one fetus (table 8.1). One additional adult interment, Unit 16, Layer 14, Burial 07, was left in situ for the following field season, but two teeth were collected for DNA analysis. In addition to the thirteen skeletons, numerous disturbed human remains were recovered from test excavations. These are presented in appendix 10.

(1) HP08-01: Sunken Plaza, No 4, Phase V. HP08-01 is a relatively complete skeleton of a

Table 8.3. Huaca Prieta stature estimates (in cm) compared to other samples

Sample	Period	Males n	Males Mean stature	Females n	Females Mean stature
Huaca Prieta: Dillehay and Bonavia's sample	Preceramic	1	163.8	4	150
Huaca Prieta: Bird's sample[a]	Preceramic	—	166	—	155
Paloma, central coast Peru[a]	Preceramic	—	167	—	159
Pacatnamú, Jequetepeque Valley, north coast Peru[b]	Moche	53	157.6	52	146.8
Chicama Valley, north coast Peru[c]	Late Prehistoric	1000	157.2	350	144.7
Machu Picchu[d]	Inca	8	157	10	148.3
Monsefú, Lambayeque Valley, north coast Peru[e]	Modern	67	158.6	97	145.8

[a]Farnum and Benfer 2004.

[b]Verano 1997.

[c]Hrdlička 1938.

[d]Verano 2003.

[e]Kim 2000.

young adult male. Sex is based on the morphology of the pubic portion of the left os coxae and robusticity of the cranium and mandible. Young adult age (~30 years old) is suggested by the paucity of degenerative changes of the postcranial skeleton and the lack of cranial suture closure (see fig. 7.13a). A lens of salt crystals was underneath the body.

Cranium: Red pigment is present on the right vault and the right zygomatic arch. The maxillary dentition is complete and shows occlusal wear and dentin exposure on all teeth. With the exception of the angular wear of the first molars, the tooth wear is relatively flat. No dental pathology is present (no caries, no calculus, no abscesses, no developmental variants, and no enamel hypoplasias). There is mild bilateral osteoarthritis (OA) of the mandibular fossae (temporomandibular joint). Bilateral exostoses are present in the external acoustic meati of the temporal bones. The exostosis on the right side obstructs nearly one-half of the auditory canal; the exostosis of the left ear is smaller, occluding one-quarter to one-third of the canal.

Developmental variants of the cranium include bilateral parietal notch bones, asterion ossicles, and ossicles in the midlambdoidal suture. There are also small bilateral tympanic apertures (Huschke's foramina).

Mandible: The mandibular dentition shows wear consistent with that of the maxillary teeth. There was antemortem loss of the left second molar, and a carious lesion is present on the crown of the right third molar. Both mandibular condyles have mild pitting coincident with the OA observed on the cranium.

Postcranial Skeleton: No degenerative changes were observed among the vertebrae and major joints. Many of the long bones are fragmentary, so the lengths of the lower limb bones could not be measured to estimate stature. The right humerus has a head diameter of 42.1 mm, and the left femoral head has a diameter of 44.3 mm; both of these measurements are within the ranges of males from later north coast sites (Verano 1997).

Left arm: The left ulna has a healed area of inflammation at midshaft, indicated by cortical swelling and venous tracks on the medial surface of the distal third of the shaft. The right radius and ulna are normal.

(2) HP08-02: Unit 3, Tomb 1, Phase IV. The skeleton excavated from Tomb 1 is that of a child approximately 3–4 years old, with fragile but well-preserved bones. The age estimate was based on dental calcification and eruption, bone union and epiphyseal closure, and the length of long bones. Each assessment was consistent for the

summary age estimate. The sex of the individual is indeterminate.

Cranium: The child has mild cribra orbitalia in both orbits that was active/healing at the time of death.

Dentition: There is a large carious lesion on the occlusal surface of the distal part of the crown of the upper left first deciduous molar.

Postcranial Skeleton: The following long bone measurements could be taken:

Left femur maximum length: 180 mm
Left tibia maximum length: 140 mm

Vertebrae: A developmental variant of the sacrum was observed. The first and second sacral elements have cleft or bifid neural arches, likely resulting from a developmental delay rather than a neural tube defect (Barnes 1994).

(3) HP09-01: Unit 16, Layer 04, Burial 02, Late Phase IV. The individual excavated from this disturbed burial is a nearly complete older adult female, 50–60+ years of age. Sex was determined on the basis of morphological traits of the pelvis and skull, and the age estimate was based on the morphology of the pubic symphyses, the auricular surfaces, dental wear, and postcranial degenerative changes. The basicranium and facial bones are badly fragmented, as are the ribs. Numerous bones, including the neck of the left femur, the right ramus of the mandible, the lateral side of the proximal right ulna, and the left calcaneus, have salt crystals adhering to them. A possible weaver's batten made of sea lion bone was associated with this female.

Observations include an inflammatory process on the cranium, mild to moderate degenerative changes of the postcranial skeleton, a possible healed fracture or infective process of the left third metatarsal, congenital absence of the maxillary left third molar, and minor accumulation of dental calculus.

Cranium: There is asymmetric flattening of the posterior skull between obelion and lambda to slightly below lambda. A slight occipital bun, a suprainion depression, and a faint midline ridge are present on the frontal bone. From the posterior view, the skull has a roughly pentagonal shape, which is partly due to mild biparietal thinning.

A portion of the ectocranial surface of the vault shows thickening and porosity that appears to be a healed or healing inflammatory process, possibly resulting from a scalp infection. The region extends along the sagittal plane from the coronal suture to the suprainion depression on the occipital and transversely to about 2 cm superior to each of the temporal lines. The bone surface is irregular, particularly on the posterior parietals near the sagittal suture. The left parietal foramen is slightly enlarged and is ringed by bony deposition. The endocranial surface does not show anything unusual.

There is a tympanic aperture on the right side; the left side was not observable because it was broken. No exostoses were observed in the external acoustic meati.

Dentition: Many teeth were lost antemortem, including the maxillary left first premolar, the mandibular left molars, and first incisor; and the mandibular right first and second molars. The alveoli of the mandibular left molars are nearly completely resorbed, whereas the alveoli of the mandibular right molars and the left first incisor are in the process of resorption. Although the crowns of the mandibular left canine, first premolar, right second incisor, and right canine are broken and missing, portions of roots remain in the alveoli. There may be a congenital absence of the maxillary left third molar.

The teeth that are present are heavily worn, with exposed dentin and in some cases exposed pulp chambers. There is one molar of indeterminate position; while it appears to be a first molar, it is broken, with only a portion of one root remaining, and the tooth crown is heavily worn with cementum and pulp chamber exposure. Calculus is present on the buccal aspect of the maxillary left second molar, and the roots of this tooth have resorbed such that their length is ~1 mm. The surrounding alveolar bone is porous and actively remodeling.

Postcranial Skeleton: Mild to moderate age-related degenerative changes were observed on the postcranial skeleton, with one healed fracture or area of infection on the left third toe. The left shoulder, left elbow, and left hip are fragmentary, and no observations of these joints were possible.

Right Upper Limb: The right shoulder and elbow have mild OA, observed as barely discernible lipping of the margins of the glenoid fossa of the scapula and the trochlea of the humerus. There is a septal aperture through the olecranon fossa of the distal right humerus.

Hips: The right hip has moderate OA. The acetabulum of the right os coxae is porous and sclerotic, and a small enthesophyte is present on the margin of the fovea capitis on the right femoral head.

Knees: Both knees show mild to moderate osteoarthritis, with somewhat more expression on the right knee.

Right knee: Two areas of dense, plaque-like deposition of bone are present on the femur, on the patellar articular surface (12 × 9.5 mm) and the posterior aspect of the lateral condyle (9.8 × 9.3 mm). There is a slightly elevated lip along femoral condyles and the medial edge of the patellar articular surface, which is matched by comparable lips on the tibial condyles and the articular surface of the patella. A bony spicule is present on the medial condyle of the tibia.

Left knee: There is a barely discernible lip along the femoral and tibial condyles. On the posterior lateral condyle of the left femur is a roughly circular area (7.6 × 7.1 mm) of osteochondritis dissecans that was healing at the time of death. A locus of healing porosity is present on the posterior aspect of the medial condyle of the tibia.

Feet: Mild arthritis is present on both feet, seen in barely discernible lipping of the calcaneal-talar articular surfaces and a slightly elevated lip along the cuboid-calcaneal articular surfaces. Elevated lipping of the cuboid-lateral cuneiform articular surfaces is seen in the right foot. The left foot has lipping of the cuboid-intermediate cuneiform articular surfaces and the calcaneal-fourth metatarsal and calcaneal-fifth metatarsal articular surfaces. The proximal phalanx of both great toes has a small remodeled pit on the proximal articular surface.

The left third metatarsal is thick and swollen in appearance (fig. 8.1d). There is remodeled subperiosteal bone enveloping the shaft, and the underlying cortical bone surface is sclerotic and irregular, as can be seen on a broken portion of the distal end. Possible diagnoses include healed fracture or localized infection. The adjacent bones of the foot are normal in appearance.

Vertebrae: There is mild OA of the costal facets of the thoracic vertebrae and the articular facets of most of the vertebrae. Moderate-to-marked OA is seen on the left articular facets of the fourth and fifth lumbar vertebrae. These facets have micro- and macro-porosity, with osteophytes and active new bone deposition at the time of death.

Mild vertebral osteophytosis is present on the T5, L1, and L3 vertebrae, in the form of barely elevated rings. Moderate osteophytosis is seen on T9–12 and L4–5, which have small osteophytes on the rims. Additionally, there is some compression of body of L4, particularly on the anterior right side.

Stature Estimate: This individual stood approximately 147 cm tall. From the left femur, the estimated stature is 146.4±3.8 cm. From the left tibia, the estimated stature is 148.1±3.5 cm.

(4) HP09-02: Unit 16, Ext. NW, Layer 04, Burial 04, Phase IV. HP09-02 is a relatively complete skeleton of a child, approximately 3–5 years old, based on dental development and postcranial maturation (Buikstra and Ubelaker 1994; Ubelaker 1989). Adult teeth are in their alveoli, and only the first molars have root growth (~1.1 mm). The crowns of the adult second molars have partially developed. The neural arches of the vertebrae have fused, but none of the vertebral bodies have begun to join to the arches. The sex is indeterminate.

The child was buried in a flexed position, lying on the right side, with the head oriented toward the north. Red pigment was observed on the right humerus, the anterior left humerus, and the anterior left tibia. The majority of the bones are fragile and fragmentary, and there is taphonomic destruction of a portion of the outer table of the cranium, particularly on the left parietal and frontal bone.

Cranium: The only observed pathological condition of this child is very mild bilateral cribra orbitalia, which was active/healing at the time of death.

Dentition: The deciduous dentition is worn with exposed dentin, scoring a maximum Scott Stage 7–8 (Scott 1979) for a quadrant on each of the deciduous second molars.

Postcranial Skeleton: No pathologies or anomalies were noted on the postcranial skeleton, but many bones are missing or fragmentary, so no long bone measurements could be taken.

(5) HP09-03: Unit 16, Ext. NW, Layer 04, Burial

05, Late Phase III. The human remains recovered are those of a child that was buried flexed, on its right side, with the head oriented toward the east. The child was approximately 7–8 years old, based on dental development and postcranial maturation. The sex is indeterminate. No pathological conditions or anomalies were noted.

Cranium: There is a slight flattening of the back of the cranium between obelion and lambda. The child has a slight occipital bun and mild parietal bossing. When viewed from the posterior aspect the cranium has a roughly pentagonal shape.

Dentition: There are no caries and no enamel hypoplasias. The deciduous molars are worn, with exposed dentin. The maximum wear score for a quadrant of the first molar is about an 8 on the Scott (1979) scale.

The permanent first molars are erupted and show tooth wear, about a stage 3 on the Scott (1979) scale. Root growth of the first molars is approximately two-thirds complete. The crowns of the adult second molars are fully or nearly fully formed, without root growth. Neither the first incisors nor the second incisors have complete roots. The adult second incisors I_2s are erupted and have tiny wear facets (Smith [1984] scale, Stage 1).

Postcranial Skeleton: No pathological conditions or anomalies were observed on the postcranial skeleton. Although numerous bones are fragmentary, the following long bone measurements could be taken:

Right femur maximum length: 223 mm
Left fibula maximum length: 192 mm
Right radius maximum length: 129.6 mm

(6) HP09-04, Unit 16, Ext. W, Layer 05, Burial 03, Phase III. This burial consists of the nearly complete skeleton of a middle adult female (35–45) interred flexed, on her left side, with her head oriented toward the south. The basicranium, facial bones, and ribs are fragmented due to postmortem damage, and numerous bones have salt crystals adhering to them.

Sex was determined on the basis of morphological traits of the skull and pelvis, and the age estimate was based on the morphology of the right auricular surface, degenerative changes of the postcranial skeleton, and dental wear. While observations of the auricular surface suggested an age of 40–45 years, there are few degenerative changes and the teeth are not as worn as seen in the other older individuals (such as HP09-01). The combination of aging indicators therefore suggests a skeletal age estimate of 35–45 years (middle adult).

Cranium: The cranium is mildly flattened from obelion to lambda, with a slight occipital bun. Granular foveae (pachionian depressions) are present on the endocranial surface of the parietals, in proximity to the superior sagittal sinus. There are bilateral tympanic apertures. No exostoses were observed in the external acoustic meati.

On the left temporal bone, osteoarthritis of temporomandibular joint (TMJ) is indicated by a localized circular, pitted area on the medial side of the articular eminence, approximately 3.51 mm (anterior-posterior) × 2.2 mm (medial-lateral), and by a second larger pitted area located anterior to the articular eminence, measuring approximately 8.65 (a-p) × 5.5 mm (m-l). In contrast to the temporal bone, the left mandibular condyle does not have pitting.

The frontal bone has a localized lesion in the left lacrimal fossa that was active at the time of death and exposed the underlying diploë (fig. 8.2a, b). The lesion measures 7.39 (m-l) × 6.7 mm (a-p). There is no lesion in the right orbit. While the etiology is unknown, it may be the secondary result of an infection affecting the left lacrimal gland, such as chronic trachoma, an infectious eye disease caused by the bacterium *Chlamydia trachomatis* (Euber et al. 2007; Webb 1990). If this lesion is in fact due to trachoma, then this case provides further support for the presence of this disease in the New World prior to European contact.

Dentition: No calculus, enamel hypoplasias, or dental anomalies were observed. The teeth are heavily worn, with exposed dentin. The maxillary left third molar is worn flat, but the lower third molars still have traces of their cusps. Tooth wear scores (based on Smith 1984) are incisors: 6/7, canines: 6, maxillary premolars: 5, and mandibular premolars: 4. Maximum scores per molar quadrant (based on Scott 1979) are maxillary: second molar: 8, third molar: 8, mandibular: first molar: 7/8, second molar: 7/8, third molar: 4.

Antemortem tooth loss includes the maxillary left first molar and possibly the maxillary right first molar. The alveolar bone that supported the

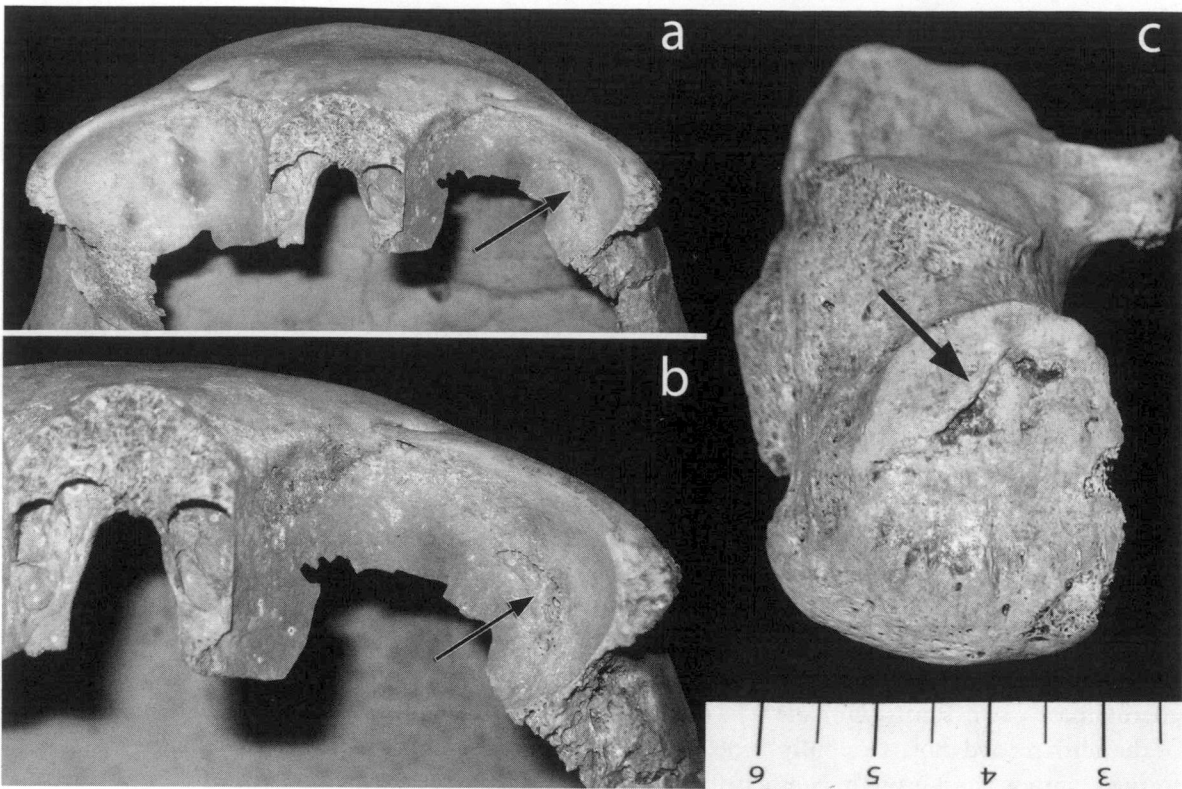

FIGURE 8.2. HP09-04 lesion in the left lacrimal fossa: *a*, right and left orbits, inferior view; *b*, detail of lesion, inferior view; *c*, possible calcaneal bursitis (left calcaneous, posterior view).

maxillary left first molar shows erosion and a healing abscess around the buccal root.

HP09-04 is the only individual with multiple caries, located on the interproximal surfaces between the molars, at the cemento-enamel junction. Caries were observed on the mandibular right first molar (distal surface) and the mandibular left second (distal surface) and third (mesial surface) molars. The mandibular right second molar (distal surface) and third molar (mesial surface), and the mandibular left third molar (mesial surface) have incipient/small caries (pits) at the cemento-enamel junction.

Postcranial Skeleton: The individual shows few degenerative changes. Pathology includes healed periostitis on the right femur, an active inflammatory process of the left tibia, and bilateral calcaneal spurs.

Vertebrae: There are few degenerative changes of the vertebrae. There is a barely discernible lip on the articular facet of the dens of the second cervical vertebra and the fifth lumbar vertebra has an elevated lip on the left superior articular facet. The

fourth and sixth thoracic vertebrae have barely discernible lips on the inferior aspect of the body (the body of the fifth thoracic vertebra is broken).

Femora: The proximal shafts of both femora are platymeric. On the right femur is a thickened area of well-healed periostitis at the attachment site of iliopsoas. Another 25 × 7.8 mm area of well-healed periostitis is found on the anterior aspect of the proximal femur.

Tibiae: The lateral condyle of each tibia has a small localized circular pitted defect (osteochondritis dissecans). The defect on the right tibia measures 4.4 (medial-lateral) × 4.9 mm (anterior-posterior), and the defect on the left tibia measures 5.3 (medial-lateral) × 4.6 mm (anterior-posterior).

Right tibia: There is an area of well-healed periostitis on the proximal end of the bone, medial to the tibial tuberosity.

Left tibia: The proximal 2/3 of the shaft is swollen, with healed, healing, and active periostitis and venous tracks. The majority of the active periostitis is found on the medial aspect of the bone. Measurements at the nutrient foramen are maximum diameter: 33.6 mm, minimum diameter: 24.2 mm, and circumference: 94 mm. In comparison, the right tibia's measurements are maximum diameter: 29.6 mm, minimum diameter: 19.3 mm, and circumference: 78 mm. The left fibula is unremarkable.

<u>Feet</u>: An area of remodeled bone on the superior part of the posterior surface of the left calcaneal tuberosity likely resulted from inflammation of the calcaneal bursa, which may indicate that the individual experienced calcaneal bursitis (Achilles bursitis) (fig. 8.2c). In addition, there is a calcaneal spur on the plantar surface of both calcaneii, extending from the medial process of the calcaneal tuberosity. More pronounced on the individual's left calcaneus, the spurs likely developed as a response to plantar fasciitis.

The left proximal phalanx of the great toe has a pit on the proximal articular surface (the right proximal phalanx is missing).

Stature Estimate: This individual stood approximately 150 cm tall. From the left femur, the estimated stature is 152.3±3.8 cm. From the left tibia, the estimated stature is 148.1±3.5 cm.

(7) HP09-05, Unit 16, Ext. SW, Layer 05, Burial 01, Phase III. This badly fragmented skeleton of a middle adult male (30–50) was discovered beneath several large blocks of polychaete tube-base (see chapter 7 and fig. 7.30b), including one that partly covered and likely crushed the cranium. It appears that the polychaete tubes were intentionally placed on the individual at the time of burial. This is the only burial at Huaca Prieta with this treatment. While the motive behind this atypical treatment is unknown, it may reflect the community's attitude toward the individual. A microlayer of salt crystals was placed underneath the body.

The pelvis was badly fragmented, and no observations were possible. Sex was assessed on the basis of morphological traits of the skull and joint size. The entire skeleton has robust features, with very large joint surfaces, and strong muscle attachment sites.

The age estimate was based on epiphyseal closure, arthritic change, and dental wear. All long bone epiphyses are closed, and the lines of fusion are obliterated. The teeth are heavily worn. Few degenerative changes were observed, but it should

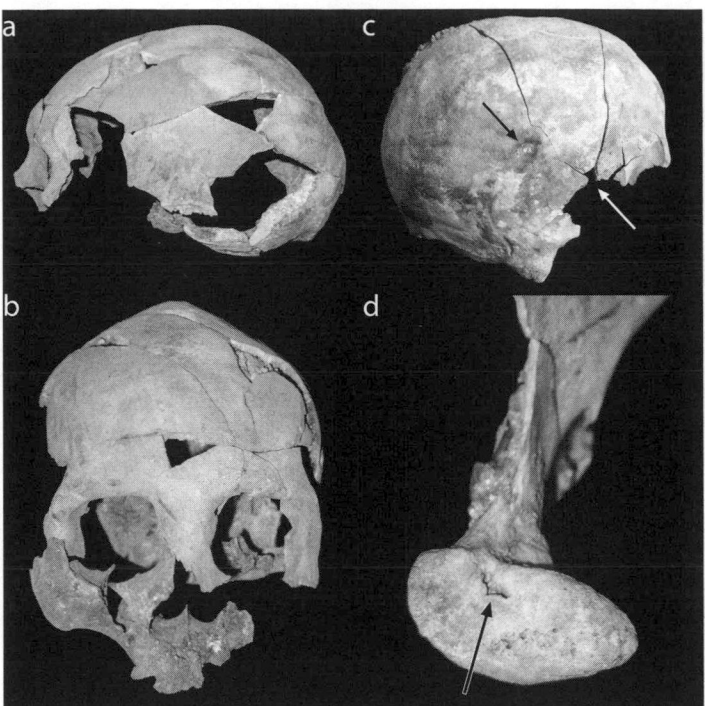

FIGURE 8.3. *a,* lateral view of HP09-05's cranium, left side; *b,* anterior view of HP09-05's cranium; *c,* postero-lateral view of right side of HP09-07's cranium (*black arrow*: healed depressed fracture; *white arrow*: possible perimortem trauma); *d,* cleft or pit on the left mandibular condyle (*black arrow*), postero-superior view, HP09-07.

be noted that most bones, including the vertebrae, are broken. Cranial suture closure appears to be pathological.

Salt crystals are present throughout the bones, including a large, 1 cm long crystal in the distal end of the right humerus. Numerous bones, including several vertebrae, are adhered together with a tenacious salt crystal and dirt matrix. The left hand is bonded in matrix and fixed in a grasping position, with the fingers flexed. The bones of the left foot are also joined together in matrix. An additional right wrist (distal ulna, distal radius, carpal bones, and 1st metacarpal) was included with the remains.

Cranium: The cranium was badly fragmented but could be largely reconstructed. The vault bones are thick and dense, and the individual has a robust orbital region, with a prominent, thick glabella and large nasal bones. The frontal bone has a low angle, giving the individual a low forehead (fig. 8.3a).

The cranium has a sagittal ridge or keel (fig. 8.3b). The bone along the entire length of the sagittal suture is very thick, with an expanded outer table. The sagittal suture is obliterated, and the other sutures are nearly obliterated, both ecto- and endocranially. From the side, and beginning with the low angle of the frontal bone, the cranium appears low and long, ending with a slight occipital bun and a well-developed nuchal crest. In addition, there is also a slight midline ridge of the frontal bone. On the endocranial surface, a thickening of the region of the sagittal suture was observed. There are numerous pacchionian depressions.

Bilateral auditory exostoses are present. The left exostosis occludes approximately one-third of the meatus, while the right exostosis occupies between one-third and one-half of the meatus.

A lesion is present on the endocranial surface of the left lacrimal bone. There is a 6 mm long by 3 mm wide locus of porosity.

Dentition: This individual lost numerous teeth antemortem, and the alveoli of both the maxillary and mandibular molars have completely resorbed. The anterior left mandibular body and the left anterior maxilla are broken and missing, so no information is available regarding most of the front teeth. It appears that the right incisors were likely lost antemortem. The only teeth present are the mandibular right premolars. The crowns of both of these teeth are completely worn down, such that the roots are the occlusal surfaces, scoring an 8 on the tooth wear scale (Smith 1984). Measuring from the top of the occlusal surface to the tip of the root, the length of the root of the first premolar is 4.4 mm, and the length of the root of the second premolar is 12.6 mm.

Two abscesses are present in the maxilla. One abscess is in the vicinity of the right canine and the other is in the region of the left first and second premolars. These abscesses were in the process of healing at the time of death.

Postcranial Skeleton: While the shoulders, knees, hips, and most of the vertebrae are too fragmented for observation, osteoarthritis is present on the elbows and feet, with healed periostitis on the anterior right femur. The individual has well-defined muscle attachments and dense cortical bone. There are large septal apertures of both humeri.

Elbows: There is mild to moderate OA in both elbows, although the OA of the right elbow is slightly more pronounced. The trochleae of both humeri have barely discernible lips, with small osteophytes along the lines that separate the trochlea from the capitulum. The ulnae have barely discernible lips along the margins of the semilunar notches, with osteophytes along the midlines of the notches. The left ulna also has a barely discernible lip on the proximal radial articular surface.

Hands: No abnormalities were noted. The left hand is held in an articulated, flexed position by the salt-dirt matrix.

Femora: Both femora are fragmented, and the proximal and distal ends are not preserved. There is a small area of well-remodeled periostitis on the antero-medial aspect of the right shaft. Posterior to the healed periostitis are venous markings, on the medial aspect of the shaft. The left femoral shaft is normal in appearance.

Feet: Both feet show degenerative changes.

Right Foot: There is marked OA on the plantar surface of the head of the first metatarsal, with lipping, eburnation, and porous areas of bone. Mild OA is present on the proximal articular facets of the fifth metatarsal, in the form of barely discernible lipping.

Left Foot: Most of the left foot is encased in the salt-dirt matrix. The plantar surface of the head of the left first metatarsal also has mild to marked OA in the form of lipping, but there is no eburnation and no porosity.

Vertebrae: All vertebrae are badly fragmented. Several cervical vertebrae and some of the lumbar spinous processes are bonded together by the salt-dirt matrix. No vertebral osteophytosis was observed on the visible vertebrae; however, there is mild osteoarthritis of the facets articulating the fourth and fifth cervical vertebrae.

Ribs: Although badly fragmented, the ribs are large, with well-defined muscle attachments.

Stature Estimate: Because the long bones are fragmented, a stature estimate from the femur and tibia is not possible.

(8) HP09-06, Unit 16, Ext. SW, Layer 05, Burial 06, Phase III. This burial consists of the remains of a young adult male, between 20 and 25 years of age. The individual was interred in a flexed position, with his head oriented toward the east. The entire skeleton is badly fragmented. Sex was assessed on the basis of the robusticity of the mastoid processes and the large size of the long

bone epiphyses. Age was estimated based on dental development and postcranial maturation. Although the RM³ is in occlusion, the epiphysis of the medial clavicle is only partially fused. These two observations suggest a skeletal age estimate of 20–25 (young adult). Observations include a developmental variant of the sternum, inflammation on the left femur, and a lesion on the left foot. Clusters of salt crystals were in the tomb suggesting that saltwater had been poured into it.

Cranium: The cranium is badly fragmented, and no observations could be made.

Dentition: Only three teeth are present: the maxillary right first and third molars and a fragment of another first molar. The third molar has mild tooth wear. The first molars are both worn with dentin exposure, with the maximum wear of a quadrant being a 7 (Scott [1979] scale). No dental pathologies were observed on these teeth.

Postcranial Skeleton: The postcranial skeleton is badly fragmented, and only limited observations could be made. No degenerative changes were observed.

Sternum: There is an aperture in the third sternal segment of the sternum. This aperture resulted from the incomplete caudal cohesion of the developing sternal bands (Barnes 1994).

Femora: An 81.4 mm long by 13.9 mm wide area of healed/healing periostitis is present on the proximal medial shaft of the left femur, distal to the lesser trochanter. The periostitis is accompanied by venous markings. Both femoral shafts have venous markings on the postero-medial surface.

Feet: There is a localized circular area of porosity on the distal articular surface of the left second cuneiform. The proximal articular surfaces of the left second and third metatarsals are normal.

Stature Estimate: The stature of this individual could not be estimated due to the fragmentary condition of the long bones.

(9) HP09-07, Unit 3N, Fill 07, Floor 07, Burial 01, Phase IV. HP09-07 is the nearly complete but fragmented skeleton of a middle adult male (35–45). The individual was found flexed, lying on his right side, with his head oriented toward the west. Although the right calcaneus and talus were recovered, the other bones of the right lower limb (femur, tibia, fibula, and patella) are missing, which suggests that the burial was disturbed.

Sex was determined on the basis of morphological traits of the skull and the pelvis. Age was estimated on the basis of the morphology of the pubic symphysis, the auricular surface, dental wear, and degenerative changes of the postcranial skeleton. This tomb also had an excessive amount of salt crystals.

Observations include antemortem and possible perimortem blunt force trauma to the cranium, a healed fracture of the distal right ulna, healed cribra orbitalia, mild to marked degenerative changes of the postcranial skeleton, marked tooth wear, numerous joint surfaces with osteochondritis dissecans, fusion of the first coccygeal element to the sacrum, and external auditory exostoses.

Cranium: Slight flattening of the posterior parietal bones and a very slight occipital bun were observed. There is healed cribra orbitalia in both orbits.

A well-healed depressed fracture is present on the right side of the cranium (fig. 8.3c). Located on the right parietal, postero-inferior to the parietal boss and near the temporal line, is an ovoid, smooth sided depression 17.6 mm (anterior-posterior) by 7.7 mm (superior-inferior), by 1.4 mm deep.

In addition to the healed depressed fracture, there is possible perimortem trauma to the skull. Numerous linear fracture lines radiating from the region of the right temporal bone were observed. Two major fracture lines cross the top of the cranium, with several short fracture lines in the proposed region of impact. None of the fractures show evidence of healing. This pattern of fractures is not typically seen in dry bone and may have occurred near the time of death, most likely due to blunt-force trauma (Burns 1999).

An exostosis occludes approximately one-third to one-quarter of the left external acoustic meatus. A small exostosis was observed in the right external acoustic meatus. There are small bilateral tympanic apertures.

Mandible: The left mandibular condyle has a small pit or cleft on the anterior aspect of the head. It appears to be a developmental variant and may be a partial bifurcation of the condyle (fig. 8.3d).

Both mandibular condyles of HP09-07 have small circular areas of healed focal necrosis,

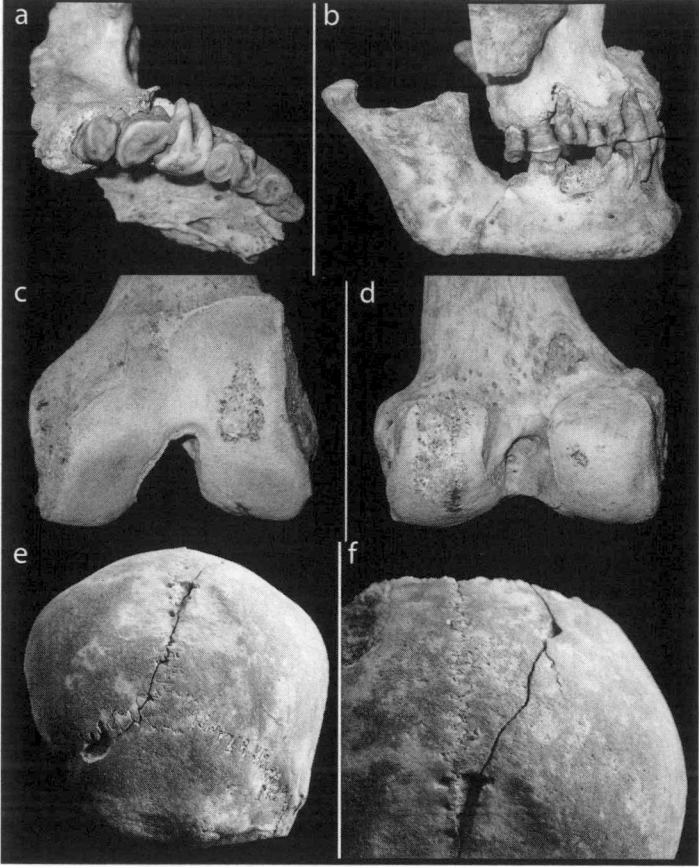

FIGURE 8.4. Dentition of HP09-07: *a*, right maxillary dentition, infero-lateral view; *b*, right maxillary and mandibular dentition, lateral view; osteochondritis dissecans on the lateral condyle of the left femur, HP09-07: *c*, antero-inferior view, *d*, posterior view; possible perimortem trauma of HP09-08: *e*, posterior view of cranium; *f*, posterior view of cranium (coronal suture is superior).

although there is no evidence of bony changes on the temporomandibular articular surfaces of the temporal bones.

Dentition: The majority of teeth are present, though some are fragmented due to postmortem damage. There is calculus on the lingual and distal root of the maxillary right second molar and the distal root of the maxillary right third molar. No caries, no enamel hypoplasias, and no developmental variants were noted. The teeth are heavily worn and show angular wear that is different from the flat wear typical of the rest of the Huaca Prieta sample. This atypical wear pattern suggests that the teeth may have been used as tools (fig. 8.4a–b). Antemortem tooth loss includes the mandibular left first molar. There appears to be a congenital absence of the mandibular left third molar.

Maxilla: All teeth are worn. Most notable is the right first molar, where the crown was entirely worn off, leaving the root as the occlusal surface. The worn surface extends onto the buccal side of the buccal roots, causing the molar to take on an arch-like form. Although broken, the mandibular right first molar appears to have comparable tooth wear.

The buccal roots of the maxillary first molars have resorbed and are much shorter than the lingual roots. The alveoli for these teeth are very porous and the alveolar bone, leaving only the lingual roots to secure the teeth, no longer holds the buccal roots. As a result, the teeth are loose in their alveoli; had the individual lived, these teeth would have likely soon been lost. Active remodeling and resorption of the alveolar bone is present around the roots of the upper right canine, both first molars, and the left third molar.

Mandible: The mandibular incisors, canines, and premolars are worn at an angle, such that the buccal edges are lower than the lingual edges of the teeth. The molars are also worn at an angle, with the distal surface worn lower than the mesial surface. The left second molar is worn flat to the root. The left first molar was lost antemortem, and the alveolus is in the process of resorption. The alveoli for the right first and third molars are very porous with active bone remodeling. The root spaces are very shallow and they are not securely holding the teeth in place. Had the individual lived, these teeth would also soon have been lost. Active remodeling and resorption of the alveolar bone is also present around the roots, the left canine, and the second molars.

Postcranial Skeleton:

Shoulders: There is mild osteoarthritis of both shoulders. Barely noticeable lips around the glenoid fossa of the left scapula and along the margin of the left and right humeral heads were observed.

Elbows: There is mild OA of the left elbow and moderate OA of the right, indicated by lipping on the trochleae of the humeri and on the semilunar notches of the ulnae. On the left humerus, small surface osteophytes were observed between the trochlea and capitulum. On the right humerus, a localized, circular pitted defect (osteochondritis dissecans) is present on the posterolateral trochlea. Additionally, there is microporosity on the anterior aspect of the proximal articular surfaces of both radii.

Wrist: The right ulna has a well-healed fracture of the distal fourth of the shaft, with a swollen cortex and a minor angulation of the shaft. There is lipping of the ulnar head, which is likely traumatic arthritis associated with the fracture. The right radius does not show trauma or OA. Although it is not conclusive without radiography, macroscopically it appears that the fracture line is transverse and not oblique, which may argue for the fracture resulting from direct force (parry fracture) rather than a fall (Judd 2008).

Hips: Both acetabula have mild OA and localized circular pitted defects (osteochondritis dissecans). The left femoral head is unremarkable, and the right femoral head is not present.

Knees: There is mild to moderate OA of the left knee (the bones of the right knee are missing). Mild lipping along the patellar surface of the left femur and the articular surface of the patella was observed. On the lateral condyle of the femur are two sizable loci of osteochondritis dissecans that can be characterized as areas of coalescing micro- and macro-porosity. One locus is found on the inferior anterior aspect of the lateral condyle, measuring 10.9 mm (medial-lateral) by 21 mm (superior-inferior) (fig. 8.4c); the second locus is on the posterior superior aspect of the lateral condyle, measuring 28.8 mm (superior-inferior) by 12 mm (medial-lateral) (fig. 8.4d). The position and manifestation of the second locus was described by Kostick (1963: 397) as an osteochondritic imprint resulting from contact between the tibial and femoral condyles in a hyperflexed knee. Such hyperflexion is seen in the position of squatting. On the medial aspect of the lateral condyle of the left tibia is a small locus of healing osteochondritis dissecans. Additionally, there is a deep stress lesion at the insertion for the medial head of gastrocnemius.

Tibia: There are two areas of well-healed periosteal deposition on the left tibia. One is located on the proximal shaft, on the medial aspect at the attachment site for the tibial collateral ligament. This locus measures 36.1 mm (superior-inferior) by 15.5 mm (medial-lateral). The second locus is found on the medial aspect of the distal shaft, measuring 40 mm (superior-inferior) by 19.3 mm (medial-lateral).

Feet: As in the case of the left calcaneous of HP09-04, there is a localized area of porosity on the posterior surface of both calcaneal tuberosities that likely resulted from inflammation of the calcaneal bursa (calcaneal bursitis). Measuring 10 mm (medial-lateral) by 7.3 mm (superior-inferior), the locus on the left calcaneal tuberosity is more pronounced and was active/healing at the time of death. The locus on the right calcaneal tuberosity was healing at the time of death and measures 9.44 mm (medial-lateral) by 5.22 mm (superior-inferior).

Ribs: The ribs are fragmented, but it is possible to observe moderate OA present on the articular facets of the tubercles of five left ribs and three right ribs.

Vertebrae: There was caudal border shifting at the sacrocaudal border. The first caudal segment has sacralized, such that the sacrum has six segments. Degenerative changes in the form of mild OA on the costal facets on the ninth and twelfth thoracic vertebrae were observed, as well as moderate to marked vertebral osteophytosis of the lower cervical, lower thoracic, and lumbar vertebrae.

Cervical: This individual appears to have suffered a herniation of the intervertebral disc between the 5th and 6th cervical vertebrae. The bodies of C5 and C6 have macroporosity. The inferior rim of the C5 body and the superior rim of the C6 body have osteophytes that articulate, but they are not fused together. The other cervical vertebrae do not show degenerative changes.

Thoracic: Moderate to marked vertebral osteophytosis of the lower thoracic vertebrae was observed. There is mild compression of the T5 and T6 bodies, as well as a long curving osteophyte that extends superiorly from the superior rim of the T6 body. The portion of the T5 body in contact with T6's osteophyte has remodeled. There are small osteophytes on the right superior rim of T5 and on the right inferior rim of T6. The T7 and T8 bodies have slightly elevated superior rims. Medium to large osteophytes are found on the right inferior rims of T8 and T9, the right superior and inferior rims of T10, the right superior rim of T11, and the left inferior rim of T11. The T12 body has a slightly elevated rim.

Lumbar: The lumbar vertebrae show moderate vertebral osteophytosis, with elevated rims of

L1–L3, and osteophytes on the right superior rims of L1 and L2 and on the left inferior rim of L2. The fifth lumbar vertebra has osteophytes on the superior and inferior rim. The inferior body of the L5 vertebra has macroporosity.

Sacrum: The superior body of the sacrum has macroporosity, and there are osteophytes on the left side.

Stature Estimate: This individual stood approximately 164 cm tall. From the left femur, the estimated stature of this individual is 162.4±3.42 cm. From the left tibia, the estimated stature is 165.1±2.82 cm.

(10) HP09-08, HP-3, West Wall, Layer 52, Burial 01, Late Phase II. HP09-08 is the fragmented remains of a middle adult female (35–40). The skeleton was flexed, on its right side, with the head oriented toward the south (fig. 7.6). Salt crystals have split apart portions of the long bones, including the humeri and distal femora, finger bones, and the ossa coxae. Salt crystals have also adhered to the left distal humerus and the left proximal ulna, fusing the left elbow in a flexed position. Red pigment was placed underneath and on top of the body.

Because the pelvis was fragmented, sex was determined on the basis of morphological traits of the skull and the size of the ephiphyses. Age was estimated from the morphology of the pubic symphysis, the auricular surface, dental wear, and degenerative changes of the postcranial skeleton.

This female has healed and healing rib fractures, possible perimortem blunt force trauma to the cranium, and minor degenerative changes of her postcranial skeleton. No exostoses were observed in the external acoustic meati.

Cranium: The cranium has fractures that may have occurred perimortem; however, these fractures are somewhat equivocal and may be the result of postmortem damage. A linear fracture runs from the right coronal suture parasagittally across the right parietal; it then crosses the sagittal suture and merges with the left lambdoidal suture (fig. 8.4e). Three fragments of bone are missing from the skull along this fracture line: one piece at the right coronal suture, superior to the squamosal suture; another at the posterior sagittal suture near obelion; and a third at the left lambdoidal suture, which appears to be the result of postmortem

damage. In addition, a short linear fracture stems from the main fracture near the coronal suture, where the piece of bone is missing. This location may indicate a point of impact or could be the result of postmortem damage. If the fractures are indeed the result of blunt force trauma, then the trauma could have been the cause of death. The left side of the skull is broken, as are the facial bones.

A flattened and slightly depressed area of the cranium extending from obelion to lambda is trapezoidal in shape (fig. 8.4e, f). It measures 26.2 mm long, 25.9 mm at its superior horizontal, and 45.6 mm at the inferior horizontal aspect. There is a small ossicle at lambda, also referred to as an apical bone, and small ossicle at asterion on the right side (the left side is damaged). These ossicles reflect a developmental delay in the closure of the fontanelles (Barnes 1994).

Dentition: Most of the teeth were present, with the exception of the maxillary first and second molars, which were lost antemortem. The maxillary left third molar is not present, but that may be due to congenital absence, as the mandibular left third molar shows very little wear. There is a thin accumulation of calculus at the anterior cemento-enamel junction of the incisors and on the buccal and lingual surfaces of the mandibular left third molar. No other dental pathologies (no caries, no enamel hypoplasias, no developmental variants) were observed.

The teeth are heavily worn, with exposed dentin. The teeth have the following scores (on the Smith [1984] scale): incisors: 5, canines: 5, first premolars: 6, and second premolars: 6. Maximum wear for a molar quadrant (based on Scott 1979) was first molars: 5/6, second molars: 5, mandibular left third molar: 2, mandibular right third molar: 5, maxillary right third molar: 7/8.

Postcranial Skeleton: This individual presents healed rib fractures, and minor arthritis was noted in the left elbow, both knees, and several thoracic vertebrae. Both clavicles show osteogenic reactions at the insertion points for the conoid ligament. There is a sternal aperture in the third sternal segment and vertebral border shifting at the sacrocaudal border.

Elbows: Very minor OA of the left elbow was observed, indicated by a barely noticeable lip on the head of the radius, where it articulates with the ulna.

Hips: What appears to be a depression or notch is present on the lunate surface of both acetabula, superior to the acetabular notch near what would clinically be described as the 12 o'clock position (Philippon et al. 2014) (fig. 8.5a). The depression may be a superior acetabular roof notch or supra-acetabular fossa, which are asymptomatic anatomical variations in the form of the acetabular roof (Dietrich et al. 2012; Johnstone et al. 1982). The notch or fossa of the left acetabulum has a greater expression than that of the right.

Knees: Both knees show very minor OA, with barely discernible lips on the lateral tibial condyles.

Feet: There is a small pit on the proximal articular surface of the proximal phalanges of both great toes.

Ribs: The majority of the ribs have postmortem damage, including three fragments with trauma. Two right rib fragments have well-remodeled fractures, and another right rib fragment has an antemortem break that was in the process of healing at the time of death, indicated by the presence of periosteal deposition (woven bone). The fragment is a segment of the vertebral end of an upper rib, from the neck to approximately the angle, and there is a moderate osteoarthritic lip on the articular facet on the tubercle.

Vertebrae: Most of the vertebrae are fragmentary.

Degenerative Changes: There are two thoracic transverse processes that display moderate OA of the costal facets, with irregularly elevated lips and spicule growth. There are small osteophytes on the left side of the inferior rim of what may be the seventh thoracic vertebra and on the superior rim of what may be the eighth thoracic vertebra. The fifth lumbar vertebra has an elevated lip on the superior rim, with a tiny osteophyte on the left side.

Border Shifting: There is also caudal border shifting at the sacrocaudal border. The first caudal segment has sacralized, such that the sacrum has six segments.

Stature Estimate: This individual stood approximately 154 cm tall. From the left femur, the estimated stature of this individual is 152.6±3.8 cm.

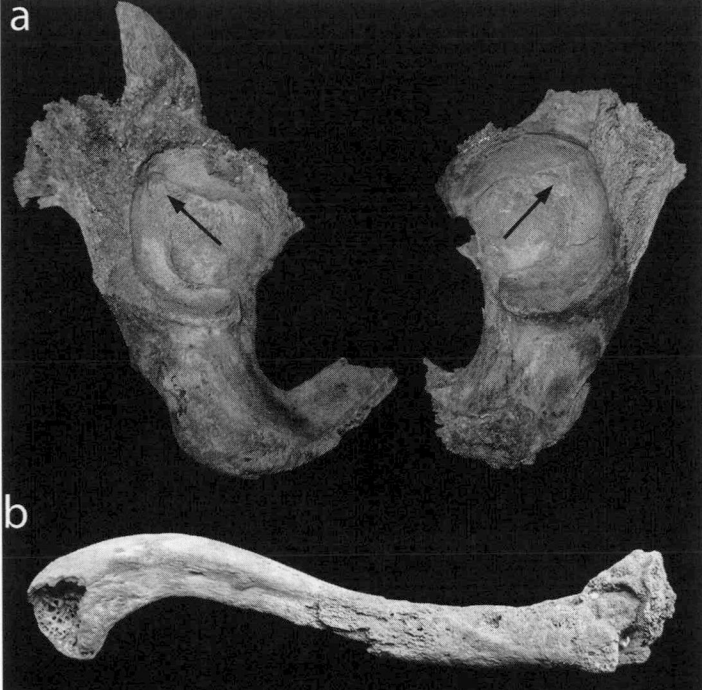

FIGURE 8.5. Views of skeleton HP09-08: *a*, lateral views of the left and right acetabulae of HP09-08 (arrows point to variation in the form of the lunate surfaces); left clavicle, *b*, inferior view (anterior is down, medial end is to the right); *c*, detail of medial end, inferior view; *d*, detail of medial end, posterior view.

From the left tibia, the estimated stature is 154.4±3.5 cm.

(11) HP09-09, Unit 10, Burial 01, Late Phase IV. This burial is the nearly complete and very well-preserved skeleton of a young adult female (20–25 years of age). The body was interred flexed, lying

on her right side, with the arms and hands placed between the flexed legs and the head oriented toward the north. Red pigment was present on most of the skeleton (a sample was collected in the field). A 7 months ±2 months in utero fetus was found near the individual's feet, described below (HP09-09A).

Sex was determined on the basis of morphological traits of the pelvis and skull. The age estimate was based on the morphology of the pubic symphysis and the auricular surface, dental development and tooth wear, and postcranial maturation. The individual has one fully erupted third molar with minimal tooth wear. The root of the M3 is complete with a closed apex. The proximal tibiae, the distal radii, the medial clavicles, and the posterior iliac crests are partly fused, with epiphyseal lines clearly apparent.

At the time of her death, this female had an active infective process affecting the medial end of her left clavicle and first rib. She also has developmental variations of her axial skeleton, such as block vertebrae (Klippel-Feil) and vertebral border shifting at the thoracolumbar and lumbosacral levels. Additionally, she has a congenital absence of three of her third molars.

Cranium: There is minor flattening of the posterior cranium, from obelion to slightly below lambda as well as a slight postbregmatic depression. No exostoses were observed in the external acoustic meati.

Dentition: All teeth are present and complete with the exception of the maxillary third molars and the mandibular right third molar. The mandibular left third molar is present, complete, and in full occlusion, so it is likely that the missing molars are congenitally absent. No caries, no abscesses, no enamel hypoplasias, and no dental calculus were observed. There is moderate to heavy tooth wear with exposed dentin on all teeth except the mandibular left third molar. The teeth scored the following (on the Smith [1985] scale): incisors: 5, canines: 5, first premolars: 4, and second premolars: 3. The molars scored the following for maximum expression per quadrant (based on Scott 1979): first molars: 7/8, second molars: 6, third molar: 1/2.

Postcranial Skeleton: Consistent with her young age, this female has no degenerative changes.

Left clavicle: There is an infective or inflam-matory process affecting the medial half of the left clavicle (fig. 8.5b–d). A combination of bone destruction and unremodeled periosteal bone mark this infection, active at the time of death. There is erosion of the medial end, with possible cloacae on the medial end and on the superodorsal surfaces. The manubrium and right clavicle are unaffected, indicating that the infection did not cross the joint space. A similar process affects the sternal end of a rib fragment (see below).

Arms: The upper limb bones are asymmetric in length. The lengths of the left humerus, left radius, and left ulna are each about 3 mm shorter than those of the right. There are septal apertures of both humeri.

Hips: A small depression on the lunate surface of both acetabula was observed, superior to the acetabular notch, near what would clinically be described as the 12 o'clock position (Philippon et al. 2014). The depression appears to be a superior acetabular roof notch, which is an asymptomatic anatomical variation in the form of the acetabular roof (Johnstone et al. 1982). The superior acetabular notch of the right acetabulum is deeper than that of the left.

Ribs: There is an infective or inflammatory process affecting a rib that was active at the time of death. Although only a fragment of the rib was recovered, it may have been a portion of the sternal end of the left first rib.

Vertebrae: Developmental variations of the vertebrae were observed, including a segmentation error and border shifting.

Block Vertebra: The second and third cervical vertebrae failed to segment and present as a single block vertebra (fig. 8.6a–b). While the bodies and spinous processes are fully joined, the transverse processes are separate. Cervical vertebral segmentation errors are clinically described as Klippel-Feil syndrome and occur due to the failure of the normal segmentation of the sclerotomes between the third and eighth weeks of embryogenesis (Aufderheide and Rodríguez-Martin 1998).

Border Shifting: Border shifting occurred at the thoracolumbar and lumbosacral borders. At the thoracolumbar border, the T12 is a transitional T12/L1 vertebra, with a rudimentary right rib. At the lumbosacral border, there is incomplete sacralization of the L5 vertebra. While the left transverse processes of the L5 and S1 are damaged,

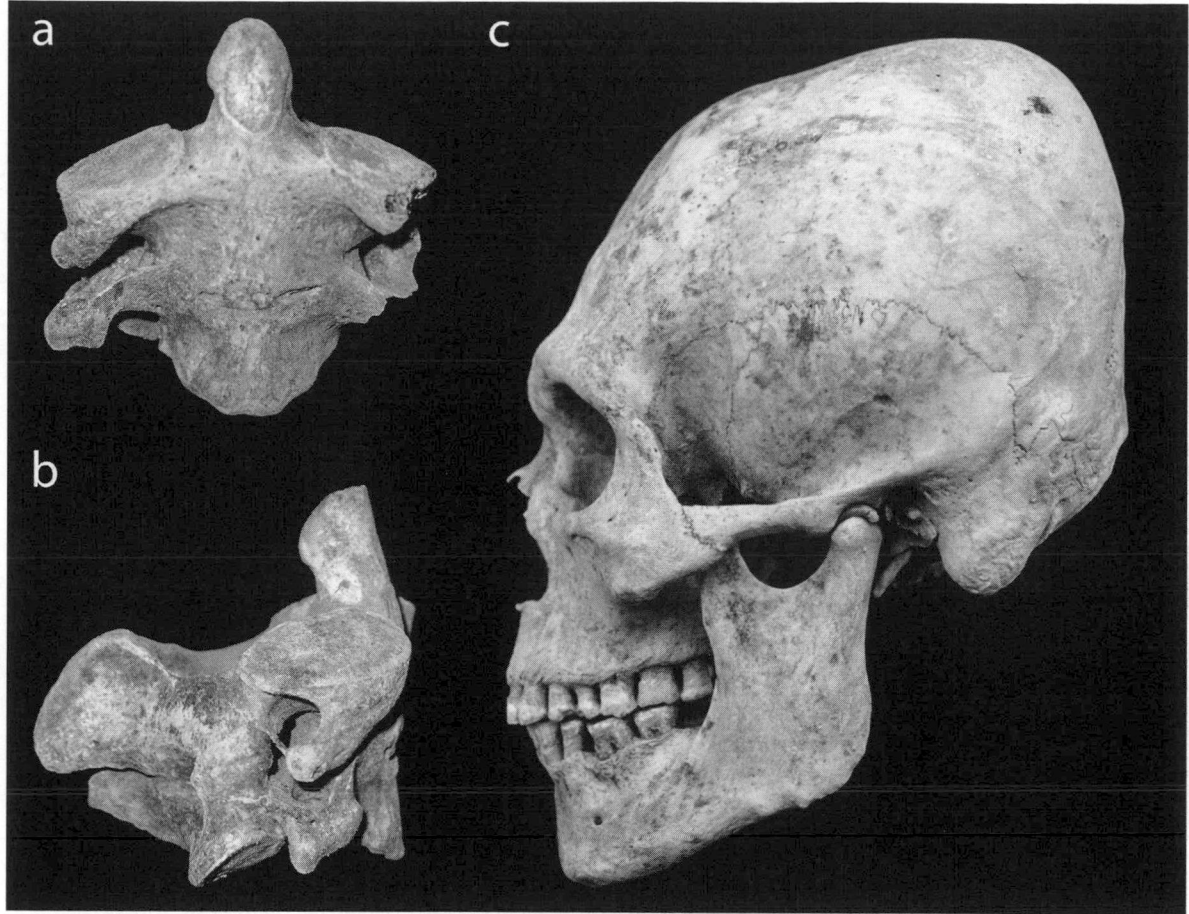

FIGURE 8.6. C2–C3 block vertebra, HP09-09: *a*, anterior view: *b*, lateral view, Cupisnique skull from the Paredones sector of the El Brujo Complex: *c*, occipital flattening and angular flattening of the frontal bone.

the morphology suggests that they had not fused together. A space persists between the bodies of L5 and S1.

Stature Estimate: This individual stood approximately 149 cm tall. From the left femur, the estimated stature of this individual is 149.2±3.8 cm. From the left tibia, the estimated stature is 148.4±3.5 cm.

(12) HP09-09A, Unit 10, Burial 01, Fetus, late Phase IV. Found at the feet of HP09-09, HP09-09A consists of the remains of a 7 months ±2 months in utero fetus. Recovered skeletal elements include cranial and mandibular fragments, including the petrous portions of both temporal bones, and a partial deciduous mandibular first incisor crown, as well as neural arches of the vertebrae, ribs, clavicles, left scapula, both arms, both legs, and both ilia. The age estimate is based on dental development and skeletal maturation. The crown of the incisor had begun to form and mea-

sures 2 mm in length. The sex is indeterminate, and no pathological conditions or abnormalities were noted.

Postcranial Skeleton: The following long bone measurements could be taken:

Right femur maximum length: 50.4 mm
Left tibia maximum length: 44.2 mm
Left fibula maximum length: 42.7 mm
Left humerus maximum length: 45 mm
Left radius maximum length: 37.2 mm
Left ulna maximum length: 42 mm

(13) HP09-10, Unit 23, Ext. 2, Layer 07, Burial 01, Phase IV. This interment contained the nearly complete skeleton of a child that was approximately 8 years of age (±2 years) at the time of death. The age estimate is based on dental development and postcranial maturation. The apices of the roots of the adult first molars are not yet

closed, the roots of the adult second molars are about 2 mm long, and the roots of the adult canines are between one-third to two-thirds complete. The sex is indeterminate.

Cranium: The facial bones demonstrate postmortem damage. The neurocranium is asymmetrical, which may be due to asymmetrical growth and development or the result of taphonomic processes. The asymmetry is seen from the posterior perspective on the left side and primarily involves the left parietal and left occipital. These bones are less expanded/inflated than the right side, giving the appearance of being underdeveloped. There are two short vessel tracks on the occipital bone: one is superior to and right of the nuchal crest, and the other is left of the nuchal crest. Other cranial features include a slight post-bregmatic depression, flattening at obelion with a slight occipital bun, and mild parietal bossing. Additionally, along the sagittal midline of the frontal bone is a slight metopic ridge.

Dentition: No dental pathology was observed: there are no caries, no dental enamel hypoplasias, and no calculus. The deciduous dentition is worn, with exposed dentin.

Postcranial Skeleton: The child has minor developmental variations of the axial skeleton involving vertebral border shifting at the thoracolumbar and lumbosacral borders. There is a singular transitional T12/L1 vertebra (instead of a T12 and L1 vertebra), where the form of the right transverse process is longer and lumbar-like, while the left transverse process is shortened and more thoracic-like. In addition, while no costal facet is present on the right side, a small protuberance at the junction of the pedicle and body on the left side of the T12/L1 vertebral body may indicate lumbar rib formation. The superior articular facets of this vertebra are flat and face posteriorly, and the inferior articular facets are convex and point antero-laterally. The fifth lumbar vertebra is incompletely sacralized. No other postcranial anomalies or conditions were noted.

The following long bone measurements could be taken:

Left femur maximum length: 228 mm
Left tibia maximum length: 192 mm
Right fibula maximum length: 182 mm

Left humerus maximum length: 174 mm
Left radius maximum length: 131.4 mm

DISCUSSION

With some exceptions, our results are consistent with osteological studies of Bird's sample of approximately thirty-three Preceramic burials from Huaca Prieta (Farnum and Benfer 2004; Lester 1965; Tattersall 1985). One difference concerns the demographic composition of the samples. While Bird's sample consists of more than twice as many females as males, the sample from 2008–2009 is even in sex distribution. The age distribution also differs somewhat, which may be due to small sample sizes or interobserver variation. Nevertheless, a commonality is that the majority of individuals in both samples are estimated to have died between the ages of 35 and 50 (table 8.1, table 8.4). Also, it appears that an initial peak of mortality occurred surrounding the time of weaning (1–4 years), but the majority once past childhood lived to middle adulthood, which is similar to what was found at Paloma (Quilter 1989).

Charles Lester (1965: 23) examined Bird's Huaca Prieta skeletons and made brief observations on disease, trauma, and deformity, including fractures, block vertebrae, dental pathology, osteoarthritis, external auditory exostoses, an osteochondroma, and one or two cases of what he called "Paget's disease (*osteitis deformans*)." He found no evidence of cranial deformation among the Preceramic burials or in burials from Huaca Prieta attributed to the later Cupisnique and Salinar cultures. We also found no cranial modification among the Preceramic burials excavated in 2008 and 2009. The lack of evidence of cranial deformation suggests that the cradle-boarding of infants was not practiced at Huaca Prieta. Cradle-boarding becomes common in populations of coastal Peru in later time periods; indeed, cranial deformation in the form of occipital flattening was observed in all six Cupisnique burials excavated by the El Brujo Project in 1997 in the nearby Paredones Sector (Mujica Barreda et al. 2007; Verano and Lombardi 1998). One of these skulls shows not only occipital flattening but angular flatten-

Table 8.4. Ages of individuals excavated: The 2008 and 2009 field seasons, Bird's samples, and Dillehay and Bonavia's samples

Age distribution in 2008 and 2009 field seasons

Identification #	Sex	Age category	Age estimate (years)
HP08-01	Male	Young adult	ca. 30
HP08-02	—	Child	3–4
HP09-01	Female	Older adult	50–60+
HP09-02	—	Child	3–5
HP09-03	—	Child	7–8
HP09-04	Female	Middle adult	35–45
HP09-05	Male	Middle adult	30–50
HP09-06	Male	Young adult	20–25
HP09-07	Male	Middle adult	35–45
HP09-08	Female	Middle adult	35–40
HP09-09	Female	Young adult	20–25
HP09-09A	—	Fetus	7±2 months in utero
HP09-10	—	Child	8±2

Age distribution (%) in other collections

	Bird	Dillehay and Bonavia
Fetus	0	8
Juvenile	18	31
Young adult	18	23
Middle adult	36	31
Older adult	27	8

Table 8.5. Percentage of individuals with cribra orbitalia

Period	Site	% of individuals with cribra orbitalia
Preceramic	Huaca Prieta (Bird)	20
Preceramic	Huaca Prieta (Dillehay and Bonavia)	23
Preceramic	Paloma	37
Preceramic	Asia	55
Ceramic	Huaca Prieta	32
Early Intermediate Period	Caral	30
Early Intermediate Period	Villa el Salvador	54

Note: Adapted from Farnum and Benfer (2004).

enamel hypoplasias and caries were infrequent, which corresponds to our observations on the 2008–2009 skeletons. They noted an increase in caries frequency in comparative samples dating to later periods (Huaca Prieta Ceramic Period, Early Intermediate Period sites), likely corresponding to an increased reliance on maize (Farnum and Benfer 2004).

NUTRITIONAL STRESS: CRIBRA ORBITALIA

Farnum and Benfer (2004) also found that 20% of the Preceramic individuals displayed cribra orbitalia, a nonspecific indicator of nutritional stress. Their finding is similar to what we observed in the 2008–2009 burials, where 23% had healing/healed cribra orbitalia. Compared to contemporary and later populations at this and other coastal sites for which data are available, the percentage of individuals with cribra orbitalia is rather low (table 8.5), which may indicate that childhood health in the Preceramic Huaca Prieta population was better than that of later populations.

ing of the frontal bone as well (fig. 8.6c), indicating that some early experimentation with binding the heads of infants occurred during the Initial Period. Occipital flattening due to cradleboard use would become common in later cultures of northern coastal Peru from the Early Intermediate Period through the Late Horizon (Verano 1997; Weiss 1962).

More recently, Farnum and Benfer (2004) reexamined Bird's Huaca Prieta burials. They observed that the teeth are very worn, but that

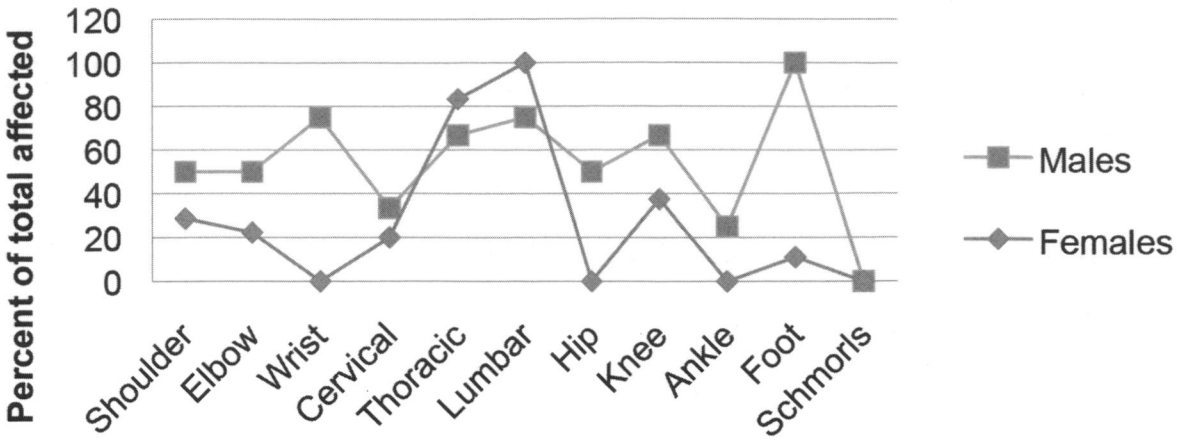

Middle Adults

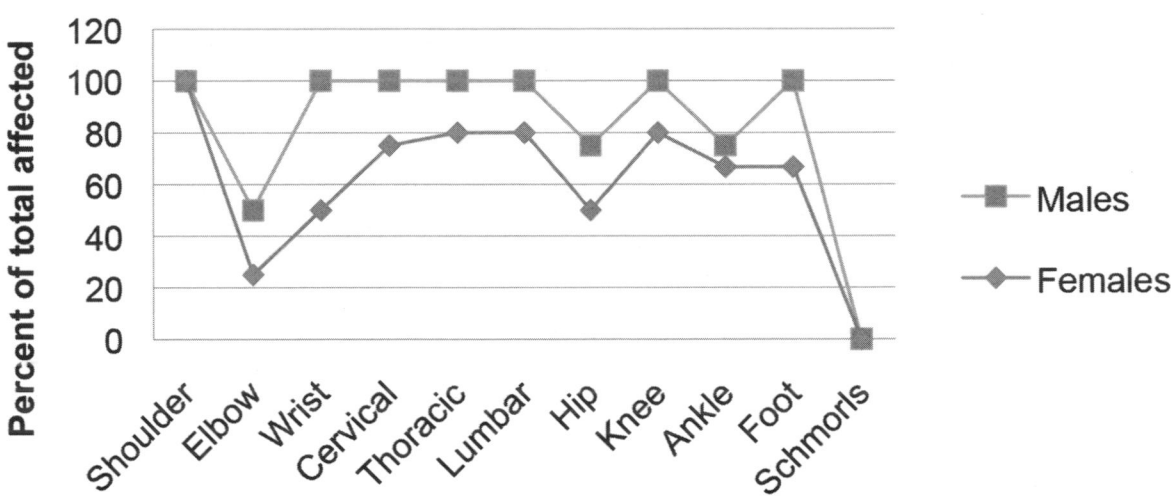

Older Adults

FIGURE 8.7. Crude prevalence comparison of frequency of degenerative changes by joint system in middle adults and older adults. From Titelbaum (2012).

Cribra orbitalia was reported to be common among the Chinchorro of northern coastal Chile (Arriaza et al. 2008). Bernardo Arriaza et al. (2008) attributed it to fish tapeworm (*Diphyllobothrium pacificum*) infection acquired by eating raw or incompletely cooked fish. Analysis of coprolites in Chinchorro mummies has identified fish tapeworm eggs (*Diphyllobothrium pacificum*) (Reinhard and Urban 2003). Raúl Patrucco et al. (1983) found *Diphyllobothrium* eggs in one of 52 coprolites recovered from the Preceramic site of Los Gavilanes in the Huarmey Valley in coastal Peru. Other

coprolites at Los Gavilanes revealed *Giardia* sp. cysts (Ortega and Bonavia 2003), and the eggs of pinworm (*Enterobus vermicularis*) and giant roundworm (*Ascaris lumbricoides*) (Patrucco et al. 1983).

Isolated coprolites collected by Bird from Huaca Prieta were analyzed by Eric Callen and Thomas Cameron (1960). Their analysis found a single coprolite that possibly contained the eggs of a species of tapeworm belonging to the genus *Diphyllobothrium*.

Given the heavy marine component of the diet at Huaca Prieta, fish tapeworm infection would not be surprising, although the low incidence of cribra orbitalia and porotic hyperostosis, and the infrequent occurrence of helminth eggs in coprolites, suggests that worm infections were not a major health problem.

NONSPECIFIC INFECTION

Examples of nonspecific infection were found in multiple individuals in the 2008–2009 sample. Six individuals had active, healing, or healed inflammatory processes at the time of death, including nonspecific periosteal reactions. Possible osteomyelitis was observed in only one individual (a young adult female, HP09-09).

One middle adult female (HP09-04) had a unilateral localized destructive lesion in the lacrimal fossa of the frontal bone. While the etiology is unknown, it may be the secondary result of an infection affecting the left lacrimal gland, such as chronic trachoma, an infectious eye disease caused by the bacterium *Chlamydia trachomatis* (Euber et al. 2007; Webb 1990). If this lesion is in fact due to trachoma, then this case provides further support for the presence of this disease in the New World prior to European contact.

One male (HP09-07) and one female (HP09-04) have lesions on the superior part of the posterior surface of the calcaneal tuberosities that likely resulted from inflammation of the calcaneal bursa, located between the calcaneal tuberosity and the calcaneal tendon (Achilles tendon). One of those individuals (female) also has calcaneal spurs that probably developed in response to plantar fasciitis. Both calcaneal bursitis (Achilles bursitis) and plantar fasciitis can result from running and high-impact activities and can cause pain posterior to the heel, under the heel, and along the medial aspect of the foot (Moore et al. 2014).

EXOSTOSES OF THE EXTERNAL AUDITORY MEATUS

Exostoses of the external auditory meatus or canal have been noted by all researchers who have examined the skeletal material (Farnum and Benfer 2004; Lester 1965; Tattersall 1985). In his observations of Bird's Preceramic skeletal sample, Ian Tattersall (1985: 60–64) identified exostoses in three categories: (1) "Slight" develop-

ment, which he described as "barely perceptible," ranging "from small longitudinal swellings to single lobular nodules"; (2) "Moderate," consisting of "a number of bony lobes developed from the anterior, posterior, and/or superior walls of the external auditory meatus"; and (3) "Severe," "consisting of multiple nodules that effectively occlude the ear canal." Tattersall found that six out of seven adult males had moderate to severe osteomas, whereas two out of nineteen adult females had slight osteomas. One additional possible female had a slight exostosis.

Among the 2008–2009 Huaca Prieta sample, we found slight to severe auditory exostoses in all of the three adult male crania that could be observed, but none in the four adult female crania. (It is interesting that these adult males also had excessive amounts of salt crystals underneath the body or clustered around them, suggesting that large amounts of seawater had been poured into the graves.) From this and the previous investigations, it is clear that exostoses occur more frequently and are more pronounced in males at Huaca Prieta. This is consistent with observations from other coastal skeletal samples in the Andean region, such as the Preceramic population of Paloma (Benfer 1990; Quilter 1989) and prehistoric populations on the northern Chilean coast, including the Chinchorro (Standen et al. 1997).

Exostoses of the external auditory meati have also been found in Cupisnique burials at the El Brujo Complex, although their frequency declines in the later Moche and Lambayeque occupations (personal observation). The decline in frequency is likely associated with shifts in subsistence patterns or in the methods used to procure marine resources. A similar decline over time has been observed at other coastal Peruvian sites, including Puémape, where frequencies declined from the Preceramic to Salinar periods (Lanfranco et al. 2009). While the etiology of these benign growths continues to be discussed (for example, Bonavia 1988; Lanfranco et al. 2009), and although some modern clinical data cited by Tattersall (1985) suggest that males may be more susceptible to exostoses than females, we concur with other researchers who hypothesize that the difference in male and female frequencies is related to the sexual division of labor associated with the extraction of cold-water marine resources (for example,

Benfer 1990; Frayer 1988; Kennedy 1986; Standen et al. 1997).

DEVELOPMENTAL VARIANTS OF THE SKELETON

The Huaca Prieta Preceramic burials have numerous developmental variations of the axial skeleton. Having familial tendencies, these variants are likely due to a combination of genetic and environmental factors (Barnes 1994). Patterns of variants among groups may suggest inheritance patterns, population affiliation, common environmental conditions, similar cultural practices, or a combination of these factors.

For example, vertebral segmentation errors clinically described as Klippel-Feil syndrome occur due to the failure of the normal segmentation of the sclerotomes between the third and eighth weeks of embryogenesis (Aufderheide and Rodríguez-Martin 1998). Involving the entire cervical spine or the fusion of two cervical segments, Klippel-Feil cases where the vertebral failure to separate is limited to two or three vertebral segments appear to have an autosomal dominant inheritance pattern (Tracy et al. 2004). The 2008–2009 sample contains one young adult female (HP09-09) with C2–C3 block vertebrae, and Bird's Preceramic skeletal sample contains three cases of young adult females with Klippel-Feil, including two C2-C3 block vertebrae (99.1/890 and 99.1/901) and one T3–T4 block vertebrae (99.1/896) (personal observation). Klippel-Feil syndrome is variably associated with other anomalies and complications, such as deafness, cardiovascular abnormalities, neurologic disturbances, genitourinary abnormalities, and musculoskeletal anomalies such as a risk for scoliosis and rib abnormalities (Klimo et al. 2007; Thomsen et al. 1997; Tracy et al. 2004). Although Klippel-Feil syndrome is underreported, based on clinical presentation, it has been estimated that it occurs in approximately 1/40,000 to 1/42,000 modern births, with a female preponderance of 3:2 (Tracy et al. 2004: 183).

In addition to vertebral segmentation errors, developmental variations observed in skeletons excavated in the 2008 and 2009 seasons include hypoplasia of the closing membrane of the tympanic plate, resulting in a tympanic aperture (Huschke's foramen) ($n = 4$; 2 female, 2 male); incomplete caudal cohesion of sternal bands, resulting in a sternal aperture ($n = 2$; 1 female, 1 male); vertebral border shifting ($n = 4$; 2 female, 1 male, 1 juvenile); cleft neural arch ($n = 1$; juvenile); unilateral malformation of the mandibular condyle (unilateral partially bifurcated condyle) ($n = 1$; male); what appears to be early fusion of cranial sutures, reflected by metopic ridges ($n = 3$; 1 female, 1 male, 1 subadult) and a sagittal ridge or keel ($n = 1$; male); early fusion of the sagittal suture ($n = 1$; male); and delays in the closure of the fontanelles resulting in ossicles at lambda ($n = 1$; female), at asterion ($n = 2$; 1 female, 1 male), and at the parietal notch ($n = 1$; male).

In a cursory examination of Bird's Preceramic skeletal sample, similar developmental variations were noted. Observed variants include tympanic apertures ($n = 6$; 4 females [99.1/883, 99.1/891B, 99.1/896, 99.1/908], 2 males [99.1/897, 99.1/899]); two cases of sternal fusion, including manubrio-mesosternal joint fusion (99.1/896, young adult female) and one case with both manubrio-mesosternal and xiphisternal joint fusion (99.1/908, a middle adult female); four examples of vertebral border shifting including a cranial shift at the thoracolumbar border (99.1/908, a middle adult female), a caudal shift of the sacrocaudal border (99.1/897, a middle adult male), and a unilateral transverse basilar cleft (99.1/891B, a middle adult female) resulting from a cranial shift at the occipitocervical border; one bifid spinous process of the first sacral vertebra (99.1/907, a young adult female); two instances of unilateral partially bifurcated condyles (99.1/891B, a middle adult female, and 99.1/902, a young adult male); and a delay in the closure of the posterolateral fontanelle resulting in bilateral parietal notch bones (99.1/891B, a middle adult female).

Similar developmental variants of the axial skeleton occasionally have been reported from prehistoric skeletons in Peru. Many, like tympanic apertures, are often observed but infrequently reported. George MacCurdy (1923) published observations from a collection of Peruvian remains from the highlands around Cuzco, describing variations of the vertebrae, ribs, and sternum. MacCurdy (1923) observed a tendency for caudal shifting of vertebrae, particularly at the lumbosacral border among females and at the sacrocaudal border among males. Indeed, while 50% of males have the caudal shift at the sacrocaudal border, not a single female had caudal vertebrae fused to the sacrum. MacCurdy (1923) also reported five instances of lumbar ribs and an additional five cases where there were reduced transverse processes on the L1, which may be rudimentary ribs. He also described two cases of manubrio-mesosternal fusion and three cases of xiphisternal fusion and noted developmental variants associated with the closing of the tympanic membrane among 30% of his highland sample. Tympanic apertures (Huschke's foramina) were also reported among a coastal sample from Pachacamac and Chincha, where it was found among 62.3% of adults (Turner and Katich 1981).

Aleš Hrdlička (1941) reported three cases of bifid mandibular condyles among the Peruvian remains in the National Museum of Natural History collection. The proveniences of the mandibles were not reported.

Roberto De La Mata and Duccio Bonavia (1980) reported the case of a six-year-old child with a supernumerary lumbar vertebra and spina bifida from the site of Los Gavilanes in the Huarmey Valley on the coast, dating to about five thousand years ago. The arches of L5, L6, and the entire sacrum remained open. More recently, Robert Mann and John W. Verano (1990) described multiple variants of the vertebrae of a 20–30 year old female from the site of Pacatnamu in the Jequetepeque Valley (AD 1000–1400). The T4–T6 vertebrae were united in a block vertebra that was asymmetrical because the left arch of T5 was aplastic, with a sagittal cleft in the body of the T8 vertebra and a supernumerary thoracic vertebra. In addition, there was no costal facet on the left transverse process of T5.

Ethne Barnes (1994) listed other reported developmental variants from Peru, including metopism (MacCurdy 1923), microcephaly (Hrdlička 1943), cleft palate (MacCurdy 1923; Ortner and Putschar 1985), aplasia of lacrimal bones (MacCurdy 1923), hypoplastic and aplastic external auditory meatii (Hrdlička 1933), cranial meningoceles at bregma from Chicama (Stewart 1975) and Ancón (Ortner and Putschar 1985), and caudal shifting of the occipitocervical border manifesting as bipartite hypoglossal canals (Mac-

Curdy 1923), paracondylar processes (MacCurdy 1923), and complete occipitalization of the atlas, from the Chicama Valley and the site of Pachacamac in the Lurín Valley (Hrdlička, in Barnes 1994: 92–93).

DEGENERATIVE CHANGE

The elbow and the knee are the most common sites of OA among the 2008–2009 Huaca Prieta sample. Generally speaking, degenerative joint disease of the elbow is relatively uncommon among modern human populations; therefore its frequency among the Huaca Prieta individuals, even if mild in form, may indicate more repetitive use of this joint. The OA seen among the knees might reflect repetitive flexion. This pattern for the Preceramic individuals differs from what has been observed among the later Early Intermediate Moche and Late Intermediate Lambayeque agricultural populations (Titelbaum 2012) and late pre-Hispanic and postcolonial coastal populations (Klaus et al. 2009), where higher frequencies of pronounced OA in multiple joints (in particular, the shoulder, elbow, wrist, hip) reflect more strenuous lifestyles associated with heavy workloads.

In an analysis of degenerative joint disease among the combined Huaca Prieta samples (Bird's and the 2008–2009 collection), Titelbaum (2012) observed that the greatest difference between the middle adult males and females is in the higher prevalence of lumbar and thoracic degenerative changes among females. At the same time, the middle adult females have a lower prevalence for wrist and foot OA (fig. 8.7). These differences in patterns may reflect a division of labor (Lieverse et al. 2007). In general, vertebral osteophytosis of the mid-to-lower back is associated with carrying heavy loads, while foot OA may be related to negotiating uneven or rocky terrain. The higher involvement of the wrist among the males may be related to activities such as manipulating nets, twining textiles, manufacturing tools, or extracting resources. In contrast to the middle adults, the Preceramic older adult males and females have nearly identical arthritic patterns, though males have an overall greater prevalence of degenerative changes for each joint system (fig. 8.7).

Titelbaum (2012) also noted that no examples

of spondylolysis were found in the combined Huaca Prieta samples. Spondylolysis refers to the separation of a vertebral body from its neural arch and is most frequently seen in the lower lumbar vertebrae (L4 or L5). Typical spondylolysis can result from repetitive strenuous loading of the lower back, and it has been associated with postures involving the hyperextension or extension and rotation of the lumbar region and activities that concentrate mechanical stress in the lumbosacral region (Merbs 1996). In an examination of a late Chinchorro fishing sample from coastal Chile (ca. 2000 BC), Arriaza (1995, 1997) observed that 18% of males had spondylolysis, whereas the condition was absent among the females. Arriaza (1997) suggested that males engaged in physically demanding tasks that involved the hyperextension and rotation of the lower back, such as throwing harpoons, using an atlatl, hunting sea mammals, collecting shellfish, and negotiating the rocky coastline. Given the similar reliance on maritime resources, it is interesting that the skeletons from Huaca Prieta have no cases of spondylolysis. The difference may be due to the use of different techniques and technology for acquiring resources or due to a greater dietary reliance on plant foods and thus less strenuous work related to obtaining marine resources (Dillehay, personal communication, 2009). Indeed the Chinchorro utilized fishing and hunting technology that late Preceramic coastal populations of Peru did not appear to have, such as harpoons, spears, and atlatls (Arriaza 1995: 71, 88; Bird et al. 1985; Ponce 2010).

TRAUMA AND INTERPERSONAL VIOLENCE

Accidental falls while negotiating slippery rocks and heavy surf may have been a concern for the population buried at Huaca Prieta, and fractures of the ribs and wrist would not be surprising. Among the 2008–2009 sample was one individual (a middle adult female) with two episodes of rib fractures, indicated by two ribs with well-healed fractures and one rib with proliferative woven bone that was actively being deposited at the time of death. Another individual (an older adult female) has a possible antemortem shaft fracture of a third metarsal.

Bird's Preceramic sample contained at least one healed rib fracture (99.1/887, a middle adult male) and one individual who has remodeled woven bone on the medial right clavicle that may mark a healed fracture (99.1/884, a young adult female) (personal observation). His sample also contained one healed colles fracture of a right radius (99.1/891b, a middle adult female) and two examples of fractures of the distal ulna (99.1/889, a middle adult female; and 99.1/894, a middle adult male). One of these individuals had an accompanying fracture of the associated radius (99.1/889), while the other had remodeled woven bone on the associated radius (99.1/894). Fractures of the distal ulna may be somewhat equivocal in their causation, particularly if accompanied by a fracture of the radius, in that they could be the result of either defending against a blow or bracing oneself during a fall (Galloway et al. 1999; Judd 2008; Phillips 2009).

In general, evidence for interpersonal conflict in Preceramic populations is rare and often indirect. For example, weapons have been reported from the sites of Paracas and Asia (Quilter 1989), rocks interpreted as piles of slingstones were found at the Ostra Camp site in the Santa Valley (Topic 1989), and massive walls were built at the site of Salinas de Chao in the Chao Valley, possibly for defensive purposes (Alva 1986).

Direct evidence of interpersonal conflict typically involves craniofacial trauma such as nasal fractures and depressed or massive fractures of the cranium, which are less likely to occur as a result of accidental falls and more likely to be associated with violence (Arkush and Tung 2013). Preceramic examples of craniofacial trauma are uncommon, and conflict during this period appears to have been localized. Elizabeth Arkush and Tiffiny A. Tung (2013) note that no craniofacial trauma was observed among sixty-nine adults at the site of Paloma in the Lurín Valley. One cranium, however, was buried separately, apparently baked in ashes (Quilter 1989: 85). A possible sacrifice was discovered at Caral in the Supe Valley (Shady 2004), and at Asia there are examples of decapitation (Engel 1963a).

In contrast, the Chinchorro tradition of northern Chile has a comparatively high frequency of interpersonal conflict. Craniofacial trauma was observed in mummies dating as early as 7500–6000 cal BP, with rates at around 23% through the Archaic period (Arriaza and Standen 2008; Standen and Arriaza 2000). Although males have higher rates of trauma than females, nasal bone and cranial vault fractures have been found among both, as well as parry fractures and two examples of fatal projectile wounds (Arriaza et al. 2008; Aufderheide 2003; Standen and Arriaza 2000). It is unclear, however, if the trauma reflects intergroup or intragroup conflict.

In the 2008–2009 Huaca Prieta burials we identified two and possibly three adult individuals that show signs of trauma that are suggestive of interpersonal violence. Healed fractures of the left and right nasal bones were observed on an adult male skull recovered from Unit 16 (Ext. W, Layer 02, Profile W), and HP09-07 (a middle adult male) and HP09-08 (a middle adult female) may have died from perimortem blunt force trauma to the head. Both HP09-07 and HP09-08 also show signs of trauma from earlier in their lives: HP09-07 has a healed depressed fracture on his cranium and a healed fracture of his right distal ulnar shaft (parry fracture), and, as noted above, HP09-08 has healed and healing rib fractures. No evidence of defensive architecture or stockpiles of weaponry has been identified at Huaca Prieta, so it is possible that the observed craniofacial trauma may reflect occasional within-group interpersonal conflict. While such violence may not have been common during the Preceramic occupation, the skeletal evidence indicates its presence.

With the exception of the Chinchorro tradition of northern Chile, the overall evidence for interpersonal conflict during the Preceramic period is low, particularly when compared with later periods (Arkush and Tung 2013). Skeletal evidence for violence on the north coast does increase over time. Of the six Cupisnique burials from the Paredones Sector of the El Brujo Site Complex, one adult male has multiple healed depressed fractures on the skull that are highly suggestive of interpersonal violence (Mujica Barreda et al. 2007; Verano and Lombardi 1998). Depression fractures and perimortem blunt force traumatic injuries have been reported among Early Intermediate Gallinazo burials in the Santa Valley (Gagné 2009), and there is well-reported interpersonal violence and perimortem trauma among the Early Intermediate Moche in the Moche and Chicama Valleys, seen among both Moche burials and sacrificial vic-

tims (Bourget 2001; Phillips 2009; Verano 1995b, 2001).

BURIAL TREATMENT

Comparing Huaca Prieta's Preceramic burials with later Cupisnique burials from Huaca Prieta, the Paredones sector at the El Brujo Complex, and Puémape to the north, it appears that the two cultural periods share a number of mortuary features. Both demonstrate an inconsistent orientation of the bodies and the general tendency for bodies to be flexed or semiflexed, wrapped in mats and interred in shallow pits in domestic settings. Both culture periods applied red pigment to a subset of the interred, placed rocks on or around certain graves, and included occasional grave good items that are not suggestive of social differentiation. The similarities between late Preceramic through Middle Cupisnique mortuary treatment argue for a north coast cultural continuity in funerary traditions (Elera 1998).

Placing rocks on or around certain graves has been observed at other coastal Preceramic sites, including Vegas, Chilca I, Piedras Negras, Río Seco, Paloma (Quilter 1989) and Alto Salaverry in the Huarmey Valley (De la Mata and Bonavia 1980) as well as at Cupisnique sites such as Puémape (Elera 1998). In general, rocks are placed on particular burials and then covered with fill. Elera (1998) found that rocks were placed on five out of twenty-four Early Cupisnique burials at Puémape and on seven out of forty-two Middle Cupisnique burials, although the actual percentage for the latter is unknown because a number of them were disturbed.

It is curious that only certain individuals had rocks placed over their graves. While it is impossible to determine the motives behind this burial practice, it may reflect the community's attitude toward the individual. Indeed, as Jeffrey Quilter (1989: 83) suggested, it may be that, rather than functioning as grave markers, such rocks may have acted as weights on the deceased "to prevent them from rising as the 'living dead' and threatening the living."

Of the 2008–2009 burials, HP09-05 is the only individual that was found beneath sizable rocks. This male (described above) is robust, with a marked sagittal ridge or keel, a low forehead, and a long and low skull. It is likely that in life this male had an unusual appearance compared to the rest of the population, and it is possible that his physical and perhaps behavioral differences in life played a role in his distinct burial treatment.

SUMMARY

The examination of the thirteen skeletons excavated from Huaca Prieta, along with the numerous human remains recovered from test excavations, has given us an opportunity to confirm and expand upon what has been previously understood about the Late Cotton Preceramic at the El Brujo Archaeological Complex. The interments conform to the common Preceramic pattern of being interred in shallow unlined pits, in generally flexed positions with no specific axial orientation, with few accompanying grave goods, and with occasional use of red pigment and rocks placed on top of or around burials. Adults and children appear to have been placed in their own graves, while fetuses were buried with adults. This manner of interment continues beyond the Preceramic on the north coast, into at least the Middle Cupisnique (Elera 1998).

Our general observations concerning dental health, indicators of nutritional stress, and trauma are similar to what has been reported for Preceramic populations of coastal Ecuador (Ubelaker 1980, 1984), and the northern highlands (Grieder et al. 1988) and central coast of Peru (Benfer 1990). Teeth are heavily worn, reflecting grit in the diet, which is unsurprising since the site is on the littoral. Dental pathology includes abscesses and antemortem tooth loss, infrequent caries and calculus, and no observed enamel hypoplasias. The low frequency of caries likely reflects not only an abrasive diet but one that was low in carbohydrates, a pattern that is distinctive from later Andean populations that were more dependent on maize, potatoes, and other starches.

Skeletal pathology includes osteoarthritis, osteochondritis dissecans, active and healed inflammation, including possible chronic trachoma, and several cases of broken and healed bones. Some of the trauma is suggestive of interpersonal violence, such as cranial fractures, nasal fractures, and parry fractures, and some of these may have been the cause of death. Indications of nutritional deficiency are uncommon, with only 23% of the sample demonstrating healed/healing cribra orbitalia, and no evidence of porotic hyperostosis or indications of dietary deficiencies. The frequency of exostoses of the external auditory meati among males may reflect the sexual division of labor, where males were likely harvesting underwater marine resources. These general patterns of skeletal health carry forward into the later Cupisnique inhabitants of the El Brujo Complex and adjacent valleys.

This chapter also presents data on developmental variations of the skeleton, including some that are frequently observed but are underreported in prehistoric north coast burials. Of the thirteen skeletons 77% have some type of developmental disturbance of the axial skeleton, 50% of these have multiple variants. Most of the variants are mild, and the majority appear to be due to genetic factors (Barnes 1994). As such, data on these developmental variations may provide another avenue for understanding population trends, such as migration and gene flow.

The human skeletal remains from Huaca Prieta present an opportunity to understand health and disease during the late Preceramic Period of northern coastal Peru. Future studies employing advances in stable isotope geochemistry and ancient DNA analysis may shed further light on these early coastal inhabitants and their challenges, adaptations, and genetic legacy.

CHAPTER 9

FAUNAL REMAINS

Víctor F. Vásquez, Teresa Rosales Tham, Tom D. Dillehay, and Patricia J. Netherly

INTRODUCTION

The faunal remains found at the Huaca Prieta and Paredones sites are numerous and reasonably well preserved. They not only bear witness to the extraordinary abundance of marine life on the Pacific coast of the Chicama Valley but also offer important insights into the economy, technology, and paleoecology found at these sites. The faunal record also reveals deliberate patterns associated with the ritual use of many of these remains.

Huaca Prieta and Paredones were intentionally located on a freestanding Pleistocene terrace where multiple resource zones were juxtaposed along the littoral and coastal plain of the Chicama Valley. The initial late Pleistocene human occupations were scattered on this terrace, which must have been a prominent landmark on the flat plain that separated the then-distant ocean (~16–18 km) from freshwater and brackish wetland and paludal environments on the inland side of the terrace (see chapters 4, 5, and 6). At this location the coast and up-valley landscapes met the seascape, giving access to the different resources within the waters of the ocean used by the maritime foragers of the Chicama littoral. The relationships between the people who utilized these sites and the faunal resources of various biotopes are implicit in the rich, varied, and well-preserved faunal remains. Except for the late Pleistocene and early Holocene periods (combined Phase I), neither Huaca Prieta nor Paredones was the locus of purely domestic occupation. With these exceptions, all other faunal remains document activities centered on the construction, ritual, and perhaps feasting use of the mounds and support locations used for food preparation. Units 13, 16, and 26, located north of Huaca Prieta at the southwestern base of the Cupisnique mound, are domestic localities, as were the premound deposits in Units 20 and 22 at Paredones (Dillehay et al. 2012a; see chapter 7).

The record of faunal remains clearly demonstrates how the inhabitants of the Chicama coast used different biotopes, some opportunistically and others as principal resource zones. In looking at the occupants of these sites over time, it is clear that this Preceramic society experienced population growth, increasing ideological elaboration, and growing social complexity, fueled in large part by the successful exploitation of resources from the sea and the littoral lagoons and wetlands and a stable population of sea lions and marine birds together with terrestrial resources, including both local wild plants and an increasing variety of imported cultivated plants (see chapter 10). The history of resource use at Huaca Prieta, Paredones, and the associated domestic sites over fourteen millennia demonstrates once again that human societies are capable of both self-organization and complex responses to chaotic perturbations of the environment whether these are cyclical or random (see chapters 4 and 5).

A number of environmental stresses recur irregularly on the Peruvian north coast: earthquakes, droughts, landslides, floods, and impacts on marine biota caused by shifts from the cool waters of the Peru Current to the warm waters of the Ecuador Current brought about by an El Niño/Southern Oscillation or ENSO event (which is relatively short in duration: up to two years) or the warm waters of a Kelvin wave, which may raise the water temperature for as long as two or three decades (Arntz and Fahrbach 1996; Bertrand et al. 2008; Hansen 1990). One of the questions that the faunal remains from Huaca Prieta and Paredones can answer is just how great a perturbation a major ENSO event really was for these maritime foragers and fishers.

While faunal and floral resources from terrestrial biotopes are present throughout the sequence at all excavated sites, the remains of mollusks, fish, and marine mammals recovered from marine and littoral biotopes are remarkably persistent, although the particular species and the biotopes from which they were taken vary. We found that ENSO disturbances, lasting no more than two or three years, were difficult to document in terms of the archaeological chronology (see chapter 5 and appendix 1). At a societal level, however, it does

not appear that dearth occurred, as might have been the case inland with a prolonged drought. Rather, the diverse faunal remains, in particular the marine fauna, testify to the steady productivity of the marine larder, its flexibility in the face of environmental change, and the quality of the foodstuffs provided.

GEOMORPHOLOGY OF THE SEA FLOOR

In a littoral environment the distribution of resources available for human use is dependent on the nature and depth of the sea floor. Depth below the surface is a primary consideration. It is estimated that ~25,000 BP at the Last Glacial Maximum the sea level was some 120 m lower than its present level (Clarke et al. 2009; Fairbanks 1989; Flood and Piper 1997). Off the Chicama coast, where the slope of the seabed is very gradual, 15,000 years ago the coastline lay some 16–18 km to the west (see chapters 4 and 5). By 12,000 years ago sea level had risen to half that amount or ~60 m below present level (Clarke et al. 2009; Flood and Piper 1997). The sea level reached its present location by ~6000 years ago and has varied by only a few meters since then, which did not affect the Huaca Prieta and Paredones sites significantly (see chapter 5).

Ocean depth is not the only consideration, however. The substrate of the sea floor is an important component in the habitat of marine biota: it can be rocky or hard, sandy or soft, or muddy with loose sediment. Each biotope supports its own faunal association, with significant differences in their productivity (Díaz and Ortlieb 1993; Vásquez Sánchez and Rosales Tham 2010). The rocky substrate, including reefs, supports the highest number of species. While no rocky outcrops or islands break the surface of the sea off the coast of the Chicama Valley, the presence of rocky substrates and reefs below the tidal zone is well known to local fishers and evident in the faunal collection. Several stretches of coast appear to have rocky substrates near the shore. The presence of water-rolled rock on the beach in front of Huaca Prieta and farther north indicates the transport of rock from the mountains by the Chicama River, which is discharged into the sea during seasonal freshets and ENSO events and carried north by the long-shore current (see chapter 5). Such mobile rocks do not support faunal associations.

Slab-like reefs of mineralized polychaete tubes create further hard substrates. Polychaetes, marine annelids, create tubes in which they live in soft substrates, which they harden with secretions. When the poychaetes die, the hardened substrate remains. This material can be found on the beach cast up by the surf. It is soft enough to be cut or worked by stone tools. Shaped and unworked blocks of this material are found in the archaeological levels at Huaca Prieta (some incorporated into the walls of structures). Fishers today call these mineralized tubes *pomiz*, apparently because in its porous structure and light weight the gray material resembles pumice. Broken pieces of rocky reef were also collected from the shore and worked into artifacts (see chapter 11).

The living polychaete bed forms a habitat that supports abundant fish and invertebrate species as well as seaweed (Glynn 2003; Glynn et al. 2015). Bivalve beds also form a hard substrate for other organisms, including seaweed. In addition to bivalves, hard substrates support marine snails and other invertebrates. The currents created by the reefs provide nutrients for fish of many species. In contrast, fewer species are found over sandy bottoms, although many are important foods for humans: clams, snails, fish such as flounders and croakers, as well as other demersal species. Sandy beaches are interspersed among the rocky reefs and predominate on the valley shore, creating a biotope mosaic.

From a human standpoint it would appear that both biotopes were exploited extensively. A third habitat is also found. Muddy bottoms and thus waters with lower salinity are found in the estuary. The fauna living on such bottoms are adapted to loose sediment, whereas those adapted to the open sea have difficulty thriving when sediment-laden river water is discharged into the sea, as during ENSO events (Arntz and Fahrbach 1996). We have found it useful to classify the fauna recovered at Huaca Prieta, Paredones, and the domestic sites in terms of their habitat: rocky, sandy, or estuarine substrates that were intensively exploited by the people at these sites. As noted later, the rocky and sandy marine biotopes were recognized and conceptualized in a relation of opposition and complementarity by the people living in the Huaca

Prieta area. Thus mussel species or the reef fish (blennies) were contrasted in even minimal ritual deposits with clams or the demersal fish (croakers) found in or over sandy substrates.

ENSO EVENTS AND REGIME SHIFTS IN THE PERU CURRENT SYSTEM

Archaeologists, interested in human habitation on land, have generally regarded the periodic incursion of warm waters along the desert coast of Peru together with persistent and sometimes heavy rainfall as potentially highly destructive if not catastrophic. For the past six millennia, El Niño/Southern Oscillation or ENSO events have occurred more frequently than in the preceding millennia (Chávez et al. 2008; Mollier-Vogel et al. 2013). These events are local manifestations of processes that are global in scope, some taking place at great distances (see chapters 4 and 5).

The incursion of warm currents, which displace the cold waters of the Humboldt Current, permits onshore rainfall, which occurs sporadically but can cause flash floods in the rivers and normally dry quebradas or washes and destroy adobe structures and irrigation infrastructure (Goldberg et al. 1987). On land, however, the rainfall can also cause the desert to bloom, bringing insects and invertebrate fauna out of estivation and providing food for the whole chain of vertebrate fauna from rodents to foxes and other predators. Farmers can plant without irrigation on the valley margins and get a crop or two. Wild fruits and tubers are abundant for some two years afterward (Netherly 2011a).

The impacts are different in the marine environment. Many organisms have a band of tolerance for changes in temperature or salinity and can withstand moderate change in either or both. More severe events affect the tightly interlinked trophic chain, beginning with the plankton, which die or move away, with dire consequences for small schooling fish, the larger fish that prey upon them, and finally the marine birds and mammals. The major changes in temperature and salinity associated with a strong ENSO event such as those of 1982–83 and 1997–98 can decimate the local populations of many species or cause them to move away by descending with the thermocline or migrating southward or westward to cooler waters. Recovery at the population level can take one to three years for most species, including the birds and sea lions, but some may need a decade or more to recover completely. Nonetheless, marine populations remain steady over the long term and appear to be adapted to these periodic bottlenecks (Arntz and Fahrbach 1996).

But the linear displacement of cold water by warmer waters of tropical origin in ENSO events is not the only perturbation suffered by the Peru Current System. The Peru Current is a group of currents: the cold waters of the Humboldt Current itself (flowing south to north), a deeper current, and countercurrents near the surface and at greater depth that carry somewhat warmer water from north to south. Other currents flow from the warmer Western Pacific and Central Pacific in the form of Kelvin waves, which move slowly from west to east (Alheit and Ñiquen 2004; Arntz and Fahrbach 1996; Bertrand et al. 2008). When they reach the continental margin, they are deflected north and south along the continental shelf. While the influence of these waves was initially seen in the alternation of high concentrations of anchovy (*Engraulis ringens*) and sardine (*Sardinops sagax*) (Chávez et al 2003; Swartzman et al. 2008), in reality, the movement of water masses affects the primary producers: the plankton upon which the anchovy and sardine feed. Thus it is not initially the fish but their primary food that is affected by the mass movement of water, as well as other marine species (Ayón et al. 2008; Espinoza and Bertrand 2008).

Resistant shark species, shifting to alternate marine species, and possibly land resources allowed the marine foragers along the Pacific Coast of the Chicama Valley to survive. Most ENSO events are less than severe, so most impacts were less dire. There is no evidence for an abandonment of Huaca Prieta, Paredones, or the domestic sites that could be attributed to a severe ENSO event (see chapter 5 and appendix 1), although we might be able to read effects into the fluctuations in frequency of certain species if we knew more. In short, normality in the marine environment of Peru involves constant change, and the marine foragers and fishers of the Chicama littoral were successful in developing strategies to deal with environmental variation.

MARINE BIOTOPES

Oceanographers divide the marine environment from the beach to the open sea into a series of zones with some overlap. Many organisms pass their lives in only one; others occupy several. The Littoral Zone in coastal environments extends from the high water mark, rarely under water, to the permanently inundated shore. The Supralittoral Zone is inundated only by the highest tides. Organisms there must adapt to temperature extremes and desiccation. The littoral also includes the Intertidal Zone (the zone between the highest and lowest tide) but can be more extensive. Estuaries, wetlands, sand dunes, and littoral drift are also found within the Littoral Zone. The rocky substrate is shaped by wave action and turbulence and provides a range of habitats for sedentary organisms such as barnacles. The substrates in intertidal zones can be hard (rocky) or soft (sandy or muddy: sandy beaches, mudflats, or salt marshes). Just beyond the limit of low tide is the Subtidal Zone of varying depths that overlaps with the Neritic Zone, the inshore zone next to the littoral, which extends to a depth of 200 m. Off the Chicama coast this lies at the edge of the continental trench distant from the shore. The Neritic Zone is rich in species. The zones are often divided into the Pelagic Zone or open sea and the Benthic Zone just above the seabed; each zone has its specific inhabitants.

The faunal and plant (seaweed) species that seek hard bottoms need fixed substrates. Sandy substrates support fewer species and a smaller variety of animals, but bivalves and crustaceans adapted to this biome are found in large numbers and are taken with relatively little effort. The muddy substrate of the estuary and the brackish water lagoons support a number of pelagic fish and shark species that approach land seasonally or are carried over the beach ridge by seasonally high tides. The occupants using the Huaca Prieta and Paredones sites exploited all these biomes.

Paleontological studies of materials from the late Pleistocene and earlier geological periods (DeVries et al. 2006; Ortlieb 1989) indicate that the Pleistocene cold water molluscan fauna was essentially the same as at present, with minor incursions of cold-tolerant warm water species during brief periods of temperature perturbation

FIGURE 9.1. *a*, local fisherfolk with nets capturing fish washed ashore overnight by storm surges; *b*, pelican hunters in reed blinds with decoys to attract live birds.

caused by ENSO events or other current perturbations (Lazareth et al. 2006).

The faunal assemblage from Huaca Prieta contains invertebrates and vertebrates (fish) from both rocky bottoms and reefs and soft bottoms like sandy substrates or the muddy sediment of the estuary. This pattern of collecting assumes an intimate knowledge of the substrates, currents, and temperature of the seawater itself, for human populations must adapt to the cyclical changes in the marine climate over time as well. The material remains recovered archaeologically did not include unequivocal evidence for watercraft, yet many pelagic fish are represented and not all of them are found close to shore. How were these fish captured and at what time of year? Probable fishnets have been identified archaeologically at Huaca Prieta (see chapter 13 for detailed description of the twining and weaving technologies). Dillehay and Bonavia observed contemporary local fishers taking fish from the surf with relatively short 3–4 m rectangular nets held between two people. Local fishers also told them that strong tides and storms cast many pelagic species of fish up onto the beach and into shallow pools of water where they can be gathered (fig. 9.1a). The harvesting of bivalves and gastropods from sandy substrates is easier to imagine: the material culture required may not have extended beyond a forked stick and a basket or bag. It also appears that foragers dove regularly to depths of 20 m in cold water for prized bivalves like the giant mussel (*Choromytilis chorus*). This practice, which requires a specialized skill, can affect the auditory canal

by leaving deposits (auditory exostosis; see chapter 8 and appendix 10). The estuary at the mouth of the river and the inland wetlands that paralleled the beach both confined the fish and mollusks that tolerate fresh to brackish water where the fish could be driven into shallower water and speared or clubbed. Marine birds such as pelicans and grebes and wetland birds such as ducks may also have been lured and taken by netting or clubbing in some quantity, as Dillehay and Bonavia observed ethnographically in the course of research (fig. 9.1b). Additionally, sea lions and the marine birds like the cormorants (*Phalacrocorax bougainvillii*) that nest near the seal rookeries could have been taken by netting and clubbing, which is still a practice today along the Chicama beaches (Dillehay, personal observation, 2008).

A consideration of the marine specialization of the inhabitants of the Chicama littoral over the long use of the Huaca Prieta and Paredones sites makes some of the choices in their subsistence strategy clear: there is a bias toward the knowledge and skill needed to harvest sessile species, an activity with relatively less risk of failure. Using the wetlands and lagoons, where large fish like mullet (*Mugil cephalus*) and sharks like the requiem (*Carcharhinus* sp.) and school sharks (*Galeorhinus galeus*) became confined and easy to capture, also lessened failure. The lagoon fauna was self-renewing through periodic seasonal high tides, which overtopped the beach ridges, or less frequently and predictably by flooding from the river when it broke its levees during floods or seasonal high water. Likewise the marine birds and seals in their rookeries constituted an almost permanent resource, easily taken and available in large quantities.

The top marine predators are sharks and some large bony fish, marine birds (penguins, albatrosses, pelicans, cormorants, boobies, gulls, and terns), marine mammals such as sea lions, dolphins, and whales—and humans. The ancient human population of the Huaca Prieta area likely did not pursue whales and dolphins in watercraft, but they evidently did scavenge whalebone and vertebrae from the beaches and these bones do appear in the faunal assemblage. Whalebones and vertebrae were incorporated into the architecture at Huaca Prieta (see chapter 7). Recently beached whales and dolphins provided opportunistic access to meat and other resources.

These conditions increased the resilience of the littoral population resulting from the relative unpredictability of terrestrial food sources and certain pelagic fish. If we consider swift-swimming fish to be "fast prey" and the sessile mollusks and gastropods as "slow prey," with a corresponding gradient of difficulty and technical expertise required for the capture of fish, then the adaptive nutritional advantage of broad spectrum marine foraging must have been a factor in the success of the marine adaptation (compare Stiner 2000).

MARINE ASSOCIATIONS

In our approach to the analysis of the faunal collections from Huaca Prieta and Paredones, we have been careful to identify the location of the habitats of marine snails and other invertebrates found on rocky and sandy bottoms together with the fish found in these habitats (see table 9.1). Organisms found in the same habitat have been identified by habitat, because mussels and marine snails could be gathered together. Demersal fish of the estuary and the near shore could have been netted easily in addition to the gathering of fish cast up on the beach by high tides. Careful attention has also been paid to the wetlands and the presence of fish tolerant of brackish water such as mullets (*Mugil cephalus*) and sharks such as *Carcharhinus* sp. or *Mustelus* sp. within wetland ponds. In this way it is possible to determine which habitats are most frequently used by faunal species and those that are most consistently exploited by human populations.

The marine associations table (table 9.1) lays out the primary habitats of the nearly 200 faunal species and seaweeds (see chapter 10) identified in the archaeological collections in order to show which ones are associated within a particular biotope. The table is also intended as a guide in the discussion of the faunal counts in the next section. It is organized in an east-to-west transect, which extends from the inland plain to the Oceanic Zone. The Inland Zone is represented by three genera of birds, none of which are very numerous in the collection. Of the land mammals, three are domesticates: the dog, the guinea pig, and the llama. It should be noted that the llama, like the wild guanaco, belongs to the genus *Lama*. It was not always possible to determine whether the samples present in the collection were from the wild or domesticated species. The Muridae, a family of small rodents, and the Sechuran desert fox (*Lycalopex sechurae* or *Pseudalopex sechurae*) are creatures of the dry forest and desert zones. The white-tailed deer (*Odocoileus virginianus*) has a range from North America into northern South America. It is very adaptable and is able to survive in dry forest without water by knocking over columnar cacti and eating their pulp. The lower valley and areas along the river and other watercourses would have provided plenty of browse for these deer.

The Lagoon and Freshwater Wetlands are described in chapter 5. These habitats were found on the inland side of the Sangamon terrace and behind the beach berms. The reeds and sedges ringing these ponds were important as a source of food, fuel, and industrial materials (see chapter 10). The freshwater snails of several genera found in archaeological contexts were probably brought in with the bundled reeds on which they feed. Their number is not sufficient to suggest that they were harvested and eaten. Egrets are found along the wetlands and the lower course of the river. A number of specimens of a freshwater crab, *Hypolobocera* sp., were probably brought downstream in the river by seasonal freshets and were gathered. The waters of the ponds and wetlands are frequently brackish and sharks such as *Carcharhinus* sp. (requiem shark) and *Sphyrna* sp. (hammerhead

Table 9.1. Marine associations of all species and habitats

INLAND and SHORE

Inland
Birds
Zenaida auriculata (eared dove)
Dives warszewiczi (scrub blackbird)
Accipitridae (family of diurnal birds of prey)

Mammals
Muridae (family of small wild rodents)
Cavia porcellus (guinea pig)
Canis familiaris (domesticated dog)
Lycalopex sechurae (Sechuran desert fox)
Odocoileus virginianus (white-tailed deer)
Lama sp. (guanaco, llama)
Phyllostomidae (leaf-nosed bat)

Lagoon and Freshwater Wetlands
Pond Snails
Lymnaea sp. (genus of freshwater pulmonate snails)
Helisoma sp. (genus of freshwater pulmonate snails; ram's horn snail)
Helisoma peruvianum (freshwater pulmonate snail; ram's horn snail)
Helisoma trivolvis (freshwater pulmonate pond snail; modern introduction to Peru)
Drepanotrema sp. (genus of freshwater pulmonate snail native to Peru)
Physa sp. (genus of freshwater pulmonate pond snails)
Physa venustula (freshwater pulmonate pond snail)
Marinula pepita (pulmonate marine snail; cobble supratidal beach)

Land Birds
Egretta sp., *E. thula* (snowy egret)
Anas sp. (genus of dabbling ducks)
Podilymbus podiceps (pied-billed grebe)
Ardeidae (family of freshwater birds; heron)
Laridae (family of seabirds; seagull)
Haematopus sp. (oystercatcher)
Charadrius sp. (wading bird; plover)

Amphibians
Leptodactylidae (family of frogs)

Riverine Environment
Crabs
Hypolobocera sp. (freshwater crab; found in rivers of the western slopes of the Andes; Pseudohelphusidae family)

Seacoast (Littoral)
Marine Birds
Spheniscus humboldti (Humboldt penguin); rocky, sandy nesting substrate above beaches
Phalacrocorax bougainvillii (guanay, cormorant); rocky, sandy nesting substrate above beaches
Sula variegata (Peruvian booby); rocky, level nesting substrate
Pelecanus thagus (Peruvian pelican); rocky, level nesting substrate
Diomedea sp. (albatross); rocky, level nesting substrate
Larus sp. (seagull); rocky, sandy nesting substrate
Laridae (family of seabirds; seagull)
Larosterna inca (Inca tern); rocky, sheltered nesting substrate
Haematopus sp. (oystercatcher)
Charadrius sp. (wading bird; plover)
Marine Mammals
Otaria flavescens (sea lion); rocky, sandy substrate for rookery

LITTORAL ZONE

Beach—Supratidal Zone
Seaweed
Chaetomorpha sp.; rocky substrate

Crabs
Ocypode gaudichaudii (painted ghost crab); rocky substrate
Platyxanthus orbignyi (violet crab); rocky, sandy substrate

Upper Tidal Zone
Barnacles
Balanus sp.; rocky, hard substrate
Chthamalus sp.; rocky, hard substrate

Crabs
Platyxanthus orbignyi (violet crab); rocky, shallow water

Intertidal Zone
Seaweed
Ahnfeltia durvillaei
Chaetomorpha
Gymnogongrus furcellatus
Gigartina chamissoi
Polysiphonia paniculata

Table 9.1. Continued

LITTORAL ZONE/Intertidal Zone (continued)

Marine Snails

Fissurella peruviana (keyhole limpet); rocky substrate
Fissurella maxima (keyhole limpet); rocky substrate
Fissurella latimarginata (keyhole limpet); rocky substrate
Fissurella limbata (keyhole limpet); rocky substrate
Fissurella crassa (keyhole limpet); rocky substrate
Collisella orbignyi (true limpet); rocky substrate
Collisella ceciliana (true limpet); rocky substrate
Scurria viridula (true limpet); rocky substrate
Scurria parasitica (true limpet); rocky substrate
Diloma nigerrima (marine snail); rocky substrate
Tegula atra (marine snail); rocky substrate
Tegula euryomphala (marine snail); rocky substrate
Tegula tridentata (marine snail); rocky substrate
Prisogaster niger (marine snail); rocky substrate
Crepipatella dilatata (marine snail); rocky substrate
Cerithium stercusmuscarum (panamic, marine snail); sandy, muddy substrate
Cerithidea mazatlanica (panamic); sandy, muddy substrate
Xanthochorus buxea (marine snail); rocky substrate
Thais haemastoma (marine snail); rocky substrate
Concholepas concholepas (marine snail); rocky substrate
Solenosteira fusiformis (marine snail); rocky substrate
Polinices uber (marine snail); sandy, gravel substrate
Bursa ventricosa (marine snail); rocky, sandy substrate
Prunum curtum (marine snail); sandy substrate
Olivella columellaris (marine snail); rocky, sandy substrate in kelp forest
Cancellaria decussata (marine snail); rocky, sandy substrate
Oliva sp. (marine snail); rocky, sandy substrate
Oliva peruviana (marine snail); rocky substrate
Anachis sp. (marine snail); rocky substrate
Diloma nigerrima (marine snail); rocky substrate
Crassilabrum crassilabrum (marine snail); rocky, sandy substrate
Thais callaoensis (marine snail); rocky substrate
Thais delessertiana (marine snail); rocky substrate
Bursa nana (marine snail); rocky substrate
Polinices cora (marine snail); rocky substrate
Crucibulum spinosum (marine snail); rocky, sandy substrate
Nodilittorina peruviana (marine snail); rocky substrate
Littoridina cummingsi (marine snail); rocky, sandy substrate

Bivalves

Semimytilus algosus (mussel); rocky substrate
Pholas chiloensis (borer); rocky substrate
Aulacomya atra (mussel); rocky substrate
Choromytilus chorus (giant mussel); rocky substrate
Perumytilus purpuratus (mussel); rocky substrate
Petricola rugosa (borer); rocky substrate
Semele corrugata (clam); sandy substrate
Semele solida (clam); sandy substrate
Spisula adamsi (clam); sandy substrate
Donax obesulus (small clam); sandy substrate
Mesodesma donacium (clam); sandy substrate
Protothaca thaca (clam); sandy substrate
Euromalea rufa (clam); sandy substrate
Protothaca zorritensis (clam); sandy substrate
Anomia peruviana (clam); sandy substrate
Argopecten circularis (scallop); sandy substrate
Spondylus princeps (clam); sandy substrate
Chama pellucida (clam); sandy substrate

Crabs

Petrolisthes sp. (porcelain crab); rocky substrate
Cancer porteri (crab); rocky, sandy substrate
Cancer polyodon (crab); rocky, sandy substrate
Callinectes arcuatus (swimming crab); sandy substrate
Platyxanthus cokeri (crab); sandy substrate

Echinoderms

Tetrapygus niger (sea urchin); rocky, sandy substrate
Caenocentrotus gibbosus (sea urchin); sandy substrate
Strongylocentrotus gibbosus (this is a species name that is synonymous with *Caenocentrotus gibbosus* and is questioned as a legitimate variety; sea urchin)

Tunicates

Pyura chiliensis; sea squirt, rocky, sandy substrate

Chitons

Chaetopleura hennahi; chiton rocky substrate
Chiton cumingsii; chiton rocky substrate
Chiton granosus; chiton rocky substrate
Enoplochiton niger; chiton rocky substrate
Acanthopleura echinata; chiton rocky substrate

Table 9.1. Continued

LITTORAL ZONE (continued)

Subtidal Zone
Marine Snails
Tegula atra; rocky substrate
Prisogaster niger; rocky substrate
Crepipatella dilatata; rocky substrate
Cerithium stercusmuscarum (panamic); muddy substrate
Xanchochorus buxea; rocky substrate
Thais haemastoma; rocky substrate
Concholepas concholepas; rocky substrate
Polinices uber; sandy, gravel substrate
Bursa ventricosa; sandy substrate
Prunum curtum; sandy substrate
Olivella columellaris; sandy substrate
Sinum cymba; sandy substrate
Mitrella sp.; sandy substrate
Nassarius dentifer; sandy substrate
Mitra orientalis; sandy substrate
Cancellaria urceolata; sandy substrate
Calyptraea trochiformis; rocky substrate
Thais chocolata; rocky substrate
Columbella paytensis; rocky substrate

Bivalves
Aulacomya ater (mussel); rocky substrate
Brachidontes sp. (mussel); rocky substrate
Choromytilus chorus (giant mussel); rocky substrate
Perumytilus purpuratus (mussel); rocky substrate
Semele corrugata (clam); sandy substrate
Semele solida (clam); sandy substrate
Spisula adamsi (clam); sandy substrate
Donax obesulus (small clam); sandy substrate
Mesodesma donacium (clam); sandy substrate
Argopecten purpuratus (scallop); sandy substrate
Trachycardium procerum (clam); sandy substrate
Protothaca thaca (clam); sandy substrate
Eurhomalea rufa (clam); sandy substrate
Gari solida (clam); sandy substrate

Crabs
Pachycheles (crab); rocky, sandy substrates to 20 m
Hepatus chiliensis (crab); sandy substrate
Cancer porteri (crab); rocky, sandy substrate to 500 m
Cycloxanthops sexdecimdentatus (crab); rocky substrate to 15 m
Paraxanthus barbiger (crab); rocky substrate
Platyxanthus cokeri (crab); sandy substrate to 15 m

Chitons
Chiton cumingsii (small mollusk); chiton rocky substrate
Chiton granosus (small mollusk); chiton rocky substrate

LITTORAL, NERITIC, OCEANIC ZONES

Near Shore and Brackish Water
Sharks and Rays
Galeorhinus sp. (school shark, 25–30 pups in litter); above seabed to 500 m
Mustelus sp. (hound shark, 5–10 pups in litter); 16–211 m above rocks
Carcharhinus sp. (requiem shark, 1–6 pups in litter); no depth data; mud, sand, rock
Rhizoprionodon sp. (sharpnose shark, 1–12 pups in litter); 500 m over mud and sand
Alopias sp. (thresher shark, 2–4 pups in litter); to 500 m
Squatina armata (Chilean angel shark, 4–5 pups in litter); sandy substrate
Rhinobatos planiceps (Pacific guitarfish, 4–5 pups in litter); sandy, rocky substrates
Urotrygon sp. (Peruvian stingray; no data on pups); soft bottom to 50 m
Myliobatis sp. (eagle ray); not known
Isurus oxyrinchus (shortfin mako); no depth data
Alopias vulpinus (thresher shark); no depth data
Lamnidae (family of white sharks); no depth data
Rajiformes (order of flattened cartilaginous fish); no depth data

Bony Fish
Galeichthys peruvianus (Peruvian sea catfish); soft bottom
Cheilodactylus variegatus (Peruvian marwong); no data
Engraulis ringens (anchovy); no data
Ethmidium maculatum (Pacific menhaden); no data
Sardinops sagax sagax (sardine); no data
Paralichthys sp. (flounder); demersal over sandy, soft bottom
Scartichthys sp. (blenny, boracho; 4 species in genus); rocky reef substrate
Labrisomus philippii (weed blenny, chalapo, trambollo); rocky reef substrate
Scorpaena sp. (scorpion fishes); sandy and rocky reef substrates
Trachurus symmetricus (Chilean jack mackerel); near kelp beds, neritic, oceanic

Table 9.1. Continued

LITTORAL, NERITIC, OCEANIC ZONES/
Bony Fish (continued)

Seriolella violacea (palm ruff, cojinova); littoral to 500 m

Centropomus sp. (robalo, snook); littoral; brackish freshwater

Stellifer minor (minor star drum); demersal, sandy, muddy substrate

Cynoscion sp. (corvina, weakfish); demersal, sandy, littoral

Sciaena deliciosa (corvina); demersal, littoral, neritic to 50 m soft bottom

Sciaena gilberti sp. (corvina, robalo); demersal, littoral; sandy? (species little known)

Sciaena starksi sp. (corvina, robalo); demersal, littoral; sandy?

Sciaena sp. (croaker, drum, corvina, etc.); benthic-pelagic; littoral, estuaries, sand, mud

Micropogonias altipinnis (highfin corvina); benthic-pelagic, littoral, estuaries sandy, muddy bottoms

Larimus sp. (drum); littoral, estuaries, pelagic sand, mud

Pareques sp. (rock croaker, *roncador*); littoral, demersal, rocky reefs

Pareques viola (shorefish); littoral, demersal, rocky reefs

Menticirrhus sp. (king croaker); demersal, littoral, sandy bays, estuaries

Paralabrax sp. (rock seabass; schooling); benthic-pelagic, above rocky reefs

Acanthistius pictus (Peruvian sea bass); over rocky reefs, neritic

Sarda chiliensis chiliensis (Pacific bonito); inshore, pelagic

Mugil cephalus (flathead gray mullet); demersal, tolerates brackish water

Trachurus symmetricus murphyi (Chilean jack mackerel); neritic

Hemilutjanus sp. (grape-eye sea bass); rocky substrate in subtidal zone

Scombridae (family of fish that includes bonito and tuna)

Merluccius gayi (merluccid hake)

Merluccius gayi peruanus (subspecies of merluccid hake; Peruvian hake)

Anisotremus scapularis (Peruvian grunt)

Pomadasyidae (family of fish that includes grunts)

Serranidae (family of fish that includes sea bass)

Paralonchurus peruanus (Peruvian banded croaker)

Clupeidae (family of ray-finned fishes; herring, sardine)

Ariidae (family of marine catfish)

NERITIC AND OCEANIC ZONES

Oceanic
Sharks

Carcharhinus sp. (requiem shark)

Sphyrna sp. (hammerhead shark)

Isurus sp. (mako shark)

Alopias sp. (genus of thresher shark)

Isurus oxyrinchus (shortfin mako shark)

Alopias vulpinus (common thresher shark)

Lamnidae (family of white sharks)

Rajiformes (order of flattened cartilaginous fish)

Bony Fish

Engraulis ringens (Peruvian anchovy)

Ethmidium maculatum (Pacific menhaden)

Sardinops sagax sagax (Peruvian sardine)

Scombridae (family of fish that includes bonito and tuna)

Merluccius gayi (merluccid hake)

Merluccius gayi peruanus (subspecies of merluccid hake; Peruvian hake)

Anisotremus scapularis (Peruvian grunt)

Pomadasyidae (family of fish that includes grunts)

Serranidae (family of fish that includes sea bass)

Thunnus albacares (yellowfin tuna)

Paralonchurus peruanus (Peruvian banded croaker)

Clupeidae (family of ray-finned fish; herring, sardine)

Ariidae (family of marine catfish)

Mammals

Balaenidae (baleen whale)

Delphinus sp. (dolphin)

Cetacea (whale)

shark) that tolerate low levels of salinity and fish such as *Mugil cephalus* (mullet), and *Galeichthys peruvianus* (Peruvian sea catfish) frequently enter the wetland ponds connected to the sea. The estuary at the mouth of the river supports these species and a number of others that are frequent in the collection, in particular the seven species of the genus *Sciaena*, including croakers, drums, and weakfish (sea bass).

The seacoast or shore is the location of what must have been vast seabird rookeries in Preceramic times, which today are found on islands at sea or on distant points in intervalley zones. A number of species nest in adjacent areas, and we find that their remains tend to show up together in the collection. Thus the Humboldt penguin, *Spheniscus humboldti*, is found on a rocky or firm sandy substrate above beaches. The cormorant or guanay (*Phalacrocorax bougainvillii*) and the Peruvian booby (*Sula variegata*) are found in adjacent areas on level, rocky nesting substrates. The Peruvian pelicans (*Pelecanus thagus*) are frequently found nearby. In contrast, the terns (*Larosterna inca*) seek sheltered areas to nest and the gulls (*Larus* sp.) nest in pairs on the beach but are often taken in significant numbers. Finally, the sea lions also seek rocky or firm sandy beaches. In contrast to the birds, they are present in large numbers only during the period of birthing and raising their young in the austral spring and summer. By the end of the fall (April or May), the adults with the now independent young have moved south. Groups of young adult or subadult males may remain in the area. The rookeries are on the beaches or just above them.

Taking the beach by its oceanographic subdivisions we have seaweed *Chaetomorpha* sp. on a rocky substrate and two crabs, the painted ghost crab (*Ocypode gaudichaudii*) on rocky substrates and the ubiquitous violet crab (*Platyxanthus orbignyi*) found on both rocky and sandy substrates in the Supratidal Zone, where only the highest tides reach. The Upper Tidal Zone, regularly wet at high tide, is where barnacles (*Balanus* sp. and *Chthamalus* sp.) are found on rocky substrates. The violet crab is present in shallow water and on rocks.

The Intertidal Zone is home to five species of seaweed (see chapter 10) and a very large number of marine snails: some four species of keyhole limpets (*Fissurella* sp.) and two genera of true limpets, *Collisella* sp. and *Scurria* sp. These keyhole limpets are very common and verge on being present in most contexts. Several species of dark or black snails found on rocks in the Intertidal Zone are frequently found in the collection. *Tegula* spp. and *Prisogaster niger* are usually found together in numbers that range from one or two to hundreds or thousands. Other snails of the Intertidal Zone are found on sandy or muddy substrates. Two brown snails (*Xanthochorus buxea* and *Thais haemastoma*) are also found on rocks and frequently occur together in large numbers in the collection. Other snails are found on more varied substrates: gravel, sand, and rocks. They occur in smaller numbers and are less common in the collection. Bivalves are also found in the Intertidal Zone: the mussels found on rocks include two species of small mussels (*Aulacomya atra* and *Perumytilus purpuratus*) as well as the giant mussel (*Choromytilus chorus*). Five clams are also found in this zone in sandy substrates: two species of *Semele*, *Spisula adamsi*, which is fairly rare, *Mesodesma donacium*, which was either not very common or not preferred, and the miniature clam, *Donax obesulus*, which is frequently represented by only one specimen but in other contexts is found in very large numbers. *Donax* can be dug up in large quantities with relatively little effort. With the exception of the porcelain crab (*Petrolisthes* sp.), which is found on rocks, all the other crabs from this zone (*Cancer porteri*, *Cancer polyodon*, *Callinectes arcuatus*, and *Platyxanthus cokeri*) are found on sandy substrates. None of these crabs are very common; it seems that the violet crab was both easier to find and preferred. Several other organisms found in the intertidal zone are of varying significance. Of the three species of sea urchins (echinoderms) recovered, *Tetrapygus niger* is by far the most important. While echinoderms are edible, it does not appear that they were eaten (or perhaps only occasionally) at Huaca Prieta. Sea urchins, in particular *T. niger*, may have had an industrial use in the construction of the mound (see chapter 7). Specimens of *T. niger* are often found in ritual or burial contexts as well. The tunicate or sea squirt, *Pyura chilensis*, is infrequently found. Although edible, it does not appear to have been eaten regularly. Occasional population blooms characterize this species, however, and there is at least one instance of a mass harvest. Chitons and sea cucumbers are found in the collection throughout the sequence in moderate numbers.

The Subtidal Zone lies below the line of the lowest ebb tide. Many of the same snails found in the Intertidal Zone are also found here, including some of the most heavily used. Species from both rocky and sandy substrates are present and are represented in the collection. They were undoubtedly eaten, but the shells of several species figure in ritual and feasting configurations as well. Many of the bivalves found in the Subtidal Zone from both rocky and sandy substrates were harvested and eaten. Of particular importance was the giant mussel *Choromytilus chorus*, which is found as deep as 20 m below the surface, requiring diving specialists for its procurement. There are six crabs from rocky and sandy substrates from this zone; they are infrequent in the collection. The two chitons found in this zone are also rare.

The Estuarine Zone is particularly rich in species, as is the Near Shore Zone (the inshore fringe of the Neritic Zone). All of these species are able to tolerate somewhat lower salinity and larger amounts of suspended sediment. Many of these fish are common in the collection, suggesting concentration of fishing in the shallow estuary and along the shore. Fish are also found above the inshore rocky reefs, which would be located along the coast away from the estuarine zone.

Many fish, but particularly the sharks, are found in the Oceanic and Neritic Zones as adults. But the females enter the Littoral Zone, where food is abundant, to give birth to live young. Since shark embryos grow for a year inside their mothers and are born live, they are fairly large at birth, ~50 cm in length. Some sharks give birth to multiple young, and some species are able to tolerate brackish water and enter the estuary and wetlands, where they can be easily taken (see table 9.1), which explains the abundance of sharks, particularly the requiem shark (*Carcharhinus* sp.) and the school shark (*Galeorhinus* sp.) together with certain large bony fish, particularly mullet (*Mugil cephalus*) and the Peruvian sea catfish (*Galeichthys peruvianus*) in the faunal collection.

SUBSISTENCE, SUSTAINABILITY, SEASONALITY, AND TECHNOLOGY

The faunal collections from Huaca Prieta, Paredones, and some domestic sites are remarkable for the length of time covered and for the preponderance of marine remains. The late Pleistocene and early Holocene Phase I remains recovered before the beginning of mound construction include snails, shellfish, and sharks as well as marine and land birds and mammals. Beginning in Phase II, with the initiation of mound construction, the faunal remains are not associated with simple subsistence. The domestic occupations at Unit 2 and Unit 16 and later Unit 20 are all associated with feeding people (feasting probably in a ritual context). What is most impressive about the collections from Phase II and the later phases is their species diversity. These are from biotopes with both rocky and sandy substrates, and from the Supratidal, Intertidal, and Subtidal and Estuarine Zones (Díaz and Ortlieb 1993; Vásquez Sánchez and Rosales Tham 2008, 2010). Some species are neritic or pelagic while others are demersal and littoral, as indicated in table 9.1.

It is not clear how the Huaca Prieta fishers and marine foragers obtained such a diversity of fish species. The assumption is that rocky substrates (including reefs) and sandy substrates were widely distributed along the shoreline of the Chicama Valley so that the communities using Huaca Prieta had access to a wide variety of marine fauna. Wetlands were disposed in a chain parallel to the shore. The estuary at the mouth of the river was a fixed place but close to Huaca Prieta. Remains of marine mammals such as whales are rare and suggest the opportunistic scavenging of beached animals rather than deliberate hunting. Seabird nesting sites and sea lion rookeries were undoubtedly found at different points along the shore and between the valleys. Sea lions were hunted with varying intensity throughout the history of Huaca Prieta and Paredones with a tendency to increase over time. Avian bones increase in frequency after Phase II. Terrestrial mammal remains are relatively infrequent after Phase I, however, although there are definite differences in frequency between terrestrial and marine mammals between Paredones and Huaca Prieta. But sharks and the larger fish such as mullet and catfish are found at both sites.

The great difference lies in the frequency of the molluscan fauna: snails and bivalves, crustaceans, and some bony fish.

Seasonality of procurement is difficult to determine, in part because the life cycles of many of the species in the collection are little known or difficult to identify. The austral spring and summer months (November through April) generally are important for reproduction and are the time when food sources are most abundant (see appendices 3 and 14). Seasonality at the level of the oceanographic shifts in water temperature associated with ENSO events that have consequences in species frequency is difficult to recognize because the duration of ENSO events is so brief in comparison with the time span of the human occupation of the site. The consequences for the human populations are ambiguous, as it appears that other species or plant foods may be substituted for species adapted to cooler water temperatures. In general, the populations appear to fluctuate and then recover without permanent perturbation. Two bivalves present in the Huaca Prieta collection are now found only in cooler waters to the south in southern Peru and Chile: the giant mussel *Choromytilus chorus* and *Mesodesma donacium*, a clam.

The technology employed by the population of the Chicama littoral over time included the strategy of broad-spectrum predation, part of which required few implements or other physical technology. It is noteworthy that the very large number of molluscan and fish species in tables 9.2–9.15 are found in the Littoral Zone. Those from sandy substrates can be obtained easily with a digging stick and a bag. The gastropods and bivalves and crustaceans from rocky substrates are more challenging beyond the Intertidal Zone. The mollusks from the Subtidal Zone required deep diving, which was likely in the hands of specialists. The primary objective may have been the giant mussel (*Choromytilus chorus*), but other mussels and marine snails were also found there.

Data presented in the tables show very clearly that a large number of demersal fish were taken from the estuarine and nearshore environments. In the nearshore case we know that high tidal and storm surges throw up fish onto the beach, where they can be easily collected. The textiles demonstrate evidence for twining technology (see chapter 12). There is now evidence for small

nets, likely 2 to 3 m by 1 m, which could have been held between two persons in the surf zone. Informants today use similar nets (Dillehay, personal communication, 2009; see fig. 9.1a). This technology does not require watercraft, although there is some evidence that reed rafts may have been in use by Phase V, as suggested by fragments of bundled totora reeds tied together. Evidence for hand lines has not been recovered at Huaca Prieta. Another procurement strategy, which has not been noted previously, is the use of decoys to lure marine birds, particularly pelicans, onto wetland ponds. Dillehay and Bonavia observed this being done today in wetland ponds, where killed pelicans were propped up on wooden poles and set out as decoys while the hunter moved the wings of a dead bird from behind a reed blind. Hunters netted the birds and wrung their necks once they had landed (see fig. 9.1b). Such strategies are technically simple but are based on close observation and knowledge. Together with the luring or fostering of fish in the wetlands, these practices made the resource base more secure.

The following sections describe the faunal remains and their associations and implications for the function of Huaca Prieta, Paredones, and domestic sites. The source areas (such as hard or soft substrate, tidal zone or pelagic), the life cycle of different species, and the relative nutritional return for effort expended are considered as well as the intensity of predation.

ANALYSIS OF THE FAUNAL REMAINS

The following data analysis is largely a translated synopsis of two large technical reports by Víctor Vásquez Sánchez and Teresa Rosales Tham (2008, 2010) on the recovered faunal remains. Analysis of the faunal remains proceeded along several lines of inquiry: (1) the patterns of use of marine and terrestrial species, by examining context, habitat of origin, frequency counts and percentages, minimum number of individuals, processing patterns, element selectivity, and any patterns of bone or shell transport, when possible and when applicable; (2) the characteristics of the animals collected, processed, and consumed at each site type (ritual, domestic, food processing), by examining their numbers and their age and sex, when possible and applicable; and (3) the post-depositional taphonomic processes, by examining the spatial distribution and density of remains, the diagenetic and geomorphic processes that may have affected the preservation and positioning of individual elements, and modification by human trampling, feasting, reburial, intrusive deposits, and architectural disturbance.

The location of the Paredones and Huaca Prieta sites placed resources from three principal environmental zones within reach of their populations: the marine environment; the estuary and the wetlands of the lower valley; and the inland environments of the lower and middle valley. The marine associations are summarized in table 9.1.

METHODS

Study of the large number of faunal remains was an integral part of the research design (see chapter 3). The unusually good preservation at sites assured a detailed faunal record from the earliest strata. In the excavations, all macrozoological remains were recovered, bagged, and labeled and sent to the laboratory for analysis. All macrozoological remains obtained from heavy and light flotation samples by manual flotation were bagged, labeled, and subsequently analyzed. Members of the project carried out flotation in the field using potable water and standard equipment and in the laboratory using a flotation machine at the Universidad Nacional de Trujillo. Microzoological remains were analyzed using a Zeiss microscope. The taxonomic identification of the mollusk remains was carried out using comparative collections, manuals, and specialized works on this group of invertebrates (Vásquez Sánchez and Rosales Tham 2008, 2010).

Taxonomic abundance for the fauna collection from Huaca Prieta and Paredones is shown in the accompanying tables by Number of Individual Specimens (NISP). While it was possible to calculate Minimum Number of Individuals (MNI) for molluscan species such as bivalves and snails by using landmarks on the shells and for the polyplacophores (chitons) by using cephalic and caudal plates, this was not feasible for the sharks, fish, birds, or mammals because multiple elements, such as vertebrae, could be from the same individual (Vásquez Sánchez and Rosales Tham 2010).

Consequently, the data presented in the tables in the detailed reports were limited to NISP and weight. Although weight has more relevance to the heavily fragmented mollusks, crustaceans, and other shells, as well as mammal bones, it is not discussed here because a majority of the shells and a significant portion of the bones had marine, *caliche*, and other encrustations on them, which differentially enhanced their weighted relevance and biased shells without these features.

The faunal collection from Huaca Prieta, Paredones, and the domestic sites consists of a total of 323,531 specimens divided among 69 vertebrate taxa and 190 invertebrate taxa (table 9.1). What is unusual about this collection is the extraordinary number of mollusk specimens at Huaca Prieta and initially at Paredones and within that group the high number of gastropod taxa (56) and individual elements. Although the total number of specimens from the bivalves is larger (223,418; mainly the small bivalve *Donax obesulus*) the number of taxa is less than half that of the snails. In contrast, for the bony fish, the total of identifiable specimens is 4035, while the total for sharks is just over three quarters of that number (3204). The cormorants dominate the total for birds (1873). The number of mammals, marine and terrestrial, is 1399, of which the sea lion is most common (1258).

In the descriptions of the fauna by phase and excavation unit given below, the counts and percentage frequencies are discussed in greater detail for each excavation unit, phase, and major species. The data from the smaller test pits and units are not given for Phases IV and V because they duplicate the trends seen in the larger units and their sample sizes are very small (total 9354) in comparison to the larger units. But the tables include all major stratigraphic units. All faunal data excavated from these units are included.

Tables 9.2–9.15, which present the quantitative data for the faunal remains from both excavated sites for each of the five phases, rely only on the information from intact layers and intact floors, use surfaces, and the features within them (see chapters 3, 6, and 7). The quantitative data from the fills between layers are not included in the table counts. Although the fills are stratigraphically intact, unlike the layers and their floors and features, they probably contain mixed material from unknown contexts such as middens and other deposits that may be earlier than the layer or floor above or below them. Therefore the fauna types and counts for a specific layer may pertain to one particular event or a series of temporally contiguous and related events, but it is virtually impossible to determine how many events over time are represented by the remains in fills. Despite this discrepancy between layers and fills, however, we have observed that the faunal data from the fills still contain counts and species proportionately similar to the layers above and below them, indicating that the fill materials are generally contemporaneous with the layers that they overlie and underlie (Vásquez Sánchez and Rosales Tham 2008, 2010).

Faunal specialists may be puzzled by the absence of detailed statistical and other quantitative studies (percentages of total specimens for all layers and units) and by little subsistence modeling here. Although more refined quantitative analyses were performed on some data, they are not presented or developed further due to several factors. First, Huaca Prieta is a very large, complex site, which required an imaginative and opportunistic sampling strategy, frequently under physically difficult conditions of deep mound recovery. Thus not all excavation units across the site and others are comparable in terms of excavated volume, because some units were probed much deeper (between 1.5 and 30 m) or were more horizontally extensive (from 1 by 2 m to 12 by 15 m) than others, sometimes making the volume of analyzable data for each cultural phase from each unit nearly incomparable with others. Second, these remains were distributed in the mound at Huaca Prieta in thousands of small contexts (such as circumscribed floors and use surfaces, pits, burials, offerings in small structures, behind architectural walls, or in small open areas of a few square centimeters or so), making this site functionally and contextually not comparable to others. Furthermore, there are multiple mixed functions within and across sites, with different mixtures of ritual, nonritual feasting, domestic, mortuary, and other activities that also make it qualitatively difficult, if not impossible, to compare the faunal results, especially in terms of subsistence practices.

For instance, true domestic contexts are found in off-mound contexts (for example, Units 13, 16, 24) so that comparisons across time or space

within and across all sites, mainly the Huaca Prieta and Paredones mounds, do not directly reflect a subsistence economy after Phase I, when ritual, mortuary, feasting, and various food preparation and consumption activities take over at the mounds. The archaeological information in the mounds thus relates more to belief systems and ideological symbolism, which can only be estimated with respect to the meaning of the combined qualitative and quantitative patterns in the faunal data for subsistence practices, but primarily the former. This makes it difficult to compare the faunal register from these sites with the domestic locales. Third, Huaca Prieta had been occupied for ~7000 years and intensively for 3500 years after the mound was first built and used ~7500 cal BP, which created a vast amount of faunal materials. The same is true to a lesser extent at Paredones and the domestic sites. Faunal remains are the largest single category of material recovered, with more than 900,000 individual elements present, including the data from test pits, cores, and other small units. Furthermore, most of these materials were deliberately broken and burned, almost without exception, making it difficult or impossible to establish MNI counts and frequencies for many species (such as mammals, birds, and fish). In the light of these preconditions, which were discovered and dealt with piecemeal in the course of nearly ten years of combined fieldwork and laboratory analyses, the following discriminations were made. We focused on the biomes from which faunal material was abstracted, the species most frequently found, the technology or method in their procurement, and the counts or numbers provided by the NISP calculations of broken and burned specimens. It is possible that a more complete taphonomic analysis of all faunal remains might alter our interpretation of some use and context patterning of some elements and species, but our preliminary study of the faunal remains suggests that we have identified the major processes and physical and cultural conditions affecting bone and shell. Finally, the strata for each cultural phase are presented in the tables from the latest to the earliest or from left to right.

Synopses of the major faunal patterns for each cultural phase are given below, with emphasis on Phases I and II because these phases provide the fundamental subsistence patterns and because the database is smaller and more manageable for descriptive purposes. Less emphasis is given to Phases III–V because they represent continuity of the prior patterns of resource exploitation. More detailed discussions of the quantitative and qualitative data and selected photographs of shell and bone remains for Phases III–V are provided in tables 9.2–9.15 and in online material presented at https://my.vanderbilt.edu/huacaprieta/.

PHASE I: ~14,500–7571 CAL BP

FAUNAL REMAINS FROM THE LATE PLEISTOCENE SUBPHASE: ~14,500–11,400 CAL BP

The faunal counts and percentage frequencies from both the late Pleistocene and the early Holocene are shown separately in table 9.2. There are several traces of late Pleistocene occupation (see chapter 7). They are not continuous, but a mobile hunting/foraging population probably lived both in the lower Chicama Valley and on the littoral, including any sites on the continental shelf that are now under water. Occupational evidence in the form of scattered middens or hearths is ephemeral. Recovery of this evidence was hampered by widespread removal of the original terrace surface by later occupations and the small areas that only could be exposed through the layers of the deep Huaca Prieta mound (see chapters 6 and 7), at times nearly 30 m below the summit of the mound.

As noted earlier, at the time of the earliest dates for this phase, sea level was still some 60 m lower than at present and the edge of the ocean was ~16–18 km west of the present-day shoreline, no great distance for a hardy hunting and foraging population (Clarke et al. 2007; Fairbanks 1989). The faunal remains provide only hints of what marine and terrestrial resources a foraging population might have utilized. The faunal remains left at these camps indicate a broad use of the resources of the littoral and adjacent inland areas (Netherly 2011a, 2011b), including wetlands, arid plains of the coast, and vegetated zones of the nearby Andean foothills and beyond. The early and later faunal remains in the Chicama collection also suggest that sea lions, a more fixed if

seasonal resource, were consistently taken. Mollusks were food resources, but their small quantity suggests that they were a minor part of the diet. Sharks (probably young and preadult), which could have been trapped in meandering estuarine channels and in the nearby wetlands by seasonal high tides and storm surges, would have been easily taken in shallow water. This pattern was also seen at some inland sites in the Nanchoc and Chaman drainages to the north, where Pleistocene foragers made periodic visits to the seacoast, returning with shells and perhaps dried fish (Dillehay 2011b; Netherly 2011b). Bony fish of the Estuary and Neritic Zones are either not present or uncommon. In addition to the plant resources of the dry forest on the valley margins and inland, the area provided faunal resources such as deer, perhaps guanacos, and land birds. Deer could have found browse along the perennial vegetation of the riverbanks and on the fringes of the dense algarrobo forests (Netherly 2011b; see chapters 4 and 5).

There is evidence for repeated, transitory visits to the littoral in the four primary excavation units that reached Pleistocene deposits on and below the surface of the Sangamon terrace. These were Unit 15/21 (Unit 15 is the portion excavated to Pleistocene levels from the bottom of the sunken circular plaza that lies within Unit 21); Unit 16, located about 40 m north of the mound at Huaca Prieta and partially underneath the nearby Cupisnique mound; Test Pit 22 on the eastern side of the Huaca Prieta mound between it and the edge of the wetland; and Unit 9 at the southeastern edge of the Huaca Prieta mound, also between it and the wetland (see fig. 3.1). The fauna are listed by macrogroups in table 9.2 and on the tables that follow with data from Phases II through V (see Dillehay et al. 2012b).

The faunal remains from all four late Pleistocene units are broken and often burned. Mollusks are represented by keyhole limpets in three units. The limpets (*Fissurella* sp.), a marine snail, are found on rocks in the Upper Tidal Zone, where they are efficient grazers on algae. In addition to serving as a food supply, their strong shells were used as scrapers (Dillehay, personal communication, 2012; see chapter 11); through time they may have acquired ritual significance as well: sev-

Table 9.2. Species type and distribution for Phase I: Late Pleistocene, early subphase (~14,500–11,400 cal BP), in excavated units at Huaca Prieta, Paredones, and domestic sites

| | Unit 9 | | Unit 15 | | | | TP-22 | | | | |
| | Layer | | Layer | | | | Layer | | | | % of Total |
Taxon	11	12	4	8	9	13a	5a	8a–b	11a	Totals	by Taxa
Chitons											
Chaetopleura hennahi										0	
Chiton cummingsii										0	
Chiton granosus										0	
Enoplochiton niger										0	
Acanthopleura echinata										0	
Total Chitons										**0**	**0.00**
Limpets											
Fissurella peruviana			3	2	4	4				13	
Fissurella maxima	2						1	2	1	6	
Fissurella latimarginata										0	
Fissurella limbata										0	
Fissurella crassa										0	
Fissurella sp.										0	
Total Limpets										**19**	**19.19**
Marine Snails/Gastropods											
Collisella orbignyi										0	
Collisella ceciliana										0	
Scurria viridula										0	
Scurria parasitica										0	
Scurria sp.										0	
Diloma nigerrima										0	
Tegula atra	2						1	3	3	9	
Tegula euryomphala										0	
Tegula tridentate										0	
Prisogaster niger										0	
Littoridina cummingsi										0	
Nodilittorina peruviana										0	
Cerithium stercusmuscarum										0	
Cerithidea mazatlanica										0	
Calyptraea trochiformis										0	
Crepipatella dilatata										0	
Crucibulum spinosum										0	
Sinum cymba										0	
Polinices uber										0	
Polinices cora										0	
Bursa ventricosa										0	
Bursa nana										0	
Xanthochorus buxea										0	

Table 9.2. Continued

Taxon	Unit 9 Layer		Unit 15 Layer				TP-22 Layer			Totals	% of Total by Taxa
	11	12	4	8	9	13a	5a	8a–b	11a		
Marine Snails/Gastropods (continued)											
Thais haemostoma										0	
Thais chocalata	2						3		2	7	
Thais delessertiana										0	
Thais callaoensis										0	
Crassilabrum crassilabrum										0	
Concholepas concholepas										0	
Solenosteira fusiformis										0	
Columbella paytensis										0	
Mitrella sp.										0	
Anachis sp.										0	
Nassarius dentifer										0	
Prunum curtum										0	
Oliva peruviana										0	
Olivella columellaris										0	
Oliva sp.										0	
Mitra orientalis										0	
Cancellaria decussata										0	
Cancellaria urceolata										0	
Marinula pepita										0	
Total Marine Snails/Gastropods										**16**	**15.15**
Freshwater Snails											
Lymnaea sp.										0	
Helisoma peruvianum										0	
Helisoma trivolvis										0	
Helisoma sp.										0	
Drepanotrema sp.										0	
Physa venustula										0	
Physa sp.										0	
Total Freshwater Snails										**0**	**0.00**
Bivalves											
Anadara sp.										0	
Aulacomya atra										0	
Choromytilus chorus										0	
Perumytilus purpuratus										0	
Semimytilus algosus										0	
Chama pellucida										0	
Brachidontes sp.										0	
Spondylus princeps										0	
Argopecten circularis										0	

Table 9.2. Continued

Taxon	Unit 9 Layer		Unit 15 Layer				TP-22 Layer			Totals	% of Total by Taxa
	11	12	4	8	9	13a	5a	8a–b	11a		
Bivalves (continued)											
Argopecten purpuratus										0	
Argopecten sp.										0	
Trachycardium procerum										0	
Anomia peruviana										0	
Protothaca thaca	2	1					7	11	1	22	
Protothaca zorritensis										0	
Euromalea rufa										0	
Petricola rugosa										0	
Gari solida										0	
Semele corrugata										0	
Semele solida										0	
Spisula adamsi										0	
Donax obesulus										0	
Mesodesma donacium										0	
Pholas chiloensis										0	
Total Bivalves										**22**	**22.22**
Barnacles											
Balanus sp.										0	
Chthamalus sp.										0	
Total Barnacles										**0**	**0.00**
Marine Crabs											
Platyxanthus orbignyi	1		1	6	2					10	
Platyxanthus cokeri										0	
Cancer porteri										0	
Cancer polyodon										0	
Paraxanthus barbiger										0	
Cycloxanthops sexdecimdentatus										0	
Hepatus chiliensis										0	
Petrolisthes sp.										0	
Pachycheles sp.										0	
Ocypode gaudichaudii										0	
Callinectes arctuatus										0	
Total Marine Crabs										**10**	**10.10**
Freshwater Crabs											
Hypolobocera sp.										0	
Total Freshwater Crabs										**0**	**0.00**

Table 9.2. Continued

Taxon	Unit 9 Layer		Unit 15 Layer				TP-22 Layer			Totals	% of Total by Taxa
	11	12	4	8	9	13a	5a	8a–b	11a		
Sea Urchins											
Tetrapygus niger										0	
Strongylocentrotus gibbosus										0	
Caenocentrotus gibbosus										0	
Total Sea Urchins										0	0.00
Ascidians (Sea Squirts)											
Pyura chiliensis										0	
Total Ascidians										0	0.00
Unidentified Crustaceans, etc.										0	0.00
Amphibians											
Leptodactylidae										0	
Total Amphibians										0	0.00
Sharks and Rays											
Galeorhinus sp.		1			1					2	
Mustelus sp.										0	
Carcharhinidae										0	
Carcharhinus sp.			2	3	2					7	
Rhizoprionodon sp.										0	
Sphyma sp.										0	
Lamnidae										0	
Alopias vulpinus										0	
Alopias sp.										0	
Isurus oxyrinchus										0	
Squatina armata										0	
Rajiformes										0	
Urotrygon sp.										0	
Rhinobatos planiceps										0	
Myliobatis sp.										0	
Total Sharks and Rays										9	9.09
Bony Fish											
Ariidae										0	
Galeichthys peruvianus										0	
Cheilodactylus variegatus										0	
Clupeidae										0	
Engraulis ringens										0	

Table 9.2. Continued

Taxon	Unit 9 Layer		Unit 15 Layer				TP-22 Layer			Totals	% of Total by Taxa
	11	12	4	8	9	13a	5a	8a–b	11a		
Bony Fish (continued)											
Ethmidium maculatum										0	
Sardinops sagax-sagax										0	
Mugil cephalus										0	
Paralichthys sp.										0	
Scartichthys sp.										0	
Labrisomus philippii										0	
Scorpaena sp.										0	
Stellifer minor										0	
Trachurus symmetricus										0	
Trachurus symmetricus murphyi										0	
Seriolella violacea										0	
Centropomus sp.										0	
Paralonchurus peruanus										0	
Cynoscion sp.										0	
Thunnus albacares										0	
Sciaena deliciosa										0	
Sciaena gilbert										0	
Sciaena starksi										0	
Sciaena sp.										0	
Pareques sp.										0	
Hemilutjanus sp.										0	
Larimus sp.										0	
Serranidae										0	
Acanthistius pictus										0	
Paralabrax sp.										0	
Pomadasyidae										0	
Micropogonias altipinnis										0	
Menticirrhus sp.										0	
Ansiotremus scapularis										0	
Merluccius gayi										0	
Merluccius gayi peruanus										0	
Sarda chiliensis										0	
Sarda chiliensis chiliensis										0	
Scombridae										0	
Total Bony Fish										0	0.00
Unidentified Fish										0	0.00

Table 9.2. Continued

Taxon	Unit 9 Layer		Unit 15 Layer				TP-22 Layer			Totals	% of Total by Taxa
	11	12	4	8	9	13a	5a	8a–b	11a		
Marine Birds											
Spheniscus humboldti										0	
Diomedea sp.										0	
Charadrius sp.										0	
Haematopus sp.										0	
Larus sp.	1				2				1	4	
Larosterna sp.										0	
Laridae										0	
Ardeidae										0	
Egretta sp.										0	
Pelecanus thagus										0	
Phalacrocorax bougainvillii	2	1	1							4	
Sula variegata										0	
Sula sp.										0	
Total Marine Birds										8	8.08
Wetland/Land Birds											
Accipitridae										0	
Podilymbus podiceps										0	
Anas sp.										0	
Zenaidura auriculata										0	
Dives warszewiczi	1								1	2	
Total Wetland/Land Birds										2	2.00
Unidentified Birds										0	0.00
Mammals											
Phyllostomidae										0	
Muridae										0	
Cavia porcellus										0	
Canis familiaris										0	
Lycalopex sechurae										0	
Otaria flavescens	2	1			2				6	11	
Balaenidae										0	
Delphinus sp.										0	
Cetacea										0	
Odocoileus virginianus					3					3	
Lama sp.										0	
Total Mammals										14	14.40

Table 9.2. Continued

Taxon	Unit 9 Layer 11	12	Unit 15 Layer 4	8	9	13a	TP-22 Layer 5a	8a–b	11a	Totals	% of Total by Taxa
Unidentified Marine Mammals										0	0.00
Unidentified Terrestrial Mammals										0	0.00
Unidentified Mammals										0	0.00
Total Faunal Phase I	15	4	7	11	16	4	12	16	15	100	

eral fragments were found as offerings in graves. Also noteworthy are two other marine gastropods: *Tegula atra*, a black snail, and *Thais chocolata*, a brown snail, are both found in the Intertidal Zone at a greater depth than the limpets (see table 9.1). Both are edible, but what is most significant is that interest in these species persists through all the later phases, when they appear not only to have been a desirable food item but also to have had persistent ritual and symbolic significance. Bivalves, represented by the clam *Protothaca thaca*, are present in modest quantity in Unit 9 and Test Pit 22. Found on sandy bottoms, these clams from the Intertidal Zone are easy to harvest with a digging stick. The shells may have been utilized as tools as well.

Only Unit 16 of the early sites shows a few remains of bony fish, suggesting that late Pleistocene foragers lacked either the opportunity or the technology or both to capture them. With this exception, all the other major groups of animals noted in table 9.1 are represented. Sharks are present in Units 9, 15/21, and 16 but absent in Test Pit 22. The violet crab, *Platyxanthus orbignyi*, was a food item available in rocky pools of the Supratidal and Intertidal Zones. Sharks of species known to tolerate the brackish waters of the estuary channels and the wetlands are found in Units 9, 15/21, and 16 but are absent in Test Pit 22. Marine birds, such as gulls (*Larus* sp.) and cormorants (*Phalacrocorax bougainvillii*), which habitually nest on the littoral were taken, as were sea lions (*Otaria* sp.), whose rookeries were also located on the shore near the water. Land birds such as the scrub blackbird (*Dives warszewiczi*) and

mammals such as the white-tailed deer (*Odocoileus virginianus*) were also hunted.

Two species of sharks, the tope or school shark (*Galeorhinus* sp.) and the requiem shark (*Carcharhinus* sp.), were recovered from Units 9, 15/21, and 16 (the 34 specimens from the latter unit probably represent only 1 or 2 individuals). Adult requiem sharks are small to large (1–3 m in length) and are found far out to sea, where they consume schooling fish like anchovies (*Engraulis ringens*), sardines (*Sardinops sagax*), and jack mackerels (*Trachurus* sp.). However, they also use warm, shallow, coastal waters as nursery areas; females, which reproduce every two years, carry their young for a year and travel to coastal waters to give birth to live young. They seek out protected bays, shallow inlets, and open beaches with abundant food for the young sharks. Births are more common in the austral spring and summer when food is abundant. The waters off the Chicama coast probably were nursery zones for these prolific sharks with a tolerance for brackish water. Both species enter estuaries and shallow inlets today, especially during storm surges when fish are tossed ashore and are trapped in pools of water behind sandy berms, where they can easily be taken (Bonavia and Dillehay, personal observation, 2009). Bony fish are represented by four species in the late Pleistocene and early Holocene records, *Mugil cephalus*, *Paralonchurus peruanus*, *Sciaena deliciosa*, and *Sciaena starksi*.

Unit 9 and Test Pit 22 each had one scrub blackbird (*Dives warszewiczi*). This bird lives in open woodland and at the edge of grassy areas. The bones were broken and burned, indicating that the birds had been eaten. The cormorant

(*Phalacrocorax bougainvillii*) is a marine bird that nests in great flocks in rookeries on rocky points and in other protected areas along the shore. Seagulls (*Larus* sp.) nest in pairs on the beach. Cormorants can be grabbed while nesting or taken in flight by slings or bolas. The gulls are more wary and may have required a weapon like a sling.

Like the shore birds, the sea lions (*Otaria flavescens*), which today are found on the offshore islands and on certain protected rocky points of the littoral, must have been present in immense numbers. While the cormorants and gulls are found in the region year round, sea lions give birth in the austral spring and early summer (December to early February). As discussed earlier, the presence of sea lions may have been seasonal. Most bones recovered are of subadults and medium-sized females, which suggests that they were taken in the austral summer.

The sea lions and cormorants appear to have been attractive prey, together with the sharks found in estuaries and brackish lagoons. Assuming the immense numbers of sea lions and seabirds that were present when competition from humans was low, the rookeries of both would have been within a reasonable distance. The shark species taken move inland along estuaries and brackish watercourses or lagoons. Only the deer are terrestrial, but these may have browsed along the river and other watercourses in the lower valley. The mollusks are interesting. While bivalves are present, the numbers do not suggest large-scale consumption. The clam *Protothaca thaca* is easily dug from the sands of the Intertidal Zone. The keyhole limpets (*Fissurella* sp.) are found on rocks in the upper Tidal Zone. They were probably sought for their shells or as food. The marine snails (*Tegula atra* and *Thais chocolata*), however, are found on rocks in the Intertidal and Subtidal Zones, requiring entry into the sea to some depth, even at low tide. Given the importance of these snails in later periods, their presence here may be significant.

For late Pleistocene foragers and hunters, it is clear that the southern end of the Sangamon terrace was a desirable location within walking distance of the littoral and with access to nearby grasslands and wetlands. Some of the resources were available year round, but the presence of sea lions, taken in large quantity, suggests that some

occupations occurred between December and April or May, when these marine mammals give birth and raise their young. Cormorants are also more abundant during these months, when they too are nesting and feeding young. Not enough is known about the biology of the sharks to understand if their presence is seasonal. What is known is that both sharks are normally pelagic; females would probably have been more abundant in the austral spring and summer. The sharks that were taken may have been juveniles. The violet stone crab is a prolific breeder year round and is commonly available on rocky shores.

In summary, the percentage frequencies of specimens by taxa in the early units show that the faunal remains were most represented by limpets (19.19%), gastropods (15.15%), bivalves (22.22%), and mammals (14.40%). Of course, the mammals dominate here in terms of total meat weight presumably. It also is likely that some marine foods were consumed near the shoreline where they were collected. Curiously, bony fish do not appear in the record, which could mean that they were consumed near the distant shoreline or that no technology was available to catch them. The presence of sharks and rays can be explained by their capture in backwater estuaries and other wetlands adjacent and connected to the sea. Today small to moderate-sized sharks swim into similar settings searching for small fish, where they are clubbed and captured by local people. Local informants claim that it is nearly impossible (and unnecessary if nets are available) to club bony fish species because they are too small and mobile. If nets were not available in the late Pleistocene, it is unlikely they were captured. There is no marine faunal record for the domestic sites and for Paredones during this early subphase.

Finally, the white-tailed deer (*Odocoileus virginianus*), found in the late Pleistocene camps on the terrace, are also present in small numbers in later phases. This indicates that both cover and browse for these animals were present in the lower valley. They would have obtained fresh water from the wetlands and river channels. Where columnar cacti are present, deer can knock them over and break open the body with their hooves to expose the succulent pulp (Netherly, personal observation, 1992). This part of the lower valley would have supported a considerable year-round deer population at this early date.

FAUNAL REMAINS FROM THE EARLY HOLOCENE SUBPHASE: ~11,400–7571 CAL BP

The faunal material for the Early Holocene comes from Units 2, 3, and 9 and HP-3, all on or at the foot of the Huaca Prieta mound. Material was also obtained from the off-mound domestic site, Unit 16 (see fig. 3.1; table 9.3). There is also material from Floors 25 and 26 of Unit 22 at Paredones. The range of species recovered for the earliest part of the early Holocene, dated between ~11,400 and 9000 calibrated years ago, is similar to the late Pleistocene material and indicates that the environmental zones had not changed substantially. The configuration of the rocky reefs and sandy bottoms may have been different, but the species recovered suggest that a mosaic littoral with both biotopes was present.

It is reasonable to assume that discernible changes occurred from the general hunting/fishing and foraging paradigm seen in the late Pleistocene materials to patterns that are precursors to those seen in the early Holocene, late Phase I, the period prior to the beginning of mound construction and its ritual use. The expectation is that the mound may have been built in a place that was already a locality of ritual or feasting significance; it may be that the faunal remains from the early Holocene layers reflect the beginning of these patterns.

One mollusk is reported from Unit 2, *Oliva* sp. Fragmented specimens of keyhole limpets (*Fissurella* spp.) are found in Unit 9 (a total of 18), in Unit 16 (3), in Unit 3 (only 1), and in Unit 22 (40). The meat presumably was consumed; the shells may have been utilized. Modestly large numbers of shells of marine snails, gastropods, and bivalves were found in Units 3, 9, 16, and 22. Marine crabs are present but in modest numbers. Sharks, bony fish, marine birds, and sea lions (based on their bulk and not so much on their numbers) are well represented by modest to significant numbers in most units (fig. 9.2).

Significantly, in the floors from Unit 22 we see clear expression of the patterning of the species and counts of mollusks, both snails and bivalves. These relations persist throughout the subsequent phases at both Huaca Prieta (Unit 9) and Paredones (Unit 22) and are presented in detail in the discussion of subsequent phases. Suffice it to say that both sites contained significant numbers of keyhole limpets, two black rock snails (*Tegula atra* and *Prisogaster niger*) that almost always occur together, two species of snails found on sand (*Crepipatela dilata* and *Polinices uber*), and three brown snails found on rocks (*Xanthochorus buxea*, *Thais haemastoma*, and *T. chocolata*), which also co-occur. There is a contrast between a group of mussel species found on rocky substrates, of which the most important is *Choromytilus chorus*, and a group of clams from sandy bottoms, of which the most prominent is *Protothaca thaca*. We return to these apparent associations in the discussion of the following phases. It is interesting that they find such clear expression at Unit 22 at this early period (see table 9.3).

In summary, the marine diet, based on the percentage of total taxa for this late or second subphase, was most characterized by marine snails and gastropods (27.19%), bivalves (21.78%), marine birds (14.76%), sharks and rays (13.60%), and bony fish (8.76%), with most of the latter species occurring in deposits dating between 9000 and 7500 cal BP. By this later time span the sea was much closer to the sites, which may account for the increased presence of bony fish in the diet (9.36%) during this subphase. Dependence on marine mammals drops significantly. These fish first appear in pre-mound levels dated around 9500–9000 cal BP in Huaca Prieta. It also is likely that nets, made with reeds or other materials, were in use by this time, although we found no hard evidence to prove this. Quantitatively speaking, the species and specimen counts for Huaca Prieta are slightly underrepresented for this subphase, which may be due to the difficulty of accessing the deeper mound levels representing this early period. The earlier cultural deposits at Unit 16 and Paredones were much less deep and thus more accessible than those in Huaca Prieta (see chapter 7). Collectively, however, the species types and counts reveal a much broader marine diet seemingly focused on more species and more biota zones than the late Pleistocene phase, which may be due to a more permanent

Table 9.3. Species type and distribution for Phase I: Early Holocene, late subphase (~11,400–7571 cal BP), in excavated units at Huaca Prieta, Paredones, and domestic sites

| | Unit 2 | | | | | | | | Unit 3 | | HP 3 | Unit 9 |
| | Layer | | | | | | | | Feature | | Layer | Layer |
Taxon	5	7	11A	12	16	8	15	24	1BA6	7	56	10
Chitons												
Chaetopleura hennahi												
Chiton cummingsii												
Chiton granosus												
Enoplochiton niger												
Acanthopleura echinata												
Total Chitons												
Limpets												
Fissurella peruviana										1		10
Fissurella maxima												8
Fissurella latimarginata												
Fissurella limbata												
Fissurella crassa												
Fissurella sp.												
Total Limpets												
Marine Snails/Gastropods												
Collisella orbignyi												
Collisella ceciliana												
Scurria viridula												
Scurria parasitica												
Scurria sp.												
Diloma nigerrima												
Tegula atra									2		1	11
Tegula euryomphala												
Tegula tridentata										1		
Prisogaster niger									6	2	2	
Littoridina cummingsi												
Nodilittorina peruviana												
Cerithium stercusmuscarum												
Cerithidea mazatlanica												
Calyptraea trochiformis												
Crepipatella dilatata												
Crucibulum spinosum												
Sinum cymba												
Polinices uber												
Polinices cora												
Bursa ventricosa												
Bursa nana												
Xanthochorus buxea									32	1		

Unit 16		Unit 22			% of Total by Taxa	Total Phase I	% Total Taxa Phase I
Layer		Floor					
11	13	25	26	Totals			
				0			
				0			
				0			
				0			
				0			
				0	**0.00**	**0**	**0.00**
			1	12			
		6	6	20			
1		7	15	23			
	1			1			
				0			
1			5	6			
				62	**4.27**	**81**	**5.22**
1			1	2			
				0			
				0			
	3			3			
				0			
				0			
38	6	19	12	89			
				0			
				1			
56	3	18	26	113			
				0			
				0			
				0			
				0			
				0			
3	1	2	1	7			
				0			
				0			
3		2	2	7			
				0			
				0			
				0			
34	1	6	8	82			

Table 9.3. Continued

| | Unit 2 | | | | | | | | Unit 3 | | HP 3 | Unit 9 |
| | Layer | | | | | | | | Feature | | Layer | Layer |
Taxon	5	7	11A	12	16	8	15	24	1BA6	7	56	10
Marine Snails/Gastropods (continued)												
Thais chocolata									2	2		5
Thais delessertiana												
Thais callaoensis												
Crassilabrum crassilabrum												
Concholepas concholepas												
Solenosteira fusiformis												
Columbella paytensis												
Mitrella sp.												
Anachis sp.												
Nassarius dentifer									1			
Prunum curtum												
Oliva peruviana												
Olivella columellaris												
Oliva sp.	1											
Mitra orientalis									4			
Cancellaria decussata												
Cancellaria urceolata												
Marinula pepita												
Total Marine Snails/Gastropods												
Freshwater Snails												
Lymnaea sp.												
Helisoma peruvianum												
Helisoma trivolvis												
Helisoma sp.												
Drepanotrema sp.												
Physa venustula												
Physa sp.												
Total Freshwater Snails												
Bivalves												
Anadara sp.												
Aulacomya atra												
Choromytilus chorus										7	3	
Perumytilus purpuratus												
Semimytilus algosus										2	2	
Chama pellucida												
Brachidontes sp.												
Spondylus princeps												
Argopecten circularis												
Argopecten purpuratus												

| Unit 16 | | Unit 22 | | | | | |
| Layer | | Floor | | | % of Total by Taxa | Total Phase I | % Total Taxa Phase I |
11	13	25	26	Totals			
9	1	12	22	53			
				0			
				0			
		1		1			
			2	2			
				0			
				0			
				0			
				0			
3		2	4	10			
				0			
				0			
				0			
				1			
1		7	1	13			
				0			
				0			
				0			
				407	**28.01**	**422**	**27.19**
				0			
				0			
				0			
				0			
				0			
				0			
				0			
				0	**0.00**	**0**	**0.00**
				0			
		1	1	2			
39	8	15	40	112			
2	3		4	9			
3	3	1	1	12			
				0			
				0			
				0			
				0			
				0			

Table 9.3. Continued

| Taxon | Unit 2 | | | | | | | | Unit 3 | | HP 3 | Unit 9 |
| | Layer | | | | | | | | Feature | | Layer | Layer |
	5	7	11A	12	16	8	15	24	1BA6	7	56	10
Bivalves (continued)												
Argopecten sp.												
Trachycardium procerum												
Anomia peruviana												
Protothaca thaca												2
Protothaca zorritensis												
Euromalea rufa												
Petricola rugosa												
Gari solida										1		
Semele corrugata												
Semele solida												
Spisula adamsi												
Donax obesulus												
Mesodesma donacium												
Pholas chiloensis												
Total Bivalves												
Barnacles												
Balanus sp.												
Chthamalus sp.												
Total Barnacles												
Marine Crabs												
Platyxanthus orbignyi												
Platyxanthus cokeri												
Cancer porteri												
Cancer polyodon												
Paraxanthus barbiger												
Cycloxanthops sexdecimdentatus												
Hepatus chiliensis												
Petrolisthes sp.												
Pachycheles sp.												
Ocypode gaudichaudii												
Callinectes arctuatus												
Total Marine Crabs												
Freshwater Crabs												
Hypolobocera sp.												
Total Freshwater Crabs												

| Unit 16 | | Unit 22 | | | % of | | % Total |
| Layer | | Floor | | | Total by | Total | Taxa |
11	13	25	26	Totals	Taxa	Phase I	Phase I
				0			
				0			
				0			
11		19	24	56			
				0			
1		1	1	3			
				0			
		21	86	108			
				0			
1		2	9	12			
				0			
				0			
2				2			
				0			
				316	**21.75**	**338**	**21.78**
				0			
				0			
				0	**0.00**	**0**	**0.00**
15		7	10	32			
1				1			
				0			
				0			
				0			
				0			
				0			
				0			
				0			
				0			
				0			
				33	**2.27**	**43**	**2.77**
				0			
				0	**0.00**	**0**	**0.00**

Table 9.3. Continued

| Taxon | Unit 2 | | | | | | | | Unit 3 | | HP 3 | Unit 9 |
| | Layer | | | | | | | | Feature | | Layer | Layer |
	5	7	11A	12	16	8	15	24	1BA6	7	56	10
Sea Urchins												
Tetrapygus niger												
Strongylocentrotus gibbosus												
Caenocentrotus gibbosus												
Total Sea Urchins												
Ascidians (Sea Squirts)												
Pyura chiliensis												
Total Ascidians												
Unidentified Crustaceans, etc.												
Amphibians												
Leptodactylidae												
Total Amphibians												
Sharks and Rays												
Galeorhinus sp.												2
Mustelus sp.												
Carcharhinidae								13				
Carcharhinus sp.			8				1					2
Rhizoprionodon sp.												
Sphyrna sp.				4	8	7						
Lamnidae												
Alopias vulpinus	1						1					
Alopias sp.												
Isurus oxyrinchus												
Squatina armata												
Rajiformes												
Urotrygon sp.												
Rhinobatos planiceps												
Myliobatis sp.												
Total Sharks and Rays												
Bony Fish												
Ariidae												
Galeichthys peruvianus												
Cheilodactylus variegatus												
Clupeidae												
Engraulis ringens				2								
Ethmidium maculatum												

Unit 16		Unit 22					
Layer		Floor			% of Total by Taxa	Total Phase I	% Total Taxa Phase I
11	13	25	26	Totals			
				0			
				0			
				0			
				0	**0.00**	**0**	**0.00**
				0			
				0	**0.00**	**0**	**0.00**
				0	**0.00**	**0**	**0.00**
				0			
				0	**0.00**	**0**	**0.00**
		4	3	9			
				0			
				13			
23	34	16	54	138			
				0			
		7	7	33			
				0			
				2			
				0			
				0			
				0			
				0			
				0			
			3	3			
1			3	4			
				202	**13.90**	**211**	**13.60**
				0			
				0			
			1	1			
				0			
				2			
				0			

Table 9.3. Continued

	Unit 2								Unit 3		HP 3	Unit 9
	Layer								Feature		Layer	Layer
Taxon	5	7	11A	12	16	8	15	24	1BA6	7	56	10
Bony Fish (continued)												
Sardinops sagax-sagax												
Mugil cephalus												
Paralichthys sp.												
Scartichthys sp.												
Labrisomus philippii												
Scorpaena sp.												
Stellifer minor												
Trachurus symmetricus												
Trachurus symmetricus murphyi												
Seriolella violacea												
Centropomus sp.												
Paralonchurus peruanus											8	
Cynoscion sp.												
Thunnus albacares												
Sciaena deliciosa											17	
Sciaena gilberti												
Sciaena starksi												
Sciaena sp.												
Pareques sp.												
Hemilutjanus sp.												
Larimus sp.												
Serranidae												
Acanthistius pictus												
Paralabrax sp.												
Pomadasyidae												
Micropogonias altipinnis												
Menticirrhus sp.												
Ansiotremus scapularis												
Merluccius gayi												
Merluccius gayi peruanus												
Sarda chiliensis												
Sarda chiliensis chiliensis												
Scombridae												
Total Bony Fish												
Unidentified Fish	3										3	
Marine Birds												
Spheniscus humboldti												
Diomedea sp.												
Charadrius sp.												

Unit 16 Layer		Unit 22 Floor			% of Total by Taxa	Total Phase I	% Total Taxa Phase I
11	13	25	26	Totals			
				0			
1	2	1	8	12			
				0			
				0			
				0			
				0			
				0			
				0			
			2	2			
				0			
				0			
8	3	4	4	27			
				0			
				0			
17	9		10	53			
			5	5			
4		2	8	14			
				0			
				0			
				0			
				0			
				0			
				0			
		1		1			
				0			
				0			
				0			
		3	15	18			
1				1			
				0			
				0			
				0			
				0			
				136	**9.36**	**136**	**8.76**
3		8	2	**19**	**1.31**	**19**	**1.22**
		2		2			
		1	1	2			
		1	7	8			

Table 9.3. Continued

| | Unit 2 | | | | | | | | Unit 3 | | HP 3 | Unit 9 |
| | Layer | | | | | | | | Feature | | Layer | Layer |
Taxon	5	7	11A	12	16	8	15	24	1BA6	7	56	10
Marine Birds (continued)												
Haematopus sp.												
Larus sp.												
Larosterna sp.												
Laridae												
Ardeidae												
Egretta sp.												
Pelecanus thagus												
Phalacrocorax bougainvillii		1			2							2
Sula variegata												
Sula sp.												
Total Marine Birds												
Wetland/Land Birds												
Accipitridae												
Podilymbus podiceps												
Anas sp.												
Zenaidura auriculata												
Dives warszewiczi												
Total Wetland/Land Birds												
Unidentified Birds												
Mammals												
Phyllostomidae												
Muridae												
Cavia porcellus												
Canis familiaris												
Lycalopex sechurae												
Otaria flavescens												4
Balaenidae												
Delphinus sp.												
Cetacea												
Odocoileus virginianus												
Lama sp.												
Total Mammals												
Unidentified Marine Mammals												
Unidentified Terrestrial Mammals												
Unidentified Mammals												
Total Faunal Phase I	5	1	8	4	10	9	2	13	48	16	37	46

| Unit 16 | | Unit 22 | | | % of | | % Total |
| Layer | | Floor | | | Total by | Total | Taxa |
11	13	25	26	Totals	Taxa	Phase I	Phase I
		1		1			
6	1	12	21	40			
				0			
				0			
				0			
				0			
7		12	4	23			
6	26	41	49	127			
	1	7	10	18			
				0			
				221	**15.21**	**229**	**14.76**
				0			
				0			
				0			
				0			
				0			
				0	**0.00**	**2**	**0.13**
7	10			**17**	**1.17**	**17**	**1.10**
				0			
				0			
				0			
				0			
				0			
18	18			40			
				0			
				0			
				0			
				0			
				0			
				40	**2.75**	**54**	**3.48**
				0	**0.00**	**0**	**0.00**
				0	**0.00**	**0**	**0.00**
				0	**0.00**	**0**	**0.00**
341	**136**	**274**	**503**	**1453**		**1552**	

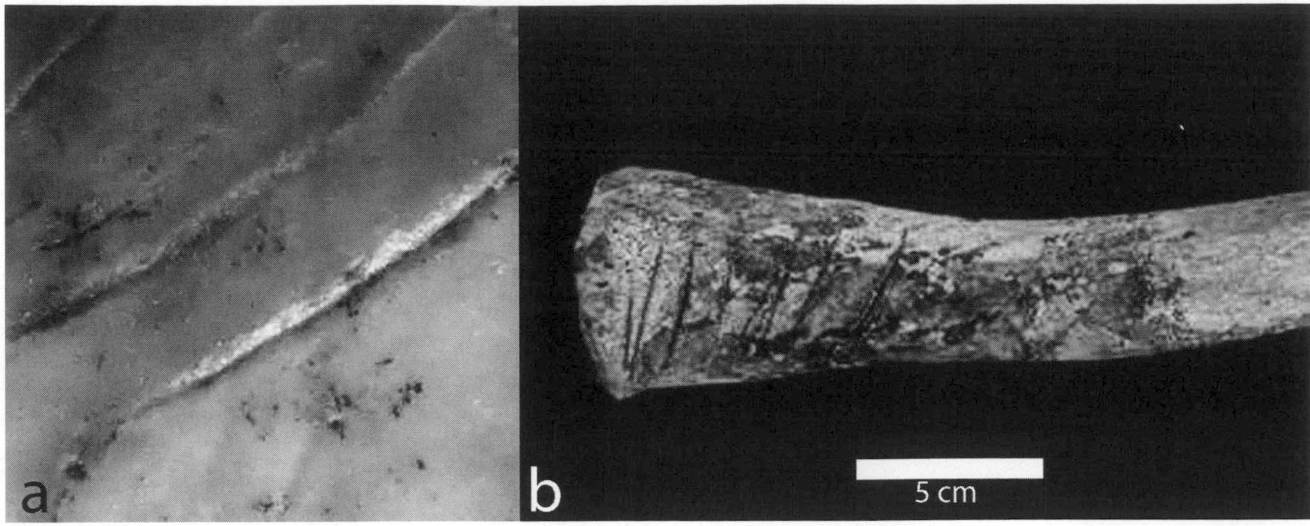

FIGURE 9.2. Cut marks on sea lion bones from premound levels at Huaca Prieta, Strata 9, Unit 15, early Phase I: *a*, V-shaped cut marks on unidentified bone fragment (20×); *b*, cut marks near epiphysis of a rib.

and perhaps larger presence of people in the area. Most of the patterning documented in this subphase represents the later cultural phases as well.

PHASE II: 7571–6538 CAL BP

We assumed that protein acquisition was primarily for consumption during Phase I. However, we have found that some species (particularly mollusks but also some bony fish during the late subphase) appear in patterns that suggest early ritual and possibly feasting use as well. Once the construction of the mound had begun at Huaca Prieta in Phase II, we looked for divergences from the consumption pattern recovered in Phase I. A number of anomalies in Phase II consumption do not recur in the later periods. For the later periods the presence of two specialized subsistence strategies (marine- and agriculture-oriented) practiced by two different populations at Huaca Prieta and Paredones, respectively, becomes evident. Beginning at the end of Phase II, the Paredones remains show greater reliance on cultivated plants and gathered terrestrial fruits and other resources and on protein from terrestrial sources, mammals, and birds and on estuarine and lacustrine fish. Mollusks, especially snails from particular species, are present in quantities that perhaps suggest ritual or commensal feasting without ritual. Grave offerings appear to extend to the principal

bivalves: mussels and clams. While certain littoral foods may have been added (such as easily gathered clams from sandy substrates, sea lions, and shorebirds instead of inland species), this subsistence pattern was more akin to that of the Nanchoc Valley population to the north on the western Andean slopes than to that of the population using the Huaca Prieta mound (Dillehay 2011a).

The Paredones site dates from ~10,500 but primarily from 6500 to 4000 cal BP. Technological advances for the later Paredones farmers include mastery of water management for wetland agriculture (raised agricultural fields) around ~5500–5000 cal BP and crop selection for higher yields. However, dependence on many gathered foods (particularly nutritionally important fruits), continued. The early Huaca Prieta populations emphasized the cultivation of industrial crops (gourds and cotton), relying primarily on gathered marine and wild plant foods, diving technologies and the development of nets, and limited cultivated plants such as squash and chile peppers (see chapter 10 and appendix 5).

Phase II at Huaca Prieta dates from ~7571 to 6538 cal BP (see chapter 6). These ten centuries cover the period when the Sangamon terrace in the vicinity of the mound ceased to be the locus of occasional or semisedentary occupations and perhaps some ritual and became a permanent place of ritual and feasting and eventually the burial place of certain individuals. There may have been a small permanent and an extensive rotating or intermittent ritual population.

The evidence for Phase II fauna at Huaca Prieta comes from the same units that produced the evidence for Phase I, especially the late subphase: Unit 2, Unit HP-3, Unit 9, and Unit 16. The evidence for Paredones comes from Layers 10 and 11 of Unit 20 and Floors 19–24 of Unit 22. The evidence from HP-3 and Unit 9 is meager but does not contradict the evidence from Unit 2 and Unit 16 (table 9.4). The faunal record documents part of the transition from the small-scale occupations of late Phase I to larger-scale resource procurement, as the construction phase of the mound moved from the involvement of small, infrequent ritual/feasting episodes by small groups of people to more frequent ritual events, including human burials, yet still at a small scale by small groups (see chapters 7, 14, and 15).

As Phase II progressed with more frequent ritual events probably in regard to the construction of the mound, both the quantity and the number of species used increased.

For instance, new species of shark are exploited in the course of Phase II but not in significant numbers, with the exception of 34 Carcharhinidae (requiem sharks) in Unit 2, Layer 7C, 24 Carcharinidae, 8 *Mustelus* sp. (thresher sharks), and 9 Laminidae (white sharks) in Layer 7B, and 32 Carcharinidae, 14 *Mustelus* sp., 35 *Rhinobatos planiceps*, and 28 *Myliobatos* sp. in Layer 7A. These animals are a source of meat. This increase may indicate that more sharks were taken from the littoral wetlands, a practice that continued through the next two phases.

Throughout Phase II new species of bony fish are caught and the increased numbers and apparent new breadth of species is tempered by the fact that some eight species of drums, croakers, and sea bass are all sciaenids, demersal inhabitants of the estuarine zone (see table 9.4). This indicates an intensification of exploitation of this habitat. While the numbers of the bony fish increase in Layer 7A, the numbers are not so dramatic as with other species. This may perhaps indicate technological innovation such as the use of different types of nets (such as small cast nets or even dip nets) in the estuary channels, in the wetlands, and at the edge of the tidal zone for exploitation (compare Chu Barrera 2011; Franco 2015; chapter

12, part 1). Marine birds are present in the collection from Unit 2 in this phase, but their numbers are not significant. In like fashion, with the exception of Layer 7C when 23 sea lions were taken, this resource is not heavily exploited.

A number of contrasts can be seen between Unit 16, the off-mound domestic site, and Unit 2, considered to be a staging area at the southeastern foot of the mound at Huaca Prieta. The presence of limpets *Fissurella* spp. and the dual opposition of the snails *Tegula atra* and *Prisogaster niger* are clear contextually and quantitatively throughout the sequence in both localities, especially at Huaca Prieta. The contrast between *Xanthochorus buxea* and *Thais haemastoma* and *T. chocolata* is also clear. While *Nassarius dentifer* and *Mitra orientalis* are both present, the patterning of opposition is not clear in Phase II at Unit 16. The contrast between mussels and clams, principally *Choromytilus chorus* and *Protothaca thaca* (each with additional species), is quantitatively evident, but the numbers are modest: for instance, 23 *C. chorus* and 54 *Protothaca thaca* specimens in Layer 5 at Unit 16 (see table 9.4).

Complementary duality (a whole is divided into two unequal but complementary parts: it can be a social group, a community, a territory, an ecological zone, and possibly aspects of the cosmos) is a powerful organizing principle in the Andean world. This principle seems to be represented in the faunal data from Huaca Prieta in the following ways.

The two most productive ecological zones are the rocky reefs and the inshore sandy bottoms and beaches. They are represented by their most characteristic fauna: snails and bivalves (see table 9.1). In the ritual offerings that make up the vast majority of the Huaca Prieta contexts, both areas are almost always represented by mussels and clams or sometimes by the rocky reef or sandy bottom species of snails.

This use of complementary duality as expressed in environmental terms as represented by characteristic fauna seems to be earlier at Huaca Prieta than what is currently known elsewhere in the Andes, as it is found in all cultural periods. Since the contexts are ritual, we must assume that the choices were deliberate. *Mustelus* sp. (thresher sharks) and *Carcharhinus* sp. (requiem sharks) are consistently present in moderate numbers, along with other shark species in lower frequency. The

Table 9.4. Species type and distribution for Phase II (~7571–6538 cal BP) in excavated units at Huaca Prieta and Unit 16

Taxon	7	7A	7B	7B1	7C	7C1	7C2	7C3	7C4	7C5	7C6	7C7
Chitons												
Chaetopleura hennahi		2	1					1				
Chiton cummingsi	31	300	1					4				
Chiton granosus	3	10	1			1		2				
Enoplochiton niger		1	1									
Acanthopleura echinata		1	2					1	1			
Total Chitons												
Limpets												
Fissurella peruviana	5	32	28			3		4				1
Fissurella maxima	1	26	17	1		14	16	4	2		1	
Fissurella latimarginata	1	23	7			4	2	2	1			1
Fissurella limbata								1				
Fissurella crassa		5										
Fissurella sp.												
Total Limpets												
Marine Snails/Gastropods												
Collisella orbignyi		43	4									
Collisella ceciliana												
Scurria viridula		2										
Scurria parasitica												
Scurria sp.		4										
Diloma nigerrima	99	1280	2						1	140		
Tegula atra	360	5256	1352	95		680	376		1065	3	463	314
Tegula euryomphala		3	16	2		13	2		4	3	1	1
Tegula tridentata	39	478	40			24	8		14	3	20	
Prisogaster niger	843	1806	721	39		163	103		707	150	558	330
Littoridina cummingsi	1		2									
Nodilittorina peruviana	3	13										
Cerithium stercusmuscarum		3										
Cerithidea mazatlanica												
Calyptraea trochiformis	5	54							1	1		
Crepipatella dilatata	19	162	6	1		2	5		11	3	1	3
Crucibulum spinosum												
Sinum cymba		2	1			1			1			
Polinices uber	15	297	47	2		8	2		2		2	1
Polinices cora		1										
Bursa ventricosa		17							2		1	1

| HP-3 | | Unit 9 | | Unit 16 | | | | | |
| Layer | | Layer | | Layer | | | | | % Total |
42	47	6b	6c	5	9	10	11	Totals	by taxa
								4	
								336	
								17	
								2	
								5	
								364	**0.14**
				1				74	
				5	1	2	1	91	
				3		1		45	
					1	2	1	5	
				1				6	
						1		1	
								222	**0.08**
				9				56	
								0	
					1			3	
								0	
								4	
								1522	
				48	63	56	27	10158	
				1				46	
				1				627	
				18	62	7	3	5510	
								3	
								16	
								3	
								0	
								61	
					2	12	14	241	
								0	
								5	
				2	3	2		383	
								1	
				1				22	

Table 9.4. Continued

	Huaca Prieta											
	Unit 2											
	Layer											
Taxon	7	7A	7B	7B1	7C	7C1	7C2	7C3	7C4	7C5	7C6	7C7
Marine Snails/Gastropods (continued)												
Bursa nana		3										
Xanthochorus buxea	213	1806	436	6		36	17		387	108	201	67
Thais haemastoma	185	3128	308	11		52	20			38	90	73
Thais chocolata	42	910	461	16		135	75		391	36	63	80
Thais delessertiana		5	1						1			
Thais callaoensis		3										
Crassilabrum crassilabrum		10	2						1	2		
Concholepas concholepas			1			1			2			
Solenosteira fusiformis												
Columbella paytensis												
Mitrella sp.	2	40										
Anachis sp.		23									105	
Nassarius dentifer	61	578	88	6		10	11		41	14		29
Prunum curtum												
Oliva peruviana												
Olivella columellaris												
Oliva sp.			1									
Mitra orientalis	5	96	97	4		10	24		107	15	59	69
Cancellaria decussata		6	1			1						
Cancellaria urceolata			1									
Marinula pepita	25	140										
Total Marine Snails/Gastropods												
Freshwater Snails												
Lymnaea sp.		1										
Helisoma peruvianum		8							1			
Helisoma trivolvis	9	36	4			1			1			
Helisoma sp.												
Drepanotrema sp.		2				1						
Physa venustula		7	1						1		1	1
Physa sp.												
Total Freshwater Snails												
Bivalves												
Anadara sp.												
Aulacomya atra		1				1	1		1		29	
Choromytilus chorus	59	567	238	16		445	460		129	23		40

HP-3		Unit 9		Unit 16					% Total
Layer		Layer		Layer					
42	47	6b	6c	5	9	10	11	Totals	by taxa
								3	
				52	6	1		3336	
				9	8	4		3926	
				6	8	5	1	2229	
								7	
								3	
								15	
								4	
								0	
								0	
								42	
								128	
				4		1		843	
								0	
								0	
								0	
								1	
					2	1		489	
								8	
						1		2	
								165	
								29862	**11.41**
								1	
								9	
								51	
								0	
								3	
								11	
								0	
								75	**0.03**
								0	
								33	
				23	14	28	8	2050	

Table 9.4. Continued

Taxon	Huaca Prieta											
	Unit 2											
	Layer											
	7	7A	7B	7B1	7C	7C1	7C2	7C3	7C4	7C5	7C6	7C7
Bivalves (continued)												
Perumytilus purpuratus	10	170	15				2		1			
Semimytilus algosus	150	2082	26			19	4		11	56	25	16
Chama pellucida												
Brachidontes sp.												
Spondylus princeps												
Argopecten circularis							2					
Argopecten purpuratus		2										
Argopecten sp.		1										
Trachycardium procerum			1									
Anomia peruviana												
Protothaca thaca	64	624	162	9		332	430		365	13	17	70
Protothaca zorritensis												
Euromalea rufa	9	84	10	1		7	14		13			1
Petricola rugosa	1	19	1									
Gari solida	2	17	2	1		7	14		2			
Semele corrugata			6									
Semele solida	2	29	12			28	36		15	2		6
Spisula adamsi	1	14	1								2	
Donax obesulus	29568	178881	1270	2		70	16					2
Mesodesma donacium												
Pholas chiloensis												
Total Bivalves												
Barnacles												
Balanus sp.												
Chthamalus sp.												
Total Barnacles												
Marine Crabs												
Platyxanthus orbignyi	443	5295	113	4		50	48	88	32	3		22
Platyxanthus cokeri		3				1						
Cancer porteri												
Cancer polyodon	13	41	4			4		2				
Paraxanthus barbiger			1					2				
Cycloxanthops sexdecimdentatus			4			2	1	5	1			
Hepatus chiliensis		1										
Petrolisthes sp.	4	33	3									
Pachycheles sp.								2				

HP-3		Unit 9		Unit 16					
Layer		Layer		Layer					% Total
42	47	6b	6c	5	9	10	11	Totals	by taxa
					2	2	1	203	
					1		1	2391	
								0	
								0	
								0	
								2	
								2	
								1	
								1	
								0	
				54		1		2141	
								0	
				2				141	
						1		22	
								45	
								6	
				1				131	
								18	
				1		1		209811	
								0	
								0	
								216998	**82.93**
								0	
								0	
								0	**0.00**
		4	3	2			15	827	
							1	5	
			1					1	
							1	65	
								3	
								13	
								1	
								40	
								2	

Table 9.4. Continued

	Huaca Prieta										
	Unit 2										
	Layer										
Taxon	7	7A	7B	7B1	7C	7C1	7C2	7C3	7C4	7C5	7C6	7C7
Marine Crabs (continued)												
Ocypode gaudichaudii												
Callinectes arcuatus												
Total Marine Crabs												
Freshwater Crabs												
Hypolobocera sp.												
Total Freshwater Crabs												
Sea Urchins												
Tetrapygus niger	74	8148	654	5		147	150	25	6	2	30	6
Strongylocentrotus gibbosus												
Caenocentrotus gibbosus	4	1190	88	1		4						
Total Sea Urchins												
Ascidians (Sea Squirts)												
Pyura chiliensis												
Total Ascidians												
Unidentified Crustaceans, etc.												
Amphibians												
Leptodactylidae												
Total Amphibians												
Sharks and Rays												
Galeorhinus sp.			4									1
Mustelus sp.		14	8	1		1	2	1		7		
Carcharhinidae		32	24	1	34	4			11			1
Carcharhinus sp.		1										
Rhizoprionodon sp.									2			
Sphyrna sp.												
Lamnidae		1	9		3	4			3			
Alopias vulpinus												
Alopias sp.												
Isurus oxyrinchus												
Squatina armata												
Rajiformes					4		7		7			
Urotrygon sp.		2						3				

| HP-3 | | Unit 9 | | Unit 16 | | | | | |
| Layer | | Layer | | Layer | | | | Totals | % Total by taxa |
42	47	6b	6c	5	9	10	11		
								0	
								0	
								957	**0.37**
								0	
								0	**0.00**
								9247	
				20				20	
								1287	
								10554	**4.03**
								0	
								0	**0.00**
								0	**0.00**
								0	
								0	**0.00**
				7	23	16	16	67	
								34	
								107	
4			1		31	46	10	93	
								2	
					1	8		9	
								20	
								0	
								0	
								0	
					3			3	
								18	
								5	

Table 9.4. Continued

	Huaca Prieta											
	Unit 2											
	Layer											
Taxon	7	7A	7B	7B1	7C	7C1	7C2	7C3	7C4	7C5	7C6	7C7
Sharks and Rays (continued)												
Rhinobatos planiceps		35	2								1	
Myliobatis sp.	5	28	2							3		
Total Sharks and Rays												
Bony Fish												
Ariidae												
Galeichthys peruvianus	11	204	1	2		6	5	1	3	2		
Cheilodactylus variegatus		21							1			
Clupeidae												
Engraulis ringens	5	22	8	1		6	42	45	92	2	130	12
Ethmidium maculatum		53					2					
Sardinops sagax-sagax	3	152	5			17		58	28		15	7
Mugil cephalus		1										
Paralichthys sp.									3			
Scartichthys sp.	4	16	2				2		1		2	
Labrisomus philippii		17										
Scorpaena sp.												
Stellifer minor		20							1	1		
Trachurus symmetricus		2				1				1		
Trachurus symmetricus murphyi												
Seriolella violacea												
Centropomus sp.		1										
Paralonchurus peruanus		47	3			11	7	1	16	2		1
Cynoscion sp.	3	15		1		1			3		1	1
Thunnus albacares?												
Sciaena deliciosa	4	59	5	1		7		1	1		1	
Sciaena gilberti					2							
Sciaena starksi					1			1				
Sciaena sp.												
Pareques sp.												
Hemilutjanus sp.												
Larimus sp.	1	8										
Serranidae												
Acanthistius pictus												
Paralabrax sp.		5										
Pomadasyidae												
Micropogonias altipinnis												
Menticirrhus sp.												
Anisotremus scapularis		11						1	1	1		

| HP-3 | | Unit 9 | | Unit 16 | | | | | |
| Layer | | Layer | | Layer | | | | | % Total |
42	47	6b	6c	5	9	10	11	Totals	by taxa
					3			41	
					7	4		49	
								448	**0.17**
								0	
								235	
								22	
								0	
								365	
					3			58	
								285	
					11	8	8	28	
				1	1		3	8	
								27	
								17	
								0	
								22	
								4	
								0	
					1		1	2	
							1	2	
2					28	17	56	191	
						2	1	28	
								0	
1				1	16	15	30	142	
								2	
					2		2	6	
				1				1	
								0	
								0	
								9	
								0	
						3		3	
						2		7	
								0	
								0	
								0	
				1	11	7	10	43	

Table 9.4. Continued

Taxon	Huaca Prieta											
	Unit 2											
	Layer											
	7	7A	7B	7B1	7C	7C1	7C2	7C3	7C4	7C5	7C6	7C7
Bony Fish (continued)												
Merluccius gayi	2	139							2	1		
Merluccius gayi peruanus												
Sarda chiliensis		12										
Sarda chiliensis chiliensis					1							
Scombridae												
Total Bony Fish												
Unidentified Fish	15	53	15	8		15	4	16	55	9	6	5
Marine Birds												
Spheniscus humboldti												
Diomedea sp.								1				
Charadrius sp.												
Haematopus sp.												
Larus sp.		1										
Larosterna sp.												
Laridae												
Ardeidae												
Egretta sp.												
Pelecanus thagus			2		7	4			1	1		
Phalacrocorax bougainvillii		11			1							
Sula variegata												
Sula sp.		1				3			1			
Total Marine Birds												
Wetland/Land Birds												
Accipitridae												
Podilymbus podiceps												
Anas sp.												
Zenaida auriculata												
Dives warszewiczi												
Total Wetland/Land Birds												
Unidentified Birds		14										
Mammals												
Phyllostomidae												
Muridae		1										
Cavia porcellus												

| HP-3 | | Unit 9 | | Unit 16 | | | | | |
| Layer | | Layer | | Layer | | | | | % Total |
42	47	6b	6c	5	9	10	11	Totals	by taxa
								144	
								0	
						3		15	
								1	
								0	
								1667	**0.64**
3				2	16	12	11	**245**	**0.09**
								0	
				1		2		4	
								0	
								0	
2					9	2		14	
					10	11		21	
								0	
								0	
								0	
					6			21	
				2	11	20	3	48	
					2	1	2	5	
								5	
								118	**0.05**
								0	
								0	
								0	
								0	
								0	
								0	**0.00**
3			2		25	13	6	**63**	**0.02**
								0	
1			2		2			6	
								0	

Table 9.4. Continued

	Huaca Prieta										
	Unit 2										
	Layer										
Taxon	7	7A	7B	7B1	7C	7C1	7C2	7C3	7C4	7C5	7C6	7C7
Mammals (continued)												
Canis familiaris												
Lycalopex sechurae												
Otaria flavescens		4	1		23	1						
Balaenidae												
Delphinus sp.		1							1	1		
Cetacea												
Odocoileus virginianus												
Lama sp.												
Total Mammals												
Unidentified Marine Mammals												
Unidentified Terrestrial Mammals												
Unidentified Mammals	6											
Total Faunal												
Phase II	32424	209540	6353	237	76	2358	1908	274	3554	646	1825	1162

bony fish appear with greater species breadth and consistently moderate numbers for mullets (*Mugil cephalus*) and the various sciaenid species. These species are demersal over soft bottoms. We see the beginning of another contrast with the appearance of *Anisotremus scapularis*, a fish of the rocky reefs, also in moderate numbers.

A significant increase is seen in the modestly higher numbers of avian fauna specimens at Unit 16, but the species are limited to the shore-roosting marine birds. The mammalian fauna, with one exception, is largely limited to occasional sea lions and beached dolphins (table 9.4).

With terminal Phase II (6538 cal BP), the archaeological record from the Paredones site begins (table 9.5). While Unit 20 is presumed to be a domestic site at these early levels (Layers 10 and 11) and had no identifiable molluscan remains, it did have comparable numbers of specimens of the same shark species as found at Unit 22. Unit 22, which is hypothesized to be a food prepara-tion site related to ritual, had a full set of molluscan remains, beginning with several species of limpet in all six floors (Floors 19–24). The patterns of species associations in the molluscan fauna, briefly outlined in Phase I for this unit, continue unchanged in Phase II. Here an association that began in late Phase I appears strongly. This is the co-occurrence of two gastropods, *Nassarius dentifer* and *Mitra orientalis*. In terminal Phase II the raw counts increase as the phase progresses, as they do in the other associations mentioned, although the specimen count increase is less marked in the mussel-clam association of the bivalves. Sharks are present; other fish are primarily the demersal sciaenids and mullets (*Mugil cephalus*) found in the estuary and in the wetlands, and *Anisotremus scapularis*, a fish of the rocky reefs. Marine birds are primarily gulls (*Larus* sp.), pelicans (*Pelecanus thagus*), cormorants (*Phalacrocorax bougainvillii*), and boobies (*Sula variegata*). The mammalian fauna is dominated by sea lions (*Otaria* sp.).

	HP-3		Unit 9		Unit 16					
	Layer		Layer		Layer					% Total
	42	47	6b	6c	5	9	10	11	Totals	by taxa
									0	
									0	
		1			1	1	1	2	35	
									0	
							10	1	14	
									0	
								1	1	
									0	
									56	0.02
							14	1	15	0.01
									0	0.00
				1					7	0.00
	16	1	4	10	281	394	349	239	261651	

In summary, the marine diet during Phase II, based on the percentage of total taxa for the phase at Huaca Prieta, was heavily dominated by bivalves (82.93%) and secondarily by marine shells and snails and gastropods (11.41%). At Huaca Prieta and less so in domestic Unit 16, limpets, marine snails and gastropods, bivalves, sea urchins, sharks and rays, and bony fish predominate. A marine subsistence economy was clearly defined during this period at these localities. At Paredones the marine diet, which is significantly less quantitatively than at Huaca Prieta, also is most represented by bivalves (77.70%) and secondarily by snails and gastropods (15.40%). Most other taxa are present at all sites but in much lower specimen counts and percentage frequencies, with heavy emphasis on bivalves, snails, and gastropods. A larger number of sea lions occur at Paredones. We believe that this narrow focus on these taxa does not imply changes in the diet or the availability of other taxa but instead reflects the increased func-

tional shift of Huaca Prieta to a nondomestic ritual place and mortuary site. The few tombs belonging to this period reveal offerings of only bivalves, snails, and gastropods, suggesting that these taxa had special symbolic meaning. Similar patterns hold for burials of Phases IV and V as well.

PHASE III: 6538–5308 CAL BP

Phase III at Huaca Prieta extends from ~6538 to 5308 cal BP (see chapter 6). After the major construction effort in Phase II, Phase III quantities are generally low, comparatively speaking (tables 9.6–9.7). Faunal remains come from Unit 2, HP-3, and Unit 9 at Huaca Prieta and Unit 16. The only molluscan remains for this phase come from Unit 16. Mollusks were recovered from Units 20 and 22 at Paredones. In general, the patterning of the molluscan fauna is similar between Unit 16 at Huaca Prieta and Layers 5–9 of Unit 20 and

Table 9.5. Species type and distribution for Phase II (~7571–6538 cal BP) in excavated units at Paredones

| | Unit 20 | | Unit 22 | | | | | | |
| | Layer | | Floor | | | | | | |
Taxon	10	11	19	20	21	22	23	24	Totals
Chitons									
Chaetopleura hennahi									0
Chiton cummingsi									0
Chiton granosus									0
Enoplochiton niger									0
Acanthopleura echinata									0
Total Chitons									**0**
Limpets									
Fissurella peruviana			14	13		9	5		41
Fissurella maxima			45	74	24	17	29	6	195
Fissurella latimarginata			19	15	7	4	13	12	70
Fissurella limbata									0
Fissurella crassa			4	10	1	3	5	4	27
Fissurella sp.									0
Total Limpets									**333**
Marine Snails/Gastropods									
Collisella orbignyi				4				3	7
Collisella ceciliana									0
Scurria viridula									0
Scurria parasitica									0
Scurria sp.									0
Diloma nigerrima									0
Tegula atra			337	863	277	154	218	42	1891
Tegula euryomphala			13	12	20	27	30		102
Tegula tridentata			2	2			1	1	6
Prisogaster niger			701	1416	873	515	843	39	4387
Littoridina cummingsi									0
Nodilittorina peruviana									0
Cerithium stercusmuscarum			1						1
Cerithidea mazatlanica									0
Calyptraea trochiformis					1				1
Crepipatella dilatata				8	2	1	1	1	13
Crucibulum spinosum									0
Sinum cymba			15	2	4	5	14		40
Polinices uber			294	95	40	41	73	6	549
Polinices cora									0
Bursa ventricosa			18	14	10	10	10		62
Bursa nana									0
Xanthochorus buxea			211	570	191	83	126	25	1206
Thais haemastoma			298	1024	377	91	254	8	2052

% Total by taxa	Total specimens Phase II	% Total by taxa Phase II
	4	
	336	
	17	
	2	
	5	
0.00	**364**	**0.13**
	115	
	286	
	115	
	5	
	33	
	1	
1.70	**555**	**0.20**
	63	
	0	
	3	
	0	
	4	
	1522	
	12049	
	148	
	633	
	9897	
	3	
	16	
	4	
	0	
	62	
	254	
	0	
	45	
	932	
	1	
	84	
	3	
	4542	
	5978	

Table 9.5. Continued

| | Unit 20 | | Unit 22 | | | | | | |
| Taxon | Layer | | Floor | | | | | | Totals |
	10	11	19	20	21	22	23	24	
Marine Snails/Gastropods (continued)									
Thais chocolata			619	524	303	193	295	22	1956
Thais delessertiana			11	13	4	1	3		32
Thais callaoensis			1	1					2
Crassilabrum crassilabrum				5	1		1	1	9
Concholepas concholepas			6	2			1	1	10
Solenosteira fusiformis				1					1
Columbella paytensis									0
Mitrella sp.									0
Anachis sp.									0
Nassarius dentifer			28	349	126	102	75	11	691
Prunum curtum									0
Oliva peruviana									0
Olivella columellaris									0
Oliva sp.									0
Mitra orientalis			48	96	57	85	118	7	411
Cancellaria decussata									0
Cancellaria urceolata				14	1	1			16
Marinula pepita									0
Total Marine Snails/Gastropods									**13445**
Freshwater Snails									
Lymnaea sp.									0
Helisoma peruvianum									0
Helisoma trivolvis									0
Helisoma sp.									0
Drepanotrema sp.									0
Physa venustula									0
Physa sp.									0
Total Freshwater Snails									**0**
Bivalves									
Anadara sp.									0
Aulacomya atra				5	2				7
Choromytilus chorus			31	100	40	31	11	13	226
Perumytilus purpuratus			56	118	37	12	21	2	246
Semimytilus algosus			13	46	30	34	30		153
Chama pellucida			1						1
Brachidontes sp.									0
Spondylus princeps									0
Argopecten circularis									0
Argopecten purpuratus									0

% Total by taxa	Total specimens Phase II	% Total by taxa Phase II
	4185	
	39	
	5	
	24	
	14	
	1	
	0	
	42	
	128	
	1534	
	0	
	0	
	0	
	1	
	900	
	8	
	18	
	165	
68.60	**43307**	**15.40**
	1	
	9	
	51	
	0	
	3	
	11	
	0	
0.00	**75**	**0.03**
	0	
	40	
	2276	
	449	
	2544	
	1	
	0	
	0	
	2	
	2	

Table 9.5. Continued

Taxon	Unit 20 Layer		Unit 22 Floor						Totals
	10	11	19	20	21	22	23	24	
Bivalves (continued)									
Argopecten sp.						1			1
Trachycardium procerum									0
Anomia peruviana									0
Protothaca thaca			679	89	39	11	13	21	852
Protothaca zorritensis									0
Euromalea rufa			5	1	1	1		1	9
Petricola rugosa				1					1
Gari solida					1			6	7
Semele corrugata									0
Semele solida			2	4		2	1	14	23
Spisula adamsi				1				1	2
Donax obesulus				1	3			5	9
Mesodesma donacium									0
Pholas chiloensis									0
Total Bivalves									**1537**
Barnacles									
Balanus sp.									0
Chthamalus sp.									0
Total Barnacles									**0**
Marine Crabs									
Platyxanthus orbignyi			67	85	34	86	70	15	357
Platyxanthus cokeri									0
Cancer porteri									0
Cancer polyodon			4	4	4	3	4		19
Paraxanthus barbiger									0
Cycloxanthops sexdecimdentatus									0
Hepatus chiliensis									0
Petrolisthes sp.									0
Pachycheles sp.									0
Ocypode gaudichaudii									0
Callinectes arcuatus									0
Total Marine Crabs									**376**
Freshwater Crabs									
Hypolobocera sp.									0
Total Freshwater Crabs									**0**

% Total by taxa	Total specimens Phase II	% Total by taxa Phase II
	2	
	1	
	0	
	2993	
	0	
	150	
	23	
	52	
	6	
	154	
	20	
	209820	
	0	
	0	
7.84	**218535**	**77.70**
	0	
	0	
0.00	**0**	**0.00**
	1184	
	5	
	1	
	84	
	3	
	13	
	1	
	40	
	2	
	0	
	0	
1.92	**1333**	**0.47**
	0	
0.00	**0**	**0.00**

Table 9.5. Continued

Taxon	Unit 20 Layer		Unit 22 Floor						Totals
	10	11	19	20	21	22	23	24	
Sea Urchins									
Tetrapygus niger			9						9
Strongylocentrotus gibbosus									0
Caenocentrotus gibbosus									0
Total Sea Urchins									**9**
Ascidians (Sea Squirts)									
Pyura chiliensis									0
Total Ascidians									**0**
Unidentified Crustaceans, etc.									**0**
Amphibians									
Leptodactylidae									0
Total Amphibians									**0**
Sharks and Rays									
Galeorhinus sp.	7	3	4	12	1	5	2	2	36
Mustelus sp.									0
Carcharhinidae									0
Carcharhinus sp.	11	14	36	22	9	5	30	3	130
Rhizoprionodon sp.									0
Sphyrna sp.		6	15	32	5	8	3	15	84
Lamnidae									0
Alopias vulpinus									0
Alopias sp.									0
Isurus oxyrinchus									0
Squatina armata			2						2
Rajiformes									0
Urotrygon sp.									0
Rhinobatos planiceps									0
Myliobatis sp.	1			1			1		3
Total Sharks and Rays									**255**
Bony Fish									
Ariidae									0
Galeichthys peruvianus									0
Cheilodactylus variegatus									0
Clupeidae									0
Engraulis ringens									0
Ethmidium maculatum									0
Sardinops sagax-sagax									0

% Total by taxa	Total specimens Phase II	% Total by taxa Phase II
	9256	
	20	
	1287	
0.05	10563	3.76
	0	
0.00	0	0.00
0.00	0	0.00
	0	
0.00	0	0.00
	103	
	34	
	107	
	223	
	2	
	93	
	20	
	0	
	0	
	0	
	5	
	18	
	5	
	41	
	52	
1.30	703	0.25
	0	
	235	
	22	
	0	
	365	
	58	
	285	

Table 9.5. Continued

Taxon	Unit 20 Layer		Unit 22 Floor						Totals
	10	11	19	20	21	22	23	24	
Bony Fish (continued)									
Mugil cephalus	16	5	9	58	24	26	19	21	178
Paralichthys sp.			33	7					40
Scartichthys sp.									0
Labrisomus philippii	2								2
Scorpaena sp.									0
Stellifer minor									0
Trachurus symmetricus									0
Trachurus symmetricus murphyi			2						2
Seriolella violacea									0
Centropomus sp.									0
Paralonchurus peruanus			17	12	1		5		35
Cynoscion sp.									0
Thunnus albacares									0
Sciaena deliciosa	3	2	11	3					19
Sciaena gilberti	1								1
Sciaena starksi	5		6	1			1	10	23
Sciaena sp.		17			1				18
Pareques sp.									0
Hemilutjanus sp.									0
Larimus sp.	2								2
Serranidae									0
Acanthistius pictus									0
Paralabrax sp.			3	2					5
Pomadasyidae									0
Micropogonias altipinnis									0
Menticirrhus sp.									0
Anisotremus scapularis	2		25	52	2	9	15		105
Merluccius gayi									0
Merluccius gayi peruanus									0
Sarda chiliensis									0
Sarda chiliensis chiliensis									0
Scombridae									0
Total Bony Fish									**430**
Unidentified Fish	9	4	21	22		5	1		62
Marine Birds									
Spheniscus humboldti	1	1	1		1	4	4		12
Diomedea sp.				31			13	11	55
Charadrius sp.							1		1
Haematopus sp.	1	1	1	2	1	1	9	1	17

% Total by taxa	Total specimens Phase II	% Total by taxa Phase II
	206	
	48	
	27	
	19	
	0	
	22	
	4	
	2	
	2	
	2	
	226	
	28	
	0	
	161	
	3	
	29	
	19	
	0	
	0	
	11	
	0	
	3	
	12	
	0	
	0	
	0	
	148	
	144	
	0	
	15	
	1	
	0	
2.19	**2097**	**0.75**
0.32	**307**	**0.11**
	12	
	59	
	1	
	17	

Table 9.5. Continued

| | Unit 20 | | Unit 22 | | | | | | |
| | Layer | | Floor | | | | | | |
Taxon	10	11	19	20	21	22	23	24	Totals
Marine Birds (continued)									
Larus sp.	14	6	28	44	26	63	77	32	290
Larosterna sp.									0
Laridae									0
Ardeidae									0
Egretta sp.									0
Pelecanus thagus	2		13	16	20	68	101	13	233
Phalacrocorax bougainvillii	12	28	57	82	80	309	314	17	899
Sula variegata	2	1	4	35	16	108	147	8	321
Sula sp.									0
Total Marine Birds									**1828**
Wetland/Land Birds									
Accipitridae									0
Podilymbus podiceps									0
Anas sp.			5	1	1	2	5	4	18
Zenaida auriculata									0
Dives warszewiczi									0
Total Wetland/Land Birds									**18**
Unidentified Birds	19	5	68	226	45	187	241	38	**829**
Mammals									
Phyllostomidae									0
Muridae									0
Cavia porcellus									0
Canis familiaris									0
Lycalopex sechurae									0
Otaria flavescens	36	14	97	72	14	75	53	103	464
Balaenidae				2		3			5
Delphinus sp.						3			3
Cetacea									0
Odocoileus virginianus			2	1					3
Lama sp.	1					1			2
Total Mammals									**477**
Unidentified Marine Mammals				1					**1**
Unidentified Terrestrial Mammals									**0**
Unidentified Mammals									**0**
Total Faunal Phase II	147	107	4012	6319	2757	2405	3307	545	19600

% Total by taxa	Total specimens Phase II	% Total by taxa Phase II
	304	
	21	
	0	
	0	
	0	
	254	
	947	
	326	
	5	
9.33	**1946**	**0.69**
	0	
	0	
	18	
	0	
	0	
0.09	**18**	**0.01**
4.23	**892**	**0.32**
	0	
	6	
	0	
	0	
	499	
	5	
	15	
	0	
	4	
	2	
2.43	**531**	**0.19**
0.01	**16**	**0.01**
0.00	**0**	**0.00**
0.00	**7**	**0.00**
	281249	

Table 9.6. Species type and distribution for Phase III (~6538–5308 cal BP) in excavated units at Huaca Prieta and Unit 16

	Huaca Prieta											
	Unit 2		HP-3				Unit 9	Unit 16				
	Layer		Layer				Layer	Layer				% Total
Taxon	5	6	26	29	31	36	6	6	7	8	Totals	by taxa
Chitons												
Chaetopleura hennahi											0	
Chiton cummingsi											0	
Chiton granosus											0	
Enoplochiton niger											0	
Acanthopleura echinata											0	
Total Chitons											**0**	**0.00**
Limpets												
Fissurella peruviana											0	
Fissurella maxima									2		2	
Fissurella latimarginata											0	
Fissurella limbata											0	
Fissurella crassa											0	
Fissurella sp.											0	
Total Limpets											**2**	**0.08**
Marine Snails/Gastropods												
Collisella orbignyi											0	
Collisella ceciliana											0	
Scurria viridula											0	
Scurria parasitica											0	
Scurria sp.											0	
Diloma nigerrima											0	
Tegula atra									4		4	
Tegula euryomphala											0	
Tegula tridentata											0	
Prisogaster niger									1		1	
Littoridina cummingsi											0	
Nodilittorina peruviana											0	
Cerithium stercusmuscarum											0	
Cerithidea mazatlanica											0	
Calyptraea trochiformis											0	
Crepipatella dilatata									1		1	
Crucibulum spinosum											0	
Sinum cymba											0	
Polinices uber											0	
Polinices cora											0	
Bursa ventricosa											0	
Bursa nana											0	

Table 9.6. Continued

	Huaca Prieta											
Taxon	Unit 2		HP-3				Unit 9	Unit 16			Totals	% Total by taxa
	Layer		Layer				Layer	Layer				
	5	6	26	29	31	36	6	6	7	8		
Marine Snails/Gastropods (continued)												
Xanthochorus buxea											0	
Thais haemastoma											0	
Thais chocolata								1			1	
Thais delessertiana											0	
Thais callaoensis											0	
Crassilabrum crassilabrum											0	
Concholepas concholepas											0	
Solenosteira fusiformis											0	
Columbella paytensis											0	
Mitrella sp.											0	
Anachis sp.											0	
Nassarius dentifer											0	
Prunum curtum											0	
Oliva peruviana											0	
Olivella columellaris											0	
Oliva sp.											0	
Mitra orientalis											0	
Cancellaria decussata											0	
Cancellaria urceolata											0	
Marinula pepita											0	
Total Marine Snails/Gastropods											**7**	**0.27**
Freshwater Snails												
Lymnaea sp.											0	
Helisoma peruvianum											0	
Helisoma trivolvis											0	
Helisoma sp.											0	
Drepanotrema sp.											0	
Physa venustula											0	
Physa sp.											0	
Total Freshwater Snails											**0**	**0.00**
Bivalves												
Anadara sp.											0	
Aulacomya atra											0	
Choromytilus chorus								2	1		3	
Perumytilus purpuratus											0	
Semimytilus algosus											0	

Table 9.6. Continued

Taxon	Huaca Prieta											Totals	% Total by taxa
	Unit 2		HP-3				Unit 9	Unit 16					
	Layer		Layer				Layer	Layer					
	5	6	26	29	31	36	6	6	7	8			
Bivalves (continued)													
Chama pellucida												0	
Brachidontes sp.												0	
Spondylus princeps												0	
Argopecten circularis												0	
Argopecten purpuratus												0	
Argopecten sp.												0	
Trachycardium procerum												0	
Anomia peruviana												0	
Protothaca thaca								58				58	
Protothaca zorritensis												0	
Euromalea rufa								1				1	
Petricola rugosa												0	
Gari solida												0	
Semele corrugata												0	
Semele solida												0	
Spisula adamsi												0	
Donax obesulus												0	
Mesodesma donacium												0	
Pholas chiloensis												0	
Total Bivalves												62	2.37
Barnacles													
Balanus sp.												0	
Chthamalus sp.												0	
Total Barnacles												0	0.00
Marine Crabs													
Platyxanthus orbignyi		138					25	4	30	50		247	
Platyxanthus cokeri									1	1		2	
Cancer porteri		2										2	
Cancer polyodon		12						2	2	6		22	
Paraxanthus barbiger												0	
Cycloxanthops sexdecimdentatus										2		2	
Hepatus chiliensis												0	
Petrolisthes sp.												0	
Pachycheles sp.												0	
Ocypode gaudichaudii												0	
Callinectes arcuatus												0	
Total Marine Crabs												275	10.52

Table 9.6. Continued

Taxon	Huaca Prieta											Totals	% Total by taxa
	Unit 2		HP-3				Unit 9	Unit 16					
	Layer		Layer				Layer	Layer					
	5	6	26	29	31	36	6	6	7	8			
Freshwater Crabs													
Hypolobocera sp.							7					7	
Total Freshwater Crabs												**7**	**0.27**
Sea Urchins													
Tetrapygus niger		718					15					733	
Strongylocentrotus gibbosus												0	
Caenocentrotus gibbosus		1										1	
Total Sea Urchins												**734**	**28.07**
Ascidians (Sea Squirts)													
Pyura chiliensis												0	
Total Ascidians												**0**	**0.00**
Unidentified Crustaceans, etc.												**0**	**0.00**
Amphibians													
Leptodactylidae												0	
Total Amphibians												**0**	**0.00**
Sharks and Rays													
Galeorhinus sp.									7	78	39	124	
Mustelus sp.		2										2	
Carcharhinidae		1							3	18	23	45	
Carcharhinus sp.						1			34	330	129	494	
Rhizoprionodon sp.					4							4	
Sphyrna sp.									5	99	7	111	
Lamnidae		1										1	
Alopias vulpinus												0	
Alopias sp.												0	
Isurus oxyrinchus												0	
Squatina armata											4	4	
Rajiformes												0	
Urotrygon sp.												0	
Rhinobatos planiceps										4	4	8	
Myliobatis sp.									1	14	2	17	
Total Sharks and Rays												**810**	**30.98**

Table 9.6. Continued

	Huaca Prieta											
	Unit 2		HP-3				Unit 9	Unit 16				
	Layer		Layer				Layer	Layer				% Total
Taxon	5	6	26	29	31	36	6	6	7	8	Totals	by taxa
Bony Fish												
Ariidae											0	
Galeichthys peruvianus		4									4	
Cheilodactylus variegatus											0	
Clupeidae											0	
Engraulis ringens	25										25	
Ethmidium maculatum											0	
Sardinops sagax-sagax	4										4	
Mugil cephalus											0	
Paralichthys sp.											0	
Scartichthys sp.											0	
Labrisomus philippii											0	
Scorpaena sp.											0	
Stellifer minor	2										2	
Trachurus symmetricus											0	
Trachurus symmetricus murphyi											0	
Seriolella violacea									1		1	
Centropomus sp.											0	
Paralonchurus peruanus		27			1		2	6	4	34	74	
Cynoscion sp.		1								4	5	
Thunnus albacares?											0	
Sciaena deliciosa	1	8						1	7	33	50	
Sciaena gilberti											0	
Sciaena starksi									1	5	6	
Sciaena sp.										7	7	
Pareques sp.											0	
Hemilutjanus sp.											0	
Larimus sp.											0	
Serranidae									1		1	
Acanthistius pictus											0	
Paralabrax sp.											0	
Pomadasyidae											0	
Micropongonias altipinnis											0	
Menticirrhus sp.											0	
Anisotremus scapularis								4	1	4	9	
Merluccius gayi		1									1	
Merluccius gayi peruanus											0	
Sarda chiliensis											0	
Sarda chiliensis chiliensis											0	
Scombridae								1			1	
Total Bony Fish											**190**	**7.27**

Table 9.6. Continued

	Huaca Prieta											
	Unit 2		HP-3				Unit 9	Unit 16				
	Layer		Layer				Layer	Layer				% Total
Taxon	5	6	26	29	31	36	6	6	7	8	Totals	by taxa
Unidentified Fish		1						2	5	6	**14**	**0.54**
Marine Birds												
Spheniscus humboldti								1		2	3	
Diomedea sp.											0	
Charadrius sp.								17	1	33	51	
Haematopus sp.											0	
Larus sp.								3	8	19	30	
Larosterna sp.									7	1	8	
Laridae											0	
Ardeidae											0	
Egretta sp.											0	
Pelecanus thagus		4	1					1	6	5	17	
Phalacrocorax bourgainvillii		1						3	69	83	156	
Sula variegata								3	9	2	14	
Sula sp.		3									3	
Total Marine Birds											**282**	**10.78**
Wetland/Land Birds												
Accipitridae											0	
Podilymbus podiceps											0	
Anas sp.											0	
Zemaoda auriculata											0	
Dives warszewiczi											0	
Total Wetland/Land Birds											**0**	**0.00**
Unidentified Birds				1		1	3	10	64	92	**171**	**6.54**
Mammals												
Phyllostomidae											0	
Muridae											0	
Cavia porcellus											0	
Canis familiaris											0	
Lycalopex sechurae											0	
Otaria flavescens	5					6			24	9	44	
Balaenidae											0	
Delphinus sp.											0	
Cetacea											0	
Odocoileus virginianus											0	
Lama sp.											0	
Total Mammals											**44**	**1.68**

Table 9.6. Continued

	Huaca Prieta											
	Unit 2		HP-3				Unit 9	Unit 16				
	Layer		Layer				Layer	Layer				% Total
Taxon	5	6	26	29	31	36	6	6	7	8	Totals	by taxa
Unidentified Marine Mammals									3	11	14	0.54
Unidentified Terrestrial Mammals											0	0.00
Unidentified Mammals							3				3	0.11
Total Faunal Phase III	37	925	1	1	1	11	56	178	788	617	2615	0.00

Floors 17 and 18 of Unit 22 at Paredones. Floors 10 through 16 of Unit 22, also Phase III, contained no identifiable faunal material (but abundant plant remains: see chapter 10).

Based on the percentage of total taxa for Phase III, marine snails and gastropods have high counts (42.66%), while sharks and rays (11.38%), marine birds (9.91%), sea urchins (8.40%), and bivalves (7.78%) are less frequent. Approximately 70% of the remains are derived from Paredones and the remainder from Huaca Prieta and Unit 16, the domestic site. The most dominant elements of the marine diet at Huaca Prieta are sharks and rays, sea urchins, marine birds, marine crabs, and bony fish. The most interesting pattern here is the sudden dominance of sharks and rays and especially the increase in sea urchins. By this time Huaca Prieta and Unit 16 are located within meters of the sea, with immediate access to all marine biozones. This also is a time when the interior littoral wetlands and lagoons are diminishing, however, which may imply fewer brackish and saltwater estuaries connected to the sea and thus fewer sharks in the littoral zone. The only explanation that we can offer here is that people had small totora reed fishing crafts by this time and were purposely capturing prey close to or slightly offshore.

The higher volume of sea urchins at Huaca Prieta are represented by only the number of shells, not spines, in the counts in table 9.6. They probably became a sacred or symbolic species and were used

as a constituent in the hardened plaster surfaces now beginning to cover the mound in some places as it grew in height and girth during this phase and appear as grave offerings as well (see chapter 7). As reported in chapter 7, enormous quantities of burned sea urchin spines are found in offerings and on floors throughout the mound during the phase. This also is the phase when approximately 60%–70% of the mound at Huaca Prieta was built.

In regard to Paredones during this phase (see table 9.7), the quantity of marine specimens is considerably higher than it is for Huaca Prieta and Unit 16, perhaps due to the shift to crop food preparation and consumption and to food production at this locale during this phase. Based on the percentage of total taxa, the marine diet is best represented by marine snails and gastropods, bony fish, sharks and rays, marine birds, bivalves, and limpets. Although the capture of sea lions had decreased considerably by this time, their presence was proportionally greater in the faunal remains during Phases I and II.

PHASE IV: 5308–4107 CAL BP

The faunal material from Phase IV comes from Units 2, 3, HP-3, 13, and 25 at Huaca Prieta and Unit 16 and from Paredones (tables 9.8–9.9). The fauna at Huaca Prieta is problematic, however. Layers 3 and 4 in Unit 2 have faunal assemblages that include most classes of animals. The repre-

Table 9.7. Species type and distribution for Phase III (~6538–5308 cal BP) in excavated units at Paredones

Taxon	Unit 20					Unit 22		Totals	% Total by taxa	Total specimens Phase III	% Total by taxa Phase III
	Layer										
	5	6	7	8	9	17	18				
Chitons											
Chaetopleura hennahi								0		0	
Chiton cummingsi								0		0	
Chiton granosus								0		0	
Enoplochiton niger								0		0	
Acanthopleura echinata								0		0	
Total Chitons								**0**	**0.00**	**0**	**0.00**
Limpets											
Fissurella peruviana		2		2	2		1	7		7	
Fissurella maxima		8		2	3	4	7	24		26	
Fissurella latimarginata		1			2	2	2	7		7	
Fissurella limbata		1		2	5		2	10		10	
Fissurella crassa		1			1		1	3		3	
Fissurella sp.								0		0	
Total Limpets								**51**	**0.83**	**53**	**0.61**
Marine Snails/Gastropods											
Collisella orbignyi		1		2				3		3	
Collisella ceciliana								0		0	
Scurria viridula								0		0	
Scurria parasitica								0		0	
Scurria sp.								0		0	
Diloma nigerrima								0		0	
Tegula atra	1	83		9	7	4	12	116		120	
Tegula euryomphala		13		3	1		3	20		20	
Tegula tridentata								0		0	
Prisogaster niger		880		63	55	17	86	1101		1102	
Littoridina cummingsi								0		0	
Nodilittorina peruviana								0		0	
Cerithium stercusmuscarum								0		0	
Cerithidea mazatlanica								0		0	
Calyptraea trochiformis								0		0	
Crepipatella dilatata		1						1		2	
Crucibulum spinosum								0		0	
Sinum cymba		2				1	2	5		5	
Polinices uber	4	83	1	15	2	13	46	164		164	
Polinices cora								0		0	
Bursa ventricosa		9		1			6	16		16	
Bursa nana								0		0	
Xanthochorus buxea		289		87	9	14	52	451		451	
Thais haemastoma		991		22	18	17	49	1097		1097	

Table 9.7. Continued

| Taxon | Unit 20 | | | | | Unit 22 | | Totals | % Total by taxa | Total specimens Phase III | % Total by taxa Phase III |
| | Layer | | | | | | | | | | |
	5	6	7	8	9	17	18				
Marine Snails/Gastropods (continued)											
Thais chocolata	2	355		39	17	32	114	559		560	
Thais delessertiana								0		0	
Thais callaoensis		2						2		2	
Crassilabrum crassilabrum		2						2		2	
Concholepas concholepas				1				1		1	
Solenosteira fusiformis								0		0	
Columbella paytensis								0		0	
Mitrella sp.		1						1		1	
Anachis sp.								0		0	
Nassarius dentifer		71		3	5	9	14	102		102	
Prunum curtum								0		0	
Oliva peruviana								0		0	
Olivella columellaris								0		0	
Oliva sp.								0		0	
Mitra orientalis		40		15	5	2	18	80		80	
Cancellaria decussata								0		0	
Cancellaria urceolata		1						1		1	
Marinula pepita								0		0	
Total Marine Snails/Gastropods								3722	60.76	3729	42.66
Freshwater Snails											
Lymnaea sp.								0		0	
Helisoma peruvianum								0		0	
Helisoma trivolvis								0		0	
Helisoma sp.								0		0	
Drepanotrema sp.								0		0	
Physa venustula								0		0	
Physa sp.								0		0	
Total Freshwater Snails								**0**	**0.00**	**0**	**0.00**
Bivalves											
Anadara sp.								0		0	
Aulacomya atra							1	1		1	
Choromytilus chorus	1	11		6	2	4	32	56		59	
Perumytilus purpuratus		9		1	7			17		17	
Semimytilus algosus		4		1		2	5	12		12	
Chama pellucida								0		0	
Brachidontes sp.		1						1		1	
Spondylus princeps								0		0	
Argopecten circularis								0		0	
Argopecten purpuratus								0		0	

Table 9.7. Continued

Taxon	Unit 20					Unit 22		Totals	% Total by taxa	Total specimens Phase III	% Total by taxa Phase III
	Layer										
	5	6	7	8	9	17	18				
Bivalves (continued)											
Argopecten sp.								0		0	
Trachycardium procerum								0		0	
Anomia peruviana								0		0	
Prototivaca thaca	1	89	44	1	5	13	365	518		576	
Prototivaca zorritensis								0		0	
Euromalea rufa							3	3		4	
Petricola rugosa								0		0	
Gari solida				1	1		1	3		3	
Semele corrugata								0		0	
Semele solida		1			1		1	3		3	
Spisula adamsi								0		0	
Donax obesulus	1	3						4		4	
Mesodesma donacium								0		0	
Pholas chiloensis								0		0	
Total Bivalves								**618**	**10.09**	**680**	**7.78**
Barnacles											
Balanus sp.								0		0	
Chthamalus sp.								0		0	
Total Barnacles								**0**	**0.00**	**0**	**0.00**
Marine Crabs											
Platyxanthus orbignyi		10		2	1		4	17		264	
Platyxanthus cokeri								0		2	
Cancer porteri								0		2	
Cancer polyodon								0		22	
Paraxanthus barbiger								0		0	
Cycloxanthops sexdecimdentatus								0		2	
Hepatus chiliensis								0		0	
Petrolisthes sp.								0		0	
Pachycheles sp.								0		0	
Ocypode gaudichaudii								0		0	
Callinectes arcuatus								0		0	
Total Marine Crabs								**17**	**0.28**	**292**	**3.34**
Freshwater Crabs											
Hypolobocera sp.								0		7	
Total Freshwater Crabs								**7**	**0.11**	**7**	**0.08**

Table 9.7. Continued

| Taxon | Unit 20 | | | | | Unit 22 | | Totals | % Total by taxa | Total specimens Phase III | % Total by taxa Phase III |
| | Layer | | | | | | | | | | |
	5	6	7	8	9	17	18				
Sea Urchins											
Tetrapygus niger								0		733	
Strongylocentrotus gibbosus								0		0	
Caenocentrotus gibbosus								0		1	
Total Sea Urchins								**0**	**0.00**	**734**	**8.40**
Ascidians (Sea Squirts)											
Pyura chiliensis								0		0	
Total Ascidians								**0**	**0.00**	**0**	**0.00**
Unidentified Crustaceans, etc.								**0**	**0.00**	**0**	**0.00**
Amphibians											
Leptodactylidae								0		0	
Total Amphibians								**0**	**0.00**	**0**	**0.00**
Sharks and Rays											
Galeorhinus sp.		12		11	2			25		149	
Mustelus sp.								0		2	
Carcharhinidae		6		6	6			18		63	
Carcharhinus sp.		22		12	66		2	102		596	
Rhizoprionodon sp.		1						1		5	
Sphyrna sp.			3	6	13	1		23		134	
Lamnidae								0		1	
Alopias vulpinus								0		0	
Alopias sp.								0		0	
Isurus oxyrinchus								0		0	
Squatina armata		1		9	1			11		15	
Rajiformes								0		0	
Urotrygon sp.								0		0	
Rhinobatos planiceps								0		8	
Myliobatis sp.		1	1	1	2			5		22	
Total Sharks and Rays								**185**	**3.02**	**995**	**11.38**
Bony Fish											
Ariidae								0		0	
Galeichthys peruvianus								0		4	
Cheilodactylus variegatus		1	3	1	6			11		11	
Clupeidae								0		0	
Engraulis ringens								0		25	
Ethmidium maculatum					2			2		2	
Sardinops sagax-sagax								0		4	

Table 9.7. Continued

| Taxon | Unit 20 | | | | | Unit 22 | | Totals | % Total by taxa | Total specimens Phase III | % Total by taxa Phase III |
| | Layer | | | | | | | | | | |
	5	6	7	8	9	17	18				
Bony Fish (continued)											
Mugil cephalus		18	28	37	121		2	206		206	
Paralichthys sp.		2		9	4		5	20		20	
Scartichthys sp.								0		0	
Labrisomus philippii								0		0	
Scorpaena sp.								0		0	
Stellifer minor								0		2	
Trachurus symmetricus								0		0	
Trachurus symmetricus murphyi					8			8		8	
Seriolella violacea								0		1	
Centropomus sp.								0		0	
Paralonchurus peruanus		1	1	2	11		2	17		91	
Cynoscion sp.				1				1		6	
Thunnus albacares?								0		0	
Sciaena deliciosa					7			7		57	
Sciaena gilberti								0		0	
Sciaena starksi								0		6	
Sciaena sp.		4			2			6		13	
Pareques sp.								0		0	
Hemilutjanus sp.								0		0	
Larimus sp.				1				1		1	
Serranidae								0		1	
Acanthistius pictus					2			2		2	
Paralabrax sp.								0		0	
Pomadasyidae								0		0	
Micropongonias altipinnis								0		0	
Menticirrhus sp.								0		0	
Anisotremus scapularis		1		2	12		2	17		26	
Merluccius gayi								0		1	
Merluccius gayi peruanus								0		0	
Sarda chiliensis								0		0	
Sarda chiliensis chiliensis								0		0	
Scombridae								0		1	
Total Bony Fish								298	4.86	488	5.58
Unidentified Fish		10	4	15	44	1		74	1.21	88	1.01
Marine Birds											
Spheniscus humboldti			1				8	9		12	
Diomedea sp.							4	4		4	
Charadrius sp.		1		1	2			4		55	
Haematopus sp.		2		1	4			7		7	

Table 9.7. Continued

Taxon	Unit 20					Unit 22					
	Layer								% Total	Total specimens	% Total by taxa
	5	6	7	8	9	17	18	Totals	by taxa	Phase III	Phase III
Marine Birds (continued)											
Larus sp.		20	17	16	96		6	155		185	
Larosterna sp.								0		8	
Laridae								0		0	
Ardeidae								0		0	
Egretta sp.								0		0	
Pelecanus thagus		11	9	3	11	1	9	44		61	
Phalacrocorax bourgainvillii		113	26	15	113		3	270		426	
Sula variegata		19	1	4	67			91		105	
Sula sp.								0		3	
Total Marine Birds								**584**	**9.53**	**866**	**9.91**
Wetland/Land Birds											
Accipitridae								0		0	
Podilymbus podiceps								0		0	
Anas sp.		3		1	2		1	7		7	
Zemaoda auriculata								0		0	
Dives warszewiczi								0		0	
Total Wetland/Land Birds								**7**	**0.11**	**7**	**0.08**
Unidentified Birds		80	23	24	132	2	9	**270**	**4.41**	**441**	**5.05**
Mammals											
Phyllostomidae								0		0	
Muridae		1						1		1	
Cavia porcellus								0		0	
Canis familiaris					1			1		1	
Lycalopex sechurae								0		0	
Otaria flavescens	5	38	7	31	161	4	18	264		308	
Balaenidae								0		0	
Delphinus sp.								. 0		0	
Cetacea								0		0	
Odocoileus virginianus								0		0	
Lama sp.						1		1		1	
Total Mammals								**267**	**4.36**	**311**	**3.56**
Unidentified Marine Mammals		13	6	1	4			**24**	**0.39**	**38**	**0.43**
Unidentified Terrestrial Mammals		1			4	4		**9**	**0.15**	**9**	**0.10**
Unidentified Mammals								**0**	**0.00**	**3**	**0.03**
Total Faunal Phase III	15	3347	175	488	1055	148	898	6126		8741	

sentational groups of gastropods and bivalves are present. Crustaceans appear in each layer, along with both sharks and bony fish, birds, and mammals, although the species are few and the numbers relatively low. But no remains of vertebrate fauna were found in Unit 25. Faunal material at Paredones comes from Layers 2–4 at Unit 20 and from Floors 4 through 9 at Unit 22 (table 9.9).

The mollusk associations were fully expressed in Unit 2, Unit 16, and Unit 25 at Huaca Prieta. The mollusks and their associations are present with low counts in Floors 4–7 at Paredones. Floor 7 has no vertebrate fauna except for 1 specimen of the sciaenid fish (*Paralonchurus peruanus*). Mollusks are very scanty on Floor 8, and not all of the association co-occurrences are present; few vertebrates are present, but all the major categories are represented. Floor 9 has only 2 snails (1 each of *Tegula atra* and *Prisogaster niger*), a minimum representation of that association. One mussel (*Perumytilus purpuratus*) is found there, but no clam to complete the association of bivalves (mussels and clams) from rocky and sandy substrates, which together appear to represent the whole marine environment. The vertebrate fauna is represented by one sea lion. Clearly the process that resulted in the absence of vertebrate fauna in Phase III continued to influence the frequency of faunal remains in Floors 7–9.

In summary, based on the percentage of total taxa for Phase IV, the marine diet at sites was focused on marine snails and gastropods (71.77%) and on bivalves (8.99%). Approximately 61% of the total collection was derived from Huaca Prieta and the domestic sites; the remainder was recovered from Paredones. The presence of sea urchin shells continues but in reduced numbers. Millions of burned sea urchin spines are present everywhere at Huaca Prieta, however, because mound building continued during this phase. Marine snails and gastropods (71.77%) predominate during this phase at Paredones, with bivalves representing a secondary item.

PHASE V: 4107–3455 CAL BP

During this phase, activity was concentrated on the summit and upper slopes at Huaca Prieta. Faunal remains suggest repeated ritual activity associated with various offerings (such as coca leaves, shells, and gourds) placed in restricted spaces on prepared or unprepared floors and only exceptionally mortuary feasting and food consumption in and around tombs, as evidenced by fragmented shells, small gourds with the remains of chile peppers and beans, and small piles of fragmented baskets, textiles, and other objects interpreted as offerings. Differences of frequency between units, however, are of interest as well as differences between Phases IV and V.

The systematic regularities described above for the mollusks persist, but their frequency decreases relative to other species. Unit 22 is the only unit at Paredones in Phase V and contains about 14% of the total specimens for this phase, with the remainder at Huaca Prieta and the domestic sites. Marine snails and gastropods, bivalves, sharks and rays, and bony fish continue to dominate at Huaca Prieta and Unit 16. Unit 22 displays relatively few changes between Phases IV and V (compare tables 9.10–9.15). While this site shares the focus on multiple species of snails, the largest specimen numbers are confined to relatively few species, with emphasis on the snails and bivalves.

Long-term fluctuations in the frequency of fauna may be the result of variations in the environment, changes in habitat, or differences in their availability or accessibility. While consistent patterns extend through several phases at Huaca Prieta and Paredones, other patterns emerge and then diminish or disappear. While in some cases it is possible to identify external causes affecting habitat or economy, some causes must lie in the social or ideological spheres. Significant among the shifts of economic origin is the disappearance of faunal remains between Floors 10 and 16 at Unit 22 in Phase III and the significant reduction in fauna seen in Floors 7–9 in Unit 22 in Phase IV, which we assume is tied to the greater emphasis on agricultural production.

The molluscan fauna (primarily gastropods, but also bivalves) appears to function as a special symbol. Habitat seems to be a factor, at least as an explanation for the consistent grouping of certain species. The bivalves appear to be divided between rock-dwelling species of mussels and several species of clams living in sandy substrates. In the case of bivalves, large quantities of remains may indicate consumption in feasts, but they occur

Table 9.8. Species type and distribution for Phase IV (~5308–4107 cal BP) in excavated units at Huaca Prieta and Unit 16

	Unit 2		Unit 3				HP-3	Unit 13			Unit 16	
	Layer		Floor				Layer	Floor			Layer	
Taxon	3	4	5	6	7	8	23–42	1	2	3	3	4
Chitons												
Chaetopleura hennahi												
Chiton cummingsi												
Chiton granosus											3	1
Enoplochiton niger												
Acanthopleura echinata												
Total Chitons												
Limpets												
Fissurella peruviana	1										3	1
Fissurella maxima	1										1	1
Fissurella latimarginata	1										4	
Fissurella limbata												1
Fissurella crassa											1	
Fissurella sp.												1
Total Limpets												
Marine Snails/Gastropods												
Collisella orbignyi											6	4
Collisella ceciliana												
Scurria viridula												
Scurria parasitica												
Scurria sp.												
Diloma nigerrima												
Tegula atra	51										156	89
Tegula euryomphala												
Tegula tridentata	3										13	8
Prisogaster niger	71										25	21
Littoridina cummingsi												
Nodilittorina peruviana												
Cerithium stercusmuscarum	1											
Cerithidea mazatlanica												
Calyptraea trochiformis												
Crepipatella dilatata	1										3	
Crucibulum spinosum											9	3
Sinum cymba												
Polinices uber	14											
Polinices cora											9	
Bursa ventricosa												
Bursa nana												
Xanthochorus buxea	109										17	25

| Unit 25 | | | |
| Layer | | | % Total |
5	6	Totals	by taxa
		0	
		0	
		4	
		0	
		0	
		4	**0.08**
1		6	
1		4	
	1	6	
2	1	4	
		1	
1		2	
		23	**0.47**
		10	
		0	
		0	
		0	
		0	
		0	
94	87	477	
1		1	
28	30	82	
371	698	1186	
		0	
		0	
		1	
		0	
1	1	2	
3	5	12	
		12	
	6	6	
7	10	31	
		9	
		0	
		0	
356	705	1212	

Table 9.8. Continued

Taxon	Unit 2 Layer		Unit 3 Floor				HP-3 Layer	Unit 13 Floor			Unit 16 Layer	
	3	4	5	6	7	8	23–42	1	2	3	3	4
Marine Snails/Gastropods (continued)												
Thais haemastoma	38										11	10
Thais chocolata	33										10	15
Thais delessertiana												
Thais callaoensis												
Crassilabrum crassilabrum												
Concholepas concholepas												
Solenosteira fusiformis												1
Columbella paytensis												
Mitrella sp.												
Anachis sp.												
Nassarius dentifer	14										1	4
Prunum curtum												
Oliva peruviana												
Olivella columellaris												
Oliva sp.	1											
Mitra orientalis	13										2	
Cancellaria decussata												
Cancellaria urceolata	1											
Marinula pepita												
Total Marine Snails/Gastropods												
Freshwater Snails												
Lymnaea sp.	1											
Helisoma peruvianum	16											
Helisoma trivolvis												
Helisoma sp.												
Drepanotrema sp.												
Physa venustula	1											
Physa sp.												
Total Freshwater Snails												
Bivalves												
Anadara sp.												
Aulacomya atra												
Choromytilus chorus	6										74	58
Perumytilus purpuratus												2
Semimytilus algosus											1	
Chama pellucida												
Brachidontes sp.												
Spondylus princeps												
Argopecten circularis												

Unit 25			
Layer			% Total
5	6	Totals	by taxa
19	35	113	
61	74	193	
		0	
		0	
	2	2	
		0	
		1	
		0	
		0	
		0	
14	39	72	
		0	
1		1	
		0	
		1	
18	39	72	
		0	
		1	
		0	
		3543	**71.63**
		1	
	1	17	
		0	
	3	3	
		0	
		1	
		0	
		22	**0.44**
		0	
1		1	
74	93	305	
		2	
1	3	5	
		0	
		0	
		0	
		0	

Table 9.8. Continued

Taxon	Unit 2 Layer		Unit 3 Floor				HP-3 Layer	Unit 13 Floor			Unit 16 Layer	
	3	4	5	6	7	8	23–42	1	2	3	3	4
Bivalves (continued)												
Argopecten purpuratus												
Argopecten sp.												
Trachycardium procerum												1
Anomia peruviana												
Protothaca thaca	26										72	21
Protothaca zorritensis												
Euromalea rufa	1										3	3
Petricola rugosa											1	
Gari solida											16	1
Semele corrugata												
Semele solida											2	4
Spisula adamsi	1											
Donax obesulus	19										11	2
Mesodesma donacium												
Pholas chiloensis												
Total Bivalves												
Barnacles												
Balanus sp.												
Chthamalus sp.												
Total Barnacles												
Marine Crabs												
Platyxanthus orbignyi	6	11				8					3	6
Platyxanthus cokeri												
Cancer porteri											1	
Cancer polyodon											1	2
Paraxanthus barbiger												
Cyclozanthops sexdecimdentatus											1	
Hepatus chiliensis												
Petrolisthes sp.												
Pachycheles sp.												
Ocypode gaudichaudii												
Callinectes arcuatus												
Total Marine Crabs												
Freshwater Crabs												
Hypolobocera sp.												
Total Freshwater Crabs												

Unit 25			
Layer			
			% Total
5	6	Totals	by taxa
		0	
		0	
		1	
		0	
15	21	155	
		0	
11	1	19	
		1	
1	2	20	
		0	
		6	
		1	
30	27	89	
		0	
		0	
		605	**12.23**
		0	
		0	
		0	**0.00**
3	29	66	
		0	
		1	
		3	
		0	
		1	
		0	
		0	
		0	
		0	
		0	
		0	
		71	**1.44**
		0	
		0	**0.00**

Table 9.8. Continued

Taxon	Unit 2 Layer 3	4	Unit 3 Floor 5	6	7	8	HP-3 Layer 23–42	Unit 13 Floor 1	2	3	Unit 16 Layer 3	4
Sea Urchins												
Tetrapygus niger						10					1	102
Strongylocentrotus gibbosus												
Caenocentrotus gibbosus												
Total Sea Urchins												
Ascidians (Sea Squirts)												
Pyura chiliensis												
Total Ascidians												
Unidentified Crustaceans, etc.												
Amphibians												
Leptodactylidae												
Total Amphibians												
Sharks and Rays												
Galeorhinus sp.											8	15
Mustelus sp.		1										
Carcharhinidae	5	23						2		3		
Carcharhinus sp.			15				1	2			2	5
Rhizoprionodon sp.												
Sphyrna sp.			7									
Lamnidae											10	
Alopias vulpinus											1	4
Alopias sp.											1	
Isurus sp.			9									
Squatina armata			5								1	
Rajiformes												
Urotrygon sp.		1										
Rhinobatos planiceps											3	
Myliobatis sp.												
Total Sharks and Rays												
Bony Fish												
Ariidae												
Galeichthys peruvianus		20										
Cheilodactylus variegatus												
Clupeidae												
Engraulis ringens		253										
Ethmidium maculatum												
Sardinops sagax-sagax		13										

Unit 25			
Layer			
			% Total
5	6	Totals	by taxa

		113	
		0	
		0	
		113	**2.28**
		0	
		0	**0.00**
		0	**0.00**
		0	
		0	**0.00**
		23	
		1	
		33	
		25	
		0	
		7	
		10	
		5	
		1	
		9	
		6	
		0	
		1	
		3	
		0	
		124	**2.51**
		0	
		20	
		0	
		0	
		253	
		0	
		13	

Table 9.8. Continued

Taxon	Unit 2 Layer		Unit 3 Floor				HP-3 Layer	Unit 13 Floor			Unit 16 Layer	
	3	4	5	6	7	8	23–42	1	2	3	3	4
Bony Fish (continued)												
Mugil cephalus												
Paralichthys sp.												
Scartichthys sp.												
Labrisomus philippii		1										
Scorpaena sp.												
Stellifer minor		5										
Trachurus symmetricus												
Trachurus symmetricus murphyi												
Seriolella violacea												
Centropomus sp.												
Paralonchurus peruanus	6	7	3					6	2	2	11	4
Cynoscion sp.		2							1			
Thunnus albacares?												
Sciaena deliciosa		3						6				
Sciaena gilberti												
Sciaena starksi				1				1				
Sciaena sp.		2										
Pareques sp.												
Hemilutjanus sp.												
Larimus sp.												
Serranidae												
Acanthistius pictus												
Paralabrax sp.												3
Pomadasyidae												
Micropogonias altipinnis												
Menticirrhus sp.												
Anisotremus scapularis												
Merluccius gayi										1		
Merluccius gayi peruanus										1		
Sarda chiliensis												
Sarda chiliensis chiliensis									1			4
Scombridae												
Total Bony Fish												
Unidentified Fish		43						5	2		5	5
Marine Birds												
Spheniscus humboldti											6	2
Diomedea sp.												
Charadrius sp.												
Haematopus sp.												

| Unit 25 | | | |
| Layer | | | % Total |
5	6	Totals	by taxa
		0	
		0	
		0	
		1	
		0	
		5	
		0	
		0	
		0	
		0	
		41	
		3	
		0	
		9	
		0	
		2	
		2	
		0	
		0	
		0	
		0	
		0	
		3	
		0	
		0	
		0	
		0	
		1	
		1	
		0	
		5	
		0	
		67	**1.35**
		60	**1.21**
		8	
		0	
		0	
		0	

Table 9.8. Continued

Taxon	Unit 2 Layer 3	4	Unit 3 Floor 5	6	7	8	HP-3 Layer 23–42	Unit 13 Floor 1	2	3	Unit 16 Layer 3	4
Marine Birds (continued)												
Larus sp.												2
Larosterna sp.												
Laridae											3	
Ardeidae												
Egretta sp.												
Pelecanus thagus											1	
Phalacrocorax bougainvillii	1		2								4	1
Sula variegata		4										
Sula sp.												
Total Marine Birds												
Wetland/Land Birds												
Accipitridae												
Podilymbus podiceps												
Anas sp.												
Zenaida auriculata												
Dives warszewiczi												
Total Wetland/Land Birds												
Unidentified Birds	3	4					2				4	2
Mammals												
Phyllostomidae												
Muridae	2											
Cavia porcellus												
Canis familiaris												
Lycalopex sechurae												
Otaria flavescens	1	2	2	6			6				2	
Balaenidae												
Delphinus sp.												
Cetacea												
Odocoileus virginianus												
Lama sp.												
Total Mammals												
Unidentified Marine Mammals												1
Unidentified Terrestrial Mammals												
Unidentified Mammals		4						1				
Total Faunal Phase IV	448	399	43	1	6	18	9	24	5	7	523	435

Unit 25			
Layer			% Total
5	6	Totals	by taxa
		2	
		0	
		3	
		0	
		0	
		1	
		8	
		4	
		0	
		26	**0.53**
		0	
		0	
		0	
		0	
		0	
		0	**0.00**
		15	**0.30**
		0	
		2	
		0	
		0	
		0	
		19	
		0	
		0	
		0	
		0	
		0	
		21	**0.42**
		1	**0.02**
		0	**0.00**
		5	**0.10**
1115	**1913**	**4946**	

Table 9.9. Species type and distribution for Phase IV (~5308–4107 cal BP) in excavated units at Paredones

| | Unit 20 | | | Unit 22 | | | | | | |
| | Layer | | | Floor | | | | | | |
Taxon	2	3	4	4	5	6	7	8	9	Totals
Chitons										
Chaetopleura hennahi										0
Chiton cummingsi										0
Chiton granosus										0
Enoplochiton niger										0
Acanthopleura echinata										0
Total Chitons										**0**
Limpets										
Fissurella peruviana	1			22	27	21	4			75
Fissurella maxima	1	1	1	24	21	26	8			82
Fissurella latimarginata	1	1		10	3	1	3			19
Fissurella limbata	1									1
Fissurella crassa				8	1	4	2	1		16
Fissurella sp.	1					1				2
Total Limpets										**195**
Marine Snails/Gastropods										
Collisella orbignyi		1		7	1	2				11
Collisella ceciliana										0
Scurria viridula										0
Scurria parasitica										0
Scurria sp.										0
Diloma nigerrima										0
Tegula atra	11		1	17	15	31	8	1	1	85
Tegula euryomphala					2	1				3
Tegula tridentata										0
Prisogaster niger	33			27	16	107	31	1	1	216
Littoridina cummingsi										0
Nodilittorina peruviana										0
Cerithium stercusmuscarum										0
Cerithidea mazatlanica						1				1
Calyptraea trochiformis						1	1			2
Crepipatella dilatata						1				1
Crucibulum spinosum										0
Sinum cymba	2					2	1			5
Polinices uber	26		4	50	23	85	16			204
Polinices cora										0
Bursa ventricosa			1			2				3
Bursa nana										0
Xanthochorus buxea	28		4	25	22	301	58			438
Thais haemastoma	37		6	24	22	126	31	3		249

% Total by taxa	Total Phase IV	% Total by taxa Phase IV
	0	
	0	
	4	
	0	
	0	
0.00	**4**	**0.05**
	81	
	86	
	25	
	5	
	17	
	4	
6.14	**218**	**2.68**
	21	
	0	
	0	
	0	
	0	
	0	
	562	
	4	
	82	
	1402	
	0	
	0	
	1	
	1	
	4	
	13	
	12	
	11	
	235	
	9	
	3	
	0	
	1650	
	362	

Table 9.9. Continued

Taxon	Unit 20 Layer			Unit 22 Floor						Totals
	2	3	4	4	5	6	7	8	9	
Marine Snails/Gastropods (continued)										
Thais chocolata	35		7	46	39	239	91	5		462
Thais delessertiana						1				1
Thais callaoensis										0
Crassilabrum crassilabrum	1									1
Concholepas concholepas										0
Solenosteira fusiformis										0
Columbella paytensis										0
Mitrella sp.										0
Anachis sp.										0
Nassarius dentifer	14		7	4	5	109	2			141
Prunum curtum										0
Oliva peruviana										0
Olivella columellaris										0
Oliva sp.										0
Mitra orientalis	8		4	4	4	46	7			73
Cancellaria decussata							2			2
Cancellaria urceolata										0
Marinula pepita										0
Total Marine Snails/Gastropods										**2288**
Freshwater Snails										
Lymnaea sp.										0
Helisoma peruvianum										0
Helisoma trivolvis										0
Helisoma sp.										0
Drepanotrema sp.										0
Physa venustula										0
Physa sp.										0
Total Freshwater Snails										**0**
Bivalves										
Anadara sp.										0
Aulacomya atra				1						1
Choromytilus chorus	2		1	6	3	15	18	2		47
Perumytilus purpuratus	4			3	1	11	5		1	25
Semimytilus algosus	1				1	2	1			5
Chama pellucida										0
Brachidontes sp.										0
Spondylus princeps										0
Argopecten circularis										0
Argopecten purpuratus										0

% Total by taxa	Total Phase IV	% Total by taxa Phase IV
	655	
	1	
	0	
	3	
	0	
	1	
	0	
	0	
	0	
	213	
	0	
	1	
	0	
	1	
	145	
	2	
	1	
	0	
71.99	**5831**	**71.77**
	1	
	17	
	0	
	3	
	0	
	1	
	0	
0.00	**22**	**0.27**
	0	
	2	
	352	
	27	
	10	
	0	
	0	
	0	
	0	
	0	

Table 9.9. Continued

Taxon	Unit 20			Unit 22						Totals
	Layer			Floor						
	2	3	4	4	5	6	7	8	9	
Bivalves (continued)										
Argopecten sp.										0
Trachycardium procerum				1						1
Anomia peruviana										0
Protothaca thaca	9		3	10	2	4	9			37
Protothaca zorritensis										0
Euromalea rufa	1		1	1	1					4
Petricola rugosa										0
Gari solida										0
Semele corrugata										0
Semele solida	3									3
Spisula adamsi										0
Donax obesulus				1		1				2
Mesodesma donacium										0
Pholas chiloensis										0
Total Bivalves										**125**
Barnacles										
Balanus sp.										0
Chthamalus sp.										0
Total Barnacles										**0**
Marine Crabs										
Platyxanthus orbignyi				24		4	1			29
Platyxanthus cokeri				1						1
Cancer porteri				1	1					2
Cancer polyodon										0
Paraxanthus barbiger										0
Cyclozanthops sexdecimdentatus										0
Hepatus chiliensis										0
Petrolisthes sp.										0
Pachycheles sp.										0
Ocypode gaudichaudii										0
Callinectes arcuatus										0
Total Marine Crabs										**32**
Freshwater Crabs										
Hypolobocera sp.										0
Total Freshwater Crabs										**0**

% Total by taxa	Total Phase IV	% Total by taxa Phase IV
	0	
	2	
	0	
	192	
	0	
	23	
	1	
	20	
	0	
	9	
	1	
	91	
	0	
	0	
3.93	**730**	**8.99**
	0	
	0	
0.00	**0**	**0.00**
	95	
	1	
	3	
	3	
	0	
	1	
	0	
	0	
	0	
	0	
	0	
1.01	**103**	**1.27**
	0	
0.00	**0**	**0.00**

Table 9.9. Continued

Taxon	Unit 20 Layer			Unit 22 Floor						Totals
	2	3	4	4	5	6	7	8	9	
Sea Urchins										
Tetrapygus niger		1								1
Strongylocentrotus gibbosus										0
Caenocentrotus gibbosus										0
Total Sea Urchins										**1**
Ascidians (Sea Squirts)										
Pyura chiliensis										0
Total Ascidians										**0**
Unidentified Crustaceans, etc.										**0**
Amphibians										
Leptodactylidae										0
Total Amphibians										**0**
Sharks and Rays										
Galeorhinus sp.	3			1	1					5
Mustelus sp.	2							1		3
Carcharhinidae	3									3
Carcharhinus sp.	47		1	10				11		69
Rhizoprionodon sp.										0
Sphyrna sp.	1	,								1
Lamnidae										0
Alopias vulpinus										0
Alopias sp.										0
Isurus sp.										0
Squatina armata	2									2
Rajiformes										0
Urotrygon sp.										0
Rhinobatos planiceps			19							19
Myliobatis sp.				2	1					3
Total Sharks and Rays										**105**
Bony Fish										
Ariidae										0
Galeichthys peruvianus										0
Cheilodactylus variegatus										0
Clupeidae										0
Engraulis ringens										0
Ethmidium maculatum										0
Sardinops sagax-sagax										0

% Total by taxa	Total Phase IV	% Total by taxa Phase IV
	114	
	0	
	0	
0.03	**114**	**1.40**
	0	
0.00	**0**	**0.00**
0.00	**0**	**0.00**
	0	
0.00	**0**	**0.00**
	28	
	4	
	36	
	94	
	0	
	8	
	10	
	5	
	1	
	9	
	8	
	0	
	1	
	22	
	3	
3.30	**229**	**2.82**
	0	
	20	
	0	
	0	
	253	
	0	
	13	

Table 9.9. Continued

Taxon	Unit 20 Layer			Unit 22 Floor						Totals
	2	3	4	4	5	6	7	8	9	
Bony Fish (continued)										
Mugil cephalus	27			2	3					32
Paralichthys sp.	1							2		3
Scartichthys sp.										0
Labrisomus philippii	1									1
Scorpaena sp.										0
Stellifer minor										0
Trachurus symmetricus										0
Trachurusmmetricus murphyi										0
Seriolella violacea										0
Centropomus sp.										0
Paralonchurus peruanus	7						1	1		9
Cynoscion sp.										0
Thunnus albacares?										0
Sciaena deliciosa	3									3
Sciaena gilberti	3									3
Sciaena starksi				8	5	13				26
Sciaena sp.										0
Pareques sp.										0
Hemilutjanus sp.										0
Larimus sp.										0
Serranidae										0
Acanthistius pictus										0
Paralabrax sp.										0
Pomadasyidae										0
Micropogonias altipinnis										0
Menticirrhus sp.										0
Anisotremus scapularis	7			6		1		2		16
Merluccius gayi										0
Merluccius gayi peruanus										0
Sarda chiliensis										0
Sarda chiliensis chiliensis										0
Scombridae										0
Total Bony Fish										**57**
Unidentified Fish	16		1	5	4	30		6		**62**
Marine Birds										
Spheniscus humboldti	1			1	2					4
Diomedea sp.	2									2
Charadrius sp.	1									1
Haematopus sp.										0

% Total by taxa	Total Phase IV	% Total by taxa Phase IV
	32	
	3	
	0	
	2	
	0	
	5	
	0	
	0	
	0	
	0	
	50	
	3	
	0	
	12	
	3	
	28	
	2	
	0	
	0	
	0	
	0	
	0	
	3	
	0	
	0	
	0	
	16	
	1	
	1	
	0	
	5	
	0	
1.79	**124**	**1.53**
1.95	**122**	**1.50**
	12	
	2	
	1	
	0	

Table 9.9. Continued

Taxon	Unit 20 Layer			Unit 22 Floor						Totals
	2	3	4	4	5	6	7	8	9	
Marine Birds (continued)										
Larus sp.	48			5	5			1		59
Larosterna sp.										0
Laridae										0
Ardeidae										0
Egretta sp.										0
Pelecanus thagus	25			13	5			1		44
Phalacrocorax bougainvillii	82			51	23			3		159
Sula variegata	24			10	2					36
Sula sp.										0
Total Marine Birds										**305**
Wetland/Land Birds										
Accipitridae										0
Podilymbus podiceps				1	1					2
Anas sp.	2									2
Zenaida auriculata										0
Dives warszewiczi										0
Total Wetland/Land Birds										**4**
Unidentified Birds	54			49	20			7		**130**
Mammals										
Phyllostomidae										0
Muridae	3									3
Cavia porcellus										0
Canis familiaris										0
Lycalopex sechurae										0
Otaria flavescens	62			31	36			12	1	142
Balaenidae										0
Delphinus sp.										0
Cetacea										0
Odocoileus virginianus										0
Lama sp.	4									4
Total Mammals										**149**
Unidentified Marine Mammals	3			65						**68**
Unidentified Terrestrial Mammals	7			4						**11**
Unidentified Mammals										**0**
Total Faunal Phase IV	661	3	62	581	318	1189	300	60	4	3178

% Total by taxa	Total Phase IV	% Total by taxa Phase IV
	61	
	0	
	3	
	0	
	0	
	45	
	167	
	40	
	0	
9.60	**331**	**4.07**
	0	
	2	
	2	
	0	
	0	
0.13	**4**	**0.05**
4.09	**145**	**1.78**
	0	
	5	
	0	
	0	
	0	
	161	
	0	
	0	
	0	
	0	
	4	
4.69	**170**	**2.09**
2.14	**69**	**0.85**
0.35	**11**	**0.14**
0.00	**5**	**0.06**
	8124	

Table 9.10. Species type and distribution for Phase V (~4107–3455 cal BP) in excavated Units 2–7 at Huaca Prieta

	Unit 2		HP-3				Unit 5					
	Layer		Layer				Floor					
Taxon	1	2	3	13	15	19	1	2	3	4	5	6
Chitons												
Chaetopleura hennahi											1	
Chiton cummingsi												
Chiton granosus												
Enoplochiton niger												
Acanthopleura echinata												
Total Chitons												
Limpets												
Fissurella peruviana								1			2	
Fissurella maxima	1							1			3	
Fissurella latimarginata	2	1					1	1			1	
Fissurella limbata												
Fissurella crassa												
Fissurella sp.												
Total Limpets												
Marine Snails/Gastropods												
Collisella orbignyi											1	
Collisella ceciliana												
Scurria viridula												
Scurria parasitica												
Scurria sp.												
Diloma nigerrima												
Tegula atra	9	3					7	5	33		94	16
Tegula euryomphala								2	1			
Tegula tridentata	1						2				20	6
Prisogaster niger	13	7					16	2	14		81	4
Littoridina cummingsi												
Nodilittorina peruviana												
Cerithium stercusmuscarum											1	
Cerithidea mazatlanica												
Calyptraea trochiformis												
Crepipatella dilatata	2	1									7	
Crucibulum spinosum												
Sinum cymba												
Polinices uber	6	2							1		12	17
Polinices cora												
Bursa ventricosa												
Bursa nana												
Xanthochorus buxea	106	56					1	2	1		8	2

	Unit 6		Unit 7	
	Floor		Floor	
1	2	1	2	
	4	4		
1	1	5	3	
	3	5	2	
	1			
	1	14	4	
		3		
1	41	343	150	
	1	1	1	
	1	122	54	
37	1855	400	210	
		1		
		17	5	
2	21	38	20	
1	1	1		
22	199	467	219	

Table 9.10. Continued

Taxon	Unit 2 Layer 1	Unit 2 Layer 2	HP-3 Layer 3	HP-3 Layer 13	HP-3 Layer 15	HP-3 Layer 19	Unit 5 Floor 1	Unit 5 Floor 2	Unit 5 Floor 3	Unit 5 Floor 4	Unit 5 Floor 5	Unit 5 Floor 6
Marine Snails/Gastropods (continued)												
Thais haemastoma	12	5					1				9	5
Thais chocolata	13	2						1	1		2	4
Thais delessertiana	1											
Thais callaoensis												
Crassilabrum crassilabrum												
Concholepas concholepas												
Solenosteira fusiformis												
Columbella paytensis												
Mitrella sp.												
Anachis sp.												
Nassarius dentifer	26	10							1			
Prunum curtum												
Oliva peruviana												
Olivella columellaris												
Oliva sp.												
Mitra orientalis	6	7						1				
Cancellaria decussata	2											
Cancellaria urceolata												
Marinula pepita												
Total Marine Snails/Gastropods												
Freshwater Snails												
Lymnaea sp.												
Helisoma peruvianum												
Helisoma trivolvis	1											
Helisoma sp.												
Drepanotrema sp.												
Physa venustula	1											
Physa sp.												1	
Total Freshwater Snails												
Bivalves												
Anadara sp.												
Aulacomya atra												
Choromytilus chorus	4	6					4	1	13		123	32
Perumytilus purpuratus									1		2	
Semimytilus algosus												
Chama pellucida												
Brachidontes sp.												
Spondylus princeps												

Unit 6		Unit 7	
Floor		Floor	
1	2	1	2
8	80	65	24
13	122	96	34
	1		
		4	
		1	
		1	
6	104	63	26
1	15	54	23
		1	
	2	1	1
1	13	292	149
	1	5	2
	4	12	5

Table 9.10. Continued

| | Unit 2 | | HP-3 | | | | Unit 5 | | | | | |
| | Layer | | Layer | | | | Floor | | | | | |
Taxon	1	2	3	13	15	19	1	2	3	4	5	6
Bivalves (continued)												
Argopecten circularis												
Argopecten purpuratus												
Argopecten sp.												
Trachycardium procerum												
Anomia peruviana												
Protothaca thaca	6	5					2	1	6		13	4
Protothaca zorritensis												
Euromalea rufa							1		3			
Petricola rugosa												
Gari solida												
Semele corrugata												
Semele solida		2									1	
Spisula adamsi											1	
Donax obesulus	53	22					3		3		19	12
Mesodesma donacium												
Pholas chiloensis												
Total Bivalves												
Barnacles												
Balanus sp.												
Chthamalus sp.												
Total Barnacles												
Marine Crabs												
Platyxanthus orbignyi	6	7					6		5		24	6
Platyxanthus cokeri												
Cancer porteri												
Cancer polyodon								1	1		2	
Paraxanthus barbiger												
Cycloxanthops sexdecimdentatus	1											
Hepatus chiliensis												
Petrolisthes sp.												
Pachycheles sp.												
Ocypode gaudichaudii												
Callinectes arcuatus												
Total Marine Crabs												
Freshwater Crabs												
Hypolobocera sp.												
Total Freshwater Crabs												

Unit 6		Unit 7	
Floor		Floor	
1	2	1	2
	3	76	45
	2	7	2
		1	1
1	3	7	3
		1	
1	61	108	43
		1	
24	314	161	93
		2	
			6
	7	8	1
		3	

Table 9.10. Continued

Taxon	Unit 2		HP-3				Unit 5					
	Layer		Layer				Floor					
	1	2	3	13	15	19	1	2	3	4	5	6
Sea Urchins												
Tetrapygus niger							1	6	1		57	13
Strongylocentrotus gibbosus												
Caenocentrotus gibbosus												
Total Sea Urchins												
Ascidians (Sea Squirts)												
Pyura chiliensis												
Total Ascidians												
Unidentified Crustaceans, etc.												
Amphibians												
Leptodactylidae												
Total Amphibians												
Sharks and Rays												
Galeorhinus sp.												
Mustelus sp.											4	
Carcharhinidae							3					
Carcharhinus sp.			5	7	1	3						
Rhizoprionodon sp.												
Sphyrna sp.												
Lamnidae												
Alopias vulpinus												
Alopias sp.												
Isurus oxyrinchus												
Squatina armata												1
Rajiformes										1		
Urotrygon sp.												1
Rhinobatos planiceps												
Myliobatis sp.							22		3			
Total Sharks and Rays												
Bony Fish												
Ariidae												
Galeichthys peruvianus										1		
Cheilodactylus variegatus												
Clupeidae												
Engraulis ringens		1					7		56	32	37	35
Ethmidium maculatum												
Sardinops sagax-sagax		1					3		72	7	2	5

| Unit 6 | | Unit 7 | |
| Floor | | Floor | |
1	2	1	2
	3	22	10
		2	31
		1	10
1		3	1
			1
		3	
		1	
		1	

Table 9.10. Continued

Taxon	Unit 2 Layer		HP-3 Layer				Unit 5 Floor					
	1	2	3	13	15	19	1	2	3	4	5	6
Bony Fish (continued)												
Mugil cephalus												
Paralichthys sp.												
Scartichthys sp.							1		3	5		1
Labrisomus philippii							1				1	1
Scorpaena sp.										1		
Stellifer minor												1
Trachurus symmetricus												
Trachurus symmetricus murphyi												
Seriolella violacea												
Centropomus sp.												
Paralonchurus peruanus												
Cynoscion sp.							1				1	
Thunnus albacares?												
Sciaena deliciosa		1					1		2	1		
Sciaena gilberti												
Sciaena starksi												
Sciaena sp.												
Pareques sp.												
Hemilutjanus sp.												
Larimus sp.												
Serranidae												1
Acanthistius pictus												
Paralabrax sp.												
Pomadasyidae												
Micropogonias altipinnis												
Menticirrhus sp.												
Anisotremus scapularis							2			2		
Merluccius gayi												
Merluccius gayi peruanus												
Sarda chiliensis												
Sarda chiliensis chiliensis												
Scombridae												
Total Bony Fish												
Unidentified Fish							4		6	11	6	10
Marine Birds												
Spheniscus humboldti												
Diomedea sp.												
Charadrius sp.												
Haematopus sp.												

| | Unit 6 | | Unit 7 | |
| | Floor | | Floor | |
	1	2	1	2
				1
				2
		1	27	18
			9	2
			1	
		1		
				1
				2
			1	2
			1	
			1	2
			2	3
		1	12	1

Table 9.10. Continued

Taxon	Unit 2		HP-3				Unit 5					
	Layer		Layer				Floor					
	1	2	3	13	15	19	1	2	3	4	5	6
Marine Birds (continued)												
Larus sp.												
Larosterna sp.												
Laridae												
Ardeidae												
Egretta sp.												
Pelecanus thagus											1	
Phalacrocorax bougainvillii											8	1
Sula variegata												
Sula sp.												
Total Marine Birds												
Wetland/Land Birds												
Accipitridae												
Podilymbus podiceps												
Anas sp.												
Zenaida auriculata												
Dives warszewiczi												
Total Wetland/Land Birds												
Unidentified Birds												1
Mammals												
Phyllostomidae												
Muridae		2										
Cavia porcellus												
Canis familiaris												
Lycalopex sechurae												
Otaria flavescens							1					
Balaenidae												
Delphinus sp.												
Cetacea												
Odocoileus virginianus												
Lama sp.												
Total Mammals												
Unidentified Marine Mammals												
Unidentified Terrestrial Mammals												
Unidentified Mammals												
Total Faunal Phase V	272	141	5	7	1	3	91	22	230	58	548	179

| Unit 6 | | Unit 7 | |
| Floor | | Floor | |
1	2	1	2
	2	1	6
	6		
5	20	4	2
	12	1	
	12	10	5
	4	4	8
	2	1	5
			1
	2		
	3		
	10	8	
124	**2941**	**2507**	**1240**

Table 9.11. Species type and distribution for Phase V (~4107–3455 cal BP) in excavated Unit 10 at Huaca Prieta

	Unit 10				
Taxon	Layer 1	Structure 1	Layer 2	Layer 3	Structure 2
Chitons					
Chaetopleura hennahi					
Chiton cummingsi					
Chiton granosus					
Enoplochiton niger					
Acanthopleura echinata					
Total Chitons					
Limpets					
Fissurella peruviana				5	
Fissurella maxima					
Fissurella latimarginata					
Fissurella limbata					
Fissurella crassa					
Fissurella sp.			1		
Total Limpets					
Marine Snails/Gastropods					
Collisella orbignyi					
Collisella ceciliana					
Scurria viridula					
Scurria parasitica					
Scurria sp.					
Diloma nigerrima					
Tegula atra	17		29	36	12
Tegula euryomphala					
Tegula tridentata	26		9	28	2
Prisogaster niger			112	147	1	22
Littoridina cummingsi					
Nodilittorina peruviana					
Cerithium stercusmuscarum					
Cerithidea mazatlanica					
Calyptraea trochiformis					
Crepipatella dilatata	1		1	1	
Crucibulum spinosum					
Sinum cymba					
Polinices uber	8		6	5	2
Polinices cora					
Bursa ventricosa					
Bursa nana					
Xanthochorus buxea	41		25	99	27	1
Thais haemastoma	3		1	8	1	1
Thais chocolata	2		4	24	2

Table 9.11. Continued

Taxon	Layer 1	Structure 1	Layer 2	Layer 3	Structure 2				
Marine Snails/Gastropods (continued)									
Thais delessertiana									
Thais callaoensis									
Crassilabrum crassilabrum				2					
Concholepas concholepas									
Solenosteira fusiformis									
Columbella paytensis									
Mitrella sp.									
Anachis sp.									
Nassarius dentifer	16		14	4				1	21
Prunum curtum									
Oliva peruviana									
Olivella columellaris									
Oliva sp.									
Mitra orientalis	5		3	11				4	
Cancellaria decussata									
Cancellaria urceolata									
Marinula pepita									
Total Marine Snails/Gastropods									
Freshwater Snails									
Lymnaea sp.									
Helisoma peruvianum									
Helisoma trivolvis									
Helisoma sp.	1		1						
Drepanotrema sp.									
Physa venustula									
Physa sp.									
Total Freshwater Snails									
Bivalves									
Anadara sp.									
Aulacomya atra								1	
Choromytilus chorus	5		10	91	49	28	21	47	2
Perumytilus purpuratus									
Semimytilus algosus	74		121	63				28	
Chama pellucida								1	
Brachidontes sp.									
Spondylus princeps									
Argopecten circularis									
Argopecten purpuratus									
Argopecten sp.									
Trachycardium procerum									
Anomia peruviana				1					

Table 9.11. Continued

Taxon	Unit 10						
	Layer 1	Structure 1	Layer 2	Layer 3	Structure 2		
Bivalves (continued)							
Protothaca thaca	2		2	11	2	1	5
Protothaca zorritensis							
Euromalea rufa			1	2	3	6	1
Petricola rugosa	1		1				
Gari solida				5			
Semele corrugata							
Semele solida			1	7			1
Spisula adamsi							
Donax obesulus							1
Mesodesma donacium			1				
Pholas chiloensis							
Total Bivalves							
Barnacles							
Balanus sp.							
Chthamalus sp.							
Total Barnacles							
Marine Crabs							
Platyxanthus orbignyi		10	21				
Platyxanthus cokeri							
Cancer porteri							
Cancer polyodon		2					2
Paraxanthus barbiger							
Cycloxanthops sexdecimdentatus							
Hepatus chiliensis							
Petrolisthes sp.							
Pachycheles sp.							
Ocypode gaudichaudii							
Callinectes arcuatus							
Total Marine Crabs							
Freshwater Crabs							
Hypolobocera sp.							
Total Freshwater Crabs							
Sea Urchins							
Tetrapygus niger		9	5				2
Strongylocentrotus gibbosus							
Caenocentrotus gibbosus							
Total Sea Urchins							

Table 9.11. Continued

Taxon	Unit 10				
	Layer 1	Structure 1	Layer 2	Layer 3	Structure 2
Ascidians (Sea Squirts)					
Pyura chiliensis					
Total Ascidians					
Unidentified Crustaceans, etc.					
Amphibians					
Leptodactylidae					
Total Amphibians					
Sharks and Rays					
Galeorhinus sp.			1		1
Mustelus sp.				1	
Carcharhinidae	4		6	1	
Carcharhinus sp.					
Rhizoprionodon sp.					
Sphyrna sp.					
Lamnidae					
Alopias vulpinus					
Alopias sp.					
Isurus oxyrinchus					
Squatina armata					
Rajiformes					
Urotrygon sp.					
Rhinobatos planiceps					
Myliobatis sp.			4		
Total Sharks and Rays					
Bony Fish					
Ariidae					
Galeichthys peruvianus	11		3 1	3	1
Cheilodactylus variegatus					
Clupeidae					
Engraulis ringens					
Ethmidium maculatum	6		1	3 1	4
Sardinops sagax-sagax	3		7	1 5	
Mugil cephalus					
Paralichthys sp.					
Scartichthys sp.					
Labrisomus philippii					1
Scorpaena sp.					
Stellifer minor					
Trachurus symmetricus					
Trachurus symmetricus murphyi					

Table 9.11. Continued

Taxon	Layer 1	Structure 1	Layer 2		Layer 3		Structure 2
			Unit 10				
Bony Fish (continued)							
Seriolella violacea							
Centropomus sp.							
Paralonchurus peruanus	22		9	4	4		
Cynoscion sp.					2		
Thunnus albacares							
Sciaena deliciosa	7		10		1	1	1
Sciaena gilberti							
Sciaena starksi							
Sciaena sp.		3					
Pareques sp.	1						
Hemilutjanus sp.							
Larimus sp.							
Serranidae							
Acanthistius pictus							
Paralabrax sp.							
Pomadasyidae							
Micropogonias altipinnis							12
Menticirrhus sp.							
Anisotremus scapularis							
Merluccius gayi							
Merluccius gayi peruanus	3						
Sarda chiliensis							
Sarda chiliensis chiliensis	1						
Scombridae							
Total Bony Fish							
Unidentified Fish	20	6	7	7	6	4	
Marine Birds							
Spheniscus humboldti							
Diomedea sp.							
Charadrius sp.							
Haematopus sp.							
Larus sp.			12				1
Larosterna sp.							
Laridae							
Ardeidae							
Egretta sp.							
Pelecanus thagus							
Phalacrocorax bougainvillii	4	2	3				
Sula variegata							
Sula sp.	2						
Total Marine Birds							

Table 9.11. Continued

Taxon	Unit 10				
	Layer 1	Structure 1	Layer 2	Layer 3	Structure 2
Wetland/Land Birds					
Accipitridae					
Podilymbus podiceps					
Anas sp.					
Zenaida auriculata					
Dives warszewiczi					
Total Wetland/Land Birds					
Unidentified Birds	3		6		1
Mammals					
Phyllostomidae					
Muridae					
Cavia porcellus					
Canis familiaris					
Lycalopex sechurae					
Otaria flavescens					
Balaenidae					
Delphinus sp.		3			
Cetacea					
Odocoileus virginianus					
Lama sp.					
Total Mammals					
Unidentified Marine Mammals					
Unidentified Terrestrial Mammals					
Unidentified Mammals				1	
Total Faunal Phase V	289	14	21	438 12 0	565 19 50	33 28 183 26

so consistently in small element counts that they appear to be functioning as signifiers as well. The same is true of the snails when they appear in the record in large numbers.

With the end of major mound construction projects, the practice of relatively small-scale ritual and feasting by groups of extended kin or co-residents from the communities scattered along the littoral and the need for repetitive procurement and preparation of food for gatherings may have diminished. Thus activities at locations like those in Units 2 and 9 at the foot of the mound, at Units 20 and 22 at Paredones, and even at Unit 16 seem to have declined. New areas in support of ritual activities may have emerged such as Units 5, 6, and 7 on the upper northeastern slope of the mound.

In our review of the faunal remains from these units as in the previous phases, we find definite associations of certain species forming patterns, which we are interpreting as representative of ritual or some form of symbolic activity. Due to the preconditions discussed in the methods section above, counts often appear to be less important than the presence of particular species. It is difficult to interpret why certain species in these pat-

Table 9.12. Species type and distribution for Phase V (~4107–3455 cal BP) in excavated Units 11, 12, and 16 at Huaca Prieta

Taxon	Unit 11	Unit 12	Unit 16 Layer 1	2	3	4	5
Chitons							
Chaetopleura hennahi							
Chiton cummingsi							
Chiton granosus						2	
Enoplochiton niger							
Acanthopleura echinata							
Total Chitons							
Limpets							
Fissurella peruviana			2	2	3	1	1
Fissurella maxima			1	1	1	1	5
Fissurella latimarginata			4	1	4		3
Fissurella limbata						1	
Fissurella crassa			1				1
Fissurella sp.						1	
Total Limpets							
Marine Snails/Gastropods							
Collisella orbignyi			4	23	6	4	9
Collisella ceciliana							
Scurria viridula				1			
Scurria parasitica							
Scurria sp.							
Diloma nigerrima							
Tegula atra			235	125	98	89	42
Tegula euryomphala			1				1
Tegula tridentata			12	9	12	8	1
Prisogaster niger			67	28	25	21	17
Littoridina cummingsi							
Nodilittorina peruviana							
Cerithium stercusmuscarum							
Cerithidea mazatlanica							
Calyptraea trochiformis			2				
Crepipatella dilatata			15	6	3	1	
Crucibulum spinosum							
Sinum cymba			1				
Polinices uber			12	6	9		2
Polinices cora							
Bursa ventricosa				1			1
Bursa nana							
Xanthochorus buxea			72	18	19	25	52

Table 9.12. Continued

Taxon	Unit 11	Unit 12	Unit 16				
			Layer				
			1	2	3	4	5
Marine Snails/Gastropods (continued)							
Thais haemastoma			41	13	11	10	9
Thais chocolata			38	16	10	17	6
Thais delessertiana							
Thais callaoensis							
Crassilabrum crassilabrum			1				2
Concholepas concholepas						1	1
Solenosteira fusiformis							
Columbella paytensis			2				
Mitrella sp.							
Anachis sp.							
Nassarius dentifer			2	4	1	1	4
Prunum curtum							
Oliva peruviana							
Olivella columellaris							
Oliva sp.							
Mitra orientalis			7	6	2		2
Cancellaria decussata							
Cancellaria urceolata							
Marinula pepita							
Total Marine Snails/Gastropods							
Freshwater Snails							
Lymnaea sp.							
Helisoma peruvianum							
Helisoma trivolvis							
Helisoma sp.							
Drepanotrema sp.							
Physa venustula							
Physa sp.							
Total Freshwater Snails							
Bivalves							
Anadara sp.							
Aulacomya atra			1	1			
Choromytilus chorus			87	62	74	59	26
Perumytilus purpuratus			7	3		2	2
Semimytilus algosus			17	1	4		1
Chama pellucida							
Brachidontes sp.							
Spondylus princeps							
Argopecten circularis							

Table 9.12. Continued

Taxon	Unit 11	Unit 12	Unit 16 Layer 1	2	3	4	5
Bivalves (continued)							
Argopecten purpuratus							
Argopecten sp.							
Trachycardium procerum						1	
Anomia peruviana							
Protothaca thaca			54	42	72	21	55
Protothaca zorritensis							
Euromalea rufa			10	6	3	2	1
Petricola rugosa				2	1		
Gari solida			8	4	16	1	
Semele corrugata				1			
Semele solida			2	2	2	4	1
Spisula adamsi							
Donax obesulus			3	8	6	2	1
Mesodesma donacium			2				
Pholas chiloensis							
Total Bivalves							
Barnacles							
Balanus sp.							
Chthamalus sp.							
Total Barnacles							
Marine Crabs							
Platyxanthus orbignyi	13	7	12	8	14	6	2
Platyxanthus cokeri							
Cancer porteri			1	1	1		
Cancer polyodon			1	3	2	2	
Paraxanthus barbiger							
Cycloxanthops sexdecimdentatus			2	1			
Hepatus chiliensis							
Petrolisthes sp.							
Pachycheles sp.							
Ocypode gaudichaudii							
Callinectes arcuatus							
Total Marine Crabs							
Freshwater Crabs							
Hypolobocera sp.							1
Total Freshwater Crabs							

Table 9.12. Continued

Taxon	Unit 11		Unit 12		Unit 16				
					Layer 1	Layer 2	Layer 3	Layer 4	Layer 5
Sea Urchins									
Tetrapygus niger			6	5	7	7	1	102	20
Strongylocentrotus gibbosus									
Caenocentrotus gibbosus									
Total Sea Urchins									
Ascidians (Sea Squirts)									
Pyura chiliensis									
Total Ascidians									
Unidentified Crustaceans, etc.									
Amphibians									
Leptodactylidae									
Total Amphibians									
Sharks and Rays									
Galeorhinus sp.					11	1	9	14	7
Mustelus sp.	1					5	8		
Carcharhinidae			3					8	
Carcharhinus sp.	1	1		4	5	10	2	23	52
Rhizoprionodon sp.									
Sphyrna sp.			1	4			7	10	4
Lamnidae		1							
Alopias vulpinus					2	1			
Alopias sp.							1		
Isurus oxyrinchus									
Squatina armata					1		1		
Rajiformes									
Urotrygon sp.									
Rhinobatos planiceps	1				2				
Myliobatis sp.					12	2	2		
Total Sharks and Rays									
Bony Fish									
Ariidae									
Galeichthys peruvianus									
Cheilodactylus variegatus									
Clupeidae									
Engraulis ringens									
Ethmidium maculatum					1	2			
Sardinops sagax-sagax									

Table 9.12. Continued

Taxon	Unit 11	Unit 12	Unit 16 Layer 1	2	3	4	5
Bony Fish (continued)							
Mugil cephalus							
Paralichthys sp.							1
Scartichthys sp.							
Labrisomus philippii							
Scorpaena sp.							
Stellifer minor							
Trachurus symmetricus			1				
Trachurus symmetricus murphyi							
Seriolella violacea							
Centropomus sp.			1				
Paralonchurus peruanus	1	2	9	3	11	4	
Cynoscion sp.	3						
Thunnus albacares							
Sciaena deliciosa	1		2	9	3		1
Sciaena gilberti			1				1
Sciaena starksi							
Sciaena sp.							1
Pareques sp.							
Hemilutjanus sp.							
Larimus sp.							
Serranidae							
Acanthistius pictus							
Paralabrax sp.						3	
Pomadasyidae							
Micropogonias altipinnis							
Menticirrhus sp.							
Anisotremus scapularis	1						1
Merluccius gayi							
Merluccius gayi peruanus			1				
Sarda chiliensis							
Sarda chiliensis chiliensis						4	
Scombridae							
Total Bony Fish							
Unidentified Fish			2		4	5	2
Marine Birds							
Spheniscus humboldti			2	3	6	2	
Diomedea sp.							
Charadrius sp.							1
Haematopus sp.							

Table 9.12. Continued

Taxon	Unit 11		Unit 12			Unit 16 Layer 1	2	3	4	5
Marine Birds (continued)										
Larus sp.		1				2	2		2	
Larosterna sp.										
Laridae							1	3		
Ardeidae										
Egretta sp.										
Pelecanus thagus							13	1		
Phalacrocorax bougainvillii	5					1	10	4	1	2
Sula variegata										
Sula sp.	1			3	1					
Total Marine Birds										
Wetland/Land Birds										
Accipitridae										
Podilymbus podiceps										
Anas sp.										
Zenaida auriculata										
Dives warszewiczi										
Total Wetland/Land Birds										
Unidentified Birds						7	13	5	3	
Mammals										
Phyllostomidae										
Muridae								1		
Cavia porcellus						15				
Canis familiaris										
Lycalopex sechurae										
Otaria flavescens	7							2		1
Balaenidae										
Delphinus sp.										
Cetacea										
Odocoileus virginianus										
Lama sp.										
Total Mammals										
Unidentified Marine Mammals						4	1		1	
Unidentified Terrestrial Mammals								2		
Unidentified Mammals										
Total Faunal Phase V	18	7	23	25	1	816	495	475	459	339

Table 9.13. Species type and distribution for Phase V (~4107–3455 cal BP) in excavated Unit 21 at Huaca Prieta

| | Unit 21 | | | | | | |
Taxon	Layer 1	Layer 2	Ext. 10 Feature 1	Ext. 16 Layer 1	Ext. 16 Layer 2	Ext. 17 Layer 1	Ext. 21 Feature 1
Chitons							
Chaetopleura hennahi							
Chiton cummingsi							
Chiton granosus							
Enoplochiton niger							
Acanthopleura echinata					1		
Total Chitons							
Limpets							
Fissurella peruviana			1	1	1		
Fissurella maxima	1	1					
Fissurella latimarginata			1				
Fissurella limbata							
Fissurella crassa							
Fissurella sp.			1				1
Total Limpets							
Marine Snails/Gastropods							
Collisella orbignyi							
Collisella ceciliana							
Scurria viridula							
Scurria parasitica							
Scurria sp.							
Diloma nigerrima							
Tegula atra	7	8	28	18	41	3	4
Tegula euryomphala							
Tegula tridentata			8		3		
Prisogaster niger	17	11	24	11	21	1	1
Littoridina cummingsi							
Nodilittorina peruviana							
Cerithium stercusmuscarum							
Cerithidea mazatlanica							
Calyptraea trochiformis							
Crepipatella dilatata	2	2	2		1		
Crucibulum spinosum							
Sinum cymba							
Polinices uber	8	4	4	4	8		
Polinices cora							
Bursa ventricosa		1			1		
Bursa nana							

Table 9.13. Continued

Taxon	Layer 1	Layer 2	Ext. 10 Feature 1	Ext. 16 Layer 1	Ext. 16 Layer 2	Ext. 17 Layer 1	Ext. 21 Feature 1
Marine Snails/Gastropods (continued)							
Xanthochorus buxea	64	11	71	14	39	4	35
Thais haemastoma	14	11	13	5	23		6
Thais chocolata	8	12	9	14	21	1	4
Thais delessertiana							
Thais callaoensis							
Crassilabrum crassilabrum		1					
Concholepas concholepas							
Solenosteira fusiformis				1			
Columbella paytensis							
Mitrella sp.							
Anachis sp.							
Nassarius dentifer	11		5	2	2		
Prunum curtum	1						
Oliva peruviana							
Olivella columellaris							
Oliva sp.							
Mitra orientalis	8	2	4	7	14	1	5
Cancellaria decussata							
Cancellaria urceolata							
Marinula pepita							
Total Marine Snails/Gastropods							
Freshwater Snails							
Lymnaea sp.							
Helisoma peruvianum						1	
Helisoma trivolvis							
Helisoma sp.	1						
Drepanotrema sp.							
Physa venustula			1				
Physa sp.							
Total Freshwater Snails							
Bivalves							
Anadara sp.				1			
Aulacomya atra							
Choromytilus chorus	1	5	5	1	5		1
Perumytilus purpuratus							
Semimytilus algosus		5	4				
Chama pellucida							
Brachidontes sp.							

Table 9.13. Continued

| | Unit 21 | | | | | | |
| | Layer 1 | Layer 2 | Ext. 10 | Ext. 16 | | Ext. 17 | Ext. 21 |
Taxon			Feature 1	Layer 1	Layer 2	Layer 1	Feature 1
Bivalves (continued)							
Spondylus princeps							
Argopecten circularis							
Argopecten purpuratus							
Argopecten sp.							
Trachycardium procerum							
Anomia peruviana						1	5
Protothaca thaca	3	1	9	8	6		
Protothaca zorritensis							
Euromalea rufa		1		2			
Petricola rugosa			1				
Gari solida							
Semele corrugata							
Semele solida			1				
Spisula adamsi							
Donax obesulus	13	1	1	1			1
Mesodesma donacium			1				
Pholas chiloensis							
Total Bivalves							
Barnacles							
Balanus sp.							
Chthamalus sp.							
Total Barnacles							
Marine Crabs							
Platyxanthus orbignyi	21	3	7	12	20	3	1
Platyxanthus cokeri							
Cancer porteri							
Cancer polyodon	1		1				
Paraxanthus barbiger							
Cyclozanthops sexdecimdentatus			1				
Hepatus chiliensis							
Petrolisthes sp.							
Pachycheles sp.							
Ocypode gaudichaudii							
Callinectes arcuatus							
Total Marine Crabs							

Table 9.13. Continued

| | | | Unit 21 | | | | |
| | Layer 1 | Layer 2 | Ext. 10 | Ext. 16 | | Ext. 17 | Ext. 21 |
Taxon			Feature 1	Layer 1	Layer 2	Layer 1	Feature 1
Freshwater Crabs							
Hypolobocera sp.							
Total Freshwater Crabs							
Sea Urchins							
Tetrapygus niger	3					2	
Strongylocentrotus gibbosus							
Caenocentrotus gibbosus							
Total Sea Urchins							
Ascidians (Sea Squirts)							
Pyura chiliensis							
Total Ascidians							
Unidentified Crustaceans, etc.							
Amphibians							
Leptodactylidae							
Total Amphibians							
Sharks and Rays							
Galeorhinus sp.				5	6	1	
Mustelus sp.							
Carcharhinidae							
Carcharhinus sp.			3				
Rhizoprionodon sp.							
Sphyrna sp.							
Lamnidae							
Alopias vulpinus							
Alopias sp.			2				
Isurus oxyrinchus				6			
Squatina armata							
Rajiformes							
Urotrygon sp.							
Rhinobatos planiceps							
Myliobatis sp.							
Total Sharks and Rays							

Table 9.13. Continued

			Unit 21				
	Layer 1	Layer 2	Ext. 10	Ext. 16		Ext. 17	Ext. 21
Taxon			Feature 1	Layer 1	Layer 2	Layer 1	Feature 1
Bony Fish							
Ariidae							
Galeichthys peruvianus							
Cheilodactylus variegatus							
Clupeidae							
Engraulis ringens							
Ethmidium maculatum			1				
Sardinops sagax-sagax							
Mugil cephalus							
Paralichthy sp.							
Scartichthys sp.							
Labrisomus philippii							
Scorpaena sp.							
Stellifer minor							
Trachurus symmetricus							
Trachurus symmetricus murphyi							
Seriolella violacea							
Centropomus sp.							
Paralonchurus peruanus			4	5	7		2
Cynoscion sp.							
Thunnus albacares							
Sciaena deliciosa				2	1	1	
Sciaena gilberti							
Sciaena starksi							
Sciaena sp.							
Pareques sp.							
Hemilutjanus sp.							
Larimus sp.							
Serranidae							
Acanthistius pictus							
Paralabrax sp.							
Pomadasyidae							
Micropogonias altipinnis							
Menticirrhus sp.							
Anisotremus scapularis							
Merluccius gayi							
Merluccius gayi peruanus							
Sarda chiliensis							

Table 9.13. Continued

	Unit 21						
	Layer 1	Layer 2	Ext. 10	Ext. 16		Ext. 17	Ext. 21
Taxon			Feature 1	Layer 1	Layer 2	Layer 1	Feature 1
Bony Fish (continued)							
Sarda chiliensis chiliensis							
Scombridae							
Total Bony Fish							
Unidentified Fish				2	2	4	
Marine Birds							
Spheniscus humboldti							
Diomedea sp.							
Charadrius sp.							
Haematopus sp.							
Larus sp.							
Larosterna sp.							
Laridae					1		
Ardeidae							
Egretta sp.							
Pelecanus thagus							
Phalacrocorax bougainvillii							
Sula variegata					4		
Sula sp.							
Total Marine Birds							
Wetland/Land Birds							
Accipitridae							
Podilymbus podiceps							
Anas sp.				1			
Zenaida auriculata							
Dives warszewiczi							
Total Wetland/Land Birds							
Unidentified Birds					3		
Mammals							
Phyllostomidae							
Muridae			3	2	1		
Cavia porcellus							
Canis familiaris							
Lycalopex sechurae	1						
Otaria flavescens			1				

Table 9.13. Continued

	Unit 21						
	Layer 1	Layer 2	Ext. 10	Ext. 16		Ext. 17	Ext. 21
Taxon			Feature 1	Layer 1	Layer 2	Layer 1	Feature 1
Mammals (continued)							
Balaenidae							
Delphinus sp.							
Cetacea							
Odocoileus virginianus							
Lama sp.							
Total Mammals							
Unidentified Marine Mammals							
Unidentified Terrestrial Mammals					5		
Unidentified Mammals							
Total Faunal Phase V	184	80	218	124	237	23	66

terns are present with hundreds or even thousands of specimens at some times, while at other times they are represented by only a few specimens.

The molluscan remains from Unit 22 in Paredones appear to initiate the consistent patterns of association seen in the fauna at the end of Phase I (see table 9.3) before their full expression at units from Huaca Prieta, but in Phase II patterning in the molluscan fauna is similar at Paredones, Huaca Prieta, and the domestic sites. At Paredones, however, there is an emphasis on the sharks found in wetlands or estuaries, on demersal fish, on marine birds from the beaches, and on sea lions and, in earlier phases, an occasional camelid or deer.

During Phase V, based on an average of the percentages of total taxa within all excavated units for each site, the marine diet at Huaca Prieta was focused on marine snails and gastropods (65.16%) and bivalves (13.14%) (tables 9.10–9.15). A majority of bivalves, snails, and gastropods were recovered from domestic Unit 16. Similar patterns occur at Paredones, but with many fewer species and specimens: marine snails and gastropods and bivalves. Sea lion remains continue to appear in higher numbers at Paredones than at other sites.

TEMPORAL AND SPATIAL DISTRIBUTION OF FAUNAL REMAINS

Highlighted faunal counts for certain species and distribution patterns in the major excavation units are presented below. For all quantitative data for all faunal species and excavation units, refer to tables 9.2–9.15.

PAREDONES: UNITS 20 AND 22

Units 20 and 22 extend from Phases I to V, providing an unbroken glimpse of the cultural record during that millennia-long period.

Unit 20

The deepest levels of Unit 20 are Layers 10 and 11, which date to Phase II. Layer 11 lies directly on the surface of the terrace. The fauna suggest intensive but scattered marine foraging. Present in the deeper Layer 11 were 23 shark specimens and remains from 24 bony fish, including mullet, Peruvian banded croaker, coco, and drum (*lorna*)— all demersal fish available in the estuary or river delta. A grebe (*Haematopus* sp., a freshwater diving bird), 6 gulls, and 28 cormorants, which nested on rocky areas, were found, along with 14 specimens of sea lions. One offering context of Layer 11 contained 15 cormorant remains. A similar collection in Layer 10 included specimens from 19 sharks, 16 mullets, 9 croakers, and 2 drums, a grebe, 14 gulls, 2 pelicans, 36 sea lions, and a camelid (possibly a llama). The balance between inshore, bottom-feeding fish and sharks, birds available for capture on shore, and sea lions and terrestrial game, such as guanacos, suggests a foraging/hunting pattern with intermittent occupation on the edge of the lagoon, close to the estuary, the dry thorn forest of the lower Chicama Valley, and the rich seal rookeries of the rocky littoral.

Initial construction of the Huaca Prieta mound in Phase II does not appear to have changed the activities at Unit 20. The fauna were vertebrates, although some shell was recovered. During Phases II and III, the quantity of faunal material varies from one subunit to another, which suggests that there was not a permanent place for tasks such as food preparation. Vertebrates in general are consistently more frequent than mollusks (both snails and bivalves), and crustaceans are absent. In general, the number of specimens decreases from Layers 7 to 9. Layer 7 in Unit 20 is represented by a meager number of identifiable specimens. Layer 8, Unit 20, Phase III, contained 6 different species of sharks.

Layer 9 of Unit 20 included 90 elements of sharks of different species and 121 of mullets as well as 4 grebe elements, 96 elements from gulls, 11 from pelicans, 113 from cormorants, and 132 from unidentifiable birds. Mammals were represented by 161 elements from sea lions and one from a domestic dog. Layer 9 also had 66 requiem shark elements, 13 from hammerhead sharks, 13 from smaller fish of different species, and 44 elements from unidentifiable fish. The avian fauna consisted of 96 elements from gulls, 11 from a pelican, and 113 from cormorants. Mammals were represented by 161 elements from sea lions. In one subunit of Unit 20 in Layer 9 the vertebrate elements included 72 from hound sharks (6 identified to family, Carcharhinidae, and 66 to genus, *Carcharhinus* sp.); 6 elements from demersal fish (flounders and croakers) and 44 from unidenti-

fied fish; as well as 161 elements from sea lions. The deliberate concentration on large, relatively easily obtained species and the relative paucity of bony fish, except for mullets, indicates that fishing was not a primary activity. The rookeries of large marine birds and sea lions were undoubtedly located on the littoral. The frequency and numbers of vertebrate species decreased from Layer 9 to Layers 8 and 7.

In Layer 6 the faunal counts are primarily from mollusks and vertebrates. The mollusk remains are moderate. All groups of vertebrate fauna (sharks, bony fish, birds, mammals) are present but in modest quantities. Mammals are represented by 38 sea lion elements. This same pattern is seen in Layer 8, Phase III, suggesting intermittent use by smaller groups.

Most faunal material from Unit 20 in Phase IV comes from Layer 2. All vertebrates are present but in modest quantities. The patterns seen in Layers 8 and 7 are also evident, but the distribution of species is broader.

Unit 22

In Unit 22 the earliest levels are in Phases I and II. Faunal remains include mollusks in noteworthy quantities, crustaceans, and vertebrates. For Phase I, the early Holocene subphase, only a few sea lion bones and clams were found, associated with *Capsicum* sp. seeds dated around 10,500 cal BP. Elements for the violet crab were present in modest numbers in Phase II. In Unit 22 the quantities of elements recovered were higher, particularly of sharks, birds, and sea lions. Floor 26 contained 70 shark elements, of which 54 were from a single species: hound sharks. Of a total of 92 bird elements, 49 were from cormorants and 21 from gulls. The number of elements and their distribution for Floor 25 were similar.

The mollusk, mullet, and bird species provided a moderate number of elements in Floor 24. There also are moderate numbers of limpets (with the exception of true limpets on rocky substrate at 12), snails and gastropods, bivalves, bony fish, and marine birds. But 103 sea lion elements are registered there. The mollusks follow the established pattern in Floor 23, but the numbers of elements increase greatly, except the bivalves, including the

Table 9.14. Species type and distribution for Phase V (~4107–3455 cal BP) in excavated Unit 23 at Huaca Prieta

						Unit 23								
						Structure 1			Structure 2					
	Layer					Layer			Layer					
Taxon	1	2	3	4	9	1	2	3	1	2	3	4	5	7
Chitons														
Chaetopleura hennahi														
Chiton cummingsi														
Chiton granosus														
Enoplochiton niger														
Acanthopleura echinata														
Total Chitons														
Limpets														
Fissurella peruviana	98						4	7	27	1	3		2	
Fissurella maxima	10								1					
Fissurella latimarginata	16								2		1	1		
Fissurella limbata	1													
Fissurella crassa									2					1
Fissurella sp.										1			1	
Total Limpets														
Marine Snails/Gastropods														
Collisella orbignyi														
Collisella ceciliana														
Scurria viridula														
Scurria parasitica														
Scurria sp.														
Diloma nigerrima														
Tegula atra	99						16	30	85	22	17	1	6	49
Tegula euryomphala	5													
Tegula tridentata	1									1				2
Prisogaster niger	201						5	21	99	85	10		9	7
Littoridina cummingsi														
Nodilittorina peruviana														
Cerithium stercusmuscarum														
Cerithidea mazatlanica														
Calyptraea trochiformis	1													
Crepipatella dilatata	3													4
Crucibulum spinosum														
Sinum cymba	7								2					
Polinices uber	289						3	9	54	28	4		7	3
Polinices cora														
Bursa ventricosa	7									1				
Bursa nana														

Unit 23

Structure 3	Structure 7					Structure 8									
Layer	Layer					Layer									
3	1	2	3	4	6	1	2	3	4	5	6	7	8	9	10
	54	7	14	3		3			1				3	1	
	2		2		1	1					1		1		
	5	1						1	1		3		2	1	
					1										
	1														
	280	23	69	12	14	258		243	23		3	2	28	2	1
	4		1	1											
	1	1	2	1	1	7		6					2		
	158	13	48	11	4	66		62	12		2		3	3	2
	1														
	1														
	2			1	1										
	3					1									
	109	4	28	6		5		2	1		1		4	1	
	4	2													

Table 9.14. Continued

| | Unit 23 | | | | | Structure 1 | | | Structure 2 | | | | | |
| | Layer | | | | | Layer | | | Layer | | | | | |
Taxon	1	2	3	4	9	1	2	3	1	2	3	4	5	7
Marine Snails/Gastropods (continued)														
Xanthochorus buxea	215						3	3	46	70	2		10	7
Thais haemastoma	286						1	13	55	49	8	1	2	3
Thais chocolata	287						1	5	39	21	6		4	2
Thais delessertiana														
Thais callaoensis														
Crassilabrum crassilabrum									1					
Concholepas concholepas	2													
Solenosteira fusiformis														
Columbella paytensis														
Mitrella sp.														
Anachis sp.														
Nassarius dentifer	25								7	18	1		8	
Prunum curtum														
Oliva peruviana														
Olivella columellaris														
Oliva sp.														
Mitra orientalis	73						3	17	14	20	3	1	7	2
Cancellaria decussata														
Cancellaria urceolata														
Marinula pepita														
Total Marine Snails/Gastropods														
Freshwater Snails														
Lymnaea sp.														
Helisoma peruvianum	9													
Helisoma trivolvis														
Helisoma sp.	2							4	2				1	
Drepanotrema sp.														
Physa venustula	1													
Physa sp.														
Total Freshwater Snails														
Bivalves														
Anadara sp.														
Aulacomya atra														
Choromytilus chorus	10						1	6	4	3	1	1	3	86
Perumytilus purpuratus	1													
Semimytilus algosus	11								4	1				1
Chama pellucida														

Structure 3 Layer 3	Structure 7 Layer 1	Structure 7 Layer 2	Structure 7 Layer 3	Structure 7 Layer 4	Structure 7 Layer 6	Structure 8 Layer 1	Structure 8 Layer 2	Structure 8 Layer 3	Structure 8 Layer 4	Structure 8 Layer 5	Structure 8 Layer 6	Structure 8 Layer 7	Structure 8 Layer 8	Structure 8 Layer 9	Structure 8 Layer 10
	110	14	25	4	2	2		2	10			1			1
	147	14	21		2	9		6	7		1		7	1	
	109	8	13	3	4	7		5	8		3	2	7	4	
	109														
	7	1	18	1											
	49		11	4	1	1		1	2				2		
	1														
	2														
		3	1			1									
	2	6													
	9	2	1	3	15	2		1			3		1	2	2
	2	2						1	1					1	

Table 9.14. Continued

Taxon	Layer 1	2	3	4	9	Structure 1 Layer 1	2	3	Structure 2 Layer 1	2	3	4	5	7
Bivalves (continued)														
Brachidontes sp.														
Spondylus princeps														
Argopecten circularis														
Argopecten purpuratus	1													
Argopecten sp.														
Trachycardium procerum								3	1					
Anomia peruviana														
Protothaca thaca	47								7	2	3	1	1	11
Protothaca zorritensis														
Euromalea rufa	1								1		1		1	
Petricola rugosa													2	
Gari solida														
Semele corrugata														
Semele solida	1													
Spisula adamsi	3													
Donax obesulus	7								6	4	3	3	17	6
Mesodesma donacium													1	
Pholas chiloensis														4
Total Bivalves														
Barnacles														
Balanus sp.														
Chthamalus sp.														
Total Barnacles														
Marine Crabs														
Platyxanthus orbignyi	5						1	6	7	6	11	5	7	16
Platyxanthus cokeri														
Cancer porteri														
Cancer polyodon										1	1			1
Paraxanthus barbiger														
Cyclozanthops sexdecimdentatus														
Hepatus chiliensis														
Petrolisthes sp.														
Pachycheles sp.														
Ocypode gaudichaudii														
Callinectes arcuatus														
Total Marine Crabs														

	Structure 3	Structure 7					Structure 8									
Layer	3	1	2	3	4	6	1	2	3	4	5	6	7	8	9	10
			1													
		8	2	4	3	4	2						1		1	2
		2		1		1						1			1	1
						1										
				1		1										
		16		1	1	5	1			3		2		3	2	1
		3	4	2	1	3	8		5	1		1	1	1	2	

Unit 23

Table 9.14. Continued

	Unit 23														
						Structure 1			Structure 2					
	Layer					Layer			Layer					
Taxon	1	2	3	4	9	1	2	3	1	2	3	4	5	7
Freshwater Crabs														
Hypolobocera sp.														
Total Freshwater Crabs														
Sea Urchins														
Tetrapygus niger														
Strongylocentrotus gibbosus														
Caenocentrotus gibbosus														
Total Sea Urchins														
Ascidians (Sea Squirts)														
Pyura chilensis														
Total Ascidians														
Unidentified Crustaceans, etc.														
Amphibians														
Leptodactylidae							2								
Total Amphibians														
Sharks and Rays														
Galeorhinus sp.	6														
Mustelus sp.														
Carcharhinidae														
Carcharhinus sp.	369	4					9			1	1	7	1		4
Rhizoprionodon sp.														
Sphyrna sp.	12												1		
Lamnidae														
Alopias vulpinus														
Alopias sp.	22	1												
Isurus oxyrinchus	6														
Squatina armata	5						3								
Rajiformes														
Urotrygon sp.														
Rhinobatos planiceps	6														
Myliobatis sp.														
Total Sharks and Rays														

| Structure 3 | Structure 7 | | | | | Structure 8 | | | | | | | | | |
| Layer | Layer | | | | | Layer | | | | | | | | | |
3	1	2	3	4	6	1	2	3	4	5	6	7	8	9	10
1			3												
54	3	40	26		8			1	3						
	14		7												
		3													
	1								1						
															1
			2												
			1												

Table 9.14. Continued

	Unit 23													
						Structure 1			Structure 2					
	Layer					Layer			Layer					
Taxon	1	2	3	4	9	1	2	3	1	2	3	4	5	7
Bony Fish														
Ariidae														
Galeichthys peruvianus														
Cheilodactylus variegatus														
Clupeidae														
Engraulis ringens														
Ethmidium maculatum			1						1	1				
Sardinops sagax-sagax														
Mugil cephalus	1													
Paralichthys sp.														
Scartichthys sp.														
Labrisomus philippii														
Scorpaena sp.														
Stellifer minor														
Trachurus symmetricus														
Trachurus symmetricus murphyi	10								1					
Seriolella violacea														
Centropomus sp.														
Paralonchurus peruanus	39						54	2	8	6		2		2
Cynoscion sp.	5						7			1				
Thunnus albacares	10						7			1				
Sciaena deliciosa		6												
Sciaena gilberti														
Sciaena starksi	2						1							
Sciaena sp.														
Pareques sp.														
Hemilutjanus sp.														
Larimus sp.														
Serranidae														
Acanthistius pictus														
Paralabrax sp.														
Pomadasyidae														
Micropogonias altipinnis														
Menticirrhus sp.														
Anisotremus scapularis		1								3				
Merluccius gayi														
Merluccius gayi peruanus														
Sarda chiliensis														

	Structure 3	Structure 7					Structure 8									
	Layer	Layer					Layer									
	3	1	2	3	4	6	1	2	3	4	5	6	7	8	9	10
		1	1	1						11						
			1													
			4	1						16						
			1													
												2	5			

Table 9.14. Continued

	Unit 23													
	Layer					Structure 1 Layer			Structure 2 Layer					
Taxon	1	2	3	4	9	1	2	3	1	2	3	4	5	7
Bony Fish (continued)														
Sarda chiliensis chiliensis									1					
Scombridae														
Total Bony Fish														
Unidentified Fish	16						9							
Marine Birds														
Spheniscus humboldti											1			
Diomedea sp.														
Charadrius sp.														
Haematopus sp.														
Larus sp.	17	1					2			1	2			
Larosterna sp.														
Laridae														
Ardeidae										1				
Egretta sp.														
Pelecanus thagus	6										3			
Phalacrocorax bougainvillii	22						2							5
Sula variegata	7						1							
Sula sp.														
Total Marine Birds														
Wetland/Land Birds														
Accipitridae														
Podilymbus podiceps														
Anas sp.							1							
Zenaida auriculata														
Dives warszewiczi														
Total Wetland/Land Birds														
Unidentified Birds	96	6					3	1		1	3		2	1
Mammals														
Phyllostomidae														
Muridae	8						1		3					
Cavia porcellus												10		
Canis familiaris														
Lycalopex sechurae														
Otaria flavescens	53	1				3	8	1		2	1	1		2

	Structure 3	Structure 7					Structure 8									
	Layer	Layer					Layer									
	3	1	2	3	4	6	1	2	3	4	5	6	7	8	9	10
						2							22			
											2					
		1								6		1				
								1		16						
						1			1				1			
											2					
			2							15	3					
		11	1			1		1								

Table 9.14. Continued

| | Unit 23 | | | | | Structure 1 | | | Structure 2 | | | | | |
| | Layer | | | | | Layer | | | Layer | | | | | |
Taxon	1	2	3	4	9	1	2	3	1	2	3	4	5	7
Mammals (continued)														
Balaenidae	7				4									
Delphinus sp.														
Cetacea														
Odocoileus virginianus														
Lama sp.														
Total Mammals														
Unidentified Marine Mammals	27		1		2									1
Unidentified Terrestrial Mammals							3			2				
Unidentified Mammals														
Total Faunal Phase V	2477	20	2	0	6	3	151	128	480	349	89	25	104	220

black rock snails *Tegula atra* at 218 elements and *Prisogaster niger* at 843 elements, and the brown rock snails *Thais haemastoma* at 254 elements and *Thais chocolata* at 295 elements. These numbers suggest either ritual use by a larger group of people or frequent consumption within a relatively short period. The number of elements for the violet crab increase to 70.

The counts for sharks and bony fish for Floor 23 remain moderate, but the number of avian species increases through time: 4 elements from penguins (*Spheniscus humboldti*), 13 from albatrosses (*Diomedea* sp.), 9 from grebes (*Haematopus* sp.), 77 from gulls, 101 from pelicans, 314 from cormorants, 147 from boobies (*Sula variegata*), and 241 from unidentifiable birds. There were 53 elements from sea lions. The penguins, albatrosses, and grebes as well as the sea lions are seasonal and thus relatively rare. This same context had relatively few shark elements, 19 from mullets, but relatively few from other bony fish. The snails and gastropods increase throughout time in Phase II.

Most of these patterns persist throughout Phase III and especially Phase IV, although in lower numbers. The mollusk species continue the pattern described but in elevated quantities, in some layers ascending to hundreds of elements for the species noted. Sharks were rare, with only 3 specimens. Unit 22, Phase IV, contained 27 (table 9.9) individual shark elements. There are a large number of birds and sea lions in Phase IV. In general, there is a trend toward fewer species with lower counts, except for the mollusks.

Floors 10 to 16, which correspond to late Phase III and early Phase IV, had no faunal remains other than modest amounts of highly crushed and unidentifiable shell fragments, which are not shown in the tables. This is the period when crop food production increased significantly at Paredones. This gap in the faunal record in Unit 22, however, is filled by off-mound faunal remains in Unit 20 and Test Pit 26. After Floor 3, the earliest Phase V level, significant changes occur. The mollusk species fluctuate, suggesting moderate consumption. The vertebrates and crustaceans are reduced as well as sharks. Bony fish are

	Unit 23															
Structure 3	Structure 7					Structure 8									
Layer	Layer					Layer									
3	1	2	3	4	6	1	2	3	4	5	6	7	8	9	10
						4									
										2					
	1														
55	1233	161	304	55	73	374	6	337	138	7	24	37	62	24	11

almost absent. Only two or three species of birds are present in modest numbers. Sea lions are more numerous, with 101 specimens in Floor 3 (table 9.15). The final two floors (Floor 1 and Floor 2) revert to patterns seen at the beginning of Phase V in Floor 10, with moderate numbers of elements for mollusks but a full complement of species; moderate numbers of elements for crustaceans and vertebrates, represented in Floor 2 by 29 shark elements from 3 species; 16 elements from mullets and 59 elements from additional bony fish; 107 elements for birds from 5 species; and 28 elements from sea lions. Floor 1 has fewer sea lion specimens but one from a camelid (by this date probably a llama). We believe that many of these reduced figures for marine resources reflect the increased dependence on cultigens at Paredones.

The two major units at Paredones (20 and 22) can be distinguished from the three domestic units excavated north of Huaca Prieta (Units 16, 13, and Pit 26) and from units excavated at Huaca Prieta. Paredones Unit 20 is distinguished from Unit 22 by a series of floors, although the faunal remains suggest that both functioned as areas where relatively large-scale or highly repetitive food preparation and consumption took place. But the mollusk remains at both units are identical in their patterning to those from Huaca Prieta. This suggests that the populations associated with each of these areas shared a similar ideology behind the ritual patterning of the mollusks.

The frequency of shark species, particularly those using the coastal and estuarine waters as nursery areas, suggests exploitation of these habitats. The bony fish are also predominantly estuarine and demersal. Mullets can tolerate brackish water and were probably found in lagoons and wetlands east of the terrace. There is heavy exploitation of the marine birds and sea lions. The albatrosses and penguins are present during the austral spring and summer. Cormorants and boobies are around all year but more plentiful in the spring and summer. Sea lions are highly seasonal and arrive in November and December to give birth and leave when the young are three months old in April.

Table 9.15. Species type and distribution for Phase V (~4107–3455 cal BP) in excavated units at Paredones

| | Pit 26 | | Unit 22 | | | | | | |
| | Layer | | Floor | | | | | Total specimens Phase V | % Total by taxa Phase V |
Taxon	1	2	1	2	3	Totals	% Total by taxa		
Chitons									
Chaetopleura hennahi						0			
Chiton cummingsi						0			
Chiton granosus						0			
Enoplochiton niger						0			
Acanthopleura echinata						0			
Total Chitons						0	0.00	4	0.02
Limpets									
Fissurella peruviana		3	30	8	9	50			
Fissurella maxima	1	47	11	9	29	97			
Fissurella latimarginata			1	1	7	9			
Fissurella limbata	1	1				2			
Fissurella crassa			6		2	8			
Fissurella sp.			2			2			
Total Limpets						168	5.16	548	2.30
Marine Snails/Gastropods									
Collisella orbignyi		2	3		8	13			
Collisella ceciliana						0			
Scurria viridula						0			
Scurria parasitica						0			
Scurria sp.						0			
Diloma nigerrima						0			
Tegula atra	39	53	56	4	22	174			
Tegula euryomphala	3	1	2	1	1	8			
Tegula tridentata	2	4				6			
Prisogaster niger	181	152	72	21	47	473			
Littoridina cummingsi						0			
Nodilittorina peruviana						0			
Cerithium stercusmuscarum					1	1			
Cerithidea mazatlanica						0			
Calyptraea trochiformis		2				2			
Crepipatella dilatata	3	2				5			
Crucibulum spinosum						0			
Sinum cymba		1	3	1	2	7			
Polinices uber	16	26	78	40	181	341			
Polinices cora						0			
Bursa ventricosa						0			
Bursa nana						0			
Xanthochorus buxea	132	57	37	21	36	283			

Table 9.15. Continued

Taxon	Pit 26 Layer		Unit 22 Floor			Totals	% Total by taxa	Total specimens Phase V	% Total by taxa Phase V
	1	2	1	2	3				
Marine Snails/Gastropods (continued)									
Thais haemastoma	62	48	61	36	99	306			
Thais chocolata	43	31	54	26	64	218			
Thais delessertiana			2		6	8			
Thais callaoensis						0			
Crassilabrum crassilabrum	2					2			
Concholepas concholepas						0			
Solenosteira fusiformis					1	1			
Columbella paytensis						0			
Mitrella sp.						0			
Anachis sp.						0			
Nassarius dentifer	242	119	3		3	367			
Prunum curtum						0			
Oliva peruviana						0			
Olivella columellaris						0			
Oliva sp.						0			
Mitra orientalis	14	16	5	7	6	48			
Cancellaria decussata						0			
Cancellaria urceolata	2	3			1	6			
Marinula pepita						0			
Total Marine Snails/Gastropods						2269	69.64	15542	65.16
Freshwater Snails									
Lymnaea sp.						0			
Helisoma peruvianum				1		1			
Helisoma trivolvis						0			
Helisoma sp.						0			
Drepanotrema sp.						0			
Physa venustula						0			
Physa sp.						0			
Total Freshwater Snails						1	0.03	48	0.20
Bivalves									
Anadara sp.						0			
Aulacomya atra		1				1			
Choromytilus chorus	4	9	2	2	2	19			
Perumytilus purpuratus			66		9	75			
Semimytilus algosus	1		2		1	4			
Chama pellucida						0			
Brachidontes sp.						0			
Spondylus princeps						0			
Argopecten circularis						0			

Table 9.15. Continued

Taxon	Pit 26 Layer		Unit 22 Floor			Totals	% Total by taxa	Total specimens Phase V	% Total by taxa Phase V
	1	2	1	2	3				
Bivalves (continued)									
Argopecten purpuratus						0			
Argopecten sp.						0			
Trachycardium procerum					1	1			
Anomia peruviana						0			
Protothaca thaca	6	13	10	4	2	35			
Protothaca zorritensis						0			
Euromalea rufa			2	1	1	4			
Petricola rugosa						0			
Gari solida						0			
Semele corrugata	1	2				3			
Semele solida						0			
Spisula adamsi						0			
Donax obesulus	17	24	6		1	48			
Mesodesma donacium						0			
Pholas chiloensis						0			
Total Bivalves						190	5.83	3135	13.14
Barnacles									
Balanus sp.						0			
Chthamalus sp.						0			
Total Barnacles						0	0.00	0	0.00
Marine Crabs									
Platyxanthus orbignyi	21	17	13	1	29	81			
Platyxanthus cokeri						0			
Cancer porteri						0			
Cancer polyodon				1	5	6			
Paraxanthus barbiger						0			
Cyclozanthops sexdecimdentatus						0			
Hepatus chiliensis						0			
Petrolisthes sp.						0			
Pachycheles sp.						0			
Ocypode gaudichaudii					1	1			
Callinectes arcuatus						0			
Total Marine Crabs						88	2.70	1046	4.39
Freshwater Crabs									
Hypolobocera sp.						0			
Total Freshwater Crabs						0	0.00	1	0.00

Table 9.15. Continued

Taxon	Pit 26 Layer		Unit 22 Floor			Totals	% Total by taxa	Total specimens Phase V	% Total by taxa Phase V
	1	2	1	2	3				
Sea Urchins									
Tetrapygus niger			5			5			
Strongylocentrotus gibbosus						0			
Caenocentrotus gibbosus						0			
Total Sea Urchins						**5**	**0.15**	**287**	**1.20**
Ascidians (Sea Squirts)									
Pyura chiliensis						0			
Total Ascidians						**0**	**0.00**	**0**	**0.00**
Unidentified Crustaceans, etc.						**0**	**0.00**	**0**	**0.00**
Amphibians									
Leptodactylidae						0			
Total Amphibians						**0**	**0.00**	**2**	**0.01**
Sharks and Rays									
Galeorhinus sp.				2	2	4			
Mustelus sp.	1	1				2			
Carcharhinidae						0			
Carcharhinus sp.	17	11	1	25	4	58			
Rhizoprionodon sp.						0			
Sphyrna sp.				2	8	10			
Lamnidae						0			
Alopias vulpinus						0			
Alopias sp.	2					2			
Isurus oxyrinchus						0			
Isusrus sp.					1	1			
Squatina armata						0			
Rajiformes						0			
Urotrygon sp.						0			
Rhinobatos planiceps						0			
Myliobatis sp.	2	1				3			
Total Sharks and Rays						**80**	**2.46**	**1066**	**4.47**
Bony Fish									
Ariidae						0			
Galeichthys peruvianus						0			
Cheilodactylus variegatus						0			
Clupeidae						0			
Engraulis ringens						0			

Table 9.15. Continued

| | Pit 26 | | Unit 22 | | | | | | |
| | Layer | | Floor | | | | | | |
Taxon	1	2	1	2	3	Totals	% Total by taxa	Total specimens Phase V	% Total by taxa Phase V
Bony Fish (continued)									
Ethmidium maculatum						0			
Sardinops sagax-sagax						0			
Mugil cephalus				16		16			
Paralichthys sp.				3		3			
Scartichthys sp.						0			
Labrisomus philippii						0			
Scorpaena sp.						0			
Stellifer minor						0			
Trachurus symmetricus						0			
Trachurus symmetricus murphyi						0			
Seriolella violacea						0			
Centropomus sp.						0			
Paralonchurus peruanus	2	2		11		15			
Cynoscion sp.		1		1		2			
Thunnus albacares?						0			
Sciaena deliciosa				5		5			
Sciaena gilberti						0			
Sciaena starksi					1	1			
Sciaena sp.						0			
Pareques sp.						0			
Hemilutjanus sp.						0			
Larimus sp.						0			
Serranidae						0			
Acanthistius pictus						0			
Paralabrax sp.		1				1			
Pomadasyidae						0			
Micropogonias altipinnis						0			
Menticirrhus sp.						0			
Anisotremus scapularis				11		11			
Merluccius gayi						0			
Merluccius gayi peruanus						0			
Sarda chiliensis						0			
Sarda chiliensis chiliensis				1		1			
Scombridae						0			
Total Bony Fish						55	**1.69**	**859**	**3.60**
Unidentified Fish			2	27	1	30	**0.92**	**192**	**0.80**
Marine Birds									
Spheniscus humboldti						0			
Diomedea sp.					10	10			

Table 9.15. Continued

Taxon	Pit 26 Layer		Unit 22 Floor			Totals	% Total by taxa	Total specimens Phase V	% Total by taxa Phase V
	1	2	1	2	3				
Marine Birds (continued)									
Charadrius sp.						0			
Haematopus sp.				1		1			
Larus sp.				19	2	21			
Larosterna sp.	1					1			
Laridae						0			
Ardeidae						0			
Egretta sp.						0			
Pelecanus thagus				17	4	21			
Phalacrocorax bougainvillii	1	2	6	58	31	98			
Sula variegata				12	10	22			
Sula sp.						0			
Total Marine Birds						174	5.34	456	1.91
Wetland/Land Birds									
Accipitridae						0			
Podilymbus podiceps						0			
Anas sp.						0			
Zenaida auriculata						0			
Dives warszewiczi						0			
Total Wetland/Land Birds						0	0.00	2	0.01
Unidentified Birds		2		37	20	59	1.81	261	1.09
Mammals									
Phyllostomidae		2				2			
Muridae						0			
Cavia porcellus						0			
Canis familiaris						0			
Lycalopex sechurae						0			
Otaria flavescens			4	28	101	133			
Balaenidae					1	1			
Delphinus sp.						0			
Cetacea						0			
Odocoileus virginianus						0			
Lama sp.			1			1			
Total Mammals						137	4.21	331	1.39
Unidentified Marine Mammals						0	0.00	37	0.16
Unidentified Terrestrial Mammals			2			2	0.06	15	0.06
Unidentified Mammals						0	0.00	19	0.08
Total Faunal Phase V	819	657	548	461	773	3258		23851	

OFF-MOUND DOMESTIC UNITS 13, 16, AND TEST PIT 26

UNIT 13

Very few faunal remains were recovered from Unit 13, so they are not fully reported in the tables. Because the unit is a domestic context, however, the data are mentioned briefly. Unit 13 revealed three floors from Phases IV–V, which were contemporaneous with Unit 16. Faunal remains consist of sharks and bony fish, a few birds, and unidentifiable mammals. The faunal collection primarily contains vertebrates, although shell is present. Primarily bony fish and secondarily sharks make up the most important categories. All hammerheads are pelagic as adults but probably approach the coast and give birth in coastal and estuarine waters; some were juveniles or subadults. The bony fish were also important. They are divided into large pelagic fish, such as Chilean jack mackerel or bonito, which are brought into coastal waters by heavy seas and even cast up on the beach, or the Peruvian sea catfish, which is a demersal fish found along the coast, and the smaller drums and croakers, living over sandy bottoms near the shore. Of the large pelagic fish, mackerel, bonito, hake, and catfish are present. Smaller fish of the sandy bottoms near the coast are more frequent. The Peruvian banded croaker and sciaenids were present in nearly every stratigraphic unit. The Peruvian grunt, a fish of the rocky reefs, also was present. In short, this fishery concentrated on locally available species. There also are a few bird specimens, which occur together early in the sequence.

TEST PIT 26

Test Pit 26, Phase V, also is a domestic unit. It has a full complement of fauna: mollusks, crustaceans (crabs), and vertebrates. Occasional limpets are present; in one context 47 elements were recovered. The opposition of *Tegula* spp./*Prisogaster niger* is present, expressed by elements of each species. *Polinices uber* also is present. Elements of the brown snail triad, *Xanthochorus buxea*/*Thais haemastoma*/*Thais chocolata*, were recovered in modest amounts. The opposition *Nassarius dentifer*/*Mitra orientalis*, expressed in the element count, also is present in all layers. The mussel/clam opposition appears with elements from 3 mussel species (*Aulacomya atra*, *Choromytilus chorus*, and *Semimytilus algosus*). *Choromytilus chorus*, the giant mussel, is present in all layers. Clams are represented by *Protothaca thaca* in all layers as well as by *Semele corrugata* in two layers. Elements of the tiny clam *Donax obesulus* are present in modest quantities. Elements of the violet stone crab are found in all layers. Of the 35 shark elements from 4 species, 28 are *Carcharhinus* sp. Bony fish are almost absent except for a few specimens of *Paralonchurus peruanus* and 1 specimen of *Cynoscion* sp. Specimens of only 4 birds (a tern and 3 cormorants) were found.

UNIT 16

When the numbers were removed from consideration, the profile of the fauna from domestic Unit 16 varied, although the basic patterns remained. In the late Holocene subphase of Phase I the complementary oppositions expressed by several mollusk species are present, but several are incomplete. Limpets are present in all Phase I layers. The *Tegula*/*Prisogaster niger* opposition is present. *Polinices uber*, representing snails of the sandy bottoms, is present in Phase I. All 3 members of the brown snail triad occur in all layers; *Xanthochorus buxea* is present in one layer. The mussel/clam opposition, usually *Choromytilus chorus*/*Protothaca thaca*, lacks clam species in two layers but shows both in the third. The violet stone crab *Platyxanthus orbigny* is present where there are crustaceans. The vertebrates include large numbers of shark elements, particularly *Carcharhinus* sp., with 34 and 23 specimens, respectively, for the early and late subphases of Phase I (table 9.3). The complementary opposition *Paralonchurus* sp./sciaenids (drums) is expressed with limited numbers of elements. Birds are modestly more abundant, except for one instance of 26 cormorant elements. Large-scale or highly repetitive food preparation within a short period is suggested by 18 sea lions in layers with vertebrates.

Phase II data come from four layers. The mollusks show the same patterns described above, with no clam elements in opposition to the mussels in two layers. Modest numbers of elements from several crab species are found. The frequency of vertebrates suggests moderate-scale food preparation. Sharks are prominent. The hound shark and the requiem shark are present but in varying numbers through time (table 9.4). Mullets are present in these layers, with elements numbering from 8 to 11. *Paralonchurus peruanus* is found, with from 17 to 56 elements. Sciaenid elements appear in modest numbers. Elements from several species of birds are found in larger numbers, varying between 8 and 20. Each context provides 1 or 2 elements from sea lions, but one context also has 10 dolphin specimens and another has 1 dolphin specimen. A single white-tailed deer element was found.

Phase III has three layers. Two are complete and include mussels. The previously discussed oppositions are expressed, with high counts (close to 100 elements); 2 clam species complete the opposition with the mussels. The vertebrate fauna, present in all layers, varies greatly in the number of elements for sharks, birds, and mammals. Two layers probably represent food preparation for large numbers of people, while the other three offer modest element counts. For Unit 16, *Galeorhinus* sp. is represented by 7 elements in Layer 6, 78 in Layer 7, and 39 in Layer 8. The Carcharhinidae provided 3 elements in Layer 6, 18 in Layer 7, and 23 in Layer 8. *Carcharhinus* sp. is represented by 34 elements in Layer 6, 330 in Layer 7, and 129 in Layer 8. *Sphyrna* sp. has 5 elements in Layer 6, 99 in Layer 7, and 7 in Layer 8. The bony fish are found in modest numbers. Bird counts include mainly the cormorants, with 3 in Layer 6, 69 in Layer 7, and 83 in Layer 8. The counts for unidentifiable bird remains are high: 64 in Layer 7 and 92 in Layer 8. One context yielded 24 sea lion elements.

Phase IV has two identified layers. The numbers for snails and gastropods are high while the number of mollusks is low. No crustaceans were found. The vertebrates are represented by a moderately high number of elements (52) (table 9.8). The categories are all represented, but with few species and low counts. The established patterns for species distribution persist in Phase V, with modest to moderate counts.

OFF-MOUND TO INITIAL MOUND AREAS AT HUACA PRIETA: UNITS 2, 9, AND 12

UNIT 2

Material from all five phases was recovered from Unit 2, but quantities varied. In Phase I the only fauna represented were 43 elements of shark from 4 different species (tables 9.2 and 9.3), 1 specimen of snail, 2 elements of anchovy, 3 unidentified fish elements, and 3 specimens of cormorant. Phase II has twelve stratigraphic layers, all sublayers in Layer 7. The oldest remains are found in Layer 7c-7 (table 9.4). For black snails, *Tegula atra* is represented by 314 elements and *Prisogaster niger* by 330 elements. Three species of *Tegula* sp. (*Tegula atra*, *Tegula euryomphala*, and *Tegula tridentata*) are present. *T. atra* has thousands of elements and *T. tridentata* has hundreds in the layers of this phase. *Crepipatella dilatata* is present in a single element. *Polinices uber* and *Bursa ventricosa* (from sandy bottoms) are sometimes present. The triad of brown snails from the rocky reefs has greater numbers, represented by *Xanthochorus buxea* with 67 elements, *Thais haemastoma* with 73, and *Thais chocolata* with 80 elements. The opposition *Nassarius dentifer*/*Mitra orientalis* is represented by 29 and 69 elements, respectively, along with 40 specimens of the giant mussel (*Choromytilus chorus*) and 16 of the smaller *Semimytilus algosus*. These species express the opposition between rock-dwelling mussels and clams of the sandy bottoms. The clams are represented by 70 elements from *Protothaca thaca*, 1 from *Euromalea rufa*, 6 from *Semele solida*, and 2 from the clam *Donax obesulus*.

These pairings appear to represent complementary relationships between different habitats of origin. While each is not limited to a single species, *Choromylus chorus* and *Protothaca thaca* are the most frequent and constant. The trend over time is a gradual increase in quantities, eventually reaching several hundred in the later layers (table 9.4); the black snails peak at over a thousand specimens. The complementary opposition of *Nassarius dentifer*/*Mitra orientalis* is counted in each layer by tens of elements, not hundreds. These shells appear in different layers as caches, in middens, and as small piles of offerings. While the snails were consumed, it appears that regularities are associated with shells in rituals. After

Layer 7C-3 the numbers decline until Layer 7B, when there is a major increase. Of the black rock snails, *Tegula atra* reaches 1352 specimens and *Prisogaster niger* 721. *Nassarius dentifer* and *Mitra orientalis* remain below 100 individuals each. The following Layer 7A marks an increase in species exploitation. The count for *Tegula atra* is 5256 specimens (with an additional 1280 for *Diloma nigerrima*) and for *Prisogaster niger* 1806. The count for *Polinices uber* is 297. The brown snails also show counts 2.5 times greater than in the preceding phase, with *Xanthochorus buxea* at 1806, *Thais haemastoma* at 3128, and *Thais chocolata* at 910. *Nassarius dentifer* increases to 578, although *Mitra orientalis* remains at 96. The numbers of species for mussels and clams also increase. *Choromytilus chorus* is represented by 567 elements and *Perumytilus purpuratus* by 170, but *Semimytilus algosus* provides 2082. The pattern among clams is similar. *Protothaca thaca* has 624 specimens; *Euromalea rufa* has 84; four minor clam species have counts between 14 and 30; and the tiny clam *Donax obesulus* has 178,881. It is not known whether these higher counts for some species are associated with increased food consumption during ritual, commensal feasting, or simply mound construction, also possibly associated with either or both of the other two activities.

Consumption is also indicated by an increase in the presence of species that are not common. Layer 7A contains 314 specimens of chitons distributed over 5 species (table 9.4). Crab counts increase from 113 in Layer 7B to 5295 in Layer 7A. *Cancer polyodon* and *Petrolisthes* sp. are present in much smaller quantities. The numbers of black sea urchins were first modest then moderate until Layer 7B, when the count for *Tetrapygus niger* rose to 654, and to 8148 in Layer 7A, the period roughly corresponding with initial mound building. A second echinoderm species was also found, *Caenocentrotus gibbosus*. Its counts rose from 88 in Layer 7B to 1190 in Layer 7A, most of which are fragmented exoskeletons associated with thousands of burned spines. Sea urchins are edible, but apparently were not eaten.

Sharks are present but not in large numbers. Layer 7B contained 4 specimens of the school shark; 8 of the hound sharks; 24 of the requiem sharks; 9 of the white sharks; and 2 species of rays,

with a total count of 4 elements. The count for Peruvian sea catfish was 204 specimens in Layer 7A but only 11 in Layer 7. A number of other species appear with numbers ranging from 12 to 59. Exceptions are the Peruvian hake with 139 and sardines with 152. This emphasis on bony fish implies the technology of nets, floats, hooks and lines, and also watercraft. The counts of seabirds are modest. There are few sea lion elements except for one earlier context, Layer 7C. The counts for dolphin are also modest and suggest occasional beached animals.

Significant changes occurred in Phase III, with less intense use. Identifiable mollusks are absent throughout the phase, except for the earliest stage. This suggests that the practice of obtaining and preparing the shells of gastropods and bivalves, presumably for ritual or feasting purposes, did not occur in Unit 2 during Phase III. Rather, it appears that the principal activity was food preparation. Layers 5 and 6, the earliest context in Phase III, are the exception and continue the patterns of activities described for Phase II. The count for crustaceans is high, with 138 violet stone crabs together with a few *Cancer porteri* and *Cancer polyodon*. The number of black sea urchin elements is high at 718. The vertebrate counts for sharks, bony fish, and marine birds are modest. No mammalian remains were found.

Vertebrate counts vary for Phase III. Sharks contribute only a few specimens. In contrast to Phase II, bony fish are less prominent. A few species, such as the Peruvian sea catfish, occur in low numbers. Others, like anchovies and sardines, are present but fluctuate from modest to moderate numbers. The Peruvian banded croaker also is found in modest to moderate numbers in all but one layer. Drums (Sciaenidae) appear in small numbers in both layers. *Sciaena deliciosa* is found in all but two layers. In general, a few species of fish are present in low numbers and not consistently. Important also is the slight increase in use of seabirds, particularly pelicans, cormorants, and boobies. Layer 5 has 5 sea lion elements.

Phase IV at Unit 2 is represented by two layers. The mollusk counts generally reflect the patterns described for Phase II. Counts are modest to moderate. Of interest is the appearance of freshwater snails in both Layers 4 and 3. Layer 4 contained a specimen of *Physa venustula* and 16 *Helisoma peruvianum*. It is probable that these were not deliberately collected but arrived on the stems of reeds, which had been harvested in the wetlands and brought to the mound for processing. Crustaceans are represented by modest numbers of violet stone crab elements.

The marine vertebrate counts for the earlier Layer 4 are high: 23 requiem sharks, 20 sea catfish, 253 anchovies. But the rest of the bony fish have low counts, although 43 specimens could not be identified. The avian fauna is limited to 1 cormorant in Layer 3 and *Sula variegata*. Layer 4 contained 2 sea lions and 4 unidentified mammals, but only 1 sea lion was found in Layer 3.

Unit 2 in Phase V also has two layers. The mollusk components have modest to moderate counts, similar to those from Phase IV, with the same patterning seen since Phase II. Layer 1 had 2 freshwater snail species, each represented by 1 individual. Each layer contains modest numbers of violet stone crabs. Vertebrate remains are absent in Layer 1 and represented by 3 small bony fish in Layer 2. It appears that the area of Unit 2 was used by a smaller group of people and probably intermittently in both Phases IV and V, as the principal activities were moved to the top and upper slopes of the mound.

UNIT 9

This unit lies just to the northeast of Unit 2 and was near the southeastern edge of Huaca Prieta. Excavations extended into the late Pleistocene levels, but most of the faunal remains were too fractured for our initial study (Dillehay et al. 2012b). A reanalysis of the early Phase I remains from this unit, which had sporadic occupation, found a few specimens of limpets, snails, bivalves, birds, sharks, sea lions, and marine crabs. Late subphase Phase I has elements of 18 limpets, 16 snails, 2 bivalves, 4 sharks, and 2 birds (table 9.3).

Neither mollusks nor crustaceans are registered in Phase II. In the earliest level the fauna consists of a few specimens of sharks, marine crabs, and birds. Phase III contains marine crabs, sea urchins, birds, bony fish, rodents, and a shark. No faunal remains were recovered from levels representing Phases IV and V. The emphasis on sharks and marine mammals in Unit 9 is reminiscent of patterns seen in Phase II at Unit 20 in Paredones, although the mullet is lacking in Unit 9.

UNIT 12

Unit 12 lies low on the southern slope of Huaca Prieta. It was occupied only during Phase V. The specimen remains are 20 marine crabs, 11 sea urchins, 12 sharks, 2 bony fish, and 4 birds (table 9.12).

RITUAL AND BURIAL AREAS ON THE SUMMIT OF HUACA PRIETA: UNITS 10, 19/23, AND 15/21

UNIT 10

Unit 10 is located on the southeastern side on the middle upper slope of the mound. Excavation revealed that the area was laid out on a staircase-like series of narrow terraces or platforms. Excavations followed this layout by means of a series of extensions. We excavated funerary structures. The faunal remains were primarily molluscan and followed the pattern described above. In the earlier layers (Layers 2–3, Structure 2), the molluscan assemblage has a broad distribution, although the quantities are moderate and normally fewer than 100 (tables 9.8 and 9.11). Occasionally a species of snail or a bivalve has a count larger than 100.

Crustaceans are usually present, with numbers for the violet stone crab fluctuating between 10 and 21 elements. The echinoderm *Tetrapygus niger* has counts of 5 and 9 elements (table 9.11). Occasional tomb caches with sea urchin specimens were found. As noted earlier, the regular presence of this species in a ritual context suggests that it had a symbolic significance.

Vertebrates, primarily sharks and bony fish, are present in the earlier layers but not in the later ones. The sharks are common. The bony fish are demersal species: croakers, drums, and the sciaenids. In later layers vertebrates are absent and the mollusks are restricted in species and numbers. The scale of activities in all layers is suggestive of small groups of people carrying out recurring ritual and burial acts.

UNIT 15/21

This unit contains the sunken circular plaza on the eastern side of Huaca Prieta. Unit 15 reached the deeper Pleistocene to early Holocene layers of the terrace; its numbers include a restudy of all faunal remains, including earlier counts (Dillehay et al. 2012b). In the late Pleistocene levels, there were 13 limpet fragments, 3 deer elements, 3 bird bones (seagull and cormorant), 8 shark bones (mainly *Carcharhinus* sp.), 9 fragments of spider crab, 3 deer bones, and 2 sea lion bones.

Unit 21 was excavated in the circular depression and had small stone-lined structures without secondary burials. Excavations in the tiers rising above the bottom of the plaza toward the summit of the mound indicate that this was also an area of small-scale ritual. The faunal remains are similar to those from Unit 10 but differ in several respects. The limpets, snails, gastropods, and bivalve remains are moderate in number and breadth of species. The relationships noted many times continue here. But the numbers exceed 100 only in 2 or 3 species. Thousands of burned sea urchin spines are present but no exoskeletons.

Vertebrates present include sharks, a few bony fish, and occasionally birds and rodents. Sharks are represented principally by 3 species. The bony fish are absent or represented by few individuals. Significant is the absence of mullets, whose nearby habitat may have largely disappeared with the eutrophication of the wetlands (see chapter 5), although they would have been available in the estuary and lower course of the river. The birds are principally pelicans and cormorants in small numbers.

One terrestrial mammal of interest from Layer 1, Unit 21, is a Peruvian desert fox or sechuran fox (*Lycalopex [Pseudalopex] sechurae*: table 9.13). Colonial documentation attests to the sacrality of this fox in the period after the arrival of the Spanish (Agustinos 1918). Today it continues to be incorporated into folk healing by the shamans of the north coast. Its presence in a ceremonial context is not surprising.

A relatively large area of the sunken circular plaza is represented by Unit 21. Surprisingly, relatively small numbers of faunal remains and species were present in this area, suggesting less food consumption and perhaps fewer ritual offerings.

UNIT 19/23

Units 19 and 23 are part of the same unit located on the summit of the Huaca Prieta mound, north of the plaza. The unit contained a series of structures and floors, all dated to Phase V. The faunal collection is similar to that from Units 10 and 15/21 but with some significant differences. The mollusk specimens are shown in distribution and number, following the patterns described earlier. The numbers are moderate, rarely approaching 100 or more. When they reach higher than 100 (such as in Layer 1, Structure 1), they represent small piles of ritual offerings. The patterns are present in a complex imbrication of structures, floors, and fills, which suggests that repeated events (such as rituals and feasting) took place within this area. The mollusks represent only part of the well-known patterns in some instances and are absent in others. This may suggest that the rituals requiring the shells did not take place in those layers. The crustaceans are present in most layers, almost invariably represented by the violet stone crab. A freshwater crab found in Andean rivers was present in one instance.

The principal vertebrate specimens recovered are sharks and marine mammals. Bony fish are present in small numbers. Large numbers of the Peruvian banded croaker occur in a few instances. Another bony fish, the yellowfin tuna, is found in several late layers. The principal shark represented is *Carcharhinus* sp., with 369 elements in Layer 1 in Unit 23 (table 9.14), a chamber tomb without a human skeleton. Sea lions are also numerous, especially in Layer 1, Structure 1.

Exotic vertebrate animals occur in two instances. The first is a pair of amphibians, identified only to family (Leptodactylidae), from Layer 2 of Structure 1 (table 9.14). The other is a group of 10 guinea pigs (*Cavia porcellus*) from Structure 2, Layer 5. This is one of the three instances where domesticated guinea pigs were incorporated into the fauna of locations on the summit or upper terraces of the mound in the last phase. Only a few vertebrate specimens were reported from this context: 1 requiem shark, 2 Peruvian banded croakers, the common *Paralonchurus peruanus*, and 2 unidentifiable birds. One final comment concerns whale remains in Unit 19/23, which are not shown in the table but were observed in the walls of several architectural units. These whale vertebrae were probably scavenged and brought to the mound skeletonized. Hence they would not have been a source of food but were used for some other purpose.

NUMBER OF SPECIMENS OF KEY SPECIES AT HUACA PRIETA AND PAREDONES

Long-term fluctuations in frequency of fauna may be the result of variations in the environment, changes in habitat, changing or specializing economies, or differences in their availability or accessibility. While consistent patterns extend through several phases at Huaca Prieta and Paredones, other patterns emerge and then diminish or disappear.

The molluscan fauna, primarily gastropods but also bivalves, appears to function as a signifier. Habitat may be a factor, at least as an explanation for the consistent grouping of certain species. In like fashion, the bivalves appear to be divided between rock-dwelling species of mussels and several species of clams living in sandy substrates. In the case of bivalves, large quantities may indicate consumption in feasts, whether one large-scale event or a palimpsest of repetitive small-scale events, but they occur so consistently in small quantities that they appear to be functioning as symbolic signifiers as well. The same may be said of certain snails, when these appear frequently in large numbers.

TETRAPYGUS NIGER (SEA URCHIN)

The echinoderm *Tetrapygus niger* (and to a lesser degree and episodically two other sea urchin species: *Strogylocentrotus gibbosus* and *Caenocentrotus gibbosus*) illustrates the patterning expressed above. While sea urchins are edible and are eaten today in Chile and elsewhere, there is little evidence that the population at Huaca Prieta consumed them. Today people on the north coast of Peru do not eat sea urchins. But the totals for all units in Phase II, when the mound at Huaca Prieta was first built, are different: 9256 elements for *Tetrapygus niger* and 1287 for *Caenocentrotus gibbosus*. Most of these numbers are represented by

exoskeletal fragments associated with the early habitational levels of Unit 2, suggesting that they were likely consumed. By the final Phase II levels, when this area of the site was associated with initial mound building rather than with habitation, the counts had fallen to 74 specimens of *Tetrapygus niger* and only 4 for *Caenocentrotus gibbosus* (table 9.4).

In Phase III *Tetrapygus niger* comes from Units 2 and 9. A more regular pattern of pulsating frequencies is observed. There are no echinoderms in Unit 2 in the later phases at the site. Phase IV includes 10 specimens of sea urchin (*Tetrapygus niger*) in Floor 8, Burial 7, in Unit 3 (table 9.8). This suggests an ideological or symbolic significance for sea urchins, because burials are usually the result of ritually significant acts.

Sea urchins again become extremely abundant in Phase V, especially in Units 5, 6, and 7, which are dispersed spatially along the upper northeastern portion of Huaca Prieta where the footpaths are on the entry ramp on the northeast side of the site. The recurring patterns of certain element counts suggest repetitive human activities, probably of a ritual nature. Most sea urchin fragments are exoskeletons and are found in the domestic Unit 16, indicating that they were used as a food source there.

Again, it should be noted that these counts for sea urchins are based on the presence of exoskeletons, not burned and unburned spines. Due to the large presence of burned spines throughout the site of Huaca Prieta after Phase II, it was impossible to count all of them: they are present in the millions. Furthermore, many of them are heavily fragmented, making this task even more improbable. The ubiquitous presence of burned sea urchin spines after Phase II is primarily associated with the construction of the plaster layers that prevent site erosion and with ritual events, including piles of burned sea urchin spines in and around occupied and empty tombs (see chapter 7).

Finally, the dominant species for the entire faunal collection is the small bivalve *Donax obesulus*, with more than 200,000 specimens. However, given the small amount of meat yielded by this organism, we consider its contribution over time to be roughly equivalent to 4–5 large sea lions.

NUMBER OF SPECIMENS OF KEY VERTEBRATE SPECIES

The hypothesized contrastive opposition between several species of bony fish (such as *Paralonchurus peruanus* and the sciaenid species *Sciaena deliciosa, Sciaena gilberti, Sciaena starksi,* and *Cynoscion* sp.) has been noted. In like fashion, there seems to be a contrastive opposition between bony fish of the rocky reefs such as *Anisotremus scapularis, Scartichthys* sp., and *Labrisomus philippii* and those of the sandy and muddy bottoms. Among the bony fish are the sharks, two large species of bony fish, the marine birds, and both marine and terrestrial mammals.

SHARKS AND RAYS

Ethnographic accounts from the Chicama coast indicate that sharks have been common when the coastal wetlands were more extensive, entering the brackish lagoons on the surge of unusually high tides (Dillehay, field notes, 2008).

Two shark species, *Galeorhinus* sp. and *Carcharhinus* sp., were identified in the late Pleistocene collection, indicating that they were present in the coastal waters. *Galeorhinus* sp. appears infrequently at Huaca Prieta and Paredones. *Carcharhinus* sp. is much more frequent in all phases. The total number of school sharks in Phase IV is less than half the number from Phase III. Larger numbers of these shark specimens come from domestic Unit 16.

Beginning in Phase II, the pattern of exploitation is for the largest numbers of fauna to be found at off-mound locations (Paredones and Unit 16). The same pattern continues through Phase IV, with the only change being a shift to the summit of the Huaca Prieta mound in Unit 25. In Phase V the count from Paredones is present in low to moderate specimens but remains high at Unit 16 and in the units at the mound summit.

Of the requiem sharks (Carcharhinidae, *Carcharhinus* sp.), 7 came from the late Pleistocene layers and 138 from the early Holocene portion of Phase I (tables 9.2 and 9.3). The total number of requiem sharks nearly doubles in Phase II to 200 and almost triples in Phase III to 539 (tables 9.4 to 9.7). In Phase IV the total drops significantly

to 59. Phase V had a total count of 534 specimens (tables 9.10 to 9.15).

Hammerhead sharks (*Sphyrna* sp.) are persistently present, although not as abundant as the requiem sharks. None were found in the late Pleistocene layers. In the early Holocene layers 33 specimens were recovered. In Phase II 9 were found. In Phase II at Paredones 84 more elements were recovered. For Phase III at Huaca Prieta, the total is 111 hammerheads. For Paredones the total is 23 specimens. In Phase IV the total at both sites drops to less than 10 specimens. Phase V also yielded few specimens at all sites.

Eagle rays (*Myliobatis* sp.) are consistently present in small numbers from the early Holocene to Phase V. *Myliobatis* is benthic and found close to the seabed. None were reported for the late Pleistocene. Only 1 specimen was found in Phase I in domestic Unit 16 and 3 in Unit 22. A total of 52 eagle rays came from Phase II, primarily in Unit 2 at Huaca Prieta. The total of *Myliobatis* specimens in Phase III was 22. In Phase IV the total was still smaller: only 3 at Paredones. In Phase V 3 were recovered from Test Pit 26 (table 9.15).

FISH

No mullet (*Mugil cephalus*) are reported for the late Pleistocene layers. In late Phase I 3 specimens were found in Unit 16 and 9 in Unit 22, for a total of 12 individuals during this phase. In Phase II the total is 206 specimens, mostly at Paredones. The Phase III total is 206 specimens, at Paredones. In Phase IV all mullets come from Paredones. The total for Phase IV is 32 specimens. In Phase V a notable reduction in frequency for mullets was observed (tables 9.10–9.15).

The strong association of mullets with the two units at Paredones reinforces the idea that they were fished from the nearby wetland lagoon. This is also evident in the few specimens from Unit 2, which was located in a similar situation close to the lagoon. The decline in the frequency of mullets at Huaca Prieta and Paredones in Phase V is probably due to the reduction in size of the lagoon, and perhaps its eutrophication, as the raised fields to the east were extended (see chapters 5 and 7).

No Peruvian sea catfish (*Galeichthys peruvia-*

nus) were reported from the late Pleistocene layers or from the premound layers in Phase I. In Phase II the total is 235 at Huaca Prieta. This suggests a concerted effort at procurement over time. In Phase III the number is much smaller: 4 from Unit 2. In Phase IV 20 were recovered from Unit 2. In Phase V all the sea catfish come from Huaca Prieta and from the summit and upper slopes of the mound.

While mullets are reduced in Phase V layers at Huaca Prieta and Paredones, the frequency of sea catfish increases in units on the summit of Huaca Prieta but not at Paredones, where they were not recovered. Given the eutrophication of the lagoon in this phase, it would seem that the catfish were obtained from the sea, probably at the mouth of the river.

MARINE BIRDS

At Huaca Prieta 2 specimens of albatross (*Diomedea* sp.) were found in late Phase I layers. In Phase II a total of 4 specimens was recovered at Huaca Prieta and 55 at Paredones. Only 4 specimens were reported in Phase III, both from Unit 22 in Paredones. In Phase IV 2 specimens were found at Paredones. A total of 10 albatross specimens was recovered for Phase V, all from Floor 3 in Unit 22 at Paredones. This again underlines the sporadic nature of the presence of this large bird in the Chicama region and the specificity of the interest in obtaining it.

No Peruvian brown pelicans (*Pelecanus thagus*) were reported from the late Pleistocene layers, but they were recovered from the early Holocene, with 7 specimens from Unit 16 and 16 from Unit 22. This total increased to 21 for Huaca Prieta and 233 for Paredones. In Phase III the total recovered was 17 specimens for Huaca Prieta and 44 for Paredones. In Phase IV 45 were found. The total is 21 in Phase V. The higher numbers at Paredones reflect the habitat of these birds in the nearby wetlands.

Late Pleistocene layers yielded 4 specimens of the cormorant (*Phalacrocorax bougainvillii*). The total for the early Holocene is 127. In Phase II the total is 49 at Huaca Prieta and 899 at Paredones. The number of birds taken increased and decreased in Phase III, where the total is 156 at Huaca Prieta

and 426 at Paredones. Fewer specimens are present in Phase IV, with 8 at Huaca Prieta and 167 at Paredones. In Phase V the total is 32 at Huaca Prieta and 98 in Unit 22 at Paredones.

Seagulls (*Larus* sp.) are present from late Pleistocene levels, where 4 were reported. For the early Holocene, a total of 40 specimens was recovered in Unit 16 and in Unit 22 at Paredones. At Huaca Prieta 14 were reported in Phase II and 20 in Unit 20 and 270 in Unit 22 at Paredones. In Phase III the total numbers increase to 185 at both sites. The total during Phase IV is 61 at both sites. In Phase V the numbers diminish to 21.

Paredones yielded 1 plover (*Charadrius* sp.) in Phase II and 55 in Phase III. The total is smaller in Phase IV.

LARGE TERRESTRIAL MAMMALS

The largest terrestrial mammals for Huaca Prieta are white tailed deer (*Odocoileus virginianus*) and wild guanacos or domesticated llamas (*Lama* sp.). At Huaca Prieta and Paredones sharks, marine birds, and marine mammals were the principal sources of meat.

The presence of 3 specimens of deer from the same late Pleistocene context in Unit 15 indicates that early hunter/foragers were utilizing both terrestrial and marine resources. In addition, 1 deer specimen came from Unit 16 in Phase II. At Huaca Prieta 2 deer elements were recovered from Unit 6 in Phase V.

The case of the camelids is different. Although we know that the wild camelid, the guanaco, was present on the north coast from late Pleistocene times (Lemon and Churcher 1961), it does not appear in the limited Pleistocene levels available to us. The camelid specimens from Phase II were recovered at Paredones (1 from Layer 10, Unit 20, and 1 from Floor 22, Unit 22). At Paredones 1 element was recovered from Floor 17, Unit 22, in Phase III. Layer 2 at Unit 20 in Phase IV yielded 4 specimens. These could be llamas. Huaca Prieta weavers incorporated camelid fiber into their textiles at an early stage (see chapter 12), and their potential as beasts of burden should not be overlooked. These animals may have been brought in with loads and then kept and consumed. Finally, 1 element came from Floor 1, Unit 22, and 3 from

Floor 2, Unit 6, in Phase V. These specimens are surely from llamas.

MARINE MAMMALS

The abundance and ease of capture of sea lions (*Otaria flavescens*) are evident in the late Pleistocene to early Holocene levels. In all, 11 were reported for early Phase I. A total of 40 was recovered from late Phase I. In Phase II there are 499 specimens, mainly at Paredones. In Phase III the totals are 44 for Huaca Prieta and 264 for Paredones. In Phase IV the numbers are 19 for Huaca Prieta and 142 for Paredones. Phase V yielded 87 for Huaca Prieta and 133 for Paredones. Despite the presence of Huaca Prieta and the domestic Unit 16 near the beach, the majority of the sea lion remains are at Paredones, which probably reflects its primary function as a food production and preparation site.

Guinea pigs (*Cavia porcellus*) were a rarity, with a total of 25 as follows: 15 came from Unit 16, to the north of the Huaca Prieta mound, and 10 came from Unit 23.

SPECIES OF RELIGIOUS SIGNIFICANCE: *SPONDYLUS* SP. AND *LYCALOPEX SECHURAE*

Two species are significant because they were associated with religious practice elsewhere in the Andean region. Both were found in units on or near the summit of the Huaca Prieta mound. The first is a valve of *Spondylus princeps*, the thorny oyster that came from an empty tomb in Unit 10, Phase V. This *Spondylus* valve is undoubtedly one of the earliest if not the earliest reported for Peru. It is a testimony for either direct contact or down-the-line trade with the northern coast of the Gulf of Guayaquil or the western Pacific coast of Ecuador.

The other remains of possible religious significance are those of a specimen of the Sechuran fox, *Lycalopex sechurae*, which was found in Unit 21. Today local Peruvian shamans use preserved specimens or body parts to summon "good spirits" in their rituals. Some healers use the fat of this animal to treat illness (Asa et al. 2008).

Two other exotic species appear in the context of offerings. *Anadara* sp. is a cockle found in mangroves with muddy substrates. The Huaca Prieta specimen was found in Extension 16 of Unit 21 and dates to Phase V. The nearest mangroves in Peru are east of Talara on the southern coast of the Gulf of Guayaquil (Mollier-Vogel et al. 2013). The other exotic species is the scallop *Argopecten* sp. In all, 9 specimens were recovered at Huaca Prieta. Of these 6 were found in Phase II contexts (2 *Argopecten circularis*, 2 *Argopecten purpuratus*, and 2 *Argopecten* sp.): 5 from Unit 2, Layers 7A (3) and 7C2 (2) and 1 from Unit 22, Floor 22. The other specimens were from Phase V: 1 *A. circularis* from fill in Unit 10, 1 *A. purpuratus* from Unit 23, Layer 2, and 1 *Argopecten* sp. from Structure 7 in Unit 23. All except the specimen from Unit 10 were found in offering contexts. The waters off the Chicama coast are too cool for scallops, which are found today along the southern coast of the Gulf of Guayaquil. It would appear that there was contact with that area in Phase II and again in Phase V.

COMPARISONS OF PRECERAMIC FAUNAL ASSEMBLAGES FROM OTHER NORTH ANDEAN SITES

Relatively few sites in northern Peru from the Preceramic period yielded excavated faunal collections, and none of them have the quantity of faunal remains found at Huaca Prieta and Paredones. All excavation units discussed are much smaller and less complex. More importantly, small excavation units were opened at these sites, so the question of sampling bias and the validity of comparing the types and numbers of species from each site and unit must be kept in mind. Furthermore, the majority of the contexts discussed below are associated with domestic activity rather than with ritual or mortuary activities, thus rendering their comparison to Huaca Prieta and Paredones less useful. Nonetheless, it is worth considering the species present at these sites and their general frequency. Only three sites that appear to share the same biota are considered here, including Padre Abán and Alto Salaverry on the coast of the Moche Valley, although the samples from these sites are very limited. The third site is the Preceramic occupation at Puémape on the southern coast of the Jequetepeque Valley.

PADRE ABÁN

The Moche Valley is immediately south of the Chicama Valley, and the two sites considered here have similar marine and terrestrial environments. The seabed of both is a mosaic of rocky outcrops interspersed with sandy bottoms, which gave access to the fauna of both the rocky reefs and the sandy substrates. The Padre Abán site lies north of the Moche River and north of the beach settlement of Huanchaquito. It is on the north side of a dune and consists of a stratified midden ~1.4 m deep spread over an area of 100 m². A 1 m² sample was excavated in the midden, which is a very limited sample. No structures were observed at Padre Abán, which was considered a fishing settlement with recurrent occupation. Fragments of cotton nets and cord were found but no twined textiles (S. Pozorski 1976: 17–20). Both faunal and plant remains were recovered. The fauna came from both rocky reef and sandy bottom habitats. The mollusks included chitons, gastropods, and bivalves, including clams from sandy bottoms: *Protothaca thaca, Eurhomalea rufa, Mesodesma donacium, Gari solida, Semele corrugata, Tagelus dombeii,* the razor clam, and *Donax obesulus.* By NISP and MNI *Protothaca thaca, Eurhomalea rufa,* and *Donax obseulus* (a small surf clam), were the most numerous (S. Pozorski 1976: 311–312). Mussels, found on rocky substrates, contributed a larger percentage of meat to the diet. Most came from the giant mussel, *Choromytilus chorus,* with small quantities from the much smaller *Semimytilus algosus.*

The marine snails are of more interest. Only a single keyhole limpet (*Fissurella* sp.) was found, but *Tegula atra* and *Turbo niger* (synonym for *Prisogaster niger*) were recovered in numbers similar to those from Huaca Prieta. Other snails like *Crepidula dilatata, Thais chocolata,* and *Thais delessertiana* are also found at Huaca Prieta, although *Thais haemastoma* is far more common at Huaca Prieta and *T. delessertiana* is low in frequency at the site. One snail present in quantity at Padre Abán is *Olivella columelaris*; it is rare at Huaca Prieta. Two other snails common at Huaca Prieta but represented by few specimens at Padre Abán are *Polinices* sp. and *Polinices cora.* At Huaca Prieta *Polinices uber* is common, but *Polinices cora* is rare. Two other snails from sandy substrates found at Padre Abán are *Mitra orientalis* and *Nassarius gayi.* A different species, *Nassarius dentifer,* is common at Huaca Prieta. Of interest among the crustaceans are the high number of barnacles (*Balanus tintinnabulum,* synonym for *Megabalanus tintinnabulum*) and the significant number of purple stone crabs (*Platyxanthus orbignyi*). Barnacles were absent from Huaca Prieta, but the purple stone crabs were common throughout the sequence.

Sharks, bony fish, birds, and mammals represent the vertebrate fauna at Padre Abán. *Mustelus* sp. (hound shark) and *Myliobatis peruvianus* (eagle ray) are both present at Huaca Prieta, although not the most numerous of the chondrichthyes. The sciaenid fish common at Huaca Prieta are present at Padre Abán; 2 mullets (*Mugil cephalus*) were also recovered. Birds are represented by pelicans.

It is clear that fauna from both rocky and sandy substrates were exploited. Among the mollusks the mussels are on rocky substrates, the clams on sandy bottoms; the marine snails are divided between species dwelling on rocks and those living on sandy bottoms. Of the bony fish, the sciaenids and mullets are found over soft bottoms, while others are found over rocky reefs. Shelia Pozorski (1976: 72) suggests that these bottom-dwelling coastal fish were taken with a haul seine net from the littoral.

The marine birds and mammals suggest exploitation in rookeries, but the numbers do not indicate specialization in these higher vertebrates. The high numbers of the barnacles and marine snails suggest intensive gathering. The range of fauna at Padre Abán also suggests general rather than specialized exploitation, except perhaps in the case of *Tegula* sp. and the barnacles.

ALTO SALAVERRY

This large late Preceramic site has several distinct areas of habitation refuse and several structures of a public nature. Evidence indicates the presence of more cultigens and an apparently greater dependence on horticulture. The faunal remains are in general similar to those from Padre Abán, but with changes in frequency. While both rocky and soft bottom habitats are present at Alto Salaverry, there are differences. Rather than being a mosaic bottom with rocky outcrops surrounded by a sandy seabed, Alto Salaverry has a major rocky hill (*morro*), with its corresponding underwater reefs. The sea floor is sandy. The inhabitants of Alto Salaverry appear to have preferred the rock-dwelling species and evidently traveled a longer distance to obtain them. The sandy beach was much closer. The technological gear for casting drag seine nets from shore was still in evidence, but relatively few species from this habitat were recovered. Pozorski (1976) states that dense habitation refuse midden was sampled as well as an area outside the wall of a public structure. Neither the size of the tests nor the depth of the midden is indicated in either case, and the fauna recovered from each context is not designated separately.

The mussels are the more important bivalve. The clams are greatly reduced in number despite the relative ease in getting them. The gastropods show higher frequencies. Thus the keyhole limpets and the rock-dwelling snails predominate. Crustaceans are well represented with the purple stone crab and a large number of barnacles. The chondrichthyes are represented by species found close inshore. The bony fish are from the same habitat and include the sciaenids and mullet. These fish live over sandy bottoms and were probably taken by nets from the shore. Thus, both rocky and soft bottom habitats were exploited. No birds and only a single sea lion were reported, which suggests that the marine birds and mammals were not intensively hunted.

Of the fish, chondrichthyes are represented by *Mustelus* sp. (hound shark: 1); *Rhinobatos planiceps* (guitarfish: 1), and *Myliobatis peruvianus* (eagle ray: 10). The bony fish include two sciaenids, *Paralonchurus peruanus* (2) and *Sciaena deliciosa* (21), along with *Sarda chilensis* (a large pelagic fish sometimes caught near shore: 1) and *Mugil cephalus* (mullet: 1). No birds were found. Only one individual was reported for sea lion. Neither Alto Salaverry nor Padre Abán shows a consistent pattern beyond habitat preference. The variation between Huaca Prieta and the two Moche Valley sites seems to be opportunistic. The relative paucity of shark species may be because neither site had access to extensive wetlands, where these animals would have been easier to take.

PUÉMAPE

The Preceramic occupation at Puémape, a rocky promontory and bay south of the mouth of the Pacasmayo River, is on the southern margin of

the Jequetepeque Valley (Elera 1998). Puémape lies just to the south of the now dry mouth of the Cupisnique River, which drained the highland area between the Jequetepeque and Chicama Valleys.

The faunal material recovered from the limited excavations in the Preceramic or Early Puémape levels at Puémape by Carlos Elera were cold-water species of the Peruvian Province corresponding to *Choromytilus chorus* (giant mussel) and the brown rock snails (*Thais haemastoma* and *T. chocolata*). The principal species from sandy bottoms were *Polinices uber* (white snail) and the clam *Mesodesma donacium* (Elera 1998: 196). The entire fauna found in the Early Puémape context and subsequent later contexts was, with one exception, found at Huaca Prieta, but this did not extend to the variety found there. Snails predominated, and the only other bivalves were *Semimytilus algosus*, a mussel, and *Donax obesulus*, a clam. Deposits of blocks of mineralized polychaete tubes, the "pumice stone" of local fishers, found together with dried seaweed, were apparently used as fodder for llamas, as they were also found in their dung, attesting to other similarities to Huaca Prieta (Elera 1998: 90). It is unfortunate that these early levels were not dated and that the excavations were of necessity so limited. The predominance of snails in the early levels is of interest, however, as is an apparent effort to balance mollusks from sandy and rocky habitats. It is noteworthy that the location of the site lies on the boundary between a rocky bottom seabed to the south and a sandy seabed to the north.

DISCUSSION

The faunal collections from Huaca Prieta and Paredones are large, diverse, and reasonably well preserved. They provide new insights into more than fourteen millennia of a human presence on the littoral of the lower Chicama Valley. Our approach to understanding this assemblage was to define the principal habitats in the environmental zones within the vicinity of the Sangamon terrace on which most of the sites were located. The sea is the most complex and least understood of these environments. We identified the principal marine biotopes, beginning with the basic dichotomy of hard substrates, whether rock outcrops or reefs, and soft substrates, both sandy and muddy bottoms. The rocky substrates create currents and eddies that bring nutrients to the organisms living on them. The increased nutrient load in their immediate vicinity also sustains species of fish adapted to this enhanced environment. The nutrients over the sandy substrates support fauna that bury themselves in the soft bottom, like clams and even fish such as flounders. Other demersal species feed just above the bottom. Some species of seaweeds are found on rocks, while others affix themselves to sand or shell beds in sand. In both cases the algae themselves create microhabitats.

This division contains the Supralittoral, the beach above all but the highest tides; the tidal zone between the highest and lowest tides; the Subtidal Zone lying below the lowest tide; and the Neritic Zone or open sea with a depth of up to 200 m. Within the water column some organisms are demersal, living just over the seabed, while others are found near the surface; others inhabit the middle reaches of the column.

The beaches, both rocky and sandy above the shoreline, were the locations for the rookeries of the millions of marine birds that fed on the fish found in the cold waters of the Peru Current. In the middle Holocene these birds nested and reared their young on the littoral as well as on islands in the sea. They were probably easily taken with simple weapons or bare hands because of the density of their populations. The same can be said for the sea lions, although they were seasonally available. These animals, which are awkward and slow on land, were easily taken by clubbing and provided a large return.

Other environments included the estuary of the Chicama River, which consists of the waters at the mouth of the river over a muddy bottom with reduced salinity. A number of related demersal fish species (drums and croakers) appeared in this environment. Also prominent were several species of pelagic sharks that gave birth to their young in protected bays and estuaries, leaving them to grow on the abundant resources of the coastal waters. Other fish species such as mullet and catfish were also found in this environment. As these estuarine-adapted fish entered the lower course of the river, they could be driven upstream into shallower water and taken by foragers by clubbing.

Connected to the river by overflow channels was another important area: the wetlands. These marshes had some open water, fed principally by groundwater. These wetlands also received seawater, and with it marine species of fish, during periods of unusually high surf. The brackish waters supported young sharks and mullet as well as other fish, in addition to important plant resources such as various reeds. The wetlands also provided a habitat for a number of bird species: plovers, grebes, ducks, and pelicans. This was a confined area in which taking both fish and fowl was relatively easy.

The dry forest environment of the inland valley supported both white-tailed deer and possibly guanacos in the earlier period of occupation. These animals may have been hunted by people living inland who exchanged and contributed to the food resources at Huaca Prieta. Their numbers are relatively small, but sufficient to remind us that these animals were available as well from the dry forest biomes inland from the littoral, along with a number of plant resources.

It is apparent that the sessile fauna (the bivalves) and other more mobile mollusks such as snails as well as sea urchins and chitons were heavily exploited. Most of these animals can be obtained near the shore from rocky or sandy substrates. After the earliest occupations in the late Pleistocene and early Holocene, a pattern can be observed in the faunal remains. A context that had bivalves and snails on rocky substrates would also have bivalves and snails on sandy substrates. Marine snails were taken and eaten, but not always in the quantities needed for subsistence. The shells of snails and bivalves also appear to have functioned ritually as symbols in patterns or as burial offerings, which showed considerable consistency over time. Thus the pattern of contrast between easily gathered snails and bivalves and the more mobile sharks and fish can be added to the basic dichotomy of hard or rocky substrate and soft or sandy substrate. Here too, however, it is evident that the mobility of sharks and fish in the back channels of the estuary and the brackish wetlands of the littoral was restricted to the point that they could be taken in confined areas by simple technologies. As time passed, attention shifted to demersal fishes such as mullets and the sciaenids as well as the Peruvian sea catfish, all of which could be found close to shore and near the seabed. It is probable that the use of hand-held nets made pursuit of these species possible.

We know that the food remains at Huaca Prieta were derived from marine and wetland foraging and limited fishing, with gardening of primarily gourds, squash, cotton, and chile peppers. The faunal material from Phase IV at Huaca Prieta comes from Units 2, 3, HP-3, 13, and 25 and Unit 16 (table 9.8). It showed a dependency on marine birds and sea lions, thus differing notably from the material seen at Paredones. The economy of Paredones was dependent on agriculture, with close exploitation of the wetlands for sharks and mullets and of the beaches for birds and sea lions, all probably related to food preparation. Bony fish from the sea are largely absent, and molluscan fauna seem limited to what was needed for patterned ritual, feasting, and mound construction and may have been exchanged rather than obtained directly. The faunal resources represented by sea lions (and to a lesser extent deer and camelids) together with marine birds and gulls provided a larger proportion of consumed meat. It would appear that much of the fauna recovered at Paredones was associated with food preparation, as are the plant remains. This is suggested by the stone tool technology and the types of activity areas at Paredones, including the absence of domestic features on the mound (see chapters 7 and 12). Huaca Prieta and domestic units such as Units 13 and 16 and Test Pit 26 are more complex. As foragers, the inhabitants overcame technological limitations by means of an acute understanding of the different marine species and their habitats as well as recurring natural phenomena such as strong tides, which offered unusual opportunities.

It was possible to segregate a number of excavation units on the basis of the type and frequency of faunal species over time into four groups that persisted through two or more of the phases. The most obvious are the two units at Paredones, some 600 m from Huaca Prieta itself. Initially Unit 20 was an area of domestic activity at the edge of the wetland lagoon on the eastern edge of the Sangamon terrace at the foot of Unit 22. After Phase II it became a trash area for the mound at Paredones and was associated with some food preparation activity. Unit 22 was placed in the summit of this mound. The faunal remains distin-

guish these two units from others. Patterning in the type and origin but not the abundance of the molluscan fauna is similar to that found at Huaca Prieta. At Unit 22 it is clear that moderately large quantities of mollusks were assembled, presumably for ritual and feasting activities but also possibly to prepare food for mound construction at Huaca Prieta. The principal vertebrates are sharks, mullets, marine birds, and sea lions. The smaller bony fish are largely absent. This suggests specialization in the procurement of sharks and mullets found in the nearby wetland lagoons and of the marine birds and mammals found in colonies along the littoral and in the wetlands. The second group consists of three units on the terrace to the immediate north of the Huaca Prieta mound. As opposed to Huaca Prieta and Paredones, domestic Units 13 and 16 and Test Pit 26 are defined by house structures, hearths, small storage pits, and moderately thick midden layers, among other features (see chapter 7). Unit 16 was a domestic complex, extending back to late Phase I. The molluscan fauna displayed the patterning that has been described. Sharks dominate the larger vertebrates, followed by sea lions. The bony fish, however, are also frequent throughout. Marine birds are present in constant numbers. In Phase III large quantities of food were prepared. Unit 26 to the northeast of Unit 16 has similar faunal remains. Unit 13 to the north of Unit 16 on the western side of the Pleistocene terrace was part of a fishing village, notable for the number of bony fish in the remains. The molluscan fauna is limited but follows the patterning that we have described. Marine birds and sea lions are absent from this faunal record.

The units at Huaca Prieta are service, ritual, and perhaps feasting and mortuary areas. One group of service units includes Units 2, 9, and 12. The first two lie at the northeastern foot of the mound in areas that were used before the mound was built. The fauna is notable for the large number of sharks processed here. Bony fish are also numerous, and marine birds are present. Also found in quantity are invertebrates and mollusks. Echinoderms are extremely numerous in Phase II at Unit 2, when the mound was under initial construction. Mollusks are present in large quantities for repeated ritual events and consumption. Marine birds and mammals are present in moderate amounts. Unit 9, with a long stratigraphic record, follows much the same pattern. Unit 12 (a little higher on the southern slope of the mound and later) shows a similar faunal record, with the emphasis on sharks, bony fish, and moderate amounts of marine birds and mammals. All of these areas are service areas, probably for preparing food for others. The summit and upper slopes of the mound were used for ritual or feasting. In this regard the faunal remains may be the result of ritual offerings. They are more diverse and in some cases exotic. The patterning of the mollusks is present, sometimes in abbreviated form.

Over time the frequency of particular types and species of fauna varied. In Phase V, for example, mullets disappear from the faunal remains at Paredones and also in Units 2 and 9. This appears to be the result of the eutrophication of the wetlands and consequent reduction of habitat for these fish. They were replaced in some cases by catfish, a demersal species found in the estuary. The echinoderms also have a period of high frequency in Phase II but never disappear and continue to be present in all other levels.

In general, the exploitation of the littoral, estuary, and wetlands by the populations at Huaca Prieta and Paredones suggests a particular kind of economic specialization, probably involving different segments of the littoral populations in ways similar to what was documented at Bandurria by Alejandro Chu Barrera (2011). These environments were so abundant in resources that adequate amounts could be obtained by simple means without elaborate technology: simple gathering of sandy bottom shellfish, for example, with digging stick and basket. This was apparently common at several Preceramic marine sites. The exploitation of the rocky substrates, however, required more specialization. It is clear that giant mussels and brown snails could be obtained from the Subtidal Zone only by diving. Sharks, which provided much of the protein, were probably taken in the estuary and wetlands rather than at sea. We are not sure how the demersal grunts and croakers and mullets from the estuarine zone were captured, but it seems clear from the heterogeneity of the other bony fish species that there was not a dedicated fishery directed toward those species. As the artisanal fishers of the present day have pointed out, beached fish after a high surf can be gathered up in impressive quantities, and this may have

been done. Other bony fish, including mullets, were found in the wetlands, where their mobility was limited by the shallow water and vegetation. The marine birds and the sea lions could be taken in their densely populated colonies, where the birds were immobilized by their nesting strategy and the sea lions were slow and awkward on land. Larger marine mammals such as dolphins or small whales occasionally beach themselves and die. In the case of dolphins, it would appear that humans took advantage of these relatively rare events to obtain meat, oil, and probably hides. The frequencies of dolphins in the faunal registers at Huaca Prieta and Paredones suggest this.

All of this exploitation is relatively low technology in terms of implements, nets, and weapons. We await hard evidence for the use of watercraft or fishhooks and line in the exploitation of marine resources, although Preceramic societies at other contemporary north Peruvian marine sites seem to have had one or the other of these technological advances. It may be that the evidence from Huaca Prieta and Paredones is yet to be found or is still cryptic. What is clear is that the technology considered to be essential to the successful exploitation of the marine environment does not appear so essential at Huaca Prieta and Paredones, perhaps because of the particular juxtaposition of resources in their vicinity and because of the particular resources that the population chose to exploit. This is perhaps the nature of their exceptional achievement. These populations were undoubtedly successful in terms of sustaining themselves, increasing their population, and developing moderate levels of social and economic complexity.

The most innovative and significant aspect shown by this close examination of the faunal remains from Huaca Prieta and Puémape, however, is the incorporation of certain species into the ritual and ideological structure as representatives of particular biotopes and probably as signs of abundance. Thus the *Tegula atra/Prisogaster niger* opposition and the *Xanthochorus buxea/Thais haemastoma* dyad are probably neither accidental nor random. It is easier for us to divine the opposition between mussels from a rock substrate and clams from a sandy one, even though other species can substitute for the *Choromytilus chorus/Protothaca thaca* opposition. We are left with the realization that the inhabitants of Huaca Prieta and Pare-dones not only used their rich faunal resources for sustenance but also infused them with meaning and incorporated them into their ideological constructs.

CONCLUSION

Two points should be made about this long and complex faunal study. The first has to do with the richness of the biotopes present in the marine environment and the density of the birds and mammals that it sustained along with the human population. Not every place along the Pacific coast of Peru is equally rich in resources. But the San-gamon terrace location provided access to fish and sharks in the nearshore environment, in the wet-lands, and in the estuary channels. Storm surges frequently would deposit fish on the beach or in wetland pools. Birds could have been taken by netting or clubbing in their rookeries. Sea lions served as the cattle of this economy: easily taken, present in large numbers, and highly productive. The only drawback was the departure of females and old males during four or five months, but the young males stayed behind. This was a maritime foraging economy where the shellfish and many of the fish, sharks, birds, and mammals could easily be captured with simple technology. The innovation came with the full adoption of cultivation by one segment of this society, thus creating a specialized dual economy.

The second point has to do with the social use of the fauna as symbols. Human populations are diverse in their choice of symbols and the media used to express them. The population of Huaca Prieta and Paredones had two parts: farmers, possible part-time wetland fishers, and hunters of the beach and littoral (some of whom became full time farmers) and part-time fishers, specialized shellfishers, marine hunters, and foragers unified as one social group sharing one ontology and religious practice in the form of ritual and the accouterments of ceremonial practice. The long Andean practice of creating social unity by uniting two

disparate parts can be recognized in play at Huaca Prieta. This is a principle for ordering the world found in many contexts. What is unusual is the medium in which it is expressed there. The patterning that we have recognized in the molluscan fauna is seen in the frequencies and species distribution of the faunal remains, most of which were deposited in ritual contexts over four millennia. The consistency of expression makes it possible to recognize the principle at play with a moderately high degree of confidence. At the same time, our effort to identify the faunal resources and their habitats available to the peoples of Huaca Prieta made it possible to recognize a part of the symbolic language being used. We do not know just why *Tegula atra* and *Prisogaster niger* were chosen to represent two parts of a whole, but it is clear that they do. It is easier to see that mussels living at depth on rocks contrast with clams living nearer the surface in the sandy seabed. They contrast in color as well: mussels are dark, while clams are light. (This color contrast also is evident in the deposition of light salt crystals and dark charcoal at Huaca Prieta: see chapter 15.) While the mussel *Choromytilus chorus* and the clam *Protothaca thaca* are the most common exemplars, it is clear that any variety of mussels could stand in for *C. chorus* and a variety of clams could accompany or substitute for *P. thaca*. We assume that these mollusk shells are tokens, which represent a relation. It clearly was an important principle, since we find it expressed repeatedly with different species. It is also clear that this expression of duality is very ancient: how ancient is unknown, but certainly premound and dating before the beginning of the first floors in Unit 22 in the early Holocene (late Phase I). Also significant, but only at Huaca Prieta, were hundreds of thousands of sea urchin spines, mainly burned, which were piled into offerings at times and were used in fills and in the composition of the thick plaster coverings at the site. The fauna and their contrasting habitats have led us to a recognition of basic principles for ordering the world that were no doubt applied in the social sphere and others.

CHAPTER 10

PLANT REMAINS

Duccio Bonavia, Víctor F. Vásquez,
Teresa Rosales Tham, Tom D.
Dillehay, Patricia J. Netherly, and
Kristin Benson

INTRODUCTION

The goal of the macrobotanical study was to
determine the biological and cultural importance
of plant residues recovered by the Huaca Prieta
project. Collection procedures were oriented
toward both extensive and intensive sampling. All
flotation and macrobotanical remains recovered
directly during excavations were analyzed (see
chapter 3). A total volume of 128.2 m³ of cultural
sediments was collected from 934 proveniences.
About 35.4 m³ of this volume were obtained from
floors, use surfaces, and features. The remaining
volume was from burial and miscellaneous contexts. Both heavy and light fractions from flotation were studied. The macrobotanical studies are
complemented by analyses of the macroremains
of maize (see appendix 5) and chile peppers (see
appendix 4) and by microremain studies of phytoliths, starch grains, and pollen (see appendices 7, 9,
and 12, respectively).

Excavations at Huaca Prieta and Paredones
recovered both wild and domesticated plants.
Almost all macrobotanical remains were retrieved
either directly or primarily by flotation. Selected
soil samples from all floors and use surfaces (10%
of each) and features (100%) were floated. Some
macrosamples were collected directly from
exposed floors, features, and so forth. Samples for
microscopic analysis of charcoal, phytoliths, starch
grains, and pollen were taken and sent to specialists (see appendices 1, 6, 9, and 13). Table 10.1
presents a list of all plant species for each cultural
phase for each site. Tables 10.2 to 10.24 present
the distribution of plant remains for all excavation
units. Table 10.25 shows the number of plant parts
per 1 m³ excavated at the sites.

The numbers used in this analysis are combined totals from the macrobotanical, flotation,

Table 10.1. List of all plant species by cultural phase for Huaca Prieta, Paredones, and domestic site Unit 16

Phase I: ~14,530–7571 cal BP

Huaca Prieta	U-13/U-16/TP-26	Paredones
Araceae/Arecaceae	*Phaseolus lunatus* (Beans)	*Capsicum* sp. (Chile Pepper)
Cucurbita sp. (Gourd)	*Prosopis* sp. (Algarrobo)	*Gynerium sagittatum* (*Caña Brava*)
Equisetum sp. (Horsetail)	*Tessaria intergrifolia* (*Palo Bobo*)	
Persea sp. (Avocado)		
Phaseolus lunatus (Beans)		
Salix humboldtiana (*Sauce*)		
Schinus molle (*Molle del Perú*)		
Tessaria integrifolia (*Palo Bobo*)		

Phase II: ~7571–6538 cal BP

Huaca Prieta	U-13/U-16/TP-26	Paredones
Acacia sp. (Cactus)	*Acacia* sp. (Cactus)	*Amaranthus* sp. (Amaranth)
Araceae/Arecaceae	*Cucurbita moschata* (Gourd)	*Buddleja* sp.(Butterfly Bush)
Buddleja sp. (Butterfly Bush)	*Gynerium saggitatum* (*Caña Brava*)	*Capsicum* sp. (Chile Pepper)
Chenopodium sp.(Quinoa)	*Lagenaria siceraria* (Gourd, Mate)	*Cucurbita* sp. (Squash)
Cyperus sp. (Juncus)		*Equisetum* sp. (Horsetail)
Equisetum sp. (Horsetail)		*Gynerium sagittatum* (*Caña Brava*)
Gossypium barbadense (Cotton)		
Panicum sp. (Gramalote)		
Poaceae		

Phase III: ~6538–5308 cal BP

Huaca Prieta	U-13/U-16/TP-26	Paredones
Acacia sp. (Cactus)	*Acacia* sp. (Cactus)	*Capsicum* sp. (Chile Pepper)
Cyperus sp. (Juncus)	*Cucurbita moschata* (Gourd)	*Equisetum* sp. (Horsetail)
Equisetum sp. (Horsetail)	*Gynerium sagittatum* (*Caña Brava*)	*Gigartina chamissoi* (Seaweed)
Gossypium barbadense (Cotton)	*Lagenaria siceraria* (Gourd, Mate)	*Gossypium barbadense* (Cotton)
Gynerium sagittatum (*Caña Brava*)		*Gymnogongrus furcellatus* (Seaweed)
Lagenaria siceraria (Gourd)		*Gynerium sagittatum* (*Caña Brava*)
Panicum sp. (Gramalote)		*Lagenaria siceraria* (Gourd, Mate)
Parkinsonia sp. (*Azote de Cristo*)		*Parkinsonia* sp. (*Azote de Cristo*)
Persea sp. (Avocado)		*Persea* sp. (Avocado)
Phaseolus lunatus (Beans)		*Phaseolus* sp. (Beans)
Pouteria lucuma (Lucuma)		*Phragmites australis* (Carricillo)
Prosopis sp. (Algarrobo)		*Pouteria lucuma* (Lucuma)
Salix humboldtiana (*Sauce*)		*Salix humboldtiana* (*Sauce*)
		Solanum cf. *nigrum* (*Hierba Mora*)
		Typha angustifolia (Enea)
		Zea mays (Maize)

Table 10.1. Continued

Phase IV: ~5308–4107 cal BP		
Huaca Prieta	U-13/U-16/TP-26	Paredones
Acacia sp. (Cactus)	*Acacia* sp. (Cactus)	*Acacia* sp. (Cactus)
Araceae/Arecaceae	*Cucurbita moschata* (Gourd)	*Amaranthus* sp. (Amaranth)
Arachis hypogaea (Peanut)	*Gynerium sagittatum* (*Caña Brava*)	*Annona* sp. (Chirimoya)
Canna indica (Achira)	*Lagenaria siceraria* (Gourd, Mate)	*Canna indica* (Achira)
Capparis angulata (Sapote)		*Capparis angulata* (Sapote)
Capsicum sp. (Chile Pepper)		*Capsicum* sp. (Chile Pepper)
Chenopodium sp. (Quinoa)		*Chaetomorpha* sp. (Piso)
Cucurbita moschata (Gourd)		*Cucurbita moschata* (Loche)
Cyperus sp. (Juncus)		*Cyperus* sp. (Juncus)
Equisetum sp. (Horsetail)		*Eleocharis* sp. (Velita)
Fourcroya sp. (Cabuya)		*Fourcroya* sp. (Cabuya)
Gossypium barbadense (Cotton)		*Gossypium barbadense* (Cotton)
Ipomoea batatas (Camote)		*Guadua* sp. (*Caña de Guayaquil*)
Lagenaria siceraria (Gourd, Mate)		*Gymnogongrus furcellatus* (Seaweed)
Panicum sp. (Gramalote)		*Gynerium sagittatum* (*Caña Brava*)
Persea sp. (Avocado)		*Lagenaria siceraria* (Gourd, Mate)
Phaseolus lunatus (Beans)		*Phaseolus lunatus* (Beans)
Phragmites australis (Carricillo)		Poaceae
Poaceae (Various grasses)		*Prosopis* sp. (Algarrobo)
Psidium guajava (Guayaba)		*Psidium guajava* (Guayaba)
Ruppia maritima (Ditchgrass)		*Ruppia maritima* (Ditchgrass)
Salix humboldtiana (*Sauce*)		*Schoenoplectus californicus* (Totora)
Schinus molle (*Molle del Perú*)		*Tessaria integrifolia* (*Palo Bobo*)
Schoenoplectus californicus (Totora)		*Typha angustifolia* (Enca)
Scirpus sp. (Juncus)		*Zea mays* (Maize)
Tessaria integrifolia (*Palo Bobo*)		
Trifolium (*Trébol*)		
Typha angustifolia (Enea)		
Zea mays (Maize)		

Phase V: ~4107–3455 cal BP		
Huaca Prieta	U-13/U-16/TP-26	Paredones
Acacia sp. (Cactus)	*Bunchosia armeniaca* (Wild Plums)	*Acacia* sp. (Cactus)
Araceae/Arecaceae	*Capparis angulata* (Sapote)	*Annona* sp. (Pawpaw)
Buddleja sp. (Butterfly Bush)	*Capsicum* sp. (Chile Pepper)	*Buddleja* sp.(Butterfly Bush)
Bunchosia armeniaca (Wild Plums)	*Cucurbita* sp. (Gourd)	*Canavalia maritima* (Beans)
Capparis angulata (Sapote)	*Equisetum* sp. (Horsetail)	*Capparis angulata* (Sapote)
Capsicum sp. (Chile Pepper)	*Gossypium barbadense* (Cotton)	*Capsicum* sp. (Chile Pepper)
Chloris sp. (Fingergrass)	*Lagenaria siceraria* (Gourd, Mate)	*Cucurbita* sp. (Gourd)
Commelina sp. (Dayflower)	*Nicotiana* sp. (Tobacco)	*Cucurbita moschata* (Gourd, Squash)
Cucurbita sp. (Zapallo)	*Phragmites australis* (Carricillo)	*Cyperus* sp. (Juncus)
Cucurbita moschata (Squash)	Poaceae	*Equisetum* sp. (Horsetail)
Cyperus sp. (Juncus)	*Pouteria lucuma* (Lucuma)	*Gynerium sagittatum* (*Caña Brava*)
Desmodium sp. (Tick-trefoil)	*Prosopis* sp. (Algarrobo)	*Inga feuillei* (Pacay)

Table 10.1. Continued

	Phase V: ~4107–3455 cal BP	
Huaca Prieta	*U-13/U-16/TP-26*	*Paredones*
Eleocharis sp. (Velita)	*Psidium guajava* (Guayaba)	*Lagenaria siceraria* (Gourd, Mate)
Equisetum sp. (Horsetail)	*Scirpus* sp. (Juncus)	*Parkinsonia* sp. (*Azote de Cristo*)
Erythroxilum coca (Coca)	*Tessaria integrifolia* (*Palo Bobo*)	*Phaseolus* sp. (Beans)
Fourcroya sp. (Cabuya)	*Typha angustifolia* (Enea)	*Phaseolus lunatus* (Beans)
Gossypium barbadense (Cotton)	*Zea mays* (Maize)	*Phragmites australis* (*Caña*)
Guadua sp. (*Caña de Guayaquil*)		*Pouteria lucuma* (Lucuma)
Gynerium sagittatum (*Caña Brava*)		*Prosopis* sp. (Algarrobo)
Lagenaria siceraria (Gourd, Mate)		*Psidium guajava* (Guayaba)
Panicum sp. (Gramalote)		*Scirpus* sp. (Juncus)
Parkinsonia sp. (*Azote de Cristo*)		*Tessaria integrifolia* (*Pájaro Bobo*)
Paspalum sp. (Various grasses)		*Typha angustifolia* (Enea)
Persea americana (Avocado)		*Zea mays* (Maize)
Phaseolus sp. (Beans)		
Phaseolus lunatus (Beans)		
Phaseolus vulgaris (Beans)		
Phragmites australis (Carricillo)		
Poaceae		
Pouteria lucuma (Lucuma)		
Prosopis sp. (Algarrobo)		
Psidium guajava (Guayaba)		
Ruppia marítima (Ditchgrass)		
Salix humboldtiana (*Sauce*)		
Schinus molle (*Molle del Perú*)		
Schoenoplectus californicus (Totora)		
Scirpus sp. (Juncus)		
Solanum sp. (Nightshade)		
Solanum cf. *nigrum* (*Hierba Mora*)		
Tessaria integrifolia (*Pájaro Bobo*)		
Trifolium (*Trébol*)		
Typha angustifolia (Enea)		
Zea mays (Maize)		

and anthracology studies. Due to the variation in collection methods, sample sizes varied and numbers are potentially affected by differences in fragmentation, preservation, and sampling bias (see the discussion in chapter 9 on sampling biases and interpretative meaning given to the type, quantity, and volume of faunal remains; most of that discussion also is applicable here). We also estimate that approximately only 50% of the total macrobotanical collection is represented here, especially from Paredones, because thousands of crushed and trampled plant remains other than fragments of reed matting were observed but are unidentifiable. This chapter is a survey of all identifiable botanical materials recovered by our project. Reference is made to other Preceramic sites on the north and central coast of Peru where certain species or varieties of species are found, but these lists are by no means exhaustive.

Chile peppers and maize are not covered extensively here because they are studied in appendices 4 and 5 and have been published previously (Chiou et al. 2014; Grobman et al. 2012). The most familiar common name of each plant is given

Table 10.2. Distribution of plants in Phase I (~14,530–7571 cal BP) for Units 16 and 22

Taxon		DS-Unit 16			Unit 22				
	Layer 11	Layer 13	Total Unit 16	% each species in Unit 16	Premound Level 7	Total Unit 22	% each species in Unit 22	Total Phase I	% each species in Phase I
Acacia sp.			0			0		0	
Amaranthus sp.			0			0		0	
Annona muricata			0			0		0	
Arachis hypogaea			0			0		0	
Bunchosia armeniaca			0			0		0	
Canavalia maritima			0			0		0	
Canna edulis			0			0		0	
Capparis sp.			0			0		0	
Capparis angulata			0			0		0	
Capsicum sp.			0		4	4	36.36	4	25.00
Chaetomorpha sp.			0			0		0	
Chenopodium sp.			0			0		0	
Chloris sp.			0			0		0	
Commelina sp.			0			0		0	
Cucurbita sp.			0		3	3	27.27	3	18.75
Cucurbita moschata			0			0		0	
Cyperus sp.			0			0		0	
Desmodium sp.			0			0		0	
Eleocharis sp.			0			0		0	
Equisetum sp.			0			0		0	
Erythroxylum coca			0			0		0	
Fourcroya sp.			0			0		0	
Gigartina chamissoi			0			0		0	
Gossypium barbadense			0			0		0	
Guadua sp.			0			0		0	
Gynerium sagittatum			0			0		0	
Lagenaria siceraria			0			0		0	
Manihot esculenta			0			0		0	
Nicotiana sp.			0			0		0	
Panicum sp.			0			0		0	
Paspalum sp.			0			0		0	
Persea sp.			0			0		0	
Persea americana		1	1	20.00		0		1	6.25
Phaseolus sp.			0			0		0	
Phaseolus lunatus	1		1	20.00	4	4	36.36	5	31.25
Phaseolus vulgaris			0			0		0	
Phragmites australis			0			0		0	
Poaceae			0			0		0	
Pouteria lucuma			0			0		0	
Prosopis sp.			0			0		0	

Table 10.2. Continued

Taxon		DS-Unit 16				Unit 22			
	Layer 11	Layer 13	Total Unit 16	% each species in Unit 16	Premound Level 7	Total Unit 22	% each species in Unit 22	Total Phase I	% each species in Phase I
Psidium sp.			0			0		0	
Psidium guajava			0			0		0	
Ruppia maritima			0			0		0	
Schoenoplectus californicus			0			0		0	
Scirpus sp. (*Juncus*)			0			0		0	
Solanum sp.			0			0		0	
Solanum cf. *nigrum*			0			0		0	
Tessaria integrifolia	3		3	60.00		0		3	18.75
Trifolium sp.			0			0		0	
Typha angustifolia			0			0		0	
Zea mays			0			0		0	
Total			5			11		16	
% of each phase of total remains								0.26	
% of each unit of total remains in phase			31.25			68.75		100.00	

HP = Huaca Prieta; P = Paredones; DS = Domestic Site.

in the headings. All excavated contexts are drawn from detailed reports on the archaeobotanical remains by Vásquez Sánchez and Rosales Tham (2008, 2010).

It is difficult to assess the botanical studies from Bird's excavations at Huaca Prieta. Although his major report was published in 1985, others also were produced (for example, Bird 1948a, 1948b, 1952). Not all of his excavated materials were studied and published, however.

Finally, it is important to note that tables 10.2–10.24, which present most of the quantitative data for the floral remains from all excavated sites, rely almost exclusively on the information from intact layers and the intact floors, use surfaces, and features within them. The quantitative data from the fills between layers are not always included in the table counts or mentioned in the text below. (The sedimentation associated with fills is culturally, not naturally, produced and is explained by deliberate human deposition for the purpose of leveling and filling a surface in order to build another floor or use surface on it.) Although the fills are stratigraphically intact, unlike the layers and their floors and features, they potentially contain mixed material from unknown contexts such as off-mound or nearby mound middens or other deposits that probably date earlier than the layer or floor laid above them. Therefore the floral type and count for a specific fill may pertain to one particular event, a series of temporally contiguous and related events, or many events over a long period. It is impossible to determine how many events and how much time are represented by the remains in fills. Despite this problem, however, we have observed that the content, type, and patterning of faunal remains in fills are similar to those in the intact layers and floors above and below them, indicating that fill material is generally contemporaneous with these layers.

Table 10.3. Distribution of plants in Phase II (~7571–6538 cal BP) for Units 2 and 16

| Taxon | HP-Unit 2 | | | DS-Unit 16 | | | |
	Layer 7	Total Unit 2	% each species in Unit 2	Layer 6	Layer 7	Total Unit 16	% each species in Unit 16
Acacia sp.	2	**2**	1.16	1		**1**	9.09
Amaranthus sp.		**0**				**0**	
Annona muricata		**0**				**0**	
Arachis hypogaea		**0**				**0**	
Bunchosia armeniaca		**0**				**0**	
Canavalia maritima		**0**				**0**	
Canna edulis		**0**				**0**	
Capparis sp.		**0**				**0**	
Capparis angulata		**0**				**0**	
Capsicum sp.	3	**3**	1.74			**0**	
Chaetomorpha sp.		**0**				**0**	
Chenopodium sp.	1	**1**	0.58			**0**	
Chloris sp.		**0**				**0**	
Commelina sp.		**0**				**0**	
Cucurbita sp.		**0**				**0**	
Cucurbita moschata		**0**				**0**	
Cyperus sp.	164	**164**	95.35			**0**	
Desmodium sp.		**0**				**0**	
Eleocharis sp.		**0**				**0**	
Equisetum sp.	1	**1**	0.58			**0**	
Erythroxylum coca		**0**				**0**	
Fourcroya sp.		**0**				**0**	
Gigartina chamissoi		**0**				**0**	
Gossypium barbadense		**0**				**0**	
Guadua sp.		**0**				**0**	
Gymnogongrus furcellatus		**0**				**0**	
Gynerium sagittatum		**0**			4	**4**	36.36
Lagenaria siceraria		**0**		5	1	**6**	54.55
Manihot esculenta		**0**				**0**	
Nicotiana sp.		**0**				**0**	
Panicum sp.	1	**1**	0.58			**0**	
Paspalum sp.		**0**				**0**	
Persea sp.		**0**				**0**	
Persea americana		**0**				**0**	
Phaseolus sp.		**0**				**0**	
Phaseolus lunatus		**0**				**0**	
Phaseolus vulgaris		**0**				**0**	
Phragmites australis		**0**				**0**	
Poaceae		**0**				**0**	
Pouteria lucuma		**0**				**0**	
Prosopis sp.		**0**				**0**	

Table 10.3. Continued

Taxon	HP-Unit 2			DS-Unit 16			
	Layer 7	Total Unit 2	% each species in Unit 2	Layer 6	Layer 7	Total Unit 16	% each species in Unit 16
Psidium sp.		0				0	
Psidium guajava		0				0	
Ruppia maritima		0				0	
Schoenoplectus californicus		0				0	
Scirpus sp.		0				0	
Solanum sp.		0				0	
Solanum cf. *nigrum*		0				0	
Tessaria integrifolia		0				0	
Trifolium sp.		0				0	
Typha angustifolia		0				0	
Zea mays		0				0	
Total		172				11	
% of each phase of total remains							
% of each unit of total remains in phase		82.30				5.26	

HP = Huaca Prieta; P = Paredones; DS = Domestic Site.

There are no MNI or NISP equivalents for the plant remains. The numbers presented in tables 10.2–10.24 represent those whole and fragmented specimens that could be identified. Furthermore, as noted above, thousands of crushed and broken plant parts were impossible to type (except for pieces of reed matting). Most of the crushed remains were in the Paredones mound. The specific species discussions presented are designed to provide general patterns within and across sites. Summaries of the findings for species with large numbers of plant remains in multiple contexts are provided. For the most accurate species counts and contexts, see tables 10.2–10.24. No macroremains were recovered for some species, which are nonetheless listed because carbonized or charcoal remains represent them. Data for these remains and selected photographs for charcoal and plant remains are online at https://my.vanderbilt.edu/huacaprieta/.

CULTIVATED FOOD PLANTS

ANNONA SP., CF. *ANNONA MURICATA*: SOUR SOP; *A. CHERIMOLIA*: CHIRIMOYA, CUSTARD APPLE

Environmental setting: *A. muricata* is found in coastal settings. *A. cherimolia* is reported on the temperate western slopes of the Andes between 1400 and 2000 masl (James Macbride (1936–1956: 75–76). Augusto Weberbauer (1945: 446–447) noted that in the Chicama River Valley *Annona* grows in the forest along the river at altitudes of 1100–1600 masl. *A. muricata* is reported from coastal Peru ~4500 cal BP (Dillehay and Piperno 2014).

Economic use: A fruit with medicinal properties.

Findings at Huaca Prieta/Paredones: *Annona* sp. was not reported from Bird's excavations. A single seed from *Annona muricata* was found in Layer 4,

Table 10.4. Distribution of plants in Phase II (~7571–6538 cal BP) for Unit 22 (Paredones)

Taxon	Floor				Total Unit 22	% each species in Unit 22
	20	22	23	26		
Acacia sp.	1	1			2	11.11
Amaranthus sp.					0	
Annona muricata					0	
Arachis hypogaea					0	
Bunchosia armeniaca					0	
Canavalia maritima					0	
Canna edulis					0	
Capparis sp.					0	
Capparis angulata					0	
Capsicum sp.	4			1	5	27.78
Chaetomorpha sp.					0	
Chenopodium sp.					0	
Chloris sp.					0	
Commelina sp.					0	
Cucurbita sp.					0	
Cucurbita moschata					0	
Cyperus sp.					0	
Desmodium sp.					0	
Eleocharis sp.					0	
Equisetum sp.					0	
Erythroxylum coca					0	
Fourcroya sp.					0	
Gigartina chamissoi					0	
Gossypium barbadense				1	1	5.56
Guadua sp.					0	
Gymnogongrus furcellatus	1	1	1		3	16.67
Gynerium sagittatum					0	
Lagenaria siceraria					0	
Manihot esculenta					0	
Nicotiana sp.					0	
Panicum sp.					0	
Paspalum sp.					0	
Persea sp.					0	
Persea americana				0	0	
Phaseolus sp.				7	7	38.89
Phaseolus lunatus					0	
Phaseolus vulgaris					0	
Phragmites australis					0	
Poaceae					0	
Pouteria lucuma					0	
Prosopis sp.					0	
Psidium sp.					0	

Table 10.4. Continued

Taxon	Floor 20	Floor 22	Floor 23	Floor 26	Total Unit 22	% each species in Unit 22
Psidium guajava					0	
Ruppia maritima					0	
Schoenoplectus californicus					0	
Scirpus sp.					0	
Solanum sp.					0	
Solanum cf. nigrum					0	
Tessaria integrifolia					0	
Trifolium sp.					0	
Typha angustifolia					0	
Zea mays					0	
Total					**18**	
% of each phase of total remains						
% of each unit of total remains in phase					**8.61**	

HP = Huaca Prieta; P = Paredones; DS = Domestic Site.

Table 10.5. Distribution of plants in Phase II (~7571–6538 cal BP) for Unit HP-3

Taxon	West Wall: Layer 26	West Wall: Layer 32	West Wall: Layer 33	West Wall: Layer 45	Total HP-3	% each species in HP-3	Total Phase II	% each species in Phase II
Acacia sp.					0		5	2.39
Amaranthus sp.					0		0	
Annona muricata					0		0	
Arachis hypogaea					0		0	
Bunchosia armeniaca					0		0	
Canavalia maritima					0		0	
Canna edulis					0		0	
Capparis sp.					0		0	
Capparis angulata					0		0	
Capsicum sp.					0		8	3.83
Chaetomorpha sp.					0		0	
Chenopodium sp.					0		1	0.48
Chloris sp.					0		0	
Commelina sp.					0		0	
Cucurbita sp.					0		0	
Cucurbita moschata					0		0	
Cyperus sp.					0		164	78.47

Table 10.5. Continued

Taxon	West Wall: Layer				Total HP-3	% each species in HP-3	Total Phase II	% each species in Phase II
	26	32	33	45				
Desmodium sp.					0		0	
Eleocharis sp.					0		0	
Equisetum sp.					0		1	0.48
Erythroxylum coca					0		0	
Fourcroya sp.					0		0	
Gigartina chamissoi					0		0	
Gossypium barbadense					0		1	0.48
Guadua sp.					0		0	
Gymnogongrus furcellatus					0		3	1.44
Gynerium sagittatum					0		4	1.91
Lagenaria siceraria	2	1	3	1	7	87.50	13	6.22
Manihot esculenta			1		1	12.50	1	0.48
Nicotiana sp.					0		0	
Panicum sp.					0		1	0.48
Paspalum sp.					0		0	
Persea sp.					0		0	
Persea americana					0		0	
Phaseolus sp.					0		7	3.25
Phaseolus lunatus					0		0	
Phaseolus vulgaris					0		0	
Phragmites australis					0		0	
Poaceae					0		0	
Pouteria lucuma					0		0	
Prosopis sp.					0		0	
Psidium sp.					0		0	
Psidium guajava					0		0	
Ruppia maritima					0		0	
Schoenoplectus californicus					0		0	
Scirpus sp.					0		0	
Solanum sp.					0		0	
Solanum cf. nigrum					0		0	
Tessaria integrifolia					0		0	
Trifolium sp.					0		0	
Typha angustifolia					0		0	
Zea mays					0		0	
Total					8		209	
% of each phase of total remains							3.46	
% of each unit of total remains in phase					3.83			

HP = Huaca Prieta; P = Paredones; DS = Domestic Site.

Table 10.6. Distribution of plants in Phase III (~6538–5308 cal BP) for Units 2 and 9

| | HP-Unit 2 | | | | HP-Unit 9 | | |
Taxon	Layer 5	Layer 6	Total Unit 2	% each species in Unit 2	Layer 6	Total Unit 9	% each species in Unit 9
Acacia sp.	1		**1**	0.59		**0**	
Amaranthus sp.			**0**			**0**	
Annona muricata			**0**			**0**	
Arachis hypogaea			**0**			**0**	
Bunchosia armeniaca			**0**			**0**	
Canavalia maritima			**0**			**0**	
Canna edulis			**0**			**0**	
Capparis sp.			**0**			**0**	
Capparis angulata			**0**			**0**	
Capsicum sp.			**0**			**0**	
Chaetomorpha sp.			**0**			**0**	
Chenopodium sp.			**0**			**0**	
Chloris sp.			**0**			**0**	
Commelina sp.			**0**			**0**	
Cucurbita sp.			**0**			**0**	
Cucurbita moschata			**0**			**0**	
Cyperus sp.	143	23	**166**	97.65		**0**	
Desmodium sp.			**0**			**0**	
Eleocharis sp.			**0**			**0**	
Equisetum sp.			**0**			**0**	
Erythroxylum coca			**0**			**0**	
Fourcroya sp.			**0**			**0**	
Gigartina chamissoi			**0**			**0**	
Gossypium barbadense	1	1	**2**	1.18		**0**	
Guadua sp.			**0**			**0**	
Gymnogongrus furcellatus			**0**			**0**	
Gynerium sagittatum			**0**			**0**	
Lagenaria siceraria			**0**		1	**1**	100.00
Manihot esculenta			**0**			**0**	
Nicotiana sp.			**0**			**0**	
Panicum sp.			**0**			**0**	
Paspalum sp.			**0**			**0**	
Persea sp.			**0**			**0**	
Persea americana			**0**			**0**	
Phaseolus sp.			**0**			**0**	
Phaseolus lunatus			**0**			**0**	
Phaseolus vulgaris			**0**			**0**	
Phragmites australis			**0**			**0**	
Poaceae			**0**			**0**	
Pouteria lucuma			**0**			**0**	
Prosopis sp.	1		**1**	0.59		**0**	

Table 10.6. Continued

Taxon	HP-Unit 2				HP-Unit 9		
	Layer 5	Layer 6	Total Unit 2	% each species in Unit 2	Layer 6	Total Unit 9	% each species in Unit 9
Psidium sp.			0			0	
Psidium guajava			0			0	
Ruppia maritima			0			0	
Schoenoplectus californicus			0			0	
Scirpus sp.			0			0	
Solanum sp.			0			0	
Solanum cf. nigrum			0			0	
Tessaria integrifolia			0			0	
Trifolium sp.			0			0	
Typha angustifolia			0			0	
Zea mays			0			0	
Total			170			1	
% of each phase of total remains							
% of each unit of total remains in phase			29.16			0.17	

HP = Huaca Prieta; P = Paredones; DS = Domestic Site.

Unit 20, at Paredones in Phase IV. All other remains were identified to genus, *Annona* sp.

Findings at other archaeological sites: *Annona* was found at Los Gavilanes (Popper 1982: 150).

PERSEA AMERICANA: AVOCADO, *PALTA*

Environmental setting: in northern Peru *Persea* sp. is found on the western slopes of the cordillera at 1800 masl (Weberbauer 1945: 625). It occurs at San Isidro in the upper Cauca Valley, Colombia, at 10,500 BP (Dillehay and Piperno 2014).

Economic use: The fruit is nutritious and is a source of fats. The wood can be used as fuel; the leaves have medicinal value.

Findings at Huaca Prieta/Paredones: *Persea americana* (Lauraceae) was recovered at Huaca Prieta from Phases I–V. Macroremains include 4 leaves from Floor 6, Unit 3, that date to Phase IV and 2 seeds from Unit 6 (Floor 2) correspond-

ing to Phase V. Carbonized samples of *Persea* sp. came from Unit 21 (Layer 3), Unit 23 (Structure 2, Layer 1; Structure 7, Layers 2 and 3; Structure 8, Layer 8), and Unit 25 (Sections 1 and 4, Layers 1 and 3), dating to Phases III–V. In Unit 16 carbonized remains of *Persea* sp. were recovered from Layer 5 for Phase IV and Layer 14 for early Phase I, radiocarbon dated to 10,486–10,158 cal BP (AA86632). A radiocarbon date also was assayed at 513–325 cal BP (D-AMS-013333) on an avocado seed (*Persea* sp.) from Layer 13 in Unit 16. In Phase II, Layer 8 in Unit 16 yielded 5 grams of carbonized remains. At Paredones 1.2 grams of carbonized avocado were recovered from Unit 20, Layer 6, corresponding to Phase II. Given the identification of the macroremains of avocado from Huaca Prieta as *P. americana*, it is assumed that all carbonized samples correspond to the same species. No avocado was reported from Bird's excavations.

Findings at other archaeological sites: Avocado

Table 10.7. Distribution of plants in Phase III for Units 20 and 22

| | P-Unit 20 | | | | | P-Unit 22 | | | | | | | | | | |
| | Layer | | | Total Unit 20 | % each species in Unit 20 | Floor | | | | | | | | Total Unit 22 | % each species in Unit 22 |
Taxon	5	6	6b			10	11	13	14	15	16	17	18		
Acacia sp.		4		4	12.90		2							2	0.58
Amaranthus sp.				0				1						1	0.29
Annona muricata				0										0	
Arachis hypogaea				0										0	
Bunchosia armeniaca				0										0	
Canavalia maritima				0										0	
Canna edulis				0										0	
Capparis sp.				0		1								1	0.29
Capparis angulata				0										0	
Capsicum sp.		3		3	9.68		145	110	2	20	1			278	81.05
Chaetomorpha sp.				0										0	
Chenopodium sp.				0										0	
Chloris sp.				0										0	
Commelina sp.				0										0	
Cucurbita sp.				0										0	
Cucurbita moschata				0			9	1						10	2.92
Cyperus sp.				0										0	
Desmodium sp.				0										0	
Eleocharis sp.				0										0	
Equisetum sp.				0										0	
Erythroxylum coca				0										0	
Fourcroya sp.				0										0	
Gigartina chamissoi		1		1	3.23									0	
Gossypium barbadense				0										0	
Guadua sp.				0										0	
Gymnogongrus furcellatus		1		1	3.23									0	
Gynerium sagittatum	1	4		5	16.13									0	

Taxon	P			Total	%	DS				Total	%
Lagenaria siceraria	2	3		5	16.13	5	1			6	1.75
Manihot esculenta										0	
Nicotiana sp.										0	
Panicum sp.										0	
Paspalum sp.										0	
Persea sp.										0	
Persea americana										0	
Phaseolus sp.										0	
Phaseolus lunatus									1	1	0.29
Phaseolus vulgaris										0	
Phragmites australis		2		2	6.45					0	
Poaceae										0	
Pouteria lucuma		1		1	3.23					1	0.29
Prosopis sp.									1	1	0.29
Psidium sp.										0	
Psidium guajava						20	15	1	3	39	11.37
Ruppia maritima								1		1	0.29
Schoenoplectus californicus								1		1	0.29
Scirpus sp.							1			0	0.29
Solanum sp.		1		1	3.23					0	
Solanum cf. nigrum										0	
Tessaria integrifolia										0	
Trifolium sp.										0	
Typha angustifolia		1		1	3.23					0	
Zea mays	1	5	1	7	22.58	1	1			2	0.58
Total				**31**						**343**	
% of each phase of total remains				5.32						58.83	
% of each unit of total remains in phase											

HP = Huaca Prieta; P = Paredones; DS = Domestic Site.

Table 10.8. Distribution of plants in Phase III (~6538–5308 cal BP) for Unit HP-3

Taxon	East Wall Layer		West Wall Layer			Total HP-3	% each species in HP-3	Total Phase III	% each species in Phase III
	28	34	22	23	29				
Acacia sp.						0		7	1.20
Amaranthus sp.						0		1	0.17
Annona muricata						0		0	
Arachis hypogaea						0		0	
Bunchosia armeniaca						0		0	
Canavalia maritima						0		0	
Canna edulis						0		0	
Capparis sp.						0		1	0.17
Capparis angulata						0		0	
Capsicum sp.						0		281	48.20
Chaetomorpha sp.						0		0	
Chenopodium sp.						0		0	
Chloris sp.						0		0	
Commelina sp.						0		0	
Cucurbita sp.						0		0	
Cucurbita moschata						0		10	1.72
Cyperus sp.						0		166	28.47
Desmodium sp.						0		0	
Eleocharis sp.						0		0	
Equisetum sp.						0		0	
Erythroxylum coca						0		0	
Fourcroya sp.						0		0	
Gigartina chamissoi						0		1	0.17
Gossypium barbadense	2					2	5.26	4	0.69
Guadua sp.						0		0	
Gymnogongrus furcellatus						0		1	0.17
Gynerium sagittatum						0		5	0.86
Lagenaria siceraria		1	22	11	1	35	92.11	47	8.06
Manihot esculenta						0		0	
Nicotiana sp.						0		0	
Panicum sp.						0		0	
Paspalum sp.						0		0	
Persea sp.						0		0	
Persea americana						0		0	
Phaseolus sp.						0		0	
Phaseolus lunatus					1	1	2.63	2	0.34
Phaseolus vulgaris						0		0	
Phragmites australis						0		2	0.34
Poaceae						0		0	
Pouteria lucuma						0		1	0.17
Prosopis sp.						0		2	0.34

Table 10.8. Continued

Taxon	East Wall Layer		West Wall Layer			Total HP-3	% each species in HP-3	Total Phase III	% each species in Phase III
	28	34	22	23	29				
Psidium sp.						0		0	
Psidium guajava						0		39	6.69
Ruppia maritima						0		1	0.17
Schoenoplectus californicus						0		0	
Scirpus sp.						0		1	0.17
Solanum sp.						0		1	0.17
Solanum cf. nigrum						0		0	
Tessaria integrifolia						0		0	
Trifolium sp.						0		0	
Typha angustifolia						0		1	0.17
Zea mays						0		9	1.54
Total								583	
% of each phase of total remains								9.65	
% of each unit of total remains in phase						6.52			

HP = Huaca Prieta; P = Paredones; DS = Domestic Site.

was reported at Los Gavilanes (Popper 1982: 149, 150), PV-35-6 (Bonavia 1982: 242–243), and Alto Salaverry (Pozorski and Pozorski 1977: 85).

Commentary: It is difficult to determine the species of avocado remains in Unit 16. It is probable that they are *P. americana*, which is present in other Preceramic sites.

ARACHIS HYPOGAEA: PEANUT, *MANÍ*

Environmental setting: The center of domestication was possibly southern Bolivia, lowland northwest Argentina, and/or the Matto Grosso region in Brazil, based on the distribution of the wild species *A. monticola* and *A. batizcoi* (Piperno 2011a: 276).

Economic use: The seed is nutritious, high in protein and oils.

Findings at Huaca Prieta/Paredones: At Huaca Prieta 5 hull fragments were found at Unit 25

(Layer 3) in Phase IV contexts. No remains of *Arachis hypogaea* were reported from Bird's excavations. Peanuts were recovered in contexts corresponding to the Cupisnique mound dated to the Formative period (Bird et al. 1985: 230; Whitaker and Bird 1949: 6).

Findings at other archaeological sites: *Arachis* was found at the Nanchoc Valley in northern Peru (Rossen 2011a: 106) and at Bandurria on the north-central coast of Peru (Chu Barrera 2011).

Commentary: Piperno writes that "hulls of peanuts (the nuts themselves did not survive) . . . do not exhibit some features of modern domesticated plants, nor do they conform to a known wild species" (Piperno and Dillehay 2008: 19624). Peanut starch grains recovered from human teeth are identical to those from modern varieties of *Arachis hypogaea* and are unlike starch in modern wild peanuts closely related to that species analyzed so far (Piperno and Dillehay 2008).

Table 10.9. Distribution of plants in Phase IV (~5308–4107 cal BP) for Units HP-3 and 2

| Taxon | HP-3 | | | | HP-Unit 2 | | | |
| | East Wall Layer | West Wall Layer | Total HP-3 | % each species in HP-3 | Layer | | Total Unit 2 | % each species in Unit 2 |
	22	22			3	4		
Acacia sp.			0			1	1	1.39
Amaranthus sp.			0				0	
Annona muricata			0				0	
Arachis hypogaea			0				0	
Bunchosia armeniaca			0				0	
Canavalia maritima			0				0	
Canna edulis			0				0	
Capparis sp.			0				0	
Capparis angulata			0				0	
Capsicum sp.			0				0	
Chaetomorpha sp.			0				0	
Chenopodium sp.			0		1		1	1.39
Chloris sp.			0				0	
Commelina sp.			0				0	
Cucurbita sp.			0				0	
Cucurbita moschata			0				0	
Cyperus sp.	1		1	16.67	22	44	66	91.67
Desmodium sp.			0				0	
Eleocharis sp.			0				0	
Equisetum sp.			0				0	
Erythroxylum coca			0				0	
Fourcroya sp.			0				0	
Gigartina chamissoi			0				0	
Gossypium barbadense			0			4	4	5.56
Guadua sp.			0				0	
Gymnogongrus furcellatus			0				0	
Gynerium sagittatum			0				0	
Lagenaria siceraria	1	4	5	83.33			0	
Manihot esculenta			0				0	
Nicotiana sp.			0				0	
Panicum sp.			0				0	
Paspalum sp.			0				0	
Persea sp.			0				0	
Persea americana			0				0	
Phaseolus sp.			0				0	
Phaseolus lunatus			0				0	
Phaseolus vulgaris			0				0	
Phragmites australis			0				0	
Poaceae			0				0	

Table 10.9. Continued

Taxon	HP-3				HP-Unit 2			
	East Wall Layer	West Wall Layer	Total HP-3	% each species in HP-3	Layer		Total Unit 2	% each species in Unit 2
	22	22			3	4		
Pouteria lucuma			0				0	
Prosopis sp.			0				0	
Psidium sp.			0				0	
Psidium guajava			0				0	
Ruppia maritima			0				0	
Schoenoplectus californicus			0				0	
Scirpus sp.			0				0	
Solanum sp.			0				0	
Solanum cf. nigrum			0				0	
Tessaria integrifolia			0				0	
Trifolium sp.			0				0	
Typha angustifolia			0				0	
Zea mays			0				0	
Total			6				72	
% of each phase of total remains								
% of each unit of total remains in phase			0.74				8.83	

HP = Huaca Prieta; P = Paredones; DS = Domestic Site.

More work is needed on wild peanut starch, but the "suite of phenotypic traits that characterize domesticated peanuts may not have developed all at once" (Piperno 2011b: 464).

PHASEOLUS SP.; P. LUNATUS: LIMA BEAN HABAS; P. VULGARIS: COMMON BEAN

Environmental setting: Cultivated *Phaseolus lunatus* is reported from Chilca I in coastal Peru at 6400 BP (Dillehay and Piperno 2014).

Economic use: The bean is a nutritious and high-protein food.

Findings at Huaca Prieta/Paredones: At Huaca Prieta 6 fragments were recovered from Unit 6, Floor 1; 1 fragment from Floor 1, Unit 15; 1 frag- ment from Structure 1, Unit 23; and 31 frag- ments from Unit 6, Floor 2, in Phase V contexts, and from HP-3 (Layer 28) in Phase III. At Pare- dones (Unit 22) 7 beans came from Floor 26, Phase II; 3 from Floor 15 and 5 from Floor 16 in Phase III; 1 from Floor 9, 20 from Floor 7, 57 from Floor 6, and 1 from Floor 5 in Phase IV; and 2 from Floor 2 in Phase V. Beans were found in contexts from Unit 16 (various layers) in Phase I and from HP-3 (Layer 28) in Phase III. The bean from the bottom level of Layer 16, Unit 16, was dated by radiocarbon means to 15,217–14,221 cal BP (D-AMS-013332; see table 6.2). This assay, however, is too early for a domesticated crop at this time.

Findings at other archaeological sites: Beans were reported in the Nanchoc Valley (Piperno

Table 10.10. Distribution of plants in Phase IV (~5308–4107 cal BP) for Units 3 and 13

Taxon	HP-Unit 3 Floor 6	HP-Unit 3 Floor 7	Total Unit 3	% each species in Unit 3	DS-Unit 13 Layer 2	DS-Unit 13 Layer 3	Total Unit 13	% each species in Unit 13
Acacia sp.	1	1	**2**	3.45			**0**	
Amaranthus sp.			**0**				**0**	
Annona muricata			**0**				**0**	
Arachis hypogaea			**0**				**0**	
Bunchosia armeniaca			**0**				**0**	
Canavalia maritima			**0**				**0**	
Canna edulis	1		**1**	1.72			**0**	
Capparis sp.			**0**				**0**	
Capparis angulata			**0**				**0**	
Capsicum sp.		30	**30**	51.72			**0**	
Chaetomorpha sp.			**0**				**0**	
Chenopodium sp.			**0**				**0**	
Chloris sp.			**0**				**0**	
Commelina sp.			**0**				**0**	
Cucurbita sp.			**0**				**0**	
Cucurbita moschata		1	**1**	1.72			**0**	
Cyperus sp.			**0**				**0**	
Desmodium sp.			**0**				**0**	
Eleocharis sp.			**0**				**0**	
Equisetum sp.			**0**			29	**29**	31.18
Erythroxylum coca			**0**				**0**	
Fourcroya sp.			**0**				**0**	
Gigartina chamissoi			**0**				**0**	
Gossypium barbadense			**0**				**0**	
Guadua sp.			**0**				**0**	
Gymnogongrus furcellatus			**0**				**0**	
Gynerium sagittatum	1		**1**	1.72			**0**	
Lagenaria siceraria	6	1	**7**	12.07	64		**64**	68.82
Manihot esculenta			**0**				**0**	
Nicotiana sp.			**0**				**0**	
Panicum sp.	1		**1**	1.72			**0**	
Paspalum sp.			**0**				**0**	
Persea sp.			**0**				**0**	
Persea americana	4		**4**	6.90			**0**	
Phaseolus sp.	2		**2**	3.45			**0**	
Phaseolus lunatus			**0**				**0**	
Phaseolus vulgaris			**0**				**0**	
Phragmites australis			**0**				**0**	
Poaceae			**0**				**0**	
Pouteria lucuma			**0**				**0**	
Prosopis sp.			**0**				**0**	
Psidium sp.			**0**				**0**	
Psidium guajava		2	**2**	3.45			**0**	
Ruppia maritima			**0**				**0**	

Table 10.10. Continued

Taxon	HP-Unit 3 Floor 6	HP-Unit 3 Floor 7	Total Unit 3	% each species in Unit 3	DS-Unit 13 Layer 2	DS-Unit 13 Layer 3	Total Unit 13	% each species in Unit 13
Schoenoplectus californicus			0				0	
Scirpus sp.		4	4	6.90			0	
Solanum sp.			0				0	
Solanum cf. nigrum			0				0	
Tessaria integrifolia			0				0	
Trifolium sp.		3	3	5.17			0	
Typha angustifolia			0				0	
Zea mays			0				0	
Total			58				93	
% of each phase of total remains								
% of each unit of total remains in phase			7.12				11.41	

HP = Huaca Prieta; P = Paredones; DS = Domestic Site.

Table 10.11. Distribution of plants in Phase IV (~5308–4107 cal BP) for Units 15 and 20

Taxon	HP-Unit 15 Floor 9	Total Unit 15	% each species in Unit 15	P-Unit 20 Layer 2	P-Unit 20 Layer 4	Total Unit 20	% each species in Unit 20
Acacia sp.		0				0	
Amaranthus sp.		0				0	
Annona muricata		0			1	1	6.25
Arachis hypogaea		0				0	
Bunchosia armeniaca		0				0	
Canavalia maritima		0				0	
Canna edulis		0				0	
Capparis sp.		0				0	
Capparis angulata		0				0	
Capsicum sp.		0				0	
Chaetomorpha sp.		0				0	
Chenopodium sp.		0				0	
Chloris sp.		0				0	
Commelina sp.		0				0	
Cucurbita sp.		0				0	
Cucurbita moschata		0			4	4	25.00
Cyperus sp.		0				0	

Table 10.11. Continued

Taxon	HP-Unit 15 Floor 9	HP-Unit 15 Total Unit 15	HP-Unit 15 % each species in Unit 15	P-Unit 20 Layer 2	P-Unit 20 Layer 4	P-Unit 20 Total Unit 20	P-Unit 20 % each species in Unit 20
Desmodium sp.		0				0	
Eleocharis sp.		0		1		1	6.25
Equisetum sp.		0				0	
Erythroxylum coca		0				0	
Fourcroya sp.		0				0	
Gigartina chamissoi		0				0	
Gossypium barbadense		0		2		2	12.50
Guadua sp.		0				0	
Gymnogongrus furcellatus		0				0	
Gynerium sagittatum		0		6		6	37.50
Lagenaria siceraria		0			1	1	6.25
Manihot esculenta		0				0	
Nicotiana sp.		0				0	
Panicum sp.		0				0	
Paspalum sp.		0				0	
Persea sp.		0				0	
Persea americana		0				0	
Phaseolus sp.		0				0	
Phaseolus lunatus		0				0	
Phaseolus vulgaris		0				0	
Phragmites australis		0				0	
Poaceae		0		1		1	6.25
Pouteria lucuma		0				0	
Prosopis sp.		0				0	
Psidium sp.		0				0	
Psidium guajava		0				0	
Ruppia maritima		0				0	
Schoenoplectus californicus		0				0	
Scirpus sp.		0				0	
Solanum sp.		0				0	
Solanum cf. *nigrum*		0				0	
Tessaria integrifolia		0				0	
Trifolium sp.		0				0	
Typha angustifolia		0				0	
Zea mays	1	1	100.00			0	
Total		**1**				**16**	
% of each phase of total remains							
% of each unit of total remains in phase		0.12				1.96	

HP = Huaca Prieta; P = Paredones; DS = Domestic Site.

Table 10.12. Distribution of plants in Phase IV (~5308–4107 cal BP) for Unit 22 (Paredones)

Taxon	Floor					Total Unit 22	% each species in Unit 22
	5	6	7	8	9		
Acacia sp.						**0**	
Amaranthus sp.						**0**	
Annona muricata						**0**	
Arachis hypogaea						**0**	
Bunchosia armeniaca						**0**	
Canavalia maritima		10				**10**	3.57
Canna edulis						**0**	
Capparis sp.						**0**	
Capparis angulata						**0**	
Capsicum sp.					20	**20**	7.14
Chaetomorpha sp.					1	**1**	0.36
Chenopodium sp.						**0**	
Chloris sp.						**0**	
Commelina sp.						**0**	
Cucurbita sp.		2				**2**	0.71
Cucurbita moschata		8				**8**	2.86
Cyperus sp.						**0**	
Desmodium sp.						**0**	
Eleocharis sp.						**0**	
Equisetum sp.			1			**1**	0.36
Erythroxylum coca						**0**	
Fourcroya sp.						**0**	
Gigartina chamissoi						**0**	
Gossypium barbadense						**0**	
Guadua sp.						**0**	
Gymnogongrus furcellatus			3			**3**	1.07
Gynerium sagittatum						**0**	
Lagenaria siceraria		26	36	41	1	**104**	37.14
Manihot esculenta						**0**	
Nicotiana sp.						**0**	
Panicum sp.						**0**	
Paspalum sp.						**0**	
Persea sp.						**0**	
Persea americana						**0**	
Phaseolus sp.		22			1	**23**	8.21
Phaseolus lunatus	1	35	20			**56**	20.00
Phaseolus vulgaris						**0**	
Phragmites australis			1			**1**	0.36
Poaceae						**0**	
Pouteria lucuma						**0**	
Prosopis sp.		8		2		**10**	3.57
Psidium sp.						**0**	

Table 10.12. Continued

Taxon	Floor 5	6	7	8	9	Total Unit 22	% each species in Unit 22
Psidium guajava						**0**	
Ruppia maritima						**0**	
Schoenoplectus californicus						**0**	
Scirpus sp.						**0**	
Solanum sp.						**0**	
Solanum cf. *nigrum*						**0**	
Tessaria integrifolia		6	34			**40**	14.29
Trifolium sp.						**0**	
Typha angustifolia						**0**	
Zea mays		1				**1**	0.36
Total						**280**	
% of each phase of total remains							
% of each unit of total remains in phase						**34.36**	

HP = Huaca Prieta; P = Paredones; DS = Domestic Site.

Table 10.13. Distribution of plants in Phase IV (~5308–4107 cal BP) for Unit 25 (Huaca Prieta)

Taxon	Layer C3	C4	C5	C6	3	5	6	Total Unit 25	% each species in Unit 25	Total Phase IV	% each species in Phase IV
Acacia sp.			1					**1**	0.35	**4**	0.49
Amaranthus sp.								**0**		**0**	
Annona muricata								**0**		**1**	0.12
Arachis hypogaea					5			**5**	1.73	**5**	0.61
Bunchosia armeniaca								**0**		**0**	
Canavalia maritima								**0**		**10**	1.23
Canna edulis								**0**		**1**	0.12
Capparis sp.								**0**		**0**	
Capparis angulata								**0**		**0**	
Capsicum sp.	4	7	1	1				**13**	4.50	**63**	7.73
Chaetomorpha sp.								**0**		**1**	0.12
Chenopodium sp.								**0**		**1**	0.12
Chloris sp.								**0**		**0**	
Commelina sp.								**0**		**0**	
Cucurbita sp.								**0**		**2**	0.25
Cucurbita moschata								**0**		**13**	1.60
Cyperus sp.			3					**3**	1.04	**70**	8.59

Table 10.13. Continued

Taxon	C3	C4	C5	C6	3	5	6	Total Unit 25	% each species in Unit 25	Total Phase IV	% each species in Phase IV
Desmodium sp.								0		0	
Eleocharis sp.								0		1	0.12
Equisetum sp.								0		30	3.68
Erythroxylum coca								0		0	
Fourcroya sp.					3			3	1.04	3	0.37
Gigartina chamissoi								0		0	
Gossypium barbadense		3						3	1.04	9	1.10
Guadua sp.								0		0	
Gymnogongrus furcellatus								0		3	0.37
Gynerium sagittatum						3		3	1.04	10	1.23
Lagenaria siceraria				2	128	19	56	205	70.93	386	47.36
Manihot esculenta								0		0	
Nicotiana sp.								0		0	
Panicum sp.								0		1	0.12
Paspalum sp.								0		0	
Persea sp.								0		0	
Persea americana								0		4	0.49
Phaseolus sp.								0		25	3.07
Phaseolus lunatus								0		56	6.87
Phaseolus vulgaris								0		0	
Phragmites australis								0		1	0.12
Poaceae								0		1	0.12
Pouteria lucuma								0		0	
Prosopis sp.	1					1		2	0.69	12	1.47
Psidium sp.								0		0	
Psidium guajava	22	8	3	3				36	12.46	38	4.66
Ruppia maritima	2	1		3				6	2.08	6	0.74
Schoenoplectus californicus								0		0	
Scirpus sp.	3	2		1				6	2.08	10	1.23
Solanum sp.								0		0	
Solanum cf. *nigrum*								0		0	
Tessaria integrifolia						2	1	3	1.04	43	5.28
Trifolium sp.								0		3	0.37
Typha angustifolia								0		0	
Zea mays								0		2	0.25
Total								289		815	

% of each phase of total remains 13.49

% of each unit of total remains in phase 35.46

HP = Huaca Prieta; P = Paredones; DS = Domestic Site.

Table 10.14. Distribution of plants in Phase V (~4107–3455 cal BP) for Units 1, 2, and 3

| | DS-Unit 1 | | | HP-Unit 2 | | | HP-Unit 3 | | | | |
| | Layer | Total | % each species in | Layer | Total | % each species in | Floor | | | Total | % each species in |
Taxon	4	Unit 1	Unit 1	2	Unit 2	Unit 2	1	3	5	Unit 3	Unit 3
Acacia sp.		0			0					0	
Amaranthus sp.		0			0					0	
Annona muricata		0			0					0	
Arachis hypogaea		0			0					0	
Bunchosia armeniaca		0			0					0	
Canavalia maritima		0			0					0	
Canna edulis		0			0					0	
Capparis sp.		0			0					0	
Capparis angulata		0			0				34	34	9.02
Capsicum sp.		0			0					0	
Chaetomorpha sp.		0			0					0	
Chenopodium sp.		0			0					0	
Chloris sp.		0			0					0	
Commelina sp.		0			0					0	
Cucurbita sp.		0			0					0	
Cucurbita moschata		0			0					0	
Cyperus sp.		0		18	18	100.00	9			9	2.39
Desmodium sp.		0			0					0	
Eleocharis sp.		0			0					0	
Equisetum sp.		0			0					0	
Erythroxylum coca		0			0			5		5	1.33
Fourcroya sp.		0			0				1	1	0.27
Gigartina chamissoi		0			0					0	
Gossypium barbadense		0			0					0	
Guadua sp.		0			0					0	
Gymnogongrus furcellatus		0			0					0	
Gynerium sagittatum		0			0				1	1	0.27

Taxon						
Lagenaria siceraria	0	0	149	174	323	85.68
Manihot esculenta	0	5	0	0	0	
Nicotiana sp.	5	0	0	0	0	100.00
Panicum sp.	0	0	0		0	
Paspalum sp.	0	0	0		0	
Persea sp.	0	0	0		0	
Persea americana	0	0	0		0	
Phaseolus sp.	0	0	0		0	
Phaseolus lunatus	0	0	0		0	
Phaseolus vulgaris	0	0	0		0	
Phragmites australis	0	0	0		0	
Poaceae	0	0	0		0	
Pouteria lucuma	0	0	0		0	
Prosopis sp.	0	0	0		0	
Psidium sp.	0	0	1		1	0.27
Psidium guajava	0	0	0		0	
Ruppia maritima	0	0	0		0	
Schoenoplectus californicus	0	0	0		0	
Scirpus sp.	0	0	0		0	
Solanum sp.	0	0	0		0	
Solanum cf. *nigrum*	0	0	1	1	1	0.27
Tessaria integrifolia	0	0	0		0	
Trifolium sp.	0	0	0		0	
Typha angustifolia	0	0	0		0	
Zea mays	0	0	2		2	0.53
Total	**5**	**18**			**377**	
% of each phase of total remains						
% of each unit of total remains in phase	**0.11**	**0.41**			**8.52**	

HP = Huaca Prieta; P = Paredones; DS = Domestic Site.

Table 10.15. Distribution of plants in Phase V (~4107–3455 cal BP) for Units 4 and 5

| | HP-Unit 4 | | | HP-Unit 5 | | | | | | | | |
| | Layer | Total Unit | % each species in | Floor | | | | | | Total Unit | % each species in |
Taxon	4	4	Unit 4	1	2	3	4	5	6	5	Unit 5
Acacia sp.		0							2	2	0.19
Amaranthus sp.		0								0	
Annona muricata		0								0	
Arachis hypogaea		0								0	
Bunchosia armeniaca		0								0	
Canavalia maritima		0								0	
Canna edulis		0								0	
Capparis sp.		0								0	
Capparis angulata		0					1			1	0.09
Capsicum sp.		0				109	69	238	59	475	43.94
Chaetomorpha sp.		0								0	
Chenopodium sp.		0								0	
Chloris sp.		0								0	
Commelina sp.		0								0	
Cucurbita sp.		0		1		3		12		16	1.48
Cucurbita moschata		0		2	6	51	12	21	17	109	10.08
Cyperus sp.	16	16	100.00	59	8	29	32	67	38	233	21.55
Desmodium sp.		0								0	
Eleocharis sp.		0								0	
Equisetum sp.		0					1			1	0.09
Erythroxylum coca		0								0	
Fourcroya sp.		0								0	
Gigartina chamissoi		0								0	
Gossypium barbadense		0				3	3			6	0.56
Guadua sp.		0								0	
Gymnogongrus furcellatus		0								0	
Gynerium sagittatum		0						5	4	9	0.83
Lagenaria siceraria		0			2			27	1	30	2.78
Manihot esculenta		0								0	
Nicotiana sp.		0								0	
Panicum sp.		0								0	
Paspalum sp.		0								0	
Persea sp.		0								0	
Persea americana		0								0	
Phaseolus sp.		0								0	
Phaseolus lunatus		0								0	
Phaseolus vulgaris		0								0	
Phragmites australis		0								0	
Poaceae		0								0	
Pouteria lucuma		0								0	
Prosopis sp.		0								0	

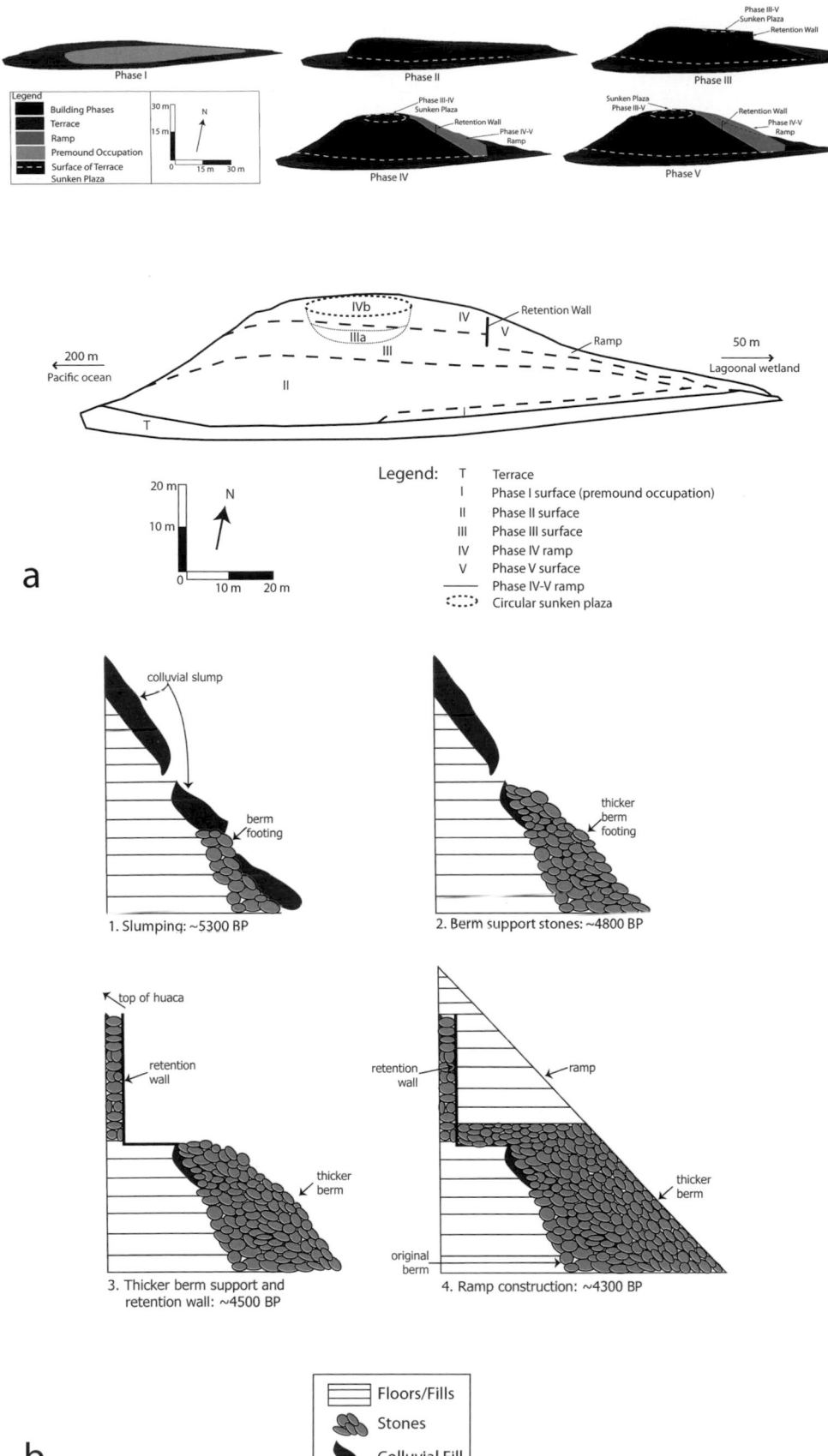

FIGURE 7.33. Schematic architectural sequences: *a*, sequence of mound building phases at Huaca Prieta; *b*, sequence of development of Phases IV–V access ramp at Huaca Prieta.

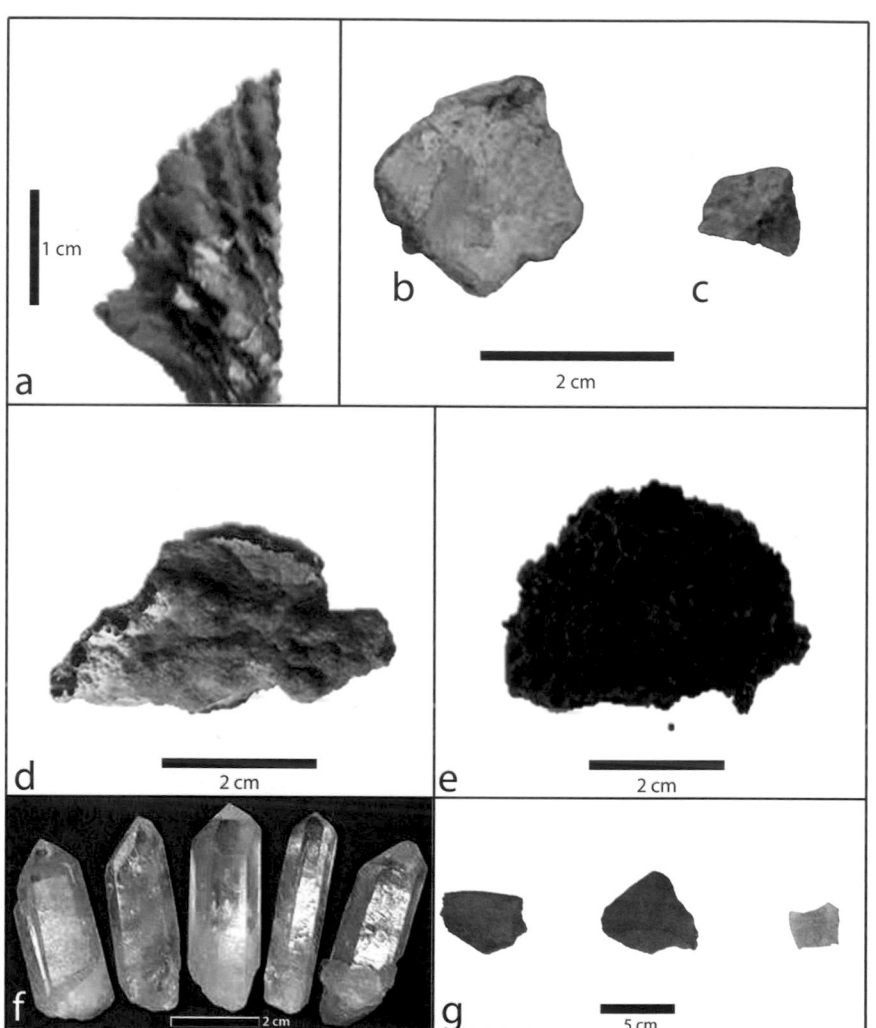

FIGURE 11.16. Various exotics: *a*, *Spondylus* fragment; *b–c*, turquoise fragments; *d*, malachite; *e*, *Scleractinia* sp. coral; *f*, rock crystals; *g*, ceramic fragments.

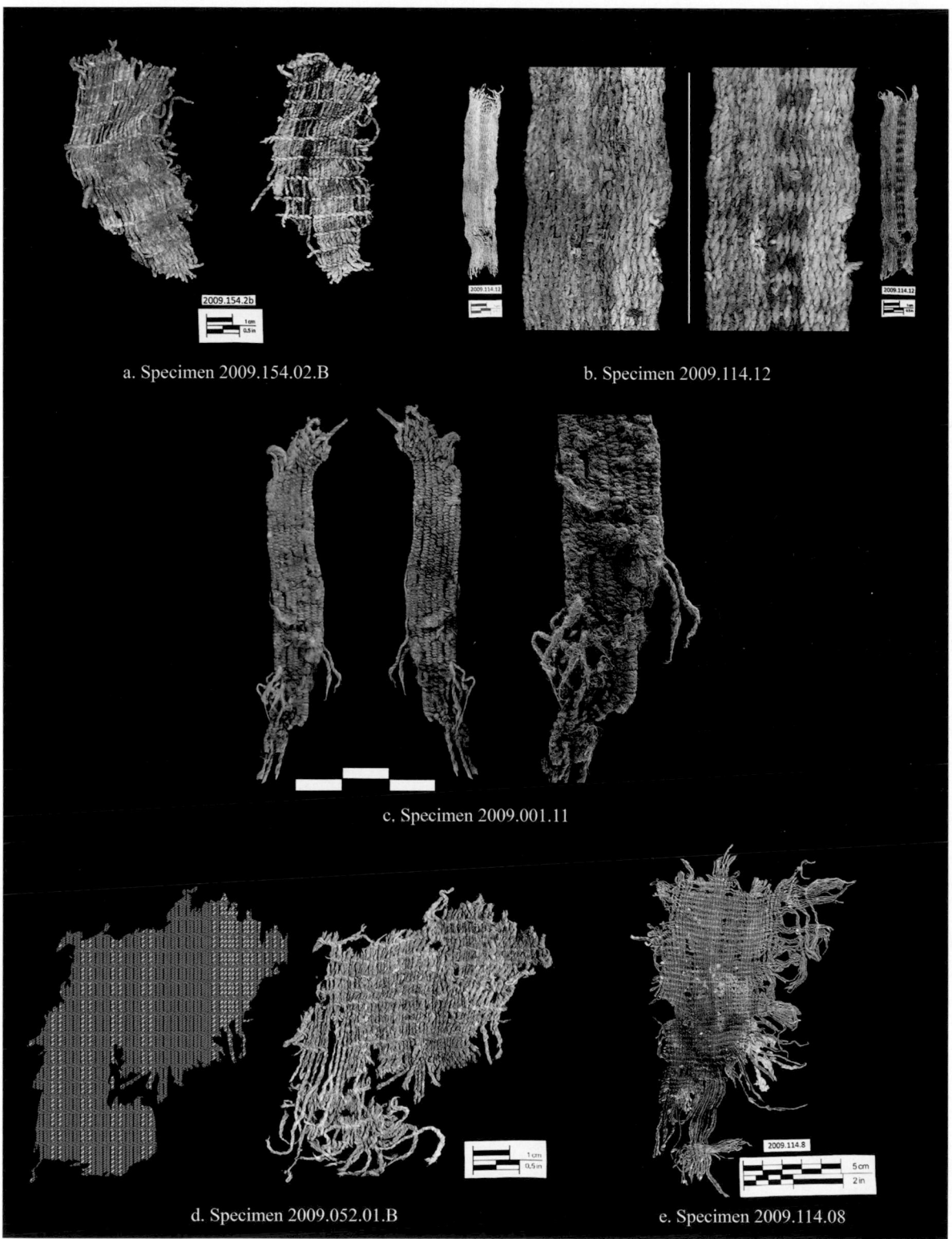

a. Specimen 2009.154.02.B

b. Specimen 2009.114.12

c. Specimen 2009.001.11

d. Specimen 2009.052.01.B

e. Specimen 2009.114.08

FIGURE 12.1. Paste and color in Huaca Prieta fabrics: *a*, Specimen 2009.154.02.B before (*left*) and after (*right*) it was washed with hexametasulfate to remove paste and reveal dark-blue warp stripes (*left*: photo by the author; *right*: photo by Lauren Badams); *b*, comparison of Specimen 2009.114.12 before (*left*) and after (*right*) washing with hexametasulfate, revealing a gold color (photos by Lauren Badams); *c*, Specimen 2009.001.11 (front, back, and detail) of a tapestry band with gold camelid hair; *d*, Specimen 2009.052.01.B, which was dyed with indigo (photo by Lauren Badams); *e*, Specimen 2009.114.08, which has an overall red color (photo by Lauren Badams).

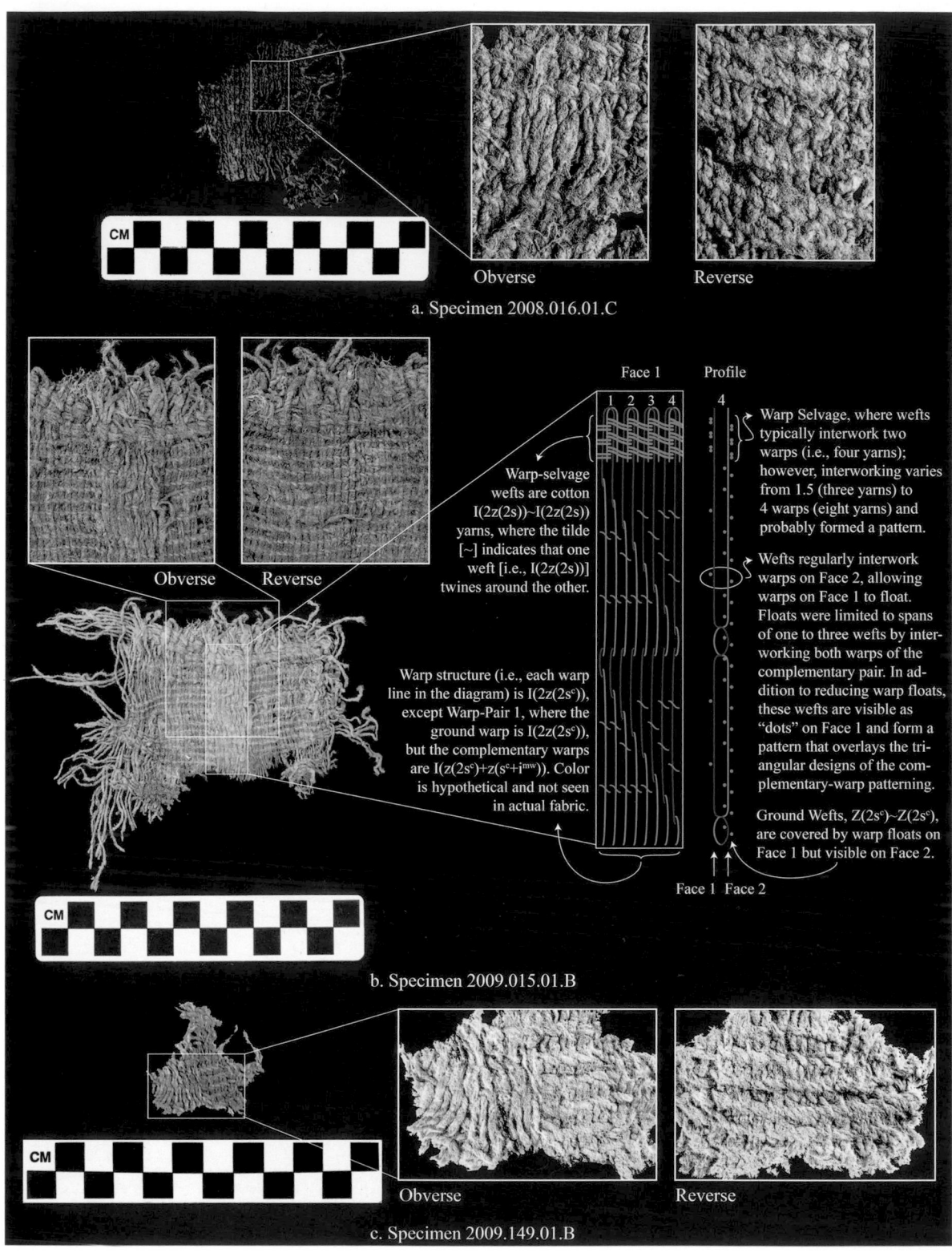

Warp-selvage wefts are cotton $I(2z(2s))\sim I(2z(2s))$ yarns, where the tilde [~] indicates that one weft [i.e., $I(2z(2s))$] twines around the other.

Warp structure (i.e., each warp line in the diagram) is $I(2z(2s^c))$, except Warp-Pair 1, where the ground warp is $I(2z(2s^c))$, but the complementary warps are $I(z(2s^c)+z(s^c+i^{mw}))$. Color is hypothetical and not seen in actual fabric.

Warp Selvage, where wefts typically interwork two warps (i.e., four yarns); however, interworking varies from 1.5 (three yarns) to 4 warps (eight yarns) and probably formed a pattern.

Wefts regularly interwork warps on Face 2, allowing warps on Face 1 to float. Floats were limited to spans of one to three wefts by interworking both warps of the complementary pair. In addition to reducing warp floats, these wefts are visible as "dots" on Face 1 and form a pattern that overlays the triangular designs of the complementary-warp patterning.

Ground Wefts, $Z(2s^c)\sim Z(2s^c)$, are covered by warp floats on Face 1 but visible on Face 2.

Face 1   Face 2

Face 1   Profile

Obverse   Reverse

a. Specimen 2008.016.01.C

Obverse   Reverse

b. Specimen 2009.015.01.B

Obverse   Reverse

c. Specimen 2009.149.01.B

FIGURE 12.9. Complementary warp patterning with warp substitution in weft twining: *a*, Specimen 2008.016.01.C; *b*, Specimen 2009.015.01.B: photos and diagram (based on specimen 2009.015.01.B, but structure is representative of all three specimens; shading added for contrast; no color was noted in the original fabric); *c*, Specimen 2009.149.01.B.

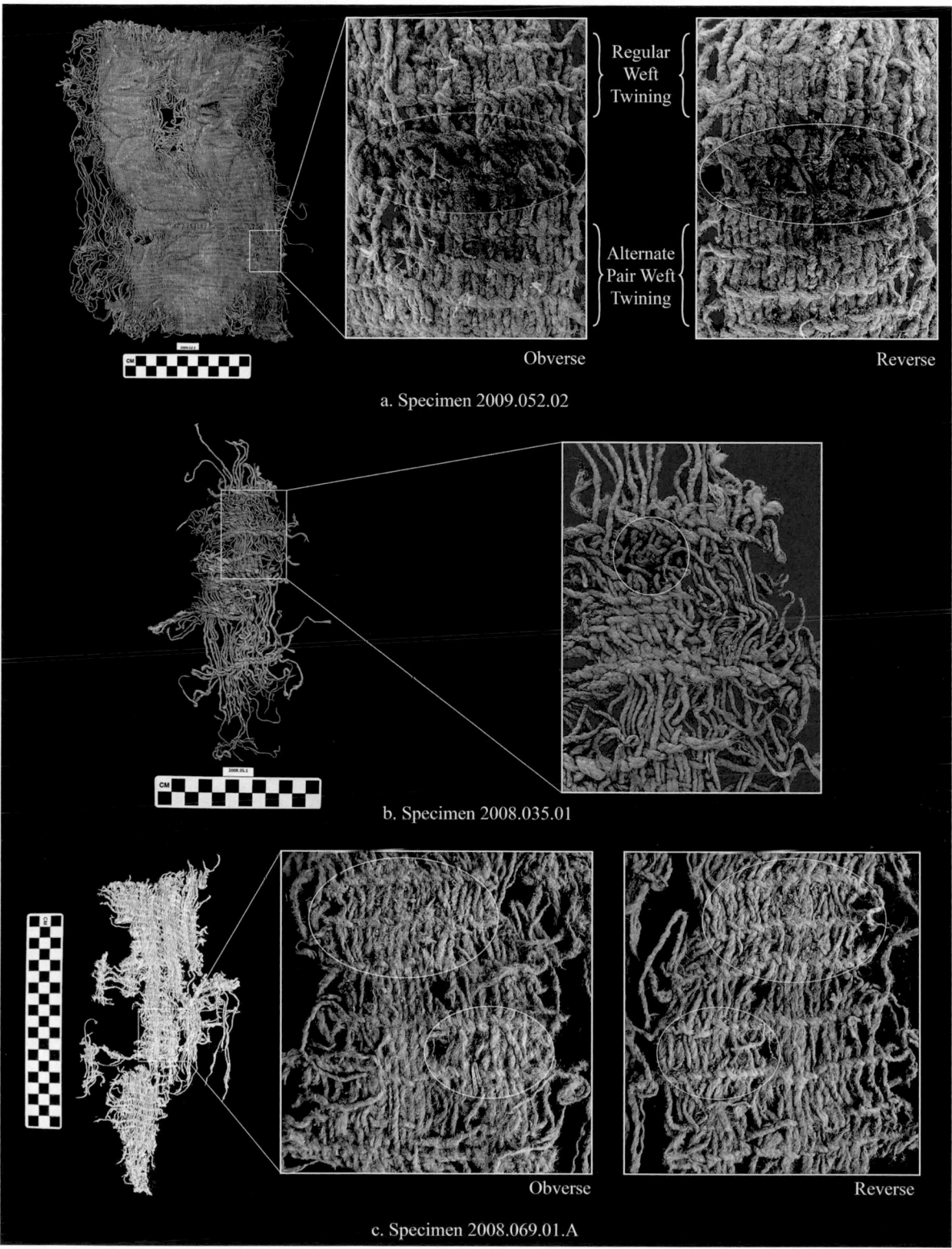

FIGURE 12.10. Structure diagram of warp crossing groups discussed in the present study: *a*, Miscellaneous and Accidental Type (Specimen 2009.052.02); *b*, Pair Transposition Type (Specimen 2008.035.01); *c*, Single Warp Transposition Type (Specimen 2008.069.01.A); *d*, Woodland Type (Specimen 2008.100.04); *e*, Condor Type (Specimen 2008.096.01) (note 360 degree twists in compact-weft bands); shading was added for contrast and is not present in the actual specimen; *f*, Geometric Type (Specimen 2008.075.03.A–B).

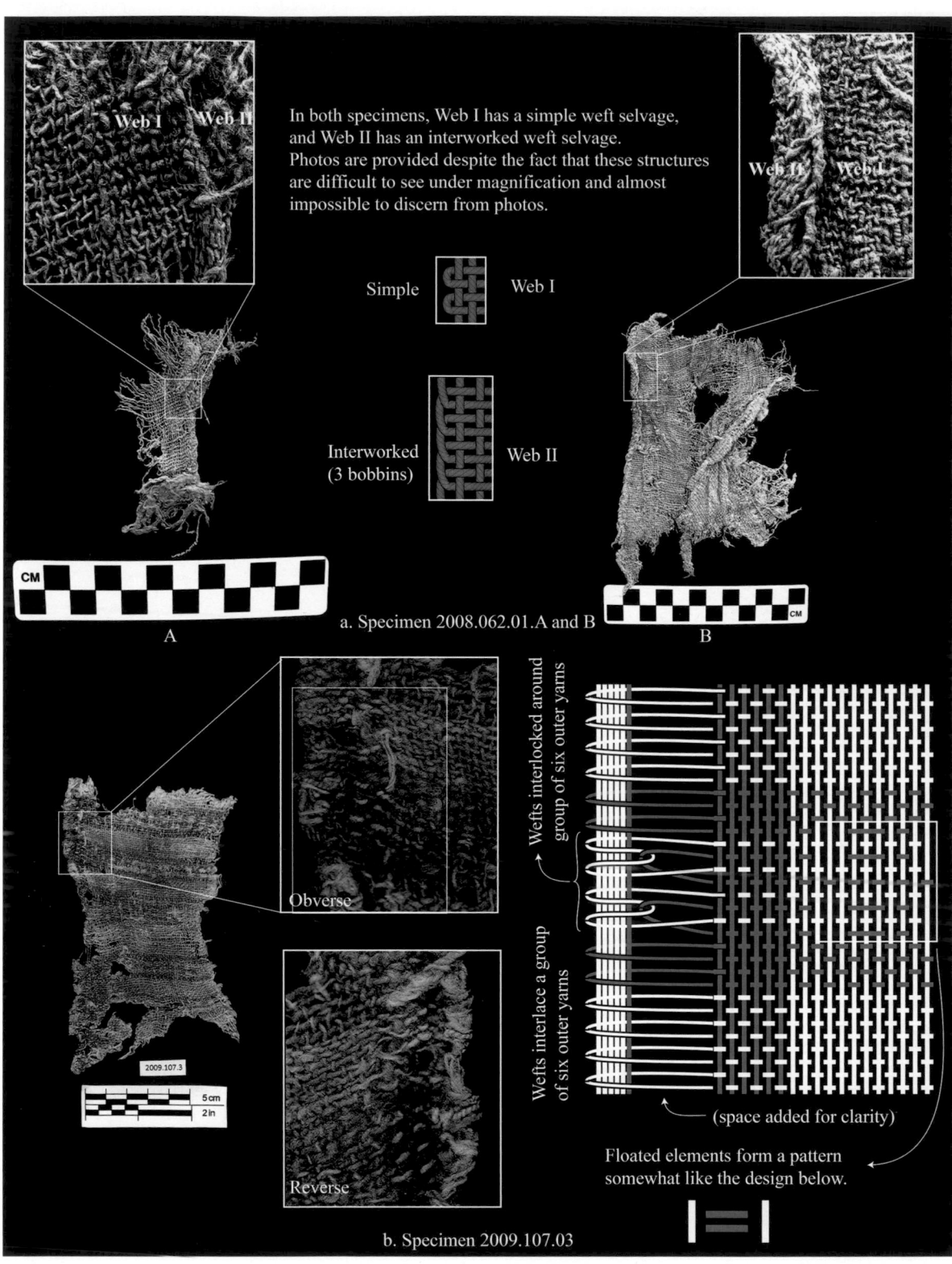

In both specimens, Web I has a simple weft selvage, and Web II has an interworked weft selvage. Photos are provided despite the fact that these structures are difficult to see under magnification and almost impossible to discern from photos.

Simple — Web I

Interworked (3 bobbins) — Web II

a. Specimen 2008.062.01.A and B

Wefts interlocked around group of six outer yarns

Wefts interlace a group of six outer yarns

(space added for clarity)

Floated elements form a pattern somewhat like the design below.

b. Specimen 2009.107.03

FIGURE 12.14. Plain-weave edge finishes: *a*, plain-weave weft-selvage finishes (Specimen 2008.062.01.A and B); *b*, weft selvage with reinforced outer warp and interlocked wefts (Specimen 2009.107.03); note that the fabric has a plain-weave-derived float-weave structure, as seen in the diagram (*right*).

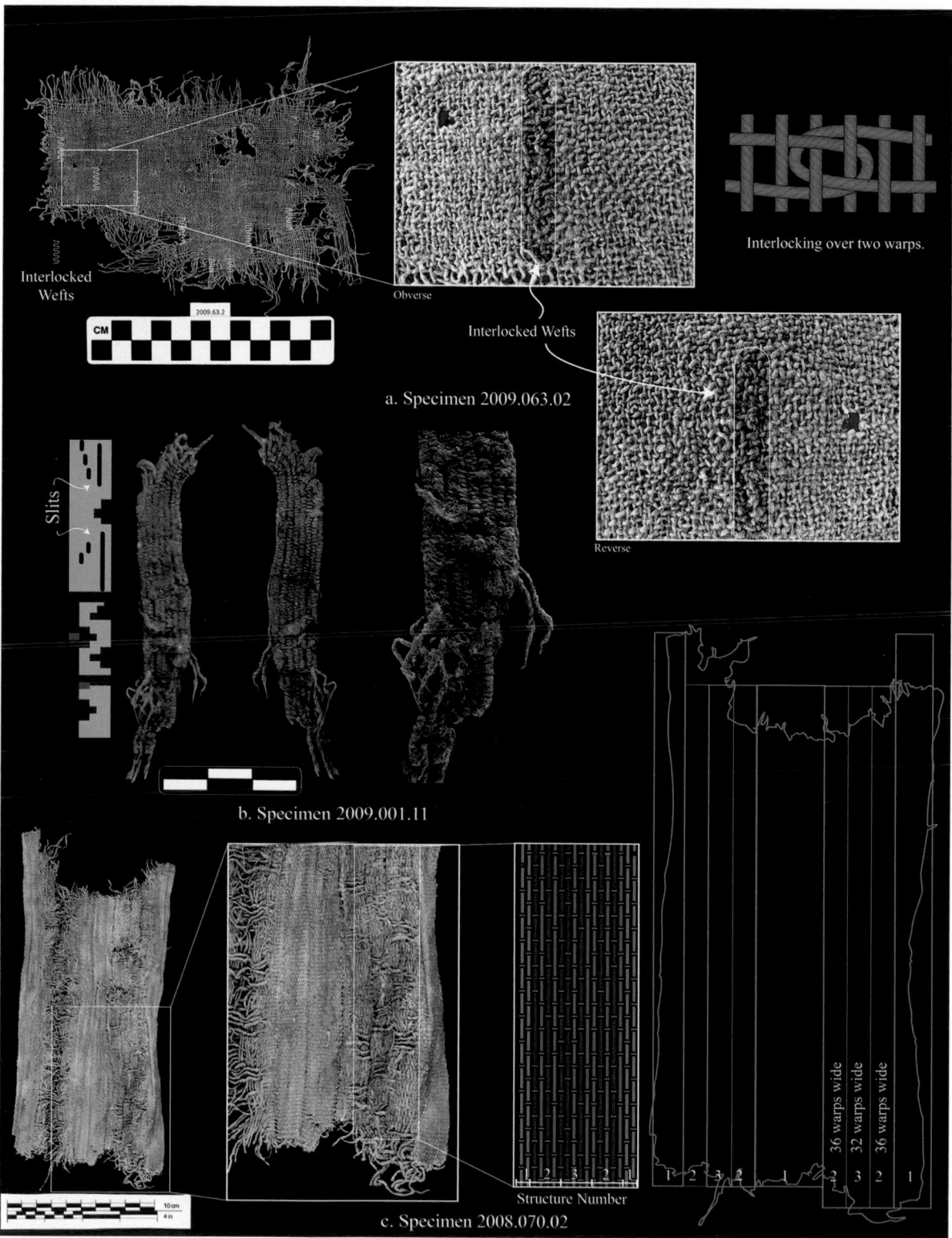

Interlocked Wefts

Interlocking over two warps.

Obverse

Interlocked Wefts

a. Specimen 2009.063.02

Reverse

Slits

b. Specimen 2009.001.11

36 warps wide

32 warps wide

36 warps wide

Structure Number

c. Specimen 2008.070.02

FIGURE 12.15. Structural diagrams of weft patterning in plain weave: *a*, discontinuous wefts (Specimen 2009.063.02); *b*, slit tapestry (Specimen 2009.001.11); *c*, plain-weave-derived float weave (Specimen 2008.070.02). Note that color is not found in the actual specimen and shading was added to the diagram for clarity. Many of the yarns that are colored in the diagram have fallen out.

FIGURE 12.19. Close simple and diagonal twining from Huaca Prieta: *a*, Type III: Close Simple and Diagonal Twining, S-Twist (paired) Wefts with Functional Wrapped Twining, obverse surface (note blue elements); *b*, reverse side of *a*; *c*, close-up of obverse surface of *a*; *d*, close-up of reverse surface of *b*.

FIGURE 12.17. Close simple twining from Huaca Prieta: *a*, Type I: Close Simple Twining, S-Twist (paired) Wefts with Auxiliary Simple Plaiting, obverse surface (note blue elements); *b*, close-up of *a*: *c*, schematic of twining selvages, all types: c1. simple 180 selvage with warps inserted into adjacent rows (Adovasio 2010: fig. 37); c2. selvage with the warp divided into two separate pieces, folded to the outside of the basket; the warps are then twill plaited (3/3 interval) with other warp segments to create a pseudo-braided appearance (compare Bird et al. 1985: fig. 60); c3. continuous weft simple self side selvage (Adovasio 2010: fig. 44); c4. an overhand-knotted simple side selvage (Adovasio 2010: fig. 42).

Table 10.15. Continued

| | HP-Unit 4 | | | HP-Unit 5 | | | | | | | | |
| | Layer | Total Unit | % each species in | Floor | | | | | | Total Unit | % each species in |
Taxon	4	4	Unit 4	1	2	3	4	5	6	5	Unit 5
Psidium sp.	0									0	
Psidium guajava	0			1		9	2	129	57	198	18.32
Ruppia maritima	0									0	
Schoenoplectus californicus	0									0	
Scirpus sp.	0									0	
Solanum sp.	0					1				1	0.09
Solanum cf. *nigrum*	0									0	
Tessaria integrifolia	0									0	
Trifolium sp.	0									0	
Typha angustifolia	0									0	
Zea mays	0									0	
Total	16									1081	
% of each phase of total remains											
% of each unit of total remains in phase	0.36									24.44	

HP = Huaca Prieta; P = Paredones; DS = Domestic Site.

2011a: 276), on the central coast of Peru (Quilter et al. 1991: 280), on the north coast at Los Gavilanes, Huaynuná (Ugent et al. 1984: 420), and at Alto Salaverry (Pozorski 1976: 85).

INGA FEUILLEI: PACAY, *PACAE*

Environmental setting: *Inga* is a genus with 350 species, of which 87 are found in Peru; 12 of these are endemic. The only one found on the north and central coasts is *Inga feuillei*, which is reported from the Nanchoc Valley at 9000 cal BP (Rossen 2011b).

Economic use: The sweet fibers surrounding large seeds in the pod are eaten as a fruit. The seeds and pods can be cooked and eaten.

Findings at Huaca Prieta/Paredones: Bird found *Inga pacae* in contexts with ceramics (Bird et al. 1985: 230).

Findings at other archaeological sites: *Inga* is reported at Aspero (Feldman 1980: 178), Cerro Lampay (Vega-Centeno 2007: table 2), Los Gavi-

lanes (Bonavia 1982), Padre Abán and Alto Salaverry (Pozorski 1976: table 5-7), Bandurria (Chu Barrera 2011), and the Nanchoc Valley (Rossen 2011a: 106). Grains of starch from pacay (*Inga feuillei*) were found in calculus on human teeth at the Nanchoc sites (Piperno and Dillehay 2008).

BUNCHOSIA ARMENIACA: CIRUELA DEL FRAILE, BUNCHOSIA

Environmental setting: *Bunchosia* is found in coastal valleys and on the western slopes of the Andes between 100 and 2600 masl. It is reported from the coast of Peru at 4500 BP (Dillehay and Piperno 2014).

Economic use: The fruit is a food source.

Findings at Huaca Prieta/Paredones: At Huaca Prieta 21 seeds from Unit 6 (Floor 2) and Unit 16 (Layer 5) in Phase V were recovered. Layer 4 in Unit 16 from Phase V yielded 4.5 grams of charcoal. Bird noted *Bunchosia armeniaca* in Layer O of

Table 10.16. Distribution of plants in Phase V (~4107–3455 cal BP) for Units 6, 7, and 8

Taxon	HP-Unit 6 Floor 1	HP-Unit 6 Floor 2	Total Unit 6	% each species in Unit 6	HP-Unit 7 Floor 1	HP-Unit 7 Floor 2	Total Unit 7	% each sp. in Unit 7	HP-Unit 8 Layer 2	HP-Unit 8 Layer 3	Total Unit 8	% each species in Unit 8
Acacia sp.		3	**3**	0.36			**0**				**0**	
Amaranthus sp.			**0**				**0**				**0**	
Annona muricata			**0**				**0**				**0**	
Arachis hypogaea			**0**				**0**				**0**	
Bunchosia armeniaca		21	**21**	2.49			**0**				**0**	
Canavalia maritima			**0**				**0**				**0**	
Canna edulis			**0**				**0**				**0**	
Capparis sp.			**0**				**0**				**0**	
Capparis angulata			**0**				**0**				**0**	
Capsicum sp.			**0**				**0**				**0**	
Chaetomorpha sp.			**0**				**0**				**0**	
Chenopodium sp.			**0**				**0**				**0**	
Chloris sp.			**0**				**0**				**0**	
Commelina sp.			**0**				**0**				**0**	
Cucurbita sp.			**0**				**0**				**0**	
Cucurbita moschata			**0**				**0**				**0**	
Cyperus sp.	1	2	**3**	0.36	231	31	**262**	80.62			**0**	
Desmodium sp.			**0**				**0**				**0**	
Eleocharis sp.			**0**				**0**				**0**	
Equisetum sp.			**0**				**0**				**0**	
Erythroxylum coca			**0**				**0**			20	**20**	95.24
Fourcroya sp.			**0**				**0**				**0**	
Gigartina chamissoi			**0**				**0**				**0**	
Gossypium barbadense	10	14	**24**	2.84			**0**				**0**	
Guadua sp.			**0**				**0**				**0**	
Gymnogongrus furcellatus		419	**419**	49.64			**0**				**0**	
Gynerium sagittatum	23	14	**37**	4.38	10	29	**39**	12.00			**0**	

Taxon											
Lagenaria siceraria	11	81	**92**	*10.90*	14	2	**16**	*4.92*	1	**1**	*4.76*
Manihot esculenta			**0**				**0**			**0**	
Nicotiana sp.			**0**				**0**			**0**	
Panicum sp.			**0**				**0**			**0**	
Paspalum sp.			**0**				**0**			**0**	
Persea sp.			**0**				**0**			**0**	
Persea americana		2	**2**	*0.24*			**0**			**0**	
Phaseolus sp.			**0**				**0**			**0**	
Phaseolus lunatus			**0**				**0**			**0**	
Phaseolus vulgaris	6	31	**37**	*4.38*			**0**			**0**	
Phragmites australis		6	**6**	*0.71*		1	**1**	*0.31*		**0**	
Poaceae			**0**				**0**			**0**	
Pouteria lucuma			**0**				**0**			**0**	
Prosopis sp.	1	2	**3**	*0.36*		7	**7**	*2.15*		**0**	
Psidium sp.			**0**				**0**			**0**	
Psidium guajava	1		**1**	*0.12*			**0**			**0**	
Ruppia maritima			**0**				**0**			**0**	
Schoenoplectus californicus			**0**				**0**			**0**	
Scirpus sp.			**0**				**0**			**0**	
Solanum sp.			**0**				**0**			**0**	
Solanum cf. nigrum			**0**				**0**			**0**	
Tessaria integrifolia			**0**				**0**			**0**	
Trifolium sp.			**0**				**0**			**0**	
Typha angustifolia			**0**				**0**			**0**	
Zea mays	27	168	**195**	*23.10*			**0**			**0**	
Total			**844**				**325**			**21**	

% of each phase of total remains | | | **19.08** | | | | **7.35** | | | **0.47** |

% of each unit of total remains in phase

HP = Huaca Prieta; P = Paredones; DS = Domestic Site.

Table 10.17. Distribution of plants in Phase V (~4107–3455 cal BP) for Units 10 and 11

	HP-Unit 10								HP-Unit 11						
	Layer		Floor		Layer				Layer 1			Layer 2	Layer 3		
									Feature						
Taxon	1	2	1	2	3	4	Total Unit 10	% each species in Unit 10	1	2	3			Total Unit 11	% each species in Unit 11
Acacia sp.							0							0	
Amaranthus sp.							0							0	
Annona muricata							0							0	
Arachis hypogaea							0							0	
Bunchosia armeniaca							0							0	
Canavalia maritima							0							0	
Canna edulis							0							0	
Capparis sp.							0							0	
Capparis angulata							0							0	
Capsicum sp.					3		3	1.12						0	
Chaetomorpha sp.							0							0	
Chenopodium sp.							0							0	
Chloris sp.							0							0	
Commelina sp.							0							0	
Cucurbita sp.							0							0	
Cucurbita moschata		2			2		4	1.49						0	
Cyperus sp.	15	7			9		31	11.57						0	
Desmodium sp.	1						1	0.37						0	
Eleocharis sp.	15				4		19	7.09	1					1	2.70
Equisetum sp.	80	20	1		28		129	48.13	12			4		16	43.24
Erythroxylum coca							0							0	
Fourcroya sp.							0							0	
Gigartina chamissoi					1		1	0.37						0	
Gossypium barbadense	3	1					4	1.49				1		1	2.70
Guadua sp.							0							0	
Gymnogongrus furcellatus					1		1	0.37						0	

Taxon									% of each unit of total remains in phase	
Gynerium sagittatum	16	3		3		3	8	11	1.12	29.73
Lagenaria siceraria	3	3	1	4	1	26	7	8	9.70	21.62
Manihot esculenta	1					0		0		
Nicotiana sp.						0		0		
Panicum sp.						0		0		
Paspalum sp.	1		2			3		0	1.12	
Persea sp.						0		0		
Persea americana						0		0		
Phaseolus sp.						0		0		
Phaseolus lunatus						0		0		
Phaseolus vulgaris						0		0		
Phragmites australis						0		0		
Poaceae	6	3		12		21		0	7.84	
Pouteria lucuma						0		0		
Prosopis sp.	1	2				3		0	1.12	
Psidium sp.						0		0		
Psidium guajava	3	2	2	1		8		0	2.99	
Ruppia maritima						0		0		
Schoenoplectus californicus						0		0		
Scirpus sp.	9			2		11		0	4.10	
Solanum sp.						0		0		
Solanum cf. *nigrum*						0		0		
Tessaria integrifolia						0		0		
Trifolium sp.						0		0		
Typha angustifolia						0		0		
Zea mays						0		0		
Total						268		37		
% of each phase of total remains						6.06		0.84		
% of each unit of total remains in phase										

HP = Huaca Prieta; P = Paredones; DS = Domestic Site.

Table 10.18. Distribution of plants in Phase V (~4107–3455 cal BP) for Units 12 and 14

| | HP-Unit 12 | | | | HP-Unit 14 | | | | | | | | | | |
| | Floor | | Total Unit 12 | % each species in Unit 12 | Floor | | | | | | | Feature | | Total Unit 14 | % each species in Unit 14 |
Taxon	2	3			1	1A	2	3	4	5	6	1	2		
Acacia sp.			0											0	
Amaranthus sp.			0											0	
Annona muricata			0											0	
Arachis hypogaea			0											0	
Bunchosia armeniaca			0											0	
Canavalia maritima			0											0	
Canna edulis			0											0	
Capparis sp.			0											0	
Capparis angulata			0											0	
Capsicum sp.			0										17	17	5.01
Chaetomorpha sp.			0											0	
Chenopodium sp.			0											0	
Chloris sp.			0								1			1	0.29
Commelina sp.			0											0	
Cucurbita sp.			0											0	
Cucurbita moschata			0										4	4	1.18
Cyperus sp.			0								7			7	2.06
Desmodium sp.			0						1					1	0.29
Eleocharis sp.		1	1	2.44			1	3	4	3				11	3.24
Equisetum sp.	12	15	27	65.85			22	3	29	34	1		4	93	27.43
Erythroxylum coca			0											0	
Fourcroya sp.			0											0	
Gigartina chamissoi			0												
Gossypium barbadense			0						1					1	0.29
Guadua sp.			0												
Gymnogongrus furcellatus			0			3									
Gynerium sagittatum			0								19		6	28	8.26

Lagenaria siceraria			**0**		4	6	10	1				35	10	**66**	19.47
Manihot esculenta			**0**												
Nicotiana sp.			**0**												
Panicum sp.			**0**												
Paspalum sp.			**0**												
Persea sp.			**0**												
Persea americana			**0**												
Phaseolus sp.			**0**												
Phaseolus lunatus			**0**												
Phaseolus vulgaris			**0**												
Phragmites australis			**0**												
Poaceae		4	**4**	9.76					2					**2**	0.59
Pouteria lucuma			**0**												
Prosopis sp.		1	**1**	2.44						2				**2**	0.59
Psidium sp.			**0**												
Psidium guajava	1	3	**4**	9.76				1	1				94	**96**	28.32
Ruppia maritima			**0**												
Schoenoplectus californicus			**0**								3			**3**	0.88
Scirpus sp.	4		**4**	9.76			1							**1**	0.29
Solanum sp.			**0**												
Solanum cf. nigrum			**0**				6							**6**	1.77
Tessaria integrifolia			**0**												
Trifolium sp.			**0**												
Typha angustifolia			**0**												
Zea mays			**0**											**0**	
Total			**41**											**339**	
% of each phase of total remains															
% of each unit of total remains in phase			**0.93**											**7.66**	

HP = Huaca Prieta; P = Paredones; DS = Domestic Site.

Table 10.19. Distribution of plants in Phase V (~4107–3455 cal BP) for Units 15 and 16

| | HP-Unit 15 | | | | | | DS-Unit 16 | | | | | | | |
| | Floor | | Total Unit 15 | % each species in Unit 15 | Floor 1 | Surface | Layer | | | | | | Total Unit 16 | % each species in Unit 16 |
Taxon	1	2					1	2	3	4	5	6		
Acacia sp.			0										0	
Amaranthus sp.			0										0	
Annona muricata			0										0	
Arachis hypogaea			0										0	
Bunchosia armeniaca			0								1		1	0.17
Canavalia maritima			0										0	
Canna edulis			0										0	
Capparis sp.			0										0	
Capparis angulata			0				3	7					10	1.72
Capsicum sp.			0			2		1			1		4	0.69
Chaetomorpha sp.			0				1	1					2	0.34
Chenopodium sp.			0										0	
Chloris sp.			0										0	
Commelina sp.			0										0	
Cucurbita sp.			0										0	
Cucurbita moschata			0				26	11					37	6.38
Cyperus sp.			0										0	
Desmodium sp.			0										0	
Eleocharis sp.	2		2	16.67	2	4							6	1.03
Equisetum sp.	7		7	58.33	35	17	1				1		54	9.31
Erythroxylum coca			0											
Fourcroya sp.			0											
Gigartina chamissoi			0											
Gossypium barbadense			0			1		1	2				4	0.69
Guadua sp.			0											
Gymnogongrus furcellatus			0					2		1			3	0.52
Gynerium sagittatum			0		8			1	1	5	4		19	3.28

Note: this is a rotated, partial data table. Column headers for the five count columns (C1–C5) are not visible in this crop; the top data row (Lagenaria siceraria: 93, 72, 35, 113, 49) falls directly under them. "P" denotes the phase-count column (total 12); "P %" is the "% of each unit of total remains in phase" for that phase.

Taxon	P	P %	C1	C2	C3	C4	C5	Total	%
Lagenaria siceraria	0		93	72	35	113	49	**362**	62.41
Manihot esculenta	0								
Nicotiana sp.	0								
Panicum sp.	0								
Paspalum sp.	0								
Persea sp.	0								
Persea americana	0								
Phaseolus sp.	0								
Phaseolus lunatus	1	8.33							
Phaseolus vulgaris	0								
Phragmites australis	0						4	**4**	0.69
Poaceae	0		6	4				**10**	1.72
Pouteria lucuma	0				5			**5**	0.86
Prosopis sp.	0		16			2		**18**	3.10
Psidium sp.	0								
Psidium guajava	1	8.33		5	23			**29**	5.00
Ruppia maritima	0								
Schoenoplectus californicus	0								
Scirpus sp.	0			3				**3**	0.52
Solanum sp.	0								
Solanum cf. nigrum	0								
Tessaria integrifolia	0		3		2		1	**6**	1.03
Trifolium sp.	0					1			
Typha angustifolia	0			1			1	**2**	0.34
Zea mays	1	8.33						**1**	0.17
Total	**12**							**580**	
% of each phase of total remains	0.27								
% of each unit of total remains in phase								13.11	

HP = Huaca Prieta; P = Paredones; DS = Domestic Site.

Table 10.20. Distribution of plants in Phase V (~4107–3455 cal BP) for Units 18, 21, and 22

Taxon	HP-Unit 18 Floor 1	Total Unit 18	% each species in Unit 18	HP-Unit 21 Structure 8	Total Unit 21	% each species in Unit 21	HP-Unit 22 Floor 1	HP-Unit 22 Floor 2	HP-Unit 22 Floor 3	Total Unit 22	% each species in Unit 22
Acacia sp.		0			0					0	
Amaranthus sp.		0			0					0	
Annona muricata		0			0					0	
Arachis hypogaea		0			0					0	
Bunchosia armeniaca		0			0					0	
Canavalia maritima		0			0					0	
Canna edulis		0			0					0	
Capparis sp.		0			0					0	
Capparis angulata		0			0				1	1	4.76
Capsicum sp.		0			0					0	
Chaetomorpha sp.		0			0				1	1	4.76
Chenopodium sp.		0			0					0	
Chloris sp.		0			0					0	
Commelina sp.		0			0					0	
Cucurbita sp.		0			0					0	
Cucurbita moschata		0			0					0	
Cyperus sp.		0			0					0	
Desmodium sp.		0			0					0	
Eleocharis sp.		0			0					0	
Equisetum sp.	7	7	77.78		0					0	
Erythroxylum coca		0		18	18	81.82				0	
Fourcroya sp.		0			0					0	
Gigartina chamissoi		0		1	1	4.55				0	
Gossypium barbadense		0		1	1	4.55				0	
Guadua sp.		0			0					0	
Gymnogongrus furcellatus		0		1	1	4.55				0	
Gynerium sagittatum		0			0					0	

Taxon							
Lagenaria siceraria					16	17	80.95
Manihot esculenta	0		0		1	0	0
Nicotiana sp.	0		0			0	0
Panicum sp.	0		0			0	0
Paspalum sp.	0		0			0	0
Persea sp.	0		0			0	0
Persea americana	0		0			0	0
Phaseolus sp.	0		0		2	2	9.52
Phaseolus lunatus	0		0			0	0
Phaseolus vulgaris	0		0			0	0
Phragmites australis	0		0			0	0
Poaceae	1	11.11	0			0	0
Pouteria lucuma	0		0			0	0
Prosopis sp.	0		0			0	0
Psidium sp.	0		0			0	0
Psidium guajava	0		1	4.55	1	0	0
Ruppia maritima	0		0			0	0
Schoenoplectus californicus	0		0			0	0
Scirpus sp.	1	11.11	0			0	0
Solanum sp.	0		0			0	0
Solanum cf. nigrum	0		0			0	0
Tessaria integrifolia	0		0			0	0
Trifolium sp.	0		0			0	0
Typha angustifolia	0		0			0	0
Zea mays	0		0			0	0
Total	**9**		**22**			**21**	
% of each phase of total remains	0.20		0.50			0.47	
% of each unit of total remains in phase							

HP = Huaca Prieta; P = Paredones; DS = Domestic Site.

Table 10.21. Distribution of plants in Phase V (~4107–3455 cal BP) for Unit 23

| | HP-Unit 23 | | | | | | | | | | | | |
| | Layer | | | | Structure | | Layer | | | | Structure | | Layer | |
Taxon	1	3	4	10	1	2	1	2	6&7	C7	3&4	7	1	3
Acacia sp.										1				
Amaranthus sp.														
Annona muricata														
Arachis hypogaea														
Bunchosia armeniaca														
Canavalia maritima														
Canna edulis														
Capparis sp.														
Capparis angulata														
Capsicum sp.														
Chaetomorpha sp.	2													
Chenopodium sp.														
Chloris sp.														
Commelina sp.								1						
Cucurbita sp.														
Cucurbita moschata														
Cyperus sp.														
Desmodium sp.														
Eleocharis sp.														
Equisetum sp.														
Erythroxylum coca														
Fourcroya sp.														
Gigartina chamissoi	1		1					1						
Gossypium barbadense	1				9		1							11
Guadua sp.														
Gymnogongrus furcellatus	1		1			1					1			
Gynerium sagittatum	6						2	1						
Lagenaria siceraria	5				2							8		
Manihot esculenta														
Nicotiana sp.														
Panicum sp.														
Paspalum sp.														
Persea sp.														
Persea americana														
Phaseolus sp.														
Phaseolus lunatus					1									
Phaseolus vulgaris														
Phragmites australis														
Poaceae		2	1	3			1	1		3				
Pouteria lucuma														

Structure	Layer				Total Unit	% each species in
8	1	8	9	10	23	Unit 23
					1	
					0	
					0	
					0	
					0	
					0	
					0	
					0	
					0	
					0	
					2	1.92
					0	
					0	
					1	0.96
					0	
					0	
					0	
					0	
					0	
					0	
					0	
					0	
					3	2.88
	4				26	25.00
					0	
					4	3.85
					9	8.65
				1	16	15.38
					0	
					0	
					0	
					0	
					0	
					0	
					0	
					1	0.96
					0	
					0	
					11	10.58
					0	

Table 10.21. Continued

| | HP-Unit 23 | | | | | | | | | | | | | |
| | Layer | | | | Structure | | Layer | | | | Structure | | Layer | |
Taxon	1	3	4	10	1	2	1	2	6&7	C7	3&4	7	1	3
Prosopis sp.	2	1												
Psidium sp.								1						
Psidium guajava		2												
Ruppia maritima		1			2			1			1			3
Schoenoplectus californicus														
Scirpus sp.									4	1				
Solanum sp.														
Solanum cf. nigrum														
Tessaria integrifolia														
Trifolium sp.								1		1				
Typha angustifolia														
Zea mays														
Total														
% of each phase of total remains														
% of each unit of total remains in phase														

HP = Huaca Prieta; P = Paredones; DS = Domestic Site.

HP-3 at Huaca Prieta (Bird et al. 1985: 234). This suggests that *pacay* was present at Huaca Prieta from at least Phase III onward.

Findings at other archaeological sites: *Bunchosia* occurred at Alto Salaverry (Pozorski 1976: 85) and at the Nanchoc sites (Rossen 2011a).

CUCURBITA SP; CUCURBITA MOSCHATA: SQUASH, LOCHE; C. MAXIMA: SQUASH, ZAPALLO; C. FICIFOLIA: SQUASH; C. ECUADORENSIS: SQUASH

Environmental setting: *Cucurbita moschata* was cultivated in the Nanchoc Valley by 10,300 cal BP (Dillehay and Piperno 2014). *C. maxima* was cultivated by 4500 BP, and *C. ficifolia* was cultivated at the Paloma site in coastal Peru at 5800 BP (Dillehay and Piperno 2014).

Economic use: The flesh and seeds are eaten.

Findings at Huaca Prieta/Paredones: The *Cucurbita* remains from Bird's excavations at Huaca Prieta correspond to the Cupisnique levels. Fragmented remains of *Cucurbita* sp. were found in the premound, early to late Phase I levels (~10,500–9000 cal BP) of Unit 22 at Paredones. Abundant remains of *Cucurbita* sp. and *C. moschata* were found in Unit 5, Phase V, at Huaca Prieta and in Unit 22, Phase IV, at Paredones. *C. moschata* also was found in domestic Units 16 and Test Pit 26 in Phase V near Huaca Prieta. The remains from Preceramic levels of Huaca Prieta are possibly *C. moschata* and *C. ficifolia* (Whitaker and Bird 1949: 12–13). These two species were present in Cupisnique times (Whitaker and Bird 1949: 13–14).

Findings at other archaeological sites: *Cucurbita* was found at Aspero and the As-8 site (Feldman 1977: 2), Los Gavilanes (Popper 1982: 153), Bandurria (Chu Barrera 2011), PV35-106 (Bonavia et al. 2001), PV35-6 (Bonavia et al. 1993: 420), and Padre Abán and Alto Salaverry on the north and north-central coasts of Peru (Pozorski 1976: 77).

Commentary: Piperno has found *Cucurbita* phytoliths in material from Siches in Piura in northernmost Peru, dated at 9533 cal BP and 9222 BP (Piperno 2011b). Both *Cucurbita moschata* and

| Structure | Layer | | | | Total Unit | % each species in |
8	1	8	9	10	23	Unit 23
		4			7	6.73
					1	0.96
	1				3	2.88
	3				11	10.58
					0	
					5	4.81
					0	
					0	
			1		1	0.96
					2	1.92
					0	
					0	
					104	
						2.35

C. ficifolia have been identified in the late Preceramic period at El Paraíso on the central coast (Quilter et al. 1991: 280). C. maxima and C. ficifolia were recovered in late Preceramic contexts at Buena Vista in the Chillón Valley (Duncan et al. 2009: 13202). Seeds from both cucurbits found at Huaynuná in the Casma Valley correspond to the late Preceramic (Whitaker 1983). Cucurbita sp. is present at Los Gavilanes in Epochs 2 and 3 (Popper 1982: 153). In the Nanchoc Valley C. moschata is present in the El Palto Phase (late Paiján subphase), dated ~10,000 BP (Rossen 2011b: 180).

PSIDIUM GUAJAVA: GUAVA, GUAYABA

Environmental setting: Psidium guajava is from lowland and lower montane environments.

Economic use: The fruit is eaten.

Findings at Huaca Prieta/Paredones: Macroremains were recovered from both Huaca Prieta and Paredones from Phase III and Phase V contexts. In Phase III 20 specimens were recovered in Floor 11, 15 in Floor 13, 1 in Floor 14, and 3 in Floor 15 in Unit 22. In Phase IV remains come from Unit 3 (Floor 7) and Unit 25 (Layers C3–C6). A single sample of Psidium sp. was recovered in Unit 23 (Structure 2). In Phase V remains were found in Unit 3 (Floor 1), Unit 5 (Floors 1 and 3–6), Unit 6 (Floor 2), Unit 10 (Layers 1–3), Unit 12 (Floors 2 and 3), Unit 14 (Floors 3 and 4 and Feature 2), Unit 15 (Floor 1), Unit 16 (Layers 2 and 3), Unit 21 (Structures 2 and 8), and Unit 23 (Layer 3 and Structure 8). Bird reported Psidium guajava from all Preceramic levels, corresponding to our Phases II–V.

Findings at other archaeological sites: Psidium sp. was excavated at El Paraíso (Quilter et al. 1991: table 3), Buena Vista (Duncan et al. 2009), Bandurria (Chu Barrera 2011), Cerro Lampay (Vega-Centeno 2007), Gavilanes, Aspero (Feldman 1977: 2), and Alto Salaverry (Pozorski 1976: 85).

CAPSICUM BACCATUM, C. CHINENSE, C. FRUTESCENS, C. PUBESCENS: CHILE PEPPER, AJÍ

Environmental setting: See appendix 4.

Economic use: Chile pepper is highly nutritious, providing essential food elements and vitamins.

Findings at Huaca Prieta/Paredones (for details see appendix 4): Bird recovered Capsicum at Huaca Prieta in almost all levels of HP-3 (from Phase II to Phase V). He indicates that C. baccatum var. pendulum was probably domesticated (Bird et al. 1985: 236). We found Capsicum in levels dated from early Phase I to Phase V.

Findings at other archaeological sites: C. baccatum was reported at El Paraíso (Quilter et al. 1991), Buena Vista (Duncan et al. 2009: 13202–13203), Cerro Lampay (Vega-Centeno 2007), Bandurria (Chu Barrera 2011), Los Gavilanes, Huaynuná (Ugent et al. 1984: 420), and Alto Salaverry (Pozorski 1976: 84).

SOLANUM SP.: POTATO, PAPAS; SOLANUM CF. NIGRUM, HIERBA MORA

Environmental setting: Various species of potato were domesticated in the Andes, probably between 10,000 and 7000 years ago. Wild and domesticated species are found from sea level to

Table 10.22. Distribution of plants in Phase V (~4107–3455 cal BP) for Units 24 and 25

| | HP-Unit 24 | | | | | HP-Unit 25 | | |
| | Layer | | | Total Unit 24 | % each species in Unit 24 | | Layer | Total Unit 25 | % each species in Unit 25 |
Taxon	1	2	3				3		
Acacia sp.		2		2	16.67			0	
Amaranthus sp.				0				0	
Annona muricata				0				0	
Arachis hypogaea				0				0	
Bunchosia armeniaca				0				0	
Canavalia maritima				0				0	
Canna edulis				0				0	
Capparis sp.				0				0	
Capparis angulata				0				0	
Capsicum sp.				0				0	
Chaetomorpha sp.				0				0	
Chenopodium sp.				0				0	
Chloris sp.				0				0	
Commelina sp.				0				0	
Cucurbita sp.				0				0	
Cucurbita moschata				0				0	
Cyperus sp.				0				0	
Desmodium sp.				0				0	
Eleocharis sp.				0				0	
Equisetum sp.				0				0	
Erythroxylum coca				0				0	
Fourcroya sp.				0				0	
Gigartina chamissoi				0				0	
Gossypium barbadense				0				0	
Guadua sp.				0				0	
Gymnogongrus furcellatus				0				0	
Gynerium sagittatum	4	1	4	9	75.00		1	1	10.00
Lagenaria siceraria				0			7	7	70.00
Manihot esculenta				0					
Nicotiana sp.				0					
Panicum sp.				0					
Paspalum sp.				0					
Persea sp.				0					
Persea americana				0					
Phaseolus sp.				0					
Phaseolus lunatus									
Phaseolus vulgaris									
Phragmites australis							1	1	10.00
Poaceae									
Pouteria lucuma									

Table 10.22. Continued

Taxon	HP-Unit 24					HP-Unit 25		
	Layer			Total Unit 24	% each species in Unit 24	Layer	Total Unit 25	% each species in Unit 25
	1	2	3			3		
Prosopis sp.								
Psidium sp.								
Psidium guajava								
Ruppia maritima								
Schoenoplectus californicus								
Scirpus sp.			1	1	8.33			
Solanum sp.								
Solanum cf. *nigrum*								
Tessaria integrifolia								
Trifolium sp.								
Typha angustifolia								
Zea mays				0		1	1	10.00
Total				12			10	
% of each phase of total remains								
% of each unit of total remains in phase				0.27			0.23	

HP = Huaca Prieta; P = Paredones; DS = Domestic Site.

above 4000 masl. *Solanum* sp. tubers from Tres Ventanas Cave have been dated to ~7600 BP and from coastal Peru to 4500 BP (Dillehay and Piperno 2014).

Economic use: Tubers provide starch.

Findings at Huaca Prieta/Paredones: Fragments of *Solanum* were found but not all identified to species. A seed was recovered from Layer 6, Unit 20, at Paredones in a Phase II context and another from Floor 3 in Unit 5, Phase V, in Huaca Prieta. Unit 14 (Floor 2) yielded 6 fragments of *S. nigrum* (not a potato but a medicinal plant) at Huaca Prieta in Phase V contexts. This is not a poisonous plant.

Findings at other archaeological sites: *Solanum* was found at El Paraíso (Quilter et al 1991: 280), Buena Vista (Duncan et al. 2009: 13202–13203), and Huaynuná (Ugent et al. 1982: 184–187).

CANNA EDULIS: ACHIRA

Environmental setting: *Canna edulis* grows on the Peruvian coast and in the temperate valleys of the Andes up to 2000 masl.

Economic use: The plant is a starchy rhizome eaten raw or boiled.

Findings at Huaca Prieta/Paredones: A single leaf fragment was recovered from Unit 3 (Floor 6), Phase IV, at Huaca Prieta. Bird recovered both leaves and rhizomes (Bird 1948a, 1948c). Margaret Towle (1961: 33–34) states: "Specimens of various parts of *canna* (locally, *achira*) were found in Test Pit 3 down through layer Q." The plant was present from Phases III–V at Huaca Prieta.

Findings at other archaeological sites: *Canna* was recorded at Aspero (Feldman 1977, 1980: 180), Cerro Lampay (Vega-Centeno 2007), Los Gavilanes (Popper 1982: table 10, 150), and Huaynuná (Ugent et al. 1984).

Table 10.23. Distribution of plants in Phase V (~4107–3455 cal BP) for Unit HP-3

Taxon	Layer													A			
	3	4	5	8	10	11	13	14	15	16	18	19	28	2	5	6	8
Acacia sp.						1											
Amaranthus sp.																	
Annona muricata																	
Arachis hypogaea																	
Bunchosia armeniaca																	
Canavalia maritima																	
Canna edulis																	
Capparis sp.																	
Capparis angulata																	
Capsicum sp.																	
Chaetomorpha sp.																	
Chenopodium sp.																	
Chloris sp.																	
Commelina sp.																	
Cucurbita sp.																	
Cucurbita moschata																	
Cyperus sp.											16						
Desmodium sp.																	
Eleocharis sp.																	
Equisetum sp.			1														
Erythroxylum coca																	
Fourcroya sp.																	
Gigartina chamissoi																	
Gossypium barbadense						1											
Guadua sp.	3																
Gymnogongrus furcellatus																	
Gynerium sagittatum						1					2						
Lagenaria siceraria	7	2	14	1	8	63	4	3	1	23	2	8		5	2	3	5
Manihot esculenta																	
Nicotiana sp.																	
Panicum sp.																	
Paspalum sp.																	
Persea sp.																	
Persea americana																	
Phaseolus sp.																	
Phaseolus lunatus																	
Phaseolus vulgaris																	
Phragmites australis						1											
Poaceae																	
Pouteria lucuma														1	2		

East-West Wall	Total HP-3	% each species in HP3
	1	0.49
	0	
	0	
	0	
	0	
	0	
	0	
	0	
	0	
	0	
	0	
	0	
	0	
	0	
	0	
	0	
	0	
	16	7.84
	0	
	0	
	1	0.49
	1	0.49
	3	1.47
	3	1.47
	151	74.02
	1	0.49
	3	1.47

Table 10.23. Continued

	HP-3																	
	Layer													A			
Taxon	3	4	5	8	10	11	13	14	15	16	18	19	28	2	5	6	8
Prosopis sp.	1					5											
Psidium sp.																	
Psidium guajava																	
Ruppia maritima																	
Schoenoplectus californicus						7											
Scirpus sp.																	
Solanum sp.																	
Solanum cf. *nigrum*																	
Tessaria integrifolia																	
Trifolium sp.																	
Typha angustifolia																	
Zea mays													1	1			
Total																	
% of each phase of total remains																	
% of each unit of total remains in phase																	

HP = Huaca Prieta; P = Paredones; DS = Domestic Site.

POUTERIA LUCUMA: LUCUMA

Environmental setting: The genus *Pouteria* has ~200 species. Of this number, 120 are found in Amazonia and in the Atlantic rainforest of Brazil. It is found in warm climates near sea level (Alves-Araújo et al. 2014). *P. lucuma* thrives in subtropical habitats in the Andean valleys 1000–2800 masl (Mostacero et al 2009: 647). *Lucuma obovata* was cultivated in coastal Peru by 4500 BP. *Pouteria lucuma* was present on the coast of Peru by 4500 BP (Dillehay and Piperno 2014).

Economic use: The fruit is highly nutritious. The wood is dense and is used for fuel.

Findings at Huaca Prieta/Paredones: At Huaca Prieta 5 seeds were recovered from Unit 16 (Layer 3) and 3 in HP-3 (Layers 8-A2 and 8-A5) in Phase V. Charcoal was recovered from Unit 13 (Floor 2) and Unit 23 (Structure 2, Layer 1) in Phase V. At Paredones an endocarp came from Unit 20 (Layer 6) in Phase II. Bird recovered lucuma from HP-3 through Layer R (Bird et al. 1985: 230, 235, fig. 179), which corresponds to our Phase III.

Findings at other archaeological sites: *Pouteria* was reported at El Paraíso (Engel 1966: 62), Buena Vista (Duncan et al. 2009), Cerro Lampay (Vega-Centeno 2007: table 2), Huaynuná (Ugent et al. 1984: 420), Alto Salaverry (Pozorski 1976: 85), and Los Gavilanes (Popper 1982: 153).

AMARANTHUS SP.: AMARANTH, *AMARANTO*

Environmental setting: This is a robust annual herb with small seeds, of which 60 species are known worldwide; 12 are found in Peru (Mostacero et al. 2009: 157).

Economic use: Amaranth seeds are nutritious

East-West Wall	Total HP-3	% each species in HP3
	6	2.94
9	16	7.84
	0	
	2	0.98
	204	
	4.61	

and contain essential proteins. The plant also has medicinal properties. The leaves and stems are eaten green.

Findings at Huaca Prieta/Paredones: A single seed was recovered from Floor 13 in Unit 22 at Paredones in Phase III. It is not clear whether they were wild plants or plants in the early stages of cultivation. Amaranth was not reported from the Bird excavations at Huaca Prieta.

Findings at other archaeological sites: Amaranth was present at El Paraíso (Quilter et al. 1991: 280) and Los Gavilanes (Popper 1982: table 10).

CHENOPODIUM SP.: QUINOA

Environmental setting: *Chenopodium* sp. was adapted to the highlands. It was widely distributed and was a component of the seasonally dry forest in the Nanchoc Valley (Rossen 2011b).

Economic use: The seeds are edible. The plant was also used medicinally, especially *C. ambrosioides* (Mostacero et al. 2009: 142).

Findings at Huaca Prieta/Paredones: A few *Chenopodium* sp. (Chenopodiaceae) specimens were recovered from Huaca Prieta. A single seed was recovered from Unit 2 (Layer 7) in a Phase II context and another from Unit 2 (Layer 3) in Phase IV. Bird does not mention the plant.

Findings at other archaeological sites: *Chenopodium* was found at Los Gavilanes and at the Nanchoc sites (Rossen (2011a: 106).

Commentary: While it is difficult to reconcile early domestication in the seasonally dry forest of the Nanchoc Valley and the larger seeded forms of the central Bolivian highlands, it may be that the Las Pircas specimens from the Nanchoc area (see Rossen 2011a) represent a predomestication phase or another place of cultivation. In any event the Las Pircas seeds are larger than those from Los Gavilanes and probably represent a form further along the path to domestication from an early date.

CULTIVATED INDUSTRIAL PLANTS

LAGENARIA SICERARIA: MATE, GOURD

Environmental setting: *Lagenaria siceraria* is a cucurbit originating in dry forest environments.

Economic use: *Lagenaria siceraria* can be used as a food, but its hard rind can also be used as a container and as a float for fishnets.

Findings at Huaca Prieta/Paredones: At Huaca Prieta 7 fragments were recovered in HP-3 and 5 were recovered in Layer 6 and 1 in Layer 7 in Unit 16 in Phase II. A single seed was recovered in Unit 9 (Layer 6) and 35 in HP-3 (Layers 22, 23, 29, and 34) in Phase III. Units 3, 13, and 25 and HP-3 in Phase IV yielded 281 fragments. In Phase V the number is much larger than in the other phases, with 1119 fragments recovered from Units 3, 5–8, 10, 11, 14, 16, 22, 23, and 25 and HP-3 and Test Pit 26. At Paredones 5 fragments were found in Floor 10 and 1 in Floor 11, Unit 22, and 5 in Layers 5 and 6, Unit 20, from Phase III. A single specimen was found in Floor 9, 41 in Floor 8, 36 in Floor 7, and 26 in Floor 6 in Unit 22, and 1 in Layer 4 in Unit 20 from Phase IV. In all 17 speci-

Table 10.24. Distribution of plants in Phase V (~4107–3455 cal BP) for Test Pit 26

| | Test Pit 26 | | | | | | | | |
| | Layer | | | Total Test Pit 26 | % each species in Test Pit 26 | Total Phase V | % each species in Phase V | Total all phases | % each species in all phases |
Taxon	1	2	3						
Acacia sp.				0		9	0.20	25	0.41
Amaranthus sp.				0		0		1	0.02
Annona muricata				0		0		1	0.02
Arachis hypogaea				0		0		5	0.08
Bunchosia armeniaca				0		22	0.50	22	0.36
Canavalia maritima				0		0	0.00	10	0.17
Canna edulis				0		0		1	0.02
Capparis sp.				0		0	0.00	1	0.02
Capparis angulata				0		46	1.04	46	0.76
Capsicum sp.				0		499	11.28	855	14.14
Chaetomorpha sp.				0		5	0.11	6	0.10
Chenopodium sp.				0		0		2	0.03
Chloris sp.				0		1	0.02	1	0.02
Commelina sp.				0		1	0.02	1	0.02
Cucurbita sp.				0		16	0.36	21	0.35
Cucurbita moschata	1	44		45	58.44	199	4.50	222	3.67
Cyperus sp.				0		595	13.45	995	16.45
Desmodium sp.				0		2	0.05	2	0.03
Eleocharis sp.				0		40	0.90	41	0.68
Equisetum sp.				0		335	7.57	366	6.05
Erythroxylum coca				0		43	0.97	43	0.71
Fourcroya sp.				0		1	0.02	4	0.07
Gigartina chamissoi				0		5	0.11	6	0.10
Gossypium barbadense				0		68	1.54	82	1.36
Guadua sp.						3	0.07	3	0.05
Gymnogongrus furcellatus						428	9.68	435	7.19
Gynerium sagittatum		7		7	9.09	176	3.98	195	3.22
Lagenaria siceraria	3	19	1	23	29.87	1138	25.73	1584	26.19
Manihot esculenta						0		1	0.02
Nicotiana sp.						5	0.11	5	0.08
Panicum sp.						0		2	0.03
Paspalum sp.						3	0.07	3	0.05
Persea sp.						0		0	0.00
Persea americana						2	0.05	6	0.10
Phaseolus sp.						2	0.05	34	0.56
Phaseolus lunatus						2	0.05	68	1.12
Phaseolus vulgaris						37	0.84	37	0.61
Phragmites australis						13	0.29	16	0.26
Poaceae						49	1.11	50	0.83
Pouteria lucuma						8	0.18	9	0.15
Prosopis sp.						47	1.06	61	1.01

Table 10.24. Continued

Taxon	Test Pit 26 Layer 1	2	3	Total Test Pit 26	% each species in Test Pit 26	Total Phase V	% each species in Phase V	Total all phases	% each species in all phases
Psidium sp.						1	0.02	1	0.02
Psidium guajava						342	7.73	419	6.93
Ruppia maritima						11	0.25	18	0.30
Schoenoplectus californicus						19	0.43	19	0.31
Scirpus sp.						26	0.59	37	0.61
Solanum sp.						1	0.02	2	0.03
Solanum cf. *nigrum*						6	0.14	6	0.10
Tessaria integrifolia	2			2	2.60	10	0.23	56	0.93
Trifolium sp.						2	0.05	5	0.08
Typha angustifolia						2	0.05	3	0.05
Zea mays				0		202	4.57	213	3.52
Total				77		4423		6045	
% of each phase of total remains						73.13		100.01	
% of each unit of total remains in phase				1.74					

HP = Huaca Prieta; P = Paredones; DS = Domestic Site.

mens came from Phase V: 1 from Floor 2 and 16 from Floor 1. Bird recovered large quantities of gourd shell fragments (Bird et al 1985; compare Whitaker and Bird 1949: 2), which corresponds to our Phase III.

Findings at other archaeological sites: Gourds were found at El Paraíso (Quilter 1991: 280), Buena Vista (Duncan et al. 2009: 13202), Aspero (Willey and Corbett 1954), Los Gavilanes (Bonavia 1982: 236), Bandurria (Chu Barrera 2011), Cerro Lampay (Vega-Centeno 2007), Huaynuná (Ugent et al. 1984: 420), Huaca Negra (Towle 1952: 355–356, 1961: 93, 106), and Alto Salaverry (Pozorski 1976: table 8).

Comments: The principal use of this plant was as a container; the fruits have also been used as floats on fishing nets (Bird et al. 1985), as spoons or serving spoons, and as enigmatic discs (Wendt 1976: 37; Bird et al. 1985: fig. 172). It was also used as an important decorative base (pyro-engraving, excision, and other techniques; Bird et al. 1985).

GOSSYPIUM BARBADENSE: COTTON, *ALGODON*

Environmental setting: The original site for the domestication of *G. barbadense* has not been determined, although it is believed to be the northern coast of Peru (Piperno 2012). It grows wild or as an escaped plant and is adapted to arid conditions.

Economic use: Cotton provides a durable, workable fiber that was used initially in cordage, fishnets and netted bags, and garments. At Huaca Prieta a great quantity was used in the production of textiles (see chapter 12).

Findings at Huaca Prieta/Paredones: Given the thousands of cotton textiles, seeds, and fibers recovered from the sites, particularly Huaca Prieta, all the information cannot be listed here (see chapter 12 for the context and study of the textiles and cordage). Thus only cotton seeds and loose fibers are mentioned here. At Huaca Prieta fibers or threads appeared in Unit 2 (Layer 4), Unit 5 (Floors 3 and 4), Unit 6 (Floors 1 and 2), Unit 10 (Layers 1 and 2), Unit 11 (Layer 2), Unit 14 (Floor 4), Unit 16 (Layers 2 and 3), Unit 20 (Layer 2), Unit 21 (Structure 8), Unit 23 (Layer 1, Structure 1; Layer 1, Structure 2; Layer 1, Structure 3; Layer 3, Structure 8), Unit 25 (Layer 4), and HP-3 (Layer 11), all in Phase IV–V contexts. At Paredones they were found in Unit 22 (Floor 26, Phase II and Floor 14, Phase III). Unit 16 (Floor 3), a domestic unit, yielded 7 thread fragments. Both carbonized seeds and fiber were recovered from Phase IV contexts.

Cotton fiber and seeds were recovered from Bird's excavations at Huaca Prieta. Much of the material came from HP-3 from the surface to his Layer R, a time equivalent to Phases II–V, in the form of fiber, string, and textiles. In HP-2 cotton was present from his Layer C to his Layer G3. Several hundred specimens of wads of brown and white lint were found (some compressed like felt) as well as seeds, bracteoles, bolls, and twigs (Bird et al. 1985: 234).

Findings at other archaeological sites: Cotton was documented at Otuma (Engel 1960a, 1960b), Ancón-Chillón (Cohen 1978a: 33), Bandurria (Chu Barrera 2011), Río Seco (Wendt 1976), Aspero (Feldman 1980), Los Gavilanes (Bonavia 1982), Huaynuná (Ugent et al. 1984: 420), Huaca Negra (Towle 1961: 106), Padre Abán (Pozorski 1976: table 8), and sites in the Nanchoc Valley (Rossen 2011b).

Comments: Genetic studies have demonstrated that "primitive domesticated *G. barbadense* has its center of domestication in the NW Peru/SW Ecuador region" (Westengen et al. 2005: 400).

RITUAL AND POSSIBLE MEDICINAL PLANTS

ERYTHROXYLUM NOVOGRANATENSE VAR. TRUXILLENSE: COCA

Environmental setting: Tropical environments.

Economic use: *Erythroxylum coca* (Erithroxylaceae) has both ritual and medicinal importance.

Findings at Huaca Prieta/Paredones: At Huaca Prieta several leaves were recovered from Unit 8 (corresponding to Phase V) and from several small ritual offerings in and around the sunken circular plaza on the south side of Huaca Prieta (see chapter 7). In recent times local shamans still come to make offerings of coca leaves at the site itself, as our local workers, one a local shaman, confirmed to us.

Findings at other archaeological sites: Coca was reported at Ancón, at Los Gavilanes (Bonavia 1982), and at the Nanchoc sites (Dillehay et al. 2010: 942).

GATHERED WETLAND PLANTS

EQUISETUM GIGANTEUM: HORSETAIL, *COLA DE CABALLO*

Environmental setting: Horsetail is a wetland plant. Weberbauer (1945: 230) notes that it is found in swamps and ponds where there is standing water.

Economic use: In the past the primary use was as fuel. The silica spicules in the epidermis were used to smooth and polish wood (Sagástegui Alva 1973: 11). Medicinal properties are also reported (Soukup 1987: 172).

Findings at Huaca Prieta/Paredones: *Equisetum* sp. was found at Huaca Prieta. Units 23 and 25 at Huaca Prieta produced minor counts of burned fragments in multiple Phase V contexts. For example, burned remains came from Unit 10 (Layers 3–4), Unit 11 (Feature 3), Unit 14 (Layers 1B, 1C, and 2A and Floor 6), HP-3 (Layer 5), Unit 16 (Layer 5), and Unit 5 (Floors 4 and 5) in Phases IV–V. Carbonized remains were recovered from Unit 2 (Layer 7) and in Unit 5 (Floor 4) in Phases II–V, respectively. *Equisetum* sp. is most abundant during Phase V. Domestic Unit 16 yielded 52 fragments from Floor 1 and Use Surfaces 1–3 in Phases IV–V; carbonized remains were recovered in Phases II–V contexts. At domestic Unit 13 several fragments were recovered in a Phase V context. At domestic Test Pit 26 carbonized material came from Floors 3 and 9, corresponding to Phase V. At Paredones a single stalk was found in Layer 8, Unit 20, in an early Phase II context.

Noncarbonized samples of *Esquisetum* sp. were also recovered, perhaps reflecting use in basketry or other material culture. A single sample was recovered in Unit 2 (Layer 7), Phase II, and 29 were recovered in Unit 13, Phase IV, at Huaca Prieta. One specimen was found in Floor 8, Unit 22, Phase IV, at Paredones. More than 200 samples were recovered in Phase V, in Units 5, 10–12, 14–16, and 18 and HP-3.

Equisetum was infrequent in Bird's excavations at Huaca Prieta (Bird et al. 1985: 238).

Findings at other archaeological sites: *Equisetum* was found at El Paraíso (Quilter et al. 1991) and Cerro Lampay (Vega-Centeno 2007: table 2).

Commentary: With regard to the use of horsetail as a fuel, Vásquez Sánchez and Rosales Tham (2010: 142) note that the "rounded root rhizomes, similar to tubers, which are burned . . . [they] are found in humid places and near swampy areas. The carbonized remains in some cases include fragments of the stalks, indicating that the population used these plants intensively as fuel. There are no comparative ethnobotanical data for this type of plant in relation to its use as fuel."

PHRAGMITES AUSTRALIS (CAV.) TRIN. EX STEUD.: COMMON REED, *CARRIZO*

Environmental setting: *P. australis* is a reed of the tidal wetlands.

Economic use: This reed was used in the construction of houses and other structures. It was also used in the manufacture of matting and baskets.

Findings at Huaca Prieta/Paredones: Phase V yielded 13 pieces of reed from Unit 6 (Floor 2), Unit 7 (Floor 1), Unit 16 (Layer 5), Unit 25 (Layer 3), and HP-3 (Layer 11). At Paredones 2 pieces came from Unit 20 (Layer 6) in Phase III and a single stem from Unit 22 (Floor 7) in Phase IV.

Findings at other archaeological sites: *Phragmites* was reported at El Paraíso (Quilter et al. 1991), Aspero (Moseley 1975: 82), Bandurria (Chu Barrera 2011), and Cerro Lampay (Vega-Centeno 2007: table 2).

GUADUA ANGUSTIFOLIA: BAMBOO, *GUADUA*, *CAÑA DE GUAYAQUIL*

Environmental setting: This bamboo is native to the Amazon rainforest. It grows well from 400 to 1200 masl.

Economic use: Bamboo has great tensile strength and is widely used in construction today.

Findings at Huaca Prieta/Paredones: 3 canes of bamboo were recovered from the HP-3 (Layer 3) at Huaca Prieta from Phase V. Vásquez Sánchez and Rosales Tham (2010: 149) note that "it has been possible to identify this graminea by the diameter of the stalk fragments, which reach 15 cm in modern specimens."

Although the species found at Huaca Prieta are not known, they were probably *G. angustifolia*, commonly known as bamboo, *guadua*, and *caña de Guayaquil*.

Findings at other archaeological sites: No information was found in reports.

TYPHA ANGUSTIFOLIA: LESSER BULRUSH, NARROWLEAF CATTAIL, *INEA*

Environmental setting: *Typha angustifolia* is an aquatic species found in muddy and flooded areas at the edge of rivers.

Economic use: Cattail may have been used for "cordage and basketry" (Vásquez Sánchez and Rosales Tham (2010: 149) or to make woven mats (Mostacero et al. 2009: 1059).

Findings at Huaca Prieta/Paredones: Phase V at Huaca Prieta yielded 2 stalks from Unit 16 (Layers 2 and 6). At Paredones a stalk was recovered from Unit 20 (Layer 6), corresponding to a Phase III context. Bird notes: "The cattail specimens (local name *jinea* [sic: *inea*]) were found in the preceramic layers of Test Pit 3 [Huaca Prieta]—flower stalks, fiber, and possibly tubers" (Bird et al. 1985). Presumably these tubers were used as food.

Findings at other archaeological sites: *Typha* was recovered at Playa Hermosa (Cohen 1978b: 120), Bandurria (Chu Barrera 2011), and Los Gavilanes (Bonavia 1982: 66). Bird (1978b) suggested the "tubers" were used for food, and Cohen (1978b) also indicates that the rhizomes are edible.

CYPERUS SP.: SEDGE, *COCO*

Environmental setting: *Cyperus* sp. is adapted to wetlands, growing from a rhizome. It would have been present in the lagoons and wetlands east of the Sangamon terrace.

Economic use: Tubers of *Cyperus esculentus* var. *sativa* Boeckler are edible, but those of other species are not (Sagástegui Alva 1973: 117). Many species are used today in matting and in folk medicine for different purposes (Mostacero et al. 2009: 1062–1064).

Findings at Huaca Prieta/Paredones: *Cyperus* sp. is present at Huaca Prieta, with 164 examples in Unit 2 (Layer 7), corresponding to Phase II. Phase III at Huaca Prieta has 166 fragments from Layers 5–6, Unit 2. Phase IV has 66 samples in Unit 2 (Layers 3–4), 3 in Unit 25 (Layer C6), and 1 in HP-3 (Layer 22). Phase V contained 595 samples from Unit 2 (Layer 2), Unit 3 (Floor 1), Unit 4 (Layer 4), Unit 5 (Floors 1–6), Unit 6 (Floors 1 and 2), Unit 7 (Floors 1 and 2), Unit 10 (Layers 1–3), Unit 14 (Floor 6), and HP-3 (Layer 18). It appears that the edible species were utilized and that the rhizomes were used as a food in Phase IV and particularly in Phase V. Stems were found in the remains from Paredones. Bird reported remains of Cyperaceae from his excavations, noting that "several hundred small sedge tubers, some carbonized, were found in layers G through P1 in Test Pit 3, most abundantly in I1. They are further distinguished by often having long, tough stolons attached as may be the case with *Scirpus*" (Bird et al. 1985: 230–231).

Findings at other archaeological sites: Sedge was found at Asia (Engel 1963c: 77), Ancón (Cohen 1978b: 114), Río Seco (Wendt 1976: 21–22), Aspero (Feldman 1980: 175), and Los Gavilanes (Popper 1982).

ELEOCHARIS SP. (CYPERACEAE): SPIKERUSH, *PISO*

Environmental setting: *Eleocharis* sp. grows in wetlands.

Economic use: Spikerush may have been used in basketry and as a fuel. Bird recovered chewed wads, indicating that it may have been consumed in this way.

Findings at Huaca Prieta/Paredones: A leaf comes from Unit 5 (Floor 6) in a Phase V context from Huaca Prieta, and seeds were recovered by flotation from this unit. Samples were found mostly in Phase V contexts, in Units 10–12 and 14–16. Only 1 seed was recovered from Paredones in Unit 20 (Layer 2) in a Phase V context. Bird

recovered stems of *Eleocharis* sp. from HP-3 down through his Layer O in the form of chewed wads (Bird et al. 1985: 231). This dates between our Phases II and III.

Findings at other archaeological sites: This plant is not mentioned in the literature.

SCHOENOPLECTUS CALIFORNICUS (= *SCIRPUS CALIFORNICUS*): CALIFORNIA BULRUSH, TOTORA; *S. CALIFORNICUS* SSP. *TATORA*: TOTORA

Environmental setting: Totora is found in wetlands with fresh or brackish water.

Economic use: The stems are used in matting, baskets, rope, and roofing and to make watercraft.

Findings at Huaca Prieta/Paredones: Modest amounts of carbonized roots of *Scirpus* sp. (*Schoenoplectus* sp.) have been recovered at Huaca Prieta and at the domestic sites. At Huaca Prieta 10 specimens were recovered from Unit 3 (Floor 7) in Phase IV contexts and 25 were recovered from Phase V contexts. Phase V contexts also yielded 1.5 grams of carbon from Floor 4, Unit 3. At Paredones 1 carbonized root was recovered from Unit 10 (Layer 1) in Phase V; 3 fragments came from Layer 2 in the same phase at Unit 16. At Unit 13 1 fragment was recovered from Floor 3 in Phase V. A fragment of carbonized root was recovered from Layer 2 in Test Pit 26, which corresponds to Phase V. Unit 14 and HP-3 in Phase V yielded 19 noncarbonized samples. Bird found specimens of *Scirpus* sp. (Bird et al. 1985: 230–231).

Findings at other archaeological sites: *Scirpus* was documented at El Paraíso (Quilter et al. 1991), Aspero (Moseley and Willey 1973: 458), Bandurria (Chu Barrera 2011), Los Gavilanes, and Alto Salaverry (Pozorski 1976: 77).

GATHERED WILD PLANTS

PROSOPIS SP., *PROSOPIS PALLIDA*: ALGARROBO

Environmental setting: The algarrobo tree is very abundant on the coast and in the western valleys of the highlands. It is resistant to drought. The abundant seeds are enclosed in pods, which have a succulent pulp. The seeds are toxic and must be leached before they can be eaten, but they are highly nutritious. Syrup is made from the pulp.

Economic use: The wood is strong and tough. It was used as fuel and as raw material to make implements. The pods and seeds were eaten.

Findings at Huaca Prieta/Paredones: At Huaca Prieta a fragment was recovered from Unit 2 (Layer 5), corresponding to Phase III; 2 fragments came from Unit 25 (Layers C3 and 5) in Phase IV. Phase V has a total of 47 fragments from Unit 6 (Floors 1 and 2), Unit 7 (Floor 2), Unit 10 (Layers 1 and 2), Unit 12 (Floor 3), Unit 14 (Floor 5), Unit 16 (Floor 1 and Layer 2), Unit 23 (Layers 1, 3 and 8), and HP-3 (Layers 3 and 11). Moreover, 2.0 grams of carbon were retrieved from Unit 16 (Layer 11) in late Phase I and 73.0 grams from Unit 23 (Layers 1, 3, 5, and 9, Structure 8) in Phase V. A few tools of algarrobo were found at Paredones (see chapter 11).

Algarrobo pods, seeds, and wood were recovered at Paredones as macroremains from Unit 22 in Phase IV and Phase V contexts. An additional specimen came from Unit 20, corresponding to Phase V. Macroremains were recovered from Floor 1 in Unit 16 and in Test Pit 26 from Phase V contexts. Unit 2 also yielded significant quantities of charcoal from Layer 7 in Phase I; a large quantity (353 grams) also came from Unit 2 in a Phase II (Layer 5) context and a small quantity from Layer 1 in Phase V. A small quantity of charcoal from Layer 1 corresponding to Phase V was recovered from Test Pit 26. In Phase IV 10 macrospecimens were recovered from Floors 6 and 8 at Unit 22 in Phase IV and 2 from Layers C3 and 5 in Unit 25, while 18 came from Floor 1 in the domestic site, Unit 16. The total for Phase V was 47 specimens. All the rest were from units on the summit of the Huaca Prieta mound. None of these units had more than 7 specimens, and most had only 1 or 2. In the material recovered by Bird no *Prosopis* sp. remains were reported. In Phase IV 2 specimens came from Floor 8 and 8 from Floor 6, Unit 22.

Findings at other archaeological sites: *Prosopis* appears at El Paraíso (Quilter et al. 1991: table 3), Buena Vista (Duncan et al. 2009: 13203), Aspero (Feldman 1977: 2), Alto Salaverry (Pozorski 1976: 86), Los Gavilanes (Weir and Bonavia 1985: table 3), Cerro Lampay (Vega-Centeno 2007: table 2), Huaca Negra (Strong and Evans 1952;

Towel 1961: 56), Nanchoc Valley (Rossen 2011b), and early Holocene sites in the Chaman and Jequetepeque Valleys (Stackelback 2011).

Commentary: In archaeological reports algarrobo is mentioned primarily as a fuel and as a raw material used to make artifacts such as perforators and fire sticks, spears, handles, or beams in structures (Lanning 1967a: 62). It is also found in midden deposits, however, as is the case at Los Gavilanes, Huaca Prieta, and the early Chaman and Jequetepeque sites in the form of seeds, pod fragments, and stems, which suggests that it was associated with food.

SALIX HUMBOLDTIANA: WILLOW, *SAUCE*

Environmental setting: This tree is widely distributed on the coast as riverbank vegetation. It is found from sea level to 4000 masl.

Economic use: The soft willow wood is used as fuel and would have uses in tools. Willow withes are an important component in the making of large baskets. Additionally, willow has medicinal properties.

Findings at Huaca Prieta/Paredones: At Huaca Prieta the remains were small quantities of charcoal from Unit 10 (Layer 1), Unit 19 (Layer 1C), Unit 25 (Section 5), and Unit 25 (Fill 1) in Phases III–V. Willow charcoal came from Layer 5, Layer 7, Layer 10, and Use Surface 2, at Unit 16, as well as a small quantity from Phase I and a larger amount from a context from Phases II–IV. At Paredones remains of willow charcoal were recovered from Unit 20 (Layers 6a and 6c) in Phase II. Bird mentions willow among the specimens found in small quantity (Bird et al. 1985: 238).

Findings at other archaeological sites: Willow was found at La Paloma (Weir and Dering 1986: table 2.2), El Paraíso (Quilter et al. 1991: table 3), Río Seco (Wendt 1976: 21–22), and Cerro Lampay (Vega-Centeno 2007: table 2).

CAPPARIS SP. [CAPPARIS ANGULATA], CAPPARIS SCABRIDA: *SAPOTE*

Environmental setting: This tree is part of the flora of the dry forest. It is adapted to prolonged drought and is found from sea level to 2500 masl (Rodríguez Rodríguez et al. 2007).

Economic use: The wood is used for artifacts and as fuel. The fruit is eaten.

Findings at Huaca Prieta/Paredones: A seed was found in Phase III at Paredones, Unit 22, in Floor 10. At Huaca Prieta in Phase V contexts 34 samples were recovered from Unit 3 (Floor 5), 1 from Unit 5 (Floor 4), and 10 from Unit 16 (Layers 1–2). At Paredones in Phase V 1 came from Unit 22 (Floor 3). As Vásquez Sánchez and Rosales Tham (2010: 118) have noted, "Bird et al. (1985) have also recorded and identified its seeds in all the levels shown in table 2, usually calling it a cherry tree (Bird et al. 1985: 237)." More than 2500 seeds, locally known as *cereza*, were found in HP-3 down through his Layer R (Bird et al. 1985: 237). The term "cherry" (*cereza* or *cerezo*) used by Bird refers to *Capparis*, however, and not to the cherry tree. Vásquez Sánchez and Rosales Tham (2010: 118) state in regard to the Phase IV finds at Huaca Prieta: "*Capparis angulata* (*Capparis scabrida* is now the accepted term) is a specialized plant of the deserts of the north coast of Peru. It is present among the remains of this phase as trunk fragments, which were identified histologically."

Findings at other archaeological sites: There is no archaeological information for other sites.

Commentary: Although we recovered 47 seeds from this plant, Bird found at least 2526 (Bird et al. 1985), which suggests that a substantial amount of this fruit was consumed.

ACACIA SP.: *FAIQUE*, "*HUARANGO*," *ESPINO*

Environmental setting: *Faique* is a member of the Leguminosae. The species of the floral material in the Huaca Prieta collection may be *A. macracantha*, which is found in the same arid environments as algarrobo.

Economic use: The pods and seeds were probably eaten. The wood was used for fuel and to make artifacts. Evidence at Huaca Prieta and Paredones suggests consumption of the fruits and or seeds.

Findings at Huaca Prieta/Paredones: At Huaca Prieta in Phase II 2 fruits were recovered from Layer 7 in Unit 2 and 1 from Layer 6 in Unit 16. For Phase II at Paredones 2 seeds came from Floors 20 and 22, Unit 22. For Phase III 1 was found in Layer 5 of Unit 1 at Huaca Prieta and 4

in Layer 6 of Unit 20 and 2 in Floor 11 of Unit 22 at Paredones. In Phase IV at Huaca Prieta 1 was recovered from Unit 2 (Layer 4), 2 from Unit 2 (Floors 6 and 7), and 1 from Unit 25 (Layer C3). At Paredones 2 were found in Floor 8 in Unit 22. More were found in Phase V, with 2 from Floor 6 in Unit 5, 3 from Floor 2 in Unit 6, 1 from Layer C7 in Unit 23, 2 from Layer 2 in Unit 24, and 1 from Layer 11 in HP-3. At Paredones fruits were recovered from Unit 22, spanning Phases II and III. In Phase II 1 fruit each was found in Floors 20 and 22. In Phase III Floor 11 of Unit 22 contained 2 fruits. Phase V contexts yielded 22 grams of carbonized material from this plant from Unit 22.

According to Bird et al. (1985: 237), "more than 30 fragments of pods identified locally as *mandaco* (fig. 183) were found in Test Pit 3 down through layer P." These finds correspond to our Phases II and III.

Findings at other archaeological sites: *Acacia* is reported from Los Gavilanes for all three epochs (Weir and Bonavia 1985: 130–131).

PARKINSONIA SP.: JERUSALEM THORN, *PALOVERDE*

Environmental setting: This member of the Leguminosae may be *P. aculeata* or *P. praecox* (Hughes et al. 2002). Both species of this small thorny tree are found in arid environments typical of the north coast away from water sources. The bean-like fruit is found in pods.

Economic use: The seeds could be eaten, and *P. aculeata* has sweet pulp when ripe. The wood served as fuel. The slender trunks provided poles. The pods and bark have medicinal properties.

Findings at Huaca Prieta/Paredones: At Huaca Prieta 4 grams of charcoal were recovered from Unit 20 (Layer 6f) in Phase II. Phase V yielded 40.9 grams of charcoal from Unit 24 (Section 1b, 3), Unit 23 (Structure 7, Layers 1 and 4), Unit 21 (Layer 3), and Unit 10 (Layers 1c1, 2, and 3, Floor 3). At Paredones, among the remains from Phase III were 4 grams of charcoal from Phase V; 16.3 grams were recovered from Unit 22 (Hearth 3) and Unit 22 (Feature 3). In Phase V the domestic site at Unit 16 contained 9.5 grams in Layer 3 and in Use Surface 3, while Test Pit 26 yielded 4.8 grams of charcoal from Layer 1.

Findings at other archaeological sites: There is no evidence of remains in other sites.

SCHINUS MOLLE: MOLLE, PERUVIAN PEPPER

Environmental setting: *Schinus molle* is a small evergreen tree common in the Andean valleys. It tolerates drought and has edible fruits (berries).

Economic use: The leaves can be used as a dye. *Schinus molle* leaves and fruits have medicinal properties, and the fruit was used for flavoring and to make a drink (*chicha*). The wood can be used as fuel.

Findings at Huaca Prieta/Paredones: At Huaca Prieta 6.9 grams of charcoal were recovered from Unit 25 (Layer 6), corresponding to Phase IV, and 22.5 grams from Unit 23 (Layer 1), corresponding to Phase V. Layer 12 in Unit 16, corresponding to Phase I, yielded 8.8 grams of carbon. In Phase V 6.8 grams came from Layer 1 and 2 grams from Test Pit 26.

Findings at other archaeological sites: *Schinus molle* was found at La Paloma (Weir and Dering 1986: 23) and Los Gavilanes (Popper 1982).

BUDDLEJA SP.: BUTTERFLY BUSH

Environmental setting: This woody evergreen bush is found from sea level to 4000 masl. Vásquez Sánchez and Rosales Tham (2010: 100–101) report *Buddleja* as a highland species that may have been carried down to the coast by high river discharge.

Economic use: This is a possible source of fuel.

Findings at Huaca Prieta/Paredones: At Huaca Prieta 6.3 grams of charcoal are present from Unit 20 (Layer 2) in Phase II; in Phase V 2.5 grams came from Unit 21 (Fill 2). At Paredones the earliest remains also correspond to Phase II, with 6.3 grams from Floor 22. Phase V yielded 21.3 grams from Unit 22 (Floors 1a, 2, 9, and 10, Feature 1, Hearth 2) as well as 22.0 grams of charcoal from Unit 16 (Layer 3 and Use Surface 3).

Findings at other archaeological sites: No information is available.

TESSARIA INTEGRIFOLIA: PALO BOBO

Environmental setting: This plant grows along riverbanks. It occasionally invades cultivated fields as a weed.

Economic use: *Palo bobo* is used as fuel and as a medicinal plant. The presence of seeds may suggest other uses.

Findings at Huaca Prieta/Paredones: At Huaca Prieta 3 samples were identified from Unit 16 (Layer 11) in Phase I, while 3 more were recovered from Unit 25 (Layers 5–6) in Phase IV. Phase V yielded 10 from Units 3 and 16 and Test Pit 16 at Huaca Prieta as well as 21 grams of charcoal from Unit 10 (Structure 2; Layer 1), Unit 21 (Feature 1), and Unit 23 (Structure 7, Layer 2). At Paredones 40 samples were recovered from Unit 22 (Floors 6 and 7) in Phase IV. This plant was not reported from Bird's excavations.

Findings at other archaeological sites: *Palo bobo* is reported from Asia (Engel 1963c: 77) and La Paloma (Quilter et al. 1991: 280).

DESMODIUM SP.: TICK-TREFOIL, PIE DE PERRO

Environmental setting: This leguminous herb is typical of the north coast of Peru (Weberbauer 1945: 279–280).

Economic use: This plant repels insects and is nitrogen-fixing in fields. It may have medicinal properties.

Findings at Huaca Prieta/Paredones: At Huaca Prieta 2 fragments of *Desmodium* sp. (Fabaceae = Leguminosae) were recovered from Unit 10 (Layer 1) and Unit 14 (Floor 4), corresponding to Phase V.

Findings at other archaeological sites: The plant is not reported from other archaeological sites.

RUPPIA MARITIMA: WIGEON GRASS

Environmental setting: *R. maritima* is a submerged aquatic herbaceous species found in lakes, ponds, and swampy areas between sea level and 180 masl in the north and central deserts of Peru (Mostacero et al. 2009: 9).

Economic use: *R. maritima* is a food for wildfowl. It may have been used in thatching or basketry.

Findings at Huaca Prieta/Paredones: At Huaca Prieta 6 seeds were recovered from Unit 25 (Layers C3, C4, and C6) in Phase IV and 11 from Unit 23 (Layer 3), Structure 1, Layer 2, Structure 2 (Layer 2), Structures 3 and 4, Structure 7 (Layer 3), and Structure 8 (Layer 1) in Phase V. At Paredones a single seed was recovered from Unit 22 (Floor 8) in Phase III and another from Floor 8, Unit 22, Phase IV.

Findings at other archaeological sites: No archaeological information is available.

Commentary: Vásquez Sánchez and Rosales Tham (2010: 119) comment that "the presence of the seeds indicates that the plants were transported to the contexts of Phase IV." They note that its presence at Paredones "indicates the exploitation of freshwater environments."

FURCRAEA SP., FOURCRAYA SP., F. PENCA, F. CABUYA (PROBABLY F. OCCIDENTALIS)

Environmental setting: This plant is found on rocky slopes between 450 and 1000 masl in northern Peru.

Economic use: Fibers from the leaves are used to make rope, cordage, string, and so forth. (Mostacero et al. 2009: 939).

Findings at Huaca Prieta/Paredones: At Huaca Prieta 3 fibers come from Phase IV and 1 from Phase V. While *Furcraea* is not on the list of plants recovered by Bird (Bird et al. 1985: 230–231), he includes a note about *penca*, probably *F. occidentalis*.

Findings at other archaeological sites: This plant was found at El Paraíso (Quilter et al. 1991: 280), Buena Vista (Duncan et al. 2009: 13202), and Los Gavilanes (Popper 1982).

COMMELINA SP.: SARA-SARA, DAYFLOWER (PROBABLY C. FASCICULATA)

Environmental setting: Found in humid places at the edges of watercourses.

Economic use: Unknown.

Findings at Huaca Prieta/Paredones: A single fragment was recovered from Unit 23 (Structure 2, Layer 2) in Phase V.

Findings at other archaeological sites: No information is available.

GYNERIUM SAGITTATUM: WILD CANE, CAÑA BRAVA

Environmental setting: This grass grows on moist organic soils where the water table is high, sometimes on seasonally flooded areas in river floodplains or sandbars. It is found from 10 to 1600 masl.

Economic use: Wild cane's culms lack strength and its stalks are not as strong as bamboo, but it is used in crude structures, drying racks, stakes, woven mats, and basketry. The canes are used in house construction; the green stalks are used for fencing.

Findings at Huaca Prieta/Paredones: At Huaca Prieta 4 samples were recovered in Unit 16, Layer 7, in Phase II, 4 samples from Units 3 and 25 in Phase IV, and 179 samples from Units 3, 5, 6, 7, 10, 11, 14, 16, 23, 24, and 25 and from HP-3 and Test Pit 26 in Phase V. Phase II yielded 9.0 grams from Floor 18 in Unit 22 and 48.4 grams from Layers 6b and f in Unit 20. Phase IV produced 66.5 grams from Units 3, 20, and 25, and Phase V yielded 1854.6 grams from Units 10, 16, 23, and 25. At Paredones 5 samples were found in Unit 20 in Phase III, while 6 samples came from Unit 20 in Phase IV. The 10.2 grams of carbon recovered in Unit 13 dated to Phases IV and V. Bird's excavations also found remains of this plant: "about 1000 specimens . . . in Test Pit 3 from layers A through R" (Bird et al. 1985: 231).

Findings at other archaeological sites: *Gynerium* is reported at El Paraíso (Engel 1966a: 62; Quilter et al. 1991), Río Seco (Wendt 1976: 21–22), Los Gavilanes (Popper 1982), Cerro Lampay (Vega-Centeno 2007), Padre Abán (Pozorski 1976: 77), and Alto Salaverry (Pozorski 1976: 86).

PANICUM SP.: GUINEA GRASS, BUFFALO GRASS

Environmental setting: This weed, which invades cultivated fields, is widely found throughout the Americas (Sagástegui Alva 1973: 78–80).

Economic use: Unknown.

Findings at Huaca Prieta/Paredones: At Huaca Prieta 1 sample was found in Unit 2 (Layer 7) in

Phase II and another in Unit 3 (Floor 6) in Phase IV. A single carbonized seed came from Unit 2 (Stratum 7B) in Phase II, another from Unit 2 (Stratum 6E) in Phase III, and 6 from Unit 5 (Floors 4–6) in Phase V, "which indicates that whole plants, including the inflorescences, were carried into the site contexts" (Vásquez Sánchez and Rosales Tham 2010: table 26). There is no evidence of *Panicum* sp. in the excavations of Bird.

Findings at other archaeological sites: The only reference is at Padre Abán and Alto Salaverry (Pozorski 1976).

PASPALUM SP.: *GRAMA*, BAHIA GRASS, DALLIS GRASS

Environmental setting: This grass is found at the edge of watercourses (Mostacero et al. 2009: 1024).

Economic use: Unknown.

Findings at Huaca Prieta/Paredones: Only 3 fragments were recovered at Huaca Prieta from Unit 10 (Layer 2 and Floor 1) in Phase V contexts.

Findings at other archaeological sites: No information has been reported.

CHLORIS SP.: FINGER GRASS

Environmental setting: The 2 species *C. virgata* (feather finger grass) and *C. halophila* (finger grass) are found in Peru. The first is an annual grass common on the north coast that is an ephemeral part of the herbaceous vegetation, commonly known as *gramilla*. It is found between 70 and 2000 masl. The second is a perennial that grows on the north coast in arid soils at the edges of roads and invades cultivated fields between 30 and 3550 masl (Sagástegui Alva 1973: 44–46).

Economic use: Unknown.

Findings at Huaca Prieta/Paredones: An inflorescence was recovered from Huaca Prieta from Unit 14 (Floor 6) in a Phase V context.

Findings at other archaeological sites: No evidence has been reported.

SEAWEEDS, *ALGAS MARINAS*

CHAETOMORPHA SP.: SEAWEED

Environmental setting: This seaweed lives in the mud of the supralittoral associated with brackish environments; it is used as a food. *Chaetomorpha* sp. is present when the biota are disturbed by some ecological or anthropogenic impact (Torres and Caille 2009: 520).

Economic use: Food plant.

Findings at Huaca Prieta/Paredones: At Huaca Prieta 4 samples of *Chaetomorpha* sp. (Cladophoraceae) have been recovered from Phase V contexts in Units 16 and 23. At Paredones 1 specimen was recovered from Floor 9, Unit 22, Phase IV, and 1 specimen from Floor 2, Phase V, also in Unit 22.

Findings at other archaeological sites: No information is available.

Commentary: The only species indicated for Peru is *Chaetomorpha antennina*, gregarious plants that "grow fixed on mollusk shells forming standing mats, exposed in the tidal zones" (Acleto Osorio 1973: 10).

GYMNOGONGRUS FURCELLATUS: SEAWEED

Environmental setting: This seaweed grows in clumps that are olive brown to blackish brown (Acleto Osorio 1971: 49–51).

Economic use: This seaweed is used for food preparation and as a laxative or to cure colds (Acleto Osorio 1971: 52).

Findings at Huaca Prieta/Paredones: At Huaca Prieta 428 samples of *Gymnogongrus furcellatus* (Phyllophoraceae) were recovered: 419 in Unit 6, Phase V. Other samples were recovered in the materials from Unit 10 (Layer 3), Unit 16 (Layers 2 and 4), Unit 21 (Structure 8) and Unit 23 (Layer 1, Structure 2; Layer 4, Structure 7) from Phase V at Huaca Prieta. At Paredones 3 came from Phase II, Unit 22; 1 from Phase III, Unit 20, Layer 6, and 3 from Phase IV, Unit 22, Floor 8.

Findings at other archaeological sites: No information on this species is available.

GIGARTINA CHAMISSOI: YUYO, UYO, MOCOCHO, SEAWEED

Environmental setting: *G. glomerata* lives only on the central coast, and *G. paitensis* is limited to the littoral of the far north (Acleto Osorio 1971:61).

Economic use: This seaweed is eaten in foods such as *ceviche*, picantes, and soups (Acosta Polo 1977: 4).

Findings at Huaca Prieta/Paredones: *Gigartina chamissoi* (Gigartinaceae) was recovered at Huaca Prieta: Unit 10 (Layer 3), Unit 21 (Structure 1), and Unit 23 (Layers 1 and 4, Structure 2) yielded 5 specimens in Phase V contexts. At Paredones 1 sample was found in Unit 20 (Layer 6) in Phase III.

Findings at other archaeological sites: No archaeological information on this seaweed is available.

BIRD'S LIST OF "SPECIMENS IN SMALL QUANTITY"

Bird's final report lists a group of plants under the title "Specimens in Small Quantity" (Bird et al. 1985: 238). The majority are identified by a common name.

No references could be found for the plants listed as *quinal* (?), *chaquira del indio*, *choloque*, and *simbolo*. Bird mentions *Sapindus saponaria*. Its identification should be correct, as this is the only species from this genus found in South America. It has many names: *choloque, tingana, chano, boliche, borlita*, and so forth. This tall tree is found on the coast and in the inter-Andean valleys from 80 to 2500 masl. The fruit, which contains saponin, is used for washing clothes. The bark and roots are used in popular medicine, and the black seeds are used in handicrafts and as toys for children (Soukup 1987: 365).

PLANTS RECOVERED BY BIRD NOT FOUND BY OUR PROJECT

Bird's excavations recovered 4 plants that were not in the botanical materials found by our project: *Calamagrostis* sp., *Tillandsia* sp., *Canavalia plagiosperma*, and *Asclepias* sp.

CALAMAGROSTIS SP.: BOBO

Calamagrostis sp. (Poaceae) was recovered from Bird's Layers D to Q in HP-3 (Bird et al. 1985: 231), that is, from our Phases II to V. Towle (1961: 17) notes that it is used for making brooms. No archaeological information about this plant is available.

TILLANDSIA SP., MOSS, MUSGO

Bird found numerous specimens of *Tillandsia* sp. (Bromeliaceae) in his excavations with "carbonized stems with closely packed leaf bases," all coming from HP-3 and from the upper levels down to his Layer Q (Bird et al. 1985: 231, 233), which corresponds to our Phases II to V.

This plant appears at La Paloma (Weir and Dering 1986), Ancón-Chillón (Lanning 1967b: 26), Río Seco (Wendt 1976: 21–22), Aspero (Moseley 1975: 82), Los Gavilanes (Popper 1982: 155), and Las Aldas and Padre Abán (Pozorski 1976: 77).

Tillandsia was used as a fuel in areas where wood was not always easily found.

CANAVALIA PLAGIOSPERMA: PALLAR DE LOS GENTILES, JACK BEAN (CF. *C. ENSIFORMIS*)

The third plant in this list is *Canavalia plagiosperma* (Fabaceae). Bird wrote: "Beans of at least three varieties (all Canavalia?)" were found (Whitaker and Bird 1949: 3). Eric Callen and Thomas Cameron (1960: 37) noted that "the most promising feature, from the point of view of identification, was the presence of strong hooked hairs, given that these occur only in some plant families, one of which is the Fabaceae (= Leguminosae) . . . or bean family, or more strictly the Papilionaceae." *Canavalia* and *Phaseolus* are the two genera of beans that have these hairs.

This plant appears in Ecuador from Valdivia I times (~5200 BP). Jonathan Damp et al. (1981: 811) comment that "the presence of the wild and possibly ancestral forms of *C. maritima* and *C. brasiliensis* in western Ecuador and of *C. maritima* extending into extreme northern Peru indicate that this region was probably a site of early *Canavalia* domestication."

ASCLEPIAS SP. (ASCLEPIADACEAE, SUBFAMILY ASCLEPIADOIDEAE): *CHIVO*, *AMARRA JUDEA*, MILKWEED

The fiber of this plant was very infrequently used in textiles at Huaca Prieta (see chapter 12). Several hundred fragments of "a fibrous material and wads" came from Bird's Layers A to G of Test Pit 2 and from his Layers C through R in Test Pit 3, corresponding to Phases II through V in our sequence. These remains were tentatively identified in the field as *Asclepias*, which Bird et al. (1985: 236) identified as *chivo* or *amarra judio*.

Archaeological remains from the central coast are described as "milkweed pods" or *Asclepias* sp. (Moseley 1975: 24; Patterson and Moseley 1968: 117). Mark Cohen (1978a: 30) wrote that it "is a shrub of the moist areas of the river valleys. There is no evidence to suggest that it was ever domesticated and it is probable that this plant is indigenous to the region."

UNIT SPATIAL ANALYSIS

Additional analysis was carried out on excavation Units 2, 10, 16, 20, 22, and 23. These were selected because they are large enough to address activity areas and intra-unit spatial analysis. There is considerable variation in the total amount of floral remains found in each unit, due to differences in preservation, discard behavior, unit function, and so forth. Units 20 and 23 stand out as having significantly fewer specimens than the other units, with only 45 and 131 specimens, respectively. This variation does not necessarily correspond to variation in the number of species represented, however. For example, Unit 20 contains 45 specimens representing 15 different species, whereas Unit 2 contains 864 specimens representing only 9 species.

UNIT 2

Unit 2 at Huaca Prieta contains floral specimens from all phases except Phase I. *Cyperus* sp. remains are the only identified species represented in significant quantity in Phases II–V (see tables 10.3, 10.9, and 10.14). This is explained by the unit's proximity to the wetlands east of the sites and its primary use as a specialized domestic area focused on the wetlands. The highest amounts are found in Phases II and III, when this area was an extensive domestic site, and decline through Phases IV and V as the mound expanded in this area and the site function became more ritualized. Overall, this species represents ~96% of the remains found in Unit 2.

Large, heavily crushed quantities of unidentified charcoal were also recovered in Unit 2, with the majority found in the domestic Phases II–III, but also present in Phases IV–V. This is significant compared to the other selected units, which do not have as much unidentified charcoal.

Remains from 6 other species were identified but are present in relatively low quantities.

UNIT 10

Unit 10 contains floral samples only from Phase V (see table 10.17). The species present in the highest quantities are gourd (*Lagenaria siceraria*) and horsetail (*Equisetum* sp.), which constitute over half (57.83%) of the floral samples in Unit 10. Unidentified stems make up another 29.3% ($n = 279$). Another 14 species are present in smaller quantities.

UNIT 16

The remains from Phases II and V in Unit 16 were grouped, leaving only two temporal groups for comparison (see tables 10.2 and 10.19). Curiously, no plant remains other than fragments of reeds were documented for Phases III and IV in Unit 16. Only marine foods were recovered from the house floors during this period. Remains from *Lagenaria siceraria* are the most prevalent in all phases in this unit. By far the majority of the remains of this species are assigned to Phase V (62.41%). This species makes up 54.55% of the remains for Phase II and 58.48% for the whole floral assemblage in this unit. Both *Equisetum* sp. and *Cucurbita moschata* were present in significant amounts, as well as 19 other species in small amounts.

UNIT 20

Unit 20, an off-mound food preparation area at Paredones, contains relatively few floral remains compared to other units, with only 47 specimens total (see tables 10.7 and 10.11). These specimens come from Phases III–IV and are evenly distributed among 15 species (and 2 unidentified stems). *Lagenaria siceraria*, *Zea mays* (maize), and *Gynerium sagittatum* (wild cane) were present in slightly larger quantities than other species, but the low overall numbers make this significant.

UNIT 22

Unit 22 at Paredones had one of the largest quantities of floral remains (excluding large quantities of crushed, unidentifiable plant material), representing 24 species, many of which are cultigens (see tables 10.4, 10.7, 10.12, and 10.20). Few remains appear during Phase II, but they increase in quantity during Phases III and IV.

Capsicum sp. is the only species that appears in a large quantity during Phase III with 278 specimens, with the combined phases making up 78.09% of the total remains in Unit 22. Phase V contains 17 specimens of *Lagenaria siceraria*, which represent 77.27% of the total floral remains in Unit 22. Another 22 species were represented in Unit 22 in smaller quantities, which were primarily comestibles and secondarily wild food species (see the conclusions below for more detailed discussion of floral remains from Unit 22).

UNIT 23

Unit 23 is an area of Huaca Prieta that consists of chamber tombs; it has few floral remains compared to the other units (see table 10.21). Those present are exclusively from Phase V, with significant percentages of *Gossypium barbadense* (25.76%), *Lagenaria siceraria* (15.84%), Poaceae (7.92%), and *Ruppia maritima* (10.89%). Another 13 species are represented in small amounts.

TEMPORAL ANALYSIS

A comparison of total remains for each phase shows a general increase in the amount of floral remains over time. This indicates an increasing use of floral resources. The substantial increase in floral remains between Phases IV and V is also significant, with more than eight times the number of specimens from Phase V found in Phase IV.

However, before Phase V is represented by 26 units, a greater number than in other phases. Table 10.1 presents a list of all plants for each phase.

PHASE I

Phase I, in both its early and late subphases, contains 15 floral specimens from Unit 16 and Unit 22 at Paredones (see table 10.2). The major species are *Phaseolus lunatus* or, most likely, *Phaseolus* spp. (5 specimens), *Tessaria integrifolia* (3 specimens), *Persea* sp. (represented by seeds and charcoal), *Capsicum* sp. (4 specimens), and *Cucurbita* sp. (3 specimens). For late Phase I 4 *Capsicum* sp. seeds and 3 *Cucurbita* sp. seeds were recovered from premound Level 7 in Unit 22 (see table 10.2). The remaining specimens were from late Phase I, early Holocene contexts.

PHASE II

Phase II contains 14 species and 191 specimens in total, a significant increase from the sparse amounts in Phase I (see tables 10.3–10.5). The majority of those specimens are *Cyperus* sp. and unidentified charcoal, which does not appear in such high quantities in any other phase. These two categories make up most of the remains from Phase II, with only a few specimens from 13 other species also represented.

Only 4 units contained remains from Phase II; Units 2, 16, and 22 and HP-3. The majority of these remains come from Unit 2. Unit 2 contains *Manihot esculenta*, *Lagenaria siceraria*, and unidentified stems. HP-3 contains *Acacia* sp., *Capsicum* sp., *Panicum* sp., *Cyperus* sp, and unidentified charcoal. Unit 16 had *Acacia* sp., *Gynererium sagittatum*, and *Lagenaria siceraria*. Unit 22 contained *Capsicum* sp., *Gossypium barbadense*, *Gymnogongrus frucellatas*, *Phaseolus* sp., and *Zea mays*.

PHASE III

Phase III contains 21 species and 594 specimens in total, which nearly triples the count for Phase II (see tables 10.6–10.8). Unit 22 provides the majority of those specimens, with *Capsicum* sp. and unidentified charcoal together making up most of the remains. The remaining specimens show more diversity than those of Phase II (see table 10.1).

It should be noted that no faunal remains were recovered from Floors 10–17, Phase III, in Unit 22, but these floors had an abundance of plant food species. This suggests that this may have been a key period when Paredones intensified agricultural production (including the appearance of the raised agricultural fields in the wetlands east of the mound) and when the site was primarily associated with the ritual economy of plant foods largely for consumption at Huaca Prieta.

PHASE IV

Phase IV contains 36 species and 667 specimens in total, which is a slightly significant increase from Phase III, as well as more diversity of species and a more even distribution from different units (see tables 10.9–10.13).

Lagenaria siceraria is the most prevalent species in Phase IV, with 386 specimens total. This species makes up 47.25% of all specimens from Phase IV. Unit 25 provides 205 of those, with Units 3, 3N, and 20 and HP-3 also contributing. *Capsicum* sp. is also present in modest quantities, mainly from Unit 22, with a few from Units 3 and 25.

Floral remains from Phase IV are more evenly distributed across the units than in earlier phases.

PHASE V

Phase V had the largest quantity of remains, with 48 species and 4426 identifiable specimens in total from 24 different units representing 45 species (including unidentified seeds, stems, threads, leaves, roots, rootlets, charcoal, and organic material). This diverse composition of floral remains is not seen in other phases (see tables 10.14–10.24). We also must keep in mind that all excavation units yielded data on Phase V and that the greatest volume of archaeological material recovered came from this phase.

Unit 5 contained the most remains, with 1081 specimens. Units 3, 5, 6, 7, 10, 14, 16, and 22 all contained significant numbers, and 15 other units contributed lesser quantities.

The great diversity of species represented in Phase V makes comparison by unit difficult, but a few patterns stand out. Only 3 species made up 60% of the total remains from Phase V, each with well over 1000 specimens. *Lagenaria siceraria* com-poses 25.86% of the total remains from Phase V, spread widely across 18 units, with the largest numbers in Units 3, 10, 16, and 22. *Cyperus* sp. makes up 13.61% of the total Phase V remains. The majority of these are from Unit 5, while the remainder are distributed in smaller quantities across 9 other units. *Capsicum* sp. constitutes 11.33% of the total remains and is found in nearly all excavated units.

CONCLUSIONS

The first observation that arises from the analysis is that Huaca Prieta, Paredones, and the nearby domestic sites (Units 13, 16, and 26) are important localities for the history of plant adoption and possibly domestication. Beginning with Huaca Prieta, 6 cultivated plants are the earliest specimens known in the region. *Phaseolus* sp., *Cucurbita* sp., and *Persea* sp. appear in early Phase I in Unit 16 near Huaca Prieta and are earlier than the Las Pircas phase specimens from Nanchoc Valley (Dillehay 2011b). *Capsicum* appears in the early Holocene at Paredones. In Phase II *Psidium guajava* (guayaba), *Capsicum baccatum* var. *pendulum* (chile pepper), *Pouteria lucuma* (lucuma), and *Canavalia plagiosperma* (jack bean) appear. In Phase III *Cucurbita ficifolia* (squash) and *Canna edulis* (achira) are present. In Phases III–V maize is found; it is oldest at Paredones, where it first appears in what seems to be popcorn. Of the cultivated industrial plants, *Gossypium barbadense* (cotton) is found in late Phase I and *Lagenaria siceraria* (gourd) is present in Phase III. Phase I has *Equisetum* sp. (horsetail), *Capparis scabrida* (sapote), *Tessaria integrifolia* (palo bobo), and *Gynerium sagittatum* (wild cane, which is equally ancient in the Paredones domestic site). Phase II has *Acacia* sp., *Buddleja* (which is equally old at Paredones), *Panicum* sp., and *Cyperus* sp. *Eleocharis* sp. appears in a context where Phases II and III are mixed, while *Scirpus* sp. is probably present in this phase, but its identification is insecure, as is the case with *Asclepias* sp. In Phase III *Parkinsonia* sp. (palo verde) is present, as it is in the same context in Paredones. Phase IV has *Capparis scabrida* (with contemporaneous material in Paredones), *Ruppia maritima* (also present at Paredones at this time), *Scirpus* sp., or *Schoenoplectus californicus* (present with the same age at Paredones). Finally,

Phase V has *Desmodium* sp. (clover), *Commelina* sp. (tick-trefoil), *Paspalum* sp. (dayflower), and *Chloris* sp. (*grama*). Phase V adds a seaweed, *Ahnfeltia durvillaei*. Additionally, 2 cultivated food plants appear at Paredones: *Zea mays* (maize), which is present in Phases III and IV, and *Annona* (*chirimoya*) from Phase IV.

The group of plants listed under "Miscellaneous" has the following chronology at Paredones. *Buddleja* and *Capparis* sp. were found in Phase II, a comparable age as at Huaca Prieta. *Parkinsonia* sp. in Phase III is in the same temporal context as at Huaca Prieta. *Phragmites australis* and *Typha angustifolia* share this temporal period with Los Gavilanes in Huarmey. In Phase IV *Capparis scabrida* (sapote), *Schoenoplectus californicus* (totora), and *Ruppia maritima* (wigeon grass) have the same date as at Huaca Prieta. Also present are *Guadua* sp. (bamboo), *Chaetomorpha* sp. (chaeto), and *Amaranthus* sp. (amaranth), which have the same dates as at Los Gavilanes in the Huarmey Valley. Finally, 2 seaweeds are found in Phase III contexts: *Gymnogongrus furcellatus* and *Gigartina chamissoi*. *Chaetomorpha* sp. was recovered from Phase IV contexts.

One of the cultivated food plants, *Persea americana* (avocado), was recovered at the domestic site of Unit 16 from early Phase I contexts. Among the miscellaneous plants also recovered in this same period were *Equisetum* sp. (horsetail) and *Gynerium sagittatum* (wild cane), which share this same age at Huaca Prieta, as well as *Salix humboldtiana* (willow) and *Schinus molle* (molle).

There is a problem with the plant remains from the domestic occupation in Unit 13. The recovery of *Phaseolus vulgaris* comes from a mixed context of Phases IV and V. If they correspond to Phase IV, they would be older than the beans from Huaca Prieta, which are the oldest known for the coast, although common beans are older in the highlands.

As mentioned earlier, the Nanchoc area in the Zaña Valley is important for the ancient plants found there. In the El Palto phase (the early Paiján subphase) 11,000–9800 cal BP, *Cucurbita moschata* (squash) was recovered, although it is not certain whether it was domesticated or in the process of domestication. There is also evidence for the use of algarrobo (*Prosopis pallida*). Chronologically, these remains correspond to the earliest occupation at Huaca Prieta. In the following

Las Pircas phase, dated between 9800 and 7800 cal BP (which corresponds to late Phase I at Huaca Prieta), remains of *Phaseolus* sp. (common bean) and *Chenopodium* cf. *quinoa* were recovered; but it has not been determined if these were domesticates or in the process of domestication. For the same period *Arachis* sp. (peanut) and *Bunchosia* sp. were already domesticated and under cultivation. In the same phase there is evidence for the use of *Erythroxylum novogranatense* var. *truxillense* (coca); these are the earliest known specimens.

Cucurbita ficifolia (squash) was found at La Paloma and is contemporaneous with Huaca Prieta Phase III. The discovery of *Solanum tuberosum* at Huaynuná is also important as a domesticated species. This is the only archaeological evidence for this plant.

Only 3 of the miscellaneous plants can be eaten: *Capparis scabrida*, *Cyperus* sp., and *Scirpus* sp. Several also were used as fuel, since their remains were found burned: *Equisetum* sp., *Capparis scabrida*, *Acacia* sp., *Eleocharis* sp., *Parkinsonia* sp., and *Salix humboldtiana*.

Some of the plants now are used in folk medicine, and we may suppose that they were used similarly in Preceramic times: *Equisetum* sp., probably *Tessaria integrifolia*, *Gynerium sagittatum*, *Cyperus* sp., *Salix humboldtiana*, and *Schinus molle*. *Cyperus* sp., *Eleocharis* sp., and *Typha angustifolia* can also be used medicinally. Of these plants, 5 can be used to make baskets: *Capparis scabrida*, *Acacia* sp., *Scirpus* sp., *Phragmites australis*, and *Schinus molle*. *Cyperus* sp., *Eleocharis* sp., and *Typha angustifolia* could also be used for this, although these three were more useful in making cordage. *Tessaria integrifolia*, *Gynerium sagittatum*, *Parkinsonia* sp., *Phragmites australis*, *Guadua* sp., *Schinus molle*, and *Salix humboldtiana* were all used in fencing and construction of shelters (huts). *Schinus molle* and *Salix humboldtiana* were also used to make various artifacts (tools and implements). The same is true for *Capparis scabrida*, *Acacia* sp., *Scirpus* sp., *Phragmites australis*, *Guadua* sp., and *Schinus molle*.

Three plants from the coast must have been important to make beverages: *Cyperus* sp., *Guadua* sp., and *Schinus molle*.

We know that *Eleocharis* sp. was chewed, as the quids have been recovered at Huaca Prieta. A second plant, *Scirpus* sp., was possibly chewed as well.

Only 3 plants could be used to make woven

mats, bags, and ties: *Scirpus* sp., *Cyperus* sp., and *Schoenoplectus* sp. They also could have served to make reed rafts (*caballitos de totora*).

Finally, *Schinus molle* could have been used as a dye. It was the plant with the most uses: as a fuel, as a medicine, to make artifacts, to build shelters, as a beverage, and as a dye.

The subcategory of wild plants or weeds that could have been associated with fields of cultivated plants includes *Panicum* sp., *Desmodium* sp., and *Amaranthus* sp. The subcategory of wild plants common on the coast that may only have been accidentally present in archaeological sites or may have been used to cover floors or fill includes *Trifolium* sp., *Ruppia maritima*, *Commelina* sp., *Paspalum* sp., and *Chloris* sp.

Buddleja sp. may be a material brought from the highlands to the coast by river discharge then gathered by the inhabitants of the coast, but it is also possible that this species was growing on the coast. What is clear is that the wood was used as fuel.

Several plants found in other Preceramic sites and not present in our sites are important: *Manihot esculenta*, *Pachyrhizus tuberosus*, *Ipomoea batatas*, *Cucurbita andreana*, *Cucurbita maxima*, *Cucurbita ecuadorensis*, and *Asclepias* sp. It is striking that *Manihot esculenta* was not known at Huaca Prieta and the nearby domestic sites, although sampling bias may have failed to produce it in our excavations. Another plant not recovered in the Huaca Prieta Project excavations was *Pachyrhizus tuberosus* (Fabaceae = Leguminosae), commonly known as *jiquima*, *achipa ajipa*, *goseo*, *namou*, *wuiso*, and *yaspo*.

Little archaeological information is available on the seaweeds. Several have been identified in the Huaca Prieta area, but the absence of others such as *Gigartina* sp., *Macrocystis pyrifera*, and *Eisenia cokeri* is of note.

The total macroplant inventory also reveals a wide array of cultigens imported from distant coastal, highland, and tropical zones, probably from various directions throughout time, and the exploitation of local seaweeds from the littoral and wild plants from wetlands and lagoons. This inventory complements and adds to the economic plants documented by microplant studies in appendices 4, 7, 9, and 12. In addition to the species presented above, the pollen record sug-gests the presence of wild grapes, probably local, and potatoes, some of which were probably highland introduced. The phytolith study indicates the addition of *lerén* (arrowroot), manihot, and passion flower fruit, all probably from distant tropical environments. All 5 of these species appear during Phase IV.

In terms of the predominant plant foods, maize seems not to be a major food item until about 5000 to 4500 years ago when meal corn appears and is associated with larger and more diverse grinding stones and manos suggestive of increased food production. Squash, beans, and chile peppers are consistently present through time and space and often appear together in small gourd eating bowls and in ritual offerings. The edible parts of *Typha*, *Scirpus*, and *Cyperus* were widely consumed and probably readily available to all populations along the littoral and inland. Additional plant types, including fruits, legumes, seaweeds, and others, appear in variable quantities and seem to be secondary foods. Cotton and reeds were significant industrial plants found in all site contexts.

Finally, the raw counts for identifiable plant species in tables 10.2–10.24 show that the greatest variety and bulk of plant remains through all cultural phases are present at Huaca Prieta, not Paredones and the domestic sites. These figures are misleading, however, because a much larger area was excavated at Huaca Prieta in comparison to other sites. This discrepancy changes significantly when the ratio of total plant parts per total m^3 excavated is calculated for each site. Table 10.25 shows that 16.5 plant parts were recovered per m^3 excavated at Huaca Prieta; this figure is 60.1 parts per m^3 at Paredones and 17.0 parts per m^3 at the domestic sites, and most of these are debris from floor mats. (These sites were exposed to similar taphonomic conditions such as trampling and foot traffic, sediment loads, and preservation, so physical elements do not explain the numerical differences.) Although not shown quantitatively, the same ratios hold for the diversity of plant species per m^3 excavated, with Paredones (0.39 species) having more variety than Huaca Prieta (0.16 species) and the domestic sites (0.11 species). In other words, it is probable that Paredones and the domestic sites would have dominated the raw count if an equal number of m^3 had been excavated there. In a similar vein, the ratio of the total

Table 10.25. Number of plant parts per 1 m³ excavated at Huaca Prieta, Paredones, and domestic sites

Site	m³ excavated	Total no. of plant parts identified	Floated plant parts per 1 m³
Huaca Prieta	584	9600	16.5
Paredones	96	5772	60.1
Domestic sites	52	885	17.0

weight of shellfish, sea snails and gastropods, fish, and sea lion remains to m³ excavated at each site is 5100 for Huaca Prieta, 3200 for the domestic sites, and 2400 for Paredones. This suggests a dual economy, with Huaca Prieta and the domestic sites focused primarily on marine foods and Paredones primarily on plant foods. The isotope studies on human teeth suggest the same pattern, although the sample size for this study is limited.

Moreover, figure 10.1 shows a comparison of the percentage of edible, industrial (for example, cotton for textiles and reeds for burial and ritual matting), and wild plants for all three type sites. At Huaca Prieta edible plants constitute about 50.2% of all plant remains, followed by industrial

plants at 29.4% (offerings of textiles and reed mats as floor covering), and then wild species at 20.4%. For Paredones edibles dominate at 93%, revealing that it was the place of food preparation, keeping in mind that there is no evidence of domestic activity on the mound and the low percentages of industrial and wild species. Domestic sites also are dominated by edibles at 73%, followed by roughly equal percentages for industrial (floor mats) and wild species.

The data in figure 10.1 and tables 10.2–10.25 make more sense when taking into account that the majority of grinding stones and manos, lithic blades for slicing, and a higher density of scattered, crushed, and discarded plant parts were recovered from Paredones. Moreover, maize was most predominant at Paredones and much less so at the domestic sites and at Huaca Prieta. A similar case was found for the chile peppers, with the count and variety being higher at Paredones (see appendix 4).

If food processing and cooking occurred primarily at Paredones, how do we explain the high variety of plant foods at Huaca Prieta, primarily a ritual place focused on the offering and consumption of marine foods and human burial? The counts at Huaca Prieta are best explained by people consuming both marine and plant food

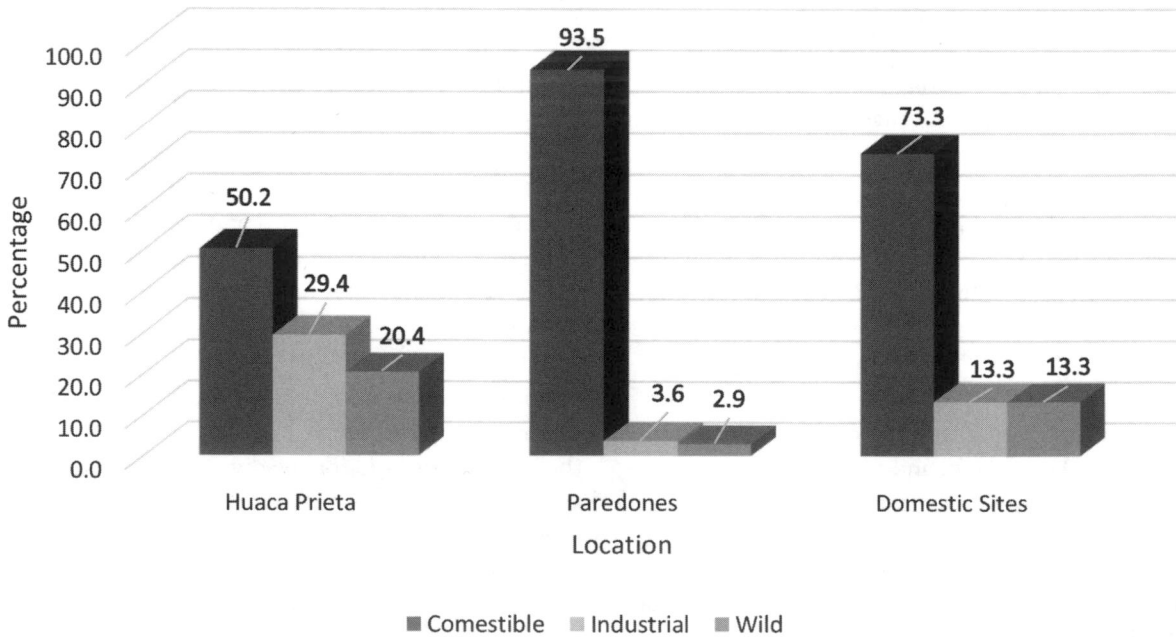

FIGURE 10.1. Bar graph showing the percentage distribution of comestible, industrial, and wild plant parts at Huaca Prieta, Paredones, and domestic sites.

while performing rituals, feasting, and probably to some extent eating and discarding food while building and maintaining the mound. Some of this diversity probably also relates to people from distant areas bringing exotic foods to Huaca Prieta as ritual offerings in much the same way they did with the exotic nonfood items. The majority of the plants on floors and use surfaces at Huaca Prieta were present in small piles, in gourd containers, and in textile bundles, sometimes in or near graves and tombs. It is possible that the bulk of the processed plant food at Paredones was transported to Huaca Prieta for consumption, which would help explain the qualitative and quantitative differences between these two sites. Given the scarcity of grinding stones and manos and the absence of slicing blades and food-processing implements at Huaca Prieta and Units 13, 16, and 26, this is a plausible conclusion. If this is the case, why was Paredones located 0.5 km north of Huaca Prieta? This may be explained by the presence of the buried raised agricultural fields located in the wetlands due east of Paredones. They are not present directly east of Huaca Prieta because this area was a deeper wetland and perhaps contained more brackish water, being located closer to the sea. Limited excavations in the Cupisnique mound, located between Huaca Prieta and Paredones, reveal only domestic occupation.

Ideally speaking, a precise calculation of the contribution of plant and marine foods to the diet would be useful, but given the large amounts of crushed and unidentifiable plant parts at sites (especially at Paredones) and the heavy fracturation of fish bone, shells, and other marine foods, it was impossible to derive reliable MNI counts for the faunal remains. Furthermore, as discussed earlier, we do not know the different behaviors at each site type (for example, domestic, food preparation, and ritual/mortuary) that may have selected for the preparation, consumption, and discard of certain food types over others. Even if we did understand these behaviors and their representation in the archaeological record better, we would still have to ask what the numbers mean. For instance, it appears that after about 5000–4500 cal BP maize became a staple crop in the diet, as suggested in both the macrobotanical and microbotanical records, in the isotope study of the human teeth, and in the analysis of grinding stone technology. But the number of maize remains is very low compared to other plant types such as squash, beans, and some fruits. Despite these issues, it remains qualitatively and quantitatively clear that the marine foods dominated at Huaca Prieta and the domestic sites and that plant foods were most important at Paredones.

CHAPTER 11

NONTEXTILE AND NONBASKETRY MATERIAL CULTURE

Tom D. Dillehay
and Duccio Bonavia

INTRODUCTION

This chapter reports the major cultural material categories from excavated sites, including stone, bone, wood, shell, gourds, and miscellaneous exotics. The textiles, basketry, and cordage are reported separately in chapter 12. Contextual inventories for most materials and more detailed study of the lithic assemblage are online at https://my.vanderbilt.edu/huacaprieta/. As stated in chapter 1, a decision was made about how much detailed information could be presented due to space limitations in the book. Given that several material culture categories provide less information on the Preceramic society in the study area than others, we chose to give only brief analyses of these artifact types. The most significant temporal, spatial, and technological aspects of these data are presented below, however, with the intent of publishing more detailed reports in the future.

Many of the objects discussed under the material categories below were ritual offerings composed of piles or pockets of seeds, shells, stones, and other materials placed in tombs, on footpaths, and in ritual spaces. Many of these objects were intentionally torn, smashed, cut, and/or broken. We have no evidence to suggest whether the broken objects were sacrificial killings, prescribed offerings to spirits and ancestors, or payments to the mound for entering a sacred domain.

STONE TOOLS

At Huaca Prieta and Paredones pebble tools are the dominant element in all levels (see Bird et al. 1985) from ~14,500 to 3500 cal BP. As reported by Bird, these are almost exclusively expedient cores, hammerstones, edge-trimmed pebble tools, and other unifacial flakes primarily made of local raw material found in the Chicama riverbed or on beaches. These tools make up ~89% of the total assemblage at both sites. The remaining percentage consists of grinding stones and miscellaneous artifacts.

The expedient pebble and unifacial tools have wider and older distributions in differing contexts throughout the prehistory of coastal Peru and beyond and raise the question of their cultural status and functions (compare Boëda et al. 2014; Collins 1997; Dillehay 2000; Richardson 1981). Pebble tools are a generalized type, as the range of forms and sizes is limited by the pebble or cobble itself: the choice of the maker was expressed as much in the selection of the original pebble as in shaping the final product. Pebble tool industries with a working edge created by the junction of either two flaked surfaces or a flaked surface with the pebble cortex are relatively common in multipurpose technologies throughout South America (for example, Bryan and Gruhn 2003; Dillehay 2000; Engel 1966a). In north coastal Peru they appear as a distinct early industry given the names Amotape and Siches (Richardson 1981).

Other than the few studies on the north and central coast of Peru (Dillehay 1997; Dillehay et al. 1989; Richardson 1981), little is known of these industries and their wider technological and economic implications. Inland distributions seem less consistent, but they are reported from noncoastal and coastal sites in southern Ecuador (Stothert 1985) and from upland sites in northern Peru (Dillehay et al. 1998). In southern Peru and northern Chile their distribution is more coastal (see Llagostera 1992; Sandweiss et al. 1998). In the central Andes these assemblages survived along the littoral zone into the Inka and colonial periods. The tools of these different areas show general similarities, as among most pebble tool assemblages, but their cultural and technological relationships remain to be tested.

Bird's work at Huaca Prieta undertook the earliest systematic research on these tools. His study highlighted several questions with these industries. What are their nature, how should they be described, what are the functions of the tools, and what are the relationships between them and the bifacial contemporaneous technologies, such as the earlier Fishtail and Paiján industries, and other pebble tool industries? The Amotape/Siches groups of north coastal Peru and the late Pleistocene Carrizal group in the abandoned wetland and delta of an ancient Zaña River bed (Dillehay 2000, 2011a) form part of a distinctive assemblage with heavy core tools, flakes, and hammerstones, while the Huaca Prieta/Paredones group is associated primarily with cores, choppers, edge-trimmed flakes, a few blades, and ground-edge artifacts (Bird et al. 1985; Dillehay et al. 2012b).

This chapter is a general study of the stone tool industry at Huaca Prieta and Paredones, defining the basic tool and debitage types and their frequency. Micro-use-wear and residue analyses of 19 stone tools from the two sites are reported in appendix 16.

THE HUACA PRIETA AND PAREDONES ASSEMBLAGE

In all, more than 20,000 lithics, including tools and debitage, were recovered in all excavations at Huaca Prieta, compared with over ~5000 lithics from fewer excavated units at Paredones and ~2300 from Unit 16. Debitage in the form of tertiary flakes and chips constitutes the majority of the lithics (~70%). The comparisons between the different site collections were made in terms of basic dimensions (length, width, thickness) and in terms of features that might reflect either technological traditions or the effects of functional demands. In measuring the artifacts, they were oriented along the long axis: length was taken as maximum on this axis, and width at right angles to this, thickness being the maximum height of the tool. In examining the position of the working edge in terms of margin retouched, we described the orientation of the tool and the position of the retouch on an end-struck flake or blade tool. Online tables present the contextual distribution of lithics at the sites (see https://my.vanderbilt.edu/huacaprieta/). Figures 11.1–11.3 present the variety of tool types from sites.

The division into typological categories describes technological distinctions between tools as a whole, that is, between those made on a complete pebble to those made on a split pebble or a large pebble flake and those made on a trun-

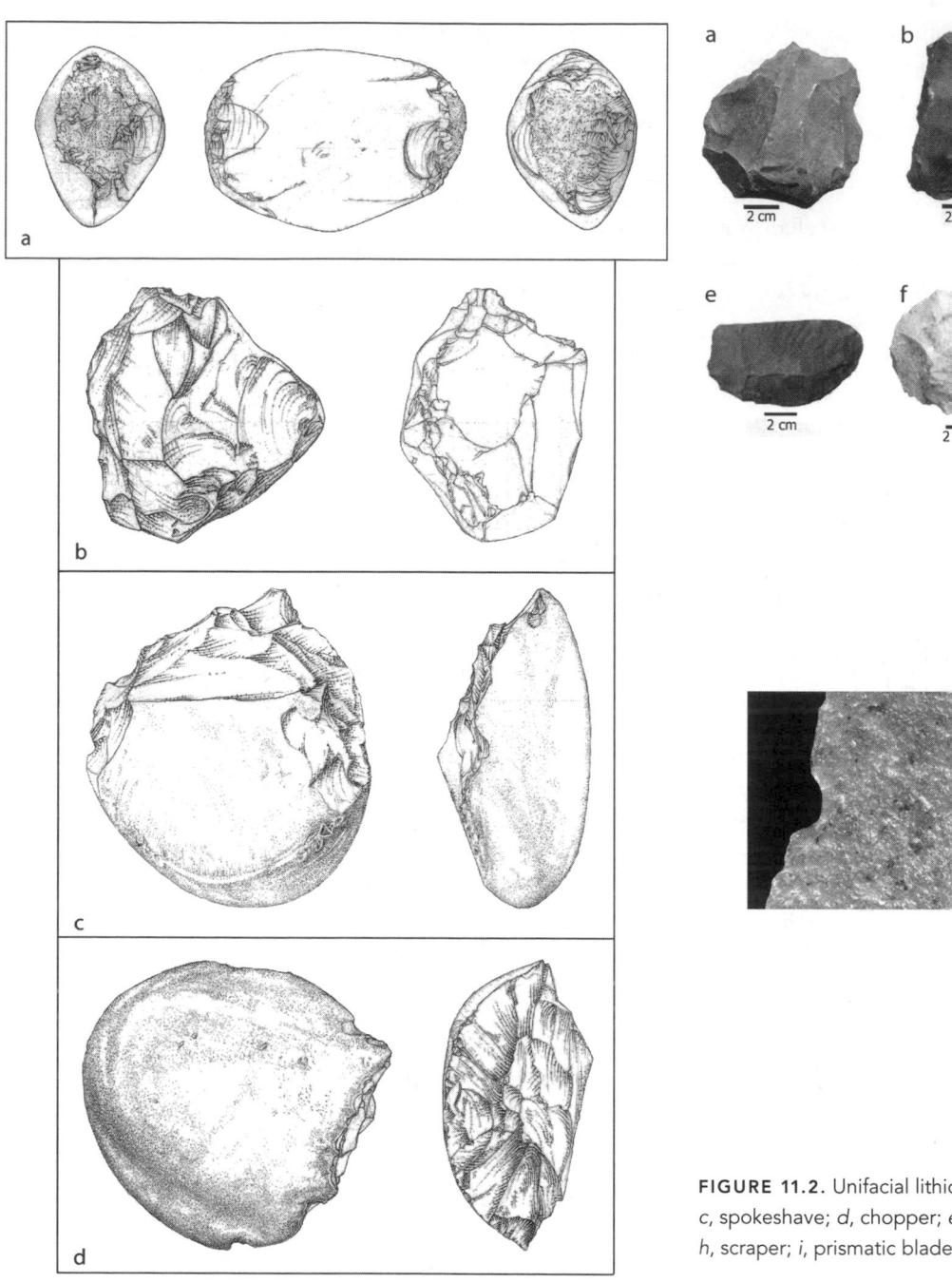

FIGURE 11.1. Unifacial lithics: *a*, hammerstone; *b–d*, choppers.

FIGURE 11.2. Unifacial lithics: *a*, secondary flake; *b*, scraper; *c*, spokeshave; *d*, chopper; *e–f*, scrapers; *g*, spokeshave; *h*, scraper; *i*, prismatic blade.

cated pebble, which corresponds to the *hache court* of the technological tradition and the functional demands influenced by this choice. In terms of selection of raw materials the collection shows a high degree of preference. Of the total debitage and tool artifacts, 63.9% were made of basalt, 9.3% of meta-andesite, 9.3% of quartz and quartz-ite, 6.7% of rhyolite, 6.7% of volcanic tuff, 3.3% of andesite, and 0.7% of dacite (fig. 11.4). Few silex, chalcedony, or other fine-grained raw materials were recovered.

The lithic types from Huaca Prieta (HP), Paredones (P), and Unit 16 (U-16) are outlined below. These are the same types recovered by Bird at Huaca Prieta. The only exception is that the prismatic blades and grinding stones were excavated only at Paredones. Bird did not describe or perhaps find either one.

Hammerstones and pounders (HP: 43; P: 21; and U-16: 13): Practically all are relatively large, oblong cobbles (12–15 cm long) that have been used extensively on one or both ends (fig. 11.1a). Some are fractured from heavy use. The majority are made of dense, heavy basalts. The blows are diagonal and not vertical (70–90 degrees).

Choppers (HP: 29; P: 34; and U-16: 12): There is a wide variety (fig. 11.1b–d, fig. 11.2d, fig. 11.3b, f). The majority are made on small cobbles

FIGURE 11.3. Unifacial lithics: *a*, stone grooved axe made of green skarn; *b*, chopper; *c*, grooved axe made of rhyolite; *d–f*, grooved spheroids.

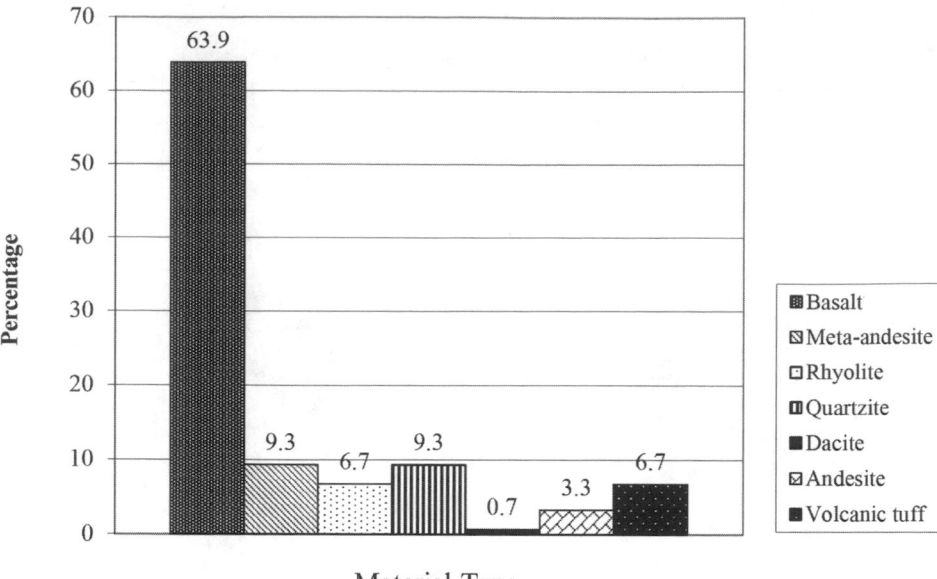

Material Type	Percentage
Basalt	63.9
Meta-andesite	9.3
Rhyolite	6.7
Quartzite	9.3
Dacite	0.7
Andesite	3.3
Volcanic tuff	6.7
TOTAL	99.9

FIGURE 11.4. Distribution of raw lithic material types in the stone tool assemblages from sites.

(9–13 cm long); fewer are made on large cobbles (>15 cm long). Many are made of quartzite. Oblong rather than round, the cobbles have active transverse edges.

Cores (HP: 56; P: 39; and U-16: 4): Some cores were abandoned after removing a number of flakes, since they were not exhausted. We found few cores with a prepared striking platform. Some were later converted into other tools (polishing stones and choppers: fig. 11.1b).

Scrapers (HP: 342; P: 188; and U-16: 34): There are many side and edge scrapers made on primary and secondary flakes (fig. 11.2b, c, e, h). In the majority of cases they exhibit small squarish flake scars. Some are carefully made and have a homogeneous active region. The majority are made on flakes of basalt. In many instances, these flakes have been used to modify the distal or side edges of large flakes.

Spokeshaves (HP: 8; P: 32; and U-16: 5): Some are made on primary flakes, using the distal or side edges of the flakes (fig. 11.2c, g). In other instances, they are made on pieces of naturally broken cobbles. In the majority of cases, the spokeshaves retain the cortex. In contrast to the scrapers, most spokeshaves show the removal of very small chips that indicate intentional retouch.

Planes (HP: 7; P: 27; and U-16: 5): A few planes were made on thick flakes or on fragments of utilized flakes with steep edges that have been retouched but have been worn away with use (figs. 11.2a, 11.3f).

Core Planes (HP: 4; P: 7; and U-16: 1): These are thick cores with steep faces that have been retouched to use as a plane.

Notched Pieces (HP: 3; P: 11; and U-16: 8): The majority are made on primary or secondary flakes. Beginning from the cortex, a relatively small active area is made.

Primary Flakes (HP: 1899; P: 766; and U-16: 212): The proportion of primary to secondary flakes is about the same (figs. 11.1c, d; 11.2c, e, f, for example). Primary flakes were made on cobbles of all sizes. The bulbs of percussion are clear and sometimes have feathering or grooves. The majority have the distal end beveled and, in a few cases, overshot.

Secondary Flakes (HP: 2111; P: 988; and U-16: 332): The majority were struck from primary flakes in order to produce a transverse fracture from the core. These flakes generally have a clear bulb scar (fig. 11.2a, b, f, h).

Prismatic Blades (P: 15): These are elongated blades of fine basalt that were found exclusively at Paredones (fig. 11.2i). Starch grain analysis on 1 blade revealed maize grains (Grobman et al. 2012; see appendix 9).

Miscellaneous Flakes (HP: 3289; P: 1286; and U-16: 489): These flakes are in the majority, representing tertiary flakes and chipping debris. There are only eight blades in this industry, two of which showed use cutting cornstalks (see Grobman et al. 2012). The bulbs are very irregular.

Manos (HP: 18; P: 34; and U–16: 14): Relatively large, oblong cobbles (13–16 cm long) have been selected that originally had a flat area used as the active grinding face. Some pebbles and small cobbles of basalt appear to have been used as both grinding and polishing stones (fig. 11.5a). Most manos are made of basalt and rhyolite. Manos were 8 to 19.2 cm in length and 6.2 to 12.1 cm in width.

Disks (HP: 16; P: 18; and U–16: 9): These are natural cobbles used with the original cortex on all sides; some have cortex on only the dorsal side. When they are worked, the blows originate on the cortical side with regular scars around the whole disk. Some disks have perforations and probably were used as net sinkers (fig. 11.5b, d).

Grinding Stones or Heating Slabs (HP: 3; P: 37; and U–16: 6): Numerous grinding stones were recovered and several grinding or heating slabs were identified (the majority at Paredones). The grinding slabs were primarily of volcanic tuff. The slabs were 14.1 to 28.3 cm in length and 17.2 to 26.3 cm in width. These materials were recovered at all depths, from Floors 2 to 22 at Paredones, from the sunken plaza on top of Huaca Prieta, and from house structures in Unit 16. Phytolith, starch, and pollen analysis was done on 2 stones, 1 from Floor 10 and 1 from Floor 18 at Paredones. The results showed preparation of maize (pop-

FIGURE 11.5. Ground stone artifacts: *a*, mano: stains are red pigment; *b*, disk; *c*, grinding stone or heating slab; *d*, fragment of stone vessel.

corn?), chile peppers, and other plants, which is confirmed by the macrobotanical remains (see chapter 10 and appendices 7 and 9). A charred heating slab in particular (fig. 11.5c) contained maize starch grains in its micropits. It appears that the increased presence of grinding stones is associated with an increase in maize and other crop food production at Paredones.

Net Sinkers (HP: 17; P: 1; and U-16: 2): At Huaca Prieta and Paredones 18 net sinkers with pecked and sawn-in grooves were recovered. A pecked waistline is found in some contexts, but only on large flat net sinkers. At Paredones, which is partly contemporary with Huaca Prieta, small net sinkers with a sawn-in waistline were found. The major type of net sinkers at Huaca Prieta seems to be the simple notched, incised or perforated pebbles (fig. 11.5b, d, e). Bird found similar perforated disks and sinkers (Bird et al. 1985: 83).

Ground Stone Vessel (HP: 1): This is a fragment of a drinking vessel made of basalt (fig. 11.4c, d) recovered from a tomb context in Unit 23 on top of the mound. Bird (Bird et al. 1985: 89) also recovered a fragmented stone bowl in his excavation on top of the mound in an area adjacent to HP-3.

Grooved Axes and Spheroids (HP: 2 and 14, respectively): 2 grooved axes, 1 complete and made of a green skarn (7.3 by 7.9 cm; fig. 11.3a) and 1 fragmented and made of rhyolite (6.3 by 8.1 cm; figs. 11.3a and c and fig. 11.6c), were recovered from Huaca Prieta, both from ritual contexts. The axes are similar to those recovered by James Richardson (personal communication, 2015) in the Siches area on the far north coast of Peru and by Karen Stothert (personal communication, 2015) at the Las Vegas site in Ecuador, which she believes came from northern Peru.

Huaca Prieta and Unit 16 also yielded 17 grooved spheroids (figs. 11.3d, e, and f and 11.5a and b; fig. 11.6a and b).

COMPARISONS

The late Pleistocene and early Holocene unifacial tool and flake assemblage excavated at Huaca Prieta is dominated by edge-trimmed flakes probably used for cutting meat (most likely sea lion, deer, guanaco, and perhaps sharks and large fish; see chapter 9) and working hides as well as slic-

ing plants (see chapter 10). Most of these tools as well as those from Phase I levels are smaller and less diverse in form than those of Phases II and III, although their morphologies and functions are generally similar. Phases II and III have a high proportion of primary flaked tools, with very little retouch. Secondary flakes with retouch increase through time, especially in Paredones, where they likely were used to process plants. A high proportion of choppers and scrapers, particularly unifacial choppers, existed during all periods, with most appearing in Huaca Prieta. Phases III–V are characterized by a high proportion of primary flakes with unprepared or plain platforms and prominent bulbs of percussion. High proportions of cores and unworked flakes characterize all phases. Blade artifacts are absent except at Paredones, where they appear throughout all phases. The majority of manos and grinding stones are found throughout all periods at all sites, but primarily in Paredones. Although this study is preliminary in nature, the frequency of specific stone tool types suggests technological and economic specialization for both sites, with chopping and cutting tools most predominant at Huaca Prieta and slicing and grinding tools at Paredones.

Except for changes in size and frequency the lithic technology at these sites is very conservative through time. Bird observed that the lack of "significant changes in the lithic assemblages from top to bottom" at Huaca Prieta "demonstrates a remarkable conservatism in the number and types of tools used" (Bird et al. 1985: 90–91). He also noted that the earlier periods relied more on basalt and the later ones more on quartz, which we also found.

Decorated Gourds

Gourds, whether decorated or not, fulfilled practical functions in the day-to-day activities of people at Huaca Prieta (Bird et al. 1985) and Paredones. Cut into containers of various shapes and sizes, they were used for serving food, as carrier vessels, as grave and ritual offerings, and as social signifiers. Although gourd bowls were important objects for the household, the decorated ones probably had additional value. Decorated gourds must have been prized objects of prestigious and aesthetic value at both sites. The etched gourds at

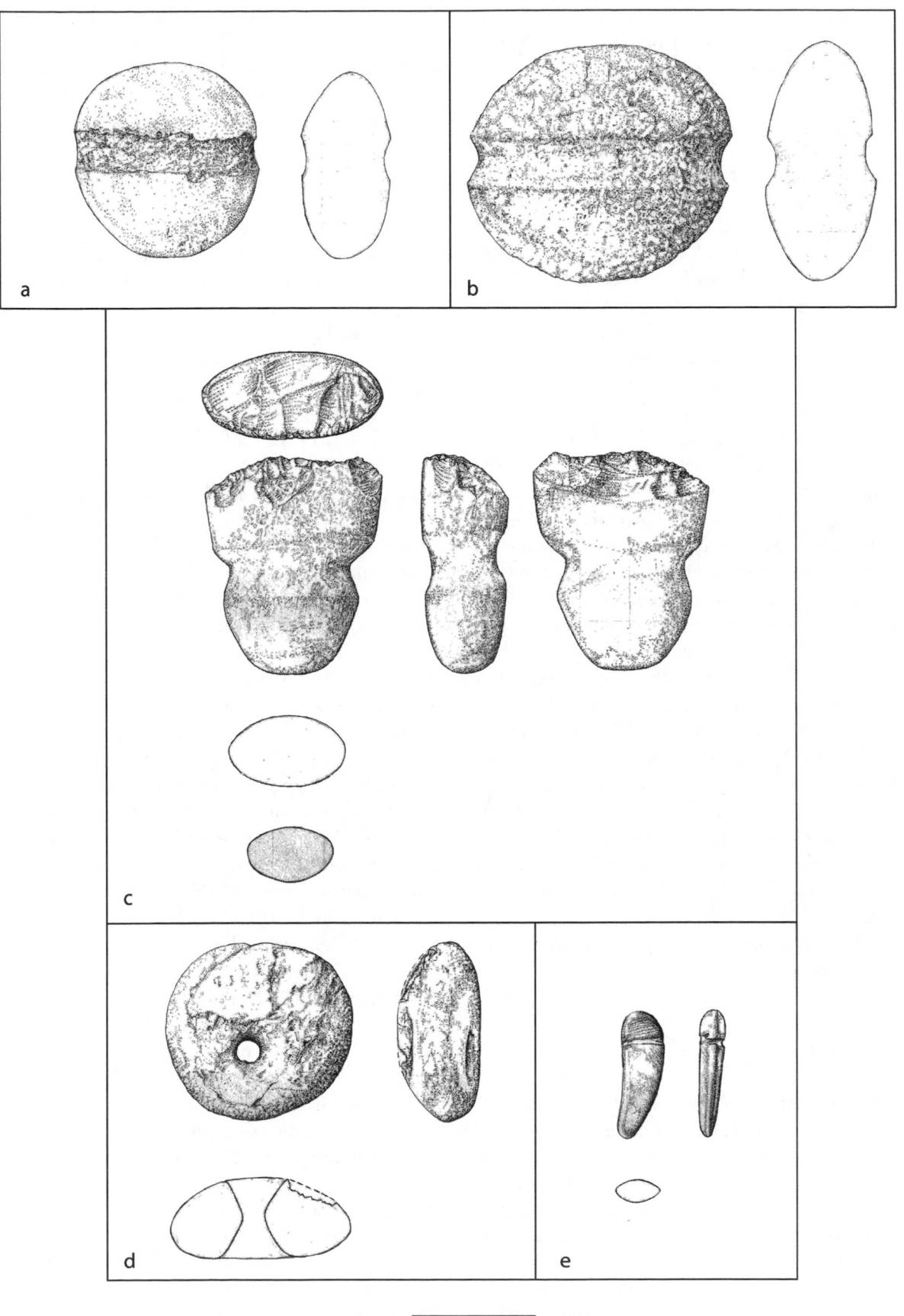

FIGURE 11.6. Pecked and grooved artifacts: *a–b*, grooved spheroids; *c*, grooved axe of rhyolite; *d*, disk; *e*, stone net sinker.

Paredones date contextually between ~5800 and 4500 cal BP, while those from Huaca Prieta appear slightly later at ~5500 to 4000 cal BP.

DESIGN TECHNIQUES AND MOTIFS

Gourds were decorated by several different techniques or methods, although a large majority of them were used without decoration and modification. Carvers employed several varieties of designs and patterns for decoration. These were achieved by applying the following main techniques: scraping, carving, scorching, pyro-engraving, and pressure-engraving. The techniques are combined in most of the collection. The basic tools for gourd decoration probably included a lithic or shell knife and engravers of different sizes and shapes, perforators, saws, and scrapers. The decoration techniques are outlined below.

Scraping: This technique involved the use of a sharp lithic knife, which sometimes had a serrated edge as suggested by micro-chatter and cut marks on some gourd fragments. This was used to scrape off the pattern motif to some depth, about 0.2–0.8 mm below the surface. As the background was scraped away, the pattern stood out in the natural beige or yellow color of the skin of the gourd against a dark brown or black background.

Carving: In this technique lines were incised with a sharp knife. The carvers made as many incisions as possible to decorate the gourd outside. Microscopic study shows some fine scorched traces in the incisions, suggesting that the cutting or engraving tool edge was often placed in a fire to heat it.

Engraving: Both pyro-engraving and pressure-engraving were used.

DISCUSSION

All decorated fragments from Paredones were retrieved from a small area on the far eastern end of the mound. Of the 24 pieces recovered, 6 were refitted pieces. No whole or larger pieces were excavated at Paredones. The 4 decorated fragments from Huaca Prieta were from tombs, ritual floors, and fills.

No decorated gourds were found in Unit 16, in other excavations (off-mound test pits), or in the debris around looters' pits at outlying household mounds.

Gourds at Huaca Prieta and Paredones were engraved with a combination of abstract and figured motifs (figs. 11.7–11.8). Gourd fragments without designs were numerous at all sites: Huaca Prieta ($n = 1389$), Unit 16 ($n = 58$), and Paredones ($n = 318$). At Huaca Prieta 4 fragments with incised lines were recovered (fig. 11.8e, ee, j, l); 54 with geometric or other designs were excavated at Paredones (fig. 11.7a–o and fig. 11.8a–d, dd, f, g, h, i, k, m–o). Bird also recovered decorated and undecorated gourds at Huaca Prieta. Most of the gourds we studied that were excavated by Bird at Huaca Prieta, housed at the American Museum of Natural History, were from the ramp in Unit HP-3 ($n = 241$). Most of our undecorated ones were from Unit 10 ($n = 12$), and a few other minor units (such as Unit 3, $n = 10$), all dating from late Phases III to V. (We examined numerous gourd fragments at the museum and observed only 7 decorated ones, which had nothing more than a few incised lines or dots.) At Paredones most were excavated in the older layers of Phase II and III ($n = 388$). Many fragments from both Huaca Prieta and Paredones were plain, but often with deliberately polished and smooth gourd bodies (table 11.1). The plain fragments are separated from the largest assemblage of unsmoothed and unpolished or modified pieces. The discussion below focuses on incised and decorated specimens. Basically all designs are combinations of various abstract motifs like circles, squares, triangles, and lines sometimes simple, broken, or wavy, although a few anthropomorphic designs are present at both sites (Dillehay, personal observation of the Huaca Prieta gourds housed at the American Museum of Natural History, 2007 and 2009).

The best-known gourds from Bird's collection are 2 complete small decorated gourd bowls from Huaca Prieta that have square-shaped geometric carved faces believed to be human and/or feline human or animal faces (Bird et al. 1985: fig. 43). The textiles found by Bird also reveal a fairly wide variety of decorative motifs, including geometric designs, stylized human figures (Bird et al. 1985: figs. 100–101, 111, 119, and 125) and faces, condors and other birds, snakes, rock crabs, felines, and several unidentified motifs that show some stylistic similarity to those found on gourds. Other than

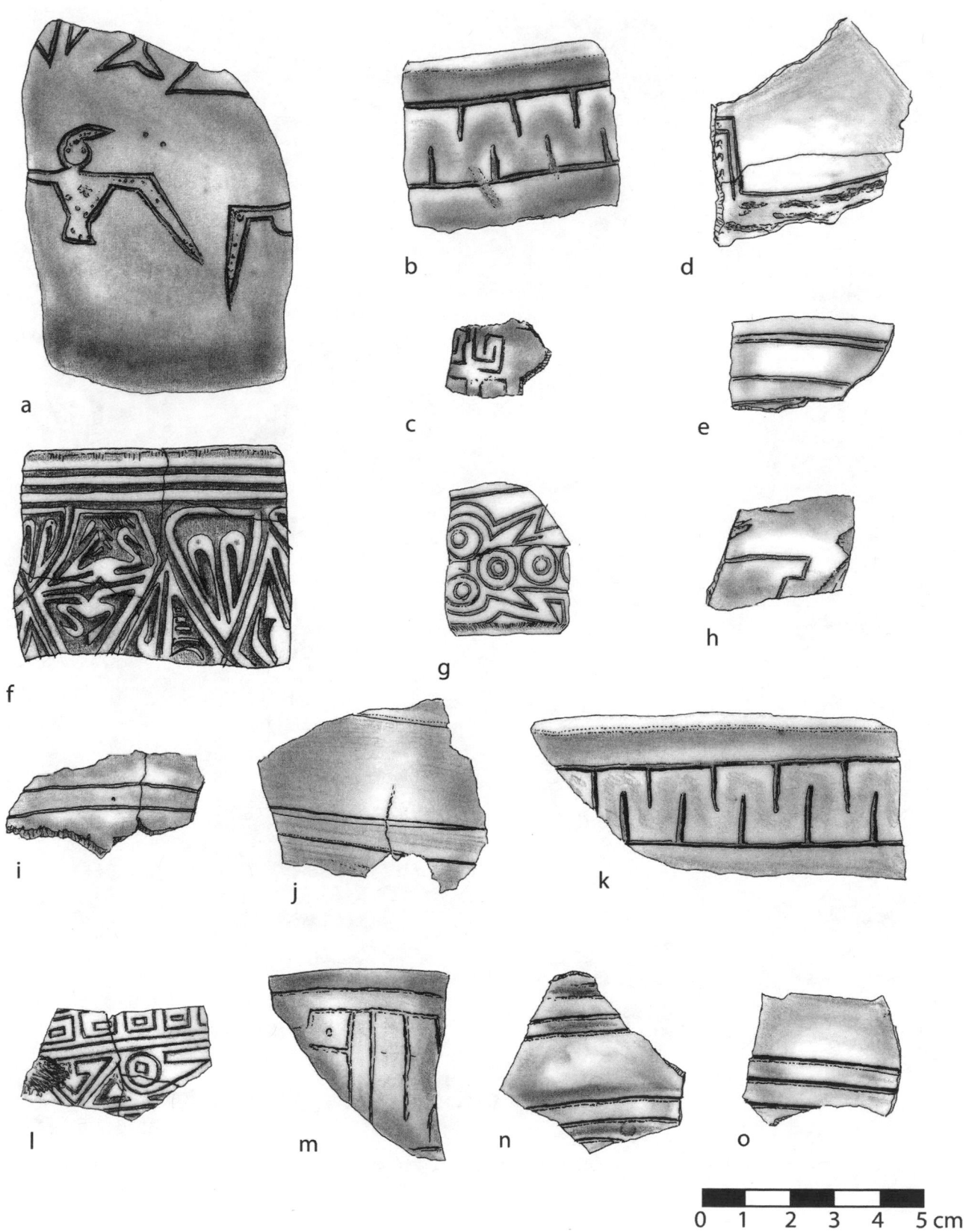

FIGURE 11.7. Decorated gourds: *a*, bird, *b–d*, *h*, *k*, *m*, geometric designs; *f*, *g*, *l*, stylized motifs; *e*, *i*, *j*, *n*, *o*, parallel incised lines.

FIGURE 11.8. Decorated gourds: *a–d, dd, ee, f, h,* geometric design; *g,* stylized design; *e, i–j, l,* and *n,* parallel incised lines; *k, m, o,* miscellaneous marks.

Table 11.1. Distribution of types of decorated and worked gourds for Huaca Prieta and Paredones

| Units | No. of gourd fragments | Gourd types | |
		Incised	Decorated
Huaca Prieta			
Unit 10			
Layer 1	1		
Layer 2	2		1
Layer 3	2		1
Layer 4	1		1
Subtotal	**6**		**3**
HP-3 Ramp			
Layer 4	31	1	3
Layer 8	23	1	4
Layer 9	32	2	
Layer 13a	22		1
Layer 17			2
Layer 19	13		1
Layer 22	20		1
Layer 24	34		
Layer 28	12		
Layer 32	10		
Layer 34	14		
Layer 39	2		
Layer 40	7		
Subtotal	**220**	**4**	**18**
Unit 3, Layer 3	5		
Subtotal	**5**		
Huaca Prieta			
Subtotal	**231**	**4**	**18**
Paredones			
Floor 1	3		
Floor 3	3	2	3
Floor 5	6	2	3
Floor 7	7		4
Floor 10	13	1	6
Floor 14	11	1	8
Floor 17	7	1	1
Floor 20	3	2	
Floor 22	3		
Paredones			
Subtotal	**56**	**9**	**25**
TOTAL	**287**	**13**	**43**

the complete bowls with the faces on them, most of the design motifs on the Huaca Prieta gourds are simple incised lines.

The designs from Paredones, in contrast, are more varied, with geometric (figs. 11.7b, c–d, h, k, m and 11.8 a–dd, f, h) or stylized motifs (fig. 11.7a, f, g, and l), ricrac, and animal motifs (such as birds: fig. 11.7a). The animal motifs probably originated from creatures and other natural aspects of the Pacific coast. A motif showing a bird with flexed wings, a long beak, and a pouch under the beak is similar to the profile and posture of pelicans (fig. 11.7a). Similar incised lines and simple geometric decorations are found at other Preceramic sites along the coast (for example, Engel 1957a, 1957b; Feldman 1980; Fung Pineda 1991; Grieder et al. 1988; Vergara Montero 2015). But they were not as stylized and perhaps not as early as those from Paredones and Huaca Prieta.

Several archaeologists have debated the origin of the designs on the 2 decorated gourds excavated by Bird. Edward Lanning (1967) thought that they were from the coast of southern Ecuador and northern Peru, similar to those seen on Phases III–V Valdivia ceramics dated between 4500 and 4200 cal BP. Henning Bischof (1999) contested this interpretation, stating that similar designs appear on several late Preceramic textiles and early ceramics at coastal and highland sites in Peru, including Asia, La Galgada, Ancón, and other sites. We generally agree with Lanning's position for two reasons. First, all sites referenced by Bischof are slightly later in age than the 2 gourd containers at Huaca Prieta, implying that Valdivia influence could have spread down the north coast of Peru to Huaca Prieta, Paredones, and other coastal sites and then dispersed from there to sites farther inland and farther south. The second factor is the presence of different styles on gourd fragments from Paredones that evidently had not yet appeared in Peru but seem to have a tropical-like influence (for instance, the stylized "ricrac" rim band on some Paredones gourd fragments may be similar to Valdivia Phase 2 styles bowl rim decorations [Karen Stothert, personal communication, 2015]), in combination with other exotics probably derived from the tropical coast of southern Ecuador and northern Peru (such as grooved green schist axes, *Spondylus* and scallop shells from warm waters, and possibly maize, squash, and other cultigens: see the discussion below).

Paredones defined more intricate spaces for design motifs on gourds. Although no whole decorated vessels were recovered at Paredones, it can be determined that individual motifs were made to define their individual spaces. In the case of geometric designs, the motifs appear to radiate from their positions on divided background spaces in all directions. These designs are made with their individual motifs linking up to form a network over a unified background. Circles, squares, and lines run into one another on their common background. A clear temporal and stylistic pattern exists at Paredones, where the most diverse and stylized motifs are early Phase III (figs. 11.7b, f, g, k, and l, 11.8a, b, dd, f, g, and h) and the less diverse and stylized are in Phases IV and V (figs. 11.7a, d, e, i, j, n, and o, 11.8m, n, and o).

FRAGMENTATION

Equally significant is the fragmented nature of the gourd pieces from both sites, which are all roughly the same size, measuring 4.9–6.4 cm by 5.1–7.2 cm. More than 200 specimens show scoring or incised lines where whole gourds were deliberately marked and snapped to produce fragments, most of which are roughly squared in form. Scored lines show sharp precise cuts; below them are uneven broken surfaces suggesting breakage and snapping. Scoring, snapping, or cutting decorated objects also is a feature of the textiles and baskets recovered from Huaca Prieta (see chapter 12).

Several gourd fragments contain coca leaf fragments or starch grains of chile peppers and beans (see chapter 10 and appendices 4 and 9). This might suggest that decorated gourds perhaps were first used as containers for eating or offerings during rituals then intentionally fragmented and deposited on the mounds. Furthermore, the absence of decorated gourds at the domestic sites suggests their exclusive ritual use at Paredones and Huaca Prieta.

In summary, the gourds were mirrors that must have symbolized certain important aspects of the world: the people themselves, their mode of life, and perhaps their households and their neighbors around them. Certainly the designs are of some decorative and expressive value, radiant with individually vital elements. It also is important to note two different decorative themes at Huaca Prieta and Paredones, perhaps indicative of a dual pattern that repeats itself in the two different weaving and twining techniques in textiles and baskets (see chapter 12), in the two coexisting populations suggested by isotope analysis of human teeth (see appendix 6), in differences in the lithic technologies and food remains at both sites, and in the symbolism expressed in the faunal remains (see chapter 9).

PAINTED STONES

At Huaca Prieta 26 green cobblestones with red painted circles were recovered from different Phase III–V contexts (fig. 11.9): 16 found in and around the chamber tombs in Units 23, 6 in Bird's backdirt piles, and 4 from Layers 22, 35, and 41 on footpaths on the entry ramp in Unit HP-3. The painted circles on individual stones were 1.9–2.4 cm in diameter and always have even numbers, usually between 2 and 10, with most stones having 6–10. Since none were found in other units off the mound, including Paredones, we presume that they are associated with ritual activities at Huaca Prieta. All painted circles are found on light green skarn stones. (The skarn stones were identified by the project geologist, Mario Pino. James Richardson reports that green schist and skarn are found in northern coastal Peru: personal communication, 2015.) The color combination of red and green and the symbolism of the red circles is not known.

SHELLS

The most common shells from which tools were manufactured are clam bivalves and gastropod shells (various species were used, indicating no preference for one over another). Several physical characteristics can be classified. The majority of shell artifacts appear to have performed utilitarian functions. This evidence does not rule out the possibility that shell hammers, adzes, scrapers, cutting tools, or other tool types were reserved for performing ritual or symbolic actions; however, there

FIGURE 11.9. Green skarn stone painted with 10 circles of a red pigment.

is little evidence to suggest this scenario. Ritual items such as decorative shell gorgets and carved shell objects have not been recovered. Even shell beads, at the very least social in nature, are underrepresented in the collections. Figure 11.10a shows a modified shell with a perforation and red pigment smeared on it.

METHODS

The literature dealing specifically with shell tools and the shell tool industry of the Preceramic period was reviewed to develop an informed concept for how to approach the collection (for example, Bird et al. 1985; Chu Barrera 2011; Engel 1957a, 1957b; Fung Pineda 1969; Quilter 1989). Recognizing that most shell tools are "expedient," we made particular efforts to identify shells with any qualities that might indicate use-wear, such as pieces with beveled or worn edges. Often these tools were quite small, sometimes under 5 cm.

We define shell artifacts on the basis of two criteria: (1) the shell exhibits deliberate shaping, such as cutting, perforation, or beveling, and/or (2) the shell shows evidence of utilization, such as smoothing from friction or chipping and spalling from hammering. Numerous shells ($n = 212$) exhibit shaping, both deliberate and nonintentional, but not all are tools or were deliberately shaped. (Numerous complete and broken limpet shells show edge damage, suggesting that they were used as scrapers.) For example, some holes in large gastropod shells were the results of animal extraction and not tool manufacture. Additionally, care was taken to differentiate between use-wear and wear due to exposure on the ground surface. We selected 126 pieces of shell for specific study based on their identification as artifacts (table 11.2), with the others classified as ecofacts. Several of these turned out not to be tools but were instead the fragmented by-products of tool manufacture (debitage).

All shells included in this study can be seen as items in themselves but also as points on a con-

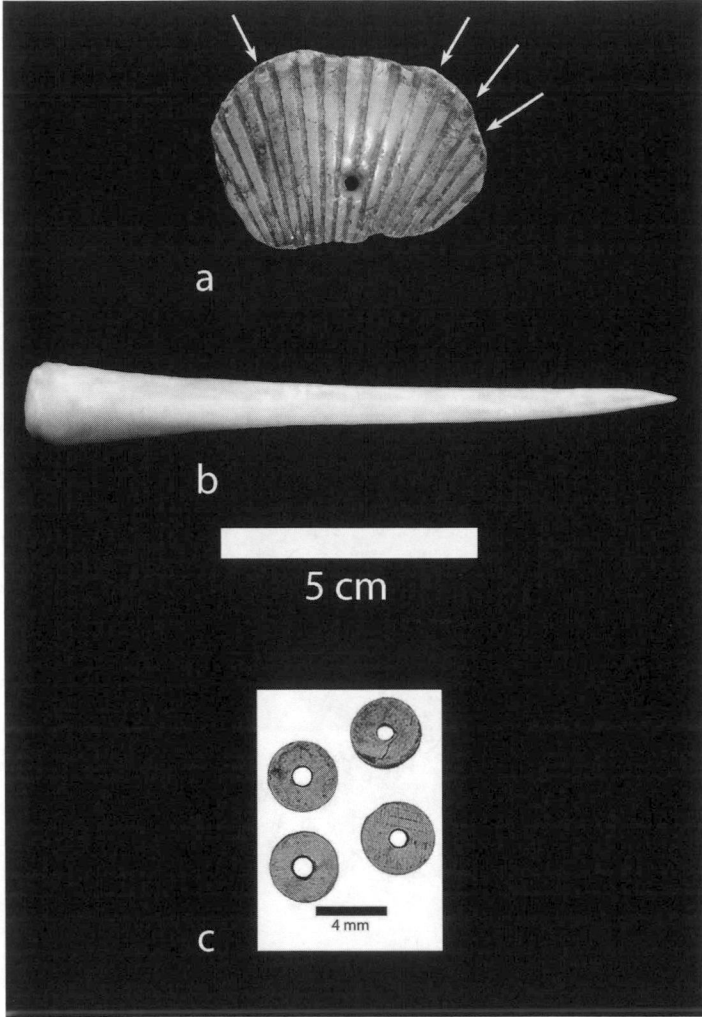

FIGURE 11.10. Shells: *a*, perforated shell with red pigment; *b*, shell awl; *c*, shell beads.

artifacts follows. The "Probable" category became a catchall for items that displayed characteristics simply too questionable to reject the specimen as a tool but that do not fit into any established category either. The "Debitage" category exists separately from "Tool Fragments" because it is composed mostly of the tips of shells. "Fragments" therefore denotes bits of shell that do not present themselves as related to tool manufacture or use, though they may very well be. In each case, not enough material was available to determine whether pieces broke off due to site formation processes or were the result of human agency. No use-wear is apparent on samples as well. The "Indeterminate" category represents shell specimens that could be seen either as artifacts or as ecofacts. These specimens usually possess more than one tool characteristic but lack a definitive aspect such as use-wear that could be used to categorize them accurately. The "Worked Shell" category is made up of ecofacts that show probable signs of activity beyond food acquisition. Shell tools and fragments were recovered from all sites but mainly from Huaca Prieta (HP), Paredones (P), and Unit 16 (U-16).

SPECIFIC TYPES

Cutting-edge tools (HP: 1; P: 13; U-16: 2): Cutting tools vary in form and size. They may include the body whorl of the gastropod. The distinctive feature is an angular cut at the basal end of the columellae, which provides a cutting edge for the tool. The distribution of these tools is shown in table 11.2. For display 3 cutting-edged tools were chosen in order to represent the widest range of this type. Cutting tools were most likely part of a plant- or fish-cutting complex that may also include adzes and planes.

Grinders/pulverizers (P: 10): The grinder is a gastropod with the entire spire and apex of the shell removed down to its shoulder and then worn smooth. The major difference between a grinder and cutting edged tools is the top end of the columella, which has been worn down and rounded, and the siphonal canal, which has suffered no chipping or spalling resulting from percussive action.

Scrapers/spatulas (P: 13; U-16: 4): These vary in size and shape and are typically made of bivalves; the pieces display beveling on one or more edges,

tinuum. Like stone tools, shell tools are made through a process of reduction. Use of the artifact continues to reduce and reshape it over time and may help transform the artifact from type to type. Items that began their use-lives as shell scoops, for instance, could have been transformed over time into smaller tools, such as scrapers (mainly limpet shells); cutting tools could become hammers and perhaps eventually bipointed punches.

There are two main classes of shell artifacts: (1) body whorl gastropod fragments and (2) whole and fragmented clam shells. The handful of bivalve shells in the collection generally fall within the whole shell category. But the presence of the majority of shells in all sites results from mere food discard.

A brief description of the categories of shell

Table 11.2. Distribution of types of worked shells for Huaca Prieta and Paredones

Units	Types of worked shells						Shells			
	Cutting-edge tool	Grinder	Scraper	Awl	Plane	Bead	Perforated shell	Indeterminate	Worked shell	Probable tool
Huaca Prieta										
Unit 10									1	
Unit 16	2		4	2			4	7	1	5
Unit 21	1			1		4				
Paredones										
Unit 22										
Floor 2	2	2	3	1	2		1	1	1	
Floor 3	1		1	1			2	2	2	
Floor 5										
Fill 6	1		1							
Floor 8	2		2						2	1
Floor 9		1			1		1	1	1	
Floor 10	1		1		2		2	2		
Fill 10		2		1	1				1	
Floor 13		1	1		2		1	1		2
Floor 14	2						1	1		3
Floor 18										
Fill 19										
Unit 20										
Layer 2	1	3	1		1		1	2		
Layer 4	2		2				1		2	1
Layer 5		1			1		1	1	2	
Layer 5a	1		1		2			2	1	
Totals	**16**	**10**	**17**	**6**	**12**	**4**	**15**	**20**	**14**	**12**

which we hypothesize results from a scraping action. They are flatter or shallower than scoops. Figure 11.10a shows a shell scraper.

Awls (HP: 1; P: 3; U–16: 2): These tools are small fragments of whorl, almost slivers, which appear to show an unusual amount of rounding or use-wear (fig. 11.10b). They could also be thought of as gravers or small chisels. The awls range in size from 3 to 6 cm long, averaging 4.7 cm long, with 6 cm as the most commonly occurring maximum length.

Planes (P: 12): These are shell tools with planning edges, most of which are broken.

Beads (HP: 4): The collection contains 4 small shell beads found in Unit 21, Structure 3 (fig. 11.10c).

Perforated shells (P: 11; U-16: 4): While numerous bivalve shells display perforations that do not appear to be the results of random accident or site-formation processes, this type is defined as shells with holes drilled or punched in them, suggesting that they were used by people (fig. 11.10a). These may have been decorative, like beads; they also may have been bead blanks. They were too small to have been used as net weights or sinkers for fishing lines. Most of the perforated shells were crafted from bivalve shells.

Indeterminates (P: 13; U-16: 7): This represents a broad category of shell fragments that might or might not be included in various tool categories. They usually possess more than one tool-like characteristic but lack a specific definitive feature.

Worked shells (HP: 2; P: 12; U-16: 1): This category holds a broad range of shell and shell pieces. Specimens in this category demonstrate a wide range of characteristics but nothing definitive. Worked shells show signs of modification but typically lack obvious use-wear.

Probable tools (P: 7; U-16: 5): These are pieces of shell ranging in size and shape that are unmistakably processed, but for which we currently have no use analogue. The probable tools may have been purely expedient, for small jobs.

Debitage and fragments: These categories are far too numerous to quantify, with thousands of fragments found at Huaca Prieta (~158,000) and Unit 16 (~38,000) and fewer at Paredones (~17,000) (keeping in mind that a much larger area was excavated at the former site, thus rendering a larger quantity of shells). This category includes all the bits and pieces of shell that show no specific evidence of use beyond food acquisition but at the same time are not large enough to be completely ruled out as having been part of the process of tool manufacture. Like fragments, the bits and pieces are not artifacts but are included in the discussion and are shown for research purposes. The essential difference is that fragments are pieces, whereas many ecofacts are nearly whole shells.

RESULTS AND DISCUSSION

Of the shell pieces studied, 19 exhibited clear signs of use-wear, while 2 others were shaped by deliberate flaking and grinding and were highly weathered, making identification of use impossible. The patterns of use-wear observed were produced mainly by scraping and cutting. In the modification of valves the dorsal or ventral edge of one lateral margin on the inferior portion of the valve appeared to be the preferred working edge: the umbo or hinge area of the valve was completely removed with two or more breaks, leaving a segment with a sharp working edge for use.

Fish-scaling is a possibility for some of these specimens, as the small size of the artifacts and the light degree of fracturing on their margins indicates that no hard materials were worked with them. Engel (1980) describes shell artifacts from various coastal sites, which seemingly functioned as cutting and scraping implements, including use in dealing with fish.

The 19 shell pieces that exhibited use traces were found in HP-3 ($n = 11$) and date to Phases III–V. The beads were found on the floor of Structure 3 in Unit 21, dated to Phase IV, in Huaca Prieta. Unit 16 yielded 6 specimens associated with graves. In Paredones ($n = 2$) shell artifacts were located mainly in Unit 20 and dated to Phase IV.

SUMMARY

The most commonly identified shell tools in the collection are made in whole or in part from bivalves. The collection contains few examples of artifacts outside utilitarian uses. Items such as beads should be considered tools, but they belong to a social category. Shell scoops for serving or eating food are harder to identify with confidence, although several limpet shells seem to have been used this way. They are far less distinctive and required less effort to produce.

People produced and used a varied utilitarian shell tool assemblage during several millennia at the sites. The presence of these tools demonstrates a complex adaptation to the marine, estuarine, and riverine environments of the Chicama area. Curiously, no shell fishhooks were recovered from our excavated sites, although Bird found 3 fragments in the deeper levels of Huaca Prieta (Bird et al. 1985: 22, 41, 220). The paucity of these elements may suggest the presence of specialized workshops where fishing equipment was produced and fish were prepared. If they exist, neither Bird nor our project found them. No worked exotic shells were recovered.

BONE TOOLS

We recovered several worked bones from Huaca Prieta ($n = 14$) and a few from Paredones ($n = 8$) and from Unit 16 ($n = 3$): 1 bone bead made of a bird long bone, a bone tube also of a bird long bone, a bone weaving tool, 7 awls and awl fragments probably from sea lion or deer bones (fig. 11.11a–d), and 3 sea lion ribs, 2 possibly used as weaving tools (fig. 11.11e and f). A small bone bead was recovered from Stratum 36, Phase IV, in Bird's HP-3. A broken, slightly incised bone tube, measuring 13 cm long, was excavated in Unit 10, a

Phase IV context. Two incisions were made on the bone tube. The complete awls ranged from 6.2 to 12.6 cm in length. We also found 78 other bones showing blunted ends or other signs of expedient use, but these are not described as formal artifacts because they were not formally shaped. A single textile bundle contained a bone-weaving tool similar to the one Bird excavated in the HP-3 trench (see chapter 12, part 1). Bird recovered several bone tools, including carved decorative pieces (Bird et al. 1985).

WOOD TOOLS

Very few wood artifacts (*n* = 6) were recovered from our excavations, although we found several pieces of long, branch fragments of algarrobo (*Prosopis* sp.) that had blunted or beveled edges, suggesting that they were used as levers or digging and poking sticks. None of these pieces had bark and branch stubs. Several revealed linear depressions or grooves, but these could result from trampling or various uses. These pieces varied in length from 14 to 34 cm. All wooden tools were recovered at Huaca Prieta and date to Phases III–V. Also excavated were 3 short tree stumps that were cut on both ends and found in a standing position in Units 21 and 22 at Paredones (see chapter 7). These may have served as posts for structures.

Finally, 4 pieces of round wood from Huaca Prieta were intentionally worked by some adzing or chopping tools, as evidenced by shave and cut marks on them; 1 of these exhibits a slightly charred and blunted end, suggesting that it may have been used as a fire poker. These objects measured between 27 and 33 cm in length.

MISCELLANEOUS FIBERS

The excavations at Huaca Prieta and in House 3, Unit 16, yielded 5 wads of plant fiber, reeds, and grasses. These had no apparent functions but were deliberately wadded or clumped to form pads or wads; they measured between 16 and 22 cm in diameter (see chapter 12, part 1, for cotton wads).

We found 3 burned torches made of long needles of an unidentified tree species (perhaps pine?). The distal tips were burned and showed

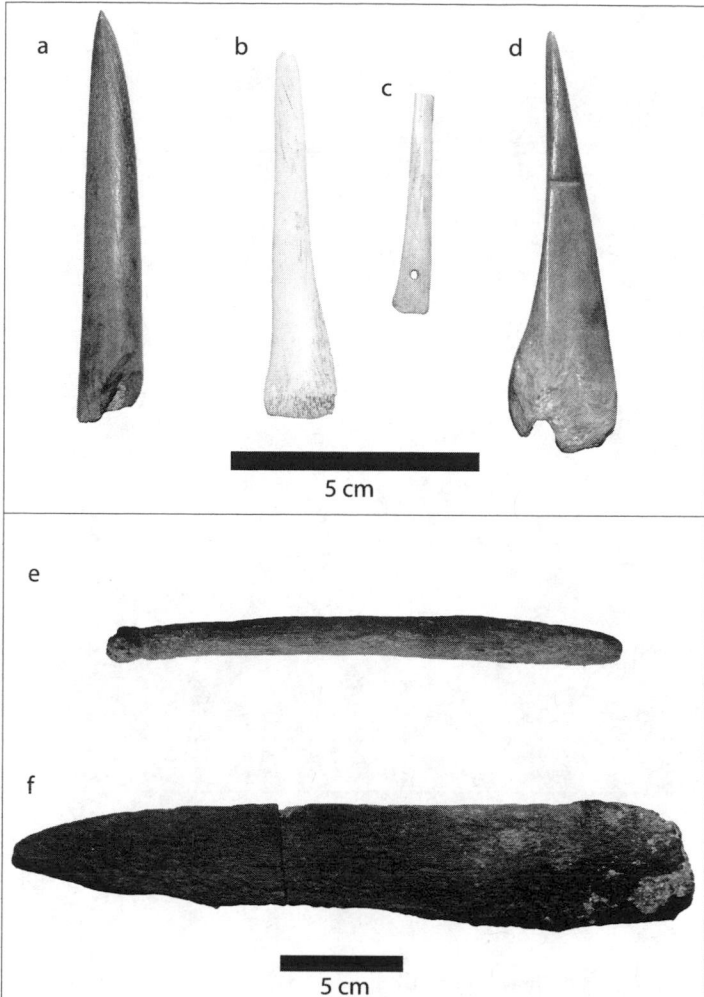

FIGURE 11.11. Bone tools: *a–d*, bone awls; *e–f*, modified long bones possibly used as weaving tools.

stains of resin. Leaves of *Typha* reeds wrapped the needles. Of these specimens 2 came from the zigzag footpath on the entry ramp in a late Phase IV layer in Unit 3 and 1 from a Phase III floor in Unit 15 (fig. 11.12).

RED PIGMENTS

A red, iron-based pigment appears on several textiles, stone tools, shells, and skeletons from Huaca Prieta (see chapter 12, part 1). A few patches of red pigment were recovered beneath the mound at Paredones and associated with burials at Unit 16 (see chapter 8). This material was recorded in the deeper late Pleistocene levels in Units 15 and 22 and from several human burials dating to Phases

FIGURE 11.12. Three burned torches from Huaca Prieta. Notice the burned tips.

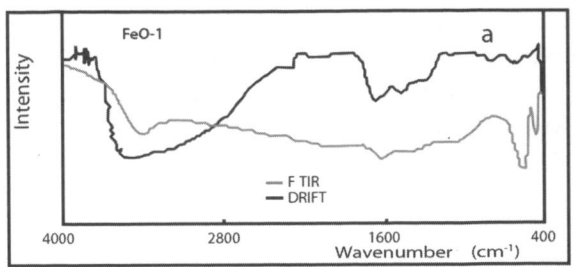

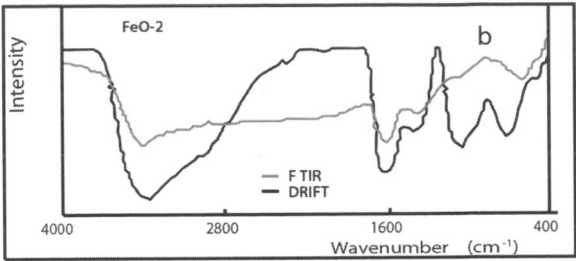

FIGURE 11.13. X-ray diffraction study of two red pigment samples: one from Stratum 13, Unit 15, and one from burial HP09-09. Diagram presents the powder X-ray diffraction pattern of FeO-1 and FeO-2 that is consistent with hematite (α-Fe_2O_3) and hematite-maghemite (α-Fe_2O_3/γ-Fe_2O_3) respectively.

IV and V (see chapters 7 and 8). Several hematite pieces were also found in various levels of the HP-3 trench. Fig. 11.13 shows an X-ray diffraction analysis of 2 red pigment samples: 1 from a burial in Unit 16 and 1 from a lens of red pigment in Stratum 9, Unit 15, dated to Phase I (see chapter 8 and appendix 11).

The nearest known hematite sources are approximately 80 km from the site, in the highlands of the Jequetepeque Valley.

A POSSIBLE COUNTING DEVICE OR GAME BOARD AND AN ANTHROPOMORPHIC FIGURE

A block of polychaete tubes in an adult male tomb in Unit 16, late Phase III (~5200 cal BP), had twenty circular depressions arranged in four rows

of five (fig. 11.14a). A complete *Semele* sp. shell was placed in one depression, and two stone spheroids of andesite were located underneath one edge of the block (fig. 11.14c). Also found underneath this block were salt crystals enclosed within a reed bundle. One stone is dark and the other light in color. Another block was shaped into a possible head of an anthropomorphic figure (fig. 11.14b, d). This burial seems to be of a distinguished individual (see chapter 7). The specimens measure 37 by 39 cm (fig. 11.14a) and 32 by 41 cm (fig. 11.14b).

Felipe Guamán Poma de Ayala's drawing of a *quipucamayoq* (quipu specialist) depicts a square device with subsquares laid out in rows of four by five that contain one to five black and white dots (Guamán Poma de Ayala and Gálvez 1956: 271). The remainder of the drawing has an individual working with a quipu, suggesting that the device is associated with record keeping. Several scholars have discussed the possible ways in which the squares of this device were used as a calculator, abacus, counting tray, or other recording instrument (D'Altroy 2014; De Pascuale and Aimi 2003; Urton 1997). Was the male buried in Unit

16 with the sculpted board with twenty depressions and the bundle of salt in charge of recording the production and exchange of items? Was he a salt trader? This type of device appears as early as the Moche period on the north coast of Peru. Although the polychaete block sculpture is about 3500 years earlier, we can ask whether it is a prototype counting or recording instrument or perhaps a game board.

OTHER POLYCHAETE TUBE PIECES

Both Bird's excavations and ours recovered several tools made of pieces of polychaete tubes that were shaped as polishers, grinders, and miscellaneous forms from Huaca Prieta and Paredones.

We also recovered a large piece of polychaete that had been sculpted into a pattern of wavy lines (fig. 11.15; we observed a similar decorated block in a looter's hole at Pulpar). Local male fisherfolk interpreted the lines as water waves and sand strandlines produced by retreating waves on the beach. Local female seaweed collectors saw them as representing human hair.

EXOTIC ITEMS

Recovered from a chamber tomb in Unit 10, Phase IV, was a cut fragment of *Spondylus princeps* shell (fig. 11.16a), which can only be from the central coast of Ecuador. Pieces of shell from a large species of clam (*Anadara* sp.), found in mangrove

20 cm

FIGURE 11.14. Polychaete tube-base artifacts: *a*, game board or counting device; *b* and *d*, anthropomorphic head or headdress; *c*, two spheroid stones associated with object in *a*.

FIGURE 11.15. Sculpted polychaete tube-base showing wavy lines.

areas of southern Ecuador and the northwest coast of Peru, were excavated from the floor of Structure 4 in Unit 21, Phase IV. Use surfaces and floors in Units 2 and 22 yielded shells from 3 species of exotic scallops (*Argopecten circularis*, *Argopecten pupuretus*, and *Argopecten* sp.), dating respectively to Phases II, IV, and V. Even when a particular unit (such as Unit 2) yields more than a single shell, they come from different contexts, primarily as offerings, from different phases. These are distinctive shells unlike any found locally. *Argopecten* comes from the Gulf of Guayaquil in southwest Ecuador. Given the presence of other exotic foods and nonfood items at Huaca Prieta, the minimal and sporadic presence of this species is very unlikely to be the result of El Niño events that shifted warm waters farther south, resulting in its growth in the Huaca Prieta area. If these species were inhabiting the coastline during a prolonged El Niño, which would be required for shell species to migrate several hundreds of km, we would expect more of these shells in midden and food deposits rather than finding a few of them in small piles of ritual offerings and in or near tombs. All of these shells appear to be exotic foods or colorful shells directly brought to Huaca Prieta by

people from coastal Ecuador or procured through direct or down-the-line exchange. A piece of hard scleractinian coral found in Unit 10, Phase IV, likely came from warm waters in northern Peru or southern Ecuador (fig. 11.16e).

At Huaca Prieta 3 copper sulfate nodules also were recovered (see appendix 19): 1 from a footpath in Unit 6 on the entry ramp that dates to late Phase IV and 2 from a floor in the sunken circular plaza of Unit 21, both of which date to Phase IV. A single piece was associated with a coca leaf (see fig. 7.21.a). Copper sulfate is found in only the Andean mountains east of Huaca Prieta. A piece of malachite from the Andean highlands to the east was excavated in Unit 21 in the sunken plaza and dated to Period IV (fig. 11.16d). Unworked green chalcedony ($n = 2$) and yellow chert ($n = 1$) were recovered from a floor in Unit 3, Phase III, at Huaca Prieta. These likely come from the foothills of the Andes east of the site. At Huaca Prieta 6 rock crystals also were recovered from footpaths: 2 on the path between the top of the mound and the sunken circular plaza and 4 on different paths of the entry ramp. All date to contexts of Phases IV and V (fig. 11.16f). These also come from the Andes to the east.

None of the exotic terrestrial and marine foods were recovered from chamber tombs. All were retrieved from Phase IV and Phase V ritual contexts, specifically the sunken circular plaza and on the footpaths from the plaza to the top of the mound and on the entry ramp.

POTTERY SHERDS

At Huaca Prieta 5 ceramic fragments were excavated in the deeper levels of the mound: 1 in the upper level of a carbonate layer of the lagoon in off-mound Test Pit 23, probably dated ~5500 cal BP; 1 from above Layer 5 in Unit 15, about 0.50 cm above the basal mound level, dated ~6000–5500 cal BP; and 2 from Layer 7b in Unit 2, dated ~6000 cal BP (fig. 11.16g). All of these sherds are from intact layers deeply buried below undisturbed stratigraphy, containing floors and stone structures in Huaca Prieta. A possible exception is the sherd from a deep carbonate layer in Test Pit 23, which may have been tossed into the lagoon sometime around 6000–5000 years ago

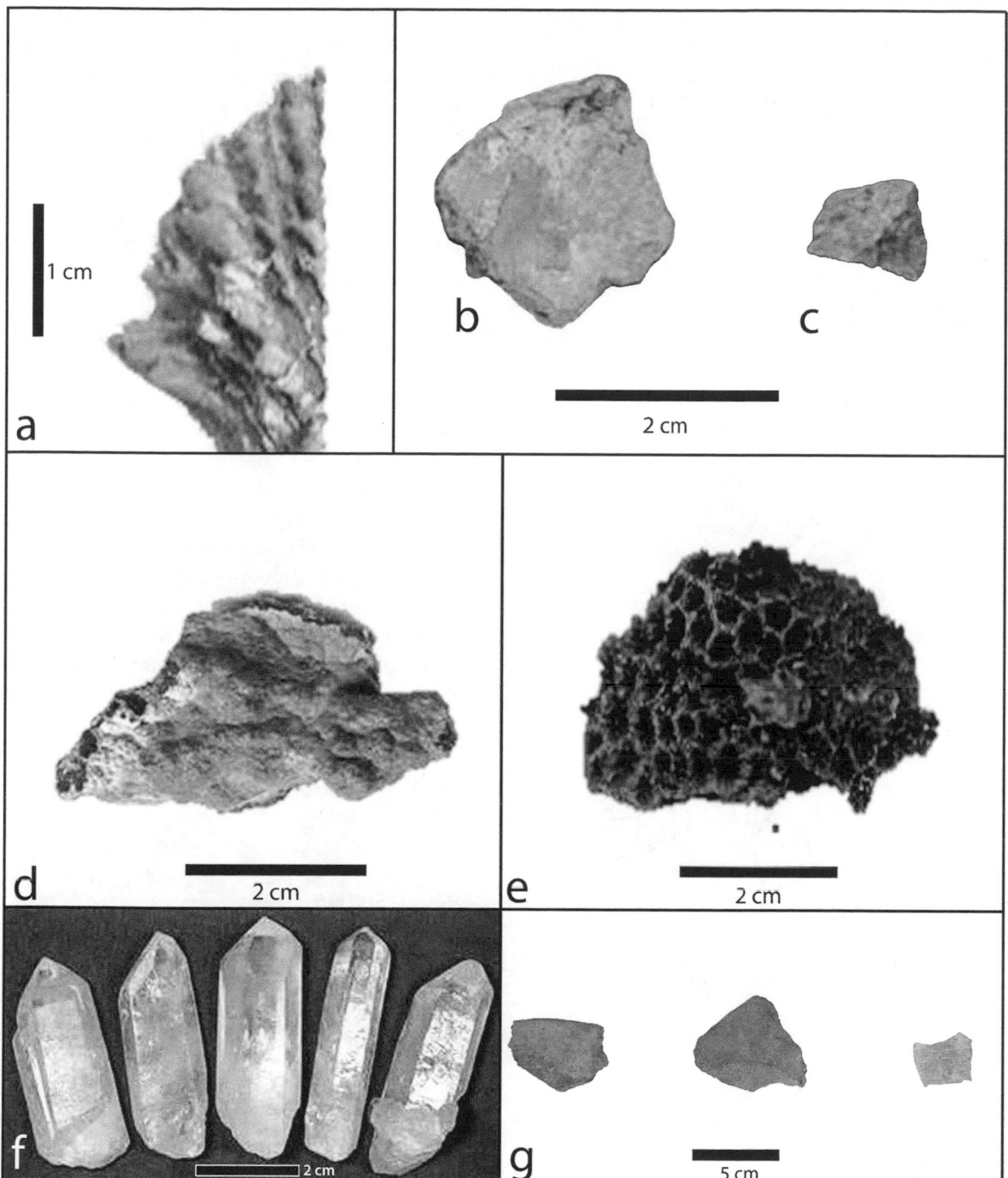

FIGURE 11.16. Various exotics: *a*, *Spondylus* fragment; *b–c*, turquoise fragments; *d*, malachite; *e*, *Scleractinia* sp. coral; *f*, rock crystals; *g*, ceramic fragments. (See color plates.)

because the sediments sealing it formed after this time (see chapter 5). No known taphonomic or other variables explain the presence of these few sherd fragments in these contexts.

None of the sherds have decoration, polish, or smoothing. All are poorly oxidized and have a

crusty paste with quartzite and sand temper. They measure between 0.8 and 1.2 cm in thickness and 3.2–4.1 cm in diameter. The sample size is too small and nondescript to compare to other early pottery collections.

In addition to the sherds from deeper layers in

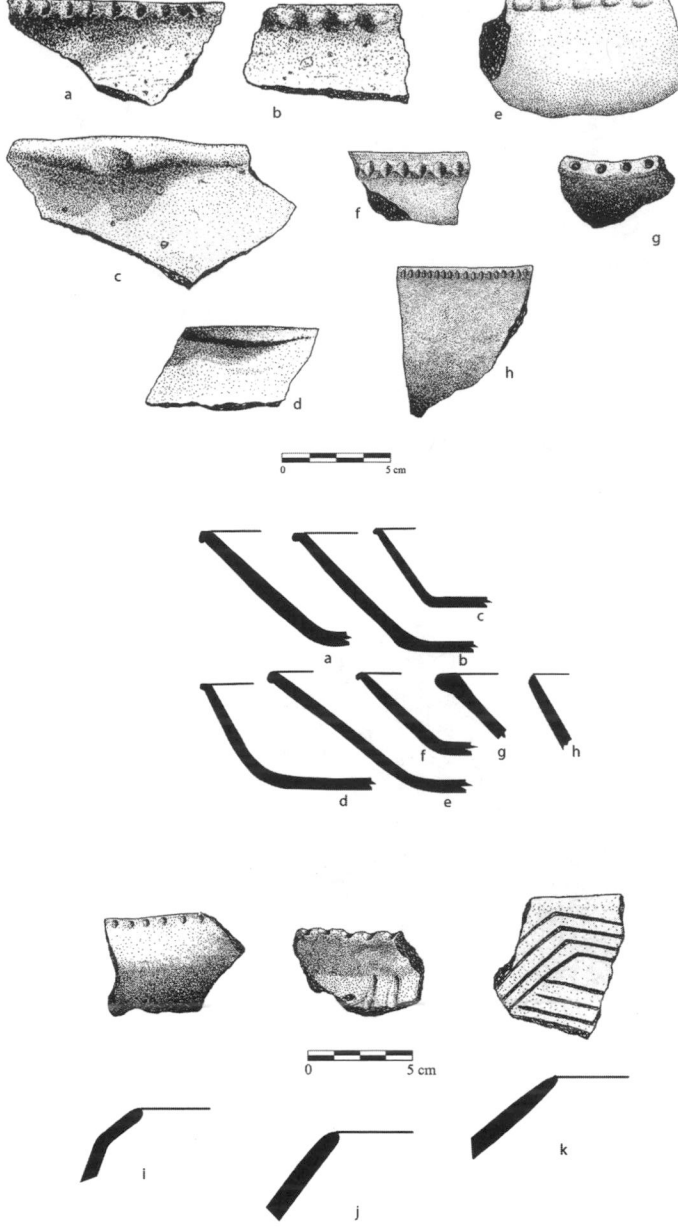

FIGURE 11.17. Various Guañape-like decorated rim sherds from Huaca Prieta, representing shallow bowls (*a–h*) and neckless jars (*i–k*).

knobs were the most common decorative motifs. Most sherds reveal burnishing or slight polish on the exterior. Temper consisted of sand and occasionally quartzite. All sherds shown in figure 11.16 were recovered from prepared floors or use surfaces that radiocarbon dated roughly from 3800 to 3400 cal BP (AA81926 or 3688–3464 cal BP on wood charcoal from soot on the interior wall of a bowl: Beta247696 or 3823–3483 cal BP on charcoal from a hearth; and AA86944 or 3614–3398 cal BP on wood charcoal from an intact floor).

The ceramics from the upper layers in and around the south side of the mound are similar in vessel form but not in decoration to Guañape types of the Initial Period in Peru, which roughly begins around 4000–3500 cal BP. However, the shallow bowl form and the appliqué and incisions on the lip of the rims are different from the Guañape style. The sample size reported here is too small to draw any conclusions other than the oddity of decorative types at Huaca Prieta. Although the meaning of this oddity is not known, it was recognized previously by Luis Lumbreras (1974: 51), who noted that the early pottery from Huaca Prieta is "so primitive that it is tempting to attribute it to independent invention." More details on these ceramics will be provided in a later publication.

CONCLUSIONS

With the exception of the lithics, shells, and textiles and cordage, the material culture assemblages are generally small, especially from Huaca Prieta, and this is likely due to the ritual and mortuary nature of the site. Nonetheless, a few other points can be made in addition to the conclusions presented above. With the exception of cultigens, all nonfood exotics are from Huaca Prieta. Very few exotic raw stone materials were recovered, which may be curiosities or come from undetected workshops in and around the excavated sites. Other raw lithic material came from abundant local sources. The nonfood exotics mentioned above, exotic dyes and pigments for use with basketry and textiles (see chapter 12), and the wide variety of cultigens imported to the site are important indicators of contact with people beyond the littoral and coastal zone. Although

and around Huaca Prieta, more than 1200 fragmented ceramics were recovered from the upper layers of Units 3, 6, 25, and HP-3 on the northeast side of the mound at Huaca Prieta and from the upper levels in Units 2 and 15 and Test Pit 9 on the south side of the mound (fig. 11.16). The few rims recovered are primarily from small neckless jars and shallow bowls (*n* = 32) and secondarily from small single-spout bottles (*n* = 4). Fingernail impressions, zoned incisions, and appliqué minor in number, the exotics suggest either direct or indirect exchange with distant areas or visits and offerings by different groups of peoples coming to Huaca Prieta from distant coastal and highland areas.

As mentioned earlier, the lithic technology is very conservative through time and changed very little. Although they are less frequent and variable in the archaeological record, the same can be said for the shell, wood, gourd, and bone technologies. The single major change among these materials, however, is the appearance of decorative motifs on gourds at Paredones around 6000–5500 cal BP. We have little evidence for another technology that appears at Huaca Prieta: the manufacture and use of dyes and pigments (see chapter 12). One notable pattern in the artifact assemblage is the absence of manos and grinding stones at Huaca Prieta and in Unit 16; the large majority were recovered from Paredones and associated with plant preparation.

Although architecture is not always included in discussions of technology, it warrants brief mention as a material component that was less conservative at Huaca Prieta (see chapter 7: conservative in the sense that since the inception of mound building people utilized loose cobblestones to make stone alignments and berm footings and to define circumscribed ritual spaces). Occasionally these alignments formed single lines of stones or low walls or small stone structures. In Phase IV, in the sunken plaza and on the summit, more formal rooms and chamber tombs were built, suggesting a more receptive approach to space and place. Associated with the architecture and stratigraphic layers at Huaca Prieta also was the technology of thick indurated or hard-plaster surfaces to conserve the mound. The most innovative and diverse technologies at Huaca Prieta, however, were twining and weaving techniques, which seem to represent at least two and maybe more different groups contributing to the textile, netting, cordage, and basketry industries (see chapter 12, part 2). As both Bird (Bird et al. 1985) and Splitstosser state (see chapter 12, part 1), cloth takes on a greater functional and social importance through time at Huaca Prieta and the wider study area, presuming that some textiles are made or exported elsewhere. As discussed in the final chapters, this probably relates to transformations taking place in the demographic and social organization of people along the littoral during the lengthy Preceramic period.

CHAPTER 12

TWINED AND WOVEN ARTIFACTS

PART 1: TEXTILES

Jeffrey Splitstoser

INTRODUCTION

Huaca Prieta first surprised the archaeological world in the 1940s when Junius Bird presented thousands of well-preserved cotton fabrics from Preceramic times that were decorated with complex invisible patterns (for example, Bird 1948a, 1948b, 1952, 1962, 1963a, 1963b; Bird et al. 1985; Bird and Mahler 1951–1952). The work that went into these fabrics hinted at a society whose inhabitants were highly skilled, technically proficient, and artistic. Since then Huaca Prieta fabrics have continued to impress the fabric and archaeology worlds with their hidden structural secrets.

Excavations by Dillehay and Bonavia expanded upon Bird's pits and trenches to reach deeper stratigraphic levels, where they found about a thousand more fabric fragments. About half of these come from intact deposits, meaning that they were excavated from new contexts; the rest came from Bird's backdirt piles, which were sifted by the recent project and included hundreds of fabrics and other fiber-based materials. A sample of approximately 75% of materials from both excavated and Bird-discarded textiles was analyzed. This chapter presents the preliminary results of this analysis.

The collection contains 825 specimens, which consist of 368 fragments of weft twining, 127 fragments of plain weave, 39 pieces of figure-8 looping, 40 fragments of knotted netting, and 251 pieces of cordage, yarns, and unspun fibers.[1] Of the weft-twined specimens, 258 are from secure archaeological contexts; 80 plain-weave fabrics have secure provenience, as do 28 fragments of figure-8 looping, 13 fragments of knotted netting, and 122 pieces of yarns, cordage, and unspun fiber.

1. These terms are defined later in the chapter.

458

The types of fabrics and their attributes and decoration are not unexpectedly similar to those encountered by Bird. Because of this, the present study does not duplicate Bird's work. The goal here is to present information about recently excavated materials, focusing on previously unknown practices and structures. Another focus is to learn about the people who made these objects by studying their choices of production.

This report consists of several parts, beginning with a discussion of past research of Preceramic fabrics and a description of the condition of the fabrics prior to conservation, followed by a discussion of conservation methods used to clean and stabilize the fabrics. Next is a section on the methodology used to analyze the textiles. This is followed by classification of the collection by fabric category according to Irene Emery (1966; Bird et al. 1985), beginning with a discussion of fabric bundles and bundling practices. Bundles are defined as one or more fabrics that constitute a unit by virtue of having been folded, bent, crumpled, and/or twisted that sometimes contain offerings such as shell, plants, and so forth. More analytical details are presented in appendices A–M online at https://my.vanderbilt.edu/huacaprieta/.

A specific interest here is the life history of textiles, examining weaving practices from making to discarding through time. Each section below ends with a discussion of practices and praxis, discussing the possible uses of fabrics and their use as ritual objects. Evidence for local versus nonlocal production as well as the presence of specialized weavers is also presented.

PREVIOUS RESEARCH

Bird first excavated and published the Huaca Prieta textiles (for example, J. Bird 1948a, 1948b, 1951, 1952, 1960, 1962: 154–161, 1963a, 1963b, 1970: 116, 1977, 1979b; Bird and Mahler 1951–1952; Bird et al. 1960a, 1960b). The most comprehensive report was published posthumously with John Hyslop and Milica Skinner (Bird et al. 1985). Preceramic fabrics have been encountered at numerous sites (although many remain unpublished) throughout present-day Peru, including Asia (Engel 1963c), Aspero (O'Neale 1954),

Bandurria (Chu Barrera 2008), Caral (Shady S. 2004), Chilca (Donnan 1964; Engel 1966a, 1970a), La Galgada (Grieder 1986, 1988), Los Gavilanes (Bonavia 1982), Guitarrero Cave (Adovasio and Lynch 1973; Adovasio and Maslowski 1980), Hacha (Gayton 1967), Huaynuná (Engel 1957b), La Paloma (Mandeville 1979; McAnulty 1977; Vallejos A. 1982), El Paraíso (Engel 1966b), Playa Culebras (Engel 1957b), Río Seco (Engel 1957b; Wendt 1964), Salinas de Chao (Olivera Alegre 2006), the Tank and Yacht Club Sites (Lanning 1963; Moseley 1975: 30–34), and others.

Most publications address textiles only briefly. Michael Moseley and Linda Barrett (1969), however, were among the first to examine chronological changes in Preceramic textile technology. In recent decades Preceramic textiles have been treated with more interest, and more studies have been produced by Peruvian scholars (for example, Bonavia 1982; Chu 2008; Fung Pineda 1988; Llagostera M. 1992; Olivera Alegre 2006; Shady S. 2004; Vallejos A. 1982).

EXCAVATION AND CATALOGUING METHODS

The vast majority of the textiles presented here were excavated from floors and fills associated with the Phase IV–V ramp on the east side of the site (see chapter 7). When textiles were excavated, they were separated from other objects and not screened. This proved to be a crucial tactic, because it allowed for the analysis of folding and bundling patterns that otherwise would have been lost.

The fiber-based objects were bagged in the field. Each bag contained one or more fabrics and was labeled with the specimen provenience (for example, date, excavators, unit, and stratum). Bags were delivered to the project's conservator, Arabel Fernández, who placed them in mounts and assigned a three-part inventory number, which consisted of the year of excavation, a three-digit number, and a sequence number.

Only one specimen is complete, and many fabrics consist of multiple fragments. For example, specimens 2009.072.31.A–C represent three pieces that were originally a single fabric that was, like many others encountered, apparently systematically fragmented. By assigning letters to fragments, Fernández's inventory allows identification of multiple fragments of what was originally a single fabric. If a lettered fragment itself multiplies, a subsequence number was assigned (for example, 2009.010.01.A.01, –02, and –03). When presenting statistical information (such as averages and standard deviations), the reference is to fragment numbers unless otherwise noted.

The term "fabric" is defined as "the generic term for all fibrous constructions" (Emery 1966: xvi), here referring to all interworked materials. Many archaeological fabrics become broken, complicating statistics and textile counts. When referring to textile numbers, "specimen" refers to the actual number of fragments, and "fabric" refers to the total number of textiles that existed prior to being broken, cut, or torn, whether in ancient or modern times.

The term "textile" refers "specifically to woven (i.e., interlaced warp-weft) fabrics" (Emery 1966: xvi). The term "web" can refer to any woven fabric but is used here specifically when multiple fabrics were stitched together to make a larger or thicker cloth.

FABRIC CONDITIONS, CLEANING, AND STABILIZATION PROCEDURES

The condition of the excavated textiles was terrible; they were thoroughly impregnated with salt, dirt, and sugar from seaweeds that formed a gummy "paste" strongly adhering to them. It obscured both colorants and fugitive fibers, making their study prior to cleaning extremely difficult or impossible. It also altered the radiocarbon dates on textiles (see chapter 6). These heavily soiled fabrics ultimately become dehydrated, acidic, and extremely brittle as the salts and carbon in their fibers absorb airborne pollutants. In other words, the paste caused long-term damage to the textiles and without intervention would ultimately destroy them. Approximately 360 fabrics were exported to the United States for study at the Conservation Lab at Mercyhurst University's Archaeological Institute in Erie, Pennsylvania. Under the terms of the export agreement with Peru, these textiles had to be cleaned prior to their return.

Traditional Cleaning

Bundles were opened prior to cleaning in order to study their folding patterns; the textiles found within the bundles were dirty and unstable and were cleaned prior to analysis.

The project's conservator, Arabel Fernández, initially applied "traditional" cleaning methods that involved flattening the textiles, brushing, blowing, vacuuming off dirt, and mounting them in an acid-free environment. Foreign materials and debris that could not be removed with either light blowing with a camera-lens duster or light suction through a screen were carefully picked off with tweezers. Flattening was done by opening and unfolding the fragment, placing Mylar sheeting over the textiles, and applying light weights to the Mylar. Dry and brittle textiles were humidified prior to flattening. Knots were not undone.

Despite Fernández's considerable skills, these methods were inadequate and ineffective on heavily soiled fabrics. Brushing inadvertently damaged the fibers of many fabrics. A method was needed that would remove the salt and other materials without removing pigments, some of which are mineral based and not fixed to the fabrics. Fernández soaked some fabrics in baths of distilled water, but the water caused the fibers to collapse, rendering them stiff and matted.

A well-known archaeologist and conservator who works with heavily soiled archaeological textiles suggested that we use percloroethelene (PCE, dry-cleaning fluid), which she believed would remove the dirt but not the colors. Despite following a strict regimen that consisted of gentle repeated agitation in diluted PCE alternating with rinses in deionized water, PCE ultimately proved ineffective. While it removed some debris, much of the salt and dirt remained even after repeated washings. More importantly, large amounts of PCE were needed, making its use impractical.

Cleaning with Cellulose Acetate and Acetone by Bird

Bird (1951) encountered the same situation (textiles heavily coated with paste), forcing him to

Table 12.1. Radiocarbon dating of three samples from AMNH Textile 41.2-3493

AMNH #	Sample #	Cellulose acetate	$\delta^{13}C$	Measured date	2-sigma calibrated BP
41.2-3493.A	OxA-28674	yes	−23.60	2802±28	2976–2803
41.2-3493.A	OxA-28654	yes	−23.75	2793±26	2961–2802
41.2-3493.F	OxA-28675	no	−23.81	2753±28	2926–2778

invent a cleaning method in the late 1940s. Considering the present-day failure of both traditional and PCE cleaning methods, it was decided to evaluate the long-term efficacy and effects of Bird's cleaning methods by studying the textiles he washed at the American Museum of Natural History (AMNH) in New York.

To summarize Bird's multistep process, it began by coating the fabrics with cellulose acetate followed by immersion in a water bath to remove the salt. This was followed by immersion in acetone to remove the cellulose acetate as well as carbon, sand, shell, and clay. Especially stubborn dirt was washed out with detergent, and sometimes the fabrics were dipped in benzene to bring out fugitive color(s) (see Bird 1951; Bird et al. 1985: 294).

Qualitative and quantitative measurements were made on several fabric specimens at the AMNH to evaluate their color, suppleness, matted fibers, unremoved pigments, and residual cellulose acetate. The results of the study showed that, despite the use of harsh chemicals and sixty years of sitting on museum shelves, the fabrics cleaned by Bird are in excellent condition. His cleaning methods were highly effective without causing stiffness, matting, or apparent loss of color.

Cellulose acetate glue is carbon-based, so its presence would adversely affect radiocarbon dating. To test whether cellulose acetate can be completely removed, an AMNH fabric (AMNH 41.2-3493) was tested at Oxford Labs for carbon dating. This fabric is from Cupisnique levels. It is in multiple pieces (A–F), some of which (such as 41.2-3493-A) were treated with cellulose acetate; others (such as 41.2-3493-F) were never treated. The results are presented in tables 12.1, 12.2, and 12.3. All radiocarbon dates overlap at the 1-sigma range, proving that cellulose acetate can be com-

pletely removed and apparently does not affect the dates.

Despite its effectiveness, however, Bird's method has significant drawbacks. Cellulose acetate, a type of glue, inhibited the removal of carbon and sand.

Cleaning with Hexametasulfate

Because of the problem inherent in cellulose acetate, Illingworth set about developing an alternative method of effectively and safely cleaning and conserving the textiles, removing the paste while leaving pigments, and salvaging detritus (such as shell, sand, dirt, and plant materials) and other materials (such as salt, carbon, clay, and pigment) dissolved in the wastewater.

Illingworth decided against methods involving percloroethelene, cellulose acetate, and acetone that involved the use of organic solvents, because they remove pigments. He experimented with sodium hexametasulfate and with a vacuum drying process. Small samples of threads were removed from 3 specimens (2009.150.01.C, 2009.151.01.B, and 2009.154.02.B) that were identified and selected because they were dirty and showed evidence of a blue color. The specimens were photographed and analyzed prior to sampling.

The results were impressive: the paste was completely removed, and no traces of sodium hexametasulfate were left on the yarns. Vacuum drying was effective too, producing fluffy and flexible yarns, while air-dried fibers had collapsed. This cleaning and vacuum drying procedure was repeated on complete fabrics with equally effective results (fig. 12.1a).

Cyclododecane, a nonreactive sublimable adhesive that provides temporary consolidation for

Table 12.2. Types, quantities, and provenience of fibers, cordage, yarns, and fabrics studied

Category	Short description	Secure provenience	Mixed provenience	Total
Bundles	Bundle	27	7	34
Loose yarns, fibers, and cordage	Unspun fiber	43	90	133
	Cordage	52	20	72
	Yarn(s)	27	18	45
	Wrapped stone	0	1	1
Subtotal		*122*	*129*	*251*
Single element	Figure-8 looping	28	11	39
	Knotted netting	13	27	40
Subtotal		*41*	*38*	*79*
Two element	Plain weave	80	47	127
	Weft twining	258	110	368
Subtotal		*338*	*157*	*495*
TOTAL (not including bundles)		**501**	**324**	**825**

Table 12.3. Number and types of fabrics and other objects composing bundles over time

Phase	Number of bundles	Number of fabrics per bundle	Fabric types	Other objects in bundle
II	1	1	Twining	
Late III	2	1	Twining	Cordage
				Yarns
Early IV	4	1–2	Twining	
Late IV	2	1	Twining & looping	
			Netting	
Early V	6	1–2	Twining	Bone tool
			Matting	Unspun fiber
V	10	1–24	Twining	Cordage
			Looping	Human hair
			Matting	Unspun fiber
			Netting	Unknown
			Plain weave	
Late V	2	1–3	Plain weave	Cordage

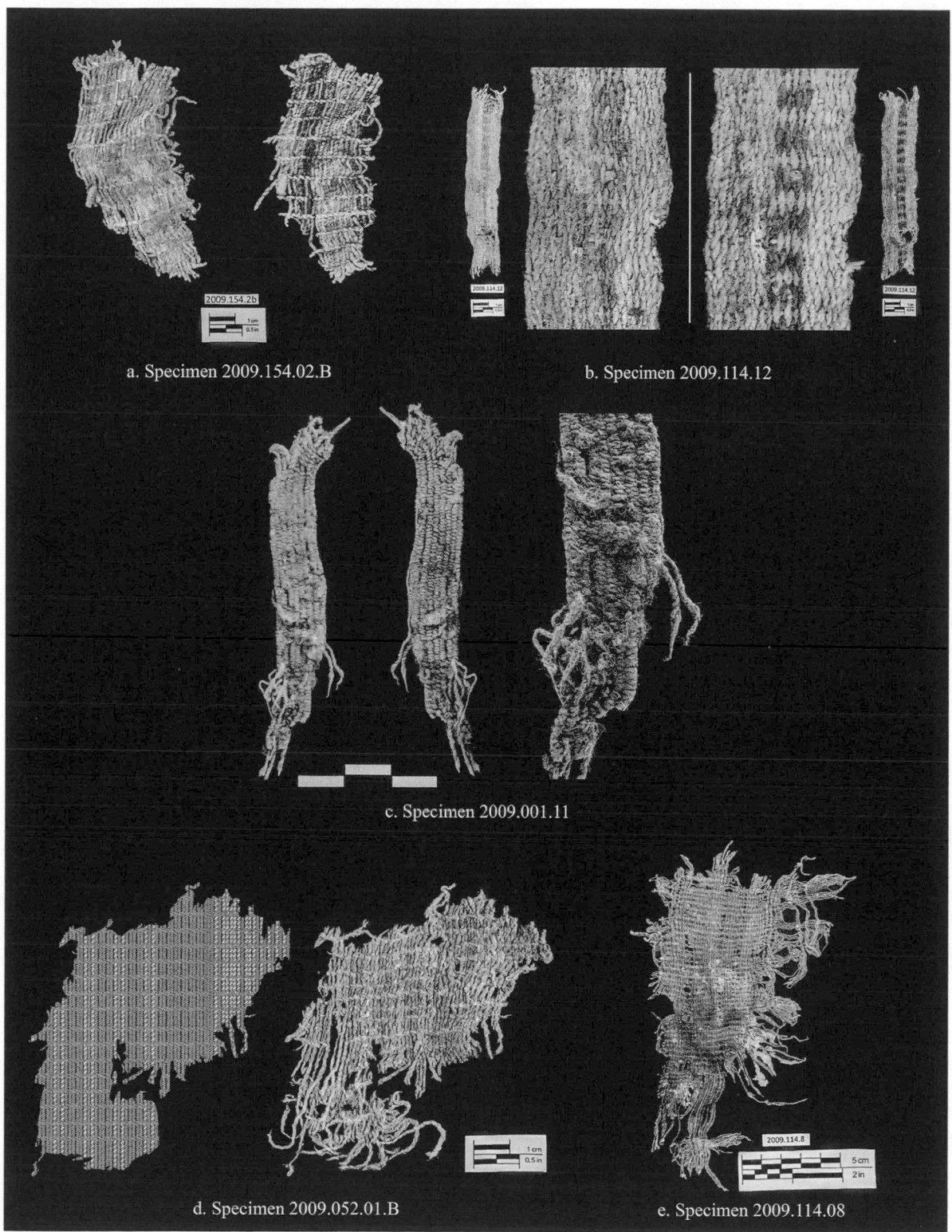

a. Specimen 2009.154.02.B

b. Specimen 2009.114.12

c. Specimen 2009.001.11

d. Specimen 2009.052.01.B

e. Specimen 2009.114.08

FIGURE 12.1. Paste and color in Huaca Prieta fabrics: *a*, Specimen 2009.154.02.B before (*left*) and after (*right*) it was washed with hexametasulfate to remove paste and reveal dark-blue warp stripes (*left*: photo by the author; *right*: photo by Lauren Badams); *b*, comparison of Specimen 2009.114.12 before (*left*) and after (*right*) washing with hexametasulfate, revealing a gold color (photos by Lauren Badams); *c*, Specimen 2009.001.11 (front, back, and detail) of a tapestry band with gold camelid hair; *d*, Specimen 2009.052.01.B, which was dyed with indigo (photo by Lauren Badams); *e*, Specimen 2009.114.08, which has an overall red color (photo by Lauren Badams). (See color plates.)

fragile textiles (for example, Kremer Pigments 2004; Smith 1999), was tested in an effort to find a drying method that would not require a vacuum chamber (Illingworth 2006).[2] Cyclododecane was not effective; even dilute solutions of it prevented water from penetrating the fibers and removing the paste.

Ultimately 296 fabrics were washed in sodium hexametasulfate and vacuum dried to remove paste. Roughly three-fourths of the fabrics (221 specimens) were analyzed prior to washing; 37% of the specimens were studied after paste was removed. The results were excellent, exposing hidden colors and materials (for example, milkweed) and making it easier to analyze the textiles.

PHOTOGRAPHY

Every textile fragment was photographed front and back. Macrophotos were taken front and back. Specimens with patterning, more than one fabric structure, or some other interesting feature (such as selvages, stains, supra-structures, or knots) were photographed in detail. The photos were archived according to specimen number. Lauren Badams photographed all the textiles washed at Mercyhurst. Unless noted, all photographs in this report were taken by the author.

TEXTILE ANALYSIS: METHOD AND THEORY

Textiles are repositories of information about the culture of the societies that made them. But textiles cannot speak to us directly; their messages must be inferred from attributes like spin, ply, selvage structures, and interworking styles. The present study follows theoretical ideas established by Marcia A. Dobres regarding technology and agency, defined as the making and using of material things and the "simultaneous making and remaking of social actors, society, and traditions, as well as their contestation and negotiation" over time (Dobres 2000: 83). The study is also rooted

in practice theory and *chaîne opératoire* analysis (for example, Splitstoser 2009: 120–122, 128–134; compare Arnold 2014). Dobres's particular form of practice theory asserts that the "functional and objective factors structuring artifact manufacture and use . . . are . . . embedded in historically antecedent contexts of value, world views, proscriptions, and social intercourse" (Dobres 2000: 108).

In other words, attributes of textiles can be used to identify choices that weavers made at each step in the creation of a textile, from gathering of fiber, spinning, and setting up a loom (or frame) to stringing the warps, interworking, and off-loom embellishing (such as hems and embroidery). Even the attributes associated with use, repair, and discard reveal choices that people made. These choices can inform us about the cultural values and worldview(s) that structured (and were in turn structured by) the choices manifested in practices (gestures) and ultimately textile attributes.

An examination of consistency/variability in yarns, fabric, and selvage structures (such as yarn diameters, structures, degree of twist, warp/weft density, and interworking order) discloses information about normative practices as well as the amount of deviation/experimentation that was attempted. Such information might suggest centralized (perhaps specialized) production practices, for instance, or it might indicate that spinning and weaving was done in nonlocalized, informal (perhaps household) settings and how they changed over time.

This approach is inherently data rich. Each specimen was drawn and photographed and the following qualitative and quantitative attributes were recorded: specimen number, specimen condition, number of fabrics and/or yarns, number of fabric structures, length and width of fabrics (length of cords), number of supra-structures, and number of knots. The material (for example, cotton, milkweed) was noted and the color, diameter, structure, and degree of twist were measured for each yarn and/or element. The number of yarns per element and their density and/or spacing characteristics was documented.

Textile practice theory is particularly concerned with skill and how spinners and weavers might have used these skills to navigate society. To gain insight into both individual and group skills, it is

2. It was hoped that a method could be found that could easily be replicated in Peru, so we wanted to eliminate the need for the vacuum chamber.

vital to take multiple measurements in every fragment of such attributes as yarn diameter, degree of twist, warp and weft densities. This provides the data needed to determine the amount of variation within a textile, which is directly related to the skill of individuals. Three measurements were made corresponding to the minimum, maximum, and visual average, where the visual average is the value that is considered the most representative of the attribute being measured. The statistical average was later calculated from the minimum and maximum values.

The amount of variation in yarn and fabric attributes provides both direct information about the consistency (or lack of it) in yarn and fabric attributes, which in turn informs us about the skills of the spinners and weavers that can be used to infer the presence or absence of specialists. A qualitative examination of patterns of wear (such as threadbare areas, holes, and felting), repair (such as darning, hemming, and patches), and discarding (such as cutting, tearing, and bundling) provided invaluable evidence about the way fabrics were used, reused, and deposited, indicating, for example, if fabrics were ritually killed before they were discarded. Examination of patterns in selvage ends and joins provides clues about the steps involved in production and repair.

Qualitative analysis of decoration recorded color, material, the presence of stripes, bands, and other treatments created with changes in color, fiber type, warp crossings, split pairing, density, and/or interworking order. Quantitative measurements of stripe and band thicknesses and so forth were also made. Finally, a narrative summary was written for each specimen that provides both a description of the specimen's weave structure and decorative patterns and an overall assessment, including observations about its context and condition.

Information about knots (including number, type, twist direction, and function) was collected. This includes warp- and weft-selvage knots, repair knots, structural knots in netting, and joins/splices in warps/wefts. Information about selvages was recorded, including their types (for example, simple, knotted, or looped) and reinforcement characteristics (such as packing or doubling).

DATABASE

All data were entered into a relational database developed in Microsoft Access. The tables used and their relationships are based on the textile classification scheme developed by Emery (1966) that begins with the yarn, the most basic element of a fabric. Fabrics are classified into types according to the number of elements that they use. For example, the most basic fabrics are single-element constructions (such as looping). Next are fabrics made with a single set of elements (such as oblique interlacing), followed by two sets of elements and compound constructions (more than two sets of elements). Supra-structural embellishments include stitching elements used to make multiweb constructions, mends, and decoration. The present study adds two categories: bundles and unspun fiber/loose yarns, which are discussed below.

When translating Emery's scheme into a database, each part of a fabric (such as yarn element and fabric structure) is an entity, and a table in the database represents each entity. The attributes of entities are measurable qualities, such as length, width, condition, and provenience. Attributes are listed in table columns, and actual specimens are represented in rows.

RESULTS

In all 825 specimens were analyzed in terms of five major categories: bundles, cordage/yarns/fibers, single-element, two-element, and compound constructions. The results are summarized in table 12.2, and more detailed descriptions of the fabrics are presented by category in appendix B online at https://my.vanderbilt.edu/huacaprieta/. These fabrics form the basis of the present study and consist of essentially the same fabric types that Bird published (Bird et al. 1985). No significant new category (such as oblique interlacing) or structure (such as gauze or brocade) was encountered. This report focuses on topics not well covered by Bird, such as knotting, bundling, and discard practices. It also presents new data, such as new selvage types.

The collection contains only a single complete specimen: 2009.160.09, a plain-weave bag found in the Bird backfill (see the section on "Plain

Weave" for a description of the bag). It could be argued that spools of yarn and bundles are also complete in the sense that they probably represent an intact unit; other than the intact bag, however, no specimen has 2 warp and 2 weft selvages. Of the fabrics, 4 have 2 warp selvages, and 11 (12 webs) have 2 weft selvages.

The majority of fabrics with complete lengths (2 warp selvages) are weft twining (75%), while the majority of fabrics with complete widths are plain weave (64%). These data are presented in appendix C online at https://my.vanderbilt.edu/huacaprieta/. Because all fabrics are fragments and only a small minority have complete lengths or widths, it is clear that people chose not to discard intact textiles. Such practices are in keeping with animistic beliefs, where all things are believed to possess a vital force and therefore must be ritually killed before discarding (see the section on "Use, Repair, and Discarding Patterns" for a discussion of discarding).

BUNDLES

Many, if not most, fabrics were discarded in the form of ritual bundles that were opened and recorded prior to conservation and mounting. In all 34 bundles were analyzed. Bundles consisted of one or more fabrics that were folded, bent, crumpled, and/or twisted into a compact unit. They were roughly brick-shaped and ranged in size from the smallest at 9.0 cm long by 5.0 cm wide by 3.8 cm high to the largest, measuring 36.0 by 28.0 by 9.0 cm, with an average size of 15.9 by 10.6 by 4.4 cm. Bundle descriptions and proveniences are found in appendix D online at https://my.vanderbilt.edu/huacaprieta/. Although Bird did not mention encountering bundles, he must have seen them, because 7 bundles in the present study came from screening Bird's backdirt; the remaining 27 bundles have secure provenience.

The simplest bundles consisted of a single weft-twined fabric, while the most complex (2009.098.01.24) contained 37 objects, including 26 pieces of weft twining, 1 piece of human hair, 2 pieces of unspun fiber, 1 piece of knotted netting, 3 pieces of figure-8 looping, and 4 pieces of cordage.

When the types of fabrics, unspun fiber, and cordage associated with bundles are examined chronologically, a pattern of change appears (table 12.3). The earliest bundles in Phases II and III consist of a single fabric made of weft twining. Bundles in Phases III and IV include twining, looping, and netting, and by Phase V the bundles include twining, looping, netting, matting, and plain weave. During late Phase V bundling practices radically changed; instead of bundling multiple fabrics with multiple techniques, bundles consisted of multiple plain-weave fabrics (one technique) that were crudely stitched together to make a single entity.

In addition to changes in the composition of bundles, the number of bundles also changed over time. Numbers rose from a single bundle excavated from Phase II contexts to 10 from early to middle Phase V, dropping to 2 in late Phase V. It could be argued, however, that 3 more late Phase V specimens (2008.038.24, 2008.038.25, and 2008.043.01) might be bundles, while Specimens 2008.038.24 and 2008.038.25 probably represent a pair of bundles. Like other late Phase V bundles, they each consist of multiple plain-weave fragments stitched together in a haphazard manner; unlike the other bundles, however, they were not folded or compressed into a packet. If they are not bundles, the presence of such crudely stitched multilayered fabric "packets" is difficult to explain.

It is worth mentioning 2 Phase V bundles, because they are larger and both structurally and compositionally different from the others. They both come from early Phase V contexts and possibly represent a single bundle that was deliberately cut or broken in two during its deposition. Bundle 2009.136 consisted of multiple parts, including whole *Semele* sp. shells, matting, unworked vegetal fiber, and cotton weft twining. The center of the bundle contained hundreds of shells that included a very small crab, a sea urchin, mollusks, and several unidentified shells that were tentatively identified as belonging to both freshwater and seawater creatures. Mixed with the shells was a perforated and worked bone and a piece of worked gourd. The gourd was carved into an almost perfect circle about 2 cm in diameter and probably functioned as a gourd stopper or plug, such as those found by Bird (Bird et al. 1985: 225–226, figs. 171, 172).

The bone is most likely a weaving tool, probably serving as both a needle and a pick (fig. 12.2a). Bird illustrates instances of nearly identical perforated bones (Bird et al. 1985: 125, fig. 176, 221, fig. 163), which he suggests functioned as bodkins, which seems logical. Similar objects are known from other Preceramic sites, including Asia and El Paraíso (Engel 1963c: 61, figs. 153, 155, 1966b: pl. 7, 2), where they were also interpreted as needles or awls.

Inside the bundle were also several wads of "folded" (bent, doubled) raw vegetal fiber that had been tied/bundled with a long ribbon-like leaf (probably a palm leaf) that had been wrapped around them three times; the wrapped bundle of raw fiber was placed over the shells. The last object in the bundle was a piece of weft twining (13 by 19 cm); now in several pieces, its structure is spaced regular two-strand ½-Z-twist weft twining with $Z(2s^c)$ wefts and two types of warp yarns making two warp structures: $I(2z(2s^c))$ and $I(z(2s^c)+z(s^c+i^{mw}))$.[3] The outer layer of the bundle consisted of matting made with weft twining, ~34 by 33 cm.

The second early Phase V bundle, 2009.137 (fig. 12.2b), contained numerous mollusk, snail, and crab shells. It also contained coca leaves. The bundle had a large piece of raw cotton fiber (~8 by 13 cm) as well as three bunches of vegetal fiber, two of which were folded very similarly to those found in Bundle 2009.136. It contained a piece of vegetal fiber tied into a square knot and a piece of matting, ~13 by 19 cm, very similar to the matting found in Bundle 2009.136. Bundles 2009.136 and 2009.137 were probably originally a single bundle consisting of matting upon which a "nest" of cotton and vegetal fiber was placed and filled with small shellfish (crabs, snails, mollusks, sea urchins) and leaves. The matting wrapped the fiber, shells, and leaves and secured them with a ribbon-like leaf. The bundle was broken in two during events associated with its deposition.

WRAPPED OBJECTS

Similar to bundles are wrapped objects. Specimen 2009.075.08 is a group of unspun unidentified reed (probably juncus reed) folded in half and wrapped three times with another unidentified vegetable fiber and secured with a square knot. Specimen 2009.123.01 is a rough green stone wrapped in an unidentified vegetable fiber (probably juncus reed) three times and tied in a S-granny knot. Similar examples of wrapped stones were found by Bird (Bird et al. 1985: 220, 223, figs. 159, 166, 167). Specimen 2009.098.02.A and B consists of human hair folded in half and wrapped twice with a cord-like piece of cotton knotted-netting that was secured by tightly twisting the netting (Z-twist). The netting has lark's-head knots with faces that alternate front and back, row by row, made with tightly twisted $Z(2s^c)$ yarns.

The literature is replete with examples of Preceramic stone wrapping and knotting with reed. For example, a roughly shaped stone wrapped and knotted with juncus (*Scirpus americanus*) was encountered by Bonavia (1982: 98) at Los Gavilanes. Bonavia (1982: 211, photo 264) also notes the presence of wrapped human hair. Quilter (1989: 27, fig. 12) found the river cobble wrapped with an unidentified fiber string capping grave fill at Paloma. Fung Pineda (1988: 78, fig. 73.73) encountered a textile-wrapped stone associated with a basket burial of a child from Bandurria.

BUNDLING PRACTICES

Bundles, including the wrapped objects noted above, can inform us about Preceramic ritual practices. The data suggest that at least three different bundling practices were employed: one represented by at least 18 examples consists of a single fabric that was folded, bunched, and/or twisted.[4] Multiple fabrics that were folded, bunched, twisted, and/or pressed together to form a packet characterize the second practice, represented by 12 examples. The third practice, of which there are 2 to 5 examples, is characterized by several (plainweave) fabrics layered like pages of a book that are

---

3. For a description of the system used to record yarn structures, see Splitstoser (2012).

4. "Folds" rarely have crisp creases; while the term "bends" might be more accurate, it is reserved for fabrics with rounded corners. Both bends and folds can be U-, N-, or W-shaped. "Bunched" refers to fabrics that look as if they were compressed in such a way as to cause numerous creases parallel to either warps or wefts that resemble but are not tidy enough to be pleats or folds.

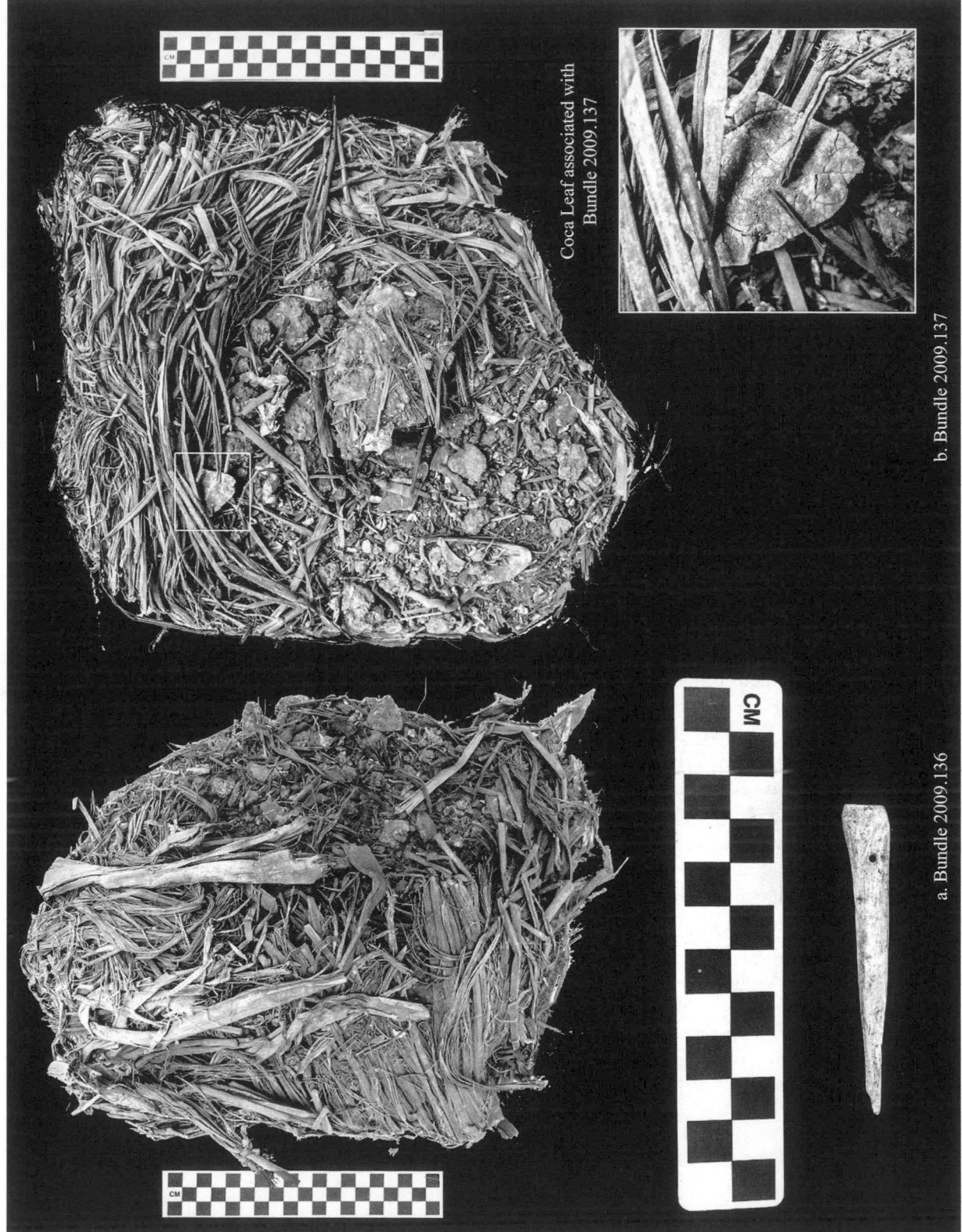

Coca Leaf associated with
Bundle 2009.137

b. Bundle 2009.137

a. Bundle 2009.136

FIGURE 12.2. Large bundle consisting of Specimens 2009.136 and 2009.137: a, Bundle 2009.136 prior to opening, with detail of perforated bone; b, Bundle 2009.137 prior to opening, with detail of coca leaf.

stitched with blue yarns to hold them together as a bundle.

Many bundles demonstrate what appear to be pairing and complementarity. For instance, most multifabric bundles (bundles composed of two or more fabrics) were formed by pressing two fabrics together, forming a two-part structure. Frequently, each part consisted of two more subparts. The number also seems to have been important in structuring other bundling practices at Huaca Prieta. For example, all but one of the wrapped stones encountered by Bird are wrapped three times and knotted. The raw fibers in Bundle 2009.136 were wrapped three times and knotted. Bundled fabrics were frequently folded or bent three times. Are instances of bending and/or wrapping three times coincidental or is there an underlying principle, value, or belief involving the number three?

Folding, pleating, bunching, and bending practices (table 12.4) suggest the existence of complementary enactments governing ritual folding and bunching. People seem to have followed loose "rules" governing proper bending and bunching techniques. For example, 32 fabrics are bunched parallel to warps (folding the fabric in a way that makes creases parallel to the warps leaving warps unbent), while only 3 are bunched parallel to the wefts. Likewise, 34 fabrics are bent parallel to the wefts (making a crease that is parallel to the wefts and leaving the warps bent), but only 3 fabrics have bends parallel to the warps. In 29 fabrics bending is combined with bunching, and in all but one instance they are bent parallel to wefts (bending the warps) and bunched parallel to warps (bending the wefts). At the same time, people apparently had no preferences governing the folding and pleating as opposed to bending.[5] Stitching might have followed complementary principles too, considering that most of the fabrics in late Phase V bundles are stitched so that the warps and wefts of adjacent fabrics are perpendicular.

Furthermore, it was common to divide the fabric conceptually into three parts when forming bundles and "sub-bundles," and one end of one

5. Pleating is the practice of making several folds, either in accordion fashion or by doubling and redoubling. Bending was almost always performed on fabrics that were already pleated or bunched.

Table 12.4. Number and types of attributes for fabrics and bundles

Attribute	Total in fabrics	Total in bundles
Bunching	41	24
Folding	31	15
Pleating	7	3
Bending	43	25
Bending elements 90° to form contrast	29	20

fabric was treated differently from the other end. For example, one end of a fabric was bunched to form folds parallel to the warps, while the other side of the same fabric was bunched parallel to the wefts; sometimes one end of the fabric was twisted S while the other was twisted Z. Sometimes an end was rotated 90° or folded in such a way that the warp and weft elements of one side or end became perpendicular to the elements of the other side/end.

The majority of fabrics that make up bundles are well preserved even though none are complete. Most making up the bundles are irregularly shaped, however, suggesting that they were stretched as a result of trauma from cutting, tearing, or excessive wear. It is not clear if the trauma occurred before or during the bundling process.

Several attributes suggest that bundling and/or discarding practices involved the application of liquids, probably saltwater. Mud, salt, sand, and soot penetrated even the innermost parts of most bundles, and most of the fabrics composing the bundles appear to have been wet at the time the bundles were made. At least 13 bundles (34%) either are covered with mud or have fibers that are matted in a way consistent with having been wet. Many of the fabrics are crumpled and/or twisted, as if a liquid had been wrung out of them.

In summary, bundling practices began simply and relatively infrequently in Phase II, peaking in complexity and frequency in early to middle Phase V, and changing abruptly in complexity and frequency late in Phase V. While the bundles might look like haphazardly formed clumps of fabric, they were intentionally made according to rules governing the number, type, and manner in which the fabrics were folded, bent, bunched, and pleated. Late Phase V bundles are almost unrecognizable as bundles compared to those made during their peak during Phase IV and early–middle Phase V; this might explain why 3 bundles were not originally recognized as such. Principles involving dualism and complementarity seem to have led to structural practices involving bunching and folding, where warps were bunched and wefts were folded, while tripartite principles permeated wrapping and bending.

COLOR, PIGMENT, AND DYE

The Pantone Textile Color Guide identified color. The guide's colored paper swatches (2 by 3 cm) were held next to the fabric and compared. Because color identification is inherently subjective, and the original color almost certainly changed from exposure to sunlight, humidity, other factors (such as exposure to pigments, stains from libations, and/or use), it was sometimes necessary to assign multiple colors to account for these inconsistencies. Pantone Color terms were translated to descriptive names that are easier to understand using a dictionary of color names (Kelly and Judd 1976). A list of all the colors and their descriptions is found in appendix A online at https://my.vanderbilt.edu/huacaprieta/.

Results suggest that Huaca Prieta weavers utilized at least three pigments with cotton yarns—red, blue, and gold—in addition to the natural white, tan, and brown of cotton and the bright white of milkweed. Essentially the same colors have been found at other Preceramic sites such as Asia where camelid hair was dyed: "there is no doubt that wool yarns were dyed a deep red, and a few small fragments of fabric were dyed in at least three shades, green or blue, yellow, and orange-red" (Engel 1963c: 25). He went on to say, "We have, of course, no way of determining the sources of the dyes: manganese, hematite, limonite, and some other oxides may have been used. Lumps of red iron-oxide are found in most pits, graves and tombs, wrapped up in fabrics and bags, and some fabrics found in the refuse are stained with a red powder. It is probable that they were stained by chance contact with a pigment which does not, of course, rule out the method of coloring fabrics by rubbing them with dry pigments" (1963c: 25). Bonavia (1982: 116–117) encountered plain weave with camelid-hair wefts dyed red and yellow at Los Gavilanes.

Gold/Yellow

Gold is less commonly reported than blue and red from Preceramic sites, perhaps because gold is easily obscured by dirt. A literature search produced only two sites other than Huaca Prieta where gold was encountered: Los Gavilanes (Bonavia 1982: 116–117) and La Galgada, where Grieder (1986: 20) noted: "One of the twined mantles has narrow yellow and brown stripes in the warp," while the looped bags also have black figures on either a red or yellow ground. As at Huaca Prieta, twining and looping at La Galgada is primarily made of cotton.

Gold has been identified in a small number of Huaca Prieta fabrics, all from late contexts. Specimen 2009.114.12 is a narrow plain-weave band or belt found in a Phase V context. It is warp predominant to warp faced and all cotton made with Z(2s) warps and S wefts interworked 1 by 1 (over-one-under-one). It has two simple weft selvages, although the second outermost warp in one selvage is paired. It has a stripe down its center, eight warps wide, with blue and white yarns alternating one by one. The white yarns were originally a gold color (fig. 12.1b, which shows the fabric before and after it was washed).

Another fabric (2009.001.11) has gold camelid-hair yarns (fig. 12.1c). This is a belt or band, that was found in Bird's backdirt. It has Cupisnique-like iconography and is woven in weft-faced plain weave with discontinuous wefts (slit tapestry). The fabric has Z(2s) warps and wefts with beige cotton warps and beige and blue cotton and gold camelid-hair wefts. It has a geometric pattern with steps and frets in blue cotton with accents in gold camelid hair.

Specimens 2009.071.31 and 2009.071.32 are cotton yarns with an overall yellowish, golden-brown color from mixed fill. Both are counter-spun: Specimen 2009.071.31 has an S(2z) structure, and specimen 2009.071.32 has a Z(2s(2z^c)) structure. Another 5 specimens stained with a gold color: Specimens 2009.093.08 and 2009.093.11 are Phase V weft twining, and the others are from mixed contexts: 2009.001.05 is plain weave; 2009.010.31 is knotted netting; and 2009.010.35 is cordage.

Gold is probably much more prevalent than imagined, because the paste imparts a gray color that makes gold nearly impossible to distinguish from natural tan or brown in cotton fabrics covered with paste. Furthermore, gold is extremely fugitive; most of it was probably washed out in antiquity. Gold was accidentally detected, because it was washed out of a fabric whose before-and-after photos revealed what had happened.

It is not unexpected that gold washes out of cotton but binds to camelid hair, because permanent colors are notoriously difficult to achieve with cellulose fibers without the use of a mordant. It is also possible that multiple pigment sources were involved. Furthermore, many fabrics have "stripes" that are essentially spaces left behind when the original warps disintegrated (see "Fugitive Stripes" below). It is possible that yarns coated with yellow ochre (an iron-based mineral) or treated with a corrosive mordant might under certain conditions cause cotton fibers to disintegrate. Without dye analysis, however, it is impossible to know with certainty.

Blue

Blue was used extensively during Preceramic times. Robert Feldman (1986: 33) noted that decoration at Aspero was "produced by the use of blue dye and applied red pigment." Huaca Prieta fabrics and basketry are the earliest known fabrics in the Americas and the world to be decorated with blue. Blue coloring comes in two hues on cotton: a light blue and a dark blue that is almost black. The dark blue is always associated with the warps of weft twining.

Bonavia (1982: 104–105) also encountered cotton weft twining with a black color that he thought was dyed. Many of the blue yarns at Huaca Prieta are almost black, suggesting that the same dye recipe was used at both Los Gavilanes and Huaca Prieta. Recent excavations produced approximately 44 specimens with blue warp stripes and/or weft bands. Of these, 7 have both blue stripes and bands, 28 have blue stripes, and 9 have blue bands. Of the fabrics with both blue stripes and bands, 5 are plain weave, 1 of which

has floated elements (see "Plain-Weave-Derived Float Weaves" below) from mixed contexts; the others are simple plain weave, 1 of which is from mixed contexts, while the other 3 are from Phase V or late Phase V. The 2 specimens with blue stripes and bands are weft twining; the first is from Phase II and the other is from Phase V contexts.

Only blue warp stripes are found on 28 specimens. Of these, 23 are made of weft twining, 1 of which also has figure-8 looping. They come from all contexts, Phases II–V, without any patterns apparent in their distributions. Of 7 specimens with blue stripes, 5 specimens (5 fabrics) are weft twined, while 2 specimens (2 fabrics) are plain weave. Blue bands occur on 9 specimens, 2 of which are from plain-weave fabrics. Traces of blue pigment or blue stains are found on 48 other specimens. Of these, 1 is from a piece of figure-8 looping, 10 are plain weave, and 37 are weft twining. Blue is further discussed in the section "Blue Stripes" below.

The Source of Blue

Bird never determined the source of blue in Huaca Prieta fabrics; however, collaborative research with Jan Wouters, a conservation scientist in Zwijndrecht, Belgium, positively identified their source as an indigoid dye, making Huaca Prietans among the earliest known people to use indigo dye (Splitstoser et al. 2016). Among the samples tested was 2009.052.01.B (fig. 12.1d), which is from Phase II (Stratum 44) contexts dated to ~6200 years cal BP, making this the earliest known fabric in the world that has been indisputably associated with indigo.

Green

Specimen 2009.093.02 has green staining and comes from Phase V contexts. The color is Pantone 15–4003 (Storm Gray). Its fabric structure is spaced ½-Z-twist two-strand weft twining with cotton $Z(2s^c)$ wefts interworking alternate pairs of cotton and milkweed $Z(s^c+s/i^{mw})$ warps. Like Specimen 2009.114.12 (the fabric with fugitive gold coloring), the fabric was washed prior to analysis, but the colors in photos taken prior to cleaning clearly show that the fabric had two pigments—gold and blue—forming stripes. The green stain is most likely the result of mixing blue and gold when the fabric was wet. The blue warps in 2009.114.12 also have a greenish hue prior to washing.

Red

Red was used extensively in Preceramic times: at Las Salinas de Chao (Olivera Alegre 2006: 46, 60), El Paraíso (Engel 1966b), Aspero (Feldman 1986: 33), and Los Gavilanes (Bonavia 1982: 104–105), where it is found in looped and knotted cotton fabrics. Approximately 84 Huaca Prieta fabrics are red either from having red stains or from having red warps, wefts, or both.

Using X-ray fluorescence (XFR) at the Mercy-hurst Archaeology Laboratory, Illingworth determined that the red found on Huaca Prieta fabrics is an iron-based mineral pigment, most likely red hematite (see appendix 11). This pigment has mostly washed off, suggesting that it was not applied as a dye. Instead the red pigment was most likely applied to fibers or yarns prior to weaving, using one of several possible methods, including (1) rubbing the pigment onto yarns somewhat like bowstring rosin; (2) grinding the pigment into a powder and applying it through pressure to unworked fibers or yarns; or (3), in a variation of (2), adding sea water to the powder to make a slurry that was applied to spun yarns (Bird 1960: 262). Bird and Mahler (1951–1952: 74) wrote that "red is fairly common and may possibly in a few instances be a dye, but in most was a pigment rubbed on the finished fabrics or on the yarns before weaving. As this brushes off, it is rather fugitive and often so faint as to be scarcely perceptible."

Stains or areas of pigment are present on 57 fabrics, including 54 specimens of weft twining (Phases III, IV, and early V), 1 piece of knotted netting (mixed contexts), and 2 specimens of figure-8 looping (both Phase V). Red warps are found on 47 specimens, of which 35 are weft twining and represent all Phases (II–V), 1 is weft twining with a band of figure-8 looping (Phase IV), 10 specimens are plain weave from Phases IV, V, and late V, and 1 specimen from mixed contexts is plain weave with floated elements.

Red weft bands without warp stripes are found on 7 specimens (5 of which are single webs), all of which are weft twining from either mixed, Phase III, or early IV. Only 1 specimen, a piece of weft twining from Phase III–IV contexts, has red warps without red wefts. 4 fabrics (10 specimens) from Phases III, IV, and V have red warp stripes and no red wefts; all are weft twining. Of the 4 fabrics (5 specimens) all have red warp stripes and red weft bands, and all are weft twining from Phase V contexts. Finally, 6 fabrics (7 specimens) have both red warps and red wefts like the fabric depicted in figure 12.1e, meaning that they are all or mostly red; 1 fabric (2 specimens) is plain weave from mixed contexts, 5 are weft twining, 1 is from Phases III–IV, and 4 are from Phase V contexts.

FIBERS

Several types of fiber were encountered at Huaca Prieta: cotton (*Gossypium barbadense*), a local milkweed known as *chivo* (*Asclepias* sp.), human hair, an unknown animal hair, camelid hair (family Camelidae), and a bulrush known as juncus (*Scirpus* sp.; see chapter 10). Several varieties of sedge were used, but it is difficult to distinguish them from one another, so they are listed as unidentified vegetal fiber (UVF). Of these, only 4 fiber types were used in fabrics (in their order of prevalence): cotton, milkweed, juncus, and camelid hair.

COTTON

Cotton is the backbone of fabric practices at Huaca Prieta. It is found in virtually all recently excavated fabrics either alone or plied with milkweed. This is not surprising, because the use of cotton (not just the presence of cotton) was well established throughout the Central Andes during Preceramic times. Cotton twined fabrics appeared on the central coast at least as early as ~3750–3700 BC at Village 1 near Chilca (Engel 1970a: 58) and at Paloma (Quilter 1989: 41), the Tank site and others near Ancón (Stephens and Moseley 1974: 112–113), and Aspero at the mouth of the Supe River (Feldman 1980; Moseley and Willey 1973).

On the south coast Engel (1981: 37–38) encountered cotton dating to 3940–3810 BC from Village 514 on the Bay of Paracas. He found early cotton elsewhere in the region at Otuma on the Paracas Peninsula and the Punta de Asma shell mounds at the mouth of the Ica River (Engel 1957a: 59–61, 1981: 30–31).

Cotton apparently entered the highlands at about the same time it appeared on the coast. Richard MacNeish (MacNeish et al. 1980: 322) found cotton yarns and plain-weave fabrics in the Ayacucho basin dating to ~3000–1750 BC. Early cotton was found in Guitarrero Cave (Adovasio and Lynch 1973) and at the site of La Galgada (Grieder 1986), where it was used in twined, woven, looped, and linked fabrics (Grieder 1988: 252).

MILKWEED

Milkweed comes from stem fibers and is therefore a bast. Single-ply milkweed yarns were frequently plied with single-ply cotton in twined and looped fabric elements; Bird also found it in plain weave and knotted netting (Bird et al. 1985: 191, 209). The present study found that milkweed was never used without cotton, but Bird (Bird et al. 1985: 210–214) encountered it alone in a group of finely knotted and finely looped pouches. The use of milkweed begins early at Huaca Prieta; it is found in warps in Phase II (for example, 2009.052.01) and in wefts in Phase III.

The use of milkweed was seemingly less widespread than the use of cotton or *Furcraea* (agave), although it was found at Asia in knotted nets and pouches, looped fabrics, twined fabrics, and a piece of tapestry (Engel 1963c: 24). Engel found twined fabrics made of an unidentified "bast" fiber that was probably milkweed (possibly *Furcraea*) from Paracas Site 104 AL-I, a cemetery associated with a permanent fishing village next to Cabezas Largas dating to ca. 3000 BC (Engel 1960b: pl. 4.3; Lanning 1963). Milkweed might be present but unrecognized at many more sites, because bast fibers are difficult to identify with certainty. Illingworth recognized them because of his extensive experience with North American fabrics, in which milkweed is occasionally used.

BULRUSH/JUNCUS

Juncus is widely used in Preceramic matting and basketry and is far too extensively found to describe its early distribution. Its use in textiles, however, is limited, and at Huaca Prieta it was rare. No fabrics have juncus warps or even warps made of juncus mixed with cotton. One weft-twined fabric, Specimen 2009.072.15, has what are probably juncus wefts (see online appendix M at https://my.vanderbilt.edu/huacaprieta/).

HUMAN HAIR

Human hair was not made into fabric at Huaca Prieta. Bird did not find any, but recent excavations encountered several specimens of unspun human hair and human-hair cordage.

ANIMAL HAIR

Camelid hair was not used to make fabrics at the majority of Preceramic sites. It was found in fabrics at Asia (Engel 1963c) and Los Gavilanes (Bonavia 1982: 132) but not at Caral or Las Salinas de Chao (Olivera Alegre 2006). Its usage probably co-occurred with the introduction of domesticated camelids, though fiber from wild camelids could easily have been transported from one place to another even without llama caravans.

At Huaca Prieta 7 camelid-hair specimens were found in the form of unspun fiber and cordage, and camelid hair is present in the gold discontinuous wefts in a Phase V tapestry specimen (2009.001.11; see fig. 12.1c and the section "Gold/Yellow" above).

FURCRAEA

No vegetal fiber from the agave leaf known as *Furcraea occidentalis* was encountered at Huaca Prieta, although it is frequently found in fabrics from Preceramic sites. *Furcraea* and cotton were used to make spaced looping and spaced linking (both nets) at La Galgada (Grieder 1988: 252–257). *Furcraea* was not found at Asia, but Engel encountered it at Otuma, Paracas (Engel 1981: 30–31), and El Paraíso (Engel 1966b).

YARNS AND CORDAGE

Yarns and cordage are the fundamental components of fabrics. Their attributes (listed online in appendix E at https://my.vanderbilt.edu/huacaprieta/) represent choices that can be used to inform us about the people who made them. The discussion below analyzes 139 specimens of yarns, cordage, and unspun fiber.

UNSPUN FIBER

The collection contains 26 specimens of unspun fiber. Of these, 4 are from secure contexts: a strand of unspun human hair from Phase II and clumps of unspun human hair, milkweed, and junco from Phase V. As a group, the 26 specimens of unspun fiber consist of 4 specimens of human hair alone, 1 of human hair with cotton, 1 of milkweed, 1 of milkweed with cotton, 1 of cotton, 3 of an unidentified animal hair, and 15 of junco.

Among the earliest specimens of unworked fiber are 2 hanks of human hair (see online appendix M).

YARNS

The analysis included 37 yarns. The difference between yarns and cordage (discussed below) is somewhat subjective, although cordage is typically thicker and stiffer than yarn. Yarns and cordage thicknesses are influenced by their structures (the twist direction and number of elements twisted together to make a larger element) and the amount and type of fiber. All 37 yarn specimens at Huaca Prieta are cotton (including 6 that are spooled around sticks and reeds). Of these 25 are from secure contexts.

Regarding their structures, 11 specimens (including the spools of yarn) are S-spun single-ply yarns. Of the other 26, 1 is S(2z), 24 are Z(2s), and 1 specimen consists of 4 yarns: 2 Z(2s), 1 S(2z), and 1 Z(2s(2z)). The 11 single-ply yarns have an average diameter of 0.34 mm, and the other yarns have a combined average diameter of 1.21 mm. Among the earliest specimens encountered was a yarn (see online appendix M).

CORDAGE

The analysis included 76 cordage specimens. Most have diameters greater than or equal to 1.5 mm,

with an overall average diameter of 3.43 mm. Cordage fiber types include cotton (24 specimens), cotton and junco (1 specimen), juncus (46 specimens), human hair (2 specimens), and milkweed (4 specimens).

These have structures as varied as their materials, ranging from unspun (2 specimens made of junco) to single-ply (1 S and 1 Z, both cotton), multi-ply (1 S(23–25z)), and very complex (1 Z(s(7z(2s))+s(5z(2s)))), the latter two being all cotton. Human hair has two structures, S(2z) and S(2z(2s)). Of the cordage specimens, 13 are counter-spun (those with an initial spin of Z) and represented by all material types (cotton, human hair, milkweed, and juncus).

FABRIC YARNS

The vast majority of weft-twining, looping, and knotted-netting yarns are $Z(2s^c)$, while the majority of plain-weave yarns are S. This "rule" is consistently followed. The exceptions are found in weft-twining supplementary and discontinuous wefts that are thicker, frequently milkweed, and structurally different from ground wefts. For example, 4 specimens have wefts that are $S(z(2s^c)+Z(s^c+?^{mw}))$, $S(2z(s^c+i^{mw}))$, $Z(3s^c)$, and $Z(2s(2z^c))$.

Nearly all warp yarns in weft twining are $Z(2s)$ or, when milkweed is present, $Z(s^c+i^{mw})$, $Z(s^c+s^{mw})$, or $Z(s^c+z^{mw})$, but in 2 specimens warps include $Z(3s^c)$ yarns. Specimens 2009.085.01 and 2009.114.07 have $Z(z(2s^c)+z(3s^c))$ and $S(z(2s^c)+z(3s^c))$ warp yarns, respectively. The majority of knotted netting yarns are also $Z(2s^c)$, with the exception of 6 specimens that have $Z(2s^{cuvf})$, $Z(3s^c)$, and $S(2z(2s^c))$ yarns. The same is true for looping, where the majority of yarns are $Z(2s^c)$ or $Z(s^c+s^{mw})$. But 1 specimen, 2009.098.14, incorporates $Z(3s^c)$ and $S(2z(2s^c))$ yarns, and 2 fragments (1 specimen), 2008.101.01.A–B, which both have figure-8 looping in weft twining, have $Z(4z(2s^c))$ yarns.

Table 12.5 presents the average diameters and twists for yarns and cordage broken down by fabric category and yarn structure. The yarn attributes from each category of fabric are fairly distinct, suggesting that yarns were tailor-made according to their purpose even at this early age. In fact, Z(2s) yarn diameters and twist, for example, are distinct enough that it is theoreti-

Table 12.5. Average diameters of elements for fabrics, loose yarns, and cordage

Category	Fabric type or element	Structure	No. samples	Average diameter (mm)	Average twist (°)
Weft twining	Warps	Cotton Z(2s)	357	0.87	41
		Cotton & Milkweed Z(2s), Z(s+z), Z(s+i)	164	0.86	39
	Wefts	Z(2s), Z(s+z), Z(s+i)	333	0.94	31
		S(2z)	64	0.90	38
		S(2z(2s)), Z(2s(2z)), Z(3s)	3	1.55	26
		S	7	0.48	37
		Z	1	1.70	45
Plain weave	Warps	S	118	0.43	54
		Z	4	0.45	53
		Z(2s)	8	0.76	38
	Wefts	S	125	0.46	53
		Z	7	0.47	49
		Z(2s)	2	0.70	35
Looping	Figure-8	Mostly Z(2s)	39	0.95	43
Knotted netting	Type 1	Mostly Z(2s)	8	1.23	54
	Type 2	Mostly Z(2s)	27	0.83	51
	Other	Mostly Z(2s)	3	1.13	43
Yarns and cordage	Cordage	All types	76	3.43	35
	Single-ply yarns	Mostly S	11	0.34	43
	Complex yarns	Mostly Z(2s)	26	1.21	43

cally possible to use them as a tool or guide to suggest the category of fabric for which loose yarns/cordage were meant to be used. For example, the table shows that the average warp and weft diameters of Z(2s) yarns in weft twining, looping, and 3 types of knotted netting (described below) are 0.86, 0.94, and 0.95 and 1.23, 0.83, and 1.13 mm, respectively. The average diameter of Z(2s) Type 1 knotted-netting yarns (1.23 mm) most closely approximates the average diameter of Z(2s) loose yarns (1.21 mm); however, loose-yarn average twist is 43 degrees, while the average twist of Type 1 knotted netting is 54 degrees. Loose yarns frequently lose their twist, suggesting that the majority of Z(2s) loose yarns might have either sloughed off or were intended for use in Type 1 knotted netting.

The data in table 12.5 suggest that yarns were deliberately produced with attributes that varied in accordance with the needs of the fabrics that they would make. This is apparent even in the earliest yarns and fabrics. For example, the attributes of yarns used in weft twining (see the diameter and twist in table 12.5) are quite different from the yarns used in plain weave, looping, and knotted netting. The earliest (Phase II) plain-weave fabrics have yarns as fine as and consistent with later plain-weave fabrics. This is true for yarns for all fabric categories. In other words, the differences in yarn diameter and twist are interpreted as intentional and conforming to the functional needs of fabrics.

For example, the yarns in looping and both Type 1 and Other-Type knotted netting are considerably thicker than the yarns in plain weave, weft twining, and Type 2 netting. In fact, Type 1 netting yarns are the thickest and most tightly twisted yarns of all categories. While Type 2 netting yarns have the thinnest two-ply yarns of any category, they also have some of the hardest twist, on a par with single-ply plain-weave yarns and two-ply Type 1 netting yarns. Twisting imparts friction, making tightly twisted yarns stronger than loosely twisted yarns. This suggests that both Type 1 and Type 2 nets required very strong yarns, which is not surprising. Their different mesh size, knot type, and yarn diameters can be used to infer the net's use, as discussed in "Knotted Netting" below.

The yarns used in two-element fabrics are subjected to greater strains during fabric construction than looping and netting yarns. This is because two-element fabrics are made on frames or looms to keep warps rigid and under tension. Weft-twining yarns, both warp and weft, are thicker than plain-weave yarns, suggesting that twining is exposed to greater stresses than plain weave either during production, use, or both. If both fabric types were made on looms or frames where warp ends were fixed and had roughly equal tensions, then the differences in yarn thickness most likely reflect usage, where weft-twined fabrics required greater strength.

While the data indicate that spinners were aware of the need to produce yarns with qualities consistent with the function of the final fabric, they did not seem to apply these principles to distinguish between warps and wefts, at least not in plain weave. It is generally believed that weaving has been done on looms with heddles only since Initial Period times. Heddles impart significant strain on warps, and spinners typically overspin warps to make them tighter and smoother to withstand these pressures resulting in warps and wefts with different attributes. The differences between warps and wefts in plain weave at Huaca Prieta, however, are negligible. This is in contrast to twining warps and wefts, where warps are definitely thinner and harder spun than weft yarns. These differences, however, can be explained as the result of the unique stresses involved with weft twining. For instance, Z-twining unwinds Z-twisted yarns and makes them slightly thicker as the twist is relaxed. Similarly, Z-twisting tightens and thins S-twisted yarns. These are exactly the patterns found in the archaeological record. Z(2s) weft-twined yarns are the loosest of all yarn categories and S(2z) wefts are thinner and more tightly twisted than Z(2s) wefts in weft twining. Wefts are thicker than warps in weft twining, although these data are influenced by the fact that decorative (for example, supplementary and discontinuous) wefts were not separated from ground wefts when calculating the data presented in table 12.5. Decorative wefts are usually thicker than ground warps and wefts as a way to add contrast.

Loose single-ply yarns are the thinnest yarns of all categories and are among the least twisted single-ply yarns. Single-ply plain-weave yarns are the second thinnest yarns and have a relatively hard twist. Thus it would seem the attributes of single-ply loose yarns are incompatible with those found in single-ply plain weave, so the original purpose of loose single-ply yarns remains enigmatic. The attributes of complex loose yarns are similar to those found in Type 1 and some Other-Type netting yarns, however, suggesting that some high-order loose yarns were either intended for or sloughed off Type 1 and/or Other-Type netting.

MAKING YARNS AND CORDAGE

The process of making yarns and cordage begins with spinning. The hallmark of spinning is the spindle whorl; however, none were excavated by Bird and Dillehay. The earliest known undisputed spindle whorls were excavated by MacNeish along with cotton yarns and plain-weave fabrics from the Ayacucho basin dating to ~3000–1750 BC (MacNeish et al. 1980: 322).

The lack of spindle whorls is not surprising, however, considering that until recent times north coast spinners did not always use them, employing horizontal spindles without whorls, frequently made of natural objects that could go unnoticed as spindles. When whorls were used on the north coast, they were often made of natural objects like avocado pits, fruit, or potatoes (Bird 1979a: 15; Vreeland 1986: 368). Spinners today also use a chalky substance to maintain friction.

Twisting fiber with a horizontal spindle where the fingers twist the spindle in a clockwise motion (meaning that the rod rotates clockwise when viewed from the proximal end and the yarn is attached to and extends from the distal end) produces an S-spun yarn. The majority of yarns are S-spun, which conforms to the ancient tradition of S-spinning on the north coast (for example, Grieder 1988; Olivera Alegre 2006; Shady S. 2004).

FABRICS

The analysis included 574 fabric fragments (originally 401 fabrics), 195 of which are from Bird's backdirt pile and 379 from secure stratigraphy. This includes 40 specimens of knotted netting, 39 of figure-8 looping, 127 of plain weave, and 368 of weft twining. Fabrics are classified by construction type and include single element, single set of elements, two sets of elements, and compound weaves. Fabric constructions are further subdivided into types.

SINGLE-ELEMENT CONSTRUCTIONS

Single-element constructions consist of one element interworked with itself to form a fabric. Single-element constructions are classified into three types: knotting, looping, and linking. Two types of single-element constructions were encountered: figure-8 looping and knotted looping (knotted netting).

Figure-8 Looping

Looping is a single-element construction in which a single yarn is interworked to form rows of loops, where each row forms the foundation for the succeeding row (Emery 1966: 31). Looping varieties are based on density (spaced and compact), complexity (simple and complex), pattern (plain and patterned), and yarn type-variety (structure, material, color). A diagram of figure-8 looping with extended loops is shown in figure 12.3a.

The analysis included 39 specimens (originally 26 fabrics) of figure-8 looping. Their technical descriptions are provided online in appendix F at https://my.vanderbilt.edu/huacaprieta/. All are of the figure-8 variety, and most are all-cotton, monochrome, made with Z(2s) yarns

patterned with spaced and compact areas that make diamond-like designs, such as specimen 2009.098.19 (fig. 12.3a). No examples of the variants Bird called open-work and narrow-looped were encountered (Bird et al. 1985: 203, fig. 147, 206, fig. 149). A single fabric, 2008.101.01.A–C, which is now in three pieces, differs from other examples of figure-8 looping, where figure-8 looping was most likely added to the warp ends of a weft-twined fabric during the warping process. After the finished fabric was removed from the frame, the looping formed a band. The figure-8 looping is made with natural-cotton Z(2s) yarns.

Looping produces either flat or circular fabrics depending on whether the element is interworked back and forth (flat) or in a spiral (circular), producing diagnostic attributes, such as circular areas at the start of a circular fabric (for example, Bird et al. 1985: 199–201, figs. 143, 144, 145). No recently excavated specimens have finished edges or rings, so it is impossible to determine their original shape or manufacture.

Recently excavated looping specimens have an average length of 15.1 cm, width of 12.6 cm, and area of 237.4 cm² , putting them on par with the size of Type 1 and Other-Type Netting fabrics but smaller than Type 2 netting. Specimen 2009.028.05 is 99.55 cm long and is the longest looping specimen (16.5 cm wide) in the collection. It is considerably longer than the other looping specimens (the next longest piece is 38.0 cm).

DECORATION

Patterning was made in figure-8 looping in two ways: geometric patterns were created by spacing the lengths of the loops as in specimen 2009.098.19 (fig. 12.3a) or by adding contrast through the use of color, yarn material, or yarn structure. All examples of decorated figure-8 looping, both banded and geometric patterned, are from Phase V contexts except for 2009.028.05 (fig. 12.3c), which is from Phase III–IV contexts and is the longest specimen of the collection, with two blue bands running down its entire length. It is unusual for being the only specimen in the entire collection that was repaired.

The analysis showed that 12 specimens (7 fabrics) were decorated with compact and spaced

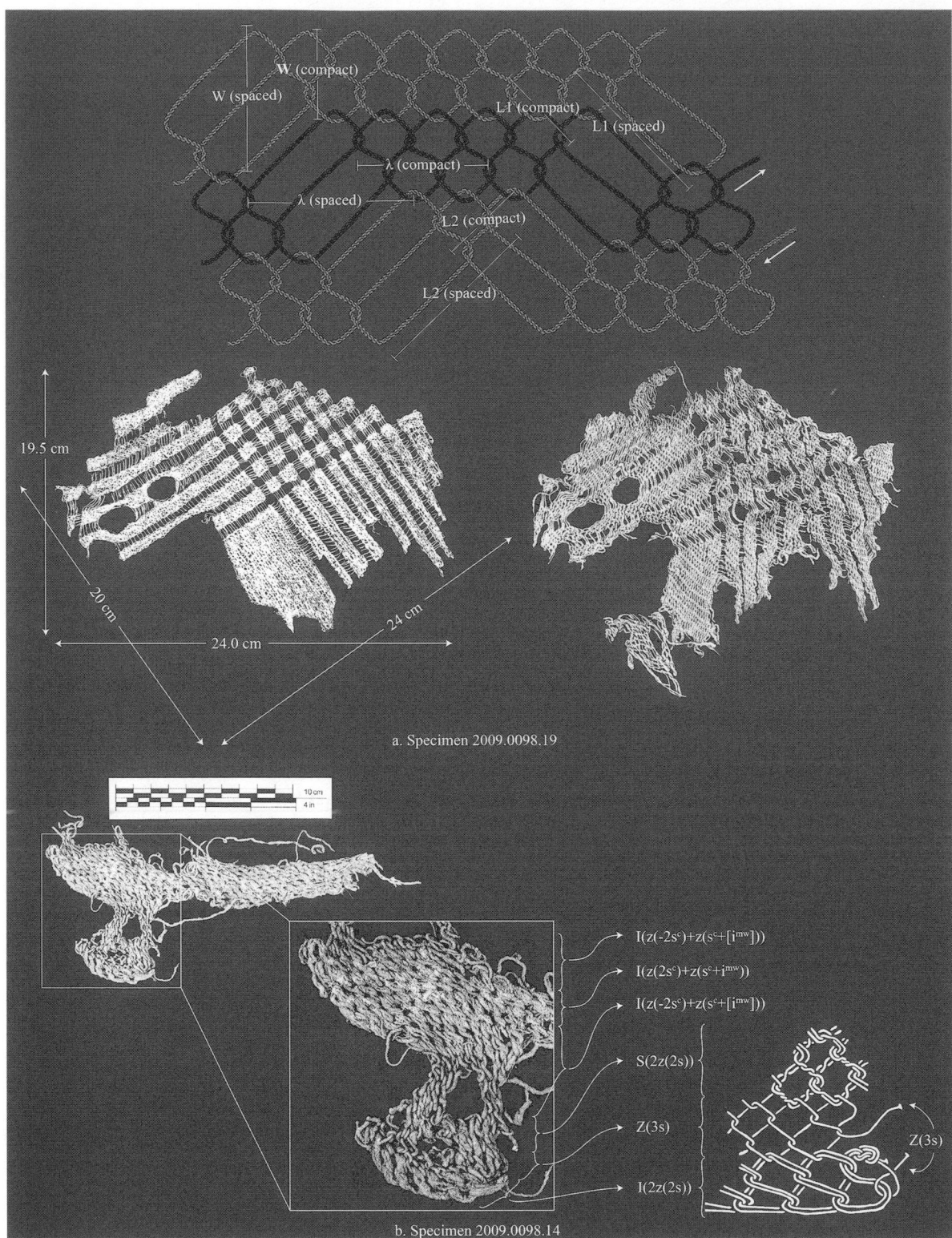

FIGURE 12.3. Looping: *a*, figure-8 looping with diamond-like design made by extending the length of the loops (Specimen 2009.098.19; drawing by the author; photo by Lauren Badams; *b*, striped looping made with contrasting yarn structures (Specimen 2009.098.14); note that contrasting shades are also present (photos by Lauren Badams); *c*, striped looping made with contrasting shade (Specimen 2009.028.05) (photo left and drawing right). Photographic details (*left*) and accompanying drawings (*right*) indicate four instances of mending and color changes.

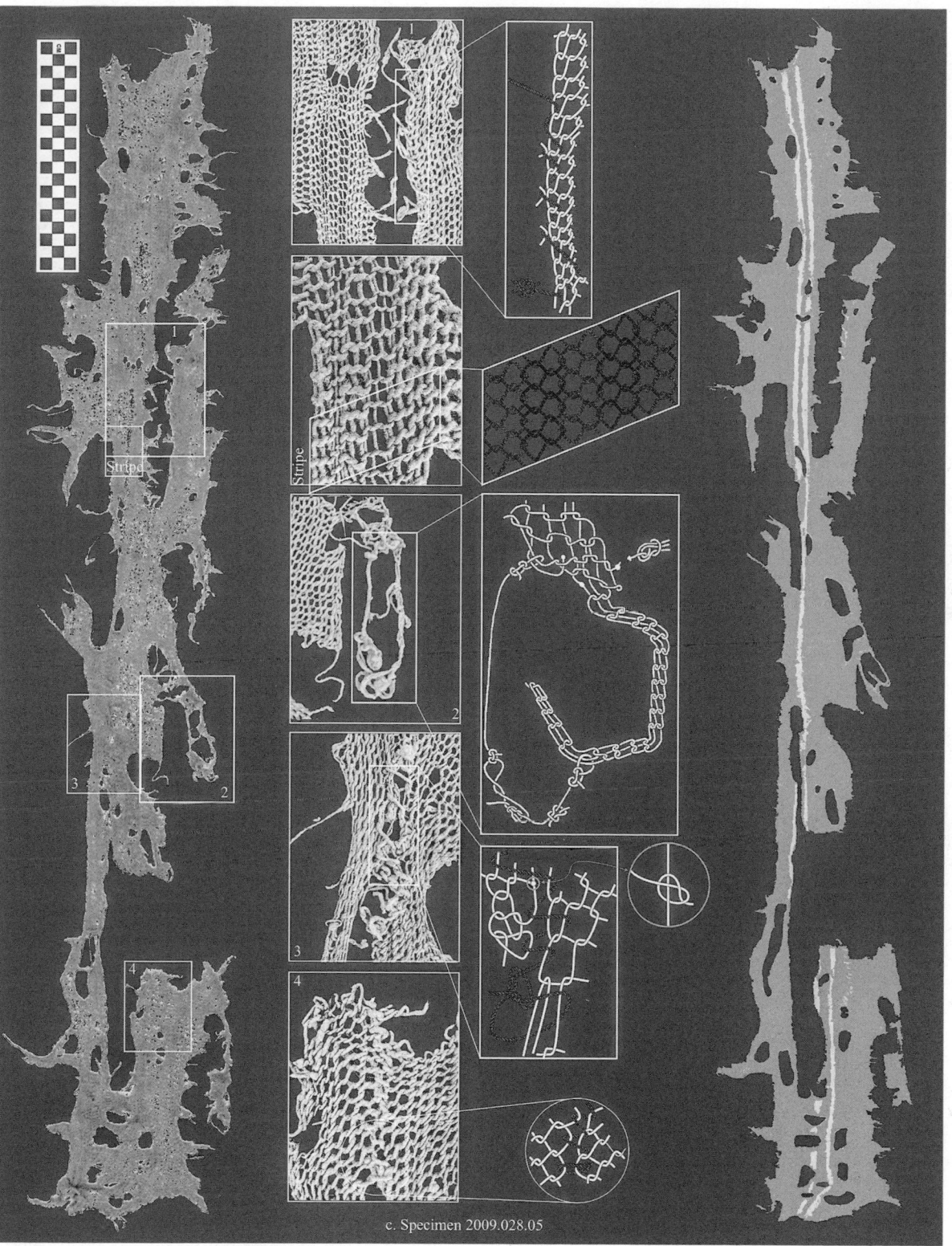

c. Specimen 2009.028.05

looping (see appendix G online at https://my.vanderbilt.edu/huacaprieta/). Of these, 4 specimens (6 fragments) have bands of contrasting color, material, and/or structure. Specimens 2008.017.01, 2009.028.05, 2009.098.09, and 2009.098.14 have bands made of cotton and cotton plied with milkweed (see online appendix M).

Specimen 2009.098.14 (fig. 12.3b) has five yarn structures: $Z(2s^c)$, $Z(3s^c)$, $S(2z(2s^c))$, $I(2z(2s^c))$, and $I(z(2s^c)+z(s^c+i^{mw}))$. Specimen 2009.098.09 has remnants of two bands, one blue and one red, made with cotton $Z(2s)$ elements. Colored yarns were added to make bands in specimens 2009.098.14 and 2009.028.05 (see online appendix M).

ELEMENT KNOTS AND THE MAKING OF FIGURE-8 LOOPING

During the process of making figure-8 looping, the working end of the element passes through the loops of adjacent figure-8 loops. The mesh size of Huaca Prieta figure-8 looping is between 2–5 mm and thus precludes the use of a bobbin (a spool wound with yarn); hence any tools that were used, such as bodkins or needles, would have to be thin, and the length of the working element would have been relatively short to keep the yarn from twisting and tangling (probably no more than double the length of the practitioner's arm). Therefore the working yarn would have to be extended frequently, which should show up in a pattern of relatively uniform knots throughout the fabric.

This is exactly what is found in the archaeological record. Excluding the smallest fragments of figure-8 looping, all 6 specimens (5 fabrics) have several knots in their elements, the majority of which are either joins or mends. In these specimens, the knots appear to be randomly placed, like the pattern seen in 2009.142.02 (fig. 12.13c below), suggesting that the knots are joins used to extend the working element. This practice is used to make simple-looping bags, called *shicra*, in highland Ecuador, where the yarns are made as the work proceeds about a meter at a time (Miller 2003–2004: 63).

The practice of adding yarns as work progresses is frugal, allowing yarns to be made as needed and reducing excess. Such practices were probably important during Preceramic times, when cot-

ton was probably not as abundant as it would later become. The practice of making small lengths that are added to as work progresses requires close coordination with spinners and works most efficiently when the spinner and "looper" are the same person. This is in contrast with weaving practices, such as interlacing, where all the yarns making a fabric are spun prior to weaving, and spinners, warpers, and weavers are typically different people (for example, Franquemont and Franquemont 1987).

USE, REPAIR, AND DISCARDING PATTERNS

Looping is frequently associated with head coverings and/or containers in the ancient Andes. Specimens of figure-8 looping in the present study were from ritual, nonmortuary contexts and were not found containing other objects, however, so their function remains unknown.

Specimen 2009.028.05 is the only fabric in the entire collection that was repaired, where mends are here defined as stitching that joins two or more broken nonselvage edges of fabric (see online appendix M at https://my.vanderbilt.edu/huacaprieta/).

Damage provides significant clues about fabric function, and looping has the highest percentage of torn edges of all categories (table 12.6). At the same time, its percentage of distorted yarns—an indicator of trauma from cutting and/or tearing—is about the same as that of plain weave but not as high as that of weft twining. While the results are inconclusive, the distortion, cuts, and holes are consistent with the specimen having been used as a container; its torn edges appear intentional and are thus consistent with ritual destruction.

FIGURE-8 LOOPING ELSEWHERE

Figure-8 looping at Huaca Prieta is similar to that found throughout Preceramic Andean sites, where it was encountered at Salinas de Chao (Olivera Alegre 2006), Los Gavilanes (Bonavia 1982), and Asia (Engel 1963c). Figure-8 looping at Los Gavilanes is all-cotton and comes in both compact (Bonavia 1982: 121–122, fig. 137) and spaced vari-

Table 12.6. Fabric conditions: Holes and cut and torn edges

Category	Total		Holes		Cut edges		Torn edges		Distorted yarn elements	
	No. of specimens	Fabrics	No. of specimens (%)	Fabrics (%)	No. of specimens (%)	Fabrics (%)	No. of specimens (%)	Fabrics (%)	No. of specimens (%)	Fabrics (%)
Figure-8 looping	39	26	18 (46.2%)	13 (50.0%)	11 (28.2%)	7 (26.9%)	30 (76.9%)	17 (65.4%)	15 (38.5%)	8 (30.8%)
Knotted netting	40	35	5 (12.5%)	5 (14.3%)	19 (47.5%)	16 (45.7%)	22 (55.0%)	18 (51.4%)	7 (17.5%)	5 (14.3%)
Weft twining	368	269	166 (45.1%)	132 (49.1%)	96 (26.1%)	72 (26.8%)	250 (67.9%)	189 (70.3%)	208 (56.5%)	156 (58.0%)
Plain weave	127	71	79 (62.2%)	43 (60.6%)	22 (17.3%)	17 (23.9%)	81 (63.8%)	47 (66.2%)	44 (34.6%)	23 (32.4%)

eties (Bonavia 1982: 125–126, fig. 144). Figure-8 looping at Asia comes in multiple varieties involving loop-and-twist techniques (Engel 1963c: 38–39, figs. 71, 72; for a definition of the loop-and-twist technique, see Emery 1966: 31, fig. 11); its I-type seems most similar to Huaca Prieta figure-8 looping, but it is usually made of human hair or bast, rarely cotton (Engel 1963c: 34, 37, fig. 56). At La Galgada the figure-8 looping is open and made of "bast fiber" and has the appearance of netting, which is interesting, because knotted netting was not encountered at La Galgada (Grieder et al. 1988: 155–156, fig. 105). As at Asia and Los Gavilanes, the figure-8 looping at Aspero was not made of cotton.

KNOTTED NETTING

The analysis found 35 knotted-looping fabrics (40 specimens), also called knotted netting, or netting (for a description of knotted looping and netting, see Emery 1966: 34–39). Their provenience, dimensions, and other technical descriptions are presented online in appendix H at https://my.vanderbilt.edu/huacaprieta/. Varieties of netting include those made with lark's-head (cowhitch) and sheet-bend knots (fig. 12.4a–c). Within the lark's-head variety (fig. 12.4c) are cotton nets made with Z(2s) yarns and others made of Z(3s) yarns. Their average length is 17.9 cm, their width is 17.5 cm, and their area is 526.7 cm. Standard deviations are high, because the actual sizes range a great deal, where the longest and widest fabrics are 67.0 and 85.0 cm, respectively, and the shortest and narrowest are 2.5 and 1.1 cm, respectively. Bird encountered significant amounts of netting similar to the netting discussed here.

TYPE 1 NETS

The analysis found Type 1 nets (9 fragments; fig. 12.4a), defined by having simple half-hitch knots, thick Z(2s) cotton yarn elements with an average diameter of 1.2 mm ranging from 1.1 to 1.4 mm (and a standard deviation [STD] of 0.18), an average twist of 54 degrees, and a relatively small mesh size, less than 1 cm on a side (average of 0.6 cm, ranging from 0.5 to 0.8).

Net dimensions, like looping specimens, are difficult to measure accurately. Nets not only are unwieldy—always curling, twisting, and recoiling but are "shape shifters," distorting with the slightest tension and making them difficult to measure. Type 1 nets are on average smaller than Type 2 and Other nets, and they are longer than they are wide (that is, in strips) with an average length of 7.0 cm, an average width of 4.3 cm, and an average area of 40.9 cm².

TYPE 2 NETS

The 24 Type 2 nets (27 fragments) are characterized by having a large mesh size, greater than 1 cm on a side (average 2.81 cm ranging from 1.3 to 5.7 cm), secured with lark's-head knots using cotton yarns, the majority of which are Z(2s), although 5 are made of Z(3s) cotton yarns (fig. 12.4c). Type 2 yarns—both Z(2s) and Z(3s)—are thinner than Type 1 yarns, with an average diameter of 0.8 mm, ranging from 0.5 to 1.3 mm (STD of 0.21) and an average twist of 51 degrees.

Type 2 nets are on average significantly larger than Type 1 nets, with an average length of 21.1 cm, average width of 22.6 cm, and average area of 737.4 cm². Their average lengths and widths are almost equal, and many are roughly square. Those net fragments that are rectangular or strips are likely to be short and wide more than long and thin, which is in contrast to Type 1 nets, which are typically long and thin.

Specimen 2009.057.01 is a yarn from Phase II contexts (Pit 3, Muro W, Stratum 52) and is one of the earliest yarn-based artifacts excavated. Its color, diameter, and structure are consistent with Type 2 netting (see online appendix M at https://my.vanderbilt.edu/huacaprieta).

OTHER-TYPE NETS

The analysis classified 4 fabrics (5 fragments) as "Other," because they do not fit into either the Type 1 or Type 2 categories. Like Type 1 nets, the Other-Type nets are longer than they are wide, with an average length of 17.6 cm, average width of 9.8 cm, and average area of 161.3 cm².
Two of the Other-Type net fragments (Speci-

mens 2009.077.01.A and 2009.077.01.B) are made of a thick Z(2s) unidentified vegetal fiber (probably juncus), making both lark's-head and Z-half hitches (overhand knots, not sheet bends) that are inconsistently placed (fig. 12.4b) with variable mesh sizes. Together these attributes—inconsistent knotting patterns and uneven mesh sizes—suggest a hasty, unplanned construction. Perhaps the netting was made around an object to contain it, like a *shicra* bag.

The three remaining Other-Type nets have an average mesh length of 0.75 cm, an average yarn diameter of 1.1 mm, and average twist of 43 degrees. For a description of Specimens 2009.072.33 and 2009.114.15, see online appendix M at https://my.vanderbilt.edu/huacaprieta/.

Other-Type specimen, 2009.010.31, is a complex net made with multiple yarn structures with both sheet-bend knots and linking. The fabric consists of essentially three interconnected strips that are longer than wide and connected with simple linking (S twist) to make panels with multiple fabric structures, as depicted in fig. 12.5. The fabric might have a complete width, but it is cut on its top and bottom edges. It has essentially four different structures defined by yarn structure and knotting/linking practices (see online appendix M at https://my.vanderbilt.edu/huacaprieta/).

DECORATION

Decoration in netting is rare. It was encountered in a single fabric, 2009.010.31 (fig. 12.5), as noted above.

NET MAKING

All nets except Specimens 2009.077.01.A and 2009.077.01.B are made of cotton yarns or cotton plied with milkweed. These specimens are made of sedge or a sedge-like material. Netting yarns have a look and feel that is different from twining and looping yarns. Netting yarns are on average more tightly and evenly twisted, with a more consistent diameter than twining and looping yarns (see online appendix E). The majority of yarns are Z(2s); however, 5 Type 2 nets as well as Specimen 2009.010.31 are made of Z(3s) cotton yarns.

All knots involve one or more interworked elements that form one or more crossings (twists), each with a direction of S or Z. Their patterns of interworking impart a face, meaning that the knot has a front (obverse, recto) and back (reverse, verso) as well as sides. Knots have orientations, meaning that they can be rotated perpendicularly (90/−90 degrees) and upside down (180 degrees). Type 1 netting knots typically have Z-twist with faces that alternate obverse/reverse row by row (one row of obverse followed by one row of reverse, and so forth). What does this tell us about the steps and practices involved in making nets?

The outer rows of Type 2 nets (but apparently not in Type 1 nets) usually (7 specimens) have one or two rows of knots that are perpendicular. This pattern was also encountered at Los Gavilanes (Bonavia 1982: 124–125, fig. 143). Perpendicular knots are described by Graumont and Wenstrom (1976: 145–154), who note that the first two rows of mesh established the width of the net (fig. 12.4c), after which the net is rotated 90 degrees and attached to a rigid body, such as a rod or frame. Specimen 2009.079.01 is such a net. It is almost complete and has two rows of perpendicular knotting along one side and a single column of perpendicular knotting on the top.

If the presence of rows of perpendicular knots indicates that Type 2 nets were rotated during the process of net making, the lack of perpendicular knots in Type 1 nets suggests that they were not rotated. This may indicate that Type 1 nets were started, ended, and possibly used on the same rod or frame. Both Type 1 and Type 2 nets have faces that alternate row by row, which strongly suggests that they were made on rectangular frames or rods; nets made on circular frames have knots with faces that are all the same direction. This implies that Huaca Prieta nets were not made on circular frames, but they might have been mounted afterward and thus could have been used for fishing.

USE, REPAIR, AND DISCARD PRACTICES

Bird believed that the Huaca Prieta nets were used in water, as evidenced by watermarks, which presumably means they had matted yarns, salt deposits, and/or stiff textures. Type 2 nets have more salt crystals and matted and stiff fibers than

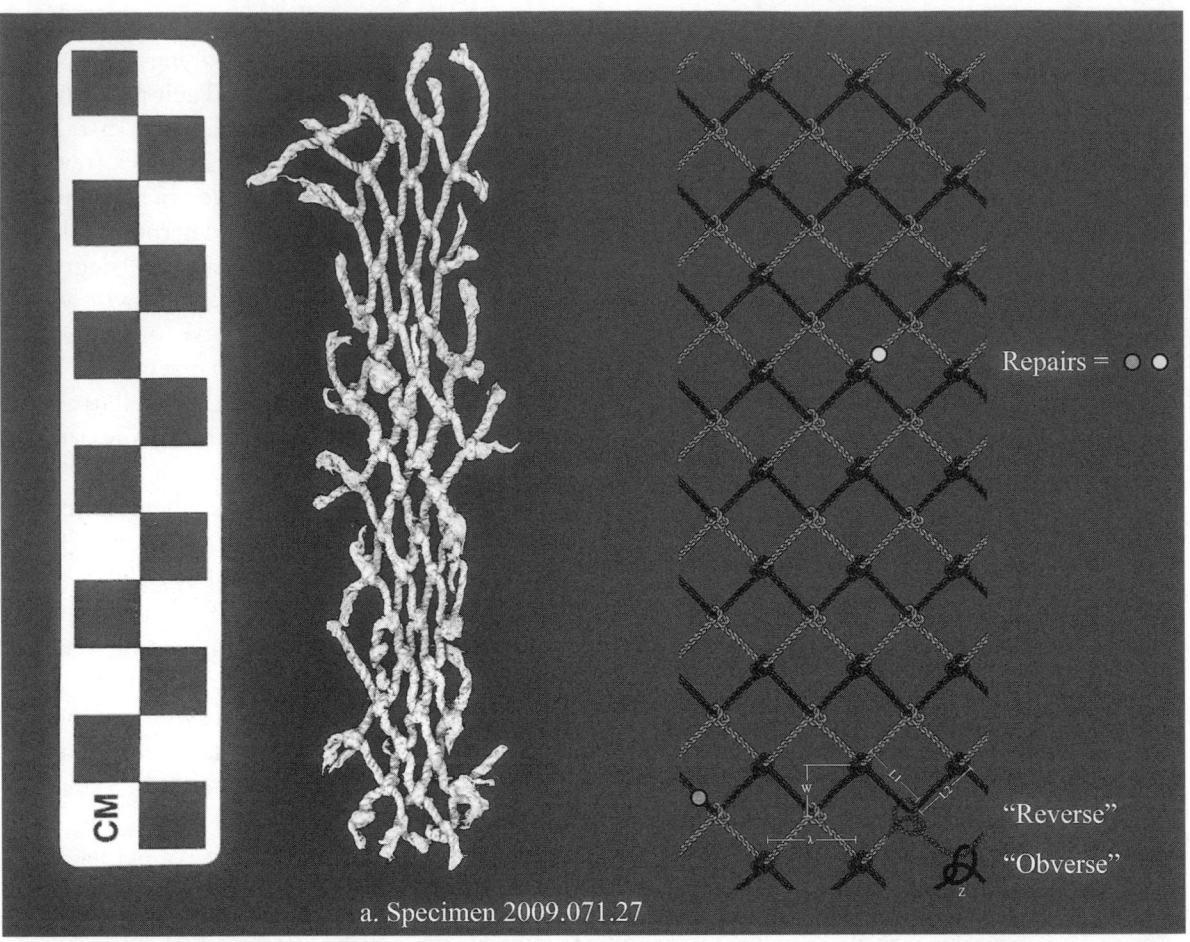

Repairs = ● ●

"Reverse"

"Obverse"

a. Specimen 2009.071.27

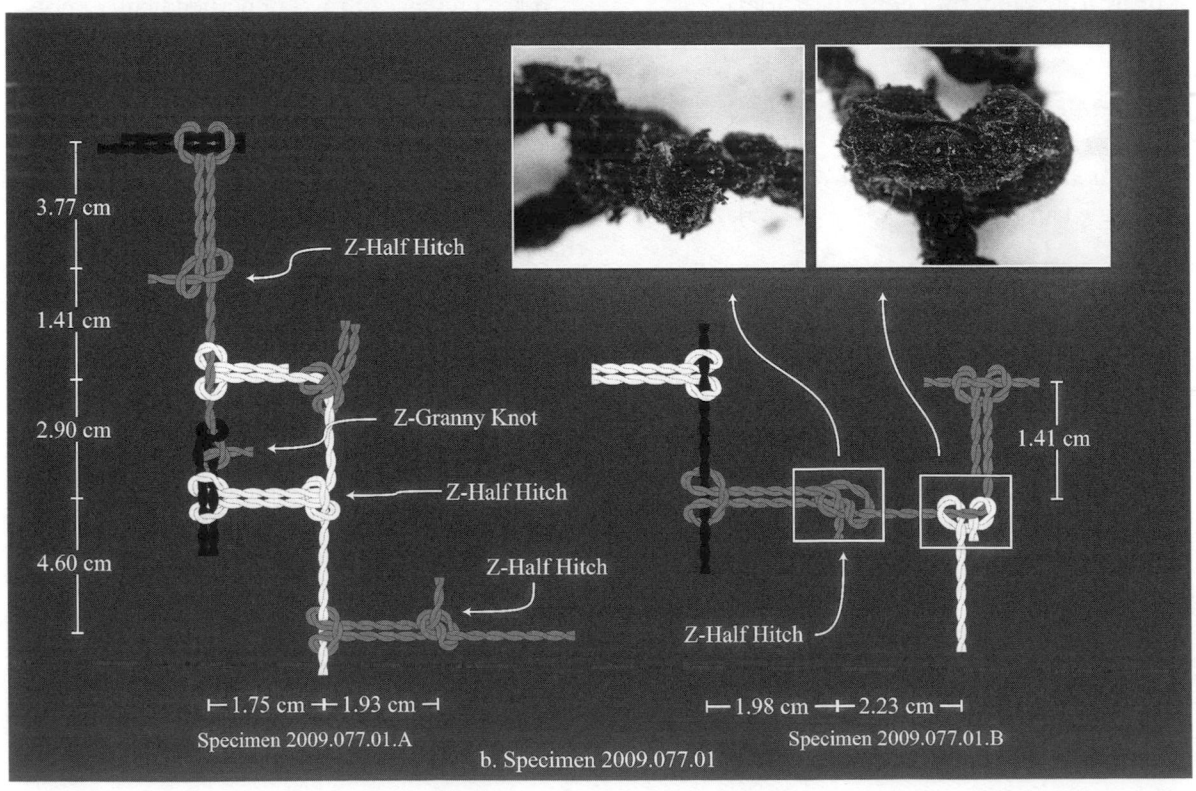

3.77 cm

Z-Half Hitch

1.41 cm

Z-Granny Knot

2.90 cm

Z-Half Hitch

Z-Half Hitch

4.60 cm

1.41 cm

Z-Half Hitch

⊢ 1.75 cm ⊣ 1.93 cm ⊣

Specimen 2009.077.01.A

⊢ 1.98 cm ⊣ 2.23 cm ⊣

Specimen 2009.077.01.B

b. Specimen 2009.077.01

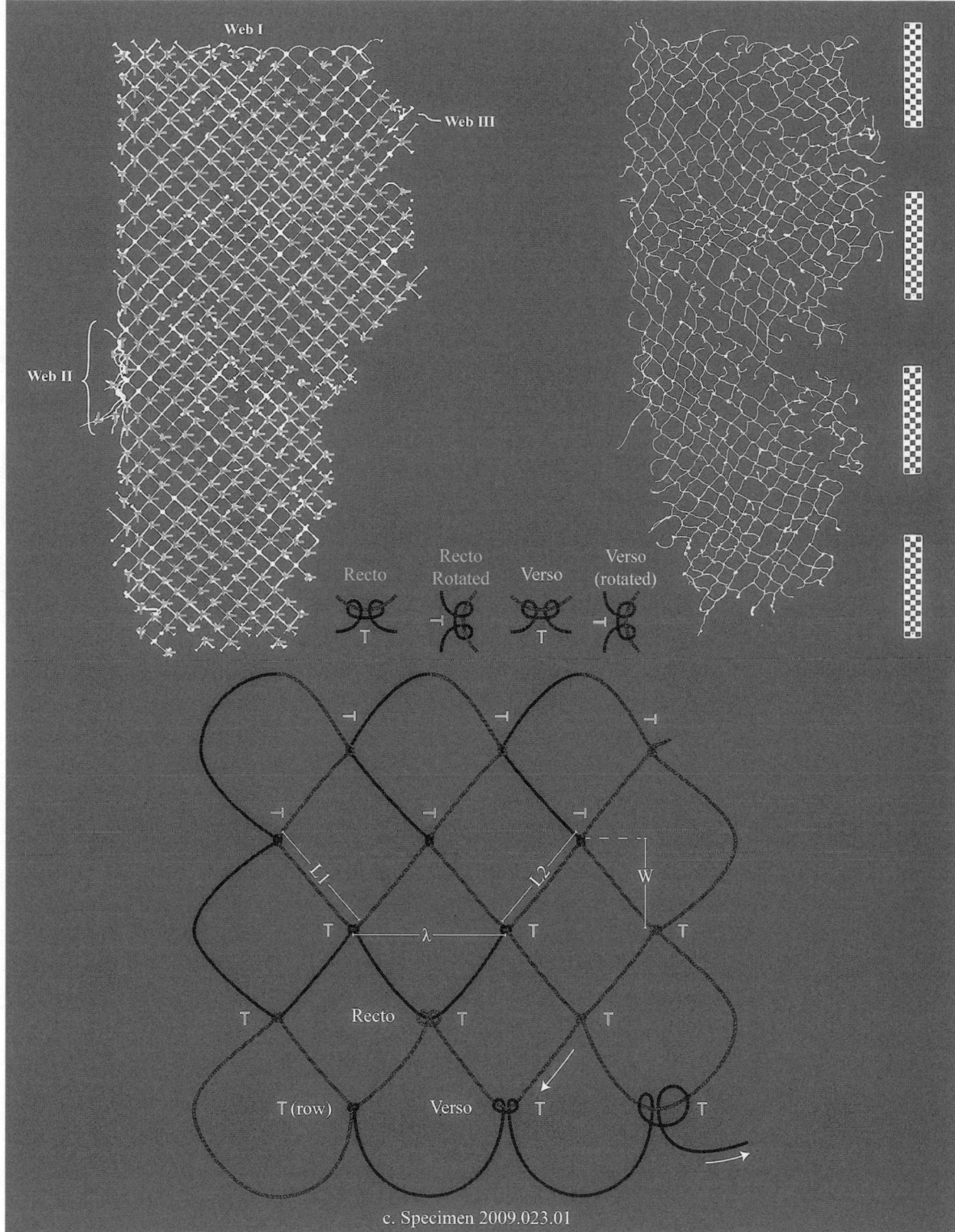

FIGURE 12.4. Knotted netting types and attributes: *a*, Type 1 netting, depicting its structure, the attributes that were measured, and obverse and reverse knot faces using Specimen 2009.071.27 as an example (shading added for clarity, not in actual net); *b*, example of Other-Type netting, Specimens 2009.077.01.A–B, which are made of juncus fiber and two types of knots (*left*: Specimen 2009.077.01.A; *right*: Specimen 2009.077.01.B; shading added for clarity; actual net is monochrome); *c*, Type 2 netting depicting its structure, the attributes that were measured, and obverse and reverse lark's-head knot faces using Specimen 2009.023.01 (which has remnants of three knotted-netting webs) as the example. The drawing (*left*) and photo (*right*) are rotated 90 degrees counter clockwise. The drawing depicts knot faces and directions, showing that the knots in the first two rows are perpendicular to the rest of the net, which is common in Huaca Prieta nets (shading added for clarity and not present in actual specimen).

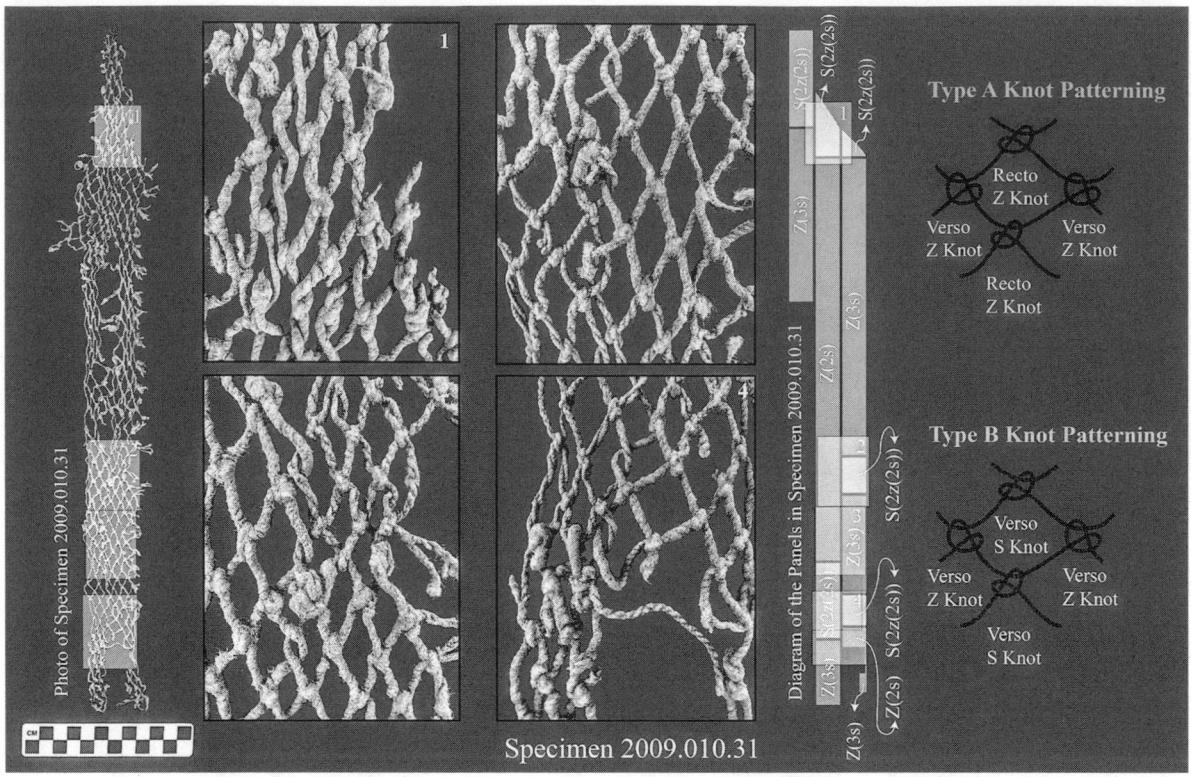

Type A Knot Patterning

Type B Knot Patterning

Specimen 2009.010.31

FIGURE 12.5. Decorated nets: example of Other-Type netting made with multiple yarn structures and both sheet-bend knots and linking that forms a pattern (Specimen 2009.010.31). A photo of the complete fabric is on the left, with details of parts 1–4 in the center. A diagram of the net's parts is on the center right, with diagrams of knot patterns on the far right. Bands differ in their yarn structure and their knotting patterns. Yarn structures are listed in the panels, which are shading coded according to their knotting pattern. Photos of the various yarn structures and knotting patterns are also provided on the right (yarn shading added for clarity and not seen in the actual specimen).

Type 1 nets, suggesting that Type 2 nets were almost certainly used in saltwater, while Type 1 nets might have been used more predominantly in freshwater (XRF analysis suggests that some textiles were never exposed to water; see appendix 18).

All net types show multiple signs of wear and repair, as seen in table 12.6. All are fragmentary. While this might be the result of ritual destruction at the time of deposition, almost all nets have mending knots, presumably for repairing holes. Many of the nets, such as 2009.102.27, –28, –31, –32, and –33, have knots that were pulled out of alignment, turning them from lark's-head knots to cow hitches and square knots. In 2009.079.01 the knots in an entire row at the edge of the net were pulled out of alignment, converting them all from obverse to reverse knots. Perhaps cutting the net from a frame with a dull object caused the trauma.

Although it is difficult to know how and for

what activities the nets were used (see "Making Yarns and Cordage" above), it is likely that the two types were used for very different purposes. Type 1 nets, with their thicker yarns, tight twist, and small mesh size, presumably were involved in catching or holding something that was small and presumably strong, sharp, or heavy and were perhaps attached to a circular frame to make a dip net for scooping up shellfish in sharp rocky areas. Perhaps they were attached to small fish weirs. Type 2 nets, with their fine, strong yarns and large mesh size, presumably were used to catch larger and perhaps less sharp and heavy objects.

Bird believed that "the majority of netted items are fishnets" (Bird et al. 1985: 207). He noted: "Both [Guañape, another Preceramic site, and Huaca Prieta] are near sections of beach which are good for net fishing but not for hand lines" (Bird 1948c:26). But no nets encountered are large enough to be used as fishing nets. Bird might have been referring to a large, seine-like net that he encountered with gourd floats (Bird et al. 1985: 225, fig. 171); however, this net came from relatively late, possibly Initial Period, levels.

No recently excavated nets are comparable to the large net with floats excavated by Bird. They are all significantly smaller, not large enough to have served as a drag net or a seine, suggesting that the nets in the present study were probably used as dip nets or perhaps attached to small weirs. Small modern weir fishing nets have small meshes with thick yarns (for example, for shrimp) resembling Type 1 nets, although modern nets have lark's-head knots (for example, Ashley 1944: 586, fig. 3787; Graumont and Wenstrom 1976), and Huaca Prieta Type 1 nets have half hitches.

None of the nets have a complete width or length (none have two finished selvages that provide a length or width). Some Type 2 nets (2009.079.01, 2009.102.33, and 2009.115.03) and some Type 1 nets have two or more edges that are nearly straight and look as if they were cut from a frame, suggesting that they are mostly complete (fig. 12.4a, c). Table 12.6 shows that nets have the highest percentage of cut edges and the lowest percentage of torn edges of all fabric categories, strongly supporting the idea that nets were cut, not torn, from frames prior to discarding.

If this is true and if the nets were not cut again prior to discarding, many (perhaps most) nets are complete or nearly so and made for ritual deposition. Many Type 2 nets have three straight cut edges, many of which have twenty-five or twenty-six rows of knots, including 2009.115.03 (twenty-five knotting rows), 2009.079.01, and 2009.102.33 (each with twenty-six rows). Specimen 2009.114.15, which looks cut, has thirty-three rows.

Several nets with two or three relatively straight edges have a rough fourth edge, which supports the idea that at least some nets were attached to small weirs or dip nets, with the uneven edge representing the bottom of the net that might have suffered damage. The relatively small size of Huaca Prieta nets of both Types 1 and 2 further supports this. Their construction, however, suggests that they were used to catch and/or carry different things.

KNOTTED NETTING ELSEWHERE

Netting is commonly found at most Preceramic sites. Unlike Huaca Prieta netting, however, knotted netting elsewhere is not usually made of cotton. Engel (1963c: 46–48, figs. 102–106) described and illustrated two types of netting at Asia, all made of milkweed with lark's-head knots, where one variety is made with open meshes and fine yarns (0.1 mm diameter), like Type 2 netting, and the other is made of thicker yarns (1.5 mm diameter) and smaller mesh size (Engel 1963c: 37–38, figs. 68, 69, 70) like Type 1 netting. While more than a continent away and five millennia distant in time, Papago men made nets from agave fiber with wide meshes similar to Huaca Prieta Type 2, which they used to carry deer meat (Underhill 1940: 16–17).

No nets from Asia have half hitches. Other sites, however, have their own knot patterns. At Los Gavilanes, where nets were made of either cotton or camelid hair, Bonavia (1982) encountered both half hitches and lark's-head knots, but he did not note a correlation between mesh size and knot type. He used the terms "cabeza de alondra" and "red china" (Chinese netting) when referring to the two faces of lark's-head knots, where "red china" refers to the reverse face.

The practice of alternating knot faces was not consistently practiced throughout the ancient Andes. Photos of Asia netting—including those with thick yarns and small mesh and thin yarns with open mesh—indicate that knot faces alternated row by row. Bonavia (1982: 124, figs. 142, 143) found lark's-head knots at Los Gavilanes that alternated every two rows, while half hitches did not alternate. Knotted netting at Aspero follows the pattern of Los Gavilanes, where nets were made of both cotton and noncotton fibers, and nets have both open-mesh and closed-mesh varieties using lark's-head or half-hitch knots, where half hitches do not alternate faces but lark's-head knots do (for example, Feldman 1980: 226–227, table 210, 1986: 46, figs. 48, 49). These other Preceramic sites do not seem to show the same correlation between mesh size and knot type as at Huaca Prieta. No knotted netting was reported from La Galgada (apparently replaced by types of looping with open meshes).

SINGLE-SET-OF-ELEMENT CONSTRUCTIONS

No constructions were made with a single set of elements as defined by Emery (1966). Common varieties of this category include three-strand braiding like the braids that people make in their hair. Bird encountered five single-set-of-element constructions, all fragments of three-strand braiding (Bird et al. 1985: 216).

Oblique interlacing is apparently uncommon at Preceramic sites. For instance, Grieder (1988) did not report oblique interlacing from La Galgada other than basketry or matting; he found no braided cordage either. Similarly, Gloria Olivera Alegre (2006) did not report braiding from Salinas de Chao. Engel (1963b) encountered several pieces of "braided rope" (three-strand oblique interlacing) at Asia; however, he did not report obliquely interlaced fabrics. Oblique interlacing apparently was not used to make fabrics until after the Preceramic period. Considering that braiding is easy—even small children in Western cultures do it—its rarity in Preceramic times is puzzling.

TWO-ELEMENT CONSTRUCTION

The analysis showed that 505 specimens have two or more sets of elements, meaning that they have at least one stationary, fixed set of elements called warps and one active set called wefts (the two are usually perpendicular to one another). These fabrics are classified in the present study according to categories defined by Irene Emery (1966), including weft twining, plain weave, compound weaves (such as fabrics with complementary-warp elements), float weaves, and fabrics with crossed/recrossed elements.

All fabrics with complementary elements are weft twining with complementary warps. All crossed elements are associated with weft twining too. Both complementary warps and crossed warps are discussed below in the section on weft-twining decoration. Similarly, all float weaves were associated with plain weave and are discussed in the section on plain-weave decorative techniques.

WEFT TWINING

The most common fabric construction technique was weft twining (fig. 12.6). The primary difference between interlacing and twining is the way in which the weft is inserted. Twining is a fabric construction that requires at least two weft yarns per shot, because the wefts enclose the warps and twist around each other between warps, producing a Z- or S-twist (for example, Bendure and Pfeiffer 1946: 286; Emery 1966: 11). Warp elements consist of one or more yarns, but Huaca Prieta warps, like much Preceramic weft-twist twining, are always handled in pairs or groups of pairs.

The process of twining requires many choices resulting in a large number of attributes and a great many styles. Huaca Prieta "twiners" seem to have had significant leeway in their choices, creating a situation where no two fabrics are alike. At the same time, some "rules" appear to govern the right and wrong ways of making twining, resulting in a situation where most twined fabrics have two-strand, cotton, spaced weft twining with Z(2s) warp and weft yarns.

As the wefts twist around each other (and at the same time as they interwork the warps), they can make a half twist (180 degrees, notated as a ½ or half twist) or more. This is done to produce patterning, either by using the twists to make a space or, when the wefts have different colors, by changing the color on the fabric's two faces. The wefts in most Huaca Prieta weft twining textiles make half twists with a Z slant (noted as ½-Z twist) around regular (parallel) pairs of warp yarns. The majority of recently excavated weft-twining specimens are similar to those described by Bird. The present study focuses on techniques and structures not described by him.

The analysis included 368 twined specimens (269 original fabrics). The average length of twined specimens is 16.5 cm; the average width is 11.8 cm, and average area is 292.4 cm², which is slightly larger than figure-8 looping and smaller than knotted netting. The longest twined specimen (2008.066.02) is 81.5 cm. The widest weft-twined specimen (2009.142.02) is 106.0 cm. The shortest and narrowest specimens are both 0.7 cm. The technical traits, provenience, and dimensions of all twining specimens are in the online appendices B and I.

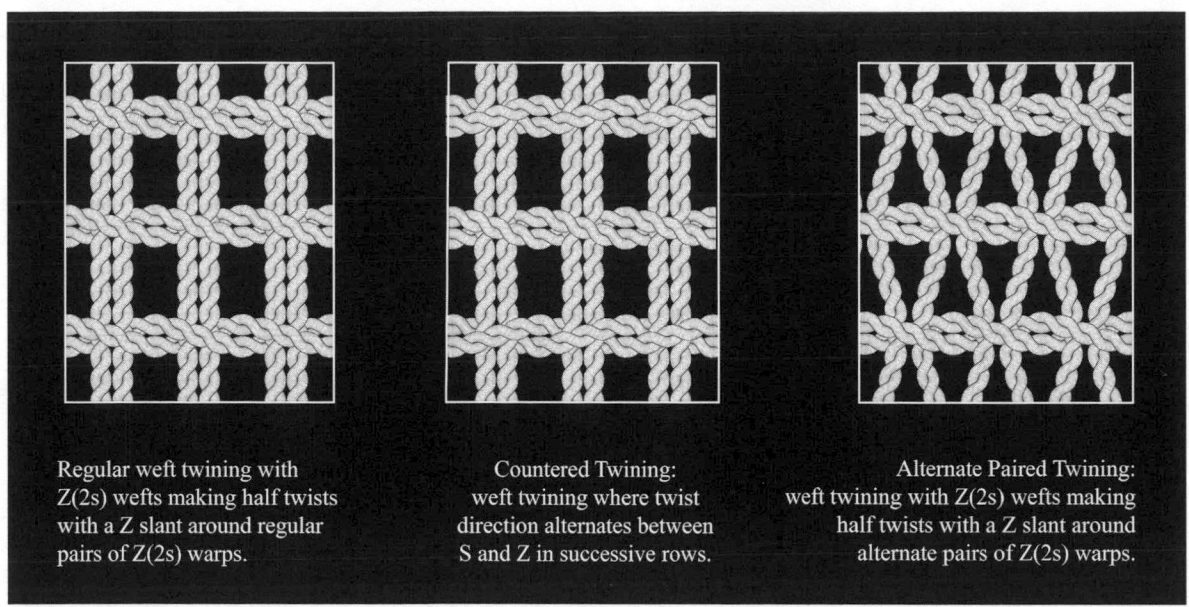

Regular weft twining with Z(2s) wefts making half twists with a Z slant around regular pairs of Z(2s) warps.

Countered Twining: weft twining where twist direction alternates between S and Z in successive rows.

Alternate Paired Twining: weft twining with Z(2s) wefts making half twists with a Z slant around alternate pairs of Z(2s) warps.

FIGURE 12.6. Structural diagram of weft twining.

SELVAGES

Warp selvages are found on 39 weft-twined specimens (37 fabrics), while 85 specimens (71 fabrics) have weft selvages and 13 have both warp and weft selvages. Specimens 2008.075.03.A and 2008.100.04 have two weft selvages representing complete widths of 10.7 and 22.0 cm, respectively; 2008.066.05.A has two weft selvages, because it consists of two webs stitched together, where each web has its own (single) weft selvage. Weft-twined fabrics 2009.043.01, 2009.098.13, and 2008.066.02 each have two warp selvages, representing complete loom lengths of 81.5 cm, 39.0 cm, and 8 cm, respectively.

Weft Selvages

Bird described 14 weft-passage practices and 22 different weft-selvage treatments (such as knotting and doubling: Bird et al. 1985: 279–280, fig. 193, 287–288, fig. 197). The majority of weft selvages (63 specimens, 53 fabrics) are identical to Bird's Code XIII.B (Bird et al. 1985: 280, fig. 193), where each weft was knotted prior to inserting into the fabric and after finishing the shot. Without having both selvages, however, it is impossible to know if this accurately describes the majority of weft-selvage practices. Of the 63 with selvage Code XIII, the majority (36 specimens, 25 fab-

rics) have overhand knots (Bird's Code XXIII.D, XXIII.E, XXIII.N), while 4 specimens/fabrics end in a loop around the outer warp (Bird Code XXIII.B); 9 specimens (8 fabrics) end in half hitches (Bird Code XXIII.K) about the outer warp; 15 specimens (11 fabrics) are new selvage types (fig. 12.7); and 6 were either not analyzed (1) or could not be analyzed (5).[6] In Specimen 2009.010.16, and possibly 3 others, a single weft interworks back and forth across the fabric. In all others with weft selvages the ends were knotted.

Most of the weft-end selvage knots have a beadlike, shiny appearance. They almost look like they were polished (for example, 2008.030.01.A), suggesting that they might have been decorative. Certainly packing the knots with mud and polishing them would have helped keep the knots from unraveling. Perhaps it had both functional and decorative purposes.

The presence of knots at the edges of weft-twined fabrics suggests that wefts were individually made (see "Making Weft Twining" below). This is in stark contrast to interlacing practices, where the weft—typically a single yarn wound onto a bobbin—was passed back and forth through

6. The total number of specimens listed associated with the various knotting structures is greater than the number of fabrics with selvage Type XXIII.B because 7 specimens have multiple knotting types.

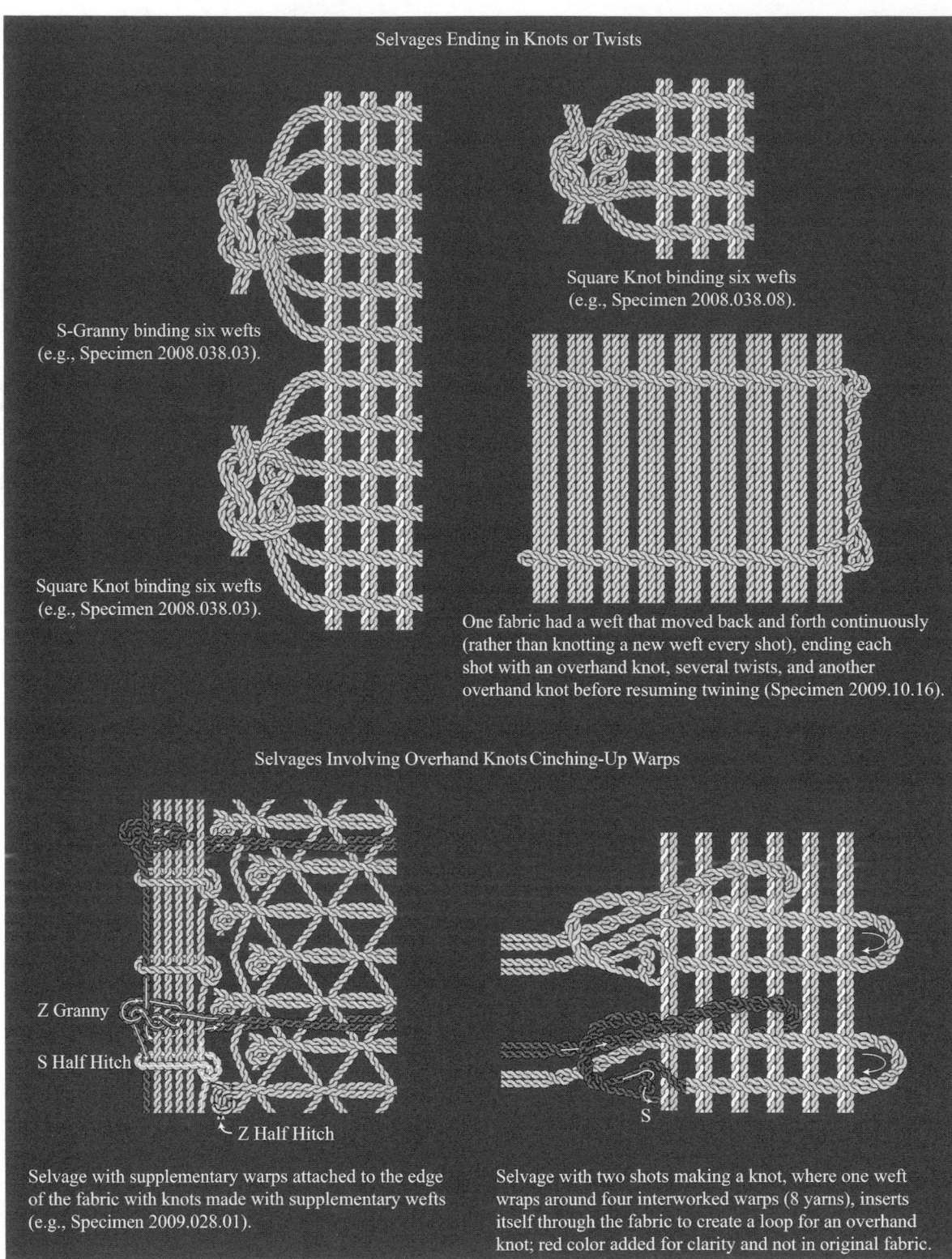

Selvages Ending in Knots or Twists

S-Granny binding six wefts
(e.g., Specimen 2008.038.03).

Square Knot binding six wefts
(e.g., Specimen 2008.038.03).

Square Knot binding six wefts
(e.g., Specimen 2008.038.08).

One fabric had a weft that moved back and forth continuously
(rather than knotting a new weft every shot), ending each
shot with an overhand knot, several twists, and another
overhand knot before resuming twining (Specimen 2009.10.16).

Selvages Involving Overhand Knots Cinching-Up Warps

Z Granny

S Half Hitch

Z Half Hitch

S

Selvage with supplementary warps attached to the edge
of the fabric with knots made with supplementary wefts
(e.g., Specimen 2009.028.01).

Selvage with two shots making a knot, where one weft
wraps around four interworked warps (8 yarns), inserts
itself through the fabric to create a loop for an overhand
knot; red color added for clarity and not in original fabric.

FIGURE 12.7. Newly encountered weft selvage structures.

sheds controlled by heddles. While it is possible that bobbins were used in weft twining, it seems unlikely, given that they were subsequently cut at the start and end of every shot. Cutting yarns and fabrics goes against well-documented Prehispanic and modern Andean beliefs that all things, both animate and inanimate, have a life force.

New Weft Selvage Types

The present study encountered at least 29 specimens (22 original fabrics) with selvage treatments not described by Bird. They differ from selvages previously encountered primarily in their use of supplemental yarns to reinforce and/or decorate weft edges (see fig. 12.7).

New Warp Selvages and Their Implications for Warping Practices

The analysis showed that 37 fabrics (39 specimens) have warp selvages. It was not possible to analyze 4 of the fabrics, while 33 have warp selvages made of compact-weft twined bands in a variety of yarn structures, interworking orders, colors, and materials generally like those described by Bird (Bird et al. 1985: 287–290, fig. 198). The selvage types from 2008.101.01.A–B, 2009.093.11, and 2009.043.01 are newly described. All structures support Bird's belief that both woven and twined fabrics were made on frames with fixed circular warps (Bird et al. 1985: 119–121). For instance, Specimens 2008.101.01.A–B are from phase 4 contexts and made of weft twining where the two warp ends are connected with figure-8 looping (fig. 12.8a; see online appendix M).

The tightness of the interworking suggests that the looping must have preceded the weft twining. This implies that it was done during warping, a process that created a circular warp and imparted elasticity to the warps during twining. Bird found a single fabric (41.2/2425) that had the same structure: weft twining with a central band of figure-8 looping. Like the specimens recently excavated, he noted that the looping "runs through the warp end-loops of the twined end-finishes" (Bird et al. 1985: 207), which not only suggests that this was a relatively well established warp-end treatment but confirms the use of a circular loom for at least some weft twining.

The warp ends in Specimen 2009.093.11 from Phase V contexts are tied in square knots (fig. 12.8b), which very well could have been tied during the warping process to create a circular warp. Another weft-twined fabric (2009.043.01) from Phase II contexts has warps with looped ends. The remnants of yarns are found in many of these loops, which suggests the loops were interlocked around a frame (fig. 12.8c). This is consistent with attributes of circular warps where the ends are interlocked. The fabric's structure is described online in appendix M.

The bands of figure-8 looping in 2008.101.01.A–B and the interlocked-looped ends of 2009.043.01 are compatible with Bird's belief that people used the same frame technology for both twining and interlacing, which consisted of two fixed sticks or cords. Warps were wound around the sticks/cords, turning about a locking cord. It is believed that heddles were not used at this early time (Bird 1979b: 121–125; Bird et al. 1985: 119–122). While this is true for weft twining, specimens of interlacing support the idea that true looms were in use as early as Phase III (discussed below in the section "Making Plain Weave and the Implications for Loom Type").

DECORATIVE TECHNIQUES

The majority of Huaca Prieta textiles were decorated: only 64 twined specimens (54 fabrics) have no traces of decoration. Considering that paste obscured the color of the majority of fabrics at the time they were analyzed, the actual number of decorated fabrics is almost certainly higher (see online appendix G).

Decoration was added to twined fabrics in various ways, from structural methods involving warp and/or weft manipulations to the addition of color (both natural and pigment) and materials other than cotton (such as milkweed). Although all types of patterning encountered in the present study (except random stripe patterning and element-knotting) were described by Bird, his focus was on warp patterning:

> Very rarely some color differences can be detected in different weft rows, but with this minor exception, the weft is not utilized for any patterning

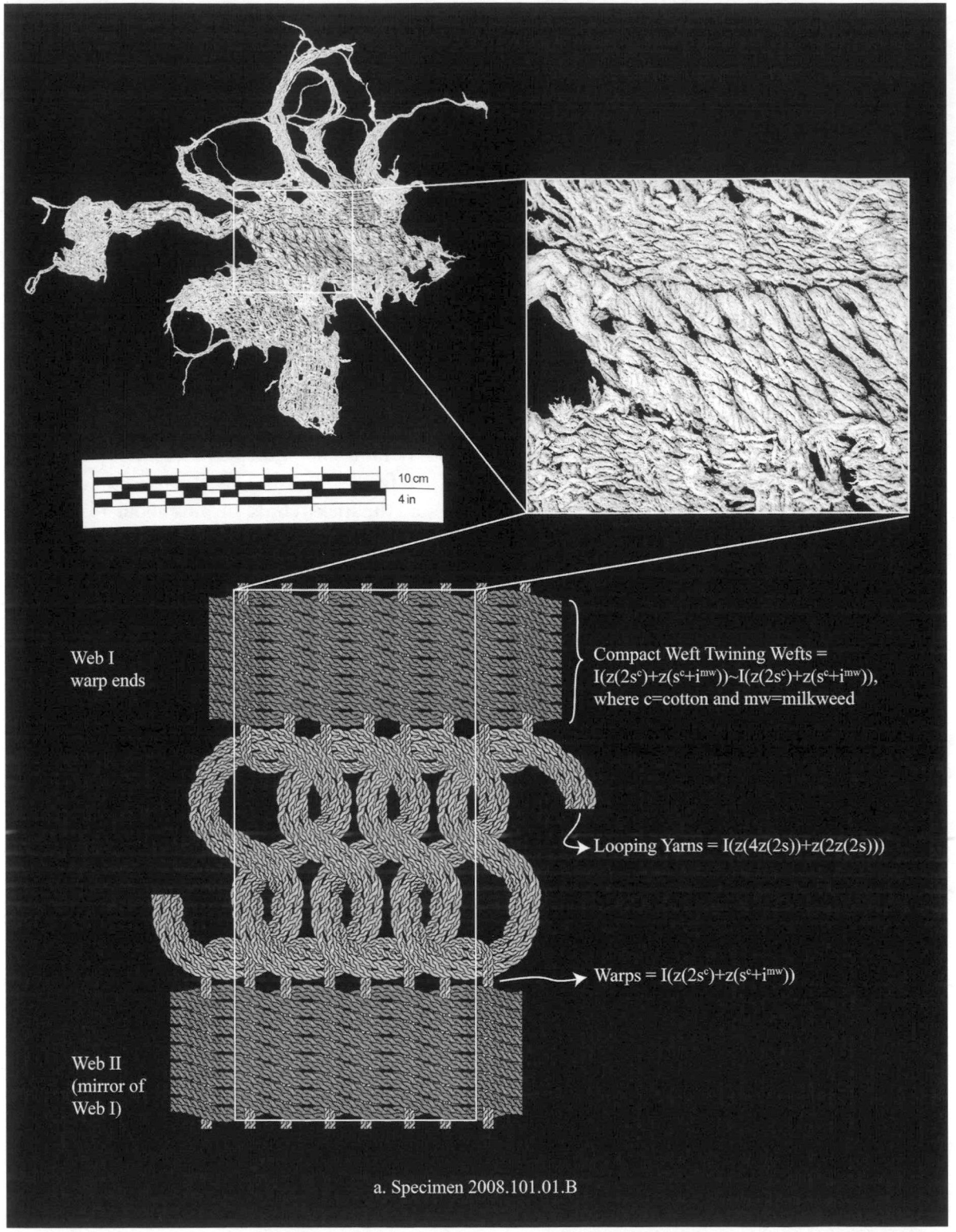

Web I
warp ends

Compact Weft Twining Wefts =
$I(z(2s^c)+z(s^c+i^{mw}))\sim I(z(2s^c)+z(s^c+i^{mw}))$,
where c=cotton and mw=milkweed

Looping Yarns = $I(z(4z(2s))+z(2z(2s)))$

Warps = $I(z(2s^c)+z(s^c+i^{mw}))$

Web II
(mirror of
Web I)

a. Specimen 2008.101.01.B

FIGURE 12.8. Possible warp end structures that indicate weft twining with circular warps on frames: *a*, figure-8 looping (Specimen 2008.101.01.B; photos by Lauren Badams); *b*, knotting (Specimen 2009.093.11; photos by Lauren Badams); *c*, interlocking (Specimen 2009.043.01; photos by author).

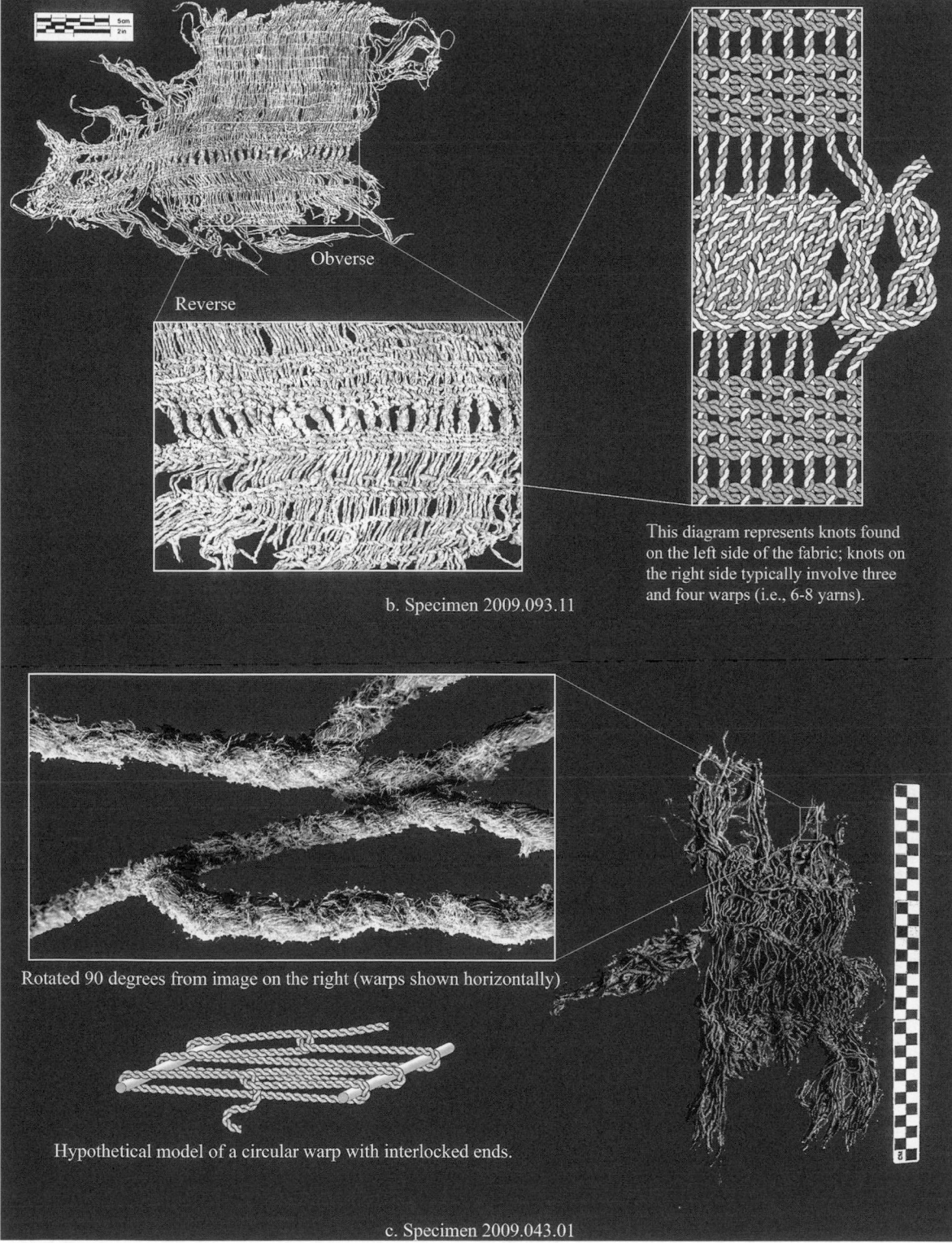

Obverse

Reverse

This diagram represents knots found on the left side of the fabric; knots on the right side typically involve three and four warps (i.e., 6-8 yarns).

b. Specimen 2009.093.11

Rotated 90 degrees from image on the right (warps shown horizontally)

Hypothetical model of a circular warp with interlocked ends.

c. Specimen 2009.043.01

effect. Patterning was achieved with the warp—either, in its simplest form, by varying the color or fiber, or by warp manipulation. Change in texture sometimes was produced by setting groups of several yarns in a field of paired warps. (Bird and Mahler 1951–1952: 75)

WARP PATTERNING

Warp patterning was encountered in many twined fabrics (see the types listed in appendix G online). Warp patterning is categorized by warp stripes, compound warps, and crossed warps.

WARP STRIPES

Warp stripes are the most common type of decoration. They are found in 183 weft-twining specimens (half of them). Warp-stripe patterning was achieved in several ways, including the use of natural colors of cotton, incorporating milkweed (for example, in bright white), and pigmenting yarns.

Natural Colors of Cotton

Natural hues of cotton found in Huaca Prieta fabrics include whites, tans, and browns; however, the present study found very little evidence for their use as stripes in textiles. Paste made it difficult to distinguish between white and tan and between tan and brown hues, but this was unimportant, because only two fabrics have used natural colors to create warp stripes. Bird found the same situation in his collection, where the passage of warps across the warp ends determined the presence of warp stripes, thereby avoiding the need to distinguish between now almost nonexistent colors.

Specimens 2009.157.01 and 2008.067.02 in the current study (from Phase II and early Phase V, respectively) were striped with natural colors of cotton. In both specimens, one color was natural tan or brown, while the other was a lighter color that was fugitive. The section on "Color, Pigment, and Dye" above notes that gold pigments might have been based on a mineral that was destructive to cotton over time. If this is the case in these specimens, then no textiles were decorated with only natural-cotton stripes. Adding milkweed or yarns with a mineral or dye pigment makes the majority of stripes in twined fabrics.

Pigments in Warp Stripes

Three colors were most likely used to make warp stripes: yellow-gold, red, and/or blue.

Yellow-Gold Stripes

No twined fabrics have been identified with yellow-gold stripes; however, this is almost certainly an error, because (1) the paste obscured the gold-yellow color, making it look brown; (2) the yellow-gold pigment was probably a mineral ochre that was rubbed on and easily washed off; and (3) there is some evidence that mineral ochre damaged fabrics, causing cotton yarns rubbed with pigment to disintegrate and leaving many fabrics with phantom stripes. As a result, I propose that fabrics with fugitive stripes (discussed below) might have been yellow-gold.

Red Stripes

The present study found that 21 twined specimens (12 fabrics) have warp stripes pigmented red, 18 (9 fabrics) of which are all-cotton warps, and some have fugitive cotton. Because red pigment washes away and is rarely present to form visible stripes, 8 more specimens (7 fabrics) are thought to have red warp stripes based on their association with traces of red pigment. Adding the number of fabrics known to have red stripes with those inferred to have them, potentially, 30 specimens (20 fabrics) have red stripes.

In addition, 5 specimens (5 fabrics) have red (or reddish) warps that are not striped, meaning that these fabrics were probably red all over. As noted earlier, red was probably rubbed onto fabric yarns but is fugitive, washing away over time. Therefore the likelihood is high that many more fabrics were originally red or red striped.

Blue Stripes

Analysis showed that 14 weft-twined specimens (10 fabrics) have blue warp stripes. Of these,

5 specimens (4 fabrics) are all-cotton-warp constructions and 9 specimens (6 fabrics) have warps with both cotton and milkweed. A single all-cotton specimen (2 fabrics) might also have red and blue stripes.

Milkweed Stripes

Milkweed was always added to warps by plying it with a single-ply cotton yarn, producing two-ply yarns. The milkweed-cotton warps give the fabric a white-speckled look (see appendix J online). Of the 169 specimens with milkweed stripes, only 11 (10 fabrics) also have red coloring, while 9 fabrics/specimens have milkweed with blue stripes. No fabrics with both red and blue warp stripes also have milkweed.

Fugitive Stripes

In many fabrics warp yarns are clearly missing. When remnants of the missing fiber are still present, they are always light-colored cotton. Bird encountered these fugitive stripes and found that the missing fiber was a lighter shade of cotton (Bird et al. 1985: 35, 137, 143, fig. 181). As noted earlier, several specimens of fugitive cotton also had remnants of a yellow-gold mineral, hinting that the fugitive cotton was associated with this mineral pigment, which might subsequently have caused their deterioration. If so, then the fugitive stripes might have been yellow-gold.

Invisible (Structural) Stripes

This study found 17 fabrics with cotton warps that have an S(2z) structure and are invisible to the naked eye. The practice of adding decoration that cannot be seen with the naked eye was apparently widely practiced in the ancient Andes but is relatively little discussed in the literature. Invisible structures are found at Cerrillos, where they are typically found in the wefts. At Cerrillos and probably elsewhere, they were probably involved with dualism and vitalistic principles (Splitstoser 2009: 243–245, 423–425, 463–467). The earliest examples are found in Phase III contexts at Huaca Prieta, but invisible structures were added through late Phase V times. They generally form no obvious patterns; their placement seems to intentionally avoid repetition, symmetry, or other patterning.

Stripe Patterns

Simple stripes involving a change in material (cotton and milkweed), color (either natural or applied or dyed), and/or yarn structure were identified in 180 specimens (130 fabrics), the majority of which are from Phase V contexts, although 35 are from mixed contexts, 14 come from early to late Phase IV, 11 fabrics are from middle and late Phase III contexts, and 3 are from Phase II contexts. The warp patterns of practically all warp-striped fabrics were recorded, even in fabrics whose sequence of warp patterns was obscured by the paste or confounded by fugitive fibers. The warp-stripe patterns for several fabrics are charted in table 12.7. Each column represents an individual stripe; warp structures are entered in the first row, and the number of warps in the stripe associated with that structure is listed below in the second row.

The table shows that several fabrics have repetition and/or symmetry in their sequence of warp structures, while stripe widths seems intentionally random. For example, 2009.072.03 and 2009.095.01 are charted in table 12.7a and table 12.7b, respectively. Both have three warp structures whose sequences repeat in predictable and quintessentially Andean ways,[7] and both specimens have stripe widths that are random. Warp-patterning tables reveal that the majority of warp-stripe width patterns are without predictable pattern, while warp structures sometimes have a pattern of repetition such as those in tables 12.7a–d and h. Sometimes the pattern of repetition is interrupted (table 12.7f) or breaks down (tables 12.7e and g).

The tables indicate that stripe widths (the number of warps that make up the width of a warp stripe) are both independent of warp structure and free of repetitive or symmetrical patterning. They are essentially without pattern other than some-

---

7. In some specimens, Structure 2 alternates with the other two (Structures 1 and 3), while Structures 1 and 3 alternate with each other.

Table 12.7. Warp stripe patterns in weft twined fabrics

a: Specimen 2009.072.03 (stripes with 1-2-3-2-3-2-1 structure symmetry and stripe widths made of even numbers of yarns seemingly randomly distributed)

Selvage	Structure*	1	2	3	2	3	2	1
	# Warps	1	6	2	2	2	6	4

*Structure 1 = $I(2z(2s^c))$; Structure 2 = $I(z(2s^c)+s^c)$; and Structure 3 = $I(2z(2s^c)+i(2s^c))$.

b: Specimen 2009.095.01 (1-2-3-2-3-2-1 structure symmetry; random # warps)

Selvage	Structure*	2	1	2	3	2	1	2	3	2	3	2	1	2	3	...
	# Warps	2	7	4	1	1	1	2	6	1	3	1	1	4	1	...

*Structure 1 = $I(2z(2s^c))$; Structure 2 = $I(z(2s^c)+z(s^c+i^{mw}))$; and Structure 3 = $I(2z(s^c+i^{mw}))$.

c: Specimen 2009.097.06 (repetitive structure pattern; random # warps that are all prime numbers)

Selvage	Structure*	3	1	3	4	3	4	3	2
	# Warps	5	5	3	1	3	1	5	29

*Structure 1 = $I(2z(2s^c))$; Structure 2 = $I(z(2s^c)+s^c)$; Structure 3 = $I(z(2s^c)+z(s^c+i^{mw}))$; and Structure 4 = $I(z(s^c+i^{mw})+i(3z(2s^c)))$.

d: Specimen 2009.071.09 (repetitive structure; random # warps that are all even numbers)

Selvage	Structure*	2	1	2	1	2
	# Warps	6	4	8	4	2

*Structure 1 = $I(2z(2s^c))$; Structure 2 = $I(z(2s^c)+z(s^c+z^{mw}))$.

e: Specimen 2009.098.20 (interrupted structure pattern; random # warps that are almost all even numbers)

Selvage	Structure*	2	3	2	3	2	3	4	2	4	5	1	2
	# Warps	3+	4	4	4	4	4	2	12	2	4	3?	4+

*Structure 1 = $I(2z(2s^c))$; Structure 2 = $I(z(2s^c)+z(s^c+i^{mw}))$; Structure 3 = $I(2z(s^c+i^{mw}))$; Structure 4 = $I(z(s^c+i^{mw})+i(2z(2s^c))+s^c)$; Structure 5 = $I(z(2s^c)+z^c)$.

Table 12.7. Continued

f: Specimen 2009.094.01 (interrupted structure pattern; random # warps): Web I

Selvage	Structure*	1	2	1	2	1	3	4	1	4	1	5	1
	# Warps	7+	2	20	3	13	1	1	2	2	2	2	68

*Structure 1 = I(2z(2s^c)); Structure 2 = I(z(2s^c)+z(s^c+z^{mw})); Structure 3 = I(2z(s^c+i^{mw})+z(2s^c)); Structure 4 = I(z(s^c+i^{mw})+i(2z(2s^c))); Structure 5 = I(3z(2s^c)).

Specimen 2009.094.01 (repetitive structure of interruptions): Web II

Selvage	Structure*	1	2	1	2	1	2	5	1	2	5	2	5	2	4	2	5	2	1	2	1	2	1	2
	# Warps	20	9	11	13	8	3	2	1	1	2	1	1	1	1	2	2	2	4	12	8	12	7	5+

*Structure 1 = I(2z(2s^c)); Structure 2 = I(z(2s^c)+z(s^c+z^{mw})); Structure 3 = I(2z(s^c+i^{mw})+z(2s^c)); Structure 4 = I(z(s^c+i^{mw})+i(2z(2s^c))); Structure 5 = I(3z(2si^{mw})).

g: Specimen 2009.098.15.A (interrupted structure pattern; random # warps)

Selvage	Structure*	3	2	4	3	4	3	1	3	4	3
	# Warps	6	6	2	16	2	5	2	6	2	6

*Structure 1 = I(2z(2s^c)); Structure 2 = I(z(2s^c)+z(s^c+i^{mw})); Structure 3 = I(z(2s^c)+s^c); Structure 4 = I(z(s^c+i^{mw})+z(2s^c)+s^c).

h: Specimen 2009.107.02 (plain weave with repetitive structure and random # warps, which are all odd and prime numbers)

Selvage	Structure*	1	2	1	2	1
	# Warps	29	13	7	17	23

*Structure 1 = I(2s^c)); Structure 2 = Z(2s^c).

times demonstrating all odd (tables 12.7c and h) or all even numbers (table 12.7d), while tables 12.7e and g are almost all even but with some odd numbers randomly interspersed. Tables 12.7c and 12.7.h chart textiles with stripes whose widths consist of all prime numbers.

Is the lack of patterning intentional or merely coincidental? I suspect the former, even though proving it is difficult given the small sample size and incomplete nature of the majority of fab-rics under study here. Repetition in warp-stripes is actually difficult to avoid, given the way warp yarns are (and presumably were) wrapped around stakes during the process of making the warp.

Could the patterns found in warp stripes be due to human error rather than to ancient pre-occupation with random patterning? Of course human error, including those made by textile ana-lysts, is always possible; however, warp patterns were checked and double-checked, yet the lack of pattern persists even when attempts are made to correct for possible inaccuracies inherent in data collection.[8]

These data strongly suggest that people might have striven for repetition in the structural makeup of warp stripes while avoiding repetition in stripe width. This goes against the vast majority of warp patterning found in other Prehispanic textiles, yet the idea that people created fabrics intentionally lacking repetitive patterning is tantalizing and mirrors other decorative practices observed at the site, such as the patterns of randomly placed knots in warp and weft elements of weft-twined fabrics (discussed in the section "Element Knots" below).

While intentional lack of pattern might seem to be an unusual decorative strategy, it was practiced elsewhere in the Andes. For example, color patterns were broken in both Wari and Inka tunics, perhaps as a way to draw attention to particular aspects of the design (for example, Stone 1986, 2007). Could the Huaca Prieta stripe patterns be the earliest known example of this practice?

COMPLEMENTARY WARPS

Complementary warps are compound structures. Compound weaves are fabrics that have more than two sets of elements, either warp or weft or both (Emery 1966: 140). The extra set(s) can be complementary (meaning that the set is an integral part of the ground weave) or supplementary (where removal of the extra element would not alter the ground). Compound constructions can be single-faced (only one finished face), double-faced (the fabrics are identical on either face, but the colors on one face are the opposite of the colors on the other face), or two-faced (two finished but different faces).

Fabrics 2008.016.01.A–C, 2009.015.01.A–B, and 2009.149.01.A–B have stripes made with complementary-warp structures as defined for woven fabrics by Emery (1966: 150). All three structures involve warp substitution as discussed for woven fabrics by Ann Rowe (1977: 50–52). Complementary-warp weft twining with warp substitution at Huaca Prieta essentially means that a pattern was created by using two contrasting warp types (differing in material and/or color) that interworked ground wefts. When one of the pair of contrasting warps was interworking the ground wefts, the other warp was floated on the opposite face, creating a two-faced fabric. Floated warps never span more than three wefts; when the design calls for longer color spans of color, warps are intermittently bound by wefts (fig. 12.9).

The three fabrics with complementary warp with warp substitution are reported online in appendix M.

CROSSED WARPS

Weft twining with crossed-warp patterning is a hallmark of textile-making practices at Huaca Prieta. Much attention is paid to this particular technique not only by Bird (Bird 1952, 1962, 1963a; Bird et al. 1985; Bird and Mahler 1951–1952) but by others, who are intrigued by the art it produced (for example, Bischof 1994; Grieder 1986; Lumbreras 1974). The use of crossed-warp patterning is essentially limited to Phase IV; except for Specimens 2009.052.01.A from a Phase II context and 2008.069.01.A from an early Phase V context. The number of twined fabrics decreased from Phase IV to V (see appendix L online), which might explain why crossed warp patterning did not persist to the end of the Preceramic period at Huaca Prieta.

This study found that 23 specimens (13 fabrics) of weft twining have crossed-warp patterning. In the majority of these fabrics, warp crossings either created geometric patterning or shifted colored and/or milkweed warps to change stripe patterns: see "Miscellaneous and Accidental Type (Bird Group I)." Figurative designs were encountered only in the Condor Type (Bird Group V).

The analysis showed that 16 specimens (7 fabrics) with warp crossings are associated with pigments and represent Groups I (Miscellaneous and Accidental), III (Single-Warp Transport), and V (Condor): 5 specimens (1 fabric) have red; 2 specimens (2 fabrics) have blue; and 9 specimens (4 fabrics) have both blue and red pigment. Of these, 5 fabrics (8 specimens) have colored warp stripes, and 5 (13 specimens) have weft bands. The study found that 5 crossed-warp specimens (4 fabrics),

---

8. In one exercise the numbers of warp yarns in a stripe were replaced with symbols indicating qualitative values of thin, medium, and wide (and so forth) yarns.

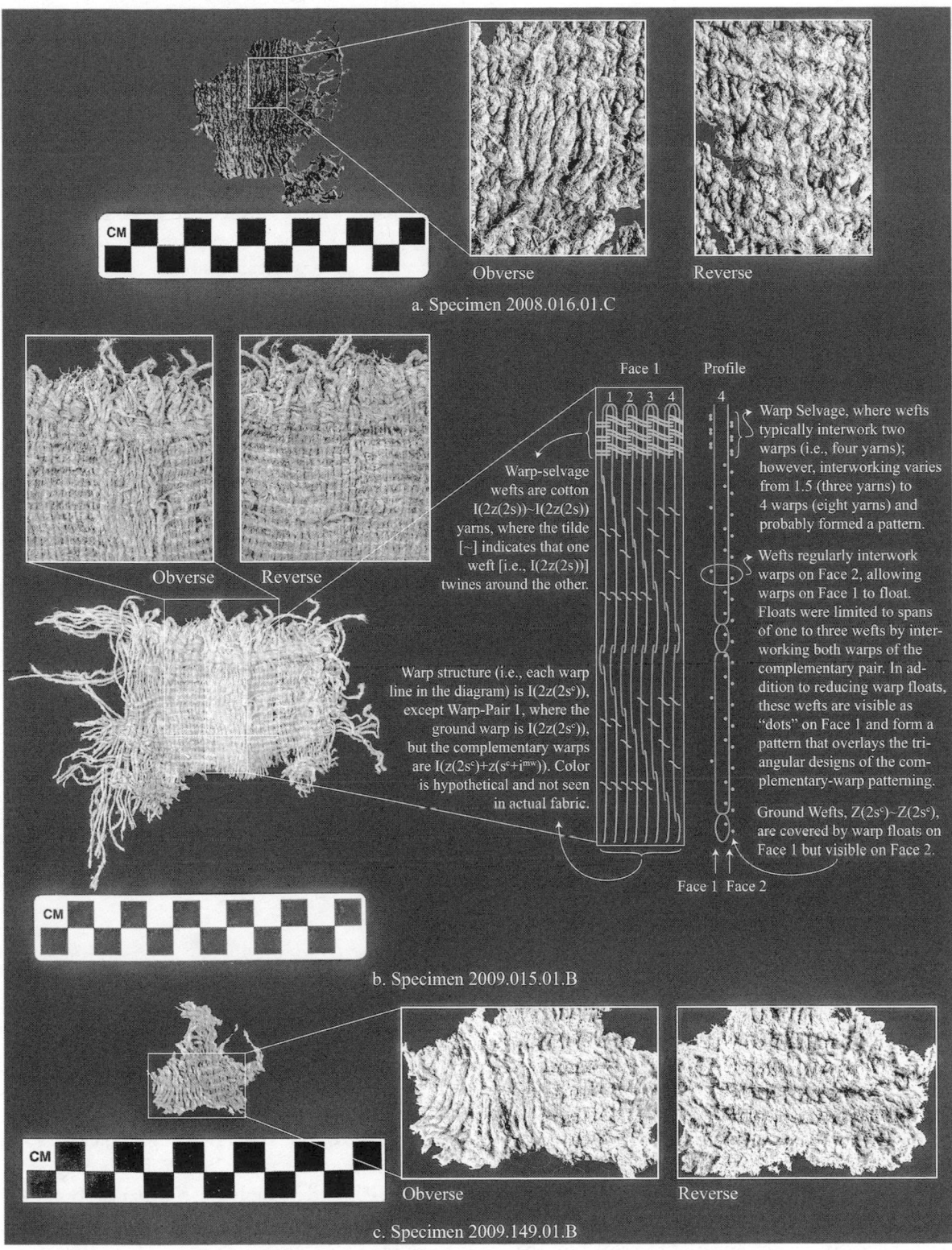

Obverse

Reverse

a. Specimen 2008.016.01.C

CM

Obverse

Reverse

Face 1   Profile

1 2 3 4   4

Warp-selvage
wefts are cotton
I(2z(2s))~I(2z(2s))
yarns, where the tilde
[~] indicates that one
weft [i.e., I(2z(2s))]
twines around the other.

Warp structure (i.e., each warp
line in the diagram) is I(2z(2s^c)),
except Warp-Pair 1, where the
ground warp is I(2z(2s^c)),
but the complementary warps
are I(z(2s^c)+z(s^c+i^{mw})). Color
is hypothetical and not seen
in actual fabric.

Warp Selvage, where wefts
typically interwork two
warps (i.e., four yarns);
however, interworking varies
from 1.5 (three yarns) to
4 warps (eight yarns) and
probably formed a pattern.

Wefts regularly interwork
warps on Face 2, allowing
warps on Face 1 to float.
Floats were limited to spans
of one to three wefts by interworking both warps of the
complementary pair. In addition to reducing warp floats,
these wefts are visible as
"dots" on Face 1 and form a
pattern that overlays the triangular designs of the complementary-warp patterning.

Ground Wefts, Z(2s^c)~Z(2s^c),
are covered by warp floats on
Face 1 but visible on Face 2.

Face 1 Face 2

CM

b. Specimen 2009.015.01.B

CM

Obverse

Reverse

c. Specimen 2009.149.01.B

FIGURE 12.9. Complementary warp patterning with warp substitution in weft twining: *a*, Specimen 2008.016.01.C; *b*, Specimen 2009.015.01.B: photos and diagram (based on Specimen 2009.015.01.B, but structure is representative of all three specimens; shading added for contrast; no color was noted in the original fabric); *c*, Specimen 2009.149.01.B. (See color plates.)

representing all types except Group IV (Woodland), have milkweed warp stripes.

Data on milkweed and pigments suggest that crossed-warp patterned fabrics were highly decorated and originally had (in addition to figures and/or patterns made with crossed warp patterning) stripes and/or bands made with pigments and/or milkweed. The use of color with crossed warps typically results in double-faced fabrics, where the design on one face would have the opposite color from the other face, presuming that they used two colors. Most of this color today has vanished.

Crossed-warp patterning is commonly found at Preceramic sites, such as Asia (Engel 1963c: 27, fig. 30), Salinas de Chao (Olivera Alegre 2006: 71, fig. 78), Gavilanes (Bonavia 1982: 107, figs. 122, 123), Aspero (Feldman 1986: 34), and La Galgada (Grieder 1988: 158, fig. 110). Complex figurative designs made of crossed-warp patterning, however, are rare. The scarcity of figurative designs might be due to uneven preservation conditions, where not enough of a fabric remains to determine its structure or design.

Another possible explanation might be the difficulty in plotting warp crossings to determine the "design." Virtually all pigments that might have been rubbed onto the yarns to add color to crossed-warp patterning are gone, leaving monochrome fabrics, whose patterning can only be "seen" today by plotting each and every warp crossing. Technical descriptions of specimens with crossed-warp patterning are described below according to group types developed by Bird (fig. 12.10).

Miscellaneous and Accidental Type (Bird Group I)

Specimens 2009.052.02 (fig. 12.10a), 2009.071.16, and 2009.154.02B have crossed-warp patterning defined by Bird et al. (1985: 149–151, 275–276) as Miscellaneous and Accidental Type. Specimens 2009.071.16 and 2009.154.02.B are of the subtype code 10, which means that the fabric is "either too poorly preserved or too small for specific group classification" yet has "evidence of some transposed-warp movement either accidental or deliberate" (Bird et al. 1985: 275). Specimen 2009.052.02 is of subtype 12, in which the warp crossings were most likely made to redistribute

warps to create a color patterning, where warps changed from alternate paired to regular twining. Each specimen is described online in appendix M.

Pair Transposition Type (Bird Group II)

Specimen 2008.035.01 (fig. 12.10b) has crossed warps that resemble Bird Group II Code 21 (Bird et al. 1985: 151, 275–277), where all the warps cross at the same weft shot, similar to gauze crosses in plain weave. Damage to the textile appears to have degraded one of the weft yarns in the shot, making the crossed-warp structure look like gauze. If there was never a second weft yarn, then the structure is gauze and is a unique instance of weft twining combined with gauze, but this is unlikely.

Single Warp Transposition Type (Bird Group III)

The Single Warp Transposition Type described by Bird et al. (1985: 151–152, 276–277, fig. 194) is found on 5 specimens (4 fabrics). Their structures are described online in appendix M.

Woodland Type (Bird Group IV)

In this study 1 specimen is classified as having Woodland Type warp crossings as defined by Bird et al. (1985: 154, 276–277). The specimen (fig. 12.10d) also has Single Warp Transposition Type crossings (Group III).

Condor Type (Bird Group V)

In the present study 11 specimens (6 fabrics) are classified as having Condor Type (Code V.51) warp crossings as defined by Bird et al. (1985: 160–161, 277–278, fig. 192). The Condor Type was made famous at Huaca Prieta (see the description online in appendix M) but is found at other Preceramic sites, including Salinas de Chao (Olivera Alegre 2006: 70–71) and possibly Los Gavilanes (Bonavia 1982: 109, photo 119).

Geometric Type (Bird Group VI)

The analysis showed that 6 specimens (2 fabrics) are interworked in a style called the Geometric Type (Bird Code VI.61) as defined by Bird

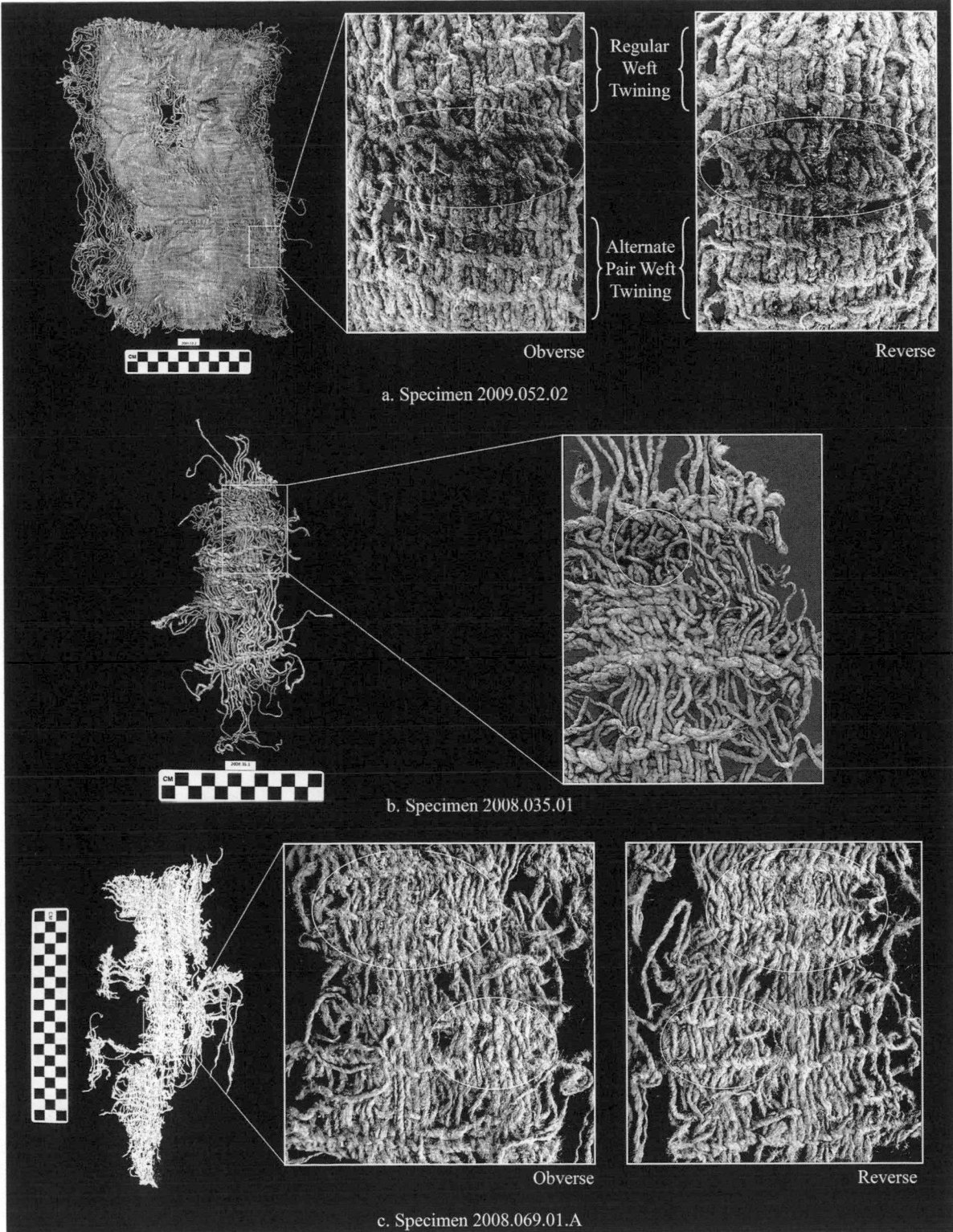

FIGURE 12.10. Structure diagram of warp crossing groups discussed in the present study: *a*, Miscellaneous and Accidental Type (Specimen 2009.052.02); *b*, Pair Transposition Type (Specimen 2008.035.01); *c*, Single Warp Transposition Type (Specimen 2008.069.01.A); *d*, Woodland Type (Specimen 2008.100.04); *e*, Condor Type (Specimen 2008.096.01) (note 360 degree twists in compact-weft bands); shading was added for contrast and is not present in the actual specimen; *f*, Geometric Type (Specimen 2008.075.03.A–B). (See color plates.)

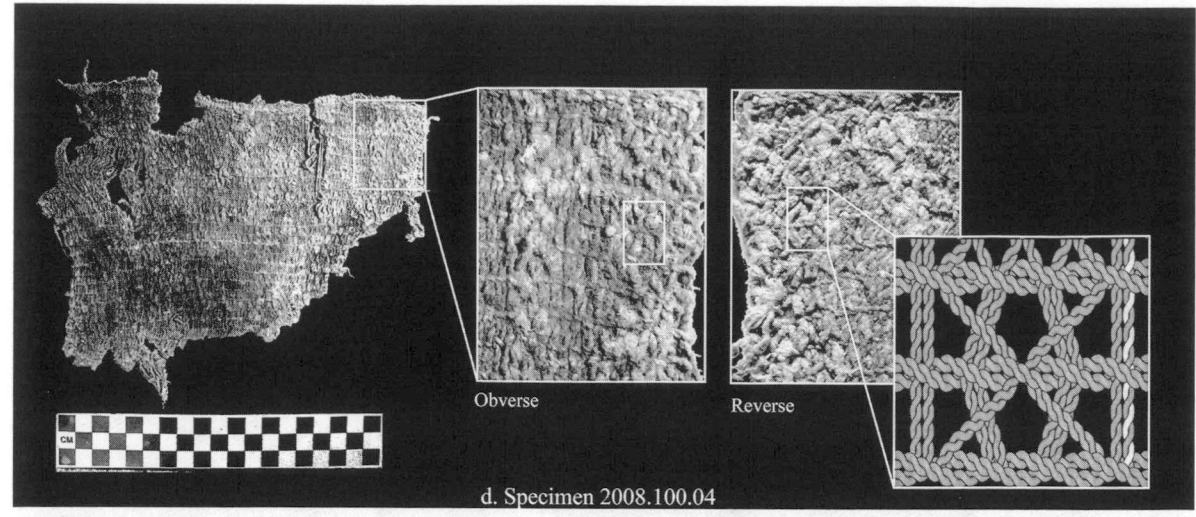

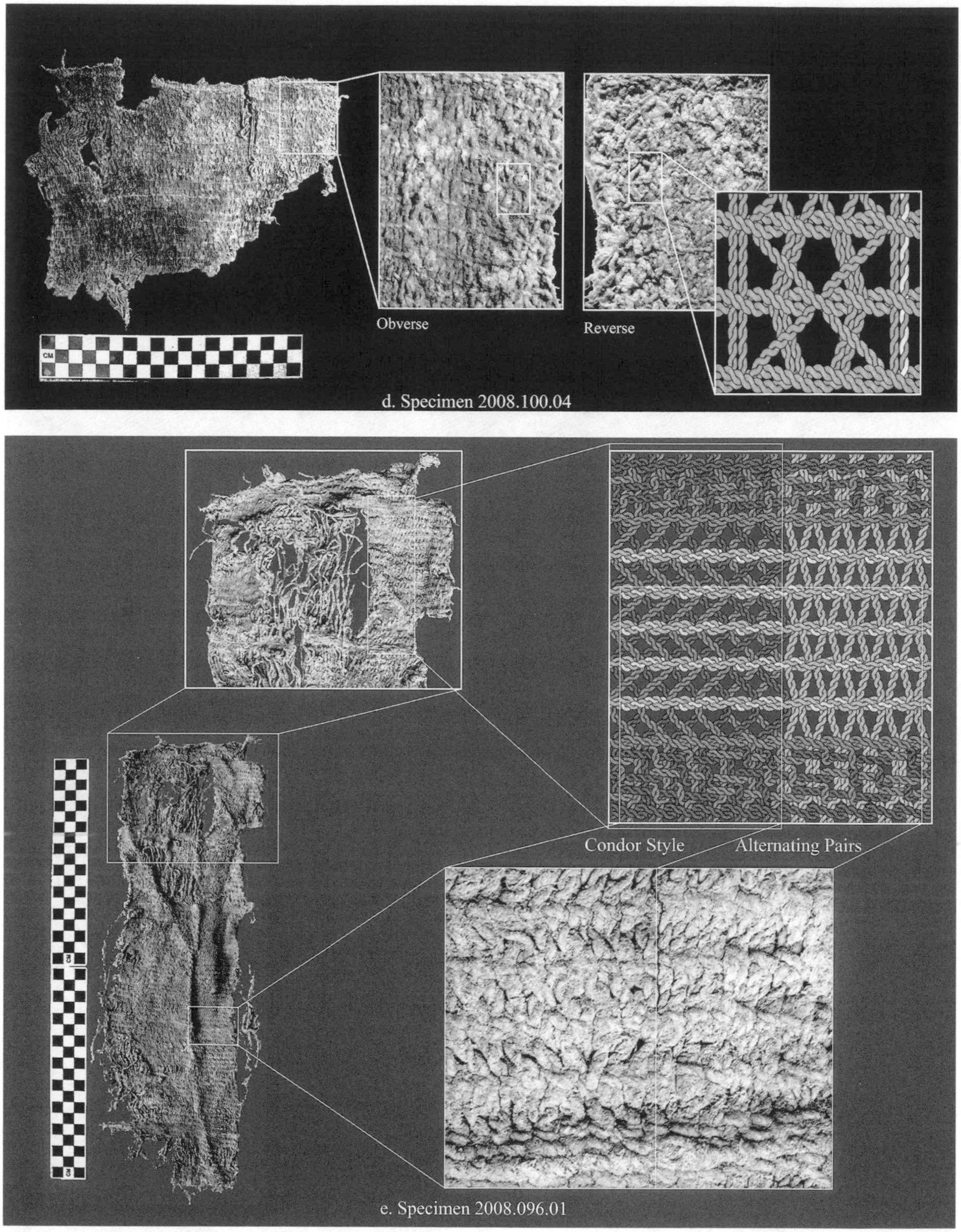

d. Specimen 2008.100.04

Obverse Reverse

Condor Style Alternating Pairs

e. Specimen 2008.096.01

FIGURE 12.10. Continued

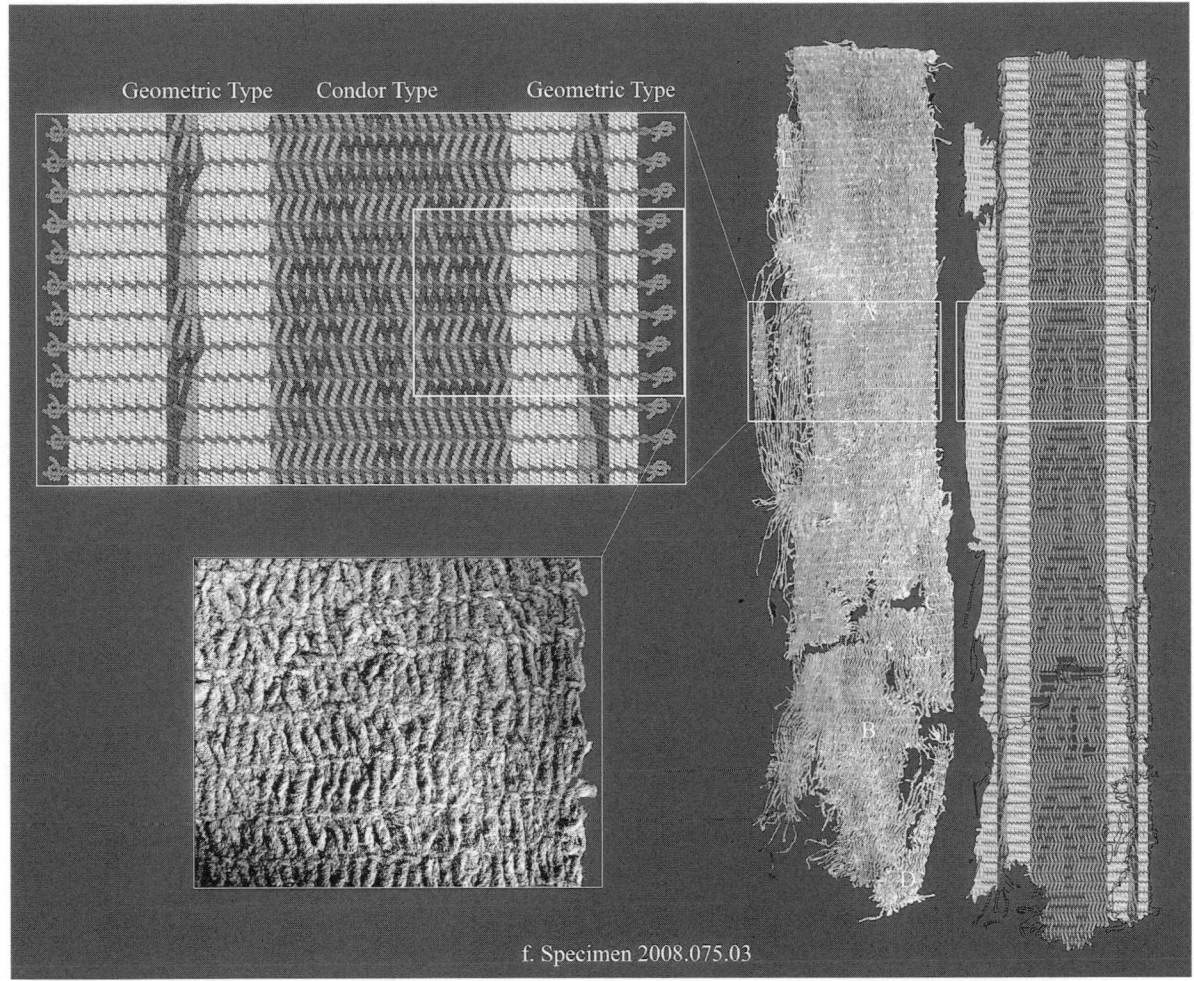

Geometric Type   Condor Type   Geometric Type

f. Specimen 2008.075.03

FIGURE 12.10. Continued

et al. (1985: 187, 277–279). Their structures are described online in appendix M. Most fabrics decorated with the Geometric Type have geometric designs. The warp crossings in Specimen 2009.071.19 formed a vertical diamond pattern across the left side of the fabric.

Shift and Return Type (Bird Group VII)

No fragments were encountered interworked with crossed warps of the Shift and Return Type (Bird et al. 1985: 279). This is surprising, because it was commonly used to make diamond patterns at such Preceramic sites as Asia (Engel 1957b: pl. 22b), Caral (for example, Shady S. 2004: 109), and Los Gavilanes (Bonavia 1982: 107–108, photo 119, fig. 125).

WEFT PATTERNING

Weft patterning in weft twining is accomplished through a diverse number of techniques. This is largely because wefts, unlike warps, whose patterns are established during the warping process (although Huaca Prietans avoided this through the use of crossed-warp patterning described above), can be changed at any time during the process of interworking. Wefts were easily changed at any time during the twining process.

The weft-patterning practiced at Huaca Prieta are presented in eight categories that include multiple types of wefts (such as color, material, diameter, and structure); discontinuous wefts; compound wefts (for example, using supplementary and/or complementary sets of wefts); eccentric wefts (that are inserted in a diagonal and/or cut across other weft shots, and so forth); multiple interworking orders (such as the number of interworking warp elements); regular versus alternating pairs of warps; half and/or full twists; and combinations of these. Huaca Prietans created diverse patterned effects from simple colored bands to complex geometric patterns (described below). Their structures are diagrammed in fig. 12.11.

SIMPLE CHANGES IN WEFTS: WEFT BANDS

Perhaps the simplest way to add texture and contrast is through a change in weft color, structure, and/or material. For example, many Huaca Prieta fabrics have bands created by using thick wefts. This is in contrast to many Preceramic sites, such as Asia and Caral, where wefts were somewhat finer than the warps (for example, Engel 1963c: 30, fig. 40; Shady S. 2004: 109, 204–205), perhaps to reduce the visibility of wefts and keep patterning in the warps, since weft-twining is already a warp-dominant fabric structure. At Huaca Prieta the majority of ground weft diameters are the same as warp diameters; but weft diameter is greater in fabrics with simple weft patterning, perhaps to increase their visibility.

COLOR

Blue wefts were used in a large number of Huaca Prieta fabrics. These wefts frequently were also supplementary, thicker in diameter, and often of a different structure than the ground wefts. The blue in twined fabrics is typically much darker (some almost black) than the blue found in plain weave. Because the earliest plain weave fabrics with blue are light blue, and plain-weave is found as early as weft twining at Huaca Prieta, the differences in color between plain-weave and weft twining is probably the result of different dye processes rather than age. This suggests that different groups of people might have been responsible for dying plain-weave and weft-twining fibers. This idea is further supported by differences found in plain-weave and weft-twining yarn attributes.

STRUCTURE

A widespread feature found in textiles at sites like Los Gavilanes and La Galgada involved the use of both Z- and S-spun yarns in weft-twined fabrics (and plain weave) to create patterns (for example, Bonavia 1982: 102–103, table 105; Moseley and Barrett 1969: 163; Shady S. 2004: 204–205). The majority of weft yarns at Huaca Prieta are Z(2s); when they are combined with yarns different from Z(2s), they are here considered decorative. Decoration involving weft structures includes any type of weft structure that creates contrast, such as any counter-spun wefts, single-ply wefts, and multi-plied high-order weft yarns, all of which are found in Huaca Prieta weft twining.

Several specimens have counter-spun weft yarns at Huaca Prieta, including Specimens 2009.028.01 and 2009.028.04.A, whose structures are depicted in fig. 12.11a and described online in appendix M. These bands in Specimen 2009.028.01 consist of single shots of $S(2z^c)\sim S(2z^c)$ in a fabric with ground wefts that are otherwise $Z(2s^c)\sim Z(2s^c)$.[9] Specimen 2009.028.04.A–C has bands consisting solely of $Z(2s^c)\sim Z(2s^c)$ shots as well as bands of $Z(2s^c)\sim Z(2s^c)$ alternating with $S(2z^c)\sim S(2z^c)$ shots.

COUNTERED TWINING

Countered twining produces a spiral that is opposite to the prevailing twist. All twining in recently excavated Huaca Prieta fabrics with a single exception has a Z-twist or a Z-spiral. Specimen 2008.067.01 (fig. 12.11b) has both S- and Z-twist twining that alternates throughout the fabric. The specimen also has supplementary discontinuous wefts inserted between the ground wefts (described in the section "Supplementary Wefts" below). Bird encountered 5 examples with alternating twist and found 19 examples of it in compact bands either as selvages (15 examples) or in the body of the fabric (4 examples). Engel (1963c: 30, fig. 40) frequently encountered countered weft twining at Asia.

9. When describing fabric structures, I use "~" to designate interworking involving twining.

MATERIAL

The use of wefts with both cotton and milkweed plied together was very common. Pure milkweed and occasionally juncus yarns, however, were occasionally used to create simple weft patterning. These milkweed and juncus wefts are also of a different structure, diameter, and color from cotton wefts: the milkweed and juncus wefts are typically single-ply and significantly thicker than the others. Furthermore, they are usually discontinuous and/or supplementary, as discussed below.

COMPACT WEFT TWINING

Compact weft twining was used to create weft-faced bands. Such bands occur most frequently at warp selvages (20 specimens/18 fabrics), which was done to strengthen the warp end while at the same time adding a decorative touch. Compact weft twining was added to make decorative weft bands in 13 specimens (10 fabrics), 1 of which has a compact-weft-band warp selvage. Structurally compact bands have wefts that usually interwork alternate pairs of warps (or three warps) in fabrics with regular weft twining.

Compound Weft Constructions

Two categories of compound-weft constructions were encountered: complementary wefts and supplementary wefts, where complementary-weft patterning is discussed in the section "Full versus Half Twist." Supplementary wefts are further classified into three subcategories: supplementary discontinuous wefts, regular supplementary wefts, and supplementary eccentric wefts. All compound-weft constructions typically incorporate wefts with materials, diameters, yarn structures, and colors different from ground wefts.

SUPPLEMENTARY DISCONTINUOUS WEFTS

The majority of weft-twining with supplementary wefts at Huaca Prieta involve discontinuous wefts that are almost always supplementary. Supplementary discontinuous wefts were frequently used to make weft patterning at Huaca Prieta (fig. 12.11c). One of the more interesting structures with discontinuous wefts is spaced weft twining with ground wefts that span the fabric, selvage to selvage, with discontinuous wefts that interwork only one side of the fabric, where each weft turns back at the same warp thus dividing the fabric in half (for example, Specimens 2008.027.01.A and C). In other fabrics discontinuous wefts create patterns, as in 2009.094.01, which was mentioned in the section "Stripe Patterns."

REGULAR SUPPLEMENTARY WEFTS

Regular supplementary wefts are defined here as elements that travel from edge to edge and are thicker and sometimes of a different material (such as milkweed or juncus) and/or different interworking pattern than ground wefts (such as interworking multiple warps). If the supplementary weft were removed, the fabric would lose none of its integrity. A common regular supplementary-weft practice is the use of thick, Z-spun (single-ply) wefts interworking three warp yarns (1.5 warps); above and below them are cotton Z(2s) ground wefts that interwork warps 1~1. Specimen 2008.100.05 has regular supplementary wefts in a compact weft band that create a chevron design (fig. 12.11d).

Often weft patterning involves both supplementary and discontinuous weft elements, such as Specimen 2008.067.01, described online in appendix M.

SUPPLEMENTARY ECCENTRIC WEFTS

The term "eccentric wefts" normally refers to a specific type of discontinuous weft found in tapestry. At Huaca Prieta, however, eccentric wefts are not confined to weft-faced constructions. They are not common, but when they occur they meander across ground wefts (fig. 12.11e) forming diagonals, although not enough of any of them are left to determine an overall pattern. An example is Specimen 2009.093.01, whose structure is described online in appendix M.

CHANGES IN INTERWORKING ORDER

Normal interworking order at Huaca Prieta is 1~1, which means that wefts interwork one warp (two yarns) over one and under one. Typical changes to

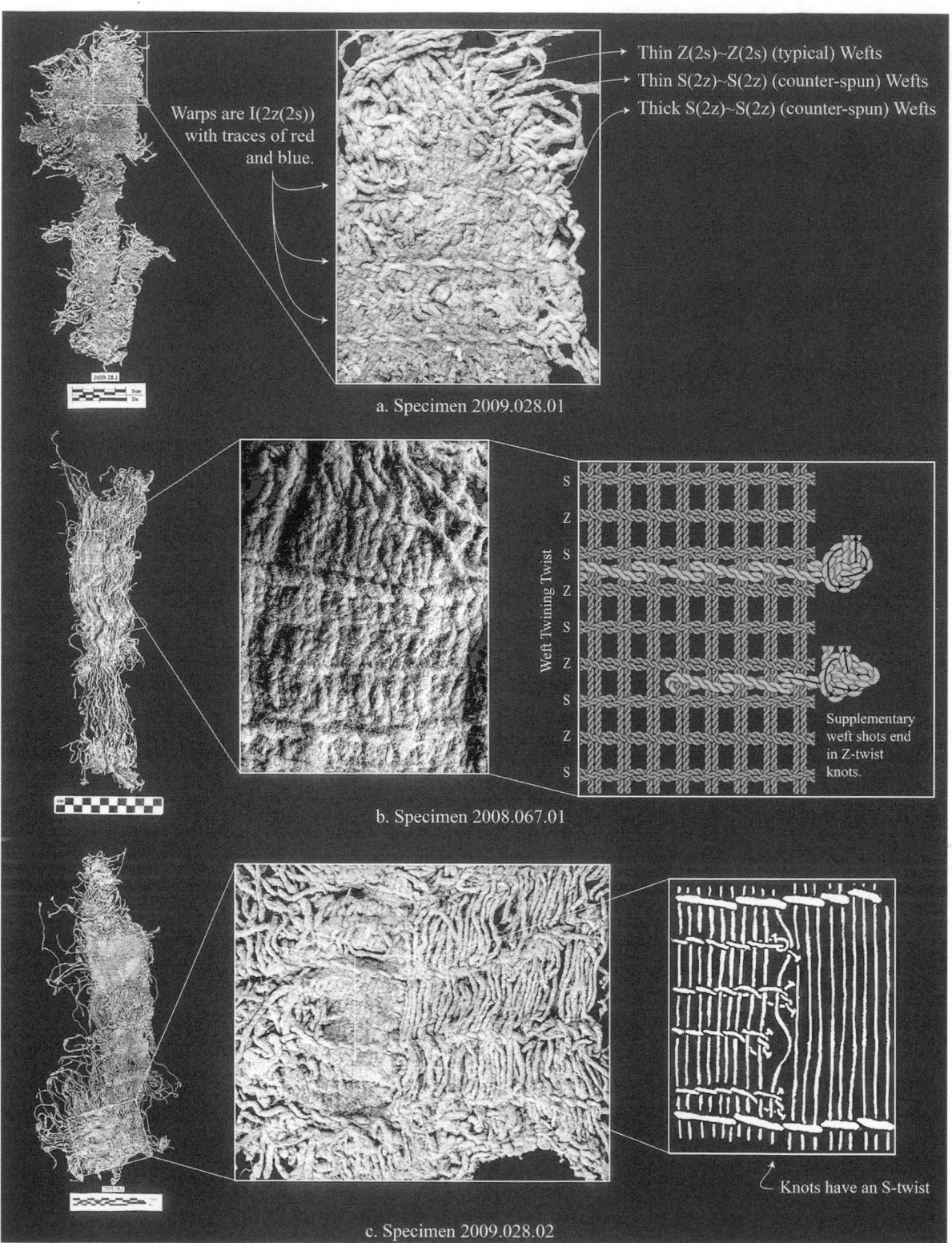

Warps are I(2z(2s)) with traces of red and blue.

Thin Z(2s)~Z(2s) (typical) Wefts
Thin S(2z)~S(2z) (counter-spun) Wefts
Thick S(2z)~S(2z) (counter-spun) Wefts

a. Specimen 2009.028.01

Weft Twining Twist

S
Z
S
Z
S
Z
S
Z
S

Supplementary weft shots end in Z-twist knots.

b. Specimen 2008.067.01

Knots have an S-twist

c. Specimen 2009.028.02

FIGURE 12.11. Structural diagrams of categories of weft patterning: *a*, yarn structure (wefts with counterspun yarns) (Specimen 2009.028.01; photos by Lauren Badams); *b*, countered twining (Specimen 2008.067.01); *c*, supplementary discontinuous wefts (Specimen 2009.028.02; photos by Lauren Badams; note that supplementary wefts of left side are alternate-pair weft twining); *d*, eccentric supplementary wefts (Specimen 2008.100.05); *e*, eccentric supplementary wefts (Specimen 2009.093.01; photos by Lauren Badams); *f*, changes in interworking order (Specimen 2009.072.04).

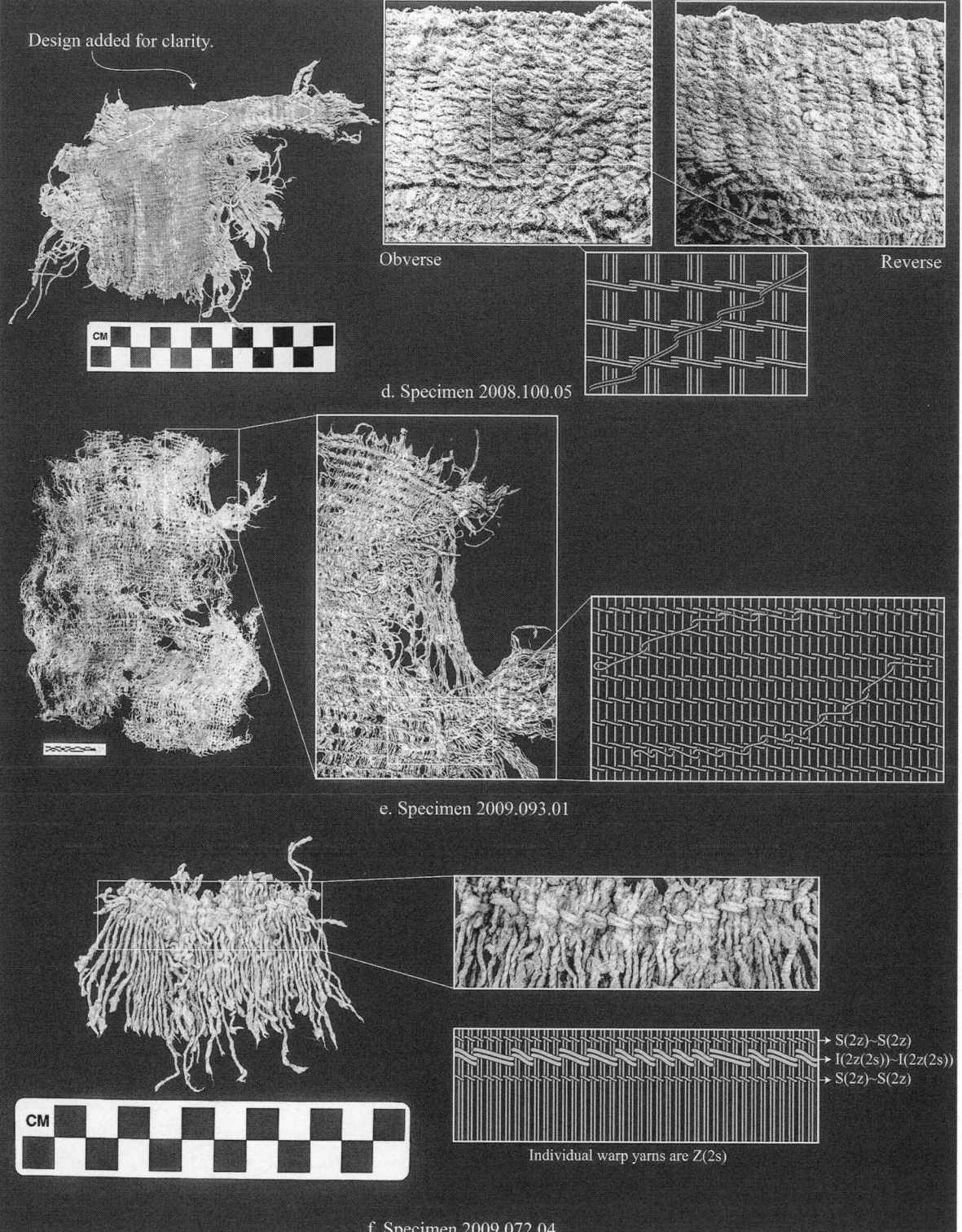

Design added for clarity.

Obverse

Reverse

d. Specimen 2008.100.05

e. Specimen 2009.093.01

S(2z)~S(2z)
I(2z(2s))~I(2z(2s))
S(2z)~S(2z)

Individual warp yarns are Z(2s)

f. Specimen 2009.072.04

interworking order involve groups of 1.5 (three yarns) or 2 warps (four yarns); however, interworking of 3 (six yarns, and so forth), and 4 warps is encountered, rarely more, unless it involves groups of warps at the weft selvage.

Interworking order was plotted to look for patterning. For example, Specimen 2009.072.04 (fig. 12.11f) has a single weft shot that interworks warps in multiple interworking orders: [2–4–2–3 –3–3–2–2–2–2–2–4–2–3–2], where the brackets represent the edges of the fabric. Some patterns are regular, while others (like the example above) seem random like some warp-stripe patterns. Their significance is unclear. When wefts interwork multiple warps, the effect is to make the weft more visible. Perhaps that is why wefts that interwork multiple groups of warps frequently have a different color, material, diameter, structure, and so forth, and they are often discontinuous, supplemental, and/or complementary.

CHANGE IN GROUPING OF WARP ELEMENTS FROM REGULAR TO ALTERNATE PAIRS

Wefts used in weft twining at Huaca Prieta most commonly enclose regular pairs of warps (such as 2008.069.01.A fig. 12.10c). But 63 specimens (46 original fabrics) have weft twining around alternate pairs of warps representing all chronological phases. At other Preceramic sites, including Los Gavilanes, Asia, and Salinas de Chao, wefts routinely interwork both regular and alternate pairs of warps (for example, Bonavia 1982: 106, fig. 121 [regular], 108, fig. 124 [alternate, crossed]; Engel 1963c: 30, figs. 39, 40 [regular], fig. 38 [alternate]; Olivera Alegre 2006: 62, fig. 22 [regular], 70, fig. 30 [alternate, crossed]). In the Ancón-Chillón area of coastal Peru, Moseley and Barrett (1969) found that the weft twining techniques between ~2500 and 1300 BC could be divided into three phases characterized first by single-warp constructions, next by the use of multiple warps interworked as both regular and alternate pairs, then by the sole use of plural-warp constructions and alternate pairing. This evolution is not found at most other Preceramic sites, where single-yarn warps are very rare, and both regular and alternate-paired twining is practiced through time at Huaca Prieta and other sites including Aspero (Feldman

1986: 32), Asia (Engel 1963c: 29), Salinas de Chao (Olivera A. 2006), Los Gavilanes (Bonavia 1982: 104), and La Galgada (Grieder 1988); see, however, Piedra Parada (Feldman 1986: 33).

FULL VERSUS HALF TWIST

Twining by its nature requires two weft yarns. Pattern is easily introduced simply by using two weft colors, textures, diameters, twists, and/or materials. A half twist (180°) causes the two yarns to alternate faces and is similar to the use of two-color complementary weft structures in warp-faced plain weave, both of which create dashed-line effects. Full twists (360°) prevent weft yarns from alternating faces, making solid lines of color (see compact weft band areas of 2008.096.01 in fig. 12.10e).

Twist is most effective when used in weft twining with compact weft elements (weft faced), where it creates complex two-color designs. Only a single specimen (2008.096.01, a fabric that was excavated as a folded and twisted bundle) was encountered in recent excavations that has weft twining with full twists. The design is simple, consisting of an undulating line. The fabric is described online in appendix M.

KNOTS AND APPLIQUÉ

Like all nautical people, Huaca Prietans were highly skilled in making nets and knots. But it seems that the people who made the fabrics deposited at the site appreciated knots aesthetically and tied knots not purely for functional necessity but in order to make patterns. Most of these knots are essentially invisible today, which might explain why they went unnoticed by Bird (or perhaps he did not consider them important).

Element knotting is the practice of tying knots in warps and/or wefts and is found only in weft-twined fabrics and 1 specimen of figure-8 looping. The present study discusses it as a decorative technique apart from appliqué, mends, and fabric knots, (for example, fabric knots are tied with the fabric itself, like tying the corner of a fabric). Huaca Prietans incorporated a large number of knots into their fabrics (see fig. 12.12).

ELEMENT KNOTS

Among the most perplexing possible forms of decoration (unmentioned by Bird) are fabric-element knots, which are defined as knots found in the elements (warps and wefts) that cannot be understood as anything other than decorative, even though they are invisible to the naked eye (fig. 12.13). They are found in about 25% of weft-twined textile specimens (90 specimens and 83 fabrics), but they are not found in interlaced fabrics or looped fabrics.[10] Knotted-netting fabrics have so many knots that it is impossible in the present study to distinguish decorative element knots (presuming that they exist) from mends or mesh knots. Over 95 element knots were counted in a single twined fabric alone (2009.142.02).

Element knots found in weft twining are tightly pulled, fragile, and dirty, which prevented their analysis in the majority of cases. Of those that were analyzed, the majority have no loose ends. Thus they are some sort of knob knot (more precisely defined as single or double stopper knots: see, for example, Ashley 1944: 12, figs. 14, 18). Of these knots, 58 specimens have weft-element knots, 18 have warp-element knots, and 28 have both warp and weft element knots.

Several clues suggest that some element knots are decorative. First, most lack visible ends, so technically they cannot be joins or mends. Bird et al. (1985: 135) also noted that "the joining of lengths of warp yarn by knotting was more frequent at an end selvage than within the fabric area." While several fabrics have knots that can be identified as joins, selvage, and antislippage knots (whose function was presumably to keep elements from shifting within the fabric), the knots discussed here are different and did not function in that way.

No element knots have remnants of pigment, although a small minority *might* have held some sort of fugitive fiber. For example, Specimen 2009.093.11 has many element knots, including two wefts with slip knots (both tied with a Z twist) that most likely held an appliqué-like

object. Feathers have been found at Huaca Prieta (for example, in bundle 2008.100.01) and Engel (1963c: 33) found featherwork at Asia, where wefts caught the bent quills. So we can suggest that some element knots might have been used to attach feathers, but at the present time this is speculation. The majority of element knots are not associated with any applied material.

If element knots are decorative, they have no obvious pattern across the face of the fabric, meaning that the knots do not form identifiable designs or patterns. Furthermore, they are barely visible. While they might have been more eye-catching in the past, it seems doubtful that they were visual standouts. In Fabrics 2008.067.02 and 2009.097.01.A the knots seem to form lines; in 2008.093.01 they form a small cluster; and in 2009.093.01 they form both a line and a cluster.

In some cases the knots are more predominant on one side of the fabric than on the other (2009.142.02). In most fabrics the knots are much more apparent on one face than on the other, so there might be many more fabrics with element knots that went unnoticed. The knots appear to be randomly spread out across the fabrics, as in 2009.142.02.

In sum, it would appear that element knots were intentionally added to weft-twined fabrics as a means of decoration. In some instances the knots might have attached an object like a feather to the fabric, but their purpose remains enigmatic in the majority of fabrics. Their random patterning might simply reflect an aesthetic that prized the lack of predictable pattern (as discussed in "Stripe Patterns" and "Changes in Interworking Order" above). In other words, perhaps the Huaca Prieta aesthetic prized highly texturized fabrics, and adding knots was one way of making proper appealing twining.

INTERWARP KNOTS

Interwarp knots (in Specimens 2009.010.12.A–B and 2009.093.08) were found to create decorative spaces (fig. 12.12a). In all examples, weft yarns make two half hitches between warps to create a gap. This technique is also found at Asia (Engel 1957b: pl. 21a, 1963c: 29, figs. 36–37).

In addition to decorative interwarp knots, people inserted single half hitches between

10. As noted earlier, element knots are found in figure-8 looping, but only a single specimen has knots that *might* be decorative; the rest are joins that were used to extend the working length of the looping-element yarn.

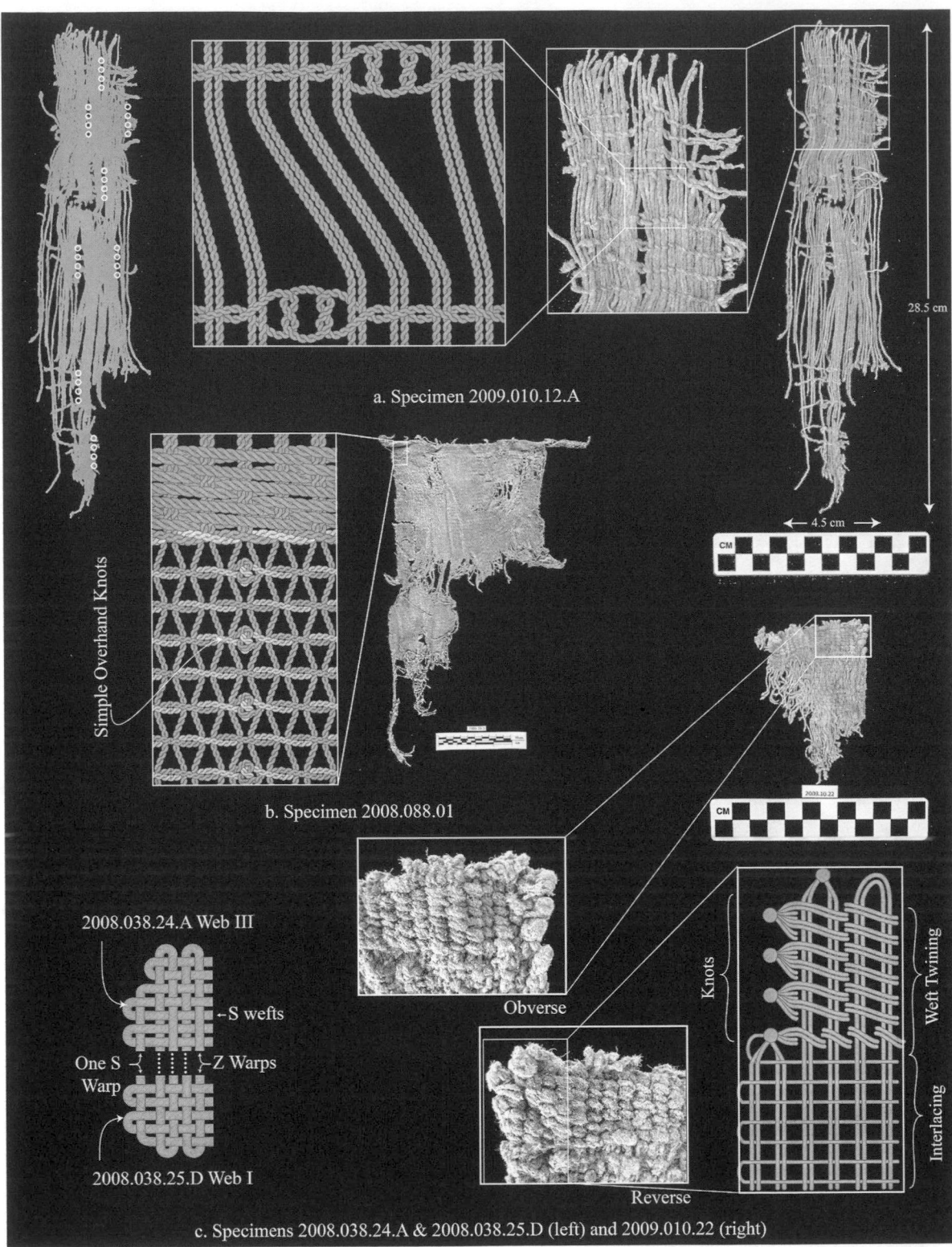

FIGURE 12.12. Knots, stitching, and end finishes encountered at Huaca Prieta: *a*, decorative spacing interwarp knots (Specimen 2009.010.12.A); *b*, interwarp knots preventing color change and/or maintaining weft alignments (Specimen 2008.088.01); *c*, warp and weft finishes: outer S warps shown in diagrams of two specimens indicates 180-degree rotation of fabrics during weaving (Specimens 2008.038.24.A and 2008.038.25.D and Specimen 2009.010.22, in which twining wefts became warps).

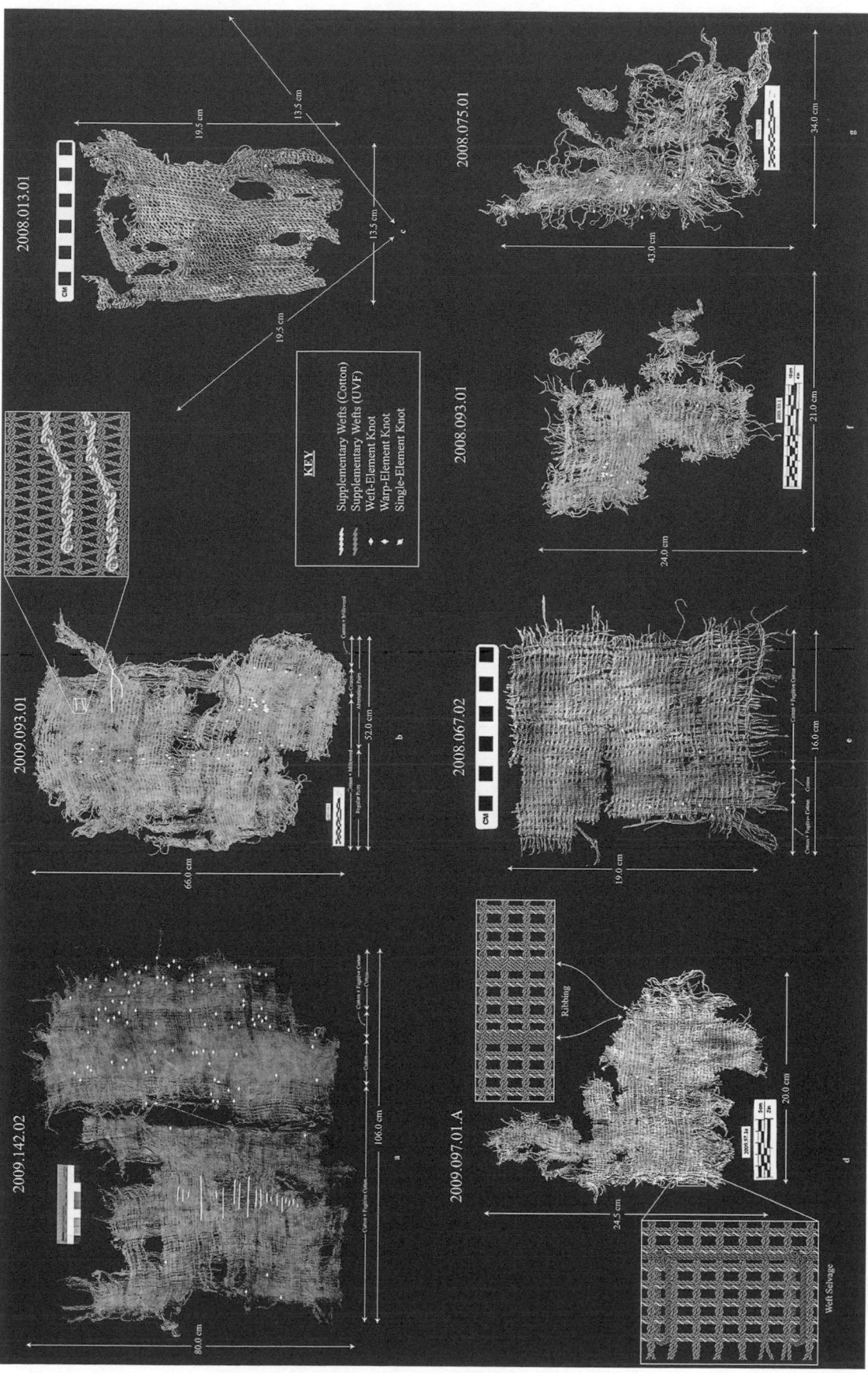

FIGURE 12.13. Element knots found in several specimens, including *a*, Specimen 2009.142.02; *b*, Specimen 2009.093.01; *c*, Specimen 2008.013.01; *d*, Specimen 2009.097.01.A; *e*, Specimen 2008.067.02; *f*, Specimen 2008.093.01; *g*, Specimen 2008.075.01 (photos for Specimens 2008.067.02, 2008.075.01, 2008.093.01, 2009.093.01, and 2009.097.01 by Lauren Badams).

warps that were not visible, such as in Specimen 2008.088.01. Single half-hitches might have been inserted to reinforce fabrics in case of tears, in which case the fabric would cease to unravel at the half hitch, which would serve more or less like a weft-end selvage knot. Such interwarp knots would serve to keep the weft from slipping under the stress of carrying heavy loads and would keep the fabric's warp and weft alignments in place. Bird et al. (1985: 130, 286–287, fig. 196) also commented on interwarp knots, finding them difficult to explain.

In addition to reinforcing fabric structure, interwarp knots were probably used instead of a 360-degree twist to create color effects. This suggests that fabrics with interwarp knots had two weft colors to make patterns. In normal twining with half twists, the weft yarns and their corresponding colors alternate from one face to the other. Half knots prevent color change, creating a solid color. This can also be done with full twists, but if tension between the two weft-element yarns is not perfectly equal full twists result in lines of one element on one face and dots of the other element on the other face. Interwarp knots prevent this from occurring (fig. 12.12b).

MAKING WEFT TWINING

Many aspects of the process of making weft twining have been discussed elsewhere (see "Selvages" within the section "Weft Twining"). This section will revisit questions regarding the use of a frame or loom and discuss who made weft twining at Huaca Prieta. Attributes of warp selvages seem to confirm Bird's hypothesis that weft twining was probably made on frames with two bars that secured circular warps. This setup allows for the greatest warp length possible in a hand-held portable frame. Many cultures with traditions of twining, such as the Chilkat of the northwestern United States, however, prefer to use upright stationary looms on which the warps are not fixed but attached to bags that keep warps clean and prevent them from tangling and unraveling (Samuel 1990: 134–135). In the Chilkat loom, warps move about freely so that bobbins can easily move through and around them.

The frame used at Huaca Prieta was significantly different. To keep warps from tangling and unraveling, both ends of the warp were probably fixed, making it difficult if not impossible to pass bobbins like those that were excavated between warp yarns. Wefts were probably made in relatively short lengths, essentially one weft at a time, so they could easily be inserted between warps while minimizing tangling and unraveling.

The presence of knotted weft-selvages supports the suggestion that wefts were individually made and inserted; long weft lengths were not used. Furthermore, no spools of yarn were encountered holding yarns compatible with those used in weft twining (or figure-8 looping or knotted netting either). Single-ply yarns of the type used in weaving were found around spindles that could have served as bobbins.

The practices involved with the production of weft twining seem much like those involved with figure-8 looping. Perhaps both categories of fabric were produced by the same people, which is supported by the average diameter of looping yarns (0.95 mm), which is similar to the average diameter of two-ply weft yarns in weft-twining (0.94 mm) (table 12.5). The diameters and other attributes of both looping and weft twining Z(2s) yarns are different enough from those found in plain weave and knotted netting to suggest that they represent two separate technologies and two different groups of people.

So who were these people? Who made the Huaca Prieta twined (and probably the figure-8 looping) fabrics? Were they specialists or homemakers, men or women, adults or children? The section on selvages shows that people produced a large number of different warp-selvage and weft-selvage types, especially weft-selvage types. This suggests that people had significant leeway in starting and finishing fabrics; they had a large number of choices or significant freedom to innovate them. This indicates a society in which innovation and individuality were encouraged or a society without rigidly imposed uniformity. It suggests that specialized groups or guilds probably did not exist. People probably learned by watching, the way weavers learn today to make incredibly complex warp-patterned fabrics in the Andes (Torrico 2014). The gender and age of the people making twined fabrics are impossible to know for certain, but arguments are nonetheless presented below.

USE, REPAIR, SUPRA-STRUCTURES, AND DISCARDING PRACTICES

All Huaca Prieta fabrics are fragmentary and look like they were cut and/or torn prior to deposition, making analysis of use-wear challenging. But a limited study derived from the attributes of supra-structures that were added as tailoring and/or repair is illuminating. Only 4% of weft-twined fabrics have supra-structures of any type, which sets them apart from plain weave but is similar to looping and knotted netting. A list of all supra-structures listed by fabric category is presented in table 12.8.

Mends are conspicuously absent from all fabric categories in general, suggesting that fabrics were not commonly tailored, decorated with stitching, or repaired prior to discarding. All fabrics show signs of trauma. But none of the damage inflicted on them (from whatever cause) was repaired except for one looped fabric previously discussed (Specimen 2009.028.05). The most prevalent form of supra-structures in weft twining are edge embellishments, which are stitches associated with edges: 38% of all edge embellishments are associated with weft-twining specimens (53% of all fabrics). A paucity of edge embellishments is associated with plain weave. The function of edge embellishments in weft twining is quite different from in plain weave; in weft twining they are used as weft selvage reinforcements where they typically pass along the selvage knotting the outer warps and wefts. Plain-weave edge embellishments, in contrast, are most often whip-stitches used to join fabric edges. Both categories might have been decorative as well as functional.

Two weft-twined fabrics are associated with joins, which are stitches used to unite multiple webs. The only other fabric category with multiweb constructions is plain weave. But, unlike plain weave, weft-twined multiweb constructions have no hems, which are typically added to reinforce exposed fabric edges, strengthening them or hiding frayed areas. The lack of hems in weft twining suggests that the function of multiweb twined fabrics was very different from the function of multiweb plain weave.

These attributes of supra-structures in weft twining, combined with twining's relatively thick yarn elements compared to plain weave, suggest that weft twining was a method of making a working, utilitarian fabric. The people who made them were probably the same people who made figure-8 looping, considering the yarn attributes of both are similar. Both have many element knots, suggesting that they were made with relatively short, manageable lengths of yarn made as needed. Both processes rely exclusively on hand manipulations, where yarns wind around one another and are inserted into tight spaces where bobbins and/or spools of yarn cannot fit.

PLAIN WEAVE

There are 127 plain-weave specimens (71 original fabrics), all of which are all-cotton. The average plain weave is 12.6 cm long by 10.8 cm wide with an average area of 301.9 cm², which makes them on average larger than looping, about the same size as weft twining, and smaller than knotted netting. The longest specimen is 54.0 cm, and the shortest is 0.6 cm; the widest piece is 42.0, and the narrowest is 1.1 cm. Only a single plain-weave fabric (2009.160.09: a bag and the only complete fabric in the collection) has two warp selvages with a length of 17.0 cm. The technical traits, provenience, and dimensions of all plain-weave specimens are described online in appendices B and K.

Plain weave is the second most common fabric structure. It is almost always woven 1 by 1 with fine (0.2–0.8 mm) S-spun, single-ply warps and wefts, although paired wefts are encountered in 41 specimens (26 fabrics) and paired warps in 37 specimens (25 fabrics). In 4 specimens (3 fabrics) wefts consist of pairs of S and Z yarns.

Plain weave appears as early as twining in Phase II. A single specimen (2009.056.01) is among the oldest fabrics found at the site, yet its fibers are very fine. Its structure is described online in appendix M. The fabric had been bundled, suggesting that it was ritually deposited. The fabric was folded in thirds, after which the center third was pleated, fanlike, so that the warps and wefts of the final third were shifted 90 degrees from the first.

Among the only complete objects in the collection is Specimen 2009.160.09, which is described online in appendix M.

Table 12.8. Supra-structures presented by function and fabric categories

	Edge embellishment		Hem		Join		Mend	
Fabric category	Spec. (%)*	Fabric (%)	Spec. (%)*	Fabric (%)	Spec. (%)*	Fabric (%)	Spec. (%)*	Fabric (%)
Weft twining	9 (*38*)	8 (*53*)	—	—	2 (*6*)	2 (*11*)	—	—
Figure-8 looping	—	—	—	—	—	—	1 (*100*)	1 (*100*)
Knotted netting	—	—	—	—	—	—	—	—
Plain weave	15 (*63*)	7 (*47*)	7 (*100*)	5 (*100*)	33 (*94*)	17 (*89*)	—	—
Total	**24**	**15**	**7**	**5**	**35**	**19**	**1**	**1**

Note: Spec. = No. of specimens.

* % refers to the percentage of supra-structures.

MAKING PLAIN WEAVE AND THE IMPLICATIONS FOR LOOM TYPE

Much information regarding the making of plain weave can be inferred from the attributes of fabrics. For example, Huaca Prieta plain weave has an average warp diameter of 0.45 mm, with an average range of 0.21–0.76 mm and an STD of 0.13 mm; wefts have an average diameter of 0.46 mm and an average range from 0.22 to 0.79 mm (STD = 0.12 mm). Warps have an average twist of 52.71 degrees, with an average range of 30.73 to 76.07 (STD = 7.52); average weft twist is 51.89 degrees, with an average range of 30.23 to 77.18 degrees (STD = 7.35). Average warp density is 12.08 warps/cm, with an STD of 3.46 and a range of 9.18 to 18.65. Average weft density is 9.40 wefts per cm, with a range of 7.57 to 13.01 wefts/cm (STD = 2.9).

The attributes of Specimen 2009.056.01, the oldest plain-weave fabric, are nearly identical to the average attributes for all plain-weave fabrics, suggesting that plain-weave practices did not change much, if at all, during the site's entire use (or else 2009.056.01 was exceptionally well made for its time, but that is not the case).

In addition to the relative conservative nature of weaving practices at the site, the attributes of plain-weave fabrics also indicate that warp and weft diameters and twists—even their variations and standard deviations—are nearly identical. This suggests that both warp and weft yarns were made the same way and probably by the same people without specialization. Warp and weft plain-weave element alignments are remarkably straight, with low standard deviations in their densities. In addition, the weft-density STD is lower than that of the warps, which argues against darning, a process where wefts are sewn in with a needle but without heddles. Furthermore, 7 spindles wound with single-ply yarns of the type used in plain weave were recovered from Phase V contexts, which suggests that yarns were prepared beforehand and textiles woven with bobbins.

Together, this evidence suggests the presence of a shed, a device that creates an opening within the warps that both mechanizes and speeds up the weaving process but also allows a thick bobbin to pass through. Thus plain weave and weft twining were probably made with different loom/frame technologies sometime after Phase III, when at least some plain weave might have been woven on a loom. This suggestion is further supported by the percentage of plain weave produced at the site, which rose considerably between Phases IV and V (see online appendix K).

| | | | | All specimens/ fabrics w/ supra-structure | |
| Unknown | | Total supra-structures | | | |
Spec. (%)*	Fabric (%)	Spec. (%)*	Fabric (%)	Spec. (%)*	Fabric (%)
—	—	10 (13)	10 (17)	13 (20)	12 (29)
—	—	1 (1)	1 (2)	1 (1)	1 (2)
1 (7)	1 (8)	1 (1)	1 (2)	1 (1)	1 (2)
14 (93)	12 (92)	68 (85)	46 (79)	52 (78)	28 (67)
15	13	80	58	67	42

WEFT SELVAGES

Weft selvages provide another important source of information about weaving practices, from the number of warps used for reinforcements to the number of wefts (bobbins) used. All but 2 weft-selvage structures are simple, meaning that a single bobbin was used and the weft interworked the outer warp as a single yarn (without reinforcement). Single bobbins were used to create both 1 by 1 and 2 by 2 fabric structures. However, 2 specimens (1 fabric of 1 by 1 plain weave) have interworked weft edges, which can only be made with three bobbins (fig. 12.14a: 2008.062.01.A and B, Phase V). 1 specimen, 2009.107.03, has a weft selvage made with two wefts that interlock around a group of reinforcing outer warps (fig. 12.14b).

Web III of 2008.038.24.A and 2008.038.24.D is Phase III plain-weave fabric with selvage structures suggesting that the practice of turning fabrics 180 degrees to weave the ends first is ancient, going back to Preceramic times. Both webs are simple cotton plain weave with S wefts and S and Z warps that form invisible stripes (invisible structures are discussed in "Warp Stripes" within the section on "Weft Twining"). At the upper corner of specimen 2008.038.24.A the third weft shot is turned 90 degrees to become the outer warp (fig. 12.12c).

In the lower corner of Specimen 2008.038.24.D, which was once part of 2008.038.24.A, the outer warp bends 90 degrees to become the first weft shot. The simplest explanation for the presence of these two structures would be that they show a weaving practice in which, after placing the warps, the first three weft shots were inserted; then the weft traveled as the outer warp to the other end of the fabric, which was rotated 180 degrees. The weft-become-outer-warp traveled as a warp to the other warp end of the fabric, at which point it turned 90 degrees to become the first weft shot of the second warp end.

A similar pattern is found in Specimen 2009.010.22, where a twining weft became an outer warp (fig. 12.12c). The warp selvage is made of compact weft twining (see "Weft Twining with Plain Weave").

WARP SELVAGES

The warp ends of the previously discussed fabrics suggest that they could have been made on a loom with a circular warp with a locking (or scaffold) cord like that depicted by Bird et al. (1985: 121–122, figs. 170, 172); however, Web I of Speci-

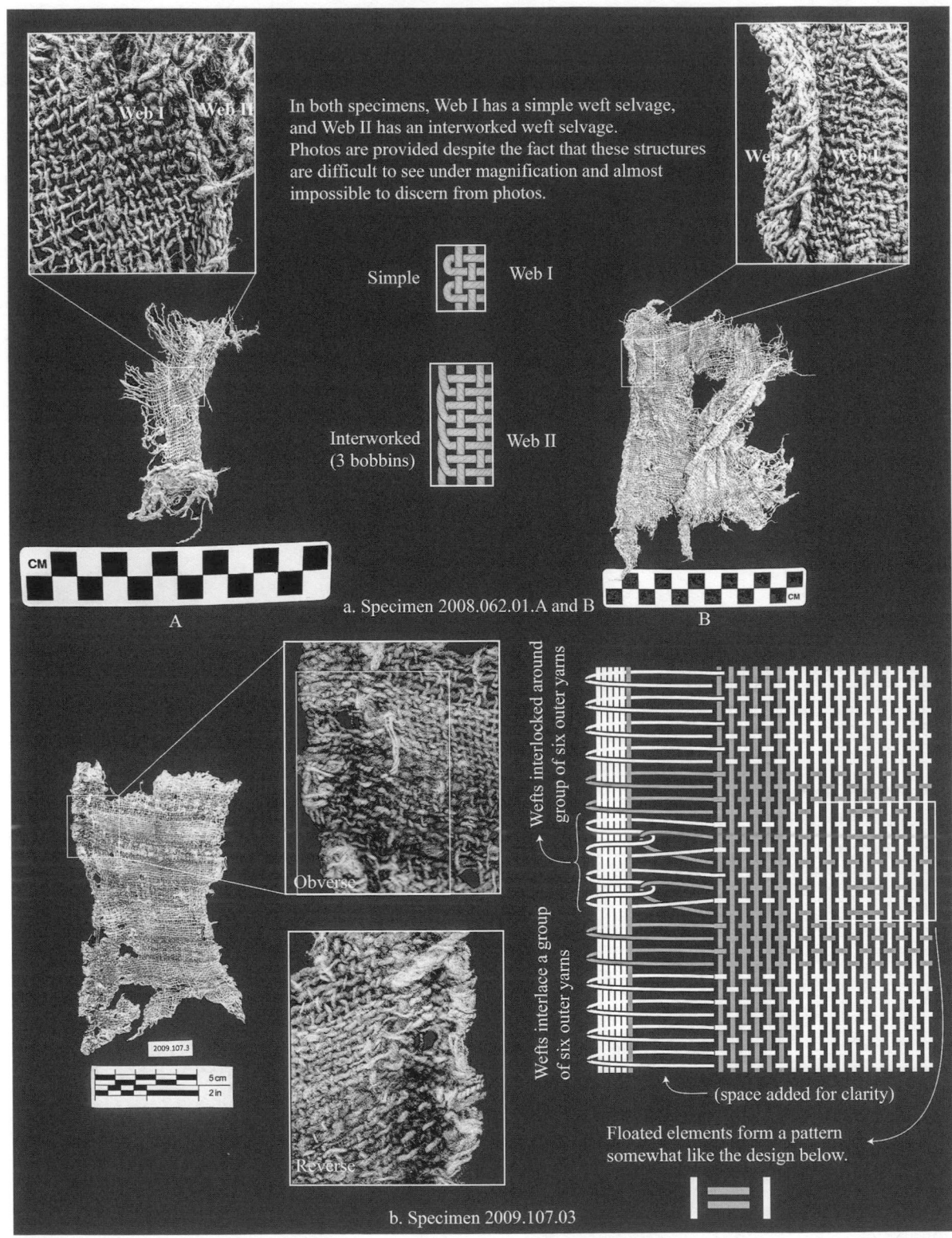

In both specimens, Web I has a simple weft selvage, and Web II has an interworked weft selvage.
Photos are provided despite the fact that these structures are difficult to see under magnification and almost impossible to discern from photos.

Simple   Web I

Interworked (3 bobbins)   Web II

a. Specimen 2008.062.01.A and B

Wefts interlocked around group of six outer yarns

Wefts interlace a group of six outer yarns

(space added for clarity)

Floated elements form a pattern somewhat like the design below.

b. Specimen 2009.107.03

FIGURE 12.14. Plain-weave edge finishes: *a*, plain-weave weft-selvage finishes (Specimen 2008.062.01.A and B); *b*, weft selvage with reinforced outer warp and interlocked wefts (Specimen 2009.107.03); note that the fabric has a plain-weave-derived float-weave structure, as seen in the diagram (*right*). (See color plates.)

men 2008.038.24.A has a warp selvage with a very short fringe made from the warp ends extending past the terminal weft. This type of warp-extension fringe could be produced on either a frame with a circular warp or a frame with warps attached directly to it. The fringe is produced by removing the scaffold yarn that secured the dovetailed warp ends of a circular warp or by removing the fabric from the frame and allowing the warps to twist (Splitstoser 2009: 945).

SELVAGE STRUCTURES

Only 3 specimens/fabrics have warp selvages. Specimen 2009.160.09 has two, making a complete length. Warp selvages are simple and essentially indistinguishable from weft selvages. Neither warp nor weft selvages have fringes either as warp or weft extensions or as appliqué, which is common practice in later (especially Early Horizon) plain weave. Selvage structures are discussed in more detail in the following section.

DECORATIVE TECHNIQUES

Decoration in plain weave was more restricted than in weft twining, both in the number of techniques used to decorate fabrics and in the number of fabrics that were decorated. While the majority of twined fabrics were decorated, the opposite is true of plain-weave fabrics, of which only 21 specimens (8 original fabrics) are decorated. The number of specimens includes 3 webs that were part of a single-fabric, multiweb bundle (see online appendix G).

WARP STRIPES

Stripes are found in Huaca Prieta plain-weave fabrics either as yarns colored blue or red or in the form of invisible counter-spun (Z) yarns. The practice of making stripes (and/or bands) in which contrast is created completely from structure, usually from the use of counter-spun yarns, creates invisible stripes (presuming the yarns were never dyed; see the discussion of invisible structures in the section "Warp Stripes" within the section on "Warp Patterning").

This study found that 3 plain-weave specimens (3 fabrics) have paired warps where one yarn is Z and the other is S. The analysis showed that 20 specimens (12 fabrics) have blue stripes, and 9 specimens (5 fabrics) have red stripes. Fewer red stripes might be due to the fugitive red pigment that washed out, while blue is indigo and much more colorfast. No specimens have both red and blue stripes.

Specimen 2009.114.12 with warp-striped patterning is unusual for Huaca Prieta, because it is made in warp-faced plain weave. It is described online in appendix M.

Weft Patterning

Unlike weft twining, weft patterning in plain weave is relatively simple. The study found that 13 specimens (11 fabrics) have weft patterning, which comes in weft bands and discontinuous wefts (fig. 12.15).

Weft Bands

There are 11 specimens (9 fabrics) with weft-band patterning. Like warp stripes, weft patterning in plain weave at Huaca Prieta is either structural—formed by using S and Z yarns—or achieved through the use of color. And 5 specimens have blue and natural weft bands, all of which are from either mixed or Phase V contexts. "Invisible" bands made of S and Z cotton wefts are found on 2 fabrics, while 4 specimens/fabrics have bands made of paired wefts. Another 8 specimens have both warp stripes and weft bands created through combinations of structure and color. For example, Specimen 2009.001.08 has both S and Z warps and wefts, and 2008.038.24.A has blue stripes and Z weft bands.

DISCONTINUOUS WEFTS

Specimens/fabrics 2009.065.01.A and 2009.063.02 from Late Phase V contexts are nearly balanced plain weave with discontinuous, interlocked wefts. In both cases, the interlocks are over two warps (fig. 12.15a). They are described

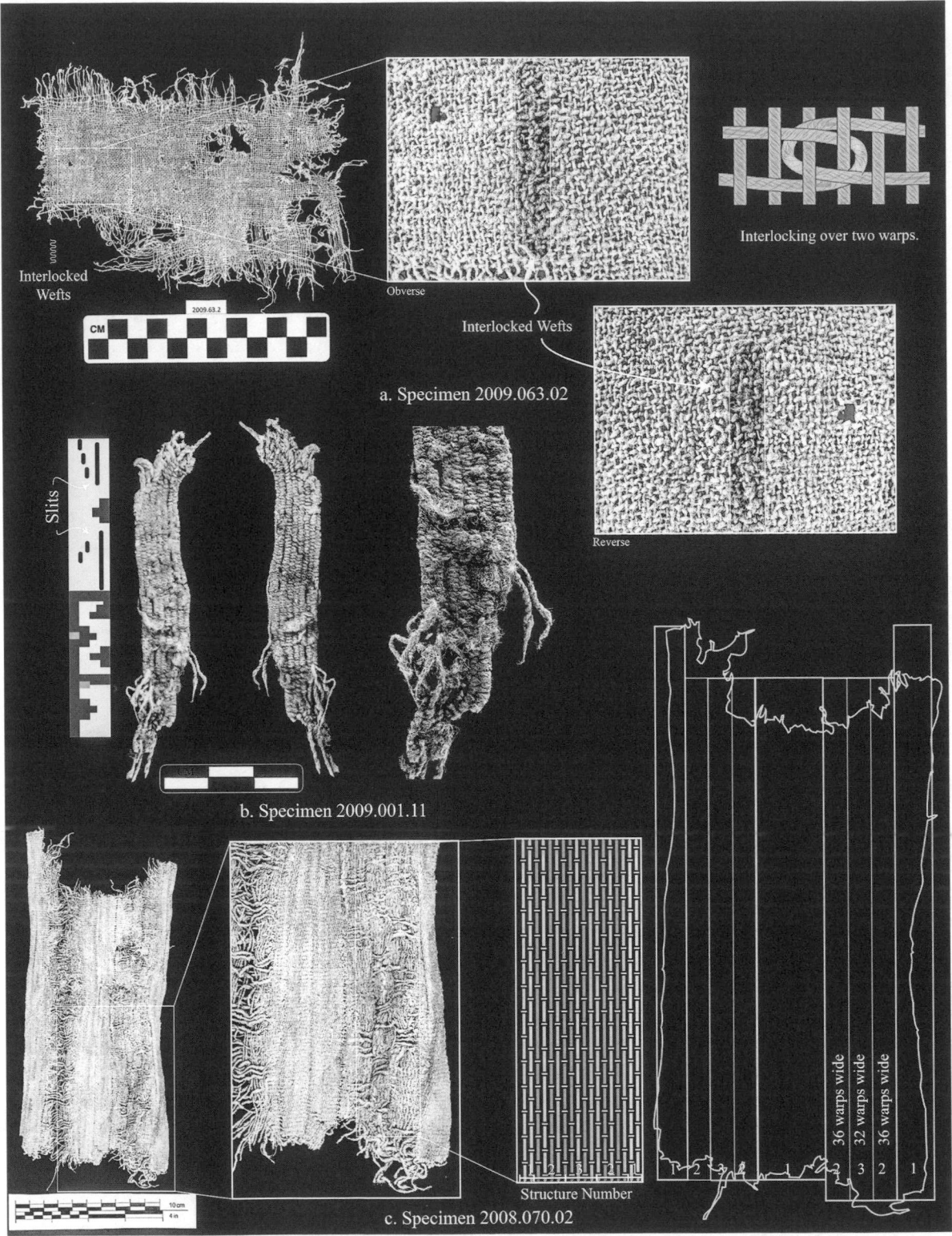

Interlocked Wefts

Obverse

Interlocking over two warps.

Interlocked Wefts

a. Specimen 2009.063.02

Reverse

Slits

b. Specimen 2009.001.11

36 warps wide

32 warps wide

36 warps wide

Structure Number

c. Specimen 2008.070.02

FIGURE 12.15. Structural diagrams of weft patterning in plain weave: *a*, discontinuous wefts (Specimen 2009.063.02); *b*, slit tapestry (Specimen 2009.001.11); *c*, plain-weave-derived float weave (Specimen 2008.070.02). Note that color is not found in the actual specimen and shading was added to the diagram for clarity. Many of the yarns that are colored in the diagram have fallen out. (See color plates.)

online in appendix M. Neither specimen has any color today, but they probably did in the past.

SLIT TAPESTRY

Specimen 2009.001.11 (fig. 12.15b) is from Bird backdirt and the only example of slit tapestry, which is defined as plain weave with discontinuous weft in the weft face. It has Z(2s) light-yellow camelid-hair wefts as well as bluish gray and beige cotton Z(2s) wefts that make the pattern. The structure is described online in appendix M.

PLAIN-WEAVE-DERIVED FLOAT WEAVES

Cotton plain-weave fabrics 2008.070.02 and 2009.107.03, from Phase V and Bird backdirt contexts, respectively, are patterned with plain-weave-derived float weaves, in which an element on one face skips an interlace, creating a three-span float on that face and a three-span float of the opposite element on the other face. Emery (1966: 114–116) calls this technique "alternating float weave," which is derived from plain weave. For a more detailed description of the technique and its history, see Rowe (1977: 53–66). Bird encountered the technique (Bird et al. 1985: 194–197; Bird and Mahler 1951–1952: 76, 78). The structure of plain-weave-derived float weave is depicted in fig. 12.15c (see also 2009.107.03 in fig. 12.14b).

In Specimen 2009.107.03 blue warps were used to create a contrast with natural-white cotton; it also has blue weft bands. Specimen 2008.070.02 today has no visible color other than natural cotton, and many warps involved in the float-derived area have disintegrated, suggesting that the yarns were at one time colored with a fugitive pigment that was corrosive to cellulose. Upon plotting the floats a geometric pattern could be seen; perhaps this fabric had gold yarns pigmented with ochre, which caused their disintegration (see "Gold/Yellow" above). Detailed descriptions of both fabrics with plain-weave-derived float weave are described online in appendix M.

PLAIN-WEAVE USE, REPAIR, SUPRA-STRUCTURES, AND DISCARD PRACTICES

As noted earlier, 6 spools of yarn were encountered, all of which were finely made, single-ply, S-spun cotton yarns; this is the same structure found in the yarns used in plain weave. Weft yarns are typically wound onto spindles that serve as bobbins to keep the yarns from tangling during the process of weaving, suggesting that these spools of yarn were probably intended for plain weave. This is in dramatic contrast with the loose yarns prepared for twining, looping, and netting, of which there are none, suggesting that plain-weave yarns were prepared ahead of time, while looping, netting, and twining yarns were made as needed.

As noted for netting, the best clues regarding a fabric's use typically come from its original shape and tailoring, but the fabrics at Huaca Prieta are nearly all incomplete fragments, missing their selvages, making their original shapes difficult if not impossible to discern. In this case the best source of tailoring information comes from the existence of supra-structures, including the stitches from multiweb constructions, holes for heads and appendages, straps for handling, folds and hems involved with making containers, and so forth.

A significant amount of information about the process of weaving can be inferred from an examination of supra-structures. Of the 67 specimens with supra-structures, 13 specimens (12 fabrics) are weft twining, 1 specimen/fabric is looping, and 1 specimen/fabric is netting. The other 52 specimens (28 fabrics) with supra-structures are plain weave, indicating that a far higher percentage of plain-weave fabrics are made of multiple webs than any other category of fabric. The majority of all supra-structures—from joins involving multiweb constructions (94%) to edge embellishments (62%) and hems (100%)—are found in plain weave (see table 12.8).

To date, however, no supra-structures clearly represent tailoring of the type found in tunics (for example, neck slits, arm holes, and embroidered edges). The majority are stitches involved in making bundles, where fabrics were layered and sloppily stitched together.

The attributes of multi-web constructions can inform us about fabric use. The study found that 33 specimens (17 fabrics) are associated with

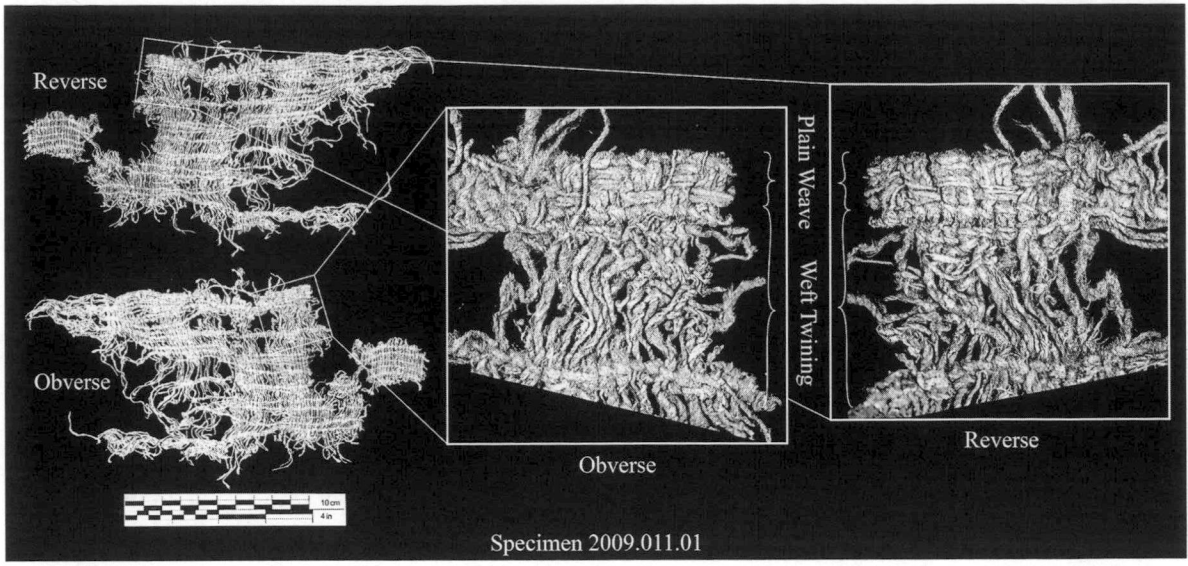

Reverse

Obverse

Plain Weave

Weft Twining

Obverse

Reverse

Specimen 2009.011.01

FIGURE 12.16. Weft twining with plain weave (Specimen 2009.011.01).

joins; of these, 17 specimens (15 fabrics) have edge-to-edge constructions making larger fabrics from smaller ones. The remaining 22 specimens (8 fabrics) have layered joins, where fabrics are stacked and crudely stitched with whipping and/ or running stitches, suggesting that it was done in a hurry. These multi-web fabrics lack any sort of logical structure customarily found in multi-web constructions, like bags or tunics, and lack any coherency, making analysis immensely time consuming.

The function of these multiweb, stacked-and-stitched fabrics was initially baffling. Some were clearly folded and bundled.

COMPOUND CONSTRUCTIONS AND FABRICS WITH MULTIPLE FABRIC CATEGORIES

There are 5 specimens (4 fabrics) made of two fabric categories: weft twining with plain weave and weft twining with figure-8 looping. Their fabric structures are depicted in fig. 12.16 and fig. 12.8a, respectively.

WEFT TWINING WITH PLAIN WEAVE

Specimens 2009.010.22, 2009.011.01.A–B, and 2009.149.01.A–B (5 fragments) from Bird back-

dirt combined spaced weft twining and plain weave. Bird et al. (1985: 198–199) also found 3 fabrics that combined both interlacing and twining. Specimens 2009.149.01.A and B from Phase IV contexts have been described in the section "Complementary Warps" within the section on "Weft Twining." Their technical descriptions are presented online in appendix M. The structure, based on Specimen 2009.011.01, is presented in fig. 12.16.

WEFT TWINING WITH FIGURE-8 LOOPING

Specimen 2008.101.01.A–B (2 fragments) from Phase IV contexts combines weft twining and figure-8 looping (fig. 12.8a), where the looping might have been added to the warp ends during the process of warping, creating a circular warp (see an illustration of a circular warp by Bird et al. 1985: 121, fig. 170). The looping might take the place of the cord or stick and might have been added as the stick or cord was removed.

DISCUSSION

Fabrics are uniquely able to inform us about the values and practices of the people who made them. What have we learned about the people of Huaca Prieta? One of the research questions posed involved structure and agency: what were the rules of making fabrics, if any, and how well and how often were they adhered to? The present study has identified several new twining weft-selvage structures, indicating that the people making them had significant choice in their production or else were encouraged to innovate and experiment.

Huaca Prieta weavers apparently valued random-like patterning, which appears in multiple attributes, from yarn element knots and weft interworking order to warp-stripe patterning. Randomness is inherently innovative; no two patterns were the same. This might imply that Huaca Prieta weavers had leeway and possibly encouragement to experiment and innovate.

This is not to say that there were no rules. To the contrary, spinners almost always made S-spun yarns, and twining twist is almost 100% Z twist. The diameters and degree of twist of the yarns have relatively low standard-of-deviation values through time, suggesting that the same methods of processing and spinning fiber were used for centuries. Weft twining, with few exceptions, used paired two-ply warps and wefts, and wefts were consistently spaced and interworked warps making half twists with a Z slant. Plain weave almost always employed single-ply, S warps and wefts interlacing 1 by 1. Nearly all plain-weave selvages are simple; those that are not are either interlocking or interlacing, also commonly found at other Preceramic sites.

Other than these factors, Huaca Prieta fabric practitioners followed few rules when making fabrics: a culture of innovation that I refer to as ordered "chaos" that made their study a challenge. This goes against people's general perception of Huaca Prietans as the makers of the first representational art that was produced with weft twining with crossed-warp patterning and plain-weave-derived float weaves (Bird and Mahler 1951–1952). Luis Lumbreras (1989: 178) called this early art, whose designs are heavily influenced by textile structures, the "Huaca Prieta Style," which is defined as rigidly symmetrical. Figures often repeat in pairs, perhaps indicating an early pre-occupation with bilateral symmetry, dualism, complementarity, and reciprocity.

Looking at patterning more generally, a technical study of the decorative practices found at

the site is found online in appendix K. In summary: (1) half of the decorative techniques practiced over time at Huaca Prieta experienced a decline between Phases II and III; (2) the majority of decorative techniques peaked in Phase IV and declined significantly in Phase V; (3) the use of weft twining mirrors these two trends; (4) the pattern for plain weave is the inverse; and (5) only five out of sixteen techniques, all associated with weft twining, experienced an increase in frequency between Phases IV and V.

These trends point to a decrease in the number of decorated fabrics from Phases II to V, as is the case for decorated gourds (see chapter 11). The majority of techniques that decreased are generally associated with twining, such as the use of milkweed fiber, fugitive cotton fiber, and interwarp knots. These data indicate a tremendous change that took place between Phases IV and V. This is also seen in bundling practices, where bundles from late Phase V contexts are completely different from earlier bundles (see "Bundling Practices" above).

Huaca Prieta fabric production seems to have peaked in Phase IV when all but two examples of crossed-warp patterning were produced; there was only one example of crossed-warp patterning from Phase II, one from Phase V, and none from Phase III contexts. Concurrently, when weft twining was at its peak in Phase IV plain weave is almost nonexistent. This pattern strongly supports the argument discussed throughout the chapter that (at least) two groups of people with different fabric-making traditions lived and left fabrics at the mound.

Regarding the function of the fabrics, they generally show little evidence of wear, having no threadbare areas and no mends other than those found in a single fabric. This is odd. Suprastructural evidence suggests that the majority of fabrics, even plain weave, were not tailored, at least not much. Only two twined fabrics consisted of two fabrics stitched together, and it is possible that the two webs might have been one fabric that was once folded and stitched to make a container. This was the case for the only complete fabric found at the site (a plain-weave bag) and suggests that fabrics were not meant to be worn; the evidence (or lack of it) suggests that most fabrics, including looping, plain weave, and twined fabrics, were used to wrap and/or carry things. Netting was probably also similarly used but attached to frames and used as dip nets.

While showing no signs of wear, almost all the fabrics show signs of trauma consistent with having been torn (for example, 2008.066.02). The edges have characteristically jagged saw-blade edges, where groups of wefts are bunched together separated by spaces without wefts; this pattern is characteristic of cutting with a relatively dull implement, such as a crudely chipped stone, of which there are many at the site. Many of the fabrics are rectangular strips characteristic of textiles that had their edges torn or cut off. They may indicate acts of ritual sacrifice. Many, if not most, fabrics were found as packets of offerings, which suggests that they were ritually bundled and deposited.

CONCLUSIONS

The 825 specimens making up the collection of fibers, cords, yarns, and fabrics excavated by Dillehay and Bonavia and analyzed by Splitstoser have provided a unique set of data to study. The present study combines *chaîne opératoire* analysis with practice theory to infer information from the attributes of the textiles (such as yarn diameter and selvage structures) about Preceramic society in general and the textile technology of Huaca Prieta in particular.

The collection of fabrics presented here is similar to the collection studied by Bird over fifty years ago. The application of improved methodologies—both in the field and the lab—and advanced analytical tools (such as XRF and GCMS), however, allowed us to learn much more from the data. For example, we now know that the blue encountered by Bird is the earliest known use of indigo in the world; and we have positively identified milkweed, which was one of the unknown vegetal fibers that Bird could not name. The washing technique developed by Illingworth at Mercyhurst University made it possible to detect a yellow-gold color that was hidden by the paste covering.

No new primary structures (such as gauze or brocade) were encountered. But similarities in the attributes of at least two technologies—figure-8

looping and weft twining—suggest that they shared a common practice of making short lengths of fiber that were interworked rather than using long spools of yarn. Furthermore, the attributes of the yarns used to make both twining and looping are so similar that it is probable that they were made and possibly interworked by the same people.

In addition to establishing a link between twining and looping, the present study has identified two distinct contemporary traditions involving fabrics with warps and wefts: plain weave and weft twining. These two fabric types not only employed distinct technologies that involved vastly different interworking skills and practices (twining and interlacing) but used yarns with different attributes (such as two-ply versus single-ply) and most likely involved different types of looms.

The present study also has identified two distinct netting traditions: Type 1 nets are made with overhand knots and have a small mesh size and thick yarns; and Type 2 nets are made with lark's-head knots and have a larger mesh size with thin yarns. Yarns in nets from both traditions show evidence that they were used in water, but nets in both traditions are small and square, which may indicate that both traditions were making square dip nets. Was one net tradition used in freshwater (inland), while the other was used in seawater? Type 2 nets have more salt crystals and stiff, matted fibers than Type 1 nets, suggesting that Type 2 nets were probably used in seawater.

These facts and inferences hint at the existence of two societies, each with its own sets of knowledge, skills, and traditions concerning fabrics, possibly representing fisherfolk and farmers. One group is associated with fabrics that have thick two-ply yarns that were probably made with short lengths of yarn made on demand. Members of the first tradition probably made looping, weft twining, and possibly Type 1 netting. Evidence from the warp ends of three fabrics suggests that weft twining was done on frames with circular warps. These people may have been farmers.

The second tradition was closely associated with finely spun single-ply yarns that were wound on spools. These people made plain weave and probably Type 2 nets and might have lived near the sea, because Type 2 nets seem to have been used in saltwater. Several lines of evidence suggest that they might have used looms (or devices that could create a shed) sometime after Phase III, including the use of bobbins and the habit of turning fabrics. This was done so that fabrics could be woven from the selvages to the center, making it easier to insert the final weft shots. These practices were in use during Preceramic times, making their study highly relevant to the evolution of weaving practices even if they are not proof of the use of a loom.

The question regarding who made the Huaca Prieta fabrics still remains. Were they specialists or nonspecialists, individuals or groups, men or women? The significant variety in weft-end treatment and the lack of an overarching style suggest that the fabrics were made at the household level and brought from multiple places to the site for ritual deposition. Warp-crossed fabrics are the most consistent fabric type, but even they display significant structural variation. Most Huaca Prieta fabrics share a "look and feel" that is probably the result of both competitive copying (Torrico 2014) and the adherence to the few simple rules discussed above.

The significant amount of variation in decorative practices and the lack of a common style suggest that nonspecialists made the Huaca Prieta fabrics. The wide array of variations in warp-end and weft-end selvage treatments, which are good indicators of standardization in both setting up warps and making fabrics, also suggests that nonspecialist individuals made the fabrics.

The final question concerns the role of gender within the two fabric-making communities. Another explanation for the existence of two fabric traditions, in particular the inverse relationship between plain weave and weft twining, could indicate a division of labor based on gender, although the two explanations are not mutually exclusive. Possible scenarios are discussed for each fabric type below.

FIGURE-8 LOOPING

It is difficult to make any kind of definitive statement about the role of gender in the making of figure-8 looping. First, among the many difficulties is the relative rarity of the technique, which does not require any special tools other than a needle and a spacer of some sort to maintain even loop distances. These tools can be made of almost anything from sticks to palm-leaf strand, so archaeological evidence from sexed tombs—the best source of evidence for associating gender with technological practices—is difficult to use. It is difficult to apply direct historical methods, too, because figure-8 looping is not commonly made by modern Andean people, and we do not know who the descendants of the Huaca Prietans might be.

That said, ethnographic evidence suggests that looping in at least some indigenous communities is made by women today. For example, *shicra* bags made with a simple-looping structure with maguey fiber are encountered in highland Ecuador. They are made by women who use them to hold water jars, seeds, and crops (Miller 2003–2004). Among the Jívaro people of the Amazon region of eastern Ecuador, however, men spin yarns from the inner bark of a palm tree that they make into bags using looping and netting techniques that were not identified (Harner 1984: 68–69). The women of Chachapoyas in Amazonas and Tupicocha in the Huarochirí region of Peru make bags out of *Furcraea* fiber (locally called *casca*) using the loop-and-twist technique (Del Solar 2007: 112–113, 2011: 40). Yagua women and unmarried girls of northeastern Peru make bags of *chambira* fiber (a palm leaf) in an interconnected looping technique in which loops pass through the crosses of the previous row, in addition to lateral linking with adjacent loops in the same row (Fejos 1943: 62, fig. 23, pl. 47).

KNOTTED NETTING

As in the situation with figure-8 looping, it is difficult to know archaeologically who was making the nets at Huaca Prieta without actual evidence from sexed burials. Net remains are relatively abundant at Huaca Prieta and throughout the Andes, where nets are encountered wrapped around bodies. Ethnographic evidence for net making, however, is scarce. What little there is suggests that netting on the north coast was both made and used by men (Vreeland 1986: 368), but the nets referred to in the literature are large and very different from types recovered from Huaca Prieta, which are small and were probably attached to frames. A similar type of net is made and used by the women of the Matsigenka, a tribe who live in the Amazon basin of present-day Peru. The nets are made of natural and dyed cotton yarns, are attached to a circular piece of cane, and have a mesh size, knot structure, and striped design technically identical to Type 1 nets at Huaca Prieta; unfortunately, no mention was made of their use (Shepard 2006: 52–53). Thus the ethnographic evidence is contradictory and of little use.

TWINING

Like figure-8 looping, twining is not commonly found ethnographically. The best-known examples are probably Chilkat dancing blankets from the northwestern United States. They are made by women, although the goat hair and cedar bark used for the warp and weft elements are collected by men, who also make the looms (Samuel 1990).

Like the other techniques discussed above, weft twining does not require any special tools other than a needle and possibly some sort of spacer like a palm leaf strand. The frame on which they were made could be just a straight stick, of which many were encountered. As far as I know, no unfinished twining still on its frame has been found from a sexed tomb. Until it is, it will be difficult to say anything with certainty about the gender of the people who made the twining at Huaca Prieta.

INTERLACING

Unlike the cases of twining, looping, and netting, a significant body of archaeological evidence suggests that most interlacing weaving was done by women. This comes in the form of weaving baskets, which are almost never associated with men (however, the sex of an individual is often determined by the presence of weaving baskets and female garments, so it is possible that anatomical males who were buried dressed as women have been missed). In addition, there is ethnographical support that spinning and weaving on the north coast were primarily women's activities (Vreeland 1986: 368).

The only Preceramic weaving tool found at Huaca Prieta was probably used as a composite weaving tool—part pick and part batten—and was associated with the burial of a woman (HP09-01, see chapter 8 for the burial description and chapter 11 for a description of the tool). We should be cautious, however, about concluding that women were indeed weaving at Huaca Prieta. Women do not weave in every indigenous population. For example, a very similar tool was encountered in use by the Heta, a now extinct tribe of the Parana of southern Brazil, where men used it to make plain-weave fabrics on a loom with a circular warp (Kozak et al. 1979: 430, fig. 465).

Whether the Huaca Prieta fabrics were made by one or two populations, specialists or nonspecialists, men or women, their quality and sophistication suggest that they developed from an even older fabric-making tradition(s), clues of which have been found at such sites as Guitarrero Cave (for example, Adovasio and Lynch 1973). Huaca Prieta is special in the sheer number of specimens that it produced and their remarkable preservation and overall sophistication.

ACKNOWLEDGMENTS

I wish to thank Tom Dillehay for offering me the opportunity to analyze the Huaca Prieta textiles as well as William Conklin and Ann Rowe for their recommendations. I could not have finished my work without the assistance of Arabel Fernández and Patricia Landa, who helped me greatly while I was working in Peru. I would like to thank both Mary Frame and Ann Rowe for sharing their time and considerable expertise in the field of Andean textile studies. I would also like to acknowledge the late Duccio Bonavia for his support and advice. He was a "textile person" too. I will miss him and was privileged to have worked with him, however short the time was. Finally, I need to thank both Tom Dillehay and Chris Calvert for their incredible patience with me while I worked on this project.

PART 2: BASKETRY AND CORDAGE FROM HUACA PRIETA

Jeff Illingworth
and J. M. Adovasio

INTRODUCTION

This chapter addresses a sample of the basketry and cordage assemblages recovered during recent excavations at Huaca Prieta and selected materials from Bird's excavations. In the present context, basketry encompasses several distinct kinds of items, including rigid and semirigid containers or basketry proper, matting, and bags. Matting includes items that are essentially two-dimensional or flat, while baskets are three-dimensional. Bags can be viewed as intermediate forms, because they are two-dimensional when empty and three-dimensional when filled. As Harold Driver (1961: 159) points out, these artifacts can be treated as a unit because the overall technique of manufacture is the same in all instances. Specifically, all forms of basketry are manually woven without any frame or loom. While all forms of basketry are usually treated as varieties of textiles, in the present context the term "textile" denotes plant fiber–derived constructions that include infinitely flexible materials of theoretically unlimited length or lineal dimensions. In practice such items are generally made on some variety of hanging or horizontal frame or loom, whereas most varieties of basketry are not.

Three major kinds or subclasses of basketry are generally mutually exclusive: twining, coiling, and plaiting. Two of these subclasses, twining and plaiting, were recovered from Huaca Prieta. Additionally and unusually, some of the recovered basketry is a "hybrid" variety that utilizes both twining and plaiting technology.

Twining denotes a subclass of basket weaves manufactured by moving (active) horizontal elements called wafts around stationary (passive) vertical elements or wraps. Twining techniques can be employed to produce containers, mats, and bags as well as sandals, cradles, hats, items of clothing, fish traps, or other "atypical" basketry forms.

The term "plaiting" denotes a subclass of basket weaves in which all elements pass over and under each other without any engagement. For this reason, plaited basketry is technically described as unsewn. Plaiting can be used to make containers, bags, and mats as well as a wide range of other less "standard" forms. As noted above, the Huaca Prieta hybrid specimens combine both twining and plaiting in the same form, which is usually a type of container.

The term "cordage" denotes a class of elongated fibers and/or hair constructions with components generally subsumed under the terms "string" and "rope." As discussed below, most of the cordage recovered from Huaca Prieta appears to be detached fragments of textiles or basketry rather than string or rope *sensu stricto*.

HISTORY OF RESEARCH

Bird's excavations at Huaca Prieta produced a large corpus of basketry, cordage, and textiles. However, a comprehensive and detailed report on these materials did not appear until after Bird's death (Bird et al. 1985). The perishable plant fiber–derived artifacts reported in Bird et al. (1985) are among the first to accurately (in all but one case!) describe the depth and diversity of Preceramic perishable technology from Peru.

In order to familiarize himself with the Huaca Prieta basketry and cordage, Adovasio perused the collections in the American Museum of Natural History (AMNH) in the spring of 2009. That summer Adovasio analyzed the basketry recovered by Dillehay at the project field laboratory in Magdalena de Cao. A second trip to the AMNH occurred in 2012 and included Adovasio, Illingworth, and Dillehay. The object of this second visit was to ascertain whether the Bird collections contained any basketry or cordage types not represented in the Dillehay collections and vice versa. The analysis of the Dillehay-excavated cordage from Huaca Prieta was conducted by Illingworth at the R. L. Andrews Perishables Analysis facility at Mercyhurst University on specimens transported from Peru by J. Splitstoser. At the AMNH, Illingworth

conducted additional analysis of selected elements of the Bird cordage assemblage in 2012.

ANALYTICAL PROCEDURES

The vast majority of the analyzed specimens from this project did not require additional cleaning and were analyzed in an "as is" condition. The few specimens that did require cleaning were treated according to the protocols outlined in part 1 of this chapter.

Visual analysis was accomplished with the unaided eye and where warranted with the aid of either 10× magnification hand lens, 10–40× dissecting microscopes or with the aid of a Leica Wild M10 variable power stereomicroscope.

Macrophotographs of all of the basketry and a large portion of the cordage were produced in digital format with either a Nikon D90, Nikon D35, or Nikon D4 camera with variable DSLR lenses. All microphotographs were obtained with a Nikon D90 attached to a Leica Wild M10 stereomicroscope.

All measurements were obtained with either a Starrett Digital Caliper or a Helios Needle-Nosed Dial Caliper. All measurements and analytical data were recorded onto standardized analytical forms and are reported in millimeters unless otherwise noted.

CRITERIA OF CLASSIFICATION

The authors analyzed a total of 690 plant fiber–derived artifacts that were assigned to the basketry and cordage subclasses. Significantly, this total includes all representatives of all but one basketry type excavated by Dillehay and company and selected specimens excavated by Bird. As noted elsewhere in this chapter, a large collection of one basketry type was *not* available for analysis and an unspecified amount of cordage may remain unanalyzed. Significantly, only 18 specimens of Type II: Open Simple Twining Z-twist (paired) Wefts matting representing 15 individual forms were analyzed. As discussed further below, more than 50,000 fragments of this twining type, often heavily degraded, were recovered from all levels of the site but were *not* part of this study. Despite these lacunae, the analyzed collection *may* be considered generally representative of the perishable plant fiber–derived artifact assemblage from Huaca Prieta. Additionally, Bird specimens do not include all items recovered by him, but the sample does include representatives of all varieties of basketry or cordage reported in Bird et al. (1985).

BASKETRY

A total of 45 specimens of basketry were analyzed during this project. These include 44 pieces of twining and a single piece of plaiting. Twined specimens were allocated to three structural types based on the protocols outlined in Adovasio (2010), including the number and sequence of warps engaged at each weft crossing and the spacing of the weft rows. Additionally, all twined specimens were analyzed, where feasible, for selvage, method of starting, method of insertion of new warp and weft elements, method of preparation of warps and wefts, form, wear patterns, function, decorative patterns and mechanics, type and mechanics of mending, and raw materials.

The solitary plaited basketry specimen was allocated to a single structural type based on the interval of element engagement. Additionally, the specimen was analyzed for selvage treatment, shifts, methods of preparation of elements, form, wear patterns, function, type and mechanics of mending, and decorative patterns and mechanics.

CORDAGE

A total of 645 specimens were analyzed in the present study. While this analysis includes most of the specimens excavated by Dillehay, it only includes a selected sample of the Bird-collected assemblage. The analyzed cordage has been allocated to twenty structural types based on three interrelated construction attributes: (1) the number of penultimate ply elements; (2) the direction of twist (S, Z, or untwisted) of those penultimate elements; and (3) the method by which these elements are engaged (S-twist, Z-twist, or braided) to each other to create the finished product.

These attributes may require elucidation for some readers, particularly because identical terms are employed by some authors to designate quite different phenomena. The term "ply" as used here

denotes a strand or bunch of fibrous material that is twisted, spun, or, rarely, left untwisted. These strands may be used alone to form single-ply cordage or in groups to form multiple-ply cordage. When spun, they may be used to form warps or wefts of loom woven textiles, as noted above and below.

An individual ply can be homogeneous or simple in that it consists of a single strand or bunch of materials with the same twist or spin or may be compound. Compound plies are constructed with multiple strands or bunches of material that are individually twisted or spun and then retwisted or respun with each other, usually in the opposite direction. Compound plies are actually separate elements that form technically distinct finished products or types when combined with other such elements.

The Huaca Prieta cordage collection includes both actual string or rope specimens whose plies were not produced by spinning in the literal sense (compare Emery 1966: 9). Rather, these specimens are produced with "fibers of limited length" whose length or lineal dimension is increased by some form of splicing. Such items are in the distinct minority in the Huaca Prieta collection.

In describing such specimens, it is conventional to describe the initial twist as "spun" even though this is not technically accurate. Conversely, most specimens of certain types are spun via whorls and almost certainly represent disaggregated warps or wefts of loom- or frame-woven textiles.

The direction of initial twist or spin as well as final twist or spin can only be S or Z; these terms have exactly the same meaning as those specified in Emery (1966: 11). They are also the same as those employed in part 1 of this chapter.

In addition to these construction attributes, each cordage specimen was scrutinized for the presence and type of splices; the presence, type, and spacing of knots; and the angle of final twist or spin and any ancillary manipulations such as rat-tailing, crepe-twisting, and so forth. Finally, each specimen was analyzed for the presence of dyes or colorants, wear patterns, and any adhering or inorganic residues.

Knot terminology follows Geoffrey Budworth (2003). Angle of twist or spin measurements were taken according to procedures specified in Emery (1966: 11).

HUACA PRIETA BASKETRY

TYPE I: CLOSE SIMPLE TWINING, S-TWIST (PAIRED) WEFTS WITH AUXILIARY SIMPLE PLAITING (FIG. 12.17A–B)

Number of specimens: 8
Type of specimens: wall and rim fragments
(2009.116 [n = 4], 147, 2009.119); wall and
possible rim fragment, 1 (no number); wall
fragment, 1 (2009.130)
Number of individual specimens represented: 6
Type of forms represented: basket of indeterminate configuration, 5; bag, 1 (2009.130)

Technique and comments: Single warps of
either whole, undecorticated rush (*Juncus* sp.)
(147, unnumbered specimen, and 2009: 130) or
accidentally split, undecorticated rush are engaged
by paired weft elements composed of whole,
undecorticated rush (*Juncus* sp.), which alternate
with rows of simple plaiting 1/1 interval also of
whole, undecorticated rush (*Juncus* sp.). Wefts are
closely spaced so as to conceal the warps. None of
the specimens exhibit centers, although 4 exhibit
rim/end selvages. The rim/selvage of Specimen
147 is of the simple 180° variety with the warps
inserted into adjacent rows (fig. 12.17c1). On this
specimen three rows of simple S-twist twining
are present before the warp folds. The rim/selvage
treatments on Specimens 2009.116 and 2009.119
are more elaborate versions of the treatment on
Specimen 147. Specifically, on these specimens the
warp is divided into two separate pieces, folded to
the outside of the basket. The warps are then twill
plaited (3/3 interval) with other warp segments to
create a pseudo-braided appearance (fig. 12.17c2).
As on Specimen 147, three rows of simple S-twist
twining are effected before the selvage. The rim/
selvage of the specimen with no number is heavily
decayed and damaged but appears to have been
similar to that of Specimen 147. None of the specimens exhibit warp splices and weft splices of the
laid-in variety are observed only on the unnumbered specimen. Specimens 147 and 2009.116
were decorated by dying or painting some of the
warp and weft (both twined and plaited) elements
blue (Munsell dry 10B6/1); however, damage and
decay to the specimen make the determination
of any pattern impossible. None of the specimens

a

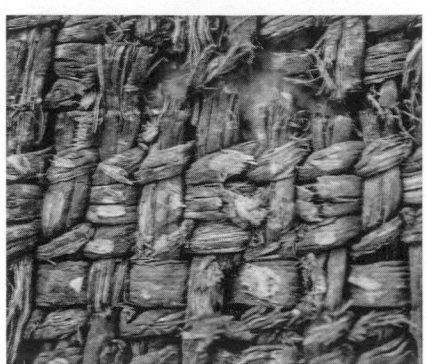

b

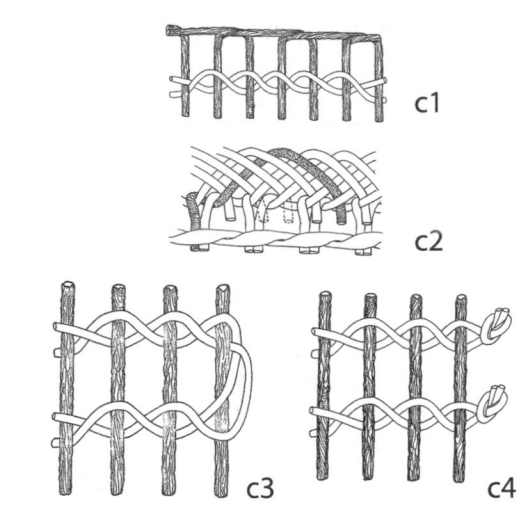

c

FIGURE 12.17. Close simple twining from Huaca Prieta:
a, Type I: Close Simple Twining, S-Twist (paired) Wefts with
Auxiliary Simple Plaiting, obverse surface (note blue elements);
b, close-up of *a; c,* schematic of twining selvages, all types:
c1. simple 180 selvage with warps inserted into adjacent rows
(Adovasio 2010: fig. 37); c2. selvage with the warp divided
into two separate pieces, folded to the outside of the basket;
the warps are then twill plaited (3/3 interval) with other warp
segments to create a pseudo-braided appearance (compare
Bird et al. 1985: fig. 60); c3. continuous weft simple self side
selvage (Adovasio 2010: fig. 44); c4. an overhand-knotted
simple side selvage (Adovasio 2010: fig. 42). (See color plates.)

exhibit mends. All specimens exhibit extensive postdepositional decay as well as varying degrees of predepositional or peridepositional distress that may have been intentional.

These specimens correspond to what Bird et al. (1985: 93–97) called "baskets with alternate rows of twining and weaving."

Measurements:
Warp diameter (range): 3.26–5.86 mm
Warp diameter (mean): 4.58 mm
Weft diameter (range): 2.43–4.16 mm
Weft diameter (mean): 3.33 mm
Warps/cm (range): 2–2
Warps/cm (mean): 2
Wefts/cm (range): 3–3
Wefts/cm (mean): 3
Weft row gap (range): 0.0–3.45 mm
Weft row gap (mean): 2.29 mm

TYPE II: OPEN, SIMPLE TWINING, Z-TWIST (PAIRED) WEFTS (FIG. 12.18A–B)

Number of specimens: 18
Type of specimens: wall with side selvage, 3 (2008.06.1, 2008.99.2 [n = 2]); wall fragment, 15 (2009.29.117, 2008.06.0, 2008.52.1, 2008.50.6 [n = 2], 2008.05.5, 145 [n = 9])
Number of individual specimens represented: 15
Type of forms represented: petate, 17; mat or petate, 1 (2008.06.1)

Technique and comments: Single warps of whole, undecorticated rush (*Juncus* sp.) are engaged by paired wefts of whole, undecorticated rush (*Juncus* sp.). Wefts are widely spaced in order to expose the warps. None of the specimens exhibits centers and only 2 exhibit selvages (both side selvages). Specimen 2008.06.1 has a continuous weft simple self-side selvage, while 2008.99.2 has an overhand-knotted simple side selvage. Warp splices are only observed on a single specimen (2008.50.6) and are accomplished by simply inserting a new warp into a preexisting weft crossing. Weft splices are found on 4 of the specimens. Specimens 2008.05.5 and 145 F2 exhibit simple, laid-in weft splices. Specimen 145 F6 has a weft

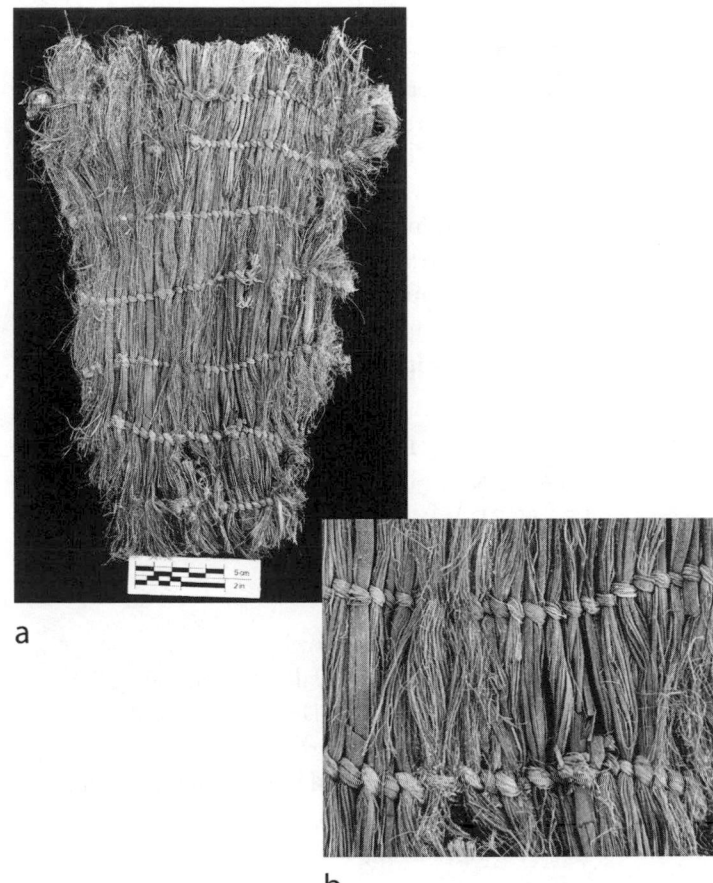

a

b

FIGURE 12.18. Open simple twining from Huaca Prieta: *a*, Type II: Open Simple Twining, Z-Twist (paired) Wefts, obverse surface; *b*, obverse side of *a*.

splice that is wrapped around a warp and then overhand-knotted to the exhausted weft. Specimen 2008.52.1 has a weft splice where the new material is overhand-knotted around a warp. All specimens exhibit extensive postdepositional decay. None of the specimens are decorated or mended.

An example of this type was directly dated to 11,159–10,600 cal BP (Beta235952) (see chapter 6). This specimen was not analyzed but, based on a field photo, appears to be a "typical" representative of this twining variety. The raw material employed in the warps is almost certainly *Juncus* sp., while the source of the wefts is not determinable from the image.

These specimens correspond to what Bird et al. (1985: 99–100) called "plain twining" and, as noted by Bird, constitute by far the most common twining type recovered from Huaca Prieta.

Measurements:
Warp diameter (range): 3.50–7.50 mm
Warp diameter (mean): 4.98 mm
Weft diameter (range): 2.41–6.45 mm
Weft diameter (mean): 4.37 mm
Warps/cm (range): 1–3
Warps/cm (mean): 1.9
Wefts/cm (range): 1–1
Wefts/cm (mean): 1
Weft row gap (range): 2.38–20.0 mm
Weft row gap (mean): 8.32 mm

TYPE III: CLOSE SIMPLE AND DIAGONAL TWINING, S-TWIST (PAIRED) WEFT WITH FUNCTIONAL WRAPPED TWINING (FIG. 12.19A–D AND 12.20A–B)

Number of specimens: 18
Type of specimens: wall fragments, 4
   (2008.91.2, 2009.118 [*n* = 12], 75.2, 75.1
   [*n* = 4])
Number of individual specimens represented: 4
Type of forms represented: basket of unknown
   configuration, 4

Technique and comments: Warps of rhetted and very loosely S-spun rush (*Juncus* sp.) are engaged singly (simple twined) and in pairs (diagonal twined) by paired weft elements composed of rhetted rush (*Juncus* sp.) and/or specimens of Type III cordage constructed of cotton (*Gossypium* sp.). These paired weft elements alternate between "normal" twining and wrapped twining to create intricate patterns.

Specimen 75.2 consists of a single fragment and was probably once part of Specimen 75.1. This specimen exhibits three rows of close-simple twining with paired S-twist wefts followed by six courses of finger-gauge wefts that are close-diagonal wrapped twined. This wrapped twined section uses one weft element of rhetted rush as the "stationary" weft and another weft element of Type III cordage, composed of either bluish cotton or cotton dyed blue, as the "moving" weft. All of the wrapping occurs on the presumed outside surface of the specimen. Following these six rows is a single row of diagonal twining composed of paired rhetted rush wefts. Directly below this are two rows of close, simple wrapped twining

using one rhetted rush weft as the stationary weft and a bluish (or blue-dyed) cotton as the moving weft. Following these two rows are a minimum of twenty-four rows (the specimen is broken) of close diagonal wrapped twining using the same weft combination as in the preceding wrapped twined rows. This specimen is without a center or rim. No warp splices were observed, while weft splices are laid-in. Decoration consists of the aforementioned changes in weft patterns, which probably produced an elaborate geometric pattern on the original specimen. It exhibits moderate abrasion wear on the presumed external surface and mild abrasion wear on the presumed interior surface. Both surfaces have moderate amounts of adherent sediment. The specimen is unmended but may have been intentionally cut or torn along one side prior to deposition.

Specimen 75.1 consists of four fragments and was probably once also part of Specimen 75.2. This specimen exhibits twelve rows of simple, paired weft twining composed of rhetted rush. Immediately below this section are three rows of decayed diagonal wrapped twining using one weft of rhetted rush and another weft of bluish or blue-dyed cotton. This specimen is without a center or rim and is also without warp or weft splices. Decoration may consist of the variation in weft manipulation, though the extent and nature of this is indeterminate due to the fragmentary nature of the specimen. It exhibits moderate abrasion wear on the presumed external surface and mild abrasion wear on the presumed interior surface. Both surfaces show moderate amounts of adherent sediment. The specimen is unmended but may have been intentionally cut or torn along at least one side.

Specimen 2008.91.2 consists of a single fragment and was presumably not part of any other specimens described in this report. It appears to be a wall fragment of a round or circular construction and is described from the apparent top (outer curve) to the apparent bottom (inner curve). The specimen consists of twenty-four extant weft rows. These are mostly diagonal wrapped twining, but several rows change within their course and incorporate limited lengths of simple wrapped twining, yielding a wall with intermittent diamond and triangular patterns. This wrapped twining employs rhetted rush as the stationary element

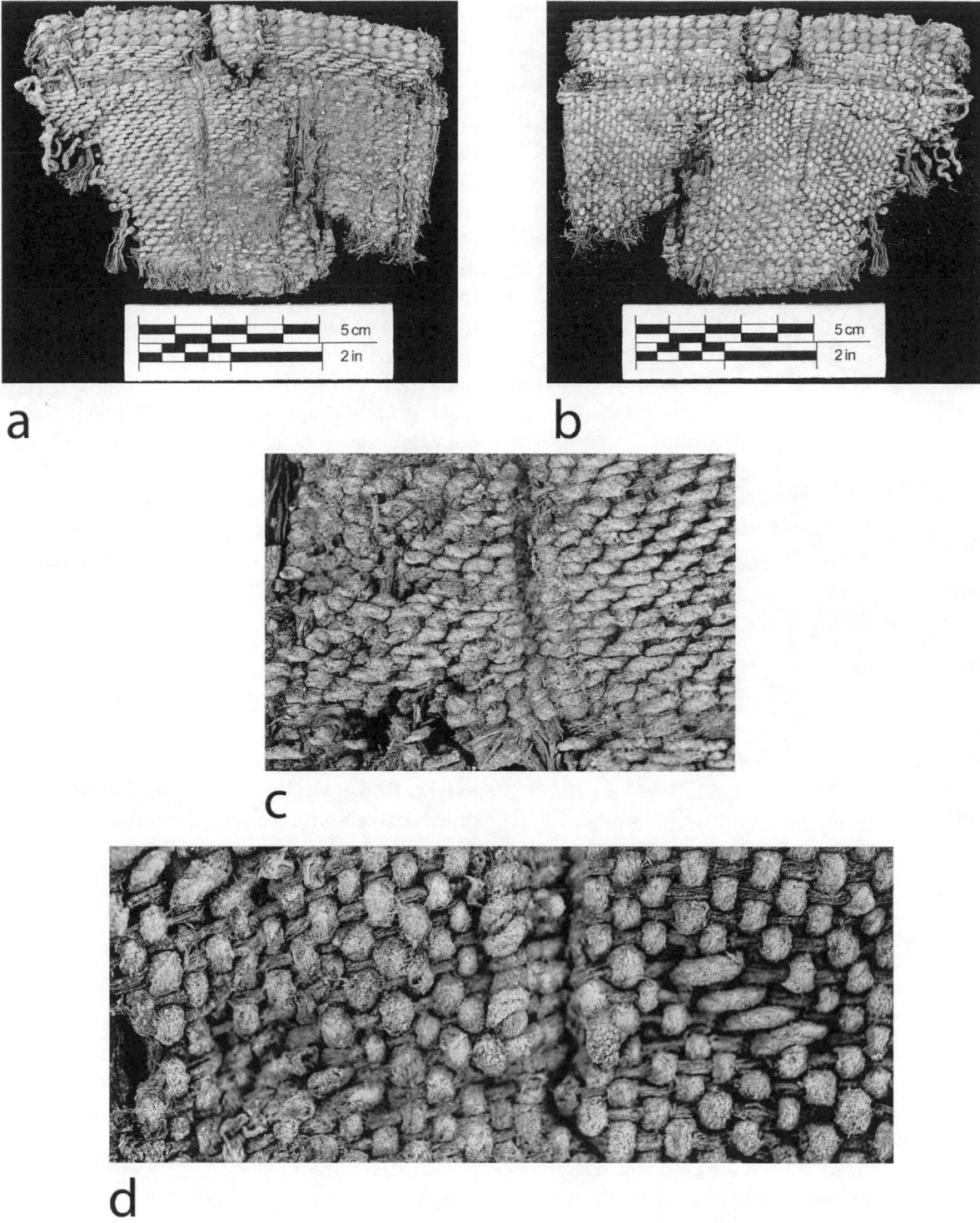

FIGURE 12.19. Close simple and diagonal twining from Huaca Prieta: *a*, Type III: Close Simple and Diagonal Twining, S-Twist (paired) Wefts with Functional Wrapped Twining, obverse surface (note blue elements); *b*, reverse side of *a*; *c*, close-up of obverse surface of *a*; *d*, close-up of reverse surface of *b*. (See color plates.)

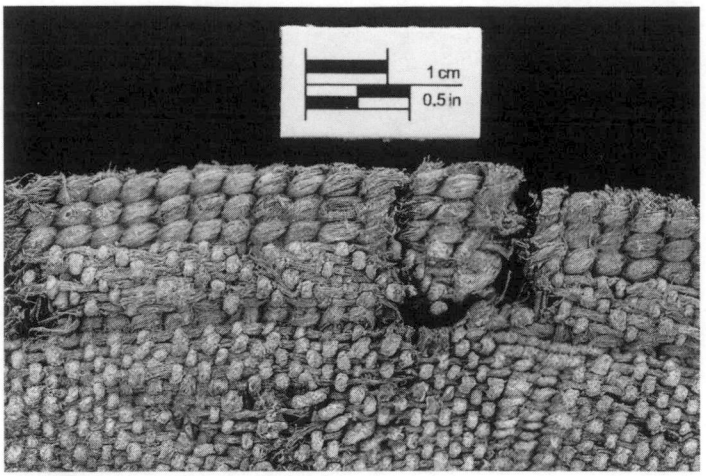

a

b

FIGURE 12.20. Close simple and diagonal twining from Huaca Prieta: *a*, Type III: Close Simple and Diagonal Twining, S-Twist (paired) Wefts with Functional Wrapped Twining, close-up obverse surface (note intentionally cut edge); *b*, Type IV: Simple Plaiting, 1/1 Interval, obverse surface.

and bluish or blue-dyed cotton as the moving element. The specimen is without center or rim. While the specimen does not exhibit warp splices, it does show weft splices that are overhand-knotted to the exhausted weft element. The aforementioned weft manipulations result in a decoration. The specimen exhibits moderate abrasion wear on the presumed external surface and mild abrasion wear on the presumed interior surface. Both surfaces have moderate amounts of adherent sediment. The specimen is unmended but does appear to have been intentionally cut or very neatly torn across the warp rows at both the top and bottom.

Specimen 2009.118 (fig. 12.20a) consists of eleven fragments that were presumably all once part of a single construction, though it is unclear how each of these fragments relates to any of the others. These fragments are sections of simple twining using paired, rhetted rush fibers and sections of diagonal wrapped twining wherein the stationary weft is rhetted rush fiber and the moving weft blue or blue-dyed cotton. Sections of this diagonal wrapped twining intermittently "shift" to two simple wrapped twined crossings in order to create a visual division between sections of the specimen. The item is too fragmentary to determine the nature of the intended visual effect. The specimen is without center or rim. While it does not exhibit warp splices, it does have weft splices that vary from laid-in to being looped around warps. It is decorated through the aforementioned weft manipulations. The specimen exhibits moderate abrasion wear on the presumed external surface and mild abrasion wear on the presumed interior surface. Both surfaces have moderate amounts of adherent sediment. The specimen is unmended but does appear to have been intentionally cut or very neatly torn across the warp rows at both the top and bottom.

All of these specimens generally correspond to what Bird et al. (1985: 97–98; figs. 56 and 62) called "baskets with patterns and cotton wefts." As discussed below, the original description of the wrapping appears to be incorrect.

Measurements:
Warp diameter (range): 1.44–2.81 mm
Warp diameter (mean): 2.10 mm
Weft diameter (range): 1.13–3.91 mm
Weft diameter (mean): 2.43 mm
Wrapped weft diameter (range): 0.90–1.70 mm
Wrapped weft diameter (mean): 1.27 mm
Warps/cm (range): 2.5–3
Warps/cm (mean): 2.9
Diagonal warps/cm (range): 4–6
Diagonal warps/cm (mean): 5
Wefts/cm (range): 3–6
Wefts/cm (mean): 3.8
Weft row gap (range/mean): 0

TYPE IV: SIMPLE PLAITING, 1/1 INTERVAL (FIG. 12.20B)

Number of specimens: 1
Type of specimen: wall fragment, 1 (151)
Number of individual specimens represented: 1
Type of form represented: circular mat or base of container, 1

Technique and comments: single elements of Type III Cordage, composed of rush (*Juncus* sp.) fibers, pass over and under an alternate set of elements, composed of now badly decayed rush (*Juncus* sp.) leaves in a 1/1 interval that evenly exposes both sets of elements. The specimen exhibits no shifts, decorations, or mends. It is sufficiently decayed so as to not retain any center or rim elements.

This specimen does not correspond to any form or type reported by Bird et al. (1985).

Measurements:
Pseudo-warp diameter (range/mean): 5.11 mm
Pseudo-weft diameter (range): 3.70–4.0 mm
Pseudo-weft diameter (mean): 3.85 mm
Angle of element crossing (range/mean): 90°

HUACA PRIETA CORDAGE

TYPE I: SINGLE PLY, Z-SPUN (FIG. 12.21)

Number of specimens: 2
Type of specimens: fragment, 2 (2009.69.10, 41.2/1840D)
Number of individual forms represented: 2
Type of form represented: generic cordage, 2

Technique and comments: A single bundle of either cotton (*Gossypium* sp.) or an indeterminate bast fiber are Z-spun together. Neither specimen exhibits splices, mends, decoration, knots, or diagnostic wear. The cotton-based specimen (2009.69.10) appears to be spindle-spun stock weaving material.

Measurements:
Length (range): 4.55–6.25 mm
Length (mean): 5.40 mm

Cord diameter (range): 1.45–1.65 mm
Cord diameter (mean): 1.55 mm
Ply diameter (range): n/a
Ply diameter (mean): n/a
Angle of twist (range): 28.5°–31.5°
Angle of twist (mean): 30°
Twist/cm (range): 1.5–1.5
Twist/cm (mean): 1.5

TYPE II: SINGLE PLY, S-SPUN (FIG. 12.21)

Number of specimens: 1
Type of specimen: fragment, 1 (2007.24.01)
Number of individual forms represented: 1
Type of form represented: cord-wrapped stick (spindle?), 1

Technique and comments: A single bundle of cotton (?) (*Gossypium* sp.) fibers are S-spun together. The cord exhibits no splices, mends, knots, decoration, or diagnostic wear. The specimen is haphazardly wrapped, generally from left to right, around a decorticated stick of indeterminate taxon. This stick is broken in several places, and the cord actually holds it together. While the stick exhibits no tool marks or diagnostic wear, it is possible that this represents a discarded spindle for spinning weaving stock.

Measurements:
Length (range/mean): 27.55 mm
Cord diameter (range/mean): 0.50 mm
Ply diameter (range/mean): n/a
Angle of twist (range/mean): 27°
Twist/cm (range/mean): 1.5

TYPE III: TWO PLY, S-SPUN, Z-TWIST (FIG. 12.21)

Number of specimens: 547 (minimum)
Type of specimens: fragment (2007.02.02, 2007.02.04, 2007.18.07, 2007.18.08, 2007.22.01, 2007.22.04, 2007.32.01, 2008.02.1, 2008.36.1, 2008.38.15a–b, 2008.38.20, 2008.38.22, 2008.73.1, 2008.88.3a, 2008.88.3a, 2008.88.3b, 2009.102.36, 2009.113.3, 2009.115.4, 2009.133.1, 2009.133.4, 2009.133.5, 2009.141.1, 2009.141.3, 2009.141.4,

Type I Z

Type II S

Type III $Z\genfrac{}{}{0pt}{}{S}{S}$

Type IV $S\genfrac{}{}{0pt}{}{Z}{Z}$

Type V $Z\genfrac{}{}{0pt}{}{S}{\genfrac{}{}{0pt}{}{S}{S}}$

Type VI $S\genfrac{}{}{0pt}{}{Z}{\genfrac{}{}{0pt}{}{Z}{Z}}$

Type VII $S\genfrac{}{}{0pt}{}{Z}{\genfrac{}{}{0pt}{}{Z}{\genfrac{}{}{0pt}{}{Z}{Z}}}$

Type VIII $Z(S)^{12}$

Type IX $Z\genfrac{}{}{0pt}{}{S}{Sz}$

Type X $Z\genfrac{}{}{0pt}{}{SI}{\genfrac{}{}{0pt}{}{SI}{SI}}$

Type XI $Z\genfrac{}{}{0pt}{}{Sz}{Sz}$

Type XII $S\genfrac{}{}{0pt}{}{Zs}{\genfrac{}{}{0pt}{}{Zs}{Zs}}$... $S\genfrac{}{}{0pt}{}{Zs}{Zs}$

Type XIII $Z\genfrac{}{}{0pt}{}{Ss}{\genfrac{}{}{0pt}{}{Ss}{Ss}}$

Type XIV $S\genfrac{}{}{0pt}{}{Zs}{Zs}$

Type XV $Z\genfrac{}{}{0pt}{}{Sz}{\genfrac{}{}{0pt}{}{Sz}{\genfrac{}{}{0pt}{}{Sz}{Sz}}}$

Type XVI $Z\genfrac{}{}{0pt}{}{S(Z)^3}{\genfrac{}{}{0pt}{}{S(Z)^3}{S(Z)^3}}$

Type XVII $Z\genfrac{}{}{0pt}{}{S(Zs)^3}{S(Zs)^3}$

Type XVIII $Z\genfrac{}{}{0pt}{}{S(Zs)^8}{S(Zs)^8}$

Type XIX $\#I$

FIGURE 12.21. Ply formulae of all identified Huaca Prieta cordage types.

2009.148.4, 2009.156.1, 2009.233.2, 2009.44.2, 2009.65.1b–c, 2009.68.10, 2009.68.10, 2009.68.13, 2009.68.14, 2009.68.15, 2009.68.16, 2009.68.17, 2009.68.18, 2009.68.19, 2009.68.2, 2009.68.20, 2009.68.21, 2009.68.4, 2009.68.5, 2009.68.6, 2009.68.7, 2009.68.8, 2009.69.12a–c, 2009.69.15, 2009.69.16, 2009.69.17, 2009.69.19, 2009.75.11, 2009.75.12, 2009.93.13, 2009.96.6, 2009.96.7, 2009.98.25, 2009.98.26, 2009.98.27, 2009.98.28, 2009.98.29, 2009.98.30, 41.1, 9238 and 9239, 41.1/9096, 41.1/9113A–E, 41.1/9115, 41.1/9115A, 41.1/9240A, 41.1/9242, 41.1/9431A–C, 41.1/9535, 41.1/9577G, 41.1/9631A, 41.1/9688A, 41.1/9884A, 41.2/1201, 41.2/129F, 41.2/1751 B2, 41.2/1751 C1, 41.2/1751B2, 41.2/1751C1, 41.2/1751D, 41.2/1840A, 41.2/1841A, 41.2/1841B, 41.2/1859, 41.2/1861, 41.2/2495A,B, 41.2/2542, 41.2/2543, 41.2/2587A, 41.2/2588, 41.2/2602A, 41.2/2602A, 41.2/2608, 41.2/3067A, 41.2/3068D, 42.1/1841A). These specimen numbers represent multiple specimens under the same number, often in wadded masses of 50+ cords.

Number of individual forms represented: 547 (minimum)

Type of form represented: Generic cordage, 547 (minimum)

Technique and comments: Two bundles of fibers composed of cotton (*Gossypium* sp.) (2009.148.4, 2009.156.1, 2009.98.30, 41.1 9238, 41.1 9239, 41.1/9113A–E, 41.1/9240A, 41.1/9431A–C, 41.2/1840A, 41.2/1859, 41.2/2587A, 41.2/2588 41.2/2608), rush (*Juncus* sp.) (41.1/9096, 41.1/9115, 41.1/9115A, 41.1/9242, 41.1/9535, 41.1/9577G, 41.1/9631A, 41.1/9688A, 41.2/129F, 41.2/1751 C1, 41.2/2495A,B, 41.2/2543, 41.2/3068D, 41.2/1751C1, 2007.02.02, 2007.18.07, 2007.18.08, 2007.32.01, 2009.113.3, 2009.115.4, 2009.133.1, 2009.141.1, 2009.141.3, 2009.93.13, 2009.98.27), or bast fibers of an indeterminate taxa are S-spun and subsequently Z-twisted together. None of the specimens are crepe-twisted. Specimens 41.2/1751C, 41.2/2588, and 41.2/2608 are rat-tailed. Where present, splices are either laid-in (41.1/9115A, 41.1/9242, 41.2/1201, 41.2/1751B2, 41.2/1751C1, 41.2/2588, 41.2/26082009.69.15); S-twisted (41.2/1841A, 41.2/1841B, 42.1/1841A); or looped (2009.68.13). None of the specimens are mended or decorated. Overhand knots are present on specimens 41.1/9431A–C, 41.2/1841A, 2008.36.1, 41.1/9240A, 2009.69.15, 2009.141.3, 2009.69.16, 2009.69.19, 2009.68.2, 2008.38.15a–b, and 2009.69.17. Square knots are present on specimens 42.1/1841A, 41.1/9115, 2008.88.3a, 41.2/2542, and 41.2/1751D. Specimen 41.2/1859 is chain looped. Wear is variable throughout these specimens. 42.1/2588 and 2009.69.12a–c exhibit heavy abrasion wear, while 41.2/1861, 41.2/2587A, 41.2/1751B2, 41.2/1751D, 2009.148.4, 2008.38.22, 2009.68.13, 2009.98.26, and 41.2/1751B2 exhibit moderate or medium levels of abrasion wear. 41.2/1751C1, 2008.38.20, 41.1/9096, 41.1/9240A, 41.2/1751C1, 2009.68.2, 2007.22.01, 2007.18.08, 41.2/1859, and 41.2/1840A show mild abrasion wear. The remaining specimens are generally coated in a mix of organic and inorganic detritus. The vast majority of these specimens appear similar to weaving element material described in part 1 of this chapter.

Measurements:
Length (range): 10.0–249.20 mm
Length (mean): 26.21 mm

Cord diameter (range): 0.70–9.40 mm
Cord diameter (mean): 2.72 mm
Ply diameter (range): 0.20–5.95 mm
Ply diameter (mean): 1.57 mm
Angle of twist (range): 21°–52°
Angle of twist (mean): 36.6°
Twist/cm (range): 1–14
Twist/cm (mean): 4.6

TYPE IV: TWO PLY, Z-SPUN, S-TWIST (FIG. 12.21)

Number of specimens: 21 (minimum)
Type of specimens: fragment, 21 (2007.03.07, 2007.13.01a, 2008.100.11, 2009.126.1, 2009.127.1, 2009.26.1a, 2009.26.1b, 2009.68.10, 2009.69.11, 2009.69.13, 41.2/1840A [*n* = 3], 41.2/1861, 41.2/2587D [*n* = 4], 41.2/2602B [*n* = 3])
Number of individual forms represented: 14 (?)
Type of form represented: bracelet (?), 3; sling (?), 1; generic cordage, 16

Technique and comments: Two bundles of cotton (*Gossypium* sp.) fibers (41.2/2587D, 2007.13.01a), rush (*Juncus* sp.) fibers (2007.03.07), or bast fibers of an indeterminate taxa are Z-spun and subsequently S-twisted together. None of the specimens have crepe-twisting, rat-tailing, mending, or decoration. Specimens 41.2/2602B, 2009.26.1a, and 2009.68.10 exhibit Z-twisted ply splices. Specimen 2007.13.01a is replete with laid-in ply splices using Z-spun plies as new material. The remaining specimens are unspliced. Specimen 41.2/1840A has two lark's-head knots and one overhand knot. Specimen 2008.100.11 exhibits a single overhand knot.

Specimens 2009.26.1a, 2009.26.1b, 2009.69.11, and 2009.69.13 appear to have been bracelets or something similar. Specimen 2009.26.1b is folded on itself four times and overhand knotted to complete the loop series (the specimen appears to have broken during or shortly after excavation). Specimen 2009.69.11 is doubled or quadrupled and overhand knotted on itself. Specimen 2009.69.13 is doubled on itself and then tied with an overhand-on-a-bight stacked on a standard overhand (shoe knot). Specimen 2009.26.1a is coiled but currently unknotted and was probably a bracelet construction as well.

Specimen 2007.13.01a is looped on itself three times, with the base of all three loops bound by an overhand knot. The specimen is generally similar to the "sling shots" described by Bird et al. (1985: 214) and is presumed to be one of these forms.

*Wear is variable among these specimens of this type. Specimens 41.2/1840A, 41.2/2602B, 2007.03.07, 2009.126.1, and 2009.68.10 exhibit no discernible wear. Specimens 41.2/1861 and 2009.69.11 have mild abrasion while 2009.69.11 also has adherent red ochre staining. Specimens 2009.127.1 and 2008.200.11 are both heavily abraded, while 2009.100.11 is also encrusted in a concretion of matrix and indeterminate organic residue. The remaining specimens are encrusted in a concretion similar to that of 2009.100.11.

Measurements:
Length (range): 60.05–140.0 mm
Length (mean): 27.25 mm
Cord diameter (range): 0.75–7.20 mm
Cord diameter (mean): 2.14 mm
Ply diameter (range): 0.45–4.60 mm
Ply diameter (mean): 1.28 mm
Angle of twist (range): 19°–46°
Angle of twist (mean): 33.14°
Twist/cm (range): 1–14
Twist/cm (mean): 4.86

TYPE V: THREE PLY, S-SPUN, Z-TWIST (FIG. 12.21)

Number of specimens: 19
Type of specimens: fragment, 19 (2007.03.08, 2007.22.02, 2007.22.03, 2008.38.16, 2008.38.18, 41.1/9115B [n = 9], 41.1/9243, 41.1/9535, 41.1/9688B, 41.1/9884G, 41.2/1294)
Number of individual forms represented: 19
Type of form represented: generic cordage, 19

Technique and comments: Three bundles of rush (*Juncus* sp.) (41.1/9115B, 41.1/9243, 41.1/9535, 41.1/9688B), sedge (Cyperaceae) (41.1/9884G), or an indeterminate bast fiber are S-spun and subsequently Z-twisted together. None of the specimens are crepe-twisted, rat-tailed, spliced, mended, or decorated. Specimen 2007.22.03 exhibits an overhand knot on one end. None of the remaining specimens are knotted.

Wear is generally minimal to nonexistent. Specimens 41.1/9688B and 2008.38.18 exhibit mild abrasion. Specimen 2008.38.16 exhibits wear consistent with having once been knotted. Specimen 2007.03.08 is encrusted with a concretion of sedimentary matrix and an indeterminate organic residue.

Measurements:
Length (range): 27.25–200.00 mm
Length (mean): 18.18 mm
Cord diameter (range): 1.20–17.55 mm
Cord diameter (mean): 6.63 mm
Ply diameter (range): 0.70–8.35 mm
Ply diameter (mean): 02.93 mm
Angle of twist (range): 29°–50°
Angle of twist (mean): 38.09°
Twist/cm (range): 01–8
Twist/cm (mean): 03.5

TYPE VI: THREE PLY, S-SPUN, Z-TWIST (FIG. 12.21)

Number of specimens: 20 (minimally)
Type of specimens: fragments, 20 (minimally) (41.1/9430A–C [n = 20+])
Number of individual forms represented: 1
Type of form represented: mass of weaving stock, 1

Technique and comments: Three S-spun plies, constructed from cotton (*Gossypium* sp.) fibers, are Z-twisted together. The specimen consists of at least twenty pieces of cordage in a loosely wadded mass that appears to have been weaving stock. None of the specimens exhibit crepe-twisting, rat-tailing, splices, decoration, mends, or knots. The specimens are essentially without wear and appear to have been abandoned/deposited prior to use.

Measurements:
Length (range): 9.25–12.35 mm
Length (mean): 11.16 mm
Cord diameter (range): 0.55–1.05 mm
Cord diameter (mean): 0.70 mm
Ply diameter (range): 0.05–0.25 mm
Ply diameter (mean): 0.10 mm
Angle of twist (range): 18°–25°
Angle of twist (mean): 22.5°

Twist/cm (range): 10–17
Twist/cm (mean): 14

TYPE VII: FIVE PLY, Z-SPUN, S-TWIST CORDAGE (FIG. 12.21)

Number of specimens: 1
Type of specimen: fragment, 1 (2009.146.1)
Number of individual forms represented: 1
Type of form represented: generic cordage, 1

Technique and comments: Five Z-spun plies, each composed of the same indeterminate bast fiber, are S-twisted together. This specimen is neither crepe-twisted nor rat-tailed. The specimen is without splices, knots, decoration, or mends. It is heavily stained, though the staining appears to be the result of postdepositional processes as opposed to use-related.

Measurements:
Length (range/mean): 22.5 mm
Cord diameter (range/mean): 1.45 mm
Ply diameter (range/mean): 0.85 mm
Angle of twist (range/mean): 35.5°
Twist/cm (range/mean): 7.5

TYPE VIII: TWELVE PLY, S-SPUN, Z-TWIST (FIG. 12.21)

Number of specimens: 1
Type of specimen: fragment, 1 (2008.62.2)
Number of individual forms represented: 1
Type of form represented: damaged textile fragment, 1

Technique and comments: Twelve S-spun bundles of cotton (*Gossypium* sp.) fibers are Z-twisted together. Interestingly, all of these "plies" are actually the warp units of a very heavily damaged 1/1 Interval plaited textile. As a piece of cordage, the specimen does not exhibit crepe-twisting, rat-tailing, splices, mends, knots, or decoration. The specimen exhibits no wear attributable to its post-twisted state.

Measurements:
Length (range/mean): 212.55 mm
Cord diameter (range/mean): 2.65 mm
Ply diameter (range/mean): 0.45 mm

Angle of twist (range/mean): 36°
Twist/cm (range/mean): 13

TYPE IX: COMPOUND, TWO PLY, S-SPUN, Z-TWIST (FIG. 12.21)

Number of specimens: 1
Type of specimen: fragment, 1 (2009.68.11)
Number of individual forms represented: 1
Type of form represented: generic cordage, 1

Technique and comments: One strand of Type II Cordage and one strand of Type VI (Three Ply, S-Spun, Z-Twist) cordage, both composed of an indeterminate bast fiber, are Z-twisted together. The specimen is neither crepe-twisted nor rat-tailed and is without splices, knots, decoration, or mends. The specimen exhibits abrasion wear consistent with having once been knotted.

Measurements:
Length (range/mean): 29.75 mm
Cord diameter (range/mean): 2.26 mm
Ply diameter (range/mean): 1.85 mm
Angle of twist (range/mean): 34°
Twist/cm (range/mean): 4.5

TYPE X: COMPOUND, TWO PLY, S-SPUN, Z-TWIST (FIG. 12.21)

Number of specimens: 2
Type of specimens: fragments, 2 (2007.02.01, 2007.02.03)
Number of individual forms represented: 2
Type of form represented: generic cordage, 2

Technique and comments: Two cords composed of unspun bundles of rush (*Juncus* sp.) fibers are S-spun together and subsequently Z-twisted together. Neither specimen is crepe-twisted or rat-tailed. Specimen 2007.02.03 exhibits a laid-in ply splice, while Specimen 2007.02.01 is without splices. Neither specimen is knotted, decorated, or mended. Both specimens are without diagnostic use wear but are encrusted in a conglomeration of sediment and indeterminate organic residue.

Measurements:
Length (range): 15.60–25.55 mm
Length (mean): 20.58 mm

Cord diameter (range): 7.00–9.20 mm
Cord diameter (mean): 8.10 mm
Ply diameter (range): 4.00–4.30 mm
Ply diameter (mean): 4.15 mm
Angle of twist (range): 31°–42°
Angle of twist (mean): 36.5°
Twist/cm (range): 1.5–2
Twist/cm (mean): 1.75

TYPE XI: COMPOUND, TWO PLY, S-SPUN, Z-TWIST (FIG. 12.21)

Number of specimens: 12
Type of specimens: complete (?), 1
    (41.1/9700A); fragment, 11 (2007.18.06,
    2009.129.1, 2009.68.12, 2009.68.3,
    2009.68.9, 2009.69.9, 41.1/9096,
    41.2/1750E, 41.2/1751C1, 41.2/2587E,
    41.2/2605)
Number of individual forms represented: 12
Type of form represented: net float holder (?),
    1 (41.1/9700A); generic cordage, 11

Technique and comments: Two segments of
Type IV (Two Ply, Z-Spun, S-Twist) cordage
composed of cotton (*Gossypium* sp.) (41.1/9096,
41.1/9700A, 41.2/1750E, 41.2/2587E,
41.2/2605) fiber, an indeterminate bast
(2006.68.12, 2009.129.1, 2007.18.06, 2009.68.3,
2009.68.9, 2009.69.9) fiber, or rush (*Juncus* sp.)
(41.2/1751C1, 2009.129.1) are S-twisted together.
None of the specimens exhibit crepe-twisting or
rat-tailing. Specimen 41.1/9700A exhibits a laid-
in ply splice, while the remaining specimens are
unspliced. None of the specimens are mended
or decorated. Specimen 41.2/1750E has a square
knot, and Specimen 2009.129.1 has an overhand
knot on one end. Specimen 41.1/9700A is looped
on itself four times with additional cords of
equivalent characteristics looped and subsequently
lark's-head knotted to the core cord. The museum
tag claims that this was part of a net float structure. None of the other specimens exhibit knots.
Specimen 41.1/9700A shows mild abrasion wear,
and Specimen 41.2/1750E shows heavy abrasion.
The remaining specimens, while without diagnostic wear, are generally filthy and are heavily
encrusted with sediment and/or organic residue.

Measurements:
Length (range): 68.70–184.65 mm
Length (mean): 51.88 mm
Cord diameter (range): 1.50–4.50 mm
Cord diameter (mean): 2.92 mm
Ply diameter (range): 0.20–3.00 mm
Ply diameter (mean): 1.75 mm
Angle of twist (range): 28°–43°
Angle of twist (mean): 40°
Twist/cm (range): 2–5.5
Twist/cm (mean): 3.5

TYPE XII: COMPOUND, TWO PLY, Z-SPUN, S-TWIST (FIG. 12.21)

Number of specimens: 6
Type of specimens: fragment, 6 (2009.69.14,
    41.2/1201, 41.2/1751B2, 41.2/2496,
    41.2/2587B, 41.2/2587C)
Number of individual forms represented: 6
Type of form represented: sling (?), 1
    (2009.69.14); generic cordage, 5

Technique and comments: Two segments of
Type III (Two Ply, S-Spun, Z-Twist) cordage
composed of cotton (*Gossypium* sp.) (41.2/1201,
41.2/2587B, 41.2/2587C) fiber, an indeterminate bast (41.2/1751B2, 2009.69.14) fiber,
or human (*Homo sapiens*) hair (41.2/2496) are
S-twisted together. Specimens 2009.69.14 and
41.2/2587C are re-plied on themselves, yielding a
crepe-twisted appearance. None of the specimens
have splices, mends, or decorations. Specimen
41.2/2496 exhibits two roughly evenly spaced
overhand knots, and Specimen 2009.69.14 is overhand knotted on itself twice (possibly as part of
its formation into a sling). Specimens 41.2/2487B,
41.2/2487C, and 2009.69.14 are encrusted in a
mix of sediment and indeterminate organic residue. Specimen 41.2/2587B also exhibits mild
abrasion. Specimen 41.2/1751B2 has medium
abrasion. The remaining two specimens do not
exhibit diagnostic wear.

Measurements:
Length (range): 28.55 mm–175.05 mm
Length (mean): 87.5 mm
Cord diameter (range): 2.0–3.65 mm
Cord diameter (mean): 2.67 mm

Ply diameter (range): 1.20–1.80 mm
Ply diameter (mean): 1.58 mm
Angle of twist (range): 22°–40°
Angle of twist (mean): 33.3°
Twist/cm (range): 3–5.5
Twist/cm (mean): 3.9

TYPE XIII: COMPOUND, TWO PLY, S-SPUN, Z-TWIST (FIG. 12.21)

Number of specimens: 1
Type of specimen: fragment, 1 (42.2/1291)
Number of individual forms represented: 1
Type of form represented: generic cordage, 1

Technique and comments: Two segments of four-ply S-spun, S-twist cordage composed of rush (*Juncus* sp.) are Z-twisted together. The specimen is without splices, mends, decoration, or knots. It exhibits no diagnostic wear.

Measurements:
Length (range/mean): 27.50 mm
Cord diameter (range/mean): 6.60 mm
Ply diameter (range/mean): 3.55 mm
Angle of twist (range/mean): 54°
Twist/cm (range/mean): 2

TYPE XIV: COMPOUND, TWO PLY, Z-SPUN, S-TWIST (FIG. 12.21)

Number of specimens: 1
Type of specimen: fragment, 1 (2009.69.20)
Number of individual forms represented: 1
Type of form represented: generic cordage, 1

Technique and comments: Two segments of four-ply S-spun, Z-twist cordage composed of an indeterminate bast fiber are S-twisted together. The specimen is without splices, mends, or decoration. It exhibits a single overhand knot on one end. The specimen, while filthy with a concretion of sediment and indeterminate organic residue, is without diagnostic wear.

Measurements:
Length (range/mean): 160.0 mm
Cord diameter (range/mean): 1.55 mm
Ply diameter (range/mean): 0.70 mm

Angle of twist (range/mean): 28°
Twist/cm (range/mean): 4

TYPE XV: COMPOUND, THREE PLY, S-SPUN, Z-TWIST (FIG. 12.21)

Number of specimens: 2
Type of specimens: fragment, 2 (2008.38.21, 41.1/9431D)
Number of individual forms represented: 2
Type of form represented: generic cordage, 2

Technique and comments: Three segments of Type IV (Two Ply, Z-Spun, S-Twist) cordage composed of either an indeterminate bast fiber (2008.38.21) or cotton (*Gossypium* sp.) (41.1/9431D) are Z-twisted together. Specimen 2008.38.21 is re-plied on itself and exhibits a moderately crepe-twisted appearance. Neither specimen is spliced, mended, decorated, or knotted. Specimen 41.1/9431D has medium abrasion; the other specimen is generally without wear.

Measurements:
Length (range): 27.20–52.05 mm
Length (mean): 39.63 mm
Cord diameter (range): 1.90–2.85 mm
Cord diameter (mean): 2.38 mm
Ply diameter (range): 1.20–1.40 mm
Ply diameter (mean): 1.30 mm
Angle of twist (range): 22°–31°
Angle of twist (mean): 26.5°
Twist/cm (range): 3–6
Twist/cm (mean): 4.5

TYPE XVI: COMPOUND, THREE PLY, S-SPUN, Z-TWIST (FIG. 12.21)

Number of specimens: 1
Type of specimen: fragment, 1 (41.2/1751 B3)
Number of individual forms represented: 1
Type of form represented: generic cordage, 1

Technique and comments: Three segments of Type VI (Three Ply, S-Spun, Z-Twist) cordage, composed of an indeterminate bast fiber, are Z-twisted together. The specimen is without splices, mends, decoration, or knots. It is heavily abraded and generally filthy from a mixed concretion of sediment and unidentified organic residue.

Measurements:
Length (range/mean): 27.55 mm
Cord diameter (range/mean): 4.65 mm
Ply diameter (range/mean): 2.60 mm
Angle of twist (range/mean): 35.5°
Twist/cm (range/mean): 4

TYPE XVII: COMPOUND, TWO PLY, S-SPUN, Z-TWIST (FIG. 12.21)

Number of specimens: 2
Type of specimens: fragment, 2 (41.2/1751A, 41.2/2551C)
Number of individual forms represented: 2
Type of form represented: generic cordage, 2

Technique and comments: Two S-twisted cords, each constructed of three pieces of Type III (Two Ply, S-Spun, Z-Twist) cordage composed of cotton (*Gossypium* sp.) fibers, are Z-twisted together. Splices, which are laid-in Z-spun plies, are apparent only on Specimen 41.2/2551C. Neither specimen exhibits mends, decoration, or knots. Specimen 41.2/1751A is heavily abraded, while Specimen 41.2/2551C exhibits decay generally consistent with that caused by decomposing flesh.

Measurements:
Length (range): 155.60 mm–240.10 mm
Length (mean): 179.85 mm
Cord diameter (range): 2.70–4.00 mm
Cord diameter (mean): 3.35 mm
Ply diameter (range): 1.75–2.95 mm
Ply diameter (mean): 2.35 mm
Angle of twist (range): 23.5°–38°
Angle of twist (mean): 30.75°
Twist/cm (range): 1.5–2
Twist/cm (mean): 1.75

TYPE XVIII: COMPOUND, TWO PLY, S-SPUN, Z-TWIST (FIG. 12.21)

Number of specimens: 1
Type of specimen: fragment, 1 (41.2/129J)
Number of individual forms represented: 1
Type of form represented: generic cordage, 1

Technique and comments: Two S-twisted cords, each constructed of eight pieces of Type III Cordage composed of cotton (*Gossypium* sp.) fibers, are Z-twisted together. The specimen is without splices, knots, decoration, or mends. The specimen is moderately abraded and generally coated in an adherent mix of sediment and organic residues of an indeterminate nature.

Measurements:
Length (range/mean): 53.30 mm
Cord diameter (range/mean): 3.65 mm
Ply diameter (range/mean): 2.15 mm
Angle of twist (range/mean): 8°
Twist/cm (range/mean): 3

TYPE XIX: THREE STRAND, UNSPUN, BRAID (FIG. 12.21)

Number of specimens: 4
Type of specimens: fragments, 4 (2008.38.17, 41.1/9115C, 41.1/9884C, 41.2/2547)
Number of individual forms represented: 4
Type of form represented: generic cordage, 4

Technique and comments: Three unspun plies of rush (*Juncus* sp.), sedge (Cyperaceae), or an indeterminate bast fiber are plaited in a 1/1 interval to form a three-strand braid. None of the specimens exhibit splices, mends, or decoration. Specimen 41.2/2547 has two stacked square knots in the approximate center of the cord. It is unclear whether the specimen was tied on itself or represents two equivalent pieces tied together. None of the other specimens exhibit knotting. Diagnostic wear, in the form of knot-related abrasion, was observed only on Specimen 2008.38.17. Specimen 41.2/2547 may be associated with a human burial (Skeleton 99.1/900 of Test Pit 3, Layer 1).

Measurements:
Length (range): 102.55–498.75 mm
Length (mean): 324.85 mm
Cord diameter (range): 2.75–13.15 mm
Cord diameter (mean): 8.06 mm
Ply diameter (range): 1.75–7.15 mm
Ply diameter (mean): 5.06 mm

INTERNAL CORRELATIONS

A total of 690 specimens of plant fiber–derived artifacts were analyzed from Huaca Prieta. As noted elsewhere in this volume, this total is only a fraction of the total fiber inventory from the site. It does, however, contain *all* of the types recovered by Bird as well as several "new" variants. These include 45 examples of basketry and 645 examples of cordage. A synopsis and an assessment of these materials are presented below by subclass.

BASKETRY

TECHNOLOGY

As a class of artifacts, basketry accounts for 6.5% of the analyzed Huaca Prieta nontextile perishable artifact assemblage. If the unanalyzed 50,000+ specimens of Type II: Open Simple Twining, Z–Twist (paired) Wefts matting were added to the total, basketry would constitute more than 95% of the Huaca Prieta plant fiber–derived artifact suite. Summary comments on the production of basketry at Huaca Prieta are offered below by technological attribute within each subclass.

Twining

Twining is represented by three structural types. It accounts for nearly 98% of the analyzed Huaca Prieta basketry sample. If the unanalyzed Type II: Open Simple Twining, Z–Twist (paired) Wefts matting were added to this total, the twining percentage of the basketry sample recovered from Huaca Prieta would approach 100%.

Of the three twining types represented in the analyzed sample, two are simple twining variants and one is a simple and diagonal variant with functional wrapped twining. Collectively, simple twining varieties account for 59% of the analyzed twining sample, while the mixed simple and diagonal type constitutes the remaining 41% of the sample.

The 44 twining fragments from the analyzed sample appear to represent 25 separate items. Based on the frequency of forms by type, Type II: Open, Simple Twining, Z–Twist (paired) Wefts accounts for 57.29% (*n* = 15) of the forms, followed by Type I: Close Simple Twining, S–Twist (paired) Wefts with Auxiliary Simple Plaiting, which constitutes 23.07% (*n* = 6) of the forms. The mixed simple and diagonal variety, Type III: Close Simple and Diagonal Twining, S–Twist (paired) Wefts with Functional Wrapped Twining, represents the remaining 15.38% (*n* = 4) of the individual forms. We stress again that if the unanalyzed Type II: Open Simple Twining, Z–Twist (paired) Wefts matting were added to this total, this type would constitute *by far* the dominant twining variety.

Warps

The warps in two of the twining types, Type I: Close Simple Twining, S–Twist (paired) Wefts with Auxiliary Simple Plaiting and Type II: Open Simple Twining, Z–Twist (paired) Wefts, are unspun and untwisted single elements. The warps in these two types are semiflexible to flexible.

The warps in twining Type III: Close Simple and Diagonal Twining, S–Twist (paired) Wefts with Functional Wrapped Twining are loosely S–spun elements that are single in the simple twined sections and paired single elements in the diagonal twined sections. In both the simple and diagonal segments warps are semiflexible to flexible.

Wefts

In all three twining types wefts are paired. In Types I and II individual wefts are single, flexible, unrhetted elements. Wefts are also flexible single elements on most of the simple and diagonal twined body or wall fragments of the Type III specimens, but they are rhetted. In the wrapped twined portions of the wall or body of Type III specimens, a single flexible, rhetted weft serves as the moving element while a second, slightly less flexible, single rhetted weft functions as a stationary element.

Interestingly, both weft slants, S and Z, are represented in the analyzed Huaca Prieta twining sample. S slant is the only slant represented in Types I and III, while Z slant is the only slant represented in Type II. The existence of two different weft slants in the same assemblage is somewhat unusual, as is the restriction of opposing slants to particular twining types. This situation may reflect differential production by different cohorts of artisans and/or different functions for the different weft slant specimens. In this regard, the restriction of Z-twist wefts to the matting forms and S-twist wefts to the decorated basketry is probably *not* coincidental.

Method of Starting

All 18 of the Type II: Open Simple Twining, Z-Twist (paired) Wefts specimens are mat-petate fragments for which it is impossible to determine the method(s) of initiation of twining.

Similarly, it is impossible to determine the method(s) of starting in any of the examples of Type I: Close Simple Twining, S-Twist (paired) Wefts with Auxiliary Simple Plaiting or Type III: Close Simple and Diagonal Twining, S-Twist (paired) Wefts with Functional Wrapped Twining. All of the Type I and III specimens lack "centers," precluding any observations about the initiation of twining.

Selvages

Selvages (rim or edge finishes) are rare in the analyzed Huaca Prieta basketry sample. Two of the Type II: Open Simple Twining, Z-Twist (paired) Wefts specimens exhibit side selvages. One is of the continuous weft, simple self variety (fig. 12.17c3), while the other exhibits an overhand knot weft termination (fig. 12.17c4). Rim or edge selvages are found on 4 of the Type I: Close Simple Twining, S-Twist (paired) Wefts with Auxiliary Plaiting specimens. All 4 are variants of the 180° warp fold variety (fig. 12.17c1). As noted in the type description, on 1 specimen single warps are simply folded into adjacent rows after the final three weft rows. On the other 3 specimens the warp is bifurcated, folded, then twill plaited (3/3 interval) to produce a false braid.

All Type III: Close Simple and Diagonal Twining, S-Twist (paired) Wefts with Functional Wrapped Twining lack any selvages.

Splices

Splicing techniques for both warps and wefts are relatively simple in the Huaca Prieta twining assemblage. Only a single specimen of Type II:

Open Simple Twining, Z-Twist (paired) Weft twining exhibits a warp splice, which is effected by inserting a new warp into a preexisting weft crossing. Examples of weft splices are observed in all three Huaca Prieta twining types. In Type I: Close Simple Twining, S-Twist (paired) Wefts with Auxiliary Simple Plaiting new wefts are simply laid in. In Type II: Open, Simple Twining, Z-Twist (paired) Wefts 2 specimens exhibit laid-in weft splices, while 2 others exhibit slightly more complicated knotted splices. In one case the new weft is knotted to the exhausted weft and in the other the new weft is knotted around a warp. In Type III: Close Simple and Diagonal Twining, S-Twist (paired) Weft with Functional Wrapped Twining weft splices are either laid-in ($n = 1$), overhand knotted to exhausted wefts ($n = 1$), or multiple variety ($n = 1$), with both weft knotted and warp looped versions.

Mending and Decoration

None of the Huaca Prieta twined specimens are mended. Two examples of Type I: Close Simple Twining, S-Twist (paired) Wefts with Auxiliary Plaiting are decorated with some of the twined warps and wefts and auxiliary plaited elements dyed or painted blue. However, the dyed/painted specimens are too degraded to discern any patterning to the colored sections.

Though no example of Type II: Open Simple Twining, Z-Twist (paired) Wefts is decorated, all specimens of Type III: Close Simple, and Diagonal Twining, S-Twist (paired) Wefts with Functional Wrapped Twining are decorated. In all cases, the alternation of various weft manipulations with wrapped twining produces or results in geometric designs or patterns. Additionally, the "moving" wefts in the functional wrapped twining are either naturally bluish in color (see "Raw Materials" below) or are dyed blue, which enhances the geometric patterning.

Form and Function

Only two basic forms are represented in the Huaca Prieta twined assemblage. These include baskets or containers of indeterminate configuration and mats/petates. Twining Type II: Open Simple Twining, Z-Twist (paired) Wefts is employed

FIGURE 12.22. *a*, Mat fragment associated with a 6500-year-old burial; *b*, a modern-day mat weaver.

exclusively to produce mats or petates, while the other two types are used to manufacture decorated baskets or containers of unknown configuration. As noted in the type descriptions and discussed below, many, if not all, of the decorated examples of Type I: Close Simple Twining, S-Twist (paired) Wefts with Auxiliary Simple Plaiting and Type III: Close Simple and Diagonal Twining, S-Twist (paired) Wefts with Functional Wrapped Twining appear to have been intentionally cut, torn, or otherwise disarticulated. This same condition is inferred for some of the Huaca Prieta textiles.

It should be stressed that the dominant twining form at Huaca Prieta is flat matting, generally rectangular to square in plan. Specimens observed and/or analyzed are generally fragmentary, with the largest measuring 45 × 90 cm. While many specimens are associated with burials (fig. 12.22a), others appear to be "floor" or living surface coverings with purely attendant utilitarian functions.

Raw Materials

Only two plant genera are employed for the production of the Huaca Prieta twined basketry. Whole, split, undecorticated *Juncus* sp. leaves are employed for all warps and most wefts. In Type III: Close Simple and Diagonal Twining, S-Twist (paired) Wefts with Functional Wrapped Twining warps and some wefts are made of rhetted *Juncus* sp., while the running or moving wefts are made of *Gossypium* sp. The *Gossypium* sp. wefts are either a variety of naturally bluish cotton or, more likely, are dyed blue.

Though *not* represented in the analyzed collection, a handful of matting specimens may have been produced with split or whole totora (*Schoenoplectus* sp.) reed warps. The composition of the wefts in such specimens is unknown.

Plaiting

Plaiting is represented by a single structural type at Huaca Prieta. The sole plaiting type is a simple variant and represents only 2.2% of the Huaca Prieta basketry sample. It should be noted that, though baskets produced exclusively by plaiting are very rare in the analyzed sample from Huaca Prieta, courses of simple plaiting are employed somewhat more commonly in twining Type I: Close Simple Twining, S–Twist (paired) Wefts with Auxiliary Simple Plaiting.

Types

As only a single type of plaiting is represented at Huaca Prieta, it is impossible to speculate on its relative frequency/popularity vis-à-vis other plaiting types. It is perhaps significant that the simple plaiting 1/1 interval is not only the solitary type plaiting type found in the baskets but also the only plaiting type encountered as an auxiliary technique in the twined basketry assemblage.

Shifts, Selvages, Mending, and Decoration

As the lone Type IV: Simple Plaiting, 1/1 Interval specimen from Huaca Prieta lacks any shifts, selvages, or evidence of mending and decoration, it is not possible to comment on these attributes.

Form and Function

The solitary plaiting specimen from Huaca Prieta is too fragmentary and devoid of construction features to specify form or presumed function. The use of cordage plaiting elements is somewhat unusual and suggests that the final form was flexible. As noted in the type description, the specimen may have been part of a circular mat or the base of some kind of cylindrical container.

Raw Materials

The plaiting elements of Type IV: Simple Plaiting, 1/1 Interval are composed of cordage made from split *Juncus* sp. leaves.

CHRONOLOGY

The chronological distribution of the analyzed basketry sample from Huaca Prieta is presented by numbered cultural phase in table 12.9. It should be stressed that only 6 of the 45 basketry specimens, representing 13.33% of the analyzed sample, could not be assigned to a particular phase because they were derived from Bird's backdirt pile. Furthermore, as the table indicates, 5 of the basketry specimens representing three types (Type I: Close Simple Twining, S–Twist [paired] Wefts with Auxiliary Simple Plaiting; Type II: Open Simple Twining, Z–Twist [paired] Wefts; Type III: Close Simple and Diagonal Twining, S–Twist [paired] Wefts with Functional Wrapped Twining) in the analyzed sample have been directly dated by AMS assay (those results are presented in table 12.9).

Significantly, heavily fragmented and decayed pieces of Type II: Open Simple Twining, Z–Twist (paired) Wefts matting were recovered and/or observed in Phase I (9000–7500 BP) and Phase II (7572–6538 BP) contexts at Huaca Prieta but were unavailable for analysis. Additionally, as noted above, an unanalyzed example of this type from the premound construction/early Holocene levels at Huaca Prieta was radiometrically assayed to 11,159–10,600 cal BP. As of this writing, this is the oldest directly dated basketry from lowland South America.

It is also probable that for reasons discussed elsewhere in this volume that at least some of the basketry may be older than the direct or associated ^{14}C assays due to contamination issues (see chapter 6).

TYPES

As table 12.9 indicates, twining is represented continuously in the analyzed sample from Phase III (6538–5308 cal BP) through Phase V (4107–3455 cal BP) at Huaca Prieta. However, no single type is represented through those phases.

Though table 12.9 does not indicate that this type exists throughout the late Pleistocene and Holocene sequences at Huaca Prieta in the analyzed sample, as noted elsewhere in this contribution, Type II: Open Simple Twining, Z–Twist (paired) Wefts is not only the numerically preponderant basketry type at this site but also appears in

Table 12.9. Chronological distribution of the analyzed basketry samples from Huaca Prieta by cultural phase

Type	Quantity	% of total in phase	% of type across phases	Accession number
				Phase Ascription of Huaca Prieta Basketry
Phase V (4107–3455 cal BP) [n = 30; 66.7%]				
Type I	3	10.3	37.5	2009.130; 147[a]; 2009.119[b]
Type II	13	44.8	77.8	2008.06.0; 2008.06.1; 2008.50.6[c] (*n* = 2); 145 (*n* = 9)
Type III	13	44.8	77.2	2009.118[d] (*n* = 12); 2008.91.2[e]
Type IV	0	0	0	—
Phase IV (5308–4107 cal BP) [n = 4; 8.9%]				
Type I	5	100.0	50	2009.116 (*n* = 4); 2009.29.117
Type II	0	0	0	—
Type III	0	0	0	—
Type IV	0	0	0	—
Phase III (6538–5308 cal BP) [n = 5; 11.1%]				
Type I	0	0	0	—
Type II	0	0	0	—
Type III	5	100	27.8	75.1 (*n* = 4); 75.2
Type IV	0	0	0	—
Indeterminate Provenience/Chronology [n = 6; 13.3%]				
Type I	1	16.7	12.5	unknown
Type II	4	66.7	22.2	2008.05.5; 2008.52.1; 2008.99.2 (*n* = 2)
Type III	0	0	0	—
Type IV	1	16.7	100	151

[a]UCIAMS-96024, 3515±16 ^{14}C. (See table 6.2 in chapter 6.)

[b]UCIAMS-96027, 3515±15 ^{14}C.

[c]UCIAMS-96026, 3550±15 ^{14}C.

[d]OxA-28650 and OxA-28651, 3797±27 and 3777±26 ^{14}C.

[e]OxA-28652, 3765±27 ^{14}C and A10:E37A8:E37A2:E37E8A15:E37A1:E37.

all phases of site occupancy/use. Type III: Close Simple and Diagonal Twining, S-Twist (paired) Wefts with Functional Wrapped Twining, appears in Phase III (6538–5308 cal BP) and persists with a "hiatus" in Phase IV (5308–4107 cal BP) through Phase V (4107–3455 cal BP). Significantly, the decorated examples of this type are presently the oldest decorated baskets in South America (see "External Correlations" below) and among the oldest decorated baskets in the Americas. Indeed, if one excludes the designs produced by over-laying weft elements in the ancient Great Basin of North America (compare Fowler and Hattori 2008; Hattori and Fowler 2009), the Huaca Prieta Type III: Close Simple and Diagonal Twining, S-Twist (paired) Wefts with Functional Wrapped

Twining baskets are the oldest decorated basketry in the New World. At the very least, the Type III specimens with their bluish *Gossypium* sp. running wefts are, potentially, the oldest dyed specimens in the New World. Even if the running wefts of the Type III specimens are naturally blue in color, they still represent the earliest use of color distinctions to effect basketry decoration in South America.

Interestingly, the other complex close twining variety at Huaca Prieta also includes decorated specimens. Type I: Close Simple Twining, S-Twist (paired) Wefts with Auxiliary Simple Plaiting initially occurs during Phase IV (5308–4107 cal BP) and thereafter Type I persists through Phase V (4107–3455 cal BP). In the case of the Type I twining, there is no question that the twined warps and wefts as well as the auxiliary plaiting elements on two examples were painted or dyed blue.

In the case of the Type I twining, there is no question that the twined warps and wefts as well as the auxiliary plaiting elements on two examples were painted or dyed blue.

The last twining variety to appear at Huaca Prieta is Type II: Open Simple Twining, Z-Twist (paired) Wefts, which is exclusive to Phase V (4107–3455 cal BP). Within the Phase V twining subassemblage, Type II is the co-dominant twining variety (46.7%). In contrast with the rather more complex and often decorated twining varieties, Types I and III, Type II is not only a much more simple variety of twining to produce but is also devoid of any decoration and exhibits a reverse weft slant.

PLAITING

The single specimen of Type IV: Simple Plaiting, 1/1 Interval plaiting is of unknown provenience and hence indeterminate phase ascription.

WARPS

Though not represented in the analyzed sample, the earliest warp treatment at Huaca Prieta and one that persists throughout the sequence is the use of semiflexible to flexible whole or split, undecorated leaf elements, usually composed of *Juncus* sp. Indeed, this plant is still employed for the production of twined mats and basketry (fig.

12.22b). In the analyzed sample, the use of *Juncus* sp. warps is first evident in Phase III (6538–5308 cal BP) and thereafter continues through Phase V (4107–3455 cal BP), with a probably illusory hiatus in Phase IV (5308–4107 cal BP).

The other warp treatment represented in the analyzed Huaca Prieta sample includes flexible warps of loosely S-spun, rhetted *Juncus* sp. fibers employed singly or in pairs. These warp variants occur in Phase III (6538–5308 cal BP) and again in Phase V (4107–3455 cal BP), with a hiatus in Phase IV (5308–4107 cal BP).

WEFTS

Paired semiflexible to flexible wefts represent the "standard" weft treatment at Huaca Prieta. In the analyzed sample, this variation appears in Phase III (6538–5308 cal BP) but is observed in the unanalyzed sample from as early as early Holocene contexts.

The other Huaca Prieta weft manipulation, functional wrapped twining, again exhibits paired wefts made of rhetted *Juncus* sp. leaves, but one is moving and the other is stationary. This variant initially appears in the analyzed sample in Phase III (6538–5308 cal BP) and reappears in Phase V (5308–4107 cal BP), after a hiatus in Phase IV (4107–3455 cal BP). Another variation of the same basic paired running weft pattern does occur in Phase IV and employs whole or split rush leaves as weft elements. This weft treatment is also represented in Phase V. Interestingly, all of the paired weft treatments except those associated with twining Type II: Open Simple Twining, Z-Twist (paired) Wefts are S-slant wefts.

METHOD OF STARTING

No data are available to delineate or elucidate trends in twining start methods at Huaca Prieta in any way.

SELVAGES

None of the twined basketry specimens in the analyzed sample assigned to Phase III (6538–5308 cal BP) exhibit end selvages or rims and all of the other documented end selvage/rim manipulations occur together in Phase V (4107–3455 cal BP).

Using only the analyzed sample, it is impossible to delineate any trends in rim/selvage treatments at Huaca Prieta. However, based on the observed profusion of Type II: Open Simple Twining, Z-Twist (paired) matting, throughout the sequence, the simple transverse cutting or truncation of leaf elements employed as warps is both the oldest and the longest-lived end selvage/rim treatment evidenced at Huaca Prieta.

Similarly, the earliest and most common side selvage treatment at Huaca Prieta is the self-variety, though in the analyzed sample this side/lateral weft termination is only reported in Phase V (4107–3455 cal BP).

SPLICES

Only a single Huaca Prieta twined basket in the analyzed sample exhibits a warp splice. As this splice is restricted to Phase V (4107–3455 cal BP), it does not clarify trends in warp splicing through time. Laid-in weft splices occur in all phases at Huaca Prieta that have produced twined basketry. Slightly more complex weft splicing techniques occur in insufficient quantities to determine trends in weft splicing mechanics.

MENDING AND DECORATION

As none of the Huaca Prieta twined baskets are mended, nothing can be said about chronological trends in repairs. Conversely, many of the twined baskets in the analyzed sample are decorated. If the auxiliary plaiting elements in Type I: Close Simple Twining, S-Twist (paired) Wefts with Auxiliary Simple Plaiting are considered a form of decoration, then all examples of this type are decorated. Of course, the specimens with dyed or painted warps, wefts, and plaiting strips are also clearly decorated. Similarly, all of the examples of Type III: Close Simple and Diagonal Twining, S-Twist (paired) Wefts with Functional Wrapped Twining may be considered decorated with or without the bluish or blue-dyed running wefts. As noted above, the decorated Type III specimens initially appear in Phase III (6538–5308 cal BP) and are also represented in Phase V (4107–3455 cal BP), with a hiatus in Phase IV (5308–4107 cal BP).

The decorated Type I: Close Simple Twin-ing, S-Twist (paired) Wefts with Auxiliary Simple Plaiting specimens occur in Phase IV (5308–4107 cal BP) and Phase V (4107–3455 cal BP) but are not found in Phase III (6538–5308 cal BP). If the chronological distributions of the various forms of decorated baskets accurately reflect their prehistoric incidence, then some form of decoration in twined basketry is evidenced from 6538 cal BP to 3455 cal BP. Furthermore, it appears that the use of functional wrapped twining as a decorative device predates the use of auxiliary plaiting for similar purposes. As discussed further below and elsewhere (see chapters 14 and 15), it is probably not coincidental that virtually all of the decorated baskets appear to have been intentionally dismembered or damaged. In contrast, none of the Type II: Open Simple Twining, Z-Twist (paired) Wefts specimens in the analyzed sample or observed in the field are decorated or exhibit indications of intentional damage.

FORM AND FUNCTION

All of the Type II specimens are fragments of flat, probably rectangular mats or petates of indeterminate size. As noted above in the type descriptions, none are decorated. These specimens probably served purely utilitarian functions for most of their life history but were also employed in lining graves and tombs or as burial accoutrements. All of the examples of Type I: Close Simple Twining, S-Twist (paired) Wefts with Auxiliary Simple Plaiting and Type III: Close Simple and Diagonal Twining, S-Twist (paired) Wefts with Functional Wrapped Twining represent containers of indeterminate configuration or size. Furthermore, all appear to have been purposefully fragmented, cut, disarticulated, or damaged by cutting/slicing/tearing. It is suggested that these items may have served socioritual integrative functions that are discussed elsewhere in this volume.

In this context, mention should be made of the reversal of weft slant between the decorated examples of Types I and III (both S-twist) and the more prosaic specimens of Type II (Z-twist). The use of S-twist wefts in the decorated specimens may be part and parcel of their "special" function(s), while the Z-twist weft slant was reserved for more utilitarian items. The two different weft slants may also reflect different cohorts or learning communities of weavers or even artisans of different genders.

RAW MATERIALS

Weaving elements of *Juncus* sp. are evidenced in the analyzed sample at Huaca Prieta from Phase III (6538–5308 cal BP) to Phase V (5308–4107 cal BP) without interruption and clearly constitute the preferred construction medium or plant fiber source at the site. Based on the observed occurrence of this plant source, in late Pleistocene contexts and in all later deposits, *Juncus* sp. was the earliest and preferred construction medium throughout the Huaca Prieta sequence. The running wefts of *Gossypium* sp. are likewise documented in Phase III and V, but with a hiatus in Phase IV (4107–3455 cal BP).

PLAITING

Given the circumscribed sample size (*n* = 1), the absence of diagnostic attributes, and the inability to ascribe the Type IV: Simple Plaiting, 1/1 Interval specimen to a phase, nothing can be said about temporal trends in plaiting technology at Huaca Prieta.

CORDAGE INTERNAL CORRELATIONS

As a class of artifacts, cordage accounts for 93.5% of the analyzed Huaca Prieta nontextile perishable artifact assemblage. If a large but untallied corpus of twined matting recovered by Dillehay were included here, the relative ratios of cordage specimens to basketry specimens would, per force, change. Similarly, there *may* be some specimens of cordage that were not available for analysis. Any untabulated cordage totals would necessarily alter the figures presented here. Both major subclasses of cordage, twisted and braided, are represented in the Huaca Prieta assemblage. Summary comments on the production attributes of these items follow (table 12.10).

FINAL TWIST DIRECTION

Cordage exhibiting a final S-twist accounts for 15.24% of the total analyzed cordage assemblage

Table 12.10. Distribution of Dillehay-excavated cordage by phase

Type	Quantity	% of total in phase
Moche (AD 400–700)		
III	1	100.00
Phase V (4107–3455 cal BP)		
II	1	3.57
III	18	64.29
IV	2	7.14
V	3	10.71
VII	1	3.57
VIII	1	3.57
X	2	7.14
Phase IV (5308–4107 cal BP)		
I	1	0.98
III	83	81.37
IV	6	5.88
V	2	1.96
IX	1	0.98
XI	5	4.90
XII	1	0.98
XIV	1	0.98
XV	1	0.98
XIX	1	0.98
Phase III (6538–5308 cal BP)		
IV	1	50.00
XI	1	50.00

and is generally equally represented in the initial Bird excavations and the subsequent Dillehay excavations. Within this subassemblage of the cordage, single-ply cordage accounts for 8% of the sample; two-ply accounts for 64%; and compound constructions account for 28%.

Cordage exhibiting a final Z-twist accounts for 82.32% of the total analyzed cordage assemblage and is generally equally represented between the Bird and Dillehay excavations. Within this subassemblage of the cordage, single-ply cordage accounts for 0.75% of the sample; two-ply accounts for 83.46%; and compound constructions account for 15.79%.

Braided analyzed cordage accounts for 2.44% of the total cordage assemblage and is slightly more common (*n* = 3) from the Bird excavations and less common (*n* = 1) from the Dillehay excavations. All braided cord specimens are three-ply and may also be considered 1/1 interval plaiting.

NUMBER OF CORDAGE PLIES

Single-ply cordage represented the least numerous and presumably the least popular form of cordage at Huaca Prieta, accounting for only 1.22% of the analyzed cordage assemblage.

Two-ply cordage (cordage with two levels of engagement) is the most numerous and presumably the most popular form of cordage at Huaca Prieta, accounting for 77.44% of the analyzed cordage assemblage. Arguably, braided cordage may be added to this category, as it has only two levels of engagement. If braiding is included with the two-ply twisted cordage, the incidence of two-ply rises to 81.71% in the analyzed cordage assemblage.

Compound-ply cordage (cordage with three or more levels of engagement) accounts for 17.07% of the analyzed cordage assemblage.

TWIST MANIPULATION

Variations in twist manipulation, specifically including crepe-twisting and rat-tailing, are relatively rare in the analyzed Huaca Prieta cordage assemblage. Crepe-twisting, which may also be representative of a form of re-plying, is evidenced in only 4 of the analyzed cordage specimens. Interestingly, 3 of these are final S-twist cords and 3 of these crepe-twisted specimens occur in compound-ply cordage, while the only noncompound crepe-twisted cord occurs on a single-ply variety.

Rat-tailing is even less common, with only 3 specimens represented in the total assemblage. All of these specimens are of the Type III: Two Ply, S-Spun, Z-Twist variety. Interestingly, crepe-twisting and rat-tailing are mutually exclusive.

SPLICES

Splices, while more common than twist manipulation variations, are still relatively rare in the Huaca Prieta cordage assemblage, with only 11.59% (*n* = 19) of the analyzed specimens exhibiting splices. Laid-in ply splices are the most common variety (*n* = 11), followed by twisted ply spices (*n* = 7). Looped splices (*n* = 1) are the least common.

Only 4 of these splices, all of the twisted ply variety, occur within final S-twist cordage; all of these are Type IV: Two Ply, Z-Spun, S-Twist specimens. All of the remaining splices occur in final Z-twist cordage.

Splices, where observed, are isolated to single occurrences within a given cord with only one exception. A single specimen of Type IV cordage (2007.13.01a) exhibits numerous laid-in ply splices. While it would be expected that an unusually long cord may exhibit more splices than a shorter one, this specimen is only 72.5 mm in length (of average length for these specimens).

RAW MATERIALS

Raw material use is relatively nonhomogeneous within the Huaca Prieta cordage assemblage, with five different materials represented. Of these, the least common by far is human (*Homo sapiens*) hair with only a single specimen represented. This single specimen (41.2/2496) derives from the Bird excavations. It should be noted that Bird et al. (1985) report several additional human hair specimens. Illingworth observed several, but these were not analyzed as part of the Bird subassemblage reexamination. Interestingly, no human hair cordage was observed among the more recent Dillehay subassemblage. The next least common raw material choice is a sedge (Cyperaceae) of indeterminate taxonomic ascription. This material accounts for only 2.03% of the cordage subassemblage and is used in the construction of 2 specimens of final Z-twist and 1 specimen that is braided.

Cotton is a moderately common raw material choice and accounts for 18.92% of the analyzed cordage. Interestingly, cotton (*Gossypium* sp.) is observed exclusively on cordage specimens that appear to have been part (or an intended part) of textile constructions, "sling shots," or knotted loops (bracelets). Specimens of cordage exhibiting a final S-twist account for 25% of the cotton-based specimens: final Z-twist cords account for the remaining 75%.

The most common identifiable raw material within the analyzed cordage subassemblage is rush (*Juncus* sp.), which accounts for 25% of the analyzed specimens. Interestingly, while rush is used in the construction of braided cordage (5.41%) and in the construction of final Z-twist cordage (94.59%), it was not observed in the construction of any of the analyzed final S-twist cordage. It should be noted, however, that some of the unidentifiable raw material samples (see below) used to construct final S-twist cordage may be rush.

The most common raw material observed in the construction of the analyzed Huaca Prieta cordage subassemblage is a bast fiber of indeterminate taxonomic ascription. A total of 53.38% of the analyzed cordage specimens are sufficiently worn, encrusted in various forms of filth, and/or constructed of a raw material sufficiently well processed that the raw material cannot be identified. The appearance of this raw material appears to be consistent across the specimens, and Adovasio suspects that this material is some form of rush (*Juncus* sp.) that has been very heavily processed.

KNOTTING

Knots or knot-related wear are observed on 24.39% of the analyzed cordage specimens. Of these knots, 52.1% are of the overhand variety. Of all the knot variants known to Illingworth, overhand knots are among the very, very few that may form through accident or happenstance whenever cords are handled without care. Despite this, the majority of the overhand knots observed in this assemblage were clearly intentionally tied and in many cases were used as an expedient knot to secure a bunch or bundle of cords together, particularly in those specimens that appear to have been manufactured to serve as weaving stock.

Square knots are the second most common knot forms, representing 37.85% of the analyzed knot population. The use of these knots is most often indeterminate due to the small size and/or heavy wear of the specimens. In several instances the square knots appear to have been used to join lengths of cord together for unknown reasons. In three cases square knots are used to form loops or bracelet structures. In only a single instance, based on knot morphology, does a square knot appear possibly to have been part of a net construction.

Three lark's-head knots are observed in the total analyzed collection. It is uncertain whether these knots were intentionally tied to form a lark's-head knot (which is a movable knot) or whether they are the not uncommon result of square knots that have been pulled in an asymmetric manner and caused to "shift" form.

A single surgeon's knot is present in the analyzed assemblage. Surgeon's knots may be considered similar to square knots and in fact are formed by making an extra loop in the square knotting process. This knot may have been part of a net construction.

The remaining 8.57% of these analyzed specimens exhibit wear consistent with having been knotted during their use-life. However, the wear is either sufficiently vague or further degraded due to postdepositional processes to render identification of the knot likely to have been tied indeterminate.

MENDING OR DECORATION

None of the analyzed Huaca Prieta cordage specimens exhibit mends or decoration. Though none are mended, a single example appears to be a complete specimen. Specimen 41.1/9700A derives from the Bird subassemblage and was identified by him (Bird et al. 1985) as part of a net float.

FORM AND FUNCTION

The overwhelming majority of the analyzed Huaca Prieta cordage specimens are of indeterminate form and function, as they exhibit no diagnostic wear (though almost all of the specimens are worn), diagnostic knots, or consistent lengths (which may indicate having been part of a net).

While indeterminate, approximately 75% of the examined cords appear to be consistent with material used in the construction of textiles and those nets described in part 1 of this chapter. Of the remaining 25%, an additional 5.46% of the analyzed assemblage is consistent with having been part of a knotted structure (such as netting), though likely of a slightly larger gauge than the aforementioned specimens.

Knotted loops and/or bracelet forms account for 7.51% of the analyzed cordage forms. These items were discussed and described by Bird et al. (1985), though their actual use is indeterminate.

Only 3 specimens appear to be parts of sling shots or similar stone-flinging devices. One of them is of a sufficiently diminutive size to suggest its use by children or as a toy.

A single specimen is described by Bird et al. (1985: 216) as part of a net float. Presumably, this can be considered a small net used to secure a hollowed, buoyant gourd to a net body. While Illingworth observed no attributes that would challenge Bird's ascription, he also did not observe any attributes to support this ascription. This analysis noted no attributes to support or challenge Bird's posited ascription.

The remaining 8.73% of the analyzed assemblage is composed of bunched and wadded groups of cordage exhibiting very ragged ends that are heavily encrusted with organic and inorganic residue. In most situations it would be assumed that these specimens were simply bunched and wadded detritus. However, based on the high observed frequency of presumably intentionally damaged and deposited textiles and basketry, it is possible that these specimens represent separate components of either of these subclasses of perishables "offerings" or are in and of themselves similarly intentionally damaged and deposited items.

CHRONOLOGY

For the purpose of this section of the cordage discussion, only analyzed specimens deriving from the recent excavations are presented (table 12.10).

No cordage specimens were directly analyzed from late Pleistocene to early Holocene, Phase I (14,500–7500 cal BP) or Phase II (7572–6538 cal BP) contexts. As it is most unlikely that cordage was not manufactured or used during these horizons, particularly given the observed occurrence of basketry (see below), it is confidently assumed that the absence of cordage in the analyzed sample is *not* representative of the actual absence of this

subclass of plant fiber artifacts from earliest Huaca Prieta.

Phase III (6538–5308 cal BP)

Phase III is represented by only 2 analyzed cordage specimens: 1 specimen is final S-twist (Type IV: Two Ply, Z-Spun, S-Twist) and the other is final Z-twist (Type XI: Compound, Two Ply, S-Spun, Z-Twist). No crepe-twisting, rat-tailing, decoration, or mending is evident on these pieces.

Bast fibers are the exclusive raw material within this Phase with the Type XI specimen composed of rush (*Juncus* sp.) and the Type IV specimen composed of an indeterminate bast fiber. A single overhand knot, of indeterminate use, is present on the Type XI specimen. The form and function of the Phase III cordage are indeterminate though paired Z-twist wefts were employed in the production of Type II: Open Simple Twining Z-twist (paired) Wefts matting.

Phase IV (5308–4107 cal BP)

Phase IV is represented by 70.65% of the analyzed cordage specimens. Of these, 0.98% are braided, 12.31% are final S-twist, and the remaining 86.71% are final Z-twist. While a total of eight types are observed during Phase IV, this variation is generally unimodal. Type III: Two Ply, S-Spun, Z-Twist accounts for 70.77% of the cords deriving from this Phase; 9.23% are Type IV: Two Ply, Z-Spun, S-Twist; 7.69% are Type XI: Compound, Two Ply, S-Spun, Z-Twist. Types XII: Compound, Two Ply, Z-Spun, S-Twist, XIV: Compound, Two Ply, Z-Spun, S-Twist; and XV: Compound, Three Ply, S-Spun, Z-Twist each account for 1.54%.

While no decoration, rat-tailing, or mending was observed in the Phase IV cordage suite, 2 analyzed specimens do exhibit rat-tailing. Interestingly, both rat-tailed specimens are minority (1.54%) types (Types XII and XV).

Splices during Phase IV are relatively diverse, though not numerous: 2 specimens exhibit laid-in ply splices, 2 specimens exhibit twisted ply splices, and the only looped splice in the entire cordage assemblage occurs during Phase IV.

Raw material use during Phase IV is almost exclusively bast fiber (98.2%). While some of these bast-fiber specimens (13.57%) are identifiable as rush (*Juncus* sp.), the majority are of indeterminate taxonomic ascription. The remaining 1.8% of the analyzed specimens are composed of cotton seed (*Gossypium* sp.) hair.

Knotting within the analyzed Phase IV sub-assemblage is not uncommon. A total of 20% of the cordage specimens exhibit overhand knots, and 6.15% of the specimens are square knotted. No other knot forms are represented during Phase IV.

The form and function of the analyzed Phase IV cordage are generally indeterminate. Of the specimens with determinable form and function, 2 appear to have been parts of nets and 2 are of the bracelet/knotted looped form.

Phase V (4107–3455 cal BP)

Phase V is represented by 19.79% of the analyzed Huaca Prieta cordage assemblage. Of these, 21.05% are final S-twist variants and 78.95% are final Z-twist variants. None of the specimens are braided. The final S-twist variants are represented by 1 example of Type II (Single Ply, S-Spun), 1 example of Type VII (Five Ply, Z-Spun, S-Twist), and 2 examples of Type IV (Two Ply, Z-Spun, S-Twist). Among the final Z-twist variants, 9 of them are Type III (Two Ply, S-Spun, Z-Twist), 3 are Type V (Three Ply, S-Spun, Z-Twist), 2 are Type X (Compound, Two Ply, S-Spun, Z-Twist), and 1 is Type VIII (Twelve Ply, S-Spun, Z-Twist).

While rat-tailing, decoration, and mending were not observed on any of the analyzed Phase V cords, a single specimen does exhibit crepe-twisting. This is the only single-ply (Type II: Single Ply, S-Spun) specimen observed in this Phase and 1 of the only 2 single-ply specimens in the analyzed cordage assemblage.

Splicing is apparently very rare during Phase V and is represented by a single laid-in ply splice on a single example of Type X cordage.

Raw material use is generally circumscribed during Phase V. A total of 17.65% of the analyzed specimens are constructed of cotton seed (*Gossypium* sp.) hair. The remaining specimens are composed of bast fibers either of an indeterminate taxonomic ascription (79.25%) or of rush (*Juncus* sp.) (3.1%).

Compared to the preceding phase, Phase V exhibits remarkably few knotted specimens. In fact only 1 specimen is definitely knotted (an overhand knot) and only 1 specimen exhibits wear consistent with having once been knotted. The knotted specimen is on a fragment of Type V cordage and the knot-wear specimen is an example of Type IV cordage.

The form and function are generally indeterminate for the analyzed specimens deriving from Phase V contexts. The single specimen of Type II is part of a cord-wrapped stick structure that may be an abandoned spindle whorl shaft.

Moche (AD 400–700)

A single analyzed specimen of Type III: Two Ply, S-Spun, Z-Twist cordage derives from later Moche contexts. This specimen is without crepe-twisting, rat-tailing, mending, decoration, splices, knots, or diagnostic use-wear. It is constructed of bast fibers of indeterminate taxonomic ascription. Its form and function are indeterminate.

EXTERNAL CORRELATIONS

The basketry and cordage from Huaca Prieta exhibits technical and stylistic attributes that may be compared with other plant fiber–derived collections of broadly similar age. However, though a number of Preceramic sites have yielded basketry, cordage, cordage by-products, and textiles, very few of these assemblages have been adequately described, illustrated, or discussed (for example, Asia [Engel 1963c]; Aspero [O'Neale 1954]; Bandurria [Chu 2008]; Caral [Shady S. 2004]; Chilca [Donnan 1964; Engel 1966a]; La Galgada [Grieder 1986, 1988]; Los Gavilanes [Bonavia 1982]; Hacha [Gayton 1967]; Huaynuná [Engel 1957b]; La Paloma [Vallejos A. 1981, 1982]; El Paraíso [Engel 1966b]; Playa Culebras [Engel 1957b]; Río Seco [Engel 1957b; Wendt 1964]; Salinas de Chao [Olivera Alegre 2006]; the Tank and Yacht Club sites [Lanning 1963; Moseley 1975]). Moreover, the basketry and cordage assemblages that have been described and published are often incompletely or inadequately dated, if at all. As a result of these descriptive and chronological lacunae, comparison of the Huaca Prieta basketry and cordage to other Preceramic assemblages is per force abbreviated.

The production of basketry, textiles, cordage, and cordage by-products such as netting is well documented in the Old World by 29,000–24,000 ^{14}C yr BP (Adovasio et al. 2004; Soffer et al. 2000) and, as of this writing, even earlier (Hardy et al. 2013). Indeed such technologies are evidenced, albeit in the form of impressions, on the very threshold of the Bering Platform by no later than 12,860 ^{14}C yr BP (Hyland et al. 2002). Based on these and other Old World occurrences, it was concluded long ago (Adovasio 1977: vii) that plant fiber–derived industries were undoubtedly "part and parcel of the armamentarium of the first colonists to the New World." Additionally, these interrelated industries may have well played critical roles in the colonization of both the northern and southern reaches of the hemisphere (Adovasio et al. 2004).

A recent summary of the antiquity of perishable plant fiber industries in North America is available in Adovasio et al. (2014). As that document indicates, the manufacture of both twined and plaited basketry as well as cordage extends back into the early Holocene. Furthermore, in most regions of North America and South America the oldest basketry is usually twined.

In South America the production of cordage, cordage by-products, and basketry is well established by the early tenth millennium BP. Presently the oldest well-dated cordage in the Western Hemisphere derives from Monte Verde in Chile (Adovasio 1997). At that location, 33 individual specimens of cordage and at least 11 separate cordage impressions were identified in a context firmly dated between 14,600 and 14,200 cal BP. The average age of the Monte Verde perishable materials is 14,500 cal BP, rendering this the largest and earliest perishable plant fiber assemblage (as opposed to individual specimens) from the entire New World. One structural type is apparently represented in the Monte Verde assemblage: single ply, S-twist. However, regular indentations on several examples of this type strongly suggest that some of these specimens are individual plies of two ply, S-spun, Z-twist cords that have come untwisted. Several knots are also represented,

including simple overhands and overhand nooses. Interestingly, all of the actual specimens of cordage from Monte Verde are made of *Juncus* fiber.

In upland South America the oldest plant fiber–based artifacts derive from Guitarrero Cave in the north-central highlands of Peru (Lynch 1980a). Elements of this assemblage have more recently been directly dated via AMS (Adovasio 1997; Jolie et al. 2011). A two ply, S-spun, Z-twist cord yielded a date of 12,130–11,300 cal BP, while a second such cord produced a date of 11,400–11,090 cal BP. A close simple twined Z-twist (paired) wefts fragment of either indeterminate flexible basket or textile form was dated to 11,330–11,100 cal BP, and an open simple twined, Z-twist (paired) wefts fragment of a mat or flexible container was only slightly younger at 11,280–11,080 cal BP. The cordage was composed of Agavaceae/Bromeliaceae fiber, as were the warps and wefts of the close simple twining. Wefts of the open simple twining were also produced of Agavaceae/Bromeliaceae fiber, while warps were possibly made of cut rush (Cyperaceae, cf. *Schoenoplectus* sp.). Significantly, in both the Monte Verde and Guitarerro caves the recovered assemblages are presumed to be only a small fraction of the nondurable repertoire of their respective populations.

As noted above, the unanalyzed specimen of Type II: Open Simple Twining, Z-Twist (paired) Wefts matting from Huaca Prieta was directly dated to the 11th millennium cal BP and represents the oldest specimen of basketry of any form from lowland South America.

Thereafter basketry, cordage, cordage by-products, and textiles have been reported from a variety of coastal and interior South American contexts. Fragments of knotted cordage with little to no associated descriptive data were reported from Quebrada Jaguay and date to ca. 10,600 cal BP (Sandweiss et al. 1998). These items are most likely portions of fishing nets, which in turn suggest the early development of a maritime-focused economy. As noted by Edward Jolie et al. (2011: 299), the recovery of small fish bones at Quebrada Jaguay as well as maritime bird bones and anchovy bones from Quebrada Tacuay (compare De France 2005) also suggests the existence of netting and a maritime-focused economy.

Not surprisingly, a very different economic focus is reflected by excavations in the high desert of northwestern Argentina (Pintar 2014). Excavations at the residential campsite of Cueva Salamanca 1 (CS-1) yielded both cordage specimens and what is currently the oldest example of coiled basketry from South America. This unique item exhibits a bundle foundation, sewn with noninterlocking stitches in a right-to-left work direction with some accidental splitting of the stitches. The bundle is apparently made of *Cortaderia* sp. leaves and dates to ~7400 cal BP. At least some of the cordage is also of similar age but is allegedly made of animal fibers.

Between ~7400 cal BP and the initial recovery of basketry, cordage, and textiles at Huaca Prieta, ~6500 cal BP, only a few sites have yielded plant fiber–derived artifacts. Of these, the most extensively published and illustrated as well as potentially the most important is Paloma in the Chilca Valley of Peru.

Excavations conducted at Paloma between 1973 and 1975 by Frederic Engel and between 1976 and 1979 by Robert Benfer yielded a large assemblage of basketry, cordage, cordage by-products, and textiles. Radiocarbon dates range from 7735±100 to 6000±150 ^{14}C years BP, with the most intensive use of the site apparently occurring between 7060 and 6000 BP. The perishable collection from Paloma thus overlaps Phase II (7572–6538 cal BP) and Phase III (6538–5308 cal BP) at Huaca Prieta.

Miriam Vallejos A. (1988) reports a substantial corpus of plant fiber–based artifacts assigned to nine analytical categories, such as specimens of string and rope, detached warps and wefts from textiles, finished textiles of various configurations including looped and linked items as well as twined pieces, knotted forms, and open twined mats or bags. Of these forms, by far the most common are mats.

Perhaps significantly, the dominant cordage type is two ply, S-spun, Z-twist and includes both detached warp and weft fragments as well as string/rope *sensu stricto*. The netting assemblage is diverse, with a variety of netting knot types represented (Vallejos A. 1988: figs. 7–11). While the basketry assemblage includes numerous examples of flat, open simple twined mats and what appear to be flexible bags with predominately S-twist weft slants, neither of the decorated Huaca Prieta

twining types (Type I: Close Simple Twining, S-Twist [paired] Wefts with Auxiliary Plaiting or Type III: Close Simple and Diagonal Twining, S-Twist [paired] Wefts with Functional Wrapped Twining) is represented at Paloma.

Perhaps very significantly, the complex, decorated twined basketry types from Huaca Prieta are also unreported at all published later Preceramic sites. Though this "absence" may reflect sampling/preservation issues and/or may be attributed to inadequate or missing descriptions (for example, Bandurria [Chu Barrera 2011] and others), the absence of these types at other contemporary or later sites may be real.

If genuinely unique to Huaca Prieta, as presently seems to be the case, the decorated baskets may reflect the escalation of cultural complexity at this locality, albeit in a highly perishable medium. Put simply, the decorated baskets may be emblematic of a mode or level of sociocultural integration, heretofore unrepresented or at least undetected in the greater study area.

OVERVIEW

The basketry and cordage from Huaca Prieta described and discussed above consists of 690 specimens that, minimally, span the use of the site from ~6538–3455 cal BP. As such, it is presently one of the largest plant fiber–based assemblages from this period to be analyzed and described from all of South America. If the observed abundance of Type II: Open Simple Twining, Z-Twist (paired) Wefts matting is added to this total, then the Huaca Prieta perishable assemblage is the largest of its kind yet recovered in all of South America. In retrospect, the salient aspects of the Huaca Prieta basketry and cordage collections are enumerated below.

1. Not atypically, cordage specimens are far more numerous in the analyzed sample at Huaca Prieta than basketry. In all likelihood, cordage fragments probably exceeded basketry or textile specimens in the unanalyzed sample, although this is not verifiable at present. While the analyzed cordage suite appears to be typologically diverse, the range of types is actually somewhat limited. The vast majority of

the cordage is represented by a single type (Type III: Two Ply, S-Spun, Z-Twist), and the next three most common varieties are reverse or mirror versions of the dominant type or each other. These include Type IV: Two Ply, Z-Spun, S-Twist and the compound manipulations (Type XI: Compound, Two Ply, S-Spun, Z-Twist and Type XII: Compound, Two Ply, Z-Spun, S-Twist). The remaining cordage types are rarely represented by more than 5 specimens, and several of them may actually be splices from one of the more common types. Curiously, no cordage or basketry were found at the Paredones site.

2. From a functional perspective, most of the coarser cords probably represent binding/lashing/tying devices. A few others may be portions of composite constructions such as slings, so-called net floats (Bird et al. 1985), or knotted loops/bracelets. However, by far the great majority of the cords are disaggregated warps and wefts from textiles or construction materials intended but never used for textile production.

3. Braided cordage is rare in the Huaca Prieta assemblage, as is typical throughout the New World, and is generally characterized by the use of coarser raw material and the production of a thicker and presumably stronger cord. Again, as is also the case in other New World cordage collections, the braided segments from Huaca Prieta are usually so short as to preclude any assignment of function.

4. The range of knots represented in the cordage assemblage is circumscribed. The great majority are overhand manipulations that are also common in the textiles. A few of these knots are used to bundle groups of cords (weaving stock) together. While some of the overhand knots on the textiles may be splices, none of the overhand knots on the cordage are so employed. Many of the overhand knots are probably the result of hurried production or careless handling of long cords. Most of the remaining knots are typical Preceramic forms (such as square knots and surgeon's knots) used for conjoining lengths of cordage or for net production. A few knots, such as the lark's heads, would have been tied intentionally only for netting. Interestingly, there are no granny knots, half hitches, or sheet bend/weaver's knots.

5. The analyzed and observed basketry assemblage is dominated by twining, with plaiting restricted to a single specimen of unknown configuration or to supplementation elements in twined constructions.

6. As in many other Preceramic basketry assemblages from South America, the most common forms of twining are flat mats or petates of unknown dimensions. These items are undecorated and clearly intended and used for utilitarian as well as mortuary functions. The antiquity of matting production is directly supported by the dated specimen of Type II from Huaca Prieta.

7. Though typologically restricted, the analyzed Huaca Prieta twined basketry assemblage does include two types (Type I: Close Simple Twining, S-Twist [paired] Wefts with Auxiliary Plaiting and Type III: Close Simple and Diagonal Twining, S-Twist [paired] Wefts with Functional Wrapped Twining) that are unique to that site and not reported from any other Preceramic sites in South America. One of these types, Type III, incorporates a form of functional wrapped twining that is exceedingly rare in the hemisphere at large.

8. The occurrence of Type I (Close Simple Twining, S-Twist [paired] Wefts with Auxiliary Plaiting) and Type III (Close Simple and Diagonal Twining, S-Twist [paired] Wefts with Functional Wrapped Twining) at Huaca Prieta may be a function of reporting or may be real. As noted above, while many Preceramic sites have yielded basketry, these collections are often poorly reported and/or illustrated, if at all. Under these circumstances, Types I and III may exist at other sites, but their presence may not be documented. If these two types are actually unique to Huaca Prieta, however, they may represent perishable artifact innovations associated with or expressing early sociocultural complexity at that locale.

9. The two complex twining types from Huaca Prieta include dyed, painted, or naturally colored decoration elements and are the oldest such items in South America. They are also, as noted above, among the oldest decorated baskets in the New World.

10. An extremely circumscribed range of raw materials was employed to manufacture cordage and basketry at Huaca Prieta, including rush (*Juncus* sp.), cotton (*Gossypium* sp.), and a bast fiber of indeterminate taxonomic ascription. All three fiber sources are represented from Phase III through Phase V (6538–3455 cal BP). Further, as noted above, *Juncus* sp. was probably the principal medium of basketry production from late Pleistocene times.

11. Interestingly, the locus of at least some of the basketry production in the greater study area may have been at nearby Paredones. Though no basketry in any form was recovered there, the occupational levels of that site are suffused with *Juncus* sp. pollen. This in turn suggests that *Juncus* sp. was extensively processed into basketry at this locality, perhaps for ultimate use and/or disposal at Huaca Prieta.

12. As indicated above, though congruent in many ways with basketry (and cordage) collections from other Preceramic sites in Peru, the plant fiber–derived artifact collection from Huaca Prieta does contain forms presently known or reported *only* from that locality. Moreover, the depositional context and condition of these pieces—often intentionally dismembered and in ritual bundles associated with access ramps or "staircases"—are also unprecedented. It should be stressed that the intentional fragmentation of some of the basket sample is paralleled in other artifactual media and doubtless served some sort of ritual function. Again, as noted above, the mound at Huaca Prieta was built initially solely for ritual purposes. However, it was later associated with the practices of both a ritual and a mortuary place, which amplified its meanings historically. That is, over a period of several millennia the internal spatial and stratigraphic record and the fragmented or whole material content of Huaca Prieta reflect thousands of recursive behavioral episodes, material depositions, and building and ritual moments, not all necessarily associated with the same specific practices and meanings. But these episodes must have been sieved through different or similar ontologies through time and, above all, collectively formed a cohesive, coherent, and meaningful archaeological material record at the site.

CHAPTER 13

OUTLYING DOMESTIC HOUSE MOUND SITES

Greg Maggard
and Tom D. Dillehay

This chapter reports the settlement pattern of domestic sites recorded on the Sangamon terrace and along the littoral and in the lower valley wetlands of the project area. On the north coast of Peru where Preceramic household mounds make an early appearance, it is not their presence alone that suggests permanent settlement but the combination of the structures, the intact and continuous stratigraphy, and the material culture that they contain. It is the investment in constructing house mounds and the dense domestic middens and continuous strata that implies sedentism. The presence of outlying domestic sites dating to the middle to late Preceramic period and containing material culture similar to that found at Huaca Prieta and Paredones suggests that these sites were related to and likely supported the activities at these mounds. One reason we carried out the settlement pattern survey was to understand the relationship between ritual nodes like Huaca Prieta and domestic sites. The relationship between ceremonial or ritual centers and domestic sites in the Central Andes is poorly understood. We hope that the information presented here contributes to this understanding.

The chronology of the Preceramic domestic occupation was obtained through a few radiocarbon assays and the presence of diagnostic lithic and other artifacts in domestic Units 13, 16, and 20 and Test Pits 26–28 and in exposed looter's pits at outlying domestic sites. Evidence of modern looting was observed at all sites and varied in extent from relatively minor damage to nearly complete destruction. Aside from the damage to sites, the looting exposed buried stratigraphy and artifacts, including textile and net fragments, floral and faunal remains, and human burials. A few charcoal samples for assays were obtained from intact hearths in exposed house floors (see chapters 6 and 7). Although several of the household sites presented here contain limited evidence for reuse through the presence of surface scatters (including debris tossed from numerous looter holes) of later Cupisnique, Moche, or Chimú ceramics, the vast majority of artifactual and depositional evidence is indicative of a middle to late Preceramic age (7000–4000 cal BP). Because of the scarcity of dates, no subphases are defined for these sites.

The house mounds appear as single and clustered sites on terraces overlooking the interior wetlands and at the mouths of wetlands draining into the ocean. In some cases three to six tightly clustered house mounds are found in one location on one side of a wetland terrace, while in others fifteen to twenty house mounds appear to form a semicircular or oval arrangement, and in still others three to four house mounds are positioned on opposite sides of the mouth of the drainage.

Most of the household mounds are low, accretional deposits located on top of stabilized paleodunes along the littoral that have their origins in the middle Preceramic period (~7500–5500 cal BP). Accretional deposition of domestic middens is suggestive of relatively intensive or long-term use of individual settings. It is difficult to estimate the sizes of the structures in and on top of these mounds. Based on observations in looter's holes, which reveal midden debris and preserved cane and pole side-walls of structures, the houses appear to be between 8 and 12 m in length, 4–5 m in width, 0.5–1.8 m high, and roughly rectangular in shape, perhaps housing eight to ten people. Although much smaller in scale, the intentionality in location, persistent reuse, and inclusion of the dead in the fills of the house mound reflect different mortuary processes than those operating at Huaca Prieta. It could be determined from looter activity that burials were placed in shallow pits either inside or outside of house mounds or sometimes below house floors. The few semi-intact burials suggest that they were both flexed and extended, a pattern also seen in and around Huaca Prieta.

Survey results also indicate the types of microenvironments that attracted the most intense activity, and comparisons between locations with different types of artifact assemblages give some indication of the nature of this activity. Results from preliminary studies of surface materials (for example, faunal and floral remains, stone, bone and shell implements) suggest the importance of fishing and gathering along the littoral, with contributions from terrestrial gathering and horticulture around interior coastal wetlands.

An opportunistic survey area extended 30 km along the ocean shore and 1–4 km inland from the shoreline to the north and south of Huaca Prieta. A total of thirty-three Preceramic sites were identified along the littoral, twenty-two of which are described below, and thirty-four others in the interior wetlands (see fig. 13.1 survey area). The distribution of these Preceramic sites highlights the varied patchwork of microenvironments that constituted a littoral/coastal ecological system. In this case the site distribution reflects the importance of coastal lagoon and estuarine settings, with access to both the shoreline and lagoon and estuarine settings having been the primary focus of site location. The orientation of local settlement toward these resource-rich locations is not surprising, but it does suggest that Preceramic subsistence strategies emphasized the collection of food resources from the relatively easily accessible tidal and coastal lagoons in conjunction with the exploitation of nearshore, offshore, and inland resources.

Field methods consisted of pedestrian reconnaissance of the shoreline and nearshore interior that extended north and south from the mouth of the Chicama River. In the course of the survey, each site location was mapped by hand, photographed, recorded with different GPS instrumentation, and described by landform and setting. Dimensions of the surface artifact scatters or mounds were recorded in the field notes, along with inventories and descriptions of the types and relative densities of different artifacts and cultural materials observed. No artifacts were collected from these surface sites. The sites presented here are described in several groups (Salamanca, Salamanca Norte, Malabrigo 1, Pulpar, Lower Coastal Plain, and Santiago de Cao) based on the nomenclature assigned during the survey. Although none of the surveyed sites reported here were extensively excavated by us, we placed 1 by 2 m test pits in several (see chapter 7) and carried out extensive observations on the stratigraphy and discarded materials around looter holes in many of these

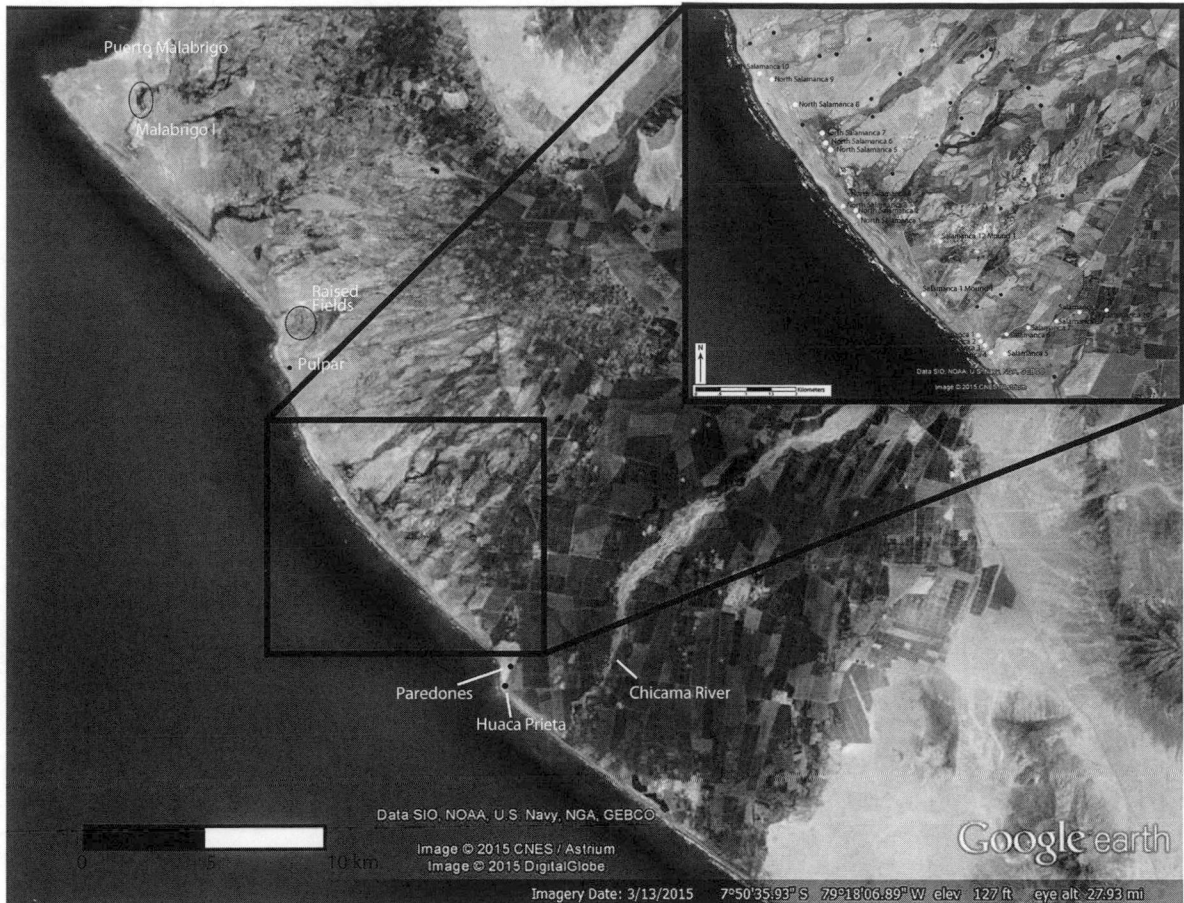

FIGURE 13.1. General location of outlying domestic sites north and east of Huaca Prieta and Paredones. The inset shows the major concentration of sites in the Salamanca area.

sites, which provided valuable data on community patterns and chronology. The survey of interior areas where ancient wetlands are located was more opportunistic and less systematic than the littoral area because several landowners did not permit us to enter their lands due to conflicts that they had with private corporations attempting to buy their properties.

SALAMANCA

SALAMANCA 1 (17M 0683513/ 9127896; 90 M NS/100 M EW)

Salamanca 1 is a low, dark gray accretional mound situated among the nearshore dunes approximately 230 m east of the modern shoreline. The mound has an ovate form measuring approximately 22 m north-south by 16 m east-west, with an altitude of 2–3 m. A dense surface scatter of artifacts and

marine shells is present across the mound and surrounding terrace, covering an area roughly 90 by 100 m. Surface artifacts included Chimú, Moche, and Cupisnique ceramics, along with a large amount of basalt and andesite lithic tools and fragments of polychaete tube-base. Substantial looting of the site had disturbed numerous human burials and exposed textile fragments similar to those recovered at Huaca Prieta. Marine shell and fauna were also observed in the disturbed graves and tombs. None of the disturbed graves were associated with ceramic artifacts, suggesting that the mound deposits and burials are of Preceramic age.

SALAMANCA 2 (17M 0683549/ 9127758; 60 M NS/90 M EW)

Salamanca 2 is a low, small accretional mound located approximately 140 m south of Salamanca 1 (fig. 13.2c). There is a continuous scatter of lithic

FIGURE 13.2. Outlying domestic sites: *a*, general view of the Malabrigo 1 site, showing the late Preceramic raised agricultural fields in the background and a domestic site around their border in the foreground; *b*, view of a garden plot in a wetland near Huaca Prieta (the sandy terrace in the right background has 1–2 m high Preceramic household mounds); *c*, view of a Preceramic house mound in the Salamanca area; *d*, aerial view of the Pulpar site and wetland north of Huaca Prieta (*arrow*); the site is located on an isolated remnant of the Sangamon terrace, similar to but much smaller than the terrace where Huaca Prieta and Paredones are located; *e*, view of *caballito* reed boats still used by fishers today near Pulpar; *f*, looted chamber tomb at Pulpar similar in architectural style to those of Phase V at Huaca Prieta.

implements and marine shell between the two mounds. Salamanca 2 is located at the edge of the nearshore dunes approximately 165 m east of the modern shoreline. The site has been intensively looted and partially destroyed by a bulldozer that leveled portions of the site. The original dimen-

sions of the mound are unknown, but the extant portion measures 14 by 19 m with a height of approximately 2 m. A dense surface scatter of artifacts was present across the extant mound surface and disturbed areas, extending roughly 60 m by 90 m in size. Basalt tools and cores, modified polychaete tube-bases, large gourd fragments, textile fragments, and a limited amount of Moche and Chimú ceramics were observed. A dense scatter of marine shell and fauna was also present. Intensive looting had resulted in the disturbance of a large number of Preceramic human burials.

SALAMANCA 3 (17M 0683614/ 9127668; 125 M NS/120 M EW)

Salamanca 3 is a cluster of low mounds located approximately 110 m south of Salamanca 2. The northernmost mound has been nearly completely leveled by a bulldozer. Two other low and elongated, accretional mounds (both measuring approximately 30 by 25 m with a height of 2 m) are located to the south of the destroyed mound. These mounds are situated at the edge of the near-shore dunes approximately 160 m east of the modern shoreline and have also been intensively looted. A dense surface scatter of artifacts extends 125 by 120 m in size. Surface artifacts are dominated by basalt lithic implements, including scrapers, choppers, and cores. Marine shells and faunal remains are ubiquitous. A relatively dense scatter of Cupisnique ceramics is also present. Looters in the mounds have exposed Preceramic human burials.

SALAMANCA 4 (17M 0683778/ 9127580; 20 M NS/40 M EW: ONLY THE PRECERAMIC COMPONENT)

Salamanca 4 is a buried Preceramic site identified in a stratigraphic profile exposed in a terrace edge erosional feature on the southern bank of a drainage channel from the interior of the valley. The site is located approximately 210 m east of the modern shoreline and 175 m southeast of Salamanca 3. A buried zone of dark sediment was documented along approximately 40 m of the north end of the terrace, beneath the thick, yellow silty sand layer that forms the modern surface. The dark zone extended from 30–200 cm below the surface and included multiple lithic tools and fragments and abundant marine shells and faunal remains exposed in the profile. The buried portion of the site is located just past a line of stabilized dunes and paleodunes.

In addition to the buried Preceramic compo-
nent that defines Salamanca 4, a double wall of blocks of polychaete tube-bases is associated with a small adobe mound approximately 50–75 m south of the exposed stratigraphic profile. A relatively dense distribution of textile fragments, looted human burials, and Moche ceramics are present in this portion of the site and indicate a later reoccupation of Salamanca 4.

SALAMANCA 5 (17M 0684019/ 9127650; 45 M NS/45 M EW: ONLY THE PRECERAMIC COMPONENT)

Salamanca 5 is a small accretional mound characterized by dark sediment with an abundance of marine shell and faunal remains and blocks of polychaete tube-bases. The site is situated in an area of coastal dunes ~250 m east of Salamanca 4 and ~375 m from the modern shoreline. The low, elongated mound is approximately 26 by 12 m. A low wall constructed of blocks of polychaete tube-bases (22 m in length) crosses the mound. Looter's pits in the mound revealed human burials, concentrations of marine shell, lithic artifacts, and textile and net fragments. The artifact scatter continues around the mound and covers an area of roughly 45 by 45 m. A light scatter of Cupisnique ceramics was also observed around the mound.

SALAMANCA 6 (17M 0684238/ 9127847; 20 M NS/50M EW)

Salamanca 6 is a low, small mound with Cupisnique and Moche ceramics covering the surface. The mound measures 20 by 50 m and has been cut roughly in half by a bulldozer for the clearing and preparation of cane fields. As a result, the northern end of the site has been completely destroyed. Salamanca 6 is situated on the edge of an interior terrace that overlooks an ancient coastal lagoon and is located 350 m northeast of Salamanca 5 and approximately 750 m from the modern shoreline. The bulldozer cut revealed a stratigraphic profile of the mound suggesting the presence of a buried Preceramic component beneath later Cupisnique and Moche occupations. This lower, buried zone consisted of dark sediment at the base of the mound that contained marine shells and lithic artifacts.

SALAMANCA 7 (17M 06846611/ 9128007; 200M NS/150 M EW)

Salamanca 7 is a complex of seven small, low accretional mounds situated on an interior terrace that overlooks an ancient coastal lagoon. The site is located approximately 460 m northeast of Salamanca 6 and 1 km from the modern shoreline. Each of the low mounds is of a slightly different shape. Three low, elongated mounds (approximately 20 by 6–8 m and roughly 0.5–1 m in height) are located in the southern part of the cluster. Four higher mounds (12 by 10 m and ~3 m in height) are located on the northern end of the cluster. These four mounds appear to be roughly aligned along an east-west axis. The site is under active cane planting. Multiple looter's holes in the mounds revealed dark sediment, an abundance of marine shells and faunal remains, and lithic artifacts. The artifact scatter covers the area between and around the mounds.

SALAMANCA 8 (17M 06852071/ 9128185; 40M NS/30 M EW)

Salamanca 8 is a small site located approximately 540 m northeast of Salamanca 7 and 1.5 km from the modern shoreline. The site is situated on the edge of an interior terrace that overlooks an ancient coastal lagoon and is characterized by a series of adobe walls and looted human burials. The majority of the surface artifacts reflect a Moche and Chimú occupation. Some of the looter's pits, however, exposed buried dark sediment containing dense concentrations of marine shells. It is possible that a buried Preceramic component is located beneath the later occupations, though this is speculative.

SALAMANCA 9 (17M 0685611/ 9128359; 90 M NS/100 M EW)

Like Salamanca 8, this site consists of a dense surface scatter of Moche and Chimú ceramics and textiles, associated with disturbed human burials. This site is located approximately 440 m northeast of Salamanca 8 and is situated on the edge of the same interior terrace overlooking an ancient coastal lagoon. The surface of the site has been heavily impacted by recent cane farming and loot-

ing. A few of the looter's holes revealed buried dark sediment and marine shells, possibly indicating a buried Preceramic component at the site.

SALAMANCA 10 (17M 0686136/ 9128384; 250 M NS/300 EW)

Salamanca 10 is a relatively large complex of ten (possibly twelve) small, accretional mounds located along the edge of a low interior terrace that overlooks the eastern end of an ancient coastal lagoon. The site is located approximately 530 m northeast of Salamanca 9 and 2.4 km from the modern shoreline. The mounds range between 1 and 3 m in height, and the largest measures approximately 38 by 20 m. Several ancient raised fields probably date to the late Preceramic period. Abundant marine shell and faunal remains, lithic artifacts, and disturbed human burials were observed on the mounds and in looter's pits as well as a dense scatter of Moche and Chimú ceramics.

SALAMANCA 11 (17M 0682593/ 9128782; MOUND 1: 90 M NS/70 M EW AND MOUND 2: 40M NS/30 M EW)

Salamanca 11 is located 1.2 km northwest of Salamanca 1 and approximately 180 m east of the modern shoreline. Two relatively large accretional mounds characterize the site. Mound 1 measures ~90 by 70 m and is 3–4 m in height. Mound 2, located 75 m northwest of Mound 1, measures 40 by 30 m and is ~2–3 m in height. The mounds are located on a narrow beach terrace covered with sand dunes between the shoreline and edge of an ancient interior lagoon/coastal wetland. Minimal looter disturbance was observed at the site. Surface artifacts included abundant marine shell and faunal remains and lithic artifacts. A few Cupisnique ceramics were also noted. These appear to be Preceramic mounds.

SALAMANCA 12 (MOUND 1: 17M 0682824/9129786; 400 M NS/250 M EW)

Salamanca 12 is a complex of twelve small accretional mounds located on a low, interior terrace that overlooks the northern edge of an ancient coastal lagoon/wetland. The site is located ~1 km north of Salamanca 11 and 1 km east of the modern shoreline. A small U-shaped mound (Mound 1) is located near the center of the mound complex. This structure (30 m east-west by 22 m north-south) opens to the east and is ~4 m in height. The southern arm is slightly higher than the northern arm. Six smaller mounds (Mounds 2–7) are located to the south and west of Mound 1. Each of these mounds is circular to ovate in shape. The largest of these mounds (Mound 2) measures 14 m north-south by 15 m east-west with a height of 1–2 m.

An additional five mounds (Mounds 8–12) are located to the east and north of Mound 1. Mound 10 is the closest to Mound 1 and is also the largest, measuring 26 m north-south by 22 m east-west with a height of ~2–3 m. The remaining mounds are all small, circular to ovate in shape, and 1–2 m in height.

The site has experienced only minor looting, so subsurface profiles were limited. Surface artifacts included a dense scatter of lithic artifacts and marine shell. The artifact distribution is densest around the small mounds on either side of Mound 1 but does extend over the entire site area (roughly 400 by 250 m). A few Cupisnique ceramics were observed on the surface of the site; the limited presence of ceramics, general absence of looting, and dark midden deposits in looter's holes, however, strongly suggest that this is a Preceramic mound complex.

SALAMANCA NORTE

SALAMANCA NORTE 1–4 (SALAMANCA NORTE 1: 17M 0681290/9130260; SALAMANCA NORTE 2: 17M 0681247/9130386; SALAMANCA NORTE 3: 17M 0681111/9130634; SALAMANCA NORTE 4: 17M 0680883/9130536)

Salamanca Norte 1–4 are Preceramic accretional mounds situated among the sand dunes on an upper beach terrace adjacent to the mouth of a large estuary/coastal lagoon. Salamanca Norte 1 and 2 are located on the southern side of the drainage, while Salamanca Norte 3 and 4

are located on the northern side. The mounds are between 130 and 300 m from one another. Salamanca Norte 1 is located ~2 km northwest of Salamanca 11 and 210 m from the modern shoreline.

Salamanca Norte 1 is an ovate-shaped accretional mound with an approximate height of 2.5–3 m and dimensions of 65 by 30 m. The top of the mound has been looted, exposing abundant marine shell and lithic artifacts. In general the density of surface artifacts was very low.

Salamanca Norte 2 is a relatively small, circular accretional mound with a height of 2 m and dimensions of 48 by 32 m. This mound was located ~80 m northeast of Salamanca Norte 1. A low density of surface materials consisting of marine shell and faunal remains and a few lithic artifacts was observed.

Salamanca Norte 3 is a small, elongated accretional mound with a height of 1.5 m and dimensions of 28 by 16 m. The only materials observed on the surface were marine shells. Several lithic flakes and cobbles were observed next to a looter's hole on the mound.

Salamanca Norte 4 is a roughly circular accretional mound with a height of approximately 1.5–2 m and dimensions of 60 by 65 m. The mound is situated only 80 m from the modern shoreline. Heavy looting has occurred at this mound. As a result a relatively large quantity of human remains, textile fragments, marine shell and faunal remains, and lithic artifacts have been exposed on the surface.

SALAMANCA NORTE 5–7 (SALAMANCA NORTE 5: 17M 0680735/9131628; SALAMANCA NORTE 6: 17M 0680602/9131803; SALAMANCA NORTE 7: 17M 0680530/9131984)

Salamanca Norte 5, 6, and 7 are relatively large accretional Preceramic (and later) deposits on stabilized paleodunes situated on the western edge of a coastal lagoon/estuary. Salamanca Norte 5 is located ~1 km north of Salamanca Norte 4 and 600 m east of the modern shoreline. Dense linear surface scatters of lithic materials and marine shells and faunal remains that are spaced ~200 m apart characterize each of these three sites.

Salamanca Norte 5 is an accretional deposit measuring 180 by 21 m. Lithic materials were observed on the surface, along with a large concentration of marine shells and faunal remains. The very northern end of the dune contained a large concentration of human remains, marine fauna and shells, and lithic artifacts exposed by looters. A light scatter of Cupisnique and Moche ceramics was observed on the southern end of the site.

Salamanca Norte 6 measures 85 by 41 m. A large concentration of marine shell and faunal remains, lithic artifacts, and a few heavily weathered and eroded ceramics was observed on the surface. As at Salamanca Norte 5, a large concentration of human remains on the northern end of the site had been exposed by looters.

Salamanca Norte 7 is an accretional deposit with dimensions of 40 by 35 m. Abundant marine shell and faunal remains were observed on the surface, along with textile fragments, lithic artifacts, and a light scatter of Cupisnique ceramics.

SALAMANCA NORTE 8
(17M 0679981/9132631; 45 M NS/36 M EW)

Salamanca Norte 8 is a Preceramic accretional deposit located on a stabilized coastal paleodune situated on a high beach terrace. The site is ~850 m northwest of Salamanca Norte 7 and 600 m east of the modern shoreline. The surface artifact scatter (45 by 36 m) consisted of lithic artifacts and marine shell. A large but shallow bulldozer cut (16 by 8 m) has been excavated across the site. The upper portion (upper 60 cm) of the exposed profile contained a layer of dark sediment with burned sediment and charcoal (likely hearths). Marine shell and lithic artifacts also were observed in the exposed profile. The lower portion of the profile appeared to be the finely sorted sand of the paleodune.

SALAMANCA NORTE 9
(17M 0679481/9133029; 85 M NS/25 M EW)

Salamanca Norte 9 is a Preceramic accretional deposit with dimensions of ~85 by 25 m. The site is located 645 m northwest of Salamanca Norte 8 and 380 m east of the modern shoreline. The deposit appears to cap a stabilized coastal paleodune that is situated on a high beach terrace. The site surface is heavily eroded, with the surface elevation varying by 40–60 cm in places. A relatively dense scatter of marine shell and faunal remains, lithic artifacts, and textile and net fragments was observed on the surface. A light scatter of Cupisnique ceramics also was observed.

SALAMANCA NORTE 10
(17M 0679248/9133154; 42 M NS/18M EW)

Salamanca Norte 10 is a Preceramic accretional deposit located on a stabilized coastal dune on an upper beach terrace. It is situated 260 m northwest of Salamanca Norte 9 and 170 m east of the modern shoreline and sits along the southwestern margin of a coastal lagoon/estuary. A dense surface scatter of lithic cobbles and artifacts and marine shell and faunal remains characterize this site (42 by 18 m). A light scatter of Cupisnique ceramics was also noted.

MALABRIGO 1 (7425851S; 75760342W)

This is an extensive Preceramic site associated with numerous lithics, shells, and other debris along the west side of a large wetland defined by ~5 hectares of raised agricultural fields that we have dated by OSL means to ~2200 years ago (fig. 13.2a; see chapter 7). The domestic area stretches around the west side for about 1.2 km and is associated with a small hill that has siliceous raw material used as a quarry site. Another area of possible Preceramic raised fields is located farther south at 7475775S and 75223545W.

PULPAR (7485136S; 79225231W)

This is a smaller version of the Huaca Prieta site, located ~15 km north of the latter also on a remnant of the Sangamon terrace (fig. 13.2d and f). The site is ~200 by 220 m and situated on the south side of a finger-like wetland running east to west and draining into the ocean. The west face of the terrace is associated with mortared, cobblestone chamber tombs identical to those for Phases IV–V at Huaca Prieta. The east side slopes into a residential area with scattered shell, lithic, and other debris spread over an extensive area. We surmise a similar economic and mortuary scenario during Phases II–III at Huaca Prieta. Although the relationship between Huaca Prieta and Pulpar is unknown, it is likely that Pulpar is a Phase V northward extension of Huaca Prieta, as suggested by similar chamber tombs and diagnostic artifactual debris. In contrast to Huaca Prieta, Pulpar seems to be more residential and mortuary than ritual in function. This also may be the case with other late Preceramic dark mounds along the Peruvian littoral, such as Huaca Negra in the Virú Valley to the south.

LOWER COASTAL PLAINS

Our cursory survey south of Huaca Prieta along the beach and about 3–4 km into the interior beyond the littoral zone located and briefly registered thirty-four other Preceramic sites, suggesting that the most typical sites on the lower coastal plain to the south are located on old, highly eroded dune ridges, sandy hummocks, or shorelines overlooking wetlands. It seems reasonable to infer that these sites are the remains of households used by people perhaps more specialized in the exploitation of varied wetland resources. Although not detailed here because they have been heavily destroyed by modern-day activity (or we did not have time to record them properly because most of these sites are on lands of owners who would not give permission to continue the survey or would give us a limited time to examine their terrain), most of these sites seem to be scatters of lithics and some shell debris similar to those found at Huaca Prieta and Paredones. Only four of these sites were associated with low house mounds (0.5–1.1 m high). These are interpreted as small homesteads exploiting the wetland environments, though here the sites seem smaller in areal extent, with the buried deposits not as thick as at the shoreline sites and with artifacts that are generally fewer in number, suggesting that occupa-

tion may have been less intensive than it was along the littoral zone. Eight of these sites also are associated with light scatters of Cupisnique ceramics and occasionally Moche sherds.

SANTIAGO DE CAO, SOUTH SIDE OF THE CHICAMA RIVER

Immediately south of the Sangamon terrace across from the small irrigation drainage at the south end of the mound along the elevated dune terraces fronting the beach are eleven low Preceramic accretional mounds similar to those described for the Salamanca area. Additional low household mounds are scattered farther south along the dune formations south of the Chicama River to Santiago de Cao and farther toward Cerro Campana. Due to heavy destruction of the interior by cane fields, we did not survey the interior zones here. However, we were informed by locals that lagoons and wetlands similar to those seen in the Salamanca area once existed in the Santiago de Cao area as well, suggesting that more Preceramic sites may have been present on the low coastal and littoral plain south of the Chicama River. Most of these sites measure between 35 by 60 m and 1.0–1.4 m high and are situated on low paleodunes along the littoral. They contain the same kinds of lithics, shells, and textiles as Huaca Prieta. Inspection of looter's holes and a few test pits placed by our project indicate that all of these sites have Preceramic occupation, sometimes overlaid by later ceramic sites.

DISCUSSION

The above sites are primarily single and clustered house mounds probably associated with a mixed littoral and interior wetland economy. The presence of these sixty-seven sites (and others that we did not record or that were destroyed by modern-day activity) reveals the density of Preceramic sites in the area. Not all of these are presumed to be associated with Huaca Prieta, but many of them probably supported and used the mound there for ritual, burial, or other purposes. Scattered human burials associated with these sites and exposed by looter activity indicate the placement of tombs below house floors and outside of houses in the mounded midden debris. Furthermore, these sites seem to begin to appear when the wetlands and lagoons east of the shoreline started to form between ~7200 and 6200 cal BP. Whether some of these site areas were abandoned or shifted in response to minor climatic changes is not known. Given the location of these sites at the mouth of several wetlands draining the interior lands and on low terraces overlooking lagoons and wetlands as far as 3–4 km inland, we hypothesize that some of these sites were associated with specialized littoral and inland economies and that the spatial organization may suggest a segmented kinship structure (see chapters 14 and 15).

Finally, in several of these areas some local people today continue to practice certain traditions of a Preceramic subsistence lifestyle, such as inhabiting what are called *quincha* huts made of cane walls. They farm in seasonal wetlands behind the terraced beaches, where they grow cotton, corn, chile peppers, and avocados among other crops (fig. 13.2b). A few families continue to collect seafood and to fish in the small *caballito* reed boats (fig. 13.2e).

CHAPTER 14

CONTINUITY, CHANGE, AND THE CONSTRUCTION OF THE EARLY SANGAMON SOCIETY

Tom D. Dillehay

INTRODUCTION

We have proposed a five-phase model for the construction and use of the Huaca Prieta and Paredones mounds. This model also serves to place the domestic Units 13, 16, and 26 and outlying household mound sites to the north and south chronologically. We found evidence that the mound at Huaca Prieta overlies an earlier late Pleistocene and early Holocene occupation (Phase I), focused largely on maritime and terrestrial foraging, and that the subsequent mound construction proceeded in gradual multilevel stages, initially spanning the entire south end of the Sangamon terrace and later expanding to the north. The maritime and terrestrial lifeway of the early Holocene period was similar to that of the late Pleistocene but with a slightly different array of plant and animal species and with a different frequency of their exploitation. The unifacial stone technology of the entire Holocene period at all sites also was morphologically similar to that of the late Pleistocene but slightly expanded in tool diversity and size throughout time, with a wider variety of flakes and grinding stones added.

Data supporting these early phases illuminate an interesting anomaly that should be pursued. Work done at other middle to late Holocene monumental sites on the coast does not reveal millennia-long site use, but in some cases this may be the result of not fully probing their basal or premound deposits both horizontally and vertically. Even though there is a dearth of well-excavated late Preceramic locales along the Central Pacific coast of South America, it is not unreasonable to assume that the earliest occupation at some of them conformed to a generalized maritime pattern seen throughout the late Pleistocene and early Holocene period, but this also depends on the environmental setting and other factors. The archaeological data also point to small populations moving up and down the coast and occasionally into the interior (perhaps only short distances) over the span of several millennia (see Sandweiss 2012).

As noted at the outset of this volume, the archaeological data from Huaca Prieta represent fourteen millennia of a human presence in the study area. The period between roughly 14,500 and 8000 years ago pertains to intermittent occupations by maritime foragers and terrestrial hunters and gatherers. Between about 7500 and 3400 cal BP, the mound at Huaca Prieta was built and used for ritual and mortuary purposes. Paredones was constructed and used between ~6500 and 3800 cal BP, primarily for food preparation. After this period Huaca Prieta was used by early ceramic cultures, as evidenced by the presence of Guañape-like, Cupisnique, and Moche ceramics (and occasionally burials) in the upper levels of the ramp on the northeast side of the mound (see Bird et al. 1985). From the Moche period to colonial times, the mound at Huaca Prieta was occasionally used as a cemetery place. The major findings for each cultural period are summarized below.

PHASE I: EARLY ARRIVALS AND SETTLING IN, ~14,530–7571 CAL BP

This period encompasses two major subphases between ~14,500 and 7500 cal BP, the terminal Pleistocene and the early Holocene, the premound levels at Huaca Prieta and Paredones. Shell, bone, and lithic debris as well as burned features, a few plant remains, and a red pigment yielded information about technology, chronology, and subsistence practice at Huaca Prieta and Paredones (see chapters 6, 9, 10, and 12). The coastline at the outset of early Phase I was ~30 km farther west, and the elevated, 2.5 km long Sangamon terrace would have been a very prominent place on the landscape: surrounded by braided streams, wetlands, and grassy plains, with access to many different habitats. About 15 km east into the interior were the Andean foothills, locating the site roughly an equal distance between two major ecological zones. Early exploitation of sea organisms is revealed at both sites, including

abundant remains of sharks and sea lions, both of which were probably captured in backwater estuaries close to the sea and on beaches, respectively (see chapter 9). Marine fauna recovered from late Pleistocene levels and subsequent early Holocene deposits indicate that the exploitation of shellfish was incorporated into the coastal subsistence strategy at an early stage. Also present are a few deer remains, wild plant foods, and squash, chile peppers, and avocado, suggesting a mixed diet of marine and terrestrial resources in the transition between these two early subphases (see chapter 10 and appendix 4). The lithic technology is very conservative during these subphases, with fewer worked tool types (pebble tools such as scrapers and cutting and pounding implements) than in later phases (see chapter 11). Collectively, these data represent sporadic visits to the Sangamon terrace by maritime and terrestrial foragers, probably as early as 14,500 years ago, who left behind an ephemeral record and laid the foundation for the later, more complex adaptations associated with the mounds. Although they were probably modified or destroyed by later mound building, it is probable that more scattered early remains of these foragers were once present across the entire terrace. No human burials were recorded for this early phase. Until more evidence is obtained on the late Pleistocene and early Holocene deposits in the study area, caution should be taken in relying too heavily on the chronology and cultural patterns described for this period here.

PHASE II: MOUND BUILDING AND INCIPIENT SPECIALIZATION ALONG THE LITTORAL, ~7571–6538 CAL BP

The southern and eastern portions of the Huaca Prieta mound first rose during Phase II, probably because they are on the lower southeast side of the terrace, not only protected from winds off the ocean but also in close proximity to different types of wetlands along the littoral and into the coastal interior that began to form ~7500–7200 cal BP (see chapters 3, 4, and 5 for discussion of the littoral zone). Mound construction began in this area by at least 7500 and possibly as early as 7800 cal BP (see chapter 6). Although people lived on the southern end of the terrace, exploiting both marine and terrestrial resources prior to development of the wetlands, it probably was the appearance of several new exotic cultigens, a slight population increase, and initial mound building that stimulated the beginning of a mixed economy of specialized maritime and wetland foraging and low-intensity gardening or farming. A population increase is suggested by the presence of several individual household mounds along the littoral and interior wetlands, some dated to ~7000 cal BP or earlier (see chapters 6, 7, and 13). Interactions between foraging and farming communities were probably in flux during this period. Given the absence of weapons and physical trauma on the few skeletons of this period (see chapter 8 and Bird et al. 1985), the social relations among scattered populations appear to have been amicable, which may have fostered economic specialization and short- and long-distance exchange of resources from different production zones, as suggested by the presence of exotic cultigens and a few nonfood items (green schist, nonlocal shells; see chapter 11). Amicable interaction between different littoral and wetland economic groups explains the similarities in material culture that they shared, with the exception of the type and frequency of food remains, as seen at Huaca Prieta, Paredones, and Unit 16, for instance.

Phase II deposits were encountered in Units 2, 9, 15/21, 19, 20, 22, 23, and 25, Bird's HP-2 and HP-3, and Test Pit 22. The elevation of the mound at Huaca Prieta and the thickness of its Phase II deposits vary and are not known in all areas across the south end of the terrace because so few of our excavation units reached the bottom of this large, deep mound. The upper elevation of the initial deposits observed in Units 2 and 15 and Test Pit 22 is between 1.8 and 2.1 m higher than those on the eastern edge of the northern and western areas in Units 19 and 25 and in Bird's HP-2 and HP-3 units, corresponding to the natural west-to-east decline of the terrace upon which the mound was built (see chapter 7 and appendix 1).

Evidently a communal decision was made ~7500 cal BP to build the Huaca Prieta mound vertically and horizontally in an elongated, serial accretional form oriented from south to north, first along the eastern edge of the terrace. There appears to be no physical or other reason to suggest why the mound was built up artificially and deliberately other than for ritual and mortuary

activities and perhaps for commensal feasting in and around mounds. If people sought a higher mound for residency, then we would expect to see the same accretional buildup in other areas along the coast and particularly along the Sangamon terrace, where there is laterally spread early Preceramic occupancy. The initial 2 m of the Huaca Prieta mound was constructed slowly and associated with a series of probable mixed residential and ritual and feasting uses, primarily by maritime and wetland foragers, as evidenced by numerous burned features, lithics, and floral and faunal remains placed alongside the southeast corner of the mound (see chapter 7). The next 5 m of the mound appear to have been built as a continuous project over a long time, ~7500–6500 cal BP.

More specifically, the mound during this phase was stacked in a layer-cake manner or built up by the addition of hundreds of blanket mantles of sediment. Where these occurred, they were highly circumscribed and generally 2 to 3 m by 4 to 5 m in size (see chapter 7). The first cobble berms in late Phase II (see Unit 2 and HP-3 in chapters 6 and 7) were later additions designed to shore up the southern and eastern slopes of the initial mound layers. (As noted above, the terrace slopes from west to east, which served as a naturally inclined berm for the west side of the mound; cobble support-footings were not observed on this side.) People deliberately engineered this arrangement of berms to keep the basal layers of sediment well supported as the mound grew in size, presumably until it reached a height and form that eventually required longer and thicker berms along its entire lower eastern base in addition to the later thin but fairly extensive plaster covers to prevent surface erosion (see Units 2 and HP-3 in chapter 7). The first thick plaster coating appears in early Phase III, as seen in HP-3, Units 9 and 15/21, and Test Pit 22. Only one human burial pertains to this phase (HP09-08: see chapters 7–8).

As at Huaca Prieta, the premound levels at Paredones contain early hunter-gatherer domestic debris dating to the early Holocene and maybe earlier. Stratigraphy and material evidence from the basal deposits of the Paredones mound, which was built nearly a thousand years later than the first layers at Huaca Prieta, including a few low cobblestone berms, suggests a functional equivalent to the lower Phase II levels of Huaca Prieta, which are associated with habitation, food preparation, ritual (such as a few burned areas and small offerings of food, shells, decorated gourds), and perhaps feasting. These early mound layers do not contain the hearths, density of midden debris, ash, and charcoal, and stains and postholes found in the early to late domestic deposits at Units 13, 16, and 26 and at outlying household mounds. However, the domestic units do not contain decorated gourds, textiles, and berms and the intense burning of material observed at Huaca Prieta and Paredones. Around 6500 cal BP, when Phase II at Huaca Prieta leaves off and Phase III begins, Paredones seems to focus on the preparation of plant food for rituals, perhaps those taking place at Huaca Prieta. Although the initial layers in both mounds, albeit temporally separated by ~1000 years, were associated with ritual and other activities, they do not reveal the circumscribed private or individual ritual spaces seen later in Phases III–IV at Huaca Prieta. That is, during early Phase III, stone architecture in the form of rock alignments and small stone-lined rooms with ritual offerings and burned areas first appear at Huaca Prieta.

After the construction of the mound core at Huaca Prieta during Phase II, subsequent additions of thousands of thin, spatially limited use stages were made on what appears to be a continuous ritual basis. Yearly or seasonal additions to the mound added to its overall height and girth in an appreciable manner. This suggests at least 5–6 m of additional mound height at Huaca Prieta by the end of Phase II, less than 25% of the mound's total height, with additional stages during Phases III–V. Paredones also grew upward and outward at the same time by the addition of blanket mantles of sediment and cultural debris. By the end of Phase II the type, diversity, and frequency of marine and plant foods revealed an economic dichotomy whereby marine foods are primarily associated with Huaca Prieta and plant foods with Paredones.

PHASE III: MOUND GROWTH AND LITTORAL ECONOMIC INTENSIFICATION, ~6538–5308 CAL BP

The subsequent 14–16 accretional m of the following Phase III at Huaca Prieta were built as a series of roughly level surfaces for small-scale circumscribed rituals, some of which were associated with human burials. As discussed in chapters 7 and 9–12, substantial changes took place in the mound strata, architecture, technology, material culture, and food during Phase III, all suggestive of numerous small-group rituals rather than habitation. Most notable was the appearance of painted cobbles, fragmented textiles and gourds, exotic novelties such as copper sulfate, and possibly pottery or at least ceramic sherds (as offerings?).

Huaca Prieta continued to expand in size to a low elongated oval mound that reached farther to the north. However, Phase III deposits represent a different content and texture than those of Phase II. Phase III sediments were composed of a much darker, ashy, charcoal-laden mass of sediments with marine shells, burned sea urchin spines, other faunal and floral debris, and more extensive and thicker stone berms. It appears that burning plants, sea urchins, and other organisms and pouring seawater on the mound became more essential activities in ritual, as evidenced by the high content of charcoal, salt crystals, and burned sea urchin spines in discrete spaces in all strata. A few human burials are present in shallow, informal graves (see chapters 7 and 8), but the chamber tombs had not yet appeared. Also present for the first time are numerous walls of aligned stones and small stone structures. The co-appearance of burials, individual stone alignments, and excessive burning suggests an ontological shift or development in the relationship among the living, the dead, the memorialization of the dead in sacred places, and the use of fire and its meaning. The mound at Paredones, in contrast, was beginning to be built around ~6500 cal BP: as with Huaca Prieta, the site shifted from being a domestic forager locale to a food preparation and ritual site. Although a common sequential and equivalent planned staging is found in the lower strata of both mounds (especially at Huaca Prieta, as revealed by the berm footings to preserve the site), differences are seen throughout the stratigraphic columns and artifact and feature content. Most notably, at Paredones all floors and use surfaces are relatively thin (~2 and 8 cm in thickness), whereas all floors and use surfaces after Phase II in Huaca Prieta are much thicker (~0.5 to 1 m) and composed of coarse materials such as rocks, polychaete blocks, whalebones, and so forth (see chapter 7) and occasionally of stone-walled architecture (for example, Units 9 and 15). It is not known whether these differences reflect larger groups participating in rituals or whether the rituals were more frequent and prolonged, thus resulting in thicker floors and use surfaces. During and after Phase III more burials appear in Huaca Prieta, indicating a functional shift from Phase II occupation to both ritual and mortuary practices during Phase III. At Paredones the thin use surfaces and fills continue in an incremental and rather even fashion, as if they were sequentially arranged, if not on a seasonal basis then on an annual one. Human burials do not appear in Paredones except for a single Moche burial in the upper layer of Unit 2 and three individual teeth placed with piled food remains as offerings in Preceramic levels (see appendix 6).

It is important to note that space and activity were clearly segmented (fragmented) into individualized or private compartments of similar but still different scales and material content during these early phases of mound construction at Huaca Prieta, patterns also seen at later Formative ritual sites such San Luis in the Zaña Valley (Dillehay 2004) and Kotosh in the Andean highlands (Izumi and Sono 1963). At Huaca Prieta this is indicated by the many small, individual use surfaces and/or prepared floors, often marked by a line of stones to define them or simply revealed by a different type of sand, clay, or sediment layer composing the use surface or floor. These features are not present in any phase at Paredones (see chapter 7).

At Huaca Prieta the end of Phase III is also represented by a series of short, fragmented cobble-lined walls and stone alignments covered by a ~0.5 m thick yellowish sediment cap, which is a structural and depositional shift associated with the beginning of Phase IV (see chapter 7). Both Phase III and especially Phase IV were associated with floors and use surfaces sealed by laterally extensive plaster coatings that were similar to roof shingles, as evidenced by their overlapping appearance. Excavations revealed some gaps between the shingled layers of plaster, suggesting that the coverings were a thick liquid apparently poured quickly in some areas and not filling all spaces. These individual surfaces also were multiple single-use, rebuilding, and preservation epi-

sodes. Numerous fill episodes were found between these surfaces.

Phase III also is characterized by the incorporation of new cultigens into the diet of the people using Huaca Prieta and Paredones. Solid evidence of systematic and specialized exploitation of diverse marine and plant foods was found during Phase III at Huaca Prieta and Paredones, respectively. There also was an increase in the number of tools for processing more plant foods at Paredones (grinding stones, manos, and prismatic slicing blades). This indicates that the target food resources associated with this site expanded even more to plant foods, many of which were the focus of subsistence specialization by people using the site area, including gardens and crop fields in the nearby wetlands to the east (see chapter 7). The same thing was occurring at Huaca Prieta, but with marine rather than plant foods. During this phase, three new cultigens (primarily as offerings) appeared at Huaca Prieta and one and two at Unit 16 and Paredones, respectively (see table 10.1). Despite the signs of increased exploitation of marine and plant foods, people still used the wetlands, as evidenced by the presence of reeds, sedges, acacia pods, and other wild plants in sites. Also present are camelid bones and camelid hair in textiles, perhaps indicative of low-level animal husbandry or the exchange of camelid products from distant groups.

At the end of Phase III the yellowish sediment layer spanning and recapping nearly all of Huaca Prieta signaled the onset of the construction of the chamber tombs, the entry ramp on the northeast side of the mound, and the sunken circular plaza during early Phase IV. This event suggests another major social and ontological shift, with greater group formality toward ritual and mortuary practice and perhaps feasting. (Curiously, this was the only time that a nearly mound-long layer was placed across the site and that a yellowish sediment was used: see chapter 7.) With the exception of the exotic cultigens at Paredones and Huaca Prieta, most of which were probably derived from tropical environments to the north in present-day Colombia and Ecuador or to the east of the Andes, the majority of the cultural material and expression at these sites is associated from the littoral zone. This does not imply that there were no major exchange networks with neighboring coastal and distant highland groups; it means that the cultural influence from these areas is minimal or unidentifiable, except during Phases IV and V when the ramp and sunken circular plaza appear.

PHASE IV: BECOMING MORE COASTAL, ~5308–4107 CAL BP

After Phase III mound building was pursued by the addition of layers atop the yellowish cap foundation. The Phase IV building stage was constrained by the initial footprint of the mound. More single-plaster layers were placed over Huaca Prieta during this phase as an additional 4–5 m of height were added. All layers continued to be serial-use episodes, possibly on the order of weeks, months, seasons, and years, with brief hiatuses in construction. In this phase multiple small chamber tombs were placed on top and along the sloping upper sides of the mound (Units 10, 19, 21, 23) and stone-like burial niches constructed along the upper rim of the sunken circular plaza (Unit 8). Phases IV and V represent fewer additional mound layers though the placement of the chamber tombs, each supported by small retention walls that are present throughout the mound, gives the impression that individual groups of people (families from outlying households?) defined their own ritual and burial areas.

Of all mound phases at Huaca Prieta, only Phase IV is partially laterally level and associated with the initial construction of agglutinated formal chamber tombs (Units 10, 11, 19, and 23 and around the rim of the sunken plaza), most of which were roofed and empty. Above the yellowish sediment are the majority of the burial chambers, which transformed the mound for the first time into a near-whole or near-single function — a ritual and mortuary complex. During this phase, the economy of both mounds became even more specialized with the addition of different cultigens, mainly food crops, now with a total of thirteen (as offerings) at Huaca Prieta, one at Unit 16, and eleven at Paredones. The isotope data and abrasion patterns on human teeth indicate a clear difference in the diet between the maritime consumers at Huaca Prieta and the plant eaters at Paredones (see appendix 6). Although the size of the teeth sample ($n = 3$) for isotopic studies is limited at Paredones, the analysis suggests that the teeth (presumably

from secondary burials) are from local people who primarily ate plant food, from individuals who resided farther inland when they were young and later in life moved to the Paredones area, or from distant persons who were reburied in or near the mound for unknown reasons. The isotope study from Huaca Prieta individuals is different from the data from Paredones and from other coastal populations in that the teeth show a primary seafood diet but with less abrasion than expected. This is surprising, because people residing in sandy coastal areas such as Huaca Prieta generally show more wear due to substantial amounts of sand in their diet (see appendix 6). These data may suggest that some people buried at Huaca Prieta lived more inland, away from the littoral, but primarily consumed seafood.

As for the possible seasonality of activities, both mound sites contain plant and animal species that indicate year-round use during Phases II–V, although any one stratum or use episode may have been seasonally based. The only suggestion of a specific season of activity is offerings of *Semele corrugata* and *Semele solida* possibly gathered during the winter months and deposited in chamber tombs dating to Phases IV and V (see appendix 3).

Other than chamber tombs, the major additions of Phase IV were the sunken circular plaza on the upper south side and the access ramp and its zigzag footpaths on the northeast side of the mound. The plaza was a purposefully constructed feature of the mound that was sunk yet elevated above the natural ground level by about 12 m. Construction of the ramp did not preclude the possibility of an earlier ramp or entry paths anywhere else on the mound.

Another defining characteristic of Huaca Prieta during Phases III–IV is mortuary ritual, suggesting that the construction of parts of the mound and the furnishing of burials in it may have provided a context for more elaborate ritual behavior. The inhabitants of Huaca Prieta (the combined mound and off-mound areas) seemingly created a landscape that not only was altered for food and ritual production but was set with a large permanent monument and a formal cemetery for a select type of dead that persisted across generations and millennia (see chapter 15). Not yet fully understood is the degree to which the mound was ritualized, related to mortuary practices (and perhaps commensal feasting as well), linked with off-mound residential areas and outlying sites, and related to inland and other maritime economies and exchange systems. It is likely that during this phase Huaca Prieta had more cultural linkages with interior coastal groups and that the ramp and sunken plaza emulated similar features at contemporary religious centers farther south, such as Alto Salaverry, Bandurria, and sites of the Norte Chico area. In other words, Huaca Prieta seems to have shifted culturally and perhaps ontologically from an Andean littoral site to an Andean coastal locality ("coastal" here implies the grassy plains and interior lower to middle floodplain of the river valley).

During late Phase IV, the underlying design principles of the outlying domestic sites probably became more evident. The domestic sites appear to be arranged according to recognizable geographic and ecological relationships in close proximity to the small deltas of the east-to-west trending wetland drainages (see chapter 13). This is to say, there is a clear orientation to the layout of the various domestic groups based on the location of the wetlands. After 5000 cal BP construction at both Huaca Prieta and Paredones increased in both quantity and scale.

PHASE V: BECOMING MORE ANDEAN, ~4107–3455 CAL BP

Phase V is more intensive than Phase IV, distinguished by increased lateral construction of more elaborate chamber tombs on the summit (Units 11 and 23 and Bird's excavation on top of the mound next to HP-3) and the eventual abandonment of Preceramic activities, although later cultures continued to bury people there. The economy continued to be mixed and specialized, but with fewer natural resources from the wetland environments, although these environments were continuously used for agricultural production and expanded farther east into the lower valley coastal plain. Eighteen and twelve cultigens now appear at Huaca Prieta (as offerings) and Paredones, respectively; nine are present at Unit 16.

Phase V also saw the construction of the Pulpar mound ~15 km to the north, which also was built next to a rich wetland area that still survives today (see chapter 13). The tomb architecture at Pulpar is very similar to that of late Phase IV and early

Phase V at Huaca Prieta, suggesting that Pulpar dates to at least ~4100–3500 cal BP. A major similarity between Huaca Prieta and Pulpar is that both have adjacent residential sectors, although the domestic sector at Pulpar is more visible because it is not covered by subsequent mound building by Guañape-like and Cupisnique occupations, which was the case at Huaca Prieta. A similar pattern may be seen farther north at Puémape in the southern Jequetepeque Valley, where Carlos Elera (1998) recorded late Preceramic habitation overlaid by Cupisnique deposits. Site location and landscape usage along the littoral north and south and into the interior wetlands of Huaca Prieta clearly indicate a trend toward demographic expansion and growth evident in Phase V.

By the end of Phase V early Guañape-like and Cupisnique deposits are on the northeast side of the mound, indicating continued ritual use and human burial. These deposits in addition to the earlier ramp and sunken plaza features of Phase IV suggest that Huaca Prieta continued to become part of a wider Andean coastal and a coastal/highland sphere of interaction, probably involving shared ritual beliefs and practices as well as the exchange of food and other products.

The final plaster capping and Preceramic abandonment of Huaca Prieta came at the end of Phase V. We assume that the first appearance of pottery (Guañape-like and Cupisnique styles) from the upper layer of the north end of the mound is contemporaneous with several terminal capping layers, especially those on the northeast side of Huaca Prieta, with the final capping occurring as late as ~3500 BP. As nonmortuary ritual mounds, both Huaca Prieta and Paredones were abandoned about the same time, marking the end of their Preceramic activities. Abandonment also coincided with the gradual reduction of the paludal wetlands in the lower valley ~3800–3500 cal BP and with the maximum transgression of the sea, which extended inland ~200–300 m more than it does today (see chapter 5). Such transgression would have placed the sea against the west base of Huaca Prieta and also would have flooded the low-lying raised agricultural fields east of it, at least making this area of the lower valley less hospitable for perhaps a few centuries. The transgression also affected the water table along the littoral zone by generating more interior wetlands and less habitational space close to the shoreline. Together, these results correlate maximum transgression at both the river mouth and Huaca Prieta, while also correlating this period with the major environmental transition from a low-lying floodplain to a more arable high floodplain, all occurring ~3800–3500 cal BP. Taken together, the increased water management system (such as raised agricultural fields and canals), the ramp and sunken circular plaza, the wider array of cultigens, and the presence of Initial period and Formative ceramic styles point to increased contact with and influence by contemporaneous coastal and highland Andean cultures.

A SENSE OF LONG-TERM PLANNING AT HUACA PRIETA

Prior publications on Huaca Prieta imply a residential mound with a few late "house" structures (see Bird et al. 1985). Although there is some evidence of site modification and thin to thick layers of fill upon which floors and use surfaces were constructed, numerous intact short segments of stone alignments and small wall units were also recorded throughout the site from early Phase III to Phase V (see chapter 7). Most of these features are associated with retention walls, chamber tomb walls, stone alignments defining individual ritual spaces, and perhaps reserved burial spaces (empty tombs?). The burial areas evolved over time, with the earliest in Phases II–III composed of numerous small, informal depressions used as tombs. These areas and the numerous walls, the chamber tombs (although largely empty of burials), the nontomb rooms in the sunken circular plaza, and the access ramp of Phases IV and V all reveal a sense of planning. Planning is also suggested by the cobblestone berm footings and the haystacking construction technique beginning in Phase II and by the plaster coatings in all subsequent phases, all designed as retention features for architectural expansion and preservation.

Huaca Prieta undoubtedly rose slowly and incrementally, and the final form of the mound is a detailed palimpsest of its long construction and use history. The same holds true to a lesser extent for Paredones, because it is smaller and later and probably contains no or fewer burials. Funda-

mentally, these two mounds were built through thousands of temporally and spatially discrete events where construction was undertaken as a high-frequency series of very small individual or small group activities, each designed to create an immediate and circumscribed ritual and occasionally a mortuary surface. Despite what may appear to be a distinction between these activities over time, a consensual grand plan or design seems to have existed for the mound at Huaca Prieta: a diachronic continuation to demarcate the circumscribed ritual spaces used by these activities and to build the mound higher and longer and occasionally seal it with thick plaster covers to protect it. As noted earlier, after its Preceramic use, Huaca Prieta was used continuously by all cultures from the Guañape-like to the colonial periods for placement of special burials. These burials do not dominate the upper mound surface but are scattered across the top of its summit.

Although the internal structure of Huaca Prieta exhibits many types of construction methods rather than a single rigid plan, it was built as an ongoing transgenerational mound, with knowledge of how and when to use and construct it evidently passed from generation to generation. Mound building was at a slow temporal and small spatial scale that would not have required a large population or a centralized authority. Its growth was more organic through ritual repetition without an apparent fixed ending point. The mound must have had ritual, social, and ontological functions. The rituals behind its construction were probably created and supported primarily by outlying support households but also by distant groups, as suggested by the variability of food and nonfood exotics at the site. Cosmological and ontological associations of construction materials, such as the types of materials (such as yellow sediment and sea urchins) or the environments (for example, littoral and wetlands) they represent, also are expected. In this regard the mound probably was an embodiment of ideas embedded in local group-oriented ritual processes rather than a demonstration of individual elite-based power (see chapter 2).

By ~7500–7200 cal BP the basic elongated, oval layout of Huaca Prieta was in place. During Phases II–III, no logic for cardinal orientation is apparent. During Phases IV–V, the access ramp (and perhaps the aperture in the sunken circular plaza?) orients the mound to the east. (Prior research on late Preceramic coastal sites demonstrates that cardinal orientation was a fundamental concept in the later Andean world [Moore 1996; Williams 1985].) Before the ramp and sunken plaza appeared, people at Huaca Prieta must have had other ontological concepts related to space and architecture to which they added the later one.

Radiometric assays from cultural deposits beneath Paredones indicate that mound building commenced no later than ~6500 cal BP. Discrete mound episodes at this site are identifiable by the existence of multiple floors, use surfaces, and fills. Each of the twenty-eight building stages or floor/fill sequences represents successive ritual and food preparation activities, as evidenced by the absence of domestic features such as postholes, hearths, and burials. The premound levels at this site indicate occupational debris, as do those at Huaca Prieta. Paredones also has a long chronology of ~3000 years of use, and apparently none of its stages are associated with burials, which differs from Huaca Prieta. But, much as at Huaca Prieta, a deliberate decision was made to build the mound vertically, when the use of this space could have been continuously extended horizontally. As was the case with domestic units around Huaca Prieta (for example, Units 13, 16, and 26 and several test pits), off-mound areas around Paredones (such as Units 20 and 30 and Test Pits 28–29) also indicated domestic activity in the form of hearths, postholes, a wide variety of tools, and thick trash debris.

The smaller incremental events at both mounds cannot be subdivided by radiocarbon dating. The precise template by which the mounds were built and used incrementally is unknown, because they were constructed to fit the space of the specific terrace area where they were erected. But there must have been some agreement and transgenerational knowledge over time among many different social groups in the area regarding the specific place of mound-use and building-design, the size and shape of new ritual, feasting, and mortuary levels, where their activities and burials could be placed, and how the mounds would be used and preserved. This knowledge probably resided with ritual specialists.

Despite differences in detail, both Huaca Prieta and Paredones are crucial for asking questions about and understanding the culture history, social organization, specialized economies, technology, and ontology of the larger Preceramic population of the lower valley during the Preceramic period. For example, does the stratigraphy of Huaca Prieta and Paredones and the presence of outlying domestic sites in the lower valley imply the existence of a society divided by economically specialized and demographically distinct social segments beginning sometime between ~7500–6500 cal BP? Does it also imply the existence of a differentiated or segmented social structure capable of organizing the labor for continuous long-term, high-frequency, but small-scale ritual and mortuary construction projects within the large-scale, long-term plan or design represented at these mounds? The first evidence for deliberate plastering to preserve the form and surface of Huaca Prieta was in Phase III, but the widest and thickest plaster application, covering almost the entire mound, was in late Phase IV. (The first plaster was not applied until the mound was ~12–14 m high, although support footings or berms of cobblestones at the base of the mound were placed earlier in late Phase II to begin the haystacking design for vertical accretion and preservation of the structure.) Although the mound was built of earth layers, no plaster was observed at Paredones, perhaps because it had not yet reached a height requiring its preservation (its maximum height in Phase V was 6 m) or simply because its long-term preservation was not a concern or it was not as sacred as Huaca Prieta. The domestic sites (Units 13 and 16, Test Pit 26, and the outlying household mounds) were not built up vertically but did spread horizontally. They also do not have the dark charcoal appearance found at Huaca Prieta and Paredones, suggesting different functions for them.

The specific relationship between Huaca Prieta and Paredones is not known. As discussed earlier, there are similarities between their earlier stratigraphy and material content. Does this similarity imply a laterally expanded building sequence of mounds? That is, when new ritual and mortuary functions developed at Huaca Prieta at the end of Phase II, were the preceding food preparation and ritual activities transferred to the newly constructed Paredones? Or was Paredones independently created to accommodate the socioeconomic and demographic changes associated with the rise of farming in the area? Or perhaps both or other possibilities are correct.

A LONG SUMMARY

First, stratigraphy from Huaca Prieta indicates that it was constructed as a series of smaller levels of sediment and debris, which were interconnected to form a single larger structure. The presence of berms, haystacking, a ramp and sunken plaza, and the single continuous mound form all indicate a planned transgenerational structure. Similar construction techniques have been noted in Paredones but not at the same degree and scale. This construction method does not imply a specialized class of mound engineers and rulers to build the mound. Nor does it imply that a relatively large corporate labor force was spread out over the entire mound at any one point in time. In this model, leaders would not need to have knowledge of how to place soils according to physical properties. Nor would sediment placement be a function of coordinating many relatively small work groups over time. Relative to engineering concerns, the only centralized or common knowledge among fisherfolk needed for sediment placement would come from knowing the required or agreed techniques and copying those observed by prior participation in rituals or perhaps maintenance projects. Analyses of sediments and plaster of the mound demonstrated that saltwater and heavy burning of plants and sea urchin spines and exoskeletons, primarily the toxic, nonedible black species (see chapter 9), were components of construction and maintenance (see appendix 8). These elements hardened and preserved layers.

Second, as described in chapter 7, specific sediments and plasters were utilized for their physical properties to construct shingled plaster retention or recapping surfaces in a deliberate attempt to keep the site from eroding. Large amounts of labor went into these surfaces, especially in the later periods. It is clear that the plaster was chosen and emplaced specifically for its ability to resist erosion. The yellowish sediment encountered between Phases III and IV is a good example of exotic sediment probably used to commission or decommission construction phases, if not simply to signal a new building and behavioral phase. The use of plaster to stabilize the middle and upper slopes is similar to the use of mortared cobblestones for berm footings and repairs as well as capping.

Third, mound-wide stratigraphy at Huaca Prieta shows a minimal presence of slumps, erosion, and faulting (see chapter 7). The timing of mound repair was a continual process or something that occurred in a series of relatively high-frequency events. This may imply that both construction and maintenance were likely aspects of ritual events. Slope erosion was a minor process, with each individual deposition being the result of a specific set of circumstances. Although each depositional episode was individual, thick plaster was laid most regularly in areas where differing sediments and a high angle were juxtaposed. Slope failures seem to have most frequently occurred at the boundaries between coarse and fine sediments and architecture, such as along the slope identified in the east wall where several chamber tombs are located (for example, Unit 10). At least in some cases, slope angle appears to be a function of the method used for construction, because optimal sediment types (such as clays) were not chosen or soils with differing resistance to wind and water (such as sand and silt) were deposited near one another. Plaster was a structural element designed to hold sediments in place until subsequent layers were deposited. (The point here is that caution should be used when evaluating unexpected features within the mounds, as the construction process did not only involve the repetitive act of building floors and piling layers and fills.)

Although the excavations indicate a slow but continuous construction sequence, mound building took a long time. Some slope wash and erosion were seen in the stratigraphy (see chapter 7 and appendix 1). These deposits suggest that some degree of weathering took place, but this is expected, because the scale indicates that the construction extended over thousands of years. In short, any model of Huaca Prieta needs to consider a reasonable construction time, likely punctuated by short hiatuses due to demographic, social, environmental, and/or economic changes.

Fourth, the available information suggests a different function for the mounds at Huaca Prieta and Paredones. There is no secure analogy to other Preceramic or later mound constructions across the Central Andes. Even though it is not possible to say that the elevated sunken plaza and access ramp in Phases IV and V were elements required for participation within a wider circuit of coastal exchange and ritual movements taking place during the late Preceramic period, they nonetheless do not represent traditional stepped, stone platforms typical of the monumental sites of the late Preceramic period on the Peruvian coast.

Fifth, these data lend support to the model that the mound was not built by design as a definite project with a beginning and an end but was planned in a different way. The project was somewhat discontinuously undertaken. Labor, probably at the extended family level, must have required constant reinforcement and encouragement through frequent small-scale rituals. Building Huaca Prieta was a conscious, extended diachronic process. The data support a model of labor organization that was not centralized but was a continuous, high-frequency series of small work and/ or kin groups, each pursuing mound construction and private ritual use for a limited time.

AN EARLY SETTLEMENT HISTORY OF THE LOWER CHICAMA VALLEY

The lower Chicama Valley is a special place. In addition to the obvious scale of pre-Hispanic activities over the past 14,500 years and the central place that it held for local societies, archaeologists have produced a varied amount of data that allow for much finer-scale interpretation than is possible in many other archaeological areas. Even understanding the construction chronology of Huaca Prieta and Paredones requires the use of perspectives from numerous projects in the area, including Bird's prior work and the recent research at the later El Brujo archaeological complex on the north end of the Sangamon terrace (see fig. 1.2b). Although relying primarily on stratigraphic and radiometric data, we combined as many sources of data as possible to understand the temporal, cultural, social, and geological circumstance of the sites under study here. Even though the data are far from complete, they provide a clearer picture of Huaca Prieta than was previously provided and a new view of Paredones and other sites in the lower valley.

The project data also present a different per-spective on Preceramic domestic sites than past work had proposed. Concurrent with the non-linear nucleation of littoral settlements were cultural and social changes whereby growing Preceramic populations created new ways of living. We see a growing population as a necessary condition contemporary with monumental construction at Huaca Prieta. In this view, building Huaca Prieta and Paredones partially integrated the local population dispersed along littoral and wetland areas in the lower valley and perhaps outlying ones as well. Ritual, social, and other relationships created during this fusion process must have formed the basis for a new ontological understanding of the growing society and its relationship to the wider coastal environment. At the same time, the local population would have needed to incorporate any preexisting social harmony and economic specialization, in effect creating a complex yet noncentralized political and economic organization.

Making a single model of the settlement pattern requires an understanding of how the built landscape developed through time as a consequence of a chain of causes and effects. Accordingly, we use different large-scale categories: the spatial scale is restricted to the Sangamon terrace and littoral and wetland sites to the north and south: extending on the east approximately 2 km from Huaca Prieta just beyond the terrace, on the west to the limits of the ocean, north to include the Malabrigo and Pulpar wetland areas, and south to the northern extent of Cerro Campana (see chapter 13).

Because this framework is based solely on this data set, it may be the most appropriate for a site-specific discussion. This is not to say that the Chicama sites developed in the absence of regional transformations. On the contrary, Huaca Prieta and especially Paredones probably developed because of interregional developments, as suggested by the numerous exotic cultigens and other items imported to these sites. Understanding how the history of the lower Chicama Valley fits into the history of the region and beyond first requires an understanding of the history of the lower valley area as well. We specifically want to highlight the uniqueness of the area and of the Sangamon terrace as a place and a cultural phenomenon, given that the entire known history of the region and Central Andes from ~14,500 BP to the present day is represented there.

If uninterrupted periods of use of Huaca Prieta spanned more than fourteen thousand years, then we might expect similar circumstances at sites such as Bandurria, Aspero, Caral, and a few other Norte Chico sites on the coast (see chapter 2), with multiple, stacked occupations represented by superpositioning of use surfaces. While later use of these sites is certainly present after about ~5000–4000 cal BP, earlier superpositioning is presently lacking, especially when compared to Huaca Prieta. Because of the apparent lesser degree of superpositioning at other places, a similar or even shorter-term pattern is expected. Although other portions of the lower Chicama Valley appear to have been occupied from at least the seventh millennium (Malabrigo 1, Salamanca Norte; see chapters 6 and 13), thus establishing a historical continuity, it is likely that not all of them were occupied during this long period. This suggests a discontinuous geographic distribution across the terrace and beyond, perhaps explained by social or other factors.

Using data from Huaca Prieta and Paredones as a model, several long-standing traits linked to social and economic organization make an initial appearance. First, a general pattern of settlements with low household mounds comes into being along the littoral zone by at least 7000 to 6500 years ago (as it also does on the central coast; see Engel 1966a, 1966b; Lavallée 2000). (Prior to this period sites seem to have been smaller, scattered, and not characterized by house mounds.) Related to the settlement layout, a communal or community-based pattern often is found at the small deltas and inland shorelines of the east-to-west trending wetlands that drain to the ocean (see fig. 13.1).

Second, social differentiation and leadership are not archaeologically evident. At Huaca Prieta there is differentiation in tomb chamber size (especially during Phases III and IV), but many of these tombs are unoccupied, though almost all were sealed and contain *Semele corrugata* shells and occasionally a lithic or fragmented textile offering. Most were never used. If these structures represent tombs and designated ritual areas, then they may have been the burial places of missing bodies or may have marked other social phenomena (see chapter 15).

Third, although there is a clear community and settlement pattern, the outlying household sites were probably sedentary (meaning year-round) but perhaps not excessively long-lived (meaning many years in sequence) in any one particular configuration or location. This is because settlement plan configurations likely changed, temporally and geographically, through a fission/fusion process or movement in response to the shifting of wetlands through time. Furthermore, the stratigraphy in *huaquero* (looter) holes in these household mounds indicates periods of occupation and occasional abandonment along the coastline for reasons that are presently not fully understood.

Toward the end of Phase III and the beginning of Phase IV domestic sites seem to have expanded and people began to build the upper mound, the elevated sunken plaza, the retention wall, and the ramp at Huaca Prieta. At the end of Phase III people began modifying the landscape in substantial ways, including the first appearance of raised agricultural fields east of Paredones and building the mounded architecture at Huaca Prieta with more chamber tombs. Occupation appears to expand into littoral and inland wetlands both north to Malabrigo and south to Cerro Campana from places like the Sangamon terrace and Huaca Prieta. At this time, little in the way of overt social differentiation between littoral communities seems to have existed. Despite some variation in the size of the outlying house mounds (some locations were probably more important than others, based on the estimated size and density of household mounds: see chapter 13) at each individual community, and therefore perhaps differentiation within each community, little variation is discernible between communities near the terrace.

Research into the relationship between the mounds and domestic sites suggests that the logic of locating Huaca Prieta and Paredones is probably based on the location of access nodes to primary economic production zones, with Huaca Prieta close to the sea and Paredones overlooking the farmed wetlands. Rather than being occupied after Phase II, the mounds appear bordered by off-mound residential spaces of the terrace (such as Units 16 and 30 and Test Pits 28 and 29; see fig. 3.3). The outlying domestic sites were along the littoral and into the finger-like extensions of the coastal wetlands running from east to west. By

7000–6500 cal BP these sites probably became outlying support populations for ritual and other activities at Huaca Prieta.

THE SCALE AND SCHEDULING OF FOOD PRODUCTION

An important aspect of late Preceramic food procurement systems throughout the central Pacific coast is that the scale of production must have varied considerably in different social and environmental contexts. Simply put, food procurement was not entirely about small household units subsisting and moving about the landscape in a foraging fashion without recourse to anything but requirements for food and water. It also was about foods for public or private large-scale and small-scale ritual purposes and probably about preparing salt and salted fish and seafood for local consumption and for exchange.

The basic economic unit in the study area consisted of small groups of people at outlying household mounds, probably immediate or nuclear family groups with varying numbers of other kin and others often attached. This represents the smallest economic unit (apart from an individual) involved in resource production activities. These units probably acted less commonly as isolated residential groups and in most cases resided in multihousehold site areas on the terrace and along the coastline with a number of other similar family units (see chapter 13). Although systems of interior and littoral food redistribution probably were in operation within such residential arrangements, production in these cases was principally focused upon providing for the needs of that particular social unit. That is, production activities were scaled in relation to the economic units of small groups of closely related people operating as household units. This is suggested by the absence of storage units in the archaeological record of all sites in the study area.

Although rituals and other activities at Huaca Prieta and Paredones depended on a wide variety of marine and terrestrial food resources, including different cultigens (see chapters 9 and 10), they clearly did not rely upon a single abundant resource, a single resource habitat, or a single food category. If some activities were seasonal, they appear no different in this respect. If any season or perhaps activity (such as burials) was slightly different, it may have been the winter, as suggested by the *Semele corrugata* shells in some tombs, which seem to have been collected during the winter months. This is the period when marine foods are less abundant, so exploitation by small economic units (perhaps no more than a single or extended family) may have been the norm.

As noted above, no evidence indicates that resources were controlled by specific groups, although there was economic specialization focused on maritime fishing and gathering, farming, and initially wetland foraging. Yet even when specialization occurred (as in the case of Paredones, focused on crop production), marine foods were also available, although not yet the full complement or abundance documented at Huaca Prieta. As a result certain individuals, households, or household groups might have had some control or management over specific sites and resource zones. No evidence suggests that the prestige of a group or individuals was enhanced through hosting ritual or other events. Food production seems to have occurred at several scales and often included cooperative events that involved small groups perhaps from different areas attending particular sites. These events probably had a ritual or perhaps a commensal feasting component to them.

FROM A TRIPARTITE TO A DUAL COASTAL ECONOMY

The economy of the Huaca Prieta site previously had not been quantified through time and space to determine the degree to which the site's users relied on marine and terrestrial resources, including cultigens. Based on floral and faunal studies, stable isotope analyses of human skeletal remains, and the nature of off-mound occupation zones, we can now determine the more precise contribution of foraging and farming to the site economy and what this implies with respect to emerging social complexity (see chapters 9 and 10).

During early Phase I at Huaca Prieta, the economy was based on foraging in both maritime and terrestrial environments. During late Phase I and Phase II, the economy was unevenly focused on three resources: primarily on maritime and secondarily on cultigens and wetland flora and fauna. By Phase III the economy was becoming a dual one centered on marine and agricultural foods, although wild plant foods (edible canes and reeds) continued to contribute to the diet at all sites. By Phases IV–V more food crops had been added and a mixed dual economy was well established. The discovery of food crops at Huaca Prieta and especially Paredones indicates that the early upland cultivation of cultigens in the Nanchoc Valley (Dillehay 2011a) to the north is indicative of variable early food production systems in this part of the Andes during the early and middle Holocene. As supported by various AMS dates on squash, corn, cotton, and chile peppers at Paredones and at the Nanchoc sites, the use of cultigens in northern Peru between 10,000 and 7000 cal BP is clear, regardless of their domestication status. They were managed anthropogenic plants, and the domestication process of some crops was certainly underway somewhere in distant areas even if they were not fully domesticated.

The transition between late Pleistocene maritime/terrestrial foraging and middle Holocene agricultural systems in the Huaca Prieta/Paredones area appears not to have been rapid. Nor was there a shift from a primary maritime economy to a primary agricultural economy. By late Phase II both economies were viable and evidently practiced by at least two different (if not more) local populations. Nor was the maritime economy ever abandoned. Littoral foragers as well as farmers in the study area must have gradually adjusted to new sets of incoming cultigens that required new cultivation techniques and affected scheduling rhythms, as suggested by the introduction of different crops over several millennia. Regardless of the frequency and dependency of the changing economy, littoral gardening was a well-adapted sustainable strategy for a prolonged time, beginning by 10,000 cal BP, as evidenced by the presence of squash and chile peppers near this date. Much later, in the wetlands east of Paredones, the buried agricultural fields date to around 5200 cal BP. These reveal an actively engineered terrestrial niche for food and other resources (such as beans, cotton, and gourds). Although food crops were introduced early into the study area, wild plants were consumed during all phases, especially

Typha, *Scirpus*, algarrobo, fruits, and a few other species common in wetlands as well as seaweeds from the shoreline (see chapter 10).

Beyond the study area, Moseley (1975, 1992) once used the large number of fish bone and shellfish remains at other coastal sites of the late Preceramic period as evidence of a specialized economy focused on marine resources. A number of late Preceramic sites, however, reveal the consumption of both marine and terrestrial fauna as well as wild and cultivated plants (Bonavia 1982; Chu Barrera 2011; Quilter et al. 1991; Wendt 1964). More sites in inland coastal settings (such as floodplains and hillslopes) have also been found throughout Peru where diverse marine and particularly terrestrial resources were exploited in the late Preceramic period (Dillehay 2004; Lavallée 2000; Lavallée et al. 1999; Quilter 1989). The evidence presented by our project indicates that a marine diet was important through all periods and was an early economic specialization by certain littoral if not some inland coastal groups (for example, La Paloma), which was complemented by plant foods most likely produced by other littoral groups specializing in farming or other sections (such as lineages) in the same group.

We do not know whether the dual economic specialization and the ecological diversification that it implies led to increased social differentiation. As noted earlier, no skeletal, weapon, or other data suggest conflict between social groups, although there may have been some intergroup competition. Specialization also may have been related not only to marine and terrestrial practices but also to task or occupational specialization, with some groups or individuals focused on specific resources (such as salt production or fish as opposed to shellfish) or resource zones, and to resource exchanges among ecologically and economically intermixed groups. This may be suggested by the opposing and complementary presence of the repetitive coexistence of the shells of gastropods and clams at Huaca Prieta (see chapter 9). (Chu Barrera [2011] discovered a dual economy within the late Preceramic site of Bandurria, whereby one group exploited the sandy littoral and another the rocky littoral.) It also is likely that larger, more densely connected and specialized populations along the littoral led to more technological change and diversity.

If this was the case, it would explain the high degree of technological diversity evidenced in the basketry and textile technologies, which reveal different techniques (looping and weft twining), and the two different decorative styles seen in gourds at Huaca Prieta and Paredones. These different technologies suggest different groups coexisting in the study area, perhaps each with its own technological knowledge that was also used as an identity marker (see chapter 12). It also seems that the decorated textiles, baskets, and gourds were invested with multiple layers of local meanings, kinship relations, and narratives of small or private group quests that formed the fabric of socialization rituals (see chapter 12), cosmologies, and mythologies of origins embraced by each community, which could have been shared, to varying degrees, within and between different sites (see chapter 15).

In summary, confining the economy to a narrowly defined concept of either specialized maritime foraging or broad-spectrum subsistence, which was standard in more recent Andean archaeology, is not supported. Recent increases in archaeobotanical studies illustrate that the Preceramic period of the littoral was a complex economy beyond a single specialized subsistence based on maritime resources. Overall, early to middle Preceramic people seem to have ecologically diversified subsistence strategies into procuring available niche-specific marine and terrestrial resources (see chapter 9), possibly managing some wild plants, and tending cultigens, from at least 10,000 cal BP at Huaca Prieta and Paredones.

Finally, it is important to comment on two issues in Andean studies: the role of maize in the late Preceramic economy and the significance of a maritime economy in the development of early social complexity. An overly simplified focus on maize farming in the Andes may have blurred the real complexity of early agriculture, which means not just maize production but multiple crop production, often accompanied by herding or fishing and marine foraging. Maize farming has generally been viewed as a cure-all remedy that solved all economic problems. Maize farmers seem to be portrayed as a highly productive group that would have replaced foragers and led to a more complex society. According to the available archaeobotanical evidence, a heavy reliance on maize

probably occurred much later than the middle Holocene in the Central Andes, although maize (possibly popcorn) is present in very small quantities by 6500–6000 cal BP at Paredones and Huaca Prieta (Grobman et al. 2012; see appendix 5). Yet this early maize is popcorn, which could not produce substantial meals for a growing population (Grobman et al. 2012). Nonetheless, some studies (Haas et al. 2013) use microevidence to show the widespread production of maize by ~4500 cal BP in the Norte Chico area. Although the microevidence does not distinguish between popcorn, meal corn, and *chicha* (beer) corn, it is likely that meal corn was not in substantial production until ~5000–4500 cal BP. Missing or unreported in these recent studies, however, is an expected appearance or increase in manos and grinding stones to produce corn meal, which would indeed indicate a dietary heavy reliance on maize during the late Preceramic period.

Michael Moseley (1975) argued that the rich maritime resources of the Pacific littoral offered enough food diversity and bulk to support clusters of large sedentary communities and allow leaders to organize labor groups to construct large public monuments. This argument was later modified to include plant foods, especially maize, squash, chile peppers, beans, and fruits, as an equally important part of the early coastal economy. The floral and faunal data recovered by our project do not require a complete rethinking of the maritime foundation hypothesis, although we have shown here that the dependence on a food crop economy was much earlier and more extensive than previously believed. It also should be noted that a segment of the local littoral (if not the lower coastal valley in general) population specialized in fishing and in gathering marine resources. This suggests that focused maritime activities along with marine-related decorative motifs on textiles and gourds (crabs, fish, birds) represent an important and separate element of the local ontology and lifestyle.

INTRODUCING PLANTS TO THE LITTORAL: WHY AND HOW?

Peruvian archaeology has not yet fully examined conceptually how and why cultigens were introduced into the littoral environments during the Preceramic period. Briefly considered below are several scenarios that provide hypothetical thoughts about the possible conditions and mechanisms accounting for early crop adoption and intensification in the study area.

ADOPTION AND INTENSIFICATION

What most archaeological studies in the Andes overlook is the distinction between the first adoption of crops and the later establishment of intensive agriculture. We should consider these as two separate contexts of crop use during the Preceramic period. The late Pleistocene and early Holocene people at Huaca Prieta and Paredones had already begun to manage useful wild plants and probably three cultigens (squash, avocado, and chile peppers) by 10,000–9000 cal BP. Between 9000 and 6500 cal BP, several other cultigens were introduced (see chapter 10). From at least 6500 BP the Paredones site developed specific subsistence solutions to the narrow littoral and wetlands that involved distinctive combinations of wild, possibly managed, and domesticated species. Changes in plant use seem to have gone through similar phases in the middle to late Preceramic period (~6500–4000 BP).

Most of all, in the study area and in the Nanchoc Valley (Dillehay 2011a), the adoption of several semidomesticated or domesticated plants did not occur all together. Squash, beans, avocados, and chile peppers clearly were available as early as ~10,000–7500 cal BP, while peanuts, coca, quinoa, maize (at Paredones but not Nanchoc), and cotton arrived later, generally after 7000 cal BP. However, the dates for the initial adoption of all of these and other plants are not clear. Were they incorporated into early squash gardening individually over a number of generations during a long transitional period? Or were two to three of these crops (for example, beans and chile peppers, as suggested by their combined presence in several gourd bowls at Huaca Prieta and Paredones; see chapter 7 and appendix 4) incorporated as a package at once? Unfortunately, systematic archaeobotanical data are lacking for the critical transitional periods between the adoption of several species. Because of a lack of data from several hundred years during the transition, the question of the rate of changes

to intensive agriculture cannot be resolved. (The only possible local cultigen would have been cotton, which is native to the arid north coast.) We also must review carefully how local cultural developments and external influences and long-distance exchange were integrated into the transition rather than simplify the transition as a gradual appearance of the food production and the gradual replacement of a foraging lifeway.

CROPS AS A STRESS RESPONSE

During the early to middle Holocene, could the use of crops have been a risk-reduction strategy against sea-level shifts on the coast and a population/maritime resource imbalance from ~6000 cal BP onward? The data indicate that cultivation of various crops was practiced long before the proposed period of sea-level decline and subsequent wetland resource reduction around 6000 cal BP (see chapter 5). It is not clear whether the appearance of crops was concurrent with climatic amelioration. Goodbred's study (see chapter 5) suggests that a warming episode between 6000 and 4500 cal BP may have caused a switch to slightly more arid conditions, but this should not have had major impact on crop production. Deprivation of resources because of this condition is not evident in the archaeological record of the study area. Nor is there evidence of habitational hiatuses at any sites during periods of El Niños or other major physical events. Faunal and plant data from both our study area and the Nanchoc Valley indicate that people managed complicated scheduling of diverse marine and terrestrial resources during all periods of climatic change.

In turning to other possible environmental events, based on otolith data, appendix 13 reports slightly cooler climatic conditions and more upwelling during the early to middle Holocene period than today. (Other paleoenvironmental reports address the intermittent impacts of El Niño events and later tsunamis: see chapters 4 and 5 and appendices 13 and 14.) But these events represent very short time periods of impact, most of which seem to be minor, perhaps of one to two years in duration. The temporal resolution is so fine for these episodic events that we cannot fully detect or measure their potential impact on the human society during the long 14,000-year span under study here. It is granted that these and other major events probably stressed the local environment for a short time, perhaps killing off or reducing the number of some marine species (sea snails and mollusks) and littoral species (birds) but having little influence on the long-term survivability and sustainability of the human population. Because tsunamis, earthquakes, and El Niño events leave behind such strong and lasting physical signatures (such as sediment wasting and washout debris), archaeologists often overstate their significance for past societies. Furthermore, as Pino points out in appendix 1, the impact of a recent major tsunami on the south coast of Chile was very uneven and not as extensively damaging as we might have expected.

RESOURCE PRODUCTION DUE TO CHANGING SEA LEVELS AND POPULATION IMBALANCE

Hypothetically, a decline in marine resources due to fluctuating sea levels can be considered devastating to subsistence, which might have led to the adoption of new subsistence strategies such as farming. A growing population along the littoral, especially in times of fluctuating sea levels, also may have stimulated the adoption of more crops to increase food production. A population/resource-imbalance model depends on the assumption of an abrupt sea level decrease at the transitional period between 7000 and 4000 cal BP (see chapter 5), the period when the majority of the crop species were adopted. In the study area sea level rose almost to the present level around 6000 cal BP, decreased slightly around 4000 cal BP, increased to a maximum at 3200 cal BP, and decreased again between 3000 and 2300 cal BP, with a fluctuating height of only 1 m and a linear shift of only 150 m, which had little, if any, significant impact on the littoral population at and around Huaca Prieta. By ~3700 cal BP, however, the sea was lapping against the western edge of the site.

Unlike a common assumption of the synchronicity between the maximum sea level and shoreline transgression, our data reveal that the highest sea level and the transgression were not concurrent. Diatom and marine clay deposition suggests that the transgression had already turned to a regression at ~7000 cal BP, at least 1000 years earlier than the maximum sea-level span. Thus shoreline retreats and marine-resource fluctuations may not have occurred concurrently with the sea-level decline. Direct triangulation of sea-level fall, shoreline regression, and marine-resource decrease as explanations for the onset of farming seems not to be the case in our study area. The idea that sea-level decline might have facilitated the emergence of agriculture between 7000 and 5000 cal BP is thus unsupported at this time. Furthermore, there is no evidence in the settlement pattern of the Chicama Valley of people having responded to changing sea levels, although archaeological data show minor shifts within sites as a result of changes in wetland distributions, which probably had little, if any, impact on the mixed economy of local people.

RESOURCE SCHEDULING AND LABOR CONFLICTS

Was there incompatibility between the scheduling strategies of agricultural and marine foraging in this littoral environment? Did coastal inhabitants maintain or specialize their maritime foraging economy because of conflicts in resource scheduling that farming might have brought? This would be the case if people were both fishing and farming, but this seems not to have occurred. Any scheduling problems, if they existed, would have been resolved by economic specialization, with each specialized group dealing with its own resource schedules.

Could the low-lying, salt-saturated sediments of the littoral support crops? (See figure 1.2 for successful crop production today along the littoral.) Seafood is available year round and usually in bulk and diverse quantities but is generally more plentiful during the spring and summer months. Crops on the littoral and inland coastal areas can grow year-round: in fact families living within 300 m of Huaca Prieta today double- or triple-crop in salt-saturated soils during the entire year. Several of these crops (for instance, gourds, cotton, chile peppers, squash, and beans) are low-maintenance, quick-growing, and drought-resistant and appear to be salt-resistant.

In short, it is unlikely that littoral inhabitants were prevented from cultivation because of scheduling conflicts or the unsuitable landscape along the littoral. Yet why did coastal foragers invest their efforts in cultivation when possibly no immediate external stress existed and when they lived in one of the richest marine environments in the world, supposedly during the time of a middle Holocene climatic optimum? One reason may be that the adoption of cultigens may have provided an opportunity to expand storable food and thus to increase stability in food supply. Alain Testart (1982: 535) suggests that once foragers are practicing intensive storage and living a sedentary life, they can adopt a new crop without any immediate major changes in their way of life. We would think, however, that this depends on the required level of investment in the crops adopted and what their labor and social impacts would have been. Inhabitants along the Peruvian littoral of the north coast, in the past and present, seemingly have managed a complex seasonal foraging schedule with moderate labor-intensive techniques but without a storage strategy in an affluent and rather predictable food environment. If a new resource was acquired with minimum expense of energy and time, that resource was probably highly desirable to local people.

The varied crops introduced to the study area are primarily exotics from many distant areas. These crops were likely obtained through long-distance exchange networks connected to established socioeconomic relations among many down-the-line communities stretched over the Andes and areas to the north in Ecuador. In addition to exotic food crops, the presence of other exotics such as *Spondylus* and scallop shells, malachite, and copper sulfate suggest exchange or, less likely, migration of distant groups in different directions. Sustaining these contacts probably was an important social incentive in addition to providing a steady supply of new foods.

MIGRATION OR LONG-DISTANCE EXCHANGE AS A FORCE FOR INTENSIVE AGRICULTURE

Like the stress and conflict models, social models often emphasize a single factor—migration—as a strong impulse for a shift to farming or its increased presence in local coastal diets. The data on the late Pleistocene peopling of the Central Andes suggest that people were already on the coast by at least 14,000 years ago. We have very little information to surmise the motive for plant adoption by littoral communities and whether migration, diffusion, long-distance exchange, or a combination of these and other factors might account for the abrupt or gradual incorporation of food crops and their later intensification. No data indicate an abrupt population increase or the migration of people into the Chicama area. Most crops were probably initially obtained via long-distance exchange, more than 50 to 100 km away. It also is likely that technological ideas about crop development and conservation were derived by diffusion and/or direct contact with different groups in distant areas.

To shed some light on these issues, some of the clearest archaeological evidence for diffusion, adoption, and subsequent intensive agriculture is found in the Nanchoc Valley of northern Peru by 10,000 to 7500 cal BP. Nanchoc people devoted multiple seasons, probably year-round, to tending various wild and domesticated plants, as evidenced by a series of new crops (for example, squash, peanuts, cotton, quinoa, beans, chile peppers, manioc, and yucca) that required labor-intensive care and eventually the construction of irrigation ditches and fields (Dillehay 2011a). Here, as opposed to the Chicama littoral, there may have been a greater incentive to adopt crops because the local environment, although more diversified than the littoral, was not as productive. The evidence from Nanchoc indicates that people also were operating within a wide exchange network whereby they accessed exotic crops and noneconomic "curiosities" such as colorful stones, stingray spines, fossils, and other items, possibly trading coca leaves and lime for them.

Yet the commitment to crop production in the Nanchoc case was not simply the transition to a more intensified sedentary life structured around the shift from gardening to agriculture and long-distance exchange of goods. It also was the product of a set of decisions and responses that resulted in fundamental organizational changes in society and shifts in social and ritual roles as a result of the dependence on new technologies. Besides the shift from household gardening to multihousehold irrigation agriculture, these developments are reflected in a change from circular to rectangular structures of domestic units and in the appearance of public gatherings at small public mounds specialized in the production of lime for use with coca leaves.

SOCIAL NETWORKS AND CULTIGEN DISTRIBUTION

In the case of Huaca Prieta and especially Paredones, the introduction of non-native plants into the littoral environment suggests that the maintenance of widespread interregional communication channels probably fulfilled the important adaptive and economic task of keeping up reliable networks of raw materials, including food crops and other exotics. Furthermore, the configuration of coastal and highland routes of communication and exchange, for instance, would have the maintenance of contact points and interaction spheres on either side of the Andes and up and down the Pacific coast. The presence of a few exotic stones and the crops from distant areas certainly suggests contact with distant populations. It is not known whether this contact was direct by long-distance exchange or indirect by down-the-line exchange.

In many cases of primary origins around the world, farming seems to have appeared in complex foraging economies in affluent environments where risk was affordable (see Barker and Goucher 2015). Our study area does not seem to be an exception. Resource stress due to environmental degradation appears not to be a direct cause of the appearance of cultigens. Evidence of resource stress due to higher population density also is lacking. That is, the Paredones and Huaca Prieta data currently do not provide support for general models that incorporate environmental downturn, external environmental stress, population growth, landscape packing, constricted resource zones, and carrying-capacity imbalance in explaining the initial domestication (or adoption) process.

As an alternative explanation, could increased rituals and other activities at Huaca Prieta have spurred the adoption of more crops for increased food production to support these activities? Brian Hayden (1992) has proposed a social model for the origins of food production, which is based on competitive feasting. He notes that some hunters and gatherers occupying fluctuating environments share food, so that they have less incentive to invest time and effort in producing extra from which only others will benefit. In resource-rich areas with stable environments with adequate food to reduce such collective sharing, competition between ambitious individuals may have led to competitive feasts to gain control over labor and loyalty. The need to generate such large amounts of food in order to stage such feasts stimulated cultivation. Social models such as these, however, do not work for Huaca Prieta and Paredones for two reasons. There is no evidence of large- or small-scale public feasting, of large public spaces, or of the accumulation or display of status and wealth by ambitious individuals in and around the study area (see chapter 15). Thus social explanations must lie in the realm of kinship structure and maintaining mosaics of social networks.

The introduction of non-native plants into an insular littoral environment at Huaca Prieta and Paredones suggests that the maintenance of communication channels probably fulfilled the important adaptive and economic task of keeping up reliable supplies of exotic materials. (This implies that many more early to middle Preceramic sites on the coast and in the highlands must have had a variety of early cultigens.) As noted above, these channels would have needed exchange relations on both sides of the Andes and along the ocean corridor. These early phases of intensive interactions must have been followed by long periods of consolidation matched by low exchange volumes (or exotic food offerings made by visitors to Huaca Prieta), eventually leading to the establishment of distinct sociocultural identities, if not households or household groupings, along the littoral, on the coastal plain, and in the interior coastal valleys and perhaps of distinct technologies such as textile and basketry techniques and linguistic dialects, if not languages. These identities probably acquired their particularity from being positioned within specific socioeconomic contexts that required the investment involved in sustaining social and economic contact networks at both short and long distances. Prior terminal Pleistocene and early Holocene colonization by and contacts with outsiders might suggest such contexts, which would have been contingent upon region-specific sociocultural histories and geographical realities. The exotics at Huaca Prieta point to both the highlands to the east and the coastal areas of south Ecuador and north Peru.

However, I do not see these identities as quasi-static macroentities or markers of cultural or ethnic affiliation. They should rather be described as local-specific changeable and complex exchange networks between local kin/household groups and distant exchange partners, factions, or lineages spread among adjacent areas and communities. In turn, the objects of such exchanges cannot be interpreted primarily only as desirable food "commodities" circulating within opportunistic contact networks. Instead they probably formed active and meaningful ingredients in a broad spectrum of social relationships that occurred between and within different groups and communities, including distant highland and coastal groups. At the same time, participation in such regionally and temporally contingent networks probably did not mean that communities neglected their collective interests (ensuring their biological, sociocultural, and political reproduction). Both the maintenance of stable interregional contacts and the long-term intensive participation in extensive networks of exchange would per se have required a level of involvement and investment probably far exceeding the political outreach, intersocietal balances, and socioeconomic organization of littoral communities of the Huaca Prieta area. Conversely, the maintenance of similar contact networks could have been temporarily justified (probably in the form of reciprocal cooperation between groups inhabiting different environments), especially in the face of novel and challenging situations, such as the increased transference of cultivars to the coast. In short, the Preceramic world of the Chicama littoral constituted a very fluid universe: in the absence of a higher order unifying political framework, such networks could have emerged, peaked, and waned in the space of a few generations. Within this fluid and diverse universe, there was a single point of reference with which the inhabitants of the study area would have identified: their own household and community of households (which were themselves an agglomeration of factions, kin, and household communities), whose interests, survival, and reproduction framed the worldviews of their members, repetitively ritualized in the context of Huaca Prieta.

HUACA PRIETA: AN EARLY PILGRIMAGE SITE?

The exotic cultigens and nonfood curiosities recovered at Huaca Prieta, beginning especially in late Phase II, present several interpretative possibilities. First, no nonfood exotics were recovered from domestic units or Paredones, which contained the greatest abundance of plant foods. Second, Phases II–V reveal that Huaca Prieta contained a greater variety of cultigens than the domestic units and Paredones. Third, the human isotope studies indicate that people buried at both Huaca Prieta and Unit 16 were consumers of almost exclusively marine foods, while the few teeth from Paredones reveal plant food consumption. If this is the case, then why were there more varieties of cultigens at Huaca Prieta? Fourth, most plant foods at Huaca Prieta were offerings in small piles or folded into the pleats of textiles and placed in gourd containers or other features. Does this imply that the adoption of some or many cultigens primarily came by way of offerings by pilgrims traveling from distant lands? Did some of these individuals have special burial privileges there and, if so, for what reasons? Was Paredones part of a pilgrimage place or wider event, given its stratigraphy and mound architecture and its association with food production rather than marine food procurement? If this is the case and cultigens were introduced primarily through ritual offerings at Huaca Prieta, this is very different from the adoption of cultigens in the Nanchoc Valley. At Nanchoc independent household communities seem to have had their own exchange networks, probably exchanging coca leaves and lime for exotic food plants and other items. Nanchoc had no affiliated ritual and mortuary center like Huaca Prieta.

I suspect that many of the cultigens at Paredones and Huaca Prieta were special or magical foods that arrived by way of down-the-line exchange and that some came by way of ritual and perhaps pilgrimage-like journeys of people from distant areas. Special or mysterious foods are important in rituals, serving as exotic gifts equal to the malachite, copper sulfate, and other nonfood offerings found at Huaca Prieta. In the case of ritual processions among the Mapuche of south-central Chile, we know that special foods (such as seaweeds, piñon nuts, and dried fish) from their homeland are brought by nonlocal guests to rituals. Sometimes special dishes are made by local hosts, which do not always include the same food consumed in the household. These points are relevant not only to consider the presence of exotic foods at ritual sites like Huaca Prieta but also to suggest that we archaeologists cannot always presume that the foods consumed in ritual contexts are the same as those eaten in the households of local families who live nearby and support community-level rituals.

As table 10.1 and figure 10.1 show, the greatest variety and largest amount of comestible, industrial, and wild plant species are present at Huaca Prieta, not Paredones and the domestic sites (the industrial items are primarily reed mats placed on ritual floors). We would have expected them to be most diverse and prevalent at Paredones, where the majority of the grinding stones and manos, lithic blades for slicing, and more discarded bulk plant debris (fragmented and unidentifiable) are present (see chapter 10). Part of this discrepancy could result from sampling bias, given that approximately twenty times more cubic meters were excavated at Huaca Prieta, but it also could imply that people from distant areas were bringing exotic foods to Huaca Prieta as consumptive offerings during rituals. The majority of the nonconsumed plants on floors and use surfaces at Huaca Prieta were present in small piles, in gourd containers, and in textile bundles. Does this imply a symbolic representation involving death, burial, and the regeneration of life, the unborn, and the life cycles of food crops? Marine resources also were used as offerings, but they were not as discretely piled and spatially segmented as the way plants were. Could this mean that humans could directly partake in the life cycle and production of terrestrial food crops by managing them in fields, which they could not do with marine foods? Changes resulting from human and plant relationships and the new sociotechnological lifeway they brought were no doubt immense. Those changes must have led to wider social and economic networks, which were to become increasingly visible in Phases IV and V.

The entry of exotic foods and other items peaked during Phase IV. In Phase V long-distance exchange appears to have diminished and fewer exotic items appear in the archaeological record. This was when Huaca Prieta more strongly joined other coastal traditions, as suggested by the presence of the entry ramp and sunken plaza at the site. It also was the time when the decorative motifs on textiles, baskets, and gourds diminished in quality and variety and when the painted stones no longer appeared (see chapters 11 and 12). In other words, there seems to be less concern with symbolic social currency and iconographic identity markers in the later phases. What does this imply? Is it the appearance of individual elites or elite groups beginning to take over the economy and the long-distance exchange of exotics? Did the appearance of new groups in the area, whether they be terminal Preceramic or early Guañape-related peoples, introduce new lifestyles and ontologies?

Whatever the situation was, it is probable that social and exchange networks involved small groups of people who came on private pilgrimages or ritual processions to Huaca Prieta, perhaps a prototype of a Pachacamac-like pilgrimage node (for example, Rostworowski 2004) whereby special groups came to bury their dead, worship, and make exotic offerings from their homeland. This would explain the great diversity of cultigens (and perhaps other exotics) at Huaca Prieta over time and the absence of a political or religious authority overseeing the site.

As a final note here, in recent years I have become very dubious of so many archaeologists not just in the Andes but in many other places as well assigning ritual and ceremonial activities to so many archaeological contexts, especially those contexts that are not clearly domestic in nature.

At least for sites like Huaca Prieta, however, my colleagues and I have become convinced that at certain times and in certain places localities like Huaca Prieta were indeed primarily associated with ritual. In short, the majority of the archaeological record of this mound and perhaps Paredones as well, when compared to the domestic and other sites, is undoubtedly associated with ritual practices. But I am not willing to refer to Huaca Prieta, Paredones, and other sites that we have studied as ceremonial centers or even places where large- to small-scale public ceremonies were taking place. I perceive public ceremony as a more formal, larger-scale, and prolonged activity that is demonstrated by a different type of archaeological record, which is not evidenced here and would require much more space to discuss than is available.

SUMMARY

Most of the exotic species present at Paredones and Huaca Prieta are probably originally from the tropical environments of northwestern South America (Colombia and Ecuador) and the eastern Andean valleys or western Amazon Basin. In the case of Nanchoc, Huaca Prieta, and especially Paredones, the introduction of non-native plants into the western tropical slopes and the littoral desert environment suggests that the maintenance of widespread interregional communication channels probably fulfilled the important adaptive and economic task of keeping up reliable networks of accessing exotic food crops and other materials (such as copper sulfate, malachite, and *Spondylus*) within a large geographic network of interaction spheres. It is not known whether this contact was by direct long-distance exchange or pilgrimages or by indirect down-the-line exchange.

Curiously, it seems that we often forget the long-term persistence of widely ranging foragers from late Pleistocene and to early Holocene times; their continued presence alongside and beyond areas later inhabited by farmers, fishers, and pastoralists; and the role that they played in dispersing economic plants. As part of this persistence, the unevenness with which the initial adoption of cultigens spread throughout the continent (and more specifically the Andes) provided opportunities for foragers and nonforagers to continue a variety of exchange-based connections with each other across multiple ecological zones, connections that must have had their origin in late Pleistocene to early Holocene times.

SOCIAL HISTORY

To some archaeologists, the data from the lower Chicama area perhaps suggest the development of an increasingly differentiated society coming out of relatively simple predecessors. These views derive in part from the standard historical models giving temporal primacy to "monumentality" at Huaca Prieta and other late Preceramic mound sites along the coast of Peru, where the construction presumably served to anchor subsequent social and demographic developments. But the settlement and subsistence models to explain the emergence of social complexity, which traditionally relate to inequality, individual wealth and status, and so forth (see chapter 2), do not support the standard evolutionary view of sites like Huaca Prieta and Paredones. The Preceramic population of the Sangamon terrace and littoral certainly grew—and consequently the population became more complex—but increasing social differentiation in the form of institutionalized social inequality is not a necessary conclusion. A model for the historical development of the site that considers how and when Huaca Prieta and Paredones were constructed as vehicles for understanding the organizational changes in the Preceramic society through social processes is presented below.

As discussed elsewhere (see chapters 2 and 15), social process at the Preceramic sites under study here can probably best be described as a fission/fusion process associated with segmented egalitarian social structures, primarily household-based communities. Phases II to V of the Sangamon terrace probably consisted of at least two interrelated communities of maritime foragers and terrestrial farmers, both of which continued to forage wetland resources. The archaeological remains do not suggest either the local differentiation or nonlocal integration necessary to fit the definition of a typical emergent complex society with recognizable leaders (as suggested by house form and location, by elaborate tombs and grave offerings, and by accumulated wealth). Rather the remains suggest small-scale segmented communities, likely interrelated by kinship and necessity with little in the way of formalized leadership positions beyond those attained through age, gender status, or merit (perhaps those individuals buried at Huaca Prieta?). This pattern of course does not exclude the presence of groups or even individual ritual specialists and authority structures, based on their membership in age groups and/or individual qualities (as elders, practitioners of magic, healers, shamans, and so forth). Such figures might have mediated in the event of intracommunal and intercommunal disputes and occasionally directed public events.

Phases III to V along the coast seem to have been a time of demographic increase. The number of people along the terrace and littoral probably grew through both internal growth and perhaps the addition of a few people from farther away (although there is no direct evidence for this). By 6500–6000 cal BP the area was a burgeoning place located along the littoral and on the banks of wetlands and the Chicama River for a distance of almost 30 km north and south and at least 3–4 km east. In Phase III and especially Phase IV a notable shift in the appearance of communities occurred: mounded households along the littoral build up from occupational accretion, suggesting longer residence time in sites and replacing earlier residential locales without residential mounds. Concurrent with this change appears to be an increased occupation of the interior wetlands. An aspect of this change probably can be ascribed to an increasing ritualization of the Huaca Prieta mound. Another may be the rise of competition in the form of more inland valley populations pushing closer to the littoral as the lower valley floor developed for agricultural purposes beginning by at least 5000–4000 cal BP (see chapter 5).

Although the data are somewhat ambiguous, it is plausible that the first major iteration of the Huaca Prieta mound was built around 6500 cal BP. This structure was reused numerous times afterward, with the last iterations occurring in later phases. The stratigraphy, number of constructions, and duration of use suggest that the later plaza and ramp were renewed and maintained on a regular basis. No hearths, structures, or artifacts were found in association with floors in these structures, suggesting that these surfaces were used for special purposes outside of the realm of day-to-day domestic living. As noted in chapter 7, however, it is possible that some of the food and other debris found on floors and use surfaces at Huaca Prieta, especially during its more intensive use in Phases IV and V, are associated with attendants or special groups of individuals that lived semipermanently or permanently on or at the edge of the mound to oversee or regulate its ritual and mortuary use by local and nonlocal people. This type of stewardship residency is different from the domestic residency described for Units 13, 16, and 26 and the domestic sites located along the littoral in the sense that there are no formal living, sleep-

ing, food preparation, and other domestic activity areas such as those demonstrated in these units and sites. In short, some type of caretaking residency might account for the excessive debris and burning observed at Huaca Prieta throughout time.

Furthermore, space within the plaza was marked off or separated from view by its sunken nature. In any event, these features—the plaza, the ramp, and the chamber tombs—represent accretionary aspects of a more highly planned mound, highlighting the continually changing nature of the mound. Some degree of planning was certainly involved in the construction of the mound landscape. We can suggest that a kind of architectural inertia set in once mound building began with the initial structure in place. A "decision" to build vertically may have acted as a kind of architectural legacy effect that constrained the options for restructuring the mound in the absence of large corporate labor pools and a centralized authority. That is, Huaca Prieta developed from its initial conditions into the monument that we see today not by maintaining a master plan from generation to generation over millennia but rather by simple, repetitive, and structurally constrained acts of deposition. Given the way in which construction occurred at Huaca Prieta, it also can reasonably be asserted that the deposits and occasional offerings in the mound may be the remains of individualized construction rituals associated with building it. The offerings, whether local or nonlocal, may be items brought by individuals who had learned the building rituals performed when burying some of their dead relatives in the mound. The circumscribed scale of each individual deposit suggests that a small number of people were involved in semiprivate to private high-frequency rituals.

Set in this context, there may be two keys for a better understanding of the local Preceramic society and its relation to Huaca Prieta and Paredones. First, the act of building Huaca Prieta was a long-term generative, foundational act in the creation of a relatively well-integrated and enduring local population. (If we view some mounds as cosmologically imbued objects that reference the earth, then it is not out of line to suggest that this notion may be encoded in the repetitive transgenerational form and social history of the mound.) In addition to the labor that went into their construction, Huaca Prieta and perhaps Paredones bonded local communities together. Constructing Huaca Prieta and especially the ramp, sunken plaza, and chamber tombs in Phases IV and V may have been long-term ritual acts in their own right. That is, the construction of these types of architectural features was as important as their use. Building Huaca Prieta may have been a component of a belief system whereby its construction was the final act integrating formally unrelated peoples. Integration also would have been achieved by incorporating previously unaffiliated or loosely affiliated groups along the littoral. Fusion would have entailed expanding the number of households and communities involved in building and using the mound as a way to incorporate any newly expanded social groups. (Although the genetic data are weak, there is a slight hint that females buried in Huaca Prieta might have been more closely related than the men buried there: see appendix 17.) If so, does this imply a matrilocal society? Many more genetic and isotope data are needed from the burials to test this and other demographic and social hypotheses.

By 5500 years ago, a profusion of symbolic expression and settlement expansion within and adjacent to the Huaca Prieta area occurred, perhaps with the emergence of a new cosmology or religion centered primarily on archetypal symbols of the sea (such as crabs, fish, and birds), interaction networks characterized by shared material practices (such as exotic food crops and precious stones), cultural emulation (such as the ramp and sunken plaza), and the intensification of long-distance exchange networks (such as *Spondylus*, copper sulfate, and malachite), while at the same time continuing to display clear local characteristics. By ~4500 cal BP there was a greater degree of interregionalism, suggested by the ramp and sunken plaza as features of some contemporary late Preceramic coastal sites and the similarity in ritual expression and sociopolitical organization as a way of negotiating community cohesion. Various socioeconomic interactions, acculturations, and demic diffusions were all active at different temporal and spatial scales. But to understand these we need to know more about specific local socioeconomic contexts of intergroup and intragroup interactions and population movements, for which we presently have few data. Especially important is long-distance exchange as a socially situated process, which was probably related to the negotiation and reproduction of local group identities and perhaps to the use of Huaca Prieta as a pilgrimage-like site. In this framework, almost every element of the material culture became more regional (including sunken plazas, ramps, and animal iconography and symbolism), thus removed from its prior local context.

Around 4500 cal BP Huaca Prieta was drawn into an increasingly coastal rather than just a littoral world. One sign of a linkage with interior and distant coastal areas is seen in the construction of the east-oriented ramp and the sunken circular plaza, which we view as architectural traits of the late Preceramic monuments in the Norte Chico and other areas that date between at least 5000–4500 cal BP. But differences remained between the two areas. Huaca Prieta had no platform mound, large open spaces for public attendance, or *schira* fill. This was a time when the littoral and lower valley probably became more fully in contact, if not integrated, with the interior coast. Certainly there were continuous exchange networks with interior areas and perhaps by this time even immigrations from interior areas. Up to this time, Huaca Prieta had served as the primary place in a cosmological and ontological landscape that integrated a diverse collection of peoples who formed the constituents of the population. It was the "center" of the Chicama coastal world from 7500 to 4000 years ago.

Just as the mound's apogee was signaled by multiple events (the creation of a sacred built landscape), so was its transition to the end. The final phases of use begin with the last plaster capping of Huaca Prieta. By closing the mound, it was no longer possible to use it in the previous manner, perhaps indicating that social and cosmological relations had changed. Capping Huaca Prieta terminated its primary use as a ritual mound but not as a burial mound; Huaca Prieta's cosmological properties still existed. For all intents and purposes, the past Huaca Prieta population no longer existed, but the sacred power of Huaca Prieta—with which it was imbued from the beginning—apparently was not lost. Huaca Prieta evidently took on idiosyncratic qualities such as being the place for later burial, from Guañape-like and

Cupisnique to Inka times. Curiously, none of the subsequent burials were placed in the chamber tombs. This was a late Preceramic tradition.

In between the final use of Huaca Prieta and the appearance of the Cupisnique mound, there is a Guañape-like presence associated with households on the terrace and small homesteads on the emerging floodplain (see chapters 5 and 7). So little information is available on this period of transition that we can only guess about its nature and meaning. A Cupisnique cultural presence in the form of households may be the result of immigrations from the coastal interior. Migrations from the interior may have been entirely small-scale affairs with family or local lineages moving to the Sangamon terrace area in a piecemeal manner. After Cupisnique the terrace changed in some ways but remained important. Huaca Prieta retained an important sacred role, but its regional cosmological position diminished or disappeared.

Also, by ~4500 years ago it appears that the material, social, and symbolic resources available to the Chicama littoral communities had been mobilized across regional and areal boundaries in response to specific socioeconomic agendas whose overriding concern remained the survival, maintenance of cohesion, and reproduction of individual communities and group identities. This is to be expected during a period that saw major restructurings of economic and societal practices and relations; at this time many of the constituent elements of an early food-producing society were being established gradually in diverse environmental settings in the lower valley.

In summary, the architecture, stratigraphy, dark color, and many of the patterns documented at Huaca Prieta and Paredones have not yet been seen at other early sites along the Peruvian littoral and coast. Ideas developed at Huaca Prieta seemingly spread to only one other site: Pulpar. But these ideas probably took hold because they landed in a fertile wetland similar to Huaca Prieta where existing people were predisposed to them. The Huaca Prieta tradition disappeared by 3500 cal BP. Other than its extraordinary textile, basketry, and gourd technologies, the visual art expressed on them, and perhaps above all the specialized dual economies of marine and crop foods, it left few other lingering marks in the Andes.

The social history of Huaca Prieta and Paredones may be better discussed in relation to solving the problem of household community integration at different scales. Restated simply, these sites tell the story of how Preceramic societies were aggregating at key resource zones—where the wetlands and the river met the sea. Part of this story is the creation of a ritual landscape, the building of which was inclusive and integrative. The Huaca Prieta landscape was a conscious effort to integrate a number of social groups under the banner of a common system of beliefs about society and about the way in which it interacted with the natural environment. Decision-making was likely carried out through consensus-building rather than through economic incentives, ideological manipulation, or coercion. Flexibility allowed Huaca Prieta as a social formation to include diverse groups of people and ultimately may be the reason why the mound was so long-lived in comparison to other coastal sites.

The archaeological evidence also suggests that rituals and other activities at the mound served to integrate diverse groups of people into a single socioeconomic entity. At the same time, it seems likely that this organization was not explicitly designed to aggrandize any one individual or group. This is not to say that everybody had a roughly similar status. The society almost surely had built-in power differentials, and some people probably had more influence in the decision-making process than others.

IDENTITIES AND LEGACIES

Huaca Prieta and Paredones tell the story of building a local littoral society, not necessarily a coastal one at the outset. The initial stirrings of social integration in the Huaca Prieta area cannot be traced to a single littoral community. Integration was probably accomplished through the creation or more properly the re-creation of some aspects of a common set of beliefs about how the world worked then. People probably built Huaca Prieta and Paredones because of the social advantages afforded by shared experiences there and likely an innate desire to be part of something larger than the individual or individual household or household cluster. Later, after its abandonment, Huaca Prieta remained an important entity, moving from a large ritual mound to a burial mound.

This perspective contrasts with other views of "monumental architecture" (for example, Burger and Rosenswig 2012; Trigger 1990). Most interpretations privilege early monuments as tools of elite domination over a commoner population and the use of monuments to stage large-scale public ceremonies. Huaca Prieta is different. Although it is a large mound site, it was associated primarily with repetitive ritual acts in small, circumscribed ritual spaces built and used by small groups of people. As tempting as it is to call Huaca Prieta a large-scale monument depicting centralized power and authority, it was probably never used as a public place by a large group of people regulated by an authoritative leader. Huaca Prieta was clearly a complex place associated with a complex society, but complexity was not a consequence of its vertical presence and organization. Rather, its complexity rested with multiple social differentiations depending upon economic specialization, site location, and other variables through a dispersed and segmented lower valley. Membership in this society likely depended on circumstances: some social differentiations were determined genealogically, while others were probably occupational and merit based.

At the outset of the book I addressed some of the major social and cultural features thought to be characteristic of early complex societies around the world. I also defined those traits most typical of early Andean civilization and placed Huaca Prieta within this scheme. I now return to this theme briefly to examine some of the contributions that I think ultimately define the archaeology of the Huaca Prieta area. The mound at Huaca Prieta does not represent classic monument building because of the slow small-scale pace of its construction and the absence of a large-scale public function. Nor does its construction place emphasis on labor value and leadership; it was a long-term process construed by many self-regulating generations of people on their own and, following observed design and tradition, through participation. With increased co-dependence on the sea and on cultigens, individual household families seem to have emerged as the characteristic residential and productive

units. The archaeology of the maritime economy does not necessarily point to a strong emphasis on community-wide cohesion and cooperative effort. Such coordination may have accompanied other, practical endeavors, such as clearance and establishment of cultivated plots and raised agricultural fields near Paredones during Phase III and later. These patterns suggest social experimentation in which the wider community was more important than economy and individual display.

Furthermore, the evidence from Huaca Prieta has established the lower Chicama Valley as an early place of simultaneous maritime and agricultural development. We cannot state that this site represents all others along the littoral of the Central Andes. Other site interpretations need to be developed in terms of the practices and resources in different localities, rather than one site or region fitting all. Such an approach is important in places like the Pacific desert of the Andes, where we know the majority of the exotic plant foods come from distant areas. The southward and westward spread of propagated plants from northern and eastern South America, respectively, indicates dispersal under forms of cultivation that are currently undocumented archaeologically. In the past archaeologists often assumed that migrating farmers must have been the primary process through which domestic plants dispersed from one region to another. While several of the cultivated plants at Paredones and Huaca Prieta were not domesticated locally, it is not yet possible to establish whether we are looking at cultural diffusion, where farming was adopted by local marine and terrestrial foragers; demic diffusion, where farmers moved onto the coastal plains from elsewhere; or some combination of these two processes or others. It is most likely that many of the exotic cultigens were obtained through ritual offerings by outsiders and/or through social interaction and long-distance exchange. The strongest evidence at Huaca Prieta points to the ritual offerings of exotic foods that might have been related to social relationships between local and distant people more than to a need to increase and intensify food production to meet a growing local population. That need could easily have been met by intensifying the exploitation of marine resources. We also do not know if Huaca Prieta and Paredones advertised and promoted a form of wider communal identity that was to some extent in tension with the logic of the small-scale farmers and fisherfolk in the area by "hosting" distant peoples and whether aspects of exchange were regulated by social rules, specific types of symbolic items, and mortuary practices.

The early to middle Preceramic period was a formative threshold in the human history of the Andes. People were faced with complex patterns of cohabitation, competition, and cooperation, which arose from the social implications of novel and continuously evolving subsistence practices and the restructuring of resource use and kinship patterns. Such essentially social realities permeated every aspect of the Preceramic lifeway, from production and consumption to ritual and symbolic expression. In turn, the littoral living strategies discussed here did not develop in a vacuum or merely as adaptive responses to changing economic realities. Instead they represented the material and social outcomes of a whole spectrum of tensions operating at multiple levels and among multiple agents: among mobile hunter-gatherers, settled cultivators, and wetland foragers; between households as loci of production and reproduction and communities as productive and reproductive units; between group ancestors venerated in private community rituals, perhaps commensal feasting for the exchange of products and ideas, and emergent "private" family genealogies.

So how did the Preceramic people of the lower Chicama Valley see their world? Some littoral communities lived close together, while others were dispersed over the landscape. People seem to have valued immediate consumption, because there were no storage units and sharing and exchange. Another useful way to think about their worldview also is through their sense of time. The burials suggest temporality focused on future, present, and past (see chapter 15). The planned aspect of conservation of the mound also suggests future and continuity. Life appears to have been rich and episodic in social connections and ritual performances and in daily routine. Cooperation and sharing must have enabled the maintenance of aggregations of settlement that lacked signs of different housing or long-distance spaces between and within them. The networks of exchange and communication also suggest peaceful relations. Most people were also disease free.

I end this chapter by risking more generalizations. Despite all the recent emphasis on regional and local diversity in Andean archaeology, most scholars recognize a number of underlying common elements that characterize an entire region undergoing more or less concurrent major socioeconomic transformations such as those during the late Preceramic period on the north littoral and coast of Peru. A number of established and largely Norte Chico–centered interpretations present mounded monumental architecture as the pinnacle of the development of early complex societies (see chapter 2). It is further seen as an adaptive prelude to the linear transformation into coastal village communities of farmer-fisherfolk, followed by their expansion across the region. Contrary to such views, the picture now emerging from the archaeological record of the littoral, the coastal plains, and inland valleys of some coastal regions areas (especially in the lower Chicama area) is more complex and less linear development, which requires interpretative tools that can accommodate this nonlinear complexity. I suspect that the same holds true for many other areas of emerging complexity in the Andes, which also do not follow simple, expected linear paths to power. Finally, as part of the legacy of these early complex societies, I am not convinced that any of them were completely "Andean" at their outset. Over several centuries, if not millennia, they probably were transformationally becoming Andean, while retaining many littoral, coastal, highland, and/or tropical cultural traits.

CHAPTER 15

BEYOND MATTER TO FOUNDATIONS AND REPRESENTATIONS

Tom D. Dillehay

INTRODUCTION

In the opening chapters I stated that this book employs a socionatural approach to the study of the Huaca Prieta area, with emphasis given to social, cultural, and environmental variables in explaining the content, structure, and meaning of the archaeological record. Chapter 14 provides a summary of the major archaeological findings of this study. Two of the more important and surprising results of this study were (1) the presence of humans at Huaca Prieta in the late Pleistocene to early Holocene period, with an economy based on both marine and terrestrial/wetland resources; and (2) the broad-spectrum economy beginning at least ~9000 years ago when food crops (such as squash, chile peppers, and avocados) were added to the diet and leading eventually to the development of a specialized dual economy. In this final chapter I briefly address broader interpretive issues at Huaca Prieta and Paredones and then turn to questions about the fragmented nature of the material and stratigraphic records at these sites and why Huaca Prieta contained so much charcoal, giving it a dark appearance, and so much salt (derived from seawater). This topic requires a consideration, even if speculative, of the foundational or ontological meaning of these and other elements and the wider contribution of the Huaca Prieta area to our understanding of emergent social complexity, cosmology, and religion, given that the site is one of the longest occupied and enigmatic in human history.

The term "complexity" is becoming more widely accepted as unsatisfactory in archaeology. Nonetheless, in the absence of a better alternative, I use it briefly here to explain what I mean by it and how I use it. Most contemporary archaeological theories of the origin of complex society combine elements of both social and environmental determinism. The definition of complexity differs considerably among researchers (for example, Habu et al. 2004; Price and Brown 1985). Here "complexity" refers to both economic and social organization. "Economic organization" relates primarily to organizational complexity in subsistence and settlement, which is identified by the degree of incorporation of various economic strategies (such as specialized foraging, food production, and long-distance exchange). "Social organization" refers to the degree of vertical and horizontal differentiation (McGuire 1983) as well as the degree of integration of culturally differentiated parts (Fitzhugh 2003).

In the Andes emergent complexity is defined not only by these variables but also by site size, degree of monumentality, and display of artistic and symbolic expression, among others (see chapter 2). In an effort to correlate these variables at Huaca Prieta, we can say that the site was in its day one of the largest and most unique mounds in the Andes, but was it socially and ontologically complex or just stratigraphically and architecturally complex? Horizontal social differentiation is evidenced by diversity in burial patterns, in artistic expression, and in associated various site types. There also is social integration among these sites and complementarity of specialized economies. While subsequent late Preceramic communities in coastal Peru (such as Sechín Bajo, Caral, Aspero, and others in the Norte Chico area) were more sophisticated architecturally and in overall site design (see chapter 2), they did not endure as long as Huaca Prieta. Furthermore, although they appear to be more complex from a vertical social perspective, these other sites do not contain the number and diversity of burials and especially the variety of visual arts documented at Huaca Prieta (see chapter 11). In the context of Huaca Prieta, the thousands of vertically structured individual building and ritual episodes performed by small groups of people did not constitute large-scale public acts of monumentality coordinated by formal leaders. Over time these rituals must have been associated with many different practices and meanings, although there was likely a thread of commonality and continuity running through them. At these late Preceramic sites part-time or full-time leaders seem to have administered large-scale public acts, which occasionally included the burial of a few individuals in large mounds, but not to the extent evidenced at Huaca Prieta. Moreover, these sites reveal little clear evidence of complexity in terms of centralized political authority, elite control of corporate labor, and the gathering of bulk resources for large-scale public events. At Huaca Prieta, in contrast, "public" seems to refer to long-term, repetitive access to and ritual use of a large artificially mounded place by a wide variety of small egalitarian groups acting on their own but with certain expectations of conduct. (There is some concordance with relatively egalitarian or communitarian alternate explanations offered for the origins of monumental ceremonial centers in other times and places of the Andes, such as those in the altiplano Formative period [Bandy 2004].) Ironically, in a sense Huaca Prieta is a monument; it is large, artificially created, and visually imposing. If the rituals and burials at Huaca Prieta had been laterally rather than vertically performed across the Sangamon terrace, however, the mound would never have been produced and the site probably would never have received the archaeological attention that it has.

Social complexity also requires permanent institutions whose authority emanates from specific ideologies and worldviews. In Huaca Prieta one such institution must have been the high frequency of small group rituals at the mound; another was an ideology that must have sanctioned the continuity of building and maintaining (such as artificial berms and plaster retention surfaces) the mound by local groups but perhaps under the divine tutelage of deities and/or ancestors. The Huaca Prieta area was a sacred precinct set apart from the domestic communities. Paredones functioned in a similar capacity but was more focused on food production and preparation, perhaps serving as an ancillary ritual site to Huaca Prieta or an independent mound engaged in a ritualized agricultural economy. Separateness of the public and the domestic seems to have been an essential ingredient of intercommunity integration and the long-term building and use of the mounds.

Other than socioeconomic factors, we also can

partially credit the environment for spatially and socially structuring the community organization of the local population (expressed materially in terms of outlying household mounds) located on the terrace and dispersed along the littoral and among the inland wetlands. An apparent numerical increase and demographic concentration in these areas throughout the Preceramic period that were principal factors affecting social complexity are important too. The organization and integration of people also had to have been strongly affected by fissioning of the kinship structure: as local groups grew in size individual family units probably moved to unoccupied productive lagoonal, wetland, or littoral areas.

An integrationist view of the emergence of social complexity in the lower Chicama Valley is reflected by the presence of both short- and long-distance exchange networks connecting fisherfolk, farmers, and foragers over several millennia, from at least ~10,000 to 4000 cal BP. The idea of complexity and especially the continuous import of a wide variety of cultigens and other exotics, implying long-distance contacts and exchange networks (see chapter 14) raise a number of questions, such as the nature of the social and economic organization in these contexts and the motives for forming these networks. By ~7500–7000 years ago these networks and the specialized economies were beginning to create different types of settlement and subsistence organizations as well as a wide range of new roles and technological instruments. These developments also probably led to the creation of new types of persons and roles, in particular the farmer, the weaver, the artist, the trader, combinations of these, and so forth. These new roles would have been influenced by a wide range of new social relations, not least gendered relations, based upon these and other identities, as well as by their interplay with traditional types of persons such as shellfish collector, diver, hunter, and others. The wider communal value of new and different products and new social roles also must have led to new levels of knowledge and to new worldviews different from previous ones.

People residing in the Huaca Prieta area were acquainted with a wide variety of complementary economic strategies, including fishing, foraging, agriculture, long-distance exchange, and perhaps low-level animal husbandry (guinea

pigs and camelids; see chapter 9). The new conditions offered by the emerging alluvium in the lower valley ~5000 to 4000 cal BP certainly made life more agriculturally productive and in the long run eventually led to a new and more formal socioeconomic organization during the subsequent Guañape-like and Cupisnique periods. Rather than being caused by a confrontation between favorable maritime and terrestrial conditions, it probably was partially due to the challenge of coping with shifting wetlands ~5000–4000 cal BP, a developing floodplain in the lower valley, and other factors (see chapter 5) and to the unprecedented population and settlement density along the littoral zone that resulted in increased exchange, social complexity, and intensive agriculture during this period.

Expanded agricultural fertility must have been one of the incentives for occupying the lower floodplain and for building the raised agricultural fields east of Paredones ~5000–4500 years ago. This in turn enabled the later Guañape-like and Cupisnique populations around 3800–3500 cal BP perhaps to draw closer together, eliminating distances between communities and thus creating new social and economic relations, which demanded new solutions. On the local level economic specialization, and a division of labor between fisherfolk and farmers must have led to local exchange between people performing rituals and other activities at Huaca Prieta and those preparing food and performing rituals at Paredones, but there also must have been continued long-distance exchange with highland and other coastal regions, as suggested by the adoption of exotic cultigens and other items (such as *Spondylus* and scallop shells, copper sulfate, hematite, and indigo and other dyes and pigments on baskets and textiles) and by the introduction of new technologies (such as raised agricultural irrigation and unique textile and basketry weaving and twining techniques).

Hence local social and economic strategies did not develop in a vacuum or merely as adaptive responses to changing economic and environmental realities. Instead they represent the material and social outcomes of a wide spectrum of challenges operating at multiple levels and among multiple agents: between maritime forager and settled cultivator lifestyles; between households as loci of production and reproduction and communities as kinship units; between groups of ancestors venerated in community ceremonies and perhaps emergent "private" household genealogies; and between local people and distant maritime and highland traders, pilgrims perhaps, and inland farmers. From such a viewpoint, it is possible that the appearance of a mega-place such as Huaca Prieta could have embodied an attempt to contain several social paradoxes that in all probability formed a recurrent and defining characteristic of the littoral social life.

In summary, a mosaic of ecological niches and other factors along the Chicama littoral promoted local economic specialization by individual household communities by ~7500–6500 cal BP. Although extensive hard data are lacking, this specialization, in turn, must have promoted an exchange economy (for example, salt, dried seafood, and decorated textiles), inducing both cooperation and competition between and beyond communities and ultimately stimulating increase in social and economic diversity. Once these local economies were established, a new local and regional dynamic was created. The nature of the physical environment (combined with an increased population density over time) also constitutes a context in which all subsequent social transformations were likely nurtured and constrained. But a set of social processes explains the emergence of more complex mixed economies during the subsequent Guañape-like and Cupisnique periods, processes that are more interregional and cannot be reduced to local environmental determinism.

It is important to emphasize that the Preceramic period under study here represents an integrated economy based on uniting two distinct social segments with economic specializations. In this regard Huaca Prieta and Paredones were complementary nodes of contact between outlying communities. Their specific local ritual contexts, however, differed: Huaca Prieta was involved in achieving intercommunity social and economic integration. Paredones was probably given more to the development and incorporation of a changing economy and food production based on the import of cultigens for incipient farming and for consumption during ritual and perhaps feasting events, probably at Huaca Prieta, perhaps at Pare-

dones, and beyond to other local sites. The food assemblages obtained from the premound and mound levels at both sites, but primarily Paredones, have shown the presence of multiple cultigens from other regions (tropical lowlands, highlands; see chapter 10 and appendix 5). Increased agriculture, specialized economies, and the linear settlement nucleation that eventually resulted along the Chicama littoral and adjacent wetlands evidently helped Huaca Prieta to become a mega-place associated with outlying domestic sites and perhaps visitation by more distant people (pilgrims?). This is the best testimony for the successful creation of a shared group identity initially based on a maritime/agricultural/wetland economy and lifestyle among the littoral inhabitants. The persistent presence (beginning ~6000 cal BP) of a symbolic and cultural vocabulary in the decorated textiles and gourds rich in locally derived as well as wider Andean design motifs also must have been one key element in the creation of a shared group identity. This is further suggested by the recurrence of Huaca Prieta's material signifiers (such as protective plaster covering, painted stones, empty chamber tombs, and individual ritual spaces) inside the mound and by the presence of more formal architecture (such as the sunken circular plaza, chamber tombs, and an entry ramp) during Phases IV and V.

The appearance of the ramp and the sunken plaza architectural forms seem to bear direct parallels to prototypes known from contemporary sites such as Alto Salaverry in the adjacent Moche Valley and several sites in the Norte Chico area. Although we can only speculate about the nature and origin of these forms at Huaca Prieta, they seem to be the deliberate choice of the local population to adopting new building traditions possibly to embody concepts of a wider communally organized household society. This interpretation is consonant with views positing the Andean littoral and coast as a whole that formed an integral part of a regionwide late Preceramic cultural and historical continuum (Lavallée 2000; Moseley 1992). But within this continuum Huaca Prieta was a unique mound site. The mound is slightly earlier than others of the late Preceramic period; it is shaped differently; and it has numerous human burials in it, which form a significant part of its history.

SOCIAL DIFFERENTIATION: THE LIVING AND THE DEAD

The primary differences between Huaca Prieta and Paredones are their chronology, economy, and function. Prior to ~7500 cal BP Huaca Prieta was a premound place where foraging groups gathered intermittently to exploit maritime and wetland resources. After this period Huaca Prieta was a prominent mound of ritual and burial of certain individuals that lasted until ~3500 years ago, with burials continuing until the colonial period. Paredones was initially a forager campsite as well and later became a ritual and food-processing locality. The food consumed at Huaca Prieta and at the excavated domestic sites consisted primarily of marine resources, while the food produced and consumed at Paredones consisted primarily of crops, indicating the coexistence of two different economies and occupational specialists (see chapters 7, 9, and 10 and appendix 6). Despite specialization and probable occupational diversification, there is little evidence of social differentiation.

The human remains from both Bird's excavations and our excavations in chamber tombs and in mound fills at Huaca Prieta suggest the best evidence for social differentiation. (Differentiation within other kinds of data, such as offerings and households, is difficult.) Huaca Prieta is where individuals of various social identities and roles, different gender and kinship generations, and probably various areas were buried. Off-mound burials (such as Unit 16 and those observed in looter's holes at outlying domestic sites) had very few, if any, offerings (for example, shells and lithics). Although few in number, most burial offerings at Huaca Prieta are *Semele* sp. whole shells primarily in empty chamber tombs dating to Phases IV and V. The only burial that was distinguished from others was in the off-mound Unit 16 (HP09-08), which was an adult male associated with several large blocks of sculpted polychaete tubes. A burial of an older female (HP09-01) in Unit 16 was associated with a possible weaving batten made of sea lion bone and a textile fragment. Huaca Prieta and Unit 16 also had fetal, infant, and secondary burials. Most secondary burials represent the exhumation and reburial of bodies after the flesh had completely decayed, as

revealed by red pigment on the bones and by some missing bone elements (see chapter 8 and appendix 10). It is not understood why most burials at Huaca Prieta are females (see Bird et al. 1985), why there are formal chamber tombs and shallow informal graves, why there are so many sealed and open yet empty chamber tombs, and why none of the few burial offerings were fragmented, which is so characteristic of the vast majority of material items, including a few human skeletons. Were the empty graves designated for certain individuals who were never buried there? Or do they represent the burial places of people who died at sea while fishing whose bodies were never recovered? Do the later agglutinated chamber tombs in Unit 23 and a few in Units 8 and 10 represent tomb groups versus social groups? Why the differences between whole and fragmented objects inside and outside of tombs?

The information from Paredones and Huaca Prieta has provided some indications that role differentiation within and across generations was a major part of the life of these communities, as also suggested at the late Preceramic site of Bandurria on the central coast of Peru, where two coexisting population segments specialized in the exploitation of different marine environments near the site (Chu Barrera 2011). The occurrence of textiles, baskets, gourds, and other objects with clear traces of deliberate fragmentation (such as cutting, smashing, scoring, snapping, and tearing), perhaps as "currencies" or offerings symbolizing access to and participation in rituals and other activities at Huaca Prieta, could indicate a preoccupation with economic specialization and individual social and/or role differentiation and ultimately with the "enchainment" of individual kinship units across generations (see chapter 2 and the discussion below). Notions of achieved social differentiation may be behind the exceptional male burial in Unit 16, a domestic site situated 40 m north of Huaca Prieta, or the few single burials found on the floors of chamber tombs in Units 8, 10, and 23. Our project excavated fourteen chamber tombs, only three of which had skeletons inside. The only offerings we found in the chamber tombs were a textile fragment with one skeleton in one tomb and *Semele* sp. shells and a few gastropods and snails in six empty tombs. Three chamber tombs were excavated by Bird (see Bird et al. 1985: 65–66; field notes, American Museum of Natural History). He reported eighteen burials from three of these tombs or "houses," as he called them. Two burials were associated with fragments of cotton textile, another with perforated shells (species not identified), and another with salt crystals. Bird also excavated several empty chamber tombs. House 4, a boot-shaped tomb, was empty; he also reported finding "many subterranean structures" but mentioned no burials in them (Bird et al. 1985: 46–48).

The empty and occupied tombs could be perceived as representing the opposite ends in the local scale of obligation to the dead, perhaps from those who died on land whose bodies were recovered for burial to individuals (and bodies) lost at sea and symbolically buried in empty tombs; that is, those whose deaths were marked in an atypical way by offering complete shells of *Semele* sp. from the sea rather than the missing bodies in the tombs. The *Semele* sp. shells suggest a winter period of collection, which is the nonreproductive season of this species. It is also the season when the sea is most turbulent and dangerous (see appendix 3; personal communication with local fisherfolk, 2010). (Another shell species, *Choromytilus chorus*, and a few gastropods and snails also were present as offerings, but rarely found in the tombs as *Semele* sp. was.) Does the association between empty tombs and offerings of marine shells gathered during the winter imply that the missing bodies are fishers who died at sea during the winter whose bodies were never found? (Present-day local fisherfolk informed us that, when fishers died at sea in the early 1900s and their bodies were lost, graves were still prepared for them and some of their personal items along with shells and fishbones were placed in the graves as offerings.)

In summary, no hard data indicate major social differences among people using or supporting Huaca Prieta, suggesting that any differences may be of degree rather than kind. We thus model the development of the site as the trajectory of a few differentiated people buried at a single relatively well-placed location whose social (kin, house, or gender?) group, and maybe themselves, achieved some degree of occupational or generational dif-ferentiation over others. No evidence indicates that in this society elites who had accumulated wealth or political prestige were provisioned over others.

We also can argue that any differentiation within the burial data is a result of ancient beliefs about the nature and structure of the world and about the living, the dead, and the unborn, a continuum from the past to the future through the present. The burial patterns at Huaca Prieta appear to be not so much about individual power and a person's status in life. Rather, they seem to be an accumulative deposit in the mound designed to ensure the continuation of the population and to link the living and the dead across generations. In this model the social forces in building Huaca Prieta must have evolved from an enduring capacity to mobilize local households from generation to generation. That is, burials in the mound probably were not just about the memory of the deceased and his/her promotion but about something larger, something beyond the lingering status and memory of a single generation or person (see Kaulicke 2001 for a detailed discussion of death and memory in Peru). They likely were about the obligation of the living to the dead and about transcendence and transgenerational representation of social groups and their roles and obligations within the wider community.

CORPSES, OBLIGATION, AND REPETITION

The human body is simultaneously a physical and symbolic artifact, as both naturally and culturally produced, and is associated with a particular generation. We can assume that each skeleton in a shallow grave of the mound fill or in a chamber tomb of Units 10 and 23 at Huaca Prieta was not a singular entity but part of coherent and coordinated social relations. Once buried within a singular grave, the individual, as an object, was thus decentered from space and time and from the living to a multitude of new meanings derived from these relations (*sensu* Law: see chapter 2), including his/her membership in the past and present of the society at large. The range of meanings evoked for all burials, however, had to have been constellated in much more than decisions of tomb design and placement, the preparation of material offerings, or the use to which they were put. The wider configuration of burials must have drawn its logic and design not only from its own functions and meanings but from the larger cultural order of the littoral society to which they referred. In each instance the symbols of tomb placement, offerings, and ritual spaces must have reproduced the same organization of reality that structured every other aspect of the local society across several generations. Thus, just as the material symbols of burials and other materials were informed by the larger cultural patterns to which they referred, so too did they inform these larger cultural patterns. It was a process of mutual reflexivity in which meaning was continually created from a shared context of forms across time and across generations. This is not to say that no changes occurred in the society from one cultural phase to another, because considerable transformations were taking place materially, socially, and spatially. Although things changed, they also basically remained the same. To attempt to understand how these symbols and meanings might have operated, we must attempt to identify some of the underlying principles that united the entire system at this time and the wider importance of burying a corpse in the mound.

It is fair to say that nowadays we expect our right, as an individual member in our own society, to self-determination to extend beyond life to our dead body—where and if we or our friends and relatives will be buried, where and if our cremated ashes will be strewn. An obligation to the corpse, or to its remains, is found everywhere across the spectrum of human societies. Human remains can never be a matter of indifference where bonds of kinship exist. The obligation usually takes the form of a traditional duty, yet it has its basis in an imperative to dispose of the dead ritually and most often publicly and to mourn the loss of a relative or friend. The absence of a body, a burial, and a grave site can be a loss to kinfolk and to society at large. Thus grief cannot find its objective, the work of mourning, through which the dead were made to die.

But why bury the dead and why treat them differently, especially if the dead individual simply represents a single moment, a single life in the totality of the society—the invisible society at large over time and space, the future? One reason is because the deceased is important to his/her family and to his/her generation. Besides the individual's representation of a group's social identity and of the continuity of families, lineages, and household groups, a burial ritual also relates to the personhood of the deceased. Personhood changed throughout an individual's life, whether it was related to his/her role in society, family and kin groups, or exchange networks or simply to different life experiences in general. That is, the status and change of personhood was relational and socially produced by the individual's place and experience in society, by its social codes, and by the society's wider ideology. In this regard society had an obligation to bury the dead and what they represented to the society and its perpetuity.

Another reason is because the living were in debt to their dead ancestors for everything that kept their society going through time and still had pivotal roles. Here was the authority of the dead and of the ancestors. By passing from the realm of the engendered into the realm of the engendering, the dead became the authors and proprietors of life, personifying all that transcended and yet at the same time generating human society. In other words, the dead legitimized the living and those coming in the future: the unborn. Preoccupation with death, burial, and the continued obligatory relations between the dead and the living was a major part of the life experience and ontology of the Preceramic people building, using, and selectively being buried at Huaca Prieta.

Here I want to engage in some of the basic questions around which a local ontology (including religion and cosmology) might have revolved during the Preceramic period, in a special place like Huaca Prieta with its repetitive ritual episodes and human burials. On what foundations was the mound suddenly built upward and outward around 7500 cal BP? How did mound building define or articulate with the surrounding landscape and with outlying residential sites? Why were some people buried in the mound, either in chamber tombs or in shallow graves or their bones placed in midden debris, and others in domestic sites? Who were the people buried in the mound and why were they not buried in the outlying domestic sites? Did some buried people come from distant areas? Did the graves mark not just the resting places of the dead but the mortality of their creators and those who came in the future, the continuity and ongoingness of the society? Why was the mound saturated with salt (seawater) and charcoal (fires)? What was the meaning of these combined white and black elements, the residues of water and fire, respectively? Why are there so many offerings of fragmented objects and why are there so many individually segmented ritual spaces? How did the mound relate to the single individuals buried within it? Was it just an inalienable object that had no personal connection to the people buried in it, just a place that related to the ongoingness of the world, free of any duty to the living? Although we do not have answers to all of these questions, they are less likely to be found in the economic, technological, and environmental parameters of the site. They must be sought in ontological and social terms.

As discussed in chapter 2, people's worldviews or ontologies are spheres of human life as important as and yet somehow different from politics, economy, and social relations. Worldviews are important categories for understanding human differentiation, behavior, knowledge, and experience. In this regard ontology is something that both differentiates the world and provides a concept for understanding that differentiation. Ontology in this sense is not conceptualized as a determinant of human behavior and thought that, while perhaps culturally constructed, exists beyond human interaction. It simply helps to format the world for new kinds of rules and practices premised on concerns with all beings and things; and, as discussed in chapter 2, it sifts information for people's understanding and use. In short, ontology is a fundamental set of understandings about how the world should be and is: what kinds of beings, processes, and qualities could potentially exist in it, how these relate to each other, and how and why they are selected for understanding.

We can venture to guess that people living in the Huaca Prieta world must have had different practical understandings of the nature of that world through time and space, of its material reality, of its conceptual meaning, and of their own bodies and those of the dead, according to the situation and circumstances of changing social and environmental circumstances. We will never know how many single or multiple ontologies once existed during the long Preceramic period at the site and in the lower Chicama Valley, or whether there were contrasting ontologies. But at least one of those ontologies must have been related to both the living and the human body, and how people understood and experienced them (see Ingold 2000: 10).

Yet, whatever these ontologies might have been, within the fluid and diverse world of the Chicama Valley and beyond, the inhabitants using the mound at Huaca Prieta would have understood and identified with a single persistent point of reference or boundary: their own local communities. The interests, survival, and reproduction of these agglomerations of kin groups and households primarily framed their worldview, which was expressed over and over and in variable material forms at Huaca Prieta and for many generations. Their cosmology was probably restricted to their peculiar ontological composition(s) of a natural world and perhaps a mythical world, which we cannot access archaeologically. But a major aspect of this ontology had to have been the different mortuary patterns of the corpses, the wide variety of fragmented artifacts, the few whole objects, the natural elements accumulated for subsistence and for mound building, and the social institutions created by communities, including those that were visible, invisible, conceptual, and transcendent.

We cannot understand the social institutions of places like Huaca Prieta independently of the institutions of ritual, death, burial, and tombs. For what is a place like Huaca Prieta if not its memory and the promotion of that memory through time from one generation to another—a site or locale where time turned back upon itself and where generations both turned backward and forward onto themselves? The mound and the tombs within it mark a site on the littoral landscape where time did not merely pass through or pass over. Time was and still is inside it and gathered around it, thus immortalizing time and the place. It is this immortalization of time that gave a sacred place like Huaca Prieta its ritually articulated boundary and topography, distinguishing it from the domestic spaces beyond it, and its "monumentality"—not necessarily its size and transgenerational communalism but its meaning, perpetuity, and mound topography. (Even today this meaning continues as modern-day shamans or *curanderos* from the north coast of Peru still visit and worship at the mound, performing rituals under the light of the moon and making offerings, usually coca leaves and chicha [Dillehay and Bonavia, personal communication, 2009].)

What I want to identify here under the term "mound topography" of Huaca Prieta are aspects of the ontological foundations for the littoral community's engagement with the land, in which topology was knowledge of the sacred landscape and the continuing relations among the living, the dead, and the unborn.

Apparently not all of the dead at Huaca Prieta were necessarily buried close to their living descendants. Some may have been born and resided elsewhere and been brought to the site for burial, and some might have been placed in off-mound sites and in mound fills (see appendix 10). Wherever they came from, people had to fit their fate and to find their place in the cosmos, but first they had to disappear—that is, first they had to be buried and separated from the living. Because their bodies had places, tombs, and cemeteries to go to, we can surmise that their souls or images would have attained an afterlife among the living in the form of "social death," whereby memory of the dead eventually would have faded away among the living from generation to generation (Dillehay 1995). The dead member simply became one of many who had joined the ancestral history of the wider and longer-term community. That is, the dead could have held their social and historical place in time so that not just the living but also the unborn could inhabit the world. As a result, tombs could have become mini-monuments of projective hope for the living and the unborn of specific families or social groups. If this issue relates to the persistence of social time and not to social persistence in time, and if time has an earthly correlate, then we could say that the sight of tombs at places like Huaca Prieta (and especially tombs in large, highly visible monuments to the living in a topographic landscape like the Sangamon terrace) offered images of a covenant between the dead (the ancestors) and the living and a concept of the continuity of the society. Offerings in tombs, as meager as they were at Huaca Prieta, were prob-

ably perceived not only as offerings to the dead but as evidence of things unseen—the future and the unborn.

Most marked are the Phase IV and V chamber tombs at Huaca Prieta, which seem to take the form of small houses (which confused Bird and is probably why he called them houses; see chapter 1) and seem to define a new perspective on burial and the relationship between the living and the dead. As Ian Hodder (1990) and others have pointed out, ancient tombs often copied houses in their form and domestic meaning. The domestic interior of the house was thus in some fundamental sense mortuary, inhabited not only by the dead but also by the living (and the unborn, coming in the future) in their projective potentiality. The living and the "house" tombs that they constructed for the dead were the ties between the dead and the unborn. The house tomb, in a sense, was thus a place where the dead, through the care of the living, perpetuated their afterlives and promoted the interests of the unborn. These ties were probably most strongly realized in burial in and around the outlying "real" domestic houses (such as those observed in looter's holes and in Unit 16) and in repetitive communal mortuary rituals in the graves and tombs at Huaca Prieta.

Mortuary rituals thus would have submitted the living to the rule of rhythmic episodes that were conventionally fixed (for example, Giddens 1984), perhaps in order to depersonalize grief and provide a formal articulation between the dead and the unborn. Why is this important? The social philosopher Martin Heidegger (1927) offers an insight. He insists that human death be understood not as a logical termination of life but as a possibility that the corpse withholds a presence at the same time as it renders present an absence. Burial of the corpse is the event of passage from one state to another taking place before the living. This phenomenon of passage from the living to the dead binds past, present, and future. The past, the present, and the future all converge in the dead body, as long as it remains an object of concern for the living. In its genealogical, sentimental, and institutional relation to the living, the dead body is the personification of transcendence from generation to generation and thus toward the future.

Set in this context, we can envision a large

part of the sacredness of both the occupied and the unoccupied graves and tombs at Huaca Prieta related to transcendence and regeneration of the littoral community of the lower Chicama Valley. The female and male skeletons occupying the tombs were probably from various outlying maritime household communities, including the domestic Units 13, 16, and 26 and possibly distant coastal areas as well (as one possibility suggested by the isotope studies on their teeth, see appendix 6).

Here I return to the issue of where the bodies are that were destined for the empty tombs at Huaca Prieta. Who were these people? Were they fisherfolk or shellfish divers lost at sea? The tombs are there, the offerings are there in the form of pockets of shells, but the bodies are missing. In these cases of unoccupied tombs, the living seemingly were deprived of the dead's remains. Today we witness this in the relatives of those who are kidnapped, of soldiers missing in action, of the victims of airplane crashes, and of those who perished in death camps or became *desaparecidos* during the dictatorships of the 1970s in Latin America. Local fisherfolk informed us that when fishers die at sea an empty tomb with their netting or other fishing equipment is prepared for them in the local cemetery.

So what do such testaments tell us about the human obligation to the corpses at Huaca Prieta, whether missing or not? Do they tell us that the corpse, or its remains, possessed a kind of attraction and that in many cases the event of death remained unfinished or unrealized until a person and his/her remains were reunified and the latter disposed of ritually? I speak of death here as the completion of the life cycle, for we have seen that a person can die biologically, yet not in a full social sense (Hertz 1960; compare Dillehay 1995). This does not mean that the missing or unburied were doomed to remain dead in the memory of their living kin. Rather, it implies that the work of getting the dead to die socially was nearly impossible when the dead body was missing. To put it in terms more relevant to an earlier discussion, the contribution of the dead to the ongoing totality and continuity of the society, from past to present, could not be realized until a tomb was built and occupied. I am not concluding that the purpose of all funeral rites at Huaca Prieta was to reunify

living persons and the remains of the dead so as to perpetuate their bonds and their contribution to the society at large. On the contrary, the obligation was probably an imperative to dispose of the corpse so as to liberate and separate the living from its embrace and ritually place the corpse into the realm of the ancestors by removing it from other corpses and from the living.

In this sense burial rituals also served to effect a ritual separation between the living and the dead and to separate the image of the deceased from the corpse to which it remained bound at the moment of death. That is, before the living could detach themselves from the dead, they first had to be detached from their remains so that their images could find their place in the afterlife of the imagination. For what was a corpse if not the after-image of the person who had vanished, leaving behind a lifeless likeness of himself or herself? If the corpse embodied or held on to the person's image at the moment of death, funeral rites served to disentangle that nexus and separated the two into discrete entities with independent fates—the corpse consigned to the earth and the image assigned to its afterlife and prolonged social death (at least until its memory was no longer promoted), whatever form that afterlife imagery may have taken in any cultural framework. The difference between the dead and the living thus lies in the form of the image, whether it was a tomb, a clay or stone statue, or a photograph, in today's world. Eventually the afterlife itself would have expired, at which point biological death gave way to social death: the individual was no longer so important. Yet as long as the undead cared for the dead and for the tombs of the dead, the place of that persistence remained open. The living's obligation to the corpse was thus only one manifestation of this responsibility. The living had an obligation to "finish" the death that put an end to both biological and social life.

The secondary burials in Huaca Prieta and in Unit 16 also can be seen as a form of separation, but in a different manner. Robert Hertz (1960) views secondary burials as acts of separation or liberation of the dead, allowing them to finally die. He sees burial rituals as changing the nature of the dead so that they are more remote from the living: releasing the bond between the two and liberating the soul of the corpse from its body. The attitude of the living to the dead also changes. In the rituals that Hertz considered, the dead were separated by being removed away from the living, while the living were separated from the dead by being removed from them. To Hertz, a ritually sacrilegious attitude is forced on the living, making them consider their relatives irreversibly dead, and consequently separates the dead from the living in a definitive manner. After the secondary funeral, the soul of the dead is said to change its state and to distance itself even further from the living. Thus secondary burial can be taken as another degree of separation. It also is a form of deliberate material fragmentation of the human body: many of the secondary burials at Huaca Prieta are fragmented, with only a few skeletal bones present or most missing (see chapter 8 and appendix 10). At this point we also can ask whether fragmentation and partial skeletal loss due to secondary burial represent a further degree of separation. Did the spatial separation of primary and secondary burials represent segmentation of generations, of social groups, or of legacies? Did disarticulated or partial skeletons represent a form of alienating the corpse, creating a rupture between the living and the dead within the society, removing or separating the dead further from the living and the society at large?

REPETITION, INALIENABILITY, AND CONTINUITY

Death and corpses raise other issues of continuity, memory, and repetition, for there could not have been memory and continuity without repetition. Death and burial represent continuity that transcends the past and present to project into the future. The living had obligations to the memory of the dead. In return, the dead help the living to know themselves, to give form to their lives and to their pasts, to organize social relations through genealogical accounts, to distribute property based on ancestral rights, and to prepare for what was to come—the unborn. The dead provide the living with a social order needed to maintain institutional order. The dead are guardians of the living. In return, the living give the dead a future so that the dead in turn can give a past to the living and to the unborn. In other words, the living help

the dead live on so that they can help the living and the unborn move forward. This moving forward relates to how the personhood of the dead is individually and socially constructed and represented, with recourse to memory and ancestors, and invoked mnemonically through substances, material offerings, and ideas about the body and the way it is buried. The continuity of memory, however, requires repetition.

Although burials at Huaca Prieta have variations, they occur repetitively throughout the mound, with many of their elements being consistently repeated, especially placement within small, circumscribed ritual association with offerings and burned things and deliberate breakage of some human bones. Continuity in burial stratigraphy and in burial patterns (with the exception of the appearance of the chamber tombs in Phases IV and V, which mark a different pattern) reveals a limited but repetitive set of norms passed down through generations. In this regard burial patterns seem to have operated under the transgenerational governance of a ritually construed, rule-bound performance of tomb-making. The repetition of burial rituals in the mound must have entailed the renewal and redetermination of the legacies of ancestors.

But why so many repetitive rituals and burials at Huaca Prieta? Did repetition serve to remind people of their past and of their obligation to the future? In reflecting on death and its meaning to the living, Heidegger (1927: 23) defined repetition as a future-directed retrieval of the past that is based on a "resolute embracing" of its mortality, ongoingness, and heritage. The more resolutely people contemplate and anticipate their death, the more they are forced back upon their personal ancestry, their own life history, and the things to come in their absence. Resolute anticipation leads to greater reflection upon the roles and contributions of people's ancestors as well as their own role and accomplishment in life. It rejuvenates certain stories and selected legacies of the ancestors, drawing individuals from all generations closer together. As Heidegger (1927: 32) notes, "repetition" also implies a transfiguration based not necessarily on a recycling of the past but on "a wonderful act of selection, exclusion, juxtaposition" that gives new life to the legacies of ancestry. If we accept the possibility of similar meanings at

Huaca Prieta, then the repetition of ritual burials there would have been a way of relating to generations of the dead, to ancestry, and to projecting legacies into the future.

The people buried in the informal graves and more formal chamber tombs at Huaca Prieta were special persons, selected for burial in the mound and for perpetuation of their ancestry. The presence of burials in the outlying sites, the scattered secondary remains of human skeletons in the mound, and burials in the chamber tombs all suggest a process of selection, exclusion, and juxtaposition of certain individuals. Their presence in different places and the commitment of selecting certain persons for placement in the mound represents resoluteness in the definition of the different ancestries and legacies of people who had lived in the area, who had built portions of the mound, and who had participated in rituals there.

TRANSGENERATION AND TRANSCENDENCE

In considering ideas about memory, representation, and the transmission of knowledge and experience from one generation to another and their possible meaning, it is easy for most archaeologists to ignore these issues and the world at large of past people. However, when we aggregate types and meanings of the material archaeological record, we run the risk of emptying out the experience and knowledge of the past that people engaged in constructing in the first place. In the affective or expressive realm, apart from their functional effects, rituals and commensal feasting provide collective venues for esoteric thinking and for connecting people with their past, their memories, and their future. Rituals and feasts also convey a sense of transcendent beliefs and other practices in which transcendence can be a process of looking beyond things of the mundane world to grasp their essence in another world, but, perhaps more importantly, to envision and anticipate things to come in the next generation and in the future. It also is about individual roles and occupations within the society that endured and survived beyond the death of a single individual.

Although mortuary rituals are a significant part of the composition of the mound at Huaca

Prieta, they were not the only rituals there. In fact numerous individual ritual spaces and stone-lined structures found throughout the mound (especially those in the sunken circular plaza) are not associated with burials. These spaces and structures appear to be related to a high frequency of small-scale ritual acts performed by small groups of people leaving a wide variety of offerings ranging from coca leaves, gourd and textile fragments, and tied bundles (see chapter 12) to pockets of shells, all of which were deliberately torn, smashed, or cut and deposited. (We should keep in mind that reference to fragmented objects means only those that were recovered in ritual contexts as offerings on the zigzag footpaths on the ramp, on the floors of defined ritual spaces, and in other sacred areas. Many broken and crushed plant and faunal remains resulting from trampling and unintentional breakage in all sites do not fit within the category of deliberately fractured materials considered here.) The segmented spaces where these rituals took place are much more predominant than the graves and tombs throughout all cultural phases at Huaca Prieta (see fig. 7.34). These nonmortuary rituals may be related to overarching transgenerational social and economic concerns in the society rather than specifically to the relationship between the living and the dead of a single generation or across generations. This may be most significant in Phase II to early Phase IV, when there appear to be few graves and formal tombs in the mound. Chamber tombs begin to dominate the upper and central portions of the mound in late Phase IV and in Phase V.

In working with Mapuche shamans and their ritual world over the past four decades in south-central Chile (for example, Dillehay 1995, 2007, 2014), I have realized that most of the dead within a community are forgotten by the living within two to three generations, unless a deceased person was an exceptional leader, warrior, trader, or technician. Memory, notoriety, and celebrity in the Mapuche society are about specific contexts, events, roles, and places and not so much about the specific deceased involved. Offerings placed with the deceased in tombs are personal items usually forgotten within a single generation. Heirlooms passed from generation to generation, however, are more impersonal, more inalienable, transcending and belonging to a series of generations and thus to the society at large. The living members of the society understand and conceptualize these differences between personal offerings placed in tombs and objects that actively stay with the living and pass from generation to generation. These objects are *kuel* (sacred mounds on the landscape), ritual stones (*llanca*), and occasionally ceremonial textiles (Dillehay 2007).

At first I resisted any attempt to employ an ethnographic analogy such as the Mapuche to the archaeological record of Huaca Prieta. After all, these two societies are separated by several millennia and by several thousand kilometers. Despite differences in time and space, however, the archaeological records of both Huaca Prieta and the Mapuche are fundamentally Andean in nature and thus share certain organizing principles and beliefs (compare Dillehay 2007; Latcham 1924; Menghin 1962). I began to consider in more detail how grave offerings, heirlooms, and deliberately fragmented materials relate to beliefs about religion, social obligation, exchange networks, and other institutions extending beyond the lives of a single person or generation could be brought together to interpret the record of Huaca Prieta. In reviewing the literature on these issues beyond my experience with the Mapuche, the thinking of John Chapman (2000), Annette Weiner (1992), and Maurice Bloch (1971, 2010) (particularly their notions of fragmentation, inalienable objects, and the transcendental social, respectively) provide much of the conceptual basis for interpreting this record.

Chapman has developed a narrative on social practices related to materiality by defining several interrelated concepts, (fragmentation, enchainment, inalienability, and accumulation) that should help us to conceptualize the meaning of artifact patterning at Huaca Prieta (see chapter 2). As noted earlier, the majority of the formal artifacts (such as textiles, gourds, and baskets) at Huaca Prieta are deliberately smashed, scored, torn, cut, and snapped to create fragments (see chapters 11 and 12). For Chapman, fragmentation is the intentional breakage or burning of objects and their deliberate separation and deposition rather than discard. Fragmentation is important to his idea of "enchainment," which is the connection of social relations that are repetitively constructed through the intentional deposition of fragmented

objects that are inalienable but also imbued with the personal qualities of their collective owners through time (Chapman et al. 2007: 4). The idea is that "fragments of objects transmit not only the symbolism of their complete, once-intact form but also the enchained, the fractal, connotations of past makers and owners" (Chapman 2000: 39). What makes an object "inalienable is its exclusive and cumulative identity with particular series of owners" and their distinctive biographies across many generations (Weiner 1992: 33). In this way, inalienable possessions are transcendent things (such as heirlooms) that are kept and accumulate biographies through time. It is thus the collection of individual biographies and heirlooms that constitutes the collective history of a community. By extension, the gathering or accumulation of sets of fragmented objects that are relatively devoid of the intimate personal connotations of a single individual (although they usually possess the qualities of many individuals) also is significant to Chapman's argument. It is the recursive practice of fragmenting objects, infusing them with animacy and agency, and then accumulating them in the same place that connects or enchains people with others and with particular enactments or settings that can explain the composition of fragmented artifacts at Huaca Prieta. The continued fragmentation and accumulation of objects and how they enchained people across generations are in essence routine or repetitive behaviors, which are aspects of constructing the society and transmitting knowledge across generations and thus "necessary to maintain *ontological security* [my emphasis]" (Giddens 1984: 76).

As discussed earlier, burial patterns and rituals transcend the short time span of the lives of individual community members and represent continuity of the community, of the roles of the members within it, and of their relations and exchange networks through time. These overarching aspects of a society exist and persist independently of individual members. As Bloch (2010: 157) has pointed out, these aspects "survive irrespective of birth, death or other transformations of the members." Bloch calls this phenomenon the "transcendental social," which develops an institutional life of its own beyond the members making it up and operates on a different timescale. He also argues that despite fluctuations in the lives of individual members the transcendental social is more institutionally stable, connecting ancestors, the living and the unborn, and their histories across time to give identity to kin groups and communities. Hence the transcendental social is largely an "invisible" entity or world that achieves reality through rituals enacted by members of each generation, which develop and reiterate the roles of peoples and communities. In this regard ritual serves to remove or separate individuals from their daily routines of everyday life, shifting them away from other community leaders.

Human interaction of a normal sort, as in the case of language, depends on the mutual reading and adjustment of intentionalities. . . . It is our continually modified and adjustment understanding of others that govern our interpretation of their actions or of their words. This continuous ever-changing flux is what is denied in the transcendental world of the roles and corporate groups . . . one of the principal aspects of the usual meaning of the word "ritual" is that it makes intentionality impossible to locate. . . . This is because ritual defers intentionality in the sense that the imagined originators of the actions, or of the sounds of ritual, be they words or otherwise, are not the actors or speakers. These latter defer to others, in the sense that they *follow* those who showed them how to act in ritual circumstances. . . . Ritual thus leeches out intentionality and the tumult of a life continually created by actions to make it the static world where roles and corporate groups can exist. This is the transcendental social. (Bloch 2010: 158)

In addition to ritual, Bloch sees that the "invisible imaginary world of the transcendental social" becomes real and practical through its expressions in material culture. As one example, he cites the role of sacred landscapes in Australian Aboriginal rituals, whereby their association with rituals is "ritualized" not just because people perform spiritual and religious acts there but because the landscapes are "transcendentalized into a concept" that gives the real physical landscape meaning beyond its empirical and visible presence.

It is relevant to the argument here that the transcendental social does not belong to a single individual, group, or generation; it transcends them through time and circumstance to become both a concept and a real entity through ritual participation as individual members represent their own generation through its material expression in the form of their grave sites and their personal offerings in the mound. The transcendental social, on the other hand, which also can be considered the wider overarching and continuing society, is represented by all graves and tombs through time and by offerings of nonpersonal or inalienable materials in nontomb areas (such as pockets of shells, plant foods, and coca leaves). These inalienable offerings are different from the broken *Semele* sp. shells and the few textile fragments and stone tools placed in tombs. By belonging to no one and then to everyone and by being fragmented, they enchain all individuals of a social group, the dead, the living, and the unborn. In this regard the material record of the mound becomes a form of collective understanding and memory and the symbolic promotion of understanding and memory through time and across generations.

It is not known whether a single fragmented object offered outside of the tomb belonged to a single individual or to a single group. The whole reed bundles that contained individual fragments of textiles, gourds, shells, and other items (see chapter 12, part 1) are an exception to the fragmented objects. In Unit 3 we recovered two large intact or whole bundles wrapped and tied in reeds. Inside were broken shells, gourd fragments, and torn and pleated textiles (see chapters 7 and 12). Did these whole bundles represent a single group and the individual pieces represent single members of that group? These and other bundles were always found at the corners of the zigzag footpaths on the ramp (see fig. 7.11), suggesting that they were offerings perhaps related to processions, changing directions, or simply access to the mound.

FRAGMENTS AND COMPLEMENTARY OPPOSITES

I began this book by commenting on the snippets and material fragments of human bodies, textiles, gourds, salt, charcoal, and many other items and the segmented floors, use surfaces, and other spaces in the mound at Huaca Prieta. In chapter 2 I considered concepts relevant to fractal theory and to the possible social meaning of fragmented and accumulated artifacts beyond their inferred functions and how this meaning can be expressed in conceptual terms that have meaning for us. We can presume that value was attached to whole commodities. Yet, if so, why were so many fragmented? Or was more value attached to fragments, not whole items, in nonburial ritual contexts? (D'Altroy [2002] has discussed the treatment and value of whole and fragmented objects in the early colonial era in Peru.) The purpose here is not to just show that mounds and other artifacts were fragmented (or fractal), but to discuss why they were fragmented and why Huaca Prieta was composed of so many different and segmented building episodes and spaces. What are the implications of a prehistoric society with a segmented structure, and what role did it play in the formation of a segmentary or dual principle of organization in Andean societies (see Netherly 1990, 1993), which involved two recursive structures of opposing yet complementary social units forming a whole entity? Was this organization an aspect of Huaca Prieta ontology, and, if so, what was its wider meaning and legacy?

In turning to the most prolific case of complementary opposition, how do we explain the enormous and continuous accumulation of charcoal and salt at Huaca Prieta and their absence or rarity at other late Preceramic mounds along the coast of Peru? Charcoal appears in the form of an infinite number of flecks throughout the mound; salt appears in layers and piles of crystals that were deliberately placed in the mound, added to mortar and plaster, poured over the floors of certain tombs and bodies, and stored in large off-mound caches (see chapter 7 and appendix 1). These two opposing elements serve no obvious biological, technological, or economic purposes and must be considered in light of many repetitious acts and probably changing ontologies. We know that charcoal and salt represent the residual properties of fire and seawater, respectively, which alternatively may be seen as depicting cooperatively coexistent or antagonistic forces of nature within the local environment (or universe from a wider perspective). Certainly something about fire and water represents a dichotomous symbolism that encapsulates their contradictory powers of creation and destruction or birth and death, respec-

tively. Fire transforms and can destroy. Water creates and sustains. This signals a dialectic unity of opposites, a conflicting and dividing model of fluidity. That is, a waxing and waning, a dynamic of these properties, was created in the mound by repetitively burning plants, thus reducing them to charcoal, and pouring saltwater on the mound, thus accumulating salt (from evaporated water). This fluid cycle through these elements of nature mediates between opposite states of creation and entropy or life and death. These elements also embody a metaphysic of alternating qualitative states: hot-cold, dark-light, fire-water, water-earth, and the alternating human conditions of life (the living and the dead) and death.

Did the continuous accumulation of charcoal and salt as metaphysical icons sculpt the contours of the socially constructed ritual relationships between the living and the dead at Huaca Prieta and their cosmological and physical worlds? Were human life and the unborn dependent upon the flows of fire and water during rituals on the mound? It was not simply that life and death were relative and that the universal condition of being was one of coming-to-be (that is, the unborn). Perhaps the cosmic or universal condition reflects an ontology of the "ongoingness of things," of being: the world as an eternal becoming, ubiquitous change and conflagration (Eliade 1958: 194). Mircea Eliade thought that the fire and water in the cosmogenesis of ancient societies did not denote some basic building material but rather metaphorically referenced principles of change, a concern with the condition and finitude of the universe, with the temporality of events as a passage from life to decay, and ultimately entropy and anti-entropy. Again, we can ask whether the opposing interplay and continuous deposition of charcoal and salt/fire and water at Huaca Prieta represent a worldview that the accretion or accumulation (see the discussion on Chapman in chapter 2) of bodies and other material things entailed depletion or entropy elsewhere in the world: for instance, the depletion of natural resources such as wetlands, schools of fish, human diseases and death, or drought impacting crops? Were opposing and complementary ecological zones and their different resources (such as the rocky and sandy littorals or the sea and terrestrial resources: see chapter 9) part of this littoral worldview? Were these and other resources occasionally overexploited, which might have caused alarm in the society? Did the presence of opposing elements such as fire and water ritually depict the ebb and flow of changing social circumstances and tension?

In the southern Andean world of the Mapuche there is a continuous flow between entropic and anti-entropic forces. These flows are efficacious because they impinge upon, relate, and define the changing social ties among ancestors, the living, and the unborn; as such they constitute symbolic, referential, and communicative behavior (Dillehay 2007). That is, flows from one entropic or anti-entropic state to another in the Mapuche world are simply ontological adjustments to environmental and social changes. These adjustments help to sift and format their world for decisions, practices, and experiences premised on concerns with the potentials immanent to all beings and things. These concerns are played out in multiple, repetitive private and public rituals that tie the ancestors and deities to the living, to the unborn, and to the inevitability of the life to death cycle.

People living in the Huaca Prieta area surely were faced with the natural inevitability of their own universe, an entity that probably was often unresponsive to their intervention or agency. By contrast, transformation and change in the Huaca Prieta society were probably understood, if not mediated, by private and probably occasional small-scale public rituals. This mediation could have been effected by and necessitated roles for human and nonhuman agents, such as ritual specialists who employed esoteric and mythic knowledge (Helms 1992) and specific natural elements to mediate between the ancestral and the living world by using fire and water and other opposing and mediating forces to reconcile and understand the forces of nature. The presence of esoteric things such as exotic malachite, rock crystals, copper sulfate, and *Spondylus* and scallop shells at Huaca Prieta and the presumed knowledge associated with them suggests that they were put to use in order to make sense of or appropriate external learning while retaining local agency. From this perspective, ritual and cosmology must have provided a potential field for local people's agency to cause change in universal states or flows, including the flow and cycling of birth, life, and death. As discussed earlier, there can be no death

without life: life comes about only through cycles of death and rebirth, which brings us back to the dynamics of the human body and its wider meaning in both its forms of life and death.

The imagery of fluidity and cycling holds as true for the microworld of the self and physical body as it does for the Andean cosmos (Bastien 1985; compare Allen 2002). Whatever can be said about the hydraulics of the cosmos appears equally applicable to the systemic workings of people's biological flows. Closer attention to the body invites us to recast Joseph Bastien's accounts of the Andean cosmos and body as a conceptually unified system. That is, individual bodies can be regarded as transient rhizomatic or dendritic-like containers of fluids like inherited blood or as points along a flow of kinship or substance transformation. In a sense, it is the overall trajectory and continuity of flow that is ongoing and systemic and underwrites the structure of the Andean cosmos. Human bodies and their products, through death, decay, or entropy, are partible and transactable and eventually separated from the living. Although this decay in the form of biological death brings the physical flow of the body to an end, it does not necessarily terminate the social flow and memory of the dead. In following this line of argument, it is not simply that the bodies in the mound at Huaca Prieta emerge as an entire stratigraphic order of human burials through time, a mounded rhizomatic pattern of individual strata and the genealogical biographies of the dead connected by transgenerative rituals, births, and deaths, but rather that the decaying body fluids and the flow of seawater over them (once evaporated, leaving behind salt crystals in and around the skeletons in the tombs; see chapters 7 and 8) constituted "liquid currencies" for social transactions and for their continued negotiation of a social presence or memory and the continuity of the transcendental social through rituals. Fluid facts, the social facts about body fluids and the ecological facts about flowing (sea)water, and the mystical fluidity of factual embodiment came together in several tombs and in many other ritual contexts at Huaca Prieta. For whether the fluidity of the cosmos was etched in terms of blood, water, fire, charcoal, salt, or whatever, they all created rhizomatic flows in one form or the other in the individual sacred spaces and tombs constructed by people.

Moreover, in the ethnography of the Andes and Amazonia, the myths of origin that describe the relationship between the body and the cosmos commonly do so through the invocation of a sacred topography (Roe 1982). The notion of a sacred topography plays a critical role: the buried body becomes iconic of terrestrial and celestial geographies and the ways in which human agency intrudes into the establishment of a natural world order. In the sacred topography of Huaca Prieta, we find these lines of articulation and disarticulation of the segmented nature of the stratigraphy and ritual spaces and of the heavily fragmented nature of material things in the mound. Connections and disconnections capture the dynamics of social interchanges as mediated by hundreds of individual ritual episodes, the snippets composing the mound, the mound representing a bulletin board of transgenerational experiences, knowledge, and relations between the living and the dead. The mound is thus merely a point of segmentation, fragmentation, and accumulation that is crosscut by the lines of individual biographies over many generations, as manifested in the interconnected strata, pathways, and ritual spaces and artifacts. In this regard, there was a continuous flow of people and goods into and across the mound. It grew in a dendritic or rhizomatic form.

Moreover, we can speculate further that the mound as a rhizomatic model of local biographies and the cyclic connection among death, life, and the unborn depicts the interconnected social connections, like grass runners that in the process of mound construction and ritual accretion constantly ramified and spread out in many directions, giving the mound the repetitive elongated, oval form we see today. The mound at Huaca Prieta has no apparent center; rather, it has been decentered by multiple snippets, exits, and entries, which is precisely the spatial and architectural organization of the mound's long history. In other words, the rhizomatic pattern of the mound's interconnected physical and social history and the numerous biographies represented in it by the dead moves or flows along pathways without apparent beginnings or endings that were constantly created and formed by new connections and offshoots that were spatially segmented by related kin groups. Set in this context, what was ultimately depicted by the combined energy of seawater and fire was

harnessed in the materiality of the mound by people who were giving themselves a power to effect replenishment of both life and death, to transcend the lives of individual members of the society for the sake of continuity.

Not well understood within this context, however, is how the visual designs on gourds, painted stones, textiles, and baskets reflect these relationships or whether they even related to connections between the living and the dead, given that none of them occur as burial offerings. Perhaps it is most probable that the visual artwork on these materials expressed the identities of and was related to nonmortuary or specific work groups, social units, or lineage biographies. But this also seems not to be an acceptable explanation, because no textiles, painted stones, or baskets were found at Paredones and no decorated items whatsoever were recovered at the domestic sites, where task groups and social units were situated, respectively. There also is the issue of the invisible designs on the textiles and what they might imply (see chapter 12). Were the visible designs intended for the living and the invisible for dead, or were both intended in different ways for different segments of the public at large, including local and nonlocal people, and the invisible ones only for local people or, given their association with only the Huaca Prieta mound, only for fisherfolk? Whether the signals on textiles were invisible or visible, the interpretive stance here considers them as fields of practice reflecting a social imperative in their technological style, both in their socially embedded manufacture and in "complementary enactments" such as ritual action that involved offerings of textile bundles or wrapped objects. The presence of early artwork at Huaca Prieta is an enigma, because this type of symbolic expression is absent or weakly developed at other Preceramic mound sites in Peru.

FRAGMENTATION, ACCUMULATION, FRACTIONAL COHERENCE, AND THE INALIENABLE MOUND

Did the deliberately fragmented materials and at times human skeletons and the segmented ritual spaces at Huaca Prieta represent transgenerational heirlooms or the biographies of distinct social groups and, through their accumulative deposition in the mound, the enchainment of the living with the dead? Did the mound itself become an inalienable or impersonal object that resulted from its composition of hundreds of repetitive small-scale ritual episodes that transcended numerous generations and accumulated multiple kinship and social group biographies? Did the accumulation and enchainment of fragmented objects by the living bind transgenerational social and economic perpetuity of a segmented society? Were textiles, gourd vessels, baskets, and human skeletons deliberately broken, torn, and fragmented and their parts distributed and deposited as a way of building or sustaining a partitioned historical identity and biography of related users or owners within this society? Was a segmentary social organization part of the society's cultural logic for understanding their world?

Once again, we presently do not have answers to all of these questions. However, we perhaps can gain some understanding of the implications of these questions by considering the cultural logic, dual principle of social segmentation, and opposing numbers and social entities that have governed traditional Andean societies (for example, Allen 2002; Netherly 1993; Sallnow 1987: 145). One study in particular offers insights into principles of division and their relation to numbers and objects in the Andean world. The ethnographer Gary Urton (1997) has argued that the origin and meaning of numbers in the Andes relates to people's ideas about and formulations of gender, age, and social relations. He believes that Quechua arithmetic, for example, is based on a well-articulated body of philosophical principles and values that reflects a continuous attempt to maintain balance, harmony, and equilibrium in the material, social, and moral spheres of community life.

Urton postulates that paired numbers in the Quechua world are conjunctions of two opposite but complementary things closely bound together as something that can be one. For example, the term *yanantin* refers to a husband-wife team, a dual unit within local society that expresses part-to-whole relations. A member of this pair that is separated from the other is thought to be single, alone, and incomplete, that is, an unchained or fragmented part if we follow my usage of Chapman's logic. According to Urton, paired elements are therefore fundamental entities of ordination and enumeration and an aspect of the dual organization that is fundamental to the Andes. And enumeration is always concerned with a sense of completeness, balance, and symmetry that is a goal to be achieved by society. (See part 1 of chapter 12, where Splitstoser makes a similar argument for paired entities and numbers in the weaving technology of cotton textiles.) Urton also explains that arithmetic operations of summation, subtraction, multiplication, and division serve social principles of "rectification." When circumstances produce imbalances, incomplete sets, or disharmony, action must be taken by the society to restore balance. The arithmetic procedures of subtracting from one set, adding to the other, redividing units, and so on, are aimed at "rectifying" the imbalance. Separation, division, or fission of units can also be used to achieve rectification.

To Urton, each number or numerical symbol also defines an identical space, wherein visible realities must be perceived in order to contact the unseen forces that contribute to them. Only in this way can the forces of nature be transformed into the necessary objects of cultural use. In each instance a synthesis is achieved that brings the object into harmony not only with the other elements but also with the overarching structure of the entire culture. It is the act by which family and nature is organized into a pervasive, comprehensible pattern of reality or, as Benjamin Schneider (1976) called it, "cultural logic." Moreover, symbols used to evoke and organize acts depend on multireferential or multiple meanings that extend to every configuration of cultural expression. As such, different meanings result from a layering of experience wherein every action recapitulates the whole yet is only explained by the accumulation of all the parts. In practice the society thus seeks expressions of equilibrium, balance, and harmony in relations between and among number sets, groupings, and collections. Thus in Quechua society and culture, past and present, the goal and purpose of numerical practices seems to have been the establishment and maintenance of such harmony and balance "in the real world, which is part of people's ontology" (Urton 1997: 218). We also should note, in keeping with the logic of Bloch's arguments discussed earlier, that enumeration can be seen as an overarching institutional form of the transcendental social that has both a visible and an invisible manifestation, the former expressed in the quipu and the actual number of material objects used daily by people and the latter represented by concepts such as *yanantin* and dual division.

Furthermore, Urton's vision of the connection between Andean numbers and kinship units and their incompleteness until all parts are in harmony or form a comprehensible cultural logic is similar to the arguments that I am making about broken, smashed, or fragmented artifacts and about the individual segmented ritual spaces that were accumulated and enchained in the mound at Huaca Prieta to place and record the biographies of the dead, the living, and the unborn in a cohesive, harmonious society. Obviously, we cannot draw a direct analogy between the Quechua of today's world and the littoral Preceramic society of 7000–4000 years ago, but it is probable that several aspects of this logic and ontology are related historically. That is, the Quechuas' organizing principles of divisions, numbers, things, people, and harmony and their cohesion have their roots in earlier Andean societies. The presence of Preceramic segmented societies and their later development into more complex dual systems has been extensively documented in the Andes (for example, Bernier 2009; Netherly 1990, 1993; Netherly and Dillehay 1986). It is highly probable that sites such as Huaca Prieta were experimenting with or were one of the early expressions of dual social organization in the Andes, as seems to be expressed in the dual economy, the opposing structures in the sunken plaza (see chapter 7), the different types of weaving technologies (see chapter 12), and the dual and complementary symbolism shown in the marine faunal assemblages (see chapter 9). During the early Preceramic stages of development of society, people were probably widely experimenting with social and natural connections, sorting out things, and understanding by creating and changing their worldviews and adjusting themselves to them. But much of this experimentation began in earlier times, the late Pleistocene and early Holocene periods in many places, including other areas of northern Peru where the signs of social divisions appear in hunter-gatherer households (see Dillehay 2013).

ORGANIZING DIVISIONS IN THE LOWER CHICAMA VALLEY: A SEGMENTED OR FRACTAL ANDEAN SOCIETY

In the lower Chicama Valley the numerical increase and segmented concentration of communities in and around specific types of wetlands along with economic specialization are the principal factors organizing the Preceramic society, with opposite settlements on the north and south banks of streams and deltas (see chapter 13). Each wetland or delta community was physically separated from others by stretches of beaches or dry, open terrain. Each community apparently was divided into a number of households, as evidenced by individual household mounds and clusters of household mounds. The process of spatial differentiation among household communities probably was fundamental to the working of the littoral residential and specialized fishing and farming communities. Hypothetically, it may have permitted one segment to expand faster than another of the same group over time and yet not altered the structural relationship between them. It also may have enabled the structural alignment of social groups, established when they were mere clusters and divisions within a single community, to be maintained despite the expansion of any group to community size and beyond. As in the Bandurria site (Chu Barrera 2011), spatial separation seems to have been an index of economic specialization and social segmentation that was hierarchical, with unequal access to resources. But, in addition, spatial separation may have led to some measure of independence, including ritual independence for small groups using Huaca Prieta for burial or other ritual purposes, depositing similar types of artifacts, defining and building similar types of individualized circumscribed ritual spaces, and burning small packages of plant material. The wider concept here is a segmentary economy, settlement, and kinship system, as suggested by location and also by two (if not more) basket and textile weaving technologies (see chapter 12) and by two distinct sets of design motifs on decorated gourds and textiles (see chapters 11 and 12). A second aspect serves the purpose of stressing interpersonal links between the living and the dead and, by extension, between different living people continuously participating in rituals and other activities at Huaca Prieta.

Consideration of these linkages brings us back to division, segmentation, fragmentation, and fractal patterns. The most consistently fragmented and dispersed materials at Huaca Prieta are the textiles, baskets, and gourds but also human skeletons, shells, animal bones, and other items and, in a microsense, the millions of charcoal flecks and salt crystals. As reported in chapter 12, the cotton textiles, nets, and reed baskets show a great deal of physical trauma from deliberate tearing and cutting either prior to or during their ritual deposition on the mound. Despite this trauma, the textiles show little, if any, use wear, suggesting that they were not meant to be worn or used but to be ritually torn and deposited. Although the textiles demonstrate much technological variety and experimentation, they appear to be sensitive indicators of social and economic change (see Murra [1962] for the social importance of cloth in the Andes). It is apparent from Huaca Prieta and its material record that the textile fragments served few purposes, relating primarily to ritual practices, memory, identity construction and maintenance, and, despite their absence in the majority of tombs and a complete absence at Paredones, the enchainment of the living, the dead, and the unborn.

This allows us to observe how small elements, whether they be individual households, secondary burials, small spaces of ritual activity on the mound, or torn pieces of textiles and cut/snapped gourd fragments, were rhizomatically inserted into a continuous, accumulative, and coherent whole within the Preceramic society of the lower Chicama Valley (following Chapman and Law): the whole mound and the whole littoral settlement pattern itself. If we interpret the artificial structure of the mound, the settlement pattern, and the inferred social structure fractally (that is, all of the segmented or fractured episodes, individual layers, and fragmented objects and segmented spaces making up the mound), we do not distinguish between any of the individual episodes. All of them are essential and so perceived create a greater (fractal) coherence—a single mound with a long transcendental social history. It could be said, in this light, that the general form or "monumentality" of the mound at Huaca Prieta

is thus not what counts the most. Rather, what is important is the way in which all of the rhizomatic parts and episodes hold it together as a megasite with wider, long-term meaning, history, and purpose.

The second observation is that the set of all mound-building and ritual episodes at Huaca Prieta constitutes an approximate model of the kind of fractal society exemplified by the settlement pattern and by the specialized economies in the study area: a segmented, dispersed, but complementary one. This idea could be carried forward by hypothesizing a simple process of "budding out" or fissioning of households and littoral communities from Phases II to V, which is a realistic assumption for this early period and which gives rise to the segmented architectural composition of a similar nature at the Pulpar mound (see chapter 13) and perhaps in the Phase II levels of Paredones.

Furthermore, it would seem that any household or household group that is identified with a tomb or clustered set of tombs at Huaca Prieta would have this quality as well, although this is difficult to prove empirically. But there also seems to be segmentation in the tomb architecture, with some chamber tombs standing alone in different areas of the site (such as Unit 10) and others agglutinated (such as Unit 23: see chapter 7). We can surmise the membership of agglutinated tomb groups by speculating that a tomb group possibly consisted of closely related dead. And tomb groups may have represented outlying social groups of household clusters. (Only genetic studies of the human skeletons can resolve this issue.) As stated throughout this book, there is no hard evidence in the form of a more elaborate tomb, differentiated burial offerings (except for the one adult male with the sculpted blocks of polychaete tube-base in Unit 16), a larger house (although few were completely excavated), or the accumulation of goods by an individual to suggest the presence of an elite or social hierarchy.

Given that the mound at Huaca Prieta is not a sign of elite domination and formally organized corporate ceremony, then why and how was it built and by what kind of social organization and ontological system? In the Preceramic period people must have dealt with a changing society, a growing population, changing environments, changing relations with interior groups, and an incipient "globalizing" coastal world, especially during Phases IV and V. Integrating people for long periods in ways that were socially acceptable and establishing their presence in the natural environment must have been major concerns. Societies can be organized in one of various ways, either from the top down or from the bottom up or horizontally. As noted above, most organizational models for the Preceramic period of Peru propose that mounded sites like Huaca Prieta were designed to aggrandize leaders, the standard top-down model. People also organized from the bottom up rather than from the top down, however, where the wider community was often privileged over an individual or a small group of individuals. In bottom-up societies people are often integrated through a common system of beliefs or ideas about how the world works: cosmologies (Renfrew 2001). Preliterate societies often concretized cosmologies where the landscape took on a meaning that signified connections among society, the supernatural, space, and time. Colin Renfrew (2001) calls such places "Locations of High Devotional Expression," which are monuments to ideas rather than to people. These places can be recognized by unusual architecture, unusual scale, or unusual locations. Renfrew argues that these places were built outside of normal political economies and need to be understood as the result of powerful belief systems and worldviews rather than in the contexts of Western notions of elite power and wealth. They also can be bottom-up societies. Yet bottom-up models inherently imply a top somewhere. Although Huaca Prieta can be considered a place of High Devotional Expression, neither a top-down nor a bottom-up layer seems fully to explain its presence and construction. Instead during most of its history Huaca Prieta seems to have been more of a decentralized lateral or horizontal society composed of multiple littoral household communities. As demonstrated earlier, during its final phases of use, when an entry ramp and sunken circular plaza were built, it might have begun to have been organized following a top-down or bottom-up model.

Ethnographers have pointed out how complex yet relatively decentralized societies such as the Navajo, Mapuche, Hopi, Tikopia, and others can organize large-scale projects without the investment of power in a single individual or a solitary top-down political hierarchy, instead using ritual, ideology, and ceremony as a means of integration (for example, Adler and Wilshusen 1990; Dillehay 2007; Vega-Centeno 2007: 153). The act of building a mound is a ritual process disconnected from use of the finished monument (for example, Dillehay 2007; Knight et al. 2010; Vega-Centeno 2004). Building Huaca Prieta was a long-term transgenerational, communal ritual act that served to integrate people rather than to support individual social power. In this framework Huaca Prieta was a large "inalienable" object, important as a communal symbol justifying the existence of a wider ongoing community rather than as a badge for those few who were socially powerful.

In addition to economic, political, social, and symbolic reasons, there must have been ontological reasons as well for building Huaca Prieta (and Paredones). Understanding the site as something more than just a monument to a socioeconomic commitment to a place on the landscape and how it related to the lower Chicama Valley society requires a different view of how the people living there may have seen themselves in relation to their world. People must have seen themselves as a component of a larger natural world and structured their lives according to their place in and understanding of it. People's existence was probably more often than not conditioned by cultural practices designed to ensure harmony within their social and natural worlds (see MacCormack 1991/1993 for harmony in Andean society).

In summary, the archaeological evidence suggests that Huaca Prieta was a component of a larger landscape that concretized sacred ideals in the built environment. In doing so, members of several segmented yet transgenerationally related social units (outlying household sites?) along the littoral zone and in the interior wetlands came together to create the sacred at Huaca Prieta. Building the mound was a necessary ritual required to form a larger local community. The construction and use of the structure probably were based on the notion of an ontological whole, where numerous complementary interacting elements were required to do important cosmological (religious or ideological) work such as creating an icon like Huaca Prieta to integrate society.

Many small-scale elements and acts at the mound were probably linked through common beliefs about their necessary place in producing a harmonious local universe (not that this was ever fully achieved).

Huaca Prieta does not stand alone in human history in this regard. Vernon Knight (2006) views the large mounds constructed in the eastern United States as associated with a worldview about the underworld, birth, fertility, death, burial, the placation of spirits, emergence, purification, and supernatural protection. He suggests that mounds are related to ideas of Native American belief systems, which find objective expression in the artificial mound as an earth or world icon (compare Hall 1997). For the Mapuche of south-central Chile, cultural survival today depends on the construction of sacred landscapes and ceremonial mounds as ritual, therapeutic, symbolic, and aesthetic spaces and the effects of political policies on the physical shape of these landscapes (Dillehay 2007). These and other works argue for a more in-depth study of the historical, symbolic, and ontological importance of public ritual and meaning at large mound sites (Bradley 2000; Milner 2005; Scarre 2004). The communal architecture of these mounds must have concretized abstract notions about social, political, sacred, life/death, and/or historical beliefs and conveyed profound social meaning. They provided a communal icon that represented individual social groups and served as a connective structure that not only linked the past and the present but also created links within these dimensions on the basis of a common horizon of experience that united people and gave them orientation. When considered in these ways, megasites such as Huaca Prieta were inherently powerful not because of the labor expenditure or social order necessary for their design and construction; rather, they were powerful because of what they were and what they meant, as necessary components of the universe with the ability to link people to each other and to the natural world. This view of mounds gives Huaca Prieta a combined social, economic, and spiritual reason for being.

Despite the increasing complexity and regularity of both subsistence complementarity and ritual and ontological practice over the long term, it is effectively argued here that social differentiation and inequality and aggrandizement by factional or individual leadership, either within or between communities, are not archaeologically evident. In this social history, monument building and maintenance are seen as solving the problem of household community integration at different scales—a collective activity that mediated the stresses of settlement expansion and fission/fusion processes associated with other social changes through routinized symbolic expression. Although this interpretation stands in contrast to dominant traditional notions of "monumental architecture" as "tools of elite domination," there is some concordance with relatively egalitarian or communitarian alternate explanations offered for the origins of monumental ritual centers in other times and places, such as those in the altiplano Formative (Bandy 2004), which could be interesting for comparison.

This chapter has returned to themes of the nature of monumentality and early social complexity in societies without pronounced social inequality. A communitarian approach toward mortuary treatment is suggested, with burials seen not only as a way to manage the interface between community and ancestors but as one integral part of the larger tradition of routinized ritual at Huaca Prieta. Analogies and theoretical constructs of fragmentation, enchainment, inalienability, and accumulation have been invoked to explain how transgenerational practices of offering, prayer, and remembrance at Huaca Prieta united a community and constructed a transcendental social history over time. The mound structure and the community-affirming ritual activities within it are described here as rhizomatic, without a center, and fractal, reflecting the fractal forms of flexible and resilient segmentary social and kinship systems in the Preceramic period. This synthesis, while rather speculative compared to the rest of the volume, provides an inspirational argument for how ontological unity and incremental ritual action can enable the integration of complex yet relatively decentralized societies.

FUTURE RESEARCH

Despite the interdisciplinary research that we carried out at Huaca Prieta, many things are still not known about the site and the Preceramic period in the study area, although they are constantly being refined to ever more precise problems, such as pinpointing the geographic origins of the cultigens and other exotics, understanding how and why they arrived at Huaca Prieta and Paredones, and tracing their diffusion to other areas. More research also should be focused on the complex issues of kinship and social structure and how they are expressed materially. In particular, there is a lack of understanding of social differentiation and informal or formal leadership roles in Preceramic sites. Ritual has been at the forefront of discussion in these final chapters, but interpreting this and other topics in a more profound empirical and realistic manner remains a challenge. More precision also is required in establishing criteria for fully evaluating degrees of economic specialization, especially at the household and community levels. Particularly important in specific regard to Huaca Prieta is excavation of the outlying house mounds and the recovery and analysis of weaving and twining patterns of cotton textiles from them to determine whether they match some of the distinct textile techniques deposited in specific areas of the mound. Furthermore, despite the large number of radiocarbon dates, we still need more absolute dates and a refined chronology. Equally pressing is understanding communication and exchange along the littoral and any seafaring skills that littoral societies had. Other refinements should be directed at better definition of the nature of Preceramic interactions. In this context detailed analysis of burial data, household archaeology, gender relations, and genetic studies will be of great help. This includes the realization that the Preceramic world represents more than ideological and economic transition. Social organization and worldviews were an integral component of community interaction and ritual performance.

STRATIGRAPHY, SEDIMENTOLOGY, AND CHRONOLOGY AT HUACA PRIETA

Mario Pino

INTRODUCTION

Along the coast from Huaca Prieta and north to Huaca El Brujo are outcrops of three different geological units: the first and the second are Quaternary terraces of geological origin; the third corresponds to a mixture of natural and anthropogenic layers in the southwest and south margins of the Huaca Prieta mound. The altitudes in meters above sea level of the exposed units and layers in Huaca Prieta were calculated with a Total Station after a correction was applied to the highest position of vegetal debris on the beach that was deposited by the night high-tide water level on July 15, 2007. The altitude of the tide was obtained from tidal tables calculated by the software Tide24.

THE OLD TERRACE

The base of all landscape in the site area is a prominent Sangamon terrace (fig. A1.1a). The terrace is composed of a monotonous succession of beds made up of well-sorted cobbles, boulders, and sands well cemented by calcite. The most notorious feature of the terrace is the deep weathering of the clasts and the cement, which is over 0.5 m in depth. North of the site, near the old fishing village of the colonial period, visible in Bird's vertical image (Bird et al. 1985), the surface of the terrace is 11.6 masl, measured with respect to the current sea level. To the south, underneath the Huaca Prieta mound, the height is only 6 masl near TP-2, excavated by Bird, and 8.6 masl in Unit 1, excavated by Dillehay/ Bonavia. The degree of weathering (Lauer 1968) and the height of the terrace allow us to propose an interglacial age, probably of the Sangamon interglacial. The surface of the terrace is more than 2 m above the accepted international sea level in Sangamon times (Lambeck et al. 2002; Shackleton et al. 2003), but local and regional evidence along the coast indicates some tectonic uplift (Goy et al. 1992; Saillard et al. 2011; Wells 1996). Below the mound, the low height of the terrace surface, the completely flat morphology, and principally the absence of the upper weathered section suggest an anthropogenic transformation, implying borrowed sediments to build mounds in the area. Immediately along the border of the intertidal milieu outcrop a platform breaks the waves. That platform is formed by the same kind of layers that were observed in the terrace and thus correspond to older beds of the same feature. Bird et al. (1985) inter-

FIGURE A1.1. General profile of Sangamon terrace on the west and southwest sides of the mound at Huaca Prieta: *a*, view to the east of the old interglacial terrace with the surface at 11.6 masl; *b*, view to the east of the younger terrace on the southwest side of the Huaca Prieta mound in the foreground; the old interglacial terrace and a hill where basement volcanic rocks outcrop are in the background.

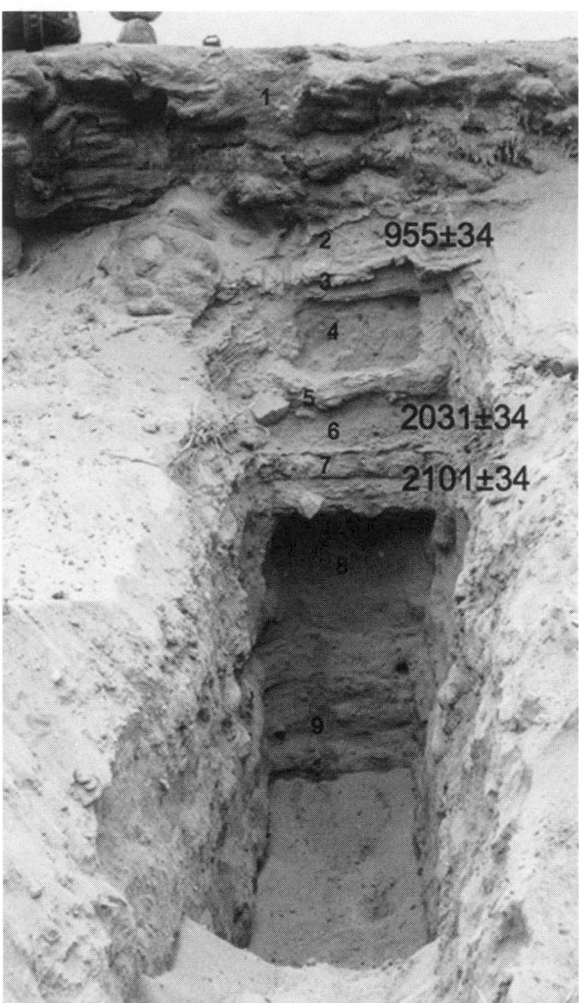

FIGURE A1.2. Close-up of stratigraphic profile of the THS pit in the younger terrace, showing the radiocarbon dates from different strata. See calibrated ages in the text. Strata numbers are referenced in figure A1.3.

preted some beds at Huaca Prieta as having been derived from tidal wave (tsunami) deposition. Geoarchaeological and archaeological work, however, reveals that these beds were not formed by tsunamis but are artificial and part of the retention architecture of the mound (see chapter 7).

After the February 27, 2010, earthquake and tsunami in central-south Chile (Moreno et al. 2010; Satake and Fujii 2010), it was possible to learn about the effects of capes and intertidal and subtidal platforms in the mitigation or cancellation of tsunamis. In the case of Chile, the town of Cobquecura (36° 08′ S) was not impacted by the tsunami, but immediately to the north and south (less than 10 km) the coast suffered waves of 20 m in height. This can help explain the absence of tsunami deposits at Huaca Prieta but their presence in the Chicama Valley at a distance of only 5 km south of the site (see chapter 5). In the Chilean 2010 tsunami the waves inundated the land with the highest wave height only in the estuaries and bays, probably due to the deeper ocean topography under the water. The same situation occurs at Huaca Prieta. Could this imply that the Huaca Prieta people learned over centuries that this location was safer from the effects of large tsunamis?

THE YOUNGER TERRACE

To the north of the site, near Huaca El Brujo, a well-defined terrace outcrops at an altitude of 3.5 masl (fig. A1.1b). The stratigraphy is very similar along the coast and can be described by profile THS (UTM 686430E 9124842S). This sequence varies between gray and light brownish gray colors (N8–N7) (fig. A1.2).

PROFILE THS

Layer 1 (60 cm thick): beach rock, moderate reddish brown (10R 4/6), well cemented by calcite, characterized by bioturbation structures, created probably by ghost crabs (*Ocypode gaudichaudii*) (fig. A1.3). A piece of charcoal recovered from a buried beach rock gave an age of 934–688 cal BP (AA76981; see tables 5.2 and 6.2 for most radiocarbon dates mentioned in appendix).

Layer 2 (20 cm): silty sand, very pale orange color (10YR 8/2), containing unidentified vegetal remains. The upper 2 cm were characterized by clean sand, similar to beach sand.

Layer 3 (5 cm): beach rock, with isolated cobbles at the base, similar to a storm or a beach berm deposit.

Layer 4 (14 cm): clean medium sand, light greenish gray (5G 8/1), with a high percentage of little (mm) carbonate fragments derived from shellfish.

Layer 5 (1 cm): dark greenish gray sand (5G 4/1), well-cemented beach rock.

Layer 6 (16 cm): yellowish gray silty sand (5Y 8/1), with vegetal remains similar to Layer 2.

Layer 7 (27 cm): dusky yellowish brown (10YR 2/2), medium to fine clean sand with remains of *Donax* sp. and unburned spines of sea urchins. This is similar to beach sand. A *Donax* shell gives an age of 2120–1899 cal BP (AA76985).

Layer 8 (40 cm): very pale orange (10YR 8/2), medium to fine clean sand with 8 intercalations of silt. In some intercalations, there are thin clay intraclasts. In the middle of the layer are only unburned spines of sea urchins.

Layer 9 (>30 cm): cobbles and boulders in a clean very light gray (N8) sand. This is similar to a beach berm.

The young terrace represents a beach environment, with some minor alluvial intercalation of fine sediments, as laminations, lenses, or intraclasts. In the field the height of the surface, the position near the actual beach, and the sedimentological composition allowed us to interpret the terrace as a middle Holocene high sea stand. The 2δ calibrated radiocarbon ages (913–751 and 1056–934 cal BP) indicate a late Holocene age. Thus the terrace was related to a drop in relative sea level (see chapter 5) and was affected by tectonic uplift. As in other parts of north Peru (Goy et al. 1992; Saillard et al. 2011; Wells 1996), the study area was constantly affected by vertical movements, probably until recent times, as evidenced by the presence of beach boulders and cobble ridges that are seen in the aerial photos in Bird (Bird et al. 1985) to the north of Huaca Prieta. The vertical uplift makes it almost impossible to recognize with precision the old stand of the sea level, at any point in time.

STRATIGRAPHY AND PALEOENVIRONMENTAL RECONSTRUCTIONS OF SOUTH AND SOUTHWEST MARGINS OF THE HUACA PRIETA MOUND

Using horizontal cords and an archaeological line-level set in accordance with the local sea level, we measured the stratigraphy of this area. Stratigraphic profiles were made by cutting and cleaning walls of the south and southeast sides of the mound. Twenty-two profiles were described at the centimeter scale, covering a total of 149 m of exposed stratigraphy. The 0 m in the horizontal scale is arbitrary and corresponds to the position of one of the first profiles, P2 (fig. A1.3). To differentiate natural from anthropogenic layers, we used the presence of charcoal, evidence of fire-cracked rock, remains of shellfish, and the presence of ceramic or stone artifacts. In general four types of sediments are found: sand, coarse gravel, organic deposits, and soils and diamictons. Some of the depositional environments were interpreted by comparison with recent deposits and experiments (for example, to differentiate effects of fire or salt on cobbles and boulders) and others by granulometric analysis of the sand fraction of the sediments (see the sedimentology discussions below). The key profiles are described below, from the north to the south. Figure A1.4a shows the extreme northern section of the stratigraphic profiles (see fig. A1.3 for numbered strata).

THE SOUTHWEST SECTION BETWEEN PROFILES 17 AND 14

Profile 17 (top at 450 cm above sea level [cmasl])

Layer 1 (5 cm thick): recent garbage and fine sediment deposit recently filled.

Layer 2 (6 cm): sandy silt, pale yellowish brown (10YR 6/2), with unidentified vegetal remains.

Layer 3 (6 cm): coarse partially cemented sand, grayish purple (5P 4/2).

Layer 4 (10 cm): clean medium sand, very light gray (N8).

Layer 5 (2 cm): beach rock.

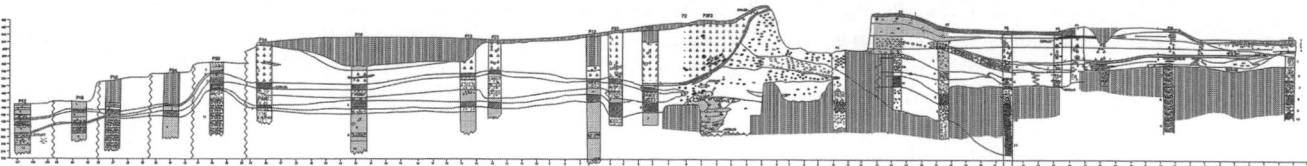

FIGURE A1.3. Close-up of stratigraphic profile along the south and southwest border of the Huaca Prieta mound referenced in the text. Strata numbers are referenced in figs. A1.4, A1.5, and A1.9.

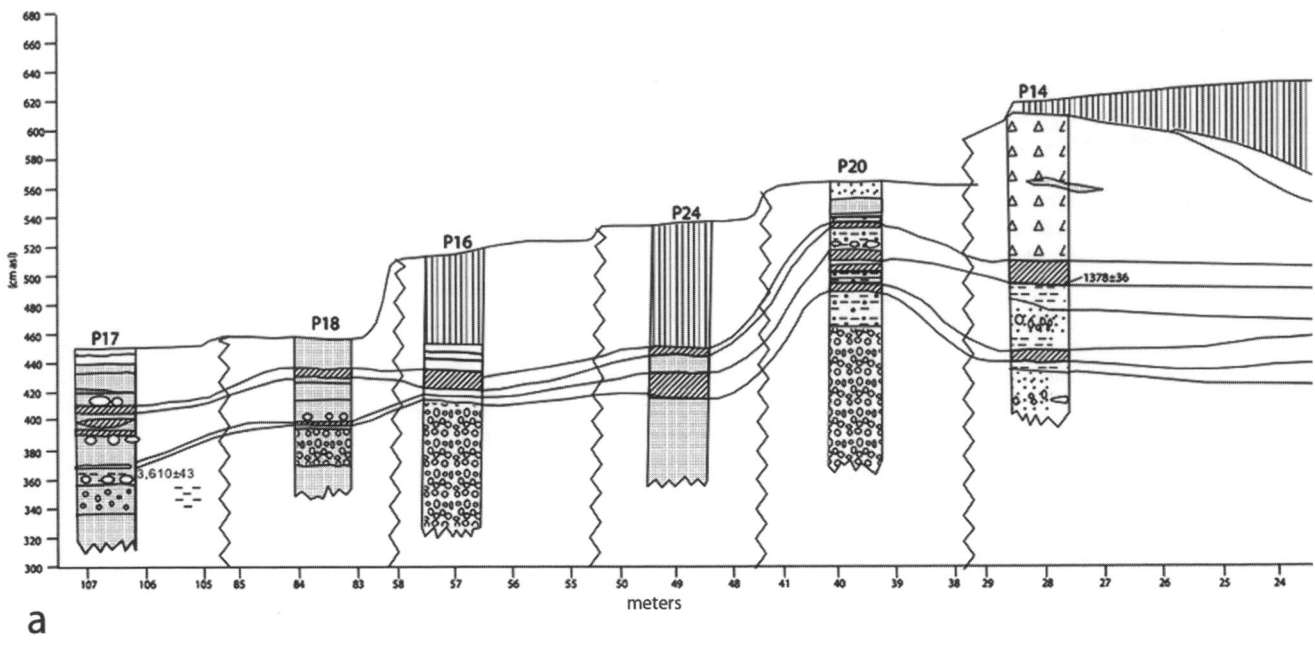

a

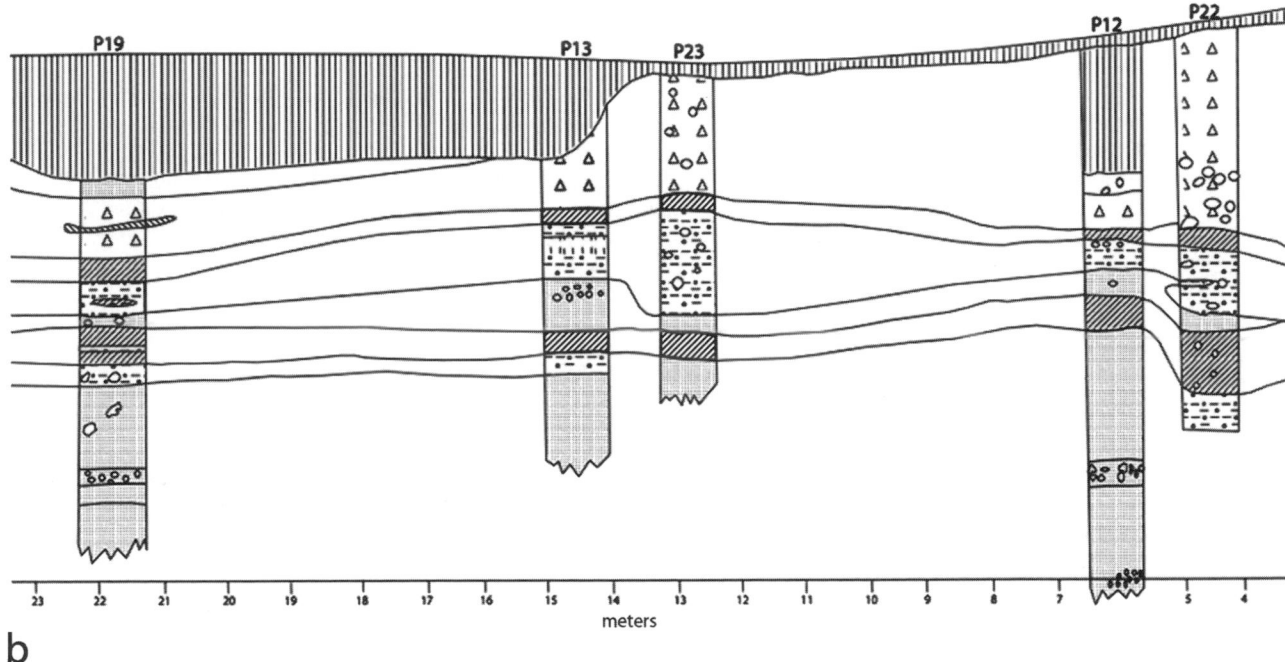

b

FIGURE A1.4. Close-up of stratigraphic profiles in the north and central sectors of the terrace: *a*, stratigraphic profiles 17, 18, 16, 24, 20, and 14 and proposed lithological correlations in the extreme north part of the section (note that the horizontal axis has two breaks); *b*, stratigraphic profiles 19, 13, 23, 12, and 22 and a proposed lithological correlation in the central part of the section (the horizontal axis is in meters; the vertical axis is in centimeters). Strata numbers are referenced in figure A1.3.

Layer 6 (5 cm): clean medium sand, medium light gray (N6), including isolated boulders with signs of heating by fire.

Layer 7 (17 cm): grayish brown (5Y 3/2) organic sediment, with two thin intercalations (lenses) of very coarse sand of very pale orange (10YR 8/2).

Layer 8 (20 cm): clean pinkish gray (5YR 8/1) sand with calcareous invertebrate remains, broken. On top are broken boulders with burning signs.

Layer 9 (2 cm): organic deposits like a peaty soil (grayish black, N2); a radiocarbon date was 3973–3702 cal BP (AA86953). In the neighboring profile, the date was 3618–3367 cal BP (AA86951).

Layer 10 (20 cm): rounded cobbles in a clean sand matrix (N8).

Layer 11 (>10 cm): clean very light gray (N8) medium sand.

Profile 16 (fig. A1.4a; see fig. A1.3 for numbered strata, top at 520 cmasl)

Layer 1 (7 cm thick): soft light brownish gray (5YR 6/1) sandy deposit, like a protosoil.

Layer 2 (3 cm): soft yellowish gray (5Y 8/1) sand.

Layer 3 (6 cm): grayish red purple (5RP 4/2), coarse sand with white inclusions due to the presence of salt crystals.

Layer 4 (10 cm): organic sediment, fine, grayish black (N2) sand.

Layer 5 (4 cm): clean medium sand, pinkish gray (5YR 8/1), in an incipient process of soil formation.

Layer 6 (5 cm): organic sediment, fine, grayish red purple (5RP 4/2) sand.

Layer 7 (>80 cm): rounded cobbles in clean sand matrix (N8, very light gray). At the top a protosoil developed.

Profile 20 (fig. A1.4a, top at 565 cmasl)

Layer 1 (12 cm): soft brownish gray (5YR 4/1) sandy deposit, like a protosoil.

Layer 2 (12 cm): grayish red purple (5RP 4/2) coarse sand, with white inclusions due to the presence of salt crystals.

Layer 3 (2 cm): beach rock.

Layer 4 (5 cm): light brownish gray (5YR 6/1) sand.

Layer 5 (2 cm): organic sediment, fine, brownish black (5YR 2/1).

Layer 6 (20 cm): greenish gray (5GY 6/1) sand, with isolated boulders showing signs of heating.

Layer 7 (8 cm): grayish black (N2) fine organic sediment.

Layer 8 (3 cm): light yellowish gray (5Y 7/2) sand.

Layer 9 (2 cm): fine, brownish black peaty sediment (5YR 2/1).

Layer 10 (5 cm): clean medium sand, light yellowish gray (5Y 7/2), in an incipient process of soil formation.

Layer 11 (3 cm): clean medium sand, light gray (N7).

Profile 14 (fig. A1.4a, top at 615 cmasl)

Layer 1 (1 cm): soft dusky brown (5YR 2/2) sandy deposit, like a protosoil.

Layer 2 (106 cm): diamictons composed of cobbles in a very pale orange (10YR 8/2) silt matrix, with irregular lenses of very light gray (N8) clean sand, similar to aeolian sand.

Layer 3 (14 cm): organic medium dark gray (N4) sediment; at the base is a concentration of charcoal, immediately below cobbles and sand with a light red color (5R 6/6) similar to a burned surface. The charcoal dated at 1302–1177 cal BP (AA81931; fig. A1.4a).

Layer 4 (5 cm): grayish orange pink (5YR 7/2) sandy protosoil.

Layer 5 (46 cm): clean pale blue (5PB 7/2) medium sand, with boulders dispersed in the layer. The upper contact is transitional to the protosoil.

Layer 6 (9 cm): anthropogenic deposit of grayish black (N2) with charcoal and fragments of calcareous invertebrates.

Layer 7 (4 cm): clean medium sand, grayish orange pink (5YR 7/2), similar to incipient protosoil.

Layer 8 (40 cm): clean very light gray (N8) medium sand; at the base is beach rock.

The stratigraphic and sedimentological descriptions of this section allow interpretations about the depositional environments and the lithological correlations. Two organic deposits are key layers to correlate all sections, which represent humid periods related to local shallow swamps perhaps developed over several seasons, in the form of organic soils, probably related to weakly developed soils over floodplain deposits (see chapter 5). This kind of deposition was developed over a general beach environment, more likely distal bars, evidenced by the presence of boulders, cobbles, and sand. The deposition of the marine sediments was interrupted many times, as registered by the weak soil formations (protosoils). In profile 14 it is possible to recognize a unique massive deposit, caused by a rapid water deposition of mixing fine (silt) and coarse (cobbles and boulders), which may be retransported colluvial sediments. The process was interrupted by the deposition of lenses of fine sand of an aeolian aspect.

SOUTHWEST SECTION BETWEEN PROFILES 19 AND 22

This section shows a change in the topographic configuration from a terrace to a low sandy hill. The upper part of the profiles is not available (see arrows in fig. A1.6).

Profile 19 (fig. A1.4b, top at 540 cmasl)

Layer 1 (10 cm thick): black (N1) coarse sand, with inclusions due to the presence of salt crystals.

Layer 2 (39 cm): diamicton conformed by fine sediments of very pale orange (10YR 8/2), including cobbles.

Layer 3 (7 cm): dark gray (N3) organic deposits, similar to a peat or organic soil; the upper cobbles have signs of heating.

Layer 4 (10 cm): olive gray (5Y 4/1) sand including a paleosoil and minor peat lenses.

Layer 5 (8 cm): clean light gray (N7) medium sand, including broken cobbles.

Layer 6 (20 cm): yellowish brown (10YR 2/2) peat, with a moderate brown medium (5YR 3/4) sand in the middle of the layer.

Layer 7 (15 cm): clean very pale orange (10YR 8/2) medium sand, including cobbles with signs of heating (5R 6/6, light red).

Layer 8 (63 cm): clean light gray (N7) medium to fine sand with 1 to 2 cm of beach rock concretions.

Layer 9 (10 cm): clean grayish black (N2) fine sand, well-laminated horizontally (mm) by light and heavy minerals.

Layer 10 (>20 cm): clean light gray (N7) medium sand.

Profile 22 (fig. A1.4b, top at 650 cmasl)

Layer 1 (155 cm thick): diamicton conformed by fine sediments of very pale orange (10YR 8/2), including cobbles.

Layer 2 (14 cm): organic deposits, similar to a peat or organic soil.

Layer 3 (44 cm): clean medium gray (N5), medium coarse sand, including broken cobbles. In the middle of the layer is a lens of sandy sediments representing the south end of Layer 4 in profile 19.

Layer 4 (12 cm): clean pinkish gray (5YR 8/1) medium sand.

Layer 5 (40 cm): dusky yellowish brown (10YR 2/2) peat, including cobbles.

Layer 6 (>20 cm): clean medium gray color (N5) medium sand.

In this section the presence of the two peat layers permits local lithological correlations under the terrace. The increase of the diamicton thickness changes the topography to the south margin of the mound. The leveling and the subsequent profile drawings show that both the organic/peat layers are declining to the north, so that the terrace in this sector is not eroded but is possibly tilted to the north by tectonic activity.

SOUTH SECTION BETWEEN PROFILES 21 AND 7 (FIG. A1.5, SEE FIG. A1.3 FOR NUMBERED STRATA)

In this section the stratigraphy is very complex because of the presence of anthropogenic layers derived from early human settlement and the subsequent growth of Huaca Prieta. Here also are key sections that allow interpretation of the environmental history of the area. (Figures A1.5–A1.7 show the vertical outcrops.)

Profile 21 (figs. A1.5, A1.6, top at 658 cmasl)

The top of the section is not exposed.

Layer 1 (115 cm thick): diamicton conformed by fine sediments of very pale orange (10YR 8/2), including cobbles and moderate olive brown (5Y 4/4) clay intraclasts.

Layer 2 (2 cm): dark gray (N3) deposit like an organic soil. At the top charcoal dated at 502–129 cal BP (AA86939); at the base the age lying immediately above another charcoal date was 3137–2793 cal BP (AA86940).

Layer 3 (5 cm): light brownish gray (5YR 6/1) coarse sand.

Layer 4 (23 cm): brownish black (5YR 2/1) organic deposit with intercalations of charcoal, sand, and thin very dusky red (10R 2/2) pure peat; at the base are pelican bones in a horizontal position (fig. A1.7).

Layer 5 (28 cm): sediment composed of a mixture of sand and cobbles, very pale orange (10YR 8/2) in the upper middle of the layer, more reddish at the base.

Layer 6 (28 cm): dusky yellowish brown (10YR 2/2) organic deposit, with isolated cobbles that increase in concentration toward the east; at the base also is a large concentration of cobbles.

Layer 7 (>34 cm): light olive gray (5Y 6/1) clean sand with thin intercalations of cobbles; the cobbles at the base of Layer 6 belong to this unit but the sandy matrix was infiltrated by organic matter.

Immediately to the east, six sand and cobble beds interfinger laterally with anthropogenic deposits; at the top of these beds is Layer 5. Many times both depositional environments made transitional lateral connections (see later discussion). Charcoal located in the anthropogenic deposit at 380 cmasl at the base of the first interfinger gave an age of 7786–7618 cal BP (Beta233651). This deposit is the first layer of the mound at Huaca Prieta. This also shows that marine transgression is age concordant with the inundation of the lower Chicama Valley (Phase II, Lagoon Stage: see chapter 5).

Profiles 2 and 3 (fig. A1.5, top at 682 cmasl)

Layer 1 (146 cm thick): diamicton conformed by fine sediments of very pale orange (10YR 8/2), including cobbles and moderate olive brown (5Y 4/4) clay intraclasts.

Layer 2 (8 cm): dark gray (N3) organic deposit like an organic soil. A bulk sample gave an age of 896–675 cal BP (AA81932).

Layer 3 (3 cm): light brownish gray (5YR 6/1) sandy deposit; the layer wedges to the east.

Layer 4 (22 cm): brownish black (5YR 2/1) deposit composed of a mixture of sand, fine organic matter, charcoal, and fragments and whole calcareous invertebrate and lithic artifacts. At the base are well-rounded

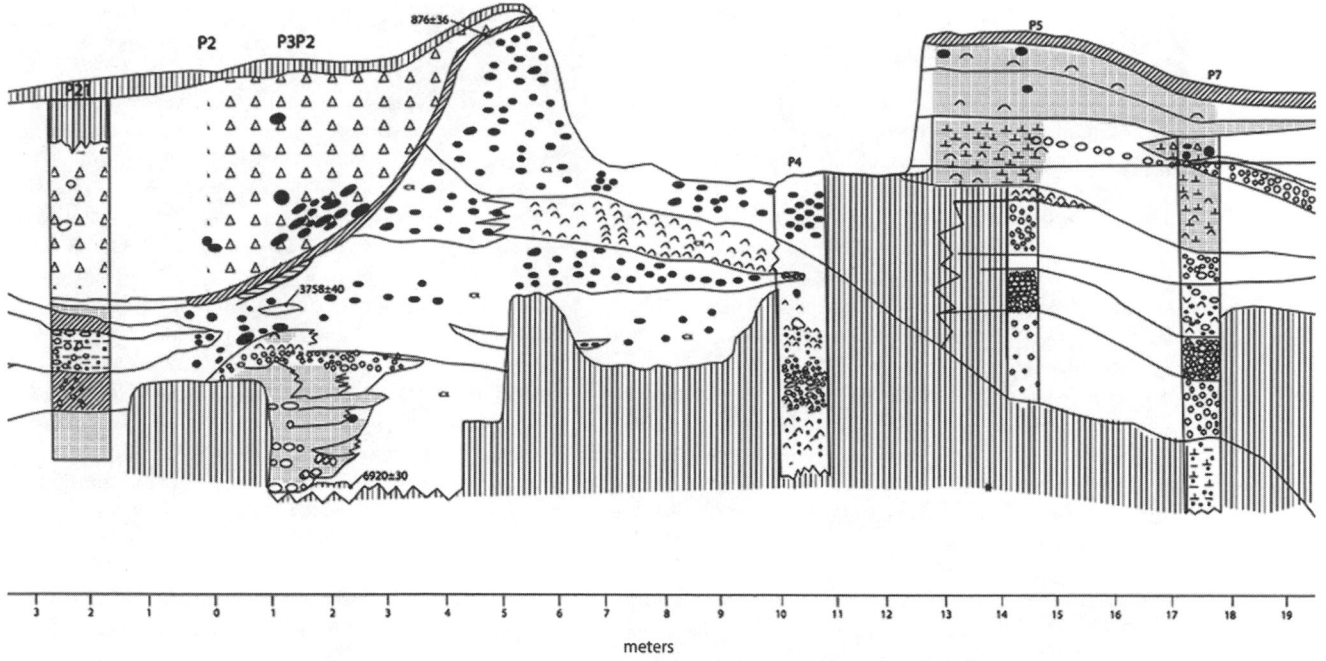

FIGURE A1.5. Close-up of stratigraphic profiles 21, 2, 2–3, 4, 5, and 7 and proposed lithological correlations in the south part of the section. The horizontal axis is in meters; the vertical axis is in centimeters. Strata numbers are referenced in figure A1.3.

FIGURE A1.6. South view of the Huaca Prieta mound. In the foreground is the terrace upon which the mound sits. The two vertical arrow lines (representing 300 cm) indicate the position of profiles 21 and 2. It is possible to observe a wedge of the orange brown layer between two beds of organic deposits (*small arrow*).

FIGURE A1.7. Details of multilayered strata in and around the mound at Huaca Prieta: *a*, details of the contact between Layers 3 and 4, showing the lamination with areas of pure peat and sand and a pelican bone at the base below the hammer; *b*, interfingering between sandy-cobble layers with anthropogenic deposits composed of organic matter, broken cobbles, charcoal, and artifacts (the sandy–cobble-gravel deposits have the characteristics of berm beaches; sometimes the beach developed farther inland, covering the cultural deposits, and at other times the cultural deposits covered the beach); *c*, details of profile 9, showing the contact between Layers 2 and 3 (Layer 3 corresponds to a diamicton with rounded boulders and clay intraclasts); *d*, comparison of the two layers of diamictons in the Huaca Prieta south sections: diamicton layer on the west side with an orange tone (*left*) and diamicton layer on the east side with an olive tone (*right*).

cobbles. Charcoal was dated at 4220–3900 cal BP (AA76982).

Layer 5 (4 cm): anthropogenic deposit composed of a moderate reddish orange (10R 6/6) mixture of ash and pieces of charcoal.

Layer 6 (12 cm): sediment composed of a mixture of sand and mud, with some cobbles and invertebrate shells.

Layer 7 (12 cm): very pale orange (10YR 8/2) coarse sand deposit, including invertebrate shells and charcoal.

Layer 8 (2 cm): broken shell invertebrates composed principally of Mytilidae.

Layer 9 (12 cm): deposits composed of cobbles (2 to 10 cm) in a clean sand matrix.

Layer 10 (26 cm): light gray (N7) clean sand with little pieces (5 mm) of beach rock.

Layer 11 (24 cm): medium gray (N5) clean medium sand, with a mixture of a beach rock at the top, including isolated boulders.

Layer 12 (8 cm): grayish olive (10Y 4/2) composed of heavy minerals like a beach placer.

Layer 13 (10 cm): medium gray (N5) medium sand tinged in some areas with yellowish tone; some isolated cobbles.

Layer 14 (20 cm): light olive (10Y 5/4) medium to fine sand with high contents of heavy minerals, with cobbles near the top.

Layer 15 (?): very well-cemented beach rock, including

cobbles. (It was not possible to excavate deeper due to water penetrating the trench.)

Profile 4 (fig. A1.5, top at 600 cmasl)

Layer 1 (66 cm): shell midden deposit with broken cobbles and fine dispersed organic matter.

Layer 2 (36 cm): blackish red (5R 2/2) organic deposit with few cobbles.

Layer 3 (7 cm): light brown (5YR 5/6) muddy deposit, with minor contents of organic matter.

Layer 4 (5 cm): deposit composed of broken cobbles.

Layer 5 (30 cm): dusky brown (5YR 2/2) organic deposit with few cobbles and invertebrate shells.

Layer 6 (26 cm): light brown (5YR 5/6) organic deposit, a few boulders, and a lot of broken invertebrate shells and charcoal pieces.

Layer 7 (>40 cm): deposit composed of cobbles and boulders with light red (5R 6/6) and black (N1) patina; there are flat clasts with soft imbrication. It is similar to beach bars with signs of present-day human-produced campfires.

Profile 5 (fig. A1.5, top at 700 cmasl)

Layer 1 (5 cm thick): caliche.

Layer 2 (20 cm): densely compacted sand with a few cobbles and a few invertebrate shells, matrix light brown (5YR 6/4).

Layer 3 (29 cm): densely compacted sand in a blackish red matrix (5R 2/2). Some invertebrate shells and cobbles.

Layer 4 (50 cm): sandy silt deposit with moderate brown (5YR 3/4) matrix. Few pebbles and a few invertebrate shells.

Layer 5 (14 cm): blackish red (5R 2/2) sandy deposit, with dense invertebrate shell fragments.

Layer 6 (80 cm): deposit of moderate brown (5YR 3/4) sand with densely packed large cobbles.

Layer 7 (60 cm): deposit of large, densely packed cobbles in a darker mud-organic matrix. Layer 6 was divided into 6a (41 cm) cobbles in a sandy matrix, 6b (10 cm) with organic matter and mud matrix, and 6c (32 cm) without a matrix. Layer 7 dips to the south to southeast.

Profile 7 (fig. A1.5, top at 660 cmasl)

Layer 1 (11 cm thick): caliche.

Layer 2 (17 cm): like Layer 2 in profile 5, densely compacted sand with a few cobbles and a few invertebrate shells; matrix is light brown (5YR 6/4).

Layer 3 (10 cm): like Layer 3 in profile 5, densely compacted sand in a very blackish red matrix (5R 2/2). Some invertebrate shells and cobbles.

Layer 4 (15 cm): grayish yellow (5Y 8/4) sandy silt matrix, including cobbles.

Layer 5 (67 cm): sand, organic matter, some shells, with a 10 cm cobble layer on top.

Layer 6 (22 cm): cobbles and pebbles in a sandy silt matrix, pale brown (5YR 5/2).

Layer 7 (40 cm): cobbles in a muddy matrix with charcoal and shells, pale brown (5YR 5/2).

Layer 8 (30 cm): cobbles and pebbles without a matrix.

Layer 9 (42 cm): cobbles and pebbles in a blackish red (5R 2/2) muddy matrix with high content of organic matter.

Layer 10 (50 cm): silty clay deposit with fine organic matter, shells, and charcoal.

In this section we observed the transition of natural deposits that composed the base of the terrace, with some cultural interventions (Phase I), to the mounded layers produced by anthropogenic activities (Phase II). Especially notable is the interfinger contact between a beach berm and human activity dated at 7784–7665 cal BP, with signs of soil formation over the sandy sediments and the advances and readvances of both environments over time. The two levels of organic deposits/peat described in the southwest sections conformed to only one bed after the disappearance of the beach sediments between them. Then the organic deposits, formed under humid climatic conditions, transformed gradually to the east to engage with the anthropogenic layers described in profiles 4, 5, and 7. The black patina on the cobbles was observed on the windward side of the beach bar in the area. They were discolored by fungus (fig. A1.8). In contrast, the reddish color of cobbles appearing over large extensions of rocks is interpreted as weathering of the local geological materials (basalts and quartzite), as observed today along the beaches. In a hearth experiment conducted by Duccio Bonavia in 2008, the pale-yellow quartzite took on a reddish color when burned (fig. A1.8); the basalts did not change color, but some were thermally broken in a parallel fashion along their natural joints. Archaeological hearths are concentrated in some parts of the deeper beds and are mixed with charcoal and seafood remains, typically associated with a mixture of fine and coarse sediments and dated 4217–3929 cal BP. The association of charcoal and shellfish denotes a cultural origin.

SOUTH SECTION BETWEEN PROFILES 8 AND 11 (FIG. A1.9, SEE FIG. A1.3 FOR NUMBERED STRATA)

Profile 8 (fig. A1.9, top at 650 cmasl)

Layer 1 (10 cm thick): caliche.

Layer 2 (9 cm): pale brown (5YR 5/2) clean medium sand with carbonate and salt cement.

Layer 3 (70 cm): moderate olive brown (5Y 4/4) diamicton, with large clay intraclasts and boulders. At the base layer of cobbles is depth weathering, which is related to the top of Layer 4.

Layer 4 (23 cm): deposit formed by pebbles, cobbles, and clean medium sand.

Layer 5 (20 cm): grayish red (10R 4/2) muddy deposit, including broken cobbles with signs of fire.

FIGURE A1.8. Black and red cobbles: *a*, black patina caused by fungi (darker stones) on the leeward side of beach berms; *b*, red colors on quartzite boulders (lighter tone) after a fire experiment; *c*, weathering of an exposed beach bar; *d*, base of profile 8 showing both the fungi patina (darker stones) and a weathered layer.

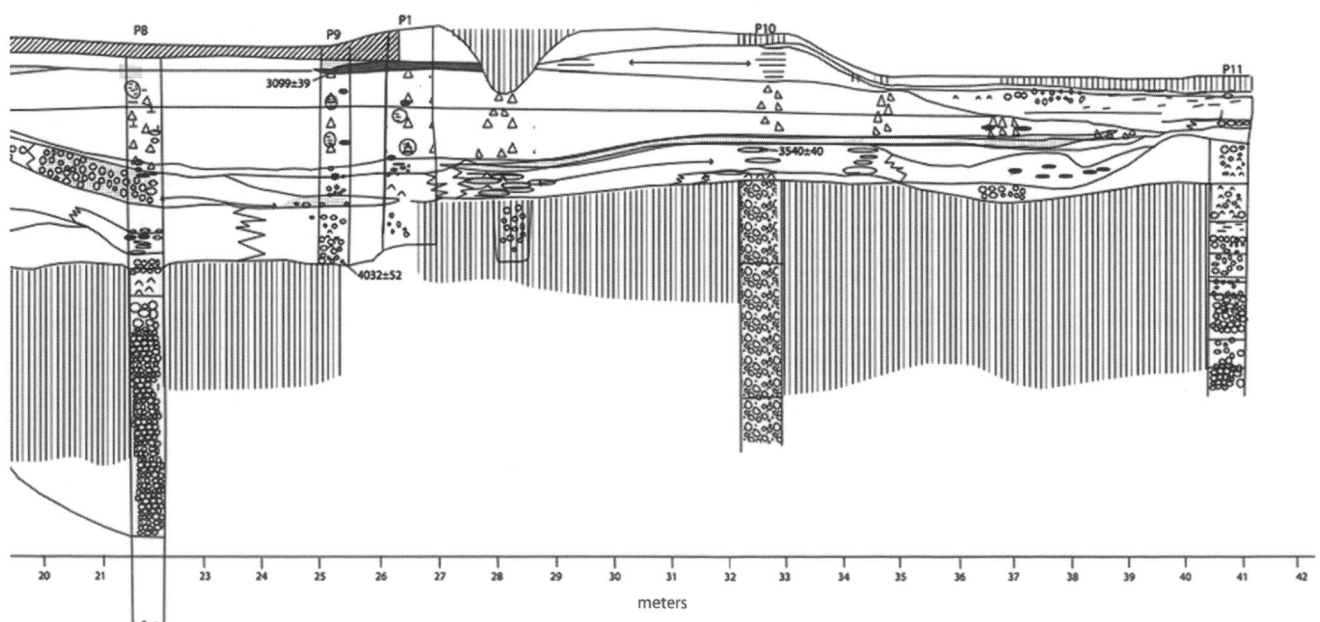

FIGURE A1.9. Stratigraphic profiles 8, 9, 1, 10, and 11 and proposed lithological correlations in the southwest part of the section. The horizontal axis is in meters; the vertical axis is in centimeters.

Layer 6 (12 cm): laminated deposit with sand and organic mud.

Layer 7 (12 cm): mixture of cobbles and organic mud interpreted as being of anthropogenic origin.

Layer 8 (17 cm): mixture of organic mud and invertebrate shells interpreted as being of anthropogenic origin.

Layer 9 (60 cm): deposit composed of light red (5R 6/6) boulders and cobbles in matrix of sand and fine organic matter.

Layer 10 (53 cm): deposit composed of pebbles and cobbles without matrix and black (N1) patina.

Layer 11 (60 cm): deposit composed of cobbles and pebbles surrounded by carbonate mud.

Layer 12 (60 cm): light greenish gray (5GY 8/1) fine carbonate muds (dated at 7457–7318 cal BP). The water table was at 6 cm over the base of the excavation.

Profile 9 (fig. A1.9, top at 644 cmasl)

Layer 1 (4 cm): caliche.

Layer 2 (4 cm): pale brown (5YR 5/2) medium sand cemented by salt.

Layer 3 (9 cm): organic soil; a charcoal at the base was dated 3366–3081 cal BP (AA76986).

Layer 4 (67 cm): diamicton with a moderate olive brown (5Y 4/4) muddy matrix; at the base is a bed of broken invertebrate shells.

Layer 5 (8 cm): cobbles with 5R 6/6 light red color by weathering or as an effect of fire.

Layer 6 (12 cm): cobbles in matrix of fine sediment, organic matter, and cultural material.

Layer 7 (7 cm): pebbles in a matrix of clean light gray (N7) sand.

Layer 8 (>20 cm): fine sediment with broken shells, pale olive (10Y 6/2). Near the base a group of twelve quartzite cobbles and pebbles was registered. Charcoal at the base dated ~4780–4243 cal BP (AA76976).

Profile 1 (fig. A1.9, top at 655 cmasl)

Layer 1 (2 cm thick): caliche.

Layer 2 (20 cm): medium to fine sand, with pale brown (5YR 5/2) and notes of white (salt) and 5P 6/2 pale purple (sea urchin spines).

Layer 3 (7 cm): blackish red (5R 2/2) paleosoil, with high contents of organic matter.

Layer 4 (62 cm): diamicton with a moderate olive brown (5Y 4/4) muddy matrix and clay intraclasts and cobbles and boulders; 2 m to the east under Layer 3 is a lens of laminated fine broken shells and organic mud; to the east in the direction of profile 10 another thin lens (1 cm in thickness) lies between Layer 3 and the laminated lens; it is composed of a coarse sand of pale purple tone (5P 6/2) over the medium gray (N5), largely due to the presence of sea urchin spines.

Layer 5 (8 cm): completely weathered boulder and cobble deposit.

Layer 6 (3 cm): medium gray (N5) clean sand with isolated pebbles.

Layer 7 (17 cm): fine organic matter deposit, without clasts.

Layer 8 (20 cm): boulders, cobbles, and shells in an organic matter matrix.

Profile 10 (fig. A1.9, top at 640 cmasl)

Layer 1 (10 cm thick): caliche.

Layer 2 (3 cm): medium to fine sand, pale brown (5YR 5/2) with lenses of white (salt) and pale purple (5P 6/2) (sea urchin spines).

Layer 3 (20 cm): blackish red (5R 2/2) paleosoil, with high contents of organic matter; intercalation sand and mud.

Layer 4 (39 cm): diamicton with a moderate olive brown (5Y 4/4) muddy matrix and clay intraclasts and cobbles and boulders.

Layer 5 (6 cm): medium gray (N5) clean medium to coarse sand.

Layer 6 (24 cm): laminated deposit with lenses of organic matter and very fine broken shells. Charcoal dated at 3828–3699 cal BP (AA76984).

Layer 7 (60 cm): quartzite boulders in an organic matter matrix, with a 5R 6/6 light red color due to fires.

Layer 8 (93 cm): boulder and cobble deposit.

Layer 9 (>50 cm): boulders and cobbles with a black (N1) patina.

Profile 11 (fig. A1.9, top at 640 cmasl)

Layer 1 (14 cm thick): caliche.

Layer 2 (2 cm): like profile 10, medium to fine sand, pale brown (5YR 5/2) with white (salt) and pale purple (5P 6/2) (sea urchin spines). At the base is 2 cm of clean sand.

Layer 3 (16 cm): blackish red (5R 2/2) paleosoil deposit, with high content of organic matter; intercalation of sand and mud.

Layer 4 (5 cm): thin cobble deposit, deep weather, making a wedge to the east.

Layer 5 (12 cm): grayish yellow (5Y 8/4) deposit composed of particles of carbonate.

Layer 6 (26 cm): boulders and cobbles in an organic matter and broken shell matrix.

Layer 7 (27 cm): organic matter deposit with high content of medium dark gray (N4) with broken shells.

Layer 8 (10 cm): moderate brown (5YR 3/4) laminated organic deposit; at the base is a deeply weathered cobble deposit.

Layer 9 (30 cm): boulders and cobbles in a moderate brown (5YR 3/4) fine matrix.

Layer 10 (20 cm): light red (5R 6/6) broken boulders and cobbles without matrix.

Layer 11 (40 cm): blackish red (5R 2/2) matter deposit with isolated cobbles.

Layer 12 (>20 cm): cobbles and boulders with black (N1) patina, without matrix.

FIGURE A1.10. Recent environments and deposits along the coast near Huaca Prieta that are similar to some of the layers described in the stratigraphic profiles: *a*, a typical beach face and berm; *b*, heavy mineral lamination on a sandy beach berm; *c*, a swamp growing over a beach berm; *d*, pelican bones of birds that died in a seasonal swamp during the 1998 El Niño.

This section is characterized by a different stratigraphy conformed by several layers of lenses with cobbles of an artificial berm deposited around 7457–7318 cal BP and associated with initial mound construction. The artificial berm is similar to natural berms in actual bars along the beach. The lagoon, represented by Layer 12 in profile 8 (fine carbonate mud), is immediately below the coarse beach deposits. There are also interbedded gravel mixtures of fine organic sediments, with or without broken shells; weathering effects are mixed with the oxidant effects of cultural fires. A second type of diamicton outcrops here, with a moderate olive brown (5Y 4/4) color very different from the very pale orange (10YR 8/2) of the diamicton on the west side of the south section (fig. A1.7). In this area the olive brown diamicton forms a little terrace attached to the mound. Over the entire area is a thin well-cemented caliche "soil" covering. There also are cobble and boulder deposits without fine matrix and a black patina (which is similar to the old beach bars of today that are not in contact with the sea). Others show broken shells, charcoal, and signs of fire, with a fine organic matter that reveals human activities. Today along the beach, as in the stratigraphic profiles, gravel bars and humid environments represented by organic paleosoils and peats coexist (fig. A1.10).

CHRONOLOGY AND ENVIRONMENTAL RECONSTRUCTIONS

The stratigraphic, sedimentological, and radiocarbon data indicate a continuous uplift similar to other areas of north Peru (Goy et al. 1992; Saillard et al. 2011; Wells 1996). Uplift possibly began during the last interglacial Sangamon in the north section of the terrace, near the historical fishing village. The surface of the terrace is 10.9 masl (~4 m above the international sea level at that time). Uplift is well recorded in the young terrace north of Huaca Prieta (at 3.5 masl), with an age in the upper layer of 913–751 cal BP. That age identifies an uplift episode that occurred less than 1000 years ago (Bird et al. [1985: 13–16] thought that the uplift had occurred prior to and after 5400 cal BP).

The first deposition recorded in the southwest and southern margins of Huaca Prieta corresponds to a fine carbonate lagoon deposit registered at the base of profile 8, which is older than ~7786–7618 cal BP in profile 21. The lagoon developed primarily between 7457–7318 and 6659–6295 cal BP (see chapter 5). Overlying the fine carbonate mud is a boulder-cobble deposit with a fungal black patina, which is interpreted as a beach bar.

Clean gray sand deposits, with heavy mineral lamination interfingered with cultural deposits (fig. A1.10), represent another event, which could be at least partially contemporaneous with Lagoon Stage Phase II. These beds record a slow lateral and vertical transition between a sandy berm of a paleobeach and a human occupation dated ~7784–7665 cal BP. This time frame corresponds to the middle of the Holocene Climatic Optimum, which is similar to the Flandriense transgression; the height of the top of the deposit (3.1 masl) makes it difficult to interpret this level as the real height of the sea at this time but as a consequence of tectonic uplift. Daniel Sandweiss et al. (2009) point out that in Peru the sea level reached a stable level 6000 years ago. Thus it is possible that in a coastal landscape similar to that of today a sandy berm beach existed about 7500–7000 cal BP with an older gravel bar to the east. Simultaneous human occupation was located along the southern and southwest side of Huaca Prieta after Lagoon Stage Phase II, as evidenced by a large number of burned cobbles mixed with organic matter over the earliest natural bar deposits. After that people began to transport and deposit berm beach boulders, cobbles, and gravel and mixed them with shellfish and charcoal from the fires. The interpretation is that people initially began to copy the gravel bars (although on a smaller scale) to form a low shelter to protect themselves from the wind and waves during storms. This same concept was later found in retention berms to support the initial mound layers in Phase II and later.

There are no radiocarbon dates for the end of the beach episode. We only know the radiocarbon age at the top of the overlying peat-cultural deposit, which indicates a minimal age of 3992–3826 cal BP. Another concordant age is located in profile 3, in a peat-cultural layer dated 4217–3929 cal years BP, which lies under the sandy gravel extending to the east. A charcoal sample dated at 3945–3680 cal BP in a cultural layer in profile 15. A fourth radiocarbon age of 4780–4243 cal BP is at the base of profile 9 from a hearth with no direct stratigraphic relationship with the old beach. We do not have environmental information about the eastern edge of Huaca Prieta for about 3000 years. The hiatus or a very slow deposition is recorded away from Huaca Prieta between 6300 and 4900 cal BP (Transitional Phase III; see chapter 5).

The next event is represented by a peat (in the west) that gradually extends to a cultural deposit to the east (gravel, charcoal, organic matter, shells). The peat is interrupted by a clean sand deposit, similar to a beach, which extended to profile 17 in the "soccer field" (100 m north of profile 2; see fig. A1.1). Several radiocarbon dates from these profiles represent the termination of late Preceramic use of this area: 3574–3268 cal BP (profile 18), 3992–3826 cal BP (profile 12), 3985–3822 cal BP (profile 21), 4217–3929 cal BP (profile 3), 4780–4243 cal BP (profile 9), and 3869–3639 cal BP (profile 10). All of these dates are overlaid by early Guañape sherds. The clean sand deposit, interpreted as a beach or a storm deposit, outcrops only west of Huaca Prieta. Afterward the transgression reached a maximum shortly after 3700 cal BP; the sand over the peaty soils and peats represents the last marine deposition. To the east and near pro-

file 1, outcrops are only cultural deposits, which are similar to those described for the second event (such as boulders, cobbles, fine organic matter, shells, and charcoal). Also, the cultural deposit in the east side is interrupted by a moderate olive brown diamicton with sand lenses. The sand lens contains only freshwater microfossils and microgastropods; this eliminates the possibility of a tsunami deposit. A radiocarbon date from the peat lens over the diamicton is 3358–3173 cal BP (profile 9). Thus the diamicton was deposited between that age and the date of the basal peat below the diamicton (3925–3700 cal BP, profile 10), possibly as a debris-flow and flood deposit of an El Niño event. In the next sections (profiles 2 and 3) after the clean sand deposition another peat layer outcrops. In the base of this stratum (fig. A1.7) are bones of pelicans lying in a horizontal position. We observed a similar situation in the wetlands to the north, where birds had died during the 1998 El Niño event due to abrupt changes in the fish abundance resulting from shifts in coastal sea currents. Thus it is possible to interpret the peats as associated with long humid periods. The age of the upper peat of this sequence is between 3167 and 2859 cal BP (profile 21) and 1302–1177 cal BP (profile 14). If all peats were developed under extraordinary humid conditions, similar to those of El Niño events, these events were very frequent between 4778–4290 cal BP and 1302–1187 cal BP, with a short interruption in the range of 3975–3817 cal BP and 3137–2793 cal BP, when a sandy beach was deposited in a short time. But this interruption did not occur if the clean sand represents a storm deposit instead. Overlying the beach or storm sand is a pedogenesis (edaphic) process forming a low-developed soil, before the second peat deposition. That process covered a geological period of over 500 years without another deposition. This also may be a humid period, which would agree with frequent El Niño events. During the same time range (3137–2793 cal BP and 1302–1187 cal BP), in the northern terrace in front of Huaca Cortada and near the historical fishing village, a sandy sequence outcrops with cultural remains (vegetable, shellfish, charcoal, and ceramics). From here two radiocarbon ages were derived from *Donax* sp. (2031±34, 2101±34) and sea urchin shells (1677–1528 and 1769–1594 cal BP). Both of these clean sandy layers correspond to the same beach sedimentation. This means that the northern terrace is not a climatic terrace deposited during the Holocene Climatic Optimum but a tectonic terrace uplifted late in the Holocene after 1000 cal BP. That uplift was a tilting movement, because the top of the terrace drops to the south near the "soccer field."

The next thousand years corresponds to a silence in the natural deposition. It is possible that the natural deposits representing this period were destroyed by massive pyramid building across the entire terrace, with a similar absence between 7784–7665 and 4299–4080 cal BP, when Huaca Prieta was flourishing and when much cultural removal of natural sediments occurred.

The fourth event is represented by an organic deposit, mainly associated with cultural remains (boulders, cobbles, shells, fine organic matter, and charcoal). Also included are many sedimentological variations (one, two, or three thin peaty levels with sandy intercalations, as in profile 16). The radiocarbon age of the base of profile 14 is 1302–1177 cal BP; the age at the top of profile 15 is 792–681 cal BP. In the same period a sandy deposit in the northern terrace is mixed with many vegetable remains and ceramics. Here a radiocarbon age on a piece of reed was dated at 913–751 cal BP. There also is a well-developed beach rock with bioturbation, similar to crab digging activities. That age is the maximal date for an important uplift and tilt, probably related to a big earthquake (perhaps a magnitude >Mw 8.5).

The fifth and last event corresponds to the deposition of the very pale orange diamicton, which is restricted to the west and southwest sides of the Huaca Prieta mound. In profile 15, at the highest point of the local natural topography overlying a cultural charcoal dated at 792–681 cal BP, is an overlying peat layer that dated at 502–129 cal BP (AA86939). We interpret the diamictons, mostly composed of an allochthonous mixture of clay and silt, with intraclasts similar to the fine carbonate sediments of the lagoon and cobbles and pebbles of an upvalley source, as perhaps representing El Niño debris-flow and flood deposits.

In Huaca Prieta there are no tsunami deposits at the same scale as in the Chicama Valley to the south of the site (see chapter 5). All the possible tsunami layers are no more than 2 cm thick layers to the south. In the area near the edge of the Huaca Prieta are several sand layers, with no mud, coarse granulometry, poor sorting, and marine fossils, which could be candidates for tsunami or tempestite deposits (the only reliable differences between these layers are the types of foraminifers and diatoms).

The first layer is located immediately over a moderate olive brown diamicton (profiles 1, 9, and 10), which dated ~3358–3173 cal BP. This corresponds to a medium to coarse sand, dark gray with a pale purple tint, due to the presence of a lot of sea urchin remains. The second deposit is located in profile 10 immediately below the same diamicton, dated after 3925–3700 cal BP. It is also a coarse dark gray sand that is poorly sorted. The third bed is intercalated in the upper peat layer (profiles 12 to 21). It has the same textural char-

acteristics, marine fossils, and a lot of salt. The basal contact is undulating, a feature of a typical erosional contact. The youngest basal age of the peat (profile 14) is 1302–1177 cal BP; another organic layer overlies it at 502–129 cal BP (profile 21).

Other clean sand layers are intercalated in very different sediments. In profile 20 a fine (like dune sand) light gray sand outcrop lies over a lower peat (after 3992–3826 cal BP). In profile 18, under the upper peat (before 1294–1185 cal BP), a coarse and poorly sorted yellow sand outcrops, with some fine gravel particles. The last two examples have no traces of marine fossils.

Bird et al. (1985) describe a tsunami layer on the east side of the Huaca Prieta mound, which is composed of cobbles and dips about 45° to the east. This layer is completely cemented by salt and organic debris (see chapter 7 and appendix 8), however, and includes an artificial berm with sorted cobblestones imbricated with long axes oriented in the same direction, much like brick-laying and layered cultural materials. We studied samples of this salt and sand matrix in the laboratory. After establishing a porosity measurement, we calculated that if the empty spaces between each cobble were filled with 35 Practical Salinity Units (PSU) of seawater it would be possible to obtain a natural content of 3.72 grams of NaCl. The samples between the cobbles yielded 583 grams of NaCl, however, which means about 157 to 160 times more than the natural NaCl content of seawater. The only possible explanation for the enormous content of salt between the cobbles is that people repeatedly used marine water on the surface of the anthropogenically deposited cobble-boulder bed to produce an artificial solid substrate or mortar to retain the steep mound surface; that is, the artificial berm served as a footing to hold the mound layers in place. In this portion of the site, as well as the southwest and south margins of Huaca Prieta, the stratigraphy thus offers a unique opportunity to understand the influence of culture activity that modified the landscape in addition to the normal humid and dry climate and sedimentation and the effect of tectonic uplift.

APPENDIX 2

CHARCOAL ANALYSIS

Isabel Rey

The consistent use of nineteen different taxa of plant species for fuel shows that people understood the qualities of each taxon for particular uses (table A2.1). A total of 13,257.7 grams of charcoal were studied, of which 4746.3 grams correspond to all phases at Huaca Prieta. Eighteen taxa were identified at Huaca Prieta. Eleven taxa weighing 4692.2 grams were identified in excavation layers corresponding to all phases of Unit 16. Twelve taxa and 3819.2 grams were studied for Paredones, representing Phases II to V (fig. A2.1). The same set of species was used throughout time in each unit, with only minor frequency variation related to sample size. A technical description and the anatomy of wood were obtained through scanning electron microscopy. As seen in the table, the majority of the charcoal represents short-lived bushes, grasses, and other vegetation. See chapter 10 for a discussion of charcoal remains and the species context. Additional SEM photographs of charcoal are at https://my.vanderbilt.edu/huacaprieta.

Table A2.1. Charcoal samples identified in the excavation units

a. Distribution and amount (grams) of charcoal in samples studied from Huaca Prieta

Taxa	Phase I		Phase II		Phase III		Phase IV		Phase V	
	Weight	%	Weight	%	Weight	%	Weight	%	Weight	%
Equisetum sp.	52.0	21.0	0.7	2.2	30.4	29.5	96.6	31.9	2027.7	23.5
Salix humboldtiana	3.5	1.4			12.9	12.5	10.0	3.3	25.0	0.3
Annona sp.									27.0	0.3
Persea sp.	8.5	3.4			1.2	1.2	12.0	4.0	85.5	1.0
Acacia sp.							3.0	1.0	17.5	0.2
Prosopis sp.	111.0	44.8							101.5	1.2
Parkinsonia sp.					4.0	3.9			52.7	0.6
Bunchosia armeniaca									4.5	0.1
Schinus molle	8.8	3.6					6.0	2.0	30.8	0.4
Pouteria lucuma									57.8	0.7
Buddleja sp.			6.3	19.4					24.5	0.3
Tessaria integrifolia									21.0	0.2
Dicotiledonea herbacea									179.0	2.1
Gynerium sagittatum	53.0	21.4	9.0	27.7	48.4	46.9	57.5	19.0	3125.6	36.3
Araceae/Arecaceae	3.5	1.4	4.0	12.3			102.9	34.0	549.2	6.4
Cyperus sp.									16.0	0.2
Scirpus sp.									1.5	0.0
Schoenoplectus californicus									8.0	0.1
Monocotiledonea									68.5	0.8
Unidentified carbon	7.4	3.0	12.5	38.5	6.2	6.0	15.0	5.0	2188.8	25.4
Total	**247.7**		**32.5**		**103.1**		**303.0**		**8612.1**	

b. Distribution and amount (grams) of charcoal in samples studied from Paredones

Taxa	Phase I		Phase II		Phase III		Phase IV		Phase V	
	Weight	%	Weight	%	Weight	%	Weight	%	Weight	%
Equisetum sp.			0.7	4.4	30.4	29.2			323.1	7.1
Salix humboldtiana					12.9	12.7				
Annona sp.									3.8	0.1
Persea sp.					1.2	1.3				
Acacia sp.									22.0	0.5
Prosopis sp.									886.0	19.4
Parkinsonia sp.					4.0	3.8			16.3	0.4
Buddleja sp.			6.3	39.4					21.3	0.5
Gynerium sagittatum			9.0	56.3	48.4	47.5			2693.0	59.1
Cyperus sp.									30.0	0.7
Unidentified carbon					5.0	4.9	15.0	100.0	529.0	11.6
Total			**16.0**		**101.9**		**15.0**		**4555.3**	

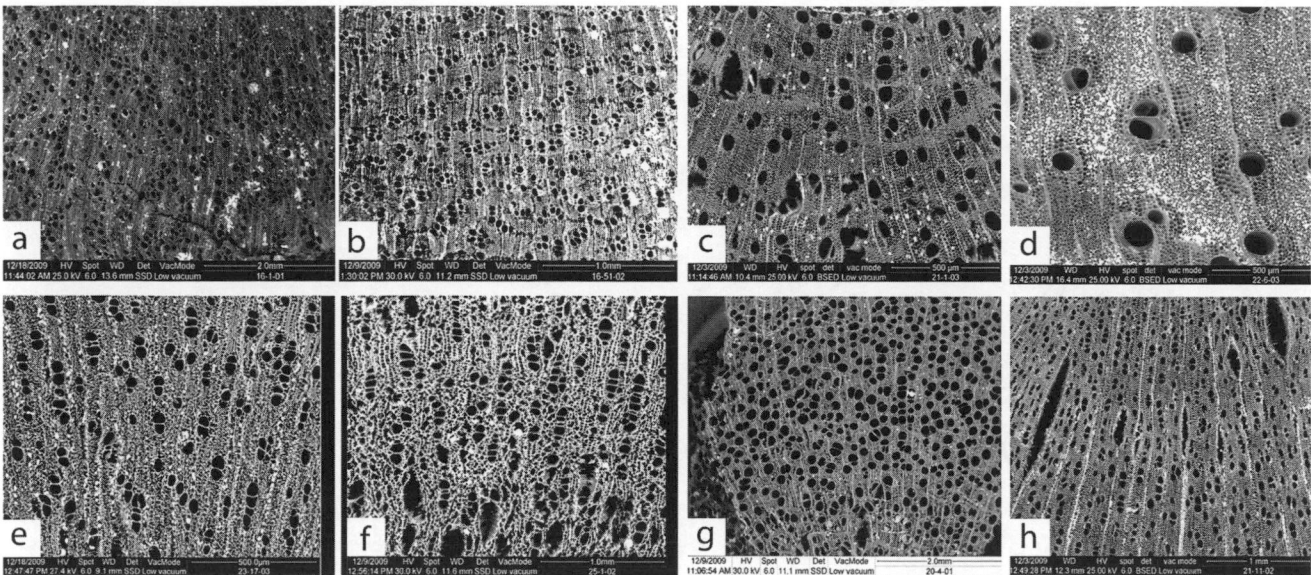

FIGURE A2.1. Various cellular features of archaeological charcoal samples: *a*, cross section of a burned *Bunchosia armeniaca* (*cansaboca*) from Unit 16, Layer 4 (growth rings are indistinguishable or absent; solitary vessels have a diagonal pattern with sharp edges and measure between 5 and 20 per mm^2; confluent axial parenchyma [50×]); *b*, cross section of burned *Schinus molle* (molle) from Unit 16, Layer 12 (vessels are diagonal and/or radial and measure 50–100 microns and 20 to 40 vessels per mm^2; axial parenchyma paratracheal are scarce [100×]); *c*, cross section of *Persea* sp. (avocado) from Unit 22, Layer 3, with diagonal solitary or radial vessels (5 to 20 vessels per mm^2, with vasicentric axial parenchyma; large rays are commonly serial and measure 4–12 mm^2 [200×]); *d*, transversal view of *Inga* sp. from Unit 22, Layer 7, with indistinguishable or absent growth rings with simple perforation plates, with different diameters (axial parenchyma are diffuse, alliforme, or alliforme with a diamond shape [200×]); *e*, transverse view of *Pouteria* sp. (lucuma), from Unit 23, Structure 8, Layer 7, at Huaca Prieta (the vessels are in a diagonal or radial pattern of 4 or more, with an average diameter of 100–200 microns and an axial parenchyma in straight lines of three cells [200×]); *f*, transversal view of *Annona cherimolia* from Unit 25, Layer 7, with solitary and multiple racime vessels and simple perforated plates of 5–20 vessels per mm^2 (with few paratracheal parenchyma and 4 to 10 large seriated rays [100×]); *g*, transversal view of *Salix humboldtiana* (sauce), from Unit 20, Layer 6c, Paredones (with radial or diagonal vessels of an average 100–200 microns in diameter and 40 to 100 vessels per mm^2, with marginal axial parenchyma or marginal bands [50×]); *h*, transversal view of *Buddleja* sp. (butterfly bush), from Unit 21, Layer R1, Huaca Prieta, with solitary vessels in radial or diagonal pattern (with 40–100 vessels per mm^2 and few paratracheal parenchyma [100×]).

MARINE SHELL ANALYSIS FOR SEASONALITY

Teresa C. B. Franco

For comparative analyses of the seasonality of shellfish procurement, both modern and archaeological shell samples of the genera *Semele* from Huaca Prieta and from the present-day seashore environment were studied. The species analyzed were *Semele solida* and *Semele corrugata*. This genus was selected over others because it has the growth ring structure suitable for this type of study. Modern shells were collected from an area close to the site of Huaca Prieta in 2008. The archaeological samples are from Phases II to V burial contexts (~7572 to 3455 cal BP; table A3.1a).

More than 75% of the studied shells were found as offerings in human burials at Huaca Prieta; the remainder were dispersed in different sectors of the site. Although shells of *Semele* are not as fragile as those of other bivalves such as *Mesodesma donacium*, all analyzed shells were broken. This could result from opening the shells and removing the mollusks, from trampling, or from deliberate breakage related to rituals or for construction purposes, such as a fill in building walls and other structures.

A total of 85 modern shells were studied. All samples were sectioned by Víctor Vásquez of the Universidad Nacional de Trujillo in a cut parallel to the umbo of the shells, or at the highest point of the middle portion. Preparation of the samples used water and sandpaper to smooth them and Brasso to polish the cut area. No samples were embedded in epoxycure resin, and acetate peels were not used (for details see Franco 2015).

The analysis followed the steps used for *Mercenaria* shells, which is based on the formation of white and dark growth bands during all seasons of the year (Quitmyer et al. 1997). A similar seasonal pattern was found on modern shells of *Semele* in a comparative attempt to identify the seasons in which shells were collected in the past.

Results of the analysis suggest no annual continuity in gathering *Semele* sp. shells at Huaca Prieta. Seasonality is indicated by the absence of shells from the late spring to late summer for all phases of site-use analyzed. Shells were probably collected mainly during the fall and winter, a period in which the clams are not at the height of their reproductive phase, and possibly during the middle spring seasons.

SHELL GROWTH RING ANALYSIS IN *SEMELE* SP.: MODERN SAMPLES

The study was performed on modern shells of *Semele solida* (Semelidae), which represent 86% of the shells studied,

Table A3.1. *Semele* sp.: Archaeological and modern shells

a. Chronological context of the archaeological samples

Cultural phase	Chronology (cal BP)	Total shells
Phase II	7572–6538	26
Phase III	6538–5308	7
Phase IV	5308–4107	9
Phase V	4107–3455	17

b. Modern shell number and percentage of dark and white bands distributed by months of the year

Month	Dark count	% Dark	White count	% White	Mirror image of %	Total
Jan	11	100.00		0.00		11
Feb	12	100.00		0.00		12
Mar	14	100.00		0.00		14
Apr	12	80.00	3	20.00	−20.00	15
May	4	26.67	11	73.33	−73.33	15
Jun	6	40.00	9	60.00	−60.00	15
Jul	7	46.67	8	53.33	−53.33	15
Aug	14	87.50	2	12.50	−12.50	16
Sep	14	100.00		0.00		14
Oct	15	100.00		0.00		15
Nov	13	100.00		0.00		13
Dec	6	35.29	11	64.71	−64.71	17

while the other 14% were shells of *Semele corrugata* (Semelidae; table A3.1).

Both species are found in shallow water at low tides partially buried in sand and gravel bottoms (Brown et al. 2002). They also are found on the subtidal zone down to 20 m (Urban and Campos 1994). An important food resource, both mollusks are highly appreciated in Chilean and Peruvian gastronomy today.

Detailed studies of these species in their north Peruvian coastal habitat are few. Their reproductive cycle can vary due to differences in ambient conditions, interspecies details, and latitudinal effects (Urban and Campos 1994). In this respect, some studies point to a continuous or biannual reproductive cycle for southern latitudes (Urban and Campos 1994). A detailed study in 1991–1992 from La Herradura Bay (29° 58′ S) in northern Chile showed a reproductive period from June to February (winter/spring/summer). Gonads were empty by March with the beginning of the fall resting period (Brown et al. 2002). Similar data

were retrieved for *S. solida* from Ditacho Bay (36° 31′ S) in Chile, which had an annual reproductive cycle that occurred during spring/summer (from October to January/February), with a second short spawning period in March/April (Urban and Campos 1994). These studies show that mollusks are sensitive to changing water conditions such as temperature, salinity, and available nutrients. It is important to know the mollusks' life cycle and its changes, which can be reflected in shell growth rings (see appendix 14 for more details).

METHODS

To establish the seasonal growth pattern for modern shells, 10 to 15 shells were sampled from each month. One valve of each selected shell was prepared for sclerochronology analyses based on the growth bands. Modern and archaeological shells were cut following a parallel plane with the shell's umbo. The polishing process flattened the surface of the cut area and highlighted its features. This allowed the lines on its surface to stand out more clearly, thereby preparing the shell for subsequent analysis. After that the polished surface of all selected shells from both collections was photographed with a metallurgical microscope (Leica DM 4000 M) at 25× magnification. A binocular microscope (Bausch and Lomb; 0.7× to 3× magnification) was also used for visual inspection.

Shells of *Semele* have an annual pattern of white and dark bands that are potential seasonal indicators.[1] The white bands (or opaque increments) and the dark bands (or translucent increments) have a well-marked alternate pattern close to the edge of the shell, which is visible at the cut zone (fig. A3.1). Shells were initially divided into groups of dark and white bands, as the tip of the shell presents one of these two classifications. Also, the size of the last band was measured in the um scale. The next step was to refine the growth stages and classify them as T1, T2, and T3 and O1, O2, and O3 following Quitmyer et al. (1997), where "T" is for translucent and "O" is for opaque. A schematic drawing of all shells was done, with a focus on the tip of the valves and its increments. The last increment was measured and then classified in one of the following categories below (fig. A3.1), as the patterns on the margins of the shells were defined. This classification scheme was used as a guide to patterns observed on the margins of the shells. Based on the analysis of modern shells, it is determined that the opaque bands relate more to winter and less to the end of spring growth. Figure A3.2.a–f shows cross-sections from modern and archaeological shells from Huaca Prieta. Alternating translucent (gray) and opaque (white or light brown on the archaeological shell) bands are visible on the shells (fig. A3.2f).

The measurements cover the width of the last band formed on the margin of the shell, from the edge of the shell to the end of the band. These measurements were used to calculate the standard deviation and the student's t-test for modern and archaeological shells, which were calculated

1. The term "band" is used here as a synonym for "increment."

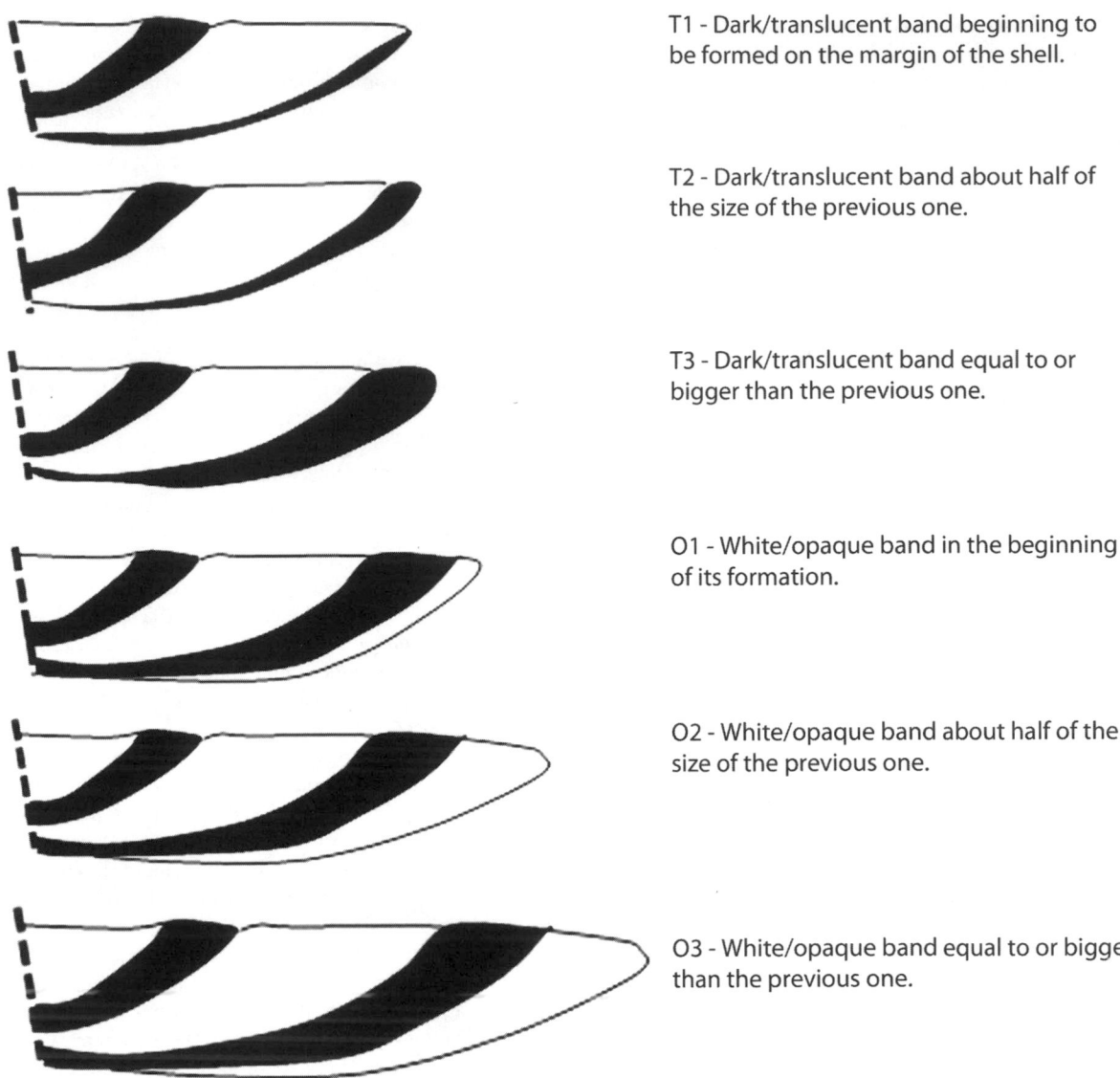

T1 - Dark/translucent band beginning to be formed on the margin of the shell.

T2 - Dark/translucent band about half of the size of the previous one.

T3 - Dark/translucent band equal to or bigger than the previous one.

O1 - White/opaque band in the beginning of its formation.

O2 - White/opaque band about half of the size of the previous one.

O3 - White/opaque band equal to or bigger than the previous one.

Adapted from Quitmyer et al. (1997)

FIGURE A3.1. Schematic cross section of shell edges and their codes.

for both collections for dark and white bands formation, arranged by months (table A3.2). This was done to verify the distribution of mean intervals and set the maximum and minimum distribution intervals. Based on the mean sizes of band formations from modern collections compared with archaeological ones from the Huaca Prieta site, a t-statistic (table A3.3) was used. This provided data confidence limits and the probable months in which archaeological shells were collected. Seasonal growth frequency histograms (fig. A3.4a) were constructed for modern shells. For comparative purposes, another growth frequency profile was done for the archaeological samples (fig. A3.4b).

RESULTS

MODERN SAMPLES

The last growth increment formed on the edge of the shell was classified in dark or white bands and organized according to the months in which they were collected. Table A3.1b provides the percentages with the occurrence of both variables distributed by month. The first numerical column (dark count) in the table refers to the number of shells with a dark or white band on the edge followed by its percentage. The column with negative numbers is the mirror image of percentage values found for white bands.

The results are significant. White bands are concen-

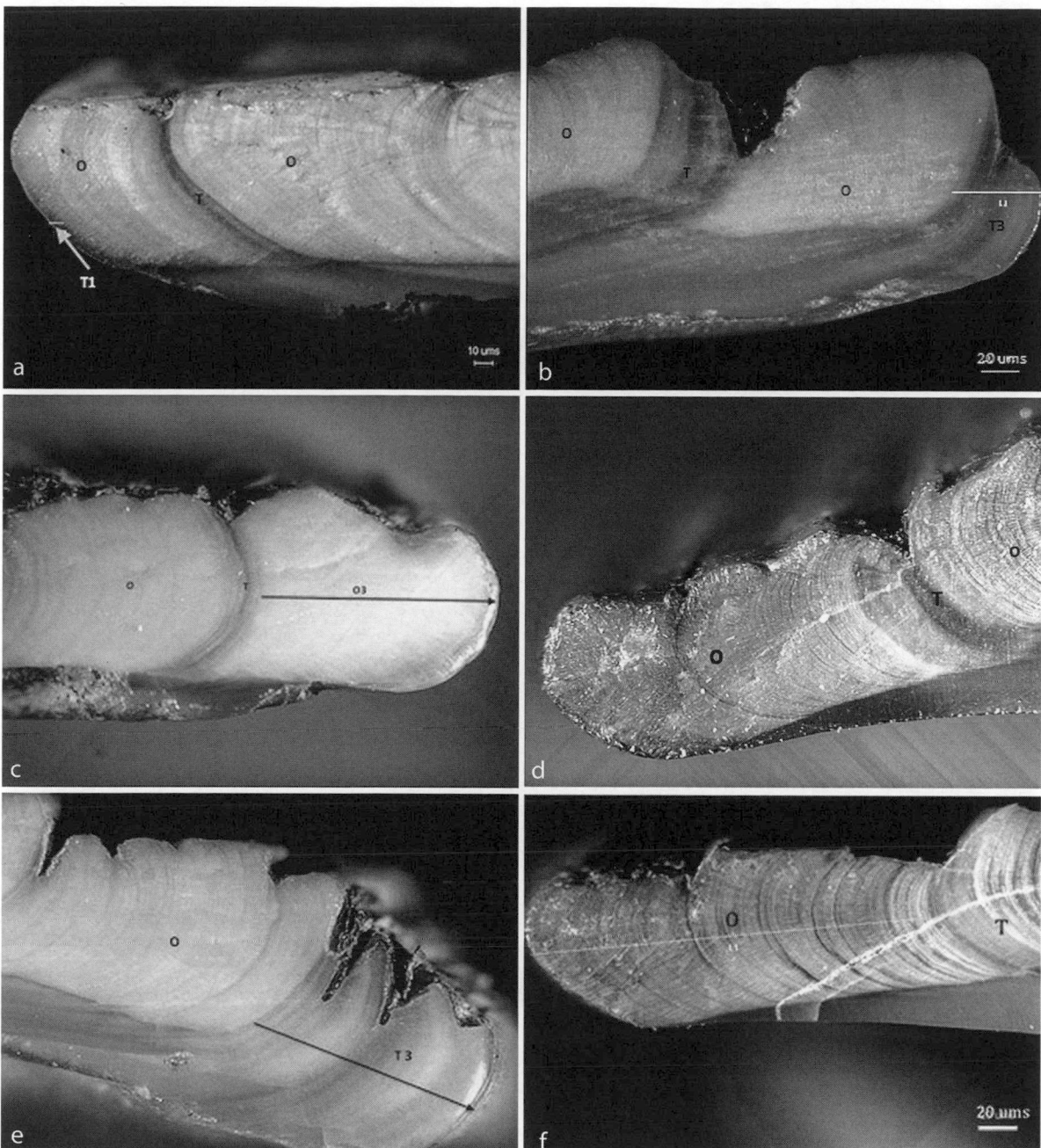

FIGURE A3.2. Dark and white bands in archaeological and modern shells of *Semele* sp.: *a*, archaeological shell sample of *Semele* sp. from Phase V, after cutting and polishing; the photo shows the extreme edge of the shell with a Translucent (T) band (dark gray) and an Opaque (O) band (light white) at the tip of a T1 band (adult sample); *b*, modern shell of *Semele* sp. collected in September 2008, after being cut and polished; the photo shows the extreme edge of the shell with the alternate bands: Translucent (T) band (light gray) and an Opaque (O) dark band; at the tip, the dark band is classified as being in the T3 category; *c*, modern shell of *Semele solida* collected in July 2008, after being cut and polished; the photo shows the extreme edge of the shell with the alternate bands: Translucent (T) band (light gray) and an Opaque (O) band (white); at the tip is the O3 band (adult sample); *d*, archaeological shell sample of *Semele solida* from Unit 22, Floor 22; the photo shows the extreme edge of the shell with a Translucent (T) band (light gray) and an Opaque (O) dark band at the tip classified as O2 (adult sample); *e*, modern shell of *Semele* collected in April 2008, after being cut and polished; the photo shows the extreme edge of the shell with the alternate bands: Translucent (T) band (light gray) and an Opaque (O) band (white); *f*, crosscut section of an archaeological shell sample of *Semele solida* (Unit 22, Floor 25); on the extreme edge of the shell an Opaque (O) dark band; behind it a Translucent (T) band (light gray).

Table A3.2. Bands on modern shells

a. Standard deviation for dark and white bands

		Dark band				Interval	
Month	No. of observed shells	Mean	Std dev	Min	Max	Mean −1 Std dev	Mean +1 Std dev
Jan	11	51.727	21.243	28.4	92.6	30.485	72.970
Feb	12	57.117	29.419	14.2	92.6	27.698	86.535
Mar	14	55.936	17.230	33.8	82.5	38.706	73.166
Apr	12	49.834	50.945	4.7	140.0	−1.111	100.779
May	4	15.560	4.498	9.7	19.8	11.062	20.058
Jun	6	32.433	21.152	12.2	57.3	11.282	53.585
Jul	7	58.343	34.596	12.0	104.0	23.747	92.938
Aug	14	38.371	21.633	9.5	78.8	16.738	60.004
Sep	14	33.421	14.651	18.9	71.9	18.771	48.072
Oct	15	33.080	15.141	13.9	62.5	17.939	48.221
Nov	13	28.219	15.487	4.3	52.7	12.733	43.706
Dec	6	19.117	6.396	13.0	29.1	12.721	25.513

		White band				Interval	
Month	No. of observed shells	Mean	Std dev	Min	Max	Mean −1 Std dev	Mean +1 Std dev
Apr	3	121.400	126.233	33.2	266.0	−4.833	247.633
May	11	48.073	37.720	13.1	115.0	10.353	85.793
Jun	9	80.956	53.064	18.4	167.0	27.892	134.019
Jul	8	168.100	118.646	83.8	444.0	49.454	286.746
Aug	2	141.600	134.067	46.8	236.4	7.533	275.667
Dec	11	28.691	11.602	13.9	52.8	17.089	40.293

b. Band formation distribution for each season

Season	Total T1	%T1	Total T2	%T2	Total T3	%T3	Total 01	%01	Total 02	%02	Total 03	%03	Total
Summer	2	5.41	14	37.84	21	56.76	0	0.00	0	0.00	0	0.00	37
Fall	2	4.44	5	11.11	15	33.33	20	44.44	0	0.00	3	6.67	45
Winter	4	8.89	10	22.22	21	46.67	2	4.44	7	16.56	1	2.22	45
Spring	3	6.67	9	20.00	22	48.89	11	24.44	0	0.00	0	0.00	45

Table A3.3. *Semele* sp.: Bands and growth stage patterns

a. Student's t-test for dark and white bands for modern and archaeological shells

Dark band modern shells

	Jan	Feb	Mar	Apr	May	Jun	Jul	Aug	Sep	Oct	Nov	Dec
Mean	51.73	57.12	55.94	49.83	15.56	32.43	58.34	38.37	33.42	33.08	28.22	19.12
Std dev	21.24	29.42	17.23	50.94	4.50	21.15	34.60	21.63	14.65	15.14	15.49	6.40

Dark band archaeological shells

	Jan	Feb	Mar	Apr	May	Jun	Jul	Aug	Sep	Oct	Nov	Dec
t-value	−7.78	−9.48	−9.11	−7.18	3.67	−1.67	−9.87	−3.55	−1.98	−1.88	−0.34	2.54

Sample
Mean 27.15
Std dev 23.01
n 53

White band modern shells

	Jan	Feb	Mar	Apr	May	Jun	Jul	Aug	Sep	Oct	Nov	Dec
Mean				121.40	48.07	80.96	168.10	141.60				28.69
Std dev				126.23	37.72	53.06	118.65	134.07				11.60

White band archaeological shells

	Jan	Feb	Mar	Apr	May	Jun	Jul	Aug	Sep	Oct	Nov	Dec
t-value				1.55	4.52	3.19	−0.34	0.73				5.30

Sample
Mean 159.70
Std dev 1.3
n 32

b. Growth stage patterns by cultural phase at Huaca Prieta

Cultural phase	Total T1	% T1	Total T2	% T2	Total T3	% T3	Total O1	% O1	Total O2	% O2	Total O3	% O3	Total
Phase II	2	7.69	3	12	11	42	3	11.5	2	7.69	5	19.2	26
Phase III	1	14.3	0	0	0	0	2	28.6	3	42.9	1	14.3	7
Phase IV	2	22.2	3	33	1	11	2	22.2	1	11.1	0	0	9
Phase V	7	41.2	2	12	3	18	2	11.8	1	5.88	2	11.8	17

Table A3.4. Exact Binomial Test of Goodness-of-Fit for modern shell samples and percentage of archaeological sample of each cultural phase at Huaca Prieta

Phase II	No. of archaeological shells	No. of modern shells in spring	% of shells identified for spring	No. of modern shells in summer	% of shells identified for summer	No. of modern shells in fall	% of modern shells for fall	No. of modern shells in winter	% of modern shells for winter
Dark count	16	34.00	75.56	37.00	100	22.00	47.83	35.00	76.09
White count	10	11.00	24.44	0.00	0	23.00	50	10.00	21.74
Total	26	45.00	100.00	37.00	100.00	45.00	100.00	45.00	100.00
Exact test p-value			0.11		0		0.171		0.058

Phase III	No. of archaeological shells	No. of modern shells in spring	% of shells identified for spring	No. of modern shells in summer	% of shells identified for summer	No. of modern shells in fall	% of modern shells for fall	No. of modern shells in winter	% of modern shells for winter
Dark count	1	34.00	75.56	37.00	100	22.00	47.83	35.00	76.09
White count	6	11.00	24.44	0.00	0	23.00	50	10.00	21.74
Total	7	45.00	100.00	37.00	100.00	45.00	100.00	45.00	100.00
Exact test p-value			0.001		0		0.126		0.001

Phase IV	No. of archaeological shells	No. of modern shells in spring	% of shells identified for spring	No. of modern shells in summer	% of shells identified for summer	No. of modern shells in fall	% of modern shells for fall	No. of modern shells in winter	% of modern shells for winter
Dark count	6	34.00	75.56	37.00	100	22.00	47.83	35.00	76.09
White count	3	11.00	24.44	0.00	0	23.00	50	10.00	21.74
Total	9	45.00	100.00	37.00	100.00	45.00	100.00	45.00	100.00
Exact test p-value			0.464		0		0.334		0.462

Phase V	No. of archaeological shells	No. of modern shells in spring	% of shells identified for spring	No. of modern shells in summer	% of shells identified for summer	No. of modern shells in fall	% of modern shells for fall	No. of modern shells in winter	% of modern shells for winter
Dark count	12	34.00	75.56	37.00	100	22.00	47.83	35.00	76.09
White count	5	11.00	24.44	0.00	0	23.00	50	10.00	21.74
Total	17	45.00	100.00	37.00	100.00	45.00	100.00	45.00	100.00
Exact test p-value			0.581		0		0.09		0.558

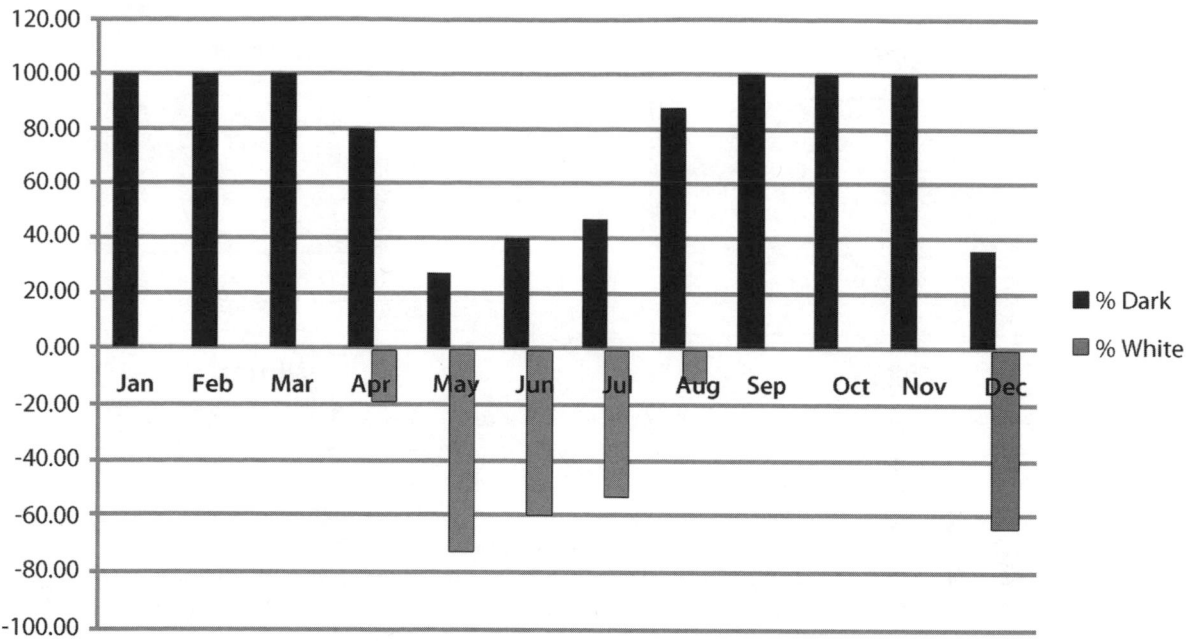

FIGURE A3.3. Monthly percentages of dark and white bands in modern shells of *Semele* sp. at Huaca Prieta.

trated in a brief interval from April to August and again in December (table A3.1b). White band formation starts in April and extends throughout August, diminishing in mid- to late winter (August) and ending in spring, followed by a rapid recovery registered at the end of spring/beginning of summer (December) with a high percentage of white increments (fig. A3.3).

The dark bands (translucent) form throughout the year, but with a sharp decline at the end of fall. Then they recover again in the middle of winter. An isolated reduction of the dark bands also occurs in December (end of spring/begin- ning of summer), which contrasts with the high percent- age of white bands at this time of the year. Dark band shell growth shows that for most of the year clams are in the slow growth cycles. A fast growth stage occurs during the fall and winter when white (opaque) bands are formed.

Table A3.2a presents the standard deviations for modern shells, showing the average values calculated from the band- widths of the shell growth. The ones for dark bands are less dispersed, while the ones for white bands are more spread out due to their fast growth and concentration in only one part of the year. The value for April shows the highest dispersion for both bands, which may reflect a transition phase between summer and fall, a period that also marks the beginning of the white band growth. In general, the values obtained are consistent with the overall patterns of shell band growth.

The next step was to classify modern shells according to their band formation (T and O), distributed seasonally (table A3.2b). Seasonal patterns stand out when percentages are plotted on histograms for each season (fig. A3.4). Trans- lucent bands, mainly T3, dominate and are collected in the spring. Opaque bands appear in late spring, with an iso- lated occurrence in December. In the fall assemblage opaque

shell growth frequency is more evident; by winter all of its subdivisions are formed and growth slows down (low fre- quency of the translucent formations).

The band analysis presented above on *Semele* sp. fits the six-part subdivision presented by Irvy Quitmyer et al. (1997) for *Mercenaria* spp. The technique is straightforward. The histograms are based on the frequency of band incre- ments for each season. This provides a baseline for the analy- sis of the archaeological collection.

As noted earlier, the period in which white bands formed coincides in part with the resting period, that is, from fall to late winter. Dark bands reflect the spawning period that extends from spring to summer, with a break between late spring and early summer.

ARCHAEOLOGICAL SAMPLES

The 59 shells from the archaeological samples were first analyzed in terms of band-width growth. For this a histo- gram with percentage values was constructed. A Student's t-test and standard deviations were calculated (table A3.3a, fig. A3.5). Samples were then analyzed by their chronologi- cal phases at the site. As a final test to verify the seasonality of shells, the Exact Binomial Test of Goodness-of-Fit was applied. This test was chosen because of the small sample sizes involved.

The growth histogram constructed for the archaeologi- cal samples with band distribution is presented in figure A3.5. The archaeological and modern histograms (figs. A3.4, A3.5) resemble each other. Both show a close resemblance to the winter growth-frequency profile in which *Semele* shells are in the Opaque stage of full development; the first

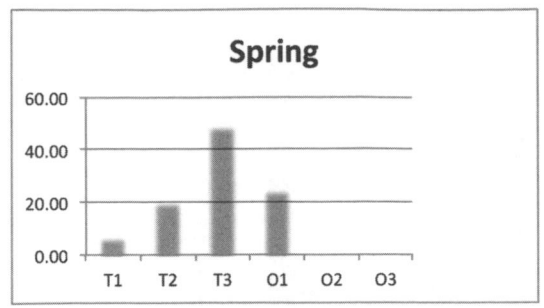

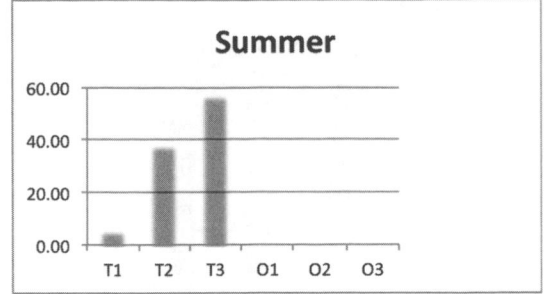

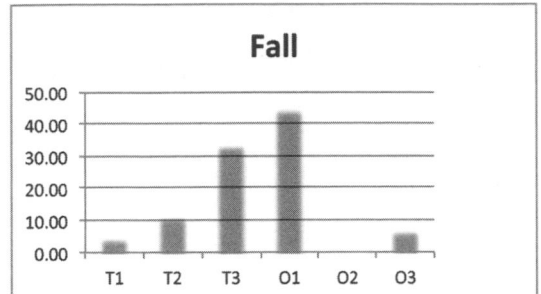

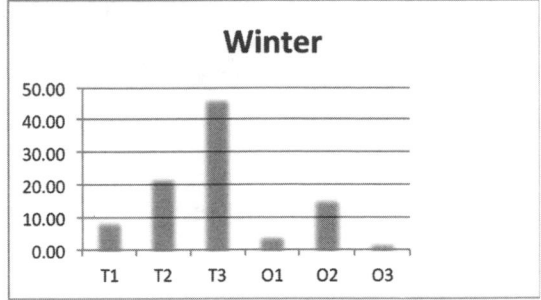

a

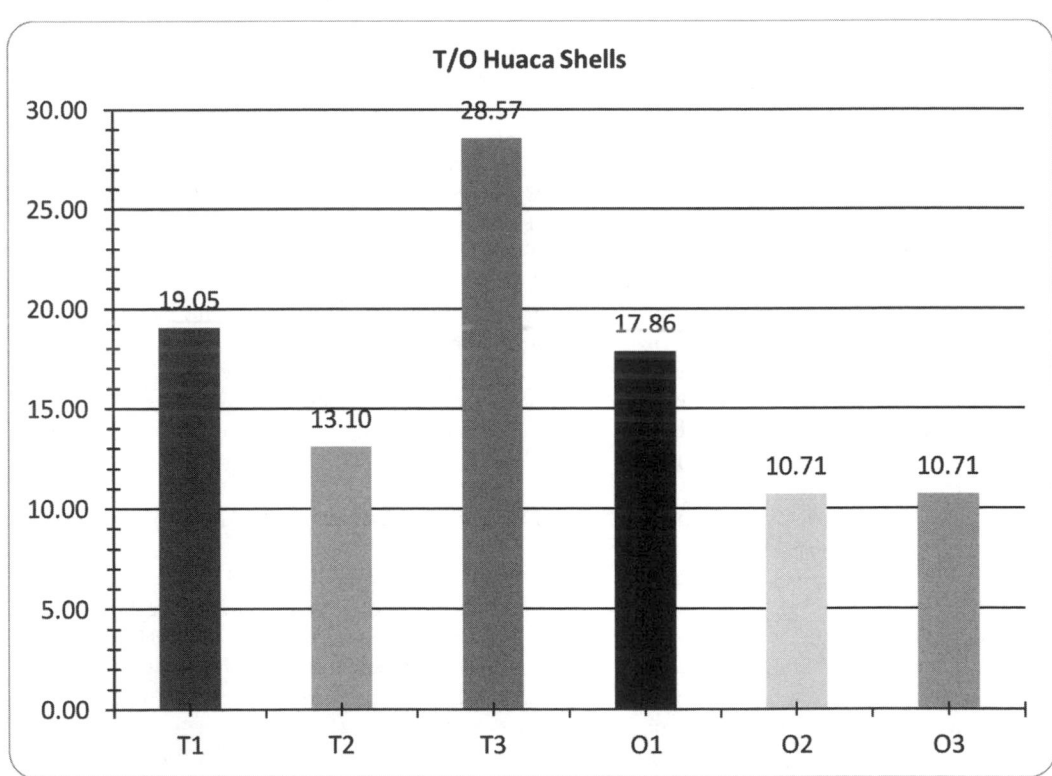

b

FIGURE A3.4. Histograms: *a*, modern shells and their distribution during the different seasons; *b*, distribution of the archaeological shell samples from Huaca Prieta.

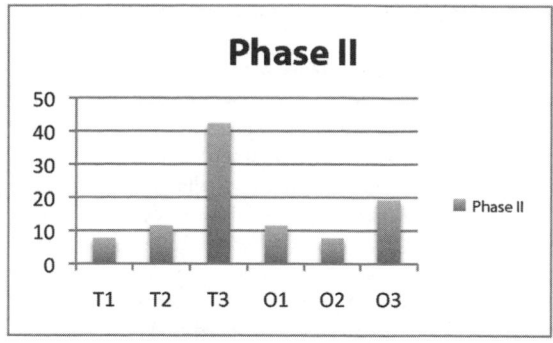

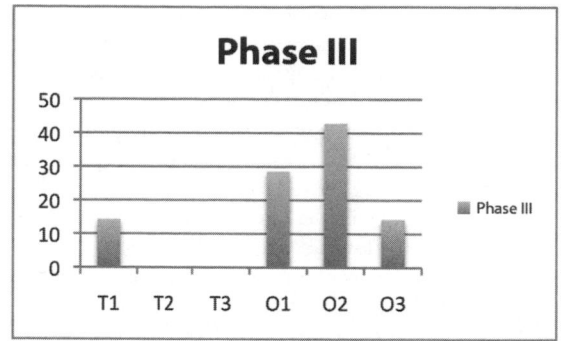

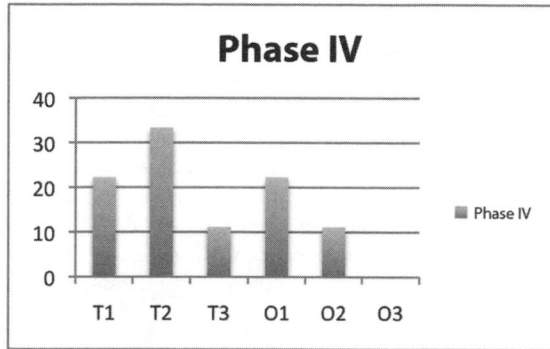

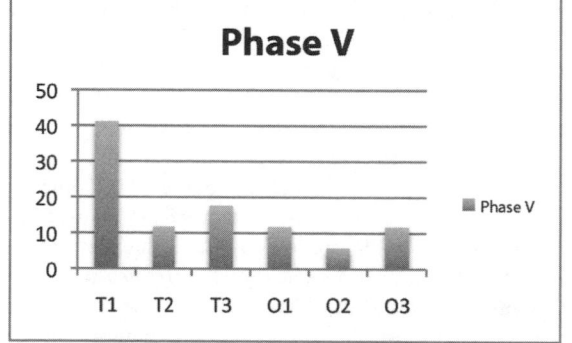

FIGURE A3.5. Histograms of the growth stage patterns of archaeological shells for each cultural phase at Huaca Prieta (*Semele* sp).

Translucent subdivision (T1) is recovering with a high frequency of shells in this stage. This suggests that most shells were collected from the end of fall through the winter season. Perhaps collection extended into early spring, considering that the frequency of T1 starts to increase.

Table A3.3a contains the means and standard deviations for band-width of both dark and white band shells in modern and archaeological samples. The Student's t-test is used to compare how close the value of the average band-width of the archaeological shells is to the value of the band-width of modern shells for each month of the year. It is important to note that the Student's t-test assumes the values found for modern shells to be the same as the true values for the entire population of modern shells and that the population of modern shells has a normal distribution.

The first set refers to shells with dark band modern samples in the first part and archaeological samples in the next part, and the second set concerns shells with white bands (modern and archaeological, respectively). Starting with modern shells, the first row shows the average band-width for each month of the year. The highest averages for dark band shells occurred in January (51.7 um), February (57.1 um), March (55.9 um) and July (58.3 um). The second row indicates the standard deviations within each month; it shows how much dispersion is observed around the average. For example, dark bands on modern shells in May have lower dispersion than in July because the standard deviation for May (4.5) is roughly one-third of the mean value for May (15.6) while the standard deviation for July (34.6) is more than half of the mean value for July (58.3). The

average band-width for modern shells for each month is also calculated by the t-statistic formula.

With a 95% confidence level, the t-statistic indicates that the average band-width of archaeological shells is not statistically different from the average of modern shells. This was the case during June and November for dark band shells, and during April, June, July, and August for the white band shells. This suggests that archaeological samples were collected from April (fall) to June to August (late fall/winter to winter), and then November (middle spring). These results apply for shells analyzed as a single unit and not classified chronologically.

The next step was to separate the archaeological samples by their chronological context at Huaca Prieta (table A3.3b). The histograms (fig. A3.5) show the growth stage pattern for each occupational stage, classified in Phases II–V. Unless noted otherwise, all shells for all phases are from tomb contexts at Huaca Prieta.

Based on frequency of the growth stage patterns, the following assertions can be made. The shells from Phase II burial contexts correspond to a period in which opaque bands are in development, O1 and O2 are shifting to the O3 phase with a high percentage of O3 bands, while translucent bands are ending their cycle with a high percentage of T3 phase and low values for T1 and T2. This could indicate the transition between fall and winter (late fall/early winter).

Phase III corresponds to autumn, in which opaque (dark) bands are at their maximum development and translucent (white) bands are just beginning to be formed.

Phase IV corresponds to early autumn, when opaque

bands initiate their formation but without reaching the O3 phase. Translucent increments are in transition to T3, starting to complete the cycle, but still with high values for T1 and T2.

Phase V is more ambiguous. It could correspond to late winter and/or spring when T bands are initiating their cycle with a high percentage in the T1 phase and starting to move into other phases, while the formation of the opaque bands is in balance with a low percentage. The t-test for the whole sample (not divided by phases) supports the appearance of shells from mid-spring, as shown in table A3.3.

The histogram for modern shells is a good reference for analysis of the archaeological shells. When the trend is not clear, it is difficult to draw a conclusion, however, as shown in Phase V. This is a problem with a small archaeological sample. In this case it is important to know the sample as a single unit. For this reason statistic tests were performed for the archaeological shells as a whole. This not only provided information on the validity of the samples and the patterns found but showed the seasonal distribution of the samples that work as a guideline, as the histograms did for modern samples. But if samples are too small, the assumption of a normal distribution cannot be made. Therefore the Exact Binomial Test was used, which is suitable when the sample size is small. A normal distribution is not a requisite for the test.

EXACT BINOMIAL TEST FOR ARCHAEOLOGICAL SHELLS

Data from both modern and archaeological shells were integrated with the quantitative analysis for comparative study using the binomial test. Bold numbers refer to positive results ($p > 0.05$) that correspond to the seasons in which archaeological shells fit. Results are presented in table A3.4, for all phases studied here.

The test shows a strong tendency toward archaeological shells collected during fall, winter, and/or spring. This is observed for Phases II, IV, and V. Only Phase III diverges from this pattern, with shells collected exclusively during the fall. There is no indication of shells collected during the summer. The samples from Phases III and IV are small (7 and 9 shells, respectively). Nonetheless, the results are consistent with the preceding tests and reinforce the idea that the shells have been seasonally harvested.

CONCLUSIONS

The biological cycle of *Semele solida* shows that this clam has a short resting period during the fall. In modern samples from Huaca Prieta the shorter cycle coincides with white bands, which occur during the fall/winter period from April to August and again in a short term in December (late spring). The dark bands seem to coincide with the spawning period that occurs with a reduction from April to August, with a break in December.

For the archaeological shells, the binomial test suggests that they were harvested in the fall, winter, and spring. Shells were collected during the reproductive cycle, which leads to two conclusions. First, no attempt to safeguard the clam population was undertaken, since the preferred period for foraging was during the period of clam reproduction. Second, a possible factor in collecting shells at this time was that clams had reached their maximum weight.

Data for the entire chronology, not separated by phases, show that shells were probably harvested in April then from June to October and in November. Another reason for the presence of clams at the site during these months may relate to specific rituals (burial?) enacted between April and August (fall/winter) and in November (spring) during the wet season and beginning of the dry season on the coast.

Studying the Huaca Prieta shells in their chronological and site context, and considering all the statistical tests, the data show that shells were probably collected in the early fall through the winter and into the spring season. Fall stands out as the most prevalent season for shell collection. The seasonal use of the site, based on the study of the shells of *Semele*, is related to the following phases:

Phase II: late fall/early winter (June/July)
Phase III: high autumn (June)
Phase IV: early autumn (April)
Phase V: middle spring (November)

There is a clear pattern in the formation of the translucent and opaque bands. Shells appear not to have been collected during the summer months.

Shellfish, especially mussels and clams, were ritual offerings throughout all phases at Huaca Prieta. Although *Semele solida* is frequent, it is not as frequent as *Protothaca thaca*. Other species were possibly collected and deposited during certain times of the year, as *S. solida* seems to have been. These other shellfish do not present the growth-ring structure of *S. solida*, however, and thus are not amenable to this type of study.

ACKNOWLEDGMENTS

This research was supported, in part, by a grant from the National Science Foundation Dissertation Enhancement (BCS-0733867). Additional support was provided by the Department of Anthropology at the Vanderbilt University. I am grateful to Isleide Zissimos (Department of Economics, Vanderbilt University) for all the discussions and help with the statistic analysis, and to Tom Dillehay for the opportunity to analyze the shells as well as for all the insights during this work. All the interpretations, however, are my full responsibility.

CHILE PEPPER DISTRIBUTION AND USE

Katherine L. Chiou, Christine A. Hastorf, Víctor F. Vásquez, Teresa Rosales Tham, Duccio Bonavia, and Tom D. Dillehay

INTRODUCTION

Chile peppers have their origins in the Western Hemisphere. Prior to Christopher Columbus's voyage to the Americas in the fifteenth century, chile peppers were cultivated to varying extents from the American Southwest to Chile. The chile pepper (*Capsicum* spp.) consists of about twenty-five species, five of which represent domesticated taxa (Andrews 1984; Basu and De 2003; Davenport 1970; Eshbaugh 1976; Eshbaugh et al. 1983; Heiser 1971; Heiser and Smith 1953; Naj 1992). These taxa include *C. annuum* L., *C. baccatum* L. var. *pendulum* (Willd.) Eshbaugh, *C. chinense* Jacq., *C. frutescens* L., and *C. pubescens* Ruiz and Pavon. The general consensus among botanists is that the nuclear origin area for the *Capsicum* genus is in highland Bolivia on the eastern slopes; from there the wild *Capsicum* species radiated outward through the Americas, dispersed by birds before people arrived in the Americas. Later they were further spread by humans after intense interaction and domestication (Andrews 1984; Eshbaugh et al. 1983; Pickersgill 1977, 2009). Figure A4.1a illustrates the distribution of *Capsicum* species prior to colonization. *C. baccatum* is thought to have been domesticated in a lowland region from coastal Peru to Brazil. *C. chinense* and *C. frutescens* have more tropical roots and likely were domesticated in the northeastern Amazon area (Moses and Umaharan 2012; Pickersgill 1972; Aguilar-Meléndez 2006; Hernández-Verdugo et al. 1999; Perry and Flannery 2007). *C. pubescens* has the most restricted homeland and is considered a highland species. Botanists believe its location of origin lies in the Andean mountains. *C. annuum* was domesticated in Mexico, perhaps even in two distinct locations (Aguilar-Meléndez 2006; Pickersgill 1972). While botanists have painted a picture of *Capsicum* domestication based on the modern distribution of wild *Capsicum* taxa in the Americas as well as the presence of preserved *Capsicum* fruits with calyx morphology intact from archaeological sites, the lack of certainty surrounding the identification of *Capsicum* seeds to species-level has hindered the effort of tracing *Capsicum* domestication and movements through the more common seed evidence. Because some scholars suggested that *Capsicum* seed identification would not work, few attempts were made to study it systematically (Andrews 1984). Based on our research on both modern and archaeological seeds, we developed an identification methodology that allowed us to assign the Huaca Prieta and Paredones seeds to their corresponding species. We believe

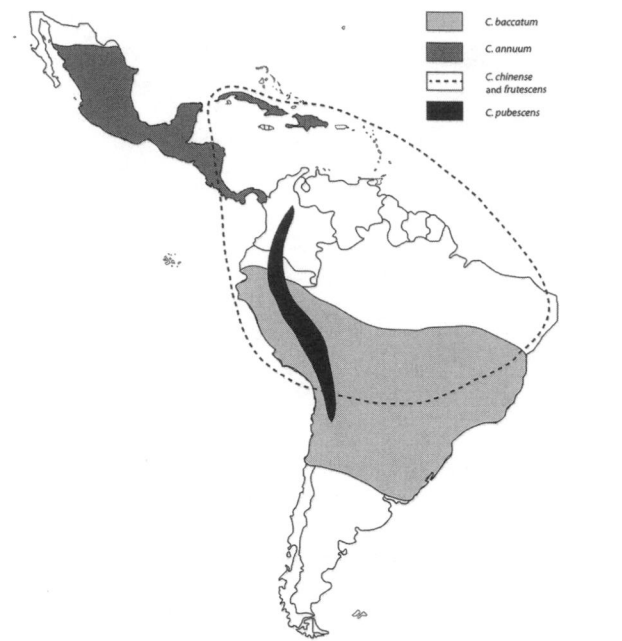

a

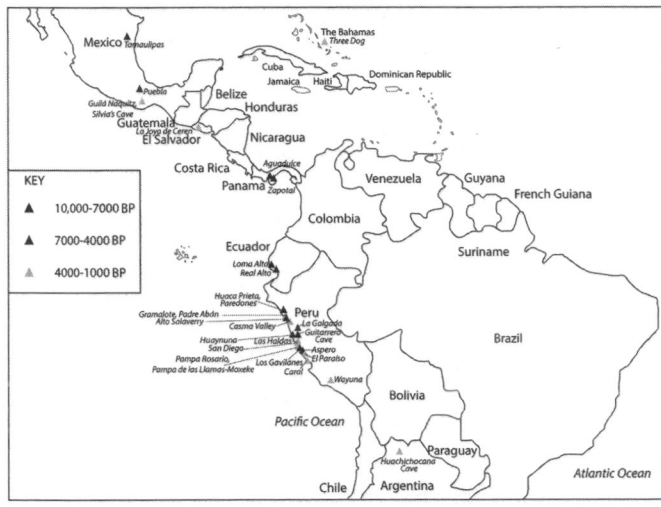

b

FIGURE A4.1. Distribution of *Capsicum*: *a*, map showing distribution of *Capsicum* domesticates at the time of European contact, ~AD 1530 (redrawn from Andrews 1984; Heiser 1976; McLeod et al. 1982); *b*, map showing early evidence for domesticated *Capsicum* in the Americas from 10,000 to 1000 BP.

that the analysis of both quantitative and qualitative traits of archaeological *Capsicum* seeds can lead to species-level identification.

Given their long history of cultivation in the Andes, it is likely that chile peppers were prized for several millennia. *Capsicum* seeds have purportedly been found in deposits dating to ~10,000 BP at Chilca and Guitarrero Cave, though this date is disputed (compare Kaplan and Lynch 1999; Moseley 2001; Pearsall 2008). Starch grains of *Capsicum* have also been recovered dating to 6000 BP from Real Alto and Loma Alta in Ecuador (Perry et al. 2007). Combined with

evidence obtained from sites like Huaca Prieta and La Galgada in Peru, the literature claims that the chile pepper was cultivated by at least 5000 BP in the central Andes (Grieder et al. 1988; Pickersgill 1969). Given the greater time-depth of our study, our reported chile pepper remains are among the earliest, if not the earliest, well-provenienced examples of cultivated *Capsicum* in the world.

The domestication of the *Capsicum* genus and its various species has long been the subject of botanical research that has informed our study. According to Barbara Pickersgill (1972), domesticated species of *Capsicum* are fairly distinct and difficult to cross, producing sterile hybrids even when fertilization is successful. Thus cultivated species of *Capsicum* had distinct wild ancestors and were characteristic of different regions where they were propagated in preconquest times (Smith and Heiser 1957). Given these traits, the *Capsicum* genus serves as a potential proxy for studying human interactions in the Americas, as "[g]enera in which several species have been domesticated may thus be useful indicators of cultural contact if the place of domestication of the individual species is accurately known and if the archaeological material can be assigned with certainty to a particular species or group" (Pickersgill 1972: 99).

Given that the presence or absence of different *Capsicum* species can reveal valuable information about cultural contact, the ability to identify *Capsicum* plant parts is crucial. The identification of *Capsicum* in the archaeological record has generally been unsystematic. Towle (1961), for example, reported that the majority of *Capsicum* remains from coastal Peru were *C. annuum*. Previous work at Huaca Prieta by Pickersgill on *Capsicum* fruits has revealed the presence of *C. baccatum* or *C. chinense* by the late Preceramic period (Pickersgill 1969). These identifications were made based on calyx morphology (Pickersgill 1972). While most of her discussion centered on chile pepper pods, Pickersgill reported the range of diameters for the seeds that were also recovered there. While her data may be useful for arriving at a general sense of seed size, they do not lend much insight into species-level identification. After our review of the literature, we decided that the best method was to create our own study to address the identity of chile peppers at Huaca Prieta from seeds.

CONTEXTUALIZING THE HUACA PRIETA AND PAREDONES CAPSICUM DATA

As of this writing, Paredones has the earliest reliably and directly dated chile pepper remains throughout the Americas (10,578–10,285 cal BP, Beta343109; Chiou et al. 2014; Chiou and Hastorf 2014). Figure A4.1b illustrates the published early *Capsicum* evidence in the Americas. These sites and their dates are listed in table A4.1. It is still clear that the residents of the coast of Peru exchanged with people who brought chile peppers to the area very early. Figure A4.1a suggests that several species are native to northeastern Amazonia, including the modern-day countries of Venezuela and Colombia (Andrews 1984).

Table A4.1. Dates associated with archaeological sites in figure A4.1 with early *Capsicum* evidence

Site	Country	Early date (BP)	Dates (BP)	Sources	Reliability of age
Guitarrero Cave	Peru	9950	9950–9450	Pearsall (2003), Pearsall (2008)	not reliable
Puebla	Mexico	9000	9000–7000	Kraft (2014); Smith (1967); Smith (1987)	dated indirectly, subsequent dating of maize to 5600
Tamaulipas	Mexico	9000	9000–7000	Smith (1997)	dated indirectly, subsequent dating of maize to 6400–6000
Huaca Prieta/ Paredones	Peru	9000	9000	Chiou et al. (2014)	direct AMS dating
Aquadulce	Panama	5600	5600	Perry et al. (2007)	Cited
Loma Alta	Ecuador	5050	5050–4080	Perry et al. (2007)	Unknown
Alto Salaverry	Peru	5000	5000	Pearsall (2003); Pearsall (2008)	7000–4000
Zapotal	Panama	4850	4850–3560	Perry ct al. (2007)	Unknown
Real Alto	Ecuador	4800	4800–4400	Perry et al. (2007)	Unknown
Los Gavilanes	Peru	4650	4650–4350	Pearsall (2003); Pearsall (2008)	Unknown
La Galgada	Peru	4612	4612–3950	Pearsall (2003); Pearsall (2008)	Unknown
Aspero	Peru	4360	4360–4350	Pearsall (2003); Pearsall (2008)	Unknown
Huaynuná	Peru	4200	4200	Pozorski and Pozorski (1990)	1000–present
Las Haldas	Peru	3960	3960–3745	Pearsall (2003); Pearsall (2008)	Unknown
Padre Abán	Peru	3930	3930–3679	Pearsall (2003); Pearsall (2008)	10,000–7000
Wayuna	Peru	3847	3847–3564	Perry et al. (2007)	Unknown
El Paraíso	Peru	3750	3750–3450	Pearsall (2003); Pearsall (2008)	Unknown
Pamapas de las Llama– Moxeke	Peru	3735	3735–2070	Pearsall (2003); Pearsall (2008)	Unknown

Table A4.1. Continued

Site	Country	Early date (BP)	Dates (BP)	Sources	Reliability of age
Gramalote	Peru	3600	3600–1250	Pearsall (2008); Pearsall (2003)	Unknown
Casma Valley	Peru	3500	3500–2500	Perry et al. (2007)	4000–1000
Caral	Peru	3050	3050–2800	Pearsall (2003); Pearsall (2008)	Unknown
San Diego	Peru	2760	2760–2400	Pearsall (2003); Pearsall (2008)	Unknown
Pampa Rosario	Peru	2500	2500–2245	Pearsall (2003); Pearsall (2008)	Unknown
Huachichocama Cave	Argentina	2450	2450–450	Pearsall (2003); Pearsall (2008)	Unknown
Guilá Naquitz and Silvia's Caves	Mexico	1500	1500–1400	Perry and Flannery (2007)	direct AMS dating
La Joya de Ceren	El Salvador	1400	1400	Perry et al. (2007)	Unknown
Three Dog	Bahamas	1265	1265–969	Berman and Pearsall (2000); Berman and Gnivecki (1995)	Unknown

GOALS OF STUDY

Huaca Prieta and Paredones are neighboring early sites. Chile pepper seeds from these sites were recovered primarily through flotation of sediment samples during recent excavations and secondarily through the retrieval of seeds from various features, especially from features and floors during excavation. More than 90% of the seeds were recovered from flotation. All feature matrix (100%) was floated. Approximately 10% of all floor sediment, depending upon floor thickness and extent, also was floated. At times, clusters of plants were excavated in floors and features. These were catalogued and stored immediately for analysis. Opportunistic sampling resulted from seeds found in bundle offerings in various contexts. The seeds were identified as *Capsicum* spp. by Víctor Vásquez and Teresa Rosales Tham of the Universidad Nacional de Trujillo. The study population here constitutes the entire collection of *Capsicum* seeds retrieved by the project; it was sent to Hastorf and Chiou at the McCown Archaeobotany Laboratory at the University of California, Berkeley, for taxon identification. The received seeds represent four out of five phases over the long history of the mounds at Huaca Prieta and Paredones (Dillehay et al. 2012b).

Out of the approximately 750 seeds recovered, 64 were studied. Table A4.2 presents the database, including the sample, site, phase, number of seeds available, number of seeds analyzed, and context from which the seeds were retrieved. Our seed selection was based on the requirement of studying complete seeds in good condition, with special concern for the preservation of the beak and a completely intact seed, including the seed margins. We selected 100% of the complete seeds from Phases II ($n = 14$) and IV ($n = 28$). The majority of seeds came from the latest period, Phase V. We analyzed 1 to 3 well-preserved seeds per sample (to gain information from all extant contexts). In total, 22 seeds were sampled from Phase V. Given the sparse nature of the literature on *Capsicum* seed identification (with exceptions such as Gunn and Gaffney 1974; Martin 1946; Minnis and Whalen 2010), we recorded both qualitative and quantitative attributes (for example, Bruno 2006; Bruno and Whitehead 2003; Langlie et al. 2011). Our first goal was to discover diagnostic traits of *Capsicum* in modern seeds that could be applied to our archaeological analysis. Our second goal was to apply these criteria to the archaeological seed data and also to offer insights into early chile pepper use in coastal Peru in the specific context of Huaca Prieta ($n = 27$) and Paredones ($n = 37$).

Table A4.2. Summary of archaeological *Capsicum* seed collection
from Huaca Prieta and Paredones

Phase	Sample no.	Site	# Available fragments	# Analyzed	Context
II	553	Paredones		0	Other
	563	Paredones	1	1	Other
	570	Paredones	13	13	Residential
IV	518	Huaca Prieta	7	3	Feasting
	519	Huaca Prieta	3	0	Feasting
	525	Paredones	9	5	Other
	526	Paredones	9	3	Other
	543	Paredones	16	5	Other
	561	Paredones	2	1	Other
	562	Paredones	6	1	Other
	568	Paredones	90	6	Other
	569	Huaca Prieta	19	4	Feasting
V	15	Huaca Prieta	220	2	Feasting
	17	Huaca Prieta	34	1	Feasting
	28	Huaca Prieta	23	2	Feasting
	32	Huaca Prieta	11	1	Feasting
	43	Huaca Prieta	33	1	Feasting
	46	Huaca Prieta	36	3	Feasting
	48	Huaca Prieta	14	1	Feasting
	49	Huaca Prieta	58	1	Feasting
	59	Huaca Prieta	22	3	Feasting
	369	Huaca Prieta	17	0	Feasting
	405	Huaca Prieta	5	1	Residential
	440	Huaca Prieta	3	1	Feasting
	460	Huaca Prieta	17	1	Feasting
	469	Huaca Prieta	1	0	Feasting
	520	Huaca Prieta	1	1	Feasting
	527	Paredones	18	1	Other
	528	Paredones	31	1	Other
	531	Paredones	5	0	Other
	575	Huaca Prieta	16	0	Residential
	601	Huaca Prieta	2	1	Residential
	602	Huaca Prieta	1	0	Residential

MODERN *CAPSICUM* SEED STUDY METHODS

We determined that studying a comparative collection of modern *Capsicum* seeds from all five domesticated species was essential to the goals of this project. To that end, we amassed 44 distinct seed collections representing *C. annuum*, *C. baccatum*, *C. chinense*, *C. frutescens*, and *C. pubescens* and several wild taxa from different sources (these are reported in Chiou and Hastorf [2012, 2014]). These modern seeds were photographed using an Olympus SZ-61 stereomicroscope (10×–30×) and an Olympus digital camera (model DP72).

Close-up electron microscopy (SEM) image scans of the testa were taken using a Hitachi TM-1000. The Olympus MicroSuite program was used to take various measurements of the whole seed, the attachment scar, and the testa in the cross-section. Qualitative assessments were also made of the seed shape and testa texture. The photography procedure can be found online as McCown Archaeobotanical Report #77 (Chiou 2014).

We recorded data for 27 attributes on each of the 44 modern *Capsicum* seeds. These attributes were generated from the *Capsicum* literature, previous research with seed

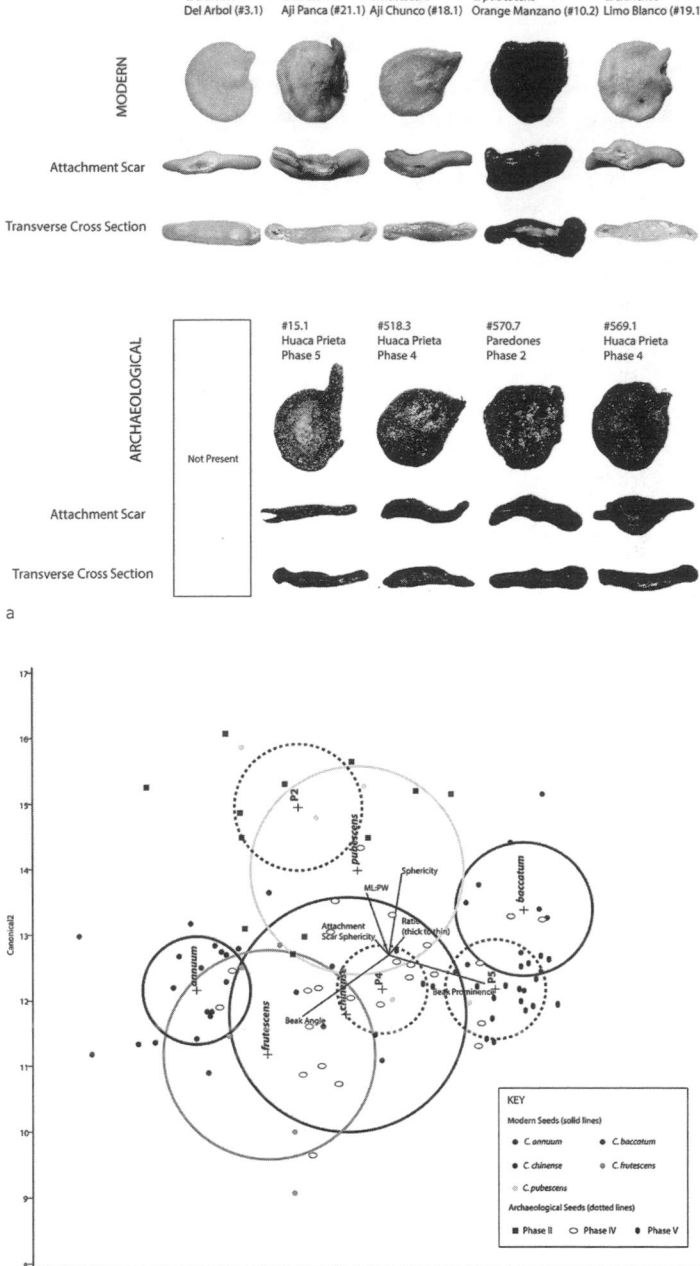

FIGURE A4.2. Modern and archaeological *Capsicum* seeds: *a*, comparison between modern and archaeological *Capsicum* seeds; photos show the seed lying flat, the attachment scar, and the transverse cross-section (note that *Capsicum annuum* seeds have not been recovered from Huaca Prieta and Paredones); *b*, discriminant analysis of modern seeds from the five domesticated *Capsicum* taxa and archaeological seeds from Huaca Prieta and Paredones using six quantitative diagnostic attributes.

identification, and observations made concerning the nature of *Capsicum* seeds. We then ran a series of exploratory data analyses to seek the most productive differentiating measurements for taxon identification, such as plotting two attributes against each other (*y* by *x*) and generating scatter plot matrices with multiple variables. From these plots we determined that six quantitative attributes combined to form diagnostic identifications of the five domestic *Capsicum* seeds to species-level. Our six quantitative attributes are (1) beak angle, (2) beak prominence, (3) the ratio of maximum seed length to perpendicular width, (4) whole seed sphericity, (5) the ratio of the thickest portion of the testa to the thinnest portion, and (6) attachment scar sphericity. In addition two qualitative attributes were important in differentiating species. These two nominal attributes are seed shape and testa texture. Combining the six quantitative attributes with the two qualitative attributes, we have eight diagnostic characteristics that distinguish the five species' seeds. (These quantitative and qualitative diagnostics are explained in Chiou and Hastorf [2012, 2014].) The photographs in figure A4.2a provide species images of both modern and archaeological species, illustrating the measured morphological differences. The attributes are defined as follows.

BEAK ANGLE

The beak is the protruding area of the seed that differentiates *Capsicum* seeds from other similar-looking seeds of the family Solanaceae (Minnis and Whalen 2010). The beak angle (fig. A4.2a) gives a sense of how much the beak diverges from the rest of the body. A high beak angle, for example, is one of the diagnostic attributes for *C. frutescens* seeds.

BEAK PROMINENCE

This term refers to how far the beak protrudes from the rest of the seed body and is recorded in an ordinal scale, based on a ranking (from 1 to 5).

MAXIMUM SEED LENGTH: PERPENDICULAR SEED WIDTH

This is a measurement of the basic length and width of a seed. The length measurement was taken from the beak, and the width measurement was taken perpendicular to the length measurement. All seeds were measured in the same manner.

RATIO OF THICK TESTA TO THIN TESTA

We made a transverse cross-section of the seed to measure the thickness of the testa, which is often an important measurement in studying domestication. Testas tend to get thinner as a result of directed selection pressure during domestication (Bruno 2006; Bruno and Whitehead 2003; Flannery 1973). Noticing a great amount of variation in the measurements of individual seed testa (especially at the outer margins), we decided to calculate a ratio of the thick portion to the thin region of the testa. Three measurements were taken for both these thick and thin testa areas and averaged to produce the score we used (Chiou and Hastorf 2014). This was a useful measurement, as a range of these ratio values are produced for each seed. For example, *C. annuum* has a low thick to thin testa ratio, whereas *C. pubescens* displays the highest thick to thin testa ratio (around 8:1).

WHOLE SEED SPHERICITY

"Sphericity" refers to how spherical (or circular in the two-dimensional sense) a seed is. Tracing the circumference of each seed and then comparing those tracings to a perfect circle using the Microsuite software measured this.

ATTACHMENT SCAR SPHERICITY

The attachment scar or hilum is the location on the seed that attaches the seed to the placental wall of the chile pepper fruit. We noticed that the shape of the attachment scar varied among these species and decided to measure sphericity of the attachment scar shape.

SEED SHAPE

The general shape of *Capsicum* seeds is relatively distinct from species to species, with some overlap. These seed shapes are shown in figure A4.2a. (Note: these names are our creations, not necessarily standardized seed shape names, and do not include all of the shapes examined.)

TESTA TEXTURE

This term refers to the topography of the seed coat. The texture of the seed coat is often diagnostic, especially in the case of *C. pubescens*, which displays an exaggerated reticulation pattern on the outer margins of the seed, particularly when compared to *C. baccatum*, which exhibits a tighter reticulation pattern (as opposed to the other four species that tend to have a smooth surface).

THE ARCHAEOLOGICAL *CAPSICUM* SEEDS FROM HUACA PRIETA (INCLUDING UNIT 16) AND PAREDONES

With these eight diagnostic criteria for *Capsicum* seeds, we turned to the 64 whole archaeological *Capsicum* seeds from Phases II, IV, and V at Huaca Prieta and Paredones (7500–3500 BP) to determine their temporal and cultural patterning. Chiou completed the exact same measurements on the archaeological seeds as she had done on the modern seeds, recording the values for these eight attributes on each whole seed.

Based on our analysis and previous experience with modern seeds, we preliminarily identified each seed to a particular species and immediately noticed temporal patterns suggesting change in species/varieties through time.

While archaeological seeds are not always in as good a shape as modern ones, the archaeological seeds chosen from the project's population were sufficiently well preserved to complete all eight measurements. A few taphonomic variables, however, hindered some qualitative assessments. One is the effect of seed browning. As mentioned above, seeds of *C. pubescens* can be readily distinguished by their dark brown to black color. Unfortunately, it is not possible to rely on color when looking at archaeological specimens (or older *Capsicum* seeds), as seed browning can occur rather quickly, depending on environmental conditions (Boonsiri et al. 2007; Lee et al. 1991). Furthermore, the testas in the archaeological seeds were not all perfectly preserved, as the epidermis was often missing, which left a distorted view of the seed surface.

CHANGES IN CHILE PEPPER PREFERENCE THROUGH TIME AND SPACE AT HUACA PRIETA (INCLUDING UNIT 16) AND PAREDONES

When all measurement data concerning diagnostic attributes are studied by phase and species (illustrated in the discriminant analysis graph of fig. A4.2b), we can connect the temporal links at sites to species, especially with *C. baccatum*. The co-variance is most strongly loaded on beak prominence and Phase V, the latest period. Phase II, the earliest, is linked to sphericity, attachment scar sphericity, and *C. pubescens*. Phase IV is weakly associated with *C. chinenese* and beak angle. *C. annuum* is the least connected with these specimens and phases. The absence of *C. annuum* is not surprising, as it is unlikely that the Mexican domesticate was present in this part of South America during these periods. The patterning seen in this figure sets the stage for a better understanding of a complex picture of the movement and introduction of *Capsicum* into these sites over thousands of years.

The history of the different species' presence at sites is shown in figure A4.3a. The bar chart clarifies the frequency of the four *Capsicum* species by the Phases II, IV, and V. We can see how evenly the four South American chile pepper taxa are present at sites in this early time, with *C. pubescens*, the highland species, dominating. This pattern strongly suggests that *Capsicum* arrived at these sites from a range of locations. Only strontium, oxygen, and sulfur stable isotopes of these seeds will tell if they were grown locally or carried into the sites. By Phase IV (~5300–4100 cal BP), there is a shift in species access, production, or exchange of these four taxa. All of these taxa could be grown on the coast, except perhaps *C. pubescens*. By Phase IV, the highland *C. pubescens* is barely present, as *C. baccatum* increases in popularity. This suggests that highland trade and/or transhumance diminished throughout Phase IV (~5300–4100 cal BP). The two eastern Amazonian taxa continue to enter into the sites, but in a lesser amount than earlier. Only *C. baccatum* increases into Phase V. At that time it dominated. This diminution of the other three *Capsicum* taxa suggests that kin, migrating groups, or trade/exchange groups who came and went from this coastal location had exchanged them into the site. But

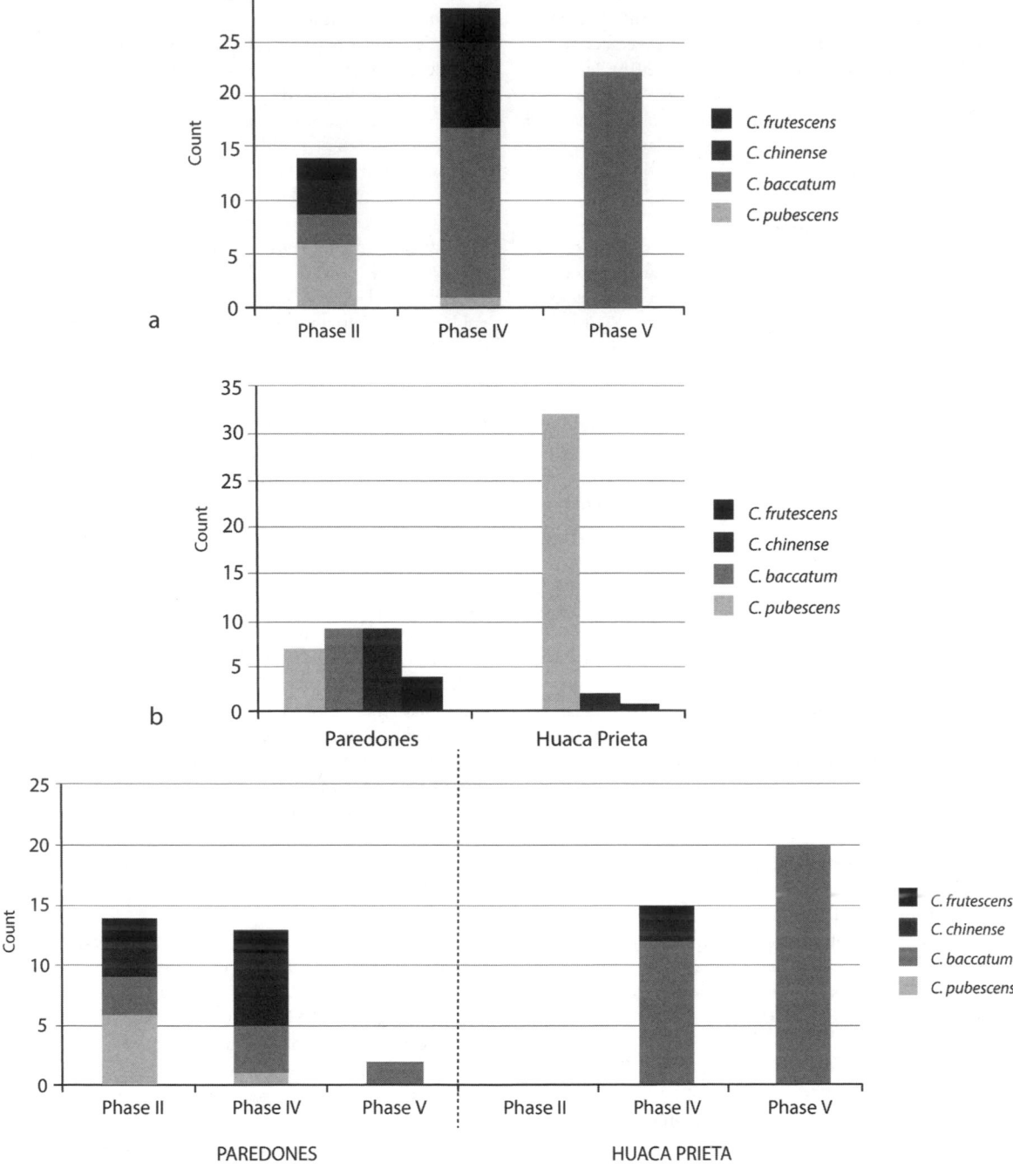

FIGURE A4.3. Presence of *Capsicum* species: *a*, species at both Huaca Prieta and Paredones by cultural phase; *b*, species at Huaca Prieta compared to Paredones; *c*, species by cultural phase and site.

by ~4000 cal BP the bringing of such foodstuffs diminished and stopped, with only *C. baccatum* entering the sites, which was probably grown around them.

Figure A4.3b helps us understand the different histories of these sites and their cultural uniqueness, through their identified *Capsicum* taxa presence. Paredones received a full and even range of the four *Capsicum* species, suggesting that the contexts sampled were engaged in a wide regional net-

work of kin and exchange partners across the Andes. Huaca Prieta, with ritual contexts sampled, looks much more focused on accessing local production, if our assumption is correct that *C. baccatum* could be and was the optimal taxon grown around these sites. Huaca Prieta contexts perhaps were more focused because these represent primarily ritual and mortuary locations.

This idea is illustrated in figure A4.3c, presenting the

taxa distribution over time at these two sites. Again, Paredones shows its strong diversity of *Capsicum* in Phases II and IV. All four taxa are present then, with Phase V contexts having only *C. baccatum*. This substantiates the idea that early Paredones residents received *Capsicum* from all over, suggesting a broad exchange network emanating from this settlement's population. When we turn to Huaca Prieta itself, we see a different picture. That site is largely receiving *C. baccatum*, but only later. No well-preserved *Capsicum* was obtained from Phase II there. *C. baccatum* dominates when we have seeds. In Phase V it is the only taxon found on that site, again supporting the idea that it was the taxon that was adopted and locally grown around the site.

SITE DATA

We plotted the locations that these specimens came from across the two sites with the hope that we could better understand the contexts of the chile peppers and therefore their different cultural use and value. Figure A4.4a presents the locations of *Capsicum* at Huaca Prieta. This figure shows the clustering of *C. baccatum* within the excavated units, suggesting a stable relationship with the source of these peppers, either by locally growing them or from stable exchange relations. The figure A4.4b map of Paredones is more complex. Because all of the samples are from one area, this is less useful for a cultural interpretation. In Paredones the samples are derived from unprepared floors in Units 20 and 22, which are associated at first with domestic activity (premound level) and later with food preparation and probably ritual. Most seeds were retrieved from flotation or from small features on the floor. No discernible spatial or activity patterns are revealed in their distributions across floors.

In figure A4.5a we plotted the distribution of the four taxa by context. Here we see that the excavations focused on feasting areas at Huaca Prieta. Few domestic areas were sampled, but in these only *C. baccatum* was identified in Unit 16, which is a domestic area off of the Huaca Prieta mound. Feasting included all of the taxa, with *C. baccatum* always dominating. These data do not suggest that the other species could not be included in ritual feasting, but through time the exchange and production patterns show how *C. baccatum* increasingly dominated in all contexts.

Figure A4.5b shows how the taxa shifted through phases, as also indicated in the other figures, and clearly depicts how *C. baccatum* slowly came to dominate the use of chile pepper at sites over time. Stable isotope analysis will allow us to say if these *C. baccatum* were grown locally or traded in, but the data we have now suggest that they were locally produced.

Focusing more on the individual floors that were sampled, figure A4.5c presents the four taxa presence by sampled floors at these two sites. Again we see how *C. baccatum* dominates all late contexts. Phase II floors, which are only represented at Paredones, contain a combination of *C. pubescens*, *C. frutescens* and *C. baccatum*, whereas Phase IV floors at Paredones have only *C. chinense* and *C. baccatum*, just like the Phase IV floors at Huaca Prieta. If the working hypothesis that *C. baccatum* was being grown nearby and

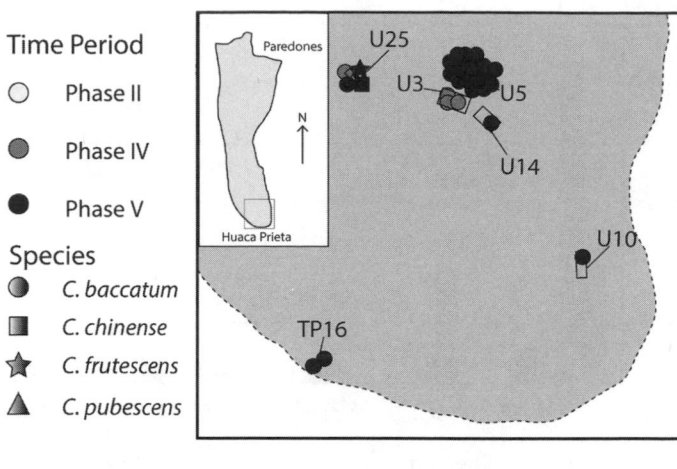

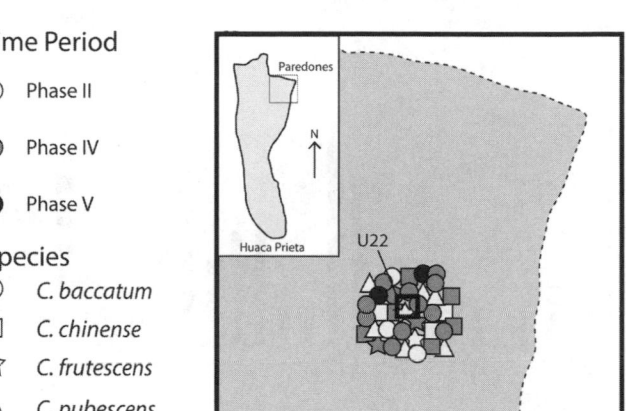

FIGURE A4.4. Occurrence of *Capsicum* spp. seeds: *a*, map showing the locations where seeds were recovered and their corresponding temporal phases at Huaca Prieta; *b*, map of Unit 22 in Paredones showing the wide array of *Capsicum* seeds recovered in Phases II, IV, and V.

the other taxa were traded in is correct, this access pattern was operating most in Phase IV, when the *C. chinense* was traded in.

The few nonfeasting samples come from Paredones, where the evidence suggests that these locations were mainly for food preparation and limited ritual. The right side of figure A4.5b displays the clear dominance of *C. baccatum* in these locations as well.

As mentioned above, upon analyzing these data, we noticed different frequencies among the phases of the archaeological *Capsicum* seeds. We observed much more variation in the earlier phases (Phases II and IV) contrasted with the homogeneity in the seed species noted in Phase V. As in the case of the modern seeds, we subjected our data (the measurements of the six quantitative attributes) to a discriminant analysis (fig. A4.2b). It is clear that the two earlier phases contain different *Capsicum* taxa than the later one. Phase II (seen only at Paredones) is most aligned with *C. pubescens* (highland *Capsicum* or *rocoto*), whereas Phase IV seems to contain equally *C. frutescens*, *C. pubescens*, and *C. chinense*. Phase V, in contrast, aligns solidly with *C. baccatum*.

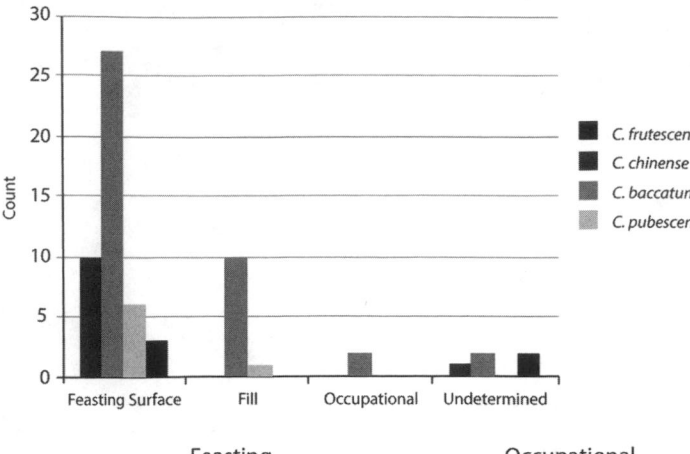

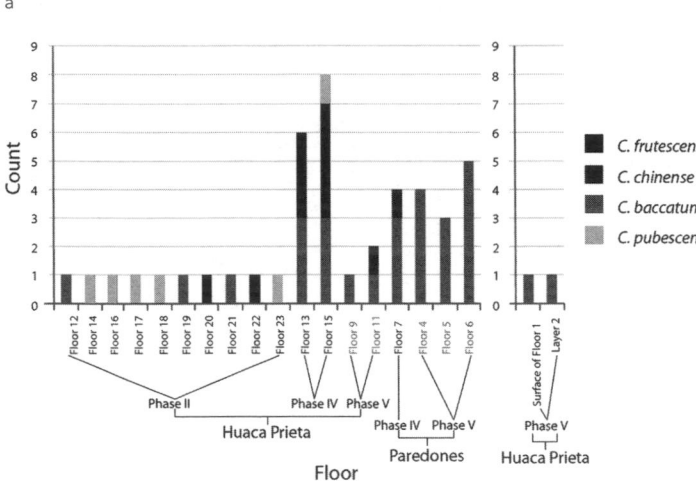

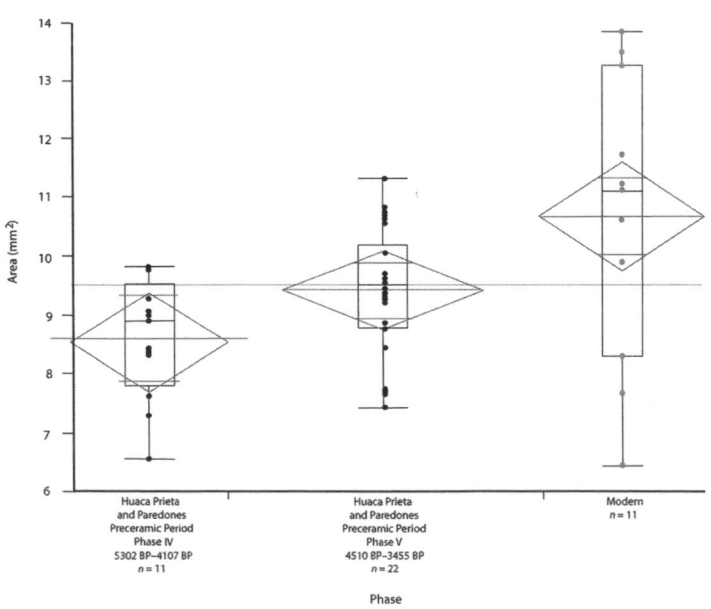

FIGURE A4.5. *Capsicum* species: *a*, presence by context; *b*, presence at Huaca Prieta and Paredones through time by floor and context; *c*, change in *Capsicum baccatum* seed size through time.

This discriminant analysis confirms our initial species-level identifications.

At this point, we can delve into these patterns regarding temporal and spatial changes at Huaca Prieta and Paredones. The map in figure A4.4a reveals the provenience of the seed specimens by phase. All seeds from late Phase II were recovered from Paredones, considered initially a domestic/habitation area, while in Phases III–V the excavated contexts were more along the line of food preparation and ritual. Chile pepper and other seeds were lightly dispersed across floors. Although occasionally found with bean remains in gourd eating bowls, they generally were not found in discrete clusters or activity patterns as they were in Huaca Prieta. Their contexts clearly relate to food preparation, consumption, and discard.

DISCUSSION

The patterns observed in the data provide much food for thought. Based on our analyses, *C. annuum* is completely absent in the archaeological collection, reaffirming our belief that this species, domesticated in Mexico, should not appear in Peru before the Spanish conquest. The bar chart in figure A4.3a shows the presence of *Capsicum* species at both sites through time. This figure reveals that the earlier phase occupations (late Phase II) contained a diversity of species including *C. chinense* (21%), *C. frutescens* (14%), *C. baccatum* (21%), and *C. pubescens* (43%). These species could have been grown on the coast, but a likelier scenario is that *C. pubescens* was grown in higher eastern slope elevations as it is today and was traded in. Figure A4.3a demonstrates that Phase IV is dominated by *C. baccatum* (57% of seeds we studied) followed by *C. chinense* (29%). Phase V contexts are filled only with *C. baccatum*.

All of these species except *C. baccatum* are originally from the eastern valleys or the highlands, suggesting that exchange and/or movement of people brought in the early chile peppers. If they were grown on the coast people had to adapt them to coastal conditions. In Phase IV (~5300–4100 cal BP) *C. baccatum* becomes far more prevalent (note: this phase corresponds to Pickersgill's research on Bird's fruit population, which identified *C. chinense* and *C. baccatum* at Huaca Prieta).

When the species are plotted at the two sites by phase (fig. A4.3c), we see differences in access and/or valuations in these two areas. Paredones contains much diversity, while Huaca Prieta has little and is always dominated by *C. baccatum*. The local *C. baccatum* is clearly valued at Huaca Prieta throughout the phases but not so much at Paredones earlier on. By ~4500 cal BP both sites are completely dominated by *C. baccatum*; in fact all the seeds that we analyzed from both sites in Phase V were identified as *C. baccatum*, suggesting to us a local production of chile peppers by this time.

Based on the contexts from which the seeds were collected, we can see that the *C. baccatum* seeds are closely tied with feasting locales in Huaca Prieta (fig. A4.4a), whereas *C. pubescens* and *C. frutescens* were encountered in domestic contexts. *C. chinense* is present throughout both sites yet seems to be found mainly in the domestic and later ceremonial areas (the context designation "other") of Paredones. With more contextual clarification, the designation "other" could allow deeper interpretation of the meanings of the species from those proveniences. Most chile pepper seeds at both sites are often associated with bean remains, especially at Paredones where they were associated with bean remains in gourd eating bowls.

C. baccatum is the species of chile pepper that is thought to have been domesticated along the western side of South America. The overwhelming presence of this species suggests that sometime after Phase II, ~6500 years ago, there was an increased focus on local production and consumption of peppers in this coastal region, whereas earlier most peppers were probably carried to the coast seasonally. We have confirmed what Pickersgill observed in the *Capsicum* fruit data; by the late Preceramic *C. baccatum* was consumed at Huaca Prieta. Based on the contexts that we have, it is clear that from Phase IV onward *C. baccatum* is so dominant in the feasting contexts, suggesting its high valuation as perhaps a more regular desired food, that the residents began growing the crop themselves.

CONCLUSIONS

Studying the archaeological *Capsicum* seeds from Huaca Prieta and Paredones has led us to develop an identification system for seeds. Applying this to the archaeological seeds allowed us to conclude that *C. baccatum* was grown successfully on the dry west coast of South America and that

exchange and transhumance occurred for many years, with people carrying plants to the coast to share and use in rituals and meals. The project allowed us to identify archaeological specimens as well as show how their production locations and probably their valuations shifted through time. We can identify trends at these two sites not only in terms of size selection but also regarding changes in taste and in particular the focus on one species, *C. baccatum*, which was indigenized as the people moved away from consuming the other exotic *Capsicum* taxa. This increased focus upon *C. baccatum* is also observed in depositional contexts, such as in feasting areas. The opposite is true for the highland *C. pubescens*, which was most often found in households at these sites. This minor pattern suggests a different valuation and use history of this species.

ACKNOWLEDGMENTS

We are grateful for Dr. Guanwei Min's training and advice concerning SEM imaging of the *Capsicum* seeds. Special thanks to the USDA Germplasm Resources Information Network (USDA-GRIN) and especially Mark Bohning, Bob Jarret, and Tiffany Fields for helping us to find rarer specimens of *Capsicum*. We also thank our chile pepper seed vendors and in particular Beth Boyd from Bayou Traders for working with us to obtain various *Capsicum* species. Last, but certainly not least, we thank our colleagues in the McCown Archaeobotany Laboratory, especially Alan Farahani, Rob Cuthrell, and Theresa Molino, for offering advice and critical insight into our project.

MAIZE ANALYSIS

Duccio Bonavia
and Alexander Grobman

INTRODUCTION

The corn remains recovered from Huaca Prieta consist of 288 cobs, 1 husk leaf, 2 fragments of stalks, 1 husk fragment, and 1 kernel (Grobman et al. 2012). For this study, samples were analyzed as a group, without differentiating between the remains found in the mounds and those from habitation sites (Unit 16 and Paredones). From a taxonomic viewpoint there is no difference between the two groups.

The corn samples from Huaca Prieta were found in excavation units 1, 3, 6, 21, 23, and 25 and in Bird's HP-3 trench. During our work, 34 Preceramic corncobs were obtained from Units 16, 20, and 22; 1 Moche cob came from Test Pit 3. Together these represent 12.5% of the total collection. Of the 252 cobs from Huaca Prieta, 195 are from Preceramic contexts, 10 are from Gallinazo contexts, and 18 are from Cupisnique contexts. The chronology of the remaining 29 could not be determined, except for 1 cob that comes from cleaning the HP-3 trench profile. We screened the backdirt of Bird's excavation and found 28 corn remains. All of these samples represented 87.5% of the total.

The samples corresponding to the Moche culture were not considered; they were in very poor condition and could not be identified to race, although they had eight rows. A sample from Unit 22, also from a Moche context, is a Proto–Confite Morocho (8-row) not included. The cobs found in Bird's backdirt also were not included due to lack of provenience. Unit 2 yielded 2 very small cob fragments that were not considered because they could not be studied.

Another 41 samples were not used in the study, because they were in poor condition and incomplete and could not be measured, including 5 from Units 16, 20, 22, and 21. The corn remains dating to Phase III (~6538–5308 cal BP) and Phase IV (~5308–4107 cal BP) have been combined because they show no differences morphologically. Most samples come from late Phase III and early Phase IV (for photographs of maize samples from sites see Grobman et al. 2012 and figs. A5.1 and A5.2).

DOMESTIC SITES

Unit 16 yielded 9 cobs dating to Phase V: 2 from Layer 1, 4 from Layer 3, and 3 from Layer 4. There was a total of 18 cobs in Unit 20, of which 11 date to Phase IV and come from Layer 4 (6 cobs), Layer 5 (4 cobs), and Layer 5/6A

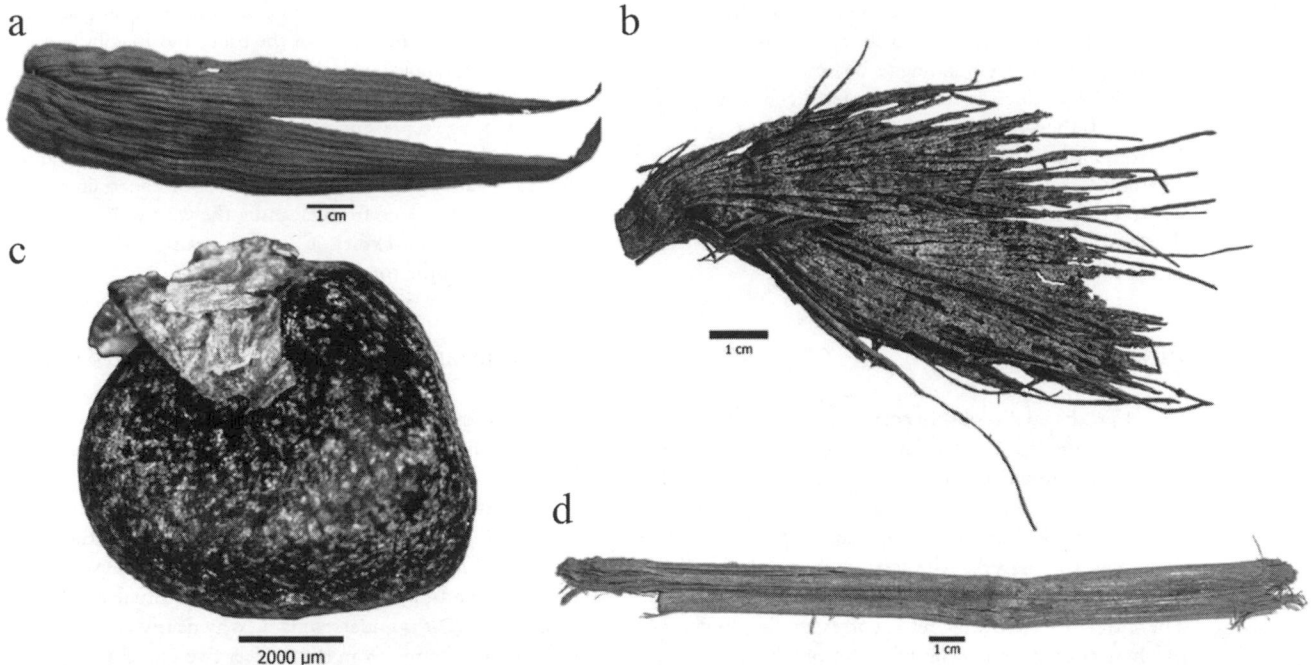

FIGURE A5.1. Various Preceramic maize elements from the Paredones site dating ~6500–4200 cal BP: *a*, husk with high venation index; *b*, tassel showing no condensation, unlike tassels from most Mexican maize; *c*, popcorn grain; *d*, stalk internode from a slender plant, probably no taller than ~1.5 m.

FIGURE A5.2. Races of Preceramic maize cobs from Paredones and Huaca Prieta: *a*, Proto-Confite Morocho cob with large soft glumes; the extreme lower right tip of the cob shows the remainder of a partially charred shank fragment (*arrow*); a portion with its attached husk fragment was removed and AMS dated to 6775–6504 cal BP; *b*, Confite Chavinense cob exhibiting fasciation and cupules underlying very small kernels; *c*, Proto-Alazan cob.

(1 cob). The other 6 cobs correspond to Phase III and come from Layer 6. A fragment of husk and 2 cornstalks were found in layers corresponding to Phase IV.

Unit 22 produced 8 maize samples: 1 cob corresponding to Floor 1, the Moche period; another cob dating to Phase IV from Floor 6; and 6 cobs dating to Phase III from Floor 18. A husk leaf was recovered from Floor 14, corresponding to Phase III. This makes a total of 36 samples from the domestic and food preparation sites, which represent 12.5% of the total.

HUACA PRIETA

Unit 1 produced 28 cobs, 18 corresponding to the Cupisnique culture and 10 to the later Gallinazo culture. The Cupisnique samples come from Layer 3 (6 samples) and Layer 4 (2 samples). In Unit 3 there was 1 sample from Feature 4, 1 sample from Feature 3, 1 sample from Layer 3, and 7 samples from Layer 2. The cobs attributed to the Gallinazo culture were found in Layer 3 ($n = 4$) and Layer 4 ($n = 6$). There were 8 cobs from Unit 3, corresponding to Phase V. Of these cobs, 2 come from Fill 1, 5 from Fill 2, and 1 from Floor 1.

Unit 6 has the largest number of maize samples: 180 cobs and 1 kernel. From Use Surface 1 came 3 cobs, all from Phase V. There were 23 cobs below Use Surface 1. Use Surface 2 yielded 125 cobs and 1 kernel; 29 cobs were found under Use Surface 2. The samples from this unit constitute 62.5% of the maize found in the mound at Huaca Prieta and 71.42% of the corn found on the whole site. Unit 21 produced 2 cob fragments: 1 in Layer 3 and the other in Floor 1. There were 2 cobs corresponding to Phase V from Unit 23, Structure 8, Layer 3. Unit 25 yielded 3 cobs, corresponding to Phase IV: 1 from Layer 1 and 2 from Layer 2. Another 28 cobs were recovered from Bird's backdirt from HP-3 and 1 from the wall of the trench. Thus 252 corncobs were found at Huaca Prieta, which, as noted above, represent 87.5% of the total maize remains found by the project.

SUMMARY OF SAMPLES BY CHRONOLOGICAL PHASE

The maize samples can be classified chronologically by the phases. The 13 cobs recovered from domestic sites date to Phase III and represent 4.51% of the total, plus 1 husk leaf. These samples came from Units 20 and 22 at Paredones. Samples dating to Phase IV from the domestic sites include a total of 12 cobs, 2 stalks, and 1 husk fragment, which come from Units 20 and 22. At Huaca Prieta 3 cobs were found in Unit 25. Added together, the total cobs recovered for this phase make up 5.20% of the total.

The largest number of specimens recovered at the site correspond to Phase V. There are more at Huaca Prieta, however, where 192 cobs and 1 kernel were found in Units 3, 6, and 23. Only 9 cobs were recovered in the domestic sites, which came from Unit 16. The maize recovered in this phase makes up 69.79% of the total.

There were 18 cobs associated with the Cupisnique culture, which make up 6.25% of the total, and 10 cobs associated with Gallinazo remains, which make up 3.4% of the total. All of this material comes from Unit 1. The 2 cobs of late Moche age represent 0.69% of the total and were both found in domestic contexts in Unit 2 at Huaca Prieta and in Test Pit 30 at Paredones. Finally, 29 cobs of uncertain cultural placement came from cleaning the west wall of the HP-3 trench and backdirt of Bird's excavation; they constitute 10.06% of the total.

CORN SAMPLES EXCAVATED BY JUNIUS BIRD

Bird found an important quantity of corn in the contexts corresponding to the Cupisnique and Gallinazo cultures. According to his report, he did not find maize in the Preceramic strata (Bird et al. 1985). In another study, Bird and Bird (1980: 325) are emphatic: "Maize is lacking in the preceramic refuse." Given that Huaca Prieta is a ritual site, Paredones is a food-processing site and perhaps ritual, and Unit 16 is domestic, it is understandable why nearly all early Preceramic corn comes from these latter two contexts.

In an early study Robert Bird (1978: 90) states that "903 Gallinazo cobs excavated from the uppermost layers of the Huaca Prieta site" and adds: "The Cupisnique material (161 specimens) come from just north of Huaca Prieta." From this it can be deduced that Junius Bird obtained a total of 1064 maize specimens. Yet his final report contains only one reference to maize: "Several hundred maize cobs being studied by Robert Bird" (Bird et al. 1985: 229). In a later publication Robert Bird mentions a find that is not cited in other reports: "a few rotted fragments in Burial 867 at Huaca Prieta." He refers to a tomb that must have corresponded to Cupisnique times. Doubt remains about the number and context of corn remains from the 1940s excavations. The published articles contain many contradictions. Thus the present study utilizes only the data from the article of Robert Bird (1978), the only report that offers concrete information (see Bonavia 2013).

MATERIALS AND METHODS

Whole cobs and fragments of cobs as well as some stalks and husks were examined, using low-level magnification. The morphological traits of the cobs were related to the pre-Hispanic races (see Grobman et al. 1961).

The external measurements of length, cob diameter, and pith diameter were taken directly. Poor preservation of the cobs prevented determination of the diameter of the rachis in the majority of cases; thus we used the index of the cob to pith diameter instead of the cob/rachis index (see Grobman 1982).

Characteristics of the glumes, cupules, and spikelets were determined. Frequency of cobs corresponding to races identifiable by morphology and the number of kernel rows and the cobs that are interracial hybrids are reported for each phase. In like fashion, the mathematical means and the weighted means are corrected for the number of cobs of each type. Examination of cupule characteristics followed procedures previously established (Cutler 1946; Grobman et al. 1961; Nickerson 1953; Roberts et al. 1957; Wellhausen et al. 1952).

BOTANICAL ANALYSIS

Advances in the recognition of variability in maize and in the varieties recovered from archaeological sites have been favored by the development of the concept of "race." In the case of maize, it is a taxonomic unit below subspecies and above variety. The concept of race was introduced by Edgar Anderson and H. C. Cutler (1942) for the study of maize variability in Mexico. The definition of race that they offered is sets of related individuals that possess sufficient common traits to allow them to be recognized as a group.

In Peru the criteria used to classify races of maize have been morphological traits of the plant, ear, and cob (including internal and external traits of the ear), complemented by cytological analysis of the presence and placement of chromosomal nodes, presence and number of supernumerary B chromosomes, and presence of the "abnormal" chromosome 10. Characterization of the frequency of genes in the plant color series (A, B, Pl, and R) and their alleles served as the defining complement in several races (Grobman et al. 1961). Rodomiro Ortiz and Ricardo Sevilla (1997) have studied the defining traits used in maize studies and have confirmed their robustness. Sevilla (1975, 1977) has confirmed and broadened the original classification of races of maize in Peru, maintaining the original races.

The defining traits of the proportion of length to cob diameter and row number are the most useful traits with the smallest coefficient of variation for highland maize races in Peru (Abu-Alrub et al. 2004), separated into types with thin, cylindrical cobs and others with conico-globular cobs, using principal component cluster analysis.

In several studies of archaeologically recovered maize in Peru it has been possible to identify the races for the periods identified in the excavations, as direct precursors of the primitive races that were cultivated at the time field observations were made in the 1950s by Grobman and his associates (Grobman et al. 1961). Many of the primitive races of the present day, with the possible exception of Enano (Dwarf) are still under cultivation (Sevilla 1984). In the case of the races of maize from the southwestern United States, the relation of present-day races with primitive ones has been questioned, as in the case of Chapalote and Proto-Maíz de Ocho (Diehl 2005). In Peru we have assigned a classification for race to the archaeological samples, giving them distinct names like Proto–Confite Morocho, Confite Chavinense, Proto-Kculli, or Proto-Alazán. These are races that have been differentiated and are undoubtedly related by cob typology to present-day races, which hypothetically were derived directly from them. Michael Diehl (2005) has questioned the use of designations like Pre-Chapalote or Proto-Maíz de Ocho, based on the resemblance of the morphology of husks and kernels to similar modern corn, proposing

instead the use of the methods of molecular biology that show the genetic distances more precisely. We agree with Major Goodman and Ernesto Paterniani (1969) that the defining morphological traits that are most useful for differentiating races of maize are precisely those that we have been using, such as cob and kernel form, number of rows, and type and height of the plant.

For this study the samples have been separated by the chronological phases. All samples were submitted to the same procedure of external and internal measurements described in Grobman et al. (1961); these were used in other studies, such as that of the corn from Los Gavilanes (Bonavia 1982; Grobman 1982). The measurements were analyzed, and lineal and weighted averages were established for each race in each phase. Comparisons of the measurements were carried out only with the samples obtained from Peruvian sites with secure contexts and dates. Study of the cupules was limited to determining their form, length, and width. The visual characteristics of the cupules in some primitive Peruvian races, such as Proto–Confite Morocho and the modern Morocho race, are unusual and can be classified using lenses with 10× or 15× magnification.

CHARACTERISTICS OF THE HUACA PRIETA CORN

CORN FROM PHASES III–IV

The analysis of the Phase III–IV maize samples was based on 2 complete cobs (2.5 and 3.1 cm in length) and 15 cob fragments; a slight majority of these belonged to the Proto–Confite Morocho race, but the sample from the Confite Chavinense race and the hybrid types together added up to almost 50% (see Bonavia 1982; Grobman 1982: 160–161, tables 11 and 12). This proportion is almost the same as that of Epoch 2 at the Los Gavilanes site. The cob length of the samples from Phases III–IV is approximately the same as that for Epoch 2 at Los Gavilanes as well. The diameter average is approximately the same or slightly less because of the relatively larger number of samples of Proto–Confite Morocho. We have used pith diameter for cob diameter because of poor preservation conditions. For this reason the values may differ from the cob/rachis index at Los Gavilanes.

The Proto–Confite Morocho race predominates slightly in Phases III–IV, so that the number of rows is slightly lower than in Epoch 2 at Los Gavilanes, where Confite Chavinense and its hybrids predominated. Thus the samples from Paredones and Huaca Prieta may be somewhat earlier than those from Los Gavilanes, as cobs with fewer rows predominate in the earliest periods.

The frequency of the color Pl (purple) is great in cobs from Epoch 2 at Los Gavilanes, almost 100%, while in Phases II–IV at Paredones and Unit 16 it comes to only 55%. This could have been caused by the longer time the plant had been on the coast, as a consequence of an earlier migration from the highlands, or it may be because the color could not be determined because of the poor preservation of the cobs. Hard glumes were 29% of the total in Epoch 2 at Los Gavilanes, while they are 36.6% of the total in Phases III–IV at Huaca Prieta and Paredones.

Fasciated cobs make up 43.3% in Phases III–IV at Huaca Prieta, compared to an average of 70% of Confite Chavinense cobs in Epoch 2 at Los Gavilanes. It can be hypothesized that Phases III–IV corn is earlier than that at Gavilanes in terms of the degree of fasciation.

In Unit 22 a husk leaf (No. 26) was found that corresponds to Phase III at Paredones. It is 13 cm long and 3 cm wide. The index of venation was 7 per cm. It was green in color, with 5 holes made by insect larvae.

In Unit 20 at Paredones 2 stalk fragments and a fragment of husk corresponding to the end of Phase IV were found. Stalk fragment No. 25 is 16.8 cm long. It has a diameter of 6 mm between nodes in the upper part and 10 mm at the base. In the basal part of the stalk on one side at least 6 points of insertion of adventitious roots were counted in a single arc. On a second level there are between 3 and 4 points of insertion of adventitious roots. The stalk has at least 3 holes where stalk-boring larvae exited. A transverse cut of the stalk has an outer segment 2 mm thick with a greater concentration of woody veins on both sides. The rind makes up 40% of the stalk thickness, which is an expression of great hardness relative to the diameter of the stalk. The small diameter of the stalk indicates that this is a plant with very small cobs. Another stem fragment (No. 24) is 19 cm long. The stalk between the nodes is 13 mm in diameter and has a rind that is 2 mm thick, so the thickness of the rind is 30% of the stem diameter. There are 2 nodes present and several possible exit holes of borer insects. The length of the stem between the nodes is 9.8 cm. The stem appears to have been red. Husk fragment No. 13 is in a state of very poor preservation and is heavily impregnated with salts. The peduncle of the cob is 1 cm in diameter. There are up to 11 veins per cm in the external husk leaf, which provides considerable rigidity against insect attack, indicated by at least 17 holes made by larvae, which suggests a long coexistence with insects that attack maize. There are signs of a rudimentary branching of the cob. The length of the husk from the base of the insertion of the cob is 7 cm. The total length could have been 12 cm.

CORN FROM PHASE V

The Proto-Kculli race appears during this phase as well as the Proto-Alazán race, with a low number of specimens. The percentages for Proto–Confite Morocho are 21.7% for whole cobs and 37.5% for incomplete cobs, with a general average of 35.6% for Proto–Confite Morocho. This becomes 45.7% if the cobs of hybrids with Confite Chavinense are included. In Phases III–IV the percentage is 58.8% for Proto–Confite Morocho compared to Epoch 3 at Los Gavilanes, which has 60.8% of Proto–Confite Morocho. This observation implies a selection for a larger number of kernel rows from Phases III–IV to Phase V, indicating efficiency in selection for a higher potential yield.

The presence of the Proto-Alazán race coincides with its zone of geographic distribution from the Chao Valley northward and is the first archaeological evidence for the origin of the modern race of Pagaladroga or its successor, Alazán, which has been identified for Moche times (Grobman et al. 1961: figs. 29, 30, 99–100).

Cob length, with a weighted average of 4.27 cm, is slightly less in Phase V, comparatively speaking, than in Epoch 3 in Los Gavilanes (4.67 cm) and is within the limits of variation for Phases III–IV. Cob diameter is greater than in Phases III–IV because the cobs included Proto-Alazán, which has the largest diameter of the races recovered. Moreover, in comparing the specimens from Phase V with those from Epoch 3 at Los Gavilanes, average cob diameter is greater in Phase V. This is evidence that Phase V is later than Epoch 3 at Los Gavilanes.

The diameter of the rachis is lower because the measurement was taken on the pith because of the poor preservation. The average number of rows on the ears is greater than in Phases III–IV but the same as in Epoch 3 at Los Gavilanes. In the populations of Proto–Confite Morocho from Phases III–IV and V and those from Epoch 3 at Los Gavilanes the averages for row number are almost identical. The populations of Confite Chavinense in Phase V and in Epoch 3 from Los Gavilanes have averages of 12.3 and 9.85 rows, respectively, indicating that this race has more rows at Huaca Prieta and Paredones than in Huarmey. Proto-Alazán, which is the most improved highly evolved race, reaches 14 rows, increasing the potential for kernel yield.

In Phase V the color Pl (purple) has an average of 62.8%, with 54–55% in Proto–Confite Morocho and Confite Chavinense, while in Phases III–IV the average for Pl is 55%. Nevertheless, this differs from Epoch 3 at Los Gavilanes, with 91.6% of the samples. This may be because of the greater ease in identifying Pl at Gavilanes due to the better preservation conditions.

The l/w (length/width) index of the cupules is an important value for determining the level of evolution of samples from the different periods, both at Paredones and Huaca Prieta and at Los Gavilanes. A higher l/w index in the populations of Preceramic maize in Peru is evidence that the cupules belong to older races, if we consider Proto–Confite Morocho, with long, narrow, naviform cupules, as the most primitive (or least evolved) type of maize.

During Phases III–IV at Paredones and Huaca Prieta the length/width index of the cupules averages 0.896, while during the more recent Phase V it is 0.778, as is expected from the higher yield of a more modern and selected maize with a higher number of rows, as noted in the shift from Phases III–IV to Phase V. In contrast, Epoch 2 at Los Gavilanes has an average length/width index for the cupules of 0.946, a higher value than for the more recent Epoch 3, at 0.639. From this it can be seen that at Los Gavilanes Epoch 2 and Epoch 3 differ most from each other. During Phases III–V at Paredones and Huaca Prieta, however, the differences are as expected but lie between the greater differences between Epoch 2 and Epoch 3 at Los Gavilanes.

As expected, corn from Phases III–IV has the highest cupule length/width index, from 0.896 to 0.778. In Epoch 3 at Los Gavilanes the cupule length/width index is 0.639. This index is slightly later in time, comparatively speaking, but it is coincident in relative age with both phases. The same change occurs in the cupule length/width indices across the races. For example, in Phase IV the index for the length/width of the rachis for Proto–Confite Morocho is 0.913, while in Phase V it is 0.758, which means that the Proto–Confite Morocho specimens from Phase IV are more primitive. The cupule length/width index for Proto–Confite Morocho in Epoch 3 at Los Gavilanes is 0.729, which would make it contemporaneous or slightly more recent than the index of Phase V. There are very few specimens of Confite Chavinense from Phase IV. This gives a cupule length/width index of 1.11, which is unusually high, while the relation of cupule length to width of 0.550 in Epoch 3 from Los Gavilanes is narrower: the cupules are shorter compared to the width, a form of more highly evolved maize in the racial group Confite Chavinense. A single specimen of Proto-Alazán has 18 rows.

Comparing the percentages of fasciated cobs, Phase V has a lower percentage (21.6%) than Phases III–IV (71.4%), although with a larger number of rows. This observation indicates the presence of two different genetic mechanisms for the increase in kernel rows. One is based on fasciation (the flattening of the cob) to increase the number of kernel rows (Confite Chavinense race), which appears earlier. The other is based on an increase in the diameter of the cob (Proto-Alazán race), which is later.

A larger percentage of hard glumes appear in Phases III–IV than in Phase V: 36.6% compared to 15.4%. This figure is 30% during Epoch 3 at Los Gavilanes. It would seem that the percentage of hard glumes becomes less with the passage of time. In Phases III–IV cupules with spikelets make up 20% of the total, while in Phase V they represent 6.7%.

The only kernel recovered is ~7 mm in width and in length. It is red and from its size appears to be a flint corn. The kernel was not destroyed; a small portion of the endosperm was extracted through a perforation.

CORN CORRESPONDING TO THE CUPISNIQUE PHASE

Only a few specimens (1 complete cob, 3 almost complete cobs, and 18 incomplete cobs) were recovered. The length of the complete cobs is 4.3 cm, compared to 3.7 cm for Phase V. The cobs are longer in Cupisnique times. Cob diameter is 4.50 cm, compared to 4.27 cm in Phase V (that is, the cob is thicker). Rachis diameter is greater in Cupisnique material than in Phase V. The cob/pith index of 5.60 in Cupisnique is greater than the 4.23 index for Phase V. Row number is the same in Cupisnique as it was in Phase V. The purple color (Pl) is less frequent, dropping from 54.27% in Phase V to 40.91% in the following Cupisnique times. The average number of fasciated cobs is similar to the number in Phase V. There do not appear to be more changes in fasciation, unless the weighted average of 27.27% for Cupisnique compared to 21.65% for Phase V is considered. The percentage of hard glumes (Grobman et al. 1961) is slightly greater in Cupisnique: 20% compared to 17.7% for Phase V.

Cobs with soft glumes make up 20% in the Cupisnique material, compared to only 5.2% in Phase V. Among other reasons, this may be due to the better state of preservation of the cobs from the later Cupisnique phase.

The situation for the glumes that are crested and at the same time are soft is similar, changing from 11.17% in Phase V to 41.17% in Cupisnique. The percentage of the Cupisnique material with hairs is 30%, while in Phase V it is 6.7%.

Table 1 of Bird et al. (1985) shows 161 cobs corresponding to the Cupisnique culture north of the Huaca Prieta mound. Robert Bird identified material characterized as having small cobs, between 3.5 cm and 6.2 cm in length, with the majority falling between 4.5 cm and 5.7 cm and having a relatively high number of rows, between 14 and 24. Of the 18 specimens studied, only 3 have 12 rows; the rest have between 14 and 24 (the majority with the larger number of rows). Comparing this information with the data obtained from Huaca Prieta, the lengths of the cobs recovered by the project and those studied by Robert Bird are very similar. Nevertheless, there are large differences in the number of rows. In the project samples cobs with 8 rows are most common (corresponding to the Proto–Confite Morocho race), along with cobs of the Confite Chavinense and Proto-Alazán races. The proportions are reversed in the samples analyzed by Bird, with no cobs typical of Proto-Confite Morocho but a small number derived from this race, while the great majority correspond to Confite Chavinense, with a possible appearance of Proto-Alazán, none of which were identified by Bird in a racial sense.

CORN CORRESPONDING TO THE GALLINAZO PHASE

No complete cobs were recovered from this phase. Cob diameter data is influenced by the sample of 6 cobs related to Proto–Confite Morocho or its racial hybrids; for this reason it is close to the average for Proto–Confite Morocho. The average rachis diameter does not differ from that of the earlier periods. The cob/pith index is between the averages for Phases III–IV and Phase V. The average row number of 9.43 is also between the averages for Phases III–IV and V. The frequency of the color purple (Pl) is greater than in the other phases. The frequency of fasciation in the cobs is 100%. This is greater than in the other phases. The occurrence of hard glumes is 100%, much higher than in the other phases. The occurrence of soft glumes is higher than in the other phases. Hairs are also more frequent than in the earlier phases.

The sample analyzed was made up of only 7 incomplete cobs. Of these, 4 are Proto–Confite Morocho, 2 are a Proto–Confite Morocho/Confite Chavinense hybrid, and 1 is Confite Chavinense. Thus the biometric measurements of the sample are biased toward Proto–Confite Morocho compared to the early phases, with frequent predominance of this race.

Using the data from Bird's 1978 report, several comparisons can be made. Of the 903 cobs excavated from the upper layers of Huaca Prieta corresponding to the Gallinazo culture, Robert Bird analyzed 88 cobs. There is a significant reduction in the number of rows on the cobs from the Gallinazo complex, compared to a Salinar period sample that he includes in his database (although it comes from a different locality, Puerto Morín, in the Virú Valley). But the row number is not very different than in the Cupisnique phase, the earliest at Huaca Prieta. The project's sample of cobs from Gallinazo times is more consistent in showing a low number of rows, without much difference in the Cupisnique samples. Our average for kernel row number in this Gallinazo complex is 10.66, based on only 7 specimens. This is evidence for a high presence of maize races derived from Proto–Confite Morocho. In Bird's samples most of the cobs have 10 to 14 rows, with very few at the extremes of 8 and 18 rows. This indicates that our data and Bird's coincide.

ABSOLUTE DATES OF THE HUACA PRIETA/ PAREDONES SAMPLES

Several corn samples were submitted for AMS radiocarbon assays (see chapters 6 and 10). On the Huaca Prieta mound an unburned cob from Unit 3, Floor 3 (Beta233649) gave a date of 1080±40 BP that corresponds to 1052–809 cal BP. This date, which in our chronostratigraphic sequence corresponds to Phase V, is obviously an error. During our profiling of the west wall of Bird's HP-3 trench, a burned corncob was recovered from our Layer 23. The burned cob fragment was submitted for radiocarbon dating. The result was 4180–3839 (Beta278050), which corresponds to Phase V.

Dates on corn come from 3 units in the domestic sites. In Unit 16 an unburned cob fragment from Layer 3 was dated, which is from our Phase V. The date obtained is anomalous, 830±40 (Beta263319) or 767–664 cal BP. Of 2 unburned cob fragments sent for dating from Unit 20, the cob from the transition between Layers 5–6 gave a date of 1130±27 (AA86938) or 1055–831 cal BP. The other was from Layer 6 and gave a date of 1310±40 (Beta263322) or 1279–1076 cal BP. Both dates are considered anomalous, because they correspond to Phase IV according to our chronostratigraphic sequence.

A burned cob fragment from Floor 2 from Unit 21 at Huaca Prieta was assayed and gave a date of 3956–3704 cal BP (AA86941). Subsequently a burned cob in Floor 9 was dated at 4235–3928 cal BP (AA86946). It is worth noting that several other dates were obtained on different materials in floors in this same unit. Thus for Floor 26 (Unit 15) a piece of wood charcoal gave a date of 5911–5488 cal BP (AA75322). A piece of wood charcoal from Floor 3 gave a date of 3982–3728 cal BP (AA86931).

It is clear that the dates obtained on maize burned remains agree among themselves and accord with our Phase V. They are also coherent with respect to the other dates obtained on wood charcoal, although one of these dates is slightly earlier. They are equivalent to Phases IV and V.

Samples from Unit 22 at Paredones provided a series of dates. For Floor 6 a burned cob fragment was dated at 4821–4527 cal BP (AA86934). This date agrees with the context, which corresponds to Phase IV. A fragment of cornhusk from Floor 16 also was assayed and dated at 5574–5048 cal BP (AA86847). A fragment of an unburned corncob from Floor 10 was dated at 133–34 cal BP (Beta263988). According to our sequence, this context corresponds to Phase III, so the first date is correct while the second is erroneous.

Floor 18 provided five dates. A fragment of burned cob peduncle and husk gave a date of 6775–6504 cal BP (OS7730; see Grobman et al. 2012). Four unburned fragments from the same sample dated between post-bomb to 563 cal BP (Beta27823,27804,282127, and AA88761; see Grobman et al. 2012). The date obtained on the burned fragment of peduncle is undoubtedly correct, while the dates on the unburned cob fragments are in error. Floor 18 corresponds to Phase III. We consider that this is proved indirectly by two other dates obtained for other strata in this same excavation. Wood charcoal from Floor 10 provided a carbon date of 5435–5044 cal BP (AA86947). The remains of a burned plant from Floor 15 gave a date of 5585–5325 cal BP (Beta263321).

Certain conclusions can be drawn from these results. In the first place all valid dates are coherent in their stratigraphic temporal sequence and are in agreement with the classification of phases at the site. Moreover, as shown below, they are also in agreement with the dates from other Preceramic sites with maize.

The five dates from Floor 18 of Unit 22 indicate a serious problem that has yet to be resolved (see chapter 6). What is the explanation for a burned cob peduncle fragment with a husk fragment attached giving a correct date, while fragments of the same unburned cob give anomalous dates? This would seem to support the possibility that the more porous tissues of the unburned cobs could absorb some substance that does not affect the harder tissue of the burned peduncle and the husk.

COMPARISON OF HUACA PRIETA AND PAREDONES CORN WITH CORN FROM OTHER PRECERAMIC SITES

CERRO EL CALVARIO

At the Cerro El Calvario site in the Casma Valley a fragment of the upper portion of a cob was classified as intermediate between Confite Chavinense and Proto–Confite Morocho. The cob is fasciated ($\sim$1.7 × 1.2 cm in diameter on its two axes). The cupules are interlocking and the glumes are purple (see Bonavia 2008: 158–159). This corncob is roughly contemporary with Phase IV. It is related to the maize races from Los Gavilanes.

ASPERO

The first Preceramic maize was found at Aspero in the Supe Valley (Willey and Corbett 1954) and was studied by Towle

(1954). The material examined by Towle (1954) consisted of 49 cobs. The majority of these are of a length that fits within the upper and lower limits of 10.6 to 3.0 cm, with an average of 5.8 cm. For Phase V at Huaca Prieta they are 2.1 cm to 5.32 cm, with an average of 3.75 cm. The cob diameter at Aspero is 1.92 cm, while the weighted average is 1.37 cm at Huaca Prieta.

Towle (1954: 132) found naviculate "lower glumes" (possibly cupules?) associated with the Proto–Confite Morocho race, with a frequency of 26%. The average number of rows in the cob sample from Aspero is 13.2, while for Phase V at Huaca Prieta the weighted average is 10.9. Based on the photographs included in the text of Towle's 1954 report, it is possible to identify the races Confite Chavinense and Proto-Kculli (based on the definition of the purple color of the cob and its size) and also a more evolved race of maize that could be Proto–Alazán because of the greater length of the cob. Based on this information, the maize from Phase V at Huaca Prieta can be distinguished by the abundance of slender cobs with few rows, which correspond to the Proto–Confite Morocho. This differentiates it from the Aspero corn, where a more evolved maize population with a greater number of rows, evidently later than that from Huaca Prieta, confirms our evaluation of the cobs subsequently excavated by Robert Feldman (1980). Given these characteristics, these samples from Aspero do not differ greatly from those from Phase V at Huaca Prieta (see Bonavia 2008: 176–177).

ROSAMACHAY (AC-117)

There is a cob with a secure date from a good context from Rosamachay (Ac-117) in the Ayacucho Valley and also a photograph (Galinat 1975: plate 2, no. 2). It has not been described, but the length could be estimated from the scale in the photograph (Bonavia 2008: 190–192). Galinat (1975: 23) states that "the lowest layer, zone D, had a few Chihua-type artifacts, a single corncob in a good stratigraphic position, and stick remains that yielded [a] radiocarbon determination of 3520 BC ±110 (I-5685) and 3300 BC ±105 (I-5685) [n.b. this sample number repeats the first]." A corn leaf was dated at 3520±110 BC radiocarbon years (I-5685) [5470±110 BP; Ziolkowski et al. 1994: 332]. Based on an examination of the photograph (Galinat 1975), it is a typical Proto–Confite Morocho cob with navicular cupules. The cob length of 4.7 cm corresponds exactly with the same length of the Proto–Confite Morocho samples that were recovered at Huaca Prieta in Phases III–IV. The date corresponds to Phase III.

DISCUSSION

It is evident that maize in Peru is ancient and that its presence before 6000 years ago is secure. All the primitive maize are popcorns, with very small cobs, a small number of kernels, small plants, and all the characteristics of maize. The races that have been identified as present in the earliest archaeological periods are Proto–Confite Morocho with

8 rows of kernels, Confite Chavinense with many kernel rows and fasciated cobs, and Proto-Kculli.

We may conclude that Phases III–IV at Huaca Prieta and Epoch 2 at Los Gavilanes are similar in the racial composition and frequency of Proto–Confite Morocho and Confite Chavinense. It should be noted that in this early phase the Proto–Confite Morocho race is characterized by slender cobs with 8 to 10 rows of small kernels. All the specimens examined are of a reduced cob length and correspond to small kernels, which are undoubtedly popcorns. The greater presence of Proto–Confite Morocho in the total sample leads to the conclusion that Phases III–IV at Huaca Prieta were possibly earlier than Epoch 2 at Los Gavilanes.

Towle's (1954) description of the types of maize at the Aspero site shows a very high percentage of cobs with 12 to 16 rows and only 12.2% of the cobs with 8 to 10 rows, which would indicate that it is younger than Huaca Prieta. She also divides the lower glumes into three types: naviform, collar-like, and intermediate. We have classified these forms as the forms of the cupules themselves. Only 25% are naviform; 63% are intermediate in form, as might be expected for the period from which they come (a little later than Phase V at Huaca Prieta); and only 9% have a collar-like form. She assigns the cobs a brown color, which she admits could have changed through time due to the state of preservation. Our determinations of color on the samples from Huaca Prieta, which are clearly distinguishable, found purple, which is on a very high proportion of the cobs and is very visible at only 10× magnification. This high proportion of purple, which is attributed to the combination of the genes A, B, Pl, and R and their several alleles, is characteristic of earlier highland maizes and indicates their route down the river valleys, where the purple color of the plant stalks, and consequently the cob, confers a selective advantage, in contrast to the green color that predominates in tropical lowland races of corn.

The husks covering the studied cobs have a high number of parallel veins. This indicates a very long period of selection for rigidity and toughness as a measure of defense of the husks against perforation by insect larvae. We have encountered evidence in previous studies for the presence of the cob larvae of *Heliothis zea*. In the husks from Huaca Prieta we found several perforations made by larvae that could belong to this already identified species or to other Lepidopterae. The size of the husks suggests the presence of branched cobs, and a rudimentary branched cob was found in this sample. More developed branching cobs were recovered at Los Gavilanes. This could have been an ancestral form more common in primitive maize (Grobman 1982: figs. 60, 167).

In the passage from Phases III to V at Huaca Prieta, a notable increase in the percentage of cobs with a higher number of rows is evident, which reveals selection for a greater yield potential for growth that can be seen in the larger number of fasciated cobs corresponding to the Confite Chavinense race. This progressive selection is already notable in the presence of longer cobs and the increased number of rows acquired through a process of condensation and by a genetic mechanism different from that for fasciation. This could be indicated in the final derivation, either the Proto-Pagaladroga race or its derived race, Proto-Alazán. These are found in the cobs of the more modern phases studied in precisely the geographic areas where the modern races Pagaladroga and Alazán are found (Grobman et al. 1961: 201–205, 232–237).

As we measured the index of cupule length/width (or thickness), we found that the difference between Phases III–IV and Phase V at Huaca Prieta is less than that found between Epochs 2 and 3 at Los Gavilanes. The higher index is indicative of less condensed cobs, which we identify as belonging to a more primitive cob phenotype, corresponding to Proto–Confite Morocho.

A single kernel was found that has the characteristics of a flinty or popcorn endosperm type. Flour was extracted with a microdrill, which enabled the study of the starch grains. According to Piperno's analysis (appendix 9), they probably belong to a kernel of hard consistency, which is typical of a popcorn because of the kernel size.

Cob size increases in the Cupisnique phase, which is expected. The number of purple cobs decreases as the maize becomes more distant from the founding population. In the following Gallinazo phase we note the presence of fasinated cobs in a greater relative proportion.

It is worth noting that the presence of 100% hard glumes in a late phase represents evidence for the introduction of tripsicoid maizes in the Gallinazo phase. The lower presence of hard glumes in early phases is evidence contrary to the theory of an early migration of maize with remnant teosinte (triipsacoid) traits to the Andean area in very early times.

It is also important to comment on Piperno's study of the starch grains that she has identified. Her results are consistent with the results of the analyses of the maize remains recovered at Paredones for the earliest phases. It is no surprise that starch grains are found in later periods, as it is well known that the Pagaladroga and Alzán races are essentially used for chicha (corn beer) in periods when all the races of corn had small high endosperm protein-matrix kernels (low in starch, useful only for popping). Although only a single maize kernel was recovered, as has been noted, the data from the cobs make it very clear that the maize from Huaca Prieta during Phases III–IV and V had small, hard kernels

that would lead to its consumption as popcorn, probably popped in hot sand or hot stones or by the heat of fire. This is also consistent with the findings at Los Gavilanes.

As the size of the grains increased, the following stage of evolution in the use of maize on the Peruvian coast was toasting or parching it. Given that the size of the kernels increased, the partition of the metabolites that reached the kernels favored the accumulation of starch relative to the protein matrix in the kernel.

It is possible that as the size of the kernels increased in later phases they were used for the preparation of chicha. This could have occurred with an early race such as Proto-Pagaladroga evolving toward Proto-Alazán, which was found in the late phases at Huaca Prieta. The absence of starch grains at Huaca Prieta may indicate that corn was not ground, due to the presence of primitive types with small kernels with a high protein and low starch content. These were not useful for grinding and were essentially used for popping.

It is possible that chicha production could have been discovered early (although certain factors suggest the difficulty of achieving it in Preceramic times, such as the problem of maintaining a prolonged period of boiling without ceramic vessels). In early times this was possibly inefficient because of the low starch content and high protein level of popcorn. No discernible starch grains would be left on milling stones, as would be the case with the floury corns of later races.

All early corn in Peru is of three quite distinct popcorn-type races, as defined by their morphological, genetic, cytologenetic (analysis of their derived races; Grobman et al. 1961), and biomolecular characteristics. This indicates a very long presence on the Peruvian coast (Grobman 2013). The association of early archaeological coastal corn with high altitude corn of the same races and the anthocyanic pigmentation present in cobs and plant remains from several archaeological sites (including Huaca Prieta and Paredones) point to a previous long adaptation to a highland environment before appearing on the coastal plain. No systematic study was made of the sample, only a superficial examination with no report (Grobman, personal communication, 2009). That was the case when Grobman et al. (1961: 44) referred to the corn remains from Huaca Prieta following Towle (1961: 22).

DIETARY ECOLOGY, STABLE ISOTOPE, AND DENTAL MICROWEAR TEXTURE ANALYSIS

Larisa R. G. DeSantis, Tom D. Dillehay, Steven L. Goodbred Jr., and Robert S. Feranec

INTRODUCTION

Early archaeological evidence at Huaca Prieta suggested that the major portion of their diet was marine based, including fish, sea urchins, crabs, clams, starfish, and less frequently sea birds, sea lions, and porpoises (Bird 1948a). Huaca Prieta has provided some of the earliest evidence of maize consumption via the presence of cobs, husks, stalks, and tassels (Grobman et al. 2012). Additionally, different races of Preceramic maize cobs were discovered from Huaca Prieta and Paredones, while phytolith and pollen evidence of *Zea mays* was also found at Paredones (Grobman et al. 2012; see appendix 5). Husks, cobs, and shanks were dated to between 6775 and 6504 cal BP, suggesting the early consumption of maize resources. But maize was likely not a staple before ~4500–4000 cal BP, as maize macrofossils and microfossils are scarce and discontinuous prior to this time (Grobman et al. 2012). While plant macrofossil and phytolith evidence have proved critical to dietary interpretations of early Peruvians, additional proxies including stable isotope analysis and dental microwear texture analysis can help clarify the dietary behavior of humans from the Huaca Prieta and Paredones mounds. Here, we aim to assess dietary behavior in Preceramic populations by testing the following hypotheses: (1) individuals from Huaca Prieta consumed primarily marine resources during Phases III and IV; (2) Huaca Prieta individuals consumed food items with minimal abrasives, as is consistent with a marine-based diet; and (3) Huaca Prieta and Paredones individuals had similar diets.

BACKGROUND

CLARIFYING DIETARY BEHAVIOR FROM STABLE CARBON AND NITROGEN ISOTOPES

Specifically, stable carbon and nitrogen isotopes are used to infer the isotopic composition of food consumed during the time of tissue formation (for example, DeNiro and Epstein 1978, 1981; Schoeninger et al. 1983). Nitrogen isotopes are useful in assessing if early humans were eating a significant amount of fish and/or marine animals (see DeNiro and Epstein 1981). For example, individuals who consume large proportions of marine protein have greater nitrogen isotope values than terrestrial meat consumers, as there are more rungs on the ladder in marine food webs and thus opportunities for consumers to become increasingly enriched in ^{15}N relative to the lighter ^{14}N isotope.

Carbon isotopes can help clarify maize consumption and/or help decipher between terrestrial and marine protein consumption when analyzed in conjunction with nitrogen isotopes (DeNiro and Epstein 1978; Schoeninger et al. 1983). Greater δ^{13}C values can be indicative of maize consumption and/or marine resources, as both are enriched in δ^{13}C. Alternatively, low δ^{13}C values suggest primarily terrestrial meat and/or nonmaize consumption (Tucker 2002). Nitrogen isotopes also can help decipher between these individuals. Individuals with high δ^{13}C values and low δ^{15}N values are consistent with maize consumption (Finucane et al. 2006; Schoeninger et al. 1983), while high δ^{13}C values and high δ^{15}N values occur in individuals who primarily consume marine resources (Schoeninger et al. 1983; Walker and DeNiro 1986; Yesner et al. 2003). Individuals with low δ^{13}C values and low δ^{15}N values are consistent with non-maize plant consumption, while those with low ^{13}C values and high δ^{15}N values would imply consumption of terrestrial meat.

Carbon isotopes from tooth enamel (carbonate) are used to assess an individual's whole diet during the time when sampled teeth were mineralized, while dentine collagen is representative of dietary protein consumed (Ambrose and Norr 1993). Additionally, carbonate and collagen reflect an individual's diet with different offsets; δ^{13}C$_{carbonate-diet}$ is 9.4‰, while δ^{13}C$_{collagen-diet}$ is 5.0‰ (Ambrose and Norr 1993). Thus carbon isotope values from bioapatite (such as enamel) and collagen (such as dentin or bone) can also be compared to assess if the isotopic signatures of protein are similar or different from the whole diet (as in Ambrose et al. 1997; Finucane et al. 2006). For example, if dietary protein and whole diet sources have similar δ^{13}C values, then the difference between collagen and carbonate δ^{13}C values (Δ^{13}C$_{carbonate-collagen}$, here referred to as Δ^{13}C$_{enamel-dentin\ collagen}$) should equal 4.4‰ (9.4–5.0‰; Ambrose et al. 1997). However, if Δ^{13}C$_{enamel-dentin\ collagen}$ is >4.4‰ then dietary protein is less enriched in ^{13}C than the whole diet and may suggest a diet with some C$_3$ protein and C$_4$ carbohydrates (such as maize). In contrast, if Δ^{13}C$_{enamel-dentin\ collagen}$ is <4.4‰, then dietary protein is less enriched in ^{13}C than the whole diet and may suggest a diet with marine protein and C$_3$ carbohydrates (such as terrestrial plants; Ambrose et al. 1997).

INFERRING TEXTURAL FOOD PROPERTIES FROM DENTAL MICROWEAR TEXTURE ANALYSIS

The microscopic wear patterns resulting from the processing of food are an effective proxy for inferring past diets. As dental microwear records food consumption during the last few days to weeks of an individual's life, it can be used to clarify ancient diets, including the degree to which food items or food preparation techniques involved abrasives. While microwear has been commonly used by anthropologists and paleontologists since the late 1970s (for example,

Walker et al. 1978) via scanning electron microscopes, more recent advances have enabled dental microwear to be assessed in three dimensions using a scanning white light confocal microscope and scale-sensitive fractal analysis (DeSantis et al. 2013; Scott et al. 2006; Ungar et al. 2003).

Dental microwear textures are assessed via anisotropy, complexity, and textural fill volume and can distinguish between disparate diets in mammals, including bovids, carnivorans, marsupials, xenarthrans, and primates, including humans (DeSantis et al. 2013). Anisotropy (epLsar) represents the degree to which features of similar depth share a similar orientation (for example, many parallel striations yield more anisotropic surfaces; Scott et al. 2006; Ungar et al. 2003). Complexity (Asfc) distinguishes taxa that consume brittle foods from taxa that consume softer and/or tougher ones, by assessing the change in surface roughness across a changing scale of observation (Scott et al. 2006; Ungar et al. 2003). Organisms that consume harder and/or more brittle food items have higher complexity (DeSantis et al. 2013; Donohue et al. 2013; Schubert et al. 2010; Scott et al. 2006; Ungar et al. 2003). Finally, texture fill volume (Tfv) measures the volume filled by large (10 μm diameter) and small (2 μm diameter) square cuboids, with high Tfv values indicating potentially deeper and/or larger features (Donohue et al. 2013; Scott et al. 2006).

Dental microwear textures can also reveal significant differences in diet in prehistoric and historic populations (El-Zaatari 2010). Most notably, differences between meat-eaters and mixed diet hunter-gatherers can be detected. For example, the dental microwear of Chumash (Mediterranean environments, such as the island of Santa Cruz, Channel Islands, California) and Fuegian (cold-steppe environments, such as the southwestern region of Tierra del Fuego, Chile) individuals are indicative of a diet low in abrasives and consistent with a diet of predominately marine meat (with few extraneous particles on the meat; El-Zaatari 2010). In contrast, Tigara (arctic/tundra, such as Point Hope, Alaska) and Andamanese (tropical climates, such as Port Blair, South Andaman) individuals are known to ingest abrasives attached to their food as a result of food preparation techniques and exhibit dental microwear textures consistent with these diets (El-Zaatari 2010). Prehistoric/historic hunter-gatherers from Africa (such as the Khoe-San) had mixed diets that were also intermediate in dental microwear textures, as compared to the above-mentioned populations (El-Zaatari 2010). Collectively, these data provide further evidence of the efficacy of dental microwear texture analysis (DMTA) and are essential to our interpretation of the dental microwear textures from the Huaca Prieta and Paredones individuals.

METHODS

STABLE CARBON AND NITROGEN ISOTOPES

A total of 20 individuals from Huaca Prieta and 3 from Paredones (2 lower right molars from different adult individuals and a child's molar) were analyzed for stable carbon and nitrogen isotopes (table A6.1). At Huaca Prieta 9 individuals were from Phase III and 11 were from Phase IV. Approximately 2 mg of tooth enamel powder was collected from individual teeth using a low-speed dental-style drill and carbide dental burrs. All enamel powder was pretreated with 30% hydrogen peroxide for 24 hours and 0.1 N acetic acid for 18 hours to remove organics and secondary carbonates, respectively (DeSantis et al. 2009, slightly modified from Koch et al. 1997). These samples were analyzed at the Department of Geological Sciences at the University of Florida, where they were run on a Finnigan-MAT 252 isotope ratio mass spectrometer coupled with a Kiel III carbonate preparation device. All results are reported using the delta notation, $\delta = [(R\text{sample}/R\text{standard}-1) * 1000]$. For oxygen isotope values, $R = {}^{18}O/{}^{16}O$ and values are reported against V-SMOW (Coplen 1994). The obtained oxygen V-PDB values were converted using the following equation: $\delta\text{VSMOW} = 1.03086 * \delta\text{VPDB} + 30.86$ (Friedman and O'Neil 1977). For carbon isotope values, $R = {}^{13}C/{}^{12}C$ and all values are reported against V-PDB (Coplen 1994). All 23 teeth enamel samples yielded both stable carbon and oxygen isotope values from the carbonate portion of tooth enamel hydroxyapatite. As significant differences in stable oxygen isotope values were not present between Phase III and Phase IV at Huaca Prieta or between Paredones and Huaca Prieta individuals (fig. A6.1), however, these results are only briefly discussed below.

Stable carbon and nitrogen isotopes were also analyzed from the collagen of tooth dentin, extracted from the roots and/or the interior of individual teeth. Sufficient collagen from tooth dentin was successfully extracted from 20 individuals from Huaca Prieta and all 3 individuals from Paredones (table A6.1); however, the collagen extraction protocol was performed on all individual samples (Brown et al. 1988; Bronk Ramsey et al. 2004). Specifically, samples were decalcified (typically over a 24-hour period) using 0.5N HCl. Collagen was gelatinized at 58°C for 17 hours, filtered to remove any remaining solids, and then ultrafiltered to remove the 30-kD fraction, which was lyophilized. Approximately 1 mg of the lyophilized collagen was analyzed by continuous flow (CF) dual isotope analysis using a CHNOS Elemental Analyzer interfaced to an IsoPrime100 mass spectrometer in the Center for Stable Isotope Biogeochemistry at the University of California, Berkeley. As stated above, all results are reported using the delta notation, $\delta = [(R\text{sample}/R\text{standard}-1) * 1000]$; for carbon isotope values, $R = {}^{13}C/{}^{12}C$ and all values are reported against V-PDB (Coplen 1994). For nitrogen isotope values, $R = {}^{15}N/{}^{14}N$ and values are reported against atmospheric N_2 (AIR). Diagenesis was assessed by evaluating percent carbon, percent nitrogen, and atomic C:N ratios (table A6.1). All but 2 individual dentin collagen samples had carbon to nitrogen (C:N) ratios between the preferred range of 2.9 and 3.6 (DeNiro 1985). The 2 exceptions have C:N ratios of 2.6; both have high %C and %N (as compared to degraded collagen), however, and did not have anomalous $\delta^{13}C$ or $\delta^{15}N$ values.

Statistical comparisons between Huaca Prieta individuals during Phase III and Phase IV, and between Huaca Prieta individuals and Paredones individuals, employed pri-

marily nonparametric Mann-Whitney U tests. However, $\delta^{15}N_{\text{dentinc collagen}}$, $\delta^{13}C_{\text{dentinc collagen}}$, and $\delta^{18}O_{\text{enamel}}$ from individuals from Huaca Prieta (Phase III and Phase IV) were compared using parametric t-tests, as these data were normally distributed (Shapiro-Wilk tests).

DENTAL MICROWEAR TEXTURE ANALYSIS

Molars from all individuals exhibiting wear were molded and subsequently cast for dental microwear texture analysis (DMTA). As only 1 tooth from Paredones was a molar with antemortem microwear, in contrast to all teeth examined from Huaca Prieta, we only conducted DMTA on individuals from Huaca Prieta ($n = 20$, the same individuals analyzed for stable isotopes; tables A6.2 and A6.3).

All teeth were cleaned with cotton swabs soaked in ethyl alcohol. Once they were dry, a mold was made using polyvinylsiloxane dental impression material (President's Jet regular body, Coltène-Whaledent Corp., Cuyahoga Falls, Ohio). Tooth casts were then prepared using Epotek 301 epoxy resin and hardener (Epoxy Technologies Corp., Billerica, Massachusetts), allowing resulting casts to reproduce microscopic features with a resolution of a fraction of a micron. Further, all dental microwear molds were made prior to any drilling for stable isotope analyses.

Dental microwear texture analysis was performed on crushing/grinding facets (for example, facet 9) of all tooth casts that preserved antemortem microwear using whitelight confocal profilometry and scale-sensitive fractal analysis (SSFA; Scott et al. 2006; similar to Ungar et al. 2003). All specimens were scanned in three dimensions in four adjacent fields of view at 100× magnification, for a total sampled area of $204 \times 276~\mu m^2$. Scale sensitive fractal analysis software (ToothFrax and SFrax, Surfract Corp., www.surfrait.com) was used to analyze all resulting scans and characterize tooth surfaces according to the following attributes: anisotropy, complexity, and texture fill volume. All attributes were statistically compared to the raw data from Sireen El-Zaatari (2010), allowing individuals from Huaca Prieta to be compared to five historic/prehistoric hunter-gatherer populations with diverse dietary behaviors (all acquired from the same confocal microscope in the Department of Anthropology at the University of Arkansas). While El-Zaatari (2010) notes seven populations, she combines the Khoe-San samples (specifically combining the prehistoric sites of Matjex River and Oakhurst Shelter with the historic site of Riet River) for subsequent comparisons after no significant differences were observed between subpopulations; thus we have also combined all Khoe-San samples into one population for statistical analyses.

Statistical comparisons used Kuskal-Wallis tests and multiple comparisons using Dunn's procedure, as DMTA data are nonnormally distributed (as indicated via Shapiro-Wilk tests).

Table A6.1. Stable carbon, oxygen, and nitrogen isotope data from individuals at Huaca Prieta and Paredones

Site	Specimen ID	Phase	$\delta^{13}C_{enamel}$ (‰)	$\delta^{18}O_{enamel}$ (‰)	$\delta^{13}C_{collagen}$ (‰)	$\delta^{15}N_{collagen}$ (‰)	$\Delta^{13}C_{enamel-collagen}$ (‰)	%C	%N	C:N ratio
Huaca Prieta	AMNH6	III	−12.7	26.5						
	AMNH7	III	−13	26.9						
	AMNH8	III	−12.6	26.7	−17.1	13	4.5	26.9	10.1	3.1
	AMNH9	III	−12.5	25.6	−15.4	15	2.9	26.1	10.2	3
	AMNH10	III	−10.8	26.9						
	HP-1	III	−10.9	27.4	−15.4	15	4.5	33.9	12.7	3.1
	HP-5	III	−12.9	26.4	−16.2	15.8	3.3	39.4	14.2	3.2
	HP-7	III	−11.9	25.8						
	HP-9	III	−11.8	27.1	−17.6	14.6	5.8	46.4	15.9	3.4
	AMNH1	IV	−12.4	26.2	−18.1	13.1	5.7	36.7	13.2	3.2
	AMNH2	IV	−14	25.3						
	AMNH3	IV	−11.4	26.2	−16	15.5	4.6	44.8	16.1	3.3
	AMNH4	IV	−12.7	26.8						
	AMNH5	IV	−12.8	26.5	−16.5	14.7	3.7	42.6	15.1	3.3
	HP-11	IV	−12.3	27.6	−15.6	16.5	3.3	30.8	11.3	3.2
	HP-2	IV	−12.1	27.4	−18.3	11.7	6.2	18.2	8.2	2.6*
	HP-3	IV	−12	27.6	−17	13.3	5	34.1	13	3.1
	HP-4	IV	−12	27	−15.9	15.1	3.9	33.3	12.4	3.1
	HP-6	IV	−13.6	27.4	−18	11.4	4.4	28	12.4	2.6*
	HP-8	IV	−12.6	27.5						
Paredones	Paredones1		−4.7	26.3	−10.9	11.5	6.2	36.8	13.4	3.2
	Paredones2		−7	26.4	−10.8	11.2	3.8	40	13.9	3.3
	Paredones3		−5.8	25.1	−12.6	10.2	6.8	25.6	9.4	3.2

*Samples with C:N ratios outside of the preferred 2.9 to 3.6 range (DeNiro 1985) for collagen.

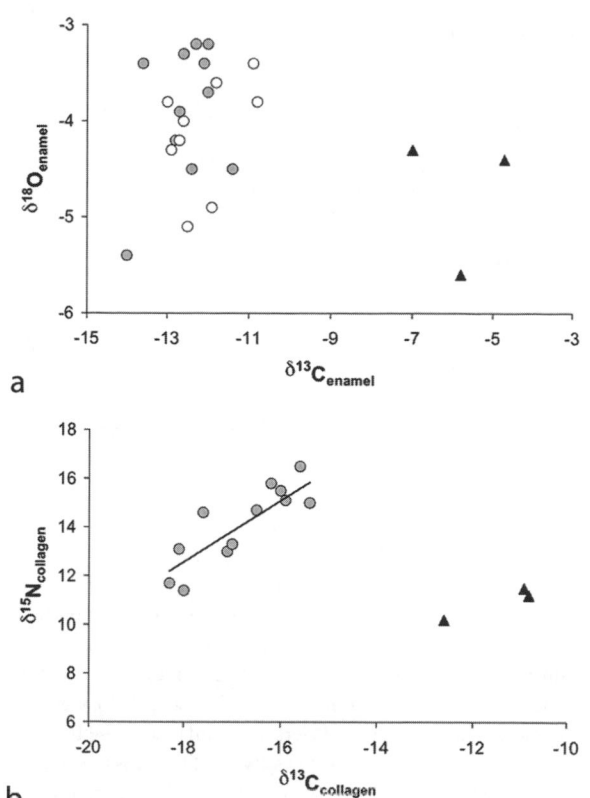

a

b

c

FIGURE A6.1. Isotope values for various individuals: a, biplot of $\delta^{13}C_{enamel}$ and $\delta^{18}O_{enamel}$ values; Huaca Prieta (*circles*) individuals have significantly lower $\delta^{13}C_{enamel}$ values than individuals from Paredones (*black triangles*; $p < 0.01$); oxygen isotope values are indistinguishable between individuals from Phase III (*open circles*) and Phase IV (*gray circles*) at Huaca Prieta ($p = 0.30$) and between Huaca Prieta and Paredones individuals ($p = 0.08$); b, stable carbon and nitrogen isotope values from dentin collagen; at Huaca Prieta there is a significant relationship between $\delta^{13}C_{collagen}$ and $\delta^{15}N_{collagen}$ ($p < 0.001$; $R^2 = 0.71$); stable carbon and nitrogen isotope values are also significantly lower ($p = 0.01$) and higher ($p < 0.01$), respectively, at Huaca Prieta as compared to Paredones, indicating greater reliance on maize reliance on marine resources at Paredones; c, relationship between $\Delta^{13}C_{enamel-collagen}$ and $\delta^{15}N_{collagen}$ values at Huaca Prieta (*gray circles*) and Paredones (*black triangles*); $\Delta^{13}C_{enamel-collagen}$ values are negatively correlated with $\delta^{15}N_{collagen}$ values ($p < 0.01$; $R^2 = 0.42$).

DIETARY ECOLOGY OF INDIVIDUALS FROM HUACA PRIETA

STABLE ISOTOPE EVIDENCE

Individuals from Huaca Prieta have $\delta^{15}N_{dentin\ collagen}$ values that range from 11.6‰ to 16.5‰, with a mean value of 14.2‰ (±1.6 standard deviation, SD; table A6.1, figs. A6.2, A6.3). These values are consistent with a diet of predominately marine resources. For comparison, historic populations with primarily marine diets (for example, Eskimo, Haida, and Tlingit) have $\delta^{15}N_{bone\ collagen}$ values ranging from 17‰ to 20‰, while those with values between 6‰ and 12‰ are predominantly agriculturalists (Schoeninger et al. 1983). Furthermore, early and middle Holo-

Table A6.2. DMTA data from all individuals sampled from Huaca Prieta

Individual ID	Phase	Asfc	epLsar	Tfv
AMNH1	IV	1.529	0.0007	11263
AMNH2	IV	0.760	0.0033	2672
AMNH3	IV	1.246	0.0020	13994
AMNH4	IV	1.354	0.0022	7152
AMNH5	IV	1.272	0.0027	9986
AMNH6	III	1.418	0.0042	4077
AMNH7	III	0.803	0.0019	8590
AMNH8	III	0.816	0.0025	11255
AMNH9	III	1.193	0.0027	15151
AMNH10	III	1.164	0.0036	8379
HP-1	III	1.686	0.0024	15698
HP-2	IV	1.661	0.0023	8660
HP-3	IV	1.288	0.0018	5705
HP-4	IV	0.577	0.0027	1556
HP-5	III	0.511	0.0042	14614
HP-6	IV	1.078	0.0034	718
HP-7	III	2.120	0.0029	8615
HP-8	IV	1.080	0.0023	2831
HP-9	III	1.800	0.0049	10659
HP-11	IV	1.054	0.0026	10947

Table A6.3. Descriptive statistics of DMTA data from Huaca Prieta as compared to historic/prehistoric populations

Population	n	Asfc mean	SD	epLsar mean	SD	Tfv mean	SD
Andamanese*	30	6.345	4.219	0.0026	0.0012	10293	4746
Chumash*	13	2.787	2.344	0.0023	0.0007	6636	3192
Fuegians*	6	0.948	0.291	0.0044	0.0014	5225	3523
Khoe-San*	43	3.616	2.360	0.0026	0.0013	10869	4622
Tigara*	25	6.569	5.807	0.0029	0.0015	11912	4657
Huaca Prieta	20	1.220	0.414	0.0028	0.0010	8626	4563

*DMTA data from El-Zaatari (2010).

cene humans from the central California coast have mean $\delta^{15}N_{bone\ collagen}$ values of 13.6‰ and 12.5‰, respectively (Newsome et al. 2004). Using isotope mixing models (a concentration-dependent IsoSource model), the above-mentioned $\delta^{15}N_{bone\ collagen}$ values from California suggest 70%–84% marine food source contributions during the early Holocene and 48%–58% during the middle Holocene (Newsome et al. 2004). Similarly, $\delta^{13}C_{dentin\ collagen}$ values from Huaca Prieta are consistent with predominantly marine resource consumption, ranging from −18.3‰ to −15.4‰, with a mean value of −16.7‰ (±1.1, SD; table A6.1, fig. A6.2). Additionally, there is a significant positive correlation between $\delta^{13}C_{dentin\ collagen}$ and $\delta^{15}N_{dentin\ collagen}$ in Huaca Prieta individuals ($p < 0.001$; $R^2 = 0.71$; fig. A6.2), further suggesting that individuals with higher $\delta^{13}C_{dentin\ collagen}$ values consumed marine resources, in contrast to C_4 plants such as maize.

Similarly, Huaca Prieta individuals have $\delta^{13}C_{enamel}$ values that range from −14‰ to −10.8‰ with a mean value of −12.4‰ (±0.8, SD; table A6.1, fig. A6.1). Assessing $\Delta^{13}C_{enamel-collagen}$ can reveal if protein versus whole diet food items had dramatically different isotopic sources. The mean $\Delta^{13}C_{enamel-collagen}$ value is 4.4‰, the published cut-off value above or below which suggest protein and whole diet sources are different (Ambrose et al. 1997). Thus, both protein and whole diet components (including carbohydrates) of an individual's diet were very similar, suggesting a heavy reliance on marine resources. If individuals with high nitrogen values ($\delta^{15}N_{dentin\ collagen} \geq 15‰$) are separated from those with lower values ($\delta^{15}N_{dentin\ collagen} < 15‰$), $\Delta^{13}C_{enamel-collagen}$ values are 3.8‰ and 5.0‰, respectively. Furthermore, there is a significant negative relationship between $\Delta^{13}C_{enamel-collagen}$ values and $\delta^{15}N_{dentin\ collagen}$ values ($p = 0.024$; $R^2 = 0.38$; fig. A6.3). These data collectively suggest that individuals who consumed a larger proportion of marine-based resources (higher $\delta^{15}N_{dentin\ collagen}$ values) may have also consumed C_3 terrestrial plants, while those individuals with lower $\delta^{15}N_{dentin\ collagen}$ values may have consumed some C_4 plant resources (potentially some maize) or more ^{13}C enriched carbohydrates from marine sources (such as seaweed).

Despite individual variation (fig. A6.1) in carbon and nitrogen isotope values at Huaca Prieta, all geochemical data from Huaca Prieta individuals are consistent with prior archaeological evidence that suggested a predominantly marine-based diet, potentially also including C_3 plant resources (Bird 1948a; Dillehay et al. 2012a, 2012b). Geochemical data from Huaca Prieta are similar to those for other coastal populations, especially the Fuegians (Yesner et al. 2003). Specifically, $\delta^{15}N_{collagen}$ and $\delta^{13}C_{collagen}$ values from Huaca Prieta and Fuegians are statistically indistinguishable from one another, with nearly identical mean $\delta^{15}N_{collagen}$ values (14.2‰ and 14.8‰, respectively) and mean $\delta^{13}C_{collagen}$ values (−16.7‰ and −15.3‰, respectively). These similarities suggest that these populations likely had similar diets, specifically diets consisting of primarily marine resources.

Diets of individuals from Phases III and IV are indistinguishable, via $\delta^{13}C_{enamel}$ values, $\delta^{13}C_{dentin\ collagen}$ values, and $\delta^{15}N_{dentin\ collagen}$ values. Furthermore, $\delta^{18}O_{enamel}$ values are indistinguishable and suggest the consumption of similar water resources. Collectively, the absence of differences between phases may indicate the absence of profound environmental, climate, and/or cultural dietary practices between Phases III and IV.

DENTAL MICROWEAR TEXTURAL EVIDENCE

Examples of dental microwear of Huaca Prieta individuals are shown in figure A6.3 and all primary data are noted in table A6.2 and summarized in table A6.3. All DMTA variables assessed (anisotropy, complexity, and texture fill volume) yielded statistical differences between Huaca Prieta individuals and prehistoric/historic populations (table A6.3). Complexity and texture fill volume were the most revealing. Huaca Prieta individuals had complexity values indistinguishable from Fuegians and significantly lower than all other populations (Chumash, Khoe-San, Andamanese, and Tigara, listed in order of ascending mean Asfc values, $p < 0.05$; tables A6.2 and A6.3; fig. A6.3). These differences cor-

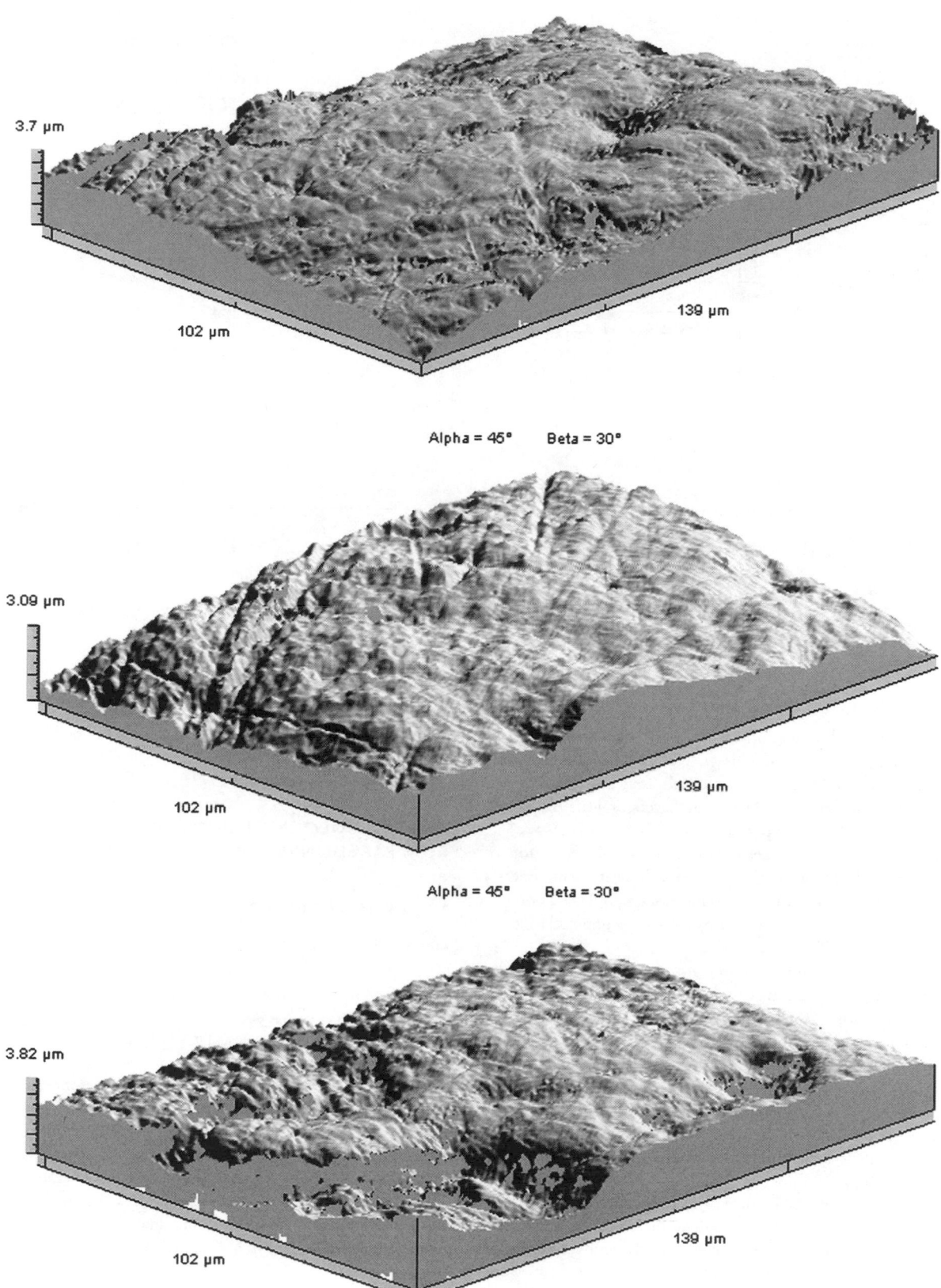

FIGURE A6.2. Examples of microscopic tooth wear from individuals at Huaca Prieta.

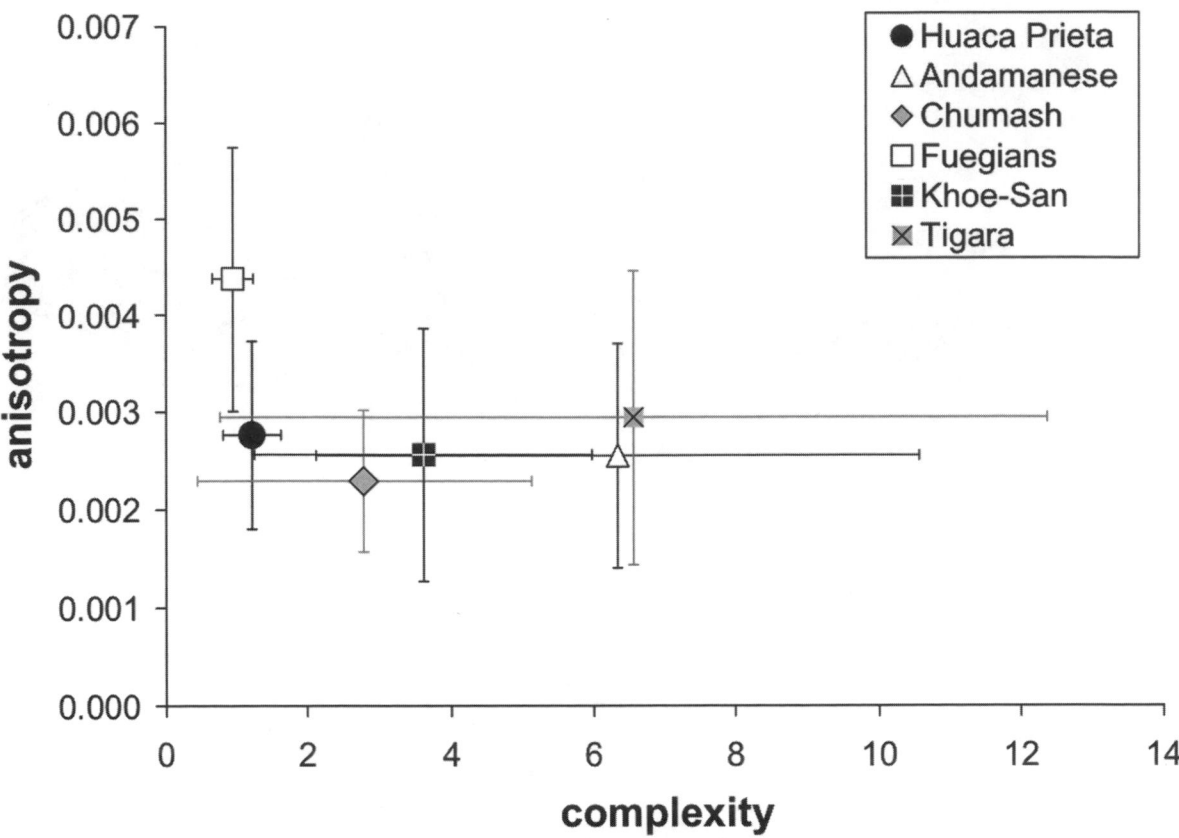

FIGURE A6.3. Dental microwear textural data of individuals from Huaca Prieta as compared to historic/prehistoric populations (mean values, with error bars denoting 1 SD; baseline data from El-Zaatari 2010).

respond with known differences in diet and food preparation techniques, with the Fuegians and Chumash primarily consuming marine meat with low abrasives, the Khoe-San being intermediate hunter-gatherers, and the Andamanese and Tigara preparing/storing their food in ways that allowed for the ingestion of significant abrasives (for example, the incorporation of sand into meat during freezing on open racks or underground storage by Tigara populations or uncovered cooking by Andamanese populations; El-Zaatari 2010).

Texture fill volume values from Huaca Prieta individuals cluster with the Fuegians and Chumash; however, they are only statistically indistinguishable from the Tigara individuals ($p < 0.05$; tables A6.2, A6.3). Anisotropy only distinguishes Fuegians from all other populations (including Huaca Prieta) that have lower values ($p < 0.05$; tables A6.2 and A6.3); it is unable to resolve differences between any other populations, so it is potentially the least revealing test and unable to differentiate between disparate diets in human populations.

Collectively, DMTA data suggest that Huaca Prieta individuals consumed diets most similar in textural food properties as populations known to heavily rely on marine resources (including the consumption of marine meat). Subsequently, Huaca Prieta individuals are most different from populations known to store or prepare their food on sandy

beaches, as there is little evidence of significant abrasives in their consumed food.

DIETARY ECOLOGY OF INDIVIDUALS FROM PAREDONES

STABLE ISOTOPE EVIDENCE

Only 3 individual teeth from Paredones individuals were geochemically analyzed (table A6.1, figs. A6.2, A6.3). Despite the limited sample size, these individuals exhibit significantly lower $\delta^{15}N_{dentin\ collagen}$ values ($p < 0.01$) and significantly greater $\delta^{13}C_{dentin\ collagen}$ ($p = 0.01$) and $\delta^{13}C_{enamel}$ ($p < 0.01$) values. Lower nitrogen isotope values (a mean value of 11.0‰) suggest less reliance on marine resources and increased consumption of plant and/or terrestrial protein sources. Increased carbon isotope values can indicate increased maize consumption or marine resources; in combination with lower nitrogen isotope values, however, maize is the more likely explanation. Furthermore, maize may have been a staple for Paredones individuals, based on the degree of ^{13}C enrichment in $\delta^{13}C_{enamel}$ and $\delta^{13}C_{dentin\ collagen}$ values.

Evidence of maize consumption at Paredones is consistent with macroscopic archaeological evidence from the site (the presence of cobs, husks, and tassels; Grobman et al. 2012; see appendix 5). It is interesting, however, that the diets of these individuals are distinct from individuals found only 0.5 km away and overlapping temporally (Dillehay et al. 2012b). These data may suggest that human remains from Paredones were from individuals that resided farther inland and were potentially transported to Paredones for burial or migrated to coastal regions later in life (after tooth enamel and dentin formation had occurred), while Huaca Prieta individuals represented more local populations that both resided on the coast and relied on coastal resources, or there were two locally specialized economies. Further work is needed to resolve hypotheses regarding reasons for profound dietary differences between Huaca Prieta and Paredones individuals. For example, the analysis of strontium isotopes in enamel and bone apatite of adults from Paredones and Huaca Prieta could help reveal if populations were indigenous to the local area, both as children and adults, or if Paredones individuals immigrated from elsewhere (see Turner et al. 2009).

SUMMARY

Human remains of early Peruvians from Huaca Prieta and Paredones can help clarify ancient diets. All geochemical and dental microwear data from Huaca Prieta individuals suggest a diet consisting of primarily marine resources, including those low in abrasives. Interestingly, Huaca Prieta individuals have isotopic and DMTA data similar to Fuegian populations (El-Zaatari 2010; Yesner et al. 2003), sug-

gesting that these populations shared a similar reliance on coastal resources. Stable isotope and dental microwear textural data are consistent with early interpretations of Huaca Prieta being largely based on a marine economy, although the degree to which cultivated plant resources played a role is more difficult to evaluate. Surprisingly, Huaca Prieta individuals had significantly different diets from individuals found at Paredones (despite being spatially and temporally similar), with Paredones individuals exhibiting carbon isotope values consistent with significant maize consumption. Thus maize may have been a staple for early Peruvians sometime between ~4500–4000 cal BP (Dillehay et al. 2012b). Further work is needed to examine reasons for the disparate diets of Huaca Prieta and Paredones individuals, including the analysis of additional individuals from Paredones.

ACKNOWLEDGMENTS

We would like to thank S. El-Zaatari for generously sharing her DMTA data from El-Zaatari (2010), allowing for the statistical comparisons included here. We also thank the American Museum of Natural History for access and permission to sample teeth, Peter Ungar for access to a white-light confocal microscope at the University of Arkansas, James Curtis for analyzing the enamel samples at the University of Florida, and Saril Mambelli for analyzing the collagen samples at the University of California, Berkeley. This work was funded by Vanderbilt University.

PHYTOLITH ANALYSIS

José Iriarte and Jennifer Watling

INTRODUCTION

A total of 39 phytolith samples from the Huaca Prieta and Paredones sites (table A7.1) were analyzed with the main objective of identifying plants of economic importance. Samples were processed, identified, and counted at the University of Exeter Archaeobotany Laboratory. Phytolith extractions from the archaeological sediments followed standard procedures. Samples were deflocculated in a shaker with sodium hexametaphosphate for 24 hours. Clays were washed by gravitational sedimentation, carbonates were removed using hydrochloric acid, and organic matter was removed with nitric acid and potassium chlorate when necessary. Samples were floated in a zinc bromide solution at a specific density of 2.3 grams/ml, dried in acetone, and mounted in Permount (see Piperno 2006b: 119–129). In order to maximize the recovery of phytoliths of different size classes, such as those derived from the rinds of *Cucurbita* fruits and leaves and cobs of maize (*Zea mays* L.), sediments were separated by wet-sieving into fine silt (fraction A, 2–25 μm), coarse silt (fraction B, 25–50 μm), and sand (fraction C, 50–2000 μm) fractions. The entire extract from the sand fraction was scanned for *Cucurbita* phytoliths and other large arboreal and economic plant forms. Extended counts of the fine silt fraction were searched for cross-shaped phytoliths in order to detect the presence of maize leaf phytoliths (Iriarte 2003; Pearsall 2000; Piperno 2006b). Similarly, since wavy-top maize rondel types constitute a minor part of the prolific rondel assemblages produced by maize cobs and may be absent in some maize races (Mulholland 1993; Pearsall et al. 2003; Piperno and Pearsall 1993), the samples were subjected to an intensive search. Phytoliths were identified under the light Zeiss Axioscope 40 microscope at 500 × magnifications. Identification was based on the modern phytolith reference collection curated at the Laboratory of Archaeobotany and Palaeoecology at the Department of Archaeology, Exeter University, which contains more than 500 species of tropical and subtropical plants, as well as atlases and catalogues (Dickau et al. 2013; Iriarte and Paz 2009; Piperno 2006b; Watling and Iriarte 2013).

Identification of Poaceae phytoliths was based on a morphological classification first proposed by Page Twiss et al. (1969) and later modified by various researchers by taking into account criteria based on three-dimensional morphology and other micromorphological features (Mulhol-

Table A7.1. Archaeological samples analyzed for phytoliths from Huaca Prieta and Paredones

Lab #	Provenience	Lab #	Provenience
PL–HP–19	Unit 2 West profile, Layer 2	PL–HP–15	Unit 3, South profile, Floor 2
PL–HP–21	Unit 2 West profile, Layer 2	PL–HP–10	Unit 3, South profile, Floor 3
PL–HP–16	Unit 2 West profile, Layer 3	PL–HP–11	Unit 3, South profile, Floor 4
PL–HP–20	Unit 2 West profile, Layer 3	PL–HP–8	Unit 3, South profile, Floor 5
PL–HP–18	Unit 2 West profile, Layer 5b	PL–HP–9	Unit 7, Floor 1
PL–HP–25	Unit 2 West profile, Layer 5b	PL–HP–2009–7	Unit 16, Layer 11
PL–HP–23	Unit 2 West profile, Layer 6	PL–HP–2009–5	Unit 16, Layer 19
PL–HP–14	Unit 2 West profile, Layer 7a	PL–HP–2009–6	Unit 16, Layer 9
PL–HP–24	Unit 2 West profile, Layer 7a	PL–HP–2009–35	Unit 18, Layer 12
PL–HP–17	Unit 2 West profile, Layer 7b	PL–HP–2009–13	Unit 18, Layer 13
PL–HP–22	Unit 2 West profile, Layer 7b	PL–HP–2009–33	Unit 18, Layer 14
PL–HP–6	Unit 2 West profile, Layer 7c1	PL–HP–2009–17	Unit 18, Layer 18
PL–HP–5	Unit 2 West profile, Layer 7c2	PL–HP–2009–12	Unit 18, Layer 20
PL–HP–2	Unit 2 West profile, Layer 7c3	PL–HP–2009–16	Unit 18, Layer 23
PL–HP–7	Unit 2 West profile, Layer 7c3	PL–HP–2009–16	Unit 18, Layer 23
PL–HP–4	Unit 2 West profile, Layer 7c4	PL–HP–2009–15	Unit 18, Layer 25
PL–HP–1	Unit 2 West profile, Layer 7c5	PL–HP–2009–1	Unit 20, Layer 6C
PL–HP–3	Unit 2 West profile, Layer 7c7	PL–HP–2009–21	Unit 22, Floor 11
PL–HP–13	Unit 2, Layer 6c	PL–HP–2009–24	Unit 22, Floor 17
PL–HP–12	Unit 3, South profile, Floor 1		

land 1989; Twiss 1992); neotropical grasses (Pearsall 2000; Piperno 2006b; Piperno and Pearsall 1998; Sondahl and Labouriau 1970); and the Río de la Plata Grasslands (Bertoli de Pomar 1971; Zucol 1999).

RESULTS

In the 39 contexts analyzed we documented the presence of squash, bottle gourd, and maize as well as the presence of phytoliths that can potentially represent the consumption of beans and Marantaceae tubers. A description of each particular plant of economic importance follows.

Squash: We documented 55 squash (*Cucurbita* spp.) phytoliths from 11 of the 39 samples analyzed. The majority (7 out of 11) were recovered from Unit 2, Layers 7c1, 7c2, 7c3, 7c5, 7c6, and 7c7 and Layers 7a1 and 7a2, in addition to 1 from Unit 2, Layer 6, 1 from Unit 7, Floor 1, 1 from Unit 18, Layer 25, and 1 from Unit 22, Layer 17. In terms of size (fig. A7.1), the samples have *Cucurbita* phytoliths that fall in the wild/domesticated overlap zone and some that are clearly domesticated (length >80μm and thickness >70μm) (Piperno and Stothert 2003; Piperno et al. 2000a). In morphological terms, several phytoliths that are thicker than they are long probably correspond to the species *C. moschata* (fig. A7.2a, c, e) and others with very grainy surfaces that are possibly from *C. maxima* (fig. A7.2d). The definitive identification of the latter requires more work with modern reference

material. Combined metric and morphological attributes indicates that the *Cucurbita* assemblage corresponds to domesticated species of squash (figs. A7.1, A7.2). In chronological terms, squash phytoliths are present in all phases at Huaca Prieta, beginning in the terminal Pleistocene/early Holocene and in Phase I in Unit 2. It first appears in radiocarbon-dated levels in Paredones around ~10,000 cal BP.

Bottle gourd: A single phytolith from a bottle gourd (*Lagenaria siceraria*) with its characteristic elongated scallops (Piperno et al. 2000a) was recovered from Unit 2, Layer 7c7, and contextually radiocarbon dated around 7000 cal BP (fig. A7.3a).

Zea mays: The wavy top rondels produced in the glumes of maize cobs (*Zea mays* L.) (Piperno and Pearsall 1993; Pearsall et al. 2003) were detected in Paredones, Unit 18, Layers 13 and 23 (fig. A7.3b–e). In addition to these diagnostic phytoliths, we detected the characteristic silica bodies with speculate projections called IRPs (bodies with irregular projections), which are the product of epidermal silicification in the fruit case, cupule, glume, and other inflorescence tissues of maize and other grasses. The type of IRP found in these samples is not restricted to maize (it is also produced by other Panicoideae and Bambusoideae grasses), but it is the type of phytolith associated with maize cob phytoliths (fig. A7.3f–g).

Despite complete and intensive scanning of samples and of other contexts, no Variant 1 cross-shaped phytoliths produced by a maize leaf were found. The phytolith data com-

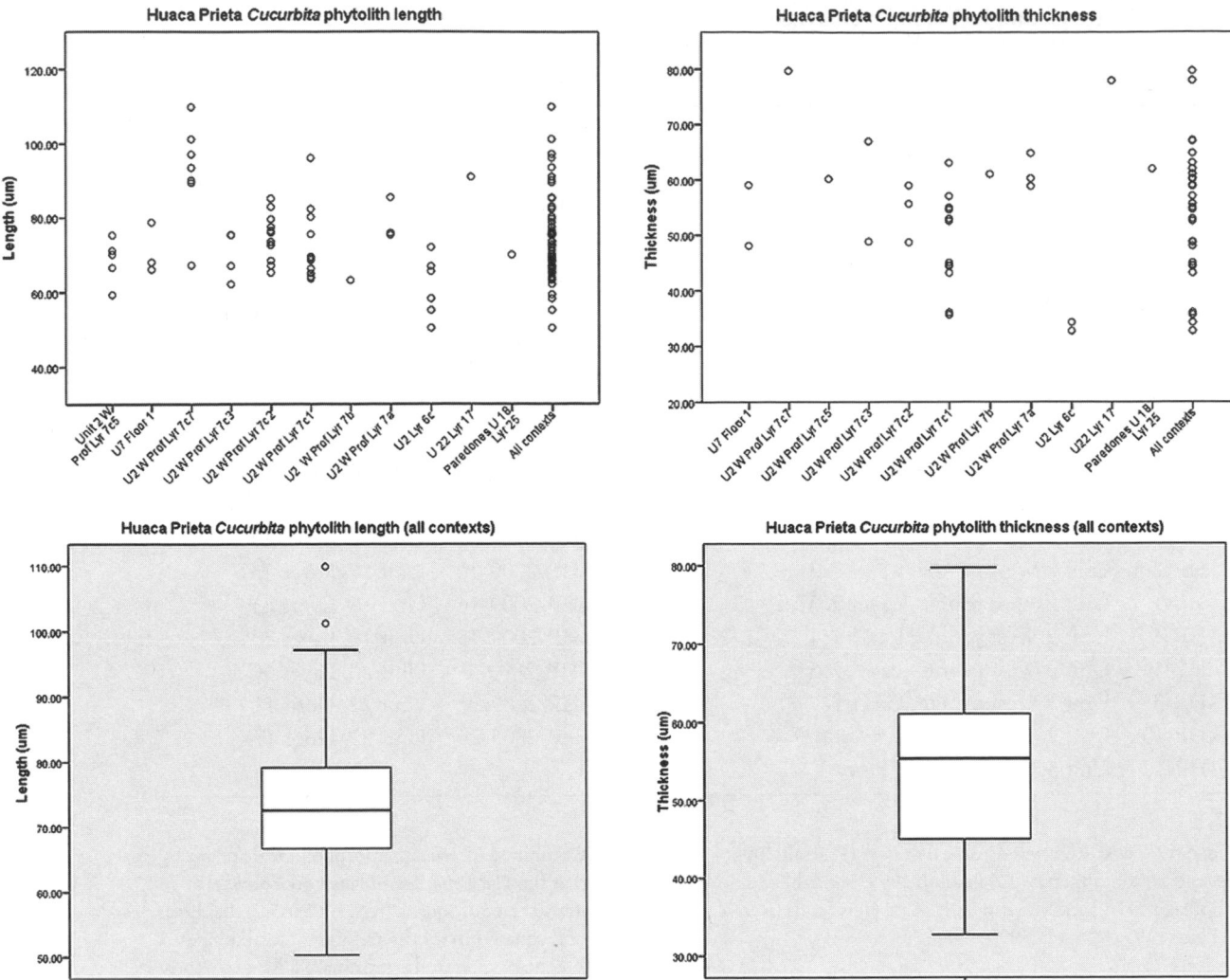

FIGURE A7.1. *Cucurbita* phytoliths length and thickness dot and box-plot graphs.

plement the large assemblage of macrobotanical remains found at different contexts of the sites dating between ~6700 and 3000 cal BP (Grobman et al. 2012; see chapter 10 and appendix 5).

TENTATIVE IDENTIFICATION OF BEAN POD SILICIFIED HAIRS

Unit 18, Layer 22, and Unit 22, Floor 11, yielded 2 samples that contained abundant hook-shaped phytoliths that appear to be characteristic of domesticated *Phaseolus* spp. pod hairs (fig. A7.3h–l). This type of curved nonsegmented hairs was found by Piperno (1988) in the Aristolochiaceae, Boraginaceae, Moraceae, Leguminoseae, and Urticaceae families. Stephen Bozarth (1990) demonstrated that the hook-shaped hairs of domesticated *Phaseolus vulgaris* are wider than ones produced in other families of plants in the Great Plains, allowing for their identification using phytolith analysis. Bozarth (1990) arrived at this conclusion based on the

measurement of the width of the hair at 6 μm from its tip. He found that the average width of *Phaseolus vulgaris* hairs is above 4.63 μm, while the widths of wild *Phaseolus* and other plant families producing hook-shaped hairs do not exceed 4.0 μm. The width of 12 nonsegmented curved hairs from Unit 18, Layer 22, was measured at 6 μm from the tip, which averaged 4.99 μm (min. 2.17 μm; max. 7.79 μm). Similarly, the width of 30 nonsegmented curved hairs from Unit 22, Floor 11 was measured at 6 μm from the tip. Those hairs averaged 5.04 μm (min. 3.37 μm; max. 7.14 μm). The large average widths of nonsegmented curved hairs from both contexts and the fact that most of the other plant families in which this type of hair occurs are not native to the Peruvian coast suggest the presence of domesticated *Phaseolus* in these contexts. However, no definite confirmation of its presence can be made at the moment. These phytolith remains date from Phase III to Phase V at Huaca Prieta.

Identification of Marantaceae Phytoliths: Marantaceae spheres (globular nodulose phytoliths) (Piperno 2006b) were present in all analyzed samples from Units 16 and 18.

These phytolith morphotypes (fig. A7.4f) cannot be identified beyond the family level, but they could have been produced by Marantaceae roots of economic importance, such as lerén (*Calathea allouia*) or arrowroot (*Maranta arundinacea*). Despite intensive search for the diagnostic that phytoliths produce in the seeds (Piperno 1989) and roots (Ezell et al. 2006) of *Calathea allouia* and *Maranta arundinacea*, none of these phytoliths were detected. These remains are derived from Phase IV and V contexts.

Phytoliths from Grasses (Poaceae), Sedges (Cyperaceae) and Herbs (Asteraceae): In addition to the plants of economic importance a variety of phytoliths were identified (fig. A7.4). Several samples, including examples from Unit 2, Layer 2, and Layer 7c5, have abundant thick, narrow rondels exhibiting two or three spikes in one end (fig. A7.4d) while others contain a low abundance (see appendix 12 for pollen comparison). These phytolith morphotypes are generally called "towers" or "spools" in the Old World (for example, Boyd et al. 1998; Kondo et al. 1994). In the New World this type of phytolith has been found in the Pampa grass *Cortaderia* sp. (Danthonideae) (Zucol 1999), in the seashore salt-grass *Distichlis spicata* (Chloridoideae), and in some bamboos like *Guada* sp. (Bambusoideae) (Pearsall 2000: 452–453). Given the absence of other phytoliths diagnostic of the bamboo family (Bambusoideae) and the proximity of Huaca Prieta to the seashore, it is likely that these "spiked towers" represent background vegetation from a local lagoon or from the mouth of the Chicama River, possibly seashore saltgrass or *Cortadeira* sp. Large ridged saddles from the red reed *Phragmites* sp. (Ollendorf et al. 1988; Piperno and Pearsall 1998), which is well adapted to brackish water estuaries, were present in Unit 16, Layer 19 (Fig. A7.4a). The presence of *Phragmites* could represent reeds brought to the site from the nearby brackish estuary. Similarly, the typical polygonal epidermal phytoliths from the wetland family of sedges Cyperaceae was recovered from most contexts (fig. A7.4e). All other contexts analyzed contain trace amounts of panicoid (crosses and bilobates) (fig. A7.4c), chloroid (saddles), and pooid (circular) (fig. A7.4b) grass phytoliths, as well as perforated opaque bladelets from Asteraceae herbs (fig. A7.4g). Most samples contain phytoliths produced by arboreal and herbaceous dycotiledons, such as globular granulate

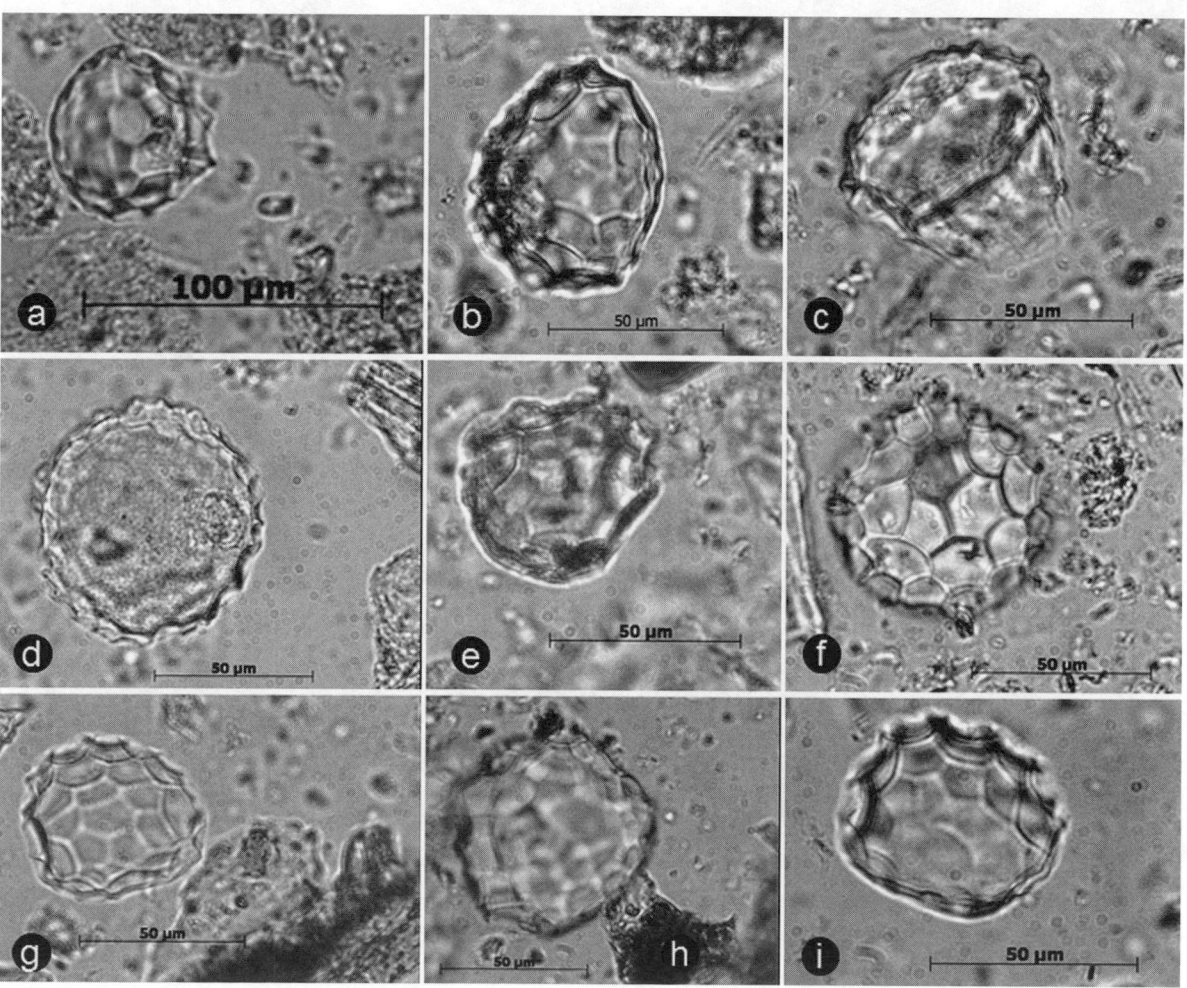

FIGURE A7.2. Samples of *Cucurbita* scalloped spheres: *a* and *e*, Unit 2, Layer 7c1; *b*, *c*, and *d*, Unit 2, Layer 7c2; *f*, Unit 2, Layer 7c3; *g*, *h*, and *i*, Unit 2, Layer 7c5.

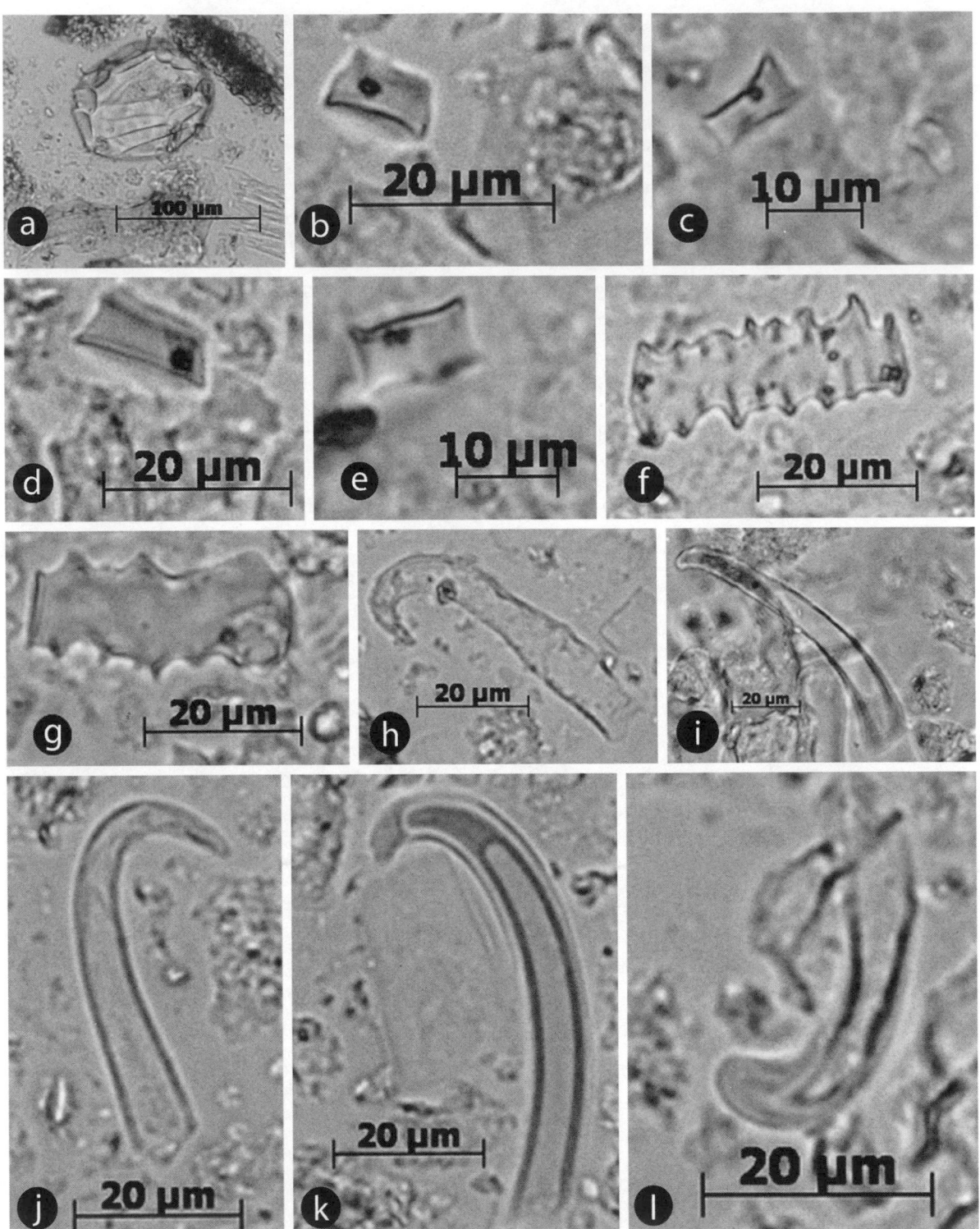

FIGURE A7.3. Sample of phytoliths from domestic plants: rind: *a*, *Lagenaria siceraria*, Unit 2, Layer 7c7; *b–e*, Zea mays cob wavy-top rondels; *d* and *c*, Unit 18, Layer 13; *d* and *e*, Unit 18, Layer 23; *f–g*, Zea mays IRPs bodies; *f*, Unit 18, Layer 13; *g*, Unit 18, Layer 23; *h–l*, curved nonsegmented hairs (possibly *Phaseolus vulgaris*), Unit 22, Floor 11.

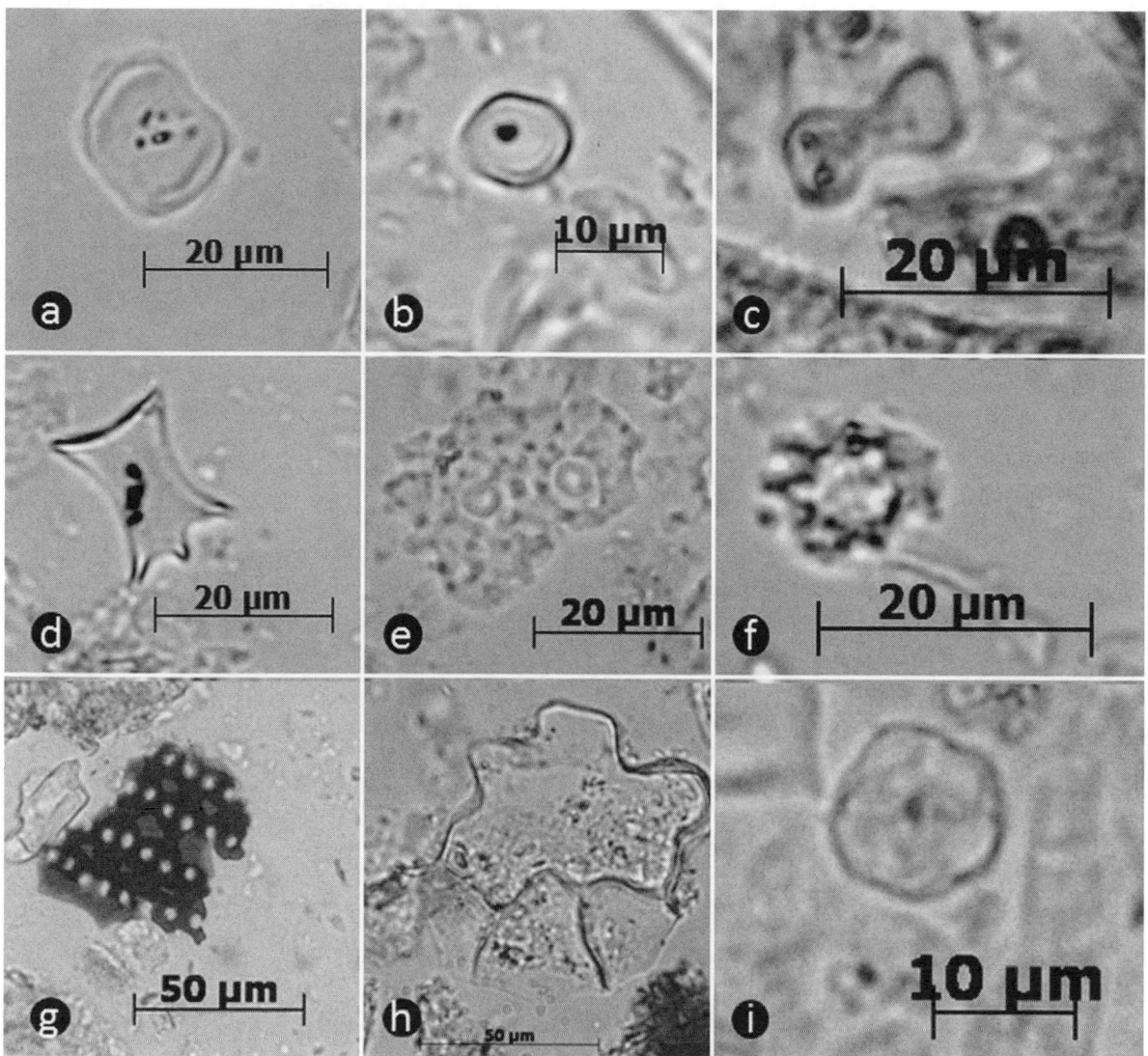

FIGURE A7.4. Phytolith morphotypes: *a*, *Phragmites* saddle; *b*, pooid circular; *c*, panicoid bilobate; *d*, "spiky tower rondel; *e*, Cyperaceae polygonal; *f*, Marantaceae nodular; *g*, Asteraceae opaque perforated bladelet; *h*, anticlinal epidermal cell; *i*, arboreal globular granulate.

(fig. A7.4i) and psilate phytoliths and anticlininal epidermal cells from dycots (fig. A7.4h). The samples also contain radiolarians, sponge spicules, and diatoms in trace amounts related to the location of sites close to the sea. The majority of these remains come from the deeper levels of units dated between 7500 and 6000 cal BP.

CONCLUSIONS

The phytolith analysis from the different contexts at Huaca Prieta and Paredones documented the presence of large scalloped sphere phytoliths produced in the rinds of domestic squash, possibly representing *C. moschata* and *C. maxima*. More work with modern reference material is necessary to produce conclusive identification at the species level. *Cucurbita* phytoliths were particularly abundant in Unit 2 Layers 6 and 7 but were also represented in Units 6, 7, 18, and 22. The phytolith of another cucurbit, bottle gourd (*Lagenaria siceraria*), showing the characteristic elongated scallops, was detected in one context in Unit 2, Layer 7c7.

We also documented the presence of phytoliths produced in the glumes of maize (*Zea mays*) cobs, including wavy top rondels and bodies with irregular projections. These phytoliths were only documented at Paredones Unit 18, Layers 13 and 23. This analysis complements previously published maize macrobotanical remains in the Huaca Prieta site.

We identified a type of hook-shape phytolith called nonsegmented curved hairs, which is consistent in terms of morphology and dimensions with ones that grow in the epidermis of bean pods. They were present in Unit 18, Layer 22, and Unit 22, Floor 11. There are a few neotropical families that can produce similar hairs but do not grow today on the northern coast of Peru. Therefore we suggest the presence of domestic *Phaseolus* beans at the site, but we cannot make a definite confirmation of the identification.

We also recovered typical Marantaceae nodular spheres in most contexts that raised the possibility that the Huaca Prieta inhabitants were consuming Marantaceae tubers such as *lerén* or arrowroot. However, we did not find the phytolith diagnostic of the seeds or root epidermis of these cultivars.

Finally, we found phytoliths that may have been used as a construction material or could represent background vegetation related to the brackish water estuary that the Chicama River creates when it meets the Pacific Ocean. We detected the idiosyncratic ridged saddles produced by reed red (*Phragmites* sp.) as well as the so-called "spiky towers" that were likely produced by the seashore saltgrass *Distichlis spicata* or the pampa grass *Cortadeira* sp.

SAND AND SALT SAMPLES FROM HUACA PRIETA

Mario Pino

Junius Bird interpreted the cobble layers with salt and sand at the base of his HP-3 trench as having been deposited by tsunamis (Bird et al. 1985: 17–18). He reasoned that the only explanation for the stone layers to have been imbricated the way they were with sand and salt fill between them and to have arrived to the east side of the mound was as the result of forceful waves driven over the mound by powerful tsunamis. To test whether these deposits were tsunami derived, we studied the elemental composition of these strata by taking sand samples from between the stones.

Three samples of sand were analyzed: two from stone berms in Layers 25 and 38 of the east profile of the HP-3 trench and one from a nonberm and noncultural Layer 8 in Unit 2. The two samples in HP-3 were derived from what are called retention footings or berms at the base of the mound to prevent erosion and to provide support for building the layers higher. The samples were dried at 40°C for 12 hours. After that a small subsample was separated from each sample. Then both were weighed. Distilled water was added to the larger sample; after 24 hours the water was evaporated at 50°C and salt crystals formed. This operation was performed until only salt crystals were present. The larger sample was sieved to remove mud from the sand. Thus the salt, sand, and mud fractions were separated, each characterized by its own weight. Finally, the subsample from each of the large samples of 45.64 cm³ was placed in a container. The volume of each subsample was weighed and then added with precision-burette water to saturate the subsample. The color of the samples was calculated (before processing) with the software ImageJ 1.3.9t, using artificial white light. The sample composition was described by the binocular microscope. Figure 7.3 shows the profile where samples from Layer 25 (5.80–5.86 m) and Layer 38 (8.14 m) were taken. The base of Layer 8 (6.27–6.36 m) was taken from noncultural level in Unit 2 (see salt-filled mortar in fig. 7.3).

Sample 1, Layer 25, Binocular Description: In this sample the color varies between 91 and 151, with an average of 116. It is white quartz sand with angular grains and very few ferromagnesian minerals. Abundant fragments of marine shells and unidentified rock, perhaps limestone or quartzite, were present.

Sample 1 totals: depth is 5.80–5.86 m in HP-3.

Sand	265.83 gr	27.064%
Mud	132.90 gr	13.530%

Salt	583.50 gr	59.406%
Total	982.23 gr	100.00%

The subsample of washed sand is 61.94 grams, with a volume of 45.64 cm³ and a laboratory porosity (H₂O content) of 24.80 cm³.

The total sample is 265.83/61.94 relative to the subsample (4.29 times). Therefore the total sample can contain up to 4.29 cm³ of 24.80 * H₂O (106 392 cm³). Such a volume of water, if it is seawater with a salt concentration of 35 g l⁻¹ (0.035gr/cm³) 106 392 * 0035, should result in 3.72 grams of salt. However, the sample has 583.50 grams, which is 157 times more salt than is normally contained in beach sand of this type.

Sample 2, Layer 38, Binocular Description: The color in this sample varies between 95 and 148, with an average of 113. It is also white quartz sand with angular grains and a few ferromagnesian minerals. Numerous fragments of marine shells and unidentified rocks, perhaps limestone or quartzite, were present.

Sample 2 totals: depth is 8.14 m in HP-3.

Sand	272.04 gr	24.77%
Mud	133.45 gr	12.12%
Salt	713.45 gr	64.02%
Total	1098.94 gr	100.91%

The subsample of washed sand is 60.34 grams, with a volume of 44.05 cm³ and a laboratory porosity (H₂O content) of 23.56 cm³.

The total sample is 272.04/60.34 relative to the subsample (4.51 times). Therefore the total sample can contain up to 4.58 cm³ of 23.56 * H₂O (106 392 cm³). Such a volume of water, if it is seawater with a salt concentration of 35 g l⁻¹ (0.035gr/cm³) 106 392 * 0035, should result in 3.72 grams of salt. The sample has 593.45 grams, however, which is 190 times more salt than is typically contained in beach sand of this type.

Sample 3, Layer 8, Binocular Description: In this sample the color varies between 90 and 204, with an average of 120. It is composed mainly of sand remains of crab shells and sea urchins, with unpolished white quartz. It contains no ferromagnesian minerals. There is a small percentage of fine gravel composed of a very fine-looking white limestone rock or grain quartzite.

Sample 3 totals: depth is 2.80–2.86 m in HP-2.

Sand	339.0 gr	38.20%
Mud	124.0 gr	14.00%
Salt	425.5 gr	47.99%
Total	888.5 gr	100.19%

The subsample of washed sand is 60.0 grams, with a volume of 45.64 cm³ and a laboratory porosity (H₂O content) of 22.50 cm³. The total sample is 1339.0/60.20 relative to the subsample (22.24 times). Therefore the total sample can contain up to 22.24 cm³ 22.50 * H₂O (500 400 cm³). Such a volume of water, if it is seawater with a salt concentration of 35 g l⁻¹ (0.035g/cm³) 500 400 * 0035 grams, should result in 17.514 grams of salt. In this case, the sample is 25.5 grams, which is only 1.46 times more salt than is normally contained in beach sand of this type, a number of the same order of magnitude. This sample was derived from a noncultural layer below Unit 2 and contains an expected amount of salt in marine sediments.

Finally, although not quantified in detail here, similar ratios of artificially high salt content to the salt content of natural sediments (158–167 times higher) were recorded for salt lenses in several tombs at Huaca Prieta (see chapter 7). Furthermore, large caches of salt were found at the base of the southwest side of the Huaca Prieta mound in Test Pit 4.

CONCLUSIONS

By their nature, tsunamis wash away all silt and clay fraction, which is not the case here. Moreover, the amount of salt in samples 1 and 2, which is derived from the "mortar" between the stone berms of the ramp on the east side of the site, is 157 and 190 times more than in marine sediments. It appears that these sediments in the mound were "watered" multiple times with seawater, taking advantage of evaporation from these climatic conditions to produce a cement-like substance to hold the cobbles in place.

Sample 3 from Unit 2 has less than 1% of fine sediment, many marine calcareous pieces, and only a normal (referring to marine water) amount of salt within its pores.

Preliminary study of five other samples from across the mound at Huaca Prieta reveal similar results, suggesting that the findings here are probably representative of the endurated plaster mortar within most or all of the mound.

STARCH GRAINS

Dolores R. Piperno, Timothy Messner, and Irene Holst

INTRODUCTION

This appendix reports the results of an analysis of starch grains from the sites of Huaca Prieta and Paredones. The following samples were analyzed: 13 residues removed from macrobotanical specimens of bottle gourds; residues from 7 grinding stones; 9 human teeth from Bird's original excavations; 11 human teeth from the new excavations; 24 stone tools; 33 sediment samples; and a maize kernel from Paredones.

METHODS

Starch grain analysis of sediments, stone tools, and human teeth followed standard procedures (Piperno and Dillehay 2008; Piperno et al. 2000b, 2009), with the exception of the grinding stones that were sampled in Peru by Dillehay without the multistage processing protocol described in Piperno et al. (2000b, 2009). Inserting a thin needle through the outer layer into the endosperm, removing the needle, and then washing it with water in a plastic container to collect the adhering residue sampled the maize kernel examined. The residue was then mounted directly in water on a microscope slide. Archaeological starch grains were compared with a modern reference collection consisting of about 500 species of neotropical plants.

The crop plant reference collection includes 24 traditional maize races from Central and South America, a diverse collection of modern traditional lima and common bean races from Peru, Mexico, and other areas of Latin America, and traditional land races of domesticated *Cucurbita* species. Starch keys and classification systems used herein emphasize shape, surface, and size attributes known to be useful in identification (for example, Chandler-Ezell et al. 2006; Dickau et al. 2007; Pearsall et al. 2004; Piperno et al. 2000b, 2009; Reichert 1913; Torrence and Barton 2006; Zarrillo et al. 2008).

RESULTS

SEDIMENT SAMPLES

Sediment samples from excavations carried out from 2007–2010 were analyzed. No starch was recovered from a total of

Table A9.1. Material of major starch grain types from Huaca Prieta and Paredones

Material	Provenience	Age BP	Maize	Phaseolus	Cucurbita	Pacay	Unknown
Sediment	HP-3, Capa 17	4100		P			P
Sediment	HP-3, Capa 16	5900–5600		P			P
Sediment	Paredones, U-22, Floor 11	5500–5400		P			
Sediment	Paredones, U-20, Layer 6A	3200	P*				
Sediment	Pit 18, Layer 13	7000	P*				
Sediment	U-16, Layer 11	6800–6200	P*				
Sediment	U-23	5900–5600	P				
Bottle gourd	Paredones, U-22, Floor 18	6500–6400		P**	P		
Grinding stone	Paredones, U-22, Floor 1	4000		P**			
Grinding stone	Paredones, U-22, Floor 20	6600–6500			P		P
Chipped stone tools	U-16, Layer 16	7000	P				
	U-22, Floor 20	6600–6500	P		P†		
	U-16, Layer 11	6800–6200	P				
	U-20, Floor 8	5000	P				
	U-20, 6F	3500	P				
	U-16, Layer 12	6800–6600			P†		
Human teeth	U-3, Fill 7, Floor 7	4200		P**			
	Field 7-2-2#	4500		P**	P††		
	Field 2-G2-4#	6000		P**			
	Field 3-0-1#	4200		P**			

P = Present.

*Sample size is small; identification is maize.

**Grains showed heat damage, probably from cooking.

#Grains appear to be highly diagnostic and some may be from underground plant organs (roots, rhizomes, tubers).

†One grain from *C. moschata* and one from cf. *C. ficifolia*.

††The grains are like those found in *C. ecuadorensis*, but additional modern reference work is needed to rule out other domesticated species. Other *Cucurbita* grains are identified as *C. moschata*.

8 samples analyzed from the 2007 excavations. The samples came from floors and levels from Units 2, 3, and 7 at Huaca Prieta. Of the 15 samples analyzed from the 2008 excavations, starch grains were recovered from 7. In 4, only 1 to 3 grains were recovered. The following samples yielded starch, with chronological associations in calibrated carbon-14 years in parentheses (if not listed in table A9.1, the tool did not have identifiable starch types): Unit 2: Layer 6 (10–20 cm) with 3 grains (~6538–5308 cal BP); Unit 2: Layer 2 with 2 grains (~4088–3485 cal BP); HP-3: Layer 4B with 1 grain (~3500 cal BP); HP-3: Layer 10 with 2 grains (~4000 cal BP); HP-3: Layer 19 with 10 grains (~4200–3800 cal BP); HP-3: Layer 39A with 11 grains (~6700–5900 cal BP); HP-3: Layer 17 with 60 grains (~4100 cal BP); HP-3: Layer 40 with 13 grains (~6800–6000 cal BP); and HP-3: Layer 36 with 9 grains (~5600 cal BP). All of these contexts are ritual and burial in the mound at Huaca Prieta.

Phaseolus starch is present in 2 samples that date from ~5900 to 4100 cal BP (table A9.1; fig. A9.1a, b). Because of the substantial size and morphological overlap between starch from the common and lima beans (Piperno and Dillehay 2008), it is not possible to make a species-specific identification of the *Phaseolus* starch. Remains of the lima bean are the only *Phaseolus* species recovered from the macrofossil remains at sites, suggesting that the starch remains are most likely to be from this species. In many samples starch grains that were recovered do not match those from taxa presently in our modern reference collections. Some may be from underground storage organs; this needs to be confirmed with further work. Of particular interest in this regard are large oval to ovate grains with eccentric hila and lamellae and sometimes with a fissure that were found along with *Phaseolus* in the sample from HP-3, Layer 17 (fig. A9.1c–e) and in other samples (table A9.1). Other unknown grains were small with centric and eccentric hila and largely without fissures or other surface features (fig. A9.1f, g). As seen from this and from other results described below, future starch studies would benefit from increasing a modern reference collection by way of focusing on economic taxa identified in the macrobotanical analysis of the sites' plant remains

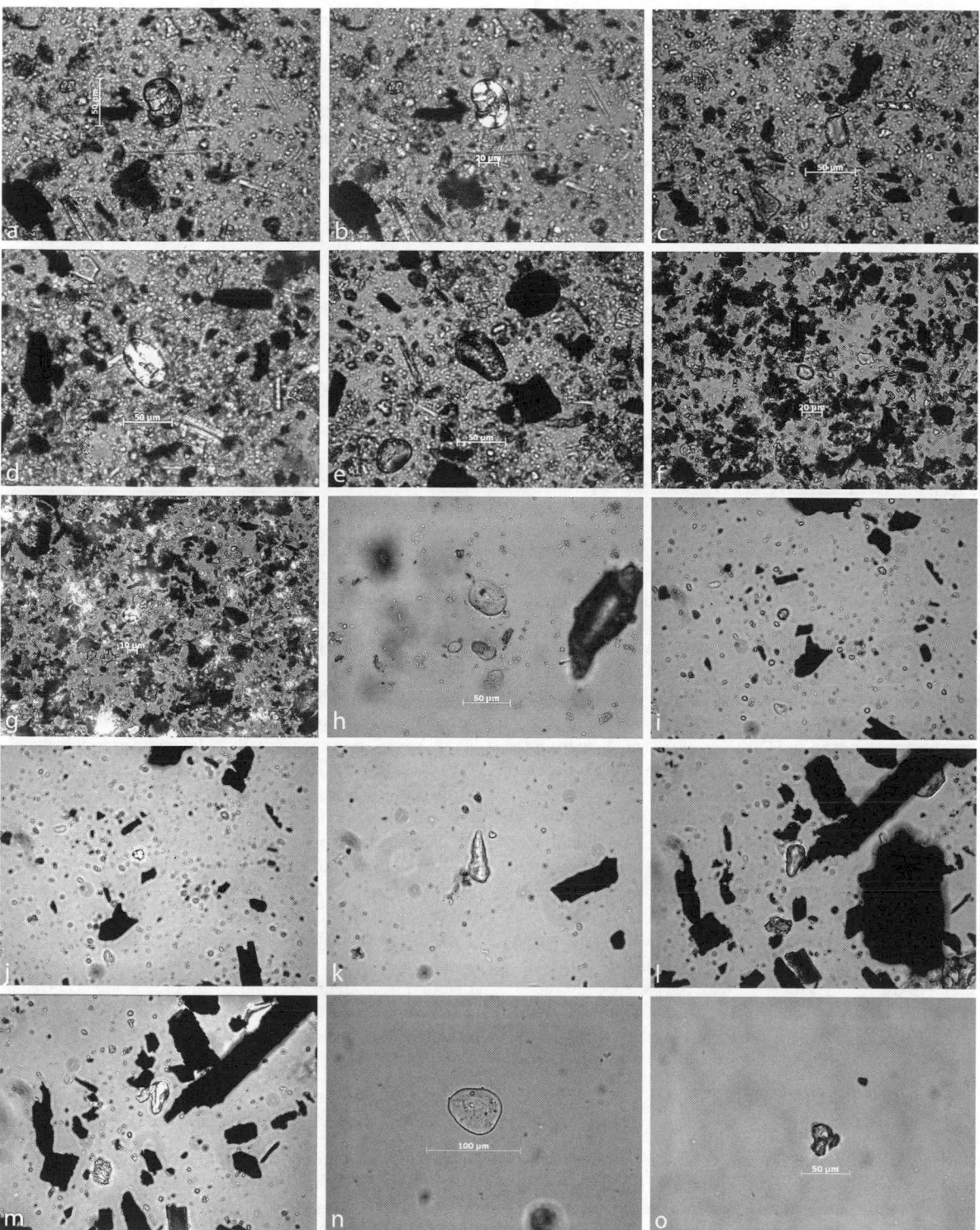

FIGURE A9.1. Various examples of archaeological starch grains: *a*, a starch grain from *Phaseolus* beans from Trinchera NS, Capa 17; *b*, a grain showing cross-polarization and the extinction cross characteristic of starch grains; *c*, large oval to ovate grains with eccentric hila and lamellae and sometimes with a fissure from NS Trench, Layer 17; *d*, grain with cross-polarization; *e* and *f*, another type of unknown starch grain from NS Trench, Layer 19; *g*, a *Phaseolus* starch grain from the bottle gourd sample, Floor 15-2, showing damage from heat, probably from cooking; *h*, a starch grain from the fruit flesh of *Cucurbita moschata* from a grinding stone from Floor 20 at Paredones; *i*, the grain with cross-polarization; *j*, unknown starch grains from the grinding stone from Floor 20 at Paredones (they may be from underground plant organs); *k* and *l*, unknown starch grains from a grinding stone from Floor 20 in Paredones (they may be from underground plant organs), showing the grains with cross-polarization; *m*, the grain with cross-polarization; *n*, *Phaseolus* starch grain damaged from heat, most probably from cooking, from a human tooth; *o*, starch grains removed from the maize kernel that was recovered from the floor of Paredones.

and on other plants native to the study region. No maize was identified in these samples.

Of the samples analyzed from the 2009 excavation, 8 had starch grains, often in low numbers ranging from 1 to 3 grains. *Phaseolus* was recovered from Paredones, Unit 22, Floors 1, 11, 18, and 20 (table A9.1). A few starch grains consistent with those from maize kernels were recovered from 3 samples: Unit 20, Layer 6A; Test Pit 18, Layer 13; and Unit 16, Layer 11, which is bracketed by dates of 6800 and 6200 cal BP. Layer 6A dates to ~5500 cal BP and Layer 13 to ~5400 cal BP. Starch securely identified as derived from maize kernels occurred in a sediment sample from Unit 23 at Huaca Prieta and dated to ~5902–5606 cal BP. A total of 7 starch grains with size and morphological attributes of maize (mean length: 18 μm; range of length: 10–24 μm) were isolated from this sample. All contexts except Unit 16 here relate to ritual activity.

RESIDUES COLLECTED FROM HUACA PRIETA BOTTLE GOURD FRAGMENTS

Starch occurred in 5 of the 13 samples from bottle gourds recovered from Unit 22 floors and other contexts analyzed, which date from ~7000 to 3500 cal BP, but starch content was generally poor when present. Samples containing starch were from Floor 10, Sector 4B (1 grain), Floor 12-2 (6 grains), Floor 15-2 (14 grains), Floor 15-1 (1 grain), and Floor 12-1 (3 grains). The sample Floor 15-2 had 7 grains from *Phaseolus* beans that show heat, most probably cooking damage, which are hereafter referred to as "cooked grains" (fig. A9.1g) (Piperno and Dillehay 2008), and 2 are from the fruit of *Inga feuillei* (pacay). Other starch grains that occurred in the residues cannot be identified; many showed heat or other damage, leading, in part, to the difficulty in assigning them to taxa. No maize starch was recovered, a finding that may suggest that the function of the gourds was not to consume *chicha* in social ceremonies. A caveat with this interpretation is that experimental work needs to be carried out to determine if maize starch survives the *chicha*-making process. Nonetheless, the presence of *Phaseolus* and pacay fruit starch in the residues together with the presence of heat-damaged grains suggests that the gourds may have been used as food plates.

RESIDUES COLLECTED FROM GRINDING STONES

Residues from 6 grinding stones from Paredones were analyzed. They yielded little starch, probably because the intensive, multistep recovery process typically used for these types of lithic artifacts (Piperno et al. 2000b) was not carried out. A single unidentifiable starch grain was present in a sample from Floor 18 at Paredones, and cooked *Phaseolus* bean grains were among the 3e grains recovered from a sample from Unit 22, Floor 20, at Paredones (table A9.1). The evidence is slim at this point, but cooked foods may have been among the items mashed with one of the stones.

A grinding stone from Paredones, Floor 20, dated to ~6500 cal BP, was analyzed using the standard, multistep protocol for removal of residues (Piperno et al. 2000b). The stone yielded a total of 32 starch grains, some of which were highly damaged. Most are presently unidentifiable. A bell-shaped grain with an eccentric hilum and a "capped" pressure facet diagnostic of *Cucurbita* sp. fruit flesh occurred (fig. A9.1h, i). The grain can be identified as *C. moschata* (Piperno and Dillehay 2008). Some of the unknown grains may be from underground plant organs and appear highly diagnostic and representative of at least more than one taxon (fig. A9.1j–m); others are of the same types found in other contexts studied, as described above.

RESIDUES FROM CHIPPED STONE TOOLS

A total of 24 flaked stone tools from Huaca Prieta and Paredones were analyzed. Starch content was absent to low (0 to 4 grains) on many. But 5 yielded significant numbers of maize kernel starch (maize grains: n = 9, 11, 12, 20, and 6 on the tools; table A9.1); their proveniences, respectively, are Unit 16, Layer 16; Unit 22, Floor 20; Unit 16, Layer 11; Unit 20, Floor 8; and Unit 20, Floor 6. Another tool from Unit 20, Layer 6, had 6 maize grains. Also, as previously described (Grobman et al. 2012), a blade cutting tool (12.7 cm long) made of andesite from Floor 18, Unit 22, directly associated with 4 maize cobs of the Proto–Confite Morocho race had 9 maize-like grains on one of its sharp lateral edges (mean length: 14 μm; range of length: 6–18 μm). The mean and maximum lengths of the grains are consistent with modern Latin American maize races. But a few wild grasses contribute starch grains as large, so the archaeological grains cannot be definitively identified as maize. Nonetheless, given their context, the grains are likely to be from maize.

Starch grains from *Cucurbita* fruit flesh were found on 2 of the chipped and ground stone tools (table A9.1). They are typical of those found in some varieties of *C. ecuadorensis*, but further modern reference work is needed to make a positive identification and rule out other domesticated species. Also present on some tools were unknown grains that may be from underground plant organs and occurred in other contexts studied (for example, *lerén* or arrowroot: see appendix 7).

HUMAN TEETH FROM THE 2009 EXCAVATION

A total of 9 teeth from 9 different individuals and contexts dating from ~6500 to 4000 cal BP were analyzed. All were molars, evenly divided among adult males, adult females, and juveniles. Just 2 teeth yielded starch remains: 1 from Unit 3, Floor 7 (6 grains), and another from Unit 16, Layer 2 (1 damaged grain). Among the grains from the Unit 3 tooth was a cooked *Phaseolus* (fig. A9.1n). The other grains present were some of the same types recovered from other contexts and cannot be identified at the present time.

HUMAN TEETH FROM THE ORIGINAL HUACA PRIETA EXCAVATION

A total of 8 molars from 9 different individuals were studied. Starch was recovered from 3 of them. Of these, 1 (field number 7-2-2) had 2 grains from the flesh of squash fruits, 1 of which may be from *Cucurbita ficifolia*; the other is from *C. moschata*. This tooth also yielded 3 grains from cooked *Phaseolus* beans. Another 2 grains on the tooth could not be identified. Another molar (field number 2-G2-4) had 6 grains from cooked *Phaseolus* beans and 5 other grains damaged by heat that could not be identified. A third molar (field number 3-0-1) had a grain from cooked *Phaseolus* and 1 unidentifiable cooked grain.

THE MAIZE KERNEL FROM A FLOOR OF PAREDONES

The maize kernel from Floor 18, Unit 22, of Paredones that dates to ~6500 cal BP provided the opportunity to study starch grains directly from an ancient variety of popcorn (Grobman et al. 2012). Dozens of starch grains were observed in a tiny sample of the endosperm (fig. A9.1o). Many grains were in clumps and could not be accurately measured. Measurements of a total of 23 grains yielded an average size of 19 μm (range: 12.8–27 μm). It is not possible to suggest any racial affinity from the starch. In shape and surface features, however, the grains display the characteristic attributes of popcorn (such as irregular polyhedral shapes, rough surfaces, and fissures), which is consistent with the identifications of macrofossil cob remains from the deposits (Grobman et al. 2012). The starch grains are like those previously recovered from archaeological stone tools and sediments from Mexico, Panama, and Ecuador that were identified as hard endosperm-popcorn types (Pearsall et al. 2004; Piperno et al. 2000b, 2009; Zarrillo et al. 2008).

DISCUSSION

It is clear from the variety of starches recovered from the different contexts and materials studied that plant exploitation at Huaca Prieta and Paredones involved a diverse range of taxa, a finding mirrored from the analysis of the sites' macrobotanical and phytolith remains that has revealed the presence of an even wider array of plants in the economy. Maize, *Phaseolus*, *Cucurbita*, and *Inga feullei* starch occurred in sediments, on human teeth, and on lithic artifacts, providing further evidence that they were part of the complex of domesticated plants processed and consumed in Peru during the Preceramic period (see also Piperno and Dillehay 2008; Dillehay 2011a). From all contexts examined, starch grains identified as maize were like those found in hard endosperm varieties of maize, such as the popcorns that were identified from the macrobotanical remains at Huaca Prieta and Paredones dating as early as 6775–6504 cal BP (Grobman et al. 2012). No evidence has been found (such as drinking cups, boiling vessels, or storage bins) to suggest that maize was

used as a fermentable drink in late Preceramic times, as suggested by some investigators (for example, Solis et al. 2001).

Persistent presence of starch from the flesh of *Cucurbita* fruits on human teeth and in other materials studied further indicates that at other Preceramic sites in Peru (Piperno and Dillehay 2008) and Ecuador (Piperno, personal notes, 2014) domesticated *Cucurbita* varieties had nonbitter flesh, were routinely consumed, and thus were not used primarily as a utilitarian or industrial plant (for example, as containers and fishnet floats). At least 2 different species of domesticated *Cucurbita* appear to be present on the teeth, including *C. moschata* and possibly *C. ficifolia*, although more comparisons between modern *C. ficifolia* and other *Cucurbita* species must be carried out to confirm the identification of *C. ficifolia*. Starch grains from *Cucurbita* fruit flesh clearly have considerable potential to provide information on the origins and early distributions of all the domesticated squash species native to South America (*C. moschata*, *C. ficifolia*, *C. maxima*, *C. ecuadorensis*) (Piperno and Dillehay 2008; Duncan et al. 2009). Fruit flesh starch provides information on fruit edibility and agricultural practices through time (for example, human selection for the major domestication gene controlling for nonbitter fruits) not attainable through the seed and the often fragmented rind and peduncle remains that form the macrofossil components of archaeological *Cucurbita*. Starch and phytolith microfossil work to date increasingly suggests that *C. moschata* and *C. ecuadorensis* were not the only species domesticated and consumed in northern South America during the Preceramic period (Piperno 2011b).

Maize starch grains were relatively uncommon, which may have to do with the overall poor survival of starch in the material studied as well as with the importance of the plant in the local economy. The dates on the materials yielding maize starch are concordant with those directly from, and closely associated with maize cobs and other macrofossils of the plant, which indicate that maize was present at sites by ~6500–6200 cal BP. The analysis of the maize kernel revealed that the size and morphology of the grains are completely consistent with those found in modern races of popcorns from Latin America, demonstrating a close association between archaeological specimens and the modern reference collections used to identify them. More such work examining starch grains and also phytoliths retrieved from ancient macrofossil food remains should be carried out. It may sometimes be the case that land race diversity of crops has decreased during the past 500 years and that knowledge of ancient crop characteristics will add important information to identification keys not obtainable through modern collections.

Phaseolus starches were the most common type recovered from most materials studied. Many showed evidence of heat from cooking. These starches appear to be able to survive cooking heat in a still identifiable form; they were also common components of teeth residues studied from the Nanchoc Valley culture sites in northern Peru (Piperno and Dillehay 2008) and from human teeth studied from OGSE-80, the type-site of the Preceramic Las Vegas culture in southwestern Ecuador (Piperno, personal notes, 2014).

Because the size and morphological characteristics of the lima and common bean starches overlap considerably, it is not possible to assign a species-specific identification to the *Phaseolus* grains. But the macrobotanical record from the sites indicates the presence solely of lima beans. At the Nanchoc Valley sites, *Phaseolus* starches recovered similarly could not be identified to species, but for a number of reasons the remains were more likely to be from the lima rather than the common bean (Piperno and Dillehay 2008). Therefore evidence is increasing that *Phaseolus* beans (probably lima beans) were important components of early crop systems in northwestern South America along with squashes, some tree crops, peanuts, and manioc (Piperno and Dillehay 2008; Dillehay 2011a; Piperno 2011b).

Finally, some potentially important food sources thought or documented to have been used in the study region and indeed directly evidenced at Huaca Prieta and Paredones from macrobotanical remains do not produce starch or have nondiagnostic grains, so their dietary contribution cannot be evaluated (see chapter 10). They include domesticated tree fruits of various *Annona* species (guanabana, custard apple) and guava (*Psidium guajava*), other fruits (*Bunchosia armeniaca* and *hartwegiana*; *Solanum quitoense* or *naranjilla*), and the lupine bean (*Lupinus mutabilis*). The value of having multiproxy botanical evidence wherever possible is apparent once again through these studies at Huaca Prieta and Paredones.

HUMAN SKELETAL REMAINS FROM VARIOUS EXCAVATIONS

Anne R. Titelbaum
and John W. Verano

This appendix reports isolated or fragmented human remains recovered from middens, fills, or features in and around Huaca Prieta. Bird also reported loose bones that were not part of graves (Bird et al. 1985: 74–76).

1. Bird's HP-3 trench yielded the fragmentary remains of at least 1 subadult, one young adult male between 25–35 years of age at the time of death, and 1 fetus with an age estimate between 7 months in utero and birth. Also recovered were textile fragments and human hair.
   a. HP-3, Floor 3, Phase V: one long bone diaphysis from a fetus, possibly a right tibia shaft.
   b. HP-3, Fill below Floor 4, Phase V: human hair was recovered.
   c. HP-3, Layer 5, Phase V: 1 adult left calcaneus and 1 maxillary 3rd molar. The molar shows relatively minor tooth wear, suggesting that the individual was a young adult, with an age estimate between 25 and 35 years. The large size of the calcaneus suggests that the individual was male. Salt crystals were placed underneath the body.
   d. HP-3, Layer 4B, Phase V: textile fragments and remains of a fetus, including long bones (right and left femora, right and left tibiae, 1 fibula, 1 ulna), the right ilium, 3 cranial fragments, 2 rib fragments, 5 vertebral centra, 9 vertebrae fragments, and 5 hand phalanges. The maximum length of the left tibial diaphysis is 57 mm; the maximum length of the fibula is 55.4 mm.
   e. HP-3, Layer 5, Phase V: adult cranial bones, including a fragment of a sphenoid, a portion of a left maxilla, and a portion of a right maxilla. The left maxilla includes the 2nd and 3rd molars, which demonstrate moderate dental wear. Based on the wear, the individual is estimated to be between 25 and 35 years old. The right maxilla only includes a portion of the root of the 1st molar; all other teeth were lost postmortem.
   f. HP-3, Layer 10, Phase IV: human hair was recovered.
   g. HP-3, Layer 11, Phase IV: a single adult thoracic vertebra (T1).
   h. HP-3, Layer 16, Phase IV: adult remains consist of 27 cranial fragments (basilar, temporal, frontal, indeterminate) and 2 mandibular fragments. Fetal remains include 42 small cranial fragments and 4 primary tooth crowns (1 incisor, 2 molars, 1 indeterminate).

The tooth crowns are unerupted; based on dental development, they derived from a fetus with an age estimate between 7 months in utero and birth.

i. HP-3, Layer 40B, Phase II: 1 adult right 1st metatarsal and 1 subadult lumbar vertebra (either L2 or L3). The rims had not yet fused to the centrum of the vertebra.

j. HP-3, Layer 40B, Phase II: fetal remains consisting of arm bones (right and left humeri, left ulna, and one radius fragment), 24 vertebrae fragments, 4 rib fragments, 5 cranial fragments (1 right zygomatic and 4 miscellaneous fragments), and 2 primary teeth (1 incisor crown and 1 molar crown). The maximum length of the ulna is 53.7 mm. Based on long bone length and dental development, the remains are that of a fetus, with an age estimated between 7 months in utero and birth.

2. Geological Trench 1: Layer 4, Phase III: adult male human remains. Included are 1 right calcaneus, 2 rib fragments, the proximal epiphyses and diaphyses of a left ulna and radius, 1 left 5th metacarpal, a portion of a left maxilla (including the canine, 1st premolar, 1st molar, and 2nd molar), and 1 miscellaneous cranial fragment. Based on size, the proximal ulna and radius are probably from a single male individual of indeterminate adult age. Salt crystals were placed underneath the body.

3. Unit 10: Layer 2, Phase IV: 1 human bone: the distal portion of an adult right humerus. Based on size, the humerus is probably from an adult female.

4. Unit 12: Layer 3, Phase IV: at least 1 juvenile about 3 years old at the time of death and at minimum 2 adults, 1 male and 1 female.

a. Unit 12, Layer 4, Phase IV: A juvenile right mandibular 2nd molar. Based on dental development, the tooth indicates that the child was approximately 2 to 4 years old.

b. Unit 12, Ash Lens under Layer 4, Phase IV: a complete juvenile right ulnar diaphysis (maximum length of 125.7 mm).

c. Unit 12, Fill of Floor 3, Phase IV: 32 bones representing a minimum of 2 adult individuals (1 male and 1 female). Included are foot bones, leg bones, and 1 hand bone: 1 left calcaneus (male), 2 left tali (1 male, 1 female), the right 1st, 2nd 3rd, and 5th metatarsals, the 5th metatarsal and proximal phalanx of the great toe (male) of the left foot, 1 metatarsal fragment, 1 proximal femur (male), 1 femoral diaphyseal fragment, 1 hand phalanx, and 19 unidentifiable bone fragments. The only observed pathological condition was minor osteoarthritis of the ankle and foot, indicated by minor lipping on the male talus.

5. Unit 14: Unit 14 yielded 72 bones, the majority of which represented adult hands and feet.

a. Unit 14, Fill 1B, Phase V: 2 adult foot phalanges.

b. Unit 14, Fill below Layer 2, Phase V: adult bones from a right foot (cuboid, navicular, 1st–3rd cuneiforms, 1st–5th metatarsals, the proximal and distal phalanges of ray 1), bones from a left foot (1st metatarsal and the distal phalanx of ray 1), bones of the right hand (trapezium and 2nd metacarpal), and bones of the left hand (trapezium, trapezoid, capitate, scaphoid, and 1st–4th metacarpals). Also recovered were 13 foot phalanges and 1 sesamoid bone from a foot, 13 hand phalanges, 1 left patella, 1 fragment of a vertebra, and 17 miscellaneous bone fragments. The only observed pathological conditions were very minor osteoarthritis on the patella and a minor abnormality of shape of the medial inferior shaft of the right 3rd metatarsal.

6. Unit 16: Unit 16 produced numerous human remains, representing a juvenile, a young adult, and at least 1 middle adult. The juvenile was about 10 years of age at the time of death. Salt crystals were placed around and underneath the body.

a. Unit 16, Use Surface 2, Phase V: fragment of an adult right 4th metatarsal.

b. Unit 16, Use Surface 3, Phase IV: a right mandibular 3rd molar. The root apex is closed, but the tooth shows very little wear, suggesting an age of 20–25 years.

c. Unit 16, Fill of Use Surface 3, Phase IV: human remains pertaining to a juvenile (ca 10±2.5 years old) and at least 2 adult individuals, 1 of whom was of middle adult age. The 8 juvenile bones excavated included 1 proximal thumb phalanx, 1 hand phalanx, 1 coracoid process of a scapula, 4 pelvic fragments, a 5th lumbar vertebra (rims are not fused to the centrum), and 1 unerupted mandibular left 2nd premolar (age estimate: 10±2.5 yrs). The 76 adult remains consist of 3 long bone fragments (1 left fibula, 1 fibula diaphyseal fragment, 1 femoral condyle fragment with minor osteoarthritic lipping), a right scapula, 13 rib fragments, a fragmented sacrum, 8 vertebrae (3 cervical [C1, C7, C7] vertebrae, 1 thoracic vertebra [T9?], 3 lumbar vertebrae [L1, L2, and indeterminate], and 1 vertebral fragment; both of the C7s demonstrate moderate vertebral osteophytosis, the T9 shows very minor vertebral osteophytosis, and the L2 displays marked vertebral osteophytosis), 13 foot bones (1 left talus [probably male, based on size], a left 1st cuneiform, a right 1st cuneiform, a right scaphoid, a right 1st metatarsal, a left 2nd metatarsal [probably male, based on size], a left 3rd metatarsal; a left proximal phalanx of the great toe, a right distal phalanx of the great toe [probably male, based on size], a left phalanx, 2 miscellaneous phalanges), 12 hand bones (right 2nd metacarpal, right 5th metacarpal, right distal thumb phalanx, and 9 miscellaneous hand phalanges), 8 cranial fragments (a fragment from a left temporal bone, a fragment from a right temporal bone, a right temporal/sphenoid fragment with very minor osteoarthritis of the temporomandibular joint, and 5 miscellaneous cranial fragments), 13 indeterminate bone fragments, 3 teeth (1 maxillary left 2nd molar and 2 premolars of indeterminate position), and a mandible with all teeth present except for the right 2nd incisor and the left 2nd premolar that were lost postmortem. The teeth are worn with exposed dentine, and there is minor calculus on the buccal aspect of all teeth. The mandible is of indeterminate sex: while the mental eminence appears female, the gonial eversion suggests male.

d. Unit 16, Fill of Use Surface 3, Phase IV: adult and juvenile remains. Adult bones included a worn maxillary premolar (with exposed dentine), 2 cranial bone fragments (parietal), bones from a right foot (3rd metatarsal, a proximal phalanx, and a distal phalanx), 3 cervical vertebrae (C2, C5, C6), a right 2nd metacarpal, a manubrium, and 3 rib fragments. Juvenile remains consist of a sacrum (S1–S3 are fused together, but the lines of fusion are not obliterated), a femoral fragment (the epiphyses are not fused to the diaphysis), and a tibial fragment (the epiphyses are not fused to the diaphysis).

7. Unit 18: Fill of Layer 4, Phase III: 2 weathered adult bones: a distal portion of a left humerus and a distal portion of a left tibia. Both bones are sun-bleached white and are splitting, indicating prolonged exposure. Based on robusticity and the size of the epiphysis, the humerus appears to be male.

PIGMENT ANALYSIS

Jeff Illingworth, Jack Williams, and Michelle L. Farley

A number of the basketry and textile samples from Huaca Prieta exhibit the use of colored elements (see chapter 12). These colors specifically include blue or dark gray on basketry elements and blue, dark gray, yellow, and red within textile specimens. In an attempt to determine the origin of these colors, selected specimens of basketry and textiles were subjected to gas chromatography and X-ray fluorescence (XRF).

BASKETRY

Initially, 3 samples of blue-colored basketry elements were shipped to Mercyhurst Archaeological Institute for assay. These specimens were subjected to X-ray fluorescence analysis using a Bruker Tracer III–V+ handheld X-ray fluorescence analyzer. These specimens were originally run without cleaning or processing and with the blue pigment still adhering to the basketry material. A second assay was run with the blue pigment removed from the basketry material prior to submitting the pigment for gas chromatography analysis.

All basketry samples produced XRF signatures that were generally equivalent. The signatures suggested a strong, relatively homogeneous mineral component with a strong organic background signature that did not vary significantly in magnitude whether the assay was run while the pigment was still adherent to the basketry element or removed from it.

A selection of blue mineral samples housed by the Department of Geology at Mercyhurst University was also assayed via XRF in order to find a likely inorganic match for the blue pigment. While none of the assayed samples were a strong match, sodalite produced the elemental signature with the closest similarity.

Concurrent with the XRF analysis, samples of the blue pigment were also subjected to gas chromatography to determine the nature of the strong organic signature observed during the XRF study. The chromatography study suggested the presence of an animal-derived fat of indeterminate origin. This fat did not match any of the available samples to which it was cross-referenced and may in fact be sea-mammal derived.

In sum, the blue pigments observed on the Huaca Prieta basketry samples are posited to be a finely crushed indeterminate mineral (similar to sodalite) mixed in a fatty emulsion (probably from a sea mammal, such as a seal or sea lion) and applied to selected basketry elements to create patterns of indeterminate design and meaning.

TEXTILES

INSTRUMENTATION

A Bruker TRACeR III–V Handheld X-Ray Fluorescence Analyzer operated with a vacuum system was used for all elemental analysis. No filter was used for calibration of the TRACeR III–V. The S1PXRF Spectrum analysis tool software was used to collect all data. ARTAX software was then used to translate raw data into net results based on the suite of observed diagnostic elements.

ANALYSIS

Our X-ray fluorescence analysis included 39 textiles and 1 sediment sample. Of the 39 textiles, 34 were assayed both before and after cleaning, 2 were assayed only before cleaning, and 3 were assayed only after cleaning. The XRF system's high voltage was kept at 40 kV, and the anode current was kept at 10.5 uA. The pulse length was maintained at 200 with a pulse period of 254. The vacuum was kept at 5 Torr or less. Each run lasted 120 seconds. This time was determined to be adequate based on previous lithic research with the same instrument and software. Only one run was administered unless a pigment or foreign object was visible to the researcher. Multiple runs were then conducted until sufficient information was obtained. The research focused on 16 elements based on ARTAX auto-selections as well as the analysts' perception of possible noteworthy elements. These elements included sodium (Na), aluminum (Al), chloride (Cl), potassium (K), calcium (Ca), titanium (Ti), manganese (Mn), iron (Fe), nickel (Ni), copper (Cu), bromine (Br), strontium (Sr), zirconium (Zr), molybdenum (Mo), ruthenium (Ru), and rhodium (Rh). All elements were line L1 except for Ru and Rh, which were line L1 and K12.

RESULTS

RED PIGMENTS

Red pigments were visible to the naked eye on 3 of the textiles: 2008.83.2a, 2009.93.12, and 2009.98.20. The red areas, when compared to the nondyed areas of the textiles, show greater Fe concentrations (fig. A11.1a). This higher concentration of Fe could indicate the use of hematite (red ochre). Red ochre has a blood-red color and has been known to be used as a paint pigment. In the Huaca Prieta collection the average Fe level of all the red pigment areas is 53.72%. The average Fe level of the pigments before cleaning is 43.73%, whereas the average Fe level of the pig-

ments after cleaning is 59.97%. The pure form of red ochre (Fe_2O_3) contains roughly 70% of Fe. The pigment may not have been pure red ochre, the textiles have been buried for thousands of years, the textiles have been cleaned/treated, and the TRACeR XRF instrument is reading the pigment as well as the textile itself, so the ~10% difference between the cleaned pigment and the red ochre Fe levels would not seem to be a significant variance.

BLUE PIGMENTS

Blue pigments were visible to the naked eye on 2 textiles: 2008.38.4 and 2009.64.1a. When assayed with XRF, the blue pigment area does not register with the system, in marked contrast to the basketry blue pigmentation. There seems to be no drastic difference in percentages of elements between noncolored (light) and blue (dark) areas (fig. A11.1b).

Due to the apparent organic nature of the textile blue pigment, these specimens were subject to gas chromatography with particular interest in determining whether indigo may have been the source of this color. Following a protocol used by Jennifer Poulin of the Canadian Conservation Institute (Poulin 2007) for detection of indigo (indogotin) all samples were treated with a 1:1 mixture of m-(trifluoromethyl) phenyltrimethylamonium hydroxide (TMTFTH) and toluene and heated at 65°C for one hour in a capped 2 mL glass vial. Samples were then centrifuged for 2 minutes.

Fiber analysis was performed using an Agilent Technologies 7890A Gas Chromatograph equipped with a 5975C Mass Selector Detector from the same company. Analysis conditions are identical to those previously reported (Ferreira et al. 2004) except for a shorter temperature program (all important compounds elute under 20 minutes). The data were processed using Agilent Chemstation software (E.02.01.1177).

None of the marker compounds of indigo (Methyl Anthranilate, Methyl N-Methylanthranilate, 2-Benzyl-3-indolinone and 2-bis-[N-methylindole-3-methoxy]) could be detected using the NIST (National Institutes Standards and Technology) data base or by ion extractions of the entire mass spectra chromatogram, which is necessary for compound identity (fig. 11.1c).

There appear to be four possibilities regarding the use of indigo as a dye for fibers from Huaca Prieta. (1) Indigo was not used as a dye for these fibers. (2) Indigo was used as a dye, but the marker concentrations have decreased to a point where their concentrations are below the detection limits of GCMS. (3) Indigo was used as a dye, but long-term decomposition and storage has changed the identity of the marker analytes. Without samples known to have been dyed, the identification of these new marker compounds would be difficult. (4) Another material was used as a dye for artifacts from Huaca Prieta.

With respect to point 4, logwood (*Haematoxylon campechianum*) may be a likely candidate. The range of colors for this substance is the most extensive of all vegetable dyes

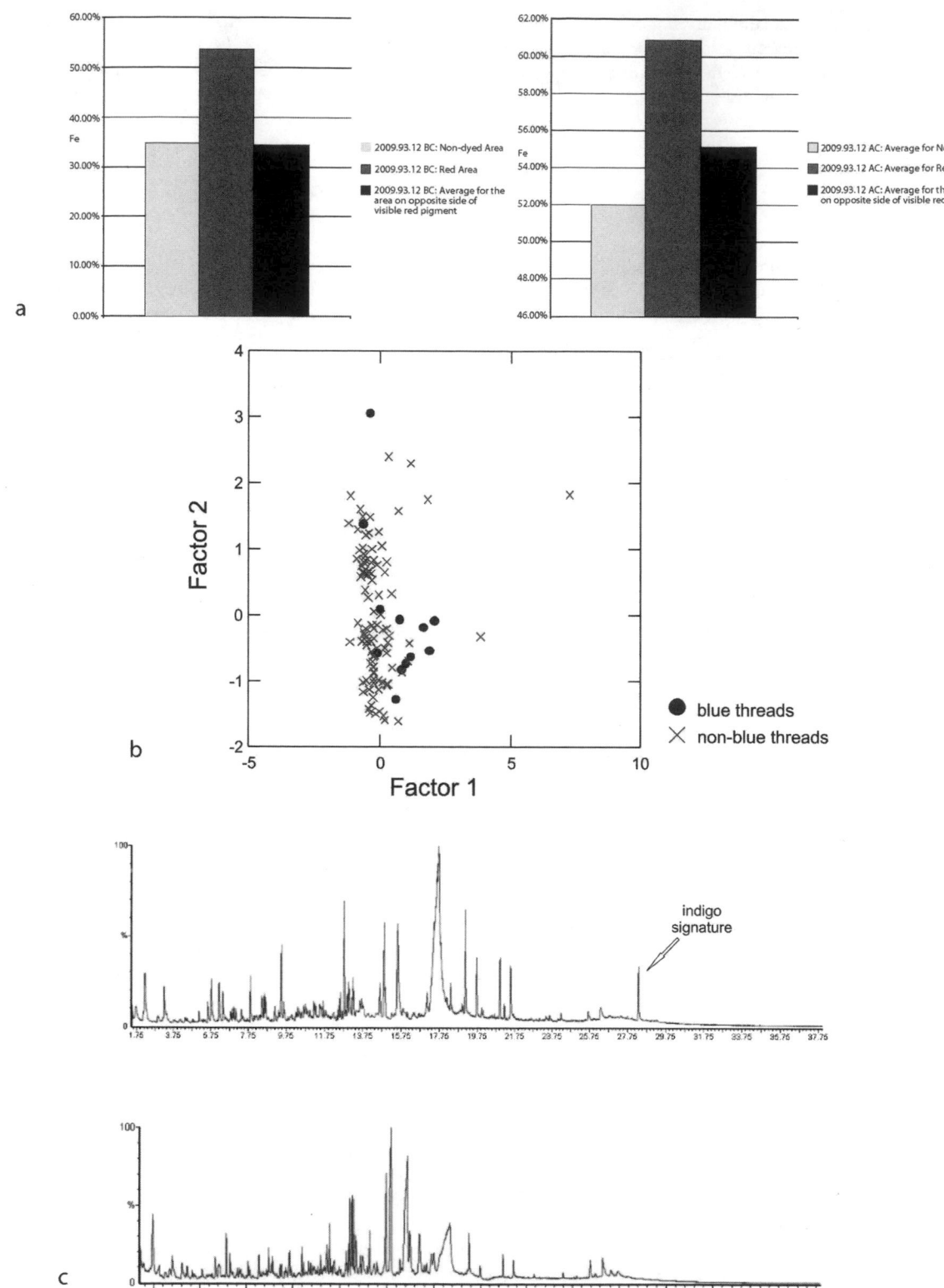

FIGURE A11.1. Physical appearance of textiles: *a*, typical iron (Fe) content before (*left*) and after (*right*) cleaning; note that red-colored sections of the fabrics (*gray column*) are consistently higher than areas that are either not red-dyed (*light gray column*) or are on the opposite side of the fabric from the red-colored areas (*black column*); this supports the use of red ochre in red pigmentation; *b*, scatter plot of factor analysis of pXRF results of blue-colored and not blue-colored textiles; generally there is no significant difference in inorganic elements between the two samples, suggesting that the cause of the blue pigmentation is organic in origin; *c*, typical mass spectra chromatogram results of indigo-dyed fabrics (*top*) and blue-pigmented Huaca Prieta fabrics (*bottom*).

(Hammeke 2004). It is also possible that a variety of cotton (*Gossypium* sp.) that is naturally blue may have been used to affect the colored textile elements.

SEAWATER USE

During the course of analysis, several of the researchers expressed interest in the possibility that some of the textiles and nets were used in seawater. If some of the textiles were used in this setting, the salt content should be higher. In general, however, the Na and Cl proved to be low. The Na levels did not exceed 0.0012%, while the Cl levels did not exceed 6%. Additionally, iodine (a possible seawater signifier) is generally not observed in any of the assayed samples.

While a higher concentration of iodine or NaCl would support the hypothesis that these specimens were used in seawater, their absence does not exclude this possibility. The high solubility of NaCl and iodine could easily cause them to leach out of the specimens postdepositionally. Or they could have been washed out prior to deposition during some interment ritual.

APPENDIX 12

POLLEN ANALYSIS

Linda Scott Cummings

INTRODUCTION

Huaca Prieta and Paredones were examined for pollen evidence of local vegetation. Of the 12 pollen samples studied from Huaca Prieta, 6 were recovered from geological contexts to provide a record of the local vegetation through time. The other samples were recovered from excavated contexts in the mound. All samples from this site contained large quantities of charcoal. Pollen samples were also collected and examined from Unit 22 at Paredones. This site did not exhibit the extensive burning that characterized Huaca Prieta.

METHODS

A chemical extraction technique based on flotation is the standard preparation used at PaleoResearch Institute for removal of pollen from large volumes of sand, silt, and clay. It is important that it is not the repetition of specific and individual steps in the laboratory but rather mastery of the concepts of extraction and how the desired result is best achieved, given different sediment matrices, that produces successful recovery of pollen for analysis.

Hydrochloric acid (10%) was used to remove calcium carbonates present in the soil, after which the samples were screened through 250-micron mesh. The samples were rinsed until neutral by adding water, letting samples stand for 2 hours, then pouring off the supernatant. A small quantity of sodium hexametaphosphate was added to each sample once it reached neutrality, then the samples settled according to Stoke's Law in settling columns. This process was repeated with ethylenediaminetetraacetic acid (EDTA). These steps remove clay and soluble humics prior to heavy liquid separation. The samples then were freeze-dried. Sodium polytungstate (SPT), with a density of 1.8, was used for the flotation process. The samples were mixed with SPT and centrifuged at 1500 rpm for 10 minutes to separate organic from inorganic remains. The supernatant containing pollen and organic remains was decanted. Sodium polytungstate again was added to the inorganic fraction to repeat the separation process. The supernatant was decanted into the same tube as the supernatant from the first separation. This supernatant was centrifuged at 1500 rpm for 10 minutes to allow any remaining silica to be separated from the organics. The supernatant was decanted into a 50-ml conical tube and diluted with reverse osmosis deionized (RODI) water. These samples were centrifuged at 3000 rpm to concentrate the organic fraction in the bottom of the tube. After rinsing the pollen-rich organic fraction obtained by this separation with RODI water several times, all samples received a 20–30 minute treatment in hot hydrofluoric (HF) acid to remove any remaining inorganic particles. The samples then were acetolated for 5 minutes to remove any extraneous organic matter.

A light microscope was used to count pollen at a magnification of 500×. Pollen preservation varied from good to poor. Comparative reference material collected at the Intermountain Herbarium at Utah State University and the University of Colorado Herbarium as well as reference books were used to identify the pollen to the family, genus, and species level, where possible (see chapter 10 for a study of the macroplants that provide the species level for families identified here).

Pollen aggregates were recorded during identification. Aggregates are clumps of a single type of pollen and represent either pollen dispersal over short distances or the introduction of portions of the plant represented in an archaeological setting. Aggregates were included in pollen counts as single grains (noted by an "A" next to the pollen frequency on the pollen diagram). A plus sign (+) on the pollen diagram indicates that the pollen type was observed outside the regular count while scanning the remainder of the microscope slide. Pollen diagrams were produced using Tilia 2.0 and TGView 2.0.2. Total pollen concentrations are calculated in Tilia using the quantity of sample processed in cubic centimeters (cc), the quantity of exotics (spores) added to the sample, the quantity of exotics counted, and the total pollen counted and expressed as pollen per cc of sediment. Total pollen concentration is used to evaluate pollen deposition and recovery. Low total pollen concentrations often are associated either with poor preservation or very rapid deposition. Pollen concentrations of individual pollen grains, however, have not proven useful for interpreting either the environment or economic activity when no information is available about the time span represented by each sample. In cases with no independent temporal control it is not possible to assign environmental or cultural significance to values of individual pollen taxa that vary even by an order of magnitude, as they might represent vastly different periods of pollen accumulation. Therefore pollen frequencies are presented and interpreted.

"Indeterminate pollen" includes pollen grains that are folded, mutilated, and otherwise distorted beyond recognition. These grains are included in the total pollen count because they are part of the record. The microscopic charcoal frequency registers the relationship between pollen and charcoal. The total number of microscopic charcoal was divided by the pollen sum, resulting in a charcoal frequency that reflects the quantity of microscopic fragments observed, normalized per 100 pollen grains. Due to the abundance of microscopic charcoal in samples from sites, they required several applications of additional treatment that included centrifugal spins at high rpms for a short period and a gravity swirl method. These additional steps reduce the quantities of charcoal in the residue examined for pollen. Therefore direct comparisons of quantities of charcoal are gross estimates at best.

Pollen analysis includes identification of starch granules to general categories, if they are present.

RESULTS

HUACA PRIETA

The 12 pollen samples representing Huaca Prieta were derived from two different contexts (table A12.1a). Pollen samples designated HP were collected from off-mound geological contexts. The samples recovered from Unit 2 (U-2, Ext-Oeste) represent materials recovered from archaeological contexts on the east side of the mound within 30 m of a wetland.

Surprisingly, the samples from the geological contexts, many of which were located in former off-mound activity areas as well as the cultural contexts, all exhibited large quantities of microscopic charcoal relative to pollen. In fact the quantities of microscopic charcoal were so large and the total pollen concentrations so small that all of these samples apparently represent burned contexts. Total pollen concentrations are between 50 and 550 pollen per cubic centimeter (cc) of sediment for Unit 2. Larger concentrations of pollen were found in 2 samples. Sample PS-HP-15, collected from Layer 5b, exhibited a total concentration of nearly 2100 pollen per cc of sediment, while sample PS-HP-16 yielded over 6000 pollen per cc of sediment. The low count for sample PS-HP-15 is the result of an overabundance of microscopic charcoal. Samples PS-HP-8 and PS-HP-16 were unusual in containing slightly less charcoal than other samples.

Artemisia pollen (fig. A12.1a, table A12.1b) is dominant in the lowest (PS-HP-6) and uppermost (PS-HP-1) samples, indicating growth of shrubby sagebrush in the area. Poaceae pollen, representing local grasses, is most abundant in samples PS-HP-5 and PS-HP-2. Sample PS-HP-4 exhibited pollen that was particularly deteriorated. Moderate quantities of *Artemisia*, High-Spine Asteraceae, Brassicaceae, cheno-am, and Malvaceae pollen were present, although ~35% of the pollen was too poorly preserved to identify. Finally, sample PS-HP-3 was dominated by Santalaceae and *Typha angustifolia*–type pollen, representing trees in the sandalwood family and cattails. The signature for cattails is better in the lower than in the upper strata. The lower strata are associated with development of the nearby wetland between ~7000–6200 cal BP (see chapter 5). Frequencies of *Typha* pollen increase through time, culminating in ~20% *Typha* pollen in sample PS-HP-3 after an absence in sample PS-HP-4.

Other types of pollen in geological samples represent trees, including *Alnus*, which grows along streams, in running water, or in wetlands; Myrtaceae, representing a member of the myrtle family; and *Pinus*, which might be present through long-distance wind transport. Recovery of Low-Spine Asteraceae and High-Spine Asteraceae pollen rep-

Table A12.1. Pollen in sediment samples from Huaca Prieta

a. Provenience data

Sample no.	Test unit	Depth (cm below surface)	Provenience/description	Analysis
PS-HP-1	HP P2	5.00	HP P2 5.00	Pollen
PS-HP-2	HP P2	5.05	HP P2 5.05	Pollen
PS-HP-3	HP P2	5.10	HP P2 5.10	Pollen
PS-HP-4	HP P2	5.15	HP P2 5.15	Pollen
PS-HP-5	HP P2	5.20	HP P2 5.20	Pollen
PS-HP-6	HP P2	5.25	HP P2 5.25	Pollen
PS-HP-8	HP	5.30	Layer 7c-7	Pollen
PS-HP-9	HP	5.35	Layer 7c3/below layer of ash	Pollen
PS-HP-12	HP	5.40	Layer 6	Pollen
PS-HP-14	HP	5.45	Layer 7b	Pollen
PS-HP-15	HP	5.50	Layer 5b	Pollen
PS-HP-16	HP	5.55	Layer 3	Pollen

b. Pollen types observed

Scientific Name	Common Name
ARBOREAL POLLEN	
Alnus	Alder
Myrtaceae	Myrtle family
Pinus	Pine
Santalaceae	Members of *Santalales* family
NONARBOREAL POLLEN	
Apiaceae	Umbel family
Asteraceae:	Sunflower family
Artemisia	Sagebrush
Low-spine	Includes ragweed, cocklebur, sumpweed
High-spine	Includes aster, rabbitbrush, snakeweed, sunflower, etc.
Liguliflorae	Chicory tribe, includes dandelion and chicory
Brassicaceae	Cruciferae, also known as crucifers, the mustard family
Caryophyllaceae	Pink family
Cheno-am	Includes the goosefoot family and amaranth
Corylaceae	Hazel family
Cressa-type	Alkali weed
Cyperaceae	Sedge family
Euphorbia	Spurge
Fabaceae	Bean or legume family
Malvaceae	Mallow family
Plantago	Plantain
Poaceae	Grass family
Rubus	Bramble
Scrophulariaceae	Figwort family

Table A12.1. Continued

Scientific Name	Common Name
NONARBOREAL POLLEN (*continued*)	
Solanaceae	Potato/tomato family
Trichopetalum-type	Flor de la plumilla-type (Lily family)
Typha angustafolia	Cattail
CULTIGENS	
Cucurbita	Squash, pumpkin, gourd
Indeterminate	Too badly deteriorated to identify
HAIR	
Hair: sheep-type	Hair from a sheep
Phaseolus hook-shaped hair	Hook-shaped hair from a bean/wild bean
STARCHES	
Solanum starch	Starch produced by potato or tomato
Spheroid starch with centric hilum	
Dot starch	Typical of starches produced by grass seeds
Lycopodium	Clubmoss
Monolete smooth	Fern
Trilete smooth	Fern
Total pollen concentration	Quantity of pollen per cubic centimeter of sediment

resents members of the sunflower family. The presence of Brassicaceae pollen indicates that members of the mustard family grew in the area, probably as a result of disturbance. Cheno-am pollen also reflects weedy plants that commonly colonize disturbed areas. *Cressa*-type pollen represents a weedy member of the Convolvulaceae or bindweed family. Cyperaceae pollen comes from sedges, which often grow in wetlands, although some species favor drier habitats and grow with grasses there. *Euphorbia* pollen comes from spurge and related plants, which also are weedy annuals. Fabaceae pollen could not be identified to the genus level but represents members of the legume family. Malvaceae pollen, which comes from the mallow family and was recovered in samples PS-HP-6 and PS-HP-4, also suggests weedy plants.

Solanaceae pollen recovered in the uppermost sample (PS-HP-1) represents the presence of a member of the nightshade family. This pollen was not typical of the cultivars *Lycopersicon*, *Solanum*, or *Nicotiana* and exhibited a smooth surface, so the identification was left at the family level. Recovery of a single *Trichopetalum*-type pollen represents local growth of a member of the lily family. A single large grass pollen, measuring approximately 60 microns in diameter and presenting a large pore, was recovered in sample PS-HP-5. This pollen is too small for maize but is an appropriate size and pore morphology to represent *Agropyron*. A *Solanum*-type starch (elongated with a very eccentric hilum) was recovered from sample PS-HP-3, suggesting the

presence of potatoes. Recovery of a spherical starch with a centric small hilum might represent either deterioration of grass seeds or perhaps a very immature potato starch. A single hair similar to the wool of sheep was recovered in sample PS-HP-5. (It is probable that this fiber is intrusive to the sample as a loose wool fiber from a sweater worn by a field or lab worker.) Fern spores were recovered in most samples and are noted as both monolete and trilete forms. A *Lycopodium*-type spore with a rugulate surface existed in sample PS-HP-3.

This diversity of pollen frequencies in samples from geological contexts suggests several possibilities. First, seasonal deposition signatures might be present, meaning that sediment accumulation was relatively rapid. This is an unlikely scenario. It is more likely that the local vegetation is highly variable and dependent on moisture received during the previous or existing season for annuals to grow and perennials and trees to flower.

The samples collected from cultural proveniences in U-2 exhibit a far more consistent record. Sample PS-HP-16, collected from Layer 3, is dominated by Poaceae pollen and exhibits a small quantity of *Typha angustifolia*-type pollen, reflecting the presence of cattails growing near the site and perhaps used or processed in this area. In addition, this sample yielded a single *Phaseolus*-type hook-shaped hair. Although not silicified, this hair is diagnostic of legumes, including cultivated beans. Other pollen types present in this sample include small quantities of *Pinus*, *Artemisia*, Low-

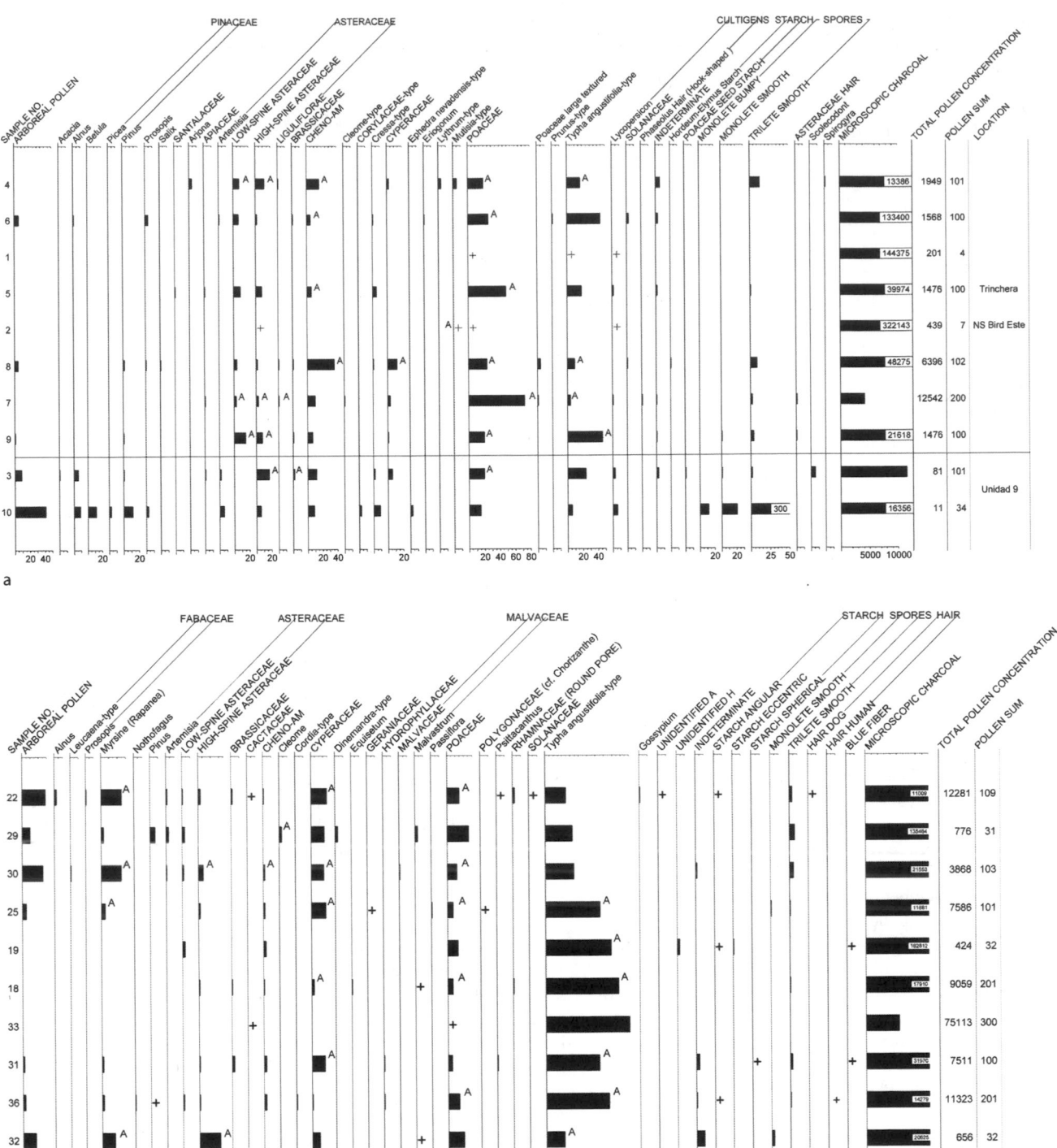

FIGURE A12.1. Pollen diagrams: *a*, Huaca Prieta; *b*, Paredones.

Spine Asteraceae, and High-Spine Asteraceae. Liguliflorae and cheno-am represent a combination of wind pollen transport and local weedy plants. The remainder of the samples examined from cultural proveniences are dominated by *Artemisia* pollen with moderate quantities of High-Spine

Asteraceae and/or Poaceae pollen, from sagebrush, various members of the sunflower family, and grasses. Cheno-am pollen is present in all samples in small quantities and probably comes from weedy plants. Other pollen types noted in the cultural samples that probably come from local plants include Low-Spine Asteraceae, Brassicaceae, Caryophyllaceae, Corylaceae, *Plantago*, and Scrophulariaceae, belonging to members of the sunflower, mustard, pink, and hazel families, respectively; plantain; and a member of the figwort family. In addition, a small quantity of *Rubus*-type pollen was observed in sample PS-HP-8, Layer 7c7. The genus *Rubus* includes raspberries and similar edible berries. Identification of this pollen is left at the "-type" level, because I do not have the familiarity with the project area to substantiate that these fruits might have grown in the area.

PAREDONES

At Paredones 10 floors within Unit 22 were sampled for pollen and starch (table A12.2a). Although the sediments were not dark, the samples contained large quantities of microscopic charcoal that necessitated aggressive charcoal removal. Quantities of microscopic charcoal were calculated on the posttreatment samples, meaning that the charcoal was more abundant than is portrayed here.

The pollen records from the floors were dominated, to varying extents, by *Typha* pollen (fig. A12.1b, table A12.2b), probably representing cattails growing at the edge of the nearby lagoon (see chapter 10). This was particularly true for samples 36 through 25, representing periods 7 through 4, ~6700–6200 cal BP. Sample 33 in particular was heavily dominated by *Typha* pollen, to the near exclusion of all other types. Cactaceae and Poaceae were also noted. Recovery of such large quantities of *Typha* pollen in samples suggests that the floors were wet and that cattail pollen was deposited seasonally while these sediments were exposed, although the possibility that cattail reeds were used as flooring material cannot be discounted. Reeds are used today by locals for flooring.

These samples yielded varying quantities of pollen, all of which were more than sufficient to produce counts of 200–300 pollen per sample had the presence of microscopic charcoal not been such a severe problem. The largest total pollen concentration was noted in sample 33, representing Floor 23B, at more than 75,000 pollen per cubic centimeter (cc) of sediment. This large quantity of pollen is consistent with the hypothesis that cattail pollen concentrated artificially on wet floors. The greater concentrations of cattail pollen in samples between periods 7 and 4 suggest that the local cattail population was large between ~6700 and 6200 cal BP and that at the time they pollinated (in early to middle summer) conditions were wet at the site or floors were covered in cattail reed mats. This also is the period when the nearby lagoon existed (see chapter 5). It is likely that the ground was tinged yellow with the accumulating pollen. The record for other periods reflects accumulations of pollen that represent more local vegetation. It contains moderate quantities of Cyperaceae, Poaceae, and *Typha* pollen, reflecting sedges, grasses, and cattails, all probably growing on margins of the lagoon. When not overwhelmed by large quantities of *Typha* pollen, these frequencies suggest that the margins of the lagoon probably supported locally abundant clusters of sedges and grasses. In addition, the most abundant tree growing in this area appears to have

been *Myrsine* (formerly *Rapanea*), which grows in coastal areas and may become weedy. *Prosopis* (mesquite or algarrobo) was present in the area at least toward the end of the occupation of this site. Recovery of small quantities of *Alnus* and *Leucaena*-type pollen in the upper samples indicates that alder and guaje grew locally. Guaje trees are legumes that were used for a variety of purposes such as fuel, crafts, lumber, and pulp. The presence of *Pinus* pollen might be the result of long-distance atmospheric transport. *Nothofagus* pollen was observed only in low numbers (sample 36 in period 7), indicating that southern beech trees grew in the area, although they do not appear to have been abundant.

This area supported a few members of the sunflower family. Low-Spine Asteraceae and High-Spine Asteraceae pollen, as well as *Artemisia* pollen, was noted in the upper samples. They were present rarely in the lower samples, with the exception of the lowest sample, which exhibited a large quantity of High-Spine Asteraceae pollen. Plants in the Brassicaceae (mustard family) also grew locally. Cactaceae pollen was noted occasionally. This pollen is not readily wind transported, so it is possible that cacti were more abundant locally away from the lagoon than they appear to be from this record. Cheno-am pollen is observed in many samples, suggesting that one or more members of the goosefoot family grew locally. *Cleome* pollen was noted only in sample 29. This pollen, like that of Cactaceae, is not readily wind transported, so it is possible that beeweed grew more abundantly than is suggested by this single recovery. *Cordia*-type pollen represents a member of the borage family that grows either as a shrub or as a tree. This pollen was observed only once in sample 36.

Pollen types noted in only a few samples include *Dinemandra*-type, *Eriogonum*, Geraniaceae, *Halgoris*, Hydrophyllaceae, Malvaceae, *Malvastrum*, cf. *Nierembergia* (a member of the nightshade family), *Passiflora*, *Psittaecanthus*, and *Vitis*. *Psittaecanthus* is a parasitic plant. Recovery of a single *Gossypium* pollen fragment in sample 22, from the most recent period, suggests growth of cotton at the site. *Equisetum* pollen is observed rarely even when horsetail plants grow in an area. Horsetail usually grows in moist sediments and is likely part of the wetland. Pollen preservation was very good in these samples, suggesting the possibility that the sediments remained wet and anoxic for long periods. The visibility of pollen was hampered primarily by the presence of large quantities of microscopic charcoal mentioned above.

Starches were recovered in 4 samples (22, 19, 31, and 36) representing layers, not floors. The angular starch observed in samples 22, 19, and 36 is consistent in morphology with that produced by *Zea mays*, but it is not considered to be diagnostic of maize, as similar angular starches are produced in the seeds of other grasses. An exhaustive study of the morphology of starches produced in seeds of all grasses known to grow in this area is required prior to assigning diagnostic status to these starches. In light of the recovery of *Zea mays* in the macrofloral and phytolith records (see chapter 10 and appendices 5 and 7), however, it is likely that these starches represent *Zea mays*. Scanning in search of *Zea mays* pollen and/or pollen representing other cultigens

Table A12.2. Pollen samples from Unit 22 at Paredones

a. Provenience data

Unit 22 floor	Sample no.	Period	Description	Analysis
Floor 7E	22	1	~4600–4500 cal BP	Pollen
Floor 8	29	2	~4600–4400 cal BP	Pollen
Floor 14	30	3	~5400–5000 cal BP	Pollen
Floor 17	25	4	~5500–5300 cal BP	Pollen
Floor 21	19	5	~6500–6200 cal BP	Pollen
Floor 22	18	5	~6500–6200 cal BP	Pollen
Floor 23B	33	6	~6500–6200 cal BP	Pollen
Floor 24	31	7	~6600–6300 cal BP	Pollen
Floor 24	36	7	~6600–6300 cal BP	Pollen
Floor 26	32	8	~6800–6700 cal BP	Pollen

b. Pollen types observed

Scientific Name	Common Name
ARBOREAL POLLEN	
Alnus	Alder
Fabaceae:	Legume family
Leucaena	Guaje
Prosopis	Algarrobo
Myrsine (Rapanea)	No common name
Nothofagus	Southern beech
Pinus	Pine
NONARBOREAL POLLEN	
Asteraceae:	Sunflower family
Artemisia	Sagebrush
Low-spine	Includes ragweed, cocklebur, sumpweed
High-spine	Includes aster, rabbitbrush, snakeweed, sunflower, etc.
Brassicaceae	Mustard family
Cactaceae	Cactus family
Cheno-am	Includes the goosefoot family and amaranth
Cleome	Beeweed
Cordia	Too many common names
Cyperaceae	Sedge family
Equisetum	Horsetail
Geraniaceae	Geranium family
Hydrophyllaceae	Waterleaf family
Malvaceae:	Mallow family
Malvastrum	Mallow
Poaceae	Grass family
Polygonaceae	Knotweed family
Psittacanthus	Parasitic plant

Scientific Name	Common Name
NONARBOREAL POLLEN (*continued*)	
Rhamnaceae	Buckthorn family
Solanaceae	Nightshade family
Typha angustafolia	Cattail
CULTIGENS	
Gossypium	Cotton
Indeterminate	Too badly deteriorated to identify
STARCHES	
Angular starch	Typical of starches from grass seeds such as those from bluestem (*Andropogon*) or ricegrass (*Achnatherum*) and maize (*Zea mays*)
Eccentric starch	Root starch
Spherical starch	Typical of starches produced by grass seeds
SPORES	
Monolete smooth	Fern
Trilete smooth	Fern
HAIR	
Hair, dog	Dog hair
Trilete smooth	Hair, human
Blue fiber	Fiber dyed blue

produced a record of other types, but no further evidence of cultigens. It is highly likely that difficulties arising from the density of microscopic charcoal created a problem in locating *Zea mays* pollen.

A starch with an eccentric hilum was observed in sample 19, suggesting the possibility that an edible root or tuber was processed in this area. The morphology is not consistent with that of potato starch. This starch remains unidentified to genus or family, so the interpretation is very tentative. Recovery of a spherical starch with a centric hilum in sample 31 probably represents deterioration of grass seeds in this area and is not considered to have interpretive value.

These samples contained 2 types of hair fragments. Dog hair was recovered in sample 22, and a human hair fragment was noted in sample 36. Blue fibers that appeared to be synthetic rather than cotton were noted in samples 19 and 31, probably from a loose fiber on a worker's sweater. The possibility of local growth of indigo and its prehistoric use as a dye is acknowledged (see chapter 12, part 1, and appendix 11).

CONCLUSION

While analysis recovered pollen from the Huaca Prieta samples, finding pollen in the extreme quantity of micro-

scopic charcoal fragments was extremely tedious and time consuming. Evidence of cultigens that included *Cucurbita* (squash), *Gossypium*, and *Phaseolus* (beans) suggests an active Preceramic agricultural community. Samples yielding larger quantities of indeterminate pollen were unusually poorly preserved. Samples collected from cultural proveniences do not exhibit the variety of pollen observed in the geological samples. The context of these samples is largely unknown, so it is difficult to speculate on the reasons for this difference. Interpretations remain at a preliminary stage.

Pollen and starch analysis of samples from the Paredones produced a record heavily dominated by *Typha* pollen, probably representing cattails growing along the margins of the nearby ancient lagoon. This substantiates the existence of the lagoon during most of the site use but should not be seen only as an indication that cattail pollen was processed. Wind transport of cattail pollen onto wet surfaces or floors with mats made from cattail reeds are the likely methods of pollen distribution and concentration in these locations. This does not diminish the possibility that cattails might have been used as food.

No pollen evidence of *Zea mays* was recovered from these samples, although angular starches that are consistent with those produced in maize kernels were recovered in samples 22, 19, and 36. Combined with the macrofloral record, this suggests processing and/or use of maize at ~6700–6600 cal BP, ~6600–6500 cal BP, and ~4500–4200 cal BP. These starches are not considered to be diagnostic of maize, however, but rather are consistent with those produced in maize, so they should not be seen as direct evidence of maize unless they are corroborated by other irrefutable remains such as macrofloral or phytoliths, which was the case at both Paredones and Huaca Prieta. Recovery of a *Gossypium* pollen fragment in sample 22 at the top of this record suggests cotton growing in this area by ~4000 cal BP. The presence of *Passiflora* pollen is considered unusual because only small quantities of pollen are contained in each flower, which is insect-pollinated. This documents the availability and probable use or processing of passiflora fruits during period 4. *Vitis* pollen also was observed in the uppermost sample, suggesting the availability of grapes. *Cleome* pollen was present in sample 29, representing period 2. It is not known whether or not beeweed had a cultural use in this area.

FISH OTOLITHS FROM HUACA PRIETA

Elise Dufour, Olivier Trombret, and
Philippe Béarez

INTRODUCTION

Although the eastern side of the Pacific plays a key role in the tropical atmospheric circulation and in the global carbon cycle, past interannual climatic variability over time has been primarily observed in the western and central Pacific. Elemental and isotopic analyses of fossil corals record tropical Pacific SST with seasonal, decadal, and millennial resolution (Cole and Fairbanks 1990; Corrège et al. 2000; Evans et al. 2002; Tudhope et al. 2001). Marine observations in the eastern region are limited by the scarcity of corals (Dunbar et al. 1994), so paleoclimatic reconstructions mostly rely on continental past precipitation proxies (Conroy et al. 2008; Moy et al. 2002; Rodbell et al. 1999). Mollusk shells and fish otoliths present in anthropologic and natural contexts constitute alternative marine archives (Sandweiss et al. 2001, 2007). The brevity of their timespan compared to corals characterizes mollusks and fish, but they have strict ecological preferences (Béarez et al. 2011). They record SST by growth marks and $\delta^{18}O$ measurements in shells and otoliths (Carré et al. 2005, 2012; Lazareth et al. 2006; Perrier et al. 1994; Piner et al. 2004) and upwelling conditions by radiocarbon content (Etayo-Cadavid et al. 2013). Studies of mollusk assemblages as well as isotopic measurements of shells and otoliths from sites localized at different latitudes of the Peruvian and Chilean coasts have brought insight into east Pacific marine conditions. Some studies have led to controversial interpretations of mid-Holocene climate evolution (Andrus et al. 2002a; Béarez et al. 2003; Carré et al. 2012; Dufour 2012; Perrier et al. 1994; Wells and Noller 1997).

The present study reports the identification of Huaca Prieta otoliths and the environmental conditions indicated by the assemblage. $\delta^{18}O$ values bagre (*Galeichthys peruvianus*) otoliths from 6 strata and that of modern counterparts were analyzed. Mean annual and seasonal temperature reconstructions were compared to published data to assess marine conditions during the mid-Holocene and early late Holocene on the northern coast of Peru.

HUACA PRIETA OTOLITHS

Fish otoliths are aragonitic ($CaCO_3$), acellular, and metabolically inert structures that precipitate within the inner ear. Shape and size are usually species-specific (Nolf 1985). Otoliths grow continuously by accretion from hatching to death

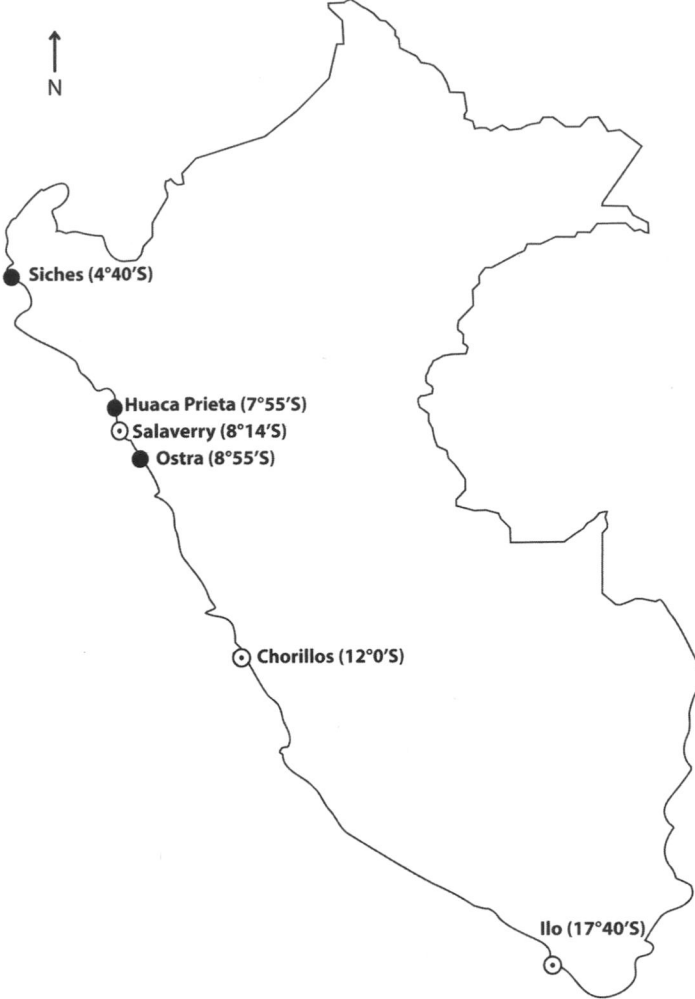

FIGURE A13.1. Map of Peru with location of sites and places of fish collection mentioned in the text.

Among fish species present at the site, the bagre was chosen because of its abundance and potential ability to record local marine coastal conditions due to its ethology and ecology. The bagre is a benthopelagic fish that is widely distributed along the Peruvian coast, from 6° S to about 18° 30′ S (Béarez 2012; Béarez et al. 2003). The species spends its whole life cycle in marine water and does not migrate long distances during El Niño events. Moreover, it usually inhabits waters between 5 and 40 m deep, although it can go deeper (down to 140 m) according to oxycline depth (Carbajal et al. 2006). A sample of 12 archaeological specimens of bagre was selected from Layers 7C-3 to 5a, dated from ~7571–7424 to ~3956–3694 cal BP (table A13.2), along with 3 modern counterparts collected at Salaverry (8° 14′ S) in 2005, Chorillos (12° 0′ S) in 2005, and Ilo (17° 40′ S) in 2002 by P. Béarez (table A13.2). Archaeological and modern otoliths were embedded in a polyester resin and cut by a precision saw equipped with a diamond wire to obtain transversal thin sections. Transverse sections were polished to reveal growth banding (fig. A13.2b).

Diagenetic alteration of ancient otoliths might modify their geochemistry and subsequently compromise paleoclimatic reconstructions (Dufour et al. 2000). Aragonite was the only form of $CaCO_3$ detected in Huaca Prieta otoliths by powder XRD analysis (Inel, 0.03 degree of accuracy). Preservation was also checked through microstructure and mineralogy observation. Scanning electronic microscope (Vega II LSU Tescan) observation of slightly decalcified thin sections showed long needle-like crystals of aragonite, which are typical otolith microstructural features (fig. A13.2c and d). No recrystallization between regular aragonite crystals was present. Due to the lack of evidence of diagenetic alteration, Huaca Prieta otoliths were considered valuable archives for isotopic analysis.

The individual age of both archaeological and modern specimens was estimated in order to assess the time window provided by isotopic analysis. Fish individual age is commonly estimated by counting yearly growth marks of calcified structures (Panfili et al. 2002). Otolith yearly marks are defined as the combination of an adjacent opaque zone and a translucent zone, which appear either dark or light depending on illumination light (fig. A13.2b). Archaeological and modern thin sections presented growth structures best observed in transmitted light. However, there was no clear pattern of alternating opaque and translucent zones allowing reliable age estimation, contrary to the interpretation of growth marks on the same species by C. Fred T. Andrus et al. (2002a, 2002b). Donna Surge and Karen Walker (2005) experienced the same issue with otoliths of the catfish *Ariopsis felis*. Finally, the age of the studied specimens was estimated from growth mark observation in whole otoliths immersed in a mix of alcohol and distilled water for enhancing the contrast between growth zones. The 3 modern specimens were estimated to be 6/7 years old and the archaeological specimens 4 to 7 years old (table A13.2).

and present daily and annual microstructural increments. Because of these shape and growth characteristics, otoliths have long been used in fishery sciences (Campana and Nielson 1985) and have been useful for archaeological studies (Béarez 2000).

Excavations at Huaca Prieta, mostly Layer 7A from Unit 2, provided a total number of identified specimens (NISP) of 256 otoliths. All were identified to species level, separating 11 belonging to 6 families (table A13.1). Otoliths were measured and weighed, and laterality was determined in order to estimate the minimum number of individuals (MNI). The marine catfish or bagre (*Galeichthys peruvianus*) dominates the assemblage (37.9%) (fig. A13.2a), followed by several species of drums (Sciaenidae) and the hake (*Merluccius gayi*). All identified species are common coastal inhabitants of the actual Humboldt Current Ecosystem.

FIGURE A13.2. Bagre otolith from Huaca Prieta: *a*, external view; *b*, micrograph of a polished thin section showing growth marks; *c* and *d*, SEM view of the etched thin section showing growth marks and needle-like aragonite crystals. Bar = 100 μm (*c*) and 20 μm.

Table A13.1. Frequency of identified species in the otolith assemblage at Huaca Prieta

Family	Species	NISP	% NISP	MNI	% MNI
Ariidae (sea catfishes)	*Galeichthys peruvianus*	97	37.9	54	32.5
Sciaenidae (drums)	*Sciaena deliciosa*	43	16.8	28	16.9
	Robaloscion wieneri	26	10.2	24	14.5
	Cynoscion analis	34	13.3	22	13.3
	Stellifer minor	21	8.2	12	7.2
	Paralonchurus peruanus	14	5.5	11	6.6
Merlucciidae (hakes)	*Merluccius gayi*	14	5.5	9	5.4
Haemulidae (grunts)	*Anisotremus scapularis*	3	1.2	2	1.2
Sciaenidae (drums)	*Cilus gilberti*	2	0.8	2	1.2
	Cheilotrema fasciatum	1	0.4	1	0.6
Engraulidae (anchovies)	*Engraulis ringens*	1	0.4	1	0.6
TOTAL		256		166	

Table A13.2. Archaeological otolith samples from Huaca Prieta and modern Peruvian bagre (*Galeichthys peruvianus*) studied for stable isotope analysis

Specimens	Provenience	Conventional radiocarbon (years BP)	2-sigma calibrated age range (years BP)	Estimated individual age (years)
HP-1	Unit 2 Ext West, stratum 5a	3588±36	3956–3694	7
HP-2	Unit 2 Ext West, stratum 5b-1		—	7
HP-3	Unit 2 Ext West, stratum 6a		—	4
HP-4	Unit 2 Ext West, stratum 6a		—	7
HP-5	Unit 2 Ext West, stratum 7a	3748±40	4151–3898	6
HP-6	Unit 2 Ext West, stratum 7a	3748±40	4151–3898	7
HP-7	Unit 2 Ext West, stratum 7a	3748±40	4151–3898	7
HP-8	Unit 2 Ext West, stratum 7a	3748±40	4151–3898	7
HP-9	Unit 2 Ext West, stratum 7a	3748±40	4151–3898	7
HP-10	Unit 2 Ext West, stratum 7a	3748±40	4151–3898	7
HP-11	Unit 2 Ext West, stratum 7c-1	—	—	7
HP-12	Unit 2 Ext West, stratum 7c-3	6641±49	7571–7424	7
GP-409	Salaverry (8° 14′ S)	Modern	2005/05/23	7
GP-292	Chorillos (12° 0′ S)	Modern	2002/03/26	6
GP-215	Ilo (17° 40′ S)	Modern	2002/03/13	6

OTOLITH MICROSAMPLING, STABLE ISOTOPES ANALYSIS, AND DETERMINATION OF MEAN $\delta^{18}O$ VALUES

Stable isotope measurements of otolith aragonite were performed at the Service de Spectrométrie de Masse Isotopique of the Muséum National d'Histoire Naturelle (SSMIM). $\delta^{18}O$ values were determined using a Thermo Advantage mass spectrometer directly coupled to a KIEL-IV automated carbonate preparation device. Isotopic values are reported (per mil) relative to the Vienna Pee Dee Belemnite (VPDB) international reference standard. Accuracy and precision were checked by routine analysis of a NBS-19 standard and were determined to be better than ±0.05‰.

For seven archaeological and three modern specimens, thin sections were serially microsampled using a semiautomated microdrilling system (Micromill, NewWave) to generate high-resolution isotopic profiles. Serial microsampling consisted in a series of contiguous grooves of 50 to 150 μm depth adjacent for a continuous sampling (Dufour et al. 2007). From 36 to 85 microsamples of aragonite weighing from 25 to 50 μg were obtained spanning the fish's whole life.

Intra-otolith variations in $\delta^{18}O$ obtained by the serial microsampling method and calculation of mean life $\delta^{18}O$ value are exemplified for the modern specimen captured at Salaverry (GP-409) in figure A13.3a. The isotopic profile exhibits a sinusoidal pattern of variation with a large excursion at the beginning of life followed by regular variations. Otolith $\delta^{18}O$ depends on both the temperature and the $\delta^{18}O$ of ambient water (for example, Patterson et al. 1993; Thorrold et al. 1997). Seawater $\delta^{18}O$ values can vary slightly on the temporal and spatial scales. But factors that usually cause short timescale variations are virtually nonexistent along the Peruvian coast, with almost no precipitation and minimal river discharge. It has been shown that seawater $\delta^{18}O$ variability was weak along the central and southern coasts on both intra- and interannual time scales (Carré et al. 2013). A similar situation is expected in the northern coast. Ambient temperature variation thus represents the first-order control of variation of $\delta^{18}O$ in biogenic carbonate value, and the 9 cycles observed in GP-409 profile are interpreted to be annual. This is in accordance with estimated age by growth mark counting. The most extreme (highest and lowest) $\delta^{18}O$ values of each annual cycle were used to calculate seasonal variations (0.1 to 1.7‰) and mean seasonal values. A decrease in seasonal variation is observed during the last 3 years of life. It does not reflect a decrease in seasonal SST over time but a methodological bias linked to a variation in temporal resolution among microsamples. Microsample size was adjusted not to represent a constant temporal duration but to provide the minimum amount of carbonate to generate a valid mass spectrometry assay. As the fish growth rate decreases over ontogenesis, the microsample temporal duration increases. The 2 last annual cycles of GP-409 were likely affected and were missing minimum and maximum extreme seasonal values. Mean seasonal values varied from 0.15 to 0.55‰ and provided an averaged mean life isotopic record of 0.3‰ for GP-409 (fig. A13.3b). Mean individual values were calculated in the same way for other modern and serially microsampled archaeological specimens. Figure A13.3b presents extreme maximum and minimum values for typical seasonal cycles (−0.1 and 0.7‰ for GP-409, fig. A13.3a), as well as extreme values for the early life excursion (−0.7 and 1.0‰ for GP-409, fig. A13.3a). Change in polar ice volume has a long-term effect on marine water $\delta^{18}O$ values. A correction of 0.1‰ was applied for the oldest specimen (HP-12), following Kurt Lambeck and John Chappell (2001).

Averaged life isotopic values for 5 additional specimens of Layer 7A are also presented in figure A13.3b. For these specimens, a single groove following the main axis was performed to collect a single microsample.

RECORD OF AMBIENT TEMPERATURE BY BAGRE OTOLITHS

The reliability of bagre otoliths in recording environmental conditions is assessed by estimating temperatures from $\delta^{18}O$ of the three modern otoliths using the equation developed by Høie et al. (2004), which are compared to monthly SSTs variations measured at or nearby the fish capture locations at Salaverry, Callao and Ilo (www.imarpe.gob.pe). Fish thermal history can be reconstructed on the condition that water $\delta^{18}O$ values are known or can be reasonably constrained. Mean seawater isotopic composition shows some geographical variations along the Peruvian coast. A mean $\delta^{18}O$ value of 0.2±0.14‰ was measured at Ilo between 2001 and 2004 and a single value of 0.2‰ at Callao (12° 04′ S) (Carré et al. 2013). For the north coast the analysis of 2 samples collected in July 1998 and 1999 provides a value of 0.1% Vienna Standard Mean Ocean Water (VSMOW).

The range of typical seasonal variations in $\delta^{18}O$ is 0.7–0.8‰, which corresponds to a variation of ~3.5°C, in close relation with seasonality at the three locations. Mean annual reconstructed temperatures are ~17°C, 16°C, and 15.5°C for fish captured respectively at Salaverry, Chorillos, and Ilo (fig. A13.3b). They slightly underestimate mean recorded SST at the three localities. However, the trend in decreasing mean reconstructed temperatures (or increasing $\delta^{18}O$ values) from the north to the south is in accordance with the general latitudinal SST gradient over the coast of Peru. Two profiles contain negative $\delta^{18}O$ excursions with extreme negative values corresponding to estimated temperatures of 22°C (GP-409) and 23°C (GP-292) (fig. A13.3b). They far exceed the normal seasonal warm extremes recorded on the coast of Peru. Given the position of the excursions within profiles and the estimated age for the two individuals, the negative $\delta^{18}O$ excursions reflect the warm phase of the 1997–1998 El Niño event. The cold phase of the El Niño 1997–1998 event is also recorded by the highest values exhibited by GP-409 (fig. A13.3b).

Andrus et al. (2002a, 2000b) previously used bagre otoliths as proxies of SST in northern Peru, but the reliability of

the species was questioned (Béarez et al. 2003). The present data suggest that $\delta^{18}O$ measurements of bagre otoliths record geographic (latitudinal) variation in SST but underestimate reconstructed temperature. Comparison of otolith-specific temperature-fractionation relationships established for different species (for example, Høie et al. 2004; Patterson et al. 1993; Thorrold et al. 1997) showed that they make it possible to estimate ambient temperature with a precision and accuracy better than 1°C with some variation in $\delta^{18}O$-derived temperature (Høie et al. 2004). Physiology and phylogeny-related factors are suspected of being responsible for this variation (Godiksen et al. 2010). Furthermore, bagre otolith–based temperatures were compared to SST recorded at stationary points. Fish are mobile organisms that can swim freely within local waters, and during part of their life cycle bagre stay at a depth of less than 40 m (Carbajal et al. 2006). Consequently, bagre might record a both more regional and deeper signal over at least part of their life cycle than more (or completely) sessile organisms such as bivalves.

As long as no specific temperature fractionation equation has been specifically developed for bagre it might be difficult to estimate SST directly from $\delta^{18}O$ measurements. Even if the present database is still limited, however, it suggests that intra-individual variation in the $\delta^{18}O$ of modern bagre otoliths reflects the general latitudinal SST gradient (note that nearshore SST gradients along the Peruvian coast are determined more by the position of the upwelling centers than by latitude), while the interindividual variation reflects the seasonality or ENSO events. Therefore the comparison of archaeological and modern otolith values allows characterization of climatic variation over time at a given latitude.

TEMPERATURE CONDITIONS RECORDED AT HUACA PRIETA

Archaeological specimens exhibit mean annual $\delta^{18}O$ values ranging from 0.3 to 1.0‰ and typical seasonal ranges similar to those of modern specimens (fig. A13.3b). The specimens dated from the mid-Holocene (HP-12) present the same value as the modern specimen from the north coast, while late Holocene specimens (HP1–HP11) present similar or more negative values than modern specimens from the central and southern coast (fig. A13.3b). At the latitude of the Huaca Prieta mound this corresponds to a cooling as high as 3°C. Four specimens exhibited negative $\delta^{18}O$ excursions (fig. A13.3b). The specimen (HP-12) that dates from the mid-Holocene presents a negative excursion value (−0.7‰) that is equivalent to the value measured in the two modern specimens recognized to have experienced an El Niño event (figs. A13.3a–b). Several specimens dated from the early late Holocene also present negative excursions. While their extreme values are lower than those of modern specimens, these individuals also experienced warm events during one year of life.

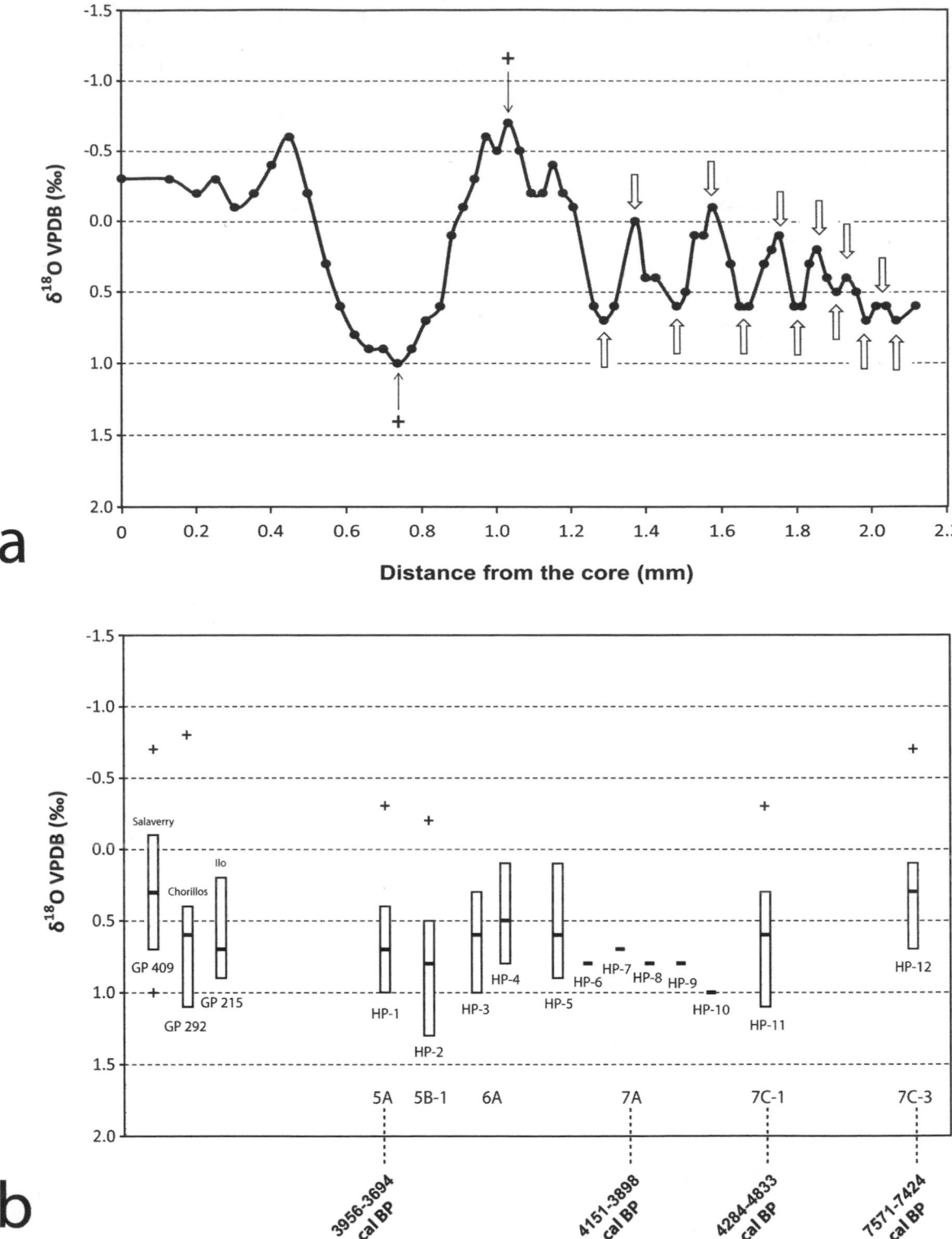

FIGURE A13.3. *a,* intra-otolith profile in δ^{18}O of a modern bagre captured in Salaverry in 2005; δ^{18}O data are plotted following ontogeny, with core microsample values on the left and edge (end of life) microsample values on the right (note that vertical δ^{18}O-axis is reversed; white arrows identify extreme values of regular seasonal range; crosses indicate negative and positive excursion interpreted as reflecting the 1997–1998 ENSO events); *b,* comparison of mean annual and typical seasonal range of δ^{18}O values of modern Peruvian and Huaca Prieta otoliths. (Note that the vertical δ^{18}O-axis is reversed.)

EVOLUTION OF CLIMATIC CONDITIONS DURING THE MID-HOLOCENE TO EARLY LATE HOLOCENE

Bagre otolith $\delta^{18}O$ values from Huaca Prieta indicate a similar or cooler mean SST than today and a similar seasonality during the mid-Holocene and beginning of the late Holocene. For the northern coast and mid-Holocene, most direct comparative data come from the sites of Ostra (8° 55′) and Siches (4° 10′ S). The presence of warm-water mollusk assemblages (Sandweiss et al. 1997) and relatively low isotopic values for bagre otoliths and cockle (*Trachycardium procerum*) shells were interpreted as the result of warmer conditions (~2–3°C warmer at Ostra) of the open sea. Geomorphology studies, various shell $\delta^{18}O$–based studies (Béarez et al. 2003; Carré et al. 2012; Perrier et al. 1994; Wells and Noller 1997), and the unique value obtained for the mid-Holocene at Huaca Prieta do not support this interpretation and suggest an alternative environmental explanation. At Siches and Ostra anomalous mollusk assemblages reflect habitats that no longer exist at these latitudes. A former mangrove existed in Siches, while in Ostra a shallow bay with limited connection to the open sea where warm conditions—and warm-water fauna—could persist locally was certainly present (Béarez et al. 2003; Carré et al. 2012; DeVries and Wells 1990; Perrier et al. 1994; Wells and Noller 1997). Matthieu Carré et al. (2012) recently compiled and critically reviewed available marine records for the mid-Holocene from northern Peru to northern Chile that yield consistent cooler SST along the coast, suggesting a shallower mean position of the thermocline and a strengthened Walker circulation with increased wind stress and coastal upwelling, as observed today during La Niña conditions. Coastal records are consistent with paleoclimatic evidence from the equatorial Pacific (for example, Colinvaux 1972; Koutavas et al. 2002) and terrestrial evidence (Fontugne et al. 1999). Records of cooler temperatures at Huaca Prieta and at the site of Los Vilos (31° 52′ S) by $\delta^{18}O$ analysis of *M. donacium* shell (Carré et al. 2012) data yield consistent evidence that the conditions persisted after the mid-Holocene over the southeastern Pacific.

CONCLUSIONS

In summary, ancient assemblages of mollusk shells and fish otoliths (ear stones) and their isotopic measurements provide the most direct proxy of past environmental and climatic conditions on the eastern side of the tropical Pacific (fig. A13.1). Recent excavations at Huaca Prieta provided otoliths in levels dated from ~7572–7424 to ~3956–3694 cal BP. We identified 11 species, which are all common coastal inhabitants of the current Humboldt Current Ecosystem. The marine catfish or bagre (*Galeichthys peruvianus*) dominates the assemblage. The quality of preservation of the bagre otoliths makes them reliable archives for measuring oxygen isotope values ($\delta^{18}O$). Serial sampling was performed for 7 archaeological and 3 modern specimens from Salaverry (8° 14′ S), Chorillos (12° 0′ S), and Ilo (17° 40′ S) for which typical seasonal range and mean annual $\delta^{18}O$ values were calculated. An additional 5 specimens provided mean annual values. Despite some limitations of bagre $\delta^{18}O$ as proxy of SST, the comparison of modern and archaeological otoliths allows reconstruction of the variation of climatic conditions over time. Intra-individual variation in $\delta^{18}O$ of Huaca Prieta otoliths indicates a seasonality similar to today and suggests ENSO-like events. Mean annual values of $\delta^{18}O$ indicate similar or cooler temperatures than today. Cooler SSTs were previously recorded for the mid-Holocene by different proxies from northern Peru to northern Chile and for just after the mid-Holocene in Chile. Together these data yield consistent evidence of persistent cooler conditions and an increase of the coastal upwelling activity during and after the mid-Holocene over the southeastern Pacific.

ACKNOWLEDGMENTS

We thank Michel Lemoine and Vincent Rommevaux for their help during thin-section preparation, Sylvain Pont for SEM examination at SEM-EDS facility of the Direction des Collections (Muséum National d'Histoire Naturelle), and Joël Ughetto for stable isotope measurement at the SSMIM. This work was partly supported by the Action Thématique du Muséum (ATM) BIOMINERALISATION and LabEx ANR-10-LABX-0003-BCDiv within the "Investissements d'avenir" program reference n° ANR-11-IDEX-0004-02 (Olivier Tombret).

SEMELE CORRUGATA MICROSTRUCTURE AND OXYGEN ISOTOPE PROFILES AS INDICATORS OF SEASONALITY

Jeixin Wei, C. Fred T. Andrus, and Alberto Pérez-Huerta

INTRODUCTION

This study examines mollusk shells as a potential archive of proxy data for the archaeological season of capture and/or paleoclimate at Huaca Prieta (compare Andrus 2011; see appendix 3). Before such analysis can be applied to archaeological materials, the methods used on each new species must be validated using modern examples (Andrus 2012). The goal of the research presented here is to demonstrate whether *Semele corrugata*, a common clam species in Peru, records season of capture and/or seasonal climate data in the oxygen isotope ($\delta^{18}O$) chemistry of the clam's carbonate shell. However, oxygen isotope profiles may not be interpreted solely in terms of seasonal temperature variation. Other key points to be considered include timing of shell growth, biomineralogy and shell structure, and environmental variation in ambient water $\delta^{18}O$.

Oxygen isotope analysis is among the most widely applied geochemical methods in the sclerochronological study of mollusk shells (Andrus 2011). The fundamental mechanism is that $\delta^{18}O$ shell varies with $\delta^{18}O$ water and ambient water temperature (Urey 1947) in most species (Andrus 2011), and $\delta^{18}O$ water often corresponds with changing precipitation (for example, Kennett and Culleton 2009) and other freshwater mixing such as river runoff (Andrus and Thompson 2011). The amplitude of the sinusoidal annual oxygen isotope profile depends on how different the summer and winter SSTs are: how distinctive the seasonality is in a given location. But not all mollusk shells are in constant equilibrium with seawater (for example, Fenger et al. 2007). In some instances $\delta^{18}O$ shell is influenced by various factors such as kinetic and vital effects, and $\delta^{18}O$ water is changed by freshwater mixing and various rates of evaporation (for example, Hallmann et al. 2009), which will cause inaccuracy in later interpretations if *these* factors are not considered.

Prior to the application of geochemical analysis, key points concerning shell growth must be addressed. Most shells lengthen and thicken in layers with variable timing depending on the species, biological processes, and/or local environmental conditions, so it is important to understand the timing of growth and growth cessations. Shell growth rate does not remain constant over ontogeny but often decreases with age (Schöne and Surge 2012). One well-established approach is the individual growth model (Bertalanffy 1934), which accounts for a systematic slowing of growth rate over ontogeny. Additionally, shells grow rapidly (producing wider growth increments) in favorable environments and grow slowly or even stop growing (producing growth lines or narrower growth increments) in unfavorable conditions (Andrus et al. 2008). Growth checks (lines that denote growth cessation) are caused by unfavorable conditions, such as temperature (Urban 1994), tidal variation (Andrus and Rich 2008; Hallmann et al. 2009), food availability (Sato 1997), pollution and water quality (Ravera et al. 2007), and interrupting weather events like storms (Hallmann et al. 2009; see Wei 2014 for more details).

Furthermore, since not all mollusks can serve as equally useful environmental and/or paleoclimate proxies, the possibility exists that *S. corrugata* might not be useful as a season of capture indicator. This project therefore is the first to collect and reveal the growth patterns, mineralogy, shell microstructure, and oxygen isotope profiles of *S. corrugata*, using sclerochronological and geochemical methods, for the purpose of demonstrating whether it is an applicable new proxy for paleoclimate and/or season of capture.

LOCAL CLIMATE

In general the study region is a coastal desert with an average air temperature of ~20°C (http://www.metoffice.gov.uk/media/pdf/c/r/Peru.pdf). The climate is extremely arid, with scarce rainfall in El Niño–free years. The seasonal SST shows as little as 3°–5°C variation throughout a typical year (Andrus et al. 2008; Urban 1994) with an average SST of 16.8°C (from Puerto Chicama, where the ancient samples were excavated, calculated from the local historical data: http://jisao.washington.edu/data/chicama_sst) and 18.7°C (Chimbote, where modern samples were derived and calculated from the database at http://www.seatemperature.org/south-america/peru/chimbote-october.htm). The assumption is that the seasonal amplitudes of the sinusoidal oxygen isotope profiles are limited.

The archaeological site of Huaca Prieta is 4–5 m above sea level and ~100 m away from the shoreline today, while this distance was as much as 20 km during the earliest occupation in the late Pleistocene (Dillehay et al. 2012a, 2012b). The main freshwater source is the comparatively small and braided Chicama River, which is ~3 km from the site today. The $\delta^{18}O$ water in this and similar rivers in the region is quite negative (often <−10‰ VSMOW, Andrus, unpublished data, 2015); freshwater mixing may influence shells living proximally to river mouths.

SEMELE CORRUGATA

S. corrugata (fig. A14.1a) is a common bivalve species distributed in coastal Ecuador, Peru, and Chile from ~2° S to ~45° S (average ~14° S: Urban 1994), but it may be misidentified due to its morphological similarity with *S. solida* in the southern portion of this range (Coan 1988; Urban 1994). The ancient sample suite might include more than one *S. solida*, which may have been treated as *S. corrugata* due to the unreliable differentiation between the species on the basis of the shells alone. The LT_{50} (lethal temperature for 50% of the population) of *S. corrugata* is 30.6°C (Urban 1994), and the species suffered significant mortality during the 1982–1983 El Niño, indicating that it is sensitive to warm water and may be climatologically useful and a potential environment proxy. This species grows in shallow marine environments and typically buries in sands from the intertidal zone to 9 m (5 m on average: Coan 1988; http://shell.sinica.edu.tw), which may indicate fine-scale growth patterns corresponding to the tidal variation.

METHODOLOGY

A sample of seven modern and two archaeological shells (table A14.1a) was used for SEM and isotope analyses. All modern and archaeological *S. corrugata* shells were collected by Dillehay. The total suite of samples contains 36 modern shells collected from the seawaters in Playa El Dorado, Chimbote, Peru (9° 10′ S, 78° 33′ W, 180 km southeast from Huaca Prieta), from August 2008 to July 2009, with three samples collected each month. The two archaeological shells were age-dated using associate terrestrial carbon sources. The size of each shell was determined by a digital caliper from umbo to edge along the axis of maximum extension. All modern samples were bisected along the shell length in prior analysis (fig. 14.1b), which decreased values of the shell size by 1–2 mm and produced gaps in imaging and in oxygen isotope sampling.

All described preparation and analysis took place at the University of Alabama Department of Geological Sciences laboratories.

XRD AND SEM ANALYSIS

A modern *S. corrugata* shell (sample name UA-1, collected from the Chicama Valley, Peru, on October 18, 2008) was used for XRD analysis. The specimen was ground to fine powder with an iron mortar and pestle. The sample material was loaded and packed into an XRD powder holder designed to promote random grain orientation. The sample was analyzed using a Brücker D8 X-ray diffractometer. Seven modern *S. corrugata* shells were prepared for SEM imaging and oxygen isotope analysis. Shells were bisected from the umbo to the ventral margin using a Hillquist SF-8 trim saw. One half of each shell was used for SEM analysis, while the other half was micromilled for oxygen isotope analysis (for details of specific treatment and analysis techniques, see Wei 2014).

MICROSAMPLING AND STABLE ISOTOPE ANALYSIS

The opposite halves of seven modern shells plus two ancient shells (epoxied and thin-sectioned in the same method with SEM analysis but without acid rinsing or gold coating) were micromilled using a Merchantek micromill for oxygen isotope analysis through the following procedures. An ontogenetic sequence of a 300–600 μm deep pits with a diameter of ~200 μm was drilled in the outer layer of each shell. Pits

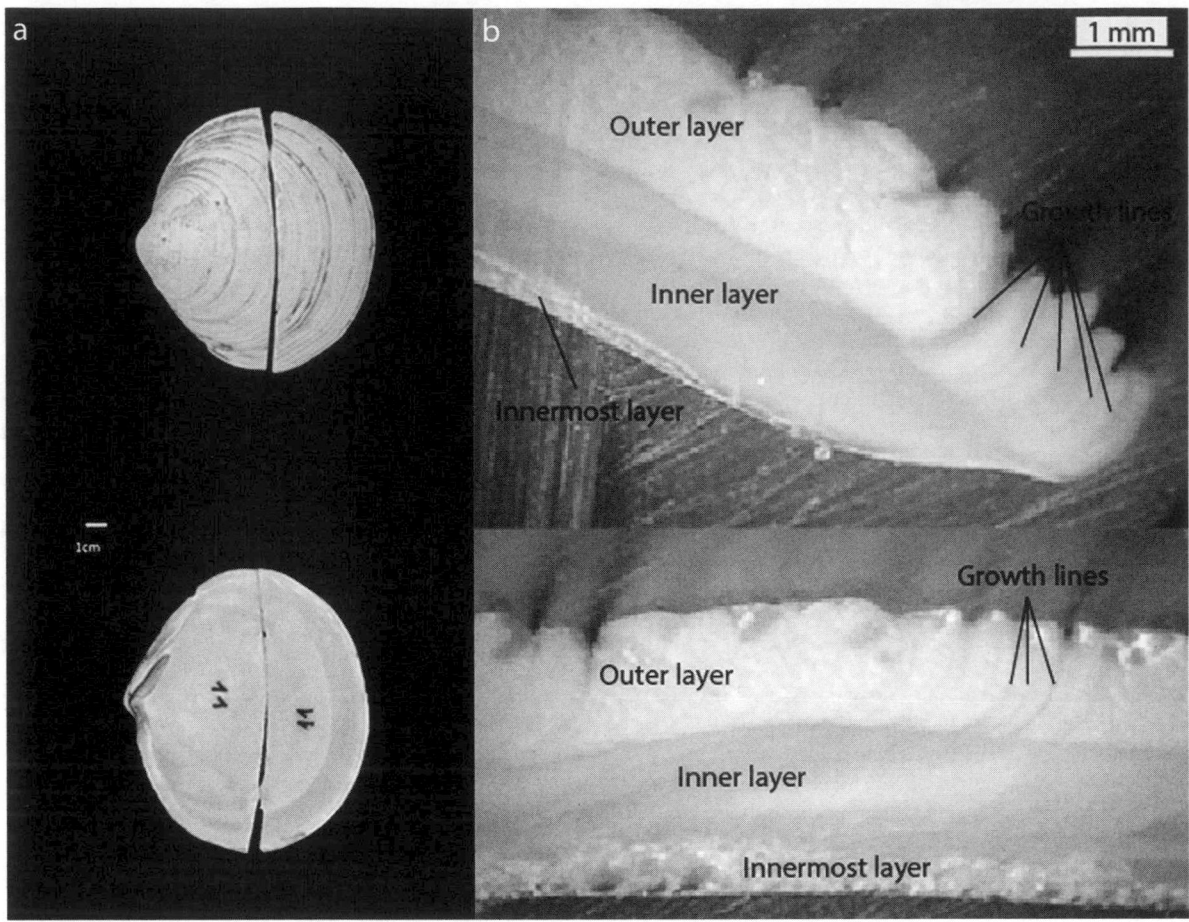

FIGURE A14.1. Various views of *Semele corrugata* shells: *a*, external and internal views of a modern *S. corrugata* shell collected from Chimbote, Peru, by Tom D. Dillehay on January 24, 2009; all modern samples were bisected along the shell length in prior analysis by other researchers; *b*, reflected light photomicrographs, showing three shell layers as well as growth increments and lines in outer shell layers that guided sampling for time-series oxygen isotope profiles.

Table A14.1. *Semele* sp. shells studied from Huaca Prieta

a. Measurements and information

	Sample name	Date collected	Height (mm)	Pigment present?	Distinct growth lines?	Calibrated ^{14}C age
Modern	Jan-4	24–Jan–2009	78.8	Yes	Yes	NA
	Feb-3	13–Feb–2009	76.2	Yes	Yes	NA
	Mar-13	13–Mar–2009	77.1	Yes	Yes	NA
	May-3	23–May–2009	58.4	No	No	NA
	Jul-11	11–Jul–2009	70.4	Yes	Yes	NA
	Sep-10	13–Sep–2008	73.6	Yes	Yes	NA
	Nov-6	12–Nov–2008	65.7	Yes	Yes	NA
Ancient	278	15–Jan–2008	24.1	No	yes	<~3705
	57	11–Jul–2007	43.4	No	No	~3933–3873

Table A14.1. Continued

b. Key $\delta^{18}O$ values of all studied shells

Shell	$\delta^{18}O$ ranges	$\delta^{18}O$ profile amplitude	$\delta^{18}O$ profile median	Mean $\delta^{18}O$
Jan-4	−1.1 to 0.4	1.5	−0.1	−0.1
Feb-3	−1.1 to 0.6	1.7	−0.1	−0.1
Mar-13	−1.3 to 0.4	1.7	0.0	−0.1
May-3	−1.2 to 0.7	1.9	0.2	0.2
Jul-11	−2.0 to 0.2	2.3	−0.7	−0.7
Sep-10	−0.7 to 0.3	1.0	−0.2	−0.2
Nov-6	−0.8 to 0.2	1.0	−0.2	−0.2
278	−0.2 to 0.7	0.9	0.2	0.2
57	−0.7 to 0.7	1.4	0.2	0.2

Data reported in parts per mil (‰) relative to VPDB.

c. Key $\delta^{13}C$ values of all studied shells

Shell	$\delta^{13}C$ range	$\delta^{13}C$ profile amplitude	$\delta^{13}C$ profile median	Mean $\delta^{13}C$
Jan-4	−1.2 to 0.3	1.5	0.0	0.0
Feb-3	−0.9 to −0.1	0.7	−0.5	−0.5
Mar-13	−0.7 to 0.4	1.0	0.0	−0.1
May-3	−0.6 to 0.2	0.8	−0.2	−0.2
Jul-11	−1.1 to 0.2	1.3	−0.4	−0.4
Sep-10	−1.4 to 0.3	1.7	0.0	−0.1
Nov-6	−1.7 to 0.4	2.0	0.0	−0.1
278	−1.1 to −0.1	1.0	−0.7	−0.6
57	−1.9 to 0.4	2.2	−0.1	0.0

Data reported in parts per mil (‰) relative to VPDB.

d. Results of predicting season of capture key $\delta^{13}C$ values of all studied shells

Shell	Date of capture	True season of capture	Predicted season of capture
Jan-4	24-Jan-2009	Spring	Spring
Feb-3	13-Feb-2009	Summer	Summer
Mar-13	13-Mar-2009	Summer	Winter
May-3	23-May-2009	Fall	Spring
Jul-11	11-Jul-2009	Fall	Fall
Sep-10	13-Sep-2008	Winter	Winter
Nov-4	12-Nov-2008	Spring	Summer

Data reported in parts per mil (‰) relative to VPDB.

were spaced equidistantly (~500–700 μm, depending on the individual shell). Modern shell Feb-3 was milled in transects instead of drilling spots for the purpose of comparing methods. An ontogenetic sequence of 300 μm deep transects with a diameter of ~200 μm was milled in the outer shell layer (each two transects were equally spaced, with a distance of ~660 μm). For both sampling methods ~50–100 μg of sample powder from each pit was collected into a 4.5 ml Labco exetainer (borosilicate glass vial) (for details on specific treatment and analysis techniques, see Wei 2014).

RESULTS

The height of modern shells is from 54 to 78.8 mm, with an average of 67.3 mm, while the average size of archaeological shells is 42.9 mm, measured from 24.1 to 63.4 mm. The height and physical characteristics of nine shells used for SEM and isotopic studies are listed in table A14.1a.

MINERALOGY AND MICROSTRUCTURE

XRD analysis indicates that *S. corrugata* is monomineralic aragonite to within the detection limits (~5%) of the technique. Cross-sectioned shells (fig. A14.1b) reveal three distinct layers, defined as the outer, inner, and innermost layer. The outer layer is white in modern shells and becomes thinner near the umbo; the ancient shells have darker outer layer colors. A yellow-orange pigment is present in most inner layers of modern *S. corrugata*, while no inner layers of ancient shells display this pigment. The white innermost layer is present in only parts of the internal shell surface (not consistently distributed along ontogeny), with a limited width and more coarse-grained texture (fig. A14.1b).

SEM images revealed the microstructure of each layer (figs. A14.2–A14.4). There are several common aragonitic crystal habits in bivalve mollusk shells, including aragonite prismatic, nacreous, composite prismatic, crossed lamellar, and homogeneous structure with limited combinations (Kobayashi and Samata 2006). The SEM images indicated the *S. corrugata*'s shell microstructure is composed (from outer to innermost layer) of composite prismatic structure, crossed lamellar structure, and complex crossed lamellar structure.

STABLE ISOTOPE ANALYSIS

The stable isotope profiles of the seven modern and two ancient shells are plotted in figure A14.5, with statistical summaries in tables A14.1b–d (for full data see Wei 2014). The average $\delta^{18}O$ of ancient samples 278 and 57 are both 0.2‰, and average $\delta^{13}C$ values are −0.6‰ and 0.0‰, respectively. The average $\delta^{18}O$ values for modern shells are −0.1‰ for Jan-4, Feb-3, and Mar-13; 0.2‰ for May-3, Sep-10, and Nov-6; and −0.7‰ for Jul-11. Average $\delta^{13}C$ values are more variable, which are 0.0‰ (Jan-4), −0.5‰ (Feb-3), −0.1‰ (Mar-13), −0.2‰ (May-3), −0.4‰ (Jul-11), −0.1‰ (Sep-10), and −0.1‰ (Nov-6). The ranges of $\delta^{18}O$ and $\delta^{13}C$ values of all shells are shown in table 14.1b and c. The $\delta^{18}O$ values

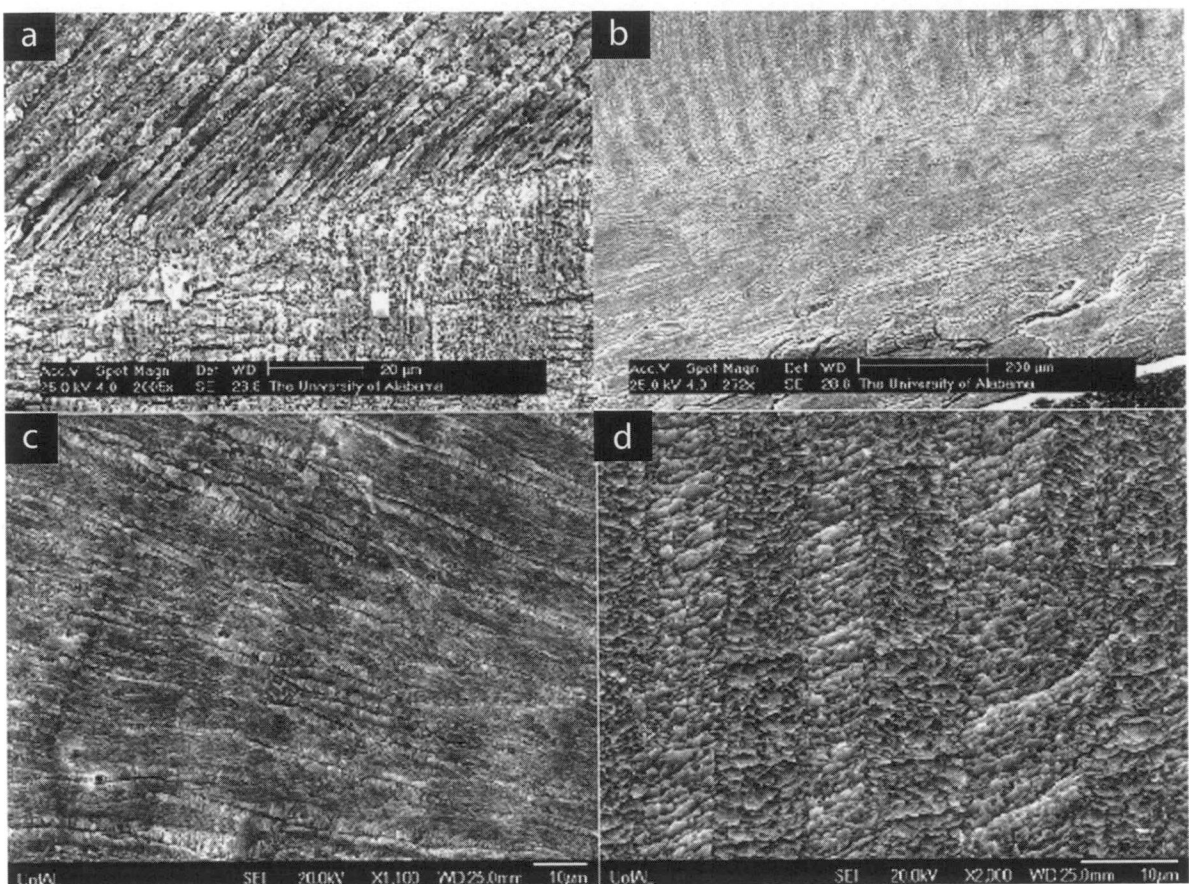

FIGURE A14.2. SEM images of the microstructure of *S. corrugata*: *a*, composite prismatic structure in outer layer and crossed lamellar structure in inner layer of sample Mar-13 (dashed line indicates the contact point between layers); *b*, crossed lamellar structure in inner layer and complex crossed lamellar structure in innermost layer of sample Jan-4 (dashed line suggests the contact point between the two layers); *c*, outer layer of composite prismatic structure of sample May-3; *d*, inner layer of crossed lamellar structure of sample May-3.

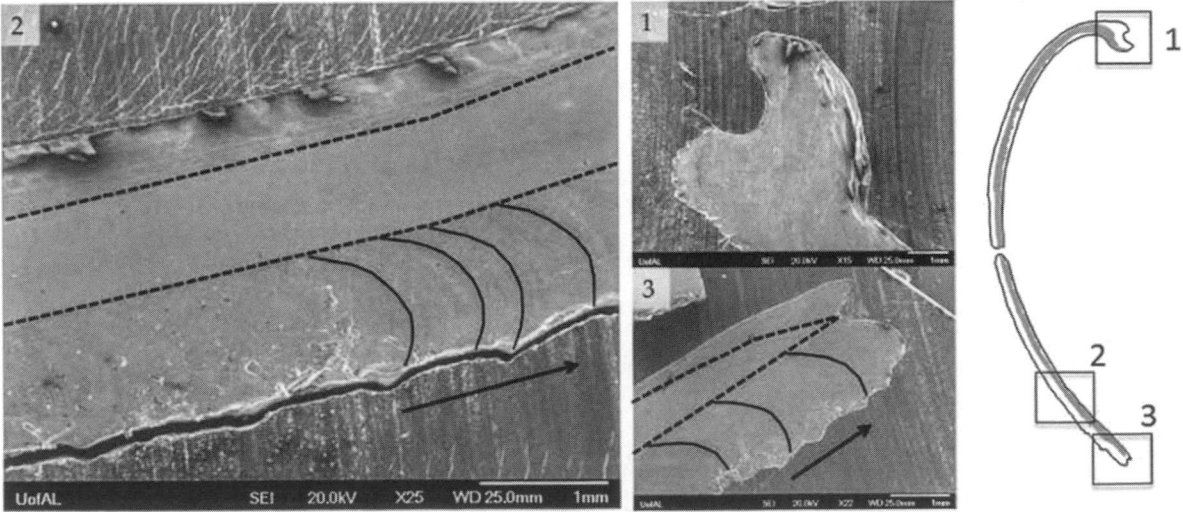

FIGURE A14.3. SEM images of a modern *S. corrugata* shell highlighting (*gray band*) three shell layers (1–3) as well as some growth increments and lines. Arrows indicate direction of growth.

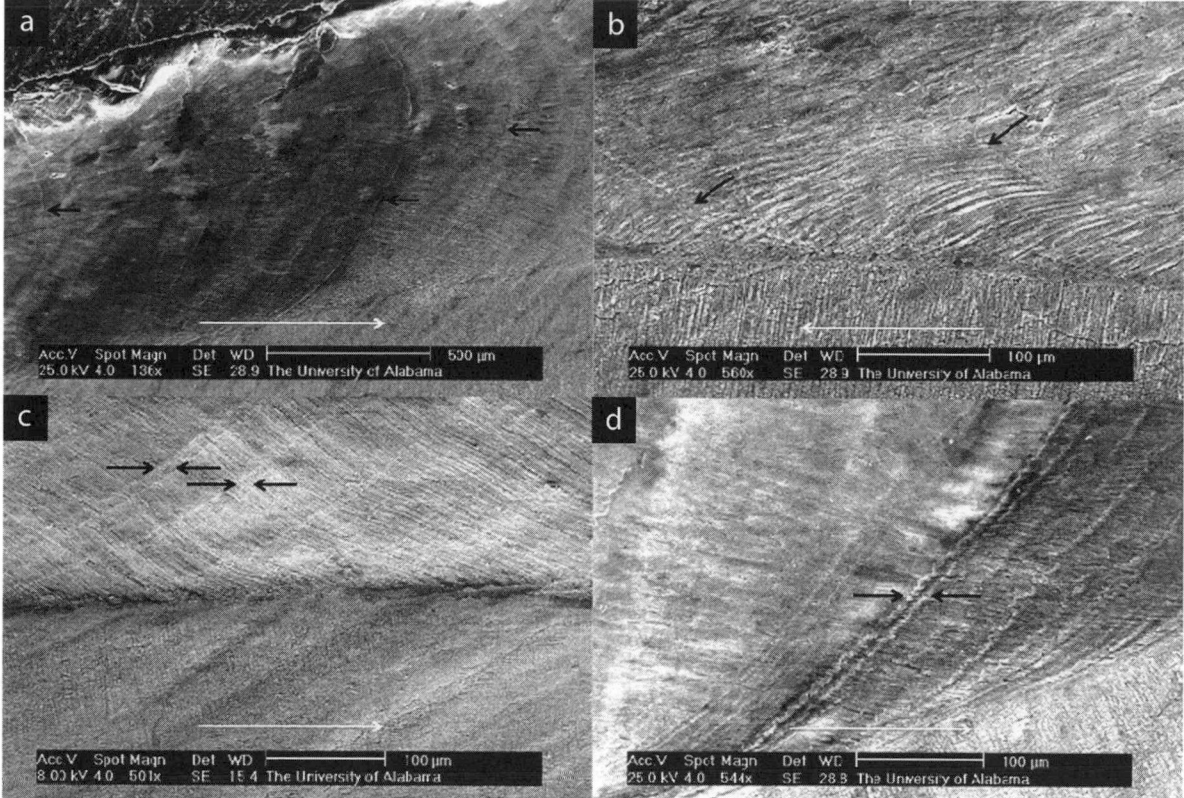

FIGURE A14.4. SEM images of different types of growth lines of *S. corrugata* with arrows pointing to distinct growth lines: *a–b*, single periodic growth checks of samples Jan-4 and Jul-1; *c–d*, paired periodic growth checks in samples May-3 and Jan-4.

of the sample closest to the edge of each modern shell are 0.1‰, 0.0‰, 0.1‰, −0.2‰, −0.8‰, −0.1‰, and −1.0‰ for the January to November sequence. None of the oxygen isotope profiles display a clear sinusoidal shape throughout ontogeny. Ancient shells have more positive average value in $\delta^{18}O$.

DISCUSSION

MINERALOGY AND MICROSTRUCTURE

Prior to the interpretation of oxygen isotope analysis, several key points are addressed here, including mineralogy and microstructure. Defining shell microstructures and different types of growth patterns (timing of shell growth) is useful to help explain the patterns of oxygen isotope profiles. The shell structure also influences practical methodology, in that growth structures were clearly delineated in the outer shell's layer, which usually represented shell lengthening. The inner shell layer contained visible growth that also suggests shell thickening, but the lines were tightly compacted and less readily visible. No growth lines were detected in the innermost layer at all.

A yellow-orange pigment is present on most modern shell interior surfaces; on some ontogenetically young modern shells (such as shell May-3) no pigment is present, which

may suggest that the inner shell layer pigment appears as the organism matures. Additionally, none of the ancient *S. corrugata* inner shell layers has the pigment, which may suggest that the inner shell layer pigment may disappear through digenetic alternation in archaeological sites.

A distinctive line (figs. A14.1b and A14.3) that separates the inner and outer shell layers is present on all specimens. SEM images revealed three layers with microstructure as composite prismatic structure, crossed lamellar structure, and complex crossed lamellar structure in the outer, inner, and innermost shell layers, respectively (fig. A14.2).

Different patterns of growth lines were observed on both the external surface and the cross-sectioned shell (figs. A14.3 and A14.4). The line spacing varies considerably, making it difficult to distinguish the causes of the growth checks (annual or subannual). At least four types of growth patterns were defined. (1) No apparent annual growth cessations occurred through ontogeny (May-3, fig. A14.5b). (2) Growth lines are present at lower $\delta^{18}O$ values, possibly indicating cessations due to warm SST (summer). (3) Growth lines are present at higher $\delta^{18}O$ values, suggesting that growth was interrupted by low SST (winter). (4) Other disruptive events appear noncyclical or subseasonal, perhaps caused by nontemperature driven events. Growth checks usually appeared more often and more closely spaced on ontogenetically older regions of shells. This might be due to the higher frequency of shell growth cessations on ontoge-

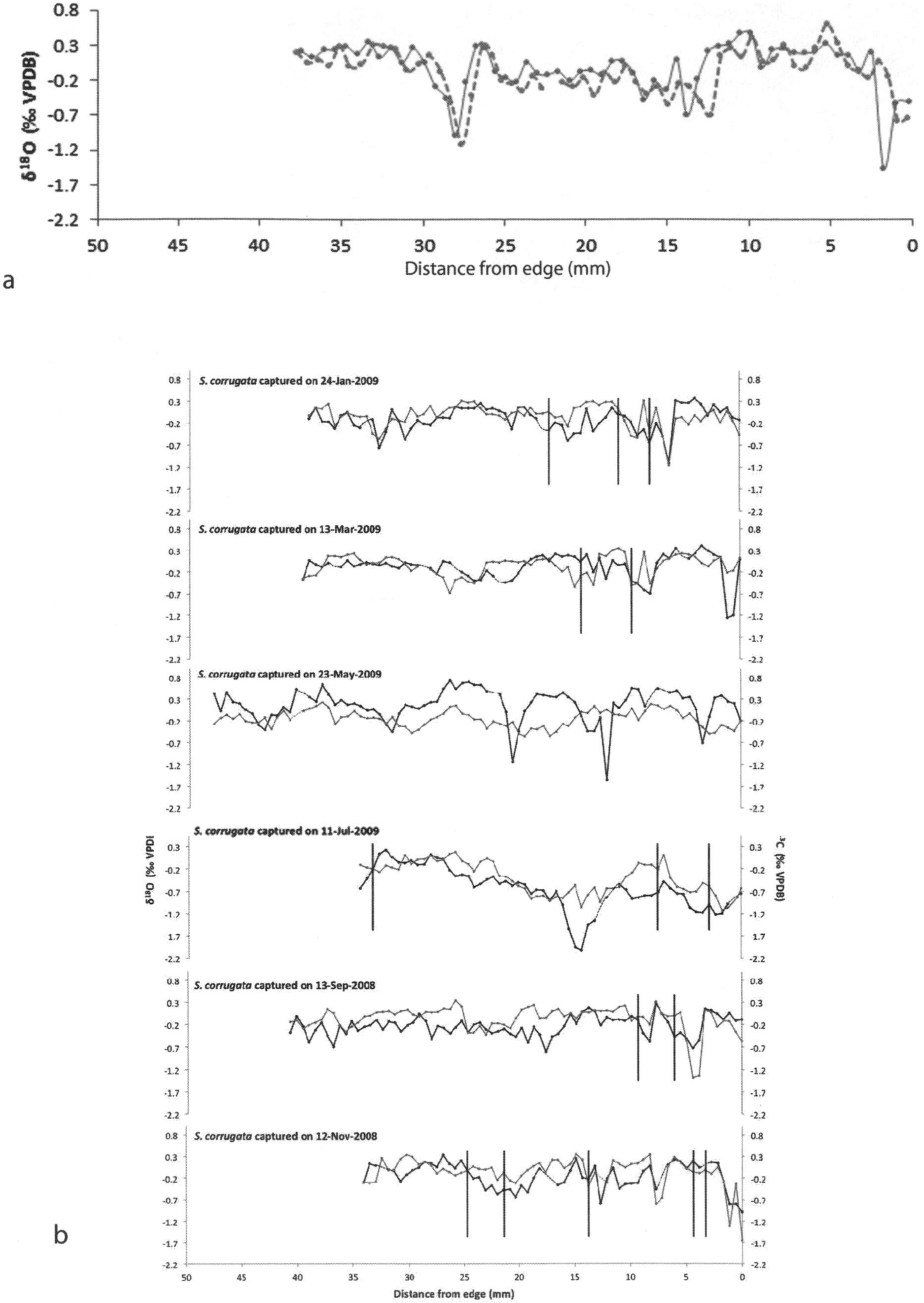

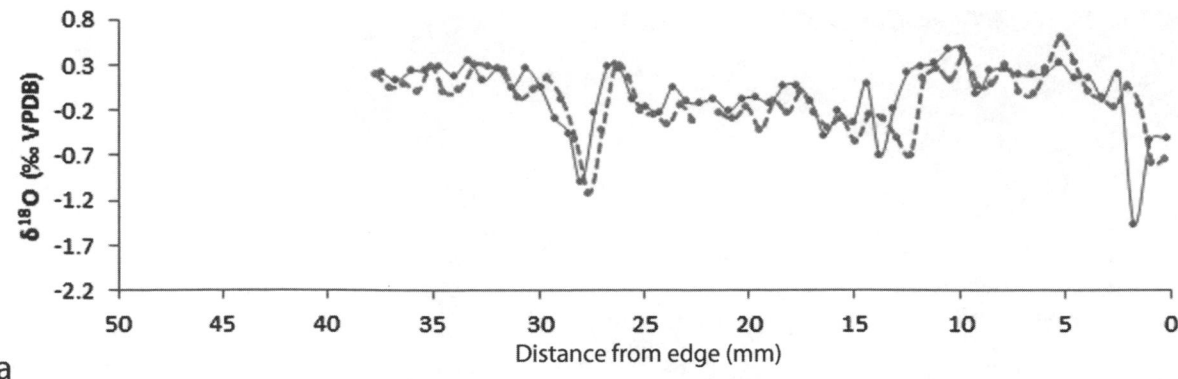

FIGURE A14.5. Comparative oxygen isotope results: *a*, comparison of oxygen isotope profile between milled transects sampling (*solid line*) and drilled spot sampling (*dashed line*) on Shell Feb-3; *b*, oxygen isotope and carbon isotope profiles of six modern shells: Jan-4, Mar-13, May-3, Jul-11, Sep-10, and Nov-6; vertical black lines indicate obvious (macroscopically visible) dark bands or lines (growth cessations) observed and recorded during microsampling (missing data are replaced by dashed lines); there are no distinct growth checks on sample May-3.

netically older shells and/or the fast growth rate during the younger ages and decreasing rate in later ontogeny.

For a better understanding of the growth patterns, the observed growth lines are categorized as single periodic growth lines, paired periodic growth lines, and interrupting growth lines.

Single periodic growth lines (figs. A14.4a–b) can be spaced narrowly (several μm apart) or widely (mm to cm apart), possibly representing tidal/daily growth and annual growth checks, respectively. Tidal/daily growth lines are narrow, difficult to observe with the unaided eye, and more distinct in the ontogenetically younger shell portions than in older shell material. Young clams' rate of shell growth appears to be as fast as 150 μm per day (fig. A14.4b) in some cases. In contrast, apparent annual growth lines are wide and more visible during microsampling. They usually are more abundant and closely spaced in the ontogenetically older shell, which can be explained by the decreasing shell growth with age. A shell without easily visible single periodic growth lines might indicate that it died at less than one year old or that the shell grows all year round without cessations corresponding with seasonal SST variation (possibly shell May-3).

Paired growth lines (figs. A14.4c–d) are two growth lines occurring with a distance of less than 10 μm in between, versus single growth lines. The distances between each vary significantly in the shells observed in this study. This type of growth pattern might demonstrate daily tidal variations for two possible reasons. (1) The region's tides are semidiurnal and partially mixed, meaning that tidal amplitude can vary significantly between oscillations. (2) This type of growth line alternates with the fine-scale single growth lines (assumed to be daily growth lines) in the ontogenetically younger parts of the shell. The irregular alternations of these two types of growth lines might be caused by the inconstant submonthly shell growth rate in the juvenile years, caused by many factors. For example, the irregular heights of daily tides can change the shell growth rate by bringing different amounts of food, making the shells grow faster in some tidal cycles than in others.

The interpretation of interrupting growth lines is largely complicated by mixing with periodic growth lines; therefore it is subjective to distinguish such lines based on visual data alone. Unlike periodic growth checks, this type is comparatively more unpredictable and aperiodic because it can be generated by various factors, such as food unavailability, diseases, freshwater mixing, including river runoff and more precipitation (for example, during El Niño episodes, but unlikely in this case), and so forth. The exact factors that generated the interrupting growth lines are not generally clear, so lines identified as neither single periodic or paired periodic growth lines were assumed to be interrupting growth lines.

OXYGEN ISOTOPE ANALYSIS

Only the outer and inner shell layers contain clear growth increments. The outer layer was chosen for micromill sampling because the growth increments were more clearly

visible and more fine growth lines were detected. The determination of shell growth patterns ensured that the microsampling method followed ontogeny and improved interpretations of the resulting oxygen isotope profiles.

The δ^{18}O profiles are not continuous and do not include the entire growth history of the shell. Incomplete sampling has two causes. (1) The bisection of each modern shell along the shell length during prior research caused one to two samples to be lost in between and produced gaps in oxygen isotope profiles. (2) The width of the outer shell layer decreases nearer the umbo, making it more difficult to drill, so sampling could not take place in the ontogenetically youngest portions of the shells.

Seasonality Proxy Assessment: No absolute SST could be reconstructed for a quantitative assessment of whether the shell δ^{18}O profiles accurately represent seasonality due to the lack of δ^{18}O water and SST data collected with shells. Qualitatively analyzing the amplitudes and the shapes in oxygen isotope profiles, however, permits assessment of potential seasonality proxy utility. Sinusoidal curves in δ^{18}O values in between two annual growth lines were expected to indicate seasonality. Assuming that δ^{18}O water remains constant, every 1‰ shift in δ^{18}O shell indicates ~4.3°C of SST variations (Epstein et al. 1953; Grossman and Ku 1986; and others). The local annual SST range is 5.7°C (for details see Wei 2014). Therefore we would expect one year of continuous shell growth to contain a sinusoidal δ^{18}O profile amplitude of ~1.3‰ Vienna Pee Dee Belemnite (VPDB) if using monthly time averaged δ^{18}O shell values. At least some of the δ^{18}O shell data points reported may represent less than one month of growth, however, which could increase annual amplitude. Furthermore, daily or submonthly environmental and growth pattern "noise" may also contribute to this observed difference. This may partially explain why the average amplitude of all tested modern shells is ~1.6‰ (averaged from each oxygen isotope profile amplitude listed in table A14.1b), ~0.3‰ higher than the expected value. Part of this difference may also result from the shell data being compared to average data for the region, not the specific period in which the shells grew.

Almost no sinusoidal curves are evident in the δ^{18}O profiles. They each differ from one another, although the shells all grew in the same area (figs. A14.5 and A14.6). This deviation from expected patterns and variation within the population may be caused by a combination of factors. (1) Decreasing growth rate with age might cause the drilled pits in later ontogeny to involve longer time-averaging of δ^{18}O, thus making the profiles insinusoidal and decreasing profile amplitudes. (2) Subseasonal environmental or biological disturbances might generate short-term growth rate changes and/or growth cessations that may change the oxygen isotope profile shapes. (3) The annual variation in SST is fairly narrow, so a comparatively small variation in short-term SST and/or δ^{18}O water can change the shape of the profile.

All shells were captured in the same general area and thus exposed to nearly identical variability of water temperature. But the δ^{18}O profiles appear noticeably different. Modern shells Mar-13 and Sep-10 (fig. A14.5b) have similar sizes (77.1 and 73.6 mm) and are most likely to be the

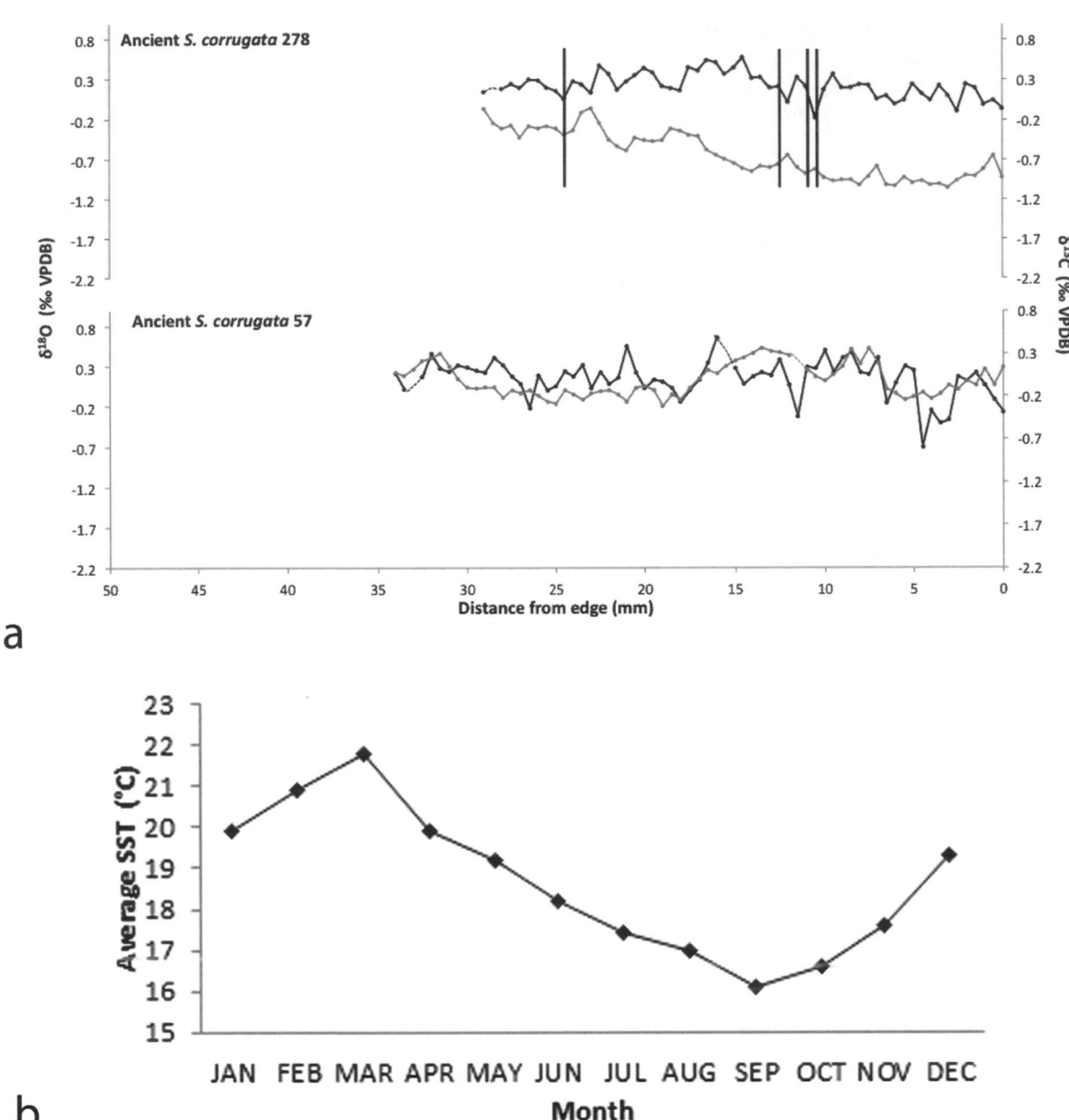

FIGURE A14.6. Oxygen and carbon isotope profiles: a, oxygen isotope and carbon isotope profiles of two archaeological shells 278 (a) and 57 (b), dated to ~3700 and ~3900 cal BP, respectively (estimated from data published in Dillehay et al. 2012b) (black vertical lines marked prominent growth checks on shell 278, while no visible growth lines were detected on shell 57); b, average monthly SST at Chimbote, Peru (calculated from data at http://ingrid.ldgo.columbia.edu).

same age and share similar growth rates. These two shells have the most similar $\delta^{18}O$ profiles. Both profiles display little $\delta^{18}O$ shell variability in earlier ontogeny, and both lack distinct growth checks with greater $\delta^{18}O$ amplitudes later in ontogeny. The $\delta^{18}O$ values measured between two large growth lines (assumed to be annual) show rough sinsusoidal curves, which suggest one year's carbonate deposition. The ranges of $\delta^{18}O$ shell in these two parts are 0.8‰ and 1.0‰, which reveal ~3.5°C and ~4.4°C SST differences. The pre-

dicted ranges of SST values are close to the local SST yearly range of 5.7°C. The differences between the predicted and observed data might be caused by growth due to temperature peaks beyond the species tolerance and time-averaging effects related to sampling strategy. These are the only two shells that seem to archive data similar to what may be expected on a seasonal timescale. The other modern shells' oxygen isotope profiles did not indicate close correspondences with the environment or one another.

Shell Jul-11 (fig. A14.5b) was the only modern sample in which the oxygen isotope profiles had a relatively clear seasonality curve in the earlier ontogeny. The oxygen isotope values range from −2.0 to 0.2, however, which corresponds to a predicted SST amplitude of ~9.7°C (assuming constant $\delta^{18}O$ water), which is almost twice the difference as the local SST range of 5.7°C over one year.

Another modern shell, May-3 (fig. A14.5b), has a relatively small size of 58.4 mm and is the only shell used in this research that does not have any distinct growth lines and thus was considered to be young (less than one year old). The $\delta^{18}O$ values ranged from −1.2 to 0.7‰ VPDB, suggesting a higher predicted SST amplitude of ~8.1°C.

The ancient shell 278, unlike most modern $\delta^{18}O$ shell values, has a notably smaller range of predicted SST of 3.8°C, as compared to the average annual SST range today in the Puerto Chicama area of 6.8°C. This is explained by the small shell size (24.1 mm), indicating that the shell was less than a year old before being captured and thus cannot record the whole annual SST range.

$\delta^{13}C$ shell profiles were plotted with $\delta^{18}O$ shell in figure A14.5 to display possible correlations. Although the relationship between $\delta^{13}C$ and $\delta^{18}O$ is inconsistent, in several instances correlations in negative excursions might suggest possible freshwater mixing (such as fig. A14.5b), because $\delta^{13}C$ in mollusk shell has been noted to be driven by changes in dissolved inorganic carbon $\delta^{13}C$ related to mixing of fresh and marine waters (Andrus and Rich 2008; McConnaughey and Gillikin 2008). The factors that control $\delta^{13}C$ shell are complex, and simple interpretations are not possible without greater knowledge of local environmental $\delta^{13}C$ values and metabolic contributions to shell $\delta^{13}C$ (McConnaughey and Gillikin 2008). The arid local conditions limit the possible input of freshwater to the open coastal habitats of these shells.

To summarize, one out of seven modern profiles shows a relatively clear sinusoidal curve that might indicate seasonality in the ontogenetically younger parts of the shell, while another two out of seven have sinusoidal curves in ontogenetically older parts. However, 57% of the modern profiles do not display clear evidence of seasonality curves, while 70% of the $\delta^{18}O$ shell profile amplitudes indicate a higher predicted SST compared to the Chimbote modern annual SST range of 5.7°C.

Collectively these observations indicate that modern *S. corrugata* $\delta^{18}O$ profiles as measured here cannot serve as a trustworthy seasonality proxy. This is likely due to growth rate variations, which in turn distort seasonal $\delta^{18}O$ cyclicity, coupled with a habitat in which short-term temperature and environmental variability mask the narrow annual SST amplitude.

The ranges of $\delta^{18}O$ values of archaeological *S. corrugata* shells 1278 and 57 (fig. A14.6a) are −0.2 to 0.7‰ VPDB and −0.7 to 0.7‰ VPDB, making the reconstructed SST ranges from 3.8°C and 5.8°C. Compared to the modern oxygen isotope profiles (fig. A14.5b), the ancient shells have more positive $\delta^{18}O$ values and relatively narrower amplitudes, which may suggest a cooler and/or more saline environment,

but no clear sinusoidal curves that might indicate seasonality were observed as in the modern shells. The small sample size and high apparent variability between modern contemporaneous shells limit the potential significance of these observations, so no trustworthy conclusions can be drawn.

Season of Capture: Qualitative tests were applied to predict season of capture from the trends of each oxygen isotope profile and compare to the capture date of each shell. Due to the inverse relationship between $\delta^{18}O$ shell and SST values (for example, the equation in Grossman and Ku 1986), season of capture can be predicted from the oxygen isotope profiles. For instance, the average monthly SST plots in figure A14.6b show that March has the highest average SST, which indicates summer peak temperatures that should result in the most negative $\delta^{18}O$ shell if the species is a valid season of capture proxy data source. Similarly, September, which has the lowest average SST, indicating the winter temperature minimum, should result in the most positive $\delta^{18}O$ shell (see Andrus and Crowe 2008 for more details).

Season of capture is predicted qualitatively from each modern shell's oxygen isotope profile. However, only 57% of the modern shells yielded the accurate season of capture (table A14.1d). A likely explanation for this high failure rate might be the lack of clear sinusoidal seasonality curves. Additionally, ontogenetically older shells grow more slowly and appear to undergo more growth cessations than younger shells, which may cause the discrepancy of the predicted and accurate season of capture. Consequently, younger shells with known ages are needed to better define this season of capture, but *S. corrugata* cannot be reliably used in season of capture studies under the current data.

CONCLUSIONS

1. *S. corrugata* is composed only of aragonite. The pigment present on most of the modern inner shells does not indicate variation in its mineralogy.
2. *S. corrugata* has three shell layers. The growth increments and lines are most clearly expressed on the outer layer, though present in the inner layer. The innermost shell layer is not present throughout the entire ontogeny like the other two layers and is relatively thin.
3. The microstructure patterns of the outer, inner, and innermost layers are defined as composite prismatic, crossed lamellar, and complex crossed lamellar, respectively.
4. Seasonality curves are not clearly revealed on the $\delta^{18}O$ profiles of most modern shells, possibly obscured by sub-monthly/aperiodic interrupting events and growth evident in growth lines.
5. $\delta^{18}O$ values in *S. corrugata* cannot be confidently applied as a season of capture proxy. Ontogenetically younger shells may contain more reliable seasonal $\delta^{18}O$ variations.
6. More accurate assessment of this shell's utility as a season of capture proxy will require in situ monitoring of time series SST and $\delta^{18}O$ water data from the location where the shells were captured.

ACKNOWLEDGMENTS

We thank Tom Dillehay for funding the project and providing samples. Invaluable assistance was provided by Joe Lambert and Paul Aharon of the Alabama Stable Isotope Laboratory, Rob Holler, Johnny Goodwin, and Rich Martens at the Alabama Central Analytical Facility, and Jim Donahoe at the Alabama X-ray diffraction laboratory.

GEOPHYSICAL PROSPECTION AT HUACA PRIETA AND PAREDONES

Phillip Mink

INTRODUCTION

In 2009 a geophysical survey of portions of Huaca Prieta and Paredones was completed for the purpose of identifying subterranean Preceramic domestic deposits in off-mound areas and below-ground chamber tombs on the mounds. Magnetometry and electrical resistance were the techniques applied. "Magnetometry" is a common term for a set of geophysical techniques used to measure slight variations in the earth's magnetic field. Magnetometry can either be passive and measure changes in the earth's magnetic gradient across a landscape (fluxgate gradiometer) or active and induce an electromagnetic current into the matrix to measure its potential to become magnetized (magnetic susceptibility). A fluxgate gradiometer was used to measure magnetic field variations in this study.

Interpreting magnetic data begins by identifying anomalies, which may have high and low magnetic gradient values (Bevan 1998: 23). Anomalies with strong narrowly spaced dipoles, or strong monopoles, are usually produced by ferrous material. The depth below surface of a magnetic gradient target is hard to discern from magnetic gradient data. In some cases a half-width rule can be used to estimate the depth of an anomaly. This rule depends on the drop-off of readings over the anomaly and assumes the buried material relating to the anomaly is simple and regular in shape (Bevan 1998: 25).

Electrical resistance survey works on the principle that anomalies beneath the ground can be detected by differences in their resistance to the flow of an electrical current (Clark 2003). These surveys measure the distortion of an induced electrical field caused by a subsurface phenomenon. If the sediments are completely uniform, there is no contrast in the electrical data and the resulting map will be featureless. When the archaeological or geological feature differs from sediments in various properties, however, then the induced electrical field is no longer uniform and the resistance either increases or decreases. Differences in the electrical properties or contrast combined with the size and depth of archaeological features produce a record that can be mapped and interpreted (Somers 1998).

Resistance to the flow of electrical current in sediments and soils depends on several variables, including soil moisture, soluble salts (mobile ions), soil permeability, and temperature (Gaffney and Gater 2004). There is rarely a one-to-one correspondence between an individual variable and

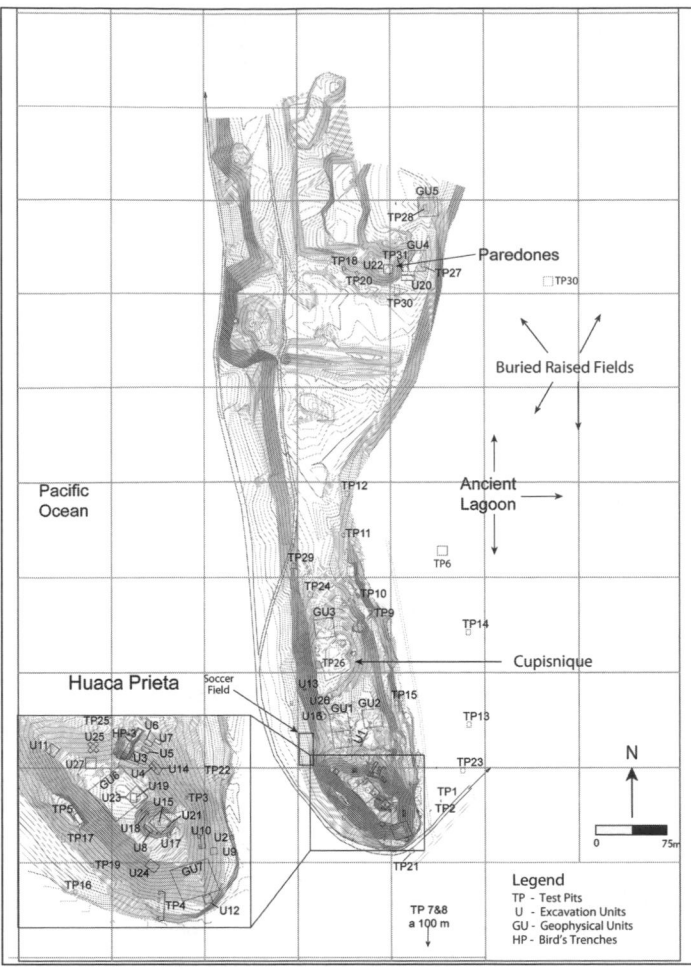

FIGURE A15.1. Location of the fifteen geophysical survey units throughout the El Brujo Archaeological Complex.

vals. The magnetic gradiometer survey was conducted with a GeoScan Research FM 256 fluxgate gradiometer to a depth of 50 cm to 1 m. The FM256 is capable of detecting anomalies up to 1 m below the surface (features that experience intense heating, such as kilns, may be detected up to a depth of 3 m) (Geoscan Research 2006). Data were collected using the zigzag method on 50 cm transects with 1 m intervals and a sample interval of 12.5 cm. Following collection, the data were downloaded to a computer using the Geoplot 3.0 software that presents the quantified data as a grayscale image.

The data were initially processed in the field using interpolation and general filters and then later more fully processed at the University of Kentucky. The standard electrical resistance processing consisted of despiking the data if any very high or low single points of data were recorded, running a low pass filter employing Gaussian weighting and a 2 by 2 pixel window, and finally running both a Sin x/y and linear interpolations in both the x and y directions. The standard magnetic gradiometer processing for these data consisted of running a zero-mean traverse and then both Sin x/y and linear interpolations of the data in both the x and y directions.

RESULTS

The geophysical prospection of the fifteen grids provided a large sample of data to employ in the testing strategies of the site. The Geophysical Units (GU) that provided the most intriguing data were GU-1, GU-4, GU-5, and GU-6, all of which had anomalies that were tested by excavation and dated to Phase IV and V contexts. While the other geophysical survey units did contain anomalies, it was unclear whether they were natural or cultural in origin.

GU–1

Figure A15.2 illustrates the results of the electrical resistance survey of Geophysical Unit-1, a 40 by 20 m survey block, collected to a depth of 50 cm below the surface. The area is located several meters north of Huaca Prieta, between it and another small mound. The low area between these mounds was hypothesized to contain off-mound habitation areas, and the geophysical grids were placed over recent excavation units (Unit-1). A series of anomalies (represented by darker spots) occur on the western edge of the grid near the excavation units. The size, shape, and patterning of these anomalies as well as their location in close proximity to excavated habitation remains (Unit-1) hint that they are likely also habitation remains such as structures. Excavation of a small test pit (TP-26) within these anomalies (fig. A15.3) recovered dark ash and beige-yellow mortar, compacted fill, and possible foundation rocks that together indicate a possible off-mound structure.

GU–4

Figure A15.4 illustrates the results of an electrical resistance and magnetic gradiometer survey of Geophysical Unit 4, two adjacent 20 by 20 m survey blocks. The area is located

the resultant resistance data. On the contrary, these variables show wide spatial variation, depending on environmental conditions (Clark 2003).

METHODOLOGY

A total of fifteen 20 by 20 m grids were examined with both electrical resistance and magnetic gradiometry (fig. A15.1). The geophysics grids were placed on or near features dating to the Preceramic period. The features chosen to investigate are diverse and include both the top of the Huaca Prieta mound and its sloping south face as well as a number of other mounds and off-mound areas thought to have vestiges of habitation.

A GeoScan RM15-D resistance meter configured using the MPX15 multiplexer with a single twin array on a 1 m beam was used to complete the resistance survey. The depth below surface at which the resistance meter collects data is proportionate to the distance between the probes, so a 1 m beam was chosen to achieve this depth. Data were collected using the zigzag method on 1 m transects with 1 m inter-

Electrical Resistance

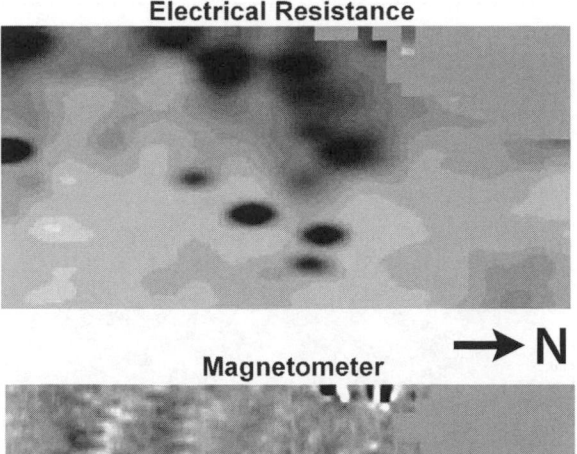

Magnetometer

→ N

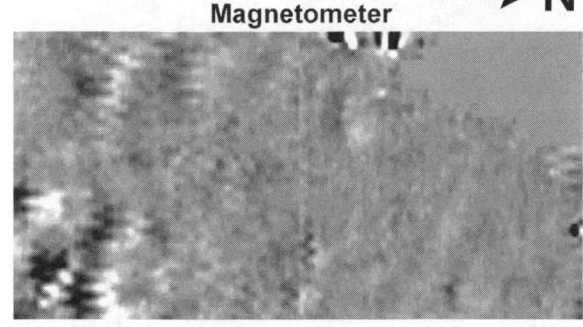

FIGURE A15.2. Results of electrical resistance and magnetometer surveys of Geophysical Unit 1, Unit 26.

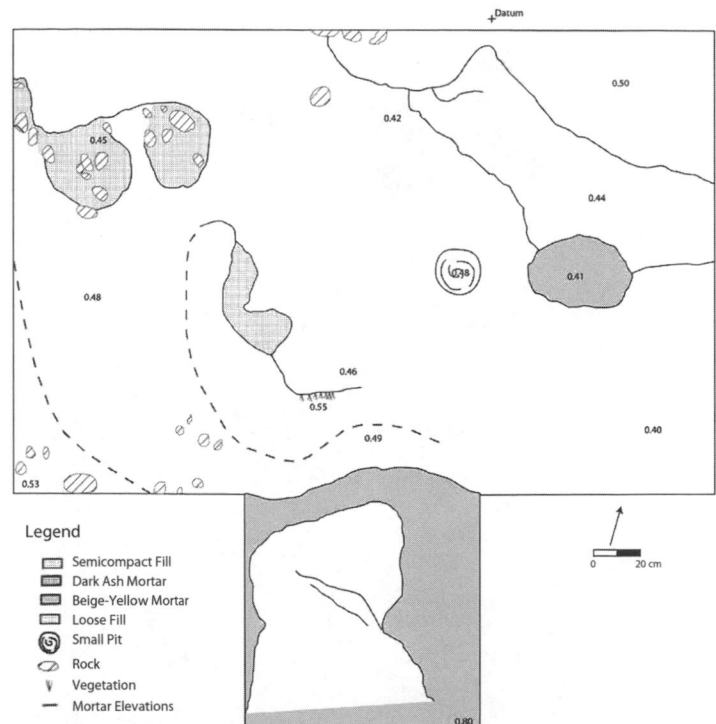

Legend

- Semicompact Fill
- Dark Ash Mortar
- Beige-Yellow Mortar
- Loose Fill
- Small Pit
- Rock
- Vegetation
- Mortar Elevations

FIGURE A15.3. Results of the excavation of Test Pit 26.

approximately 0.6 km north of Huaca Prieta and adjacent to the Paredones mound, where two large excavation units (Unit 20 and Unit 22) were investigated. Figure A15.3 illustrates the results of the first 20 by 20 m survey block. An anomaly in the northeastern/north-central portions of both the electrical resistance and magnetometer results is intriguing. An adjacent 20 by 20 m survey block was later investigated with both techniques to determine if the anomalies continued. The southwestern and central western portions of the grids contain continuations of the anomalies found in the original survey. It was hypothesized that this anomaly was a feature associated with off-mound habitation. A test pit (TP-27) excavated within the anomaly confirmed this hypothesis and recovered dark burned soil that was anthropogenic.

GU–5

Figure A15.5a–b illustrates the results of an electrical resistance and magnetic survey of Geophysical Unit 5, a 20 by 20 m survey block. The area is located several meters northwest of Geophysical Unit 4 and encompasses most of a small mound approximately 25 m in diameter. Two distinct anomalies occur in the northwest portion of both the resistance and magnetic gradiometer datasets (blocks indicate that data were not collected due to the presence of looter holes). The shape and depth of these anomalies indicate a possible habitation feature, and the large size of these anomalies is likely due to overlap of two separate features. A small test pit (TP-28) was excavated into the anomaly and recovered dark burned soil of an anthropogenic origin that is probable evidence of a habitation feature.

→ N

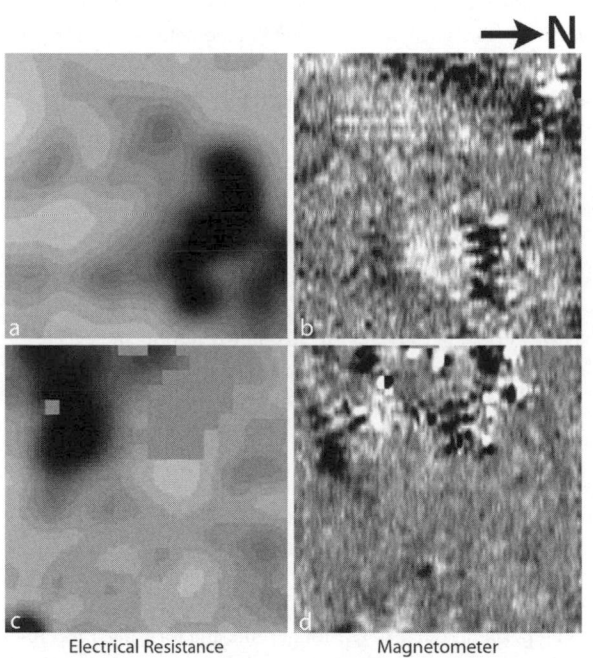

Electrical Resistance   Magnetometer

FIGURE A15.4. Results of electrical resistance (a) and magnetic gradiometer (b) survey of first grid at Geophysical Unit 4; results of electrical resistance (c) and magnetic gradiometer survey (d) of additional grid at Geophysical Unit 4.

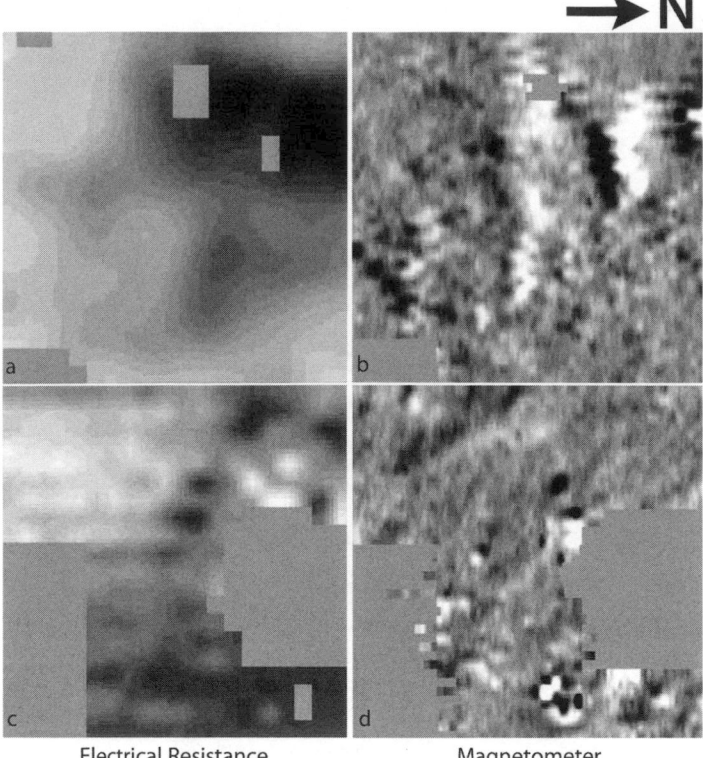

→ **N**

Electrical Resistance   Magnetometer

FIGURE A15.5. Results of Geophysical Survey Investigation studies: *a*, results of electrical resistance and magnetic gradiometer survey; *b*, grid at Geophysical Unit 5; *c*, magnetic gradiometer survey and results of electrical resistance; *d*, grid at Geophysical Unit 6.

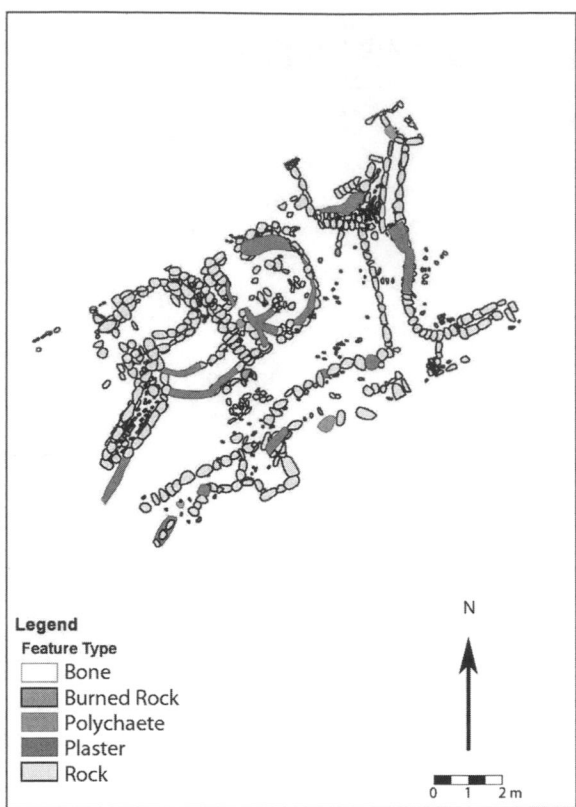

Legend
Feature Type
☐ Bone
▨ Burned Rock
▨ Polychaete
▨ Plaster
▨ Rock

N

0   1   2 m

FIGURE A15.6. Results of the excavation of Unit 23, a structure on the top of Huaca Prieta.

GU-6

Figure A15.5c–d illustrates the results of an electrical resistance and magnetic survey of Geophysical Survey Unit 6, a 20 by 20 m survey block. The area is located on the top of Huaca Prieta between both current excavation and earlier pits dug by Bird. Current excavations are ongoing in the data blocks in the southeastern portion of the grid, while the data block on the north-central portion of the grid is where data were not collected due to the presence of both backdirt piles and the top of an earlier trench dug into the side of the mound by Bird. The most intriguing anomaly located in the electrical resistance data is a line of anomalies starting in the northwest corner of the grid and running to the center of the grid and a separate linear anomaly running perpendicular to the longer line and forming a rectangular anomaly. It was hypothesized that this was the location of a series of walls that extend from a stone wall found in a portion of this grid excavated prior to the geophysical survey. Several interesting anomalies occur in the magnetometer results. First, a linear anomaly that is adjacent to the anomaly in the electrical resistance data is associated with the same feature and is likely anthropogenic and probably a stone wall. There are also two clusters of anomalies on both

the southeast and southwest corners of the Bird trench. It is likely that these are some type of modern metal. Excavation of Unit 23 confirmed that these anomalies indeed were part of a wall (fig. A15.6). In fact, the anomalies were part of a series of chamber tombs located on top of the mound.

DISCUSSION

The application of geophysical survey at Huaca Prieta and Paredones area proved to be successful. Numerous anthropogenic variances were found, and testing of these anomalies determined that they were associated with habitation features. These techniques were successful in a variety of contexts, from the top of both the large mound and smaller mounds to off-mound locales. On top of Huaca Prieta both the electrical resistance and magnetic gradiometry surveys (GU-6) identified a series of walls that were part of a series of chamber tombs. In addition, both techniques were equally successful at locating habitation features on a smaller mound (GU-5). In off-mound locations (GU-1 and GU-4) the techniques were also productive in locating anthropogenic anomalies. In both locales test excavations uncovered evidence for likely off-mound habitation areas, which guided many of the test pits placed in the study area for identifying subterranean domestic deposits.

PRELIMINARY USE-WEAR STUDY OF STONE TOOLS

Tom D. Dillehay

INTRODUCTION

Lithic micro-use-wear analysis is the examination of surfaces on experimental and/or archaeological stone tools to determine tool use. It is primarily used to determine the functions of chipped stone tools (for example, Aoyama 2009; Keeley 1980; Lerner 2007). Analysis of use-wear patterning, including edge damage, polish formation, residues, and linear gouges (striations) on tool faces, is recognized as an essential component of any microscopic study (Dillehay 1997; Odell 2001). In Peru microwear investigations have largely been limited to the Preceramic period in areas along the coast (Dillehay and Rossen 2001).

The main objectives for use-wear analysis of stone tools from Huaca Prieta and Paredones were to identify the method of use and the worked material by selected tools and to compare the typological groups with the determined functional results (see chapter 11 for a description of the stone assemblage at Huaca Prieta and Paredones). Interpretation of the contact materials at these sites was based on the structure of polishes, striations, and edge damage and on comparison with the use-wear traces on experimental tools. The reliability of the method and my ability to interpret observed use-wear traces were confirmed by blind tests performed previously on similar raw materials from the north coast of Peru, using an extensive collection of 100 experimental tools (Dillehay 1997). In addition to these experiments, 30 additional experiments were done on plants, fish, shells, and clam meat from the study area for use as a blind test for further accuracy in identification. These experiments were arbitrarily distributed among the 6 use-actions in proportions unknown to me. Use-actions were correctly identified for 24 out of 30 tools. Table A16.1 shows the tools and use-wear examined in this study.

Although the numerical specifications of the amount of material-working implements observed in a given assemblage may reflect an average of several independent occupation episodes, this is a lesser problem with expedient unifacial stone tools (such as those from the study area) that are discarded after immediate use and where an abundance of raw material is readily available (as it is in the study area).

The use-wear analysis was done on 19 flaked expedient tools from the Huaca Prieta (dated ~12,000–7500 cal BP and ~6000–4500 cal BP) and Paredones (dated ~6500–4500 cal BP) lithic assemblage. The tools, including primarily basalt,

Table A16.1 Percentage distribution of worked material by specimen

Worked material	Total %
Hide	15
Soft/fresh plants	22
Fish or other marine tissue	27
Wood	2
Unspecific hard (wood or dry bone)	8
Unspecific medium hard (plants?)	6
Unsure	15
No traces	5

andesite, and secondarily quartz and quartzite, were selected based on context, size, the presence of flake scars that might indicate retouch or use-wear, and the edges or areas potentially used as a tool, with 5 tools representing the late Pleistocene to the middle Holocene periods.

USE-WEAR ANALYSIS

Microscopic analysis was conducted by using both bright and dark field illumination. Artifacts were not cleaned prior to analysis in order to avoid loss of residues. Once it was determined that there were no residues on the edges of tools, they were cleaned for further analysis. Identification of any residues to class or species level was based on observation of diagnostic anatomical features.

High magnification microscopy (100–1000×) formed the core of the combined residue and use-wear study, although initial macroscopic and low magnification (10–50×) inspection was undertaken to discern gross use-wear and residue deposits. All facets of each artifact were examined in incident (from above) white light using a Leitz microscope fitted with 10× magnification eyepieces, with 5×, 10×, and 20× objective lenses and with 50× to 1000× long working distance (LWD) objective lenses. This allowed a maximum resolution on the artifact's surface of ~1/1000 mm or ¹⁄₁₀₀₀. The microscope is also fitted with bright and dark field illumination, rotatable polarizing filters, and a movable (X-Y) stage. The majority of scanning was conducted using the 50× and 100× magnifications, with higher magnifications used whenever necessary to allow closer inspection of possible archaeological features. Transects were used to cover the complete artifact surface, not just suspected working edges, as residues may accumulate away from those areas of an artifact directly in contact with a worked material. In addition, several stones were sent to Dolores Piperno at the Smithsonian Institution Tropical Research Laboratory for cleaning and study of residues (see appendix 9).

In conclusion, the use-wear analysis added more details to our picture of daily life at the sites, but interpretation must be made responsibly. The method does not provide quick and secure answers to whatever questions were asked concerning the use of specific artifacts, but it is an approach founded on interpretation analogy and based on observations of the clusters of wear attributes that are considered to be relevant to functional inference.

USE-ACTIONS

Some of the common actions anticipated on the stone tools are:

Slicing: Use-wear is parallel to the working edge.
Incising: Use-wear is parallel to the working edge.
Whittling: Use-wear is perpendicular to the working edge.
Scraping: Use-wear is perpendicular to the working edge.
Planing: See scraping.
Boring: Use-wear is perpendicular to the long axis of the tool and confined to the tip.
Hafting: Hafting traces, with the sole exception of identifiable adhesives, are not recognized on the artifact surface but rather are deduced according to the observed traces that were not likely to be the result of the use or any other circumstances, such as manufacture or deposition within the site soil.

In some cases it was possible to recognize diagnostic elements of plant anatomy on tools, which allowed the identification of the origin of the residue. Most residues seen on tool surfaces, however, have no visible diagnostic anatomical features.

UNIFACIAL FLAKES: 17 SPECIMENS

Specimen: HP-1, Layer 13, Unit 9, Early Phase I: Aspect 1: This reveals a slight dull to semibright polish and diagonal to perpendicular tiny striations at the base of the distal end that suggest possible hafting polish. Aspect 2 is located along a sharp edge near the lateral edge. It shows parallel and diagonal striations and semibright polish and tiny (200 ×) step fractures, all of which are suggestive of either penetration upon impact into a target or slicing/cutting motion on fresh hide or meat. Aspect 3 shows semibright polish and tiny subparallel and diagonal striations and step fractures indicative of slicing and scraping (fig. A16.1a).

Specimen HP-2, Floor 3, Unit 16, Phase IV: Aspect 1: This reveals slight polish suggestive of wood or hard plant polish. Aspects 2, 3, and 4 along the sides show localized flat areas of bright to semibright polish and a few minor nicks and scratches. All of this evidence suggests one use episode on a target or no use, with the damage due to trampling or other taphonomic variables (fig. A16.1b).

Specimen HP-3, Layer 7c, Unit 2, Phase II: This is a flake fragment with dull, pitted polish along the distal area indica-

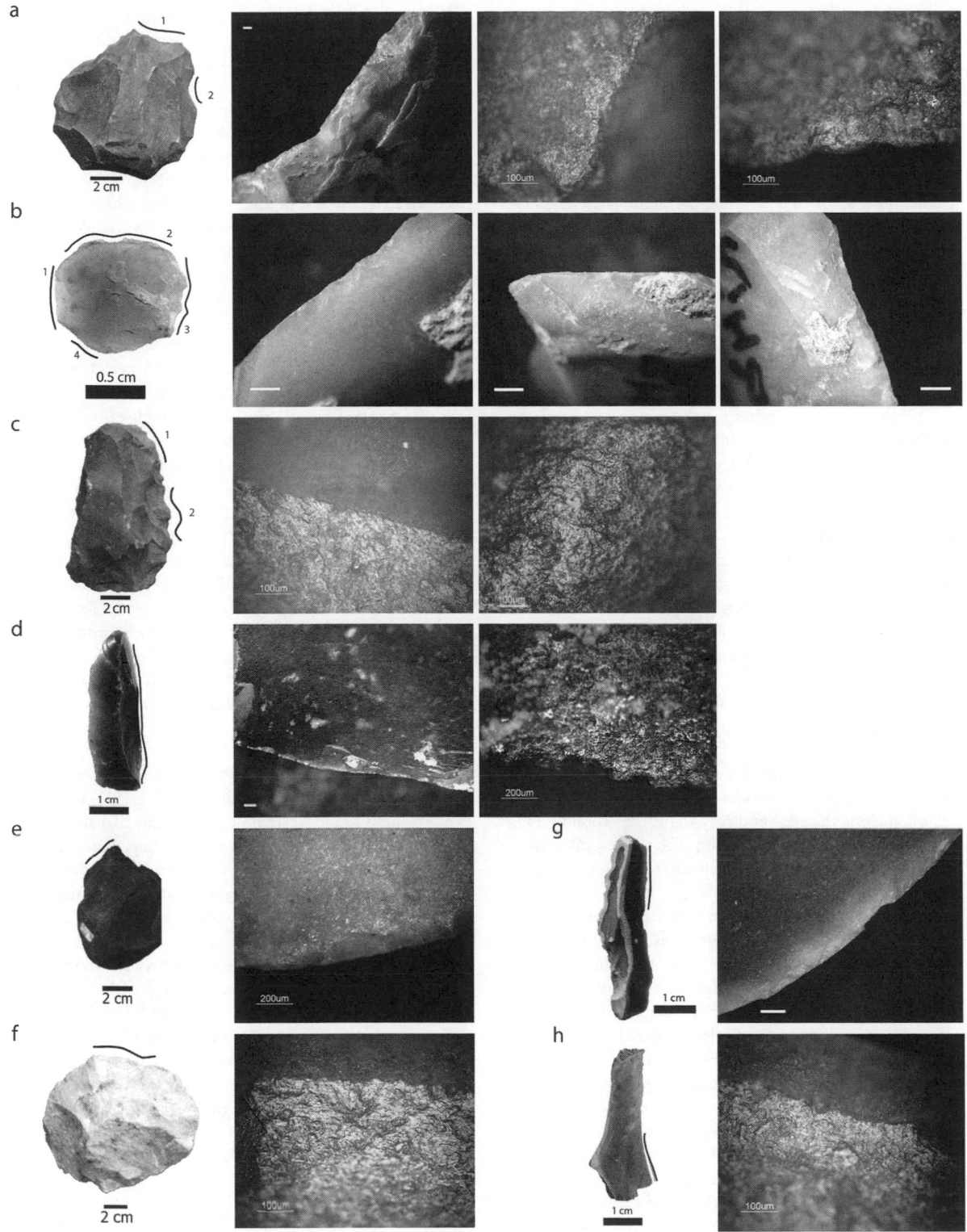

FIGURE A16.1. Microscopic shots of use-wear on various tool types from Huaca Prieta and Paredones: *a–h* represent various unifacial tools identified and discussed in the text.

tive of gouging and scraping (Aspect 1). A few nicks and polish spots could be seen along the edges at 100×–200× (Aspect 2), but they are so minor that they could be attributed to any cultural or natural cause (fig. A16.1c).

Specimen HP-4, House 3, Unit 16, Phase III: This flake shows spotty bright polish and minor scratches along a lateral edge indicative of use. One long aspect reveals discontinuous but extensive semibright to bright polish and subparallel nicks and striations along the edges. These suggest use as a cutting/slicing tool perhaps more than a scraping function. Use may have been related to cutting soft fresh plant material. There also are several scratches, nicks, and polish spots that are indeterminate in function (fig. A16.1d).

Specimen HP-5, Layer 2, Unit 21, Phase V: This flake reveals polish similar to the others along a distal edge. One aspect shows slight damage in the form of a light, dull polish and slight nicking at 100× and 250×, but there is no convincing evidence of use other than possibly being employed briefly as a slicing tool (fig. A16.1e).

Specimen HP-6, Layer 2, Unit 21, Phase V: A lateral aspect shows a few parallel streaks and dull polish, which also suggests slicing. The tips are intact and show no impact damage (fig. A16.1f).

Specimen HP-7, Floor 5, Unit 16, Phase II: This is a worked lateral edge of an elongated flake or microblade. The edge shows slight grinding and a dull polish. The edge also contains slight nicking, scarring, and polish but nothing determinate. This could have been used to slice dry plants (fig. A16.1g).

Specimen HP-9, Layer 5, Unit 2, Phase III: This tool is a quartz fragment with no apparent use polish or scarring, mainly because of the hardness of the material and the refraction of light from its surface, although the probable utilized edge (Aspect 1) has distinctive smears of light reflection along the edge and very slight edge rounding suggestive of a possible slicing motion. The worked material is indeterminate. Aspect 2 is slightly notched, but no clear use wear was observed.

Specimen HP-10, Layer 9, Unit 15, Early Phase I: This tool has two possible aspects. Aspect 1 is a straight beveled edge with slight polish and a few short striae running perpendicular to the edge. Slight edge rounding also appears, which is similar to patterns associated with working or adzing/scraping hard wood or plant material. Several small flake scars and tiny spurs were observed along a lower angle edge of Aspect 2. This edge has both subparallel and subperpendicular striae and dull polish on high points to suggest scraping or slicing dry hide or possibly bone.

Specimen HP-11, Floor 56, HP-3, Late Phase I: This tool is a flake with several aspects. All edges show semibright to dull polish, extensive edge rounding, and a few subparallel striae. This tool was interpreted to be primarily used to slice/cut hide or meat.

Specimen P-1, Floor 18, Unit 22, Phase II: This is a microblade too. There is a dull polish on a slightly worn lateral edge. The polish is discontinuous in some areas, with minor perpendicular and subparallel striae along the edge suggestive of cutting/slicing dried plants (fig. A16.1h).

Specimen P-2, Floor 21, Unit 22, Phase II: This is a small flake with light polish smear along the stem base (Aspect 1), which is possibly due to hafting, and small localities of streaked polish along Aspects 2 and 3. The use of this tool is indeterminate.

Specimen P-4, Floor 12, Unit 22, Phase III: This is an elongated flake with a notch near the proximal end and a long convex working edge extending from the notch to the distal tip. The notch (Aspect 1) reveals perpendicular and diagonal striae, both long and short, and semibright domed polish on the interior edge reminiscent of working wood or hard plants. The long convex edge shows intermittent polish streaks and edge rounding on the high or prominent points along the edge, suggesting some scraping but mostly cutting action.

Specimen P-5, Floor 18, Unit 22, Phase II: This tool also has a slight notch on the distal edge (Aspect 1) and an adjacent sharp edge with small flakes struck from the surface edge to form a semiserrated straight edge (Aspect 2). The raw material refracts light strongly, making it difficult to determine cultural polish. The notch (Aspect 1) showed no clear edge scarring or use polish. However, there was some polish and edge damage in the form of rounding and nicking along the serrated edge (Aspect 2), suggesting a slicing motion. The type of material worked is indeterminate.

Specimen P-6, Floor 9, Unit 22, Phase IV: This is a well-formed flake with a sharp distal edge (Aspect 1). This aspect has a few specks of residues that may be plant (or soft tissue?), with striations running parallel to the edge. Subparallel streaks of polish and a few striae as well as slight edge rounding are also observed on this edge. The tool is interpreted as a cutting/slicing edge for working soft, low silica plant material.

Specimen P-7, Layer 6b, Unit 20, Phase III: This is an elongated core flake with a small notch (Aspect 1) that exhibits slight to moderate polish, perpendicular striations, and edge rounding suggesting woodworking. Aspect 2 is a long rugged edge with large stepped fractures produced when manufactured. Edge rounding and a few polish points are present, but the action and material are indeterminate.

Specimen P-8, Floor 24, Unit 22, Phase II: This tool has a small notch on one edge (Aspect 1), which shows semibright polish on a few high points and slight edge rounding. This notch seems to have been used to work fresh wood.

Specimen P-9, Floor 14, Unit 22, Phase III: This tool has obvious edge scarring on both aspects. Both aspects are long continuous edges with pronounced edge rounding and extensive polish streaks roughly running parallel to the edges. This tool is interpreted as a general-purpose cutting/slicing tool, probably used on plants.

CHUNKS: 2 SPECIMENS

Specimen P-3, Floor 10, Unit 22, Phase III: This tool has a long-convex edge (Aspect 2) that is well worked and slightly retouched and a short-convex edge that is much steeper (70–80 degrees). A weakly developed polish, edge scarring, and slight rounding at 100× are visible along the interior spurred tips of Aspect 3. Aspect 2 shows more localized polish on the interior edge, which is semibright to bright and associated with minor perpendicular striae that are not well developed. On the basis of the weakly developed polish and edge scarring the tool is tentatively interpreted as an implement, which was probably used for working a hard siliceous plant, possibly wood. This tool seems to have been used for scraping and possibly adzing.

Specimen HP-8, Floor 26, Unit 22, Late Phase II: This is a large tool that has several seminotched or concave flake scars forming three long worked aspects (2–4). The edge was moderately rounded and displayed microscopic edge scarring and moderate polish on the inner and outer edges. Aspect 2 reveals similar but much less scarring and polish. Aspect 4 also reveals moderate to heavy polish and scarring and diagonal striae. Aspect 1 has extensive rounding that may be due to use, hafting, or some natural cause. Aspects 2–3 were probably related to processing some animal material, most likely fresh bone and hide, but the nature of this material was not clearly indicated by the use-wear. The function was recorded as scraping to indeterminate.

DISCUSSION

In this study flakes were the most plentiful tool category in the analyzed samples. More than 50% of them showed traces of use. Although the sample size is limited, the proportional frequency of working plants, relative to the other interpreted contact materials, suggests a change in use patterns when comparing early to middle Holocene materials, with more work with plants at all sites from Phase III to Phase V. Maize starch grains were recovered from the edge of one blade tool (Grobman et al. 2012; see chapter 10, appendix 7). Blades appear around 5000 cal BP at Paredones and are likely associated with increased crop production.

Of the artifacts analyzed, 11 possessed a combination of use-wear and residue traces. A further 20 artifacts possessed wear patterns that showed the use-action and hardness of the worked material but did not exhibit residues that would allow for more precise identification. The remaining artifacts did not show evidence of use-wear.

Plant working and/or woodworking were evident on several edges and surfaces. Use polish was generally well developed, and extensive edge scarring was not common. Exceptions were tools with semibright to bright polish streaks. However, plant tissue and fibers were not common residues distinctive of material worked. Any plant residues also may be fortuitous adherences. The most common function observed among the artifacts from Paredones was some form of plant or oily meat processing (fish or mammal), recovered in the premound late Pleistocene and early Holocene levels where many sea lion bones were recovered (see chapter 9). One activity identified was the cutting, slicing, and scraping of soft to moderately hard plant materials. Some of these tools may have been used to work soft and hard woods, but the low amount of edge scarring and poor use polish development made more precise determinations impossible. Other activities may have involved the scraping of fresh hide and bone and the cutting/slicing of meat. Several tools had moderately to heavily utilized edges, which were interpreted as used for woodworking or for working bone.

Clear residue and use-wear evidence for woodworking on two of the smaller flakes from Paredones (Specimens P-2 and P-6), each measuring less than 4 cm in maximum dimension, raises interesting interpretive questions. These artifacts are not large enough (and do not possess the requisite use-wear patterns) to have been used for chopping or large-scale curation (planing, adzing) of wooden objects. Instead they appear to have been used to carve or drill small portions of wood or gourd pieces, suggesting that they were used for incising decorations or other fine work. A tradition of craft activity in decorative gourd carving has been documented at Huaca Prieta and Paredones (see chapter 11).

Apart from plants, the other major finding was 3 tools with residues of bone/skin. There is no archaeological evidence for large animals other than sea lions, deer, and camelids. These tools were recovered from contexts dating to late Phase I at Paredones.

Contact with fish and bird bone is also likely. Shell residues also were observed, and bone carving may have occurred during prehistory. Except for a few small items such as possible shanks, shell tools did not call for meticulous shaping. Whittling down and carving bone into awls and needles, however, could have required the stone artifacts examined.

A few tools had multiple edges used for several tasks, such as plant working and hide manufacture. Unfortunately, the relationship between these different kinds of tasks cannot be determined. Several tools also may have been recycled, or the tasks may be related to a single complex activity. Several worked edges had clear evidence of use, but the material worked could not be determined with any degree of confidence.

A few edges were interpreted as having been used exclusively for butchering. Butchering tools were indicated mainly by heavy edge damage and dull polish. Quartz and quartzite would have been most efficient for these tasks. However, the quartz and quartz artifacts from sites rarely showed any distinct form of edge scarring or distributions of polishes. Bone working was interpreted as the primary function of 2 tools.

CONCLUSION

The small sample size of this study prevents any secure interpretation of activity areas across sites and through time. Many tools seemed to be used expediently; very little retouch and resharpening is evident on the stones. A few tools suggest multiple tasks. Alternatively, particular tasks may have involved manipulation of several materials. Based on this preliminary study, it is speculative to infer the importance of any one activity over another, because of the small sample size and the proportion of tools whose function could not be determined to material worked.

Several tasks were identified by the use-wear study. These were primarily plant cutting and scraping, skin scraping, and bone working. The actual tasks identified probably represent the range of simple domestic activities rather than a single complete task. The activities identified include plant processing, probably to extract starch, and simple butchering. The wood, skin, and bone working probably relate to maintenance of organic equipment such as spears, clothing, and animal gutting tools, respectively.

Finally, in addition to these 19 tools, 40 others from various contexts at both sites were also examined in a preliminary fashion. Although not reported here, the results were similar to those described above, suggesting that the collection studied here is fairly representative of the use-wear history of stone tools in the study area.

ESTIMATING HAPLOGROUP AFFILIATION THROUGH ANCIENT MTDNA ANALYSIS FROM THE HUACA PRIETA BURIALS

Tiffiny A. Tung, Jessica Blair, Marshal Summar, Raúl Tito, and Cecil Lewis

INTRODUCTION

A total of 21 dental samples from 21 individuals from Huaca Prieta (and Paredones) underwent ancient mtDNA analysis in an attempt to establish haplogroup affiliation and address questions about biological relatedness among the burial population. Dillehay's research team excavated 11 of the samples (10 from Huaca Prieta and 1 from Paredones), and another 10 samples from Huaca Prieta were obtained from Bird's collection at the American Museum of Natural History (AMNH) in New York City. Jessica Blair at the Vanderbilt University Medical Center and Center for Human Genetics and Raúl Tito at the University of Oklahoma Laboratory for Molecular Anthropology and Microbiome Research attempted to extract and amplify the ancient mtDNA from those samples. The process of analysis and the results are detailed below. Although our study did not result in any individuals being assigned to a Native American haplogroup, we present the phases of analysis and the specific mutations that were observed in particular samples.

CODING SYSTEM

The samples exported from Peru are referred to as HP1, HP2, HP3, and so forth; the samples from the AMNH are referred to as AMNH1, AMNH2, and so forth; and the single sample from Paredones is coded as PAR1 (see table A17.1).

In the section that provides specific information on amplification and sequencing, the coding system is as follows:

- The first portion is the sample ID (a numeral in front of letters indicates 2nd or 3rd extract);
- The 2nd portion is the fragment "chunk" (1st, 2nd, 3rd, 4th);
- The 3rd portion is the primer used for that specific fragment's data.

Example: 2HP3-1-15986 = 2nd extract of HP3, 1st fragment, primer 15986.

Table A17.1. Summary data on the Huaca Prieta mtDNA samples exported from Peru

Sample no.	Arch. code	Museum code	Tooth	Sex	Age (years)	Extraction 1
HP-1	Burial 1		Md RM2	F	Adult	failed
HP-2	Burial 1		Md RM2	M	35–45	failed
HP-3	Burial 3		Mx LM2	F	35–45	failed
HP-4			Mx RM1	?	12–15	failed
HP-5	Burial 2		Md RM3	F	50–60+	failed
HP-6	Burial 1		Mx RM2	F	Adult	failed
HP-7	Burial 6		Mx RM3	M	18–25	failed
HP-8	Burial 4		Mx RM2	?	3–5	failed
HP-9	Burial 1		Md RM1	?	6–10	failed
HP-11			Md RM1		7–8	amplified when incubated for longer time
PAR-1			Md RM 1 or 2			chelexed; failed
AMNH1	7-2-2	99.1/890	Mx RM2			failed
AMNH2	3-D3	99.1/896	Md RM3			failed
AMNH3	3-F	99.1/897	Mx LM3			chelexed; failed
AMNH4	3J	99.1/900	Mx LM3			chelexed; failed
AMNH5	3-0-3	99.1/901	Md LM2			chelexed; failed
AMNH6	3-0-2	99.1/902	Md RM3			chelexed; mutations at 16129A, 16169T, 16173T
AMNH7	3-0-1	99.1/903	Md RM3			chelexed; mutation at 16266T and 16223T
AMNH8	2-G1-2	99.1/906B	Md LM3			chelexed; failed
AMNH9	2-G2-4	99.1/908	Md RM3			chelexed; mutation at 16266T and 16129A.
AMNH10	3-T	99.1/904	Md RM2			chelexed; amplified

RESULTS

The preliminary ancient mtDNA testing of these samples shows that 62% of the samples that were tested (13 out of 21) have mtDNA, albeit in low counts and in low quality. Additional techniques to clean the samples and increase the quantity may result in more successful identification of haplogroups and sequence data, so that questions about biological affiliation among the individuals at Huaca Prieta can be addressed.

The initial attempt to obtain mtDNA from samples HP1 through HP9 yielded no results (fig. A17.1a).

The second attempt (fig. A17.1b) tested whether or not samples HP1–HP5 were inhibited (that is, whether some material in the sample such as metal ions was inhibiting the mtDNA from amplifying). Results showed that HP2 was indeed inhibited. This was demonstrated by combining HP2 with a well-preserved ancient sample with a known haplogroup (MC5, Malata Chullpa sample 5 from the site of Malata in southern Peru), and the HP2 sample did not

Sample no.	Extraction 2	Extraction 3	Unit	Floor	Layer	Pit	Wall
HP-1	chelexed; not Hg D; mutation at 16129A and 16294T				15	3	W
HP-2	chelexed; sample inhibited and contaminated; no data		3	7			
HP-3	chelexed; not Hg B	not Hg A, B, C, or D; mutations at 16311C and 16362C	16		5		
HP-4	chelexed; no data.		16		2		
HP-5	chelexed; not Hg A; mutations at 16362C, 16266T, 16129A, and 16080G		16		2		
HP-6	chelexed; mutation at 16129A; this is seen in Hg A5c, A7, A9; B4c1a1a, B5a2; C4a1; Z1, D2, D4a		10				
HP-7	chelexed; mutation at 16044C; possible contamination		16				
HP-8	chelexed; failed		16		2		
HP-9	chelexed; mutation at 16325C and 16223T	contamination from J. Blair	23		7		
HP-11	failed		16	NW muro	2		
PAR-1	chelexed; failed						
AMNH1	chelexed; mutations at 16295T and 16319A						
AMNH2	chelexed; mutation at 16111T						
AMNH3	chelexed; failed						
AMNH4	chelexed; mutation at 16223T						
AMNH5	chelexed; failed						
AMNH6							
AMNH7							
AMNH8	chelexed; failed						
AMNH9							
AMNH10	mutations at 16261T and 16304C						

amplify. There is no band in the gel in the right lane of HP2, thus confirming inhibition (fig. A17.1b). It is unknown what is inhibiting the mtDNA, but salt is a likely factor among other possible inhibitors, such as metal ions.

Chelex resin was then added to the samples to increase the likelihood of mtDNA amplification. Chelex resin "cleans" the sample; they are resin beads that remove inhibitory metal ions remaining in the DNA solution, while leaving the DNA intact so that amplification is possible. The addition of Chelex to each sample led to some promising results; faint bands appeared in lanes 2 and 3 (fig. A17.1c). Given the likelihood that these samples contained some mtDNA, they were sent to the Sequencing Core at the Vanderbilt University Medical Center for sequencing.

Although one of the tests on HP3 suggested that it had the 9-base pair deletion characteristic of Haplogroup (Hg) B (fig. A17.1a), the sequence data from HP3 did not show the 9-base pair deletion, suggesting that the individual does *not* belong to Hg B. Subsequent runs were unable to obtain data for any of the known Native American haplogroups

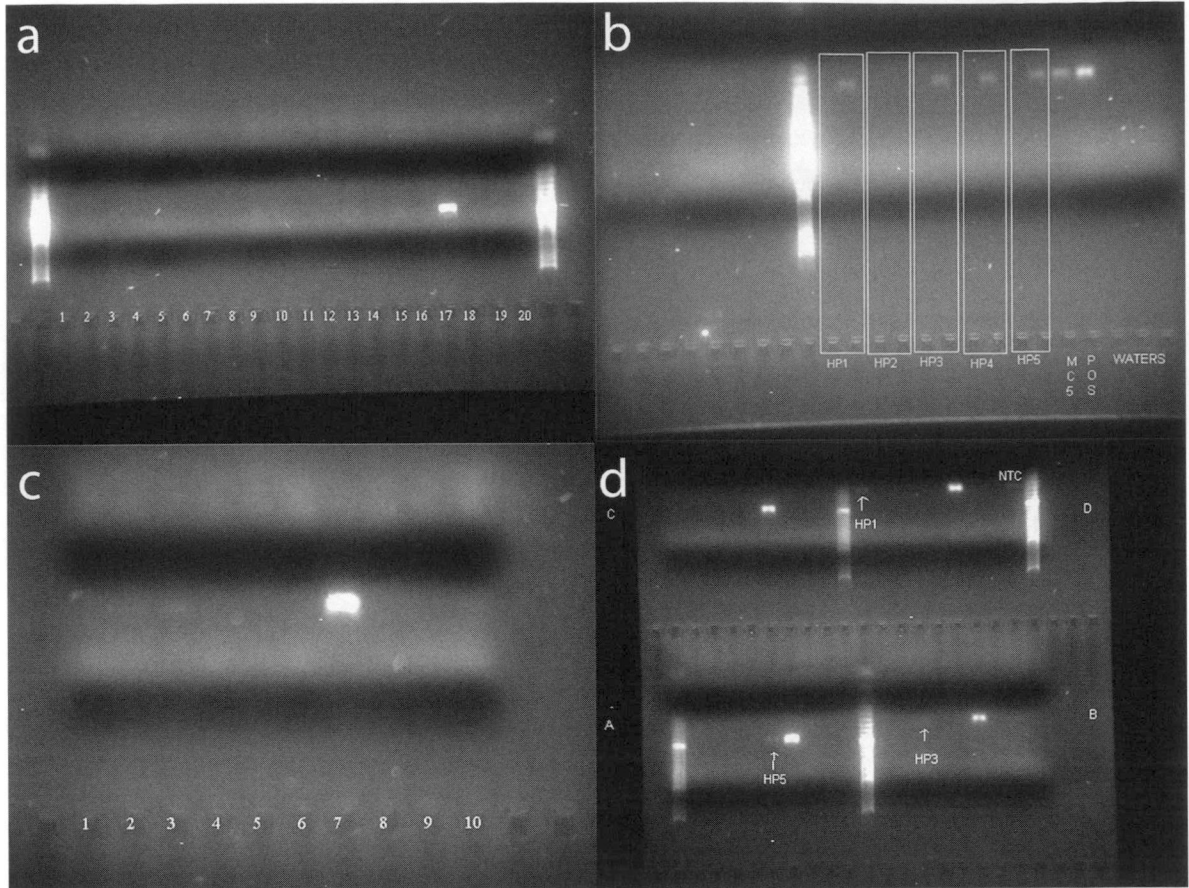

FIGURE A17.1. DNA results from Huaca Prieta tooth studies: *a*, initial attempt to obtain mtDNA from HP samples 1–9 (lanes 1–9) post–DNA extraction; the bright band is positive modern control (lane 17); no HP samples had any indication of amplification, nor did any negative controls (lanes 16, 18–20); *b*, inhibition testing for HP1–HP5; within each box, the left lane contains the HP sample only and the right lane contains the HP sample plus positive ancient DNA (MC5); a diminished or no band in the right lane indicates inhibition of the HP sample, as compared to the lane marked MC5: HP2 has no band in the right lane and thus is inhibited; the bright band on the far right is the positive modern control; *c*, image of a gel showing the faint bands in lane 2 (sample HP2) and lane 3 (sample HP3); the bright band is the positive control (lane 7); lanes 8–10 are negative controls; *d*, image of gel showing bands from HP1, HP3, and HP5; letters correspond to the haplogroups being tested for in that set; bright bands are positive modern controls; lanes to the right of the positive control are negative controls.

(Hg A, C, or D) (fig. A17.1d). The inability to identify one of the traditional Native American haplogroups (A, B, C, D) (Schurr 2004) in HP3 could suggest that it is a contaminated sample. There is also a very low possibility that HP3 belongs to haplogroup X or a heretofore unknown haplogroup in ancient South America. In sum, HP3 is *not* Hg B; nor could it be confidently assigned to Hg A, C, or D.

As seen in figure A17.1d, after Chelex cleaning, HP1 was amplified for haplogroup D and HP5 was amplified for Hg A. However, sequencing data from these amplifications indicate that neither belongs to the respective haplogroup that each was amplified in. That is, HP1 is *not* Hg D, and HP5 is *not* Hg A.

All of the HP samples underwent three extractions, described in more detail below. Among the AMNH samples,

AMNH1–AMNH3 underwent two extractions, AMNH4 and AMNH5 went through three extractions because the first extraction failed, and AMNH6–AMNH10 underwent two extractions. PAR1 went through two extractions.

The specific details of the amplification and sequence process for each sample are presented below.

HP1 (Adult female, Sample Mand RM2): The first amplification yielded no results. It was then chelexed, and the sample amplified. This individual does *not* belong to Hg D. Sequence data show that on the first fragment (primer 15986) a mutation is present at 16129A [2HP1-1-15986 (16153frag rCRS).[1] There is also a mutation at 16294T. This sample was subsequently examined by the Laboratory for

1. rCRS = Revised Cambridge Reference Sequence.

Molecular Anthropology and Microbiome Research at the University of Oklahoma, which concluded that there was not enough mtDNA preserved for analysis.

HP2 (35–45 yr old male, Sample Mand RM2): The first amplification yielded no results. It was then chelexed, but the sample remained inhibited, so the haplogroup is unknown. The second attempt at amplification of the third fragment (primer 16355) shows that the sample was contaminated by the lab technician, Jessica Blair. The one exception is at 16278T, which is not from Blair [2HP2-3-16355]. Although all precautions were taken to prevent modern contamination, Blair's mtDNA contaminated a sample in two or possibly three cases, which are always noted.

HP3 (35–45 yr old female, Sample Max LM2): The first amplification yielded no results. It was then chelexed, and the subsequent sequence data showed that this individual does not belong to Hg A, B, C, or D. It is likely that this sample is contaminated, with a low possibility that it belongs to Hg X or some other unknown haplogroup in South America. Sequence data show that the 4th fragment (primer 16232) has two mutations: 16311C 16362C [3HP3-4-16232]. Sequence data of the 4th fragment (primer 16404), also showed the mutation at 16311C.

HP4 (12–15 yr old, sex unknown, Sample Max RM1): the first amplification yielded no results. It was then chelexed, but no mtDNA was retrieved.

HP5 (50–60+ yr old female, Sample M and RM3): The first amplification yielded no results. It was then chelexed, and the sample amplified. This individual does not belong to Hg A.

Sequence data show that on the 4th fragment (primer 16232), signs of a mutation (double peak) are found at 16362C [2HP5-4-16232], and on the 4th fragment (primer 16404) there is a sign of a mutation at 16266T. Also, the first fragment (primer 15986) shows signs of a mutation at 16129A [2HP5-1-15986], and both primers for the first fragment show signs of a mutation at 16080G [2HP5-1-both].

HP6 (Adult female, Sample Max RM2): The first amplification yielded no results (no mtDNA was retrieved). The sample was then chelexed, and it amplified. The sequence data showed that on the first fragment (primer 15986) there was a sign of a mutation at 16129A [2HP6-1-15986].

HP7 (18–25 yr old male, Sample Max RM3): The first amplification yielded no results (no mtDNA was retrieved). The sample was then chelexed, and it amplified. The sequence data showed that on the first fragment (both primers) there was a sign of a mutation at 16044C [2HP7-1-both]. This mutation is not observed in Hg's A, B, C, D, or X, so this sample may be contaminated.

HP8 (3–5 yr old, sex unknown, Sample Max drm2): The first amplification yielded no results (no mtDNA was retrieved). The sample was then chelexed, but there was no amplification, so the haplogroup is unknown.

HP9 (6–10 yr old, sex unknown, Sample Mand RM1): The first amplification yielded no results (no mtDNA was retrieved). It was then chelexed. The sequence data show a sign of a mutation at 16325C on the 3rd fragment (primer 16190) [2hp9-3-16190] and a sign of a mutation at 16223T

on the 3rd fragment (primer 16355) [2hp9-3-16355]. The sequence data obtained from the third extraction showed contamination from Jessica Blair (16192T).

HP10: This code was used for a carbon sample that was radiocarbon dated.

HP11 (5–9 yr old, sex unknown, Sample Mand RM1): The first extraction amplified, but subsequent attempts to get sequence data failed.

PAR1 (Site of Paredones, Adult, sex unknown, Sample Mand RM): The first and second extractions were chelexed, but both failed to amplify. No data on haplogroup.

THE AMNH SAMPLES

AMNH1 (99.1/890): The first extraction did not amplify. The second extraction was chelexed, and the sample amplified. This second extraction was sequenced and the 2nd fragment (primer 16190) had mutations at 16295T and 16319A [2amnh1-2-16190]. Also, the 2nd fragment (primer 16355) showed a mutation at 16295T [2AMNH1-2-16355]. This sample was also examined by the Laboratory for Molecular Anthropology and Microbiome Research at the University of Oklahoma, which concluded that there was not enough mtDNA preserved for analysis.

AMNH2 (99.1/896): The first extraction did not amplify. The second extraction was chelexed, and the sample amplified. This second extraction was sequenced, and the 1st fragment (both primers) showed mutation at 16111T [2AMNH2-1-both].

AMNH3 (99.1/897): The first and second extractions were chelexed, but both failed to amplify. No haplogroup data were obtained. This sample was also examined by the Laboratory for Molecular Anthropology and Microbiome Research at the University of Oklahoma, which concluded that there was not enough mtDNA preserved for analysis.

AMNH4 (99.1/900): The first extraction was chelexed, but it failed to amplify. The second extraction was also chelexed, and it amplified. This second extraction was sequenced. The third fragment (primer 16355) showed a sign of a mutation at 16223T [2AMNH4-3-16355], and the third extraction (primer 16404 and both primers) showed that it matched the rCRS.

AMNH5 (99.1/901): The first extraction was chelexed, but it failed to amplify. The second extraction also failed.

AMNH6 (99.1/902): The first extraction was chelexed, and it amplified. This first extraction was sequenced, and the 2nd fragment (primer 16251) showed mutations at 16129A, 16169T, and 16173T. A fourth mutation at 16192T could be contamination from Jessica Blair [AMNH6-2-16251]. This sample was also examined by the Laboratory for Molecular Anthropology and Microbiome Research at the University of Oklahoma, which concluded that there was not enough mtDNA preserved for analysis.

AMNH7 (99.1/903): The first extraction was chelexed, and it amplified. This first extraction was sequenced. The 3rd fragment (primer 16190) showed a mutation at 16266T [AMNH7-3-16190] and the 3rd fragment (primer 16355) showed mutation at 16223T and 16266T [AMNH7-

3-16355]. The fourth fragment (primer 16404) also showed a sign of a mutation at 16266T [AMNH7-4-16404].

AMNH8 (99.1/906B): The first and second extractions were chelexed, but both failed to amplify, so no data were obtained on the haplogroup designation.

AMNH9 (99.1/908): The first extraction was chelexed, and it amplified. This first extraction was sequenced, and the 3rd fragment (both primers) showed signs of a mutation at 16266T [AMNH9-3-both]. The 1st fragment (primer 15986) showed signs of a mutation at 16129A [AMNH9-1-15986]. This sample was also examined by the Laboratory for Molecular Anthropology and Microbiome Research at the University of Oklahoma, which concluded that there was not enough mtDNA preserved for analysis.

AMNH10 (99.1/904): The first extraction was chelexed, and it amplified. The second extraction also amplified, and sequence data from the second extraction of the 3rd fragment (primers 16190 and 16355) showed mutations at 16261T [2AMNH10-3-16190] and 16304C [2AMNH10-3-16355].

DISCUSSION AND CONCLUSIONS

The inability to replicate the results in a second lab is cause for concern, though it should be noted that the University of Oklahoma Lab did not chelex samples, which may explain at least some of the failure to amplify the mtDNA. Although every additional step in the analysis introduces possibilities for contamination (such as the chelex step), the clean controls suggest that those run by the Center for Human Genetics Research Laboratory at Vanderbilt University may have yielded accurate albeit incomplete results. Thus, while some specific mutations were documented, none of the samples could be assigned to a specific Native American haplogroup.

BIOLOGICAL KINSHIP UNKNOWN

Based on the archaeological context of the human burials, we were interested in establishing whether or not individuals from Unit 16 shared the same maternal lineage (Samples HP 3, 4, 5, 7, 8, and 11). The poor DNA preservation prevented the identification of haplogroups, however, so this particular question could not be addressed. But the sequence data did reveal that HP3 (adult female) and HP5 (adult female) both have the same mutation at 16362C. This mutation is observed in haplogroups/haplotypes A2, A4, A4d, A6, B4b1b, and D.

Additionally, we investigated whether the individuals from separate burial contexts (separate units) were more distantly related than those found in proximity (in the same units). There were three individuals from units other than Unit 16: Units 3, 10, and 23. The mtDNA from the adult (HP2) in Unit 3 was inhibited, so his haplogroup is unknown and could not be compared to different units.

One mutation (16129A) was shared by HP1 (adult female), HP5 (adult female), HP6 (adult female), and AMNH6 (sex unknown). Although the goal was to evaluate whether females were closely related, as might be expected in matrilocal societies, this question could not be addressed because this particular mutation is seen in all four Native American haplogroups: A, B, C, and D. Thus, while those individuals appear to belong to one of the traditional Native American haplogroups, it does not reveal whether they are closely related on the maternal line. This hypothesis clearly requires further testing. It is unknown whether or not the males at Huaca Prieta were closely related, because only one male provided sequence data.

HP5 and AMNH9 share two mutations: 16266T and 16129A. Mutation 16266T is seen in Hg D5a2, and no other Native American haplogroups, but it should be accompanied by 1438A, which was not tested for in these samples. Mutation 16129A is seen in all haplogroups. Within Hg D it is specifically seen within D2 and D4a. The particular mutation (16266T) was further shared by AMNH7 (HP5 and AMNH9 also have it).

Granted, there is much biological homogeneity in the Andes (Kemp et al. 2009; Lewis et al. 2007; Shinoda et al. 2006), so specific haplogroup designations and additional sequence data are needed before any claims of maternal relatedness can be made among the Huaca Prieta burials.

HP7, a young adult male, has a mutation 16044C, but none of the other 11 burials with sequence data showed that particular mutation. Moreover, mutation 16044C is not typically seen in any of the Native American haplogroups (A, B, C, D, X), so this sample may be contaminated, but it is not contamination from Jessica Blair.

SOIL CHEMISTRY
ANALYSIS

Table A18.1. Soil sample data: Huaca Prieta (HP), Paredones (U-20 and U-22), and Units 9, 15, 16 (U-16), and 18

Sample ID	Lab #	Sample	pH	BU pH	P (lbs/ acre)	K (lbs/ acre)	Ca (lbs/ acre)	Mg (lbs/ acre)	Zn (lbs/ acre)	Organic matter %	Na %
HP-3, Layer 5	25067	2	7.19	7.51	31	1335	2186	1957	3.8	0.62	0.083
HP-3, Layer 12	25066	1	7.01	7.45	79	1575	4365	3101	4.5	1.1	0.12
HP-3, Layer 30	25071	6	8.36	7.5	27	383	21636	2973	5.3	4.7	0.054
HP-3, Layer 34	25076	11	8.56	7.79	218	1365	15722	5616	11.1	3.53	0.082
HP-9, Layer 11	25079	14	7.89	7.67	15	2908	8292	3552	3.6	0.76	0.12
U-9, Layer 15	25080	15	8.17	7.56	10	1763	12528	3053	2.2	1.53	0.099
U-9, Layer 16	25081	16	8.15	7.7	36	3386	14791	4853	1.6	3.42	0.061
U-15, Basal layer	25075	10	8.28	7.7	41	1654	9321	5865	2.5	0.93	0.064
U-16, Layer 5	25070	5	8.22	7.51	27	279	18857	1697	5.1	3.04	0.063
U-18, Basal layer	25074	9	8.08	7.51	55	2256	5062	3163	3	0.64	0.06
U-20, Layer 5	25069	4	8.06	7.5	2	178	12008	1343	2.9	3.16	0.061
U-20, Layer 6	25072	7	8.33	7.55	2	170	14266	1525	1.1	2.13	0.038
U-20, Layer 8	25073	8	8.14	7.52	12	223	12201	1652	2	0.95	0.044
U-22, Floor 15	25068	3	7.7	7.56	16	2194	1560	3104	3	0.72	0.078
U-22, Floor 20	25077	12	8.82	7.88	21	642	30801	5318	3.2	2.94	0.065
U-22, Floor 24	25078	13	9.22	7.86	24	373	50313	4789	3.8	6.02	0.056

Soil sample results from Huaca Prieta and Paredones.

Source: University of Kentucky, College of Agriculture, Division of Regulatory Services—Soil Lab.

SEM-XRF ANALYSIS OF GREEN STONE

Steven L. Goodbred Jr.
and Tom D. Dillehay

The sample shown in figure A.19.1 (see chapter 11), which initially was believed to be copper or turquoise, has been determined by SEM-XRF analysis to be copper sulfate with a matrix of copper silicate (chrysocolla) and smatterings of gypsum, Fe-rich oxide, and organics. This sulfate/silicate–based copper ore is ordinary and widespread in the Central Andes, so its source could be 100 km to several km away. No phosphorous was detected, so it is not turquoise.

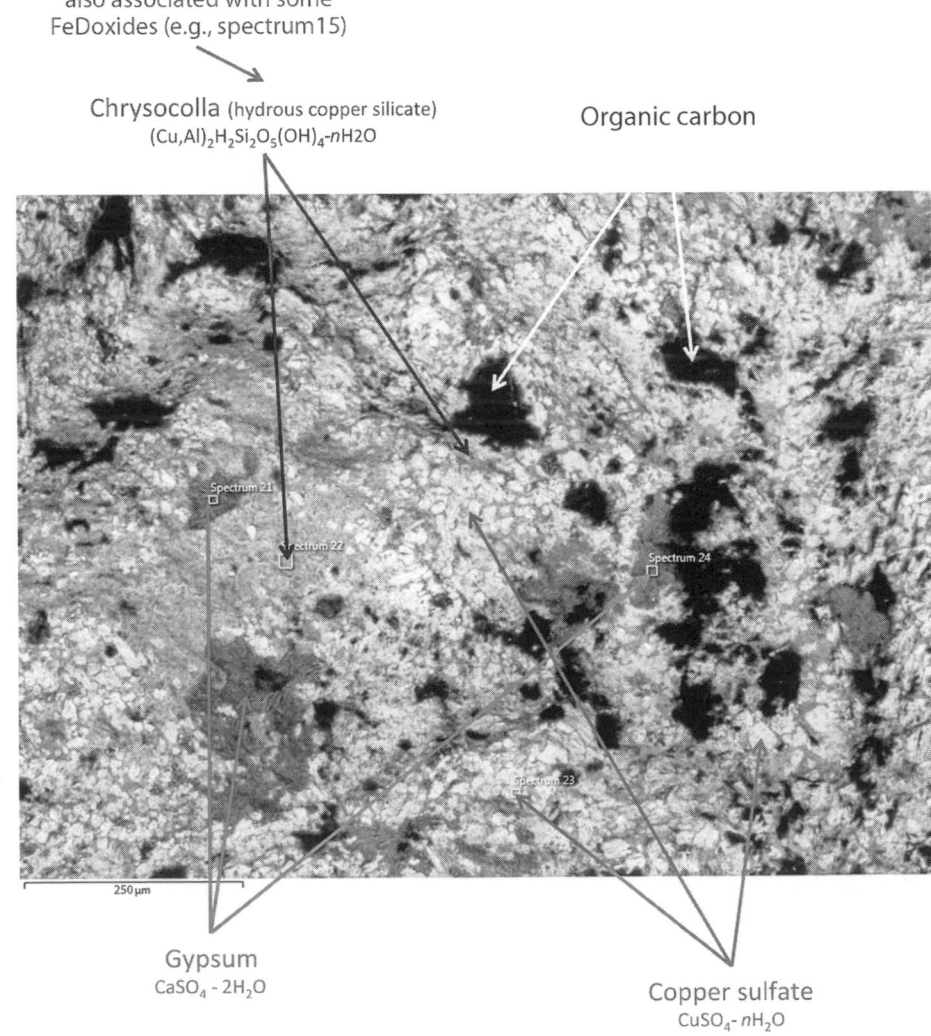

also associated with some FeDoxides (e.g., spectrum15)

Chrysocolla (hydrous copper silicate)
$(Cu,Al)_2H_2Si_2O_5(OH)_4$-$nH2O$

Organic carbon

Gypsum
$CaSO_4 - 2H_2O$

Copper sulfate
$CuSO_4$- nH_2O

250 μm

FIGURE A19.1.
Principal components
of copper sulfate.

REFERENCES

ABRILES, J., AND J. NEGRI

1973   *Manual de malezas en el Perú, comunes en Caña de Azúcar.* Cooperativa Agraria de Producción Casagrande Ltda No. 32. Hortus S. A. Lima: May and Baker.

ABU-ALRUB, I., J. CHRISTIANSEN, S. MADSEN, R. SEVILLA, AND R. ORTIZ

2004   Assessing Tassel, Kernel and Ear Variation in Peruvian Highland Maize. *Plant Genetic Resources Newsletter* (FAO-Biodiversity) 137:34–41.

ACATOS, S.

1990   *Pueblos: Prehistoric Indian Cultures of the Southwest.* Translated by B. Fritzemeier. New York, Oxford: Facts on File.

ACLETO OSORIO, C.

1971   *Algas marinas del Perú de importancia económica.* Lima: Museo de Historia Natural "Javier Prado," Departamento de Botánica, Universidad Nacional Mayor de San Marcos.

1973   Las algas marinas del Perú. *Boletín de la Sociedad Peruana de Botánica* 6(1–2):1–164.

ACOSTA POLO, J.

1977   *Nombres vulgares y usos de las algas en el Perú.* Lima: Museo de Historia Natural "Javier Prado," Departamento de Botánica, Universidad Nacional Mayor de San Marcos.

ADAMIEC, G., AND M. AITKEN

1998   Dose-Rate Conversion Factors: Update. *Ancient TL* 16(2):37–50.

ADLER, M., AND R. WILSHUSEN

1990   Large-Scale Integrative Facilities in Tribal Societies: Cross-Cultural and Southwestern US Examples. *World Archaeology* 22(2):133–145.

ADOVASIO, J. M.

1977   *Basketry Technology: A Guide to Identification and Analysis.* Chicago: Aldine.

1997   Cordage and Cordage Impressions from Monte Verde. In *Monte Verde: A Late Pleistocene Settlement in Chile*, vol. 2, edited by T. D. Dillehay, pp. 221–228. Washington, DC: Smithsonian Institution Press.

2010   *Basketry Technology: A Guide to Identification and Analysis.* Walnut Creek, CA: Left Coast Press.

ADOVASIO, J. M., D. C. HYLAND, AND O. SOFFER

2004   Perishable Fiber Artifacts and the First Americans: New Implications. In *New Perspectives on the*

First Americans, edited by B. T. Lepper and R. Bonnichsen, pp. 157–164. College Station: Texas A&M University Press.

ADOVASIO, J. M., AND T. F. LYNCH
1973   Preceramic Textiles and Cordage from Guitarrero Cave, Peru. *American Antiquity* 38(1):84–90.

ADOVASIO, J. M., AND R. F. MASLOWSKI
1980   Cordage, Basketry, and Textiles. In *Guitarrero Cave: Early Man in the Andes*, edited by T. F. Lynch, pp. 253–290. Studies in Archaeology, Stuart Struever (general editor). New York/London: Academic Press.

ADOVASIO, J. M., O. SOFFER, J. S. ILLINGWORTH, AND D. C. HYLAND
2014   Perishable Fiber Artifacts and Paleoindians: New Implications. *North American Archaeologist* 35(4):331–352.

AGUILAR-MELÉNDEZ, A.
2006   Ethnobotanical and Molecular Data Reveal the Complexity of the Domestication of Chiles (*Capsicum annuum* L.) in Mexico. PhD dissertation, Department of Plant Biology, University of California, Riverside.

AGUSTINOS, LOS PRIMEROS
1918   Relacíon de la religión y ritos de Perú (1550). In *Informaciones acerca de la religión y gobierno de los Incas*, edited by H. Urteaga. Lima: Imprenta y Librería Sanmartí.

AITKEN, M. J.
1961   *Physics and Archaeology*. New York: Interscience Publishers.
1998   *An Introduction to Optical Dating: The Dating of Quaternary Sediments by the Use of Photon-Stimulated Luminescence*. Oxford: Oxford University Press.

ALHEIT, J., AND M. ÑIQUEN
2004   Regime Shifts in the Humboldt Current Ecosystem. *Progress in Oceanography* 60:201–222.

ALLEN, C.
2002   *The Hold Life Has: Coca and Cultural Identity in an Andean Community*. Washington, DC: Smithsonian Institution Press.

ALLEN, R. G., AND R. D. ROBERTSON
1994   *Fishes of the Tropical Eastern Pacific*. Honolulu: University of Hawaii Press.

ALVA, W.
1986   *Frühe Keramik aus dem Jequetepeque-Tal, Nord-Peru*. Materialien zur Allgemeinen und Vergleichenden Archäologie 32. Munich: Verlag Beck.

ALVES-ARAÚJO, U. SWENSON, AND M. ALVES
2014   A Taxonomic Survey of *Pouteria* (Sapotaceae) from the Northern Portion of the Atlantic Rainforest of Brazil. *Systematic Botany* 39(3):915–938.

AMBLER, J. R.
1977   *The Anasazi: Prehistoric People of the Four Corners Region*. Flagstaff: Museum of Northern Arizona.

AMBROSE, S., B. M. BUTLER, D. B. HANSON, R. L. HUNTER-ANDERSON, AND H. W. KRUEGER
1997   Stable Isotopic Analysis of Human Diet in the Marianas Archipelago, Western Pacific. *American Journal of Physical Anthropology* 104:343–361.

AMBROSE, S., AND L. NORR
1993   Experimental Evidence for the Relationship of the Carbon Stable Isotope Ratios of Whole Diet and Dietary Protein to Those of Bone Collagen and Carbonate. In *Prehistoric Human Bone: Archaeology at the Molecular Level*, edited by J. B. Lambert and G. Grupe, pp. 1–38. Berlin: Springer.

AMES, K. M.
1985   Review of *Archeology: Marxist Perspectives in Archaeology*, edited by M. Spriggs. *American Anthropologist* 87(2):453–455.

ANDERSON, D. L., G. W. THOMPSON, AND F. POPOVICH
1976   Age of Attainment of Mineralization Stages of the Permanent Dentition. *Journal of Forensic Sciences* 21: 191–200.

ANDERSON, E., AND H. C. CUTLER
1942   Races of Zea Mays: I. Their Recognition and Classification. *Annals of the Missouri Botanical Garden* 29(2):69–86, 88.

ANDREWS, J.
1984   *Peppers: The Domesticated Capsicums*. Austin: University of Texas Press.
1992   The Peripatetic Chili Pepper: Diffusion of the Domesticated Capsicums since Columbus. In *Chilies to Chocolate: Food the Americas Gave to the Rest of the World*, edited by N. Foster and L. S. Cordel, pp. 81–93. Tucson: University of Arizona Press.

ANDREWS, J. E., P. COLETTA, A. PENTECOST, R. RIDING, S. DENNIS, P. F. DENNIS, AND B. SPIRO
2004   Equilibrium and Disequilibrium Stable Isotope Effects in Modern Charophyte Calcites: Implications for Palaeoenvironmental Studies. *Palaeogeography, Palaeoclimatology, Palaeoecology* 204: 101–114.

ANDRUS, C.
2011   Shell Midden Sclerochronology. *Quaternary Science Reviews* 30(21):2892–2905.
2012   Isotope Sclerochronology in Southeastern US Archaeology to Estimate Season of Capture. In *Seasonality and Human Mobility along the Georgia Bight: Proceedings of the Fifth Caldwell Conference, St. Catherine's Island, Georgia, May 14–16, 2010*. Issue 97 of *Anthropological Papers of the American Museum of Natural History*, edited by Elizabeth J. Reitz, Irvy R. Quitmyer, and David Hurst Thomas, pp. 123–133. New York: American Museum of Natural History.

ANDRUS, C., AND D. CROWE
2000   Geochemical Analysis of *Crassostrea virginica* as a Method to Determine Season of Capture. *Journal of Archaeological Science* 27:33–42.
2002   Alteration of Otolith Aragonite: Effects of Prehistoric Cooking Methods on Otolith Chemistry. *Journal of Archaeological Science* 29:291–299.
2008   Isotope Analysis as a Means for Determining Season of Capture for Mercenaria. In *Native American*

Landscapes of St. Catherine's Island, Georgia, vol. 88, edited by D. H. Thomas, pp. 498–518. New York: American Museum of Natural History.

ANDRUS, C., D. CROWE, D. SANDWEISS, E. REITZ, AND C. ROMANEK

2002a Otolith $\delta^{18}O$ Record of Mid-Holocene Sea Surface Temperature in Peru. *Science* 295:1508–1511.

2002b Oxygen Isotope Record of the 1997–1998 El Niño in Peruvian Sea Catfish (*Galeichthys peruvianus*) Otoliths. *Paleoceanography* 17:1053–1060.

ANDRUS, C., AND K. RICH

2008 A Preliminary Assessment of Oxygen Isotope Fractionation and Growth Increment Periodicity in the Estuarine Clam *Rangia cuneata*. *Geo-Marine Letters* 28(5–6):301–308.

ANDRUS, C., D. SANDWEISS, AND E. REITZ

2008 Climate Change and Archaeology: The Holocene History of El Niño on the Coast of Peru. In *Case Studies in Environmental Archaeology*, edited by E. J. Reitz, S. J. Scudder, and C. M. Scarry, pp. 143–157. New York: Springer.

ANDRUS, C., AND V. THOMPSON

2011 Determine the Habitats of Mollusk Collection at the Sapelo Island Shell Ring Complex, Georgia, USA, Using Oxygen Isotope Sclerochronology. *Journal of Archaeological Science* 39:215–228.

ANGELL, M.

1981 *A Field Guide to Berries and Berrylike Fruits*. New York: Macmillan.

AOYAMA, K.

2009 *Elite Craft Producers, Artists, and Warriors at Aguateca: Lithic Analysis*. Salt Lake City: University of Utah Press.

APARECIDO DO CARMO, D., R. C. WHATLEY, AND S. TIMBERLAKE

1999 Variable Noding and Palaeoecology of a Middle Jurassic Limnocytherid Ostracod: Implications for Modern Brackish Water Taxa. *Palaeogeography, Palaeoclimatology, Palaeoecology* 148:23–35.

ARKUSH, E. AND T. A. TUNG

2013 Patterns of War in the Andes from the Archaic to the Late Horizon: Insights from Settlement Patterns and Cranial Trauma. *Journal of Archaeological Research* 21:307–369.

ARMSTRONG, H. A., AND M. D. BRASIER

2005 *Microfossils*. 2nd ed. Oxford: Blackwell Publishing.

ARNOLD, D.

2014 Introduction. In *Textiles, Technical Practice and Power in the Andes*, edited by D. Y. Arnold and P. Dransart, pp. 1–20. London: Archetype Publications.

ARNOLD, D., AND C. HASTORF

2008 *Heads of State Icons, Power, and Politics in the Ancient and Modern Andes*. Walnut Creek, CA: Left Coast Press.

ARNTZ, W., AND E. FAHRBACH

1996 *El Niño: experimento climático de la naturaleza*. Mexico City: Fondo de Cultura Económica.

ARRIAZA, B.

1995 *Beyond Death: The Chinchorro Mummies of Ancient Chile*. Washington, DC: Smithsonian Institution Press.

1997 Spondylolysis in Prehistoric Human Remains from Guam and Its Possible Etiology. *American Journal of Physical Anthropology* 104:393–397.

ARRIAZA, B., AND V. STANDEN

2008 *Bioarqueología: Historia biocultural de los antiguos pobladores del extreme norte de Chile*. Santiago: Editorial Universitaria.

ARRIAZA, B., V. STANDEN, V. CASSMAN, AND C. SANTORO

2008 Chinchorro Culture: Pioneers of the Coast of the Atacama Desert. In *Handbook of South American Archaeology*, edited by H. Silverman, and W. H. Isbell, pp. 45–58. New York: Springer.

ASA, C., E. COSSIOS, AND R. WILLIAMS

2008 *Pseudolopex sechurae*. Version 2015.2. Electronic document: www.iucnredlist.org.

ASHLEY, C. W.

1944 *The Ashley Book of Knots*. New York/London: Doubleday.

ASPINALL, A., C. GAFFNEY, AND A. SCHMIDT

2008 *Magnetometry for Archaeologists*. New York: AltaMira Press.

AUFDERHEIDE, A.

2003 *The Scientific Study of Mummies*. Cambridge: Cambridge University Press.

AUFDERHEIDE, A., AND C. RODRÍGUEZ-MARTIN

1998 *The Cambridge Encyclopedia of Human Paleopathology*. Cambridge: Cambridge University Press.

AVARIA, S., J. CARRASCO, J. RUTLAND, AND E. YÁÑEZ (EDS.)

2004 *El Niño–La Niña 1997-2000: Sus efectos en Chile*. Valparaiso: Comité Oceanográfico Nacional.

AYÓN, P., G. SWARTZMAN, A. BERTRAND, M. GUTIÉRREZ, S. BERTRAND

2008 Zooplankton and Forage Fish Species off Peru: Large-scale Bottom-Up Forcing and Local-Scale Depletion. *Progress in Oceanography* 79:208–214.

BAAB, K., S. FREIDLINE, S. WANG, AND T. HANSON

2010 Relationship of Cranial Robusticity to Cranial Form, Geography and Climate in *Homo sapiens*. *American Journal of Physical Anthropology* 141:97–115.

BALEE, W., AND C. ERICKSON (EDS.)

2002 *Time and Complexity in Historical Ecology Studies in the Neotropical Lowlands*. Symposium on Neotropical Historical Ecology, Tulane University. New York: Columbia University Press.

BANDY, M.

2004 Fissioning, Scalar Stress, and Social Evolution in Early Village Societies. *American Anthropologist* 106(2):322–333.

BARD, E., B. HAMELIN, AND R. G. FAIRBANKS

1990 U-Th Ages Obtained by Mass Spectrometry in Corals from Barbados: Sea Level during the Past 130,000 Years. *Nature* 346:456–458.

BARKER, G., AND C. GOUCHER (EDS.)
2015   *The Cambridge World History, Volume II: A World with Agriculture, 12,000 BCE-500 CE*. Cambridge: Cambridge University Press.

BARNES, E.
1994   *Developmental Defects of the Axial Skeleton in Paleopathology*. Niwot: University Press of Colorado.

BARTON, C., J. BERNABEAU, J. AURA, E. O. GARCÍA, S. SCHMICH, AND L. MOLINA
2004   Long-term Socioecology and Contingent Landscapes. *Journal of Archaeological Method and Theory* 11: 253-291.

BAR-YOSEF, O., AND R. H. MEADOW
1995   The Origins of Agriculture in the Near East. In *Last Hunters-First Farmers: New Perspectives on the Prehistoric Transition to Agriculture*, edited by T. D. Price and A. B. Gebauer, pp. 39-94. Santa Fe: School of American Research Advanced Seminar Series.

BASTIEN, J.
1985   *Mountain of the Condor: Metaphor and Ritual in an Andean Ayllu*. Long Grove, IL: Waveland Press.

BASU, S., AND A. DE
2003   *Capsicum*: Historical and Botanical Perspectives. In *Capsicum: The Genus Capsicum*, edited by A. K. De, pp. 1-15. New York: Taylor and Francis.

BÉAREZ, P.
2000   Archaic Fishing at Quebrada de los Burros, Southern Coast of Peru: Reconstruction of Fish Size by Using Otoliths. *Archaeofauna* 9:29-34.

2012   Los peces y la pesca. In *Prehistoria de la costa extremosur del Perú: Los pescadores arcaicos de la Quebrada de los Burros (10000-7000 a. P.)*, edited by D. Lavallée and M. Julien, vol. 297, pp. 99-123. Lima: Instituto Francés de Estudios Andinos (IFEA), Pontificia Universidad Católica del Perú (PUCP).

BÉAREZ, P., T. DEVRIES, L. ORTLIEB
2003   Comment on "Otolith δ180 Record of Mid-Holocene Sea Surface Temperature in Peru." *Science* 299(5604):203.

BÉAREZ, P., E. DUFOUR, J. CREDOU, AND C. CHAUCHAT
2011   Les Paijaniens de la Pampa de los Fósiles (nord du Pérou, 11,000-8,000 BP): Pêcheurs, chasseurs ou opportunistes? In *Peuplements et préhistoire en Amériques*, edited by D. Vialou, pp. 233-246. Paris: Comité des Travaux Historiques et Scientifiques (CTHS).

BÉAREZ, P., M. GORRITI, AND P. EECKHOUT
2003   Primeras observaciones sobre el uso de invertebrados y peces marinos en Pachacamac (Perú) en el siglo XV Período Intermedio Tardío. *Boletín del Instituto Francés de Estudios Andinos* 32(1):51-67.

BELL, C.
1997   *Ritual: Perspectives and Dimensions*. New York: Oxford University Press.

BENDER, B.
1978   Gatherer-Hunter to Farmer: A Social Perspective. *World Archaeology* 10(2):204-222.

BENDURE, Z., AND G. PFEIFFER
1946   *America's Fabrics: Origin and History, Manufacture, Characteristics and Uses*. New York: Macmillan.

BENFER, R., JR.
1990   The Preceramic Period Site of Paloma, Peru: Bio-indications of Improving Adaptation to Sedentism. *Latin American Antiquity* 1(4):284-318.

2012   Monumental Architecture Arising from an Early Astronomical-Religious Complex in Peru, 2200-1750 B.C. In *Early New World Monumentality*, edited by R. Burger and R. Rosenswig, pp. 313-363. Gainesville: University Press of Florida.

BEREZINA, N.
2003   Tolerance of Freshwater Invertebrates to Changes in Water Salinity. *Russian Journal of Ecology* 34(4):261-266.

BERMAN, M. J., AND P. L. GNIVECKI
1995   The Colonization of the Bahama Archipelago: A Reappraisal. *World Archaeology* 26:421-441.

BERMAN, M. J., AND D. M. PEARSALL
2000   Plants, People, and Culture in the Prehistoric Central Bahamas: A View from the Three Dog Site, An Early Lucayan Settlement on San Salvador Island, Bahamas. *Latin American Antiquity* 11: 219-240.

BERNIER, H.
2009   Dualism in Andean Art. In *Heilbrunn Timeline of Art History*. New York: Metropolitan Museum of Art, New York. Electronic document: http://www.metmuseum.org/toah/hd/dual/hd_dual.htm.

BERTALANFFY, L. VON
1934   Untersuchungen über die Gesetzlichkeit des Wachstums: I. Teil: Allgemeine Grundlagen der Theorie; Mathematische und physiologische Gesetzlichkeiten des Wachstums bei Wassertieren. *Wilhelm Roux' Archiv Für Entwicklungsmechanik der Organismen* 131:613-652.

BERTOLI DE POMAR, H.
1971   Ensayo de clasificación morfológica de los silico-fitolitos. *Ameghiniana* 3-4:317-328.

BERTRAND, S., B. DEWITTE, J. TAM, E. DÍAZ, AND A. BERTRAND
2008   Impacts of Kelvin Wave Forcing in the Peru Humboldt Current System: Scenarios of Spatial Reorganization from Physics to Fishers. *Progress in Oceanography* 79:278-289.

BEVAN, B.
1975   A Magnetic Survey at Les Forges du Saint Maurice. *MASCA Newsletter* (Museum Applied Science Center for Archaeology) 11(2):1.

1998   *Geophysical Exploration for Archaeology: An Introduction to Geophysical Exploration*. Midwest Archaeological Center, Special Report No. 1. Lincoln, NE: National Park Service.

BEVAN, B., AND J. KENYON
1975   Ground-Penetrating Radar for Historical Archaeology. *MASCA Newsletter* (Museum Applied Science Center for Archaeology) 11(2):2-7.

BINFORD, L.

1980 Willow Smoke and Dogs' Tails: Hunter-Gatherer Settlement Systems and Archaeological Site Formulation. *American Antiquity* 45(1):4–20.

1982 The Archaeology of Place. *Journal of Anthropological Archaeology* 1(1):5–31.

BIRD, J.

1948a America's Oldest Farmers. *Natural History* (New York, American Museum of Natural History) 57(7):296–303, 334–335.

1948b The Most Ancient Peruvian Farmers. *Transactions of the New York Academy of Sciences* 10(5):180–181.

1948c Preceramic Cultures in Chicama and Viru. In *Memoirs of the Society for American Archaeology*, no. 4, *A Reappraisal of Peruvian Archaeology*, pp. 21–28. Washington, DC: Society for American Archaeology.

1951 Recent Developments in the Treatment of Archaeological Textiles. In *Essays on Archaeological Methods: Proceedings of a Conference Held under Auspices of the Viking Fund*, edited by James B. Griffin, pp. 51–58. Ann Arbor: University of Michigan Press.

1952 Before Heddles Were Invented. *Handweaver and Craftsman* 3(3):5–8, 45, 50.

1960 Techniques: Textiles. In *Andean Culture History*, edited by W. C. Bennett and J. B. Bird, pp. 257–293. Handbook Series 15. 2nd revised ed. New York: American Museum of Natural History.

1962 *Art and Life in Old Peru: An Exhibition.* New York: American Museum of Natural History.

1963a Pre-Ceramic Art from Huaca Prieta, Chicama Valley. *Ñawpa Pacha* (Instituto de Estudios Andinos, Berkeley) 1:29–34.

1963b Technology and Art in Peruvian Textiles. In *Technique and Personality*, edited by the Museum of Primitive Art, pp. 45–77. New York: Museum of Primitive Art.

1970 Culturas precerámicas en Chicama y Virú. In *100 años de arqueología en el Perú*, edited by R. Ravines, pp. 111–121. Translated by J. Matos Mar and F. Fuenzalida. Fuentes e Investigaciones para la Historia del Perú 3. Lima: Instituto de Estudios Peruanos.

1977 Pre-Ceramic Art from Huaca Prieta, Chicama Valley. In *Pre-Columbian Art History: Selected Readings*, edited by A. Cordy-Collins and J. Stern, pp. 277–286. Palo Alto, CA: Peek Publications.

BIRD, J., G. ECKHOLM, AND W. FAGG

1960a *The Lipchitz [Jacques, Yulla, and Lolya] Collection.* New York: Museum of Primitive Art.

1960b *The Raymond Wielgus Collection.* New York: Museum of Primitive Art.

BIRD, J., J. HYSLOP, AND M. SKINNER

1985 *The Preceramic Excavations at the Huaca Prieta, Chicama Valley, Peru.* Anthropological Papers, vol. 62, pt. 1. New York: American Museum of Natural History.

BIRD, J., AND J. MAHLER

1951–1952 America's Oldest Cotton Fabrics. *American Fabrics* 20:73–78.

BIRD, R.

1978 Archaeological Maize from Peru. *Maize Genetics Cooperation Newsletter* (Maize Genetics and Genomics Database) 52:90–92.

1979a Fibers and Spinning Procedures in the Andean Area. In *The Junius B. Bird Pre-Columbian Textile Conference, May 19th and 20th, 1973*, edited by A. P. Rowe, E. P. Benson, and A. L. Schaffer, pp. 13–17. Washington, DC: Textile Museum and Dumbarton Oaks.

1979b New World Fabric Production and the Distribution of the Backstrap Loom. In *Irene Emery Roundtable on Museum Textiles 1977 Proceedings: Looms and Their Products*, edited by I. Emery and P. Fiske, pp. 115–126. Washington, DC: Textile Museum.

1983 A Tsunami, a Head, Maize and Dates in the Peruvian Early Horizon. *American Antiquity* 45:325–332.

1987 A Postulated Tsunami and Its Effect on Cultural Development in the Peruvian Early Horizon. *American Antiquity* 52:285–303.

1988 Preceramic Archaeobotany of Huaca Prieta: Investigations from 1946 to 1986. In *Economic Prehistory of the Central Andes*, edited by E. S. Wing and J. C. Wheeler, pp. 3–17. British Archaeological Reports International Series 427. Oxford: British Archaeological Reports.

1990 What Are the Chances of Finding Maize in Peru Dating before 1000 B.C.?: Reply to Bonavia and Grobman. *American Antiquity* 55(4):828–840.

BIRD, R., AND J. BIRD

1980 Gallinazo Maize from the Chicama Valley, Peru. *American Antiquity* 45(2):325–332.

BIRDLIFE INTERNATIONAL

2015 BirdLife International Species Factsheet: Guanay Cormorant *Phalacrocorax bougainvilliorum*. Electronic document: http://www.birdlife.org/datazone/speciesfactsheet.php?id=3683.

BISCHOF, H.

1994 Toward the Definition of Pre- and Early Chavín Art Styles in Peru. *Andean Past* 4:169–228.

1999 The Carved Gourd Vessels of Huaca Prieta: Evidence of Valdivia Art in Central Andean Archaic? *Boletín de Arqueología PUCP* 3:85–119.

BLOCH, M.

1971 *Placing the Dead: Tombs, Ancestral Villages, and Kinship Organization in Madagascar.* London: Seminar Press.

2010 Is There Religion in Çatalhöyük . . . or Just Houses? In *Religion in the Emergence of Civilization: Çatalhöyük as a Case Study*, edited by I. Hodder, pp. 146–163. New York/London: Cambridge University Press.

BLOCH, M., AND J. PARRY

1982 *Death and the Regeneration of Life.* Cambridge: Cambridge University Press.

BLUCK, B.

2011   Structure of Gravel Beaches and Their Relationship to Tidal Range. *Sedimentology* 58:994–1006.

BODDY, J., AND M. LAMBEK

2013   *A Companion to the Anthropology of Religion.* Malden, MA: Wiley Blackwell.

BOËDA, E., I. CLEMENTE-CONTE, M. FONTUGNE, C. LAHAYE, M. PINO, G. DALTRINI FELICE, N. GUIDON, ET AL.

2014   A New Late Pleistocene Archaeological Sequence in South America: The Vale da Pedra Furada (Piaui, Brazil). *Antiquity* 88:927–955.

BOIVIN, N.

2008   *Material Cultures, Material Minds: The Impact of Things or Human Thought, Society, and Evolution.* Cambridge: Cambridge University Press.

BONAVIA, D.

1982   *Precerámico peruano: Los Gavilanes—Mar, desierto y oásis en la historia del hombre.* Lima: Corporación Financiera de Desarrollo, SA and Instituto Arqueológico Alemán.

1984   La importancia de los restos de papas y camotes en época precerámica hallados en el valle de Casma. *Journal de la Société des Américanistes* 52:7–20.

1988   Exostosis del conducto auditivo externo: Notas adicionales. *Chungará* 20:63–68.

1993   La papa: Apuntes sobre sus orígenes y su domesticación. *Journal de la Société des Américanistes* 79(1):173–187.

1996   Letters to the editor. *SAA Bulletin* 14(4):3.

2006   Origen y domesticación de la papa. *Boletín Jaka Tinkuy*, special edition 4(7):12.

2008   *El maíz: Su origen, su domesticación y el rol que ha cumplido en el desarrollo de la cultura.* Lima: Universidad de San Martín de Porres, Fondo Editorial.

2013   *Maize: Origin, Domestication, and Its Role in the Development of Culture.* Cambridge: Cambridge University Press.

BONAVIA, D., L. JOHNSON, E. REITZ, E. WING, AND G. WEIR

1993   Un sitio Precerámico de Huarmey (PV35-6) antes de la introducción del maíz. *Bulletin de l'Institut Français d'Études Andines* 22(2):409–442.

BONAVIA, D., L. JOHNSON-KELLY, E. REITZ, AND E. WING

2001   El Precerámico medio de Huarmey: Historia de un sitio (PV35-106). *Bulletin de l'Institut Français d'Études Andines* 30(2):265–333.

BONAVIA, D., C. OCHOA, Ó. TOVAR S., AND R. PALOMINO

2004   Archaeological Evidence of Cherimoya (*Annona cherimolia* Mill.) and Guanabana (*Annona muricata* L.) in Ancient Peru. *Economic Botany* 58(4):509–522.

BOONSIRI, K., S. KETSA, AND W. VAN DOORN

2007   Seed Browning of Hot Peppers during Low Temperature Storage. *Postharvest Biology and Technology* 45:358–365.

BOSERUP, E.

1965   *The Conditions of Agricultural Growth: The Economics of Agrarian Change under Population Pressure.* London: Allen and Unwin.

BOURGET, S.

2001   Children and Ancestors: Ritual Practices at the Moche Site of Huaca de la Luna, North Coast of Peru. In *Ritual Sacrifice in Ancient Peru*, edited by E. P. Benson and A. G. Cook, pp. 93–118. Austin: University of Texas Press.

BOYD, W. E., C. J. LENTFER, AND R. TORRENCE

1998   Phytoliths Analysis for a Wet Tropics Environment: Methodological Issues and Implications for the Archaeology of Garua Island, West New Britain, Papua New Guinea. *Palynology* 22:213–228.

BOZARTH, S.

1990   Diagnostic Opal Phytoliths from Pods of Selected Varieties of Common Beans (*Phaseolus vulgaris*). *American Antiquity* 55:98–104.

BRADLEY, R.

2000   *An Archaeology of Natural Places.* London: Routledge.

2007   *The Prehistory of Britain and Ireland.* Cambridge: Cambridge University Press.

BRAKO, L., AND J. ZARUCCHI

1993   Catalogue of the Flowering Plants and Gymnosperms of Peru. In *Monographs in Systematic Botany*, pp. i–xl, 1–1286. St. Louis: Missouri Botanical Garden.

BRICEÑO, J., AND M. MILLONES

2000 (1999)   The First Human Remains of Northern Peru: Balances and Perspectives. *Boletín de Arqueología PUCP* 1999(3):55–67.

BRONK RAMSEY, C., T. HIGHAM, A. BOWLES, AND R. HEDGES

2004   Improvements to the Pretreatment of Bone at Oxford. *Radiocarbon* 46:155–164.

BROOKS, S., AND J. SUCHEY

1990   Skeletal Age Determination Based on the Os Pubis: A Comparison of the Acsádi-Nemeskéri and Suchey-Brooks Methods. *Human Evolution* 5:227–238.

BROWN, C., W. WITSCHEY, AND L. LIEBOVITCH

2005   The Broken Past: Fractals in Archaeology. *Journal of Archaeological Method and Theory* 12(1):37–78.

BROWN, D., B. CAMPOS, AND H.-J. URBAN

2002   Reproductive Cycle of the Bivalve Clams *Semele solida* (Gray, 1828) (Semelidae) and *Gari solida* (Gray, 1828) (Psammobiidae) from Chile. *Journal of Shellfish Research* 21(2):627–634.

BROWN, T., D. NELSON, J. VOGEL, AND J. SOUTHON

1988   Improved Collagen Extraction by Modified Longin Method. *Radiocarbon* 30:171–177.

BRÜCK, J.

2006   Death, Exchange and Reproduction in the British Bronze Age. *European Journal of Archaeology* 9(1):73–101.

BRUNO, M.

2006   A Morphological Approach to Documenting the

Domestication of *Chenopodium* in the Andes. In *Documenting Domestication*, edited by M. Seder, D. G. Bradley, E. Emshwiller, and B. D. Smith, pp. 32–45. Berkeley: University of California Press.

BRUNO, M., AND W. WHITEHEAD
2003   *Chenopodium* Cultivation and Formative Period Agriculture at Chiripa, Bolivia. *Latin American Antiquity* 14:339–355.

BRYAN, A., AND R. GRUHN
2003   Some Difficulties in Modeling the Original Peopling of the Americas. *Quaternary International* 109/110:175–179.

BRYAN, N., AND S. YOUNG
1978   *Navajo Native Dyes: Their Preparation and Use*. Chilocco, OK: Chilocco Agricultural School.

BUDWORTH, G.
2003   *The Ultimate Encyclopedia of Knots and Ropework*. London: Hermes House.

BUIKSTRA, J. E., AND D. H. UBELAKER
1994   *Standards for Data Collection from Human Skeletal Remains*. Arkansas Archeological Survey Research Series No. 44. Fayetteville: Arkansas Archeological Survey.

BULDYREV, S. V., A. L. GOLDBERGER, S. HAVLIN, C. K. PENG, AND H. E. STANLEY
1994   Fractals in Biology and Medicine: From DNA to the Heartbeat. In *Fractals in Science*, edited by Armin Bunde, pp. 49–87. New York: Springer.

BURGER, R.
1992   *Chavín and the Origins of Andean Civilization*. New York: Thames and Hudson.

BURGER, R., AND R. ROSENSWIG (EDS.)
2012   *Early New World Monumentality*. Gainesville: University Press of Florida.

BURGER, R., AND L. SALAZAR
2012   Monumental Public Complexes and Agricultural Expansion on Peru's Central Coast during the Second Millennium BC. In *Early New World Monumentality*, edited by R. L. Burger and R. M. Rosenswig, pp. 399–430. Gainesville: University Press of Florida.

BURGER, R., AND L. SALAZAR-BURGER
1991   The Second Season of Investigations at the Initial Period Center of Cardal, Peru. *Journal of Field Archaeology* 18(3):275–296.

BURKLE-ELIZONDO, G., AND R. VALDEZ-CEPEDA
2006   Fractal Analysis of Mesoamerican Pyramids. *Nonlinear Dynamics, Psychology, and Life Sciences* 10(1):105–122.

BURNS, K.
1999   *Forensic Anthropology Training Manual*. Upper Saddle River, NJ: Prentice Hall.

BUTZER, K.
1996   Ecology in the Long View: Settlement Histories, Argosystemic Strategies, and Ecological Performance. *Journal of Field Archaeology* 23(2):141–150.

CALLEN, E., AND T. CAMERON
1960   A Prehistoric Diet Revealed in Coprolites. *New Scientist* 8(190):35–37, 39–40.

CAMPANA, S., AND J. NEILSON
1985   Microstructure of Fish Otoliths. *Canadian Journal of Fisheries and Aquatic Sciences* 42:1014–1032.

CARBAJAL, W., J. GALÁN, J. CASTAÑEDA, AND M. GUTIÉRREZ
2006   Spatio-Temporal Distribution, Abundance, and Habits of Catfish (Bagre *Galeichthys peruvianus*) in the Peruvian Coast between 1998 and 2006. Paper presented at the Humboldt Current System International Conference, Lima.

CÁRDENAS, C., J. TORRES, AND J. RODAS
2001   Productividad primaria durante El Niño 1997–98 en los bosques secos de Piura, Perú. In *El Niño en América Latina: Impactos biológicos y sociales*, edited by J. Tarazona, W. Arntz, and E. Castillo de Maruenda, pp. 199–211. Lima: Consejo Nacional de Ciencias y Tecnología.

CÁRDENAS, M.
1999   The Preceramic Period in Chao Valley. *Boletín de Arqueología PUCP* 3:141–169.

CARDINAL, D., B. HAMELIN, E. BARD, AND J. PATZOLD
2001   Sr/Ca, U/Ca and δ^{18}O Records in Recent Massive Corals from Bermuda: Relationships with Sea Surface Temperatures. *Chem. Geol.* 176:213–233.

CARRÉ, M., M. AZZOUG, I. BENTALEB, B. CHASE, M. FONTUGNE, D. JACKSON, M.-P. LEDRU, A. MALDONADO, J. SACHS, AND A. SCHAUER
2012   Mid-Holocene Mean Climate in the South Eastern Pacific and Its Influence on South America. *Quaternary International* 253:55–66.

CARRÉ, M., I. BENTALEB, M. FONTUGNE, AND D. LAVALLÉE
2005   Strong El Niño Events during the Early Holocene: Stable Isotope Evidence from Peruvian Sea-Shells. *Holocene* 15:42–47.

CARRÉ, M., AND E. DUFOUR
2012   Seasonal Strategies of Exploitation of the Marine Environment: The Contribution of Sclerocronology and Isotopic Study. Prehistory of the Extreme South Coast of Peru. The Archaic Fisherman of the Quebrada de los Burros (10000–7000 a. P.). Edited by D. Lavallée and M. Julien. Chapter 5. IFEA. 297:195–205.

CARRÉ, M., J. SACHS, A. SCHAUER, W. RODRÍGUEZ, AND F. RAMOS
2013   Reconstructing El Niño: Southern Oscillation Activity and Ocean Temperature Seasonality from Short-Lived Marine Mollusk Shells from Peru. *Palaeogeography, Palaeoclimatology, Palaeoecology* 371:45–53.

CARROLL, M., AND J. REMPEL (EDS.)
2011   *Living through the Dead: Burial and Commemoration in the Classical World*. Oakville, CT: David Brown Book Company, Oakville.

CARTER, G.
1945   Some Archeological Cucurbit Seed from Peru. *Acta Americana* 3(3):163–172.

CASTEEL, R.

1976 *Fish Remains in Archaeology and Paleo-environmental Studies.* London: Academic Press.

CASTETTER, E., AND W. BELL

1942 *Pima and Papago Indian Agriculture.* Albuquerque: University of New Mexico Press.

CHANDLER-EZELL, K., D. PEARSALL, AND J. ZEIDLER

2006 Root and Tuber Phytoliths and Starch Grains Document Manioc (*Manihot esculenta*), Arrowroot (*Maranta arundinacea*), and Llerén (*Calathea* sp.) at the Real Alto Site, Ecuador. *Economic Botany* 60: 103–120.

CHAPMAN, B.

2002 Archaeological Studies of the Social Practices of Death. *Current Anthropology* 43(4):685–686.

CHAPMAN, J.

2000 *Fragmentation in Archaeology: People, Places and Broken Objects in the Prehistory of South-Eastern Europe.* London: Routledge.

CHAPMAN, J., AND B. GAYDARSKA

2009 The Fragmentation Premise in Archaeology: From the Paleolithic to More Recent Times. In *The Fragment: An Incomplete History*, edited by W. Tronzo, pp. 131–153. Los Angeles: Getty Research Institute.

CHAPMAN, J., B. GAYDARSKA, A. RADUNCHEVA, AND B. KOLEVA

2007 *Parts and Wholes: Fragmentation in Prehistoric Context.* Oxford: Oxbow Books.

CHAUCHAT, C.

2006 *Prehistoria de la costa norte del Perú: El paijanense de Cupisnique.* Translated by S. Uceda. Trujillo, Peru: Instituto Francés de Estudios Andinos.

CHAUCHAT, C., M. GÁLVEZ, R. BRICEÑO, AND S. UCEDA

1998 *Sitios arqueológicos de la zona de Cupisnique y margen derecha del Valle de Chicama.* Trujillo, Peru: Instituto Nacional de Cultura La Libertad.

CHÁVEZ, F., A. BERTRAND, R. GUEVARA-CARRASCO, P. SOLER, AND J. CSIRKE

2008 The Northern Humboldt Current System: Brief History, Present Status and a View towards the Future. *Progress in Oceanography* 79(2–4):95–105.

CHÁVEZ, F., J. RYAN, S. LLUCH-COTA, AND M. ÑIQUEN

2003 From Anchovies to Sardines and Back: Multidecadal Change in the Pacific Ocean. *Science* 299: 217–221.

CHIOU, K.

2014 *Capsicum* spp. Project Procedure for Seed Photography. University of California McCown Archaeobotany Laboratory Report No. 77. Electronic document: http://archaeobotany.berkeley.edu/Research/LabReport/lab77/lab77.pdf.

CHIOU, K., AND C. HASTORF

2012 *Capsicum* spp. at the Preceramic Sites of Huaca Prieta and Paredones, Chicama Valley, Peru. University of California McCown Archaeobotany Laboratory Report No. 74. Electronic document:

http://archaeobotany.berkeley.edu/Research/LabReport/lab74/lab74.pdf.

2014 A Systematic Approach to Species-Level Identification of *Capsicum* spp. Seeds: Establishing the Groundwork for Tracking the Domestication and Movement of Chile Peppers through the Americas and Beyond. *Economic Botany* 68(3):316–336.

CHIOU, K., C. HASTORF, D. BONAVIA, AND T. DILLEHAY

2014 Documenting Cultural Selection Pressure Changes on Chile Pepper *Capsicum baccatum* Seed Size through Time in Coastal Peru (7600 B.P.–Present). *Economic Botany* 68(2):190–202.

CHU, A.

2008 *Bandurria: Arena, mar y humedal en el surgimiento de la civilización andina.* Huacho, Peru: Proyecto Arqueológico Bandurria–Huacho.

CHU BARRERA, A.

2011 Household Organization and Social Inequality at Bandurria, a Late Preceramic Village in Huaura, Peru. PhD dissertation, University of Pittsburgh, Pittsburgh. University Microfilms, Ann Arbor.

CLARK, A.

2003 *Seeing beneath the Soil, Prospecting Methods in Archaeology.* New York: Routledge.

CLARK, K.

1983 Prehistoric Coprolite Remains from Chaco Canyon, New Mexico: Inferences for Anasazi Diet and Subsistence. Master's thesis, Department of Anthropology, University of New Mexico, Albuquerque.

CLARKE, P. U., A. S. DYKE, J. D. SHAKUN, A. E. CARLSON, J. CLARK, B. WOHLFARTH, J. X. MITROVICA, S. W. HOSTETLER, AND A. M. MCCABE

2009 The Last Glacial Maximum. *Science* 325:710–714.

CLEMENT, A., AND M. CANE

1999 A Role for the Tropical Pacific Coupled Ocean-Atmosphere System on Milankovitch and Millennial Timescales. Part I: Modeling Study of Tropical Pacific Variability. In *Mechanisms of Global Climate Change at Millennial Time-Scales*, edited by P. U. Clark, R. S. Webb, and L. D. Keigwin, pp. 363–371. Washington, DC: American Geophysical Union.

CLEMENT, A., R. SEAGER, AND M. CANE

2000 Suppression of El Niño during the Mid-Holocene by Changes in the Earth's Orbit. *Paleoceanography* 15(6):731–737.

COAN, E.

1988 Recent Eastern Pacific Species of the Bivalve Genus *Semele. Veliger* 31(1/2):1–42.

COHEN, M.

1978a Archaeological Plant Remains from the Central Coast of Peru. *Ñawpa Pacha* (Instituto de Estudios Andinos, Berkeley) 16:23–50.

1978b Population Pressure and the Origin of Agriculture: An Archaeological Example from the Coast of Peru. In *Advances in Andean Archaeology*, edited by D. L. Browman, pp. 91–132. The Hague: Mouton.

COLE, J., AND R. FAIRBANKS
1990   The Southern Oscillation Recorded in the $\delta^{18}O$ of Corals from Tarawa Atoll. *Paleoceanography* 5:669–683.

COLETTA, P., A. PENTECOSTA, AND B. SPIRO
2001   Stable Isotopes in Charophyte Incrustations: Relationships with Climate and Water Chemistry. *Palaeogeography, Palaeoclimatology, Palaeoecology* 173:9–19.

COLINVAUX, P.
1972   Climate and the Galapagos Islands. *Nature* 240: 17–20.

COLINVAUX, P., M. BUSH, M. STEINITZ-KANNAN, AND M. MILLER
1997   Glacial and Postglacial Pollen Records from the Ecuadorian Andes and Amazon. *Quaternary Research* 48:69–78.

COLINVAUX, P., P. DE OLIVEIRA, AND M. BUSH
2000   Amazonian and Neotropical Plant Communities on Glacial Time-Scales: The Failure of Aridity and Refuge Hypotheses. *Quaternary Science Reviews* 19: 141–169.

COLLINS, M.
1997   The Lithics from Monte Verde, A Descriptive-Morphological Analysis. In *Monte Verde: A Late Pleistocene Settlement in Chile*, vol. 2, edited by T. D. Dillehay, pp. 383–506. Washington, DC: Smithsonian Institution Press.

CONROY, J., J. OVERPECK, J. COLE, T. SHANAHAN, AND M. STEINITZ-KANNAN
2008   Holocene Changes in Eastern Pacific Climate Inferred from a Galápagos Lake Sediment Record. *Quaternary Science Reviews* 27:1166–1180.

COPLEN, T.
1994   Reporting of Stable Hydrogen, Carbon, and Oxygen Isotopic Abundances. *Pure and Applied Chemistry* 66:173–276.

CORRÈGE, T., T. DELCROIX, J. RÉCY, R. BECK, G. CABIOCH, AND F. LE CORNEC
2000   Evidence for Stronger El Niño-Southern Oscillation (ENSO) Events in a Mid-Holocene Massive Coral. *Paleoceanography* 15:465–470.

COUTURE, N.
2004   Monumental Space, Courtly Style, and Elite Life at Tiwanaku. In *Tiwanaku: Ancestors of the Inca*, edited by Margaret Young-Sánchez, pp. 127–135, 139–143, 146–149. Denver/Lincoln: Denver Art Museum/University of Nebraska Press.

CREEL, D., AND A. LONG
1986   Radiocarbon Dating of Corn. *American Antiquity* 51(4):826–837.

CUSHING, F.
1920   *Zuni Breadstuff*. Indian Notes and Monographs, vol. 8. New York: Heye Foundation.

CUTLER, H.
1946   *Races of Maize in South America*. Botanical Museum

Leaflets, vol. 12, no. 8. Cambridge, MA: Harvard University.

DALAN, R.
2006   Magnetic Susceptibility. In *Remote Sensing in Archaeology: An Explicitly North American Perspective*, edited by Jay K. Johnson, pp. 161–204. Tuscaloosa: University of Alabama Press.

D'ALTROY, T. N.
2002   *The Incas*. Malden, MA: Blackwell.
2014   *The Incas*. 2nd ed. Peoples of America. Somerset, NJ: Wiley.

DAMP, J., D. PEARSALL, AND L. KAPLAN
1981   Beans for Valdivia. *Science* 212(4496):811–812.

DAVENPORT, W.
1970   Progress Report on the Domestication of *Capsicum* (Chile Peppers). *Proceedings of the Association of American Geographers* 2:46–47.

DAVIS, S.
1989   *The Archaeology of Animals*. New Haven: Yale University Press.

DE FRANCE, S.
2005   Late Pleistocene Marine Birds from Southern Peru: Distinguishing Human Capture from El Niño–Induced Windfall. *Journal of Archaeological Science* 32:1131–1146.

DE LA MATA, R., AND D. BONAVIA
1980   Lumbosacral Malformations and Spina Bifida in a Peruvian Preceramic Child. *Current Anthropology* 21:515–516.

DEL SOLAR, M.
2007   *La trama y la urdimbre: Textiles tradicionales del Perú*. Translated by M. E. Del Solar and A. Soldi. Lima: Universidad Ricardo Palma and the Instituto Cultura Peruano Norteamericano.
2011   *Las Shicras de Casca: El arte del tejido anillado en la sierra de Lima*. Lima: Ministerio de Comercio Exterior y Turismo (MINCETUR).

DENIRO, M.
1985   Postmortem Preservation and Alteration of in Vivo Bone Collagen Isotope Ratios in Relation to Palaeodietary Reconstruction. *Nature* 317: 806–809.

DENIRO, M., AND S. EPSTEIN
1978   Influence of Diet on the Distribution of Carbon Isotopes in Animals. *Geochimica Cosmochimica Acta* 42:495–506.
1981   Influence of Diet on the Distribution of Nitrogen Isotopes in Animals. *Geochimica Cosmochimica Acta* 45:341–351.

DE PASQUALE, NICOLINO, AND A. AIMI
2003   Come funzionano le yupane 1 e 2 di Milano. In *Le culture del Perù da Chavín agli Inca*, edited by A. Aimi, pp. 148–155. Milan: Cinisello Balsamo, Silvana.

DESANTIS, L., R. FERANEC, AND B. MACFADDEN
2009   Effects of Global Warming on Ancient Mammalian Communities and Their Environments. *PLoS ONE* 4:e5750.

DESANTIS, L., J. SCOTT, B. SCHUBERT, S. DONOHUE,
B. MCCRAY, C. VAN STOLK, A. WINBURN,
M. GRESHKO, AND M. O'HARA

2013   Direct Comparisons of 2D and 3D Dental Micro-
        wear Proxies in Extant Herbivorous and Carnivo-
        rous Mammals. *PLoS ONE* 8:e71428.

DESCOLA, P.

2005   *Beyond Nature and Culture.* Chicago: University of
        Chicago Press.

2012   *The Ecology of Others: Anthropology and the Question of
        Nature.* Chicago: Prickly Paradigm.

2014   Beyond Nature and Culture. *American Anthropolo-
        gist* 116(2):445.

DESCOLA, P., AND J. LLOYD

2013   *Beyond Nature and Culture.* Chicago: University of
        Chicago Press.

DESCOLA, P., AND G. PÁLSSON (EDS.)

1996   *Nature and Society: Anthropological Perspectives.* New
        York/London: Routledge.

DEVRIES, T., L. ORTLIEB, A. DÍAZ, L. WELLS, AND
C. HILLAIRE-MARCEL

1997   Determining the Early History of El Niño. *Science*
        276(5314):965–967.

DEVRIES, D., R. WRIGHT, AND A. PEER

2006   First-Year Growth and Recruitment of Coastal
        Largemouth Bass (*Micropterus salmoides*): Spatial
        Patterns Unresolved by Critical Periods along a
        Salinity Gradient. *Canadian Journal of Fisheries and
        Aquatic Sciences* 63:1911-1924.

DEVRIES, T., AND L. WELLS

1990   Thermally-Anomalous Holocene Molluscan
        Assemblages from Coastal Peru: Evidence for
        Paleogeographic, Not Climatic Change. *Palaeo-
        geography, Palaeoclimatology, Palaeoecology* 81:11–32.

D'HARCOURT, R.

1960   Les textiles dans l'ancien Pérou. *Cahiers Ciba*
        8(86):2–40.

DÍAZ, A., AND L. ORTLIEB

1993   El fenómeno "El Niño" y los moluscos de la
        Costa peruana. *Bulletin de l'Institut Français d'Études
        Andines* 22(1):159–177.

DÍAZ, H., AND V. MARKGRAF (EDS.)

2000   *El Niño and the Southern Oscillation: Multiscale Vari-
        ability and Global and Regional Impacts.* New York:
        Cambridge University Press.

DICKAU R., A. RANERE, AND R. COOKE

2007   Starch Grain Evidence for the Preceramic Dis-
        persals of Maize and Root Crops into Tropical
        Dry and Humid Forests of Panama. *Proceedings of
        the National Academy of Sciences of the United States of
        America* 104:3651–3656.

DICKAU, R., B. WHITNEY, J. IRIARTE, F. MAYLE,
D. SOTO, P. METCALFE, F. STREET-PERROT,
N. LOADER, K. J. FICKEN, AND T. KILLEEN

2013   Differentiation of Neotropical Ecosystems by
        Modern Soil Phytolith Assemblages and Its Impli-
        cations for Palaeoenvironmental and Archaeologi-
        cal Reconstructions. *Review of Palaeobotany and Paly-
        nology* 193:15–37.

DIEHL, M.

2005   Morphological Observations on Recently Recov-
        ered Early Agricultural Period Maize Cob Frag-
        ments from Southern Arizona. *American Antiquity*
        70(2):361–375.

DIETLER, M.

2001   Theorizing the Feast: Rituals of Consumption,
        Commensal Politics, and Power in African Con-
        texts. In *Feasts: Archaeological and Ethnographic
        Perspectives on Food, Politics, and Power,* edited by
        M. Dietler and B. Hayden, pp. 65–114. Tuscaloosa:
        University of Alabama Press.

DIETRICH, T., A. SUTER, C. PFIRRMANN, C. DORA,
S. FUCENTESE, AND M. ZANETTI

2012   Supraacetabular Fossa (Pseudodefect of Acetabu-
        lar Cartilage): Frequency at MR Arthrography and
        Comparison of Findings at MR Arthrography and
        Arthroscopy. *Radiology* 263:484–491.

DILLEHAY, T.

1995   Mounds of Social Death: Mapuche Mortuary
        Practice. In *Tombs for the Living: Andean Mortu-
        ary Practice,* edited by T. D. Dillehay, pp. 281–313.
        Dumbarton Oaks: Harvard University Press.

1997   *Monte Verde: A Late Pleistocene Settlement in Chile.*
        Vol. 2. Smithsonian Institution Press, Washington,
        DC.

2000   *A New Settlement of the Americas.* New York: Basic
        Books.

2004   Social Landscape and Ritual Pause: Uncertainty
        and Integration in Formative Peru. *Journal of Social
        Archaeology* 4:239–268.

2007   *Monuments, Empires, and Resistance: The Araucanian
        Polity and Ritual Narratives.* Cambridge: Cambridge
        University Press.

2011a   *From Foraging to Farming in the Andes: New Perspec-
        tives on Food Production and Social Organization.* Cam-
        bridge: Cambridge University Press.

2011b   Introduction. In *From Foraging to Farming in the
        Andes, New Perspectives on Food Production and Social
        Organization,* edited by T. D. Dillehay, pp. 1–27.
        Cambridge: Cambridge University Press.

2013   Entangled Knowledge: Old Trends and New
        Thoughts in First South American Studies.
        In *Paleoamerican Odyssey,* edited by K. Graf,
        C. Ketron, and M. Waters, pp. 377–396. College
        Station: Texas A&M University Press.

2014   *The Teleoscopic Polity: Andean Patriarchy and Materi-
        ality.* New York: Springer.

DILLEHAY, T., D. BONAVIA, S. GOODBRED, M. PINO,
V. VÁSQUEZ, AND T. ROSALES THAM

2012a   A Late Pleistocene Human Presence at Huaca
        Prieta, Peru, and Early Pacific Coastal Adapta-
        tions. *Quaternary Research* 77(3):418–423.

DILLEHAY, T., D. BONAVIA, S. GOODBRED, M. PINO,
V. VÁSQUEZ, T. THAM, W. CONKLIN, ET AL.

2012b   Chronology, Mound-Building and Environment
        at Huaca Prieta, Coastal Peru, from 13700 to 4000
        Years Ago. *Antiquity* 86:48–70.

DILLEHAY, T., D. BONAVIA, C. HASTORF, K. CHIOU
2014 Documenting Cultural Selection Pressure Changes on Chile Pepper (*Capsicum baccatum* L.) Seed Size through Time in Coastal Peru (7,600 B.P.–Present). *Economic Botany* 68(2):190–202.

DILLEHAY, T., D. BONAVIA, AND P. KAULICKE
2004 The First Settlers. In *Andean Archaeology: Blackwell Studies in Global Archaeology*, p. 1634. Malden, MA: Blackwell.

DILLEHAY, T., AND A. KOLATA
2004 Long-term Human Response to Uncertain Environmental Conditions in the Andes. *Proceedings of the National Academy of Sciences of the United States of America* 101:4325–4330.

DILLEHAY, T., P. NETHERLY, AND J. ROSSEN
1989 Middle Preceramic Public and Residential Sites on the Forested Slope of the Western Andes, Northern Peru. *American Antiquity* 54(4):733–759.

DILLEHAY, T., AND D. PIPERNO
2014 Agricultural Origins and Social Implications in South America. In *The Cambridge World Prehistory*, edited by C. Renfrew, and P. Bahn, pp. 970–985. Cambridge: Cambridge University Press.

DILLEHAY, T., AND J. ROSSEN
2001 The Nanchoc Lithic Tradition of Northern Peru: Microscopic Use-Wear Analysis. *Andean Past* 6:7–36.

DILLEHAY, T., J. ROSSEN, T. ANDRES, AND D. WILLIAMS
2007 Preceramic Adoption of Peanut, Squash, and Cotton in Northern Peru. *Science* 316:1890–1893.

DILLEHAY, T., J. ROSSEN, AND P. NETHERLY
1997 The Nanchoc Tradition: The Beginnings of Andean Civilization. *American Scientist* 85:46–56.
1998 Middle Preceramic Household, Ritual, and Technology in Northern Peru. *Chungará: Revista de Antropología Chilena* 30(2):111–124.

DILLEHAY, T., J. ROSSEN, D. UGENT, A. KARATHANASIS, V. VÁSQUEZ, AND P. NETHERLY
2010 Early Holocene Coca Chewing in Northern Peru. *Antiquity* 84(326):939–953.

DILLON, M.
1994 Bosques húmedos del norte del Perú. *Arnaldoa* 2:29–42.
2003a Checklist for Bosque Cachil. Electronic document: http://www.sacha.org/envir/bosques/cachil/cachil.html.
2003b Checklist for Bosque Monteseco. Electronic document: http://www.sacha.org/envir/bosques/monte/monte.html.

DILLON, M., A. SAGÁSTEGUI ALVA, I. SÁNCHEZ VEGA, S. LLATAS QUIROZ, AND N. HENSOLD
1995 Floristic Inventory and Biogeographic Analysis of Montane Forests in Northwestern Peru. In *Biodiversity and Conservation of Neotropical Montane Forests*, edited by S. Churchill, H. Balslev, E. Forero, and J. Luteyn, pp. 251–269. New York: New York Botanical Garden.

DOBRES, M.-A.
2000 *Technology and Social Agency: Outlining a Practice Framework for Archaeology*. Malden, MA: Blackwell.

DONNAN, C.
1964 An Early House from Chilca, Peru. *American Antiquity* 30:137–144.

DONOHUE, S., L. DESANTIS, B. SCHUBERT, AND P. UNGAR
2013 Was the Giant Short-Faced Bear a Hyper-Scavenger?: A New Approach to the Dietary Study of Ursids Using Dental Microwear Textures. *PLoS ONE* 8:e77531.

DRESSLER, R.
1953 Las plantas cultivadas en el México Precolombino (Resumen). *Ciencias Sociales* (Washington, DC) 7(40):277–316.

DRIVER, H.
1961 *Indians of North America*. 2nd ed. Chicago: University of Chicago Press.

DUFOUR, E., H. CAPPETTA, A. DENIS, Y. DAUPHIN, AND A. MARIOTTI
2000 La diagenèse des otolithes par la comparaison des données microstructurales, minéralogiques et géochimiques: Application aux fossiles du Pliocène du Sud-Est de la France. *Bulletin de la Société Géologique de France* 171:521–532.

DUFOUR, E., D. GERDEAUX, AND C. WURSTER
2007 Whitefish (*Coregonus lavaretus*) Respiration Rate Governs Intra-Otolith Variation of $\delta^{13}C$ Values in Lake Annecy. *Canadian Journal of Fisheries and Aquatic Sciences* 64:1736–1746.

DUNBAR, R., G. WELLINGTON, M. COLGAN, AND P. GLYNN
1994 Eastern Pacific Sea Surface Temperature since 1600 A.D.: The $\delta^{18}O$ Record of Climate Variability in Galapagos Corals. *Paleoceanography* 9:291–315.

DUNCAN, N., D. PEARSALL, AND R. BENFER JR.
2009 Gourd and Squash Artifacts Yield Starch Grain of Feasting Foods from Preceramic Peru. *Proceedings of the National Academy of Sciences of the United States of America* 106(32):13202–13206.

EBELING, W.
1986 *Handbook of Indian Foods and Fibers of Arid America*. Berkeley: University of California Press.

EGLASH, R.
1999 *African Fractals: Modern Computing and Indigenous Design*. New Brunswick, NJ: Rutgers University Press.

ELERA, C.
1998 The Puémape Site and the Cupisnique Culture: A Case Study on the Origins and Development of Complex Society in the Central Andes, Perú. PhD dissertation, Department of Archaeology, University of Calgary, Canada. Ann Arbor: University Microfilms International.

ELERA, C., J. PINILLA, AND V. VÁSQUEZ
1992 Bioindicadores zoológicos de eventos ENSO para el Formativo Medio y Tardío de Puémape—Perú. *Pachacamac* 1(1):9–19.

ELIADE, M.
1958   *Patterns in Comparative Religion*. London: Sheed and Ward.

EL-ZAATARI, S.
2010   Occlusal Microwear Texture Analysis and the Diets of Historical/Prehistoric Hunter-Gatherers. *International Journal of Osteoarchaeology* 20:67–87.

EMERY, I.
1966   *The Primary Structures of Fabrics: An Illustrated Classification*. Washington, DC: Textile Museum.

EMMONS, L.
1990   *Neotropical Rainforest Mammals*. Chicago: University of Chicago Press.

ENGEL, F.
1957a   Early Sites on the Peruvian Coast. *Southwestern Journal of Anthropology* 13(1):54–68.

1957b   Sites et établissements sans céramique de la côte péruvienne. *Journal de la Société des Américanistes*, n.s. 46:67–155.

1960a   Datos con referencia al estudio de sitios prehistóricos en su contexto morfológico y climatológico. In *Antiguo Perú, espacio y tiempo: Trabajos presentados a la Semana de Arqueología Peruana, 9–14 de noviembre de 1959*, pp. 119–127. Lima: Librería-Editorial J. Mejía Baca.

1960b   Un group humain datant de 5000 ans à Paracas, Pérou. *Journal de la Société des Américanistes*, n.s. 49:7–35.

1963a   Datations à l'aide du Radio-Carbon 14, et problèmes de la préhistoire du Pérou. *Journal de la Société des Américanistes* 52:101–131.

1963b   *Notes relatives à des explorations archéologiques à Paracas et sur la côte sud du Peróu*. Paris: Travaux de L'Institut Français d'Études Andines.

1963c   *A Preceramic Settlement on the Central Coast of Peru: Asia, Unit 1*. Vol. 53, pt. 3. Philadelphia: American Philosophical Society.

1964   El Precerámico sin algodón en la costa del Perú. In *Actas y memorias, XXXV Congreso International de Américanistas, México 1962* (International Congress of Americanists), pp. 141–152. Mexico City: Instituto Nacional de Antropología e Historia.

1966a   *Geografía humana prehistórica y agricultura precolombina en la quebrada de Chilca*, vol. 1: *Informe preliminar*. Lima: Universidad Agraria.

1966b   Le complexe précéramique d'El Paraiso (Pérou). *Journal de la Société des Américanistes* 55-1:43–95.

1967   El complejo El Paraíso en el valle del Chillón, habitado hace 3,500 años: Nuevos aspectos de la civilización de los agricultores del pallar. *Anales Científicos de la Universidad Agraria* 5(3–4):241–280.

1969   Eléments de géographie humaine precolombienne. *L'Homme: Revue Française d'Anthropologie* 9(4):96–102.

1970a   Exploration of the Chilca Canyon, Peru. *Current Anthropology* 11(1):55–58.

1970b   La Grotte du Mégathérium à Chilca et les écologies du Hauth-Holocene, Péruvien. In *Échanges et communications: Mélanges offerts à Claude Lévi-Strauss à l'occasion de son 60eme anniversaire*, by C. Lévi-Strauss, J. Pouillon, and P. Maranda (contributors), pp. 413–436. The Hague: Mouton.

1970c   *Las lomas de Iguanil y el Complejo de Haldas*. Lima: Universidad Nacional Agraria, Departamento de Publicaciones.

1970d   Recolección y cultivo en los Andes precolombinos. *Anales Científicos* (Universidad Nacional Agraria, La Molina, Lima) 8(1–2):122–136.

1973   New Facts about Pre-Columbian Life in the Andean Lomas. *Current Anthropology* 14(3):271–280.

1980   *Prehistoric Andean Ecology: Man, Settlement and Environment in the Andes*, vol. 2: *The Deep South*. Prehistoric Andean Ecology. Lausanne, Switzerland: Centro de Investigaciones de Zonas Áridas (CIZA)/Fondation pour L'Étude des Problèmes de Terres Arides. Paperback 1981.

ENGELS, S., AND M. ROBERTS
2005   The Architecture of Prograding Sandy-Gravel Beach Ridges Formed during the Last Holocene Highstand: Southwestern British Columbia, Canada. *Journal of Sedimentary Research* 75:1052–1064.

EPSTEIN, S., R. BUCHSBAUM, H. LOWENSTAM, AND H. UREY
1953   Revised Carbonate Water Isotopic Temperature Scale. *Geological Society of America Bulletin* 2:417–425.

ESHBAUGH, W.
1976   Genetic and Biochemical Systematic Studies of Chili Peppers (*Capsicum*-Solanaceae). *Bulletin of the Tory Botanical Club* 102:396–403.

ESHBAUGH, W., S. GUTTMAN, AND M. MCLEOD
1983   The Origin and Evolution of the Domesticated *Capsicum* Species. *Journal of Ethnobiology* 3:49–54.

ESPINOZA, P., AND A. BERTRAND
2008   Revisiting Peruvian Anchovy (*Engraulis ringens*) Trophodynamics Provides a New Vision of the Humboldt Current System. *Progress in Oceanography* 79:215–227.

ETAYO-CADAVID, M., C. ANDRUS, K. JONES, G. HODGINS, D. SANDWEISS, S. UCEDA-CASTILLO, AND J. QUILTER
2013   Marine Radiocarbon Reservoir Age Variation in *Donax obesulus* Shells from Northern Peru: Late Holocene Evidence for Extended El Niño. *Geology* 41:599–602.

EUBER, J., S. SPENCER, AND D. COOK
2007   Incidence of Trachoma in Two Prehistoric Lower Illinois River Valley Populations. *Paleopathology Newsletter* 138:9–12.

EVANS, M., A. KAPLAN, AND M. CANE
2002   Pacific Sea Surface Temperature Field Reconstruction from Coral $\delta^{18}O$ Data Using Reduced Space Objective Analysis. *Paleoceanography* 17(1):7-1–7-13.

EZELL, K., D. PEARSALL, AND J. ZEIDLER
2006   Root and Tuber Phytoliths and Starch Grains

Document Manioc (*Manihot esculenta*) Arrowroot (*Maranta arundinacea*) and Llerén (*Calathea* sp.) at the Real Alto Site, Ecuador. *Economic Botany* 60: 103–120.

FAEGRI, K., J. IVERSEN, AND H. WATERBOLK
1964   *Textbook of Pollen Analysis*. New York: Hafner.

FAIRBANKS, R.
1989   A 17,000–Year Glacio-Eustatic Sea Level Record: Influence of Glacial Melting Rates on the Younger Dryas Event and Deep-Ocean Circulation. *Nature* 342:637–642.

FARNUM, J., AND R. BENFER
2004   Diet, Health, and Human Adjustment to Sedentism on the North Coast of Peru: New Evidence from Huaca Prieta. Paper presented at the 2004 Northeast Conference on Andean Archaeology and Ethnohistory, Yale University, New Haven, CT.

FEJOS, P.
1943   *Ethnography of the Yagua*. Viking Fund Publications in Anthropology, No. 1. New York: Viking Fund.

FELDMAN, R.
1977   Preceramic Corporate Architecture from Aspero: Evidence for the Origins of the Andean State. Paper presented at the 76th Annual Meeting of the American Anthropological Association's Andean Preceramic Symposium, Houston, TX.
1980   Aspero, Peru: Architecture, Subsistence Economy, and Other Artifacts of a Preceramic Maritime Chiefdom. PhD dissertation, Department of Anthropology, Harvard University, Cambridge, MA.
1986   Early Textiles from the Supe Valley, Peru. In *The Junius B. Bird Conference on Andean Textiles, April 7th and 8th, 1984*, edited by A. P. Rowe, pp. 31–46. Washington, DC: Textile Museum.

FENGER, T., D. SURGE, B. SCHÖNE, AND N. MILNER
2007   Sclerochronology and Geochemical Variation in Limpet Shells (*Patella vulgata*): A New Archive to Reconstruct Holocene Coastal Sea Surface Temperature. *Geochemistry Geophysics Geosystems* 8(7):Q07001.

FERNALD, M.
1950   *Gray's Manual of Botany*. 8th ed. New York: American Book Company.

FERNÁNDEZ D., A. ALICIA
1980   Los fechados radiocarbónicas en la arqueología de la provincia de Jujuy: Fechas radiocarbónicas de la Cueva CH III de Huachichocana, Tiniyan e Inca-Cueva. *Argentina: Radiodcarbono en Arqueología* 1(4/5):89–100.

FERREIRA, E., A. HULME, H. MCNAB, AND A. QUYE
2004   The Natural Constituents of Historical Textile Dyes. *Chemical Society Reviews* 33(6):329–333.

FINUCANE, B., P. AGURTO, AND W. ISBELL
2006   Human and Animal Diet at Conchopata, Peru: Stable Isotope Evidence for Maize Agriculture and Animal Management Practices during the Middle Horizon. *Journal of Archaeological Science* 33: 1766–1776.

FIRTH, R.
1951   *Elements of Social Organization*. London: Watts.

FITZHUGH, B.
2003   *The Evolution of Complex Hunter-Gatherers: Archaeological Evidence from the North Pacific*. New York: Kluwer Academic/Plenum.

FLANNERY, K. (ED.)
1986   *Guilá Naquitz: Archaic Foraging and Early Agriculture in Oaxaca, Mexico*. Orlando, FL: Academic Press.

FLANNERY, K.
1973   The Origins of Agriculture. *Annual Review of Anthropology* 2:271–310.

FLOOD, R., AND D. PIPER
1997   Amazon Fan Sedimentation: The Relationship to Equatorial Climate Change, Continental Denudation, and Sea-Level Fluctuations. In *Proceedings of the Ocean Drilling Program, Scientific Results, 155*, edited by R. Flood, D. Piper, A. Klaus, and L. C. Peterson, pp. 653–675. College Station, TX: Ocean Drilling Program.

FONTUGNE, M., P. USSELMANN, D. LAVALLÉE, M. JULIEN, AND C. HATTÉ
1999   El Nino Variability in the Coastal Desert of Southern Peru during the Mid-Holocene. *Quaternary Research* 52:171–179.

FORTES, M.
1949   *The Web of Kinship among the Tallensi*. International African Institute. London: Oxford University Press.

FORTES, M., AND E. EVANS-PRITCHARD (EDS.)
1940   *African Political Systems*. London: Oxford University Press.

FOUCAULT, M.
1972   *The Archaeology of Knowledge*. New York: Pantheon Books.

FOWLER, C. S. AND E. M. HATTORI
2008   The Great Basin's Oldest Textiles. In *The Great Basin: People and Place in Ancient Times*, edited by C. Fowler and D. Fowler, pp. 60–67. Santa Fe: School for Advanced Research Press.

FRANCO, T.
2015   Paleoecology and Sedentism of Early Coastal Hunter-Gatherers in North Chile. PhD dissertation, Vanderbilt University, Nashville, TN.

FRANQUEMONT, C., AND E. FRANQUEMONT
1987   Learning to Weave in Chinchero. *Textile Museum Journal* 26:55–78.

FRAYER, D.
1988   Auditory Exostoses and Evidence for Fishing at Vlasac. *Current Anthropology* 29:346–348.

FRIEDMAN, I., AND J. O'NEIL
1977   *Compilation of Stable Isotope Fractionation Factors of Geochemical Interest*. Washington, DC: U.S. Government Printing Office.

FRITZ, G.
1994   Are the First Farmers Getting Younger? *Current Anthropology* 35(3):305–308.

FUNG PINEDA, R.
1969   Las Aldas: Su ubicación dentro del proceso histó-

rico del Perú antiguo. *Dédalo: Revista de Arte e Arqueologia* (Museu de Arte e Arqueologia, Universidade de São Paulo), year 5(9–10):5–208.

1988 The Late Preceramic and Initial Period. In *Peruvian Prehistory: An Overview of Pre-Inca and Inca Society*, edited by R. W. Keatinge, pp. 67–96. Translated by Margaret Brown. Cambridge and New York: Cambridge University Press.

1991 El Precerámico Tardío en la costa. In *Los incas y el antiguo Perú*, pp. 152–167. Serie Catálogos, Colección Encuentros Quinto Centenario. Vol. 1. Madrid: Ayuntamiento de Madrid, Concejalía de Cultura: Centro de Cultura de la Villa.

GAFFNEY, C., AND J. GATER

2004 *Revealing the Buried Past, Geophysics for Archaeologists.* Stroud, Gloucestershire, UK: Tempus.

GAGNÉ, G.

2009 Gallinazo Disposal of the Dead and Manipulation of Human Remains at El Castillo de Santa. In *Gallinazo: An Early Cultural Tradition on the Peruvian North Coast*, edited by J.-F. Millaire and M. Morlion, pp. 207–222. Los Angeles: Cotsen Institute of Archaeology Press, University of California.

GALBRAITH, R., R. ROBERTS, G. LASLETT, H. YOSHIDA, AND J. OLLEY

1999 Optical Dating of Single and Multiple Grains of Quartz from Jinmium Rock Shelter, Northern Australia: Part I. Experimental Design and Statistical Models. *Archaeometry* 41:339–364.

GALINAT, W.

1975 Identificación del maíz de Tiliviche 1.B. MS.

GALLOWAY, A., S. SYMES, W. HAGLUND, AND D. FRANCE

1999 The Role of the Forensic Anthropologist in Trauma Analysis. In *Broken Bones: Anthropological Analysis of Blunt Force Trauma*, edited by A. Galloway, pp. 5–34. Springfield, IL: C. Thomas.

GÁLVEZ, C.

1999 Nuevos datos y problemas sobre el Paijanese en el Chicama: Aportes para una evaluación de la ocupación temprana en el norte del Perú. *Boletín de Arqueología PUCP* 3:41–54.

2012 Adobe, tiempo y arquitectura en el valle de Chicama: 1300 a.c.–1100 d.c. *Arkinka: Revista de Arquitectura, Diseño y Construcción* 16/195:88–97.

GÁLVEZ, C., J. CASTAÑEDA M., AND M. RUNCIO

2012 Geoglifos, ocupación y uso del espacio en el valle medio de Chicama, costa norte del Peru. In *Arqueología y antropología en la encrucijada*, edited by M. Teresita de Haro, A. Rocchietti, M. Runcio, O. Hernández de Lara, and M. Fernández, pp. 87–108. Buenos Aires: Centro de Investigaciones Precolombinas.

GAMBLE, C.

2007 *Origins and Revolutions: Human Identity in Earliest Prehistory.* Cambridge: Cambridge University Press.

2013 *Settling the World: The Archaeology of Deep Human History.* Cambridge: Cambridge University Press.

GARCÍA, A.

1974 El origen del sedentarismo en el área de Ayacucho, Perú. *Boletín del Instituto Nacional de Antropología e Historia, México* 11:15–30.

1994 Charophyta: Their Use in Paleolimnology. *Journal of Paleolimnology* 10:43–52.

GAYTON, A.

1967 Textiles from Hacha, Peru. *Ñawpa Pacha* (Instituto de Estudios Andinos, Berkeley) 5:1–14.

GEERTZ, C.

1973 *The Interpretation of Cultures: Selected Essays.* New York: Basic Books.

GENOVÉS, S.

1967 Proportionality of Long Bones and Their Relation to Stature among Mesoamericans. *American Journal of Physical Anthropology* 26:67–78.

GENTRY, A.

1993 *A Field Guide to the Families and Genera of Woody Plants of Northwest South America.* Chicago: University of Chicago Press.

1995 Diversity and Floristic Composition of Neotropical Dry Forests. In *Seasonally Dry Tropical Forests*, edited by S. Bullock, H. Mooney, and E. Medina, pp. 148–194. New York: Cambridge University Press.

GEOSCAN RESEARCH

2006 *Fluxgate Gradiometer, FM256, Instruction Manual Version 1.7.* Heather Brae, Chrisharben Park, Clayton, Bradford, Yorkshire: Geoscan Research.

GEPTS, P. (ED.)

1988 *Genetic Resources of Phaseolus Beans.* Dordrecht, Netherlands: Kluwer Academic Publishers.

GEPTS, P., K. KMIECIK, P. PEREIRA, AND F. BLISS

1988 Dissemination Pathways of Common Bean (*Phaseolus vulgaris*, Fabaceae) Deduced from Phaseolin Electrophoretic Variability: I. The Americas. *Economic Botany* 42(1):73–85.

GIDDENS, ANTHONY

1991 *Modernity and Self Identity: Self and Society in the Late Modern Age.* Cambridge.

GIOVANETTI, M., V. LEMA, C. BARTOLI, AND A. CAPPARELLI

2008 Starch Grain Characterization of *Prosopis chilensis* (Mol.) Stuntz and *P. flexuosa* DC, and the Analysis of Their Archaeological Remains in Andean South America. *Journal of Archaeological Science* 35(1):2973–2985.

GLYNN, P.

2003 Coral Communities and Coral Reefs of Ecuador. In *Latin American Coral Reefs*, edited by J. Cortes, pp. 449–472. Amsterdam: Elsevier.

GLYNN, P. W., B. RIEGL, S. PURKIS, J. M. KERR, AND T. B. SMITH

2015 Coral Reef Recovery in the Galápagos Islands: The Northernmost Islands (Darwin and Wenman). Coral Reefs DOI 10.1007/s00338-015-1280-4.

GODDE, K.

2010 An Examination of Proposed Causes of Auditory

Exostoses. *International Journal of Osteoarchaeology* 20:486–490.

GODELIER, M.

1999 *The Enigma of the Gift*. Chicago: University of Chicago Press.

GODIKSEN, J., M.-A. SVENNING, J. DEMPSON, M. MARTTILA, A. STORM-SUKE, AND M. POWER

2010 Development of a Species-Specific Fractionation Equation for Arctic Charr (*Salvelinus alpinus* (L.)): An Experimental Approach. *Hydrobiologia* 650: 67–77.

GOLDBERG, R., G. TISNADO M., AND R. SCOFIELD

1987 Characteristics of Extreme Rainfall Events in Northwestern Peru during the 1982–1983 El Niño Period. *Journal of Geophysical Research* 92(c13):14, 225–241.

GOLDSTEIN, D., AND R. COLEMAN

2004 *Schinus molle* L. (Anacardiaceae) *Chicha* Production in the Central Andes. *Economic Botany* 58(4):523–529.

GOODMAN, M., AND E. PATERNIANI

1969 The Races of Maize: III. Choices of Appropriate Characters for Racial Classification. *Economic Botany* 23:265–273.

GOY, J., J. MACHARE, L. ORTLIEB, AND C. ZAZO

1992 Quaternary Shorelines in Southern Peru: A Record of Global Sea-Level Fluctuations and Tectonic Uplift in Chala Bay. *Quaternary International* 15–16:99–112.

GRAUMONT, R., AND E. WENSTROM

1976 *Fisherman's Knots and Nets*. Centreville, MD: Cornell Maritime Press.

GRIEDER, T.

1986 Preceramic and Initial Period Textiles from La Galgada, Peru. In *The Junius B. Bird Conference on Andean Textiles, April 7th and 8th, 1984*, edited by A. P. Rowe, pp. 19–29. Washington, DC: Textile Museum.

1988 La Galgada Textile Specimens. In *La Galgada, Peru: A Preceramic Culture in Transition*, edited by T. Grieder, A. Mendoza, C. Smith Jr., and R. Malina, pp. 249–269. Austin: University of Texas Press.

1997 On Two Types of Andean Tombs. In *Arquitectura y civilización in the Andes*, edited by H. Bischof and E. Bonnier, pp. 107–119. Heidelberg, Germany: Reiss-Museum Mannheim, Peruvian-German Archaeological Society.

GRIEDER, T., A. BUENO MENDOZA, C. SMITH JR., AND R. MALINA

1988 *La Galgada, Peru: A Preceramic Culture in Transition*. Austin: University of Texas Press.

GROBMAN, A.

1982 Maíz (*Zea mays*). In *Precerámico Peruano: Los Gavilanes—Mar, desierto y oasis en la historia del hombre*, edited by D. Bonavia, pp. 157–180. Lima: Corporación Financiera de Desarrollo S.A. COFIDE, Instituto Arqueológico Alemán, Comisión de Arqueología General y Comparada.

2004 El origen del maíz. In *Cincuenta años del Programa Cooperativo de Investigaciones en maíz (PCIM), 1953-2003*, edited by W. F. Wilfredo Salhuana, pp. 426–470. Lima: Universidad Nacional Agraria, La Molina.

2013 Origin, Domestication and Evolution of Maize: New Perspectives from Cytogenetic, Genetic and Biomolecular Research Complementing Archaeological Findings. In *Maize: Origin, Domestication and Its Role in the Development of Culture*, edited by D. Bonavia, pp. 329–488. Cambridge: Cambridge University Press.

GROBMAN, A., D. BONAVIA, T. D. DILLEHAY, D. R. PIPERNO, J. IRIARTE, AND I. HOLST

2012 Preceramic Maize from Paredones and Huaca Prieta, Peru. *Proceedings of the National Academy of Sciences* 109:1755–1759.

GROBMAN, A., W. SALHUANA, AND R. SEVILLA, IN COLLABORATION WITH P. C. MANGELSDORF

1961 *Races of Maize in Peru*. Publication 915. National Academy of Sciences. Washington, DC: National Research Council.

GROSSMAN, E., AND T.-L. KU

1986 Oxygen and Carbon Isotope Fractionation in Biogenic Aragonite: Temperature Effects. *Chemical Geology* 59:59–74.

GUAMÁN POMA DE AYALA, F., AND L. BUSTÍOS GÁLVEZ

1956 *La nueva crónica y buen gobierno*. Lima: Editorial Cultura, Dirección de Cultura, Arqueología e Historia del Ministerio de Educación Pública del Perú.

GUMAER, D. R.

1985 Preliminary Report of Geophysical Surveying at the Nanchoc Cemetery Site. MS on file, Department of Anthropology, University of Kentucky, Lexington.

GUNDERSON, L., AND C. HOLLING

2001 *Panarchy: Understanding Transformations in Human and Natural Systems*. Washington, DC: Island Press.

GUNN, C., AND F. GAFFNEY

1974 Seed Characteristics of 42 Economically Important Species of Solanaceae in the United States. *USDA Technical Bulletin* 1471:1–33.

GUSHIKEN, S., T. ACUÑA, AND J. TORRES

2001 Dinámica poblacional de los algarrobales (*Prosopis pallida*) y El Niño en la costa norte del Perú. In *El Niño en América Latina: Impactos biológicos y sociales*, edited by J. Tarazona, W. Arntz, and E. Castillo de Maruenda, pp. 213–223. Lima: Consejo Nacional de Ciencias y Tecnología.

GUSTAFSON, G., AND G. KOCH

1974 Age Estimation Up to 16 Years of Age Based on Dental Development. *Odontologisk Revy* 25: 297–306.

GUZMÁN B., V.

1951 *Informe del viaje de exploración sobre la chirimoya y otros frutos tropicales: Otras exploraciones sobre la chirimoya.*

Lima: Ministerio de Agricultura, Dirección General de Agricultura, Centro Nacional de Investigación y Experimentación Agrícola "La Molina."

HAAS, J., AND W. CREAMER

2012   Why Do People Build Monuments?: Late Archaic Platform Mounds in Norte Chico. In *Early New World Monumentality*, edited by R. Burger and R. Rosenswig, pp. 289–312. Gainesville: University Press of Florida.

HAAS, J., W. CREAMER, L. HUAMÁN MESÍAC, D. GOLDSTEIN, K. REINHARDE, AND C. RODRÍGUEZ

2013   Evidence for Maize (*Zea mays*) in the Late Archaic (3000–1800 B.C.) in the Norte Chico Region of Peru. *Proceedings of the National Academy of Sciences of the United States of America* 110:4945–4949.

HABU, J.

2004   *Ancient Jomon of Japan (Case Studies in Early Societies).* Cambridge: Cambridge University Press.

HALL, R.

1997   *An Archaeology of the Soul: North American Indian Belief and Ritual.* Urbana: University of Illinois Press.

HALLMANN, N., M. BURCHELL, B. SCHÖNE, G. IRVINE, AND D. MAXWELL

2009   High-Resolution Sclerochronological Analysis of the Bivalve Mollusk *Saxidomus gigantea* from Alaska and British Columbia: Techniques for Revealing Environmental Archives and Archaeological Seasonality. *Journal of Archaeological Science* 36:2353–2364.

HAMMEKE, E.

2004   Logwood Dye on Paper. University of Texas at Austin. Electronic document: https://www.ischool.utexas.edu/~cochinea/html-paper/e-hammeke-04-logwood.html.

HANSEN, B., D. RODBELL, G. SELTZER, B. LEÓN, K. YOUNG, AND M. ABBOT

2003   Late-Glacial and Holocene Vegetational History from Two Sites in the Western Cordillera of Southwestern Ecuador. *Palaeogeography, Palaeoclimatology, Palaeoecology* 194:79–108.

HANSEN, D.

1990   Physical Aspects of the El Niño Event of 1982–1983. In *Ecological Consequences of the 1982-83 El Niño-Southern Oscillation*, edited by P. W. Glynn, pp. 1–20. Amsterdam: Elsevier.

HARDY, B.L., C. DAUJERDAD, P. FERNANDES, P. BÉAREZ, E. DESCLAUX, M. G. C. NAVARRO, S. PUAUD, AND R. GALLIOTTI

2013   Impossible Neanderthals? Making String, Throwing Projectiles and Catching Small Game during Marine Isotope Stage IV (Abri du Maras, France). *Quaternary Science Reviews* 82:23–40.

HARMANSAH, Ö.

2014   *Place, Memory, and Healing: An Archaeology of Anatolian Rock Monuments.* London: Routledge Press.

HARMS, H.

1922   Übersicht der bisher in altperuanishen Gräbern gefundenen Pflanzenreste. In *Festschrift Eduard Seler*, edited by W. Lehmann, pp. 157–186. Stuttgart: Strecker und Schröder.

HARNER, M.

1984   *The Jívaro: People of the Sacred Waterfalls.* Berkeley: University of California Press.

HARRINGTON, H.

1964   *Manual of the Plants of Colorado.* Chicago: Sage Books.

1967   *Edible Native Plants of the Rocky Mountains.* Albuquerque: University of New Mexico Press.

HARRIS, E.

1975   The Stratigraphic Sequence: A Question of Time. *World Archaeology* 7(1):109–121.

HARRIS, O., AND J. ROBB

2012   Multiple Ontologies and the Problem of the Body in History. *American Anthropologist* 114(4):668–679.

HASTORF, C., AND S. JOHANNESSEN

2009   Pre-Hispanic Political Change and the Role of Maize in the Central Andes of Peru. *American Anthropologist* 95(1):115–138.

HATTORI, E. M., AND C. S. FOWLER

2009   Recent Advances in Great Basin Textile Research. In *Past, Present, and Future Issues in Great Basin Archaeology: Papers in Honor of Don D. Fowler*, edited by B. Hockett, pp. 203–224. Nevada Cultural Resource Series No. 20. Elko: USDI Bureau of Land Management.

HAUG, G., K. HUGHEN, D. SIGMAN, L. PETERSON, AND U. RÖHL

2001   Southward Migration of the Intertropical Convergence Zone through the Holocene. *Science* 293:1304–1307.

HAWKES, J.

1989   The Domestication of Roots and Tubers in the American Tropics. In *Foraging and Farming: The Evolution of Plant Exploitation*, edited by D. R. Harris and G. C. Hillman, pp. 481–503. London: Unwin Hyman.

HAWKES, J., AND J. HJERTING

1969   *The Potatoes of Argentina, Brazil, Paraguay and Uruguay.* London: Oxford University Press.

HAWKES, K., AND J. O'CONNELL

1981   Affluent Hunters?: Some Comments in Light of the Alyawara Case. *American Anthropologist* 83(3):622–626.

HAYDEN, B.

1992   Models of Domestication. In *Transitions to Agriculture in Prehistory*, edited by A. Gebauer and T. Price, pp. 11–19. Madison, WI: Prehistory Press.

2001   The Dynamics of Wealth and Poverty in the Transegalitarian Societies of Southeast Asia. *Antiquity* 75:571–581.

HEDRICK, U. (ED.)

1972   *Sturtevant's Edible Plants of the World.* New York: Dover Publications.

HEIDEGGER, M.

1927   *Being and Time.* Translated by J. Macquarrie and E. Robinson. Oxford: Basil Blackwell. Reprint 1962.

HEIP, C.
1976   The Life-Cycle of *Cyprideis torosa* (Crustacea, Ostracoda). *Oecologia* 24:229–245.

HEISER, C.
1971   The Domestication of *Capsicum*: A Reply to Davenport. *Professional Geographer* 23:169–170.
1976   Peppers: *Capsicum* (Solanaceae). In *Evolution of Crop Plants*, edited by N. Simmonds, pp. 265–268. London: Longman.

HEISER, C., AND P. SMITH
1953   The Cultivated *Capsicum* Peppers. *Economic Botany* 7:214–227.

HELMS, M.
1992   Long-Distance Contacts, Elite Aspirations, and the Age of Discovery in Cosmological Context. In *Resources, Power, and Interregional Interaction*, edited by E. Schortman and P. Urban, pp. 157–174. New York: Plenum Press.

HENDERSON, A., S. CHURCHILL, AND J. LUTEYN
1991   Neotropical Plant Diversity. *Nature* 351:21–22.

HENRICH, J., AND R. BOYD
2008   Division of Labor, Economic Specialization, and the Evolution of Social Stratification. *Current Anthropology* 49(4):715–724.

HENRY, E. R.
2011   A Multistage Geophysical Approach to Detecting and Interpreting Archaeological Features at the LeBus Circle, Bourbon County, Kentucky. *Archaeological Prospection* 4:231–244.

HERNÁNDEZ-VERDUGO, S., P. ARANDA, AND K. OYAMA
1999   Síntesis del conocimiento taxonómico, origen y domesticación del género *Capsicum*. *Boletín de la Sociedad Botánica de México* 64:65–84.

HERTZ, R.
1960   *Death and the Right Hand*. Translated by R. Needham and C. Needham. New York: Free Press.

HESSE, R.
2009   Do Swarms of Migrating Barchan Dunes Record Paleoenvironmental Changes?: A Case Study Spanning the Middle to Late Holocene in the Pampa de Jaguay, Southern Peru. *Geomorphology* 104:185–190.

HEUSSER, C.
1971   *Pollen and Spores of Chile: Modern Types of the Pteridophyta, Gymnospermae, and Angiospermae*. Tucson: University of Arizona Press.

HODDER, I.
1982   *Symbols in Action*. Cambridge: Cambridge University Press.
1990   *The Domestication of Europe: Structure and Contingency in Neolithic Societies*. Cambridge: Cambridge University Press.

HØIE, H., E. OTTERLEI, AND A. FOLKVORD
2004   Temperature-Dependent Fractionation of Stable Oxygen Isotopes in Otoliths of Juvenile Cod (*Gadus morhua* L.). *ICES Journal of Marine Science* 61:243–251.

HOLLING, C.
1973   *Resilience and Stability of Ecological Systems*. Laxenburg, Austria: International Institute for Applied Systems Analysis.

HORKHEIMER, H.
1958   *La alimentación en el Perú Prehispánico y su interdependencia con la agricultura*. Lima: UNESCO, Programa de la Zona Árida Peruana.
1973   *Alimentación y obtención de alimentos en el Perú Prehispánico*. Lima: Universidad Nacional Mayor de San Marcos, Comentarios del Perú.

HOWE, M. A.
1914   The Marine Algae of Peru. *Memoirs of the Torrey Botanical Club* 15:1–185.

HRDLIČKA, A.
1933   Seven Prehistoric American Skulls with Complete Absence of External Auditory Meatus. *American Journal of Physical Anthropology* 17:355–379.
1938   The Femur of the Old Peruvians. *American Journal of Physical Anthropology* 23:421–462.
1941   Lower Jaw Double Condyles. *American Journal of Physical Anthropology* 28:75–90.
1943   Skull of a Midget from Peru. *American Journal of Physical Anthropology* 1:77–82.

HU, S., Q. CHENG, L. WANG, AND S. XIE
2012   Multifractal Characterization of Urban Residential Land Price in Space and Time. *Applied Geography* 34:161.

HUGHEN, K., J. SOUTHON, S. LEHMAN, AND J. OVERPECK
2000   Synchronous Radiocarbon and Climate Shifts during the Last Deglaciation. *Science* 290:1951.

HUGHES, C., C. BAILEY, AND S. HARRIS
2002   Divergent and Reticulate Species Relationships in *Leucaena* (Fabaceae) Inferred from Multiple Data Sources: Insights into Polyploid Origins and nrDNA Polymorphism. *American Journal of Botany* 89:1057–1073.

HUTCHINSON, D., C. DENISE, H. DANIEL, AND G. KALMUS
1997   A Reevaluation of the Cold Water Etiology of External Auditory Exostoses. *American Journal of Physical Anthropology* 103:417–422.

HUTCHINSON, J.
1959   *The Application of Genetics to Cotton Improvement*. London: Cambridge University Press.
1962   Historia y relaciones de los algodoneros. *Endeavour* 21(81):5–15.

HYLAND, D., I. ZHUSHCHIKHOVSKAYA, V. MEDVEDEV, A. DEREVIANKO, AND A. TABAREV
2002   Pleistocene Textiles in the Russian Far East: Impressions from Some of the World's Oldest Pottery. *Anthropologie* 40(1):1–10.

ILLINGWORTH, J.
2006   Tips and Tricks for Perishable Analysis and Perishable Conservation. Paper presented at the 12th Annual Meeting of the European Archaeological Association, Cracow, Poland.

INGOLD, T.

2000   *The Perception of the Environment: Essays on Liveli-hood, Dwelling and Skill.* New York: Routledge, New York.

INSTITUTE OF GEOLOGY AND MINERALS

1975   *Geological Map of Peru.* Geologic map, 1:1,000,000, LEYENDA. European Digital Archive of Soil Maps. Online at http://eusoils.jrc.ec.europa.eu /esdb_archive/EuDASM/latinamerica/lists/cpe .htm.

2015   The Soil Maps of Latin America and Caribbean Islands. Electronic document: http://eusoils.jrc .ec.europa.eu/ESDB_Archive/EuDASM/Latin America/maps/pe12004_2ge.htm.

INTERNATIONAL BOARD FOR PLANT GENETIC RESOURCES (IBPGR)

1983   *Genetic Resources of Capsicum, a Global Plan of Action.* Rome: IBPGR Executive Secretariat.

IRIARTE, J.

2003   Assessing the Feasibility of Identifying Maize through the Analysis of Cross-Shape Size and Tridimensional Morphology of Phytoliths in the Grasslands of Southeastern South America. *Journal of Archaeological Science* 30:1085–1094.

IRIARTE, J., AND E. PAZ

2009   Phytolith Analysis of Selected Native Plants and Modern Soils from Southeastern Uruguay and Its Implications for Paleoenvironmental and Archeo-logical Reconstruction. *Quaternary International* 193:99–123.

ISENDAHL, C.

2011   The Domestication and Early Spread of Manioc (*Manihot esculenta*, Crantz): A Brief Synthesis. *Latin American Antiquity* 22(4):452–468.

IZUMI, S., AND T. SONO

1963   *Andes 2: Excavations at Kotosh, Peru, 1960.* Tokyo: Kadokawa.

IZUMI, S., AND K. TERADA (EDS.)

1972   *Andes 4: Excavations at Kotosh, Peru, 1963 and 1966.* Tokyo: University of Tokyo Press.

JAILLARD, E., M. FEIST, N. GRAMBAST FESSARD, AND V. CARLOTTO

1994   Senonian-Paleocene Charophyte Succession of the Peruvian Andes. *Cretaceous Research* 15(4):445–456.

JENSEN, R., M. MCLEOD, W. ESBAUGH, AND S. GUTTMAN

1979   Numerical Taxonomic Analyses of Allozymic Variation in *Capsicum* (Solanaceae) *Taxon* 28: 315–327.

JOHNSON, J. (ED.)

2006   *Remote Sensing in Archaeology: An Explicitly North American Perspective.* Tuscaloosa: University of Ala-bama Press.

JOHNSTONE, W., T. KEATS, AND M. LEE

1982   The Anatomic Basis for the Superior Acetabular Roof Notch "Superior Acetabular Notch." *Skeletal Radiology* 8:25–27.

JOLIE, E., T. LYNCH, P. GEIB, AND J. ADOVASIO

2011   Cordage, Textiles and the Late Pleistocene Peopling of the Andes. *Current Anthropology* 52(2):285–296.

JONES, A.

2005   Lives in Fragments?: Personhood and the Euro-pean Neolithic. *Journal of Social Archaeology* 5:193–224.

JONES, G.

1987   A Statistical Approach to the Archaeological Iden-tification of Crop Processing. *Journal of Archaeologi-cal Science* 14:311–323.

JONES, K.

2009   Mollusk-Shell Radiocarbon as a Paleo-Upwelling Proxy in Peru. PhD dissertation, University of Arizona, Tucson.

JONES, T., S. FORTIER, A. PENTECOST, AND M. COLLINSON

1996   Stable Carbon and Oxygen Isotopic Compositions of Recent Charophyte Oosporangia and Water from Malham Tarn, UK: Palaeontological Implica-tions. *Biogeochemistry* 34:99–112.

JUDD, M.

2008   The Parry Problem. *Journal of Archaeological Science* 35:1658–1666.

KAPLAN, L.

1965   Archeology and Domestication in American *Pha-seolus* (Beans). *Economic Botany* 19(4):358–368.

1980   Variation in the Cultivated Beans. In *Guitarrero Cave, Early Man in the Andes*, edited by T. F. Lynch, pp. 145–148. Studies in Archaeology. New York: Academic Press.

1981   What Is the Origin of the Common Bean? *Eco-nomic Botany* 35(2):240–254.

1982   Pallar (*Phaseolus lunatus*). In *Los Gavilanes: Mar, desierto y oasis en la historia del hombre: Precerámico Peruano*, by D. Bonavia and R. C. de le Mata, pp. 181–182. Lima: Corporación Financiera de Desarrollo S.A. COFIDE, Instituto Arqueológico Alemán.

1995   Accelerator Dates and the Prehistory of *Phaseolus*. Paper presented at the 63rd Annual Meeting of the Society for American Archaeology, Minne-apolis, MN.

2000   Beans, Peas, and Lentils. In *The Cambridge World History of Food*, edited by Kenneth F. Kiple, and Kriemhild Connèe Ornelas, pp. 271–281. Cam-bridge: Cambridge University Press.

KAPLAN, L., AND T. LYNCH

1999   *Phaseolus* (Fabaceae) in Archaeology: AMS Radio-carbon Dates and Their Significance for Pre-Columbian Agriculture. *Economic Botany* 53: 261–272.

KAPLAN, L., T. THOMAS, AND C. SMITH JR.

1973   Early Cultivated Beans (*Phaseolus vulgaris*) from an Intermontane Peruvian Valley. *Science* 179(4068):76–77.

KAULICKE, P.

1997   La noción y la organización del espacio en el For-mativo Peruano. In *Espacio: Teoría y praxis*, edited by H. Córdoba, pp. 113–127. Lima: PUCP.

1999   *El período Arcaico en el Perú: Hacia una definición de los orígenes*. Lima: Boletín De Arqueología PUCP.

2001   *Memoria y muerte en el Perú antiguo*. Lima: Pontificia Universidad Católica del Perú.

2010   *El Perú antiguo (9000 A.C.-200 D.C.): Los períodos Arcaico y Formativo*. Lima: Empresa El Comercio SA, Lima.

KAULICKE, P., AND T. DILLEHAY (EDS.)
1999a   El periodo Arcaico en el Perú: Hacia una definición del los orígenes. *Boletín de Arqueología*, No. 3. Lima: Pontificia Universidad Católica del Perú (PUCP).

1999b   Introducción: ¿Porqué estudiar el periodo Arcaico en el Perú? In *El periodo Arcaico en el Perú: Hacia una definición del los orígenes*, pp. 9–17. Lima: Boletín de Arqueología PUCP.

KAUTZ, R.
1980   Pollen Analysis and Paleoethnobotany. In *Guitarrero Cave: Early Man in the Andes*, edited by T. Lynch, pp. 45–49. Studies in Archaeology. New York: Academic Press.

KEARNEY, T., AND R. PEEBLES
1960   *Arizona Flora*. Berkeley: University of California Press.

KEEFER, D., M. MOSELEY, AND S. DEFRANCE
2003   A 38,000–Year Record of Floods and Debris Flows in the Ilo Region of Southern Peru and Its Relation to El Niño Events and Great Earthquakes. *Palaeogeography, Palaeoclimatology, Palaeoecology* 194:41–77.

KEELEY, L.
1980   *Experimental Determination of Stone Tool Uses*. Chicago: University of Chicago Press.

KEEN, A.
1971   *Sea Shells of Tropical West America: Marine Mollusks from Baja California to Peru*. 2nd ed. Stanford, CA: Stanford University Press.

KELLEHER, M., D. MURRAY, A. MCGILLIVARY, M. KAMEL, D. ALLCUTT, AND M. EARLEY
2006   Behavioral, Developmental, and Educational Problems in Children with Nonsyndromic Trigonocephaly. *Journal of Neurosurgery* 105:382–384.

KELLY, K., AND D. JUDD
1976   The ISCC-NBS Method of Designating Colors and a Dictionary of Color Names. In *The Universal Color Language*, edited by K. Kelly, pp. 1–158. NBS Special Publication 440. Washington, DC: U.S. Department of Commerce, National Bureau of Standards.

KEMP, B. M, T. A. TUNG, AND M. L. SUMMAR
2009   Genetic Continuity after the Collapse of the Wari Empire: Mitochondrial DNA Profiles from Wari and Post-Wari Populations in the Ancient Andes. *American Journal of Physical Anthropology* 140(1):80–91.

KENNEDY, G.
1986   The Relationship between Exostoses and Cold Water: A Latitudinal Analysis. *American Journal of Physical Anthropology* 71:401–415.

KENNETT, D., AND B. CULLETON
2009   Shellfish Harvesting Strategies at El Varal. In *Settlement and Subsistence in Early Formative Soconusco: El Varal and the Problem of Inter-Site Assemblage Variation*, edited by R. Lesure, pp. 173–178. Los Angeles: Cotsen Institute of Archaeology.

KIDDER, T., AND K. SASSAMAN
2009   The View from the Southeast. In *Archaic Societies: Diversity and Complexity across the Midcontinent*, edited by T. Emerson, D. McElrath, and A. Fortier, pp. 667–694. Albany: State University of New York Press.

KIM, S. Y.
2000   Human Growth and Development: The Physical Growth of a Rural Andean Aymara Population in Bolivia. Senior thesis, Department of Anthropology, Yale University.

KIRCH, P.
2005   III Management and Human Dimensions — Archaeology and Global Change: The Holocene Record Publication. *Annual Review of Environment and Resources* 30:409. Palo Alto, CA: Annual Reviews.

KIRK, D. R.
1975   *Wild Edible Plants of Western North America*. Happy Camp, CA: Naturegraph Publishers.

KLAUS, H. D., C. S. LARSEN, AND M. E. TAM
2009   Economic Intensification and Degenerative Joint Disease: Life and Labor on the Postcontact North Coast of Peru. *American Journal of Physical Anthropology* 139:204–221.

KLIMO, P., JR., G. RAO, AND D. BROCKMEYER
2007   Congenital Anomalies of the Cervical Spine. *Neurosurgery Clinics of North America* 18:463–478.

KNIGHT, V. J.
2006   Farewell to the Southeastern Ceremonial Complex. *Southeastern Archaeology* 25:1–5.

KNIGHT, V. J., H. E. JACKSON, AND S. L. SCOTT
2010   *Mound Excavations at Moundville: Architecture, Elites, and Social Order*. Tuscaloosa: University of Alabama Press.

KOBAYASHI, I., AND T. SAMATA
2006   Bivalve Shell Structure and Organic Matrix. *Materials Science and Engineering* C26(4):692–698.

KOCH, P. L., N. TUROSS, AND M. L. FOGEL
1997   The Effects of Sample Treatment and Diagenesis on the Isotopic Integrity of Carbonate in Biogenic Hydroxylapatite. *Journal of Archaeological Science* 24:417–429.

KOCKELMAN, P.
2014   Agent, Person, Subject, Self: A Theory of Ontology, Interaction, and Infrastructure. *American Anthropologist* 116(3):682–683.

KOEPCKE, M.
1970   *The Birds of the Department of Lima, Peru*. Revised ed. Translated by E. J. Fisk. Wynnewood, PA: Livingston Publishing Company.

KONDO, R., C. CHILDS, AND I. ATKINSON
1994 *Opal Phytoliths of New Zealand*. Lincoln, New Zealand: Manaaki Whenua Press.

KOSTICK, E.
1963 Facets and Imprints on the Upper and Lower Extremities of Femora from a Western Nigerian Population. *Journal of Anatomy* 97:393–402.

KOUTAVAS, A., P. DEMENOCAL, G. OLIVE, AND J. LYNCH-STIEGLITZ
2006 Mid-Holocene El Niño–Southern Oscillation (ENSO) Attenuation Revealed by Individual Foraminifera in Eastern Tropical Pacific Sediments. *Geology* 34:993.

KOUTAVAS, A., J. LYNCH-STIEGLITZ, T. MARCHITTO, AND J. SACHS
2002 El Niño-Like Pattern in Ice Age Tropical Sea Surface Temperature. *Science* 297:226–230.

KOVACEVICH, B., AND M. G. CALLAGHAN
2013 *The Inalienable in the Archaeology of Mesoamerica*. Archaeological Papers of the American Anthropological Society, No. 23. Malden, MA: Wiley Periodicals.

KOYAMA, T.
1963 The Genus *Scirpus* Linn: Critical Species of the Section Pterolepis. *Canadian Journal of Botany* 41(7):1107–1131.

KOZAK, V., D. BAXTER, L. WILLIAMSON, AND R. L. CARNEIRO
1979 *The Heta Indians: Fish in a Dry Pond*. Anthropological Papers of the American Museum of Natural History 55(6). New York: American Museum of Natural History.

KRAFT, K. H., ET AL.
2014 Multiple Lines of Evidence for the Origin of Domesticated Chili Pepper, *Capsicum annuum*, in Mexico. *Proceedings of the National Academy of Sciences of the United States of America* 111:6165–6170.

KRAPOVICKAS, A.
1968 Origen, variabilidad y difusión del maní (*Arachis hypogaea*). In *Actas y Memorias, XXXVII Congreso Internacional de Americanistas*, pp. 517–534. Buenos Aires: República Argentina.
1969 The Origin, Variability and Spread of the Groundnut (*Arachis hypogaea*). In *Domestication and Exploitation of Plants and animals*, edited by P. J. Ucko and G. W. Dimbleby, pp. 427–441. Chicago: Aldine Publishing.
1973 Evolution of the Genus *Arachis*. In *Agricultural Genetics: Selected Topics*, edited by R. Moav, pp. 135–151. Jerusalem/New York: National Council for Research and Development/John Wiley and Sons.

KREMER PIGMENTS
2004 87100 Cyclododecane (C12H24), Sealing Wax. Electronic document: http://www.kremerpigmente.de/englisch/87100e.htm.

KUIJT, I.
2012 Home Is Where We Keep Our Food: The Origins of Agriculture and Visibility of Late Pre-Pottery Neolithic Food Storage. *Paleorient* 37(1):137–152.

LAKOFF, G., AND M. JOHNSON
2003 *Metaphors We Live By*. Chicago: University of Chicago Press.

LAMBECK, K., AND J. CHAPPELL
2001 Sea Level Change through the Last Glacial Cycle. *Science* 292:679–686.

LAMBECK, K., T. ESAT, AND E. POTTER
2002 Links between Climate and Sea Levels for the Past Three Million Years. *Nature* 419:199–206.

LANFRANCO, L. P., S. P. LANFRANCO, AND S. EGGERS
2009 Exostosis auditiva como marcador osteológico de actividad acuática en poblaciones Formativas de la Costa Norte del Perú. *Paleopatologia Española* 6:1–18.

LANGLIE, B., C. A. HASTORF, M. C. BRUNO, M. BERMANN, R. M. BONZANI, AND W. CASTELLÓN CONDARCO
2011 Diversity in Andean *Chenopodium* Domestication: Describing a New Morphological Type from La Barca, Bolivia 1300–1250 BC. *Journal of Ethnobiology* 31:72–88.

LANNING, E.
1963 A Pre-Agricultural Occupation on the Central Coast of Peru. *American Antiquity* 28(3):360–371.
1965 Early Man in Peru. *Scientific American* 213(4):68–76.
1967a *Peru before the Incas*. Englewood Cliffs, NJ: Prentice Hall.
1967b Preceramic Archaeology of the Ancón-Chillón Region, Central Coast of Peru. Report to the National Science Foundation on Research Carried Out under Grant GS869, 1965–1966.
1974 Western South America. In *Prehispanic America*, edited by Shirley Gorenstein, pp. 65–86. London: Thames and Hudson.

LASCANO, E., P. MARTINELLI, AND A. OSELLA
2005 EMI Data from an Archaeological Resistive Target Revisited. *Near Surface Geophysics* 4:395–400.

LATCHAM, R.
1924 *Organización social y las creencias religiosas de los antiquos araucanos*. Santiago de Chile: Imprenta Cervantes.

LATHRAP, D.
1974 The Moist Tropics, the Arid Lands, and the Appearance of Great Art Styles in the New World. In *Art and the Environment in Native America*, edited by M. King and I. Traylor Jr., pp. 115–158. Special Publications 7. Lubbock: Texas Tech University.
1984 Review of "The Origins of Agriculture: An Evolutionary Perspective." *Economic Geography* 60:339–344.

LATHRAP, D., D. COLLIER, AND H. CHANDRA
1976 *Ancient Ecuador/El Ecuador Antiguo*. Chicago: Field Museum of Natural History.

LATOUR, B.
1999 *Pandora's Hope: Essays on the Reality of Science Studies*. Cambridge, MA: Harvard University Press.

2004 Whose Cosmos, Which Cosmopolitics?: Comments on the Peace Terms of Ulrich Beck. *Common Knowledge* 10(3):450–462.

LATOUR, B., AND C. PORTER
1993 *We Have Never Been Modern.* New York: Harvester Wheatsheaf.

LAUER, W.
1968 Die glaziallandschaft des südchilenischen Seengebietes. *Acta Geographica* 20:215–236.

LAVALLÉE, D.
2000 *The First South Americans.* Salt Lake City: University of Utah Press.

LAVALLÉE, D., M. JULIEN, P. BÉAREZ, P. USSELMANN, M. FONTUGNE, AND A. BOLANOS
1999 Pescadores-recolectores arcaicos del extremo sur peruano. Excavaciones en la Quebrada de los Burros (Tacna, Perú). Primeros resultados 1995–1997. *Bulletin de l'Institut Français d'Études Andines* 28(1):13–52.

LAW, J.
1991 *A Sociology of Monsters: Essays on Power, Technology, and Domination.* London, New York: Routledge.
2002 *Aircraft Stories: Decentering the Object in Technoscience.* Durham, NC: Duke University Press.
2008 *Actor-Network Theory and Material Semiotics.* Lancaster, UK: Centre for Science Studies and Department of Sociology, Lancaster University.

LAW, J., AND A. MOL (EDS.)
2002 *Complexities: Social Studies of Knowledge Practices.* Durham, NC: Duke University Press.

LAZARETH, C., G. LASNE, AND L. ORTLIEB
2006 Growth Anomalies in *Protothaca thaca* (Mollusca, Veneridae) Shells as Markers of ENSO Conditions. *Climate Research* 30:263–269.

LEA, D., D. PAK, AND H. SPERO
2000 Climate Impact of Late Quaternary Equatorial Pacific Sea Surface Temperature Variations. *Science* 289:1719–1724.

LEBEDA, A., M. WIDRLECHNER, J. STAUB, H. EZURA, J. ZALAPA, AND E. KRÍSTKOVÁ
2006 Cucurbits (Cucurbitaceae; *Cucumis* spp., *Cucurbita* spp., *Citrullus* spp.). In *Genetic Resources, Chromosome Engineering, and Crop Improvement,* edited by R. J. Singh, pp. 271–376. Vegetable Crops, vol. 3. Boca Raton, FL: CRC Press.

LEE, D., S. CHUNG, H. KIM, AND K. YAM
1991 Nonenzymatic Browning in Dried Red Pepper Products. *Journal of Food Quality* 14:153–163.

LEMON, R., AND C. CHURCHER
1961 Pleistocene Geology and Paleontology of the Talara Region, Northwest Peru. *American Journal of Science* 259:410–429.

LEON, B.
1993 Catálogo anotado de las Fanerógamas del Perú. In *Las plantas vasculares en las aguas continentales del Perú,* compiled by B. León, F. Kahn, and K. R. Young, pp. 11–128. Lima: IFEA—Instituto Francés de Estudios Andinos.

LEON, J.
1964 *Plantas alimenticias andinas.* Lima: Instituto Interamericano de Ciencias Agrícolas, Zona Andina.
1966 Central American and West Indian Species of *Inga* (Leguminosae). *Annals of the Missouri Botanical Garden* 53(3):265–359.

LERNER, H.
2007 *Lithic Raw Material Variability and the Reduction of Short-Term-Use Implements: An Example from Northwestern New Mexico.* Oxford: Archaeopress.

LESTER, C.
1965 Report on Skeletal Material from Huaca Prieta, Peru, 3 Cases from Guañape, Viru Valley, Peru. Manuscript on file, American Museum of Natural History, New York.

LEVI-STRAUSS, C.
1950 The Use of Wild Plants in Tropical South America. In *Handbook of South American Indians,* edited by H. Steward, pp. 465–486. Washington, DC: Smithsonian Institution.

LEWIS, C. M., J. E. BUIKSTRA, AND A. C. STONE
2007 Ancient DNA and Genetic Continuity in the South Central Andes. *Latin American Antiquity* 18(2):145–160.

LIEVERSE, A., A. WEBER, V. BAZALIISKIY, O. GORIUNOVA, AND N. SAVEL'EV
2007 Osteoarthritis in Siberia's Cis-Baikal: Skeletal Indicators of Hunter-Gatherer Adaptation and Cultural Change. *American Journal of Physical Anthropology* 132:1–16.

LLAGOSTERA, A.
1992 Early Occupations and the Emergence of Fishermen on the Pacific Coast of South America. *Andean Past* 3:87–110.

LONG, A., B. BENZ, D. DONAHUE, A. JULL, AND L. TOOLIN
1989 First Direct AMS Dates on Early Maize from Tehuacán, México. *Radiocarbon* 31 (3):1035–1040.

LOVEJOY, C., R. MEINDL, T. PRYZBECK, AND R. MENSFORTH
1985 Chronological Metamorphosis of the Auricular Surface of the Ilium: A New Method for the Determination of Adult Skeletal Age at Death. *American Journal of Physical Anthropology* 68:15–28.

LOVELL, N.
1997 Trauma Analysis in Paleopathology. *Yearbook of Physical Anthropology* 40:139–170.

LOZA BONIFAZ, E., AND J. SAEZ
1971 Estudio sobre la evolución del *Gossypium barbadense* Linneo. *Anales Científicos* 9(1–2):1–17.

LUMBRERAS, L.
1972 *Los orígenes de la civilización en el Perú.* Lima: Milla Batres.
1974 *The Peoples and Cultures of Ancient Peru.* Washington, DC: Smithsonian Institution Press.
1989 *The Archaeology of Andean America.* UNESCO-sponsored programmes and publications. Lima: UNDP/UNESCO Regional Project on Cultural

Heritage and Development in Latin America and the Caribbean.

LYNCH, T. (ED.)

1980a   *Guitarrero Cave: Early Man in the Andes.* Studies in Archaeology. New York: Academic Press.

LYNCH, T.

1980b   Guitarrero Cave in Its Andean Context. In *Guitarrero Cave: Early Man in the Andes*, edited by T. Lynch, pp. 293–320. New York: Academic Press.

1980c   Setting and Excavations. In *Guitarrero Cave: Early Man in the Andes*, edited by T. Lynch, pp. 3–28. New York: Academic Press.

1980d   Stratigraphy and Chronology. In *Guitarrero Cave: Early Man in the Andes*, edited by T. Lynch, pp. 29–43. New York: Academic Press.

LYNCH, T., R. GILLESPIE, J. GOWLETT, AND R. HEDGES

1985   Chronology of Guitarrero Cave, Peru. *Science* 229(4716):864–867.

MACBRIDE, J.

1936–1956   *Flora of Peru.* Chicago: Field Museum of Natural History.

1943   *Flora of Peru: Leguminosae.* Botanical Series. Chicago: Field Museum of Natural History.

MACCORMACK, S.

1991   *Religion in the Andes: Vision and Imagination in Early Colonial Peru.* Princeton: Princeton University Press. Paperback 1993.

MACCURDY, G.

1923   Human Skeletal Remains from the Highlands of Peru. *American Journal of Physical Anthropology* 6:217–330.

MACNEISH, R.

1965   The Origin of American Agriculture. *Antiquity* 39:87–93.

1969   *First Annual Report of the Ayacucho Archaeological Botanical Project.* Andover, MA: Robert S. Peabody Foundation for Archaeology, Phillips Academy.

1983   The Ayacucho Preceramic as a Sequence of Cultural Energy-Flow Systems. In *Prehistory of the Ayacucho Basin, Peru*, vol. 4, edited by R. Vierra, R. MacNeish, A. Nelken-Terner, R. Laurie, and A. Cook, pp. 236–280. Ann Arbor: Robert S. Peabody Foundation for Archaeology, University of Michigan Press.

MACNEISH, R., AND A. COOK

1981   Rosamachay, Ac 117. In *Prehistory of the Ayacucho Basin, Peru, Vol. 2: Excavations and Chronology*, edited by R. MacNeish, A. Cook, L. Lumbreras, R. Vierra, and A. Nelken-Terner, pp. 121–124. Ann Arbor: University of Michigan Press.

MACNEISH, R., AND A. NELKEN-TERNER

1983   Introduction to Preceramic Contextual Studies. In *Prehistory of the Ayacucho Basin, Peru*, vol. 4, edited by R. Vierra, R. MacNeish, A. Nelken-Terner, R. Laurie, and A. García Cook, pp. 1–15. Ann Arbor: Robert S. Peabody Foundation for Archaeology, University of Michigan Press.

MACNEISH, R., A. NELKEN-TERNER, AND Á. COOK

1970   *Second Annual Report of the Ayacucho Archaeological Project.* Andover, MA: Robert S. Peabody Foundation for Archaeology, Phillips Academy.

MACNEISH, R., T. PATTERSON, AND D. BROWMAN

1975   *The Central Peruvian Prehistoric Interaction Sphere.* Papers of the Robert S. Peabody Foundation for Archaeology. Andover, MA: Phillips Academy.

MACNEISH, R., AND R. VIERRA

1983   *The Preceramic Way of Life in the Thorn Forest Scrub Ecozone.* In *Prehistory of the Ayacucho Basin*, vol. 4, edited by R. MacNeish, R. Vierra, A. Nelken-Terner, R. Laurie, and A. Cook, pp. 130–187. Ann Arbor: Robert S. Peabody Foundation for Archaeology. University of Michigan Press.

MACNEISH, R., R. VIERRA, A. NELKEN-TERNER, R. LURIE, AND A. COOK

1983   *Prehistory of the Ayacucho Basin, Peru.* Robert S. Peabody Foundation for Archaeology, vol. 4. Ann Arbor: University of Michigan Press.

MACNEISH, R., R. VIERRA, A. NELKEN-TERNER, AND C. PHAGAN

1980   *Prehistory of the Ayacucho Basin, Peru: Vol. 3, Nonceramic Artifacts.* Ann Arbor: University of Michigan Press.

MAJLUF, P., AND J. REYES

1989   The Marine Mammals of Peru: A Review. In *The Peruvian Upwelling: Ecosystem: Dynamics and Interactions. ICLARM Conference Proceedings*, edited by D. Pauly, P. Muck, J. Mendo, and I. Tsukayama, pp. 344–363. Manila: Instituto del Mar del Perú (IMARPE), Deutsche Gesellschaft für Technische Zusammenarbeit (GTZ), GmbH, International Center for Living Aquatic Resources Management.

MAKOU, M., T. EGLINTON, D. OPPO, AND K. HUGHEN

2010   Postglacial Changes in El Nino and La Nina Behavior. *Geology* 38:43–46.

MANDEVILLE, M.

1979   Report on Textiles from Paloma. Report on file in the Department of Anthropology, University of Missouri-Columbia.

MANGELSDORF, P., AND J. HERNÁNDEZ

1967   Prehistoric Maize from Huaca Prieta, Peru. *Maize Genetics Cooperation Newsletter* 41:48.

MANGELSDORF, P., R. MACNEISH, AND G. WILLEY

1965   Origin of Agriculture in Middle America. In *Handbook of Middle American Indians*, pp. 427–445. Austin: University of Texas Press.

MANN, R., AND J. VERANO

1990   Congenital Spinal Anomalies in a Prehistoric Adult Female from Peru. *Paleopathology Newsletter* 72:5–6.

MARTIN, A.

1946   The Comparative Internal Morphology of Seeds. *American Midland Naturalist* 36:513–660.

MARTINS, R.

1976   New Archaeological Techniques for the Study of

Ancient Root Crops in Peru. PhD dissertation, University of Birmingham, UK.

MASUDA, S.

1986 Las algas en la etnografía andina de ayer y de hoy. In *Etnografía e historia del mundo andino: Continuidad y cambio*, edited by Shozo Masuda, pp. 223–268. Tokyo: University of Tokyo.

MCANANY, P.

1998 Obscured by the Forest: Property and Ancestors in Lowland Maya Society. In *Property in Economic Context*, edited by R. Hunt and A. Gilman, pp. 73–87. Lanham, MD: University Press of America.

MCANULTY, S.

1977 Preliminary Report on the Textiles from Paloma. Unpublished manuscript.

MCCONNAUGHEY, T., AND D. GILLIKIN

2008 Carbon Isotopes in Mollusk Shell Carbonates. *Geo-Marine Letters* 28:287–299.

MCCORMAC, F., A. HOGG, P. BLACKWELL, C. BUCK, T. HIGHAM, AND P. REIMER

2004 SHCal04 Southern Hemisphere Calibration 0–1000 cal BP. *Radiocarbon* 46(3):1087–1092.

MCGLADE, J.

1995 Archaeology and the Ecodynamics of Human Modified Landscapes. *Antiquity* 69:113–132.

MCGUIRE, R.

1983 Breaking Down Cultural Complexity: Inequality and Heterogeneity. *Advances in Archaeological Method and Theory* 6:91–142.

MCLEOD, M., S. GUTTMAN, AND W. ESHBAUGH

1982 Early Evolution of Chili Peppers (*Capsicum*). *Economic Botany* 36(4):361–368.

MCNAMARA, K.

2010 *The Star-Crossed Stone: The Secret Life, Myths, and History of a Fascinating Fossil*. Chicago: University of Chicago Press.

MCVAUGH, R.

1958 Myrtaceae. In *Flora of Peru*, edited by G. Macbride, pp. 569–818. Chicago: Field Museum of Natural History.

MEINDL, R., AND C. LOVEJOY

1985 Ectocranial Suture Closure: A Revised Method for the Determination of Skeletal Age at Death Based on the Lateral-Anterior Sutures. *American Journal of Physical Anthropology* 68:57–66.

1989 Age Changes in the Pelvis: Implications for Paleodemography. In *Age Markers in the Human Skeleton*, edited by M. Iscan, pp. 137–168. Springfield, IL: Charles C. Thomas.

MENGHIN, O.

1962 *Estudios de prehistoria araucana*. Buenos Aires: Centro Argentino de Estudios Prehistóricos.

MERBS, C.

1996 Spondylolysis and Spondylolisthesis: A Cost of Being an Erect Biped or a Clever Adaptation? *Yearbook of Physical Anthropology* 39:201–228.

MIDDENDORF, E.

1890 *Wörterbuch des Runa Simi oder der Keshua-Sprache*. Leipzig: F. A. Brockaus.

MILLER, L.

2003–2004 Shigra Making in Cotopaxi. *Textile Museum Journal* 42–43:61–63.

MILNER, G.

2005 *The Moundbuilders: Ancient Peoples of Eastern North America. Ancient People and Places*. New York: Thames and Hudson.

MILSOM, J., AND A. ERIKSEN

2011 *Field Geophysics*. 4th ed. Southern Gate, Chichester, Sussex, UK: John Wiley and Sons.

MINK, P., II, AND G. MAGGARD

2011 A Technical Report of An Electrical Resistance and Magnetic Survey of Preceramic Features at the El Brujo Archaeology Complex, Magdalena de Cao, La Libertad Region, Peru. A report submitted to Tom Dillehay. Manuscript on file, Anthropology Dept., Vanderbilt University, Nashville, TN.

MINNIS, P., AND M. WHALEN

2010 The First Prehispanic Chile (*Capsicum*) from the U.S. Southwest/Northwest Mexico and Its Changing Use. *American Antiquity* 75:245–257.

MOERMAN, D.

1998 *Native American Ethnobotany*. Portland, OR: Timber Press.

MOL, A.

2002 *The Body Multiple: Ontology in Medical Practice*. Durham, NC: Duke University Press.

MOLLIER-VOGEL, E., G. LEDUC, T. BÖSCHEN, P. MARTÍNEZ, AND R. SCHNEIDER

2013 Rainfall Response to Orbital and Millennial Forcing in Northern Peru over the Last 18 ka. *Quaternary Science Reviews* 76:29–38.

MOORE, J.

1996 *Architecture and Power in the Ancient Andes: The Archaeology of Public Buildings*. New York: Cambridge University Press.

2014 *A Prehistory of South America: Ancient Cultural Diversity on the Least Known Continent*. Boulder: University Press of Colorado.

MOORE, K., A. AGUR, A. DALLEY

2014 *Essential Clinical Anatomy*. 5th ed. Philadelphia: Lippincott Williams and Wilkins.

MORÁN VAL, C.

1982 Descripción de las muestras 2. In *Precerámico peruano: Los Gavilanes—Mar, desierto y oasis en la historia del hombre*, by D. Bonavia, p. 181. Lima: Corporación Financiera de Desarrolo S.A. COFIDE.

MORENO, M., M. ROSENAU, AND O. ONCKEN

2010 Maule Earthquake Slip Correlates with Preseismic Locking of Andean Subduction Zone. *Nature* 467:198–202.

MOSCONE, E., M. SCALDAFERRO, M. GRABIELE, N. CECCHINI, Y. SÁNCHEZ GARCÍA, R. JARRET, J. DAVIÑA, D. DUCASSE, G. BARBOZA, AND F. EHRENDORFER

2007 The Evolution of Chili Peppers (*Capsicum*—Solanaceae): a Cytogenetic Perspective. *Acta Horticulturae* 745:137–170.

MOSELEY, M.

1975   *The Maritime Foundations of Andean Civilization.* Menlo Park, CA: Cummings Publishing Co.

1985   The Exploration and Explanation of Early Monumental Architecture in the Andes. In *Early Ceremonial Architecture in the Andes*, edited by C. Donnan, pp. 29–58. Washington, DC: Dumbarton Oaks.

1992   *The Incas and Their Ancestors: The Archaeology of Peru.* New York: Thames and Hudson, New York. Reprint 2001.

MOSELEY, M., AND L. BARRETT

1969   Change in Preceramic Twined Textiles from the Central Peruvian Coast. *American Antiquity* 34(2):162–165.

MOSELEY, M., AND G. WILLEY

1973   Aspero, Peru: A Reexamination of the Site and Its Implications. *American Antiquity* 38(4):452–468.

MOSES, M., AND P. UMAHARAN

2012   Genetic and Phylogenetic Relationships of *Capsicum chinense*. *Journal of the American Society for Horticultural Science* 137:250–262.

MOSTACERO, J., F. MEJIA COICO, AND O. GAMARRA TORRES

2009   *Fanerógamas del Perú: Taxonomía, utilidad y ecogeografía.* Trujillo. Peru: CONCYTEC.

MOY, C., G. SELTZER, D. RODBELL, AND D. ANDERSON

2002   Variability of El Niño/Southern Oscillation Activity at Millennial Timescales during the Holocene Epoch. *Nature* 420:162–165.

MUJICA BARREDA, E., R. FRANCO JORDÁN, C. GÁLVEZ MORA, J. QUILTER, A. MURGA CRUZ, C. GAMMARRA DE LA CRUZ, V. RÍOS CISNEROS, S. LOZADA ALCALDE, J. VERANO, AND M. AVEGGIO MERELLO

2007   *El Brujo: Huaca Cao, centro ceremonial moche en el Valle de Chicama/Huaca Cao, a Moche Ceremonial Center in the Chicama Valley.* Lima: Fundación Wiese.

MULHOLLAND, S.

1989   Phytolith Shape and Frequencies in North Dakota Grasses: A Comparison of General Patterns. *Journal of Archaeological Science* 16:489–511.

1993   A Test of Phytolith Analysis at Big Hidatsa, North Dakota. In *Current Research in Phytolith Analysis: Applications in Archaeology and Paleoecology*, edited by D. Pearsall and D. Piperno, pp. 131–145. Philadelphia: MASCA, University Museum of Archaeology and Anthropology, University of Pennsylvania.

MURPHY, R.

1925   *Bird Islands of Peru: The Record of a Sojourn on the West Coast.* New York/London: G. P. Putnam's Sons.

1936   *Oceanic Birds of South America: A Study of Species of the Related Coasts and Seas, Including the American Quadrant of Antarctica, Based upon the Brewster-Sanford Collection in the American Museum of Natural History.* 2 vols. New York: American Museum of Natural History.

MURRA, J.

1962   Cloth and Its Functions in the Inca State. *American Anthropologist* 64(4):710–728.

MURRAY, A., AND A. WINTLE

2003   The Single Aliquot Regeneration Dose Protocol: Potential for Improvements in Reliability. *Radiation Measurements* 37:377–381.

NAJ, A.

1992   *Peppers: A Story of Hot Pursuits.* New York: Alfred A. Knopf.

NATIONAL OCEANIC AND ATMOSPHERIC ADMINISTRATION (NOAA)

2012   *National Climatic Data Center.* Electronic document: https://www.ncdc.noaa.gov/.

NETHERLY, P.

1977   Local Level Lords on the North Coast of Peru. PhD dissertation, Cornell University, Ithaca, New York. University Microfilms, Ann Arbor.

1990   Out of Many, One: The Organization of Rule in the North Coast Polities, In *The Northern Dynasties: Kingship and Statecraft in Chimor*, edited by M. Moseley and A. Cordy-Collins, pp. 461–487. Washington, DC: Dumbarton Oaks Research Library and Collection.

1993   The Nature of the Andean State. In *Configurations of Power: Holistic Anthropology in Theory and Practice*, edited by J. Henderson and P. Netherly, pp. 11–35. Ithaca: Cornell University Press.

2011a   Dry Forest Biomes of the Coastal Valleys and Lower Western Slopes in Northwestern Peru. In *From Foraging to Farming in the Andes: New Perspectives on Food Production and Social Organization*, edited by T. Dillehay, appendix 2. New York: Cambridge University Press.

2011b   Pleistocene and Holocene Environments from the Zaña to the Chicama Valleys 25,000 to 6,000 Years Ago. In *From Foraging to Farming in the Andes: New Perspectives on Food Production and Social Organization*, edited by T. Dillehay, pp. 43–76. New York: Cambridge University Press.

NETHERLY, P., AND T. DILLEHAY

1986   Duality in Public Architecture in the Upper Zaña Valley, Peru. In *Perspectives on Andean Prehistory and Protohistory*, edited by D. H. Sandweiss and D. P. Kvietok, pp. 85–115. Ithaca: Cornell University.

NEWSOME, S., D. PHILLIPS, B. CULLETON, T. GUILDERSON, AND P. KOCH

2004   Dietary Reconstruction of an Early to Middle Holocene Human Population from the Central California Coast: Insights from Advanced Stable Isotope Mixing Models. *Journal of Archaeological Science* 31:1101–1115.

NICHOL, S., O. LIAN, AND C. CARTER

2003   Sheet-Gravel Evidence for a Late Holocene Tsunami Run-Up on Beach Dunes, Great Barrier Island, New Zealand. *Sedimentary Geology* 155:129–145.

NICKERSON, N.

1953 Variation in Cob Morphology among Certain Archaeological and Ethnological Races of Maize. *Annals of the Missouri Botanical Garden* 40:79–111.

NOLF, D.

1985 *Otolithi Piscium.* Handbook of Paleoichthyology, vol. 10. New York/Stuttgart: Gustav Fischer Verlag.

NÚÑEZ, L.

1974 *La agricultura prehistórica en los Andes Meridionales.* Antofagasta, Chile: Universidad del Norte.

NÚÑEZ, L., AND H. HALL

1982 Análisis de dieta y movilidad en un campamento arcaico del norte de Chile. *Boletín del Instituto Francés de Estudios Andinos* 11(3):91–113.

NÚÑEZ, L., AND C. MORAGAS

1977–1978 Ocupación arcaica temprana en Tiliviche, norte de Chile (I Región). *Boletín, Museo Arqueológico La Serena.* (Edición homenaje a Dn. Jorge Iribarren Charlín) 16:53–76.

NÚÑEZ, L., AND A. NIELSEN (EDS.)

2012 *Caravanas y pastoralismo en los Sur Andes.* La Paz: Imprenta Andina.

ODELL, G.

2001 Stone Tool Research at the End of the Millennium: Classification, Function, and Behavior. *Journal of Archaeological Research* 9(1):45–100.

ODY, P.

1993 *The Complete Medicinal Herbal.* New York: Dorling Kindersley.

OKUMURA, M., C. BOYADJIAN, AND S. EGGERS

2007 Auditory Exostoses as an Aquatic Activity Marker: A Comparison of Coastal and Inland Skeletal Remains from Tropical and Subtropical Regions of Brazil. *American Journal of Physical Anthropology* 132:558–567.

OLIVERA ALEGRE, G.

2006 *Tejidos Precerámicos de las salinas de Chao.* Lima: Universidad de San Martín de Porres.

OLLENDORF, A., S. MULHOLLAND, AND G. RAPP

1988 Phytolith Analysis as a Means of Plant Identification: *Arundo donax* and *Phragmites communis. Annals of Botany* 61:209–214.

OLSEN, B.

2010 *In Defense of Things: Archaeology and the Ontology of Objects.* Lanham, CA: Altamira Press.

OLSEN, K., AND B. SCHAAL

1999 Evidence on the Origin of Cassava: Phylogeography of *Manihot esculenta. Proceedings of the National Academy of Sciences of the United States of America* 96(10):5586–5591.

2001 Microsatellite Variation in Cassava (*Manihot esculenta*, Euphorbiaceae) and Its Wild Relatives: Further Evidence for a Southern Amazonian Origin of Domestication. *American Journal of Botany* 88(1):131–142.

2006 DNA Sequence Data and Inferences on Cassava's Origin of Domestication. In *Document-ing Domestication: New Genetic and Archaeological Paradigms,* edited by D. G. Bradley, M. A. Zeder, E. Emshwiller, and B. D. Smith, pp. 123–133. Berkeley: University of California Press.

O'NEALE, L.

1954 Textiles. In *Early Ancón and Early Supe Culture,* edited by G. R. Willey and J. M. Corbett, pp. 84–130. Columbia Studies in Archaeology and Ethnology 3. New York: Columbia University Press.

ORTEGA, Y., AND D. BONAVIA

2003 Cryptosporidium, Giardia, and Cyclospora in Ancient Peruvians. *Journal of Parasitology* 89:635–636.

ORTIZ, R., AND R. SEVILLA

1997 Quantitative Descriptors for Classification and Characterization of Highland Peruvian Maize. *Plant Genetic Resources Newsletter* 110:49–52.

ORTLIEB, L.

1989 Evolución climática al fin del Cuartenario en las regiones costeras del norte Peruano: Breve reseña. *Bulletin of the Institut Français des Études Andines* 18:143–160.

ORTLIEB, L., N. GUZMÁN, AND M. CANDIA

1994 Moluscos litorales del Pleistoceno Superior en el área de Antofagasta, Chile: Primeras determinaciones e indicaciones paleooceanográficas. *Estudios Oceanológicas* 13:57–63.

ORTLIEB, L., AND G. VARGAS

2003 Debris-Flow Deposits and El Niño: Manifestations along the Hyperarid Southern Peru/Northern Chile Coast. In *El Niño in Peru: Biology and Culture over 10,000 Years,* edited by J. Haas and M. Dillon, pp. 24–51. Chicago: Fieldiana Botany, Field Museum of Natural History.

ORTNER, D., AND W. PUTSCHAR

1985 *Identification of Pathological Conditions in Human Skeletal Remains.* Washington, DC: Smithsonian Institution Press.

OSBORN, A.

1977 Strandloopers, Mermaids, and Fairy Tales. In *For Theory Building in Archaeology,* edited by L. Binford, pp. 157–205. New York: Academic Press.

O'SHEA, J.

1984 *Mortuary Variability: An Archaeological Investigation.* Orlando, FL: Academic Press.

OSSA, P., AND M. MOSELEY

1971 La Cumbre: A Preliminary Report on Research into the Early Lithic Occupation of the Moche Valley, Peru. *Ñawpa Pacha: Journal of Andean Archaeology* 9:1–16.

OZHOVAN, M., I. DMITRIEV, AND O. BATYUKHNOVA

1993 Fractal Structure of Pores of Clay Soil. *Atomic Energy* 74:241–243.

PAICE, P.

1991 Extensions to the Harris Matrix System to Illustrate Stratigraphic Discussion of an Archaeological Site. *Journal of Field Archaeology* 18:17–28.

PANFILI, J., H. DE PONTUAL, T. HERVÉ, AND P. J. WRIGHT
2002   *Manual of Fish Sclerochronology*. Plouzané, France: Ifremer.

PARIS, H., AND E. KABELKA
2008–2009   Gene List for *Cucurbita* Species, 2009. *Cucurbit Genetics Cooperative Report* 31–32:44–69.

PASIECZNIK, N., P. FELKER, P. HARRIS, L. HARSH, G. CRUZ, J. TEWARI, K. CADORET, AND L. MALDONADO
2001   *The* Prosopis juliflora–Prosopis pallida *Complex: A Monograph*. Coventry, UK: HDRA.

PATINO, R., AND V. MANUEL
2002   *Historia y dispersión de los frutales nativos del neotrópico*. Cali, Colombia: Centro Internacional de Agricultura Tropical.

PATRUCCO, R., R. TELLO, AND D. BONAVIA
1983   Parasitological Studies of Coprolites of Pre-Hispanic Peruvian Populations. *Current Anthropology* 24:393–394.

PATTERSON, T.
1971   Central Peru: Its Population and Economy (Villages Developed in Central Peru Long before the Introduction of Agriculture). *Archaeology* 24(4):316–321.

PATTERSON, T., AND M. MOSELEY
1968   Late Preceramic and Early Ceramic Cultures of the Central Coast of Peru. *Ñawpa Pacha* (Instituto de Estudios Andinos, Berkeley) 6:115–133.

PATTERSON, W., G. SMITH, AND K. LOHMANN
1993   Continental Paleothermometry and Seasonality Using the Isotopic Composition of Aragonitic Otoliths of Freshwater Fishes. In *Climate Change in Continental Isotopic Records*, edited by P. Swart, K. Lohmann, J. McKenzie, and S. Savin, pp. 191–202. Geophysical Monograph, vol. 78. Washington, DC: American Geophysical Union.

PAULSON, A.
1974   The Thorny Oyster and the Voice of God. *American Antiquity* 39:597–607.

PEARSALL, D.
1978   Paleoethnobotany in Western South America: Progress and Problems. In *The Nature and Status of Ethnobotany*, edited by Richard Y. Ford, pp. 389–416. Ann Arbor: Anthropological Papers, Museum of Anthropology, University of Michigan.
1980   Pachamachay Ethnobotanical Report: Plant Utilization at a Hunting Base Camp. In *Prehistoric Hunters of the High Andes*, by John W. Rick, pp. 191–231. New York: Academic Press.
2000   *Paleoethnobotany: A Handbook of Procedures*. San Diego: Academic Press.
2003   Plant Food Resources of the Ecuadorian Formative: An Overview and Comparison to the Central Andes. In *Archaeology of Formative Ecuador*, edited by J. S. Raymond, R. L. Burger, and J. Quilter, pp. 213–257. Washington, DC: Dumbarton Oaks Research Library and Collection.
2008   Plant Domestication and the Shift to Agriculture in the Andes. In *The Handbook of South American Archaeology*, edited by H. Silverman and W. Isbell, pp. 105–120. New York: Springer.
2015   Paleoethnobotany. In *International Encyclopedia of the Social and Behavioral Sciences*, ed. James D. Wright, 17:456–461. 2nd ed. Oxford: Elsevier.

PEARSALL, D., K. CHANDLER-EZELL, AND A. CHANDLER-EZELL
2003   Identifying Maize in Neotropical Sediments and Soils Using Cob Phytoliths. *Journal of Archaeological Science* 30:611–627.
2004   Maize in Ancient Ecuador: Results of Residue Analysis of Stone Tools from the Real Alto Site. *Journal of Archaeological Science* 31:423–442.

PERRIER, C., C. HILLAIRE-MARCEL, AND L. ORTLIEB
1994   Paléogéographie littorale et enregistrement isotopique (^{13}C, ^{18}O) d'évènements de type El Niño par les mollusques Holocènes et récents du Nord-Ouest Péruvien. *Géographie Physique et Quaternaire* 48:23–38.

PERRY, L.
2002   Starch Granule Size and the Domestication of Manioc (*Manihot esculenta*) and Sweet Potatoes (*Ipomoea batatas*). *Economic Botany* 56(4):335–349.

PERRY, L., R. DICKAU, S. ZARRILLO, I. HOLST, D. PEARSALL, D. PIPERNO, M. BERMAN, ET AL.
2007   Starch Fossils and the Domestication and Dispersal of Chili Peppers (*Capsicum* spp. L.) in the Americas. *Science* 315:986–988.

PERRY, L., AND K. FLANNERY
2007   Precolumbian Use of Chili Peppers in the Valley of Oaxaca, Mexico. *Proceedings of the National Academy of Sciences* 104(29):11905–11909.

PERRY, L., D. SANDWEISS, D. PIPERNO, K. RADEMAKER, M. MALPASS, A. UMIRE, AND P. DE LA VERA
2006   Early Maize Agriculture and Interzonal Interaction in Southern Peru. *Nature* 440(7080):76–79.

PETERSON, LEE A.
1977   *Edible Wild Plants*. New York: Collier Books.

PHENICE, T.
1969   A Newly Developed Visual Method of Sexing in the *Os Pubis*. *American Journal of Physical Anthropology* 30:297–301.

PHILIPPON, M., M. MICHALSKI, K. CAMPBELL, M. GOLDSMITH, B. DEVITT, C. WIJDICKS, AND R. LAPRADE
2014   An Anatomical Study of the Acetabulum with Clinical Applications to Hip Arthroscopy. *Journal of Bone and Joint Surgery* 96:1673–1682.

PHILLIPS, S.
2009   Warriors, Victims, and the Merely Accident Prone: Fracture Patterns in Moche Skeletal Remains from Northern Coastal Peru. PhD dissertation, Department of Anthropology, Tulane University, New Orleans.

PICKERSGILL, B.
1969   The Archaeological Record of Chile Peppers (*Cap-

sicum spp.) and the Sequence of Plant Domestication in Peru. *American Antiquity* 34:54–61.

1971   Relationships between Weedy and Cultivated Forms in Some Species of Chili Peppers (Genus *Capsicum*). *Evolution* 25:683–691.

1972   Cultivated Plants as Evidence for Cultural Contacts. *American Antiquity* 27:97–104.

1977   Taxonomy and the Origin and Evolution of Cultivated Plants in the New World. *Nature* 268: 591–595.

1984   Migrations of Chili Peppers, *Capsicum* spp., in the Americas. In *Pre-Columbian Plant Migration*, edited by Doris Stone, pp. 105–123. Cambridge, MA: Peabody Museum of Archaeology and Ethnology.

1988   The Genus *Capsicum*: A Multidisciplinary Approach to the Taxonomy of Cultivated and Wild Plants. *Biologisches Zentralblatt* 197(4): 381–389.

2009   Domestication of Plants Revisited: Darwin to the Present Day. *Botanical Journal of the Linnean Society* 161:203–212.

PICKERSGILL, B., AND C. HEISER
1978   Origins and Distribution of Plants Domesticated in the New World Tropics. In *Advances in Andean Archaeology*, edited by D. Browman, pp. 133–166. The Hague: Mouton.

PICKERSGILL, B., C. HEISER JR., AND J. MCNEIL
1979   Numerical Taxonomic Studies on Variation and Domestication in Some Species of *Capsicum*. In *The Biology of the Solanaceae*, edited by R. Lester, A. Skelding, and J. Hawkes, pp. 679–700. The Linnean Society Symposia Series. London: Academic Press.

PILLSBURY, J.
1996   The Thorny Oyster and the Origins of Empire. *Latin American Antiquity* 7(4):313–340.

PINER, K., M. HALTUCH, AND J. WALLACE
2004   Preliminary Use of Oxygen Stable Isotopes and the 1983 El Niño to Assess the Accuracy of Aging Black Rockfish (*Sebastes melanops*). *Fisheries Bulletin* 103:553–558.

PINTAR, E.
2014   Continuidades e hiatos ocupacionales durante el Holoceno Medio en el norde oriental de la Puna Salada, Antofagasta de la Sierra, Argentina. *Revista de Antropologia Chilena* 46(a):51–71.

PIPERNO, D.
1988   *Phytolith Analysis: An Archaeological and Geological Perspective*. San Diego: Academic Press.

1989   The Occurrence of Phytoliths in the Reproductive Structures of Selected Tropical Angiosperms and Their Significance in Tropical Paleoecology, Paleoethnobotany and Systematics. *Review of Palaeobotany and Palynology* 61:147–173.

2006a   The Origins of Plant Cultivation and Domestication in the Neotropics: A Behavioral Ecological Perspective. In *Behavioral Ecology and the Transition to Agriculture*, edited by D. Kenneth and B. Whinter-

halder, pp. 137–166. Berkeley: University of California.

2006b   *Phytoliths: A Comprehensive Guide for Archaeologists and Paleoecologists*. San Diego: Altamira Press.

2007   Prehistoric Human Occupation and Impacts on Neotropical Forest Landscapes during the Late Pleistocene and Early/Middle Holocene. In *Tropical Rainforest Responses to Climate Change*, edited by M. Bush and J. Flenley, pp. 193–218. Berlin: Springer.

2011a   Northern Peruvian Early and Middle Preceramic Agriculture in Central and South American Contexts. In *From Foraging to Farming in the Andes: New Perspectives on Food Production and Social Organization*, edited by T. D. Dillehay, pp. 275–284. Cambridge: Cambridge University Press.

2011b   The Origins of Plant Cultivations and Domestication in the New World Tropics: Patterns, Process and New Developments. *Current Anthropology* 52(S2):453–470.

2012   New Archaeobotanical Information on Early Cultivation and Plant Domestication Involving Microplant (Phytolith and Starch Grain) Remains. In *Biodiversity in Agriculture: Domestication, Evolution and Sustainability*, edited by J. R. Harlan and P. L. Gepts, pp. 136–159. Harlan Symposium. Cambridge: Cambridge University Press.

2015   Early Agriculture in the Americas. In *The Cambridge World History, Vol. 2: A World with Agriculture, 12,000 BCE–500 CE*, edited by G. Barker and C. Goucher, pp. 514–538. Cambridge: Cambridge University Press.

PIPERNO, D., T. ANDRES, AND K. STOTHERT
2000a   Phytoliths in Cucurbita and Other Neotropical Cucurbitaceae and Their Occurrence in Early Archaeological Sites from the Lowland American Tropics. *Journal of Archaeological Science* 27:193–208.

PIPERNO, D., AND T. DILLEHAY
2008   Starch Grains on Human Teeth Reveal Early Broad Crop Diet in Northern Peru. *Proceedings of the National Academy of Sciences of the United States of America* 105(50):19622–19627.

PIPERNO, D., AND I. HOLST
1998   The Presence of Starch Grains on Prehistoric Stone Tools from the Humid Neotropics: Indications of Early Tuber Use and Agriculture in Panama. *Journal of Archaeological Science* 25: 765–776.

PIPERNO, D., AND D. PEARSALL
1993   Phytoliths in the Reproductive Structures of Maize and Teosinte: Implications for the Study of Maize Evolution. *Journal of Archaeological Science* 20: 337–362.

1998   *The Silica Bodies of Tropical American Grasses: Morphology, Taxonomy, and Implications for Grass Systematics and Fossil Phytolith Identification*. Smithsonian Contributions to Botany 85. Washington, DC: Smithsonian Institution Press.

PIPERNO, D., A. RANERE, I. HOLST, AND P. HANSELL
2000b   Starch Grains Reveal Early Root Crop Horticulture in the Panamanian Tropical Forest. *Nature* 407:894–897.

PIPERNO, D., A. RANERE, I. HOLST, J. IRIARTE, AND R. DICKAU
2009   Starch Grain and Phytolith Evidence for Early Ninth Millennium B.P. Maize from the Central Balsas River Valley, Mexico. *Proceedings of the National Academy of Sciences of the United States of America* 106(13):5019–5024.

PIPERNO, D., AND K. STOTHERT
2003   Phytolith Evidence for Early Holocene *Cucurbita* Domestication in Southwest Ecuador. *Science* 299: 1054–1057.

PLOWMAN, T.
1979   Botanical Perspectives of Coca. *Journal of Psychedelic Drugs* 11(1–2):103–117.

POHL, M., D. PIPERNO, K. POPE, AND J. JONES
2007   Microfossil Evidence for the Pre-Columbian Maize Dispersals in the Neotropics from San Andrés, Tabasco, México. *Proceedings of the National Academy of Sciences of the United States of America* 104(16):6870–6875.

PONCE, P.
2010   Biosocial Aspects of Sexual Division of Labour among Prehistoric Chinchorro People. *Society, Biology & Human Affairs* 75:41–65.

POPENOE, H., S. KING, J. LEÓN, L. KALINOWSKI, N. VIETMEYER, AND M. DAFFORN
1989   *Lost Crops of the Incas: Little-Known Plants of the Andes with Promise for Worldwide Cultivation, Report of an Ad Hoc Panel of the Advisory Committee on Technology Innovation*. Washington, DC: National Research Council, National Academy Press.

POPPER, V.
1979   *Analysis of Plant Remains from Huarmey Valley, Perú*. Ethnobotanical Laboratory Report, no. 526. Ann Arbor: University of Michigan.
1982   Análisis general de las muestras. In *Precerámico Peruano: Los Gavilanes—Mar, desierto y oasis en la historia del hombre*, by D. Bonavia, pp. 148–156. Lima: Corporación Financiera de Desarrollo S.A. COFIDE/Instituto Arqueológico Alemán.

PORSANI, J., G. DE MATOS JANGELME, AND R. KIPNIS
2011   Use of Ground-Penetrating Radar to Map Subsurface Features at the Lapa do Santo Archaeological Site (Brazil). *Near Surface Geophysics* 10:141–144.

POULIN, J.
2007   Identification of Indigo and Its Degradation Products on a Silk Textile Fragment Using Gas Chromatography-Mass Spectrometry. *Journal of the Canadian Association for Conservation* 32:48–56.

POZORSKI, S.
1976   Prehistoric Subsistence Patterns and Site Economics in the Moche Valley, Peru. PhD dissertation, University of Texas, Austin. Ann Arbor: University Microfilms.
1979   Prehistoric Diet and Subsistence of the Moche Valley, Peru. *World Archaeology* 11(2):163–184.

POZORSKI, S., AND T. POZORSKI
1977   Alto Salaverry: Sitio precerámico de la costa peruana. *Revista del Museo Nacional* 43:27–60.
1979a   Alto Salaverry: A Peruvian Coastal Preceramic Site. *Annals of Carnegie Museum* 48 (article 19): 337–375.
1979b   An Early Subsistence Exchange System in the Moche Valley. *Journal of Field Archaeology* 6(4):413–432.

POZORSKI, T., AND S. POZORSKI
1990   Huaynuná, a Late Cotton Preceramic Site on the Northern Coast of Peru. *Journal of Field Archaeology* 17(1):17–26.
1999   A Reexamination of the Development of the Late Preceramic Complex Society through the Radiocarbon Dates and Archaeological Researches in Casma Valley. *Boletín de Arqueología PUCP* 3:171–186.
2012   Preceramic Initial Period Monumentality within the Casma Valley of Peru. In *Early New World Monumentality*, edited by R. Burger and R. Rosenswig, pp. 364–398. Gainesville: University Press of Florida.

PRENTISS, A., I. KUIJT, AND J. CHATTERS (EDS.)
2009   *Macroevolution in Human Prehistory: Evolutionary Theory and Processual Archaeology*. New York: Springer.

PRESCOTT, J., AND L. STEPHAN
1982   The Contribution of Cosmic Radiation to the Environmental Dose for Thermoluminescence Dating: Latitude, Altitude and Depth Dependencies. *J. Council Europe PACT* 6:17–25.

PREUCEL, R.
2010   *Archaeological Semiotics*. Malden, MA: Wiley Press.

PRICE, T. (ED.)
2000   *Europe's First Farmers*. Cambridge: Cambridge University Press.

PRICE, T. D., AND J. A. BROWN
1985   *Prehistoric Hunter-Gatherers: The Emergence of Cultural Complexity*. Orlando: Academic Press.

PRIDEAUX, G., L. AYLIFFE, L. DESANTIS, B. SCHUBERT, P. MURRAY, M. GAGAN, AND T. CERLING
2009   Extinction Implications of a Chenopod Browse Diet for a Giant Pleistocene Kangaroo. *Proceedings of the National Academy of Sciences* 106:11646–11650.

PRIETO, G.
2012   Exploring Fishing Communities through Household Dimensions: The Pampas Gramalote Case. Paper presented at the 77th Annual Meeting of the Society for American Archaeology, Memphis, TN.
2014   The Early Initial Period Fishing Settlement of Gramalote, Moche Valley: A Preliminary Report. *Peruvian Archaeology* (Yamagata University Research Institute of Nazca, Peru) 1:1–46.

PRINGLE, H.
2001   The First Urban Center in the Americas. *Science*
        292 (5517):621.

PULGAR, V.
1967   *Geografía del Perú: Las ocho regiones naturales del*
        Perú. Lima: Universidad Nacional Mayor de San
        Marcos.

PURSEGLOVE, J.
1968a   *Tropical Crops: Dicotyledons 1.* London: Longmans,
        Green.
1968b   *Tropical Crops: Dicotyledons 2.* London: Longmans,
        Green.

QUILTER, J.
1989   *Life and Death at Paloma: Society and Mortuary Prac-*
        tices in a Preceramic Peruvian Village. Iowa City: Uni-
        versity of Iowa Press.
1991   Late Preceramic Peru. *Journal of World Prehistory*
        5(4):387–438.

QUILTER, J., B. OJEDA E., D. PEARSALL,
D. SANDWEISS, J. JONES, AND E. WINGS
1991   Subsistence Economy of El Paraíso, an Early Peru-
        vian Site. *Science* 251(4991):277–283.

QUINN, W., AND V. NEAL
1992   The Historical Record of El Niño Events. In *Cli-*
        mate since AD 1500, edited by R. S. Bradley and
        P. D. Jones, pp. 623–648. London: Routledge.

QUITMYER, I., D. JONES, AND W. ARNOLD
1997   The Sclerochronology of Hard Clams, *Mercenaria*
        spp., from the South-Eastern U.S.A.: A Method
        of Elucidating the Zooarchaeological Records of
        Seasonal Resource Procurement and Seasonality in
        Prehistoric Shell Middens. *Journal of Archaeological*
        Science 24:825–840.

RAMÍREZ, C.
1989   The Macrobotanical Remains. In *Monte Verde:*
        A Late Pleistocene Settlement in Chile, by T. D. Dille-
        hay, pp. 147–170. Washington, DC: Smithsonian
        Institution Press.

RAMÍREZ, R., C. PAREDES, AND J. ARENAS
2003   Moluscos del Perú. *Revista de Biología Tropical*
        51(3):225–284.

RANDALL, A., AND K. SASSAMAN
2010   Emergent Complexities during the Archaic Period
        in Northeast Florida. In *Ancient Complexities: New*
        Perspectives in Pre-Columbian North America, edited
        by S. Alt, pp. 8–31. Salt Lake City: University of
        Utah Press.

RANERE, A., D. PIPERNO, I. HOLST, R. DICKAU, AND
J. IRIARTE
2009   The Cultural Chronology Context of Early Holo-
        cene Maize and Squash Domestication in Cen-
        tral Balsas River Valley, Mexico. *Proceedings of the*
        National Academy of Sciences of the United States of
        America 106(13):5014–5018.

RAVERA, O., G. BEONE, P. TRINCHERINI, AND
N. RICCARDI
2007   Seasonal Variations in Metal Content of Two *Unio*
        pictorum mancus (Mollusca, Unionidae) Populations

from Two Lakes of Different Trophic State. *Journal*
of Limnology 66:28–29.

REDMAN, C.
2005   Resilience Theory in Archaeology. *American*
        Anthropologist 107:70–77.

REDMAN, C., AND A. KINZIG
2003   Resilience of Past Landscapes: Resilience Theory,
        Society, and the Longue Durée. *Conservation*
        Ecology 7:14.

REICHERT, E.
1913   *The Differentiation and Specificity of Starches in Relation*
        to Genera, Species, etc. Washington, DC: Carnegie
        Institution of Washington.

REIN, B., A. LÜCKGE, L. REINHARDT, F. SIROCKO,
A. WOLF, AND W. C. DULLO
2005   El Niño Variability off Peru during the Last
        20,000 Years. *Paleoceanography* 20(4):PA4003.

REINHARD, K., AND O. URBAN
2003   Diagnosing Ancient Diphyllobothriasis from
        Chinchorro Mummies. *Memórias do Instituto*
        Oswaldo Cruz 98 (Supplement):191–193.

REITZ, E.
2001   Fishing in Peru between 10000 and 3750 BP. *Inter-*
        national Journal of Osteoarchaeology 11:163–171.

REITZ, E., AND M. MASUCCI
2004   *Guangala Fishers and Farmers: A Case Study of Animal*
        Use at El Azúcar, Southwestern Ecuador. Pittsburgh:
        University of Pittsburgh Latin American Archae-
        ology Publications.

REITZ, E., I. QUITMYER, H. HALE, S. SCUDDER, AND
E. WING
1987   Applications of Allometry to Zooarchaeology.
        American Antiquity 52(2):304–317.

REITZ, E., AND E. WING
2004   *Zooarchaeology* (1999). Cambridge: Cambridge
        University Press.

RENFREW, C.
2001   Symbol before Concept: Material Engagement in
        the Early Development of Society. In *Archaeologi-*
        cal Theory Today, edited by I. Hodder, pp. 122–140.
        Cambridge: Polity Press.

RICHARDSON, J.
1978   Early Man on the Peruvian North Coast, Early
        Maritime Exploitation and the Pleistocene and
        Holocene Environment. In *Early Man in America,*
        from a Circum-Pacific Perspective, edited by A. L.
        Bryan, pp. 274–289. Occasional Papers, Depart-
        ment of Anthropology. Alberta, Canada: Univer-
        sity of Alberta.
1981   Modeling the Development of Sedentary Mari-
        time Economics on the Coast of Peru: A Pre-
        liminary Statement. *Annals of the Carnegie Museum*
        50(5):139–150.

RICHARDSON, J., D. SANDWEISS, R. FELDMAN, J. HSU,
AND E. REITZ
1990   Tempranas adaptaciones marítimas en los Andes:
        Estudio preliminar en el sitio Ring o Anillo,
        Ilo, Perú. In *Trabajos arqueológicos en Moquegua,*

Perú, edited by L. Watanabe, M. Moseley, and F. Cabieses, pp. 139–176. Programa Contisuyo del Museo Peruano de Ciencias de la Salud. Lima: Southern Peru Copper Corporation.

RICHERSON, P., R. BOYD, AND R. BETTINGER
2001   Was Agriculture Impossible during the Pleistocene But Mandatory during the Holocene?: A Climate Change Hypothesis. *American Antiquity* 66: 387–411.

RICK, J.
1990   Review of *The Preceramic Excavations at Huaca Prieta, Chicama Valley, Peru, Anthropological Papers of the American Museum of Natural History*, vol. 61 (pt. 1), edited by J. Bird, J. Hyslop, and M. Skinner. *American Anthropologist* 92:543–544.

RICK, T., AND J. ERLANDSON
2012   Kelp Forests, Coastal Migrations, and the Younger Dryas: Late Pleistocene and Earliest Holocene Human Settlement, Subsistence, and Ecology on California's Channel Islands. In *Hunter-Gatherer Behavior: Human Response during the Younger Dryas*, edited by M. I. Eren, pp. 79–110. Walnut Creek, CA: Left Coast Press.

RIVADENEIRA-GIURIA, V., F. CARDOSO, AND J. JUSCAMAITA
1989   Ubicación de los moluscos marinos del Perú en series bioeconómicas. *Boletín de Lima* 65:85–89.

RIVERA, M.
2006   Prehistoric Maize from Northern Chile. In *Histories of Maize: Multidisciplinary Approaches to the Prehistory, Linguistics, Biogeography, Domestication and Evolution of Maize*, edited by J. Staller, R. Tykot, and B. Benz, pp. 403–413. Walnut Creek, CA: Left Coast Press.

RIZZO, E., N. MASINI, R. LASAPONARA, AND G. OREFICI
2010   Archaeo-Geophysical Methods in the Templo de Escalonado, Cahuachi, Nasca (Peru). *Near Surface Geophysics* 8:433–439.

ROBBINS, W., J. HARRINGTON, AND B. FREIRE-MARRECO
1916   *Ethnobotany of the Tewa Indians*. Bureau of American Ethnology Bulletin 55. Washington, DC: Government Publication Office.

ROBERTS, L., U. GRANT, E. RAMÍREZ, W. HATHEWAY, D. SMITH, AND P. MANGELSDORF
1957   *Races of Maize in Colombia*. National Academy of Sciences, no. 510. Washington, DC: National Research Council.

RODBELL, D.
1993   The Timing of the Last Deglaciation in Cordillera Oriental, Northern Peru, Based on Glacial Geology and Lake Sedimentology. *Geological Society of America Bulletin* 105:923–924.

RODBELL, D., G. SELTZER, D. ANDERSON, M. ABBOTT, D. ENFIELD, AND J. NEWMAN.
1999   A ~15,000–Year Record of El Niño-Driven Alluviation in Southwestern Ecuador. *Science* 283: 516–520.

RODBELL, D., J. SMITH, AND B. MARK
2009   Glaciation in the Andes during the Lateglacial and Holocene. *Quaternary Science Reviews* 28: 2165–2212.

RODRÍGUEZ, R., R. WOODMAN, B. BALSLEY, A. MABRES, AND R. PHIPPS
1993   Avances sobre estudios dendrocronológicos en la región costera norte del Perú para obtener un registro pasado del fenómeno El Niño. *Bulletin de l'Institut Français d'Études Andines* 22(1):267–281.

RODRÍGUEZ-RODRÍGUEZ, E., R. BUSSMANN, S. ARROYO ALFARO, S. LÓPEZ MEDINA, J. BRICEÑO ROSARIO
2007   *Capparis scabrida* (Capparaceae), a Species from Peru and Ecuador in Urgent Need of Conservation Plans. *Arnaldoa* 14(2):269–282.

ROE, P. G.
1982   *The Cosmic Zygote: Cosmology in the Amazon Basin*. New Brunswick, NJ, Rutgers University Press.

ROGERS, D., AND S. APPAN
1973   *Manihot and Maniothoides (Euphorbiaceae): A Computer Assisted Study*. Flora Neotropica, Monograph 13. New York: Hafner.

ROMERO, C., G. BAIGORRIA, AND L. STROOSNIJDER
2007   Changes of Erosive Rainfall for El Niño and La Niña Years in the Northern Andean Highlands of Peru. *Climatic Change* 85:343–356.

ROMERO, H.
2003   *Algae: Macroalgas del norte de Chile*. Programa de Biodiversidad. Iquiquen Chile: Universidad Arturo Prat.

RONDÓN, X., S. BANACK, AND W. DÍAZ-HUAMANCHUMO
2003   Ethnobotanical Investigation of Caballitos (*Schoenoplectus californicus*; Cyperaceae) in Huanchaco, Peru. *Economic Botany* 57(1):35–47.

ROOSEVELT, A.
2007   Geophysical Archaeology in the Lower Amazon: A Research Strategy. In *Remote Sensing in Archaeology*, edited by J. Wiseman and F. El-Baz, pp. 435–467. New York: Springer.

ROSSEN, J.
1989   Ecotones and Low-Risk Intensification: The Middle Preceramic habitation of Nanchoc, Northern Peru. PhD dissertation, University of Kentucky.

2011a   Las Pircas Phase (9800–7800 BP). In *From Foraging to Farming: New Perspectives of Food Production and Social Organization*, edited by T. D. Dillehay, pp. 95–115. Cambridge: Cambridge University Press.

2011b   Preceramic Plant Gathering, Gardening, and Farming. In *From Foraging to Farming: New Perspectives on Food Production and Social Organization*, edited by T. D. Dillehay, pp. 177–192. Cambridge: Cambridge University Press.

ROSSEN, J., T. DILLEHAY, AND D. UGENT
1996   Ancient Cultigens or Modern Intrusions?: Evaluating Plant Remains in an Andean Case Study. *Journal of Archaeological Science* 23(3):391–407.

ROSTWOROWSKI DE DIEZ CANSECO, M.

2004 *Pachacamac y el Señor de los Milagros.* Lima: Instituto de Estudios Peruanos.

ROWE, A.

1977 *Warp-Patterned Weaves of the Andes.* Washington, DC: Textile.

ROWE, J.

1966 An Interpretation of Radiocarbon Measurements on Archaeological Samples from Peru. In *Proceedings of the Sixth International Conference, Radiocarbon and Tritium Dating,* pp. 187–198. Oak Ridge, TN: U.S. Atomic Energy Commission.

ROZIN, P., AND D. SCHILLER

1980 The Nature and Acquisition of a Preference for Chile Peppers by Humans. *Motivation and Emotion* 4:77–100.

RURY, P., AND T. PLOWMAN

1983 Morphological Studies of Archaeological and Recent Coca Leaves (*Erythroxylum* spp.). *Botanical Museum Leaflets* 29(4):297–341.

RUSSO, M.

2009 Ancient Sites and Architecture on the Atlantic and Gulf Coasts. In *Archaeology in America: Northeast and Southeast,* edited by F. McManamon, pp. 217–222. Westport, CT: Greenwood Publishing Group.

SAGÁSTEGUI ALVA, A.

1973 *Manual de las malezas de la costa norperuana.* Trujillo, Peru: Universidad Nacional de Trujillo.

SAGÁSTEGUI ALVA, A., AND S. LEIVA

1993 *Flora invasora de los cultivos del Perú.* Trujillo, Peru: CONCYTEC.

SAILLARD, M., S. HALL, L. AUDIN, D. FARBER, V. REGARD, AND G. HERAIL

2011 Andean Coastal Uplift and Active Tectonics in Southern Peru: Be-10 Surface Exposure Dating of Differentially Uplifted Marine Terrace Sequences (San Juan de Marcona, ~15.4° S). *Geomorphology* 128(3–4):178–190.

SALATI, E., AND P. VOSE

1984 Amazon Basin: A System in Equilibrium. *Science* 225:129–138.

SALLNOW, M.

1987 *Pilgrims of the Andes: Regional Cults in Cusco.* Washington, DC: Smithsonian Institution Press.

SAMUEL, C.

1990 *The Chilkat Dancing Blanket.* Norman: University of Oklahoma Press.

SANDWEISS, D.

1986 The Beach Ridges at Santa, Peru: El Niño, Uplift, and Prehistory. *Geoarchaeology* 1:17–28.

2003 Terminal Pleistocene through Mid-Holocene Archaeological Sites as Paleoclimatic Archives for the Peruvian Coast. *Palaeogeography, Palaeoclimatology, Palaeoecology* 194:23–40.

2014 Early Coastal South America. In *The Cambridge Prehistory,* edited by C. Renfrew and P. Bahn, pp. 1058–1074. Cambridge: University of Cambridge Press.

SANDWEISS, D., A. CANO, B. OJEDA, AND J. R. BERNARDINO

1999 Pescadores paleoíndios del Perú. *Investigación y Ciencia* 277:55–61.

SANDWEISS, D., K. MAASCH, C. ANDRUS, E. REITZ, M. RIEDINGER-WHITMORE, J. RICHARDSON, AND H. ROLLINS

2007 Mid-Holocene Climate and Culture Change in Coastal Peru. In *Climatic Change and Cultural Dynamics: A Global Perspective on Mid-Holocene Transitions,* edited by D. Anderson, K. Maasch, and D. Sandweiss, pp. 25–50. San Diego: Academic Press.

SANDWEISS, D., K. MAASCH, R. BURGER, J. RICHARDSON, H. ROLLINS, AND A. CLEMENT

2001 Variation in Holocene El Niño Frequencies: Climate Records and Cultural Consequences in Ancient Peru. *Geology* 29:603–606.

SANDWEISS, D., H. MCINNIS, R. BURGER, A. CANO, B. OJEDA, R. PAREDES, M. SANDWEISS, AND M. GLASCOCK

1998 Quebrada Jaguay: Early South American Maritime Adaptations. *Science* 281:1830–1832.

SANDWEISS, D., AND J. QUILTER

2012 Collation, Correlation, and Causation in the Prehistory of Coastal Peru. In *Surviving Sudden Environmental Change: Answers from Archaeology,* ed. P. Sheets and J. Cooper, pp. 11–17. Boulder: University Press of Colorado, 2012.

SANDWEISS, D., J. RICHARDSON, E. REITZ, H. ROLLINS, AND K. MAASCH

1996 Geoarchaeological Evidence from Peru for a 5000 Years B.P. Onset of El Niño. *Science* 273: 1531–1533.

1997 Determining the Early History of El Niño: Response. *Science* 276:966–967.

SANDWEISS, D., R. SOLIS, M. MOSELEY, D. KEEFER, AND C. ORTLOFF

2009 Environmental Change and Economic Development in Coastal Peru between 5,800 and 3,600 Years Ago. *Proceedings of the National Academy of Sciences of the United States of America* 106:1359–1363.

SANJUR, O., D. PIPERNO, T. ANDRES, AND L. WESSEL-BEAVER

2002 Phylogenetic Relationships among Domesticated and Wild Species of *Cucurbita* (Cucurbitaceae) Inferred from a Mitochondrial Gene: Implications for Crop Plant Evolution and Areas of Origin. *Proceedings of the National Academy of Sciences of the United States of America* 99(1):535–540.

SARMIENTO, G.

1975 The Dry Plant Formations of South America and Their Floristic Connections. *Journal of Biogeography* 2:233–251.

SASSAMAN, K.

2008 The New Archaic, It Ain't What It Used to Be. *SAA Archaeological Record* 8:6–8.

SASSAMAN, K. E., AND D. G. ANDERSON
1996   *Archaeology of the Mid-Holocene Southeast.* Gainesville: University Press of Florida.

SASSAMAN, K., AND D. HOLLY JR. (EDS.)
2011   *Hunter-Gatherer Archaeology as Historical Process.* Tucson: University of Arizona Press.

SATAKE, K., AND Y. FUJII
2010   Seismic Moment and Slip Distribution of the 1960 and 2010 Chilean Earthquakes as Inferred from Tsunami Waveforms. Paper presented at 2010 Fall Meeting, American Geophysical Union, G31B-02, San Francisco, CA, December 13–17.

SATO, S.
1997   Shell Microgrowth Patterns of Bivalves Reflecting Seasonal Change of Phytoplankton Abundance. *Paleontological Research* 1:260–266.

SAUER, C.
1950   Cultivated Plants of South and Central America. In *Handbook of South American Indians*, edited by J. H. Steward, pp. 487–543. Washington, DC: Smithsonian Institution, Bureau of American Ethnology.

SAUER, J.
1964   Revision of *Canavalia. Brittonia* 16(2):106–181.
1968   Ethnobotany of *Canavalia* in the New World. In *Actas y Memorias: 32 Congreso Internacional de Americanistas* (1966), pp. 507–508. Buenos Aires: República Argentina.

SAUER, J., AND L. KAPLAN
1969   *Canavalia* Beans in American Prehistory. *American Antiquity* 34(4):417–424.

SCARRE, C.
2002   *Monuments and Landscape in Atlantic Europe.* New York/London: Routledge.
2004   Death, Emotion and Identity in Late Mesolithic Cemeteries: Embodied Rituals and Ritualized Bodies. *Cambridge Archaeological Journal* 14:149–152.

SCHLANGER, S.
1992   Recognizing Persistent Places in Anasazi Settlement Systems. In *Space, Time, and Archaeological Landscapes*, edited by J. Rossignol and L. Wandsnider, pp. 91–111. New York: Plenum Press.

SCHNEIDER, B.
1976   *Personnel Selection and Organizational Behavior: An Integrated View.* Research Report No. 14. Washington, DC: ERIC Clearinghouse.

SCHOENINGER, M., M. DENIRO, AND H. TAUBER
1983   Stable Nitrogen Isotope Ratios of Bone Collagen Reflect Marine and Terrestrial Components of Prehistoric Human Diets. *Science* 220:1381–1383.

SCHÖNE, B., AND D. SURGE
2012   Treatise Online no. 46: Part N, Revised, Vol. 1, Chapter 14: Bivalve Sclerochronology and Geochemistry. *Treatise Online* 46:1–24.

SCHUBERT, B., P. UNGAR, AND L. DESANTIS
2010   Carnassial Microwear and Dietary Behaviour in Large Carnivorans. *Journal of Zoology* 280:257–263.

SCHURR, THEODORE G.
2004   The Peopling of the New World: Perspectives from Molecular Anthropology. *Annual Review of Anthropology* 33:551–583.

SCHWEIGGER, E.
1964   *El litoral peruano.* 2nd ed. Lima: Universidad Nacional Federico Villarreal.

SCOTT, E.
1979   Dental Wear Scoring Technique. *American Journal of Physical Anthropology* 51:213–218.

SCOTT, R., P. UNGAR, T. BERGSTROM, C. BROWN, B. CHILDS, M. TEAFORD, A. WALKER
2006   Dental Microwear Texture Analysis: Technical Considerations. *Journal of Human Evolution* 51: 339–349.

SEIJO, G., G. LAVIA, A. FERNÁNDEZ, A. KRAPOVICKAS, D. DUCASSE, D. BERTIOLI, AND E. MOSCONE
2007   Genomic Relationships between the Cultivated Peanut (*Arachis hypogaea*, Leguminosae) and Its Close Relatives Revealed by Double GISH. *American Journal of Botany* 94(12):1963–1971.

SENDULSKY, T., AND L. LABOURIAU
1966   Corpos siliceos de Gramineas dos Cerrados—I. *Annais da Academia Brasileira de Ciencias* 38:159–185.

SEVILLA, R.
1974   *Razas de maíz: Sabanero.* Informativo del Maíz, no. 4. Lima: Programa Cooperativo de Investigaciones en Maíz, Universidad Nacional Agraria La Molina.
1975   *Razas de maíz: Cuzco.* Informativo del Maíz, no. 5. Lima: Programa Cooperativo de Investigaciones en Maíz, Universidad Nacional Agraria La Molina.
1977   *Razas de maíz: Cuzco Cristalino Amarillo.* Informativo del Maíz, no. 17. Lima: Programa Cooperativo de Investigaciones en Maíz, Universidad Nacional Agraria La Molina.
1984   *Evaluación del germoplasma de maíz del Cono Sur de Sudamérica con fines de agrupación racial.* Informativo del Maíz, no. 24 (September–October). Lima: Universidad Nacional Agraria La Molina.

SHACKLETON, N., M. SÁNCHEZ GONI, D. PAILLERC, AND Y. LANCELOT
2003   Marine Isotope Substage 5e and the Eemian Interglacial. *Global and Planetary Change* 36:151–155.

SHADY S., R.
2004   *Caral: La ciudad del fuego sagrado/Caral: The City of the Sacred Fire.* Lima: Interbank and Centura Sab.

SHANKS, M., AND C. TILLEY
1992   *Re-constructing Archaeology: Theory and Practice.* New York: Routledge.

SHEPARD, G. H., JR.
2006   Obsequio de la mujer araña: Hilando y tejiendo entre los Matsiguenka/Gift of the Spider Woman: Spinning and Weaving among the Matsigenka. In *Tejidos enigmáticos peruana/Enigmatic Textile Art of the Peruvian Amazon*, edited by G. L. Pardo, pp. 39–57. Lima: Cotton Knit.

SHIMOJI, T., S. SHIMABUKURO, S. SUGAMA, AND Y. OCHIAI
2002   Mild Trignocephaly with Clinical Symptoms:

Analysis of Surgical Results in 65 Patients. *Child's Nervous System* 18:215–224.

SHINODA, K.-I., N. ADACHI, S. GUILLEN, AND I. SHIMADA
2006   Mitochondrial DNA Analysis of Ancient Peruvian Highlanders. *American Journal of Physical Anthropology* 131(1):98–107.

SIELFELD, W., AND A. GUZMÁN
2002   Effect of El Niño 1997/98 on a Population of the Southern Sea Lion (*Otaria flavescens* Shaw) from Punta Patache/Punta Negra (Iquique, Chile). *Investigaciones Marinas* 30(1):158–160.

SIELFELD, W., M. VARGAS, V. BERRÍOS, AND G. AGUIRRE
2002   Warm ENSO Events and Their Effects on the Coastal Fish Fauna of Northern Chile. *Investigaciones Marinas* 30(1):122–124.

SMARTT, J.
1990   *Grain Legumes: Evolution and Genetic Resources*. New York: Cambridge University Press.

SMITH, A.
1999   An Introduction to Textile Materials: Their Structure, Properties and Deterioration. *Journal of the Society of Archivists* 20(1). Electronic document: http://search.epnet.com/direct.asp?an=1806103&db=afh.

SMITH, A., AND D. HORNE
2002   Ecology of Marine, Marginal Marine and Non-marine Ostracodes. In *The Ostracoda: Applications in Quaternary Research*, edited by J. Holmes and A. Chivas, pp. 37–64. Geophysical Monograph Series, vol. 131. Washington, DC: American Geophysical Union.

SMITH, B.
1984   Patterns of Molar Wear in Hunter-Gatherers and Agriculturalists. *American Journal of Physical Anthropology* 63(1):39–56.
1997   The Initial Domestication of *Cucurbita pepo* in the Americas 10,000 Years Ago. *Science* 276(5314):932–934.

SMITH, C. E., JR.
1967   Plant Remains. In *The Prehistory of the Tehuacán Valley*, edited by D. S. Byers, pp. 220–255. Austin: University of Texas Press.
1968   The New World Centers of Origin of Cultivated Plants and the Archaeological Evidence. *Economic Botany* 22(3):253–266.
1987   Current Archaeological Evidence for the Beginning of American Agriculture. In *Studies in the Neolithic and Urban Revolutions: The V. Gordon Childe Colloquium*, ed. L. Manzanilla, pp. 81–101. Oxford: British Archaeological Reports.
1988   Floral Remains. In *La Galgada, Peru: A Preceramic Culture in Transition*, edited by T. Grieder, A. B. Mendoza, C. Smith Jr., and R. Malina, pp. 125–151. Austin: University of Texas Press.

SMITH, C., JR., AND R. MACNEISH
1964   Antiquity of American Polyploid Cottons. *Science* 143(3607):675–676.

SMITH, C., JR., AND S. STEPHENS
1971   Critical Identification of Mexican Archaeological Cotton Remains. *Science* 25(2):160–168.

SMITH, P., AND C. HEISER
1957   Taxonomy of *Capsicum sinense* Jacq. and the Geographic Distribution of the Cultivated *Capsicum* Species. *Bulletin of the Torrey Botanical Club* 84:413–420.

SOFFER, O., J. ADOVASIO, J. ILLINGWORTH, H. AMIRKHANOV, N. PRASLOV, AND M. STREET
2000   Palaeolithic Perishables Made Permanent. *Antiquity* 74:812–821.

SOLIS R., J. HAAS, AND W. CREAMER
2001   Dating Caral, a Preceramic Site in the Supe Valley on the Central Coast of Peru. *Science* 292:723–726.

SOMERS, L.
1998   Geophysical Remote Sensing Survey of the Quartermaster Depot Dump at Fort Laramie National Historic Site. In *Archeology at the Fort Laramie Quartermaster Dump Area, 1994–1996*, edited by D. N. Walker, pp. 81–90. Cultural Resource Selections Intermountain Region, no. 13. Denver: National Park Service.

SONDAHL, M., AND L. LABOURIAU
1970   Corpos silicosos de gramineas dos Cerrados, IV. *Pesquisas Agropecuarias Brasileiras* 5:183–207.

SOUKUP, J.
1987   *Vocabulario de los nombres vulgares de la flora peruana y catálogo de los géneros*. 2nd ed. Lima: Salesiana.

SPENCE-MORROW, G.
2009   Analyzing the Invisible: Syntactic Interpretation of Archaeological Remains through Geophysical Prospection. In *Proceedings of the 7th International Space Syntax Symposium*, edited by D. Koch, L. Marcus, J. Steen, Ref. 106, pp. 1–10. Stockholm: KTH.

SPISKE, M., J. PIEPENBREIER, C. BENAVENTE, A. KUNZ, H. BAHLBURG, AND J. STEFFAHN
2013   Historical Tsunami Deposits in Peru: Sedimentology, Inverse Modeling and Optically Stimulated Luminescence Dating. *Quaternary International* 305:31–44.

SPLITSTOSER, J.
2009   Weaving the Structure of the Cosmos: Cloth, Agency, and Worldview at Cerrillos, An Early Paracas Site in the Ica Valley, Peru. PhD dissertation, Department of Anthropology, Catholic University of America, Washington, DC.
2012   The Parenthetical Notation Method for Recording Yarn Structure. In *Proceedings of the 13th Biennial Symposium of the Textile Society of America, Textile & Politics, September 19–22, Washington, DC*. Lincoln: University of Nebraska. Electronic document: http://digitalcommons.unl.edu/tsaconf/745.

SPLITSTOSER, J. C., T. D. DILLEHAY, J. WOUTERS, AND A. CLARO
2016   Early Prehispanic Use of Indigo Blue in Peru. *Science Advances*, Vol. 2, No. 9.

SPOONER, D., K. MCLEAN, G. RAMSAY, R. WAUGH, AND G. BRYAN

2005   A Single Domestication for Potato Based on Multilocus Amplified Fragment Length Polymorphism Genotyping. *Proceedings of the National Academy of Sciences of the United States of America* 102(41):14694–14699.

STACKELBECK, K.

2011   Faunal Remains. In *From Foraging to Farming in the Andes: New Perspectives on Food Production and Social Organization*, edited by Tom D. Dillehay, pp. 193–204. Cambridge: Cambridge University Press.

STANDEN, V., AND B. ARRIAZA

2000   Trauma in the Preceramic Coastal Populations of Northern Chile: Violence or Occupational Hazards? *American Journal of Physical Anthropology* 112: 239–249.

STANDEN, V., B. ARRIAZA, AND C. SANTORO

1997   External Auditory Exostosis in Prehistoric Chilean Populations: A Test of the Cold Water Hypothesis. *American Journal of Physical Anthropology* 103:119–129.

STANDLEY, P.

1937   Chenopodiaceae. In *Flora of Peru*, edited by J. F. MacBride, pp. 469–478. Botanical Series. Chicago: Field Museum of Natural History.

STEIN, G.

1998   Heterogeneity, Power, and Political Economy: Some Current Research Issues in the Archaeology of Old World Complex Societies. *Journal of Archaeological Research* 6(1):1–44.

STEPHENS, S.

1970   The Botanical Identification of Archaeological Cotton. *American Antiquity* 35(3):367–373.

1974   The Use of Two Polymorphic Systems, Nectary Fringe Hairs and Corky Alleles, as Indicators of Phylogenetic Relationships in New World Cotton. *Biotropica* 6(3):194–201.

1975   A Reexamination of the Cotton Remains from Huaca Prieta, North Coastal Peru. *American Antiquity* 40(4):406–419.

1980   Cotton. In *Aspero Peru: Architecture, Subsistence Economy, and Other Artifacts of a Preceramic Maritime chiefdom*, edited by R. Feldman, pp. 240–245. PhD dissertation, Anthropology Department, Harvard University, Cambridge, MA.

1982   Algodón (*Gossypium barbadense*). In *Precerámico Peruano: Los Gavilanes—Mar, desierto y oasis en la historia del hombre*, edited by D. Bonavia, pp. 179–180. Lima: Corporación Financiera de Desarrollo S.A. COFIDE, Instituto Arqueológico Alemán.

STEPHENS, S., AND M. MOSELEY

1973   Cotton Remains from Archaeological Sites in Central Coastal Peru. *Science* 180(4082):186–188.

1974   Early Domesticated Cottons from Archaeological Sites in Central Coastal Peru. *American Antiquity* 39(1):109–122.

STEVENSON, M.

1915   *Ethnobotany of the Zuni Indians*. Thirtieth Annual Report of the Bureau of American Ethnology. Washington, DC: U.S. Government Printing Office.

STEWARD, J.

1938   *Basin-Plateau Aboriginal Sociopolitical Groups*. Washington, DC: U.S. Government Printing Office.

STEWART, T.

1975   Cranial Dysraphism Mistaken for Trephination. *American Journal of Physical Anthropology* 42: 435–437.

STINER, M.

2000   The Tortoise and the Hare: Small Game Use, the Broad-Spectrum Revolution, and Paleolithic Demography. *Current Anthropology* 41(1):39–79.

STONE, R.

1986   Color Patterning and the Huari Artist: The "Lima Tapestry" Revisited. In *The Junius B. Bird Conference on Andean Textiles, April 7th and 8th, 1984*, edited by A. Rowe, pp. 137–149. Washington, DC: Textile Museum. Electronic document: http://www.walikioutlet.com/index.php?open=information en&cat=archiv&ID=41&PHPSESSID=43f318a7 d06a4e7c5493654d4ecbade9.

2007   "And All Theirs Different from His": The Dumbarton Oaks Inka Royal Tunic in Context. In *Variations in the Expressions of Inka Power: A Symposium at Dumbarton Oaks, 18 and 19 October 1997*, edited by R. Burger, C. Morris, and R. Matos Mendieta, pp. 385–422. Washington, DC: Dumbarton Oaks.

STOTHERT, K.

1985   The Preceramic Las Vegas Culture of Coastal Ecuador. *American Antiquity* 50(3):613–637.

STOTHERT, K., AND D. UBELAKER

1988   *La prehistoria temprana de la península Santa Elena, Ecuador: Cultura Las Vegas*. Guayaquil, Ecuador: Museos del Banco Central del Ecuador.

STRONG, W., AND C. EVANS JR.

1952   *Cultural Stratigraphy in the Virú Valley, Northern Peru: The Formative and Florescent Epochs*. New York: Columbia University Press.

STRONG, W., G. WILLEY, AND J. CORBETT

1943   *Archaeological Studies in Peru, 1941-1942*. New York: Columbia University Press.

STUIVER, M., P. REIMER, AND R. REIMER

2010   CALIB Radiocarbon Calibration 7.0. Electronic document: http://calib.qub.ac.uk/calib/.

STUMPFF, A.

2013   The Law Is a Fractal: The Attempt to Anticipate Everything. *Loyola University Chicago Law Journal* 44:649.

SUCHEY, J., AND D. KATZ

1986   Skeletal Age Standards Derived from an Extensive Multiracial Sample of Modern Americans: Abstract. *American Journal of Physical Anthropology* 69(2):269.

SURGE, D., AND K. WALKER
2005   Oxygen Isotope Composition of Modern and Archaeological Otoliths from the Estuarine Hardhead Catfish (*Ariopsis felis*) and Their Potential to Record Low-Latitude Climate Change. *Palaeogeography, Palaeoclimatology, Palaeoecology* 228: 179–191.

SWARTZMAN, G., A. BERTRAND, M. GUTIÉRREZ, S. BERTRAND, L. VÁSQUEZ
2008   The Relationship of Anchovy and Sardine to Water Masses in the Peruvian Humboldt Current System from 1983 to 2005. *Progress in Oceanography* 79:228–237.

SWEET, M.
1962   *Common Edible and Useful Plants of the West.* Healdsburg, CA: Naturegraph Company.

TAN, C., M. COHEN, D. ECKBERG, AND A. TAYLOR
2009   Fractal Properties of Human Heart Period Variability: Physiological and Methodological Implications. *Journal of Physiology* 587:3929.

TATTERSALL, I.
1985   The Human Skeletons from Huaca Prieta, with a Note on the Exostoses of the External Auditory Meatus. In *The Preceramic Excavations at the Huaca Prieta Chicama Valley, Peru,* by J. B. Bird, J. Hyslop, and M. D. Skinner, pp. 60–76. Anthropological Papers, vol. 62, part 1. New York: American Museum of Natural History.

TAYLOR, M., J. TAM, V. BLASKOVIC, P. ESPINOZA, R. MICHAEL BALLÓN, C. WOSNITZA-MENDO, J. ARGÜELLES, ET AL.
2008   Trophic Modeling of the Northern Humboldt Ecosystem, Part II: Elucidating Ecosystem Dynamics from 1995 to 2004 with a Focus on the Impact of ENSO. *Progress in Oceanography* 79: 366–378.

TAYLOR, R., A. MICOLICH, AND D. JONAS
1999   *Fractal Expressionism: Can Science Be Used to Further Our Understanding of Art?* New Brunswick, NJ: Rutgers University Press.

TELLENBACH, M.
1997   Los vestigios de un ritual ofrendatario en el Formativo peruano: Acerca de la relación entre templos, viviendas y hallazgos. In *Prehispanic Architecture and Civilization in the Andes, Archaeologica Peruana 2,* edited by E. Bonnier, and H. Bischo, pp. 162–175. Mannheim, Germany: Sociedad Arqueológica Peruano-Alemana, Reiss Museum.

TESTART, A.
1982   *Les chasseurs-cueilleurs ou l'origine des inégalités.* Mémoires de la Société d'Ethnographie, 26. Paris: Société d'Ethnographie.

THOMAS, D.
1991   *Columbian Consequences,* Vol. 3: *The Spanish Borderland in Pan-American Perspective.* Washington, DC: Smithsonian Institution Press.

THOMAS, J.
2014   What Do We Mean By "Neolithic Societies"? In *The Oxford Handbook of Neolithic Europe,* edited by C. Fowler, J. Harding, and D. Hoffmann, pp. 34–56. Oxford: Oxford University Press.

THOMPSON, V., AND J. WORTH
2010   Dwellers by the Sea: Native American Adaptations along the Southern Coasts of Eastern North America. *Journal of Archaeological Research* 25:23–45.

THOMSEN, M., U. SCHNEIDER, M. WEBER, R. JOHANNISSON, AND F. NIETHARD
1997   Scoliosis and Congenital Anomalies Associated with Klippel-Feil Syndrome Types I–III. *Spine* 22: 396–401.

THORP, J., AND A. COVICH (EDS.)
2001   *Ecology and Classification of North American Freshwater Invertebrates.* San Diego: Academic Press.

THORROLD, S., S. CAMPANA, C. JONES, AND P. SWART
1997   Factors Determining $\delta^{13}C$ and $\delta^{18}O$ Fractionation in Aragonitic Otoliths of Marine Fish. *Geochimica et Cosmochimica Acta* 61:2909–2919.

TILLEY, C., AND W. BENNETT
2004   *The Materiality of Stone: Explorations in Landscape Phenomenology.* Oxford: Berg.

TITELBAUM, A.
2012   Habitual Activity and Changing Adaptations at the El Brujo Archaeological Complex: A Diachronic Investigation of Musculoskeletal Stress and Degenerative Joint Disease in the Lower Chicama Valley of Northern Coastal Peru. PhD dissertation, Department of Anthropology, Tulane University, New Orleans.

TODD, T.
1921a   Age Changes in the Pubic Bone: I. The White Male Pubis. *American Journal of Physical Anthropology* 3:467–470.
1921b   Age Changes in the Pubic Bone: III. The Pubis of the White Female. IV: The Pubis of the Female White-Negro Hybrid. *American Journal of Physical Anthropology* 4:1–70.

TOPIC, J.
1989   The Ostra Site: The Earliest Fortified Site in the New World? In *Cultures in Conflict: Current Archaeological Perspectives,* edited by D. Tcakzuk and B. Vivian, pp. 215–227. Calgary, Canada: Archaeological Association, University of Calgary.

TORRENCE, R., AND H. BARTON (EDS.)
2006   *Ancient Starch Research.* Walnut Creek, CA: Left Coast Press.

TORRES, A., AND G. CAILLE
2009   Las comunidades del intermareal rocoso antes y después de la eliminación de un disturbio antropogénico: Un caso de estudio en las costas de Puerto Madryn (Patagonia, Argentina). *Revista de Biología Marina y Oceanografía: Nota Científica* 44(2):517–521.

TORRICO, C.
2014   Technical Competence in Weaving as a Means of Distinction among Young Macha Women from Tumaykuri, Northern Potosí, Bolivia. In *Textiles,*

Technical Practice and Power in the Andes, edited by D. Arnold and P. Dransart, pp. 195–215. London: Archetype Publications.

TOWLE, M.

1952   Descriptions and Identification of the Virú Plant Remains. In *Cultural Stratigraphy in the Virú Valley, Northern Peru: The Formative and Florescent Epochs*, by W. Strong and C. Evans, pp. 352–356. New York: Columbia University Press.

1954   Plant Remains. In *Early Ancón and Early Supe Culture: Chavín Horizon Sites of the Central Peruvian Coast*, edited by G. Willey and J. Corbett, pp. 130–138. Columbia Studies in Archaeology and Ethnology, vol. 3. New York: Columbia University Press.

1961   *The Ethnobotany of Pre-Columbian Peru*. Viking Fund Publications in Anthropology, no. 30. Chicago: Aldine.

TRACY, M., J. DORMANS, AND K. KUSUMI

2004   Klippel-Feil Syndrome: Clinical Features and Current Understanding of Etiology. *Clinical Orthopaedics and Related Research* 424:183–190.

TRIGGER, B.

1990   Monumental Architecture: A Thermodynamic Explanation of Symbolic Behaviour. *World Archaeology* 22:119–122.

TUCKER, B.

2002   Culinary Confusion: Using Osteological and Stable Isotopic Evidence to Reconstruct Paleodiet for the Ocmulgee/Blackshear Cordmarked People of South Central Georgia. MA thesis, Georgia State University, Atlanta.

TUDHOPE, A., C. CHILCOTT, M. MCCULLOCH, E. COOK, J. CHAPPELL, R. ELLAM, D. LEA, J. LOUGH, AND G. SHIMMIELD

2001   Variability in the El-Niño Southern Oscillation through a Glacial–Interglacial Cycle. *Science* 291:1511–1517.

TUNER, B.

2008   *The New Blackwell Companion to Social Theory*. Oxford: Wiley-Blackwell.

TURNER, B., G. KAMENOV, J. KINGSTON, AND G. ARMELAGOS

2009   Insights into Immigration and Social Class at Machu Picchu, Peru, Based on Oxygen, Strontium, and Lead Isotopic Analysis. *Journal of Archaeological Science* 36:317–332.

TURNER, C., AND J. KATICH

1981   Tympanic Plate Dehiscences in Crania. In *Contributions to Gran Quivira Archeology*, edited by A. C. Hayes, p. 145. National Park Service, U.S. Department of the Interior, Publications in Archeology, no. 17. Washington, DC: National Park Service.

TWISS, P.

1992   Predicted World Distribution of C3 and C4 Grass Phytoliths. In *Phytolith Systematics: Emerging Issues*, edited by G. Rapp Jr. and S. C. Mulholland, pp. 113–128. New York: Plenum Press.

TWISS, P., E. SUESS, AND R. SMITH

1969   Morphological Classification of Grass Phytoliths. *Proceedings of Soil Science of America* 33:109–115.

UBELAKER, D.

1980   Human Skeletal Remains from Site OGSE-80, A Preceramic Site on the Sta. Elena Peninsula, Coastal Ecuador. *Journal of the Washington Academy of Sciences* 70(1):3–26.

1984   Prehistoric Human Biology of Ecuador: Possible Temporal Trends and Cultural Correlations. In *Paleopathology at the Origins of Agriculture*, edited by M. N. Cohen and G. J. Armelagos, pp. 491–513. New York: Academic Press.

1989   *Human Skeletal Remains: Excavation, Analysis, Interpretation*. 2nd ed. Washington, DC: Taraxacum Press.

UCEDA, S.

1986   Le Paijanien de la region de Casma (Pérou): Industrie lithique et relations avec les autres industries précéramiques. PhD dissertation, Université de Bordeaux, Bordeaux, France.

UGENT, D., T. DILLEHAY, AND C. RAMÍREZ

1987   Potato Remains from a Late Pleistocene Settlement in Southcentral Chile. *Economic Botany* 41(1):17–27.

UGENT, D., S. POZORSKI, AND T. POZORSKI

1982   Archaeological Potato Tuber Remains from the Casma Valley of Peru. *Economic Botany* 36(2):182–192.

1984   New Evidence for Ancient Cultivation of *Canna edulis* in Peru. *Economic Botany* 38(4):417–432.

1986   Archaeological Manioc (*Manihot*) from Coastal Peru. *Economic Botany* 40(1):78–102.

UHLE, M.

1906   Los "kjoekkenmöeddings" del Perú. *Revista Histórica* 1 (trimester 1):3–23.

UNDERHILL, R.

1940   *The Papago Indians of Arizona and Their Relatives the Pima*. Sherman Pamphlets 3. Lawrence, KS: Education Department, U.S. Office of Indian Affairs.

UNGAR, P., C. BROWN, T. BERGSTROM, AND A. WALKERS

2003   Quantification of Dental Microwear by Tandem Scanning Confocal Microscopy and Scale-Sensitive Fractal Analyses. *Scanning* 25:185–193.

URBAN, H.-J.

1994   Upper Temperature Tolerance of Ten Bivalve Species off Peru and Chile Related to El Niño. *Marine Ecology Progress Series* 107:139–145.

URBAN, H.-J., AND B. CAMPOS

1994   Population Dynamics of the Bivalves *Gari solida*, *Semele solida* and *Protothaca thaca* from a Small Bay in Chile at 36 Degrees S. *Marine Ecology Progress Series* 115(1–2):93–102.

UREY, H.

1947   The Thermodynamic Properties of Isotopic Substances. *Journal of the Chemical Society*:562–581.

URTON, G.

1997   *The Social Life of Numbers: A Quechua Ontology of*

Numbers and Philosophy of Arithmetic. Austin: University of Texas Press.

USHER, G.

1974   *A Dictionary of Plants Used by Man.* New York: Hafner Press.

VALLEJOS A., M.

1981   *Textiles de Paloma, un pueblo preagrícola en las lomas de Chilca, Perú (1ra etapa).* Lima: Centro de Investigaciones de Zonas Áridas de la Universidad Nacional Agraria/La Molina.

1982   Textiles de Paloma, un pueblo preagrícola en las lomas de Chilca, Perú (1a. etapa). *Zonas Áridas* 1:37–47.

1988   Analisis y tipologia de los textiles de Paloma: Un pueblo de 7000 años en las lomas de Chilca, Peru. *Revista del Museo Nacional de Antropología y Arqueología* 3:6–37.

VAN DEN BERG, M., H. COOPS, R. NOORDHUIS, J. VAN SCHIE, AND J. SIMONS

1997   Macroinvertebrate Communities in Relation to Submerged Vegetation in Two *Chara*-Dominated Lakes. *Hydrobiologia* 342–343:143–150.

VAN DER LEEUW, S., AND C. REDMAN

2002   Placing Archaeology at the Center of Socio-Natural Studies. *American Antiquity* 67:597–605.

VÁSQUEZ SÁNCHEZ, V., AND T. ROSALES THAM

2008   *Análisis de resos de fauna y vegetales de Huaca Prieta, valle de Chicama-Temporada 2007.* Trujillo, Peru: Universidad Nacional de Trujillo.

2010   *Resumen final 2010: Restos de fauna y vegetales de Huaca Prieta y Paredones, valle de Chicama.* Trujillo, Peru: Universidad Nacional de Trujillo.

VEGA-CENTENO, I.

2004   *Costumbres indígenas, administración de bienes y normas eclesiásticas (s. XVI-XIX): Catálogo de la Sección Eclesiástica del Archivo Regional del Cusco: José Romualdo Vega Centeno, notario y archivista.* Cusco: Centro de Estudios Regionales Andinos Bartolomé de Las Casas (CBC).

VEGA-CENTENO, R.

2007   Construction, Labor Organization, and Feasting during the Late Archaic Period in the Central Andes. *Journal of Anthropological Archaeology* 26(2):150–171.

VELARDE, L.

1997   Problemática de las dataciones C14 y su calibración. *Boletín* (Hanan Pacha, Instituto de Investigaciones de Arqueología Aplicada) 15(4):17–18.

VERANO, J.

1995a   Osteological Analysis of Guañape Period Burials at Huaca El Gallo, Virú Valley, Peru. Paper presented at the sixty-first annual meeting of the Society for American Archaeology, New Orleans.

1995b   Where Do They Rest? The Treatment of Human Offerings and Trophies in Ancient Peru. In *Tombs for the Living: Andean Mortuary Practices,* edited by T. D. Dillehay, pp. 189–227. Washington, DC: Dumbarton Oaks Research Library and Collection.

1997   Physical Characteristics and Skeletal Biology of the Moche Population at Pacatnamu. In *The Pacatnamu Papers, Volume 2: The Moche Occupation,* edited by C. B. Donnan and G. A. Cock, pp. 189–214. Los Angeles: Museum of Cultural History, University of California.

2001   The Physical Evidence of Human Sacrifice in Ancient Peru. In *Ritual Sacrifice in Ancient Peru,* edited by E. P. Benson and A. G. Cook, pp. 165–184. Austin: University of Texas Press.

2003   Human Skeletal Remains from Machu Picchu: A Reexamination of the Yale Peabody Museum's Collections. In *The 1912 Yale Peruvian Scientific Expedition Collections from Machu Picchu: Human and Animal Remains,* edited by R. L. Burger and L. C. Salazar, pp. 65–117. Yale University Publications in Anthropology, no. 85. New Haven: Yale University.

VERANO, J., AND G. LOMBARDI

1998   Report on Bioanthropological Research Conducted at the El Brujo Archaeological Complex: The 1997 Field Season. Manuscript on file, Tulane University, New Orleans.

VERGARA MONTERO, ENRIQUE

2015   *Mates: Corpus iconográfico Perú prehispánico.* Lima: Imprenta Gami.

VIDAL-FERNÁNDEZ, J., E. LARCO-LEÓN, M. ÑIQUE-ÁLVAREZ, AND B. ALVA-PÉREZ

1993   Conservación ex-situ de *Schoenoplectus californicus* (C. A. Mey) Soják en Huanchaco (Trujillo, Peru). *Revista Anteonor Orrego* 2(2):17–27.

VIVEIROS DE CASTRO, E.

1998   Cosmological Deixis and Amerindian Perspectivism. *Journal of the Royal Anthropological Institute* 4(3):469–488.

VREELAND, J., JR.

1986   Cotton Spinning and Processing on the Peruvian North Coast. In *The Junius B. Bird Conference on Andean Textiles, April 7th and 8th, 1984,* edited by A. Rowe, pp. 363–383. Washington, DC: Textile Museum.

VUILLEUMIER, B.

1971   Pleistocene Changes in the Fauna and Flora of South America. *Science* 173:771–780.

WALKER, A., H. HOECK, AND L. PÉREZ

1978   Microwear of Mammalian Teeth as an Indicator of Diet. *Science* 201:908–910.

WALKER, P., R. BATHURST, R. RICHMAN, T. GJERDRUM, AND V. ANDRUSHKO

2009   The Causes of Porotic Hyperostosis and Cribra Orbitalia: A Reappraisal of the Iron-Deficiency-Anemia Hypothesis. *American Journal of Physical Anthropology* 139:109–125.

WALKER, P., AND M. DENIRO

1986   Stable Nitrogen and Carbon Isotope Ratios in Bone Collagen as Indices of Prehistoric Dietary Dependence on Marine and Terrestrial Resources in Southern California. *American Journal of Physical Anthropology* 71:51–61.

WALLINGA, J., A. MURRAY, AND L. BØTTER-JENSEN
2002   Measurement of the Dose in Quartz in the Presence of Feldspar Contamination. *Radiation Protection Dosimetry* 101:367–370.

WANG, Y., H. CHENG, R. EDWARDS, Y. HE, X. KONG, Z. AN, J. WU, ET AL.
2005   The Holocene Asian Monsoon: Links to Solar Changes and North Atlantic Climate. *Science* 3008:854–857.

WANG, Y., H. CHENG, R. LAWRENCE, X. KONG, K. SHAO, S. CHEN, J. WU, ET AL.
2008   Millennial- and Orbital-Scale Changes in the East Asian Monsoon over the Past 224,000 Years. *Nature* 451:1090–1093.

WATLING, J., AND J. IRIARTE
2013   Phytoliths from the Coastal Savannas of French Guiana. *Quaternary International* 287:162–180.

WATSON, R. P.
1979   Water Control and Land Use on the Arid North Coast of Peru: Prehispanic Agricultural Systems in the Chicama Valley. Master's thesis, University of Texas, Austin.

WEBB, S.
1990   Prehistoric Eye Disease (Trachoma?) in Australian Aborigines. *American Journal of Physical Anthropology* 81:91–100.

WEBER, W.
1976   *Rocky Mountain Flora.* Boulder: Colorado Associate University Press.

WEBERBAUER, A.
1945   *El mundo vegetal de los Andes peruanos, estudio fitogeográfico.* Lima: Estación Experimental Agrícola de la Molina, Dirección de Agricultura, Ministerio de Agricultura.

WEI, J.
2014   Sclerochronological and Geochemical Study of Modern and Ancient *Semele corrugata* from North Coastal Peru. Master's thesis, Department of Geological Sciences, University of Alabama, Tuscaloosa.

WEIJIAN, Z., AND P. SHIYAO
1991   The Changes of the Morphology and Structure of Cotyledon Storage Cell and Their Relation to the Accumulation of Oil and Protein in Peanut. *Scientia Agricultura Sinica* 24(3):8–13.

WEINER, A.
1980   Reproduction as a Replacement for Reciprocity. *Mankind* 7:71–85.

1992   *Inalienable Possessions: The Paradox of Keeping-While-Giving.* Oakland: University of California Press.

WEIR, G., AND D. BONAVIA
1985   Coprolitos y dieta del Precerámico tardío de la costa peruana. *Boletín del Instituto Francés de Estudios Andinos* 14(1–2):85–140.

WEIR, G., AND J. PHILIP DERING
1986   The Lomas of Paloma: Human-Environment Relations in a Central Peruvian Fog Oasis: Archaeobotany and Palynology. In *Andean Archaeology: Papers in Memory of Clifford Evans,* edited by

S. Turpin, R. Matos M., and H. Eling, pp. 18–44. Los Angeles: Institute of Archaeology, University of California.

WEISS, P.
1962   Tipología de las deformaciones cefálicas de los antiguos peruanos, según la osteología cultural. *Revista del Museo Nacional* 31:15–42.

WELLHAUSEN, E., L. ROBERTS, X. HERNÁNDEZ, AND P. MANGELSDORF
1952   *Races of Maize in Mexico.* Cambridge, MA: Bussey Institute, Harvard University.

WELLS, L.
1996   The Santa Beach Ridge Complex: Sea-Level and Progradation History of an Open Gravel Coast in Central Peru. *Journal of Coastal Research* 12:1–17.

WELLS, L., AND J. NOLLER
1997   Determining the Early History of El Niño: Comment. *Science* 276:966.

WENDT, W.
1964   Die präkeramisch Siedlung am Río Seco, Peru. *Baessler-Archiv* (Berlin), n.s., 11(2):225–275.

1976   *El asentamiento precerámico en Río Seco, Perú.* Lecturas en Arqueología, no. 3. Lima: Centro de Documentación del Museo de Arqueología y Etnología de la Universidad Nacional Mayor de San Marcos.

WEST, M., AND T. WHITAKER
1979   Prehistoric Cultivated Cucurbits from the Viru Valley, Peru. *Economic Botany* 33(3):275–279.

WESTENGEN, O., Z. HUAMÁN, AND M. HEUN
2005   Genetic Diversity and Geographic Pattern in Early South American Cotton Domestication. *Theoretical and Applied Genetics* 110(2):392–402.

WHITAKER, T.
1983   Cucurbits in Andean Prehistory. *American Antiquity* 48(3):576–585.

WHITAKER, T., AND J. BIRD
1949   Identification and Significance of the Cucurbit Materials from Huaca Prieta, Peru. *American Museum Novitates* 1426:1–15.

WHITAKER, T., AND H. CUTLER
1965   Cucurbits and Cultures in the Americas. *Economic Botany* 19(4):344–349.

1968   Pre-Historic Distribution of *Cucurbita* L. in the Americas: Unsolved Problems. In *Actas y trabajos, XXXVII Congreso Internacional de Americanistas* (1966), pp. 511–515. Buenos Aires: República Argentina.

WHITE, L. A.
1959   *The Evolution of Culture: The Development of Civilization to the Fall of Rome.* New York: McGraw-Hill.

WHITING, A.
1939   *Ethnobotany of the Hopi.* Museum of Northern Arizona Bulletin, no. 15. Flagstaff: Northern Arizona Society of Science and Art.

WILLEY, G., AND J. CORBETT
1954   *Early Ancón and Early Supe Culture: Chavín Horizon Sites of the Central Peruvian Coast.* New York: Columbia University Press.

WILLIAMS, C.

1985   A Scheme for the Early Monumental Architecture of the Central Coast of Peru. In *Early Ceremonial Architecture in the Andes*, edited by C. B. Donnan, pp. 227–240. Washington, DC: Dumbarton Oaks.

WILLIAMS, P., N. COUTURE, AND D. BLOM

2007   Urban Structure at Tiwanaku: Geophysical Investigations in the Andean Altiplano. In *Remote Sensing in Archaeology*, edited by J. Wiseman and F. El-Baz, pp. 423–441. New York: Springer.

WINSBOROUGH, B., I. SHIMADA, L. NEWSOM, J. JONES, AND R. SEGURA

2012   Paleoenvironmental Catastrophes on the Peruvian Coast Revealed in Lagoon Sediment Cores from Pachacamac. *Journal of Archaeological Science* 39: 602–614.

WINTERHALDER, D., AND B. KENNETT

2006   *Behavioral Ecology and the Transition to Agriculture*. Berkeley: University of California Press.

WOUTERS, J.

1994   Dye Analysis of Chinese and Indian Textiles, with Special Emphasis on the Recognition of *Miscanthus tinctorius* and *Sophora japonica* and the Composition of Green and Blue Colours. *Dyes in History and Archaeology* 12:12–22.

2010   HPLC High Performance Liquid Chromatography. In *Scientific Methods and Cultural Heritage: An Introduction to the Application of Materials Science to Archaeometry and Conservation Science*, edited by G. Artioli, pp. 410–413. Oxford: Oxford University Press.

WOUTERS, J., C. GRZYWACZ, AND A. CLARO

2011   A Comparative Investigation of Hydrolysis Methods to Analyze Natural Organic Dyes by HPLC-PDA: Nine Methods, Twelve Biological Sources, Ten Dye Classes, Dyed Yarns, Pigments and Paints. *Studies in Conservation* 56:231–249.

WOUTERS, J., AND N. ROSARIO-CHIRINOS

1992   Dyestuff Analysis of Precolumbian Peruvian Textiles by High Performance Liquid Chromatography and Diode-Array Detection. *Journal of the American Institute for Conservation* 31:237–255.

YACOVLEFF, E.

1933   La jíquima, raíz comestible extinguida en el Perú. *Revista del Museo Nacional* 3:51–66.

YACOVLEFF, E., AND F. HERRERA

1934   El mundo vegetal de los antiguos peruanos. *Revista del Museo Nacional* 3(3):241–322.

1935   El mundo vegetal de los antiguos peruanos. *Revista del Museo Nacional* 4(1):29–102.

YEN, T.

1961   Fossil Fresh-Water Mollusks and Ecological Interpretations. *Geological Society of America Bulletin* 62: 1375–1380.

YESNER, D., M. TORRES, R. GUICHON, L. BORRERO

2003   Stable Isotope Analysis of Human Bone and Ethnohistoric Subsistence Patterns in Tierra del Fuego. *Journal of Anthropological Archaeology* 22: 279–291.

YOUNG, S., AND W. JUDD

1992   Systematics of the *Guadua angustifolia* Complex (Poaceae: Bambusoideae). *Annals of the Missouri Botanical Garden* 79(4):737–769.

ZARRILLO, S., D. PEARSALL, J. RAYMOND, M. TISDALE, AND D. QUON

2008   Directly Dated Starch Residues Document Early Formative Maize (*Zea mays* L.) in Tropical Ecuador. *Proceedings of the National Academy of Sciences of the United States of America* 106(13):5006–5011.

ZECHENTER, E.

1998   Subsistence Strategies in the Supe Valley of the Peruvian Central Coast during the Complex Preceramic and Initial Periods. PhD dissertation, University of California, Los Angeles.

ZEIDLER, J.

2008   The Ecuadorian Formative. In *Handbook of South American Archaeology*, edited by H. Silverman and W. H. Isbell, pp. 459–488. New York: Springer.

ZIOLKOWSKI, M., M. PAZDUR, A. KRZANOWSKI, AND A. MICHCZYNSKI

1994   *Andes: Radiocarbon Database for Bolivia, Ecuador and Peru*. Warszawa-Gliwice: Andean Archaeological Mission of the Institute of Archaeology, Warsaw University/Gliwoce Radiocarbon Laboratory of the Institute of Physics, Silesian Technical University.

ZOUBEK, T.

1997   The Initial Period Occupation of Huaca El Gallo/ Huaca La Gallina, Virú Valley, Peru and Its Implications for Guañape Phase Social Complexity. PhD dissertation, Department of Anthropology, Yale University, New Haven, CT.

ZUCOL, A.

1999   Fitolitos de las Poaceae Argentinas: IV. Asociación fitolítica de *Cortaderia selloana* (Danthonieae: Poaceae), de la Provincia de Entre Rios (Argentina). *Natura Neotropicalis* 30:25–33.

CONTRIBUTORS

J. M. Adovasio, *Florida Atlantic University*

C. Fred T. Andrus, *University of Alabama*

Philippe Béarez, *Archéozoologie, Archéobotanique: Sociétés, Pratiques et Environements, Sorbonne Universités—Museum National d'Histoire Naturelle, CNRS, France*

Rachel Beavins, *Vanderbilt University*

Kristin Benson, *Vanderbilt University*

Jessica Blair, *Vanderbilt University*

Duccio Bonavia, *Academia Nacional de Historia del Perú*

Katherine L. Chiou, *University of California at Berkeley*

Linda Scott Cummings, *Paleo-Research Institute, Colorado*

Larisa R. G. DeSantis, *Vanderbilt University*

Tom D. Dillehay, *Vanderbilt University*

Elise Dufour, *Archéozoologie, Archéobotanique: Sociétés, Pratiques et Environements, Sorbonne Universités—Museum National d'Histoire Naturelle, CNRS, France*

Michelle L. Farley, *Mercyhurst University*

Robert S. Feranec, *New York State Museum*

Daniel Fernandes Moreira, *Universidad Católica del Perú*

Teresa C. B. Franco, *Vanderbilt University*

Steven L. Goodbred Jr., *Vanderbilt University*

Alexander Grobman, *Universidad Nacional Agraria, Peru*

Christine A. Hastorf, *University of California at Berkeley*

Irene Holst, *Smithsonian Institution*

Jeff Illingworth, *Florida Atlantic University*

José Iriarte, *Exeter University, England*

Claudio Latorre, *Universidad Católica de Chile*

Gerson Levi-Lazzarus, *Vanderbilt University*

Cecil Lewis, *University of Oklahoma*

Marilaura López Solís, *Universidad Nacional de Trujillo, Peru*

Greg Maggard, *University of Kentucky*

Timothy Messner, *Smithsonian Institution*

Phillip Mink, *University of Kentucky*

Patricia J. Netherly, *Vanderbilt University*

Alberto Pérez-Huerta, *University of Alabama*

Mario Pino, *Universidad Austral de Chile*

Dolores R. Piperno, *Smithsonian Institution*

Michael Ramírez, *University of Texas*

Isabel Rey, *Museo Nacional de Ciencias Naturales, Spain*

Gabino Rodríguez, *Universidad Católica del Perú*

Teresa Rosales Tham, *Universidad Nacional de Trujillo, Peru*

André Oliveira Sawakuchi, *Universidade de São Paulo*

Paige Silcox, *Office of the State Archaeologist, Tennessee*

Jeffrey Splitstoser, *George Washington University, Washington, DC*

Marshal Summar, *Children's National Health System, Washington, DC*

Anne R. Titelbaum, *University of Arizona*

Raúl Tito, *University of Oklahoma*

Olivier Trombret, *Université de Picardie Jules Verne, France*

Tiffiny A. Tung, *Vanderbilt University*

Víctor F. Vásquez, *Universidad Nacional de Trujillo*

John W. Verano, *Tulane University*

Jennifer Watling, *Exeter University, England*

Jeixin Wei, *University of Alabama*

Jack Williams, *Mercyhurst University*

INDEX

Note: Italic page numbers refer to figures and tables.

animal husbandry: and social complexity, 17, 596. *See also* camelid husbandry

anthropogenic deposits: differentiation of, 619, 622; and geophysical survey, 725, 726; and premound fill, 101; and sediments, 108, 617

anthropomorphic head or headdress, 452, *453*

apachetas, 26

appliqué: element knots distinguished from, 508, 509; in plain weave, 514

Archaic period, 3–4, 195

architecture: and interregional linkages, 16; polychaete tubes used in, 90; schematic architectural sequences, 162, *163*, color insert; segmentation in tomb architecture, 613; and social complexity, 595; stone architectural alignments, 162, *164*, 457, 570, 571, 574. *See also* monuments; ramps; sunken circular plazas

Argopecten sp., 360, 454

Arkush, Elizabeth, 194

Arriaza, Bernardo, 190, 194

arthritis, in human skeletal remains, *168*, 172–173, 174, 176, 180, 182–183, 185, 193, 196

artwork: at Huaca Prieta, 7, 11, 12, 591, 595, 610; representational artwork, 18; and social complexity, 595

Asia: basketry and cordage found at, 552; bone tools of, 467; burial treatment of, 169; and complementarity of foraging and sedentary practices, 17; crossed-warp patterning found at, 500, 503; dyes of, 470; featherwork found at, 509; fibers of, 473; and figure-8 looping, 480, 482; grouping of warp elements found at, 508; interwarp knots found at, 509; and knotted netting, 487; ornamental objects in burials, 18; *pájaro bobo* found at, 423; sedge found at, 420; single-element constructions found at, 488; textiles of, 445, 459; weapons reported in, 194; weft twining found in, 504

Aspero: *achira* found at, 411; algarrobo found at, 421; basketry and cordage found at, 552; California bulrush found at, 420; clay figurines at, 18; cotton found at, 418; crossed-warp patterning found at, 500; dyes of, 471, 472; fibers of, 472; and figure-8 looping, 482; gourds found at, 417; grouping of warp elements found at, 508; guava found at, 409; knotted netting found at, 487; lesser degree of superpositioning at, 578; maize found at, 662–663; monumental buildings of, 18, 40, 108, 595; moss found at, 426; pacay found at, 395; Preceramic stepped-platform mounds of, 8; reed found at, 419; sedge found at, 420; squash found at, 408; textiles of, 459; Valdivia settlements of, 4

Australian Aboriginals, 607

avocados (*Persea* sp.): as cultivated food plant, 279, 379, 383, 428, 430; macroremains of, 379; production of, 4

awls: bone tools as, 450, 451, *451*, 467, 731; shell tools as, *448*, 449

Bahia grass (*Paspalum* sp.), 425, 430, 431

bamboo (*Guadua angustifolia*), 419, 430

Bandurria: basketry and cordage found at, 552, 554; California bulrush found at, 420; chile pepper at, 409; cotton found at, 418; dual economy of, 580; economic special-

ization at, 365; gourds found at, 417; guava found at, 409; lesser degree of superpositioning at, 578; monumental buildings of, 18; ornamental objects in burials, 18; pacay found at, 395; peanuts found at, 383; Preceramic stepped-platform mounds of, 8; reed found at, 419; as religious center, 573; and social differentiation, 598, 612; squash found at, 408; textiles of, 459; and wrapped stones, 467

Barnes, Edward, 193

Barrett, Linda, 459, 508

Barton, Christopher, 19

basalt tools: micro-use-wear analysis of, 727; percentage of, 436, 437, 438, 439, 440; at Salamanca, 559, 560, 561; at Sangamon terrace, 100–101

baskets and basketry: analysis of, 526; chronological distribution of, 544–548, *545*; classification criteria for, 526–527; color in, 456, 471, 530, 542, 543, 546, 547, 555, 692–693; decorative patterns of, 530, 532, 542, 547, 581, 587, 610; dual patterns of, 446; dyes for, 456, 530, 532, 543, 546, 547; external correlations, 545, 552–554; forms of, 525, 526, 542–543, 547; fragmentation of, 26, 27, 123, 446, 530, 532, 543, 544, 547, 556, 598, 606, 611, 613; fragment of basket from Unit 15/21, *101*; fragments from Unit 2, 126; functional analysis of, 35, 542–543, 547–548; and horsetail, 418; innovations in technique, 457, 596; internal correlations, 541–548; material record of, 13; mats/petates, 541, 542–543, *543*, 544, 546, 547, 553, 554, 555; mending, 532, 542, 547; methods of starting, 542, 546; and molle, 430; and mortuary rituals, 90, 275; overview of, 554–556; pigments in, 169, 692–693; and plaiting, 525, 526, 527, 544, 546, 548, 555; plants for making, 430; radiocarbon dating of, 98; raw materials of, 543, 544, 548, 556; salty paste-like material saturating, 99; selvages, 542, 546–547; and sexual division of labor, 524, 548; specimens of, 527; and spikerush, 430; and splices, 529, 542, 547; and technological diversity, 581, 585, 596, 612; twining techniques, 525–526, 527, 541–543, 546, 555, 596; Type I: Close Simple Twining, S-twist (paired) Wefts with Auxiliary Simple Plaiting, 528–529, *528*, 541, 542, 543, 544, 546, 547, 554, 555, color insert; Type II: Open Simple Twining Z-twist (paired) Wefts, 526, 529–530, *529*, 541, 542, 544–545, 546, 547, 553, 554; Type III: Close Simple and Diagonal Twining, S-twist (Paired) Weft with Functional Wrapped Twining, 530, *531*, 532, *532*, 541, 542, 543, 544, 545–546, 547, 554, 555; Type IV: Simple Plaiting, 1/1 Interval, *532*, 533, 544, 548; types of, 525; warps, 541, 546; wear patterns, 530; wefts, 541–542, 546

Bastien, Joseph, 609

beans (*Phaseolus* spp.): in gourd fragments, 446; and mortuary rituals, 275; and phytolith analysis, 675, 676, *678*, 679–680; production of, 4; starch grain from, 684, *684*, *685*, 686, 687–688. *See also* common beans (*Phaseolus vulgaris*); lima beans (*Phaseolus* sp.)

Béarez, Phillipe, 36, 706

Beavins, Rachel, 36

Benfer, Robert, 166, 189, 554

benthic zone, 200

Bering Platform, 553

Beta Analytic, Inc., 88, 91

beverages, plants for making, 430, 431

Bird, Junius B.: archaeological excavations at Cupisnique mound, 153, 158; archaeological excavations at Huaca Prieta, 4, 7, 9, 30, 32–33, 38, 109, 126, 127, 142, 152, 577, 726; backdirt piles of, 446, 458, 465, 466, 470, 477, 544, 656, 658, 726; on baskets, 525, 526, 527, 529, 532, 533, 541; on bone tools, 451, 467; botanical studies from excavations at Huaca Prieta, 372, 374, 383, 395, 408, 409, 411, 414, 417, 418, 419, 420, 421, 422, 424, 426–427; on chamber tombs, 599, 602; on cobbles, 681; on colonial period at Huaca Prieta mound, 123, 164; on compound textile constructions, 520; on cordage, 525, 526, 527, 536, 548, 549, 550, 551; corn samples excavated by, 658, 661; on crossed-warp patterning, 498, 500; on decorated gourds, 442, 445, 466; on dyes, 471, 472; on erosion of Huaca Prieta mound, 164; on fibers, 473; on human skeletal remains, 152, 166, 169, 173, 188, 189, *189*, 190, 192, 194, 598, 689, 733; on initial site use of Huaca Prieta, 104; on interwarp knots, 512; on knots, 508; on knotted netting, 483, 486–487; map of Huaca Prieta showing excavation units, *33*, 103, 121; on plain-weave-derived float weaves, 519; on polychaete tubes, 453; postulated tsunami date of, 78, 85, 164, 618; radiocarbon dates of, 88–89, 103; retention wall no. 1, 103; on Sangamon terrace, 617–618; on shell tools, 450; on single-element constructions, 488; "Specimens of Small Quantity," 426; on stone tools, 435, 436, 440; on sunken circular plaza, 164; on textiles, 8, 91, 103, 458, 459, 465, 466, 477, 522, 526; textiles cleaned with cellulose acetate and acetone, 460–461; TP-5 on Cupisnique mound, 107; on tsunami deposits, 114, 117, 164, 618, 630; on warp patterning, 491, 494; on warp selvages, 515; on weaving, 457, 476; on weft bands, 504; on weft twining, 488, 489, 491, 494, 512; on wrapped stones, 467, 469. *See also* HP-2; HP-3

Bird, Robert, 658, 661–662

birds: and faunal remains, 210, 248, 352, 353, 355, 356, 364, 365, 366; habitats of, 201, 363, 366; of inland zone, 202; land birds, 208, 212, 219, 234; marine birds, 201–202, 207, 208, 209, 219–220, 221, 234, 235, 248, 268, 330, 331, 344, 345, 352, 353, 354, 355, 356, 359, 363, 364, 365; at Padre Abán, 361

Bischof, Henning, 445

black nightshade (*Solanum* sp.), 409, 411

blackware, at Unit 1, 123

Blair, Jessica, 35–36, 733, 737, 738

Bloch, Maurice, 606–607, 611–612

bobo (*Calamagrostis* sp. Poaceae), 426, 428, 674, 677, *679*

Bolivia, 645

Bonavia, Duccio: excavation of Huaca Prieta, 9; excavation of human skeletal remains, 167, *189*, 193; on knotted netting, 487; on Los Gavilanes, 40; on maize remains, 36; observation of fisherfolk, 201, *201*; observation of pelican hunters, 201, *201*, 209; on reeds, 467; at Salamanca, *560*; on stratigraphy, 625; on textiles, 458, 470, 471, 522; and tool function assessment, 35; on Unit 1, 617

bone tools: awls, 450, 451, *451*, 467, 731; beads, 450; and bundles, 466; conservative nature of, 457; weaving tools, 450, 451, *451*, 466–467, *468*

Bozarth, Stephen, 676

braiding, Type XIX cordage, 540, 549, 550, 555

Budworth, Geoffrey, 527

Buena Vista: algarrobo found at, 421; chile pepper at, 409; *Furcraea* sp. found at, 424; gourds found at, 417; guava found at, 409; lucuma found at, 414; monumental buildings of, 18; potatoes found at, 411; squash found at, 409

Buikstra, J. E., 170, 172–173

bulletin board, as metaphor for collection of fragments, 22, 23, 24, 26, 610

bunchosia (*Bunchosia armeniaca*), 395, 408, 430

bundles: Bundle 2009.136, *468*, 469; Bundle 2009.137, 467, *468*; and bundling practices, 433, 459, 460, 465, 467, 467n, 469–470, 522, 607; chile peppers found in, 648; chronology of, 466, 469–470; with coca leaf, 467, *468*; color, pigment, and dye of, 470–472; definition of, 459, 466; and discarding practices, 466, 469; exotic cultigens in, 587; folding patterns of, 460, 467, 469, *469*, 470; liquids applied to, 469; mud, salt, sand, and soot penetrating, 469; multifabric bundles, 469; number and types of attributes for fabrics and bundles, 469, *469*; number and types of fabrics and other objects composing bundles, *462*, 466; pairing and complementarity demonstrated by, 469, 470; with perforated bone, 467, *468*; plant fiber wads in, 467; plants in, 433; of reeds containing fragments of textiles, *127*, *128*, 607; and ritual offerings, 522, 605, 610; stitching of, 469, 521; wrapped objects compared to, 467, 469

burial treatment: Burial HP08-01, 169, 174; Burial HP08-02, 174–175; Burial HP09-01, 168, *169*, 171, 172, 173, 175–176, 524, 598; Burial HP09-02, 168, 169, 176; Burial HP09-03, 168, 176–177; Burial HP09-04, 177–179; Burial HP09-05, *156*, 157, 168, *169*, 179–180, *179*; Burial HP09-06, 180–181; Burial HP09-07, 168, *169*, *179*, 181–184, *182*; Burial HP09-08 near base of HP-3, 116, *118*, *182*, 184–185, *185*, 195, 569, 598; Burial HP09-09, 169, 185–187, *452*; and continuity, 604–605, 606; and faunal remains, 249; and fractured objects, 1, 26, 601; at Huaca Prieta, 7, 11, 18, 19, 26, 39, 188, 195–196, 235, 355, 432, 570, 571, 573, 574, 598–601; and mat fragments, 543, *543*, 547; meaning of, 599–600, 606; objects left with, 18, 175, 195, 212, 234, 275, 363; and orientation of bodies, 152, 168, 177, 181, 184, 186, 195, 196; and outlying domestic sites, 558; and positioning of body, 18, 26, 152, 176, 177, 181, 185–186, 195, 196, 558; and post-mortem disturbance, 168; and red pigment, 451–452; and repetition, 600, 604–605; and rocks placed over graves, 195; and secondary burials, 598, 603–604, 605, 613; and shallow unlined pits, 196; and social differentiation, 18, 195, 595, 598–599, 605, 613; and transcendence, 599, 606, 607

burning episodes: and charcoal, 1, 11, 12; at Huaca Prieta mound, 165, 576, 612; at Paredones, 165; remains of, 1, 146, 162, 165; repetition of, 608

butterfly bush (*Buddleja* sp.), 423, 429, 430, 431

caballitos de totora (reed rafts), 431, *560*, 566

Cabezas Largas, fibers of, 473

California bulrush (*Schoenoplectus californicus*), 420, 429–430, 543, 553

Callao, 709

Callen, Eric, 190, 426

camelid husbandry: and camelid fiber in textiles, 359, 470, 471, 472, 473; and faunal remains, 359–360, 571; in wetlands, 7

camellones, 83, 107, 573. *See also* raised agricultural fields

Cameron, Thomas, 190, 426

Caral: basketry and cordage found at, 552; burial treatment in, 169; clay figurines at, 18; crossed-warp patterning found at, 503; lesser degree of superpositioning at, 578; monumental buildings of, 18, 108, 595; possible sacrifice discovered in, 194; Preceramic stepped-platform mounds of, 8; textiles of, 459; Valdivia settlements of, 4; weft bands found in, 504

cardinal orientation, 574–575

Carré, Matthieu, 711

Carrizal, as late Pleistocene unifacial culture, 42, 101, 435

Center for Human Genetics Research Laboratory at Vanderbilt University, 738

Center for Stable Isotope Biogeochemistry, University of California, Berkeley, 667

Central Andes: cotton used in, 472; early development of public buildings in, 19; early development of social complexity in, 17; Preceramic period in, 3–4, 152; stone tools of, 435; ubiquity of mound-building in, 24

ceremonial practices, 16, 17. *See also* ritual practices

Cerrillos, 495

Cerro Campana: Preceramic household sites of, 10; and settlement patterns, 577, 578

Cerro Cuculicote, 142, 164

Cerro El Calvario, 662–663

Cerro Lampay: *achira* found at, 411; algarrobo found at, 421; chile pepper at, 409; gourds found at, 417; guava found at, 409; horsetail found at, 419; lucuma found at, 414; pacay found at, 395; reed found at, 419; wild cane found at, 424; willow found at, 421

Chachapoyas people, 523

Chaman Valley, 42, 212, 421

chamber tombs: architecture of, 457, 613; empty tombs, 90, 134, 135, *135*, *142*, 144, 357, 360, 572, 574, 597, 598, 599, 603, 726; at Huaca Prieta, 8, 26, 104, 123, 164, 570, 571, 572, 573, 578, 589, 590, 597, 598, 602, 604, 605, 726; mortuary rituals associated with, 90; retention walls for, 572, 574; of Unit 10, 104, 119, 131, 134, 135, *135*, 142, 152, 360, 453, 572, 576, 598, 599, 613; of Unit 23, 104, 131, 135, 140, 142, *142*, 143, 144, 152, 164, 356, 428, 446, 572, 598, 599, 613

Chao, 40

Chao Valley, 194, 660

Chapman, John, 25–26, 606, 608, 611, 613

Chappell, John, 709

charcoal: accumulation of, 608, 613; analysis of, 631; burned area in Unit 9 showing, 131, *133*; and burning episodes, 1, 11, 12; cellular features of samples, *633*; circumscribed activity areas associated with, 90; at Huaca Prieta, 8,

11, 12, 151, 570, 575, 594, 631; microscopic analysis of, 367; at outlying domestic sites, 557; at Paredones, 165, 575; and plant remains, 374, 395, 414, 421, 422–423, 427, 428, 429; and pollen samples, 697, 703; and pottery sherds, 456; radiocarbon dating of wood charcoal, 38, *58-59*, 78, 85, 88, 91, *92-97*, 98, 99, 100, 107, 662; samples identified in excavation units, *632*; sampling of, 36–37, 54, *56*, 68, *75*, 77, 85, 88, 90, 103, 107, 118, 119, 556–557, 564; at Unit 2, 124, 126, 421, 427; at Unit 9, 100, *102*, 131; at Unit 16, 106

charophyte algae, 60, 73, 82, 86

Chicama River: catchment basin of, 53, *53*; coastal sections along cutbank, 74, *75*; coastal system adjacent to river mouth, 74, *74*, 574; digital elevation model for catchment, *50*; estuary of, 363; floodplain of, 10, 38; as fluvial system, 61, 65; as freshwater source, 713; and inland coastal area, 7–8; paleoecological changes of, 38; present-day lagoon near mouth of, 47; regional location map, *50*; sampling at river mouth, 54, *55*, *56*

Chicama Valley: alluvial settings of, 59–61, *66*, 596; carbonate sediments of, 69, *72*, 73; catchment geology of, 52–53, *52*; channel deposits of, 61, 64–65, 67–69; chronology of physical environment, 39; climate during Holocene, 49–52; coastal settings of, 74, *74*, *75*, 76, 78–79, 84, 86, 197, 208, 568; dry forest zone of, 41–42; dune movement in, 48; environmental history of, *70*, *74*, 79–80, *80*, *81*, 82–85; ephemeral wetlands of, 7, 41, 42, 43–44, 61, *67*, 73–74, 83, 86, 107, 108, 162, 596; ethnographic accounts from coast, 358; floodplain sequences within, 67–69, *70*, *71*, 79, 108, 596; fluvial settings of, 61; forested foothills in Casca area, *41*; and fractional coherence of objects, 23–24; Holocene environmental settings and facies, 58–61, *62-65*, 64–65, 67–69, 73–74, 76, 78–79; Holocene paleoenvironmental history of, 10, 49, 86–87, 108; human occupation of, 87; human skeletal remains from, 193; interdisciplinary project in, 9; kin groups of, 12; lagoonal settings of, *56*, 69, *72*, 73–74, 86; late Pleistocene geography, 40–42; littoral residential sites of, 29; location of, *5*; microfossils and stable isotopes, 54, 57, *60*; model of development of, 12–13; optically stimulated luminescence, 57; Preceramic domestic site in, 4; radiocarbon sampling, 54, *58-59*, 68, *80*, 82, 83; sampling locations within, 54, *55*; sandy sediments of, 46, *48*; schematic cross section of Holocene stratigraphy, *70*; sediment coring, 54, *55*, *56*, 57; segmentary society of, 27, 571, 575, 588, 608, 611, 612–615; settlement history of, 577–579, 583; shoreline of, 208; social history of, 588–591; socio-ecosystems of, 19–20; spatially discrete mounds of, 10; sugarcane cultivation in, 44, 561, 562, 565

chicha (corn beer), 664, 686

Chilca: basketry and cordage found at, 552; chile peppers found at, 646; and complementarity of foraging and sedentary practices, 17; ornamental objects in burials, 18; textiles of, 459

Chilca I: and burial treatment, 195; fibers of, 472; lima beans cultivated at, 385

Chile: basketry and cordage of, 553; Chinchorro mummies of, 4; earthwork mounds in, 9, 24; impact of tsunami on,

583, 618; pebble tool industry in, 12. *See also* Mapuche people

chile peppers (*Capsicum* sp.): archaeological *Capsicum* seeds from Huaca Prieta (including Unit 16) and Paredones, 651; attachment scar sphericity, 651; beak angle, 650, *650*; beak prominence, 650; changes in chile pepper preference through time and space at Huaca Prieta (including Unit 16) and Paredones, 651–653; contextualizing Huaca Prieta and Paredones *Capsicum* data, 646; as cultivated plant food, 409, 428, 429, 431, 432, 580; cultivation of, 234, 363, 645–646; dates associated with archaeological sites with early *Capsicum* evidence, *647-648*, 648; distribution of, 645, 646, *646*; and flotation of sediment samples, 648; in gourd fragments, 446; macroremains of, 367, 370; maximum seed length, 650; modern and archaeological *Capsicum* seeds, 650, *650*, 653; modern *Capsicum* seed study methods, 649–651; and mortuary rituals, 275, 652; presence of *Capsicum* species at Huaca Prieta and Paredones, 651–653, *652*, 654; presence of *Capsicum* species by context, 652–653, *654*; production of, 4; ratio of thick testa to thin testa, 650–651; seed shape, *650*, 651; site data, 653, *653*, 654; and stone tools, 440; summary of archaeological *Capsicum* seed collection from Huaca Prieta and Paredones, *649*; testa texture, 651; use of, 648, 655; whole seed sphericity, 651

Chilkat culture, 512, 524

Chimú materials: in outlying domestic sites, 558, 559; at Salamanca, 561, 562

Chincha, 193

Chinchorro people, and human skeletal remains, 190, 191, 194–195

Chinchorro tradition: and maritime economy, 18; and mummification, 4, 18, 190, 194–195

Chiou, Katherine, 36, 648, 649, 651

choppers: Huaca Prieta/Paredones group associated with, 435; at Salamanca, 561; varieties of, *436*, 437–438, *437*, 440

Chorillos, 706, 709

Chu Barrera, Alejandro, 365, 580

Chumash people, 666, 670, 672

circumscribed spaces: architecture defining, 457; deposits of, 32; floors and use surfaces associated with, 30, 90, 130, 134, 165, 211; and food preparation, 131; Huaca Prieta compared to Paredones, 151; meaning of, 1; and ritual spaces, 11, 27, 146, 162, *164*, 165, 569, 570, 574, 589, 592, 604, 605, 612

Claro, Ana, 36

climate: changes in, 582, 705; of Chicama Valley during Holocene, 49–52; of Holocene period, 42–43, 44, 45–47, 48, 49–52, 629, 706, 711; late Pleistocene to late Holocene climates, 42

cobbles: burned cobbles from fire-pits, 68; cobblestone berms at Huaca Prieta, 99, 100, 102, 118, 164, 569, 570, 575, 576, 595; green schist stone painted with red pigment, 446, *447*; of HP-3, 117–118; imbricated cobblestones, 90; painted cobbles at Huaca Prieta, 7, 11, 12, 446, 570, 587, 597, 610; wrapped stones, 467

coca (*Erythroxylum novogranatense var. truxillense*): bundle with coca leaf, 467, *468*; coca leaf fragments in gourd fragments, 446; as medicinal plant, 418, 430; mortuary rituals, 90; offering of coca leaf and copper sulfate in Unit 21, 140, *141*, 454; offering of coca leaves in Structure 8 of Unit 21, 140, *141*; production of lime for use with, 585; and ritual practices, 275, 418, 602, 605

Cohen, Mark, 419, 427

coiling, and basketry, 525

collectivism, 26, 615

colonial period: and fishing village north of Huaca Prieta mound, 617, 628, 629; at Huaca Prieta mound, 123, 164, 356, 574, 598; and stone tools, 435

color: in baskets, 456, 471, 530, 542, 543, 546, 547, 555, 692–693; and complementary warps, 498; and complementary weft structures, 508; and crossed-warp patterning, 498; and decorative techniques for textiles, 491, 494–495, 498; and dyes and pigments for textiles, 456, *463*, 470–472, 494, color insert; and exotic dyes, 456; in figure-8 looping, 471, 472, 477, *478*; fugitive color, 471, 472, 494, 495, 509, 517, 519, 521; and interwarp knots, *510*, 512; of maize samples, 659, 660, 661, 663, 664; natural colors of cotton, 494; in plain weave, 470, 471, 472, 504, 517; in textiles, 456, *463*, 470–472, 491, 494, 685, 692, 693, 695, color insert; in warp stripes, 494, 495, 498, 500; in weft bands, 504, 505; and weft patterning, 508; in weft twining, 470, 471, 472, 491, 494–495, 498, 504, 508

Columbus, Christopher, 645

common beans (*Phaseolus vulgaris*): as cultivated plant food, 385, 395, 428, 429, 430, 431, 433; and starch grains, 683, 684, 688

communities: collective histories of, 601, 604–605, 606; and economic specialization, 616; identity of, 607; as kinship units, 597; littoral and inland household communities, 1, 7, 26, 588, 589, 591–592, 597, 612, 613, 614; mound-building creating sense of community, 17, 589–590, 615; public activities within, 18; segmented communities, 588, 612; and social capital, 26

complementary duality: and bundles, 469, 470; and faunal remains, 235; and textiles, 446, 495, 521

complementary opposition: and enumeration, 611–612; and faunal remains, 353; and fragments, 607–610

complexity: of agriculture, 581; of Preceramic period, 15–16, 38. *See also* social complexity

Conklin, William, 35

copper sulfate: as exotic, 584, 586, 588, 590, 596, 609; offering of coca leaf and copper sulfate in Unit 21, 140, *141*, 454; principle components of, 740, *740*

cordage: analysis of, 526; average diameters for fabrics, loose yarns, and cordage, 474–475, *475*, 476; braided cordage, 488; in bundles, 466, 554, 556; chronology of, 548, *548*, 551–552; classification criteria for, 526–527; construction attributes of, 527; and crepe-twisting, 527, 538, 539, 549, 552; definition of, 526; external correlations, 552–554; as fabric component, 473–474; final twist direction, 548–549; form and function of, 550–551, 552; fragments of, 123, 458, 551, 554; innovations in, 457; internal correlations, 541, 548–552; and knots, 527, 535, 536, 538, 540, 550, 552, 555; and looping, 535, 536, 538, 550, 551, 552, 555; making of, 476–477; mending, 550;

multiple-ply cordage, 527, 549; and net floats, 550, 551, 555; overview of, 554–556; plants for making, 430; and ply elements, 527, 548–549; ply formulae for all cordage types, *534*; and rat-tailing, 527, 535, 549, 551; and raw materials, 549–552, 556; single-ply cordage, 527, 549; specimens of, 527; and splices, 527, 535, 537, 540, 549, 551, 552; and twist manipulation, 549; Type I: Single Ply, Z-spun, 533, *534*; Type II: Single Ply, S-spun, 533, *534*, 537, 551, 552; Type III: Two Ply, S-spun, Z-twist, 530, 533–535, *534*, 538, 540, 549, 551, 552, 555; Type IV: Two Ply, Z-spun, S-twist, *534*, 535–536, 538, 539, 549, 551, 552, 555; Type V: Three Ply, S-spun, Z-twist, *534*, 536, 552; Type VI: Three Ply, S-spun, Z-twist, *534*, 536–537, 539; Type VII: Five Ply, Z-spun, S-twist, *534*, 537, 552; Type VIII: Twelve Ply, S-spun, Z-twist, *534*, 537, 552; Type IX: Compound, Two Ply, S-spun, Z-twist, *534*, 537; Type X: Compound, Two Ply, S-spun, Z-twist, *534*, 537–538, 552; Type XI: Compound, Two Ply, S-spun, Z-twist, *534*, 538, 551, 555; Type XII: Compound, Two Ply, Z-spun, S-twist, *534*, 538–539, 551, 555; Type XIII: Compound, Two Ply, S-spun, Z-twist, *534*, 539; Type XIV: Compound, Two Ply, Z-spun, S-Twist, *534*, 539, 551; Type XV: Compound, Three Ply, S-spun, Z-twist, *534*, 539, 551; Type XVI: Compound, Three Ply, S-spun, Z-twist, *534*, 539–540; Type XVII: Compound, Two Ply, S-spun, Z-twist, *534*, *540*; Type XVIII: Compound, Two Ply, S-spun, Z-twist, *534*, 540; Type XIX: Three Strand, Unspun, Braid, *534*, 540; types, quantities, and provenience of fibers, cordage, yarns, and fabrics, *462*, 465, 474; at Unit 1, 123; wadded cordage, 551; wear patterns of, 527, 533, 535, 536, 538, 539, 540, 552; yarns distinguished from, 474

core planes, 438

cores: of Chicama Valley, 54, *55*, *56*, 57; in cultural phases, 440; and paleoenvironmental history, 49; at Salamanca, 560, 561; varieties of, 435, 438

corn. *See* maize (*Zea mays*); popcorn

corporate labor, 4, 575, 576, 595

corpses: burial places of missing bodies, 578; and obligation, 599–604

cosmology: and elements of fire and water, 1, 11–12, 608, 609; at Huaca Prieta, 7, 589, 590, 594, 601, 602, 614; and individual bodies as unified system, 609, 610; and social structure, 614. *See also* ontologies

cotton (*Gossypium barbadense*): and baskets, 530, 532, 543, 546, 548, 556; and cordage, 533, 535, 536, 537, 538, 539, 540, 549–550, 552, 556; as crop, 234, 363, 582; as cultivated industrial plant, 417–418, 428, 429, 431, 432, 582; as fiber, 103, 209, 472–473, 474, 480, 483; natural colors of, 494, 495, 695; soil conditions required for, 12; for weft bands, 505

cotton textiles: Bird on, 8, 91, 103, 458; geometric designs on, 18; radiocarbon dating of, 88, 91, 98–99, *99*; and rituals associated with transgenerational kin/community group identities, 16; salty paste-like material saturating, 91, 99, *99*, 460, 461, *463*, 471, 491, 494, 495, 522, color insert; twined cotton fiber, 103, 209, 472; at Unit 1, 123

cotton weaving: functional analysis of, 35, 459; at Huaca

Prieta, 7, 12; innovations of, 457; and production practices, 464–465

counting device, in Unit 16, 452–453, *453*

cradle-boarding, 188–189

craft objects, 18

cranial shape, and human skeletal remains, *169*, 170, 179–180, *179*, *182*, 184

Cretaceous Chimú Formations, 52–53, *52*, *53*

cribra orbitalia, 189–191, *189*, 196

cross-generational transmission: of meaning, 23, 24–25, 26, 599–602, 605–606, 607; and social complexity, 18

Cueva Salamanca 1, 554

Culebras, 40

cultigens: at Alto Salaverry, 361; distribution of, 585–586; exotic cultigens, 12, 41, 431, 454, 456, 569, 571, 577, 584, 585, 586–588, 592, 596, 597, 616; exploitation of, 17, 198, 431, 572, 573, 579, 580, 581, 582, 584; geographic origins of, 616; in littoral zones, 581–588; and ritual offerings, 586–588, 592; and social networks, 585–586; and terrestrial subsistence, 234, 345, 571

cultural phases: and faunal remains, 211; plant species for Huaca Prieta, Paredones, and Unit 16, 367, *368-370*, 428, 431, 571, 587; radiocarbon dates for phases and subphases by units, *92-97*, 122; radiocarbon time spans of, *89*, 107; subphases of, *89*, 90–91

culture/nature, continuum of, 20–21

Cummings, Linda Scott, 36

Cupisnique mound: absence of stone berms in, 117; archaeological evidence from, 104; Bird's TP-5 on, 107; Bird's units in, 32, 121–122, 153, 158; building of, 8, 108, 591; burial practices of, 104; ceramics of, 8, 85, 87; and domestic sector, 573; as habitational, 121; Huaca Prieta Project map of, *31*; and plant remains, 383; Preceramic village underneath, 165; present-day shoreline and sandy beach north of, *45*; reoccupation of, 87; sunken circular plaza of, 32; and test pits, 159, 160, 161; and tsunami event, 86; and Unit 16, 157

Cupisnique period: burial treatment in, 169, 170, 188, 191, 195; cobs of, 656, 658, 664; in Cupisnique mound, 121, 122; and economic practices, 596, 597; in HP-3, 116; at Huaca Prieta, 568, 573, 591; at Lower Coastal Plains, 565; maize corresponding to, 656, 658, 661, 662, 664; in outlying domestic sites, 558, 559; at Salamanca, 561, 562, 563; at Salamanca Norte, 564; textiles from, 461; in Unit 6, 130

custard apple (*Annona* sp.), 374, 379, 430, 688

Cutler, H. C., 659

cyclododecane, 461, 464

Damp, Jonathan, 426

decentering, 22, 599, 610

decoration: of basketry, 530, 532, 542, 547, 581, 587, 610; and element knots, 509; in figure-8 looping, 477, 480; of gourds, 7, 11, 12, 165, 440, 442, *443*, *444*, 445, 446, 457, 580, 587, 731; and knotted netting, 483; stone tools and gourd decoration, 442, 731; of textiles, 442, 445, 465, 521, 523, 581, 587, 597, 610, 612; and twining, 491, 494–495, 497–498, 504, 509, 515

De La Mata, Roberto, 193

dental microwear texture analysis (DMTA): data from individuals sampled at Huaca Prieta, 666, 667, *669*, 670, *670*, 672, *672*; descriptive statistics of DMTA data from Huaca Prieta, *670*; and dietary ecology, 665, 667, 670, 672; and textural food properties, 666

dentition: dental microwear texture analysis, 666, 667, *669*, 670, *670*, 672, *672*; development of, 167, 196; examination of, 170; isotope analysis of, 432, 433, 446, 572, 586, 603, 666–667, *668*, 669–670, *669*, 671, 672; microscopic tooth wear from individuals at Huaca Prieta, *671*; mtDNA analysis results from teeth studies, 734–738, *736*; pathology of, 167, 180, 188, 196; starch grains from human teeth, 683, *685*, 686, 687; wear patterns, 174, 175, 176, 177–178, 180, 181, 182, *182*, 184, 186, 188

DeSantis, Larisa, 36

Diehl, Michael, 659

dietary ecology: and dental microwear texture analysis, 665, 667, 670, 672; human diet at Huaca Prieta, 48, 190–191, 194, 221, 249, 268, 275, 330, 432, 572, 665, 669–670, 672, 673; human diet at Paredones, 48, 87, 149, 221, 249, 268, 275, 330, 432, 572, 665, 672–673; methods of, 666–667; stable carbon and nitrogen isotope analysis, 665–667, *668*, 669–670, 672–673; textural food properties inferred from dental microwear texture analysis, 666

Dillehay, Tom D.: on basketry, 526; collection of *Semele corrugata* shells, 713; and contamination effects on corn, 91; on cordage, 526, 527, 548, *548*, 549; excavation of Huaca Prieta, 9–10; excavation of human skeletal remains, 167, *189*, 733; on grinding stones, 683; observation of fisherfolk, 201, *201*; observation of pelican hunters, 201, *201*, 209; on textiles, 458, 522; tool function assessment of, 35; on Unit 1, 617; on weaving, 476

Dillon, Michael, 40

Direct-AMS, 89

discarding practices: and bundles, 466, 469; and figure-8 looping, 480; and knotted netting, 486, 487; recurrences and variability of, 111; and textiles, 465, 466, 513

disks, varieties of, 439, *439*, 441, color insert

DNA analysis, 196. *See also* mtDNA analysis

Dobres, Marcia A., 464

dolphins: and faunal remains, 248, 353, 354, 365; as predators, 202

domestic activity: chronology of, 557; as Cupisnique mound, 121; defining of, 90, 122; at Huaca Prieta, 108, 122–123, 197; outlying domestic sites, 557–566; at Paredones, 108, 197; and resource use, 198; and structures, 17. *See also* off-mound domestic units (DU); outlying domestic sites

domesticated plants, 202, 367

Driver, Harold, 525

dry forests: and ENSO events, 43; in Holocene period, 45–46, 47; in late Pleistocene period, 41–42; and mammals, 363; and wetlands of Chicama Valley, 43–44

dual economy: Huaca Prieta mound as expression of, 612; and marine foods and plant foods, 432, 570, 580, 591

Dufour, Elise, 36

Dunn tests, 667

dyes: for baskets, 456, 530, 532, 543, 546, 547; and bundles, 470–472; for cordage, 527; exotic dyes, 456; indigo dyes,

36, *463*, 471, 517, 522, 596, 693, *694*, 703, color insert; manufacture and use of, 457, 472; plants used for, 431; sources of, 470; for textiles, 456, 504

Early Intermediate Period, 189, 193, 195

earthquakes, 583, 618

economic practices: complementary multizone economy, 29, 596–597; dual economy, 432, 570, 580, 591, 612; and faunal remains, 197; and fragmentation, 28; and interregional linkages, 16; and location of Huaca Prieta and Paredones, 578; mixed foraging and farming economy, 29, 234, 569, 573, 579, 580, 581, 584, 585, 588, 592, 593, 594; and mound building, 17; and social differentiation, 580, 585, 591, 592, 612; specialization of, 27, 108, 364, 365, 366, 572, 573, 577, 579, 580, 581, 592, 595, 596, 597, 612, 613, 616; and stone tools, 440; from tripartite to coastal economy, 579–581. *See also* maritime economies

Ecuador: and exchange networks, 360; pebble tool industry in, 12; Preceramic mound cultures of, 4, 196; weaving practices in, 523

Ecuador Current, 43, 198

Eglash, Ron, 23

El Brujo Complex (Cao Viejo): Cupisnique burials from Paredones Sector of, 195, 196; Cupisnique skull from Paredones sector of, *187*, 188–189; and exostoses of external auditory meatus, 191; geophysical survey unit in, 724, *724*; research on, 577; on Sangamon terrace, 10; view of, *6*, 577

electrical resistance surveys, 723–725, *725*, 726, *726*

Elera, Carlos, 170, 195, 362, 573

Eliade, Mircea, 608

elites: competition among, indicating social complexity, 17; and corporate labor, 595; group-oriented ritual processes contrasted with, 574; Huaca Prieta mound not showing signs of, 613; and mortuary patterns, 18

El Niño: and exotics, 454; and fish otoliths, 706, 709, 711; geological analysis of, 9, 30; impact of, 582, 583, 629, 713; mid-Holocene weakening of wet phases, 50–52, *51*; and *Semele corrugata*, 713, 719; terrestrial flood records, 51, 78, 83–84, 85, 86; wet phases of, 61, 67, 79, *80*, 83, 85, 86. *See also* ENSO (El Niño/Southern Oscillation) events

El Paraíso: algarrobo found at, 421; amaranth found at, 415; basketry and cordage found at, 552; bone tools of, 467; California bulrush found at, 420; chile pepper at, 409; dyes of, 472; fibers of, 473; *Furcraea* sp. found at, 424; gourds found at, 417; guava found at, 409; horsetail found at, 419; lucuma found at, 414; monumental buildings of, 18; potatoes found at, 411; reed found at, 419; squash found at, 409; textiles of, 459; wild cane found at, 424; willow found at, 421

El-Zaatari, Sireen, 667

Emery, Irene, 459, 465, 488, 498, 519, 527

enchainment: and fragments, 26, 606, 607, 611, 612; of living and dead, 26, 611, 612–613; of living, dead, and unborn, 612, 613; and narrative of social practices, 25, 606

Engel, Frederic, 450, 470, 472–473, 487, 504, 509, 554

ENSO (El Niño/Southern Oscillation) events: effect on

marine foraging, 198, 200, 209; and fish otoliths, 706; impact of, 42–43, 44, 46, 48, 49–52, 86; and Peru Current System, 199–200; and temperature perturbation, 200–201

environmental changes: adaptation to, 29, 198, 200, 201; recent environments and deposits along coast near Huaca Prieta, 628, *628*, 629; and resource use, 198

environmental history: Alluvial Stage (Pre-Huaca Prieta), 79; of Chicama Valley, *70, 74*, 79–80, *80, 81*, 82–85; Floodplain Stage (Post-HP), 84–85; Lagoon Stage (HP Phase II), 82, 108, 622, 629; Maximum Transgression and Preceramic/Ceramic Transition (HP Phase V), 84, 86, 108, 573–574; Paludal Stage (HP Phase IV), 83–84, 573; study of, 40; Transition (HP Phase I), 79–80; Transitional (HP Phase III), 82–83, 629

environmental zones: benthic zone, 200; estuarine zone, 208, 212, 363; inland zone, 202; intertidal zone, 200, 207, 208, 209, 219, 220; and marine associations, 202, *203–206*, 207–208, 210, 212, 219, 235, 366, 612; near shore zone, 208; neritic zone, 200, 212, 363; oceanic zone, 202; pelagic zone, 200; subtidal zone, 200, 208, 209, 220, 363, 365; supralittoral zones, 200, 363; supratidal zone, 207, 208, 219; upper tidal zone, 207, 212, 220. *See also* dry forests; estuaries; highland resource zone; littoral zones; maritime resource zones; resource zones; wetlands

Ernst, Max, 23

estuaries: exploitation of, 365, 366; and faunal remains, 219, 220, 234, 330, 345, 363, 366; and marine foraging, 200, 201, 202, 207, 208, 210, 234

estuarine zone, 208, 212, 363

Evans-Pritchard, E. E., 27

exchange networks: and exotics, 16, 360, 454, 456–457, 584, 585–586, 596; and faunal remains, 360; and food production, 579, 585–586; and Huaca Prieta, 11, 573, 590; littoral and coastal sites linked through, 12, 571, 597; and monumental buildings, 18; and social complexity, 596

exostoses, of external auditory meatus or canal, 152, 173, 174, 180, 181, 191–192, 196, 201

exotics: and exchange networks, 16, 360, 454, 456–457, 584, 585–586, 596; exotic cultigens, 12, 41, 431, 454, 456, 569, 571, 577, 584, 585, 586–588, 592, 596, 597, 616; exotic items, 453–454, *455*, 456, 574, 584, 585, 586, 588, 590, 596, 609; and faunal remains, 365; introduction of, 15; and plant remains, 432

faique (*Acacia* sp.), 422, 429, 430

Farley, Michelle, 36

farming: complex foragers practicing, 17, 19; division of labor between fisherfolk and farmers, 596; and ENSO events, 199; at Huaca Prieta, 7, 9, 13, 17, 366; and knotting netting, 522; mixed foraging and farming economy, 29, 234, 569, 573, 579, 580, 581, 584, 585, 588, 592, 593, 594; in Neolithic period, 3; at Paredones, 7, 8, 17, 234, 366, 578; and percentage of diet, 19; in wetlands, 10, 17, 44, 46, 86, 571, 573, 578. *See also* agriculture

Farnum, John, 166, 189

faunal remains: analysis of, 209–210, 581; and biotypes, 197, 198; comparisons of Preceramic faunal assemblages from other North Andean sites, 360–362; diversity of, 198; and ENSO events, 199–200; and geomorphology of sea floor, 198–199, 362–363; at Huaca Prieta, 35, 46, 87, 122, 197; from late Pleistocene subphase, 210, 212, 219–221; and marine associations, 202, *203–206*, 207–208, 210, 212, 219, 235, 366, 612; and marine biotopes, 198, 199, 200–202; and material technologies, 197, 209, 220, 363; methods of analysis, 210–212; number of specimens of key species at Huaca Prieta and Paredones, 210, 211, 221, 317, 330, 331, 357, 360; number of specimens of key vertebrate species, 358–360; and off-mound domestic units 13, 16, and 26, 352–353; and off-mound to initial mound areas at Huaca Prieta, units 2, 9, and 12, 353–355; and outlying domestic sites, 557, 558; at Paredones, 197; Phase I: early Holocene late subphase, 210, 221, *222-233*, 234, 330, 352, 353, 355, 358; Phase I: late Pleistocene, early subphase, 210, 212, *213-219*, 219–221, 353, 358; Phase II, 234–235, 248–249; Phase II species type and distribution in excavated units at Huaca Prieta, 210, 235, *236-249*, 353, 354, 357, 358; Phase II species type and distribution in excavated units at Paredones, 210, 248, *250-261*, 358; Phase III, 249, 268; Phase III species type and distribution in excavated units at Huaca Prieta and Unit 16, 210, 249, *262-268*, 268, 353; Phase III species type and distribution in excavated units at Paredones, 210, 249, 268, *269-274*, 358; Phase IV, 268, 275; Phase IV species type and distribution in excavated units at Huaca Prieta and Unit 16, 210, *276-287*, 353, 355, 357, 358, 364; Phase IV species type and distribution in excavated units at Paredones, 210, *288-299*; Phase V, 275, 317, 330; Phase V species type and distribution in excavated Units 2-7 at Huaca Prieta, 210, 275, *300-311*, 330, 358; Phase V species type and distribution in excavated Units 10-16 at Huaca Prieta, 210, 275, *312-317*, 330, 355, 358; Phase V species type and distribution in excavated Units 11, 12, and 16 at Huaca Prieta, 210, 275, *318-323*, 330, 355, 358; Phase V species type and distribution in excavated Unit 21 at Huaca Prieta, 210, 275, *324-330*, 330, 356, 358; Phase V species type and distribution in excavated Unit 23 at Huaca Prieta, 210, 275, 330, *332-344*, 358; Phase V species type and distribution in excavated units at Paredones, 210, 275, 345, *346-351*, 358; quantitative and qualitative analyses of, 109; and ritual and burial areas on the summit of Huaca Prieta, units 10, 19/23, and 15/21, 355–357; at Salamanca, 561, 562; at Salamanca Norte, 563–564; and sampling biases, 360; and seasonality, 36, 209, 220, 344; and subsistence patterns, 201, 208–209, 211, 234; and sustainability, 208–209, 365, 366; temporal and spatial distribution of, 330–331, 344–345

feasting activity: and chile peppers, 653, 654, 655; and faunal remains, 197, 208, 234, 275, 317, 354; and food production, 579, 585, 597; and foodstuffs, 16; layers associated with, 90, 122; meaning of, 605; nonritual feasting, 111, 569; in Phase III, 571; in Phase IV, 572; transgenerational knowledge of, 575

featherwork, 509

Feldman, Robert, 471, 663

fencing, plants for making, 430

Feranec, Robert S., 36

Fernández, Arabel, 459–460

fibers: fragments of, 458; types, quantities, and provenience of fibers, cordage, yarns, and fabrics, *462*, 465; types of, 472–473, 521, 523; unidentified vegetal fiber (UVF), 472, 483, 550, 552. *See also* unspun fibers

figure-8 looping: average diameters of elements for fabrics, loose yarns, and cordage, *475*; and blue pigment, 471; and bundles, 466; decoration techniques, 477, 480; with diamond-like design, *478*; and element knots, 480, 508, 509n, *511*; fabric conditions, 480, *481*; and human hair, 482; in Preceramic Andean sites, 480, 482; production of, 512, 522; and red pigment, 472; repair of, 480; and sexual division of labor, 523; as single-element construction, 477; specimens of, 458, 477; striped looping, 477, *479*; supra-structures presented by function, *514–515*, 513; weft twining with, 491, *492*, 520; and yarn attributes, 512, 514

fills: characteristics of, 89–90, 162, 571; and construction sequence, 104; cultural deposits of, 122; at Paredones, 575; and plant remains, 372; quantitative data from, 210–211; of Unit 3, 129; at Unit 13, 153–154; of Unit 15, 137; of Unit 17, 137–138; of Unit 20, 165; of Unit 22, 148, 165

finger grass (*Chloris* sp.), 425, 430, 431

Firth, Raymond, 27

fish: at Alto Salaverry, 362; and faunal remains, 208, 209, 210, 212, 219, 220, 234, 235, 248, 249, 268, 275, 330, 331, 344–345, 352, 353, 354, 355, 356, 358–359, 363–364, 365, 366, 580; fish-scaling with shell tools, 450; habitats of, 202, 207, 208, 209, 363–364, 366; and marine foraging, 201, *201*, 202, 221; at Padre Abán, 361; as predators, 202; species of, 199, 200, 201, 202, 358. *See also* fish otoliths

fisherfolk: and burial treatment, 599, 603; division of labor between fisherfolk and farmers, 596; effect of major ENSO event on, 198, 200; and engineering knowledge of sediment placement, 576; and geomorphology of sea floor, 198; and invisible designs on textiles, 610; and knotted netting, 522; and marine foraging, 365; nets used by, 201, *201*, 209, 220, 221, 363; on polychaete tubes, 199; reed rafts used by, 10, 209, 268; and wetlands, 366

fish otoliths: archaeological and modern otoliths, 706, 708, *708*; archaeological otolith samples from Huaca Prieta, *708*; bagre otoliths, 706, *707*, *708*, 709; characteristics of, 706; frequency of identified species, 706, *707*; growth banding, 706, *707*, 708, 709; from Huaca Prieta, 706, *707*, 708–709, *708*, 710, 711; isotope analysis of, 708–709; location of sites, 706, *706*; and seasonal cycles, 709, 710

Fishtail, projectile points of, 42, 435

floodplains: overbank floodplain deposits, 67–69, 621; and Paredones, 105, 108; sequences within Chicama Valley, 67–69, *70*, *71*, 79, 108, 596; and Test Pit 6, 159, 162; and Test Pit 13, 160, 162; and test pits, 162

floods: and alluvial settings, 60; and ENSO events, 46, 48, 199; irregular recurrence of, 198; and marine foraging, 201; megafloods, 46; terrestrial El Niño flood records, 51, 78, 83–84, 85, 86

floors: artifact and sediment composition of, 109, 111, 576; chemical analysis of, 152; chile peppers found on, 653; and construction sequence, 104; cultural deposits of, 122; definition of, 89; and faunal remains, 210–211; Harris Matrices for, 111, *111*; of Huaca Prieta, 570–571; individual nature of prepared and unprepared floors, 165; nomenclature of, 122; and outlying domestic sites, 558; of Paredones, 106, 165, 570, 575; and plant remains, 372; prepared and unprepared floors associated with ritual offerings, 90, 162, 605; stratigraphy represented by, 91; at Unit 5, 130; at Unit 7, 130; at Unit 10, 131, 133, 134–135; at Unit 12, 136; at Unit 13, 153–154; at Unit 14, 136; at Unit 17, 137–138; at Unit 20, 150; at Unit 22, 149–152, 165, 221; at Unit 23, 144, *144*

floral remains, 35, 46, 87, 109, 122. *See also* plant remains

food debris, 90, 165

food preparation: and dental microwear texture analysis, 666, 672; and faunal remains, 197, 364, 365; mortuary rituals compared to, 90; Paredones associated with, 7, 108, 151, 152, 165, 248, 364, 427–428, 432, 568, 570, 575, 595, 596, 653; and plant remains, 364; recurrences and variability of, 111; at Unit 2, 354; at Unit 16, 352, 353; at Unit 20, 427–428

food-producing societies, 16

foodstuffs, 16, 111, 162, 165. *See also* feasting activity; food preparation

footpaths, zigzag footpaths of Huaca Prieta mound, 27, *34*, 119, 122, *127*, 128, *128*, 129, 130, 164, 451, 572

foragers and foraging: complex forager behavior as strategic, 17, 584; and faunal remains, 221; foraging/hunting pattern, 331, 359, 363, 366; and intergroup interactions, 17, 580; mixed foraging and farming economy, 29, 234, 569, 573, 579, 580, 581, 584, 585, 588, 592, 593, 594; mobility of, 17; models of, 19; and outlying domestic sites, 558; and Sangamon terrace, 220, 568; sedentary lifeways complementing, 17, 19; wetlands foraging, 7, 9, 13, 17, 19, 47, 108, 151, 363, 567, 579, 588, 593. *See also* marine foraging

Formative period: geometric designs of, 12; monumental ceremonial centers of, 595, 615; and plant remains, 383; and rise of individual elites, 18; and ritual sites, 571

Fortes, Meyer, 27

Foucault, Michel, 20

fractals: form of coastline as example of, 22, 23; as repetitive patterns, 22–23, 606, 607–608, 613; segmented socioeconomic organization as fractal system, 27, 612–615

fractional coherences: and fragmentation, 610–612; and meaning, 22–23; and objects, 23–25

fractured pieces: at Huaca Prieta mound, 7, 24, 25, 26–27, 28; meaning of, 1, 12, 23, 24, 26–27, 211, 434, 598, 601, 606, 611; and ritual offerings, 605; unintentionally broken objects, 26–27

fragmentation: and accumulation, 25, 606, 608, 610–611, 612; across artifact categories, 25; of basketry, 26, 27,

123, 446, 530, 532, 543, 544, 547, 556, 598, 606, 611,
613; and enchainment, 26, 606, 607, 611, 612; and fractional coherence, 610–612; of gourds, 26, 27, 442, 446,
570, 598, 606, 611, 613; Huaca Prieta mound as point of,
610; of human skeletal remains, 26, 116–117, 166, 167,
179, 180–181, 184, 504, 598, 605, 611, 613; of material
culture, 12, 23; and narrative of social practices, 25, 26,
27–28, 606; and plant remains, 370, 374; of shells, 27,
275, 344, 448, 450, 599, 613; of textiles, 25, 26, 27, 446,
459–460, 465, 466, 469, 513, 521, 570, 578, 598, 599,
606, 607, 611, 613
fragments: accumulation of, 610–611; cohesion of, 1; and
complementary opposition, 607–610; meaning of, 608;
metaphor of bulletin board, 22, 23, 24, 26, 610; in premound layers, 123; and sequences of use episodes, 111
Franco, Teresa, 36
Fuegian people: and dental microwear texture analysis, 666,
672, 673; isotope analysis of dietary ecology, 670
Furcraea sp., 424, 473, 523

Galinat, W., 663
Gallinazo materials: ceramics of, 85; in Cupisnique mound,
122; maize of, 656, 658, 661–662, 664
game board, in Unit 16, 452–453, *453*
gamma spectometry, 57
gardens and gardening: in littoral zones, 580; and shift to
agriculture, 584; in wetlands, *560*, 566, 571. *See also*
farming
gas chromatography, 692, 693
genetics: of cotton, 418; estimating haplogroup affiliation
through mtDNA analysis, 733–738; and Huaca Prieta
Project, 9; and human skeletal remains, 36, 170, 172, 173,
192, 196, 590, 613, 616; of maize, 659, 661
Genovés, Santiago, 167
geo-climatic processes, 19
geometric designs: on textiles and gourds from Huaca
Prieta, 12, 18; of Valdivia settlements, 12, 445
geophysical survey: GU-1, 724, *725*, 726; GU-4, 724–725,
725, 726; GU-5, 725, 726, *726*; GU-6, 726, *726*; of
Huaca Prieta and Paredones, 723–726; methodology of,
724, *724*; results of, 724–726
Giddens, Anthony, 25
Godelier, Maurice, 16
Goodbred, Steven L., 36, 38, 44, 107, 582
Goodman, Major, 659
gourds (*Lagenaria siceraria*): and bundles, 466, 586; carved
gourds at Huaca Prieta, 18; chile peppers found in, 654;
as crops, 234, 363; as cultivated industrial plants, 415,
417, 427, 428, 429, 580; decorated and etched gourds
at Huaca Prieta, 7, 11, 12, 442, *444*, 446, 580, 587, 731;
decorated gourds at Paredones, 165, 440, 442, *443*, *444*,
445, 446, 457, 580, 731; design techniques and motifs,
442, *443*, *444*, 445–446, 521, 580, 581, 597, 610, 612;
distribution of types of decorated and worked gourds for
Huaca Prieta and Paredones, 442, *445*; for food preparation, 90; fragmentation of, 26, 27, 442, 446, 570, 598,
606, 611, 613; function of, 35, 433, 440, 442, 446, 457;
gourd fragments at Huaca Prieta, 25; material record
of, 13; phytolith analysis of bottle gourds, 675, *678*; and

ritual practices, 275, 440, 446, 605; role of decorated
gourds in social exchange, 16; at Salamanca 2, 561; and
sequences of use episodes, 111; starch grains from bottle
gourds, 446, 683, *685*, 686
GPR data, and Paredones, 105
Graumont, Raul, 483
green schist: grooved axes, *437*, 440, 445; stone painted
with red pigment, 446, *447*
Grieder, Terrence, 8, 470, 488
grinding stones: from Cupisnique mound, 121; and maize,
431, 439–440, 581, 664; from Paredones, 106, 432, 436,
440, 457, 571, 587; starch grains from, 683, *684*, *685*,
686; technology of, 433; varieties of, 439–440, *439*, 457,
567
Grobman, Alexander, 36, 659, 664
grooved axes: of green schist, *437*, 440, 445; of rhyolite,
437, 440, *441*, color insert
grooved spheroids, *437*, *439*, 440, *441*, color insert
Guamán Poma de Ayala, Felipe, 452
Guañape culture: burial practices of, 104; ceramics of, 8; in
Cupisnique mound, 121, 122; domestic sector at, 573;
and economic practices, 597; in HP-3, 116; at Huaca
Prieta, 568, 573, 574, 590; knotted netting of, 486; pottery fragments of, 83, 84, 85, 105, 456, *456*, 629; socioeconomic organization during, 596; in Unit 1, 123; in
Unit 2, 123
guava (*Psidium guajava*), as cultivated plant food, 409, 429,
688
Guinea grass (*Panicum* sp.), 424–425, 429, 431
Guitarrero Cave: basketry and cordage found at, 553; chile
peppers found at, 646; fibers of, 473; textiles of, 459,
524
Gulf of Guayaquil, 360, 454
gyrogonites, 54, *60*

Hacha, 459, 552
hammerstones, 435, *436*, 437
Harris Matrices: assignment of Harris numbers to individual
strata, 111–112, *111*; correspondence between field and
Harris systems, 111–112, 115; cultural phases linked to,
91; letter designations for, 112; for primary units, 30, 89,
109, 111–114, 162; symbols used in, 89, *111*, 112–113; for
west wall of HP-3, 119, *120*, 121
Hastorf, Christine, 36, 648, 649
Hayden, Brian, 585
haystacking design, of Huaca Prieta, 99, 129, 574, 575, 576
Heidegger, Martin, 602, 604
hematite, 596
herbs, 677, 679, *679*
Hertz, Robert, 603–604
Heta people, 524
hexametasulfate, 461, *463*, 464, color insert
highland resource zone, exploitation of, 17
Hodder, Ian, 602
Høie, Hans, 709
Holocene Climatic Optimum, 629
Holocene period: and Chicama Valley, 10, 49; climates of,
42–43, 44, 45–47, 48, 49–52, 629, 706, 711; cultural
deposits of, 4, 123, 567; and faunal remains, 208; geogra-

phy of, 45–47; at Huaca Prieta, 7, 8, 9, 12, 30, 123; tsunami events in, 78, 85

Hood, Darden, 91

Hopi people, 614

horsetail (*Equisetum giganteum*), 418–419, 427, 429, 430

households: and economic specialization, 616; group identities, 16, 585–586; and littoral and inland household communities, 1, 7, 26, 588, 589, 591–592, 597, 612, 613, 614; Preceramic sites, 10–11; and sociocultural identities, 585–586, 588, 615

house mounds: clusters of, 27, 106, 569, 612, 613; and outlying domestic sites, 557–566, 616; and settlement patterns, 578, 612

HP-2: Bird's excavation of, 34, 102, 103, 114, 131; description of, 114; Phase II in, 102, 103, 569; Phases IV-V on east side of mound, 114; and plant remains, 418; and Test Pit 5, 159

HP-3: Bird's excavation of, 30, 32, 34, 88, 101, 103, 114–119, 135, 159, 573; bone tools of, 450, 451; burial from Phase II in, 116; chronology of, 91; decorated gourds of, 442; description of, 114–119, 121; east wall profile, *116*, 119, 681; entry ramp constructed in Phase IV, 116, 119, 446; and faunal remains, 221, *222-233*, 235, *236-249*, 249, *262-268*, *276-287*, *300-311*, 364; Harris Matrices for, 111; Harris Matrix for west wall, 119, *120*, 121; HP-2 compared to, 114; human skeletal remains in, 116–117, 689–690; Phase II in, 102, 103, 116, 569; Phase III in, 103; Phase IV in, 103, 116, 119, 121; Phase V in, 573; plant distribution in Phase II, *376-377*, 428; plant distribution in Phase III, *382-383*, 428–429; plant distribution in Phase IV, *384-385*, 429; plant distribution in Phase V, *412-415*, 429; and plant remains, 385, 409, 414, 415, 418, 419, 420, 421, 422, 424, 426; premound strata from, 100, 101, 115; retention walls excavated by Bird, 116, 117, *117*, 119, 126, 681; sand and salt samples from, 681–682; shell tools of, 450; spatially circumscribed strata in, 126; starch grains from, 684, *685*; stone berms at, *115*, 117, 118, 119, 121, 124, 129, 569, 681–682; unifacial tool of, *729*, 730; walled segment dating to Phase III and IV, 116; west wall of, *111*, 112–113, 184–185, 658, 662; west wall profile, 114–115, *115*, 117, 118, 119, 121; west wall's radiocarbon chronology, 115; yellow clay cap in, 145. *See also* Unit 3

Hrdlička, Alex, 193

Huaca Cortada, 107

Huaca de la Luna Project, Trujillo, 115

Huaca El Brujo, 618

Huaca El Gallo/Huaca La Gallina, 169

Huaca Negra: algarrobo found at, 421; cotton found at, 418; gourds found at, 417; residential and mortuary function of, 565

Huaca Prieta Ceramic Period, 189

Huaca Prieta mound: abandonment of, 104, 106, 108, 159, 164, 573; adobe brick mounds north of, 161; aerial view from 1940s, *33*; archaeological record of, 1, 2, 8, 13, 22, 29, 568; architectural organization of, 610; Bird's map of, *33*, 103, 121; Bird's stratigraphic profiles of, 30, 109; building phases of, 30, 46, 85, 99–100, 107–108, 121, 122, 151, 157, 162, 164, 165, 234, 589–590; burial treat-

ment at, 7, 11, 18, 19, 26, 39, 188, 195–196, 235, 355, 432, 570, 571, 573, 574, 598–601; capping episodes of, 121, 571; caretakers of, 165; cemetery of, 572; chamber tombs at, 8, 26, 104, 123, 164, 570, 571, 572, 573, 578, 589, 590, 597, 598, 602, 604, 605, 726; charcoal analysis, 631, *632, 633*; charcoal content of, 8, 11, 12, 151, 570, 575, 594, 631; chemical analysis of, 152; chronological sequence of, 30, 90–91, 98–99, 104–105, 107–108, 198, 598, 616; and complementarity of foraging and sedentary practices, 17; continuity and change within, 15–17, 29–30, 38, 610; cross-generational use of, 25, 26; cultural origins of, 12; dark appearance of, 4, 24, 146, 149, 151, 575, 591, 594; decline in use of, 84, 86, 87, 104; demographic setting of, 10–11, 28, 457; detailed topographic map and main features, *34*; distribution of comestible, industrial, and wild plant parts at, 432, *432*, 587; distributions overlapping in time and space, 23; domestic activity at, 108, 122–123, 197; economic specialization of, 27, 572; entry ramp of, 33–34, 103–104, 116, 119, 122, 123, 142, 152, 164, 454, 459, 556, 568, 571, 572, 573, 574–575, 576, 577, 578, 587, 589, 590, 597, 614; environmental history of, 79–80, *80, 81*, 82–85; exotic cultigens adopted at, 12; fractured pieces at, 7, 24, 25, 26–27, 28; function of, 8–9, 22, 24, 29; general view looking to northeast, *6*; geophysical research of, 38; geophysical survey of, 723–726; global significance of, 4; gradual building up of, 48; Harris Matrices for profiles in, *111*, 112–113, 162; Huaca Prieta Project excavations of, 34–35, 109, 151–152; Huaca Prieta Project map of, 30, *31*, 146; human diet at, 48, 190–191, 194, 221, 249, 268, 275, 330, 572, 665, 669–670, 672, 673; as inalienable object, 611, 614; incoherent nature of content and structure of, 122–123; Initial Period reuse of, 87, 104; and intercommunity social and economic integration, 597; legacies of, 591–593; littoral and marine environments of, 44–45; long-term planning at, 574–577, 578, 589; looter's hole of, 33, 136; map of excavation units and test pits at, *110*; measurements of, 4, 6, 7, 9; as mortuary site, 4, 7, 8, 164, 568, 569, 570, 571, 572–573, 574, 575, 590–591, 592, 597; natural setting of, 10; number of plant parts excavated at, 431–432, *432*; ontological understanding of materials in, 7, 12–13, 21–22, 573, 574–575, 602, 613, 614–615; ornamental objects in burials, 18; and outlying domestic sites, 557, 565–566; Phase I, premound occupation, 100–101, 104, 162, 197, 234, 235, 359, 360, 567, 568, 579–580; Phase II, mound building, 102–103, 104, 105, 106, 107, 149, 151, 164, 165, 234–235, 249, 331, 357, 358, 359, 360, 440, 568–570, 574, 579–580, 586, 605, 629; Phase III, mound expansion, 103, 105, 149, 151, 162, 165, 249, 268, 357, 358, 359, 360, 440, 569, 570–572, 574, 575, 576, 578, 580, 605; Phase IV, coastal influence, 103–104, 105, 119, 122, 129, 149, 151, 152, 162, 164, 165, 268, 275, 358, 359, 360, 364, 440, 570, 571, 572–573, 574, 575, 576, 577, 578, 580, 587, 605, 614; Phase V, termination of mound building, 104, 121, 122, 149, 151, 152, 159, 162, 164, 165, 275, 358, 359, 360, 570, 572, 573–574, 577, 580, 587, 605, 614, 648; as pilgrimage site, 11, 586–588, 590, 597; plant species by cultural phases, 367, *368-370*, 432, 571,

587; plaster covering mound layers, 32, 162, 164, 268, 357, 457, 569, 571, 572, 573, 574, 575, 576, 590, 597, 608, 682; plot of calibrated radiocarbon dates, *98*; Preceramic use of, 7–8, 104, 105; premound phase of, 30, 32, 34, 37, 123, 161; present-day shoreline and sandy beach north of, *45*; radiocarbon dates by excavation units, *92–97*, 122; record of human occupation, 39; residential zones immediately north of, 122; resource use at, 198; rhizomatic pattern of, 610; ritual spaces of, 27, 164, 432, 456, 568, 569, 570–571, 572, 573, 574, 586, 587–588, 589, 591–592, 595, 597, 605, 610, 612, 613; sanduned, raised agricultural field east of, 37, 107, *162*; and Sangamon terrace, 7, 10, 107–108; schematic architectural sequences, 162, *163*, color insert; segmented spaces of, 608, 610, 612, 613; social complexity of, 18, 146, 211; social structure of, 11–13; south view of, 622, *623*; stone tools of, 435–440, 442; stratigraphy of, 32, 35, 37–38, 91, 109, 111–114, 122–123, 151, 162, 164, 570, 575, 576, 589, 595, 609; structural nature of, 8, 9; summit of, 33, 100, 103, 104–105, 164, 212, 275, 355–357, 358, 359, 360, 421, 457, 573, 574; sunken circular plaza of, 103, 119, 123, 130, 152, 164, 571, 573, 574, 575, 578, 587, 589, 590, 597, 605, 614; synchronic and diachronic variation within, 109, 111–114, 574, 577; topography of, 602; transgenerational nature of, 574, 575, 576, 599, 601–602, 614; uninterrupted periods of use, 578; unit excavations at, 122–126, 126–131, 133–138, 140–146; Valdivia settlements of, 4; yellow sediment layer of, 121, 145, 164, 571, 572, 574, 576; zigzag footpaths of, 27, *34*, 119, 122, *127*, 128, *128*, 129, 130, 164, 451, 572, 605. *See also* south and southwest margins of Huaca Prieta mound; *and specific units*

Huaca Prieta Project: archaeological units of, 122–152; and ethnoarchaeological research, 10; field seasons of, 30; and function of Huaca Prieta, 8–9; geophysical research, 38; and interdisciplinary archaeological research, 9, 32, 35–36, 615–616; map of Paredones, Huaca Prieta, and Cupisnique mounds, 30, *31*, 146, 212; paleoenvironmental and geological analysis, 30, 32, 37–38; research design of, 29–30, 32, 38, 210; sampling excavated cultural deposits, 36–37; site excavations, 9–10, 34–35, 109; site mapping and archaeological excavation, 32–34; site survey, 37

Huanchaco, 9

Huanchaquito, 361

Huaricanga, 8

Huarmey, 660

Huaynuna: *achira* found at, 411; basketry and cordage found at, 552; chile pepper at, 409; cotton found at, 418; gourds found at, 417; lucuma found at, 414; potatoes found at, 411; squash found at, 409; textiles of, 459

human hair: in bundles, 466; in cordage, 549; as fiber, 472, 473, 474, 482; and wrapped objects, 467

human/nonhuman, continuum of, 20–21, 22

human skeletal remains: and age distribution, 167–168, *168*, 188, *189*; age indicators for, 167; analysis of, 35–36, 152, 166–167, 569, 579; Bird on, 152, 166; cranial shape, *169*, 170, 179–180, *179*, *182*, 184; degenerative changes in, *168*, 172–173, 193–194; and dental development, 167,

196; and exostoses of external auditory meatus or canal, 152, 173, 174, 180, 191–192, 196, 201; fragmentation of, 26, 117, 166, 167, 179, 180–181, 184, 504, 598, 605, 611, 613; frequency of degenerative changes by joint system in middle adults and older adults, 189–190, *190*, 192, 193; general observations, 167–173; and growth and development, 170–171, 192–193, 196; in HP-3, 116–117, 689–690; HP08-01, 131, *132*, 169, 170, 171, 173, 174; HP08-02, 170, 171, 174–175; HP09-01, 168, *169*, 171, 172, 173, 175–176, 524, 598; HP09-02, 168, 169, 171, 176; HP09-03, 168, 170, 176–177; HP09-04, 170, 171, 172, 173, 177–179, *178*; HP09-05, *156*, 157, 168, *169*, 170, 171, 172, 173, 179–180, *179*, 195–196; HP09-06, 171, 180–181; HP09-07, 168, *169*, 170, 171, 172, 173, *179*, 181–184, *182*, 195; HP09-08, 116, *118*, 170, 171, 172, 173, *182*, 184–185, *185*, 195, 569, 598; HP09-09, 169, 170–171, 185–187, *185*, *186*, 192; HP09-09A, 187; HP09-10, 170, 171, 187–188; methodology for analysis, 167; and nonspecific infection, 171, 191; and nutritional stress, 171, 189–191, *189*, 196; at Paredones, 152; pathological conditions, anomalies, and trauma, 167; preservation of, 168–169; and red pigment, 152, 169–170, 174, 176, 186, 195, 196, 451, 598; and sex distribution, 167, *168*, 188; and sex indicators, 167, 173; and social differentiation, 598–599; stature of, 167, 173, *174*, 176, 179, 184, 185, 187; teeth, 167, 170, 182, *182*, 196, 432, 433, 446, 571, 572, 586, 603; and trauma, 167, 171–172, 194–195, 196; at Unit 1, 123; of Unit 3, 174–175, 181–184; at Unit 8, 131, *132*; at Unit 10, 134, *135*, 185–187, 690; at Unit 12, 690; at Unit 16, 157, 172, 173, 175–181, 690–691; at Unit 18, 691. *See also* burial treatment

Humboldt Current, 43, 47, 50, 199, 200, 706

hunter-gatherer societies: and dental microwear texture analysis, 666, 667, 670, 672, 673; social divisions in, 612; socio-ecosystems of, 19; and terrestrial resources, 567, 568

Huschke's foramina, 192, 193

huts, plants for making, 430, 431

Hyslop, John, 459

identity markers: and burial treatment, 600; and exchange networks, 590; and household group identities, 16, 585–586, 597; inalienable objects as, 26, 606; and kin groups, 607; and legacies of Huaca Prieta and Paredones, 591–593; and material technologies, 581

ideology: and animistic beliefs, 466, 491, 495, 606; and burial practices, 18; elaboration of, 198; and elements of fire and water, 11–12; and faunal remains, 211, 275, 345, 365–366; at Huaca Prieta, 7, 591, 595; of mounds, 24; and social structure, 614; and symbols, 17

Illingworth, Jeff: on basketry and reed matting, 35, 526; on cleaning textiles with hexametasulfate, 461, 522; on cordage, 549, 550, 551; on dyes, 36, 472; on fibers, 473

Ilo, 706, 709

inalienability: and narrative of social practices, 25, 606; and repetition and continuity, 604–605; and transgenerational biographies of objects, 25, 606, 607, 610–611, 612

inalienable objects: Huaca Prieta mound as, 611, 614; as

maguey fiber, 523

Mahler, J., 472

maize (*Zea mays*): absolute dates of Huaca Prieta and Paredones samples, 662; Alazán, 660, 664; analysis methods, 658–659; botanical analysis, 659; Chapalote, 659; cobs, 91, 130, 656, *657*, 658–659, 660, 661, 662, 663–664, 665, 673, 674, 675, 687; comparison with other Preceramic sites, 662–663; Confite Chavinense, *657*, 659, 660, 661, 662, 663, 664; as cultivated plant food, 4, 429, 430, 431, 432–433, 581; cupules, 659; dating unburned corn remains, 91; and economic practices, 581; Enano, 659; flint corn, 661, 664; at HP-3, 656, 658, 662; at Huaca Prieta, 658, 659–662; and human diet at Huaca Prieta, 665; and human diet at Paredones, 672–673; husks, 91, 656, *657*, 658, 660, 663, 665, 673; hybrids, 658, 659, 660, 661; increased reliance on, 189, 196; isotope analysis of consumption, 666; kernels, 656, 658, 661, 663, 664, 683, 686, 687; macroremains of, 367, 370, 679; maize elements from Paredones, 656, *657*; meal corn, 581; Pagaladroga, 660, 664; from Phase III, 656, 658, 659–660, 661, 662, 663–664; from Phase IV, 656, 658, 659–660, 661, 662, 663–664; from Phase V, 658, 660–661, 662, 663–664; and phytolith analysis, 674, 675–676, *678*, 679, 731; pollen evidence, 665, 701, 703–704; popcorn grain, 429, 581, *657*, 663, 664, 687; Proto-Alazán, *657*, 659, 660, 661, 663, 664; Proto-Confite Morocho, *657*, 659, 660, 661, 662, 663, 664, 686; Proto-Kculli, 659, 660, 663; Proto-Maíz de Ocho, 659; Proto-Pagaladroga, 664; races of Preceramic maize cobs from Paredones and Huaca Prieta, 656, *657*, 658, 659; radiocarbon dating of, 88, 91, 656, 658, 662, 663; samples by chronological phase, 656, 658, 659; shanks, 91, *657*, 665; stalks, 123, 656, *657*, 658, 660; starch grains from, 664, 683, *684*, *685*, 687; stem fragment, 660; and stone tools, 440–441; tassels, *657*, 673; at Unit 1, 123, 656, 658; at Unit 2, 656; at Unit 3, 656, 658, 662; at Unit 6, 130, 656, 658; at Unit 16, 656, 658, 662; at Unit 20, 656, 658, 660, 662; at Unit 21, 656, 658, 662; at Unit 22, 150, 656, 658, 660, 662; at Unit 23, 656, 658; at Unit 25, 656, 658

Malabrigo 1: general view of, *560*; lagoon setting near, *72*; as outlying domestic site, 558, 564, 577, 578; Preceramic domestic sites of, 9, 10; Preceramic raised fields in wetland southeast of, 107

malachite: as exotic, 584, 586, 588, 590, 609; from Unit 21, 454, *455*

mammals: and faunal remains, 219, 220–221, 248, 352, 353, 355, 356, 359–360, 364, 365; habitats of, 202, 363; land mammals, 202, 210, 220–221, 234, 330, 331, 345, 353, 356, 359–360, 364; marine mammals, 210, 221, 248, 331, 355, 356, 360, 364, 365, 693; at Padre Abán, 361

mangroves, 360, 453–454

manioc, 688

Mann, Robert, 193

Mann-Whitney U tests, 667

manos: and maize, 431, 581; from Paredones, 432, 440, 457, 571, 587; varieties of, 439, *439*, 457

Mapuche people: and flow of entropic and anti-entropic forces, 609; and meaning of ancient mounds, 24; and

memories of deceased, 605–606; mound building of, 615; ritual processions among, 586–587; social structure of, 614; subsistence practices of, 10

Marantaceae tubers, 675, 676–677, *679*, 680

marine biotopes, 198, 199, 200–202, 362–363, 365–366

marine biotypes, 197, 198, 209

marine foraging: broad spectrum of, 202; effect of major ENSO event on, 198, 200; and faunal remains, 197, 201, 212, 366; at Huaca Prieta, 7, 8, 9, 13, 17, 29, 47, 108, 151, 234, 363, 364, 433, 567, 570, 571, 572, 579, 580; at Paredones, 330–331; as percentage of diet, 19, 190–191, 221, 248–249, 268, 432, 581; and seasonality of procurement, 209, 572, 579, 582, 583, 584; and sexual division of labor, 152, 191–192, 194, 196

marine snails. *See* sea snails

maritime cultural deposits, 4, 7, 8

maritime economies: and Chinchorro tradition, 18; and Huaca Prieta as mortuary site, 573; of Preceramic Andes, 3, 4, 7, 11, 12; and social complexity, 581

maritime resource zones: exploitation of, 17, 365, 567–568, 578, 579–580, 581; and faunal remains, 197, 198–199, 209, 210; and littoral and marine environments, 44–45, 46, 47; and sea-level changes, 582, 583; and spatial efficiency, 19

maritime societies, 4, 44–45, 581

maritime subsistence, 16, 249

material culture: fragmentation of, 12; for marine foraging, 201; and meaning, 20–21; and ontology, 16, 19, 20, 21–22; of outlying domestic sites, 557, 558; and transcendental social, 607. *See also* baskets and basketry; exotics; textiles

material technologies: at Alto Salaverry, 362; and basketry, 541–544; changes in, 19; and exploitation of resources, 365, 366; and faunal remains, 197, 209, 220, 363; at Huaca Prieta, 7, 13, 14; and identity markers, 581; at Paredones, 234

Matsigenka people, 524

McCown Archaeobotany Library, University of California, Berkeley, 648, 649

meaning: of archaeological record, 605; cross-generational transmission of, 23, 24–25, 26, 599–600, 605–606, 607; and fractional coherences, 22–23; of fractured pieces, 1, 12, 23, 24, 26–27, 211, 434, 598, 601, 606, 611; and material culture, 20–22; of numbers, 611; and ritual practices, 595, 605

medicinal plants: amaranth as, 415; avocado leaves as, 379; coca as, 418, 430; custard apple as, 374; horsetail as, 418, 430; molle as, 423, 430, 431; narrowleaf cattail as, 430; *pájaro bobo* as, 430; quinoa as, 415; sedge as, 420, 430; spikerush as, 430; wild cane as, 430; willow as, 430

mega-sites, 597, 613, 615

Mercyhurst University, Archaeological Institute, 460, 464, 472, 522, 692

Mercyhurst University, R. L. Andrews Perishables Analysis facility, 526

migration, as force for intensive agriculture, 584–585

milkweed (*Asclepias* sp.): and color in crossed-warp patterning, 498, 500; and color in twined fabrics, 491; and color in warp stripes, 494, 495, 500; as fiber, 427, 471, 472,

logical knowledge, 11, 20, 612; and segmented society, 608; sieving of, 21–22, 23; and social structure, 13, 366, 577; and sociocultural transformations, 30. *See also* cosmology; ideology; religion

Ortiz, Rodomiro, 659

OSL (optically simulated luminescence) dates: of channel deposits, 65; of ephemeral wetlands, 61, 107; at Huaca Prieta, 30, 36, *55*, 79, 89; sample preparation, 57; SAR OSL protocol for equivalent dose measurements in quartz aliquots, 57, *61*; and stratigraphy, 38; summary of dating results for age, environmental settings, and stratigraphic context, *68–69*

osteochondritis dissecans, in human skeletal remains, 172, 183, 196

Ostra Camp site, weapons reported in, 194

ostracods, 54, *60*, 73, 82

Otuma, cotton found at, 418

outlying domestic sites: deposits in, 570; excavation of, 616; horizontal extension of, 575; location of, 558, *559*, 573, 578–579; looter's pits at, 557, 558; Lower Coastal Plain, 558, 565; Malabrigo 1, 558, 564, 577, 578; off-mound domestic units compared to, 158; Pulpar, 558, 564–565, 577; Salamanca, 558, 559–563; Salamanca Norte, 558, 563–564, 578; Santiago de Cao, 558, 565; settlement patterns of, 13, 557–566, 567, 578, 579, 614; stratigraphy of, 557, 558; underlying design principles of, 573

Oxford Laboratory, 88, 461

Pacatnamu site, 193

pacay (*Inga feuillei*): as cultivated plant food, 395; starch grains from, 395, 686, 687

Pachacamac, 193, 587

Pacific littoral: communities of, 1; Huaca Prieta located on, 7, 12; as node of early Andean civilization, 13; Preceramic household sites along, 7

Padre Abán: cotton found at, 418; and faunal remains, 360, 361, 362; Guinea grass found at, 425; moss found at, 426; pacay found at, 395; and plant remains, 361; squash found at, 408; wild cane found at, 424

Paget's disease (*osteitis deformans*), 188

Paiján, 42, 435

painted stones, painted cobbles at Huaca Prieta, 7, 11, 12, 446, 570, 587, 597, 610

pájaro bobo (*Tessaria integrifolia*), 423, 428, 430

paleoecological data: of Huaca Prieta Project, 30, 32, 37–38, 48, 197; and marine biotopes, 200–202

PaleoResearch Institute, 696

palo verde (*Parkinsonia* sp.), 429

Pampas Gramalote, 169

Pantone Textile Color Guide, 470

Paracas site, 194, 472–473

parametric 6-tests, 667

Paredones mound: abandonment of, 108, 573; archaeological research on, 4, 7, 8, 9, 22, 29; archaeological units of, 122; and basketry production, 556; building phases of, 107–108, 151, 165; burial treatment at, 19; charcoal analysis, 631, *632*, *633*; charcoal content of, 149, 151; chemical analysis of, 152; chronological sequence of, 30, 90–91, 98–99, 107–108, 198, 575, 598; conti-

nuity and change within, 15–17, 29–30; and crop food production, 344, 571, 572, 576, 579, 580, 582, 586, 595, 597; cultural origins of, 12; demographic setting of, 10–11, 28, 457; distinctive features of, 151; distribution of comestible, industrial, and wild plant parts at, 432, *432*, 587; domestic activity at, 108, 197; economic specialization of, 27, 364, 572; exotic cultigens adopted at, 12, 588; floors of, 106, 165, 570, 575; food preparation associated with, 7, 108, 151, 152, 165, 248, 364, 427–428, 432, 568, 570, 575, 595, 596, 653; function of, 9; general view of, *6*; geophysical research of, 38; geophysical survey of, 723–726; gradual building up of mound, 48; Huaca Prieta Project excavations of, 34–35, 109, 151–152; Huaca Prieta Project map of, 30, *31*, 105, 146; Huaca Prieta related to, 7, 8, 9, 106, 108, 152, 575–576; human diet at, 48, 87, 149, 221, 249, 268, 275, 330, 432, 572, 665, 672–673; human occupation of, 39, 105; human skeletal remains at, 152; layout of, 105; legacies of, 591–593; littoral and marine environments of, 44–45; and long-term planning, 574; looter's hole on southwest side of, 160; map of excavation units and test pits at, *110*; measurements of, 7, 9; mound building at, 8, 9, 32, 86, 106, 575; natural setting of, 10; number of plant parts excavated at, 431–432, *432*; ontology of, 12–13, 614; and outlying domestic sites, 557; Phase I in, 100–101, 105, 197, 248, 568; Phase II in, 105, 106, 248, 358, 359, 569–570, 613; Phase III in, 358, 359, 360, 570, 592; Phase IV in, 268, 275, 358, 359, 360; Phase V in, 275, 330, 358, 359, 360, 365; plant species by cultural phases, 367, *368–370*, 432, 571, 587; plaster covering mound layers, 32, 162, 575; plot of calibrated radiocarbon dates, *98*; Preceramic village underneath, 165; premound phase of, 32, 165; radiocarbon dates by excavation units at, *92–97*, 122, 575; resource use at, 198; and Sangamon terrace, 7, 10, 107–108; social complexity of, 18; social structure of, 11–13; stone tools of, 435–440, 442; stratigraphy of, 32, 37–38, 91, 109, 162, 575; summit of mound, 33, 358, 364; and Test Pit 18, 160; and Test Pit 28, 161; and test pits, 159, 160, 161; *Typha* pollen in floors at, 123, 152; unit excavations at, 146–150. *See also specific units*

pastoral economies, 3, 4

Paterniani, Ernesto, 659

pathology: of human skeletal remains, 178, 196; of human teeth, 167, 180, 188, 196

Patterson, Thomas, 40

peanuts (*Arachis hypogaea*): as cultivated plant food, 383, 385, 430; production of, 4; and starch grains, 383, 385, 688

pebble tools: distributions of, 435; as dominant element in all levels, 434–435; at Huaca Prieta, 12, 568; typological categories of, 435–436. *See also* stone tools

pedogenic features, as markers for premound deposits, 101

pelagic zone, 200

pelicans: and faunal remains, 248, 331, 344, 354, 356, 359, 629; habitat of, 207, 359, 363; hunting of, 201, *201*, 209; as predators, 202

percloroethelene (PCE), 460, 461

Peru: archaeological sites on north coast of, *5*; burial sites in, 169; geologic map of northern Peru with local inset, *52*;

mounded platform sites in, 9; Preceramic mound cultures of, 4, 12, 108. *See also specific sites*

Peru Current System, 198, 199–200, 363

phytoliths: analysis of, 439, 674–677, 679–680, 687; from beans, 675, 676, *678*, 679–680; from bottle gourds, 675, *678*; from grasses, sedges, and herbs, 677, 679, *679*, 680; and human diet at Huaca Prieta, 665; macroremains of, 367, 431; from maize, 674, 675–676, *678*, 679, 731; microscopic analysis of, 367; and pollen analysis, 677; samples from Huaca Prieta and Paredones, 674, *675*; from squash, 674, 675, *676*, *677*, 679

Pickersgill, Barbara, 646, 654–655

Piedra Parada, 18

Piedras Negras, 168, 195

pigments: analysis of, 692–693, *694*, 695; in basketry, 169, 692–693; blue pigment, 471, 692–693, *694*, 695; and bundles, 470–472; in crossed-warp patterning, 498, 500; gold/yellow pigment, 470–471; green pigment, 471–472; in warp stripes, 494, 495; in weft bands, 517. *See also* red pigment

pilgrimages, Huaca Prieta as pilgrimage site, 11, 586–588, 590, 597

Pineda, Fung, 467

Pino, Mario, 36, 38, 100, 159, 160, 446, 583

Piperno, Dolores R., 36, 383, 408, 664, 676, 683, 728

plain weave: average diameters of elements for fabrics, loose yarns, and cordage, 475, *475*, 476, 512; and bundles, 466, 514, 519; color in, 470, 471, 472, 504, 517; dating of, 514, 521; decorative techniques, 515, 517; discarding practices, 519; discontinuous wefts, 517, *518*, color insert; and edge embellishments, 513, 519; fabric conditions, 480, *481*; fibers of, 473; float-weave structure, *516*, 519, color insert; fragments of, 458, 519; function of, 521; gauze crosses in, 500; invisible (structural) stripes, 515, 517; making of, 514, 522; and multiweb construction, 513, 519; plain-weave bag, 465–466, 514, 521; plain-weave-derived float weaves, *516*, *518*, 519, 521, color insert; repair of, 480, 519; selvage structures, 514, 521; and single-ply yarns, 476, 514, 515, 519, 521, 522; slit tapestry, *518*, 519, color insert; specimens of, 477, 514; supra-structures by function, 513, *514–515*, 519; and tailoring, 519, 521; and two-element construction, 488; use of, 519; warp selvages, 515; warp stripes in, 515, 517, 519; weft bands, 517; weft patterning, 517, *518*, color insert; weft selvages, 515, *516*, color insert; weft twining with, 515, 519, 520, *520*

plaiting: and basketry, 525, 526, 527, 544, 546, 548, 555; twining and plaiting hybrid baskets, 525, 526; and Type I basketry, 528–529, *528*, color insert

planes, 438, 449

planning, long-term planning at Huaca Prieta, 574–577, 578, 589, 595

plant remains: and collection procedures, 367, 370, 582; cultivated food plants, 374, 379, 383, 385, 395, 408–409, 411, 414–415, 429, 430, 431, 432; cultivated industrial plants, 415, 417–418, 427, 428, 429, 431, 432; distribution of comestible, industrial, and wild plant parts at Huaca Prieta, Paredones, and domestic sites, 432, *432*, 587; gathered wetland plants, 418–420; and imported

cultivated plants, 198; macrobotanical study of, 367, 370, 440; and outlying domestic sites, 557, 558; plant fiber wads, 451, 467; plant species by cultural phases for Huaca Prieta, Paredones, and Unit 16, 367, *368-370*, 428, 432, 571, 587; ritual and possible medicinal plants, 374, 379, 415, 418, 423, 430, 431; and sampling biases, 370, 431; spatial analysis of, 427–428; temporal analysis of, 428–429; and terrestrial resources, 198, 202, 363, 581; torches, 451, *452*. *See also* cultigens

platform mounds, 16, 17

Playa Culebras, 459, 552

Playa Hermosa, 419

pleating, of bundles, 469, *469*, 496n

Pleistocene period: cultural deposits of, 4; and faunal remains, 210, 212, *213-219*, 219–221; at Huaca Prieta, 7, 8, 9, 30, 100, 123, 567; late Pleistocene climates, 42; late Pleistocene geography, 40–42, 197

pollen: aggregates of, 697; analysis methods, 696–697; macroremains of, 367, 431; maize evidence, 665, 701, 703–704; microscopic analysis of, 367, 697; pollen diagrams, 697, *700*; samples representing Huaca Prieta, 697, *698-699*, 699–701, *700*; samples representing Paredones, *700*, 701, *702-703*, 703

Pollock, Jackson, 23

polychaete tubes: and burial treatment, *156*, 157, 168; definition of, 90; possible counting device or game board, 452–453, *453*; at Salamanca, 559, 560–561; sculpted blocks at Huaca Prieta, 7, 11, 12; sculpted polychaete tube-base showing wavy lines, 453, *454*; slab-like reefs creating substrates, 199; at Unit 16, *156*, 157, 179, 598, 613

popcorn, 429, 581, *657*, 663, 664, 687

population density, 17, 597

population growth: in littoral zones, 108, 588, 589; marine economy supporting, 4; in Preceramic period, 11, 198, 365, 569, 614; shifts in, 8, 573

postmodernism, 20

potatoes (*Solanum* sp.): as cultivated plant food, 409, 411; increased reliance on, 196; production of, 4

pottery sherds: at Huaca Prieta, 570; in Test Pit 23, 454–455; in Unit 2, 454, *455*, 456

Poulin, Jennifer, 693

Pozorski, Shelia, 361, 362

practice theories, 20, 21

Preceramic period: agricultural economies of, 3, 4, 8; in Central Andes, 3–4, 152; diversity and complexity of, 15–16, 38; domestic debris, 153; economic basis of societies, 16; household sites of, 10–11, 30; human skeletal remains of, 166, 188; lifeways of, 10; social structures of sites, 30; village extending north of Huaca Prieta, 158, 165

preindustrial states, 4

pre-Inka period, 3

prepared floors: characteristics of, 89, 165; in Harris Matrices, 112–113; of HP-3, 119; ritual offerings associated with, 90; at Unit 3, 129

Prescott, John R., 57

primary flakes: function of, 440; varieties of, *436*, 438, 567

prismatic blades, 438, 571, 587

proto-urbanism, 4

Puémape: biotopes of, 44; and burial treatment, 168, 169–170, 191, 195; domestic sector at, 573; and faunal remains, 360, 362, 365–366

Pulpar: aerial view of, *560*; *caballito* reed boats, *560*, 566; chamber tombs of, 565; construction of, 573; and ideology of Huaca Prieta, 591; looted chamber tomb at, *560*; looter's hole in, 453; as outlying domestic site, 558, 564–565, 577; segmented architectural composition of, 613

Punta de Asma shell mounds, 473

PV35-6 site, 408

quartz and quartzite tools, 436, 438, 440, 728, 730, 731

Quebrada Jaguay, 553

Quechua arithmetic, 611–612

Quilter, Jeffrey, 195, 467

quincha: circular houses of Unit 16 built of, 157; and outlying domestic sites, 566

quinoa (*Chenopodium* sp.): as cultivated food plant, 415; production of, 4

quipu, 452–453

Quitmyer, Irvy, 635, 641

radiocarbon dates: critiques of, 89; of cultural phases and subphases, *89*, 107; at Cupisnique mound, 121; by excavation units at Huaca Prieta, Paredones, and outlying sites, *92-97*, 122; at Huaca Prieta, 30, 32, 88–89, *92-97*, *98*, 99–105, 107, 122, 575, 616; of maize, 88, 91, 656, 658, 662, 663; of overbank floodplain deposits, 68; at Paredones, *92-97*, *98*, 105–106, 107, 122; plot of calibrated radiocarbon dates for excavated sites, *98*; problems with organic remains, 91, 98–99; radiocarbon sampling from Chicama Valley, 54, *58-59*, 68, *80*, 82, 83; of south and southwest margins of Huaca Prieta mound, 629; of textiles, 460; Unit 2 profile, 123, *124*; Unit 15 strata, *102*, 136, *137*, *139*; of Unit 21, 140; of wood charcoal, 38, *58-59*, 78, 85, 88, 91, *92-97*, 98, 99, 100, 107, 662; of younger terrace, 619

raised agricultural fields: abandonment of, 108, 573; as *camellones*, 83, 107, 573; dating of, 162; drainage ditch east of, 161, *162*; and dune earthworks, 107; east of Huaca Prieta mound, 37, 107, *162*; extension of, 358, 578, 596; in Paludal Stage, 83, 573; and Paredones, 105, 108, 234, 429, 433, 578, 592; and Test Pit 30, 161; and Test Pit 32, 161; and wetlands, 44

Ramírez, Michael, 36

ramps: entry ramp of Huaca Prieta mound, 33–34, 103–104, 116, 119, 122, 123, 142, 152, 164, 454, 459, 556, 568, 571, 572, 573, 574–575, 576, 577, 578, 587, 589, 590, 597, 614; zigzag pathway on ramp, *127*, 128, *128*, 129, 451, 605, 607

Real Alto, 4, 17, 646

realism, 20

red pigment: and baskets, 169; and burial treatment, 451–452; cobbles painted with, 446, *447*; and human skeletal remains, 152, 169–170, 174, 176, 186, 195, 196, 451, 598; perforated shell with red pigment, 447, *448*, 449, 451; and textiles, 169, 451, *463*, 471, 472, 693, *694*,

color insert; and warp stripes in textiles, 494; X-ray diffraction study of samples, 452, *452*

reed matting: and burial treatment, 117, 432; fragments of, 123, 131, 370, 374; functional analysis of, 35; at Huaca Prieta, 152; at Paredones, 152, 165; plant parts in, 431

reed rafts (*caballitos de totora*), 431, *560*, 566

reeds (*Phragmites australis*): bundle of reeds containing fragments of textiles, *127*, 128, 607; as cultivated industrial plants, 419, 430, 431, 432, 677, 680; and wrapped objects, 467

religion: and burial practices, 18; and faunal remains, 360; at Huaca Prieta, 7, 573, 594

Renfrew, Colin, 614

repetition: and accumulation, 608; and continuity, 604–605, 606; and inalienable objects, 26; and obligation, 599–604; ontological security maintained by, 25; and ritual practices, 24, 27, 28, 600, 604–605, 606, 608, 609, 611; and segmentary societies, 27

resilience, 20

resource zones: exploitation of, 21, 198, 235; of Huaca Prieta, 7, 198. *See also* highland resource zone; maritime resource zones

retention walls: for chamber tombs, 572, 574; and erosion, 162, 576, 618; in HP-3, 115–116, 117, *117*, 119, 121, 126, 681; and planning, 574, 578; retention wall no. 1, 103, 119, 126; retention wall no. 2, 103, 119, 121, 126, 129; retention wall no. 3, 103, 119, 121, 127, 129

Rey, Isabel, 36

rhizomatic patterns, 609, 610, 613, 615

Richardson, James, 440, 446

Rick, John, 8

Río Seco: basketry and cordage found at, 552; and burial treatment, 168, 195; cotton found at, 418; monumental architecture of, 40; sedge found at, 420; textiles of, 459; wild cane found at, 424; willow found at, 421

ritual floors: characteristics of, 90; circumscribed ritual spaces, 11, 27, 146, 162, *164*, 165, 569, 570, 574, 589, 592, 604, 605, 612

ritual offerings: and bundles, 522, 605, 610; and coca, 418, 605; and cultigens, 586–588, 592; and faunal remains, 360, 365–366, 587; inalienability of, 607; and material culture, 434; prepared and unprepared floors associated with, 90, 162; purpose of, 602, 607; and sequences of use episodes, 111; and shells, 454, 605; at Unit 3, 130; at Unit 10, 134; at Unit 16, 613

ritual practices: archaeological indicators of, 12; and Cerro Cuculicote, 142; and coca, 275, 418; and construction of Huaca Prieta, 577; definition of, 12, 122; and disuse of Huaca Prieta mound, 104; and elements of fire and water, 608–609; and exotics, 454; and faunal remains, 197, 212, 234, 235, 275, 317, 345, 354, 355, 356, 357, 366, 432; and food production, 579, 585; and fractured objects, 1, 26; and gourds, 275, 440, 446; group-oriented ritual practices, 574, 605; at Huaca Prieta, 7, 8, 11–12, 24, 27, 29, 108, 146, 151, 158, 162, 164, 165, 235, 249, 317, 355, 432, 556, 574, 589–590; littoral and coastal sites linked through, 12; and material culture, 16; meaning of, 595, 605; monuments as focus of, 17; mortuary rituals, 7, 20, 108, 152, 164–165, 249, 275, 456, 556, 605; mound building as, 614; at Paredones, 108, 165, 570; and plant remains, 418, 432; repetitive ritual patterns, 24, 27, 28, 600, 604–605, 606, 608, 609, 611; and rising ceremonial centers, 15; ritual processions, 119; and ritual specialists, 142, 165, 356, 575, 588, 596, 602, 609; and sea urchin spines at Huaca Prieta mound, 90, 117, 121, 124, 126, 128, 129, 133, 136, 137, 140, 142–144, 146, 158, 162, 165, 268, 275, 356, 357, 366, 570, 574, 576; and social differentiation, 612, 613, 614; and stewardship residency, 165, 589; and textiles, 521, 605, 613; and transcendental social, 607; and transgenerational experiences, 610. *See also* feasting activity

rock crystals, 454, *455*, 609

Rodríguez, Lucia, 43

Rosales Tham, Teresa, 36, 209, 372, 419, 422–424, 648

Rosamachay, 663

Rowe, Ann, 498, 519

rush (*Juncus* sp.): as baskets, 528, 529, 530, 543, 544, 546, 548, 556; as cordage, 533, 535, 536, 537, 540, 544, 550, 551, 552, 556

sacred landscapes, 24, 602, 607, 614, 615

sacred topography, 610

Salamanca: as outlying domestic site, 558, 559–563; Salamanca 1, 559; Salamanca 2, 559–561, *560*; Salamanca 3, 561; Salamanca 4, 561; Salamanca 5, 561; Salamanca 6, 561; Salamanca 7, 562; Salamanca 8, 562; Salamanca 9, 562; Salamanca 10, 562; Salamanca 11, 562; Salamanca 12, 562–563

Salamanca Norte: as outlying domestic site, 558, 563–564, 578; Salamanca Norte 1-4, 563; Salamanca Norte 5-7, 563–564; Salamanca Norte 8, 564; Salamanca Norte 9, 564; Salamanca Norte 10, 564

Salaverry, fish otoliths of, 706, 709

Salinar period: burial treatment in, 191; ceramics of, 85; in Cupisnique mound, 122; maize of, 662

salt crystals: accumulation of, 608, 613; and burial treatment, 599; and fragmentation of human skeletal remains, 166–167, 168, *169*, 609, 690; and knotted netting, 483, 486, 522, 695; and preservation of human skeletal remains, 168, 191; sand and salt samples from Huaca Prieta, 681–682; from seawater poured onto structure, 1, 11, 12, 570, 576, 594, 601, 608, 609

sambaquis (large shell mounds), 9

Sánchez, Vásquez, 36

sand dunes: dune movement in Chicama Valley, 48; and raised agricultural field east of Huaca Prieta, 37, 107, *162*

Sandweiss, Daniel, 629

Sangamon terrace: buried surface of, 30, 32, 88, 119; discontinuous geographic distribution across, 578; excavations on, 117, 119, 122; and faunal remains, 212, 220, 366; geological study of, 37, 617–618, 628; habitats of, 202, 362; Holocene occupation of, 45–46; Huaca Prieta and Paredones located on, 7, 10, 107–108, 567, 568; looter's holes and drainages across, 32, 35, 106, 442, 557; model of sites on, 14; off-mound domestic units, 152–154, 157–158, 578; outlying domestic sites, 557–566; Preceramic habitation sites on, 106–107, 153; Preceramic household mound sites along, 7; Preceramic populations of, 44; pre-

mound occupation of, 100–101, 131; profile of, 617–618, *618*; and ritual practices, 234–235; and settlement patterns, 577; spatial scale of, 577; and test pits, 159; and Unit 9, 131; and Unit 15, 137; and Unit 20, 147; view of eastern side looking north, *6*

San Luis, 571

Santa beach ridge complex, 85

Santiago de Cao, 558, 565

sapote (*Capparis* sp.), 421–422, 429, 430

sara-sara (*Commelina* sp.), 424, 431

scallops, 360, 454

scallop shells, 445–446, 584, 596, 609

Schneider, Benjamin, 611

scientific objectivism, 20

Scott system for tooth wear evaluation, 170, 176, 177, 186

scrapers: at Salamanca 3, 561; and shell tools, 448–449; and stone tools, *436*, 438, 440

sea floor, geomorphology of, 198–199, 362–363

seafood, 4, 16

sea levels: in Holocene period, 46, 76, 82, 83, 85, 619; at Last Glacial Maximum, 198; in late Pleistocene, 212; and resource production, 583; and risk-reduction strategy, 582; stability of, 629

sea lions: fatty emulsion from, 693; and faunal remains, 212, 219, 220, 221, 234, *234*, 235, 248, 249, 268, 275, 330, 331, 344, 345, 352, 353, 354, 355, 356, 360, 364, 365, 366, 568, 598, 731; habitat of, 207, 208, 220, 365, 366, 568; hunting of, 201, 208; as predators, 202; stable population of, 198

seals: fatty emulsion from, 693; and marine foraging, 201–202

sea snails: black snails, 207, 221, 344, 353, 354; and faunal remains, 212, 219, 220, 221, 235, 249, 268, 275, 330, 331, 352, 353, 355, 356, 363, 366; habitat of, 47, 199, 202, 207, 209, 220, 353, 363; at Padre Abán, 361; at Puémape, 362

sea surface temperatures (SSTs), 51–52, 198, 705, 706, 709, 711, 712

sea urchins: and faunal remains, 249, 268, 275, 354, 355, 357; habitat of, 207–208, 363; sea urchin spines at Huaca Prieta mound, 90, 117, 121, 124, 126, 128, 129, 133, 136, 137, 140, 142–144, 146, 158, 162, 165, 268, 275, 356, 357, 366, 570, 574, 576

seaweeds: habitat of, 207, 363, 425; polychaete bed forming habitat for, 199; species of, 200, 202, 425–426, 430, 431; as wild plant food, 580

Sechín Bajo, 595

secondary flakes, *436*, 438, 440

sedentary lifeways: and complex foragers, 17, 19; marine economy supporting, 4; and outlying domestic sites, 557

sedge (*Cyperus* sp.): and cordage, 540, 549, 553; economic use of, 420; environmental setting of, 419; as fiber, 472; findings as Huaca Prieta and Paredones, 420; medicinal use of, 420, 430; and net making, 483; phytolith analysis, 677, 679, *679*, 680; temporal analysis of, 428, 429; at Unit 2, 427

SEM analysis, 713, 740

Semele corrugata: analysis methodology, 713, 715; cross-sectioned shells, 713, *714*, 715, 717; indicators of season-

ality, 712–713, *714–715*, 715, 717, *718*, 719–721, *720*;
isotope analysis of, 712, 713, *714–715*, 715, 717, *718*,
719–721, *720*; microsampling of, 713, 715, 719; mineralogy of, 715, 717, 719; season of capture, 721; SEM
analysis, 713, 715, *716*, 717, *717*; and shell growth rate,
712–713, *716*, 717, *717*, 719, 720, 721; shell microstructure, 713, 715, *716*, 717, 719, 721; statistical summaries
of, 713, *714–715*, 715, 717, 721; views of shells, *714*;
XRD analysis, 713

Semele sp. shells: analysis methods, 635–636; archaeological
samples, 641, 643–644; bands and growth stage patterns,
636, *639*, 641, 643, 644; bands on modern shells, 636,
638, 641; binomial test of goodness-of-fit for modern shell samples, *640*, 644; in bundles, 466; in chamber
tombs, 578, 579, 598, 599, 607; dark and white bands of,
635–636, *636*, *637*, 641; growth ring analysis in modern
samples, 634–635, *635*, 641; histogram of archaeological shell samples and their distribution, *642*; histogram
of modern shells and their distribution, 636, 641, *642*;
histograms of growth stage patterns of archaeological
shells, 641, 643, *643*; modern and ancient samples from
Huaca Prieta, 713, *714–715*; monthly percentages of dark
and white bands, *641*; seasonality of use, 36, 572, 579,
634–636, 641, 643–644; at Unit 10, 134; at Unit 11, 136;
at Unit 14, 136; at Unit 16, 452; at Unit 23, 143

Service de Spectrométrie de Masse Isotopique of the
Muséum National d'Histoire Naturelle (SSMIM), 708

settlement patterns: factors affecting, 16–17, 20, 577, 613;
and house mounds, 578, 612; of Huaca Prieta area, 16;
linear settlement nucleation, 597; of outlying domestic
sites, 13, 557–566, 567, 578; in Preceramic period, 11, 27;
and segmentary societies, 27

Sevilla, Ricardo, 659

sexual division of labor: and degenerative changes in human
skeletal remains, 193, 194; and marine foraging, 152,
191–192, 194, 196; and weaving practices, 523–524

Shapiro-Wilk tests, 667

sharks: and ENSO events, 200; and faunal remains, 208, 210,
212, 219, 220, 235, 248, 249, 268, 275, 330, 331, 344,
345, 352, 353, 354, 355, 356, 358, 364, 365, 568; habitat
of, 200, 202, 207, 208, 219, 363, 365, 568; and marine
foraging, 201, 202, 221; at Padre Abán, 361; as predators, 202

shells: distribution of types of worked shells for Huaca
Prieta and Paredones, 447, 448, *449*; as exotic items, 140,
453–454, *455*; and faunal remains, 221, 448, 580; fragmentation of, 27, 275, 344, 448, 450, 599, 613; at Lower
Coastal Plains, 565; at Malabrigo 1, 564; and mortuary
rituals, 90; perforated shell with red pigment, 447, *448*,
449, 451; at Pulpar, 565; and ritual practices, 136, 275,
353, 363, 366, 446–447; at Salamanca, 561, 562, 563;
at Salamanca Norte, 563–564; at Santiago de Cao, 565;
seasonality of use, 36; shell beads, *448*, 449, 450; tools
manufactured from, 447–450, *448*, 457, 731; at Unit 1,
123; at Unit 2, 124, 126, 353–354. *See also Semele* sp.
shells

shoreline: aeolian dunes of, *75*, 76, *77*; coastal settings of
Chicama Valley, 74, *74*, *75*, 76, 78–79, 84, 86, 208;
gravel and sandy shoreface berms of, *75*, 76, *77*, 78, 202;
maximum trangression of, *74*, 84; present-day shoreline
north of Huaca Prieta mound, *45*; and sea-level changes,
583; tsunami surfaces and deposits, *75*, 76, 77, 78–79, 85,
86; and water table, 574; wave-swept terrace of, 76, *77*

Single-Aliquot Regenerative (SAR) dose protocol, 57, *61*

single-ply yarns: average diameters of elements for fabrics, loose yarns, and cordage, *475*, 476; and plain-weave
yarns, 476, 514, 519, 521; and S-spun, 474

site use, 19, 558

Skinner, Milica, 459

Smith scoring system for tooth wear evaluation, 170, 186

Smithsonian Institution Tropical Research Laboratory, 728

social complexity: and alliance relationships, 17; diverse
paths to, 18; factors accounting for, 17–19, 29, 48,
579, 593, 594–596, 615; at Huaca Prieta, 7, 9, 13, 365,
594–596; and innovation, 512; of maritime societies,
44–45, 581; of Preceramic period, 3–4, 15, 198, 365;
requirements of, 4, 13; and textiles, 457

social constructionism, 20

social differentiation: and burial treatment, 18, 195, 595,
598–599, 605, 613; and complex foragers, 17; and
economic practices, 580, 585, 591, 592, 612; lack of
archaeological evidence for, 578, 588, 613, 614, 615; and
leadership roles, 616

social structure: balance and harmony achieved by, 13;
bottom-up societies versus top-down societies, 614; at
Huaca Prieta, 9, 11–13, 575, 596; lateral societies, 614;
material expression of, 616; and monumental buildings,
18; and mound-building, 11; and ontologies, 13, 366,
577; reconstruction of, 16; segmented nature of, 27, 571,
575, 588, 608, 611, 612–615

socio-ecosystems, development of, 19–20, 28, 39

sociopolitical strategies, 17

soil chemistry analysis, *739*

south and southwest margins of Huaca Prieta mound: black
and red cobbles, 625, *626*; close-up of stratigraphic
profile, 619, *619*; northern section of stratigraphic profiles, 619, *620*; Profile 1, *626*, 627, 630; Profiles 2 and
3, 622, *623*, 624–625, 629; Profile 4, *623*, 625; Profile 5, *623*, 625; Profile 7, *623*, 625; Profile 8, 625, *626*,
627, 628, 629; Profile 9, *626*, 627, 629, 630; Profile 10,
626, 627, 629, 630; Profile 11, *626*, 627; Profile 14, *620*,
621, 630; Profile 16, *620*, 621, 630; Profile 17, 619, *620*,
621, 629; Profile 19, *620*, 621–622; Profile 20, *620*, 621,
630; Profile 21, 622, *623*, 628, 629, 630; Profile 22, *620*,
622; south section between Profiles 8 and 11, 625, *626*,
627–628; south section between Profiles 21 and 7, 622,
623, 624–625, *624*, 628, 629; south view of Huaca Prieta
mound, 622, *623*; stratigraphy and paleoenvironmental reconstructions of, 619, 621, 622, 624–625, 627–628,
629

Southern Oscillation, 42–43, 49–52

spatial efficiency, 19

spatial heterogeneity, 52

specialized edifices, 17

spikerush (*Eleocharis* sp.), 420, 430

spinning: and looping, 480; of plies for cordage, 476, 527;
and spindle whorls, 476; of yarns, 476–477, 480, 521

Splitstoser, Jeff, 35, 457, 526, 611

spokeshaves, 436, 438

Spondylus sp.: as exotics, 445–446, 453–454, *455*, 584, 588, 590, 596, 609; religious significance of, 360; shell ornaments, 25–26

squash (*Cucurbita* sp.): as cultivated plant food, 408–409, 427, 428, 429, 430, 431, 433, 580; cultivation of, 234, 363; and phytolith analysis, 674, 675, *676*, *677*, 679; and starch grains, 683, *684*, *685*, 686, 687

S-spun fibers: making of, 477, 521; and plain-weave yarns, 474, 514, 519; rush for baskets, 530; and single-ply yarns, 474; Type II cordage, 533; Type III cordage, 533–535; Type V cordage, 536; Type VI cordage, 536–537; Type VIII cordage, 537; Type IX cordage, 537; Type X cordage, 537–538; Type XI cordage, 538; Type XIII cordage, 539; Type XV cordage, 539; Type XVI cordage, 539–540; Type XVII cordage, 540; Type XVIII cordage, 540; and wefts, 470, 504

stable isotope geochemistry, 196

starch grains: from beans, 684, *684*, *685*, 686, 687–688; from bottle gourds, 446, 683, *685*, 686; crop plant reference collection, 683; from grinding stones, 683, *684*, *685*, 686; from human teeth, 683, *685*, 686, 687; macroremains of, 367, 683, 684, 688; from maize, 664, 683, *684*, *685*, 687, 731; material of major starch grain types from Huaca Prieta and Paredones, 684, *684*, 686; microscopic analysis of, 367; and pacay, 395, 686, 687; and peanuts, 383, 385; and pollen samples, 701, 703–704; in sediment samples, 683–684, 686; from squash, 683, *684*, *685*, 686, 687; from stone tools, 683, *684*, 686, 687, 728; from tree fruits, 688

Stephan, Larry, 57

stepped-platform mounds, 8, 103

stewardship activities, of Huaca Prieta mound, 165, 589

Stoke's Law, 696

stone berms: cobblestone berms at Huaca Prieta, 99, 100, 102, 117, 164, 569, 570, 575, 576, 595; at HP-3, *115*, 117, 118, 119, 121, 124, 129, 569, 681–682; and planning at Huaca Prieta, 574, 595; sand samples from, 681–682; at Unit 2, 117, 124, 569; at Unit 22, 149

stones. *See* cobbles

stone tools: and gourd decoration, 442, 731; at Huaca Prieta, 435–440, 442, 446; micro-use-wear analysis of, 435, 727–728, *729*, 730–732; miscellaneous flakes, 438–439; at Paredones, 364, 435–440, 442, 446; percentage distribution of worked material by specimen, 727, *728*; polychaete tubes worked by, 199; primary flakes, *436*, 438, 440, 567; raw material types of, 436–437, *437*, 456, 727; red pigment applied to, 451; residue analysis of, 435, 728, 731; secondary flakes, *436*, 438, 440; starch grains from, 683, *684*, 686, 687; typological categories of, 435–440; unifacial tools, 42, 101, 435, *436*, *437*, 440, 567, 727, 728, *729*, 730; and use-actions, 728, 730, 731–732. *See also* grinding stones; pebble tools

Stothert, Karen, 440, 445

S-twist fibers: and bundles, 469, 470; for cordage, 527, 548–549; and fabric yarns, 476; and knotted netting, 483; Type I baskets, 528–529, *528*, 547, color insert; Type III baskets, 530, *531*, 532, *532*, 547; Type IV cordage, 535–536; Type VII cordage, 537; Type XII cord-

age, 538–539; Type XIV cordage, 539; and weft twining, 488, 504

subsistence patterns: diversification of, 581; and environmental processes, 48, 582, 583; factors affecting, 16–17, 191, 593; and faunal remains, 201, 208–209, 211, 234; of Mapuche people, 10; study of, 40. *See also* maritime subsistence; terrestrial subsistence

subtidal zone, 200, 208, 209, 220, 363, 365

sunken circular plazas: architecture of, 457, 577, 612; and Bird's looter's pit at Unit 15, 136, 140; chamber tombs along upper rim, 104, 571; and coca, 418; and economic practices, 16; excavation of Cupisnique mound, 32; and exotics, 454; at Huaca Prieta mound, 103, 119, 123, 130, 152, 164, 571, 573, 574, 575, 576, 577, 578, 587, 589, 590, 597, 605, 614; and Phase II of Huaca Prieta mound, 103; and Phase III of Huaca Prieta mound, 164, 571; and Phase IV of Huaca Prieta mound, 103, 119, 164, 571, 572; and Phase V of Huaca Prieta mound, 164; photograph of burial HP08-01 on south rim, *132*; stone tools of, 439; and Unit 21, 140–142, 356, 454

supralittoral zones, 200, 363, 425

supratidal zone, 207, 208, 219

Surge, Donna, 706

symbols: of burial treatment, 600; and faunal remains, 249, 268, 275, 317, 355, 357, 366, 590; of fire and water, 608; Huaca Prieta mound as communal symbol, 614; and ideology, 17; and material culture, 20, 590, 597, 611; and social complexity, 595

Tank and Yacht Club Sites: basketry and cordage found at, 552; fibers of, 472; textiles of, 459

Tattersall, Ian, 191

teeth. *See* dentition

Tellenbach, Michael, 8

terraces: beach terraces, 566; dune terraces, 565; inland terraces, 27; sites on, 42; at Unit 10, 355; upper terraces of Huaca Prieta, 356; wetland terraces, 558. *See also* Sangamon terrace; south and southwest margins of Huaca Prieta mound; younger terrace

terrestrial biotopes, 198

terrestrial resources: and dry forest, 212; exploitation of, 579, 580, 581; and faunal remains, 209, 212, 220–221, 234, 331, 568; of Huaca Prieta area, 16; and hunters and gatherers, 567, 568; of Paredones, 234, 570; and plant remains, 198, 568; and seasonality of procurement, 582; unpredictability of, 202; wild plants as, 198, 234, 580, 581

terrestrial subsistence: and cultigens, 234, 345, 571; of Huaca Prieta area, 16; of Paredones, 234

Testart, Alain, 584

Test Pit 1, 158, 162

Test Pit 2, 158, 162, 427, 617

Test Pit 3: and cordage, 540; placement of, 141, 158–159; and plant remains, 411, 419, 420, 422, 424, 427

Test Pit 4, 159, 682

Test Pit 5, 159

Test Pit 6, 159, 162

Test Pit 7, 159, 162

Test Pit 8, 159

Test Pit 9, 159, 456

Test Pit 10, 159

Test Pit 11, 159

Test Pit 12, 160

Test Pit 13, 160, 162

Test Pit 14, 160, 162

Test Pit 15, 160

Test Pit 16, 160, 423

Test Pit 17, 160

Test Pit 18, 160, 686

Test Pit 19, 160

Test Pit 20, 160

Test Pit 21, 160

Test Pit 22: and faunal remains, 212, *213-219*, 219; feature types and distribution in late Pleistocene layers, 100, *102*; HP-2 compared to, 114; Phase II in, 102, 103, 569; profile of, 160, *161*; radiocarbon dated premound contexts in, 100, 101, *102*, 160; stone berms of, 117; stratigraphic cuts in, 88

Test Pit 23, 160, 162, 454–455

Test Pit 24, 160

Test Pit 25, 160

Test Pit 26: chronology of, 121–122, 557; and faunal remains, 344, 345, *346-351*, 352, 358, 364; geophysical survey of, 724, *725*; horizontal extension of, 575; plant distribution in Phase V, *416-417*, 429; and plant remains, 408, 415, 418, 420, 421, 423, 424; purpose of, 160

Test Pit 27, 160–161, 557, 725

Test Pit 28: chronology of, 557; and geophysical survey, 725; as off-mound area, 105, 575, 578; Paredones associated with, 161; strata and features of, 106

Test Pit 29: as off-mound area, 105, 575, 578; strata and features of, 106, 161

Test Pit 30, 161

Test Pit 31, 161

Test Pit 32, 161

test pits: description of, 158–162; and faunal remains, 211; and outlying domestic sites, 558. *See also specific test pits*

textiles: analysis of, 464–466, 520–521, 522; and animistic beliefs, 466, 491; average diameters for fabrics, loose yarns, and cordage, 474–475, *475*, 476, 512; camelid fiber in, 359, 470, 471, 472, 473; chronological changes in technology, 459; cleaning of, 460–461, *463*, 464, 522, color insert; color in, 456, *463*, 470–472, 491, 494, 685, 692, 693, 695, color insert; compound constructions and multiple fabric categories, 520; condition of, 460; consistency/variability in, 464–465; decorative motifs of, 442, 445, 465, 521, 523, 581, 587, 597, 610, 612; definition of, 460, 525; and discarding practices, 465, 466, 513; dual patterns of, 446, 495; dyes for, 456; excavation and cataloguing methods, 459–460; external correlations, 552–554; fabric conditions, 480, *481*, 486, 487; fabrics, 459–460, 465, 476, 477, 480, 521; fragmentation of, 25, 26, 27, 446, 459–460, 465, 466, 469, 513, 521, 570, 578, 598, 599, 606, 607, 611, 613; indigo dyes of, 36, *463*, 471, 517, 693, color insert; innovations in, 457, 512, 521, 596; material record of, 13; mends, 465, 508, 509, 513; and mortuary rituals, 90, 275, 578; number and types of attributes for fabrics and bundles, 469, *469*; and

outlying domestic sites, 557; photographs of, 464; previous research on, 459–461, 464; radiocarbon dating of, 460, 461, *461*; random patterning of, 521; and red pigment, 169, 451, *463*, 471, 472, 693, *694*, color insert; repair of, 465, 480; and ritual practices, 522, 605, 613; at Salamanca, 561, 562; at Salamanca Norte, 563, 564; at Santiago de Cao, 565; and sequences of use episodes, 111; single-element constructions, 477, 488; Specimen 2008.013.01, *511*; Specimen 2008.016.01.A-C, 498, *499*, color insert; Specimen 2008.017.01, 480; Specimen 2008.027.01.A, 505; Specimen 2008.027.01.C, 505; Specimen 2008.03.01.A, 489; Specimen 2008.035.01, 500, *501*, color insert; Specimen 2008.038.03, *490*; Specimen 2008.038.08, *490*; Specimen 2008.038.24.A, *510*, 515, 517; Specimen 2008.038.24.D, 515; Specimen 2008.038.25.D, *510*; Specimen 2008.062.01A-B, 515, *516*, color insert; Specimen 2008.066.02, 488, 489; Specimen 2008.066.05.A, 489; Specimen 2008.067.01, 504, 505, *506*; Specimen 2008.067.02, 494, 509, *511*; Specimen 2008.069.01.A, 498, *501*, 508, color insert; Specimen 2008.070.02, *518*, 519, color insert; Specimen 2008.075.01, *511*; Specimen 2008.075.03.A-B, 489, 500, 503, *503*, color insert; Specimen 2008.088.01, *510*, 512; Specimen 2008.093.01, 509, *511*; Specimen 2008.096.01, 500, *502*, 508, color insert; Specimen 2008.100.04, 489, 500, *502*, color insert; Specimen 2008.100.05, 505, *507*; Specimen 2008.101.01.A-C, 474, 477, 491, *492*, 520; Specimen 2009.001.05, 471; Specimen 2009.001.08, 517; Specimen 2009.001.11, *463*, 470, 473, color insert, 517, *518*, color insert; Specimen 2009.010.12.A-B, 509, *510*; Specimen 2009.010.16, 489, *490*; Specimen 2009.010.22, *510*, 515, 520; Specimen 2009.010.31, 471, 483, *486*; Specimen 2009.010.35, 471; Specimen 2009.011.01.A-B, 520, *520*; Specimen 2009.015.01.A-B, 498, *499*, color insert; Specimen 2009.023.01, 482, *485*; Specimen 2009.028.01, *490*, 504, *506*; Specimen 2009.028.02, *506*; Specimen 2009.028.04.A-C, 504; Specimen 2009.028.05, 477, *479*, 480; Specimen 2009.043.01, 489, 491, *493*; Specimen 2009.052.01.A, 498; Specimen 2009.052.01.B, *463*, 471, color insert; Specimen 2009.052.02, 500, *501*, color insert; Specimen 2009.056.01, 514; Specimen 2009.057.01, 482; Specimen 2009.063.02, 517, *518*, color insert; Specimen 2009.065.01.A, 517; Specimen 2009.071.09, *496*; Specimen 2009.071.16, 500; Specimen 2009.071.19, 503; Specimen 2009.071.27, 482, *484*; Specimen 2009.071.31, 470; Specimen 2009.071.32, 470; Specimen 2009.072.03, 495, *496*; Specimen 2009.072.04, *507*, 508; Specimen 2009.072.15, 473; Specimen 2009.075.08, 467; Specimen 2009.077.01.A, 483, *484*; Specimen 2009.077.01.B, 483, *484*; Specimen 2009.079.01, 483, 486, 487; Specimen 2009.085.01, 474; Specimen 2009.093.01, 505, *507*, 509, *511*; Specimen 2009.093.02, 471; Specimen 2009.093.08, 470, 509; Specimen 2009.093.11, 470, 491, *493*, 509; Specimen 2009.094.01, *497*, 505; Specimen 2009.095.01, 495, *496*; Specimen 2009.097.01.A, 509, *511*; Specimen 2009.097.06, *496*; Specimen 2009.098.01.24, 466; Specimen 2009.098.02.A-B, 467; Specimen 2009.098.09, 480;

Specimen 2009.098.13, 489; Specimen 2009.098.14, 474, *478*, 480; Specimen 2009.098.15.A, *497*; Specimen 2009.098.19, 477, *478*; Specimen 2009.098.20, *496*; Specimen 2009.102.27, 486; Specimen 2009.102.28, 486; Specimen 2009.102.31, 486; Specimen 2009.102.32, 486; Specimen 2009.102.33, 486, 487; Specimen 2009.107.02, *497*; Specimen 2009.107.03, 515, *516*, 519, 519, color insert; Specimen 2009.114.07, 474; Specimen 2009.114.08, *463*, color insert; Specimen 2009.114.12, *463*, 470, 471, 472, 517, color insert; Specimen 2009.114.15, 487; Specimen 2009.115.03, 487; Specimen 2009.123.01, 467; Specimen 2009.142.02, 480, 488, 509, *511*; Specimen 2009.149.01.A-B, 498, *499*, 520, color insert; Specimen 2009.154.02.B, 500; Specimen 2009.157.01, 494; Specimen 2009.160.09, 465–466, 514; supra-structures by function, 513, *514–515*, 521; and symbolic artwork at Huaca Prieta, 11, 12; and technological diversity, 581, 585, 596, 612, 613; two-element fabrics, 476, 477, 488, 498; types, quantities, and provenience of fibers, cordage, yarns, and fabrics, *462*, 465; and wear patterns, 465, 469, 513, 521, 613; webs as multifabric constructions, 460. *See also* bundles; cotton textiles; cotton weaving; weaving practices
thermally anomalous mulluscan assemblages (TAMAs), 51
tick-trefoil (*Desmodium* sp.), 423, 430, 431
Tigara people, 666, 672
Tikopia people, 614
time, sense of, 593
Titelbaum, Anne, 36, 166, 193–194
Tito, Raúl, 35–36, 733
tomatoes, 4
torches, burned torches, 451, *452*
Towle, Margaret, 411, 646, 662–663, 664
transcendence: and burial treatment, 599, 606, 607; and continuity, 610, 613; transcendental social, 606–607, 609, 612; and transgenerational concerns, 605–607, 611, 615
transgenerational concerns, and transcendence, 605–607, 611, 615
transgenerational experiences, and ritual practices, 610, 615
transgenerational nature: of Huaca Prieta mound, 574, 575, 576, 599, 601–602, 614; of inalienable objects, 25, 606, 607, 610–611, 612; of kin groups, 16; of tomb-making, 604
trauma, and human skeletal remains, 167, 171–172, 194–195, 196
Tres Ventanas Cave, 411
tripartite economy, 579–581
Trombret, Olivier, 36
tsunamis: and Bird on erosion caused by, 164, 618, 630; and Bird's analysis of HP-2, 114; and Bird's analysis of HP-3, 117; geological analysis of, 9, 30; impact of, 582, 583, 618, 630; tsunami surfaces and deposits, *75*, 76, 77, 78–79, 85, 86, 117, 618, 629, 630, 681, 682
Tung, Tiffiny A., 35–36, 194
Tupicocha people, 523
turquoise, 740
twining: analysis of, 616; and basketry techniques, 525–526, 527, 541–543, 546, 555, 596; countered twining, 504;

dating of, 514, 521; decorative techniques, 491, 494–495, 497–498, 504, 509, 515; and fabric yarns, 483, 519, 522; function of, 521; interlacing distinguished from, 488, 491, 509; interlacing with, 520, 521, 522; plaiting and twining hybrid baskets, 525, 526; and sexual division of labor, 523–524. *See also* weft twining
Twiss, Page, 674

Ubelaker, D. H., 170, 172–173
unborn: and burial treatment, 602, 604, 607; and cyclic connection among death, life, and unborn, 610; enchainment of living, dead, and unborn, 612, 613; and obligatory relations between dead and living, 600, 602; and ontology of fire and water, 608, 609; and social differentiation, 699; symbolic representation of, 587
unifacial tools, 42, 101, 435, *436*, *437*, 440, 567, 727
Unit 1: excavations at, 123, 617; and faunal remains, 219; geophysical survey of, 724, *725*; as off-mound domestic location, 123; plant distribution in Phase V, *392–393*, 429; and plant remains, 422
Unit 2: chronology of, 91; and faunal remains, 208, 221, *222–233*, 235, *236–249*, 249, *262–268*, 268, 275, *276–287*, *300–311*, 317, 353–355, 357, 358, 359, 360, 364; fish otoliths from, 706; Guañape materials in, 123; Harris Matrix for, 30, 89, 111, 123–124, *125*; HP-2 compared to, 114; layer descriptions for, 126; Moche period pots in, 122; Phase I in, 353; Phase II in, 102, 103, 353–354, 355, 364, 569; Phase III in, 354; Phase IV in, 354–355; Phase V in, 104, 355, 365; plant distribution in Phase II, *373–374*, 427, 428; plant distribution in Phase III, *378–379*, 427, 428–429; plant distribution in Phase IV, *384–385*, 427, 429; plant distribution in Phase V, *392–393*, 427, 429; and plant remains, 415, 418, 419, 420, 421, 422, 425; pollen from, 697, 699; pottery sherds in, 454, *455*, 456; premound context from, 101, 123; profile with radiocarbon dates, 123–124, *124*; sand and salt samples from, 681, 682; as service unit, 364; shells in, 454; site excavations of, 34; spatial analysis of plant remains, 427; starch grains from, 684; stone berms of, 117, 124, 569; stratigraphic cuts in, 88; submound context in, 100; unifacial tools of, 728, *729*, 730
Unit 3: bundle of reeds containing fragments of textiles, *127*, 128, 607; exotics from, 454; and faunal remains, 221, *222–233*, *276–287*, 357, 364; human skeletal remains of, 174–175, 181–184, 738; layer descriptions for, 126–130; Phase III in, 103; Phase IV in, 103, 129, 357; Phase V in, 104, 130; plant distribution in Phase IV, *386–387*, 429; plant distribution in Phase V, *392–393*, 429; and plant remains, 379, 409, 411, 415, 420, 422, 423, 424, 425; profile of, 126, *127*; and retention walls, 128, 191; shingled layers of plaster, 126, *127*, 129–130; starch grains from, 684, 686; zigzag pathway on ramp, *127*, 128, *128*, 129, 451, 605, 607
Unit 4: layer descriptions for, 130; Phase III in, 103; Phase IV in, 103; plant distribution in Phase V, *394–395*, 429; and plant remains, 420; tomb in, 130
Unit 5: and faunal remains, *300–311*, 357; layer descriptions for, 130; Phase III in, 103; Phase IV in, 103; Phase V in, 357; plant distribution in Phase V, *394–395*, 429; and

plant remains, 408, 409, 411, 415, 418, 419, 420, 422, 424, 425; and ritual practices, 317

Unit 6: exotic items in, 454; and faunal remains, *300-311*, 357, 359, 360; layer descriptions of, 130; Phase III in, 103; Phase IV in, 103, 454; Phase V in, 357, 360; plant distribution in Phase V, *396-397*, 429; and plant remains, 379, 385, 395, 409, 415, 418, 419, 420, 421, 422, 424, 425; and ritual practices, 317; stone berms of, 117

Unit 7: and faunal remains, *300-311*, 357; layer descriptions for, 130; Phase IV in, 103; Phase V in, 357; plant distribution in Phase V, *396-397*, 429; and plant remains, 415, 419, 420, 421, 424; and ritual practices, 317; starch grains from, 684

Unit 8: layer descriptions for, 130-131; Phase V in, 131; plant distribution in Phase V, *396-397*, 429; and plant remains, 415, 418; Tomb 8 in, 131, *132*; tomb structure of, 130-131, *132*, 572, 598

Unit 9: burned area showing ash and charcoal in Stratum 13a, 131, *133*; and faunal remains, 212, *213-219*, 219, 221, *222-233*, 235, *236-249*, 249, *262-268*, 317, 355, 357, 364-365; feature types and distribution in late Pleistocene layers, 100, *102*; HP-2 compared to, 114; layer descriptions for, 131; Phase I in, 355; Phase II in, 102, 103, 355, 569; Phase III in, 103, 355; Phase IV in, 355; Phase V in, 355, 365; plant distribution in Phase III, *378-379*, 428-429; and plant remains, 415; premound context from, 100, 101; radiocarbon dating of, 88, 100, 101, 102, *102*, 103, 131; as service unit, 364; stone berms of, 117, 571; stratigraphic cuts in, 88; unifacial tool of, 728, *729*

Unit 10: chamber tombs of, 104, 119, 131, 134, 135, *135*, 142, 152, 360, 453, 572, 576, 598, 599, 613; chronology of, 91; decorated gourds of, 442; exotic items in, 453-454, *455*; and faunal remains, *312-317*, 355, 356, 360; Features 1-6, 134-135; funerary structures in, 355; human skeletal remains in, 134, *135*, 185-187, 738; layer descriptions for, 131, 133-135; Phase IV in, 103, 129, 134, 453; Phase V in, 104, 360; plant distribution in Phase V, *398-399*, 429; and plant remains, 409, 415, 418, 419, 420, 421, 422, 423, 424, 425, 426; plan view of excavation extensions, structures, and plaster retention wall, 131, 135, *135*, 355; profile of tomb walls and other structures, 131, *134*; spatial analysis of plant remains, 427; Structure 1, 133, 134, 135, *135*; Structure 2, 133, 134, 135, *235*, 355

Unit 11: chamber tombs of, 135, 142; and faunal remains, *318-323*; layer descriptions for, 135-136; Phase IV in, 103; Phase V in, 573; plant distribution in Phase V, *398-399*, 429; and plant remains, 415, 418, 419, 420, 424

Unit 12: circumscribed space in, *164*; and faunal remains, *318-323*, 355, 364, 365; human skeletal remains at, 690; layer descriptions for, 136; Phase IV in, 103; Phase V in, 104, 355; plant distribution in Phase V, *400-401*, 429; and plant remains, 409, 419, 420, 421; radiocarbon dated premound contexts in, 100; as service unit, 364, 365

Unit 13: chronology of, 557; and faunal remains, 221, *276-287*, 345, 352, 364; habitation debris of, 153, 575; horizontal extension of, 165, 575; as off-mound domestic location, 122, 153-154, 158, 165, 197-198, 211, 352,

364, 567, 570, 589, 603; plant distribution in Phase IV, *386-387*, 429; and plant remains, 414, 415, 418, 419, 420, 424, 430; profile of north wall, *153*

Unit 14: human skeletal remains at, 690; layer descriptions for, 136; offering of shells in, 136, *141*; plant distribution in Phase V, *400-401*, 429; and plant remains, 409, 411, 415, 418, 419, 420, 421, 423, 424, 425

Unit 15: burned torches of, 451, *452*; and faunal remains, *213-219*, 359; layer descriptions for, 136-137; plant distribution in Phase IV, *387-388*; plant distribution in Phase V, *402-403*, 429; and plant remains, 385, 409, 419, 420; pottery sherds in, 454, 456; site excavations of, 34, 140; strata in, 136, *137*, *139*; unifacial tool of, *729*, 730

Unit 15/21: chronology of, 91; and faunal remains, 212, 219, 356; feature types and distribution in late Pleistocene layers, 100, *102*; fragment of basket from, *101*; HP-2 compared to, 114; Phase II in, 102, 103, 569; Phase III in, 103; radiocarbon dated premound contexts in, 100, 101, *102*, 137, 142; stratigraphic cuts in, 88; and Test Pit 15, 160

Unit 16: Burial HP09-05 showing polychaete tube-base, *156*, 157, 179, 598, 613; charcoal analysis, 631, *633*; chile peppers at, 653; chronology of, 91, 106, 107, 121-122, 557; and faunal remains, 208, 212, 219, 221, *222-233*, 235, *236-249*, 248, 249, *262-268*, 268, 275, *276-287*, 317, *318-323*, 330, 345, 352-353, 357, 358, 359, 360; horizontal extension of, 165, 575; house floors, 154, *156*, 157; human skeletal remains at, 157, 172, 173, 175-181, 195, 586, 690-691, 738; layer descriptions of, 154, 157; lithics of, 435; as off-mound domestic site, 106, 122, 152, 158, 165, 197-198, 208, 211, 235, 364, 567, 570, 575, 578, 589, 603; Phase I in, 352; Phase II in, 235, 352-353, 359, 569; Phase III in, 154, 157, 353; Phase IV in, 154, 353; Phase V in, 154, 353; plan of house foundations, 154, *155*; plant distribution in Phase I, *371-372*, 428; plant distribution in Phase II, *373-374*, 427, 428; plant distribution in Phase V, *402-403*, 427, 429; and plant remains, 379, 383, 385, 408, 409, 414, 415, 418, 419, 420, 421, 422, 423, 424, 425, 429, 430; plant species by cultural phases, 367, *368-370*, 432, 571, 572, 573, 587; polychaete tube-based artifacts in, 452, *453*; radiocarbon dating of, 106, 157-158; schematic profile of floors and structures, 154, *155*; spatial analysis of plant remains in, 427; starch grains from, 686; stone tools of, 435-440, 442; stratigraphic cuts in, 88; unifacial tools of, 728, *729*, 730; Unit 2 compared to, 235; Unit 13 compared to, 154, 352

Unit 17, layer descriptions for, 137-138

Unit 18: human skeletal remains at, 691; layer descriptions of, 138; plant distribution in Phase V, *404-405*, 429; and plant remains, 419; site excavations of, 140

Unit 19: chamber tombs of, 572; and faunal remains, 356-357; layer descriptions for, 138, 140; Phase II in, 569; Phase IV in, 103; and plant remains, 421; site excavations of, 34; stone aligned space in, *164*. *See also* Unit 23

Unit 20: charcoal analysis, *633*; chile peppers at, 653; chronology of, 91, 557; and faunal remains, 208, 235, 248, 249, *250-261*, *269-274*, 275, *288-299*, 317, 330-331,

344, 345, 359, 364; floors of, 150, 165; and geophysical survey, 725; Harris Matrices for, 111; layer descriptions for, 146–147; as off-mound area, 105, 106, 146, 147, 198, 427–428, 575; Phase II in, 330–331, 364, 569; Phase III in, 331, 355; Phase IV in, 103, 331, 359; plant distribution in Phase III, *380-381*, 428–429; plant distribution in Phase IV, *387-388*, 428, 429; and plant remains, 379, 411, 414, 415, 418, 419, 420, 421, 422, 423, 424, 425, 426; premound excavations in, 106, 198; site excavations of, 34; spatial analysis of plant remains in, 427–428; spatially circumscribed strata in, 124; starch grains from, 686; stratigraphic cuts in, 88; and Test Pit 18, 160; and Test Pit 27, 161; undated cultural deposits of, 105; unifacial tool of, *729, 730*

Unit 21: bundle of salt from Structure 6, 140, *141*; chamber tombs of, 572; charcoal analysis, *633*; and faunal remains, *324-330*, 356, 360; layer descriptions for, 140–142; offering of coca leaf and copper sulfate, 140, *141*, 454; offering of coca leaves in Structure 8, 140, *141*; plan of structures and pathways in, 136, *139*, 140; plant distribution in Phase V, *404-405*, 429; and plant remains, 379, 409, 418, 422, 423, 425, 426; shells in, 454; south profile of plaster floors and fills, 136, *138*; and sunken circular plaza, 140–142, 356, 454; unifacial tools of, *729, 730*; Unit 15 excavated within spatial area of, 136; west profile of structures and plaster and other floors, 136, *138*, 140. *See also* Unit 15/21

Unit 22: charcoal analysis, *633*; chile peppers at, 653; chronology of, 91; chunk specimens of stone tools, 730–731; and faunal remains, 221, *222-233*, 235, 248, 249, *250-261*, 268, *269-274*, 275, *288-299*, 317, 330, 331, 344–345, *346-351*, 358, 359, 360, 364; floors in, 149–152, 165, 221; and geophysical survey, 725; Harris Matrix for, 30, 89, 111, 147–149, *148*; layer descriptions for, 147–148; maize at, 150, 656, 658, 660, 662; as on-mound area, 105, 364; Phase I in, 331, 366; Phase II in, 106, 331, 569; Phase III in, 275, 344, 359; Phase IV in, 103, 275, 344; Phase V in, 275, 344, 345; plant distribution in Phase I, *371-372*, 428; plant distribution in Phase II, *375-376*, 428; plant distribution in Phase III, *380-381*, 428–429; plant distribution in Phase IV, *389-390*, 428, 429; plant distribution in Phase V, *404-405*, 428, 429; and plant remains, 385, 408, 409, 415, 418, 419, 421, 422, 423, 424, 425; pollen samples from, 701, *702-703*, 703; premound excavations in, 106, 198; premound habitation layer in, 100, 198; profile of, 147, *147*; shells in, 454; site excavations of, 34; spatial analysis of plant remains in, 428; starch grains from, *684, 685*, 686, 687; stratigraphic cuts in, 88; undated cultural deposits of, 105, 106; unifacial tools of, *729, 730*

Unit 23: chamber tombs of, 104, 131, 135, 140, 142, *142*, 143, 144, 152, 164, 356, 428, 446, 572, 598, 599, 613; charcoal analysis, *633*; and faunal remains, *332-344*, 356–357, 360; and geophysical survey, 726, *726*; ground stone vessel in, 440; human skeletal remains of, 187–188, 738; layer descriptions for, 142–144; Phase II in, 103, 569; Phase III in, 103, 142; Phase IV in, 103, 142; Phase V in, 104, 124, 573; plant distribution in Phase V, *406-409*, 428, 429; and plant remains, 379, 385, 409, 414, 415, 418, 421, 422, 423, 424, 425, 426; polished stone-drinking vessel in, 142; profile of multiple floors and fills of Structure 8, 144, *144*; rock crystals in, 140; site excavations of, 34; starch grains from, 686; structures of, 143–144; and Unit 19, 138, 142–144

Unit 24: and faunal remains, 211; layer descriptions for, 144–145; Phase IV in, 103, 144; plant distribution in Phase V, *410-411*, 429; and plant remains, 422, 424; profile of floors and fills in, *145*; yellow sediment layer in, 145

Unit 25: charcoal analysis, *633*; and faunal remains, 275, *276-287*, 358, 364; layer descriptions for, 145–146; Phase II in, 569; Phase III in, 103; Phase IV in, 103; plant distribution in Phase IV, *390-391*, 429; plant distribution in Phase V, *410-411*, 429; and plant remains, 379, 383, 409, 415, 418, 419, 420, 421, 422, 423, 424; stone berms of, 117

Unit 26: and faunal remains, 364; horizontal extension of, 165; layer descriptions for, 158; as off-mound domestic location, 122, 158, 165, 197–198, 364, 567, 570, 575, 589, 603; Unit 13 compared to, 154

Unit 27, 146

Unit 28, 146

Unit 29, 146

Unit 30: layer descriptions for, 150; as off-mound area, 105, 150, 575, 578; profile of west wall, 150, *151*; strata and features of, 106

United States, earthwork mounds in, 9, 615

Universidad Nacional de Trujillo, 210, 648

University of Colorado Herbarium, 697

University of Exeter Archaeobotany Laboratory, 674

University of Florida, 667

University of Kentucky, 724

University of Oklahoma Laboratory for Molecular Anthropology and Microbiome Research, 733, 736–738

unspun fibers: in bundles, 466; and camelid hair, 473; fragments of, 458; and textile analysis, 465; types of, 474

upper tidal zone, 207, 212, 220

Urana, Lauren, 464

urbanism, 4

Urton, Gary, 611–612

use surfaces: artifact and sediment composition of, 109, 111; characteristics of, 89, 162, *164*; chemical analysis of, 152; circumscribed activity areas associated with, 90; and construction sequence, 104; cultural deposits of, 122; domestic activity associated with, 90; and faunal remains, 211; in Harris Matrices, 112; of HP-2, 114; of HP-3, 119; at Huaca Prieta, 571; and incipient mound building, 103; individual nature of, 165; at Paredones, 165, 571, 575; and plant remains, 372; stratigraphy represented by, 91; of Unit 3, 129; of Unit 7, 130; of Unit 10, 134–135; of Unit 15, 137

Valdivia settlements: and complementarity of foraging and sedentary practices, 17; geometric designs of, 12, 445; jack bean found at, 426; as Preceramic mound cultures, 4

Vallejos A., Miriam, 554